The Dictionary
of Cultural Literacy

The Dictionary of Cultural Literacy

E. D. Hirsch, Jr. ❦ Joseph F. Kett ❦ James Trefil

SECOND EDITION,
REVISED AND UPDATED

HOUGHTON MIFFLIN COMPANY

Boston · New York 1993

Library of Congress Cataloging-in-Publication Data

Hirsch, E. D. (Eric Donald), date.
The dictionary of cultural literacy / E.D. Hirsch, Jr., Joseph F.
Kett, James Trefil. — 2nd ed., rev. and updated.
p.   cm.
Includes index.
ISBN 0-395-65597-8
1. United States — Civilization — Dictionaries.   2. Civilization —
Dictionaries.   3. English language — Dictionaries.   I. Kett,
Joseph F.   II. Trefil, James S., 1938–   .   III. Title
E169.1.H6   1993   93-19568
973'.03 — dc20   CIP

Printed in the United States of America

Book design by Robert Overholtzer

DOH 10 9 8 7 6 5 4 3 2 1

CONTENTS

PREFACE TO THE SECOND EDITION

Over the five years since the first edition of *The Dictionary of Cultural Literacy* was published, hundreds of readers have written us to make suggestions. The present edition has gained much in usefulness and accuracy from their generous help. To list these hundreds of coeditors and coparticipants in our project would take inordinate space, but we do wish to thank them en masse (see "Idioms"), just as we have already thanked each one individually.

Although every chapter of the dictionary has undergone some updating and fine-tuning, three areas in particular have received most of the attention: the epochal transformations in world history in the last five years, the enormous advances in science and technology, and the growing consensus over multiculturalism.

In 1988, when the first edition of the *Dictionary* appeared, the AIDS epidemic had just appeared on the horizon of public awareness. Terms like "HIV" and "AZT" were either unknown or heard only in the specialized conversation of medical biologists. Most of us were blissfully unaware that we were supposed to worry about cholesterol levels. Those who owned personal computers did not need to worry that their data banks would be wiped out by computer viruses, and concern about global warming was just starting to grow in the minds of the general public. Today, of course, all of these terms are part of cultural literacy, routinely used without explanation in newspaper articles and newscasts. New ideas flow constantly from the ferment of scientific research and technological development, and these ideas change both our lives and the way we look at the world.

The new *Dictionary* has also taken into account the recent emphasis on the ever more significant area of multiculturalism. The most numerous of such additions have been entries covering African-American culture. The strong African-American representation in the first edition has been supplemented with entries on such subjects as the AME Church, Paul Lawrence Dunbar, Toni Morrison, Josephine Baker, Benjamin Banneker, Ralph Bunche, Marcus Garvey, and Alex Haley. It will be obvious from these examples that the entries belong to American (not just African-American) cultural literacy.

Many of the changes have occurred in history and geography. The cataclysmic internal collapse of the Soviet empire and the political upheavals in Eastern Europe, the Persian Gulf War and other military conflicts, have lead to a multitude of new geographical and historical entries. Cultural literacy in the 1990s entails knowledge of a host of new republics including Kazakhstan, Kyrgyzstan, Belarus, Azerbaijan, Bosnia and Herzegovina, Slovenia, and Croatia, as well as world figures such as Nelson Mandela and Saddam Hussein, and events ranging from the violent suppression of human rights at Tiananmen Square to the dismantling of the Berlin Wall.

After taking into account these changes, we are still impressed by the remarkable stability of U.S. cultural literacy in the modern world. Educators who disparage the importance of factual knowledge on the grounds that it is always changing should take careful note. They argue that since many of the specifics we learn in school will become useless and forgotten in a few years, mere content should be subordinated to skills. This argument has sponsored a watered-down and incoherent approach to specific content in our schools. Yet a careful examination of the changes required in this dictionary over the past five years effectively demolishes that argument. Over ninety percent of what one needs to know has remained stable in all subjects except the obvious ones of recent history, science, and technology. And even in those subjects, the core of needed knowledge has remained very stable. The core contents of a first-rate school curriculum are not arbitrary elements, and in most areas of learning they do not change either rapidly or radically over time. These findings have enormous implications for schooling and school reform.

If imitation is the sincerest flattery (see "Proverbs and Sayings"), then the first edition of this work has been sincerely flattered in several countries of Europe and Asia. We single out for special admiration a fine scholarly dictionary of Dutch cultural literacy, produced in the Netherlands under the energetic editorship of Professor Dolph Kohnstamm and Dr. H. C. Kassee.

We hope that this new edition will prove to be as useful as the previous one, and we invite our readers to continue to write us to offer suggestions for its improvement.

E.D. HIRSCH, JR.
JOSEPH KETT
JAMES TREFIL

INTRODUCTION

Although it is true that no two humans know exactly the same things, they often have a great deal of knowledge in common. To a large extent this common knowledge or collective memory allows people to communicate, to work together, and to live together. It forms the basis for communities, and if it is shared by enough people, it is a distinguishing characteristic of a national culture. The form and content of this common knowledge constitute one of the elements that makes each national culture unique.

It is our contention that such a body of information is shared by literate Americans of the late twentieth century, and that this body of knowledge can be identified and defined. This dictionary is a first attempt at that task. It identifies and defines the names, phrases, events, and other items that are familiar to most literate Americans: the information that we call cultural literacy. Although few of us will know every entry, most of us will be familiar with the majority, even if we are unable to define each one exactly.

Cultural literacy, unlike expert knowledge, is meant to be shared by everyone. It is that shifting body of information that our culture has found useful, and therefore worth preserving. Only a small fraction of what we read and hear gains a secure place on the memory shelves of the culturally literate, but the importance of this information is beyond question. This shared information is the foundation of our public discourse. It allows us to comprehend our daily newspapers and news reports, to understand our peers and leaders, and even to share our jokes. Cultural literacy is the context of what we say and read; it is part of what makes Americans American.

Because this is the first time anyone has tried to identify and define the knowledge assumed in public discourse, we had to establish a number of rules for deciding what to include. First, we proposed that many things are either above or below the level of cultural literacy. Some information is so specialized that it is known only by experts and is therefore above the level of common knowledge. At the same time, some information, such as the names of colors and animals, is too basic and generally known to be included in this kind of dictionary. By definition, cultural literacy falls between the specialized and the generalized.

Our second test was to determine how widely known an item is in our culture. Only those items that are likely to be known by a broad majority of literate Americans ought to appear in this dictionary. Therefore, in selecting entries, we drew upon a wide range of national periodicals. We reasoned that if a major daily newspaper refers to an event, person, or thing without defining it, we can assume that the majority of the readers of that periodical will know what that item is. If this is true, that event, person, or thing is probably part of our common knowledge, and therefore part of cultural literacy.

Third, we proposed that cultural literacy is

not knowledge of current events, although it can help us understand those events as they occur. To become part of cultural literacy, an item must have lasting significance. Either it has found a place in our collective memory or it has the promise of finding such a place. This is one of the things that contributes to the stability of cultural literacy in America. Some of the material in this dictionary has remained unchanged in our national consciousness since our nation's beginnings.

In some cases, determining lasting significance was very difficult. In our age of communication, the lifespan of many things in our collective memory is very short. What seems monumental today often becomes trivial tomorrow. For the sake of the dictionary, we arbitrarily chose a memory span of fifteen years. If a person or event has been widely recognized for more than fifteen years or seems likely to be recognized by a majority of people fifteen years from now, that person or event deserved consideration for a place in this dictionary.

This rule of lasting significance tended to eliminate certain fields altogether, or nearly so. For example, our collective memory of most of the people and events in the fields of sports and entertainment is too ephemeral to take a permanent place in our cultural heritage. There are outstanding exceptions, however, and those are included in this dictionary.

Scientific entries presented a special problem.

Because there is little broad knowledge of science even among educated people, the criteria used to compile the lists for the humanities and social sciences simply could not be used with the natural sciences. The gap between the essential basic knowledge of science and what the general reader can be expected to know has become too large. Our criterion for choosing a science entry was that the item must be truly essential to a broad grasp of a major science. The science-related terms in this dictionary represent our best judgments, and those of our advisers, about what literate Americans ought to know to achieve the levels of communication expected for the humanities and social sciences.

We realize that many of the entries included here can be questioned. We also realize that many items that are excluded are open to similar questioning. We debated these entries at length, and we hope that this dictionary will stimulate a similar debate among our readers. American culture is not the property of the elite or even of the majority — it belongs to us all.

This attempt at creating a *Dictionary of Cultural Literacy* remains an unfinished project. We hope our readers will become our collaborators in improving and expanding it. Our culture changes constantly as new things are added and others are forgotten, and new relationships are forged and broken. Defining cultural literacy is an ongoing project, and this is only a first step. We invite your participation.

— E. D. H.
J. F. K.
J. T.

THE THEORY BEHIND THE DICTIONARY
Cultural Literacy and Education

BY E. D. HIRSCH, JR.

The conceptions that underlie this dictionary are outlined in my book *Cultural Literacy,* published in 1987. But in fact, the dictionary project was begun before I thought of writing a separate book, and the book itself was first conceived merely as a technical explanation of the ideas that led us to undertake the dictionary. The scope of the book outgrew that aim, but no one even considered the possibility that the book would become a best-seller or that it would be read outside the field of education. Although it did become a best-seller and its ideas have been widely discussed, many users of this dictionary may not be familiar with the concept of cultural literacy. So here, in brief compass, is why this project was undertaken, and why we hope it will help improve American public education and public discourse.

One good way of explaining the cultural literacy project might well be to list the points of strong agreement that have appeared in reviews of the book and in the hundreds of letters I have received from teachers and nonteachers alike. All these reviews and letters endorse the proposition that achieving high universal literacy ought to be a primary focus of educational reform in this country. They all accept the evidence that our national literacy has been declining since 1965, not only among disadvantaged

children but also among our top students. They agree that the decline has occurred at a time when truly functional literacy is becoming ever more important to our economic well-being. And they have usually stressed the idea that providing everyone with a high level of literacy is important in holding together the social fabric of the nation.

The novelty that my book introduced into this discussion is its argument that true literacy depends on a knowledge of the *specific* information that is taken for granted in our public discourse. My emphasis on background information makes my book an attack on all formal and technical approaches to teaching language arts. Reading and writing are not simply acts of decoding and encoding but rather acts of communication. The literal words we speak and read and write are just the tip of the iceberg in communication. An active understanding of the written word requires far more than the ability to call out words from a page or the possession of basic vocabulary, syntax, grammar, and inferencing techniques. We have learned that successful reading also requires a knowledge of shared, taken-for-granted information that is not set down on the page.

To grasp the practical importance of that point for our entire educational system, we need to ask a fundamental question. Why is high national literacy the key to educational progress in all domains of learning, even in mathematics and natural sciences? We have long known that there is a high correlation between students' reading ability and their ability to learn new materials in diverse fields. That sounds vaguely reasonable, even obvious, but why *exactly* should it be the case? Let's try to understand the not-so-obvious reason for the high correlation between reading ability and learning ability.

The true measure of reading ability is the ease and accuracy with which a person can understand *diverse* kinds of writing. All standardized tests of reading ability include samples from several different subject matters. But why isn't one long sample just as effective a test as several short ones? Well, if reading ability were a purely generalizable skill, one long sample would be an adequate diagnostic test. But in fact, reading ability is not a generalizable skill. If a young boy knows a lot about snakes but very little about lakes, he will make a good score on a passage about snakes, but a less good score on a passage about lakes. So to get a fairly accurate picture of his overall reading ability, we have to sample how he does on a variety of subjects.

But notice that this variability in a person's performance shows us something of utmost importance about reading ability. To have a good *general* reading ability, you need to know about a lot of things. If you know about lakes and snakes, and rakes and cakes, you will have higher reading ability than if you just know about snakes. Aha! you might say, that simply means you will read better if you have a broad vocabulary. That is true. But remember what it means to have a broad vocabulary. Knowing a lot of words means knowing a lot of things. Words refer to things. Language arts are also knowledge arts.

We have now taken a first step in understanding the correlation between reading ability and learning ability. We have established that high reading ability is a multiplex skill that requires knowledge in a wide range of subjects. It turns out that the same is true of learning ability. A basic axiom of learning is that the easiest way to learn something new is to associate it with something we already know. Much of the art of teaching is the art of associating what kids need to learn with what they already know. The process of learning often works as metaphor does, yoking old ideas together to make something new. In the nineteenth century, when people wanted to describe the new transportation technology that went *chug-chug-chug,* they called the engine an "iron horse" and the rail system "track way" (if they were Dutch) or "rail way" (if they were English) or "iron way" (if they were French, German, or Italian) or "narrow iron lane" (if they were Greek). All of these metaphors successfully conveyed a new concept by combining old concepts.

As a consequence of the fact that we learn most easily when we attach the new to the old, people who already know a lot tend to learn new things faster and more easily than people who do not know very much. Mainly this is because knowledgeable people will have less to learn; they already know many of the key elements in the new concept. In learning about a railroad, for instance, they possess whole realms of relevant knowledge that make it unnecessary to explain a lot of subordinate facts about how wheels work, what the nature of iron is, what steam engines do, and so on.

It should now be clear why reading ability and learning ability are so closely allied. They both depend on a diversity of prior knowledge. You can easily read a range of new texts if you already know a lot; so too you can easily learn a broad range of new knowledge if you already know a lot. It should not surprise us, therefore, that back in the 1950s the College Board found out that the best predictor of how well students would perform in school was their performance on a general knowledge test. "Reading, writing, and arithmetic" and the general ability to learn new things all show a high correlation with broad background knowledge.

I must ask your indulgence to take another

step along the path I am leading you. Reading and learning ability depend on something more definite than broad, unspecified knowledge. To a significant degree, learning and reading depend on *specific* broad knowledge. The reason for this goes back to my earlier point that reading is not just a technical skill but also an act of communication. When somebody is reading with understanding, communication is taking place between writer and reader. Conversely, if communication isn't taking place, the reader isn't accurately understanding what he or she is reading. Successful communication depends on understanding both the text's literal meanings and its implied meanings. These all-important implied meanings can only be constructed out of specific knowledge shared between writer and reader. Let me give a very brief example of why this is so. Here are the beginning words of a school textbook on chemistry:

You are beginning your study of chemistry at a time when growing numbers of people are concerned about the declining quality of life. Chemistry can help you gain a deeper and more satisfying understanding of your environment than you have now. If you are curious and wish to know more about natural processes, minerals of the earth, water and solutions, and gases of the atmosphere, the activities in chemistry beckon to you.

That's it. As a child, I'm supposed to know before reading the passage that chemistry has to do with minerals, water, and solutions, that numbers of people are concerned about the quality of life, that quality of life has something to do with water and solutions. Understanding that passage will be easy if I already know what "chemistry," "solution," and "declining quality of life" are supposed to signify.

But just consider the words of that last phrase one by one, "declining quality of life." They presuppose a whole realm of background knowledge that has no existence in the words themselves. To understand the phrase quickly and accurately, I need more than a knowledge of the individual words or possession of general inferencing skills. I need to know the writer's taken-for-granted information — in this case, the

widespread discussion in our culture about the pollution of rivers, atmosphere, and so on. Neither the word nor the concept of pollution is mentioned in the passage. But to understand the paragraph, I not only need to know that rivers and air are being polluted, I also need to know the unspoken convention that complaints about pollution are sometimes couched in the phrase "declining quality of life." If I don't share that background knowledge with the writer, I can't quickly understand the passage. Even someone with a good command of English and technical reading skills who happened not to know that particular background information would be baffled for a long time by the juxtaposition of quality of life with a reference to aqueous solutions.

Reading ability, then, depends not only on broad knowledge but also on shared knowledge. Communication between writer and reader always depends on implications that remain unsaid, and that must be shared by writer and reader if the communication is to proceed effectively. Since successful learning from reading depends on the effectiveness of the communicative transaction, I am led to the conclusion that both learning and reading are powerfully affected by the degree to which background knowledge is shared between writer and reader, and between teacher and student. To learn well, I need to know a lot, but I also need to know the specific things that enable me to read between the lines.

Therefore, learning depends on communication, and effective communication depends on shared background knowledge. The optimal way to fulfill this requirement of communication is simply to insure that readers and writers, students and teachers do in fact share a broad range of specific knowledge. This makes good communication possible, which in turn makes effective learning possible, and also enables a society to work. In short, we have come round to the point of my book. An important key to solving the twin problems of learning and literacy is to attain the broadly shared background knowledge I have called "cultural literacy." My book argues that the content of this literate background knowledge is not a mystery, and that it can be taught systematically to all our students. The book further claims that if we do impart this content, we can achieve the universal literacy that is a necessary foundation for further educational, economic, and social improvements. No active reading researcher — that is to say, no one who is thoroughly conversant with the empirical data in cognitive research — has challenged this analysis.

We know from the history of Europe that national schools can achieve high literacy for everyone in a multicultural population. France did so with a population that, up to the eighteenth century, spoke at least four different languages. The French school system turned illiterate "peasants into Frenchmen," to use Eugen Weber's phrase, and it was the school system, not the peasant home, that accomplished this miracle. Viewed in a long historical perspective, it has been the school, not the home, that has been the decisive factor in achieving mass literacy. Literate national language and culture are what Ernest Gellner aptly calls *school-transmitted* cultures. He observes that the chief makers of the modern nation have been schoolteachers. They helped create the modern nation-state, and they alone can perpetuate it and make it thrive. When the schools of a nation fail adequately to transmit the literate national language and culture, the unity and effectiveness of the nation will necessarily decline.

While avoiding the temptation to cast blame for our recent decline in literacy, we do need to understand and correct it. One important cause of the decline has been the use of "skills-oriented," "relevant" materials in elementary and secondary grades. The consequent disappearance from the early curriculum of literate culture (that is, traditional history, myth, and literature) has been a mistake of monumental proportions. Modern basal readers constantly update the content that young children are taught, under the theory that modern materials will be of greater interest to them than older

stories and myths, as though reading, writing, and oral communication were formal skills that could be perfected independently of specific literate content. Unfortunately, as we have seen, that theory is empirically wrong, and operating upon it has had disastrous consequences for national literacy. Research on expert performance shows a high correlation between skill and specific knowledge, and this correlation holds from the beginning stages up to the very top levels of performance.

Publishers and schools need to direct their energies to enhancing the effectiveness with which core literate content is presented. They should not try to overhaul the entire content of literate culture, which cannot successfully be done in any case. Professional linguists have often remarked on the inherent conservatism of literacy. Some of its elements do not change at all. Spelling, for example, is extraordinarily conservative, because so many people have learned the traditional forms, and so many books have recorded them, that successful spelling reform would require orthographical thought-police. This linguistic inertia induced by print and mass education also extends to other contents of literate culture.

But the conservatism of literate culture is far from total. New elements are constantly coming in, and old ones falling out of use. Americans have successfully pressed for cultural reforms, including greater representation of women, minorities, and non-Western cultures. In addition, literate culture must keep up with historical and technical change. Yet the materials of literate culture that are recent introductions constitute about a fifth of its total. The disputed territory of literate culture is much smaller still — about 4 percent. Thus, 96 percent of literate culture is undisputed territory, and, most striking of all, *80 percent of literate culture has been in use for more than a hundred years!*

Such cultural conservatism is fortunate and useful for the purposes of national communication. It enables grandparents to communicate with grandchildren, southerners with midwesterners, whites with blacks, Asians with Hispanics, and Republicans with Democrats — no matter where they were educated. If each local school system imparts the traditional reference points of literate culture, then everybody is able to communicate with strangers. That is a good definition of literacy: the ability to communicate effectively with strangers. We help people in the underclass rise economically by teaching them how to communicate effectively beyond a narrow social sphere, and that can only be accomplished by teaching them shared, traditional literate culture. Thus the inherent conservatism of literacy leads to an unavoidable paradox: the social goals of liberalism *require* educational conservatism. We only make social and economic progress by teaching everyone to read and communicate, which means teaching myths and facts that are predominantly traditional.

Those who evade this inherent conservatism of literacy in the name of multicultural anti-elitism are in effect elitists of an extreme sort. Traditionally educated themselves, and highly literate, these self-appointed protectors of minority cultures have advised schools to pursue a course that has condemned minorities to illiteracy. The disadvantaged students for whom anti-elitist solicitude is expressed are the very ones who suffer when we fail to introduce traditional literate culture into the earliest grades. Ideological partisanship on the subject of national literacy is more empirical than ideological. The overarching ideological decision has already been made in the commitment to universal literacy. What follows from that commitment is determined more by reality than ideology.

The real test of any educational idea is its usefulness. We hope this dictionary will be a useful tool. We also hope and expect that no one will be willing to stop with cultural literacy as a final educational aim. Cultural literacy is a necessary but not sufficient attainment of an educated person. Cultural literacy is shallow; true education is deep. But our analysis of reading and learning suggests the paradox that broad, shallow knowledge is the best route to deep knowledge. Because broad knowledge enables us to read and learn effectively, it is the best guarantee that we will continue to read, and learn, and deepen our knowledge. True literacy has always opened doors — not just to deep knowledge and economic success, but also to other people and other cultures.

HOW TO USE THIS DICTIONARY

The Dictionary of Cultural Literacy is a departure from all other reference works in its attempt to identify and define common *cultural* knowledge rather than to present a lexicon of words or topics. Nonetheless, for the convenience of our readers, this book incorporates some of the conventions found in standard dictionaries and encyclopedias.

ORGANIZATION

The Index
The first place to look for a particular topic in this dictionary is the alphabetically ordered index found at the end of the book.

Subject Sections
The main body of the dictionary is divided into the twenty-three sections listed in the Contents. These sections follow the traditional division of subject matter that a student should have encountered by the senior year in most high schools. Some particularly lengthy subjects have been divided into two sections according to the most common divisions used in classrooms and textbooks. For example, the year 1865 marks the dividing point between the two sections on American history because this date is traditionally used as a historical divider in American history courses. Within each section, entries are listed alphabetically. Proper names, quotations, or phrases are listed by their most commonly recognized element.

Because cultural literacy embraces more subject matter than is usually treated in an academic setting, this book contains several topics, such as proverbs and idioms, that may be encountered only indirectly in the classroom.

Definitions
Each entry provides a concise definition and also the current *cultural* sense of the term.

Cultural Associations
Most definitions make the cultural sense of an entry self-evident, but such is not always the case. Some entries require further information. Cultural associations follow the definitions and are identified by the symbol ❧. When an entry has more than one cultural association, each one is preceded by the symbol.

Cross-References
Cross-references throughout the dictionary expand the information given in each entry and indicate relationships between various entries. Set in small capitals, cross-references appear as part of a definition or cultural association, as in the example above, or are listed at the end of the definition. Cross-references refer to entry words included in the index.

Pronunciation

Some of the entries in this dictionary have unusual pronunciations; therefore, a pronunciation guide is provided. This guide appears in parentheses after the entry word. No special symbols are required for understanding these pronunciations. Instead, pronunciations rely on individual letters or familiar combinations of letters to convey their sound. Variant pronunciations are given whenever necessary. Pronunciations are broken into syllables separated by hyphens. The primary accent in a word is indicated by capital letters. In most cases the sound represented in the pronunciation is easily understood, but a key is provided here for your use.

PRONUNCIATION KEY

When A Sound Appears As	It Should Be Pronounced As In	When A Sound Appears As	It Should Be Pronounced As In
a	pat, sand, laugh	o	pot, clock, honest
ah	father, car, calm, heart	oh	go, hope, toe, coat, show, owe, sew
air	hair, fare, pear		
aw	law, caucus, all, short, talk, bought	oo	book, wood, pull, would
		ooh	boot, too, rule, suit
ay	pay, make, wait	ow	cow, town, out, house, bough,
b	bib, rubber		
ch	church, watch, cello, nature	oy	toy, point, noise
d	deed, filled	p	pop, apple
e	bet, edge, berry, bury, said	r	roar, hurry, rhythm, write
ee	bee, each, me, conceit	s	sauce, pass, city, whistle
eer	beer, ear, clear, pier, weird, cereal	sh	ship, dish, tissue, addition, anxious
eye	bite, by, aisle, buy	t	tight, attempt, stopped,
f	fife, phase, rough	th	thin, breath, nothing
g	gag, again, ghost	thh	this, breathe, other
h	hat, ahead, who	u	cut, up, above
i	bit, if, spinach, manage	uh	about, item, edible, lemon, circus, famous, better
j	jar, judge, gem, edge, manage	ur	urge, term, firm, word, heard
k	kick, cook, account, pique,	v	valve, river, of
kw	quick, acquire, choir	w	with, away, one, quick
l	let, lull, little	y	yes, onion, hallelujah
m	mum, summer, column, climb	yoo	cure, purée, uranium
		yooh	you, use, cue, few, beautiful
n	nine, sun, sudden	z	zebra, buzz, rose, anxiety
ng	sing, think, angle	zh	beige, vision, pleasure

A few foreign words that appear in this dictionary use special sounds not usually found in English. These are shown below.

When A Sound Appears As	As In	It Should Be Pronounced
eu	dans*eu*r, (French), sch*ö*n (German)	Like the sound "ay" or "e" made with the lips in position for saying the sound "oh"
kh	lo*ch*, *Ch*anukah, i*ch* (German)	Like a harsh, rasping "h" sound
nn	e*nf*a*nt* terrible (ahnn-FAHNN te-REE-bluh), S*ã*o Paulo (sownn-POW-looh)	With the vowel just before it is nasalized, or pronounced with the nasal passages open so that the breath comes out of both the mouth and nose (the "nn" is not pronounced as a consonant sound)
uu	gr*ü*n (German), t*u* (French)	Like the sound "ee" or "i" made with the lips in position for the sound "ooh"

The Bible

The BIBLE, the holy book of JUDAISM and CHRISTIANITY, is the most widely known book in the English-speaking world. It is divided into two main parts, commonly called the OLD TESTAMENT and the NEW TESTAMENT. The best-known books of the Old Testament are GENESIS, EXODUS, the PSALMS, the Book of JOB, ECCLESIASTES, the SONG OF SOLOMON, and the Book of ISAIAH. The thirty-nine books make up the holy Scripture for Judaism. Christianity at a later period built upon Judaism and included the Old Testament as the first part of its own Scripture, adding the New Testament, which consists of twenty-seven books. Its main books are the four GOSPELS — MATTHEW, MARK, LUKE, and JOHN, which relate the life of JESUS and his teachings — and the Book of REVELATION.

No one in the English-speaking world can be considered literate without a basic knowledge of the Bible. Literate people in INDIA, whose religious traditions are not based on the Bible but whose common language is English, must know about the Bible in order to understand English within their own country. All educated speakers of American English need to understand what is meant when someone describes a contest as being between DAVID and Goliath, or whether a person who has the "wisdom of SOLOMON" is wise or foolish, or whether saying "My cup runneth over" means the person feels fortunate or unfortunate. Those who cannot use or understand such allusions cannot fully participate in literate English.

The Bible is also essential for understanding many of the moral and spiritual values of our CULTURE, whatever our religious beliefs. The story of ABRAHAM AND ISAAC concerns our deepest feelings about the relations between parents and children. The story of Job is a major representation in our tradition of being patient during suffering. The PARABLES and sayings of Jesus, such as "Blessed are the meek, for they shall inherit the earth," are so often alluded to that they need to be known by Americans of all faiths.

The linguistic and cultural importance of the Bible is a fact that no one denies. Nonetheless, elementary knowledge of the Bible has declined among young people in recent years. School authorities have felt that teaching about the Bible might be offensive to some parents, and might even be illegal, in light of recent decisions of the SUPREME COURT disallowing prayer in the public schools. The dilemma for Americans is that the CONSTITUTION forbids the teaching of religion in the public schools, and even without that legal prohibition, our schools should not impose religious teaching over the objections of parents. Is there a solution to this dilemma?

No person in the modern world can be considered educated without a basic knowledge of all the great religions of the world — ISLAM, CONFUCIANISM, TAOISM, BUDDHISM, HINDUISM, Judaism, and Christianity. But our knowledge of Judaism and Christianity needs to be more detailed than that of other great religions, if only because of the historical accident that has embedded the Bible in our thought and language. The Bible is a central book in our culture, just as the KORAN is central in other nations, whose citizens need to know more about the Koran than about the Bible. The logical conclusion is that our schools need to teach more about the Bible than about the Koran, but they have a responsibility to teach about both. Far from being illegal or undesirable, teaching *about* the Bible is not only consistent with our CONSTITUTION, it is essential to our literacy.

— E. D. H.

ABRAHAM AND ISAAC. *An engraving of an angel stopping Abraham from sacrificing Isaac, by Julius Schnoor von Karolsfeld.*

Abraham and Isaac   The first two PATRIARCHS of the OLD TESTAMENT. According to the Book of GENESIS, God made a COVENANT with Abraham, telling him to leave his own country and promising to give his family (the HEBREWS) the land of Canaan. This was the PROMISED LAND. God also promised to maintain the covenant with Abraham's son ISAAC. After a time, God tested Abraham by telling him to sacrifice Isaac as a burnt offering. Abraham obediently placed Isaac on an altar and took a knife to kill him. Then an ANGEL of the Lord appeared and told Abraham to spare his son: since Abraham had proved his faith, the sacrifice of his son would not be required of him.

    ❧ Both JEWS and Arabs (*see* ARAB-ISRAELI CONFLICT) claim descent from Abraham: Jews through Isaac, Arabs through Abraham's other son, Ishmael. Abraham's devotion to God makes him a model of faith to Jews and CHRISTIANS alike. ❧ "The bosom

of Abraham" is a term used in the Gospel of LUKE, and in poetry often refers to the peace of HEAVEN.

Adam and Eve   In the BIBLE, the first man and the first woman. The Book of GENESIS tells that God created Adam by breathing life into "the dust of the ground." Later, God created Eve from Adam's rib. God placed Adam and Eve in the Garden of EDEN, telling them that they could eat the fruit of all the trees in the garden except the fruit of the TREE OF

ADAM AND EVE. The Fall of Man, *an engraving by Albrecht Dürer.*

KNOWLEDGE OF GOOD AND EVIL. They lived happily until the SERPENT (SATAN) tempted Eve to eat the FORBIDDEN FRUIT. She ate, and gave the fruit to Adam, who also ate; they immediately became aware and ashamed of their nakedness. Because of Adam and Eve's disobedience, God drove them from the garden into the world outside, where Eve would suffer in childbirth, and Adam would have to earn his livelihood by the sweat of his brow. The most dire consequence of Adam and Eve's disobedience was death: "DUST THOU ART," said God, "AND UNTO DUST SHALT THOU RETURN." After their expulsion, Eve gave birth to sons, first CAIN AND ABEL, and then Seth, and thus Adam and Eve became the parents of mankind. Adam and Eve's sin, and their consequent loss of God's grace and of the enjoyment of PARADISE, is referred to as the FALL OF MAN or simply "the Fall."

alpha and omega (AL-fuh; oh-MAY-guh, oh-MEG-uh, oh-MEE-guh)   The beginning and the end. In the Greek alphabet, in which the NEW TESTAMENT was written, alpha is the first letter and omega is the last. In the Book of REVELATION, God says, "I am Alpha and Omega, the first and the last," meaning that God remains from the beginning to the end of time.

Am I my brother's keeper?   *See* BROTHER'S KEEPER, AM I MY.

angels   Spirits who live in HEAVEN with God; also the DEVILS of HELL, who are angels fallen from goodness. In the BIBLE, angels are often sent to earth, sometimes with a human appearance, to bring the messages of God to people, to guide and protect them, or to execute God's punishments. (*See* ABRAHAM AND ISAAC, ANNUNCIATION, CHERUBIM, DANIEL IN THE LIONS' DEN, JACOB'S LADDER, LOT'S WIFE, LUCIFER, PASSOVER, PLAGUES OF EGYPT, SATAN, *and* SODOM AND GOMORRAH.)

Annunciation   An announcement made by an ANGEL to MARY, THE MOTHER OF JESUS, that she was going to bear a son, even though she was a virgin. Her son was to be called JESUS.

Antichrist   A person mentioned in the NEW TESTAMENT as an enemy of JESUS, who will appear before the SECOND COMING and win over many of Jesus' followers. The Antichrist is often identified with a beast described in the Book of REVELATION, whom God destroys just before the final defeat of SATAN.

  Since the New Testament was written, people have frequently tried to prove that an individual human being was the Antichrist. Some of the candidates have been the Roman emperors NERO and CALIGULA and the modern dictators HITLER and STALIN.

Apocalypse (uh-POK-uh-lips)   Another name for the NEW TESTAMENT Book of REVELATION; from the Greek word for "revelation."

  An "apocalypse" is a final catastrophe.   The Apocalypse is supposed to come at the end of the world or of time.

Apocrypha (uh-POK-ruh-fuh)   Religious writings that have been accepted as books of the BIBLE by some groups but not by others. ROMAN CATHOLICS, for example, include seven books in the OLD TESTAMENT that JEWS and PROTESTANTS do not consider part of the Bible. Some CHURCHES may read the Apocrypha for inspiration, but not to establish religious doctrine.

  By extension, an "apocryphal" story is one that is probably false but is nevertheless regarded as having some value.

Apostles, the Twelve   The twelve men chosen by JESUS to follow him and to spread the GOSPEL after his death. They included PETER, James, JOHN, THOMAS, MATTHEW, and JUDAS ISCARIOT (who was later replaced). PAUL, even though he was not one of the twelve, is generally considered an apostle because of his crucial role in the spread of CHRISTIANITY.

  In general usage, an "apostle" is someone who preaches or promotes a cause, particularly a religious one. The term also connotes a DISCIPLE.

Ararat (AR-uh-rat)   The mountain upon which NOAH'S ARK came to rest as the waters of the great flood receded. (*See* NOAH AND THE FLOOD.)

ark, Noah's   *See* NOAH AND THE FLOOD.

Armageddon (ahr-muh-GED-n)   In the Book of REVELATION, the site of the final and conclusive battle between good and evil, involving "the kings of the earth and the whole world," on the "great day of God Almighty."

  Figuratively, "Armageddon" is any great battle or destructive confrontation.

Ask, and it shall be given you A teaching of JESUS in the SERMON ON THE MOUNT. He continues, "Seek, and ye shall find; knock, and it shall be opened unto you."

🙠 This passage suggests that God will give whatever is needed to those who have the faith to ask for it.

Babel, Tower of (BAY-buhl, BAB-uhl) In the Book of GENESIS, a tower that the descendants of NOAH built. They intended that the tower would reach up to HEAVEN itself, increase their reputation, and make them like God. God prevented them from completing the tower by confusing their language so that they could no longer understand one another's speech. From that time forward, according to the BIBLE, the peoples of the earth would be scattered, speaking different languages.

🙠 "Babel" is confusion and noise.

Babylon (BAB-uh-luhn, BAB-uh-lon) The capital of the ancient empire of BABYLONIA, which conquered JUDAH in the sixth century B.C. The JEWS were exiled to Babylon, which they found luxurious and corrupt. The PROPHET DANIEL became a counselor to the king of Babylon (see HANDWRITING ON THE WALL), and eventually the ISRAELITES were allowed to return to their homeland. (See also DANIEL IN THE LIONS' DEN.)

🙠 A "Babylon" is any place of sin and corruption. 🙠 This event in Jewish history is known as the Babylonian captivity. 🙠 One of the most famous PSALMS begins, "By the waters of Babylon, we lay down, yea we wept."

Beatitudes (bee-AT-uh-toohdz, bee-AT-uh-tyoohdz) Eight sayings of JESUS at the beginning of the SERMON ON THE MOUNT. The word is from the LATIN *beatus*, meaning "blessed," and each of the Beatitudes begins with the word *blessed*. They include "Blessed are the meek, for they shall inherit the earth," "Blessed are the pure in heart, for they shall see God," and "Blessed are the peacemakers, for they shall be called the children of God."

🙠 In the Beatitudes, Jesus promises rewards for good living, difficult though it may be.

beginning, In the The first words of the Book of GENESIS, which contains the biblical account of CREATION: "In the beginning God created the HEAVENS and the EARTH." The GOSPEL of JOHN begins, "In the beginning was the Word."

Bethlehem The village near JERUSALEM where JESUS was born. (*See* NATIVITY.)

Bible The book sacred to CHRISTIANS, which they consider to be the inspired word of God. The Bible includes the OLD TESTAMENT, which contains the sacred books of the JEWS, and the NEW TESTAMENT, which begins with the birth of JESUS.

Besides the Christian-Jewish difference concerning the Bible, there are differences among Christians on precisely what is to be included in the book. Thirty-nine books of the Old Testament are accepted as part of the Bible by Christians and Jews alike. Some Christians hold several books and parts of books of the Old Testament to be part of the Bible also, while other Christians, and Jews, call these the Old Testament APOCRYPHA. Christians are united in their acceptance of the twenty-seven books of the New Tes-

Hebrew Scriptures

Genesis	II Kings	Micah	Song of Songs
Exodus	Isaiah	Nahum	Ruth
Leviticus	Jeremiah	Habakkuk	Lamentations
Numbers	Ezekiel	Zephaniah	Ecclesiastes
Deuteronomy	THE TWELVE	Haggai	Esther
Joshua	Hosea	Zechariah	Daniel
Judges	Joel	Malachi	Ezra
I Samuel	Amos	Psalms	Nehemiah
II Samuel	Obadiah	Proverbs	I Chronicles
I Kings	Jonah	Job	II Chronicles

Old Testament

Jerusalem Version	King James Version	Jerusalem Version	King James Version
Genesis	Genesis	Song of Solomon	Song of Solomon
Exodus	Exodus	Wisdom	
Leviticus	Leviticus	Ecclesiasticus	
Numbers	Numbers	Isaiah	Isaiah
Deuteronomy	Deuteronomy	Jeremiah	Jeremiah
Joshua	Joshua	Lamentations	Lamentations
Judges	Judges	Baruch	
Ruth	Ruth	Ezekiel	Ezekiel
I Samuel	I Samuel	Daniel	Daniel
II Samuel	II Samuel	Hosea	Hosea
I Kings	I Kings	Joel	Joel
II Kings	II Kings	Amos	Amos
I Chronicles	I Chronicles	Obadiah	Obadiah
II Chronicles	II Chronicles	Jonah	Jonah
Ezra	Ezra	Micah	Micah
Nehemiah	Nehemiah	Nahum	Nahum
Tobit		Habakkuk	Habakkuk
Judith		Zephaniah	Zephaniah
Esther	Esther	Haggai	Haggai
Job	Job	Zechariah	Zechariah
Psalms	Psalms	Malachi	Malachi
Proverbs	Proverbs	I Maccabees	
Ecclesiastes	Ecclesiastes	II Maccabees	

New Testament

Matthew	II Corinthians	I Timothy	II Peter
Mark	Galatians	II Timothy	I John
Luke	Ephesians	Titus	II John
John	Philippians	Philemon	III John
Acts	Colossians	Hebrews	Jude
Romans	I-Thessalonians	James	Revelation
I Corinthians	II-Thessalonians	I Peter	

BOOKS OF THE BIBLE

tament; Jews do not consider the writings of the New Testament inspired. The Bible is also called "the Book" (*bible* means "book").

🙠 By extension, any book considered an infallible or very reliable guide to some activity may be called a "bible."

brother's keeper, Am I my A saying from the Bible's story of CAIN AND ABEL. After Cain had murdered his brother Abel, God asked him where his brother was. Cain answered, "I know not; am I my brother's keeper?"

🙠 Cain's words have come to symbolize people's unwillingness to accept responsibility for the welfare of their fellows — their "brothers" in the extended sense of the term. The tradition of JUDAISM and CHRISTIANITY is that people *do* have this responsibility. (*See* GOOD SAMARITAN, LOVE THY NEIGHBOR AS THYSELF, *and* LOVE YOUR ENEMIES.)

burning bush A bush described in the Book of EXODUS; God revealed himself to MOSES, telling him that he must go to PHARAOH to free the ISRAELITES from slavery, and that Moses must also lead them to the PROMISED LAND. This was a miraculous appearance of God, for "the bush burned with fire, and the bush was not consumed." God told Moses, speaking out of the bush, "I am the God of thy father, the God of ABRAHAM, the God of ISAAC, and the God of JACOB." When Moses asked God for his name, "God said unto Moses, 'I Am That I Am.'"

Cain and Abel The first children of ADAM AND EVE, born after the FALL OF MAN. Once, when they were grown men, both Cain and Abel offered sacrifices to God. When Cain saw that Abel's pleased God while his did not, Cain murdered his brother out of jealousy. Soon afterward, God asked Cain where Abel was, and Cain replied, "I know not; AM I MY BROTHER'S KEEPER?" For his crime, Cain was exiled by God to a life of wandering in a distant land.

🙠 God "set a mark upon Cain" to protect him in his wanderings. The "mark of Cain" now refers to an individual's or mankind's sinful nature.

Calvary The hill near JERUSALEM on which JESUS was crucified. The name is LATIN for "Place of the Skull"; it is also called Golgotha. (*See* CRUCIFIXION.)

Cast thy bread upon the waters An expression from the Book of ECCLESIASTES in the OLD TESTA-

MENT: "Cast thy bread upon the waters: for thou shalt find it after many days."

🙠 This saying calls on people to believe that their good deeds will finally benefit them.

chapter and verse The means of locating passages in the BIBLE. Thus MATTHEW 19:18 means chapter 19, verse 18, of the Book of Matthew.

🙠 In general use, giving "chapter and verse" means giving precise evidence for a proposition.

cherubim (CHER-uh-bim, CHER-yuh-bim) *sing.* **cherub** One of the groups of the ANGELS.

🙠 God is often described in the OLD TESTAMENT as sitting on a throne supported by cherubim. 🙠 In the art of the RENAISSANCE, cherubim (or cherubs) are depicted as chubby babies with wings. Hence, a person with a chubby, childlike face may be called "cherubic."

Chosen People The HEBREWS or ISRAELITES; the nation God chose to receive his revelation, and with whom God chose to make a COVENANT.

Christ A title for JESUS meaning "MESSIAH" or "anointed one."

Christian A follower or DISCIPLE of JESUS; someone who believes Jesus is the CHRIST or MESSIAH. The NEW TESTAMENT mentions that the followers of Jesus were first called Christians within a few years after his death.

coat of many colors The special coat that JACOB gave to his son JOSEPH; the coat made his other sons jealous and resentful. (*See* JACOB AND ESAU *and* JOSEPH AND HIS BROTHERS.)

covenant Literally, a CONTRACT. In the BIBLE, an agreement between God and his people, in which God makes promises to his people and, usually, requires certain conduct from them. In the OLD TESTAMENT, God made agreements with NOAH, ABRAHAM, and MOSES. To Noah, he promised that he would never again destroy the earth with a flood. He promised Abraham that he would become the ancestor of a great nation, provided Abraham went to the place God showed him, and sealed the covenant by CIRCUMCISION of all the males of the nation. To Moses, God said that the ISRAELITES would reach the PROMISED LAND, but must obey the MOSAIC LAW. In the NEW TESTAMENT, God promised SALVATION to those who believe in JESUS.

Creation God's creation of the world as described in the Book of GENESIS, commencing in this way: "IN THE BEGINNING God created the HEAVENS and the EARTH. And the earth was without form, and void; and darkness was upon the face of the deep. And the Spirit of God moved upon the face of the waters. And God said, 'Let there be light': and there was light." According to this account, the Creation took six days, with God creating ADAM AND EVE on the sixth day, and resting on the seventh day. Genesis also gives another account of the Creation, in which God makes Adam out of clay, prepares the Garden of EDEN for him, and then fashions Eve out of Adam's rib.

crown of thorns A mock crown, made from thorn branches, that Roman soldiers put on the head of JESUS before the CRUCIFIXION. The soldiers also "bowed the knee before him, and mocked him, saying, 'Hail, King of the JEWS!'"

  ❦ In common usage, a "crown of thorns" may be anything that causes intense suffering: "The jailed South African leader bears her afflictions like a crown of thorns." Similar to the expression "cross to bear." (*See* CRUCIFIXION.)

Crucifixion The death of JESUS on the cross. After he had been betrayed by JUDAS ISCARIOT and arrested, Jesus was condemned by his fellow JEWS as a false MESSIAH and turned over to the Roman governor PONTIUS PILATE to be crucified. Pilate found no reason to condemn Jesus; he tried to convince the people that it was absurd to regard Jesus as "king of the Jews," and offered to release him. But when the people insisted that Jesus be put to death, Pilate washed his hands to indicate that Jesus' fate was no longer his responsibility, and turned Jesus over to be crucified. Roman soldiers then placed a CROWN OF THORNS on the head of Jesus, and mocked him, saying, "Hail, King of the Jews." He was made to carry a wooden cross up the hill of CALVARY near JERUSALEM, where he was nailed to the cross and was placed between two thieves, who were also crucified. Shortly before his death, he said, "FATHER, FORGIVE THEM, FOR THEY KNOW NOT WHAT THEY DO." After his death, the followers of Jesus placed his body in a tomb.

  ❦ Jesus had told his DISCIPLES that he would sacrifice his life so that believers' sins might be forgiven. CHRISTIANS believe that his death on the cross and his RESURRECTION three days later make SALVATION

CRUCIFIXION

possible. ❦ Having a "cross to bear" means any painful responsibility that is forced upon one. ❦ To "wash one's hands of it" means to refuse to take responsibility for an action or event.

Damascus An ancient city in SYRIA (and still its capital today). The APOSTLE PAUL, then an official called Saul, was on his way from JERUSALEM to Damascus to arrest CHRISTIANS. He underwent a dramatic conversion on the road, in which he fell from his horse, saw a dazzling light, and "heard a voice saying unto him, 'Saul, Saul, why persecutest thou me? . . . I am JESUS, whom thou persecutest.'"

  ❦ The "road to Damascus" is an image for a sudden turning point in a person's life.

Daniel *See* DANIEL IN THE LIONS' DEN.

Daniel in the lions' den During the captivity of the JEWS in BABYLON, in the sixth century B.C., the

PROPHET Daniel continued to pray to his God against the express command of the king. As a result, Daniel was thrown into a lions' den to be devoured. But God sent an ANGEL to protect him, and he emerged miraculously unharmed the next day.

  🙢 Daniel's situation is an image for an impossibly hostile environment.

DAVID. *The hero, as Michelangelo envisioned him, moments before slaying Goliath.*

David A great king of the ISRAELITES in the OLD TESTAMENT. David was a shepherd in his boyhood. As a youth, he asked for King Saul's permission to fight Goliath, the giant PHILISTINE warrior whom all the other Israelites were afraid to face. Despite his small size, David managed to kill Goliath by hitting him in the forehead with a stone he flung from a sling. King Saul then gave David command of his army, but he grew jealous of him and tried to kill him; David spent many years fleeing from Saul. After Saul's death, David was made king of the Israelites and served nobly, despite occasional lapses, such as an affair with Bathsheba; he had Bathsheba's husband killed so that he could marry her. Many of the PSALMS are attributed to David, who was famed as a harpist. His descendants, the House of David, included SOLOMON and the subsequent kings of ISRAEL and JUDAH; according to the GOSPELS, JESUS was descended from David.

  🙢 A "David and Goliath" contest is an unequal one in which one side is far bigger or more numerous than the other.

Day of Atonement An annual day of fasting and prayer among the ISRAELITES, still kept by their descendants, the present-day JEWS. It occurs in autumn, and its observance is one of the requirements of the MOSAIC LAW. Jews call this day YOM KIPPUR.

dead bury their dead, Let the A reply of JESUS when a new DISCIPLE of his asked for time to bury his father. Jesus said, "Follow me, and let the dead bury their dead."

  🙢 The expression often connotes an impatience to move ahead, without pausing over details or ceremonies.

Delilah, Samson and (di-LEYE-luh) *See* SAMSON.

disciples The followers of JESUS, who adhered to his teaching and transmitted it to others. The Twelve APOSTLES were the disciples closest to Jesus.

  🙢 In general, a "disciple" is an active follower of a leader or movement, religious or otherwise.

Do unto others as you would have them do unto you A command based on words of JESUS in the SERMON ON THE MOUNT: "All things whatsoever ye would that men should do to you, do ye even so to them." The MOSAIC LAW contains a parallel commandment: "Whatever is hurtful to you, do not do to any other person."

  🙢 "Do unto others . . . " is a central ethical teaching of Jesus, often referred to as the GOLDEN RULE.

doubting Thomas *See* THOMAS, THE DOUBTING APOSTLE.

Dust thou art, and unto dust shalt thou return In the Book of GENESIS, words that God spoke to ADAM in casting him and EVE out of the Garden of EDEN. In saying this, God reminded Adam that he had been made from "the dust of the ground," and confirmed that Adam and Eve had brought death upon themselves by disobeying him and eating the FORBIDDEN FRUIT. (*See* FALL OF MAN.)

Ecclesiastes (i-klee-zee-AS-teez)   A book in the OLD TESTAMENT containing the reflections of a PHILOSOPHER known as "the Preacher." "Vanity of vanity saith the Preacher, . . . all is vanity," where the word "vanity" indicates that striving is in vain, because death comes to all, and "there is no new thing under the sun." He believes that our character and achievements do not affect our fate. "The race is not to the swift nor to the strong." He concludes that one should enjoy the good things found in life until death brings oblivion. The argument and tone of this book are very unlike those of the other books of the BIBLE. (*See* NOTHING NEW UNDER THE SUN, TIME TO BE BORN AND A TIME TO DIE, A, *and* VANITY OF VANITIES; ALL IS VANITY.)

Eden, Garden of   The beautiful garden containing the tree of life, where God intended ADAM AND EVE to live in peaceful and contented innocence, effortlessly reaping the fruits of the earth. The garden also contained the TREE OF KNOWLEDGE OF GOOD AND EVIL, from which Adam and Eve were forbidden to eat. When they disobeyed and ate the FORBIDDEN FRUIT, God drove them from the garden. Their sin and consequent loss of God's grace and of their PARADISE is known as the FALL OF MAN.

🙢 Figuratively, a "Garden of Eden" (sometimes simply "the Garden," or "Eden") is any state or place of complete peace and happiness.

Egypt   An ancient empire in AFRICA that was centered on the NILE RIVER. Ruled by a PHARAOH, Egypt figures prominently in many events in the BIBLE, including the stories of JOSEPH AND HIS BROTHERS, and of MOSES and the EXODUS. (*See under* "*World Geography.*")

Elijah (i-LEYE-juh)   A PROPHET of the OLD TESTAMENT, who opposed the worship of idols, and incurred the wrath of JEZEBEL, the queen of ISRAEL, who tried to kill him. He was taken up to HEAVEN in a chariot of fire.

Esau   *See* JACOB AND ESAU.

Esther   A book of the OLD TESTAMENT that tells the story of a beautiful Jewish woman named Esther who

is chosen by the king of Persia (now IRAN; *see* PERSIAN EMPIRE) to be his queen. Esther, with the aid of her cousin Mordecai, stops a plot to massacre the JEWS in Persia, and Mordecai becomes the king's chief minister.

🙢 This event is celebrated by Jews as the feast of Purim.

Eve   In the Book of GENESIS, the first woman. (*See* ADAM AND EVE *and* CREATION.)

Exodus   The second book of the OLD TESTAMENT; it tells of the departure of the ISRAELITES out of slavery in EGYPT, made possible by the ten PLAGUES OF EGYPT and the PARTING OF THE RED SEA. MOSES led them, and their destination was the PROMISED LAND. God guided them by sending a pillar of CLOUD by day and a pillar of fire by night, to show them the way they should go. God also fed them with MANNA and gave them water out of a solid rock. Because of their frequent complaining and failure to trust him, however, God made them stay in the desert for forty years before entering the Promised Land. God gave them the TEN COMMANDMENTS and the rest of the MOSAIC LAW on Mount SINAI during the Exodus. Exodus is a Greek word meaning "departure."

🙢 By extension, "manna from HEAVEN" is any unexpected and much-needed benefit.

eye for an eye, an   The principle of justice that requires punishment equal in kind to the offense (not greater than the offense, as was frequently given in ancient times). Thus, if someone puts out another's eye, one of the offender's eyes should be put out. The principle is stated in the Book of EXODUS as "Thou shalt give life for life, eye for eye, tooth for tooth, hand for hand, foot for foot."

🙢 JESUS referred to this principle in the SERMON ON THE MOUNT, calling on his followers to TURN THE OTHER CHEEK instead.

eye of a needle   Part of a saying of JESUS: "It is easier for a camel to go through the eye of a needle than for a rich man to enter into the kingdom of God."

faith, hope, and charity   The three great virtues that the NEW TESTAMENT calls for in CHRISTIANS. Charity is often called love. According to the APOSTLE PAUL, "Now abideth faith, hope, charity, these three; but the greatest of these is charity."

Fall of Man The disobedience of ADAM AND EVE and their consequent loss of God's grace and the peace and happiness of the Garden of EDEN. When they ate the FORBIDDEN FRUIT of the TREE OF KNOWLEDGE OF GOOD AND EVIL, God punished them by driving them out of the garden and into the world, where they would be subject to sickness, pain, and eventual death. God told Eve that she would give birth in sorrow and pain; Adam's curse was that he would have to work hard to earn his livelihood.

Father, forgive them, for they know not what they do A prayer that JESUS spoke on the cross, concerning those who put him to death. (*See* CRUCIFIXION.)

fatted calf, kill the A PHRASE referring to a specially fed calf that was killed for the feast to celebrate the return of the PRODIGAL SON.

   🏿 "Killing a fatted calf" means preparing for a celebration.

forbidden fruit The fruit of the TREE OF KNOWLEDGE OF GOOD AND EVIL in the Garden of EDEN, often pictured as an apple, which God forbade ADAM AND EVE to eat. Their disobedience brought on the FALL OF MAN.

   🏿 "Forbidden fruit" is used commonly to refer to anything that is tempting but potentially dangerous. It is often associated with sexuality.

Four Horsemen Four figures in the Book of REVELATION who symbolize the evils to come at the end of the world. The figure representing conquest rides a white horse; war, a red horse; famine, a black horse; and plague, a pale horse. They are often called the Four Horsemen of the APOCALYPSE.

fruits ye shall know them, By their A teaching of JESUS in the SERMON ON THE MOUNT; it suggests that we are able to distinguish between false and genuine PROPHETS by the things they do and say. In the same passage, Jesus calls false prophets WOLVES IN SHEEP'S CLOTHING.

Genesis The first book of the OLD TESTAMENT; its first words are "In the BEGINNING" (*genesis* is a Greek word for "beginning"). It covers the time from the beginning of the world through the days of the PATRIARCHS, including the stories of the CREATION, ADAM AND EVE, the FALL OF MAN, CAIN AND ABEL, NOAH AND THE FLOOD, God's COVENANT with Abra-

ham, ABRAHAM AND ISAAC, JACOB AND ESAU, and JOSEPH AND HIS BROTHERS.

   🏿 In general, a "genesis" is a beginning.

Gentile Someone who is not a JEW. "The nations" is the common expression in the OLD TESTAMENT for non-Jews as a group, and a Gentile is a person belonging to "the nations."

   🏿 Both the Old Testament and the NEW TESTAMENT tell of numerous conflicts between Jews and Gentiles. Figuratively, a "gentile" is any nonbeliever.

Get thee behind me, Satan The reply of JESUS when SATAN offered him all the kingdoms of the world if Jesus would worship him. Jesus spoke these words on another occasion. He told his DISCIPLES that he would have to be killed and then be raised from the dead, and PETER objected that this should not happen. Jesus saw Peter as a tempter, trying to talk him out of doing what he was put on EARTH to do. He then spoke the same words, "Get thee behind me, Satan," to Peter.

give than to receive, It is more blessed to A saying quoted by the APOSTLE PAUL as a teaching of JESUS. It is commonly quoted as, "It is better to give than to receive."

go the extra mile An adaptation of a commandment of JESUS in the SERMON ON THE MOUNT: "Whosoever shall compel thee to go a mile, go with him twain" (two).

gold, frankincense, and myrrh (MUR) The three gifts that the WISE MEN brought to the infant JESUS. Frankincense and myrrh are aromatic substances. Frankincense is commonly burned as incense and myrrh is used in burial of the dead.

golden calf An idol that the ISRAELITES made during the EXODUS. While God was giving MOSES the TEN COMMANDMENTS and other provisions of the MOSAIC LAW on MOUNT SINAI, the people whom Moses was leading to the PROMISED LAND melted down their gold jewelry and ornaments and built a golden calf, which they began to worship. Moses came down from the mountain carrying two stone tablets on which the Ten Commandments were written; when he saw the calf, he smashed the tablets and made the people destroy the idol.

   🏿 By extension, a "golden calf" is any false god or anything worshiped undeservedly.

Golden Rule   *See* DO UNTO OTHERS AS YOU WOULD HAVE THEM DO UNTO YOU.

Golgotha (GOL-guh-thuh, gol-GOTH-uh)   The ancient name for CALVARY.

Good Samaritan (suh-MAR-uh-tuhn)   In one of the PARABLES of JESUS, the only one of several passersby to come to the aid of a JEW who had been robbed, beaten, and left to die on the roadside. The kindness of the Samaritan was particularly admirable because Jews and Samaritans (i.e., people of Samaria) were generally enemies. Jesus told the parable of the Good Samaritan to answer a man who had asked him, "Who is my neighbor?" He forced his questioner to admit that the Samaritan was the true neighbor of the man who had been robbed.

🕭 Figuratively, "Good Samaritans" are persons who go out of their way to perform acts of kindness to others, especially strangers.

GOOD SHEPHERD. *A fifth-century mosaic depicting Christ as the Good Shepherd.*

Good Shepherd   A title of JESUS, based on a passage in the GOSPEL of JOHN, where he says, "I am the good shepherd: the good shepherd giveth his life for the sheep," and "I am the good shepherd, and know my sheep, and am known of mine." The METAPHOR of God as a shepherd is also found in the OLD TESTAMENT. The TWENTY-THIRD PSALM begins, "The Lord is my shepherd; I shall not want," and a passage in the Book of ISAIAH says that God "shall feed his flock like a shepherd: he shall gather the lambs with his arm."

🕭 The use of the title "PASTOR" (shepherd) for certain CHRISTIAN clergymen carries on the idea.

gospel   The "good news" of SALVATION (*see* GOSPELS). Certain styles of religious music are also called "gospel." (*See* SPIRITUALS.)

Gospels   The first four books of the NEW TESTAMENT, which tell the life story of JESUS and explain the significance of his message. *Gospel* means "good news" — in this case, the news of the SALVATION made possible by the death and RESURRECTION of Jesus. The four Gospels are attributed to MATTHEW, MARK, LUKE, and JOHN.

🕭 Figuratively, anything that is emphatically true is called the "gospel truth."

handwriting on the wall, the   A PHRASE recalling an OLD TESTAMENT story about DANIEL. While a king was holding the JEWS captive in the foreign land of BABYLON, in the sixth century B.C., a mysterious hand appeared, writing on the wall of the king's palace. The king called upon Daniel, who interpreted it to mean that God intended the king and his kingdom to fall. The king was slain that night.

🕭 Figuratively, the expression means that some misfortune is impending: "His firing came as no surprise; he had seen the handwriting on the wall for months before."

He that is not with me is against me   A teaching of JESUS, which suggests that indifference to his message is the same as active opposition to it.

heaven (or heavens)   The dwelling place of God, the ANGELS, and the souls of those who have gained SALVATION; a place of the greatest peace and beauty. (*Compare* HELL.)

🕭 The term *heaven* also refers to celestial powers or divine providence, and "heavens" to the sky or UNIVERSE. 🕭 *Heavenly* can also refer to something wonderfully perfect or extremely enjoyable.

Hebrew   The language of the HEBREWS, in which the OLD TESTAMENT was written. It is the language of the modern state of ISRAEL.

Hebrews   The descendants of ABRAHAM AND ISAAC, especially the descendants of Isaac's son JACOB; the ISRAELITES.

hell   The dwelling place of SATAN, DEVILS, and wicked souls condemned to eternal punishment after death; a place of pain and torment. (*Compare* HEAVEN.)

᠍᠊᠍ "Hell" can refer figuratively to painful or extremely tough situations. ᠍᠊᠍ Hell is usually pictured as an underworld filled with heat and fire. (*Compare* HADES.)

Holy Spirit In the belief of many CHRISTIANS, one of the three persons in the one God, along with the Father and the Son (JESUS is the Son); the Holy Spirit is also called the Holy Ghost. Jesus promised the APOSTLES that he would send the Holy Spirit after his CRUCIFIXION and RESURRECTION. The Spirit came to the DISCIPLES of Jesus on PENTECOST.

In the beginning *See* BEGINNING, IN THE.

Isaac The son of ABRAHAM and the father of JACOB AND ESAU.

᠍᠊᠍ Isaac was the son Abraham was prepared to sacrifice at God's request.

Isaiah (eye-ZAY-uh) A major ISRAELITE PROPHET who foretold the coming of the MESSIAH; the Book of Isaiah in the OLD TESTAMENT is attributed to him. In the NEW TESTAMENT, his prophecies are treated as predictions of many of the details of the life and death of JESUS. (*See* GOOD SHEPHERD.)

Israel The name given to JACOB after he wrestled with God. Israel is also the name of the northern kingdom of the ISRAELITES, when their nation was split in two after the death of King SOLOMON. (*See under* "World Geography.")

Israelites The descendants of JACOB, who made up twelve tribes, including the tribes of Judah, Levi, Reuben, and Benjamin.

Jacob and Esau (EE-saw) The sons of ISAAC, who was the son of ABRAHAM. As the eldest son of Isaac, Esau should have inherited the COVENANT with God that Abraham had passed on to Isaac. But Esau traded his birthright (inheritance) to his younger brother, Jacob, for a "mess of pottage" (a meal of stew) when he was too hungry to consider what he was throwing away. Jacob also cheated Esau out of their blind father's deathbed blessing by impersonating him, a deceit prompted by their mother, Rebecca. The feud between the brothers ended many years later in a joyful reconciliation. The night before his reunion with Esau, Jacob wrestled with God and forced God to bless him. God gave Jacob the new name of ISRAEL, meaning "one who has been strong against God." (*See* JACOB'S LADDER.)

᠍᠊᠍ By extension, to trade anything of great value for "a mess of pottage," as Esau did, is to make a bad bargain.

Jacob's ladder A ladder that Jacob saw in a dream. After he had obtained his brother Esau's birthright and received his father's blessing, he had a vision of the ANGELS of God ascending and descending a ladder that extended from earth to HEAVEN. God, who stood at the top of the ladder, promised to bless Jacob and his offspring and to bring his descendants into the PROMISED LAND. (*See* JACOB AND ESAU.)

Jehovah Another name for God; an approximation of the holiest name of God in HEBREW (the name was held so sacred that it was never written or spoken, and scholars are not sure exactly how it should be pronounced). It means "I am that I am," or "I am the one who is." In the incident of the BURNING BUSH in the Book of EXODUS, God, speaking out of the bush, tells MOSES that this is his name.

Jeremiah A major ISRAELITE PROPHET; also, a book of the OLD TESTAMENT that chronicles his life and records his angry lamentations about the wickedness of his people.

᠍᠊᠍ A "jeremiad" is any long lamentation or angry denunciation.

Jericho, Battle of (JER-i-koh) *See* JOSHUA.

Jerusalem A holy city for JEWS, CHRISTIANS, and MOSLEMS; the capital of the ancient kingdom of Judah, and of the modern state of ISRAEL. The name means "city of peace." Jerusalem is often called Zion; Mount ZION is the hill on which the fortress of the city was built.

᠍᠊᠍ Jerusalem and places nearby are the scenes of crucial events in the life of JESUS. (*See* BETHLEHEM and CALVARY.) ᠍᠊᠍ The "New Jerusalem" is mentioned in the Book of REVELATION as the heavenly city, to be established at the end of time.

Jesus A PROPHET of the first century of our era; to CHRISTIANS, Jesus Christ, the son of God, a person who was both God and man, the MESSIAH sent by

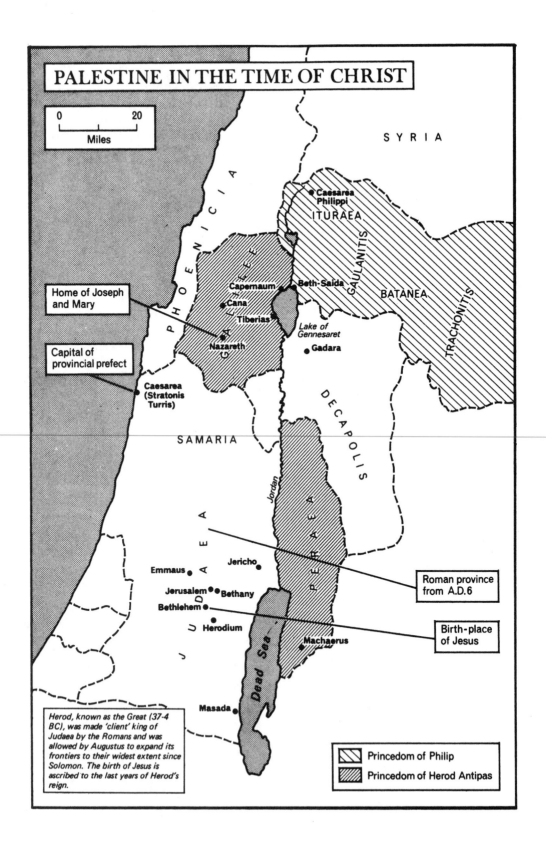

PALESTINE IN THE TIME OF CHRIST

0 — 20
Miles

SYRIA

● Caesarea
Philippi

ITURAEA

GAULANITIS

BATANEA

TRACHONITIS

PHOENICIA

GALILEE

● Capernaum

● Beth-Saida

Home of Joseph
and Mary

● Cana

Tiberias ●

● Nazareth

Lake of
Gennesaret

● Gadara

DECAPOLIS

Capital of
provincial prefect

Caesarea
(Stratonis
Turris) ●

SAMARIA

Jordan

PERAEA

J U D A E A

● Jericho

Emmaus ●

Jerusalem ●● Bethany

Bethlehem ●

● Herodium

● Machaerus

Roman province
from A.D. 6

Birth-place
of Jesus

Dead Sea

Masada ●

*Herod, known as the Great (37-4
BC), was made 'client' king of
Judaea by the Romans and was
allowed by Augustus to expand its
frontiers to their widest extent since
Solomon. The birth of Jesus is
ascribed to the last years of Herod's
reign.*

Princedom of Philip

Princedom of Herod Antipas

God to save the human race from the sin it inherited through the FALL OF MAN.

The story of the birth of Jesus in BETHLEHEM is called the NATIVITY. He was conceived by the Virgin Mary (*see* MARY, THE MOTHER OF JESUS) through the power of the HOLY SPIRIT of God, laid in a manger after his birth in Bethlehem, and raised by Mary and her husband, Joseph (*see* JOSEPH, THE HUSBAND OF MARY), in NAZARETH. As a boy of twelve, he went to the TEMPLE in JERUSALEM, where he astonished the teachers of the MOSAIC LAW with his knowledge. As a man, he chose twelve APOSTLES, with whom he traveled throughout his native PALESTINE teaching the word of God (*see* SERMON ON THE MOUNT), healing the sick, and performing miracles (*see* LOAVES AND FISHES). He attracted many followers, and also made many enemies for claiming to be the Messiah and for failing to observe all Jewish laws. He was eventually betrayed by JUDAS ISCARIOT, condemned by Pontius PILATE, and crucified by the Roman authorities who ruled his country. Christians believe that he rose again from the dead, and that his RESURRECTION makes SALVATION possible. Christians also expect a SECOND COMING of Jesus. (*See* CRUCIFIXION, GOSPEL, *and* GOSPELS.)

Jews The ISRAELITES, particularly after their return from captivity in BABYLON about five hundred years before the birth of JESUS; at that time, the Israelites were established as a religious group, founded on the MOSAIC LAW, not simply a national group.

⁊ When the Jewish nation was destroyed by the ROMANS in the year A.D. 70, and the Jews were scattered throughout the world, their religious beliefs and customs allowed them to remain one people.

Jezebel (JEZ-uh-bel) In the OLD TESTAMENT, an immoral, cruel queen of ISRAEL who attempted to kill ELIJAH and other PROPHETS of God.

⁊ A "jezebel" is a scheming and shamelessly evil woman.

Job (JOHB) In the OLD TESTAMENT, a man whose faith was severely tested by SATAN, with God's permission. Job was the most prosperous and happy of men, who faithfully praised God for God's goodness. In order to get him to curse God, Satan destroyed all that Job owned, killed his children, and struck Job himself with vile sores from head to foot. False friends of Job's suggested that he should abandon his

beliefs (*see* JOB'S COMFORTERS). But even in absolute misery, Job would not curse God, saying instead, "The Lord gave, and the Lord hath taken away: blessed be the name of the Lord." As a reward for his steadfast faith, God healed Job and "gave him twice as much as he had before."

⁊ Figuratively, any long-suffering person can be said to be "as patient as Job."

Job's comforters Three friends of JOB who visited him in his affliction, and offered him a way of making sense of his troubles: namely, that he was getting what he deserved. Job's friends maintained that misfortunes were sent by God as punishments for sin, and thus despite Job's apparent goodness, he must really be a terrible sinner. Job persistently disputed them, saying that God is supreme and mysterious — that God can send misfortunes to both good and wicked people, and may not be second-guessed.

⁊ A "Job's comforter" is someone who apparently offers consolation to another person but actually makes the other person feel worse.

John, the Gospel According to The last of the four GOSPELS in the NEW TESTAMENT; it is markedly different from the Gospels of MATTHEW, MARK, and LUKE. Many of the most famous events in the life of JESUS — including the SERMON ON THE MOUNT and the sharing of the bread and cup at the LAST SUPPER — are not mentioned in the Gospel of John, which concentrates instead on the deepest implications of Jesus' mission. John's Gospel opens, "In the BEGINNING was the Word."

John the Baptist A hermit and preacher among the JEWS of the time of JESUS, and a relative of Jesus. According to the GOSPELS, John declared, "I am the voice of one crying in the wilderness, 'Make straight the way of the Lord.'" CHRISTIANS interpret this to mean that John was sent to prepare for the coming of the MESSIAH. John was known as "the Baptist" because he called on his followers to go through a ceremony of BAPTISM to demonstrate their repentance for their sins; Jesus began his public life by submitting himself to John's baptism. John was eventually imprisoned by Herod, the ruler of the province of Galilee, for objecting to Herod's illicit marriage. At a banquet, Herod rashly promised his stepdaughter, SALOME, anything she asked; she asked for the

JOHN THE BAPTIST. *A painting entitled* Baptism of Christ, *by Andrea del Verrocchio.*

head of John on a platter. Herod, not wanting to go back on his promise, had John beheaded.

Jonah and the whale A story in the OLD TESTAMENT; Jonah was an ISRAELITE whom God had called to be a PROPHET, but who refused to accept his divine mission, and left on a sea voyage instead. God then raised a great storm as a sign of his anger with Jonah. The sailors, realizing that Jonah's disobedience had caused the storm, threw him overboard in an attempt to save their ship. Jonah was saved from drowning when he was swallowed by a "great fish." He lived for three days inside the creature, after which the fish "vomited out Jonah upon the dry land." Thankful that his life had been spared, Jonah took up his prophetic mission.

Jordan River A river in PALESTINE that empties into the DEAD SEA. JOHN THE BAPTIST baptized JESUS in the Jordan.

Joseph, the husband of Mary In CHRISTIAN belief, the foster father of JESUS, who was conceived by the power of the HOLY SPIRIT without a human father.

According to the GOSPELS, Joseph, the husband of MARY, was a carpenter; people occasionally called Jesus "the carpenter's son." Jesus apparently learned that trade at Joseph's side.

Joseph and his brothers The sons of JACOB. According to the Book of GENESIS, Joseph was Jacob's favorite son. To show his love for Joseph, Jacob gave him a COAT OF MANY COLORS, a splendid garment that aroused the jealousy of Joseph's brothers, who began to plot against him. The brothers sold Joseph into slavery in EGYPT, and pretended that he had been killed by a wild beast. Years later, PHARAOH, the Egyptian ruler, called on Joseph to interpret his troubling dreams. Pharaoh rewarded Joseph's skill in interpreting his dreams by making him second in command over the kingdom. Later, when the land of the HEBREWS was beset by famine, Jacob was forced to send Joseph's brothers into Egypt to buy grain. The official with whom they had to deal turned out to be Joseph himself. When he discovered that his brothers were truly sorry for their treachery, he forgave them.

Joshua In the OLD TESTAMENT, the leader who brought the ISRAELITES into the PROMISED LAND af-

JUDGMENT DAY. A woodcut by Albrecht Dürer.

ter the death of MOSES. Joshua is best known for his destruction of the city of Jericho. When Joshua was besieging the city, God instructed him to have his priests blow their TRUMPETS and all his troops give a great shout. At the sound of the shout, the walls of the city collapsed, and Joshua's troops rushed in. (*See* "JOSHUA FIT THE BATTLE OF JERICHO.")

Judas Iscariot (JOOH-duhs i-SKAR-ee-uht)   The DISCIPLE who betrayed JESUS to the authorities for THIRTY PIECES OF SILVER. When soldiers came to arrest Jesus, Judas identified their victim by kissing him. The next day, driven by guilt, Judas hanged himself.

❧ Figuratively, a "Judas" is a betrayer, especially one who betrays a friend. ❧ A "Judas kiss" is an act of seeming friendship that conceals some treachery.

Judge not, that ye be not judged   A command of JESUS to his followers in the SERMON ON THE MOUNT.

❧ The teaching implies that since all people are sinners, no one is worthy to condemn another.

Judgment Day   In the NEW TESTAMENT, the day at the end of time. According to the GOSPELS and the Book of REVELATION, on this day the earth and the sky will be in an uproar, the dead will rise from their graves, and JESUS will return to judge all the living and the dead. In judging their conduct, he will consider the deeds people do to each other, both good and bad, as if they had been done to him. (*See* SECOND COMING.)

Lamb of God   A CHRISTIAN term for JESUS, first used by JOHN THE BAPTIST. It carries out the image of the CRUCIFIXION and RESURRECTION of Jesus as a new PASSOVER: a lamb was killed for the Jewish Passover, and Jesus himself, in the sacrifice of his death and Resurrection, is the lamb for the new Passover.

lamb shall lie down with the lion   A misquotation. (*See* WOLF SHALL ALSO DWELL WITH THE LAMB, THE.)

land flowing with milk and honey   In the OLD TESTAMENT, a poetic name for the PROMISED LAND.

❧ Figuratively, a "land of milk and honey" is any place of great abundance.

last shall be first, The   A saying of JESUS; in the GOSPEL of MATTHEW, Jesus declares that in the world to come, "The last shall be first and the first last."

❧ The teaching implies that those who have prospered through wickedness will fail, while the good who have suffered for the sake of God will win SALVATION.

Last Supper, the   The traditional PASSOVER meal that JESUS ate with the APOSTLES the night before his

THE LAST SUPPER. Leonardo da Vinci's famous fresco, in the refectory of Santa Maria delle Grazie in Milan.

death. At this supper, according to the GOSPELS, Jesus blessed bread and broke it, telling the DISCIPLES, "Take, eat; this is my body." He then passed a cup of wine to them, saying, "This is my blood." Jesus' words refer to the CRUCIFIXION he was about to suffer in order to atone for mankind's sins. He told the apostles, "This do in remembrance of me."

☙ The actions of Jesus at the Last Supper are the basis for the CHRISTIAN sacrament of Holy COMMUNION, or the EUCHARIST, in which the faithful partake of bread and wine. ☙ The Last Supper is the subject of a famous FRESCO by LEONARDO DA VINCI, which depicts Jesus Christ and his apostles seated along one side of a long table.

Lazarus (LAZ-uhr-uhs)   A man brought back to life by JESUS after being in the tomb for four days. The incident is recorded in the GOSPEL OF JOHN. The raising of Lazarus is considered the crowning miracle or sign revealing Jesus as the giver of life. It also is the act that caused the enemies of Jesus to begin the plan to put Jesus to death. (*See* CRUCIFIXION.)

☙ Someone who makes a comeback from obscurity is sometimes called a "Lazarus rising from the dead."

Let him who is without sin cast the first stone   According to the GOSPEL OF JOHN, the PHARISEES, in an attempt to discredit JESUS, brought a woman charged with ADULTERY before him. Then they reminded Jesus that adultery was punishable by stoning under MOSAIC LAW, and challenged him to judge the woman so that they might then accuse him of disobeying the law. Jesus thought for a moment and then replied, "He that is without sin among you, let him cast the first stone at her." The crowd around him were so touched by their own consciences that they departed. When Jesus found himself alone with the woman, he asked her who were her accusers. She replied, "No man, lord." Jesus then said, "Neither do I condemn thee: go and sin no more."

letter killeth, but the spirit giveth life, The   A statement made in the NEW TESTAMENT by the APOSTLE PAUL.

☙ The general sense is that strict observance of the letter of the law is far less important than being true to its spirit.

Let there be light   The words with which, according to the Book of GENESIS, God called light into being on the first day of CREATION. (*See* BEGINNING, IN THE.)

Leviathan (luh-VEYE-uh-thuhn)   A sea monster mentioned in the Book of JOB, where it is associated with the forces of chaos and evil.

☙ Figuratively, a "leviathan" is any enormous beast. ☙ *Leviathan* is a work on politics by the seventeenth-century English author Thomas HOBBES.

lilies of the field, Consider the   Words of JESUS in the SERMON ON THE MOUNT, encouraging his followers not to worry about their worldly needs: "Why take ye thought for raiment [clothing]? Consider the lilies of the field, how they grow; they toil not, neither do they spin. And yet I say unto you that even SOLOMON in all his glory was not arrayed like one of these."

loaves and fishes   A miracle that JESUS performed; the GOSPELS record several instances of this miracle, with small differences in details. In the best known, Jesus was preaching to a crowd of thousands who grew hungry and needed to be fed, but only five loaves and two fishes could be found. He blessed the food, and then commanded his DISCIPLES to distribute it among the people. After everyone had eaten and was satisfied, twelve baskets of food remained.

Lord's Prayer   The prayer JESUS taught his followers in the SERMON ON THE MOUNT: "Our Father, which art in HEAVEN, hallowed be thy name; thy kingdom come; thy will be done, in earth as it is in heaven. Give us this day our daily bread. And forgive us our debts as we forgive our debtors. And lead us not into temptation, but deliver us from evil." Some versions of the Bible add words of praise at the end: "For thine is the kingdom, and the power, and the glory, forever. Amen."

☙ The same prayer, with slight variations, is still taught and recited in almost all CHRISTIAN CHURCHES.

Lot's wife   In the Book of GENESIS, a disobedient woman whom God punished. God sent ANGELS to destroy the cities of SODOM AND GOMORRAH for their wickedness, but chose to spare Lot and his family. The angels commanded them to flee without turning back to look at the destruction; Lot's wife did look back, and was immediately changed into a pillar of salt.

Love thy neighbor as thyself   A version of the GOLDEN RULE: Do unto others as you would have them do unto you. First found in the OLD TESTA-

MENT. JESUS tells the PARABLE of the GOOD SAMAR-
ITAN to illustrate this commandment.

Love your enemies A commandment of JESUS in
the SERMON ON THE MOUNT. The entire passage
reads: "Ye have heard that it hath been said, 'Thou
shalt love thy neighbor, and hate thine enemy.' But I
say unto you, love your enemies, bless them that
curse you, do good to them that hate you, and pray
for them which despitefully use you, and persecute
you; that ye may be the children of your Father
which is in HEAVEN: for he maketh his sun to rise on
the evil and on the good, and sendeth rain on the just
and on the unjust."

Lucifer Another name for SATAN.

Luke, the Gospel According to In the NEW TES-
TAMENT, one of the four GOSPELS that record the life
of JESUS. Luke's Gospel contains far more material
on the birth and early life of Jesus than any of the
other three, and is usually read at CHRISTMAS.

Magi (MAY-jeye) The sages who visited JESUS soon
after his birth. (*See* WISE MEN.)

mammon A NEW TESTAMENT expression for ma-
terial wealth, which some people worship as a god.
Figuratively, it simply means money. (*See* YE CANNOT
SERVE GOD AND MAMMON.)

manna from heaven Food that God gave miraculously to the ISRAELITES in the EXODUS, after the
food they had brought with them out of EGYPT had
run out. In the Book of Exodus, the Israelites found
it one morning after the dew had evaporated: "Upon
the face of the wilderness there lay a small round
thing, as small as the hoar frost on the ground."
 ❧ By extension, "manna from heaven" is any unexpected good fortune.

Man shall not live by bread alone According to
LUKE, JESUS spent forty days in the wilderness, where
he was tempted by SATAN. One of Satan's challenges
was, "If you are the Son of God, command this stone
to become bread." Jesus answered, "It is written,
'Man shall not live by bread alone,'" referring to the
words in the OLD TESTAMENT Book of Deuteronomy: "Man doth not live by bread only, but by every
word that proceedeth out of the mouth of the Lord."
 ❧ The expression is frequently used to point out
that worldy goods are not enough for most people;
they need spiritual fulfillment as well.

MARY. The Assumption, *a painting by Titian.*

Many are called but few are chosen One of the
sayings of JESUS, suggesting that SALVATION is difficult to attain.

Mark, the Gospel According to In the NEW TES-
TAMENT, one of the four GOSPELS that record the life
of JESUS. The shortest of the four, it is generally considered to be the earliest Gospel.

Mary, the mother of Jesus CHRISTIANS refer to the
mother of JESUS as the Virgin Mary, since, according
to the NEW TESTAMENT, Jesus was miraculously conceived while she was a virgin. Mary is revered for her
humility and motherly love. She is honored by all

Christians, but particularly by ROMAN CATHOLICS, who believe strongly in her mercy and her power to intercede with God. The Roman Catholic Church also teaches the doctrine of Mary's IMMACULATE CONCEPTION. (*See* NATIVITY.)

Mary Magdalene (MAG-duh-luhn, MAG-duh-leen) In the GOSPELS, a woman from whom DEVILS had been driven; she became a follower of JESUS.

Matthew, the Gospel According to In the NEW TESTAMENT, one of the four GOSPELS that record the life of JESUS. It stresses the ways in which Jesus fulfills prophecies of the OLD TESTAMENT. The SERMON ON THE MOUNT is found in Matthew's Gospel.

meek shall inherit the earth, The A saying adapted from the BEATITUDES from the SERMON ON THE MOUNT.
   🕭 The saying implies that those who forgo worldly power will be rewarded in the kingdom of HEAVEN.

Messiah (muh-SEYE-uh) For JEWS and CHRISTIANS, the promised "anointed one" or CHRIST; the Savior. Christians believe that JESUS was the Messiah who delivered mankind from its sins. Jews believe that the Messiah has not yet come.

Methuselah (muh-THOOH-zuh-luh) The oldest man mentioned in the BIBLE; according to the Book of GENESIS, he was the grandfather of NOAH, and lived to be 969 years old.
   🕭 Figuratively, a "Methuselah" is an extremely old person.

millennium A period of a thousand years foretold in the Book of REVELATION. During the millennium, those who have been faithful to JESUS and who have not worshiped the ANTICHRIST will reign with Jesus over the earth. According to the Book of Revelation, the millennium will precede the final battle for control of the universe; JUDGMENT DAY will come afterward.
   🕭 The meaning of the BIBLE's words about the millennium has been much debated by CHRISTIANS. Prophecies about the millennium are part of the basic doctrine of several denominations, including the JEHOVAH'S WITNESSES. 🕭 Figuratively, a "millennium" is a period of great justice and happiness on earth.

Mosaic law The law that, according to the OLD TESTAMENT, God gave to the ISRAELITES through MOSES. The Mosaic law begins with the TEN COMMANDMENTS, and includes the many rules of religious observance given in the first five books of the Old Testament. In JUDAISM, these books are called the TORAH, or "the Law."

MOSES. *Moses receiving the tablets inscribed with the Ten Commandments.*

Moses The great leader, lawgiver, and PROPHET of the ancient ISRAELITES (HEBREWS). According to the OLD TESTAMENT, Moses was born in EGYPT, where the Hebrews were living as slaves. When Moses was an infant, the Egyptian ruler, PHARAOH, ordered all the male children of the Hebrews slain. Moses' mother placed him in a small boat made of bulrushes, and hid him in a marsh, where he was found by the daughter of Pharaoh, who adopted him.
   When Moses was a grown man, he killed an Egyptian who was beating a Hebrew, and had to flee Egypt to escape punishment. One day, while Moses was living in exile, God spoke to him from a BURNING BUSH, commanding him to return to Egypt and bring the Hebrews out of bondage. Moses went back to Egypt and told Pharaoh of God's command; when Pharaoh refused to release the Hebrews from slavery, God sent the PLAGUES OF EGYPT to afflict the Egyptians. Pharaoh finally relented, and Moses led his

people out of Egypt across the RED SEA, on the journey that became known as the EXODUS. Shortly afterward, Moses received the TEN COMMANDMENTS from God on MOUNT SINAI. Moses and his people wandered in the wilderness for forty years; then, just as they came within sight of the PROMISED LAND, Moses died.

My God, my God, why hast thou forsaken me? Words beginning the Twenty-second PSALM. According to the GOSPELS, JESUS spoke these words during the CRUCIFIXION, after he had suffered on the cross for three hours.

NATIVITY. *A detail from Van der Goes's Portinari altarpiece.*

Naomi *See* RUTH.

Nativity The birth of JESUS, described in two of the GOSPELS (MATTHEW and LUKE). When Jesus' parents, MARY and JOSEPH, traveled from NAZARETH to BETHLEHEM to be counted in a government census, they found that there was no room for them in the local inn. Mary gave birth to Jesus in a common stable and laid him in a manger (a feeding trough for livestock). CHRISTIANS believe that Jesus' birth fulfilled many OLD TESTAMENT prophecies and was attended by miraculous events, such as a star above Bethlehem that drew local shepherds as well as the WISE MEN, or MAGI, from a distant land.

🔊 The Nativity is celebrated at CHRISTMAS. We date our present historical era from the birth of Jesus, referring to the years before his birth as B.C. (before CHRIST) and the years after his birth as A.D. (anno Domini, a LATIN PHRASE meaning "in the year of the Lord").

Nazareth The hometown of JESUS, MARY, and JOSEPH.

🔊 Jesus is often called Jesus of Nazareth or the Nazarene; the inscription above his head on the cross read "Jesus of Nazareth, the King of the JEWS."

New Testament The second part of the CHRISTIAN BIBLE. Christians believe that it records a "new COVENANT," or "new testament," that fulfills and completes God's "old covenant" with the HEBREWS, described in the OLD TESTAMENT.

No man can serve two masters A saying of JESUS. The complete passage reads, "No man can serve two masters: for either he will hate the one, and love the other, or else he will hold to the one, and despise the other." (*See also* YE CANNOT SERVE GOD AND MAMMON.)

Noah and the Flood The account in the Book of GENESIS of how, several generations after the life of ADAM, the wickedness of people made God regret that he had created them, and made him resolve to send a flood that would destroy all the living crea-

NOAH AND THE FLOOD. *Noah, his family, and pairs of animals leaving the Ark after the flood.*

tures in the world. God decided to spare Noah and his family, who lived virtuously, and to allow them to repopulate the earth. God commanded Noah to build an ark (a large, rudderless ship), and to take his wife, three sons, and three daughters-in-law into it, along with a pair of each of the earth's animals. When Noah had done so, God sent forty days and forty nights of rain, until the entire globe was flooded, and all living creatures were drowned. When the rain ended, Noah released a dove from the ark. When it returned with an OLIVE BRANCH in its beak, Noah knew that the waters had receded, and that he and his family could begin a new life. After the ark came to rest on Mount ARARAT, and Noah and the other people and animals left it, God set a rainbow in the HEAVENS as a sign that he would never again destroy the world by flood.

nothing new under the sun   A PHRASE adapted from the Book of ECCLESIASTES; the author complains frequently in the book about the monotony of life. The entire passage reads, "The thing that hath been, it is that which shall be; and that which is done is that which shall be done: and there is no new thing under the sun."

Old Testament   The first part of the BIBLE, so called by CHRISTIANS, who believe that its laws and prophecies are fulfilled in the person of JESUS, whose mission is described in the NEW TESTAMENT.

olive branch   The branch brought by a dove to NOAH's ark signifying that the Flood was receding.

‣ An olive branch is now regarded as a sign of peace, as is the dove. (See HAWKS AND DOVES.)

original sin   The eating of the FORBIDDEN FRUIT by ADAM AND EVE in the Garden of EDEN, which led to their expulsion from Eden by God. In CHRISTIAN THEOLOGY, the act by which all humans fell from divine GRACE.

parables   In the NEW TESTAMENT, the stories told by JESUS to convey his religious message; they include the parable of the GOOD SAMARITAN and that of the PRODIGAL SON.

parting of the Red Sea   See RED SEA, PARTING OF THE.

Passover   The deliverance of the ISRAELITES from the worst of the PLAGUES OF EGYPT, and the annual festival kept afterward in memory of the event.

Through MOSES, God told the Israelites to prepare a special meal to be eaten in haste the evening before their escape from Egypt (see EXODUS), with a whole roasted lamb as the main dish. The blood from the lamb was to be used to mark the Israelites' houses. That night, God would send the ANGEL of Death to kill the firstborn males of the Egyptians (this was the worst of the plagues of Egypt), but God would see the blood on the Israelites' houses, and he would command his angel to "pass over" — to kill no one there. God told Moses that the Israelites were to repeat the meal each spring on the anniversary of their departure from Egypt. The JEWS keep the festival of Passover to this day.

‣ The LAST SUPPER of JESUS and his APOSTLES was a Passover meal. The CRUCIFIXION and RESURRECTION of Jesus were explained by the apostles as the new Passover of the NEW TESTAMENT.

patience of Job   See JOB.

patriarchs   In the OLD TESTAMENT, the "founding fathers" of the ISRAELITES: ABRAHAM AND ISAAC, JACOB, and the sons of Jacob. (See JOSEPH AND HIS BROTHERS.)

Paul   Ancient CHRISTIAN preacher and teacher; along with the APOSTLE PETER, one of the foremost leaders of the early CHRISTIAN CHURCH. Paul, originally called Saul, was at first an enemy and persecutor of the early Christians. As he rode to DAMASCUS one day, seeking to suppress the Christians there, a strong light from HEAVEN blinded him, and God spoke to him; after this experience, Saul became a Christian. Going by the Greek name Paul, he spent the rest of his life bringing the GOSPEL to the peoples of the ancient world. The NEW TESTAMENT includes his many epistles (letters) to the early Christian communities.

pearl of great price   A PHRASE from one of the PARABLES of JESUS; he compares the journey to HEAVEN to a search for fine pearls conducted by a merchant, "who, when he had found one pearl of great price, went and sold all that he had, and bought it."

‣ The expression has come to mean anything that is very valuable. For example, Hester Prynne, in *THE SCARLET LETTER*, who gave birth to a daughter following an act of ADULTERY that destroyed her honor, named the child Pearl, because she had given up all that she had in bearing the child.

pearls before swine, Cast not   An adaptation of a saying of JESUS in the SERMON ON THE MOUNT. The entire passage reads, "Give not that which is holy unto the dogs, neither cast ye your pearls before swine, lest they trample them under their feet, and turn again and rend you."

⁊ The meaning of the passage is disputed, but seems generally to be that the followers of Jesus should pass his message on to those most likely to accept it. ⁊ Generally, to "cast pearls before swine" is to share something of value with those who will not appreciate it.

Pentecost   In the NEW TESTAMENT, the day that the HOLY SPIRIT descended upon the DISCIPLES of JESUS. Pentecost is the Greek name for Shavuot, the spring harvest festival of the ISRAELITES, which was going on when the Holy Spirit came. The disciples were together in JERUSALEM after Jesus' RESURRECTION and return to HEAVEN, fearful because he had left them. On that morning, however, "there appeared unto them cloven tongues like as of fire, and it sat upon each of them. And they were all filled with the Holy Ghost, and began to speak with other tongues, as the Spirit gave them utterance." Because of the festival, crowds of visitors were in Jerusalem, speaking many languages, but the disciples of Jesus moved among them and spoke to them all, and "every man heard them speak in his own language" about "the wonderful works of God." PETER then made a powerful speech to the crowds in the city, and many were baptized as new followers of Jesus.

Peter   Chief among the twelve APOSTLES of JESUS, he was a fisherman, originally named Simon (and often called Simon Peter). JESUS gave him the name Rock, of which "Peter" is a translation. Peter showed great faith, but also exhibited great failings (*see* GET THEE BEHIND ME, SATAN). In the frightening hours before the CRUCIFIXION, Peter three times denied being a follower of Jesus, just as Jesus had predicted he would. Nevertheless, Peter went on to become the leader of the early CHRISTIANS (*see* PENTECOST), thus fulfilling another prophecy of Jesus, who had said of Peter, "Upon this rock I will build my CHURCH. . . . And I will give unto thee the keys of the kingdom of HEAVEN."

⁊ Peter is often depicted holding keys. ROMAN CATHOLICS maintain a number of traditions about Peter: that he was the first of the POPES, for example,

PETER. *A detail from Perugino's fresco* Christ Delivering the Keys of the Kingdom to Saint Peter. *Found in the Sistine Chapel, Vatican City.*

and that he was martyred at ROME by being crucified upside down, since he refused to be crucified as Jesus had been. ⁊ The great church of the VATICAN, SAINT PETER'S BASILICA, was later built on what was believed to be the site of his burial.

pharaoh (FAIR-oh, FAY-roh)   The title of the kings of ancient EGYPT. In the story of JOSEPH AND HIS BROTHERS, a pharaoh puts Joseph in charge of his entire kingdom. In the Book of EXODUS, a pharaoh repeatedly refuses the request of MOSES to let the Israelites leave the country, and does not give in until after the worst of the ten PLAGUES OF EGYPT.

Pharisees (FAR-uh-seez)   A group of teachers among the JEWS at the time of JESUS; he frequently rebukes them in the GOSPELS for their hypocrisy. Jesus says they are like "the blind leading the blind," or like "whited sepulchers, which indeed appear beautiful outward, but are within full of dead men's bones, and of all uncleanness."

Philistines (FIL-uh-steenz, fi-LIS-tinz, fi-LIS-teenz) In the OLD TESTAMENT, enemies of the ISRAELITES in their settlement in the PROMISED LAND. (*See* DAVID *and* SAMSON.)

  🙿 PALESTINE, the region today split between the nations of ISRAEL, JORDAN, and EGYPT, is named after the Philistines. 🙿 A "philistine" has come to mean a person who is ignorant and uncultured.

Physician, heal thyself   A biblical PROVERB meaning that people should take care of their own defects and not just correct the faults of others. According to the GOSPELS of LUKE and MATTHEW, JESUS said he expected to hear this proverb from the people of his hometown of NAZARETH, because they would want him to work miracles there, as he had in other towns nearby. But he "did not do many mighty works there, because of their unbelief." On the same occasion, Jesus said, "A PROPHET IS NOT WITHOUT HONOR, SAVE IN HIS OWN COUNTRY."

Pilate, Pontius (PON-shus PEYE-luht)   The governor of the JEWS at the time of the CRUCIFIXION of JESUS; he was an official of the ROMAN EMPIRE, to which the Jewish nation belonged at that time. According to the GOSPELS, Pilate did not consider Jesus guilty, and wanted to release him. Under pressure from the crowds in JERUSALEM, however, Pilate sentenced Jesus to death on the cross, having first washed his hands to indicate his lack of responsibility for Jesus' fate.

plagues of Egypt   The traditional name for the set of disasters that God inflicted on EGYPT before the PHARAOH let MOSES lead the ISRAELITES out of Egypt to the PROMISED LAND. The plagues, as recorded in the Book of EXODUS, included swarms of locusts, hordes of frogs, and a scourge of boils. After the tenth and most horrible plague, in which the ANGEL of Death killed every Egyptian firstborn male child, including Pharaoh's son, Pharaoh finally freed the Israelites. (*See* PASSOVER.)

Pontius Pilate   *See* PILATE, PONTIUS.

Prodigal Son   A CHARACTER in a PARABLE JESUS told to illustrate how generous God is in forgiving sinners who repent. The Prodigal Son was a young man who asked his father for his inheritance and then left home for "a far country, and there wasted his substance with riotous living." As his money ran out, a famine occurred, and he went to work tending pigs, but even then he could not get enough to eat. He returned home, knowing that he had given up his right to be treated as his father's son, but hoping that his father would accept him as a hired servant on the farm. Seeing the Prodigal Son coming from a distance, the father rejoiced and ordered the FATTED CALF to be slaughtered for a feast to celebrate the son's return.

The Prodigal Son's elder brother returned from the fields while the feast was going on, and was angry. He complained that he had never been treated to such a feast, though he had remained and worked diligently for his father while the Prodigal Son was away. The father reassured him, saying that the elder son would still get his inheritance, but it was right to celebrate the return of the Prodigal Son: "For this thy brother was dead, and is alive again; and was lost, and is found."

Promised Land   The land that God promised he would give to the descendants of ABRAHAM AND ISAAC and JACOB; the LAND FLOWING WITH MILK AND HONEY; the land of Canaan, or PALESTINE. The ISRAELITES did not take it over until after the EXODUS, when they conquered the people already living there.

  🙿 By extension, an idyllic place or state of being that a person hopes to reach, especially one that cannot be reached except by patience and determination, is called a "Promised Land."

prophet   Someone who brings a message from God to people. The best-known prophets are those of the OLD TESTAMENT. Their most frequent THEMES were true worship of God, upright living, and the coming of the MESSIAH; they often met with bitter resistance when they spoke against the idol worship and immorality of their people. Among the prophets of the Old Testament were DANIEL, ELIJAH, ISAIAH, JEREMIAH, JONAH, and MOSES.

Prophets also appear in the NEW TESTAMENT. JESUS called JOHN THE BAPTIST a prophet; CHRISTIANS consider him a bridge between the prophets of the Old Testament and those of the New Testament. Jesus mentions "true prophets" and "false prophets" — those who present the true message of God, and those who present a counterfeit (*see* FRUITS YE SHALL KNOW THEM, BY THEIR *and* WOLVES IN SHEEP'S

CLOTHING). He himself was considered a prophet in his lifetime (see PROPHET IS NOT WITHOUT HONOR, SAVE IN HIS OWN COUNTRY, A), and is still widely revered by non-Christians as a prophet, though not as the Messiah. The New Testament also mentions that some of the early Christians were prophets who spoke inspired messages to their communities.

🙠 In general usage, a "prophet" is someone who can foretell the future. The prophets of the BIBLE often made predictions, which confirmed their authority when the predictions came true, but changing the lives of their people was a more central part of their mission.

prophet is not without honor, save in his own country, A   Words spoken by JESUS to the people of NAZARETH, the town where he grew up. They refused to believe in his teaching because they considered him one of themselves and therefore without authority to preach to them.

🙠 The expression is now used of anyone whose talents and accomplishments are highly regarded by everyone except those at home.

Psalms, Book of   An OLD TESTAMENT book containing 150 prayerful songs and songs of praise, many of them ascribed to DAVID. (See TWENTY-THIRD PSALM.)

Queen of Sheba   See SHEBA, QUEEN OF.

Rachel   The second wife of JACOB (see JACOB AND ESAU). She was sterile for many years, but eventually had two sons: JOSEPH (see JOSEPH AND HIS BROTHERS) and Benjamin.

Red Sea, parting of the   An action of God at the time of the EXODUS that rescued the ISRAELITES from the pursuing forces of EGYPT. According to the Book of Exodus, God divided the waters so that they could walk across the dry seabed. Once they were safely across, God closed the passage and drowned the Egyptians. Most scholars agree that the "Red Sea" spoken of in this account is not the deep-water RED SEA of today, but the marshy Sea of Reeds farther north, and that the opening and closing of the seabed took place through violent storms, as mentioned in the Book of Exodus.

Render unto Caesar the things which are Caesar's, and unto God the things that are God's   The response of JESUS when his enemies tried to trap him by asking whether it was right for the JEWS, whose nation had been taken over by the ROMAN EMPIRE, to pay tribute to the Roman emperor. He took a Roman coin that would be used to pay the tribute, and asked whose picture was on it; his questioners answered, "Caesar's." The reply of Jesus implied that in using Roman coins, the Jews accepted the rule of the Romans, and so the Roman government had the right to tax them, as long as the Jews were not compromising their religious duties. Jesus' more general point was, "Give to worldly authorities the things that belong to them, and to God what belongs to God."

Resurrection   The rising of JESUS from the tomb after his death; a central and distinctive belief of the CHRISTIAN faith. The GOSPELS state that after JESUS was crucified and lay in a tomb between Friday evening and Sunday morning, he rose, in body as well as in spirit, and appeared alive to his followers. His resurrection is the basis for the Christian belief that not only Jesus but all Christians will triumph over death. Christians celebrate the Resurrection on EASTER Sunday.

Revelation, Book of   The last book of the NEW TESTAMENT, also called the APOCALYPSE. In this book, traditionally attributed to the APOSTLE JOHN, the violent end of the world is foretold, and the truth of the last days is disclosed, or "revealed." It describes ARMAGEDDON, the SECOND COMING of JESUS, JUDGMENT DAY, and "a new HEAVEN and a new earth" that will be revealed at the end of time.

Ruth   The great-grandmother of King DAVID, known for her kindness and faithfulness. Not an ISRAELITE herself, she married an Israelite who had come to her country with his family. Ruth's husband died, and her mother-in-law, NAOMI, set out to return to the country of the Israelites. Ruth insisted on accompanying Naomi, saying, "WHITHER THOU GOEST, I WILL GO; and where thou lodgest, I will lodge." In the country of the Israelites, Ruth married Boaz, a rich relative of her dead husband; Boaz had been attracted to Ruth by her generosity. Her story is told in the Book of Ruth in the OLD TESTAMENT.

Sabbath   The holy day of rest and reflection observed each Saturday among the JEWS. This custom fulfills the third of the TEN COMMANDMENTS ("Remember the Sabbath day, to keep it holy"). The Sabbath commemorates the last of the seven days of CREATION as described in the Book of GENESIS, the day God rested from his labors of creating the HEAVENS and the earth.

🔊 CHRISTIANS have traditionally kept Sunday as a weekly day of rest in adaptation of the Jewish observance, and in commemoration of the RESURRECTION OF JESUS. Some denominations, such as the SEVENTH-DAY ADVENTISTS, observe Saturday as the Sabbath.

Salome (suh-LOH-mee, SAL-uh-may)   According to nonbiblical historians, the stepdaughter of Herod, the ruler of Galilee, who arranged for the beheading of JOHN THE BAPTIST. Her name is not given in the GOSPELS.

salt of the earth, Ye are the   Words of JESUS to his DISCIPLES in the SERMON ON THE MOUNT. He continues, "If the salt have lost his savor, wherewith shall it be salted?" Jesus implies that if his followers lose their dedication to the GOSPEL, no one else can give it to them.

🔊 In popular usage, "salt of the earth" means a person of admirable character.

salvation   Being "saved" among CHRISTIANS; salvation is freedom from the effects of the FALL OF MAN. This freedom comes through faith in JESUS, who is called in the NEW TESTAMENT "the author of eternal salvation unto all them that obey him." The APOSTLES taught that those who experience salvation in their lifetime on earth and continue in their friendship with God will inherit eternal happiness in HEAVEN.

Samson   In the OLD TESTAMENT, an ISRAELITE servant of God who pitted his invincible strength and his wits against the PHILISTINES on many occasions. He was eventually betrayed by his lover, the beautiful Delilah, who tricked Samson into telling her that the secret of his strength lay in his uncut hair. Delilah cut Samson's hair while he slept, and then called for the Philistines, who captured and blinded him. During his captivity, Samson's hair grew back, and he eventually pulled the Philistines' banquet hall down on their heads.

Satan   The DEVIL. In the BIBLE, Satan is identified with the tempter who encourages the fall of ADAM AND EVE; he is the accuser who torments JOB in the hope that he will curse God; the one who offers JESUS all the kingdoms of the world if Jesus will worship him (see GET THEE BEHIND ME, SATAN); and the evil one who puts betrayal in the heart of JUDAS. Satan will one day be confined in HELL, but until then he is free to roam the earth.

🔊 Satan is the power of darkness opposed to the light of CHRIST; he is thus sometimes referred to as the Prince of Darkness. 🔊 Satan has been depicted in many ways: as a man with horns, goat hooves, a pointed tail, a pointed beard, and a pitchfork; as a dragon; and sometimes as an ANGEL with large bat-like wings.

Second Coming   The return of JESUS, prophesied in the NEW TESTAMENT, to judge the living and the dead and bring about the final triumph of good over evil. The writings of the APOSTLES in the NEW TESTAMENT express the belief that the Second Coming will happen soon, and suggest that it may happen within a generation of their own time. (See JUDGMENT DAY.)

🔊 Several CHRISTIAN denominations, such as the SEVENTH-DAY ADVENTISTS and the JEHOVAH'S WITNESSES, are founded on a similar belief about the nearness of Jesus' return.

Sermon on the Mount   In the GOSPEL of MATTHEW, the first sermon of JESUS. It is a central expression of his teachings regarding the new age he has come to proclaim. Jesus tells his followers that he expects them to be even more generous than the MOSAIC LAW requires: "Be ye perfect," he says, "even as your Father which is in HEAVEN is perfect."

The Sermon on the Mount begins with the BEATITUDES. It also contains the LORD'S PRAYER; the GOLDEN RULE ("Whatsoever ye would that men should do to you, do ye even so to them"); the commandments to TURN THE OTHER CHEEK, GO THE EXTRA MILE, and CAST NOT PEARLS BEFORE SWINE; the image of false PROPHETS as WOLVES IN SHEEP'S CLOTHING; and many other well-known teachings, including: "Ye are the SALT OF THE EARTH," "LOVE YOUR ENEMIES," "NO MAN CAN SERVE TWO MASTERS," "YE CANNOT SERVE GOD AND MAMMON," "CONSIDER THE LILIES OF THE FIELD," "JUDGE NOT, THAT YE BE NOT JUDGED," "ASK, AND IT SHALL BE GIVEN YOU," and "By their FRUITS YE SHALL KNOW THEM."

serpent   The creature in the Book of GENESIS that tempts EVE to eat the FORBIDDEN FRUIT, thus committing the first act of the FALL OF MAN. In the NEW TESTAMENT, the serpent of Genesis is identified with SATAN.

Sheba, queen of (SHEE-buh)   A queen in biblical times who was famous for her beauty, splendor, and wealth. She traveled from afar to visit King SOLO-MON.

shibboleth (SHIB-uh-luhth, SHIB-uh-leth)   In the OLD TESTAMENT, *shibboleth* was a password used by the ISRAELITES. It was chosen because their enemies could not pronounce it.

   By extension, a "shibboleth" is an often-re-peated slogan. It also means an arbitrary test to prove membership in a group.

Sinai, Mount (SEYE-neye)   In the Book of EXODUS, the mountain that MOSES ascended to receive the tablets of the law (the TEN COMMANDMENTS) from God. God shrouded the mountain in a CLOUD, and made THUNDER, LIGHTNING, and TRUMPET blasts come forth from it. The ISRAELITES were commanded to stay away from it while Moses went into God's presence.

Sodom and Gomorrah (SOD-uhm; guh-MAWR-uh)   In the Book of GENESIS, the two evil cities that God destroyed with a rain of fire and brimstone (sulfur). Before the destruction, God sent two ANGELS in the form of men to advise all good men to leave the evil towns. God's messengers found only one good man, Lot, whom they transported from Sodom to the countryside with his wife and daughters, warning them not to look back. When LOT'S WIFE, not heed-ing the warning, looked back, she became a pillar of salt.

   SODOMY was supposedly practiced in the wicked city of Sodom.

Solomon   In the OLD TESTAMENT, a HEBREW king, son and successor of DAVID. The "wisdom of Solo-mon" is proverbial. Solomon is also known for his many wives, for his splendor and wealth, and for building the TEMPLE at JERUSALEM.

Song of Solomon   A collection of poems or frag-ments about sexual love and courtship, attributed to SOLOMON. In CHRISTIANITY, these poems have been interpreted as ALLEGORIES of God's love for ISRAEL, the love of JESUS for his people, and so on.

Song of Songs   Another name for the SONG OF SOL-OMON.

Temple   The central place of worship for the ISRA-ELITES. The first Temple was built in JERUSALEM by King SOLOMON. The stone tablets received by Moses on MOUNT SINAI — tablets on which the TEN COM-MANDMENTS were written — were kept in the central chamber of Solomon's Temple. Solomon's Temple was later destroyed, as were two succeeding temples built on the site.

   A wall remaining from the temples, known as the Western Wall of the WAILING WALL, is one of the most sacred places for JEWS today.

Ten Commandments   The commandments en-graved on stone tablets and given to MOSES by God on MOUNT SINAI. These commandments are the heart of the divine law in the OLD TESTAMENT: I. I am the Lord thy God; thou shalt have no other gods before me. II. Thou shalt not take the name of the Lord thy God in vain. III. Remember the SABBATH day, to keep it holy. IV. Honor thy father and thy mother. V. Thou shalt not kill. VI. Thou shalt not commit ADULTERY. VII. Thou shalt not steal. VIII. Thou shalt not bear false witness against thy neigh-bor. IX. Thou shalt not covet thy neighbor's house. X. Thou shalt not covet thy neighbor's wife, nor his manservant, nor his maidservant, nor his ox, nor his ass, nor anything that is thy neighbor's.

thirty pieces of silver   The money JUDAS ISCARIOT received for betraying JESUS to the authorities. He later threw the money into the TEMPLE of JERUSA-LEM, and the chief PRIESTS bought the "potter's field" with it, to be used as a cemetery for foreigners.

   This money is referred to as "blood money" — money received for the life of another human being.

   "Thirty pieces of silver" is also used proverbially to refer to anything paid or given for a treacherous act.

Thomas, the doubting apostle   An APOSTLE who first doubted the RESURRECTION of JESUS and then believed. He was not present when Jesus appeared alive to his DISCIPLES the evening after his Resurrec-tion. Thomas rejected their story, and insisted that he would not believe until he had seen Jesus with his own eyes and touched Jesus' wounds with his own hands. A week later, Jesus appeared again when Thomas was with the group; he invited Thomas to touch his wounds and believe. Thomas then confessed his faith, saying, "My Lord and my God." Jesus replied, "Thomas, because thou hast seen me, thou hast believed: blessed are they that have not seen, and yet have believed."

🙰 A "doubting Thomas" is someone who demands evidence to be convinced of anything, especially when this demand is out of place.

through a glass darkly To see "through a glass" — a mirror — "darkly" is to have an obscure or imperfect vision of reality. The expression comes from the writings of the APOSTLE PAUL; he explains that we do not now see clearly, but at the end of time, we will do so.

time to be born and a time to die, A A PHRASE from the OLD TESTAMENT Book of ECCLESIASTES. The passage begins, "To everything there is a season, and a time to every purpose under HEAVEN" — that is, there is a right moment for all actions.

tithe A tenth part of one's annual INCOME contributed to support the clergy or a CHURCH. The MOSAIC LAW required the ISRAELITES to pay a tithe for the support of worship.

tree of knowledge of good and evil A tree in the Garden of EDEN, the fruit of which God forbade ADAM AND EVE to eat.

🙰 They did eat the FORBIDDEN FRUIT, and their disobedience was the first event of the FALL OF MAN.

Turn the other cheek An adaptation of a command of JESUS in the SERMON ON THE MOUNT: "Ye have heard that it hath been said, 'An EYE FOR AN EYE, AND A TOOTH FOR A TOOTH'; but I say unto you, that ye resist not evil: but whosoever shall smite thee on thy right cheek, turn to him the other also."

🙰 To "turn the other cheek" is thus to accept injuries and not to seek revenge.

Twenty-third Psalm The best known of the PSALMS of the OLD TESTAMENT, often read at funerals as a profession of faith in God's protection:

The Lord is my shepherd; I shall not want.
He maketh me to lie down in green pastures;
He leadeth me beside the still waters.
He restoreth my soul;
He leadeth me in the paths of righteousness for his
    name's sake.
Yea, though I walk through the valley of the shadow
    of death,
I will fear no evil;

For thou art with me;
Thy rod and thy staff, they comfort me.
Thou preparest a table for me in the presence of
    mine enemies;
Thou anointest my head with oil; my cup runneth
    over.
Surely goodness and mercy shall follow me all the
    days of my life:
And I will dwell in the house of the Lord for ever.

valley of the shadow of death An expression from the TWENTY-THIRD PSALM ("The Lord is my shepherd").

🙰 Figuratively, the "valley of the shadow of death" stands for the perils of life, from which God protects believers.

Vanity of vanities; all is vanity A statement at the beginning of the Book of ECCLESIASTES in the OLD TESTAMENT. The pointlessness of human activity is the major theme of the book. The author, however, like JOB, insists that God's laws must be kept, whether keeping them results in happiness or sorrow.

voice of one crying in the wilderness, The A PHRASE used in the GOSPELS to refer to JOHN THE BAPTIST. It is quoted from the Book of ISAIAH; the full text reads: "The voice of one crying in the wilderness: Prepare ye the way of the Lord, Make his paths straight." The quotation is used to imply that John was preparing the way for JESUS, as foretold by the prophecy of Isaiah.

walking on water A miraculous act performed by JESUS, according to the GOSPELS. They record that Jesus walked on the Sea of Galilee to rejoin his DISCIPLES, who had departed ahead of him in a ship. When he reached the ship, the winds that had been blowing stopped, and the disciples worshiped him as the true son of God.

🙰 Figuratively, to "walk on water" is to perform an impossible or godlike task: "When I told him the project had to be done by Tuesday, he made me feel as though I were asking him to walk on water."

Whither thou goest, I will go Words of RUTH; part of a longer promise of fidelity, spoken by Ruth to NAOMI, her mother-in-law. The longer text reads: "Entreat me not to leave thee, or to return from following after thee: for whither thou goest, I will go; and where thou lodgest, I will lodge: thy people shall be my people, and thy God my God: Where thou diest, will I die, and there will I be buried: the Lord do so to me, and more also, if aught but death part thee and me."

Wise Men GENTILE sages who visited JESUS, MARY, and JOSEPH in BETHLEHEM shortly after the birth of Jesus. According to the GOSPEL of MATTHEW, they were guided by a star, and brought gifts of GOLD, FRANKINCENSE, AND MYRRH. Because three gifts were given, the traditional story is that there were three wise men. (*See* MAGI.)

wolf shall also dwell with the lamb, The From ISAIAH; this saying is part of a description of an earthly PARADISE that will follow the restoration of ISRAEL after its destruction in a series of wars. The full text reads: "The wolf shall also dwell with the lamb, and the leopard shall lie down with the kid; and the calf and the young lion and the fatling together; and a little child shall lead them." The reference to a "little child" is sometimes thought to be a prophecy of JESUS' birth.

wolves in sheep's clothing An image for false PROPHETS, adapted from words of JESUS in the SERMON ON THE MOUNT: "Beware of false prophets, which come to you in sheep's clothing, but inwardly they are ravening wolves."

Ye cannot serve God and mammon A teaching of JESUS, meaning that his followers cannot love God and money ("mammon") at the same time.

Zion, Mount The mountain in JERUSALEM on which the fortress of the city was built.

Mythology and Folklore

r. Gradgrind in *Hard Times*, by Charles DICKENS, thought that the chief staple of education should be facts, facts, facts. We take a different view. Although we think facts are important (see the scientific sections of this dictionary), we also think educated people must know myths, myths, myths. It isn't clear whether the myth of George WASHINGTON AND THE CHERRY TREE belongs in a course on history or one on mythology, but from the standpoint of literacy it doesn't matter. For purposes of communication and solidarity in a CULTURE, myths are just as important as history. And unless history achieves the vividness and memorableness of myth, it will not be very useful to shared culture. We should indeed try to discriminate between history and myth; but true or false, the stories that we share provide us with our values, goals, and traditions. The tales we tell our children define what kind of people we shall be.

The term *myth* itself implies community. In Greek, it means "what they say." The origins of most myths are lost in obscurity; they belong to the community. The myths that are shared by literate Americans are worldwide in their origins, and embrace both ancient and modern cultures. The Greek myth of PARIS and the APPLE OF DISCORD belongs to us as much as the myth of Washington and the cherry tree. According to some modern philosophers, notably NIETZSCHE, all stories, even scientific THEORIES and religious teachings, are myths. Nietzsche's view is probably wrong, but it usefully emphasizes the importance of shared myths in forming our national community and providing us with irreplaceable common points of reference. If we did not inherit myths, we would have to invent them; since we *have* inherited them, we should learn to use those we have inherited. Our traditional myths are no more true and false, wise and foolish, than those of other cultures. They are not inherently better than those of CHINA or INDIA. But being ours, they are uniquely valuable to *us*.

— E. D. H.

Achilles (uh-KIL-eez) In CLASSICAL MYTHOLOGY, the greatest warrior on the Greek side in the TROJAN WAR. When he was an infant, his mother tried to make him immortal by bathing him in a magical river, but the heel by which she held him remained vulnerable. During the Trojan War, he quarreled with the commander, AGAMEMNON, and in anger sulked in his tent. Eventually Achilles emerged to fight, and killed the Trojan hero HECTOR, but he was wounded in the heel by an arrow and died shortly thereafter.

> People speak of an "Achilles' heel" as the one weak or sore point in a person's character. > The ACHILLES TENDON runs from the heel to the calf. > Achilles is the hero of HOMER'S *ILIAD*. > The PHRASE "wrath of Achilles" refers to the hero's anger,

ACHILLES. *Achilles wounded by an arrow in his heel, the only vulnerable part of his body.*

which caused so much destruction that Homer refers to it as his main THEME in the first line of the *Iliad*.

Adonis In CLASSICAL MYTHOLOGY, an extremely beautiful boy who was loved by APHRODITE, the goddess of love.

   By extension, an "Adonis" is any handsome young man.

Aeneas (i-NEE-uhs) A famous warrior of CLASSICAL MYTHOLOGY; a leader in the TROJAN WAR on the Trojan side. After the fall of TROY, Aeneas fled with his father and son, and was shipwrecked at CARTHAGE in northern AFRICA. There DIDO, the queen of Carthage, fell in love with him, and ultimately committed suicide when she realized that Aeneas could not stay with her forever. After many trials, Aeneas arrived in what is now ITALY. The ancient Romans believed that they were descended from the followers of Aeneas.

   Aeneas is the hero of the *AENEID* of VIRGIL.   Because he carried his elderly father out of the ruined Troy on his back, Aeneas represents filial devotion and duty.   The doomed love of Aeneas and Dido has been a source for artistic creation since ancient times.

Agamemnon (ag-uh-MEM-non) In CLASSICAL MYTHOLOGY, the king who led the Greeks against TROY in the TROJAN WAR. To obtain favorable winds for the Greek fleet sailing to Troy, Agamemnon sacrificed his daughter IPHIGENIA to the goddess ARTEMIS, and so came under a curse. After he returned home victorious, he was murdered by his wife, Clytemnestra, and her lover, Aegisthus.

Amazons In CLASSICAL MYTHOLOGY, a nation of warrior women. The Amazons burned or cut off their right breasts so that they could use a bow and arrow more efficiently in war.

   Figuratively, an "Amazon" is a large, strong, aggressive woman.   The AMAZON RIVER of SOUTH AMERICA was so named because tribes of women warriors were believed to live along its banks.

ambrosia (am-BROH-zhuh) The food of the gods in CLASSICAL MYTHOLOGY. Those who ate it became immortal.

   Particularly delicious food is sometimes called "ambrosia."

Antigone (an-TIG-uh-nee) In CLASSICAL MYTHOLOGY, a daughter of King OEDIPUS. Her two brothers killed each other in single combat over the kingship of their city. Although burial or cremation of the dead was a religious obligation among the Greeks, the king forbade the burial of one of the brothers, for he was considered a traitor. Antigone, torn between her religious and legal obligations, disobeyed the king's order, and buried her brother. She was then condemned to death for her crime.

   The Greek playwright SOPHOCLES tells her story in *ANTIGONE*, a play that deals with the conflict between human laws and the laws of the gods.

Aphrodite (af-ruh-DEYE-tee) [Roman name VENUS] The Greek and Roman goddess of love and beauty; the mother of EROS and AENEAS. In what may have

APHRODITE. *Aphrodite Victorious.*

been the first beauty contest, PARIS awarded her the prize (the APPLE OF DISCORD), choosing her over HERA and ATHENA as the most beautiful goddess (*see* JUDGMENT OF PARIS). She was thought to have been born out of the foam of the sea, and is thus often pictured rising from the water, notably in *THE BIRTH OF VENUS,* by BOTTICELLI.

Apollo   The Greek and Roman god of poetry, prophecy, medicine, and light. Apollo represents all aspects of civilization and order. He was worshiped at the DELPHIC ORACLE, where a priestess gave forth his predictions. ZEUS was his father, and ARTEMIS was his sister. He is sometimes identified with Hyperion, the TITAN he succeeded.

🜚 As a representative of controlled and ordered nature, Apollo is often contrasted with DIONYSUS, the god who represents wild, creative energies.

🜚 The SUN was sometimes described as Apollo's chariot, riding across the sky.

apple of discord   In CLASSICAL MYTHOLOGY, an apple of gold thrown into a banquet of the gods and goddesses by the goddess Discord, who had not been invited. The apple had "For the Fairest" written on it. When three goddesses claimed it, the choice among them was referred to the handsome PARIS, prince of TROY. (*See* JUDGMENT OF PARIS.)

Ares (AIR-eez) [Roman name MARS]   The Greek and Roman god of war, brutal and bloodthirsty. He was the son of ZEUS and HERA, and the father of the AMAZONS.

Argonauts (AHR-guh-nawts)   In CLASSICAL MYTHOLOGY, the companions of JASON in the quest for the GOLDEN FLEECE. Their ship was the *Argo.*

🜚 *Naut* means "sailor" in Greek, and is the root of our word *nautical.* Today, the word is used to coin such terms as *astronaut* and *aquanaut.*

Argus   A creature in CLASSICAL MYTHOLOGY who had a hundred eyes. HERA set him to watch over Io, a girl who had been seduced by ZEUS and then turned into a cow; with Argus on guard, Zeus could not come to rescue Io, for only some of Argus' eyes would be closed in sleep at any one time. HERMES, working on Zeus' behalf, played music that put all the eyes to sleep, and then killed Argus. Hera put his eyes in the tail of the peacock.

🜚 *Argus* was once a fairly common name for newspapers, suggesting that the paper was constantly on the alert.

Artemis (AHR-tuh-mis)   The Greek name for DIANA, the virgin goddess of the hunt and the MOON; the daughter of ZEUS and the sister of APOLLO. Artemis was also called Cynthia.

Arthur, King   A legendary king in ENGLAND in the MIDDLE AGES. The life of King Arthur has been retold many times over the centuries; hence, most of the incidents in his life have several versions. According to one well-known story of Arthur's gaining the throne, he withdrew the sword EXCALIBUR from a stone after many others had tried and failed. Arthur established a brilliant court at CAMELOT, where he gathered around him the greatest and most chivalrous warriors in EUROPE, the KNIGHTS of the ROUND TABLE. King Arthur's knights included Sir LANCELOT,

KING ARTHUR. *A woodcut depicting King Arthur and the wizard Merlin paddling toward the sword Excalibur.*

Sir GALAHAD, Sir Percival, and Sir GAWAIN. Other CHARACTERS associated with the legends of Arthur are the wizard MERLIN, the enchantress Morgan le Fay, Queen GUINEVERE, and Arthur's enemy and kinsman, Modred, who caused his downfall. According to some legends, Arthur sailed to a mysterious island, Avalon, at the end of his life; some stories say that someday he will return. The legends of Arthur may have originated with an actual chieftain named Arthur who lived in WALES in the sixth century, but the many retellings have taken the story far away from its original place and time. Because of the belief that he will return, he is sometimes called "the once and future king."

astrology A study of the positions and relationships of the SUN, MOON, STARS, and PLANETS in order to judge their influence on human actions. Astrology, unlike ASTRONOMY, is not a scientific study and has been much criticized by scientists. (*See* ZODIAC.)

Athena (uh-THEE-nuh) [Roman name MINERVA] The Greek and Roman goddess of wisdom. She had an unusual birth, springing fully grown out of the forehead of her father, ZEUS. Athena was one of the goddesses angered by the JUDGMENT OF PARIS, a Trojan, and she therefore helped the Greeks in the ensuing TROJAN WAR. Eventually, she became the protector of ODYSSEUS on his journey home.

📎 Athena was the guardian of the city of ATHENS, which was named in her honor.

Atlantis A kingdom in CLASSICAL MYTHOLOGY. According to legend, it was once an island in the ATLANTIC OCEAN, was swallowed up in an EARTHQUAKE, and is now covered by the sea.

Atlas In CLASSICAL MYTHOLOGY, a TITAN famous for his strength. After the defeat of the Titans by ZEUS, Atlas was condemned to support the EARTH and sky on his shoulders for eternity.

📎 Since the sixteenth century, pictures of Atlas and his burden have been used as decorations on maps. Accordingly, the word *atlas* is used for a book of maps. (He is usually pictured holding up the earth rather than the sky.)

Augean stables (aw-JEE-uhn) Stables that figured in the Greek myth of the Labors of HERCULES. The stables, which belonged to King Augeas, housed a large herd of cattle, and had not been cleaned for years. Hercules was ordered to clean out these filthy stalls. He did so by diverting the course of two rivers so that they flowed through the stables.

📎 By extension, to "clean the Augean stables" is to clean up a large amount of physical filth or moral corruption, or to accomplish any large, distasteful, and arduous job.

Bacchus (BAK-uhs) The Greek and Roman god of wine and revelry. He is also known by the Greek name DIONYSUS.

📎 In painting, Bacchus is often depicted eating a bunch of grapes and surrounded by SATYRS. 📎 The followers of Bacchus were called bacchants. After overindulging in wine, they danced wildly and tore animals, and sometimes people, to pieces. 📎 A "bacchanalian" party or feast is marked by unrestrained drunkenness. The name recalls a Roman festival called Bacchanalia, held in honor of Bacchus, and marked by drunken orgies.

"Beauty and the Beast" A French fairy tale about a beautiful and gentle young woman who is taken to live with a man-beast in return for a good deed the Beast did for her father. Beauty is kind to the well-mannered Beast, but pines for her family until the Beast allows her to visit them. Once home, Beauty delays her return until she hears that the Beast is dying without her. She returns to the Beast and brings him back to health. When she agrees to marry him, the evil spell upon him is broken and he becomes a handsome prince. Beauty and her prince live happily ever after.

Blarney Stone A stone in the wall of Blarney Castle in IRELAND. According to an Irish legend, those who kiss the Blarney Stone receive a gift of eloquence that enables them to obtain, through persuasion, anything they want.

   🍂 People who talk "blarney" are saying things they do not mean. Usually the expression *blarney* is applied to flattery designed to gain a favor.

"Bluebeard" A fairy tale CHARACTER from the Charles Perrault collection. The title character is a monstrous villain who marries seven women in turn, and warns them not to look behind a certain door of his castle. Inside the room are the corpses of his former wives. Bluebeard kills six wives for their disobedience before one passes his test.

"Boy Who Cried 'Wolf,' The" One of AESOP's FABLES. A young shepherd would trick his fellow villagers by shouting for help, pretending that wolves were attacking his sheep. Several times the villagers rushed to his aid, only to find the shepherd laughing at them. One day, some wolves actually came. The shepherd cried for help, but the villagers, who had grown tired of his pranks, ignored him, and the wolves devoured his sheep.

   🍂 To "cry wolf" means to issue a false alarm.

Brünnhilde (broohn-HIL-duh) A character in NORSE MYTHOLOGY, also known by the name Brynhild. Brünnhilde, a Valkyrie, or woman servant of ODIN, loved the hero Siegfried. After she found out that he had deceived her, she had him killed and committed suicide.

Bunyan, Paul A legendary giant lumberjack of the north woods of the United States and CANADA. He was accompanied by a blue ox named Babe. The stories about him resemble traditional tall tales. One example is the story that the ten thousand lakes of MINNESOTA originated when Paul and Babe's footprints filled with water.

Camelot In the legends of King ARTHUR, the capital of his kingdom; truth, goodness, and beauty reigned in Camelot.

   🍂 The administration of President John F. KENNEDY is often idealized as an American Camelot.

carpet, magic A flying carpet that takes people anywhere they wish to go. It figures in many Asian folktales, notably in the stories of the ARABIAN NIGHTS.

Cassandra (kuh-SAN-druh) In CLASSICAL MYTHOLOGY, a prophetess in Troy during the TROJAN WAR whose predictions, although true, were never believed by those around her. APOLLO had given her the gift of prophecy, but made it worthless after she refused his amorous advances. The Greeks captured Cassandra after their victory and sacrilegiously removed her from the TEMPLE of ATHENA. As a result, Athena helped cause shipwrecks and enormous loss of life to the Greeks on their return home.

   🍂 A "Cassandra" is someone who constantly predicts bad news.

CENTAUR. *A Greek statue of a centaur.*

centaurs Creatures in CLASSICAL MYTHOLOGY who were half-human and half-horse.

Cerberus (SUR-buh-ruhs) In CLASSICAL MYTHOLOGY, the three-headed dog who guarded the entrance to HADES.

Ceres (SEER-eez) The Roman name for DEMETER, the Greek and Roman goddess of agriculture.

Charon (KAIR-uhn) In CLASSICAL MYTHOLOGY, the boatman who carried the souls of the dead across the river STYX and into HADES, the underworld.

chimera (keye-MEER-uh, ki-MEER-uh) A monster in CLASSICAL MYTHOLOGY who had the head of a lion, the body of a goat, and the tail of a dragon or serpent.

❖ Figuratively, a "chimera" is a creation of the imagination, especially a wild creation. ❖ Something "chimerical" is fictional or illusory.

"Cinderella" A fairy tale from the collection of Charles Perrault. Cinderella, a young girl, is forced by her stepmother and stepsisters to do heavy housework, and relaxes by sitting among the cinders by the fireplace. One evening, when the prince of the kingdom is holding a ball, Cinderella's fairy godmother visits her, magically dresses her for the ball, turns a pumpkin into a magnificent carriage for her, warns her not to stay past midnight, and sends her off. Cinderella captivates the prince at the ball, but leaves just as midnight is striking, and in her haste drops a slipper; as the story is usually told in English, the slipper is made of glass. She returns home with her fine clothes turned back into rags, and her carriage a pumpkin again. The prince searches throughout the kingdom for the owner of the slipper. Cinderella is the only one whom it fits, and the prince marries her.

❖ The name Cinderella is sometimes applied to a person or group that undergoes a sudden transformation, such as an athletic team that loses frequently and then starts to win steadily.

Circe (SUR-see) In CLASSICAL MYTHOLOGY, a powerful sorceress who turned people into swine. On their way home from TROY, the crew of ODYSSEUS fell prey to her spells.

classical mythology The mythology of the Greeks and Romans, considered together. A vast part of Roman mythology, such as the system of gods, was borrowed from the Greeks.

Cupid The Roman name of EROS, the god of love. In the story of Cupid and PSYCHE, he is described as a magnificently handsome young man. In many stories, he is called the son of VENUS.

❖ In art, Cupid is often depicted as a chubby, winged infant who shoots arrows at people to make them fall in love. He is also sometimes shown as blind or blindfolded.

Cyclops (SEYE-klops) *plur.* CYCLOPES (seye-KLOH-peez) One-eyed giants in CLASSICAL MYTHOLOGY. One Cyclops imprisoned ODYSSEUS and his men during their voyage back to GREECE after the TROJAN WAR. Odysseus managed to trick the Cyclops and put out his eye. Odysseus and his men were then able to escape.

Daedalus (DED-l-uhs) In CLASSICAL MYTHOLOGY, an ingenious inventor, designer of the LABYRINTH, and one of the few to escape from it. He was the father of ICARUS.

❖ Daedalus is a symbol of inventiveness and craftsmanship.

Damocles, sword of (DAM-uh-kleez) An object that figures in a legend about an actual Greek nobleman, Damocles. According to the story, Damocles frequently expressed his awe at the power and apparent happiness of his king. The king, tired of such flattery, held a banquet, and seated Damocles under a sword that was suspended from the ceiling by a single hair — thus demonstrating that kingship brought with it fears and worries as well as pleasures.

❖ Figuratively, a "sword of Damocles" is an impending danger that causes ANXIETY.

Damon and Pythias (DAY-muhn; PITH-ee-uhs) In a Greek legend, two friends who were enormously loyal to each other. When the tyrannical ruler of their city condemned Pythias to death, Pythias pleaded for time to go home and put his affairs in order. Damon agreed to stay and die in place of Pythias if Pythias did not return by the time of the execution. Pythias was delayed, and Damon prepared to be executed. Pythias arrived just in time to save Damon. The ruler was so impressed by their friendship that he let them both live.

❖ Damon and Pythias symbolize devotion between friends.

Delphic oracle The most famous oracle in GREECE, and the location of a TEMPLE of APOLLO; it was also known as the oracle of Delphi. At the oracle, a priestess went into a trance, supposedly breathed vapors from a cleft in the rocks, and delivered messages from Apollo to persons who sought her advice. These messages were often difficult to interpret.

   🙥 "Delphic utterance" is speech that is obscure or ambiguous.

Demeter (di-MEE-tuhr) [Roman name CERES] The Greek and Roman goddess of grain, agriculture, and the harvest. The story of Demeter and her daughter, Persephone, explains the cycle of the seasons. When Persephone was carried off to the underworld by HADES, Demeter was so forlorn that she did not tend the crops, and the first winter came to the earth. Eventually ZEUS allowed Persephone to rejoin her mother for two-thirds of every year, and thus the cycle of the seasons began.

Diana The Roman name of ARTEMIS, the goddess of the hunt and the MOON.

Dido (DEYE-doh) In Roman MYTHOLOGY, the founder and queen of CARTHAGE in north AFRICA. She committed suicide in grief over the departure of her lover, the hero AENEAS.

   🙥 Dido is an image of the unhappy or unrequited lover.

Dionysus (deye-uh-NEYE-suhs, deye-uh-NEE-suhs) The Greek name for BACCHUS, the Greek and Roman god of wine and revelry.

Donald Duck A loud mouthed cartoon character created by Walt DISNEY. (*See also* MICKEY MOUSE.)

Electra In CLASSICAL MYTHOLOGY, a daughter of AGAMEMNON. To avenge his death, she helped her brother, ORESTES, kill their mother and her lover.

   🙥 The "Electra complex" in psychology involves a girl's or woman's unconscious sexual feelings for her father.

Elysian Fields (i-LIZH-uhn) In CLASSICAL MYTHOLOGY, the place where souls of the good went after death: a peaceful and beautiful region, full of meadows, groves, sunlight, and fresh air.

   🙥 Figuratively, "Elysian Fields" are a place of supreme happiness and bliss. 🙥 The French translation is "CHAMPS-ÉLYSÉES," the name of the most famous boulevard in PARIS, FRANCE.

"Emperor's New Clothes, The" A story by Hans Christian ANDERSEN. An emperor hires two tailors who promise to make him a set of remarkable new clothes that will be invisible to anyone who is either incompetent or stupid. When the emperor goes to see his new clothes, he sees nothing at all — for the tailors are swindlers, and there aren't any clothes. Afraid of being judged incompetent or stupid, he pretends to be delighted with the new clothes, and "wears" them in a grand parade through the town. Everyone else also pretends to see them, until a child yells out, "He hasn't got any clothes on!"

   🙥 People who point out the emptiness of the pretensions of powerful people and institutions are often compared to the child who says that the emperor has no clothes.

Eros (ER-os, EER-os) [Roman name CUPID] A Greek and Roman god of love, often called the son of APHRODITE. He is better known under his Roman name.

   🙥 The word *erotic* comes from the Greek word *eros*, which is the term for sexual love itself, as well as the god's name.

Excalibur (eks-KAL-uh-buhr) The sword of King ARTHUR. In one version of the legends of Arthur, he proved his right to rule by pulling Excalibur out of a stone. In another version, he received Excalibur from a maiden, the Lady of the Lake, to whom he returned it at the end of his life.

fauns The Roman name for SATYRS, mythical creatures who were part man and part goat.

Fountain of Youth A fountain mentioned in folktales as capable of making people young again.

   🙥 The Spanish explorer Juan PONCE DE LEÓN discovered FLORIDA while searching for the Fountain of Youth.

"Fox and the Grapes, The" One of AESOP'S FABLES. A fox tries many times to pluck some grapes that dangle invitingly over his head, but he cannot reach them. As he slinks away in disgust, he says, "Those grapes are probably sour anyway."

   🙥 "Sour grapes" refers to things that people decide are not worth having only after they find they cannot have them.

Furies In CLASSICAL MYTHOLOGY, hideous female monsters who relentlessly pursued evildoers.

Galahad, Sir   A young KNIGHT in the tales of King ARTHUR. Galahad's exceptional purity and virtue enabled him to see the Holy GRAIL in all its splendor, while many other knights who sought it could not see it at all.

Gawain, Sir (GAH-win, guh-WAYN, GAH-wayn)   In the legends of King ARTHUR, one of the KNIGHTS of the ROUND TABLE. Gawain was a kinsman of Arthur, and was known for his integrity and decency.

*SAINT GEORGE AND THE DRAGON.
A painting by Carlo Crivelli.*

George, Saint, and the Dragon   A legendary incident concerning a real SAINT of the CHRISTIAN CHURCH. Saint George seems to have been a soldier in the army of the ROMAN EMPIRE in about the year 300. One version of the legend is that a dragon living in a pond was devouring people of the surrounding region and was about to eat the king's daughter, when George intervened and subdued the dragon. The princess tied her belt around the

dragon's neck and led it back to the city, where George killed it.

🙠 The story of Saint George and the Dragon is especially familiar in ENGLAND. George is the PATRON SAINT of that country.

Godiva, Lady (guh-DEYE-vuh)   An English noblewoman of the eleventh century. According to legend, Lady Godiva once rode naked on horseback through the streets of Coventry, ENGLAND, covered only by her long hair. Her husband, the story goes, had imposed taxes on the people of Coventry, and he agreed to lift the taxes only if Godiva took her famous ride. (*See* PEEPING TOM.)

Golden Fleece   In CLASSICAL MYTHOLOGY, the pure gold fleece of a miraculous flying ram. JASON and the ARGONAUTS made their voyage in quest of it. The fleece was kept in a kingdom on the BLACK SEA.

"Goose That Laid the Golden Eggs, The"   A story found in many forms in world literature. In one common version of the story, the owner of a goose finds that the goose can lay eggs of pure gold, and cuts the goose open to find the gold inside her. The goose turns out to be like any other goose inside, and, being dead, will lay no more golden eggs.

Gordian knot   A complex knot tied by a Greek king. According to legend, whoever loosed it would rule all ASIA. ALEXANDER THE GREAT, according to some accounts, undid the Gordian knot by cutting through it with his sword.

🙠 By extension, to "cut the Gordian knot" is to solve quickly any very complex problem, or to get to the heart of a problem.

Graces   Greek and Roman goddesses of loveliness and charm. According to most stories, there were three of them. They were supposed to be invited to every banquet.

🙠 The three Graces are a favorite subject in art, especially sculpture.

Grail, Holy   A cup or bowl that was the subject of many legends in the MIDDLE AGES. It was often said to have been used by JESUS at the LAST SUPPER. The Grail was supposedly transported to BRITAIN, where it became an object of quest for the KNIGHTS of the ROUND TABLE.

🙠 By extension, a "holy grail" is any esteemed object attained by long endeavor.

Grim Reaper   A figure commonly used to represent death. The Grim Reaper is a skeleton or solemn-looking man carrying a scythe, who cuts off people's lives as though he were harvesting grain.

Groundhog Day   February 2. The legend of Groundhog Day is that if a groundhog (a woodchuck) comes out of his hole on that day, and sees his shadow, six more weeks of winter will follow. If no shadow appears, there will be an early spring.

Guinevere (GWIN-uh-veer)   The wife of King ARTHUR. In some versions of the legends of Arthur, she has a love affair with Sir LANCELOT that leads to the end of the reign of Arthur and the fellowship of the ROUND TABLE.

Hades (HAY-deez) [Roman name PLUTO]   The Greek and Roman god of the underworld, and the ruler of the dead. Also called Dis. The underworld itself was also known to the Greeks as Hades.

⦿ The Greek and Roman underworld later became associated with the HELL of CHRISTIANITY, as in the expression "hot as Hades."

"Hansel and Gretel"   A story in the GRIMM collection of fairy tales. Hansel and Gretel, two children abandoned in the woods, are befriended by a witch, who tries to cook and eat them, but Gretel shoves the witch into the oven instead.

"Hare and the Tortoise"   See "TORTOISE AND THE HARE, THE."

Harpies   Vicious winged beings in CLASSICAL MYTHOLOGY, often depicted as birds with women's faces. In the story of JASON, they steal or spoil an old blind man's food, leaving a terrible odor behind them.

⦿ Figuratively, a "harpy" is a shrewish woman.

Hector   In CLASSICAL MYTHOLOGY, a prince of TROY, and the bravest of the Trojan warriors. At the end of the TROJAN WAR, ACHILLES killed Hector and then dragged his body behind a chariot around the walls of Troy.

Helen of Troy   In CLASSICAL MYTHOLOGY, the most beautiful woman in the world, a daughter of ZEUS by LEDA. Her abduction by PARIS led to the TROJAN WAR. Helen's was the "FACE THAT LAUNCHED A THOUSAND SHIPS": the entire Greek army sailed to TROY to get her back. (See JUDGMENT OF PARIS.)

Henry, John   A hero of American folktales and folk songs. The stories portray him as a black man, enormously strong, who worked on railroads or on steamboats, and died from exhaustion after he outperformed a steam drill in a contest.

Hephaestus (hi-FES-tuhs, hi-FEE-stuhs)   The Greek name of VULCAN, the Greek and Roman god of fire and metalworking.

Hera (HEER-uh) [Roman name JUNO]   The Greek and Roman goddess who protected marriage; she was the wife of ZEUS. Hera is best known for her jealousy and for her animosity toward the many mortal women with whom her husband fell in love. (See JUDGMENT OF PARIS.)

Hercules   One of the greatest heroes of CLASSICAL MYTHOLOGY, he is supposed to have been the strongest man on earth. He was renowned for completing twelve seemingly impossible tasks — the Labors of Hercules. One of these labors was the cleaning of the AUGEAN STABLES; another was the killing of the nine-headed Hydra. Hercules was a son of ZEUS.

⦿ Today any extraordinary effort may be called "herculean."

Hermes (HUR-meez) [Roman name MERCURY] The messenger god of CLASSICAL MYTHOLOGY. He traveled with great swiftness, aided by the wings he wore on his sandals and his cap. Hermes was a son of ZEUS and the father of PAN.

⦿ The caduceus, the wand of Hermes, is the traditional symbol of physicians. It has wings at the top and serpents twined about the staff.

Hiawatha   An actual NATIVE AMERICAN chief of the sixteenth century. In legends, he is the husband of Minnehaha. He urged peace between his people and the European settlers.

⦿ The legend of Hiawatha is best known through the poem "The Song of Hiawatha," by Henry Wadsworth LONGFELLOW.

Hymen (HEYE-muhn)   The Greek god of the wedding feast.

Icarus (IK-uh-ruhs)   In CLASSICAL MYTHOLOGY, the son of DAEDALUS. Icarus died tragically while using artificial wings, invented by his father, to escape from the LABYRINTH. When Icarus flew too close to the SUN, it melted the wax that held the wings together, and he fell to earth.

Iphigenia (if-uh-juh-NEYE-uh)   In CLASSICAL MYTHOLOGY, the eldest daughter of AGAMEMNON, and the sister of ELECTRA and ORESTES. When the Greek fleet was about to sail to fight in the TROJAN WAR, Agamemnon sacrificed Iphigenia to the goddess ARTEMIS to obtain favorable winds. According to some stories, Artemis saved Iphigenia from the sacrifice, and she was later reunited with Orestes.

Iseult (i-SOOHLT)   In English legend, the beloved of TRISTAN. In German, her name is Isolde. (*See* TRISTAN AND ISEULT.)

Janus (JAY-nuhs)   The Roman god of doors and gateways, and hence of beginnings.

🛎 Janus was pictured with two faces looking in opposite directions, one young and one old. 🛎 The month of January is named after Janus.

Jason   A hero of CLASSICAL MYTHOLOGY. Jason was the heir to a kingdom in GREECE, but his cousin seized the throne. The cousin insisted that the gods would not allow Jason to become king until Jason brought back the miraculous GOLDEN FLEECE from a distant country. After many harrowing adventures with his companions, the ARGONAUTS, and with the help of the sorceress MEDEA, he brought back the fleece. Medea, through her craft, arranged for Jason's cousin to be killed. Jason and Medea then went into exile, raised a family, and lived happily, until Jason announced plans to divorce Medea and marry a princess. Medea, enraged, killed the children she had borne Jason and Jason's bride as well, and used her magic to escape. Jason then wandered about, a man out of favor with the gods, and was eventually killed when his old ship, the *Argo*, fell on him.

Judgment of Paris   In CLASSICAL MYTHOLOGY, the incident that ultimately brought on the TROJAN WAR. When the goddess Discord threw the APPLE OF DISCORD, marked "For the Fairest," among the gods, ZEUS refused to judge which goddess was the most beautiful, but sent the three contestants — APHRODITE, ATHENA, and HERA — to the Trojan prince PARIS for a decision. Each made offers to induce Paris to give her the apple. Athena and Hera offered mili-

tary or political power, but Aphrodite said that he could have the most beautiful woman in the world. He gave the apple to Aphrodite, thereby making powerful enemies of Athena and Hera. Aphrodite led him to Helen, afterward known as HELEN OF TROY, the most beautiful woman in the world, the wife of the king of SPARTA in GREECE. Paris carried her off to TROY while her husband was away. The Greeks then combined forces to make war on Troy and bring her back. Trojan civilization was destroyed in the process.

Juno   The Roman name of HERA, the Greek and Roman goddess who protected marriage. Juno was the wife of JUPITER.

Jupiter   The Roman name of ZEUS, the most powerful of the gods of CLASSICAL MYTHOLOGY.

🛎 The fifth and largest PLANET from the SUN (the EARTH is third) is named Jupiter.

Labyrinth   In CLASSICAL MYTHOLOGY, a vast maze on the island of CRETE. The great inventor DAEDALUS designed it, and the king of Crete kept the MINOTAUR in it. Very few people ever escaped from the Labyrinth. One was THESEUS, the killer of the Minotaur. He unwound a ball of string as he passed through, and then retraced his steps by following the string backward. Daedalus, also imprisoned in the Labyrinth, escaped with his son, ICARUS, by making wings and flying over the top of the walls.

🛎 A labyrinth can be literally a maze or figuratively any highly intricate construction or problem.

Lancelot, Sir   The greatest of the KNIGHTS of the ROUND TABLE. King ARTHUR was his friend and lord. In some versions of the legend, he became the lover of Queen GUINEVERE, Arthur's wife.

Laocoön (lay-OK-oh-on)   In CLASSICAL MYTHOLOGY, Laocoön was a priest in TROY during the TROJAN WAR. When the Trojans discovered the TROJAN HORSE outside their gates, Laocoön warned against bringing it into the city, remarking, "I am wary of Greeks even when they are bringing gifts" (*see* "Beware of GREEKS BEARING GIFTS"). The god POSEIDON, who favored the Greeks, then sent two enormous snakes after Laocoön. The creatures coiled themselves around the priest and his two sons, crushing them to death. Some sources say ATHENA sent the snakes.

🛎 The squeezing to death of Laocoön and his sons

LAOCOÖN. *A statue by Agesander, Athenodorus, and Polydorus of Rhodes, showing Laocoön and his sons being crushed by serpents.*

is the subject of one of the most famous of ancient sculptures.

Leda and the swan (LEE-duh) The subject of a story from CLASSICAL MYTHOLOGY about the rape of Leda, a queen of SPARTA, by ZEUS, who had taken the form of a swan. HELEN OF TROY was conceived in the rape of Leda.

    ❧ The visit of Zeus to Leda has frequently been portrayed in art. W. B. YEATS wrote a famous poem entitled "Leda and the Swan."

leprechauns In the FOLKLORE of IRELAND, little men who resemble elves. Supposedly, leprechauns can reveal — but only to someone clever enough to catch them — the location of buried treasure, typically a crock of gold hidden at the end of the rainbow.

Lethe (LEE-thee) In CLASSICAL MYTHOLOGY, a river flowing through HADES. The souls of the dead were forced to drink of its waters, which made them forget what they had done, said, and suffered when they were alive.

Little John In English legend, one of the Merry Men who followed ROBIN HOOD. He was large and burly. At his first meeting with Robin Hood, he beat Robin in a fight with cudgels.

"Little Red Riding Hood" A fairy tale from the collections of Charles Perrault and the brothers GRIMM. A girl called Little Red Riding Hood (after the red, hooded cloak she wears) meets a wolf in the woods while traveling to visit her sick grandmother. When she tells him where she is going, the wolf takes the short way there, swallows the grandmother, puts on her clothes, and climbs into her bed to wait for Little Red Riding Hood. She arrives and exclaims, "Grandmother, what big eyes you have!" "The better to see you with, my child," says the wolf. "Grandmother, what big teeth you have!" remarks the girl. "The better to eat you with!" replies the wolf, who then devours Little Red Riding Hood. A huntsman rescues both the girl and her grandmother by cutting the wolf open.

Mars The Roman name of ARES, the Greek and Roman god of war.

    ❧ The fourth PLANET from the SUN (the EARTH is third) is named Mars, possibly because its red color is reminiscent of blood. ❧ The month of March is named after Mars.

Medea (mi-DEE-uh) In CLASSICAL MYTHOLOGY, a sorceress who fell in love with JASON and helped him obtain the GOLDEN FLEECE. When Jason abandoned her to marry another woman, she took revenge by brutally murdering his young bride as well as the children she herself had borne him.

Medusa (mi-DOOH-suh, mi-DOOH-zuh) The best known of the monster Gorgons of CLASSICAL MYTHOLOGY; people who looked at her would turn to stone. A hero, PERSEUS, was able to kill Medusa, aiming his sword by looking at her reflection in a highly polished shield.

Mercury The Roman name of HERMES, the messenger of the Greek and Roman gods.

    ❧ The PLANET nearest the SUN is named Mercury. It moves swiftly in its ORBIT like Mercury, the messenger of the gods.

Merlin In the legends of King ARTHUR, a magician who acts as Arthur's principal adviser.

Mickey Mouse A cartoon character created by WALT DISNEY. Mickey's image is so widespread that he has achieved the status of myth. (*See also* DONALD DUCK.)

MEDUSA. *A painting of Medusa's head by Caravaggio.*

MINOTAUR. *A detail from a Greek amphora showing Theseus killing the Minotaur.*

☙ Used as an adjective to connote something badly made or trivial, probably because cheap children's watches and toys carried Mickey's image.

Midas   In CLASSICAL MYTHOLOGY, a king who was granted one wish by the god DIONYSUS. Greedy for riches, Midas wished that everything he touched would turn to gold. He soon regretted his request. When he tried to eat, his food became inedible metal. When he embraced his daughter, she turned into a golden statue. On the instruction of Dionysus, he washed in a river and lost his touch of gold.

☙ A person who easily acquires riches is sometimes said to have the "Midas touch."

Minerva   The Roman name of ATHENA, the Greek and Roman goddess of wisdom.

Minotaur (MIN-uh-tawr)   In CLASSICAL MYTHOLOGY, a monster, half-man and half-bull. The Minotaur was born to the queen of CRETE, Pasiphaë, after she mated with a sacred bull. The king Minos, to hide his shame, had DAEDALUS construct the LABYRINTH in which to hide the monster. Minos then forced the Athenians to send as tribute fourteen of their young people, seven men and seven women, to be locked in the Labyrinth for the Minotaur to eat. To stop the slaughter, the hero THESEUS volunteered to enter the Labyrinth and fight the Minotaur. On the instructions of the king's daughter, Theseus brought in a ball of thread, which he unwound as he went through. He

found the Minotaur, killed it, and then used the thread to find his way out of the maze.

Morpheus (MAWR-fee-uhs)   A Roman god of sleep and dreams.

☙ Someone who is "in the arms of Morpheus" is asleep. ☙ The narcotic MORPHINE was named after Morpheus.

Muses   Nine goddesses of CLASSICAL MYTHOLOGY who presided over learning and the arts. They were especially associated with poetry. Ancient Greek or Roman writers would often begin their poems by asking for the aid of the Muses in their composition.

☙ Writers and artists to this day speak of their "muse," meaning their source of inspiration.

Narcissus   A beautiful youth in CLASSICAL MYTHOLOGY who fell in love with his own reflection in a pool. Because he was unable to tear himself away from the image, he wasted away and died.

☙ "Narcissists" are people completely absorbed in themselves. (*See* NARCISSISM.)

Nemesis (NEM-uh-sis)   In CLASSICAL MYTHOLOGY, the Greek goddess of vengeance.

☙ By extension, a "nemesis" is an avenger. One's nemesis is that which will bring on one's destruction or downfall.

Neptune (Greek name POSEIDON)   The Roman and Greek god who ruled the sea.

🔊 Neptune is frequently portrayed as a bearded giant with a fish's scaly tail, holding a large three-pronged spear, or trident. 🔊 The eighth PLANET from the SUN (the EARTH is third) is named Neptune.

Norse mythology The MYTHOLOGY of SCANDINAVIA, which was also widespread in GERMANY and BRITAIN until the establishment there of CHRISTIANITY. For the people and places most important in Norse mythology, *see* ODIN, THOR, TROLLS, *and* VALHALLA.

Nottingham, sheriff of The villain in the stories of ROBIN HOOD.

nymphs Female spirits of CLASSICAL MYTHOLOGY who lived in forests, bodies of water, and other places outdoors.

🔊 By extension, a "nymph" is a beautiful or seductive woman.

Odin (OH-din) In NORSE MYTHOLOGY, the solemn ruler of the gods. He was god of wisdom, poetry, farming, and war.

🔊 Wednesday is named after Odin, using a form of his name that begins with *W*.

Odysseus (oh-DIS-ee-uhs, oh-DIS-yoohs) [Roman name ULYSSES] A Greek hero in the TROJAN WAR. Odysseus helped bring about the fall of TROY by conceiving the ruse of the TROJAN HORSE. After Troy was ruined, Odysseus wandered for ten years trying to return home, having many adventures along the way. (*See* CIRCE, CYCLOPS, PENELOPE, SCYLLA AND CHARYBDIS, *and* SIRENS.)

🔊 The story of Odysseus' journey home is told in the *ODYSSEY* of HOMER. By extension, an "odyssey" is any long or difficult journey or transformation.

Oedipus (ED-uh-puhs, EE-duh-puhs) In CLASSICAL MYTHOLOGY, a tragic king who unknowingly killed his father and married his mother. The DELPHIC ORACLE predicted that King Laius of Thebes, a city in GREECE, would be killed by his own son. To save himself, Laius ordered his newborn son placed on a mountaintop and left to starve. The infant was rescued, however, by a shepherd, and raised in a distant city, where he was given the name Oedipus. Years later, King Laius was killed while on a journey by a stranger with whom he quarreled. Oedipus arrived at Thebes shortly thereafter, and saved the city from the ravages of the SPHINX. He was proclaimed king in

Laius' stead, and he took the dead king's widow, Jocasta, as his own wife.

After several years a terrible plague struck Thebes. The Delphic oracle told Oedipus that to end the plague, he must find and punish the murderer of King Laius. In the course of his investigation, Oedipus discovered that he himself was the killer, and that Laius had been his real father. He had therefore murdered his father and married his mother, Jocasta. In his despair at this discovery, Oedipus blinded himself.

🔊 The story of Oedipus is the subject of the play *OEDIPUS REX* by SOPHOCLES. 🔊 The OEDIPUS COMPLEX, explored by the psychiatrist Sigmund FREUD, takes its name from the character of Oedipus.

Olympus, Mount The legendary home of the Greek and Roman gods. Mount Olympus is an actual mountain in GREECE, the highest in the country. Some stories of the gods have them living on the mountain. Other stories have them living in a mysterious region above it.

🔊 The Olympians were the Greek gods. 🔊 The OLYMPIC GAMES were a celebration held every four years on the plain of Olympus in honor of ZEUS. They included athletic games and contests of choral poetry and dance. Our modern Olympic games are modeled after them.

Orestes (aw-RES-teez) In CLASSICAL MYTHOLOGY, the son of AGAMEMNON and Clytemnestra, and brother of ELECTRA. Agamemnon was killed by Clytemnestra and her lover, Aegisthus. To avenge the murder, Orestes and Electra killed them both.

Orpheus and Eurydice (AWR-fee-uhs, AWR-fyoohs; yoo-RID-uh-see) In CLASSICAL MYTHOLOGY, Orpheus was a great musician, and Eurydice was his wife. The music of Orpheus was so beautiful that it could calm the wildest animal, and even make stones rise up and follow. When Eurydice died, Orpheus went to the underworld, played his lyre for HADES, ruler of the dead, and asked that Eurydice be sent back to earth. The god was so moved that he agreed to let her return, on one condition: that Orpheus go on ahead of her and not look back until they had reached the earth again. Orpheus led Eurydice up, but at the last moment, when he had come out of the underworld and she was about to leave it, he could resist no longer and turned to look at her. She vanished, and he had lost her forever. He spent the rest of his days wandering about, playing his lyre, and singing. In the end, he was torn to pieces by crazed followers of BACCHUS, the god of wine.

Pan   The Greek god of flocks, forests, meadows, and shepherds. He had the horns and feet of a goat. Pan frolicked about the landscape, playing delightful tunes.

🐚 Pan's musical instrument was a set of reed pipes, the "pipes of Pan." 🐚 According to legend, Pan was the source of scary noises in the wilderness at night. Fright at these noises was called "panic."

Pandora's box   In CLASSICAL MYTHOLOGY, a box that ZEUS gave to Pandora, the first woman, with strict instructions that she not open it. Pandora's curiosity soon got the better of her, and she opened the box. All the evils and miseries of the world flew out to afflict mankind.

🐚 To "open a Pandora's box" is to create a situation that will cause great grief.

Paris   A prince of TROY in CLASSICAL MYTHOLOGY, whose abduction of the Greek queen Helen caused the TROJAN WAR (*see* HELEN OF TROY *and* JUDGMENT OF PARIS). Paris (or, according to some stories, APOLLO disguised as Paris) killed ACHILLES by piercing his heel with an arrow.

Parnassus (pahr-NAS-uhs)   A mountain in GREECE. According to CLASSICAL MYTHOLOGY, it was one of the mountains where the MUSES lived. The DELPHIC ORACLE was on one of its slopes.

🐚 Parnassus is known as the mythological home of poetry and music.

PEGASUS

Pegasus (PEG-uh-suhs)   In CLASSICAL MYTHOLOGY, a winged horse, tamed by the hero Bellerophon with the help of a bridle given to him by ATHENA.

🐚 As the flying horse of the MUSES, Pegasus is a SYMBOL of high-flying poetic imaginations.

Penelope (puh-NEL-uh-pee)   The wife of ODYSSEUS in CLASSICAL MYTHOLOGY. Penelope remained true to her husband for the ten years he spent fighting in the TROJAN WAR and for the ten years it took him to return from TROY, even though she was harassed by men who wanted to marry her. She promised to choose a mate after she had finished weaving a shroud for her father-in-law, but every night she unraveled what she had woven during the day. After three years, her trick was discovered, but she still managed to put her suitors off until Odysseus returned and killed them.

🐚 Penelope is an image of fidelity and devotion.

Perseus (PUR-see-uhs, PUR-syoohs)   A hero of CLASSICAL MYTHOLOGY who killed the Gorgon MEDUSA. The god HERMES and goddess ATHENA helped him in this brave deed by giving him winged shoes, a magical sword, and a polished shield. With the help of these, he swooped down on Medusa from the air, used the shield as a mirror, and cut off her head without looking at it directly — for anyone who looked at a Gorgon turned to stone.

PHOENIX

phoenix (FEE-niks)   A mythical bird that periodically burned itself to death and emerged from the ashes as a new phoenix. According to most stories, the rebirth of the phoenix happened every five hundred years. Only one phoenix lived at a time.

🐚 To "rise phoenixlike from the ashes" is to overcome a seemingly insurmountable setback.

Pluto   The Roman name of HADES, the Greek and Roman god of the underworld and ruler of the dead.

🐚 The PLANET PLUTO is the most forbidding and usually the most distant planet in the SOLAR SYSTEM.

Poseidon (puh-SEYED-n)   The Greek name for NEPTUNE, the Greek and Roman god who ruled the sea.

Priam (PREYE-uhm)   The king of TROY and father of HECTOR and PARIS. The Greeks killed him at the end of the TROJAN WAR, when they sacked the city.

"Princess and the Pea, The"   A story by Hans Christian ANDERSEN. A prince insists on marrying a real princess. When a woman comes to his door maintaining that she is a real princess, the prince's mother tests her by burying a pea under a huge stack of mattresses and then ordering the woman to sleep on the mattresses. The woman cannot sleep, and therefore passes the test: being a true princess, she is so delicate that the pea keeps her awake.

Procrustes (proh-KRUS-teez)   A mythical Greek giant who was a thief and a murderer. He would capture travelers and tie them to an iron bed. If they were longer than the bed, he would hack off their limbs until they fit it. If they were too short, he would stretch them to the right size.

   A "procrustean" method is one that relentlessly tries to shape a person, an argument, or an idea to a predetermined pattern.

Prometheus (pruh-MEE-thee-uhs, pruh-MEETH-yoohs)   In CLASSICAL MYTHOLOGY, the TITAN who stole fire from the gods and gave it to humans. As punishment for the theft, ZEUS ordered Prometheus chained to a rock, and sent a great eagle to gnaw at the Titan's LIVER. Despite his torment, Prometheus refused to submit to Zeus' will. He was eventually rescued by HERCULES.

   Prometheus has become a SYMBOL of lonely and valiant resistance to authority. AESCHYLUS wrote a play, PROMETHEUS BOUND, and Percy Bysshe SHELLEY wrote a long poem entitled "Prometheus Unbound."

Proteus (PROH-tee-uhs, PROH-tyoohs)   In CLASSICAL MYTHOLOGY, a god who served POSEIDON. Proteus could change his shape at will.

   Someone or something that easily takes on several different forms may be called "protean."

Psyche (SEYE-kee)   In Roman MYTHOLOGY, a beautiful girl who was visited each night in the dark by CUPID, who told her she must not try to see him. When she did try, while he was asleep, she accidentally dropped oil from her lamp on him, and he

awoke and fled. After she had performed many harsh tasks set by Cupid's mother, VENUS, JUPITER made her immortal, and she and Cupid were married. Her name is Greek for both "soul" and "butterfly."

Punch and Judy   Two CHARACTERS, husband and wife, frequently seen in puppet shows, especially in ENGLAND. Punch has a humped back and a hooked nose, and a fierce temper. He is constantly beating people with his stick, including Judy and their baby.

"Puss-in-Boots"   A French fairy tale from the collection of Charles Perrault. A cunning cat brings great fortune to its master, a poor young man. Through a series of deceptions managed by the cat, the young man becomes a lord, and marries the king's daughter.

Pygmalion (pig-MAY-lee-uhn, pig-MAYL-yuhn)   In CLASSICAL MYTHOLOGY, a sculptor who at first hated women, but then fell in love with a statue he made of a woman. He prayed to VENUS that she find him a woman like the statue. Instead, Venus made the statue come to life.

   The play PYGMALION, by George Bernard SHAW, adapts this THEME: a professor trains a girl from the gutter to speak and behave like a lady, and then he and his new creation become attached to each other. This play became the basis for the MUSICAL COMEDY MY FAIR LADY.

Quetzalcoatl (ket-SAHL-koh-AHT-l)   A nature god of the early NATIVE AMERICAN tribes in MEXICO, represented as a plumed serpent.

Robin Hood   A legendary robber of the MIDDLE AGES in ENGLAND, who stole from the rich and gave to the poor. An excellent archer, he lived in SHERWOOD FOREST with the fair Maid Marian, the stalwart LITTLE JOHN, the priest Friar Tuck, the musician Alan a Dale, and others who helped him rob rich landlords and thwart his chief enemy, the sheriff of NOTTINGHAM.

Romulus and Remus (ROM-yuh-luhs; REE-muhs)   In Roman legend, twin brothers who were raised by a she-wolf and founded the city of ROME. They came from a city founded by the son of AENEAS. During the construction of Rome, Romulus became incensed at Remus and killed him. The Romans later made Romulus into a god.

   Rome is named for Romulus.

ROMULUS AND REMUS

Round Table, knights of the   In English legend, the fellowship of the knights of King ARTHUR. Among their adventures was the quest for the Holy GRAIL. The group dispersed after the death of Arthur.

KNIGHTS OF THE ROUND TABLE. *Sir Lancelot (top center) is seated among the knights; the Holy Grail is held above the table by two angels. From an illuminated manuscript.*

"Rumpelstiltskin"   A fairy tale from the collection of the brothers GRIMM. The title CHARACTER, a dwarf, tells a woman who has promised him her first-born child that he will not hold her to her promise if she can guess his name. She finds it out, and Rumpelstiltskin, furious, destroys himself.

Saturn   The Roman name for one of the TITANS, the father of ZEUS. In Roman MYTHOLOGY, Saturn fled from MOUNT OLYMPUS after Zeus defeated the Titans. He settled in ITALY, and established a golden age, in which all people were equal and harvests were plentiful.

☙ Saturday ("Saturn's day") is named after Saturn.
☙ The sixth PLANET from the SUN (the EARTH is third) is named Saturn. Saturn, with its rings, is one of the most beautiful planets.

satyrs (SAY-tuhrz, SAT-uhrz) [Roman name FAUNS] Creatures in CLASSICAL MYTHOLOGY who were part man and part goat. Satyrs were famous for being constantly drunk and for chasing NYMPHS. They were companions of DIONYSUS.

☙ By extension, a "satyr" is a lecherous male.

Scylla and Charybdis (SIL-uh; kuh-RIB-dis)   In CLASSICAL MYTHOLOGY, Scylla was a horrible six-headed monster who lived on a rock on one side of a narrow strait. Charybdis was a whirlpool on the other side. When ships passed close to Scylla's rock in order to avoid Charybdis, she would seize and devour their sailors. AENEAS, JASON, and ODYSSEUS all had to pass between Scylla and Charybdis.

☙ Figuratively, to be "caught between Scylla and Charybdis" is to be forced to choose between two unpleasant options.

Sherwood Forest   An actual forest in ENGLAND. According to legend, it was the home of ROBIN HOOD and his companions.

Sirens   In CLASSICAL MYTHOLOGY, evil creatures who lived on a rocky island, singing in beautiful voices in an effort to lure sailors to shipwreck and death. ODYSSEUS ordered his crew to plug their ears in order to escape the Sirens' fatal song.

☙ Figuratively, a "siren" is a beautiful or tempting woman; a "siren song" is any irresistible distraction.

Sisyphus (SIS-uh-fuhs)   A king in CLASSICAL MYTHOLOGY who offended ZEUS and was punished in HADES by being forced to roll an enormous boulder to the top of a steep hill. Every time the boulder neared the top, it would roll back down, and Sisyphus would have to start over.

☙ A difficult and futile task may be called a "labor of Sisyphus."

"Sleeping Beauty"   A fairy tale from the collection of Charles Perrault, about a beautiful princess cast into a deep sleep through a jealous fairy's curse. Sleeping Beauty is awakened at last by the kiss of a prince.

"Snow White and the Seven Dwarfs" A fairy tale in the GRIMM collection, about a beautiful young princess whose jealous stepmother tries to kill her. She avoids being killed, and hides in a forest cottage occupied by dwarfs. The stepmother finds out where Snow White is, visits her in disguise, and gives her a poisoned apple; Snow White eats it and falls into a deathlike sleep. When a prince kisses her, she awakens from her sleep, and he marries her.

  The wicked stepmother consults a magical mirror several times throughout the story, often saying to it, "Mirror, mirror, on the wall, who is the fairest one of all?" The mirror tells her that Snow White is fairer than she is, and discloses Snow White's hiding place in the woods. In the 1930s, Walt DISNEY made a very popular animated film adaptation of the story of Snow White, in which the dwarfs sing, "Heigh ho, heigh ho, it's off to work we go."

Sphinx (SFINGKS) In the story of OEDIPUS, a winged monster with the head of a woman and the body of a lion. It waylaid travelers on the roads near the city of Thebes, and would kill any of them who could not answer this riddle: "What creatures walk on four legs in the morning, on two legs at noon, and on three legs in the evening?" Oedipus finally gave the correct answer: human beings, who go on all fours as infants, walk upright in maturity, and in old age rely on the "third leg" of a cane.

  The sphinx of Greek MYTHOLOGY resembles the sphinx of Egyptian mythology but is distinct from it (the Egyptian sphinx had a man's head). (*See under "Fine Arts."*)

Styx (STIKS) In CLASSICAL MYTHOLOGY, one of the rivers of HADES, across which CHARON ferried the souls of the dead. The gods occasionally swore by the river Styx. When they did so, their oath was unbreakable.

Tantalus (TAN-tuh-luhs) A king in CLASSICAL MYTHOLOGY who, as punishment for having offended the gods, was tortured with everlasting thirst and hunger in HADES. He stood up to his chin in water, but each time he bent to quench his thirst, the water receded. There were boughs heavy with fruit over his head, but each time he tried to pluck them, the wind blew them out of reach.

  Something is "tantalizing" if it is desirable but unattainable.

Tell, William A legendary hero of SWITZERLAND, famous for his skill as an archer. A tyrannical official forced him to shoot an apple off his son's head.

Theseus (THEE-see-uhs, THEE-syoohs) In CLASSICAL MYTHOLOGY, a hero of the city of ATHENS. He killed PROCRUSTES and the MINOTAUR, and made war on the AMAZONS, subsequently marrying their queen, Hippolyta.

Thor The god of thunder in NORSE MYTHOLOGY. He wielded a hammer.

  Thursday (Thor's day) is named after Thor.

Tiresias (teye-REE-see-uhs) In CLASSICAL MYTHOLOGY, the blind prophet who revealed the truth of the crimes of OEDIPUS. According to the Roman poet OVID, Tiresias spent part of his life as a man and part of it as a woman, so he knew the act of love from both points of view. When asked by JUPITER and JUNO who enjoyed sex more, he answered that women did. This so enraged Juno that she blinded Tiresias.

Titans The gods in CLASSICAL MYTHOLOGY who ruled the UNIVERSE until they were overthrown by ZEUS. ATLAS and PROMETHEUS were Titans.

  Any great and powerful person can be called a "titan." "Titanic" means great or large as a titan.

"Tortoise and the Hare, The" One of AESOP'S FABLES. A tortoise and a hare hold a race. The hare is so confident of winning that he lies down halfway through and goes to sleep. The tortoise, knowing he must work hard to win, plods along without stopping until he passes the sleeping hare and wins.

Tristan and Iseult (TRIS-tuhn, TRIS-tahn, TRIS-tan; i-SOOHLT) Two lovers in the legends of BRITAIN and IRELAND. A common version of their story is that Tristan brought the maiden Iseult from Ireland to Britain to be the bride of his uncle, King Mark. On the voyage they drank a potion that made them eternally in love with each other. When King Mark learned of their love, he banished Tristan. Tristan sent for Iseult as he was dying, but she arrived after his death, and died herself beside his corpse.

TROJAN HORSE. *An engraving after a painting by Henri Motte, showing the Greek army emerging from the Trojan Horse.*

Trojan horse In CLASSICAL MYTHOLOGY, a large, hollow horse made of wood used by the Greeks to win the TROJAN WAR. The resourceful ODYSSEUS had come up with the plan for the horse. The Greeks hid soldiers inside it, left it outside the gates of TROY, and set sail, apparently for GREECE. They anchored their ships just out of sight of Troy, and left a man behind to say that the goddess ATHENA would be pleased if the Trojans brought the horse inside the city and honored it. The Trojans took the bait, against the advice of CASSANDRA and LAOCOON. That night the Greek army returned to Troy. The men inside the horse emerged and opened the city gates for their companions. The Greeks sacked the city, thus winning the war.

&❧ The story of the Trojan horse is the source of the saying "Beware of GREEKS BEARING GIFTS." (*See also* LAOCOON.)

Trojan War In CLASSICAL MYTHOLOGY, the great war fought between the Greeks and the Trojans. The Greeks sailed to TROY in order to recover HELEN OF TROY, the beautiful wife of a Greek king. She had been carried off to Troy by PARIS, a prince of Troy. (APHRODITE had promised Helen to Paris following the JUDGMENT OF PARIS.) The fighting continued for ten years, while ACHILLES, the greatest warrior of the Greeks, refused to fight because he had been offended by the commander, AGAMEMNON. Achilles finally took to the field and killed the greatest Trojan war-

rior, HECTOR. Having seriously weakened the Trojan defense, the Greeks achieved final victory through the ploy of the TROJAN HORSE. They burned Troy to the ground and returned to GREECE.

&❧ The story of the Trojan War is told in the *ILIAD* of HOMER.

trolls In NORSE MYTHOLOGY, repulsive dwarfs who lived in caves or other hidden places. They would steal children and property, but hated noise. The troll in the children's story "The Three Billy Goats Gruff," for example, lives under a bridge, and is enraged when he hears the goats crossing the bridge.

&❧ Figuratively, a "troll" can be any mean-spirited person.

Troy The ancient city inhabited by the Trojans; the site of the legendary TROJAN WAR of CLASSICAL MYTHOLOGY. The ruins of Troy were found in the nineteenth century in the western part of what is now TURKEY.

"Ugly Duckling, The" A children's story, told by Hans Christian ANDERSEN. One young bird in a family of ducks is constantly mocked by the other ducks for his ugliness. Eventually, though, he grows up to be a swan — the most beautiful of all birds.

&❧ An "ugly duckling" is someone who blossoms beautifully after an unpromising beginning.

Ulysses The Roman name of the Greek hero ODYSSEUS.

&❧ In the *AENEID* of VIRGIL, which was written in LATIN, Odysseus is called Ulysses. &❧ The Irish author James JOYCE adopted the name for the title of his masterpiece of the early twentieth century, which is, in part, a retelling of the myth of Odysseus. Alfred Lord TENNYSON also wrote a famous poem called "Ulysses."

unicorn A mythical animal resembling a small horse but with a long, straight horn growing out of its forehead. It often was described as having the legs of a deer and the tail of a lion. Some sources claim it was visible only to virgins.

Valhalla (val-HAL-uh) In NORSE MYTHOLOGY, a dwelling in Asgard, the Norse heaven, reserved for the souls of those who died heroic deaths.

vampires Originally part of central European FOLKLORE, they now appear in horror stories as living corpses who need to feed on human blood. A vampire will leave his coffin at night, disguised as a great bat, to seek his innocent victims, bite their necks with his long, sharp teeth, and suck their blood.

&. The most famous vampire is Count DRACULA, from the NOVEL *Dracula* by Bram Stoker.

Venus   The Roman name of APHRODITE, the Greek and Roman goddess of love and beauty.

&. The second PLANET from the sun (the EARTH is third) is named Venus, possibly because it is one of the most beautiful sights in the night sky.

Vesta (Greek name Hestia)   The Roman and Greek goddess of the hearth and home. Roman and Greek cities were supposed to have a public hearth dedicated to Vesta, at which the fire was kept constantly burning.

&. In ROME, the sacred hearth of Vesta was attended by six maidens, the VESTAL VIRGINS.

Vulcan (Greek name HEPHAESTUS)   The Roman and Greek god of fire and metalworking; the blacksmith of the gods. He suffered bodily deformities and lameness. According to some stories, he was married to VENUS, the goddess of love and beauty; in other stories, he was married to one of the three GRACES. Vulcan was a son of JUPITER.

&. VULCANIZATION, a process for strengthening rubber, is named after Vulcan.

Washington and the cherry tree   The subject of a fanciful story by an early biographer of George WASHINGTON, Mason Weems; the source of the saying "I cannot tell a lie." According to Weems, the young Washington received a new hatchet, and used it to chop down his father's prized cherry tree. His father demanded to know how the tree had fallen. George was tempted to deny his misdeed, but then, "looking at his father with the sweet face of youth brightened with the inexpressible charm of all-conquering truth, he bravely cried out, 'I can't tell a lie. I did cut it with my hatchet.'"

werewolves   Legendary human beings who are magically transformed into wolves. Tales about werewolves appear in many countries and in many literary works. Werewolves, according to the stories, prowl at night, devouring babies and digging up

corpses, and cannot be killed with ordinary weapons. They are particularly associated with the full MOON.

Zephyr (ZEF-uhr)   The Greek and Roman god of the west wind, considered the most pleasant of the winds.

Zeus (ZOOHS) [Roman name JUPITER]   The chief of the Greek and Roman gods, who defeated the TITANS to assume leadership of the UNIVERSE. He lived atop MOUNT OLYMPUS, from which he hurled thunderbolts to announce his anger. Despite his awesome power, he had a weakness for mortal women. He frequently descended to earth to couple with some woman who had caught his eye. (*See* LEDA AND THE SWAN.)

zodiac   A band of the sky along which the SUN, the MOON, and most of the PLANETS move. It is divided into twelve parts, with each part named for a nearby CONSTELLATION.

&. The twelve constellations, or signs, of the zodiac are important in ASTROLOGY.

ZODIAC. *A rendering of the zodiac entitled* Anatomical Man, *from* Les Très Riches Heures du Duc de Berry.

Proverbs

MANY HANDS MAKE LIGHT WORK, but at the same time, TOO MANY COOKS SPOIL THE BROTH. Which of these contradictory PROVERBS shall we believe? Both, because in different contexts, both are true to experience. If they were not, they probably would not have survived. If the job to be done requires lots of unskilled labor, as picking up trash does, then many hands *do* make light work. But if the job requires intricate skill, as cooking or writing does, or if it requires a single guiding hand, then too many cooks *do* spoil the broth.

Proverbs reflect the accumulated wisdom, prejudices, and superstitions of the human race. Mainly it is the particular phrasing of the proverbs, not their ideas, that belongs to the cultural literacy of each nation and language. The ideas they express are often common to many nations. For instance, in German it is said, "Viele Hände bringt's gleich zu Ende" — literally, "many hands bring it quickly to a conclusion." But the literal sense doesn't capture the punch of the German version, which is a little RHYME:

> Viele Hände (pronounced "hen-duh")
> Bringt's gleich zu Ende (pronounced "en-duh").

In English, few would pay attention to the silly proverb "AN APPLE A DAY KEEPS THE DOCTOR AWAY" were it not for the rhyme. Indeed, it is hard to find the equivalent of this proverb in any other language, because it rhymes only in English. It sounds silly in French, and ridiculous in Italian. The rhyme alone makes us remember it — and encourages us to believe it.

The main reason we have included these little poems and nuggets of wisdom, false and true, is that they have become part of our cultural vocabulary. On many occasions when people invoke proverbs in speech and writing, they simply allude to them, rather than complete them. If someone offers you a fruit and says, "An apple a day," the communication will fail if you don't know the relevant proverb; you will be an outsider. We have included these proverbs because we want to enable everyone to be insiders. We don't wish to encourage ideas such as "BOYS WILL BE BOYS" or "FRAILTY, THY NAME IS WOMAN"; in fact, we would prefer people to question proverbial wisdom rather than accept it blindly. But we also want to give everybody the chance to be insiders in American literate CULTURE.

— E. D. H.

Absence makes the heart grow fonder   Persons, places, or things become dearer to us when they are absent.

acorns mighty oaks do grow, From little   *See* GREAT OAKS FROM LITTLE ACORNS GROW.

Actions speak louder than words   People are more impressed with our sincerity if we act on our beliefs than if we merely talk about them.

All for one and one for all   All the members of a group support each of the individual members, and

47

the individual members are pledged to support the group.

• "All for one and one for all" is best known as the motto of the title CHARACTERS in the book *THE THREE MUSKETEERS*, by the nineteenth-century French author Alexandre DUMAS.

All roads lead to Rome   All paths or activities lead to the center of things. This was literally true in the days of the ROMAN EMPIRE, when the empire's roads all radiated out from the capital city of ROME.

All that glitters is not gold   Things that appear on the surface to be of great value may be quite worthless.

All work and no play makes Jack a dull boy   A person who never takes time off from work becomes boring and bored.

All's fair in love and war   People in love and soldiers in wartime are not bound by the rules of fair play.

• This PROVERB is frequently used when two people are contending for the love of a third.

All's well that ends well   Problems that occur along the way do not matter as long as the outcome is happy.

Any port in a storm   In an emergency, we will accept help from any source and in any place, even from an unpleasant person.

apple a day keeps the doctor away, An   Apples keep us healthy.

April showers bring May flowers   Some unpleasant occurrences bring about better things.

army marches on its stomach, An   To be effective, an army relies on good and plentiful food. This saying is attributed to NAPOLEON BONAPARTE.

Bad news travels fast   People are quick to discuss the misfortunes of others.

bad penny always turns up, A   Our mistakes return to haunt us; also, nasty people have a way of reappearing.

bad workman always blames his tools, The   Our success or failure is determined not by what we have to work with but by how we employ what we have. A good workman takes care of his tools.

bark is worse than his bite, His   This person makes a great many threats, but doesn't follow through on them.

Beauty is only skin deep   Physical beauty is superficial, and is not as important as a person's intellectual, emotional, and spiritual qualities.

Beggars can't be choosers   People who depend on the generosity of others are in no position to dictate what others give them.

best of friends must part, The   No matter how much friends care for each other, they cannot be together always.

best things in life are free, The   Money can't buy the most important things in life.

best-laid plans of mice and men often go awry, The   No matter how carefully a project is planned, something may still go wrong with it. The saying is adapted from a line in "To a Mouse," by Robert BURNS: "The best laid schemes o' mice an' men / Gang aft a-gley."

Better late than never   It is better to do something after it was supposed to have been done than not to do it at all.

Better safe than sorry   It is better to act cautiously beforehand than to suffer afterward.

bigger they come the harder they fall, The   The more powerful and successful people are, the more they suffer when they experience defeat and disaster.

bird in the hand is worth two in the bush, A   The things we already have are more valuable than the things we only hope to get.

Birds of a feather flock together   People are attracted to others who are like themselves.

blood from a turnip, You can't squeeze   One can get from people only what they are willing to give.

Blood is thicker than water   Our loyalty to our family — that is, to our blood relations — is strong no matter how we may feel about them.

book by its cover, Don't judge a   Don't judge the value of a thing simply by its appearance.

Boys will be boys   Children can be expected to act in a childish way.

🙠 "Boys will be boys" is often applied to grown men who act childishly.

Brevity is the soul of wit   Intelligent speech and writing should aim at using few words. This PROVERB comes from the play *HAMLET*, by William SHAKESPEARE.

buck stops here, The   I'm the ultimately responsible person in this organization. Other people can PASS THE BUCK to me, but I can't pass the buck to anyone else.

🙠 President Harry TRUMAN kept a sign on his desk that read, "The buck stops here."

burnt child fears the fire, The   A person who has suffered in a situation will avoid that situation in the future.

Business before pleasure   We must take care of our responsibilities before enjoying ourselves.

bygones be bygones, Let   Let past offenses and problems stay in the past; don't let them taint the present.

Carpe diem (KAHR-pay DEE-em, DEYE-em)   LATIN for "Seize the day": take full advantage of present opportunities. This sentiment is found not only in classical literature but in much of English literature as well (*see* "GATHER YE ROSEBUDS WHILE YE MAY" *and* "HAD WE BUT WORLD ENOUGH, AND TIME, / THIS COYNESS, LADY, WERE NO CRIME.")

cart before the horse, Don't put the   Begin at the proper place; do things in their proper order.

cast your pearls before swine, Do not   Do not waste good things on people who will not appreciate them. This PROVERB is adapted from a saying of JESUS from the GOSPELS, "Cast not PEARLS BEFORE SWINE." Jesus appears to be warning his DISCIPLES to preach only before receptive audiences.

cat's away, the mice will play, When the   When a person in authority is away, those under the person's rule will enjoy their freedom.

chickens have come home to roost, The   The consequences of earlier actions are making themselves felt.

Cleanliness is next to godliness   Cleanliness is a great virtue.

Close, but no cigar   Even a near miss is still a miss. The saying probably originated with carnival contests in which a cigar was the prize for hitting a target.

close the barn door after the horse runs away, Don't   It's foolish to take precautions after the damage they would have prevented has already been done. Another version of this saying is "Don't LOCK THE STABLE (OR BARN) DOOR AFTER THE HORSE HAS BEEN STOLEN."

cloud has a silver lining, Every   Every misfortune has its positive aspect.

cobbler should stick to his last, The   People should not make judgments in areas about which they are not informed.

Cold hands, warm heart   Cold hands indicate affection, possibly because the emotions affect BLOOD circulation.

Comparisons are odious   It is wrong to compare different people or things in order to establish some as superior to others.

count your chickens before they hatch, Don't   Don't assume that you'll get the things you want until you have them.

course of true love never did run smooth, The   True love always encounters difficulties. This PROVERB comes from the play *A MIDSUMMER NIGHT'S DREAM*, by William SHAKESPEARE.

cross that bridge when we come to it, Let's   Let's face difficulties as they happen and not worry uselessly about them beforehand.

cry over spilt milk, Don't   It doesn't do any good to be unhappy about something that has already happened or that can't be helped.

cut off your nose to spite your face, Don't   Don't engage in an act of anger or revenge that will hurt you more than it hurts anyone else.

death and taxes, In this world nothing is certain but   Death and taxes are the only things that we can be sure of. This saying comes from the letters of Benjamin FRANKLIN.

devil can cite Scripture for his purpose, The   Even things that are good in themselves (such as the BIBLE) can be twisted to serve bad purposes. This PROVERB comes from the play *THE MERCHANT OF VENICE*, by William SHAKESPEARE.

Discretion is the better part of valor Caution is preferable to rash bravery. Said by FALSTAFF in *King Henry the Fourth, Part One*, by William SHAKESPEARE.

Do unto others as you would have them do unto you Treat other people with the concern and kindness you would like them to show toward you. This saying has come to be called the GOLDEN RULE.

dog has his day, Every Even the lowest of us enjoys a moment of glory.

dog is a man's best friend, A A dog is more faithful than most other animals — and more faithful than many people.

Don't give up the ship Don't surrender; a favorite motto of the United States Navy. These were the dying words of Commander James Lawrence during a battle in the WAR OF 1812.

early bird catches the worm, The If we want to achieve our goal, we must get an early start.

Early to bed and early to rise makes a man healthy, wealthy, and wise A saying of Benjamin FRANKLIN in *POOR RICHARD'S ALMANACK*.

East is East, and West is West, and never the twain shall meet The CULTURE of the West (EUROPE and the Americas) will always be very different from that of the East (ASIA). (*Twain* means "two.") This saying is part of the REFRAIN of "The Ballad of East and West," a poem by Rudyard KIPLING.

Easy come, easy go Things easily acquired may be lost just as easily.
　🞕 This saying is often used after something has been lost.

Eat, drink, and be merry, for tomorrow we die We should enjoy life as much as possible, because it will be over soon. This saying is based on verses from the biblical Books of ECCLESIASTES and ISAIAH.

eggs in one basket, Don't put all your Don't concentrate all your prospects or resources in one thing or place, or you could lose everything.

err is human, to forgive divine, To All people commit sins and make mistakes. God forgives them,

and people are acting in a godlike (divine) way when they forgive. This saying is from "An ESSAY on Criticism," by Alexander POPE.

Everybody talks about the weather, but nobody does anything about it This saying is usually attributed to Mark TWAIN, but actually seems to have originated with a friend of his, Charles Dudley Warner.

Experience is the best teacher Life teaches more effectively than books or school.

Familiarity breeds contempt The better we know people, the more likely we are to find fault with them.

famous for fifteen minutes, Everybody will be world A statement by ANDY WARHOL, who actually wrote "In the future everyone will be world-famous for fifteen minutes."

Feed a cold; starve a fever Eating will help cure a cold; not eating will help cure a fever.

Finders keepers, losers weepers A person who finds something can keep it, and the loser has no right to it. This PROVERB is of dubious ethical merit.

fish in the sea, There are plenty of There are lots of potential mates in the world.
　🞕 This saying is often used to console a person who has lost a girlfriend or boyfriend.

fit night out for man or beast, It ain't a The night is terribly cold and stormy. This line was used several times by the comedian W. C. FIELDS in the film *The Fatal Glass of Beer*.

Fish or cut bait Make a decision now; stop hesitating. To cut bait is to stop fishing.

flies with honey than with vinegar, You can catch more You can win people to your side more easily by gentle persuasion and flattery than by hostile confrontation.

fool and his money are soon parted, A Foolish people do not know how to hold on to their money.

fool like an old fool, There's no The most extreme fools are people whose age should have made them wise.

foolish consistency is the hobgoblin of little minds, A A great person does not have to think consistently from one day to the next. This remark comes from the ESSAY "SELF-RELIANCE" by Ralph Waldo EMERSON. Emerson does not explain the difference between foolish and wise consistency.

Fools rush in where angels fear to tread Foolish people are often reckless, attempting feats that the wise avoid. This saying is from "An ESSAY on Criticism," by Alexander POPE.

Forewarned is forearmed Those who know that something is coming are better prepared to face it than those who do not know.

Frailty, thy name is woman! From *HAMLET* by William SHAKESPEARE; this PROVERB is taken to mean that women are weaker than men.

friend in need is a friend indeed, A A friend who helps out when we are in trouble is a true friend — unlike others who disappear when trouble arises.

game is not worth the candle, The What we would get from this undertaking is not worth the effort we would have to put into it. The saying alludes to a game of cards in which the stakes are smaller than the cost of burning a candle for light by which to play.

Genius is one percent inspiration and ninety-nine percent perspiration Great accomplishments depend not so much on ingenuity as on hard work. This is a saying of the American inventor Thomas EDISON.

gift horse in the mouth, Don't look a Don't question the value of a gift. The PROVERB refers to the practice of evaluating the age of a horse by looking at its TEETH. This practice is also the source of the expression "long in the tooth," meaning old.

Give him enough rope and he'll hang himself A person will bring about his or her own misfortune if given the opportunity.

Give the devil his due Admit it when there is some good even in a person you dislike. This saying appears in *DON QUIXOTE*, by Miguel de CERVANTES.

go home again, You can't You can't recover the past. This saying is the title of a NOVEL by the twentieth-century American author Thomas Wolfe.

God helps those who help themselves God will not come to the aid of those who refuse to try; we must exert ourselves if we want to succeed.

God and mammon, You cannot serve Being virtuous is not compatible with being greedy (*mammon* means "money"). This is a saying of JESUS in the GOSPELS. It explains "NO MAN CAN SERVE TWO MASTERS."

Good fences make good neighbors Good neighbors respect one another's property. Good farmers, for example, maintain their fences in order to keep their livestock from wandering onto neighboring farms. This PROVERB appears in the poem "Mending Wall," by Robert FROST.

good man is hard to find, A Dependable, trustworthy help is not easy to get.

good or bad but thinking makes it so, There is nothing The significance of an event or situation depends on our perspective. This saying is spoken by the title CHARACTER in the play *HAMLET*, by William SHAKESPEARE; Hamlet, however, is joking at the time, and may not believe what he says.

grass is always greener on the other side of the fence, The People are never satisfied with their own situation; they always think others have it better.

Great oaks from little acorns grow Great things or people often have humble origins.

Greeks bearing gifts, Beware of Do not trust enemies who bring you presents — they could very well be playing a trick. The saying is adapted from the words of LAOCOON in the story of the TROJAN HORSE.

gustibus non est disputandum, De (day GOOS-ti-boos nohn est dis-poo-TAHN-doom) LATIN for "There's no disputing about taste." Another version of this saying is "There's no accounting for taste." (*See* TASTE, THERE'S NO ACCOUNTING FOR.)

Half a loaf is better than none Something is better than nothing at all.

Haste makes waste Acting too quickly may actually slow things down.

have your cake and eat it too, You can't The things people want are often incompatible. This PROVERB is easier to grasp if it is understood to mean "You can't eat your cake and have it too."

Hell hath no fury like a woman scorned No one is angrier than a woman who has been rejected in love. This PROVERB is adapted from a line in the play *The Mourning Bride*, by William Congreve, an English author of the late seventeenth and early eighteenth centuries. (*See also* MUSIC HAS CHARMS TO SOOTHE A SAVAGE BREAST.)

Here today, gone tomorrow What is present or important now may be absent or irrelevant in the future.

hesitates is lost, He who A person who spends too much time deliberating about what to do loses the chance to act altogether.

Hitch your wagon to a star Aim high; hope for great things. This advice appears in the works of Ralph Waldo EMERSON.

Honesty is the best policy Honesty is more effective than dishonest scheming. This saying appears in *DON QUIXOTE*, by Miguel de CERVANTES.

Hope springs eternal in the human breast People always hope for the best, even in the face of adversity. This saying is from "An ESSAY on Man," by Alexander POPE.

If at first you don't succeed, try, try again Keep trying.

If wishes were horses, then beggars would ride If wishing could make things happen, then even the most destitute people would have everything they wanted.

If you can't stand the heat, get out of the kitchen Don't take on a job if you are unwilling to face its pressures.
  ❧ This saying was a favorite of President Harry TRUMAN.

Ignorance is bliss Not knowing something is often more comfortable than knowing it.
  ❧ This PROVERB resembles "What you don't know cannot hurt you." It figures in a passage from "On a Distant Prospect of Eton College," by the eighteenth-century English poet Thomas Gray: "Where ignorance is bliss, / 'Tis folly to be wise."

Imitation is the sincerest form of flattery To imitate someone is to pay the person a genuine compliment — often an unintended compliment.

Knowledge is power The more one knows, the more one will be able to control events. This sentence is found in the works of Francis BACON.

Laugh, and the world laughs with you; weep, and you weep alone People prefer cheerfulness in others. A person who is cheerful will have company, but someone who is gloomy will often be alone. A poet of the late nineteenth and early twentieth centuries, Ella Wheeler Wilcox, is the author of this saying.

laughs last, laughs best, He who You may laugh now, thinking you have won, but you may not prevail in the end.

Leave well enough alone If things are going tolerably well, leave them alone; your efforts to improve the situation may make things worse.

leopard cannot change its spots, The We cannot change our basic nature. This saying is adapted from words in the biblical Book of JEREMIAH: "Can the Ethiopian change his skin, or the leopard his spots?"

Let them eat cake A saying that shows insensitivity to or incomprehension of the realities of life for the unfortunate. ROUSSEAU, in his *CONFESSIONS*, tells of a great princess who, on being informed that the country people had no bread, replied, "Let them eat cake." This statement is often, and incorrectly, attributed to MARIE ANTOINETTE.

life, there's hope, While there's Never give up. (*Compare* It's NEVER OVER TILL IT'S OVER.)

Life is short; art is long Good work takes a long time to accomplish. The earliest version of this famous saying that we know of is by the great Greek medical doctor HIPPOCRATES. It was repeated by many artists and writers including Seneca, CHAUCER, GOETHE, LONGFELLOW, and BROWNING.

Lightning never strikes twice in the same place Misfortune does not occur twice in the same way to the same person.
  ❧ In the actual world, LIGHTNING can strike twice in the same place.

light under a bushel, Don't hide your Do not conceal your talents or abilities. This PROVERB is taken from the SERMON ON THE MOUNT; JESUS is telling believers not to hide their faith.

little learning is a dangerous thing, A People who know only a little do not understand how little they know and are therefore prone to error. First said by Alexander POPE.

Little pitchers have big ears Adults must be careful about what they say within the hearing of children. The saying refers to the large handles (ears) sometimes attached to small vessels.

Little strokes fell great oaks Limited strength, when persistently applied, can accomplish great feats. This PROVERB is found in *POOR RICHARD'S ALMANACK*, by Benjamin FRANKLIN.

Live and learn Learn from experience and from your mistakes.

Live and let live We should live the life we choose and allow others to do the same.

lock the stable door after the horse has been stolen, Don't It's foolish to take precautions after the damage they would have prevented has already been done. Another version of this saying is "Don't CLOSE THE BARN DOOR AFTER THE HORSE RUNS AWAY."

Look before you leap We should know what we are getting into before we commit ourselves.

Love conquers all Love overcomes all obstacles. This saying is found in the works of the ancient Roman poet VIRGIL.

Love makes the world go 'round Love is the principal force behind human life. In MEDIEVAL THEOLOGY, it was held that love literally set the UNIVERSE in motion.

love of money is the root of all evil, The All wrongdoing can be traced to an excessive attachment to material wealth. This saying comes from the writings of the APOSTLE PAUL. It is sometimes shortened to "MONEY IS THE ROOT OF ALL EVIL."

made your bed, now lie in it, You've You made a decision and now must accept its consequences.

&. This expression is commonly used as a response to people who have been complaining about problems they have brought on themselves.

Make haste slowly The quickest way to accomplish something is to proceed deliberately.

Make hay while the sun shines Take advantage of favorable circumstances; they may not last.

Man does not live by bread alone People have spiritual as well as physical needs. In the BIBLE, these words are spoken by MOSES to the ISRAELITES in the EXODUS; they are also used by JESUS in disputing with SATAN.

man is known by the company he keeps, A Our character is reflected in our choice of friends.

Man proposes, God disposes People can make plans; God determines how things will turn out.

man's home is his castle, A People enjoy the position of king or queen in their own home, and others have no right to enter without the householder's permission.

&. The legal doctrine "A man's home is his castle" is reflected in the BILL OF RIGHTS: "The right of the people to be secure in their ... houses ... against unreasonable searches and seizures shall not be violated."

many a slip 'twixt the cup and the lip, There's Between the time we decide to do something and the time we do it, things often go wrong.

Many hands make light work Large tasks become small when divided among several people.

Marry in haste, repent at leisure If we marry without thinking about the decision, we will have a lifetime to regret the choice.

meek shall inherit the earth, The Pushy people do not succeed in the end. This saying is adapted from the BEATITUDES of JESUS.

Misery loves company People who are unhappy may get some consolation from knowing that others are unhappy too.

miss is as good as a mile, A A near miss is still a miss and therefore no better than missing by a great margin. Losing a game by one point is still losing.

Money is the root of all evil A more extreme version of "The LOVE OF MONEY IS THE ROOT OF ALL EVIL."

more the merrier, The The more people there are involved in something, the more fun it will be.

🖎 "The more the merrier" is often used to welcome those who wish to participate in an activity but hesitate to join in uninvited.

more than one way to skin a cat, There's Many tasks can be accomplished in several ways.

mountain labored and brought forth a mouse, The These results are disappointing after all the buildup they were given.

mountain will not come to Mohammed, then Mohammed will go to the mountain, If the If someone won't do this thing for me, I'll do it for myself. The PROVERB can also be interpreted this way: We may find a way to make a difficult situation better if we simply think about the situation in different terms.

Murder will out Crime or wrongdoing will eventually come to light.

Music has charms to soothe a savage breast Music has the power to enchant even the roughest of people. This PROVERB comes from the play *The Mourning Bride*, by William Congreve, an English author of the late seventeenth and early eighteenth centuries.

nail the kingdom was lost, For want of a Something of great importance may depend on an apparently trivial detail. The saying comes from a longer PROVERB about a battle during which the loss of a nail in a horseshoe leads to the loss of a horse, which leads to the loss of the rider, which leads to the loss of the battle, which in turn leads to the loss of a whole kingdom.

Necessity is the mother of invention A need or problem encourages creative efforts to meet the need or solve the problem. This saying appears in the dialogue *REPUBLIC*, by the ancient Greek PHILOSOPHER PLATO.

Never give a sucker an even break Don't hesitate to take advantage of a fool.
🖎 This saying served as the title for one of the films of the comedian W. C. FIELDS.

never over till it's over, It's Don't give up too soon; there may still be a chance to succeed. Various forms of the saying have been attributed to professional baseball manager Yogi Berra.

Never put off until tomorrow what you can do today Don't procrastinate.

Never say die Never give up.

never too late to mend, It's It is never too late to change your ways.

never too old to learn, You're Learning is always possible. (*Compare* TEACH AN OLD DOG NEW TRICKS, YOU CAN'T.)

new broom sweeps clean, A New leadership injects energy.

Nice guys finish last Winning requires toughness, even ruthlessness; attributed to professional baseball manager Leo Durocher.

No man can serve two masters One's loyalties must be undivided. This is a saying of JESUS from the GOSPELS. Jesus goes on to say, "YE CANNOT SERVE GOD AND MAMMON" — that is, God and money.

No man is an island No one is self-sufficient; everyone relies on others. This saying comes from a sermon by the seventeenth-century English author John DONNE.

No news is good news Not hearing about a situation suggests that nothing bad has happened.

No one ever went broke underestimating the intelligence of the American people People can easily be persuaded to accept the most inferior ideas or useless products; attributed to H. L. MENCKEN.

no place like home, There's Home is the best of all places. This saying comes from the song "HOME, SWEET HOME."

Nothing succeeds like success Success breeds more success.

Nothing ventured, nothing gained If you don't risk anything, you won't gain anything.

Nothing will come of nothing You will gain nothing if you invest nothing. This saying is spoken by the title CHARACTER in the play *KING LEAR*, by William SHAKESPEARE. King Lear is telling his daughter CORDELIA that she will gain no favors from him if she does not make elaborate speeches saying she loves him.

Oil and water don't mix Certain qualities or personalities are incompatible.

Old soldiers never die; they only fade away A line from a song popular among soldiers in BRITAIN in WORLD WAR I.

2. This PROVERB became particularly famous when General Douglas MACARTHUR quoted it after being relieved of his command in the KOREAN WAR.

omelet without breaking eggs, You can't make an We have to give up or destroy something to gain something.

Once bitten, twice shy An injury makes a person wary of its cause. (*Compare* BURNT CHILD FEARS THE FIRE, THE.)

One good turn deserves another A kindness is properly met with another kindness.

One man's meat is another man's poison What is good for one person may be bad for another; what is pleasant to one person may be unpleasant to another.

One picture is worth a thousand words A visual image can convey an idea or an emotion more effectively than words.

One rotten apple spoils the barrel A single bad influence can ruin what would otherwise remain good.

One swallow does not make a summer One piece of evidence doesn't prove the case.

ounce of prevention is worth a pound of cure, An A little precaution before a crisis occurs is preferable to a lot of fixing up afterward. (*See also* STITCH IN TIME SAVES NINE, A.)

Out of sight, out of mind We often forget about things or people who are absent.

pays the piper calls the tune, The one who The person who hires another determines the SERVICES to be rendered.

pen is mightier than the sword, The Human history is influenced more by the written word than by warfare.

penny saved is a penny earned, A Money not spent is money that is in one's pocket.

People who live in glass houses shouldn't throw stones We shouldn't complain about others if we are as bad as they are.

place for everything and everything in its place, A Things should be kept in order.

Poets are born, not made Poets, like all true artists, possess talent that cannot be taught.

Politics makes strange bedfellows Political interests can bring together people who otherwise have little in common. This saying is adapted from a line in the play *THE TEMPEST*, by William SHAKESPEARE: "Misery acquaints a man with strange bedfellows." It is spoken by a man who has been shipwrecked and finds himself seeking shelter beside a sleeping monster.

Practice makes perfect Doing something over and over makes one better at it.

Practice what you preach Do yourself what you advise others to do.

Pride goeth before a fall People who are overconfident or too arrogant are likely to fail. This saying is adapted from the biblical Book of PROVERBS.

Procrastination is the thief of time Putting things off robs us of the opportunity to accomplish something.

proof of the pudding is in the eating, The Actual use is the best test. This saying appears in *DON QUIXOTE*, by Miguel de CERVANTES.

rains but it pours, It never When misfortunes occur, they seem to occur all at once.

Render unto Caesar the things which are Caesar's Keep politics separate from certain other fields, such as religion. This is part of a saying of JESUS in the GOSPELS; the full version is "RENDER UNTO CAESAR THE THINGS WHICH ARE CAESAR'S, AND TO GOD THE THINGS THAT ARE GOD'S."

road to hell is paved with good intentions, The Merely intending to do good, without actually doing it, is of no value.

rolling stone gathers no moss, A This PROVERB now has two meanings: people pay a price for being always on the move: they have no roots in a specific place (the original meaning); or people who keep moving avoid picking up responsibilities and cares.

Rome wasn't built in a day Valuable projects take time.

round peg in a square hole, You can't fit a   People can't be forced into roles for which they are not suited.

royal road to learning, There is no   People prepare a smooth path for a king to move on, but no one can make it easy for a king or anyone else to learn. If we wish to learn, we must work hard for ourselves. According to tradition, this was said by EUCLID to the king of EGYPT.

Seeing is believing   I'll believe it when I see it with my own eyes.

show must go on, The   People are counting on us to do this, and we must not disappoint them.
   ❧ This notion is supposed to be a fundamental principle of entertainers.

Sic transit gloria mundi (SIK TRAN-sit GLAWR-ee-uh MOON-dee)   LATIN for "Thus passes away the glory of the world"; worldly things do not last.

Silence is golden   Silence is of great value.

Silence is golden; speech is silver   Speaking is fine, but silence is better yet.

silk purse from a sow's ear, You can't make a   It is impossible to make something excellent from poor material.

sleeping dogs lie, Let   Do not stir up a problem that has lain quiet for some time.

Slow but steady wins the race   Consistent, effective effort leads to success. This is the moral of one of AESOP'S FABLES, "The TORTOISE AND THE HARE."

smoke there's fire, Where there's   Rumor means that something is afoot, even if not exactly what is rumored.

snows of yesteryear, Where are the   Why does life fade so quickly? This saying comes from the works of the fifteenth-century French poet François VILLON.

soft answer turneth away wrath, A   A gentle reply to someone who is angry will pacify that person. This saying comes from the Book of PROVERBS in the BIBLE.

Spare the rod and spoil the child   Children need physical punishment in order to develop.

Speech is silver; silence is golden   *See* SILENCE IS GOLDEN; SPEECH IS SILVER.

spilt milk, Don't cry over   *See* CRY OVER SPILT MILK, DON'T.

spring a young man's fancy lightly turns to thoughts of love, In the   Spring is the season for love. This line is from a poem "Locksley Hall," by Alfred, Lord TENNYSON.

Step on a crack, break your mother's back   Bad luck will come from stepping on the seams of a sidewalk.

Still waters run deep   A person's calm exterior often conceals great depths of character, just as the deepest streams can have the smoothest surfaces.

stitch in time saves nine, A   A little preventive maintenance can eliminate the need for major repairs later. (*See also* OUNCE OF PREVENTION IS WORTH A POUND OF CURE, AN.)

Stone walls do not a prison make   External constraints cannot imprison someone whose spirit and thoughts are free. This saying is taken from a poem, "To Althea: From Prison," by the seventeenth-century English poet Richard Lovelace.

Strike while the iron is hot   Take advantage of favorable circumstances while they last. The image is from a blacksmith's shop; the smith can shape iron only by striking it with his hammer when it is red hot.

sublime to the ridiculous is but a step, From the   In life, things that are noble and magnificent are never far from things that are trivial and laughable. This saying has been attributed to both NAPOLEON BONAPARTE and the French statesman Talleyrand.

Take the bitter with the sweet   Accept life's misfortunes as well as its joys.

take it with you, You can't   We all must leave worldly wealth behind when we die.
   ❧ This PROVERB was used as the title of a COMEDY by the twentieth-century American playwrights Moss Hart and George S. Kaufman. *You Can't Take It with You* concerns an unconventional family fiercely opposed to materialistic values.

takes a heap o' livin' in a house t' make it home, It   A house is just a building until we have lived in it long enough for it to feel like "home," a place intimately associated with life's trials and joys. This saying is from a poem by the twentieth-century American author Edgar A. Guest.

takes a thief to catch a thief, It Only a thief knows how a thief thinks and acts.

takes two to tango, It Certain activities cannot be performed alone — such as quarreling, making love, and dancing the TANGO.

taste, There's no accounting for Personal preferences are not debatable. This saying is a version of a LATIN PROVERB, *DE GUSTIBUS NON EST DISPUTANDUM.*

teach an old dog new tricks, You can't People who have long been used to doing things in a particular way will not abandon their habits. (*Compare* NEVER TOO OLD TO LEARN, YOU'RE.)

Those who cannot remember the past are condemned to repeat it Studying history is necessary to avoid repeating past mistakes. This saying comes from the writings of George Santayana, an American author of the late nineteenth and early twentieth centuries.

throw out the baby with the bath water, Don't In getting rid of waste, don't also discard what is worth keeping.

Time and tide wait for no man The processes of nature continue, no matter how much we might like them to stop. The word *tide* meant "time" when this PROVERB was created, so it may have been the ALLITERATION of the words that first appealed to people. Now the word *tide* in this proverb is usually thought of in terms of the sea, which certainly does not wait for anyone.

Time heals all wounds People eventually get over insults, injuries, and hatreds.

Time is money If we don't use our working time to earn money, we are in effect losing money.

Too many cooks spoil the broth When too many people work together on a project, the result is inferior.

Truth is stranger than fiction Sometimes what actually happens is more bizarre than anything that could have been imagined.

Truth will out One way or another, in spite of all efforts to conceal it, the truth will come to be known.

Turnabout is fair play You had your turn; now it's only fair that I should have mine. (*Compare* DOG HAS HIS DAY, EVERY.)

Two heads are better than one Some problems may be solved more easily by two people working together than by one working alone.

two masters, No man can serve *See* NO MAN CAN SERVE TWO MASTERS.

Two wrongs don't make a right An evil act can't be corrected with more evil.

Two's company, three's a crowd One companion is better than two.
   This saying is often used by lovers who want to be by themselves.

Uneasy lies the head that wears a crown A person who has great responsibilities, such as a king, is constantly worried and therefore doesn't sleep soundly. This saying is a line from the play *King Henry the Fourth, Part Two*, by William SHAKESPEARE.

unscramble an egg, You can't Some processes are irreversible. (*See* ENTROPY.)

Variety is the spice of life Changes and new experiences make life delightful.

Walls have ears We may be overheard without our knowing it.
   This saying is a warning to persons with secrets.

Waste not, want not If we don't waste what we have, we'll still have it in the future and will not lack (want) it.

watched pot never boils, A Something we wait for with impatient attention seems to take forever.

way to a man's heart is through his stomach, The A woman can best endear herself to a man by feeding him well.

Well begun is half done A good beginning almost assures success.

What will be, will be Some things cannot be prevented from happening.

When the going gets tough, the tough get going The way to overcome adversity is to try harder.

When in Rome, do as the Romans do   When visiting a foreign land, follow the customs of those who live in it.

When it rains, it pours   *See* RAINS BUT IT POURS, IT NEVER.

whites of their eyes, Don't fire until you see the   Don't react to a situation too early. This saying comes from an order allegedly given by an American officer, William Prescott, at the Battle of BUNKER HILL in the American REVOLUTIONARY WAR.

will, there's a way, Where there's a   If you want something badly enough, you can find the means to get it.

win or lose, it's how you play the game, It's not whether you   Reaching a goal is less important than giving our best effort. (*Compare* WINNING ISN'T EVERYTHING; IT'S THE ONLY THING.)

Win this one for the Gipper   Do this in memory of somebody you revere; attributed to Knute Rockne, coach of the Notre Dame football team, during a half-time pep talk at the 1928 Army–Notre Dame football game. Rockne told his team that a former player, George Gipp, had said on his deathbed, "Rock, someday when things look real tough for Notre Dame, ask the boys to go out there and win for me." The incident was made famous in a movie in which Ronald REAGAN played George Gipp.

Winning isn't everything; it's the only thing   Attributed to the professional football coach Vince Lombardi, this PROVERB stresses the importance of reaching a goal no matter what effort is required. (*Compare* WIN OR LOSE, IT'S HOW YOU PLAY THE GAME, IT'S NOT WHETHER YOU.)

wish is father of the deed, The   Desire leads to action.

word to the wise is sufficient, A   Intelligent people can take hints; they don't need to have everything explained to them at great length.

  ঌ The PHRASE "a word to the wise" frequently accompanies a warning of some sort.

Work expands to fill the time available for its completion   A PROVERB coined by the twentieth-century British scholar C. Northcote Parkinson, known as PARKINSON'S LAW. It points out that people usually take all the time allotted (and frequently more) to accomplish any task.

worm turns, The   One's luck or fortune changes. (*Compare* DOG HAS HIS DAY, EVERY.)

Yes, Virginia, there is a Santa Claus   Our fantasies and MYTHS are important, and often are spiritually if not literally true. This saying originated in 1897 in a newspaper EDITORIAL by Francis Pharcellus Church, written in reply to a girl named Virginia who said that her friends had told her there was no Santa Claus. Church also said about Santa Claus that "ten times ten thousand years from now, he will continue to make glad the heart of childhood."

You can lead a horse to water, but you can't make him drink   You can show people the way to do things, but you can't force them to act.

Idioms

It isn't always the non–native speaker's accent (which may be perfect) that enables people to recognize instantly an outsider who is learning their language, but the odd mistakes that no native speaker would make. The foreigner's little words — PREPOSITIONS such as *to*, *for*, and *with* — are often wrong. The idiomatic use of these words varies from language to language. Just as each person has a unique, characteristic signature, each language has unique idioms. In fact, the word *idiom* comes from the Greek root *idio*, meaning a unique signature. Thus, each language contains expressions that make no sense when translated literally into another tongue. Art Buchwald wrote a famous column, often reprinted, in which he translated some of our Thanksgiving (Merci-donnant) terms into literal French, with comic results. If a German or Spaniard or Italian literally translated BIRTHDAY SUIT and GET DOWN TO BRASS TACKS, the terms would make no sense, or the wrong sense. Even a native speaker of English who is not used to hearing literate idioms like FITS AND STARTS, COCK-AND-BULL STORY, HUE AND CRY, and TOUCH AND GO will not be able to make sense of them. Our purpose in defining these idioms is to LET THE CAT OUT OF THE BAG for those who haven't heard them often enough to catch their meanings.

Other idioms are really allusions or foreign-language terms that make no sense unless you know what the allusions or terms mean. CARRY COALS TO NEWCASTLE obviously translates adequately into any language, but it makes no sense to a person who hasn't run across the fact that Newcastle is a coal-mining city. Knowing the *literal* meaning of idioms won't enable you to understand them unless you also know what they allude to. Such ignorance is your ACHILLES' HEEL and an ALBATROSS AROUND YOUR NECK. Nothing can take the place of simply knowing the allusion or the foreign-language term; that is the ALPHA AND OMEGA of comprehending such idioms. Moreover, just knowing a BAKER'S DOZEN of them is not enough; you have to know them EN MASSE. Educators who complain about the illiteracy of the young but pay no attention to teaching idioms are just weeping CROCODILE TEARS. We have therefore decided to CUT THE GORDIAN KNOT by systematically defining some of the most widely used idioms in American literate CULTURE.

— E. D. H.

according to Hoyle (HOYL) With strict adherence to a set of rules; fairly and honorably: "We don't want to lose this case over any legal technicalities; everything must be done strictly according to Hoyle." Hoyle was the author of a book on whist in the eighteenth century; his name has since been used in the titles of many books of rules for card games.

ace in the hole A hidden advantage or resource kept in reserve until needed: "The coach was certain that his new trick play would turn out to be his ace in the hole." This term comes from the game of stud poker, in which one or more cards are turned face down, or "in the hole," as bets are placed. The ace is the card with the highest value.

Achilles' heel (uh-KIL-eez)   A point of vulnerability. (*See* ACHILLES.)

act of God   An event beyond human control — e.g., HURRICANE, EARTHQUAKE, volcanic eruption (*see* VOLCANO), etc. — for which there is no legal redress. The PHRASE is frequently used by insurance companies and lawyers.

ad absurdum (ad uhb-SUR-duhm)   An argument whereby one seeks to prove one's position by pointing out the absurdity or foolishness of an opponent's position. Also, an argument carried to such lengths that it becomes silly or ridiculous. (*See* REDUCTIO AD ABSURDUM.) *From* LATIN, *meaning "to absurdity."*

ad hoc (ad HOK, ad HOHK)   A PHRASE describing something created especially for a particular occasion: "We need an ad hoc committee to handle this new problem immediately." From LATIN, meaning "toward this (matter)."

ad hominem (ad HOM-uh-nem, ad HOM-uh-nuhm)   A LATIN expression meaning "to the man." An ad hominem argument is one that relies on personal attacks rather than reason.

ad nauseam (ad NAW-zee-uhm)   To go on endlessly; literally, to continue "to seasickness": "The candidate told us the details of how he overcame his childhood problems *ad nauseam.*"

adieu (uh-DYOOH, uh-DOOH)   French for "goodbye."

adios (ad-ee-OHS, ah-dee-OHS)   Spanish for "goodbye."

albatross around one's neck   An annoying burden: "That old car is an albatross around my neck." Literally, an albatross is a large sea bird. The PHRASE alludes to Samuel Taylor COLERIDGE's poem "The RIME OF THE ANCIENT MARINER," in which a sailor who shoots a friendly albatross is forced to wear its carcass around his neck as punishment.

all thumbs   Clumsy or awkward: "Where plumbing is concerned, Walter is all thumbs."

alma mater (AL-muh MAH-tuhr, AHL-muh MAH-tuhr)   The school or university from which one graduated. The term also refers to a school's official song: "The reunion began with everyone singing the alma mater." From LATIN, meaning "nurturing mother."

aloha (uh-LOH-hah)   Hawaiian for "love," used to express greeting or farewell.

alpha and omega (AL-fuh; oh-MAY-guh, oh-MEG-uh, oh-MEE-guh)   The beginning and the end. In the NEW TESTAMENT Book of REVELATION, God says, "I am Alpha and Omega," meaning that he is the beginning and end of all things. In the Greek alphabet, alpha is the first letter and omega is the last.

A.M.   An ABBREVIATION for the LATIN PHRASE *ante meridiem*, meaning "before noon," or midday; the twelve hours from midnight to noon. "In the A.M." means "in the morning." (*Compare* P.M.)

And thereby hangs a tale   An expression, taken from *As You Like It*, by William SHAKESPEARE, that means roughly "There's a real story behind this." It is commonly used by someone who is about to give the background of an interesting object, incident, or idea: "The colonel remarked, 'See that umbrella over the mantelpiece? It saved my life during the war, and thereby hangs a tale.'"

annus mirabilis (AN-uhs mi-RAB-uh-lis)   A LATIN expression meaning "miraculous year." The term is used to refer to a year in which an unusual number of remarkable things occurred: "'THE WASTE LAND' and *ULYSSES* both appeared in 1922, the *annus mirabilis* of modern literature."

anon.   An ABBREVIATION for *anonymous*, used to indicate unknown or unacknowledged authorship. Without the period, *anon* means "at another time" or "again."

apple of one's eye   The favorite object of a person's love or affection: "Linda was fond of all the horses on the ranch, but the little palomino was the apple of her eye."

arrivederci (ah-ree-ve-DER-chee)   Italian for "goodbye" or "until we meet again."

as the crow flies   The most direct route between two places: "The sea voyage from NEW YORK to SAN FRANCISCO is a long one, though it's not so far as the crow flies."

at loggerheads   Engaged in a head-on dispute: "Labor and MANAGEMENT are at loggerheads in this affair, and it may be some time before they can negotiate a settlement."

at sixes and sevens In a state of confusion or disorder: "Trying to cram for this math test has me all at sixes and sevens."

au revoir (oh ruh-VWAHR) French for "good-bye" or "until we meet again."

auf Wiedersehen (owf VEE-duhr-zay-uhn) German for "good-bye" or "until we meet again."

back to the drawing board A saying indicating that one's effort has failed, and one must start all over again: "The new package we designed hasn't increased our sales as we'd hoped, so it's back to the drawing board."

baker's dozen Thirteen; bakers once provided an extra roll with every dozen sold.

beat around the bush To avoid getting to the point of an issue: "Your worries have nothing to do with the new proposal. Stop beating around the bush, and cast your vote!"

bee in one's bonnet A chronic preoccupation, often fanciful or eccentric: "Cohen has a bee in his bonnet about the rudeness of local cabdrivers; he's written four letters to the editor on the subject."

beg the question To assume what has still to be proved: "To say that we should help the democratic movement in Ilyria begs the question of whether it really is democratic."

behind the eight ball A term, referring to the game of pool, meaning in an unfavorable or uncomfortable position: "After his unkind remarks were repeated to the boss, Gary really ended up behind the eight ball."

bête noire (BET NWAHR) A "bête noire" is a thing or person one views with particular dislike: "The new candidate for governor is the bête noire of all the LIBERALS in the state." From French, meaning "black beast."

beyond the pale Totally unacceptable: "His business practices have always been questionable, but this last takeover was beyond the pale." The Pale in IRELAND was a territorial limit beyond which English rule did not extend.

birthday suit To be "in one's birthday suit" is to be completely naked (as people are at birth): "The rock star was not pleased to learn that the magazine had published old photos of him in his birthday suit."

bit between one's teeth To "take the bit between one's teeth" means resolutely to face up to a hard task: "Ralph is having a difficult time in medical school now, but once he takes the bit between his teeth, there's no stopping him." The bit is the part of a bridle that controls a horse by allowing the rider to pull on its mouth. If the horse takes the bit between its teeth, it can't be controlled.

bite the bullet To adjust to unpleasant circumstances: "The severe drought is forcing everybody to bite the bullet and use less water." Before anesthesia, surgeons operating on the wounded gave them a bullet to bite to help them withstand the pain.

bite the dust To suffer a defeat: "Once again, the champion wins, and another contender bites the dust."

black sheep A person who is considered a disgrace to a particular group, usually a family: "Uncle Jack, who was imprisoned for forgery, is the black sheep of the family."

blarney Smooth, flattering talk, often nonsensical or deceptive. Based on an Irish legend that those who kiss the BLARNEY STONE will become skilled in flattery.

blind leading the blind An expression applied to leaders who know as little as their followers, and are therefore likely to lead them astray: "When it comes to science and technology, many politicians know as little as the average citizen; they're the blind leading the blind."

blow hot and cold To change one's mind constantly about the value of something: "The administration should stop issuing such contradictory statements on taxes; they are alienating the voters by blowing hot and cold on tax reform."

blow one's own horn To brag about oneself: "While usually modest, Marilyn had to blow her own horn a bit during the job interview." Sometimes phrased as TOOT ONE'S OWN HORN.

bolt from (out of) the blue   An unexpected event that strikes like LIGHTNING from the sky: "He had been with the company for eighteen years; when he was fired, it must have felt like a bolt from the blue."

bona fide (BOH-nuh feyed, boh-nuh FEYE-dee, BON-uh feyed)   Genuine: "The offer was a bona fide business opportunity: they really meant to carry it through." From LATIN, meaning "in good faith."

bone to pick   Having a "bone to pick with someone" means having a grievance that needs to be talked out: "I have a bone to pick with you, Wallace; I heard how you criticized me at the meeting last night."

bonjour (bohn-ZHOOHR)   French for "good day" or "hello."

born with a silver spoon in one's mouth   Born into a wealthy family: "He may have a lot of money, but he earned every penny himself; he wasn't born with a silver spoon in his mouth."

brain trust   A group of experts who serve as advisers to a government or organization: "Before being appointed to the CABINET, Brown had been a leading figure in a financial brain trust."

break the ice   To remove the tension at a first meeting, at the opening of a party, etc.: "That joke about the car salesman really broke the ice at the conference; we all relaxed afterward."

burn the candle at both ends   To do more than one ought to; to overextend oneself: "His doctor said that his illness was brought on by STRESS, and recommended that he stop burning the candle at both ends."

burn the midnight oil   To stay awake late at night to work or study: "Jill has been burning the midnight oil lately; I guess she has a big exam coming up."

burn your bridges behind you   To eliminate any possibility of a retreat to a former position: "In his ruthless pursuit of success, Sloane offended all his co-workers and effectively burned his bridges behind him."

bury the hatchet   To agree to end a quarrel: "Jerry and Joe had been avoiding each other since the fight, but I saw them together this morning, so they must have buried the hatchet."

busman's holiday   A vacation during which a person engages in activity that is the same as or similar to his or her usual employment: "Our Spanish professor had a busman's holiday this year; she spent her entire vacation doing research in SPAIN."

butter someone up   To praise or flatter someone excessively: "Percy was always buttering up the boss, so he was surprised when he failed to get a promotion."

buy a pig in a poke   To buy something sight unseen (a "poke" is a bag): "The mail-order offer sounded like a bargain, but I didn't want to buy a pig in a poke."

by the book   According to established rules: "The inspector will be visiting the plant today, so let's make sure we do everything by the book."

by hook or by crook   By whatever means possible, fair or unfair: "Ed was determined to get an A on the exam by hook or by crook."

call a spade a spade   To speak directly and bluntly; to avoid EUPHEMISM: "The prosecutor said, 'Let's call a spade a spade; you didn't borrow the money, you stole it.'"

call the tune   To be in control. The PHRASE comes from the PROVERB "The one who PAYS THE PIPER CALLS THE TUNE."

can't hold a candle to   An expression describing a person or thing that is distinctly inferior to someone or something else: "Senator Nelson is extremely knowledgeable, but as a speaker, he can't hold a candle to Senator Delano."

can't see the forest for the trees   An expression used of someone who is too involved in the details of a problem to look at the situation as a whole: "The congressman became so involved in the wording of his bill that he couldn't see the forest for the trees; he did not realize that the bill could never pass."

carry coals to Newcastle   To do something that is obviously superfluous; Newcastle is a city in ENGLAND where coal is mined: "Karen wanted to give

Dad a magazine subscription for his birthday, but I said that would be like carrying coals to Newcastle, since he already has fifteen or twenty subscriptions."

carry a torch for To be infatuated with: "Frank may be engaged to Helen, but I think he still carries a torch for Laura."

carry the torch To carry on a cause: "The columnist feels that he is carrying the torch of LIBERALISM in a CONSERVATIVE period."

carte blanche (kahrt BLAHNSH, kahrt BLAHNCH) To be given "carte blanche" is to receive the power and authority to do as one wishes: "The PRIME MINISTER herself did not take any action on the refugee issue but gave her MINISTER of the interior carte blanche to deal with the situation." *Carte blanche* is French for "blank card," meaning one that can be filled in as a person wishes.

cash in one's chips An expression referring to gambling, meaning to quit: "Since his argument wasn't convincing the committee, Tony decided to cash in his chips and go home." Also, a EUPHEMISM for dying.

castles in the air Extravagant hopes and plans that will never be carried out: "I told him he should stop building castles in the air and train for a sensible profession."

catch-as-catch-can A PHRASE that describes a situation in which people must improvise, or do what they can with limited means: "We don't have enough textbooks for all of the students, so it'll be catch-as-catch-can."

cause célèbre (kohz say-LEB-ruh, kawz suh-LEB) A cause or issue, generally political, that arouses public opinion: "The question of the DRAFT was a *cause célèbre* in the 1960s." From French, meaning "celebrated cause."

C'est la vie (se lah VEE) An expression used to play down some minor disappointment: "So we lost a softball game by twenty-two runs. What can you do; *c'est la vie*." From French, meaning "that's life."

cheek by jowl Situated side by side or in close contact: "The commuters were packed in the subway cheek by jowl."

chip off the old block An expression used of people who closely resemble their parents in some way: "Mark just won the same sailboat race his father won twenty years ago; he's a chip off the old block."

chip on one's shoulder To "have a chip on one's shoulder" is to invite conflict by being extremely touchy: "Joe really has a chip on his shoulder; every time I say something to him, he takes it the wrong way." In the past, a young boy would place a wood chip on his shoulder and dare anyone to knock it off as a way of showing how tough he was.

chutzpah (KHOOT-spuh, HOOT-spuh) Yiddish term for courage bordering on arrogance, roughly equivalent to "nerve" (in the SLANG sense): "It took a lot of chutzpah to make such a controversial statement."

clean bill of health To "get a clean bill of health" is to be told by some authoritative source, generally a doctor, that one is perfectly healthy. The PHRASE is sometimes used figuratively to indicate that a person or organization has been found free of any sort of irregularity: "After looking into her financial background, the SENATE gave the nominee a clean bill of health."

clean slate A new start; especially to make a new start by clearing the record. This PHRASE comes from the use of chalk and slates in classrooms in the past. By wiping the slate clean, a student could remove any evidence of a mistake.

climb on the bandwagon To join a particular cause or political party: "When the party leader saw how popular the opposition was becoming, he decided to climb on the bandwagon and offer his full support to his opponent."

cock-and-bull story A story that is false: "When John came home at 3:30 A.M., he gave his mother some cock-and-bull story about having a flat tire on the way home." Probably connected to fables in which animals talk.

cockles of the heart, warm the To cause a feeling of affectionate happiness: "The thought of his grandmother was enough to warm the cockles of his heart."

cold feet To "have cold feet" is to be too fearful to undertake or complete an action: "The backup quarterback was called into the game, but he got cold feet and refused to go in."

cold shoulder, the   To "give someone the cold shoulder" is to ignore someone deliberately: "At the party, Carl tried to talk to Suzanne, but she gave him the cold shoulder."

cold turkey   To "go cold turkey" is to withdraw suddenly and completely from an addictive substance or some other form of dependency: "The majority of those who attempt to quit smoking do so by going cold turkey rather than by gradually cutting down."

come full circle   When something "comes full circle," it completes a cycle, returns to its beginnings: "The novelist's vision of human life has come full circle — from optimism to pessimism and back to optimism again."

comme il faut (kum eel FOH)   A French expression meaning "as it should be." It describes an action that is properly or correctly performed according to some code of manners: "Everyone agreed that Andrea's behavior at the dinner party was not *comme il faut*."

cool one's heels   To wait for a long time: "The doctor kept her cooling her heels for almost an hour."

cotton to   To take a liking to someone or something: "I was afraid Janet wouldn't like my brother, but she cottoned to him immediately."

coup de grâce (kooh duh GRAHS)   The final blow: "He had been getting deeper and deeper in DEBT; the fates delivered the coup de grâce when he died." The PHRASE is French for "stroke of mercy." It originally referred to the merciful stroke that put a fatally wounded person out of his misery or to the shot delivered to the head of a prisoner after he had faced a firing squad.

creature comforts   The basic physical things that make life pleasant — good food, warm clothing, etc.: "The poor frequently lack the creature comforts the rest of us take for granted."

crème de la crème (KREM duh lah KREM)   The best of the best: "Our school's marching band is acknowledged as the *crème de la crème*." From French meaning, "cream of the cream."

crocodile tears   An insincere show of sympathy or sadness; crocodiles were once thought to "weep"

large tears before they ate their victims: "Don't shed any crocodile tears for Fisher; I know you were responsible for his firing."

Croesus, rich as (KREE-suhs)   Extremely wealthy. Croesus was an ancient Greek king whose wealth was legendary.

cross the Rubicon (ROOH-bi-kon)   to make an irrevocable decision; it comes from the name of the river JULIUS CAESAR crossed with his army, thereby starting a civil war in ROME. (*See* RUBICON.)

cruel to be kind, be   To cause someone pain for his or her own good. The PHRASE is used by HAMLET after he has berated his mother for her infidelity to the memory of her deceased husband.

cry over spilt milk   To dwell pointlessly on past misfortunes: "I know you wish that you'd handled the project more efficiently, but there's no use crying over spilt milk."

cultivate one's own garden   To take care of one's own needs before trying to take care of others: "The mayor ought to cultivate his own garden before he starts telling the governor what to do." This is the moral of *CANDIDE*, by VOLTAIRE: take care of your own and the world will take care of itself.

curry favor   "Currying favor" with someone means trying to ingratiate oneself by fawning over that person: "The ambassador curried favor with the dictator by praising his construction projects."

cut the Gordian knot   To solve a notoriously difficult problem in a quick and decisive manner: "The president hoped that his bold new anti-INFLATION plan would cut the Gordian knot." According to Greek legend, an oracle declared that the man who could untie the GORDIAN KNOT would become the ruler of all ASIA. ALEXANDER THE GREAT impatiently cut it with a single stroke of his sword and proceeded to conquer Asia.

damn with faint praise   To criticize someone or something indirectly by giving a slight compliment: "When the critic remarked that Miller's book was 'not as bad as some I've read,' she was obviously damning it with faint praise."

Danke schön (DAHNG-kuh SHEUN, DAHNG-kuh SHURN)   German for "thank you."

Davy Jones's Locker Sailors' SLANG for the bottom of the ocean. Someone drowned at sea may be said to have "gone down to Davy Jones's Locker."

de facto (di FAK-toh, day FAK-toh) Something generally accepted or agreed to without any formal decision in its favor: "They never elected him; he became their leader de facto." From LATIN, meaning "in fact." (*Compare* DE JURE.)

de jure (di JOOR-ee, day YOOR-ay) Determined by law. In the South, racial SEGREGATION was *de jure*, but in the North, it was DE FACTO.

de rigueur (duh ree-GUR) A French term meaning necessary according to convention: "Formal dress is *de rigueur* at weddings."

déjà vu (DAY-zhah VOOH) The strange sensation that something one is now experiencing has happened before: "I knew I had never been in the house before, but as I walked up the staircase, I got a weird sense of déjà vu." From French, meaning "already seen."

devil to pay, the Trouble to be faced as a result of one's actions: "When the principal hears of Bobby's pranks, there will be the DEVIL TO pay."

diamond in the rough Someone or something with potential or talent but lacking training or polish: "Her singing voice is beautiful, but she needs help with her gestures; she's a diamond in the rough." This PHRASE refers to the fact that diamonds found in nature are rough and uneven. They must be cut and polished to bring out their true beauty.

dog days The hot, muggy days of summer. The Romans associated such weather with the influence of Sirius, the dog STAR, which is high in the sky during summer.

dog in the manger A person who spitefully refuses to let someone else benefit from something for which he or she has no personal use: "We asked our neighbor for the fence posts he had left over, but, like a dog in the manger, he threw them out rather than give them to us." The PHRASE comes from one of AESOP'S FABLES, about a dog lying in a manger full of hay. When an ox tries to eat some hay, the dog bites him, despite the fact that the hay is of no use to the dog.

dog-eat-dog Ruthlessly competitive: "You have to look out for your own interests; it's a dog-eat-dog world."

Don Juan (don WAHN, don HWAHN, don JOOH-uhn) An obsessive and unscrupulous pursuer of women: "He charms all the secretaries; he is the Don Juan of the office." From the legendary nobleman who seduced hundreds of women and was eventually damned for his immoral ways. This nobleman is the subject of many works of music, literature, and art, among them MOZART's *DON GIOVANNI* and BYRON's *Don Juan*.

down in the dumps In a gloomy or depressed mood: "After losing the student election, Jack really felt down in the dumps."

draw the line To set a limit, as of acceptable behavior: "Phil sometimes drank a few beers, but generally he knew when to draw the line."

drive a nail into one's coffin To do something that causes you serious and permanent harm: "My uncle has a bad liver; I tell him that every time he drinks, he's driving another nail into his coffin."

Dutch treat An outing or date on which each person pays his or her own way. To "go Dutch" is to go on such a date.

dyed-in-the-wool Thoroughgoing or complete. "The door-to-door EVANGELISTS were wasting their time with Evans; he was a dyed-in-the-wool atheist."

easy come, easy go A PHRASE suggesting lack of concern over how things turn out, and particularly over money: "She never took things very seriously; 'easy come, easy go' was her motto."

eat crow To suffer a humiliating experience: "The organizers had to eat crow when the fair they had sworn would attract thousands drew scarcely a hundred people."

eat humble pie To be forced to acknowledge one's deficiencies or errors: "Professor Norris had to eat humble pie when the reviewers pointed out numerous factual errors in his book."

eat someone out of house and home To consume a great deal of someone's food: "Mrs. Baker complained that her three teenagers were eating her out of house and home."

elbow grease   Strenuous physical effort: "If you're going to get this job done, you'll need to apply a little elbow grease."

El Dorado (el duh-RAH-doh)   A place of fabulous wealth, or an opportunity to obtain it. During the GOLD RUSH many adventurers believed that CALIFORNIA would be their El Dorado. The name comes from the name of a legendary South American city of stupendous riches sought by Spanish CONQUISTADORES.

eleventh hour   The last minute: "The water bombers arrived at the eleventh hour — just in time to prevent the forest fire from engulfing the town."

éminence grise (ay-mee-NAHNS GREEZ)   A person who wields power behind the scenes: "The king's brother-in-law is his *éminence grise*; he has enormous influence, though he is rarely in the public eye." A French term meaning "GRAY EMINENCE."

en masse (ahn MAS)   A French PHRASE meaning "in a large body": "The protestors left en masse for the WHITE HOUSE."

end of one's rope   Out of options: "Having tried everything he could think of to get admitted to law school, Robert finally found himself at the end of his rope."

enfant terrible (ahn-FAHN te-REE-bluh)   A person who stirs things up in an irresponsible or indiscreet way or has unconventional ideas: "Doctor Hill keeps writing articles that criticize his fellow physicians; he is becoming known as the enfant terrible of his profession." From French, meaning "terrible child."

ergo (ER-goh, UR-goh)   LATIN word meaning "therefore"; usually used to show a logical conclusion: "BIRDS are WARM-BLOODED, and REPTILES are COLD-BLOODED; ergo, no bird is a reptile."

esprit de corps (es-PREE duh KAWR)   The feeling of camaraderie among members of a group or an organization: "The campers have been together for only one week, but they are already bound by a strong esprit de corps." From French, meaning "group spirit."

Eureka! (yoo-REE-kuh)   A Greek word meaning "I have found it!" An exclamation that accompanies a discovery: "When he finally located the rare book, the scholar cried, 'Eureka!'" (*See* ARCHIMEDES.)

every inch a ———   "Every inch a ———" describes someone whose appearance seems perfectly fitting to his or her profession or STATUS: "The general stood straight and tall at the podium, looking every inch a soldier."

ex cathedra (eks kuh-THEE-druh)   Descriptive term for an official pronouncement from the POPE. *Ex cathedra* is LATIN for "from the chair." ROMAN CATHOLICS believe that the pope speaks infallibly when speaking ex cathedra on questions of faith or morals. The pope has done so once in the last hundred years, when Pope Pius XII declared in 1950 that MARY, THE MOTHER OF JESUS, was physically taken up to HEAVEN after her death.

€ Figuratively, any authoritative pronouncement may be called "ex cathedra."

ex post facto (eks pohst FAK-toh)   An explanation or regulation concocted after the event, sometimes misleading or unjust: "Your ex post facto defense won't stand up in court." (*See* EX POST FACTO LAW.) From LATIN, meaning "after the deed."

Fabian tactics (FAY-bee-uhn)   To "win like Fabius" or to win by "Fabian tactics" is to wear out an opponent by delay and evasion rather than confrontation, in the style of the ancient Roman general Fabius.

face the music   To accept unpleasant consequences: "After several years of cheating his employer, the embezzler finally had to face the music."

fair-weather friend   A friend who supports others only when it is easy and convenient to do so: "I thought Gene would always stick by me, but when I got into trouble, he turned out to be a fair-weather friend."

fait accompli (fayt uh-kom-PLEE, fet ah-kohnn-PLEE)   Something that has already been done: "The company president did not discuss the new hiring policy with his board of directors; instead he put it into effect and presented the board with a *fait accompli*." From French, meaning "an accomplished fact."

far from the madding crowd   To be "far from the madding crowd" is to be removed, either literally or figuratively, from the frenzied actions of any large crowd or from the bustle of civilization. (*See under* "*Literature in English.*")

🍂 The main reason for the currency of this PHRASE is that it was used as the title of a popular NOVEL by the English author Thomas Hardy.

Faustian bargain (FOW-stee-uhn) Faust, in the legend, traded his soul to the DEVIL in exchange for knowledge. To "strike a Faustian bargain" is to be willing to sacrifice anything to satisfy a limitless desire for knowledge or power.

feather in one's cap An accomplishment a person can be proud of: "The negotiator's success in getting the terrorists to release their hostages was a real feather in her cap."

feather one's own nest To look after one's own interests, especially material ones: "The director was supposed to distribute the money to various charities; instead, he used it to feather his own nest."

feet of clay People are said to have "feet of clay" if they are revealed to have a weakness or flaw that most people were unaware of: "When the coach was arrested for drunken driving, the students realized that their hero had feet of clay."

fiddle while Rome burns To do something trivial and irresponsible in the midst of an emergency; legend has it that while a fire destroyed the city of ROME, the emperor NERO played his VIOLIN, thus revealing his total lack of concern for his people and his empire.

fifth wheel A hanger-on; a person who serves no function: "The vice president felt like a fifth wheel after his exclusion from the committee."

fine kettle of fish A troublesomely awkward or embarrassing situation: "Gurnley usually managed to worm his way out of trouble, but this time he found himself in a fine kettle of fish."

first come, first served Those who are first to arrive will be the first to be waited on.

fits and starts To do something in "fits and starts" is to do it intermittently or sporadically: "Martin has been working on his master's thesis in fits and starts; he needs to buckle down to work on it."

flash in the pan Someone or something that promises great success but soon fails: "The rock group that was all the rage last year turned out to be just another flash in the pan."

fly the coop To get away or escape: "The Hendersons found the cocktail party rather dull and decided to fly the coop."

fly in the ointment A drawback, especially one that was not at first apparent: "Joe's lack of experience turned out to be the fly in the ointment when he applied for the job."

fly off the handle To become suddenly enraged: "When Jack's father found out about the car, he really flew off the handle."

fly-by-night Shady or untrustworthy: "Before buying STOCK in a newly formed company, the prudent investor will check its owners' credentials to make sure it's not a fly-by-night operation."

footprints on the sands of time A PHRASE from a poem by Henry Wadsworth LONGFELLOW, describing the mark that great individuals leave on history.

for the birds Worthless: "The last scheme you cooked up was really for the birds."

forty winks A nap; a short sleep: "If you're feeling drowsy, take forty winks; I'll wake you when our guests arrive."

four-letter words EUPHEMISM for the lowest and most common verbal OBSCENITIES.

from pillar to post From one place or thing to another in rapid succession: "Abernathy couldn't stick to one project and was always dashing from pillar to post."

gamut, run the (GAM-uht) To cover a whole range: "The students' reactions to the NOVEL ran the gamut from delight to loathing."

garden path *See* PRIMROSE PATH.

gauntlet, fling (throw) down the (GAWNT-luht) To issue a challenge: "The candidate flung down the gauntlet and challenged his opponent to a debate." A gauntlet was a glove; the wearer would throw it to the ground to show that he was challenging an opponent to fight.

Gesundheit (guh-ZOONT-heyt) German for "good health." Like the English PHRASE "Bless you," it is conventionally said to someone who has just sneezed. This reflects the superstition that a sneeze can cause the soul to fly out of the body; saying the phrase prevents this from happening.

get a dose of one's own medicine To receive the same unpleasant treatment one has given others: "Bart got a dose of his own medicine when everyone in the office started playing practical jokes on him."

get down to brass tacks Get to the real issue; deal with the task at hand: "After avoiding the thorny question of tax reform for months, CONGRESS finally got down to brass tacks last week and drafted a preliminary proposal."

get in somebody's hair To annoy or hinder someone: "Mary tried to ignore Bill and go on with her work, but he was really getting in her hair."

get one's dander up To lose one's temper or to become aroused to some form of action: "The boxer finally got his dander up and went after his opponent with a vengeance."

get someone's goat To make someone annoyed or angry: "Gavin may seem unflappable, but I know a way to get his goat."

get something off one's chest To confess something: "I know something is troubling you; I'm sure you'll feel better if you tell me and get it off your chest."

get up on the wrong side of the bed To act unpleasant because the day got off to a bad start: "Steer clear of the boss today; he got up on the wrong side of the bed this morning."

ghost town A town, especially a boomtown in the old American West, that has been completely abandoned and deserted: "If you drive through the desert, you can still see the main street of Dry Gulch, a ghost town."

gild the lily To adorn unnecessarily something that is already beautiful or perfect: "Morty had us all believing his TALL TALE until he couldn't resist gilding the lily."

gilded cage To be like "a bird in a gilded cage" is to live in luxury but without freedom: "Because the movie star could not go out without being recognized and pursued, she stayed in her penthouse, living like a bird in a gilded cage."

glad-hander An excessively friendly or familiar person: "A glad-hander like Patterson offends more people than he charms."

go against the grain To go contrary to someone's natural disposition: "Having to be up this early in the morning really goes against my grain." This refers to the fact that someone who rubs his hand against the grain on a piece of lumber will get splinters.

go haywire To break down or cease to function properly: "The COMPUTER was running smoothly until something started to go haywire."

go off the deep end To act recklessly or hysterically: "The students were behaving themselves at the party, but then a couple of kids started to go off the deep end."

go to pot To decline or deteriorate: "Since most of the businesses moved out to the suburbs, my old neighborhood has really gone to pot."

go the whole hog To engage in something without reservation or constraint: "At first, the general had his doubts about the plan, but finally he decided to go the whole hog."

golden mean The desirable middle ground between any two extremes, according to the PHILOSOPHY of ARISTOTLE.

goose is cooked, one's One's chances are ruined: "After the recent disclosures of foul play, political analysts feel that the candidate's goose is now thoroughly cooked."

gracias (GRAH-see-uhs, GRAH-thee-uhs) Spanish for "thank you."

grain of salt To "take something with a grain of salt" is to ignore or not worry about it, to treat it as trivial, as worth less than a grain of salt: "The producer took the bad reviews with a grain of salt when her film broke all attendance records."

grasp (clutch) at straws To make a final, desperate effort: "The candidate made a few last attempts to discredit his opponent, but it was clear he was just grasping at straws."

gravy train A job or project that requires little effort but yields considerable profits: "His father worked hard to build the company, but all Percy has to do is sit back and ride the gravy train."

gray eminence See ÉMINENCE GRISE.

green thumb A knack for growing plants and keeping them healthy: "All my houseplants are in sorry shape; it's clear I don't have a green thumb."

green-eyed monster, the Jealousy: "Carl has really been bitten by the green-eyed monster; he gets jealous if his wife so much as talks to another man." This METAPHOR was coined by SHAKESPEARE in his play OTHELLO.

gringo In LATIN AMERICA, a foreigner, especially a North American or Englishman; usually a term of contempt.

gung-ho Extremely enthusiastic or zealous: "He was gung-ho about going on a vacation to the beach."

hail-fellow-well-met A term describing a person who is superficially friendly and is always trying to gain friends. Such a person may also be referred to as a "back-slapper" or a "GLAD-HANDER."

hair of the dog that bit you A remedy that contains a small amount of whatever caused the ailment: "When Anne had a bad hangover, Paul offered her a Bloody Mary and said, 'Have a little of the hair of the dog that bit you.'"

halcyon days (HAL-see-uhn) Times of peace and tranquillity; the expression refers to a mythical bird that had the power to calm the waves when it nested on the sea during the winter SOLSTICE. "Compared to the utter turmoil of last month, these are certainly halcyon days."

have an ax to grind To have a selfish motive or personal stake in a matter: "When the lobbyist approached the senators, they suspected he had an ax to grind."

high horse, on one's Disdainful or conceited: "Sally got tired of Peter's snobbery and finally told him to get off his high horse."

hit below the belt To say something that is often too personal, usually irrelevant, and always unfair: "To remind reformed alcoholics of their drinking problem is to hit below the belt." The expression comes from boxing, in which it is illegal to hit an opponent below the belt.

hit the ceiling To become extremely angry: "When Corey found out someone had stolen his stereo, he really hit the ceiling."

hoi polloi (HOY puh-LOY) The masses, the ordinary folk; the PHRASE is often used in a derogatory way to refer to a popular preference or incorrect opinion: "The hoi polloi may think that Oswald is a great director, but those who know about film realize that his work is commercial and derivative." From Greek, meaning "the many."

hoist with one's own petard (pi-TAHRD) To be caught in one's own trap: "The swindler cheated himself out of most of his money, and his victims were satisfied to see him hoist with his own petard." A "petard" was an explosive device used in MEDIEVAL warfare. To be hoisted, or lifted, by a petard literally means to be blown up.

hold water To seem logical and consistent: "At first I was persuaded by the politician's speech, but upon reflection, I decided that his arguments didn't hold water."

hook, line, and sinker Completely and without reservation: "Mary doubted that her ruse would fool the boss, but he fell for it hook, line, and sinker." The reference is to fishing tackle.

horns of a dilemma, caught on the To be divided between two seemingly equal options, and to be undecided as to which option to choose: "When Mary was offered two equally attractive jobs, she found herself on the horns of a dilemma."

horse of a different color A different matter entirely: "You might be able to convince Devin's father, but as for his mother, that's a horse of a different color."

how many angels can stand (dance) on the head of a pin? Scornful description of a tedious concern with irrelevant details; an allusion to medieval religious controversies. In fact, the medieval argument was over how many ANGELS could stand on the *point* of a pen.

hubris (HYOOH-bris) Arrogance or overbearing pride; from the Greek, meaning "insolence."

hue and cry Any loud clamor or protest intended to incite others to action: "In the 1980s, there arose a great hue and cry for educational reform."

in the doghouse Temporarily out of favor or in trouble: "Tyrone forgot his wife's anniversary, and now he's really in the doghouse."

in hot water   In deep trouble: "When Marjorie flunked algebra, she knew she would be in hot water with her folks."

in loco parentis (in LOH-koh puh-REN-tis)   To assume the duties and responsibilities of a parent: "Because Jack's parents were out of town, his sister acted in loco parentis and punished him for drinking." From LATIN, meaning "in the place of a parent."

❧ At one time, colleges and universities acted in loco parentis for their students, but this is no longer true.

in memoriam (in muh-MAWR-ee-uhm)   A LATIN PHRASE meaning "in memory of." This phrase often precedes a name in obituaries and on tombstones.

in the pink   In good health: "Marsha has recovered from the flu and is feeling in the pink again."

in situ (in SEYE-tooh, in SIT-ooh)   In the original place or arrangement: "The body was left in situ until the police arrived." From LATIN, meaning "in position."

in toto (in TOH-toh)   Totally or completely: "We reject your demands in toto." From LATIN, meaning "in all."

In vino veritas (in VEE-noh VER-ee-tahs)   A LATIN PHRASE suggesting that people are more likely to say what they really feel under the influence of alcohol. It means "There is truth in wine."

Indian summer   A period of unusually warm weather in the fall.

ivory tower, live in an   To lead an impractical existence removed from the pressures and troubles of everyday life: "Like most college professors, Rasponi lives in an ivory tower."

Jack of all trades, master of none   Someone who is good at many things but excellent at none.

je ne sais quoi (zhuh nuh say KWAH)   That little something; that quality that eludes description. "The MONA LISA's smile has a certain *je ne sais quoi.*" From French, meaning "I don't know what."

John Doe, Jane Doe   Fictitious names used in legal proceedings and advertising campaigns to represent the average person.

John Hancock   A signature: "Please help us out and put your John Hancock on our petition." The expression refers to the bold signature that John HANCOCK wrote on the DECLARATION OF INDEPENDENCE.

joie de vivre (zhwah duh VEEV-ruh, VEEV)   A love of life. From French, meaning "joy of living."

jump down someone's throat   To answer or respond sharply or angrily: "It's fine if you don't agree with me, but you don't have to jump down my throat."

keep one's fingers crossed   To hope that nothing will happen to bring bad luck or to ruin one's plans: "Helen will soon find out whether she got into law school; in the meantime, she is keeping her fingers crossed."

keep the wolf from one's door   To ward off poverty or hunger: "The job won't provide him with any luxuries, but it should keep the wolf from his door."

keeping up with the Joneses   Striving to achieve or own as much as the people around you: "If you want to keep up with the Joneses in this neighborhood, you will have to own at least three cars."

kick the bucket   To die: "Scarcely anyone was sorry when the old tyrant finally kicked the bucket."

kill two birds with one stone   To accomplish two objectives with a single action: "If we can get gas and have lunch at the next rest stop, we will be killing two birds with one stone."

kingdom come   The next world; the afterlife: "The superpowers have enough NUCLEAR WARHEADS to blow the entire world to kingdom come." An ALLUSION to the LORD'S PRAYER: "Thy kingdom come, thy will be done."

King's English, the   Correct English usage and DICTION; the kind of English that would be spoken at the court of the English king: "With their mixture of JARGON and SLANG, sportscasters are constantly murdering the King's English."

knock on wood   Some people say, "Knock on wood," and then knock on something made of wood for good luck when they have made a remark that has been true up to that point, and they want it to continue to be true: "I've never had an accident yet, knock on wood."

know the ropes To be familiar with the details of an operation: "You won't have to train the new COMPUTER operator; she already knows the ropes."

kosher Food that is permitted according to a set of dietary restrictions found in the OLD TESTAMENT. For many JEWS, foods that are not kosher cannot be eaten. The term can also be used colloquially to mean anything acceptable: "I don't think it's kosher to yell at your chess opponent when he is thinking about his next move."

land of Nod To "go off to the land of Nod," or to "nod off," is to go to sleep: "What a boring speech! Half the listeners are on their way to the land of Nod."

last laugh, the The final victory or satisfaction. (See He who LAUGHS LAST LAUGHS BEST.)

last straw, the The last in a series of grievances or burdens that finally exceeds the limits of endurance: "The management has given me nothing but trouble since I took this job, and now they've cut my benefits! Well, that's the last straw: I quit!" (See also STRAW THAT BROKE THE CAMEL'S BACK.)

laugh up one's sleeve To be secretly amused at something: "Arnie acted concerned over our plight, but we knew he was laughing up his sleeve."

lay an egg To fail, or to have one's efforts fall flat: "Jim tried to tell a few jokes, but each time he laid an egg."

left-handed compliment A compliment with two meanings, one of which is unflattering to the receiver: "The SENATOR said that his opponent was quite competent for someone so inexperienced; you hear nothing but left-handed compliments in these debates."

left holding the bag, to be To have the blame or responsibility thrust upon you: "When his partner skipped town, Harry was left holding the bag."

let the cat out of the bag To disclose a secret: "The mayor's visit was to be kept strictly confidential, but someone must have let the cat out of the bag, because the airport was swarming with reporters."

life of Riley A life of luxury: "Sheila found herself living the life of Riley after she won the lottery."

lion's share A disproportionately large segment of the whole: "Though we always divided our winnings, somehow Barton always seemed to end up with the lion's share."

lip service Insincere agreement; to "pay lip service" is to consent in one's words while dissenting in one's heart: "The boss's support of affirmative action was merely paying lip service; he never committed himself to it in any substantial way."

literati (lit-uh-RAH-tee) Intellectuals, writers, scholars. "All the literati of NEW YORK CITY came out for the book-signing party." From LATIN, meaning "the lettered ones" — those who are literate.

lock, stock, and barrel The whole of anything: "Our new manager wants to reorganize the entire operation, lock, stock, and barrel." Lock, stock, and barrel are the three parts of a rifle.

look out for number one To look after one's own interests rather than anyone else's: "When the burglar's accomplices asked why he had betrayed them to the police, he said he'd been offered a deal by the DISTRICT ATTORNEY and decided to look out for number one."

lowbrow Unsophisticated, uncultured, vulgar: "Her blind date took her to the mud-wrestling match. What a lowbrow evening!"

lunatic fringe Derogatory name for the extreme RADICAL members of a group, especially in politics — a term coined by Theodore ROOSEVELT: "The candidate referred to the JOHN BIRCH SOCIETY as being on the lunatic fringe of CONSERVATISM."

macho (MAH-choh) The often exaggerated, aggressive virility of a male: "Jim likes to wear a torn T-shirt and a black leather jacket when he rides his motorcycle. I guess he thinks it makes him look macho." The original Spanish word means "male."

madame (muh-DAM, MAD-uhm) French for "Mrs.," a title used before the name of a married woman.

mademoiselle (mad-uh-muh-ZEL, mad-mwuh-ZEL, mam-ZEL) French for "Miss," a title used before the name of an unmarried woman.

magna cum laude (MAHG-nuh koom LOW-duh, MAG-nuh kum LAW-dee) With high honors; a PHRASE applied to those who have graduated from college with great distinction. From LATIN, meaning "with great praise." (*Compare* SUMMA CUM LAUDE.)

magnum opus (MAG-nuhm OH-puhs)   The most important work in a person's career, especially in literature, art, or scholarship: "*MOBY DICK* was MEL-VILLE's magnum opus." From LATIN, meaning "great work."

make a clean breast of it   To make a full confession: "The judge will give the convict a lighter sentence if he makes a clean breast of his involvement with the crime."

make ends meet   To earn enough INCOME to provide for basic needs: "The workers complained that on their present WAGES they could hardly make ends meet, let alone enjoy any luxuries."

make a mountain out of a molehill   To blow an issue or event out of proportion: "You have only a small blister on your heel, but you complain as though you broke your leg. Why are you making a mountain out of a molehill?"

make no bones about it   To be blunt and candid about something: "The teacher made no bones about his rigorous expectations."

make a virtue of necessity   To pretend that one is freely and happily doing something one has been forced to do: "Once the mayor was forced by the voters to cut his budget, he made a virtue of necessity and loudly denounced government spending."

mañana (muhn-YAH-nuh)   A word used humorously to indicate an intention to put something off: "I've been asking you for weeks to paint the house and you always say 'Mañana.'" From Spanish, meaning "tomorrow."

McCoy, the real   The best of its kind, the real thing. "That homemade pizza was the real McCoy." The source of this expression is the story of a famous prizefighter named McCoy. He had so many imitators that no one was sure which was the real one.

mea culpa (MAY-uh KUL-puh, KOOL-puh)   An expresssion from CATHOLIC ritual that assigns blame to oneself: "I gave you the wrong directions to my house — *mea culpa*." From LATIN, meaning "my fault" or "my blame."

meet one's Waterloo   To encounter one's ultimate obstacle, and to be defeated by it: "After beating dozens of challengers, the champion finally met his Waterloo." From the Battle of WATERLOO, where NA-POLEON BONAPARTE was finally defeated.

memento mori (muh-MEN-toh MAWR-ee)   An object kept by a person as a reminder of his or her own mortality. At one time, MONKS kept human skulls for this purpose. From LATIN, meaning "Remember that you must die."

merci (mer-SEE)   French for "thank you."

method in his madness, There's   There is often a plan behind a person's apparently inexplicable behavior. Based on a line from SHAKESPEARE's *HAMLET*.

milk of human kindness   A PHRASE from *MAC-BETH*, by William SHAKESPEARE, meaning humane feeling, concern for other people: "Everyone agreed that Houston was a brilliant thinker and an excellent lawyer, but some people worried that he lacked the milk of human kindness."

mind your *p*'s and *q*'s   Pay attention to details: "We want this operation to run smoothly, so everyone please mind your *p*'s and *q*'s."

modus operandi (m.o.) (MOH-duhs op-uh-RAN-dee, op-uh-RAN-deye)   The way someone does something; a characteristic method: "Her *modus operandi* in buying a new car always included a month of research." This PHRASE, often abbreviated "m.o.," is used by police to describe a criminal's characteristic way of committing a crime. From LATIN, meaning "method of operation."

modus vivendi (MOH-duhs vi-VEN-dee, vi-VEN-deye)   A compromise between adversaries that allows them to get along temporarily: "During the separation, my parents adopted a *modus vivendi* that enabled them to tolerate each other." From LATIN, meaning a "method of living."

money burning a hole in one's pocket   Money that someone has just acquired and is eager to spend: "The day I got my allowance, I hurried down to the sporting goods store, the money burning a hole in my pocket."

monsieur (muh-SYEU, muhs-YUR)   French for "Mr.," a title used before a man's name.

more sinned against than sinning Expression used of those who, though they may be guilty of wrongdoing, think themselves the victim of a more serious wrong. From SHAKESPEARE's *KING LEAR*.

most unkindest cut of all The most painful of insults, affronts, or offenses, often so painful because it comes from a trusted friend. In SHAKESPEARE's *JULIUS CAESAR*, ANTONY describes the wound given to Caesar by his close friend BRUTUS as the "most unkindest cut of all."

Murphy's Law A rule originated by engineers that states, "If something can go wrong, it will." An addition to this law reads, "and usually at the worst time."

nine days' wonder Someone or something that is famous and celebrated for only a short time: "Last year the art critics praised Jonas as if he were a master, but he turned out to be a nine days' wonder."

nip and tuck Closely contested; neck and neck: "It was nip and tuck there for a while, but our team finally pulled through."

noblesse oblige (noh-BLES oh-BLEEZH) The belief that the wealthy and privileged are obliged to help those less fortunate than they. From French, meaning "nobility obligates."

Noël (noh-EL) French for Christmas.

non compos mentis (non KOM-puhs MEN-tis) A PHRASE used to describe someone who is out of his or her mind and therefore not legally responsible for his or her actions: "It was determined by the court that the killer was non compos mentis." From LATIN, meaning "not having control of the mind."

nose to the grindstone To work extremely hard: "Emily takes her bar exam next month, so she really has her nose to the grindstone."

nose out of joint To be in a bad mood: "Ever since Bill got that traffic ticket, he's had his nose out of joint."

nouveau riche (nooh-voh REESH) A pejorative term for one who has recently become rich and who spends money conspicuously. From French, meaning "new rich."

off-Broadway "Off-Broadway" plays are small-scale, often experimental and uncommercial dramas that are performed in any of the smaller theaters in NEW YORK. BROADWAY is NEW YORK CITY's avenue of large theaters.

Old Glory A nickname for the United States flag.

old hat Obsolete, old-fashioned: "Get with it, Murray; your methods are strictly old hat."

on the level Honest, without deception: "We doubted that the offer could be genuine, but it turned out to be on the level."

on pins and needles In a state of ANXIETY or tense expectation: "Jackie was on pins and needles waiting to hear about her job application."

on tenterhooks To be kept on tenterhooks is to be held in a state of nervous apprehension: "We've been on tenterhooks since the election results started coming in."

once in a blue moon To do something "once in a blue moon" is to do it very rarely: "That company puts on a good performance only once in a blue moon."

Open, sesame (SES-uh-mee) The magic words that open the door of a cave in the story "ALI BABA and the Forty Thieves."

paint the town red To go carousing: "Arnie and a few of his buddies drove off in a big car Friday night and really painted the town red."

pass the buck To shift blame from oneself to another person: "Passing the buck is a way of life in large BUREAUCRACIES." (*See* BUCK STOPS HERE, THE.)

pay the piper To pay the consequences for self-indulgent behavior: "If you drink heavily all night, in the morning you will have to pay the piper."

pay through the nose To pay unreasonably high prices: "If you visit any major city these days, you had better be prepared to pay through the nose for a hotel room."

pell-mell In a confused, disorderly manner: "After the assembly, the students ran pell-mell from the auditorium."

persona non grata (puhr-SOH-nuh non GRAH-tuh, GRAT-tuh)   A person who is no longer favored or welcome: "After my angry words with the manager, I am persona non grata at the record store." From LATIN, meaning "an unacceptable person."

pie in the sky   A preposterously optimistic goal: "The candidate says we can balance the budget by next year, but I think that's pie in the sky."

play fast and loose   To behave dishonorably; to make a promise and fail to deliver on it: "I hope this car salesman isn't just playing fast and loose with me."

play to the gallery   To direct a performance toward less sophisticated tastes; by extension, to attempt to gain approval by crude or obvious means: "The cast of the play was a decidedly mixed bag of youthful method actors and old hams who played to the gallery."

play it by ear   To improvise: "Rather than plan an elaborate strategy, Andy decided to play it by ear." Music played by ear does not follow written notes.

play possum   To pretend to be dead, a trick used by opossums to defend themselves from predators: "Everyone thought the old con man must have died, but it turned out he was just playing possum."

play second fiddle   To play a supporting or minor role in relation to someone else: "Tired of playing second fiddle, she resigned and started her own company." In an ORCHESTRA, the position of second violinist (FIDDLE) is not as glamorous as that of first violinist.

P.M.   An ABBREVIATION for the LATIN PHRASE "post meridiem," meaning "after noon"; the twelve hours from noon to midnight. (*Compare* A.M.)

Pooh-Bah   A self-important person of high position and great influence. Pooh-Bah is a CHARACTER in GILBERT AND SULLIVAN'S operetta *THE MIKADO*; his title is Lord-High-Everything-Else.

pop the question   To "pop the question" is to propose marriage: "They have been going out for so long; I wonder when he'll pop the question."

posthaste (POHST-HAYST)   Immediately, with great speed: "Get the flood warning to the media posthaste."

post-mortem (pohst-MAWR-tuhm)   Autopsy; figuratively, any analysis that follows an event: "When the convention is over, we'll have a post-mortem to find ways of improving it for next year." From LATIN, meaning "after death."

pot calling the kettle black   Criticizing others for the very fault one possesses: "I wouldn't call him lazy if I were you, Andy; that would be the pot calling the kettle black."

pound of flesh   Creditors who insist on having their "pound of flesh" are those who cruelly demand the repayment of a debt, no matter how much suffering it will cost the debtor: "The bank will have its pound of flesh; it is going to foreclose on our MORTGAGE and force us to sell our home." From *THE MERCHANT OF VENICE*, by SHAKESPEARE, in which SHYLOCK demands a pound of flesh from his debtor's body as the agreed compensation for a loan the debtor is unable to repay.

pour oil on troubled waters   To calm a disturbance: "His ideas caused real dissension within the party at first, but he poured oil on troubled waters in last night's speech."

prima donna (pree-muh, prim-uh DON-uh)   A vain and overly sensitive person who is temperamental and difficult to work with: "That Jenkins girl is a good gymnast, but she certainly is a prima donna." In OPERA, the prima donna is the principal female soloist. From Italian, meaning "first lady."

primrose path   A life of ease and pleasure; the easy way out of a hard situation. To "lead people down the primrose path" is to deceive them into thinking that things are easier than they actually are.

pro forma (proh FAWR-muh)   Doing something *pro forma* means satisfying only the minimum requirements of a task and doing it in a perfunctory way: "Her welcoming address was strictly *pro forma*: you could tell that her mind was a million miles away." From LATIN, meaning "by form."

pro tem (proh TEM)   *See* PRO TEMPORE.

pro tempore (pro tem) (proh TEM-puh-ree)   Temporarily: "While the president of the company is ill, the vice president will act as the leader pro tem." From LATIN, meaning "for the time being."

pull somebody's leg To tease or fool someone: "Helen had me fooled for a while, but finally I realized she was just pulling my leg."

pull strings To use personal connections to obtain a position: "Pat interviewed officially for the job, but he also had his uncle pulling strings behind the scenes."

put on the dog To make a show of wealth or elegance: "The annual ball gave everyone a chance to dress up and put on the dog."

put your foot in your mouth To make an embarrassing or tactless blunder when speaking: "Rob tries to say nice things, but he always ends up putting his foot in his mouth."

Pyrrhic victory (PIR-ik) A victory that is accompanied by enormous losses and leaves the winners in as desperate shape as if they had lost. Pyrrhus was an ancient general who, after defeating the Romans, told those who wished to congratulate him, "One more such victory and Pyrrhus is undone."

Q.E.D. *See* QUOD ERAT DEMONSTRANDUM.

quality of mercy is not strained, The Mercy is something that has to be freely given; no one can force someone else to be merciful. ("Strained" is an old form of "constrained," meaning "forced.") From *THE MERCHANT OF VENICE* by SHAKESPEARE.

quid pro quo (kwid proh KWOH) A fair exchange; the PHRASE is most frequently used in diplomacy: "The Chinese may make some concessions on trade, but they will no doubt demand a quid pro quo, so we must be prepared to make concessions too." From LATIN, meaning "something for something."

quod erat demonstrandum (Q.E.D.) (KWOD ER-aht dem-uhn-STRAN-duhm) A PHRASE used to signal that a proof has just been completed. From LATIN, meaning "that which was to be demonstrated."

raining cats and dogs Raining very heavily: "We wanted to play touch football, but now it's raining cats and dogs, so I guess we'll stay inside."

raise Cain To create a disturbance: "Alan and his buddies were always raising Cain over at the frat house."

raison d'être (ray-zohn DET-ruh) A basic, essential purpose; a reason to exist: "Professor Naylor argues that in the NUCLEAR age, infantry forces have lost their raison d'être." From French, meaning "reason for being."

rank and file The people who form the major portion of any group or organization, excluding the leaders: "The rumors of corruption at the top disturbed the party's rank and file." This PHRASE comes from military usage, where enlisted men march in ranks (close abreast) and files (one behind another), while officers march outside these formations.

read between the lines To pay attention to what is implied, though not explicitly stated, in writing or in speech.

read the riot act To chastise loudly, or to issue a severe warning: "After the students stormed the administration building, the president of the university came out and read them the riot act." In ENGLAND, unruly crowds that did not disperse after the Riot Act was read to them became subject to the force of the law.

real McCoy *See* MCCOY, THE REAL.

red herring In argument, something designed to divert an opponent's attention from the central issue. If a herring is dragged across a trail that hounds are following, it throws them off the scent.

red tape Bureaucratic procedures that delay progress: "Paula had hoped to settle the inheritance quickly but got caught up in a lot of red tape."

red-letter day A special or memorable day; the expression refers to the old custom of printing holidays in red on calendars: "John got promoted and engaged to be married yesterday; it was truly a red-letter day for him."

reductio ad absurdum (ri-DUK-tee-oh, ri-DUK-shee-oh ad uhb-SUR-duhm) To carry an idea or an argument to the point of absurdity: "The electric teaspoon is a *reductio ad absurdum* of convenient household appliances." From LATIN, meaning "reduction to absurdity."

Renaissance man An outstandingly versatile, well-rounded person. The expression alludes to such RE-

NAISSANCE figures as LEONARDO DA VINCI, who performed brilliantly in many different fields.

R.I.P.   The ABBREVIATION for "rest in peace," often found on gravestones or in obituaries. From the LATIN, *requiescat in pace.*

rob Peter to pay Paul   To harm one person in order to do good to another; by extension, to use money or resources set aside for one purpose for a different one.

R.S.V.P.   Please reply or answer. From the French, "respondez s'il vous plait," meaning "respond if you please."

rule the roost   To dominate; to be in charge: "Even though Sally has five older brothers, she still rules the roost."

rule of thumb   A practical principle that comes from the wisdom of experience and is usually but not always valid: "When playing baseball, a good rule of thumb is to put your best hitter fourth in the batting order."

run of the mill   Common, ordinary, average: "His performance in the game was neither exemplary nor disastrous; it was simply run of the mill."

Russian roulette, play (rooh-LET)   To gamble foolishly on a risky or potentially ruinous business; the expression refers to a deadly game in which a participant loads a revolver with one bullet, spins the cylinder, and fires at his own head: "If you drink and drive, you're playing Russian roulette with your life and the lives of others."

sacred cow   Figuratively, anything that is beyond criticism: "That housing project is a real sacred cow: the city council won't hear of abandoning it." In INDIA, followers of HINDUISM consider cows sacred and do not eat them because they believe the animals contain the souls of dead persons.

sail under false colors   To behave deceptively; the "colors" of a ship are its identifying flags: "It turned out that the door-to-door salesman was sailing under false colors and was actually a swindler."

salad days   An expression from SHAKESPEARE'S *ANTONY AND CLEOPATRA* that refers to the time of youth when one is inexperienced or "green" (like salad).

salt of the earth   Basic, fundamental goodness; the PHRASE can be used to describe any simple, good person: "I like Mary: she's reliable, trustworthy, and straightforward; she's the salt of the earth." In the SERMON ON THE MOUNT, JESUS tells his followers, who are mainly fishermen and other simple people, "Ye are the salt of the earth."

sanctum sanctorum (SANGK-tuhm sangk-TAWR-uhm)   LATIN for "holy of holies." The place in the Jewish temple in JERUSALEM where the Ark of the Covenant was kept. By extension, a sacred and private place.

sangfroid (sahn-FRWAH, sahn-FWAH)   Composure in the face of difficulty or danger: "We would all be dead today if our bus driver hadn't kept his sangfroid when the bus began to skid on the ice." From French, meaning "cold blood."

savoir-faire (sav-wahr-FAIR)   Ease and dexterity in social and practical affairs: "Pierre is a friendly person, but he lacks the *savoir-faire* required for a successful career in the foreign service." From French, meaning "to know how to act."

sea legs   To "have one's sea legs" is to be able to walk calmly and steadily on a tossing ship.

seamy side   The sordid, unattractive aspect of something: "Lying and stealing are part of the seamy side of life."

second wind   A new surge of energy after a period of mental or physical exhaustion: "At the midway mark, the marathoner got her second wind and left the other runners far behind." The expression refers to the fact that a person's METABOLISM changes to a more efficient mode during prolonged exercise.

see eye to eye   To be in agreement: "David and Susan found it difficult to work together since they seldom saw eye to eye on an issue."

see red   To be or become extremely angry: "When Roger realized that he had been duped, he started to see red."

semper fidelis (SEM-puhr fi-DAY-lis)   LATIN for "always faithful"; the motto of the United States Marine Corps.

señor (sayn-YAWR)   Spanish for "Mr."

señora (sayn-YAWR-uh)   Spanish for "Mrs."

señorita (sayn-yuh-REE-tuh) Spanish for "Miss."

set one's teeth on edge Something that one finds intensely irritating may be said to "set one's teeth on edge": "The mayor's sexist remark set my teeth on edge."

shalom (shah-LOHM, shuh-LOHM) A HEBREW word used to mean both "hello" and "good-bye"; literally, it means "peace."

ships that pass in the night Often said of people who meet for a brief but intense moment and then part, never to see each other again. These people are like two ships that greet each other with flashing lights and then sail off into the night. From a poem by Henry Wadsworth LONGFELLOW.

shot in the arm Something that boosts one's spirits: "After my recent financial troubles, that raise was a real shot in the arm."

siesta (see-ES-tuh) An afternoon nap or rest. Such naps are customary in the hot CLIMATE of the MEDITERRANEAN and LATIN AMERICA.

sine qua non (SIN-i kwah NON, NOHN) The essential, crucial, or indispensable ingredient without which something would be impossible: "Her leadership was the sine qua non of the organization's success." From LATIN, meaning "without which nothing."

sink or swim A sink-or-swim situation is one in which we must save ourselves by our own means or else fail. The image is that of a person thrown into the water without a life preserver; he or she must swim or drown.

sit on the fence To remain neutral, to refuse to take sides in a dispute; often used in a derogatory way about someone who is thought to lack the courage to decide: "The councilman is afraid he'll lose votes if he takes sides on the zoning issue, but he can't sit on the fence forever."

sitting duck A very easy target: "His arguments were so simple, she was able to knock them down like sitting ducks." The term comes from hunting, where it is much easier to hit ducks when they are sitting on the water than when they are in flight.

sitting pretty In a favorable position: "Abby finally got that promotion, and now she's sitting pretty."

skeleton in the closet A potentially embarrassing secret: "Before nominating the new judge, the committee asked him if he had any skeletons in the closet."

skin of one's teeth To do something "by the skin of one's teeth" is to just manage to get it accomplished: "I never thought we'd get the magazine to the printer by the deadline, but we made it by the skin of our teeth."

smell a rat To sense foul play: "They claim they will honor the terms of the CONTRACT, but I smell a rat."

soft soap Flattery: "Mary asked the boss to stop giving her a lot of soft soap about her performance and to start leveling with her like any other employee."

soup to nuts To include or cover everything, as in a full meal: "The lecture on WEATHER forecasting covered everything from soup to nuts."

sour grapes *See* "FOX AND THE GRAPES, THE."

sow wild oats To engage in youthful indiscretions, usually sexual liaisons: "Paul asked his father if he had sowed his wild oats before getting married."

split hairs To argue about an inconsequential and trivial aspect of an issue: "When you are accused of being forty-five minutes late for an appointment, you are splitting hairs to say that you were really only forty minutes late."

spread oneself too thin To engage in so many activities that one can't perform any of them well: "Last semester, Pamela tried to play basketball, serve on the student council, and work at her father's store. She quickly discovered that she was spreading herself too thin."

staff of life A basic staple food, like bread, rice, or potatoes: "Rice is the staff of life in eastern ASIA."

standing orders Orders that remain in effect until they are specifically changed: "During the year in which the troops occupied the town, they were under standing orders not to fire unless fired upon."

star-crossed lovers Lovers whose relationship is doomed to fail are said to be "STAR-crossed" (frustrated by the stars), because those who believe in ASTROLOGY claim that the stars control human destiny.

SHAKESPEARE created the PHRASE to describe the lovers in ROMEO AND JULIET.

status quo The existing order of things; present customs, practices, and power relations: "People with money are often content with the status quo." From LATIN, meaning "the state in which."

steal (someone's) thunder To upstage someone; to destroy the effect of what someone does or says by doing or saying the same thing first: "The REPUBLICANS stole the DEMOCRATS' thunder by including the most popular provisions of the Democratic proposal in their own bill."

stool pigeon An informer, especially for the police: "Lefty figured out that Mugsy was the stool pigeon when he saw him talking to the warden."

strain at a gnat and swallow a camel To take exception to a minor fault while overlooking a much larger one: "The EDITORIAL implied that the challenger was unqualified because he has lived in the state for only five years, but it overlooked the major financial scandal involving the INCUMBENT governor. The editor was straining at a gnat and swallowing a camel."

strange bedfellows Unlikely companions or allies.

straw man A made-up version of an opponent's argument that can easily be defeated. To accuse people of attacking a straw man is to suggest that they are avoiding more worthy opponents and more valid criticisms of their own position: "His speech had emotional appeal, but it wasn't really convincing because he attacked a straw man rather than addressing the real issues."

straw that broke the camel's back See LAST STRAW.

straw in the wind A small sign that hints of something that is about to happen: "It is difficult to tell whether the new regime will relax censorship, although a recent remark by the MINISTER of CULTURE may be a straw in the wind."

suffer fools gladly A person who does not "suffer fools gladly" is one who does not tolerate stupidity in others.

sui generis (SOOH-ee, SOOH-eye JEN-uh-ris) A person or thing that is unique, in a class by itself: "She is an original artist; each of her paintings is sui generis." From LATIN, meaning "of its own kind."

summa cum laude (SOOM-uh koom LOW-duh, SUM-uh kum LAW-dee) To graduate from college "summa cum laude" is to receive one's degree with the highest possible distinction. The LATIN PHRASE means "with highest praise." (*Compare* MAGNA CUM LAUDE.)

swap (switch) horses in midstream To change leaders or adopt a different strategy in the middle of a course of action: "When the coach was fired just before the playoffs, many thought it was a bad idea to swap horses in midstream."

sweeten the kitty (deal) To raise the stakes, as in a game of poker, where the pot is called the kitty: "Before you decide which job offer to accept, perhaps we can offer you a few added FRINGE BENEFITS to sweeten the kitty."

take the bull by the horns Take the initiative in confronting a difficult position: "You'll never decide what you want in life by simply thinking about it; you've got to take the bull by the horns and try out a few possibilities."

take the cake To be the most outstanding; sometimes used in a derogatory sense: "When it comes to eating like a pig, Gordy really takes the cake."

take with a grain of salt See GRAIN OF SALT.

take a powder To make a quick departure: "When he saw the police coming, the thief decided to take a powder."

take the rap To be punished, especially when innocent: "The crime boss arranged it so that his underling took the rap for the insurance scam."

talk turkey To discuss in a straightforward manner: "The time has come to talk turkey about our national DEBT."

tall tale An exaggerated, unreliable story: "My uncle claims that he was raised in a drainage ditch, but it's just another of his tall tales."

tarred with the same brush Sharing the same bad qualities: "Calhoun is a troublemaker, and I'll bet his brother Jud is tarred with the same brush."

terra firma (TER-uh FUR-muh) Dry land, as opposed to the sea: "After our stormy voyage across the ATLANTIC, we were relieved to set foot on terra firma." From LATIN, meaning "firm (or solid) ground."

tête-à-tête (tayt-uh-TAYT, tet-uh-TET) An intimate meeting or conversation between two individuals. From French, meaning "head to head."

There is no joy in Mudville A line from "CASEY AT THE BAT," describing the reaction of the hometown crowd when their hero, Casey, strikes out, losing the big game. In general, the expression is used to describe any disappointment: "My father has just lost his job; there's no joy in Mudville tonight."

three-D Three-dimensional. An object that has height, length, and width is three-dimensional.

three sheets to the wind To be "three sheets to the wind" is to be drunk.

through thick and thin To stay with someone or something "through thick and thin" is to persevere through good times as well as bad: "She stood beside her friend through thick and thin."

throw the book at someone To make as many charges as possible against an offender: "You may have gotten off lightly in the past, Mugsy, but this time we're going to throw the book at you."

throw in the towel To quit in defeat. The phrase comes from boxing, in which a fighter indicates surrender by throwing a towel into the ring: "After losing the election, he threw in the towel on his political career."

thrown to the lions Figuratively, to be thrown to the lions is to be placed in a difficult situation for which one is completely unsuited: "To put that new teacher in front of those unruly students is to throw him to the lions." During the Roman persecutions, CHRISTIANS were thrown to the lions in the COLOSSEUM.

thumbs up (down) Expressions of approval and disapproval respectively: "The two critics disagreed about the movie; one gave it thumbs up, the other thumbs down." In the gladiatorial contests of ancient ROME, the thumbs-up gesture from the crowd meant that the loser would live; thumbs down meant death.

ticker-tape parade A parade in which long strands of paper are thrown from buildings along a parade route in order to welcome a hero. Ticker-tape was the long string of paper once used to record telegraph messages. WALL STREET is famous for its ticker-tape parades.

till the cows come home For a long time: "Mr. Rowland said that as far as he was concerned, the delinquent students could stay there washing blackboards till the cows came home."

Timbuktu (tim-buk-TOOH) A remote town in western AFRICA. Figuratively, to go to Timbuktu is to go to a faraway and unknown place.

Time is of the essence Said when something must be done immediately: "The doctors need to operate right now; if they hope to save her, time is of the essence."

tip of the iceberg Only a hint or suggestion of a much larger or more complex issue or problem: "The money missing from petty cash was only the tip of the ICEBERG of financial mismanagement." This PHRASE alludes to the fact that the bulk of a floating iceberg is concealed beneath the water, leaving only a small portion, its tip, visible above.

tit for tat Giving back exactly what one receives: "If you hit me, I'll do the same to you; it's tit for tat."

to the manner born A person who is "to the manner born" is one who has acquired genteel tastes and habits by virtue of having been born into a privileged CLASS: "Rachel is charming at dinner parties — as if she were to the manner born." This expression is sometimes mistakenly rendered as "to the *manor* born." The PHRASE is from *HAMLET*, by William SHAKESPEARE.

Tom, Dick, and Harry A PHRASE referring to randomly chosen people: "I asked you to keep my plans secret, but you've told them to every Tom, Dick, and Harry."

tongue-in-cheek Ironically: "The critic's remarks of praise were uttered strictly tongue-in-cheek."

too many irons in the fire To have "too many irons in the fire" is to be engaged in too many activities: "Gomez turned down the consulting job; he felt that he already had too many irons in the fire."

toot one's own horn *See* BLOW ONE'S OWN HORN.

tooth and nail To fight "tooth and nail" is to fight with the intensity and ferocity of a wild animal: "The resistance forces fought the invading troops tooth and nail."

touch and go Uncertain or precarious: "The doctors told the patient that, even though her disease was in REMISSION, from now on it was touch and go."

tour de force (toor duh FAWRS) A feat accomplished through great skill and ability: "The speech was a *tour de force*; it swept the audience off its feet."

town and gown In a college town, the relations between "town and gown" are those between the residents of the town and the students and faculty associated with the school, who in the past wore academic gowns.

trial balloon A small campaign or test designed to gauge public response; the term originally referred to a balloon sent up to determine WEATHER conditions: "The speech on FREE TRADE that the candidate delivered in TEXAS last month must have been a trial balloon; the audience reacted with hostility, and he has not mentioned the subject since."

trial and error To "proceed by trial and error" is to experiment, rejecting what does not work and adopting what does.

trump card In general, something capable of making a decisive difference when used at the right moment; in certain card games, trump is the suit designated as having precedence over the others: "The prosecutor was about to win the case, when the defense lawyer produced his trump card: an eyewitness who testified that the accused was nowhere near the scene of the crime."

Turk, Young *See* YOUNG TURK.

turn over a new leaf To begin anew; to change one's ways: "Since he was grounded, Larry has turned over a new leaf and does his homework every night."

turn the tables To reverse a situation and gain the upper hand: "After trailing the entire first quarter, the team rallied and finally turned the tables."

two shakes of a lamb's tail Something that can be done in "two shakes of a lamb's tail" can be done very quickly: "The repairman said he could fix our tire in two shakes of a lamb's tail, and he was right: we were back on the road in ten minutes."

two strings to one's bow More than one option or set of resources: "Salinas has two strings to his bow; if his career in politics falls through, he can fall back on his law practice."

Typhoid Mary A person likely to cause a disaster; from Mary Mallen, an Irish woman in the United States who was discovered to be a carrier of TYPHOID FEVER.

UFO (yooh-ef-OH) ABBREVIATION for "Unidentified Flying Object." Often described as "flying saucers," some UFOs are believed to come from other PLANETS or GALAXIES and thus to support the idea that human beings are not the only form of intelligent life in the UNIVERSE. Few scientists agree.

uncle, to say (cry) To admit defeat, surrender: "Wilbur held his little brother in a headlock until he had to cry uncle."

under one's skin, get To affect deeply: "At first I couldn't get Wanda to notice me, but now I think I've gotten under her skin."

under the weather Indisposed, unwell: "The day after the big party, Jay had to call in sick, saying he was feeling under the weather."

under the wire Just in the nick of time: "Nancy mailed off her application, and it got in just under the wire." From horse racing, in which the wire marks the finish line.

upper crust Upper CLASS: "The upper crust tend to have at least one, and sometimes several, summer homes."

vicious circle A series of reactions that compound an initial unfortunate occurrence or situation: "A person who is overweight is likely to feel frustrated and to deal with this frustration by eating more; it's a vicious circle."

VIP (vee-eye-PEE) ABBREVIATION for "very important person": "The luncheon will be exclusive: VIPs only."

vis-à-vis (vee-zuh-VEE) Relative to; compared with: "She performed well vis-à-vis the rest of the competitors."

voilà (vwah-LAH) French for "There you have it," or "There it is": "The magician pulled a rabbit from his hat and said, 'Voilà!'"

walking papers Notice of dismissal. To "get one's walking papers" is to be fired.

wanderlust A German word for the irresistibly strong desire to travel or wander.

war horse A person or thing that has seen long service or has lived through many hardships and can be relied on: "That teacher is a real war horse; he has seen the passing of ten different principals."

warm the cockles of the heart *See* COCKLES OF THE HEART, WARM THE.

warp and woof The essential foundation or base of any structure or organization; from weaving, in which the warp — the threads that run lengthwise — and the woof — the threads that run across — make up the fabric: "The CONSTITUTION and the DECLARATION OF INDEPENDENCE are the warp and woof of the American nation."

warpath, on the From a NATIVE AMERICAN expression for war, to be "on the warpath" is to be exceedingly angry and to be inclined to take some hostile action: "Watch out! John got up on the wrong side of the bed and is on the warpath today."

wash dirty linen (laundry) in public To air private problems where they can be seen by all.

WASP An ACRONYM for "white Anglo-Saxon Protestant" — a member of what many consider to be the most privileged and influential group in American society.

water off a duck's back To fail to catch on or make a mark: "The reporter's snide comments rolled off the candidate like water off a duck's back."

wear one's heart on one's sleeve To express affection or sentiment too openly or ostentatiously: "You have to play it cool with a girl like Heidi; you mustn't wear your heart on your sleeve."

wet behind the ears To be "wet behind the ears" is to be inexperienced and naive.

wet blanket Someone who dampens enthusiasm: "We were all having a good time until Harold walked in and started acting like a wet blanket."

white elephant An unwanted or financially burdensome possession, or a project that turns out to be of limited value: "The new office building turned out to be a white elephant once the company decided to move its headquarters."

with a grain of salt *See* GRAIN OF SALT.

wolf in sheep's clothing Figuratively, anyone who disguises a ruthless nature through an outward show of innocence. JESUS taught his followers to "beware of false PROPHETS, which come to you in sheep's clothing, but inwardly they are ravening wolves."

worth one's salt Worth one's salary (a word that comes from the Latin for salt) or WAGES. From the Roman custom of paying soldiers money to buy salt.

Young Turk An insurgent person trying to take control of a situation or organization by force or political maneuver. The term originated from the mostly young Turkish officers who overthrew OTTOMAN rulers after WORLD WAR I.

World Literature, Philosophy, and Religion

Our decision to classify religious and philosophical writing under "World Literature" is a carefully considered one. During most of Western history, the term *literature* included all writing that was worthy to be known by educated people. Not only is that traditional conception theoretically justified; it is also a practical way of including important knowledge that would normally fall between the cracks in school courses. A narrow conception of literature that includes only FICTION, poetry, and drama is a recent innovation that has disadvantages as well as advantages. Since world PHILOSOPHY and religion have no clearly defined place in school courses, our classification of them as literature encourages their inclusion in the school curriculum.

World literature so conceived is an especially rich and interesting domain of knowledge. Its names are stars in the firmament of thought: PLATO and ARISTOTLE, GOETHE and CERVANTES, BUDDHA and CONFUCIUS. The kinds of writing represented cover the whole spectrum of literature. Plato wrote fictional dialogues, Aristotle technical treatises. Here one finds LYRIC poems, EPIC poems, TRAGEDIES, and COMEDIES. Here one finds the most influential ideas about ETHICS, politics, and righteousness. Several of the writers have done work that is so rich and complex that it repays a lifetime of study. Indeed, there is not a figure in this section who has not been the lifetime study of some devoted scholar.

An important feature of the writings included in this section is their almost timeless character. The world of great literature, philosophy, and religion is unlike the world of science in this important respect. In science, the latest thinking is usually the most advanced and most likely to be true, because the latest scientific theories are based on the most evidence and have withstood the most severe tests. In the sphere of thought concerning the nature and meaning of human life, however, the latest theories are not necessarily the most advanced or the most likely to be true. Knowledge about the basic character and meaning of life is not inherently progressive, as science is. The ancients had just as much evidence as we do about the basic facts of human existence. In fact, truths understood by the ancients sometimes are forgotten and have to be rediscovered. Some say, for instance, that the ancient Greeks have more to tell us about modern life than more recent thinkers do. Even if we do not all agree with this proposition, we can agree that answers to the great questions about human existence are not the exclusive property of any single place, CULTURE, or historical era.

— E. D. H.

PLATO'S ACADEMY. *An engraving called* The School of Athens, *after the fresco by Raphael.*

Abandon hope, all ye who enter here An inscription at the entrance to HELL as described by DANTE in *THE DIVINE COMEDY.*

absurd, theater of the Plays that stress the illogical or irrational aspects of experience, usually to show the pointlessness of modern life. Samuel BECKETT, Friedrich Dürrenmatt, Eugene Ionesco, Edward Albee, and Harold Pinter have written plays of this kind.

Academy, French A group of leaders in the literature and thought of FRANCE. The French Academy is supported by the government of France, and sets standards for use of the French language.

Academy, Plato's A school of PHILOSOPHY established by PLATO in ancient ATHENS, named after a legendary Greek hero, Hecademus. The Academy continued in operation for several hundred years.

☙ The *academy, academe,* and *academic life* are general terms for learning in schools, colleges, and universities.

Advent The coming of JESUS, either in the INCARNATION of biblical times or in the SECOND COMING at the end of the world. Also, a time observed in many CHRISTIAN CHURCHES in December to prepare for Christmas.

Aeneid (i-NEE-id) An EPIC in LATIN by VIRGIL. The *Aeneid* begins with the adventures of AENEAS and his men after the TROJAN WAR, and ends when Aeneas gains control of the Italian peninsula, which will eventually become the base of the ROMAN EMPIRE.

Aeschylus (ES-kuh-luhs) An ancient Greek poet, often considered the founder of TRAGEDY. He was the first of the three great Greek authors of tragedies, preceding SOPHOCLES and EURIPIDES.

Aesop's fables (EE-suhps, EE-sops) A group of stories thought to have been written by Aesop, a Greek storyteller. The main CHARACTERS in these stories are animals, and each story demonstrates a moral lesson. (*See* "THE BOY WHO CRIED 'WOLF,'" "THE FOX AND THE GRAPES," *and* "THE TORTOISE AND THE HARE.")

aesthetics The branch of PHILOSOPHY concerned with the nature of art and with judgments concerning beauty. "What is art?" and "What do we mean when we say something is beautiful?" are two questions often asked by aestheticians.

🕮 The term *aesthete* is sometimes used negatively to describe someone whose pursuit of beauty is excessive or appears phony.

agnosticism (ag-NOS-tuh-siz-uhm)   A denial of knowledge about whether there is or is not a God. An agnostic insists that it is impossible to prove that there is no God, and impossible to prove that there is one. (*Compare* ATHEISM.)

Aladdin's lamp   The subject of a story in the *ARABIAN NIGHTS*. The young boy Aladdin acquires a magic lamp that, when rubbed, brings forth a genie, a magic spirit prepared to grant his every wish. Aladdin uses his wishes to win the hand of the sultan's beautiful daughter and to build a magnificent palace. The magician who first gave Aladdin the lamp steals it back, but Aladdin regains the lamp, and he and the sultan's daughter live happily ever after.

Ali Baba (AH-lee BAH-buh, AL-ee BAB-uh)   The title CHARACTER in "Ali Baba and the Forty Thieves," a story from the *ARABIAN NIGHTS*. Ali Baba gains the treasure of the thieves, which they keep in a cave with a magical entrance.

🕮 Ali Baba opens the door of the thieves' cave with the magical password "OPEN, SESAME."

All Quiet on the Western Front   A German NOVEL by Erich Maria Remarque, published in the late 1920s, about the horrors of WORLD WAR I.

Allah   The name for God, the Supreme Being, in the Arabic language; the common name for God in ISLAM.

A.M.E. Church   The African Methodist Episcopal Church. An important denomination for African-Americans, founded in 1816 by the ex-slave and preacher Richard Allen. It is noted for education and philanthropy in the black community. An offshoot is the C.M.E. (Christian Methodist Episcopal) Church.

Amish (AH-mish, AM-ish, AY-mish)   A group of PROTESTANTS who broke away from the MENNONITES in the seventeenth century. The Amish live in close communities, farm for a living, and do without many modern conveniences, such as telephones and tractor-drawn plows.

🕮 Some of the PENNSYLVANIA DUTCH are Amish.

Andersen, Hans Christian   A Danish author of the nineteenth century, noted for his fairy tales, including the stories "The EMPEROR'S NEW CLOTHES," "The PRINCESS AND THE PEA," and "The UGLY DUCKLING."

Anglican Communion   The group of CHRISTIAN CHURCHES historically based in the CHURCH OF ENGLAND. Anglicans combine CATHOLIC and PROTESTANT elements in their teaching, worship, and government. They have BISHOPS, for example, but do not accept the authority of the POPE.

🕮 Nearly all of the churches of the Anglican Communion are in countries that once were possessions of BRITAIN, including the United States, where the Anglican Communion is represented by the PROTESTANT EPISCOPAL CHURCH. Anglicans use the BOOK OF COMMON PRAYER in worship.

animism (AN-uh-miz-uhm)   The belief that natural objects such as rivers and rocks possess a soul or spirit. *Anima* is the LATIN word for "soul" or "spirit." (*See* VOODOO.)

Anna Karenina (AN-uh kuh-REN-uh-nuh)   A NOVEL by Leo TOLSTOY; the title CHARACTER enters a tragic adulterous affair and commits suicide by throwing herself under a train.

🕮 *Anna Karenina* begins with the famous sentence "Happy families are all alike; every unhappy family is unhappy in its own way."

anthropomorphism   (an-thruh-puh-MAWR-fiz-uhm) The attributing of human characteristics and purposes to inanimate objects, animals, plants, or other natural phenomena, or to God. To describe a rushing river as "angry" is to anthropomorphize it.

Antigone (an-TIG-uh-nee)   A TRAGEDY by SOPHOCLES. It concerns the punishment of ANTIGONE for burying her brother, an act that was forbidden because he had rebelled against his own city. Antigone argues that the burial is required by divine law as opposed to human law.

Aquinas, Thomas (uh-KWEYE-nuhs)   An Italian PRIEST and PHILOSOPHER of the thirteenth century who became the most influential THEOLOGIAN of the MIDDLE AGES. Aquinas, a SAINT of the ROMAN CATHOLIC CHURCH, sought to reconcile faith and reason by showing that elements of the PHILOSOPHY of ARISTOTLE were compatible with CHRISTIANITY. His greatest work is the *SUMMA THEOLOGICA*.

Arabian Nights A famous collection of Persian, Indian, and Arabian folktales. Supposedly, the legendary SCHEHERAZADE told these stories to her husband the sultan, a different tale every night for 1001 days; therefore, the collection is sometimes called *The Thousand and One Nights*. The *Arabian Nights* includes the stories of such familiar CHARACTERS as ALADDIN and ALI BABA.

Aristophanes (ar-i-STOF-uh-neez) An ancient Greek dramatist, the author of such COMEDIES as *The Clouds* and *LYSISTRATA*.

Aristotle (AR-uh-stot-l) One of the greatest ancient Greek PHILOSOPHERS, with a large influence on subsequent Western thought. Aristotle was a student of PLATO and tutor to ALEXANDER THE GREAT. He disagreed with Plato over the existence of ideal Forms (*see* PLATO); he believed that form and matter are always joined. Aristotle's many books include *Rhetoric*, the *Poetics*, the *Metaphysics*, and the *Politics*.

Around the World in Eighty Days A NOVEL by Jules VERNE about a fictional journey around the world made in 1872 by an Englishman, Phileas Fogg, and his French servant. Fogg bets other members of his club that he can circle the world in eighty days.

asceticism (uh-SET-uh-siz-uhm) An austere, simple way of life in which persons renounce material pleasures and devote their energy to moral or religious purpose.

Ash Wednesday The seventh Wednesday before EASTER; the first day of LENT for most CHRISTIANS; the day after "Fat Tuesday," or MARDI GRAS. It is frequently observed as a day of fasting and repentance for sin. In some CHURCHES, ashes are placed on the foreheads of worshipers on Ash Wednesday as a reminder of their mortality. The words of God to ADAM in the BIBLE are often used in the ceremony: "DUST THOU ART, AND UNTO DUST SHALT THOU RETURN."

Assemblies of God A CHARISMATIC PROTESTANT denomination with about two million members in the United States.

atheism (AY-thee-iz-uhm) Denial that there is a God. (*Compare* AGNOSTICISM.)

Augustine (AW-guh-steen, aw-GUS-tin) An important teacher in the CHRISTIAN CHURCH, who lived in the fourth and fifth centuries. After a dramatic conversion to CHRISTIANITY, Augustine became a BISHOP. He is a SAINT of the ROMAN CATHOLIC CHURCH. His works include *The City of God* and his autobiography, the *CONFESSIONS*.

avatar (AV-uh-tahr) In HINDUISM, a god made visibly present, especially in a human form. The BUDDHA is considered an avatar of the god VISHNU.

🙠 By extension, an "avatar" is any new embodiment of an old idea.

Babar The elephant hero of a series of French books for children by Jean de Brunhoff.

Balzac, Honoré de (BAWL-zak, bahl-ZAHK) A French author of the early nineteenth century. In his long series of NOVELS known as *La Comédie humaine* (*THE HUMAN COMEDY*), he portrays the complexity of the society of FRANCE in his time.

baptism The ceremony of initiation into CHRISTIANITY; in most CHRISTIAN CHURCHES, it is considered a SACRAMENT. Persons baptized either have water poured on them or are immersed in water; some groups of Christians insist on immersion. The effect of baptism, in Christian belief, is to cleanse persons of their sins, so that they are born into a new life with JESUS. Most churches baptize members when they are infants, but some groups, like the BAPTISTS, insist on adult baptism. Jesus himself was baptized. (*See* JOHN THE BAPTIST.)

Baptists A group of CHRISTIAN communities marked chiefly by insistence on adult BAPTISM by immersion. Baptists regard baptism as a ceremony that accompanies and seals a conscious profession of faith in JESUS; for this reason, they do not baptize infants, but wait until candidates have reached their teen or adult years. The Baptists are the largest PROTESTANT denomination in the United States, and are particularly insistent on the SEPARATION OF CHURCH AND STATE.

bar mitzvah (bahr MITS-vuh) A ceremony in JUDAISM marking the beginning of religious responsibility for Jewish boys of thirteen. *Bar mitzvah* is HEBREW for "son of the commandment."

🙠 A bar mitzvah is an important social event in Jewish families.

bat mitzvah (baht, bahs MITS-vuh) A ceremony in JUDAISM marking the beginning of religious responsibility for Jewish girls; the counterpart of the BAR

MITZVAH. *Bat mitzvah* is HEBREW for "daughter of the commandment."

&. Although observed less frequently than a BAR MITZVAH, a bat mitzvah is often an important social event in Jewish families.

Baudelaire, Charles (bohd-LAIR) A French poet of the middle nineteenth century, whose poetry is noted for its morbid beauty and its evocative language. His famed collection of poems is called *Les Fleurs du mal* (*Flowers of Evil*).

Beatrice A woman, beloved of DANTE, who guides him through PARADISE in *THE DIVINE COMEDY*.

Beckett, Samuel A French author of the twentieth century, born in IRELAND; Beckett is best known for the play *Waiting for Godot*. (*See also* ABSURD, THEATER OF THE.)

Bhagavad Gita (BUG-uh-vuhd, BAH-guh-vahd GEE-tuh) A portion of the sacred books of HINDUISM; the name means "the song of God." It contains a discussion between the deity Krishna and the Indian hero Arjuna on human nature and human purpose.

Bible The book sacred to CHRISTIANS, containing the OLD TESTAMENT and the NEW TESTAMENT. The Old Testament contains the writings sacred to the JEWS. (*See also* KING JAMES BIBLE *and* VULGATE BIBLE.)

bishop In some CHRISTIAN CHURCHES, a person appointed to oversee a group of PRIESTS or MINISTERS and their congregations. In the ANGLICAN COMMUNION, the EASTERN ORTHODOX CHURCH, and the ROMAN CATHOLIC CHURCH, bishops are considered the successors of the Twelve APOSTLES.

Book of Common Prayer The book used in worship by the ANGLICAN COMMUNION; it has had several revisions since the REFORMATION, and different versions exist for different countries.

&. The Book of Common Prayer, widely admired for the dignity and beauty of its language, has had a strong effect on the worship of PROTESTANTS outside the Anglican Communion, many of whom have borrowed its expressions. Most traditional Protestant wedding ceremonies, for example, follow the pattern of the Book of Common Prayer very closely.

born-again Christian A CHRISTIAN who has experienced a distinct, dramatic conversion to faith in JESUS, especially a member of certain PROTESTANT groups that stress this experience. The expression recalls words of Jesus in the GOSPELS: "Except a man be born again, he cannot see the kingdom of God."

&. Someone who is "born again" in nonreligious contexts has a new enthusiasm for doing something.

Brahmins (BRAH-minz) The highest of the four major CASTES of HINDUISM. Brahmins are followers of Brahma, and were originally all PRIESTS.

&. The name is often given to socially or culturally privileged CLASSES, such as "Boston Brahmins."

Brothers Karamazov, The (kar-uh-MAH-zawf) A NOVEL by Feodor DOSTOYEVSKY; the PLOT concerns the trial of one of four brothers for the murder of his father.

&. *The Brothers Karamazov* is known for its deep ethical and psychological treatment of its CHARACTERS.

BUDDHA. *A statue of the Great Buddha in Kamakura, Japan.*

Buddha, The (BOOH-duh, BOOD-uh) A prince, originally named Gautama, who lived in INDIA several hundred years before JESUS. After years of solitary contemplation, he began to teach a religion of self-denial and universal brotherhood. (*See* BUDDHISM.)

Buddhism (BOOH-diz-uhm, BOOD-iz-uhm) A religion, founded by the BUDDHA, that emphasizes physical and spiritual discipline as a means of liberation from the physical world. The goal for the Buddhist is to attain NIRVANA, a state of complete peace in which one is free from the distractions of desire and self-consciousness. Buddhists are found in the greatest numbers in eastern ASIA.

Calvin, John A French THEOLOGIAN and religious reformer of the sixteenth century (*see* REFORMATION); the founder of CALVINISM. He directed the formation of a religiously based government in GENEVA, SWITZERLAND.

Calvinism The religious doctrines of the PROTESTANT THEOLOGIAN John CALVIN. Calvin stressed that people are saved through God's GRACE, not through their own merits. The most famous of Calvin's ideas is his doctrine of PREDESTINATION. In the United States, the PRESBYTERIANS make up the largest single group of CHRISTIANS in the Calvinist tradition.

Candide (kan-DEED, kahnn-DEED) A NOVEL of SATIRE by VOLTAIRE, in which a long series of calamities happens to the title CHARACTER, an extremely naive and innocent young man, and his teacher, Doctor Pangloss. Pangloss, who reflects the optimistic PHILOSOPHY of Gottfried Wilhelm Leibnitz, nevertheless insists that, despite the calamities, "all is for the best in this best of all possible worlds."

canonization Official enrollment of a dead person as a SAINT in the ROMAN CATHOLIC CHURCH and the EASTERN ORTHODOX CHURCH.

cardinals A group of over a hundred prominent BISHOPS of the ROMAN CATHOLIC CHURCH who advise the POPE and elect new popes.

Casanova, Giovanni Jacopo (kaz-uh-NOH-vuh, kas-uh-NOH-vuh) An Italian author of the eighteenth century, whose adventurous life and *Memoirs* gave him a permanent reputation as a lover.

    ☙ A "Casanova" is a flamboyant and irresponsible male lover.

casuistry (KAZH-ooh-i-stree) Determining right and wrong by applying general ethical principles, or applying those principles in a false or misleading way.

cathedral A CHRISTIAN CHURCH building in which a BISHOP has his official seat (*cathedra* is LATIN for "chair"). A cathedral is usually large and imposing, and many cathedrals are important in the history of architecture. (*See* CHARTRES, CATHEDRAL OF; NOTRE DAME DE PARIS, CATHEDRAL OF; *and* SAINT PAUL'S CATHEDRAL.)

Catholic Church A common ABBREVIATION for the name of the ROMAN CATHOLIC CHURCH.

Catholicism The beliefs and practices of the ROMAN CATHOLIC CHURCH.

Cervantes, Miguel de (suhr-VAN-teez, suhr-VAHN-tays) A Spanish writer of the sixteenth and seventeenth centuries; the author of *DON QUIXOTE*.

Chanukah Another spelling of HANUKKAH.

Chekhov, Anton (CHEK-awf) A Russian author of the late nineteenth century. Chekhov wrote plays, including *The Cherry Orchard* and *The Three Sisters*, and short stories.

Chosen People A term applied to the JEWS. According to the OLD TESTAMENT, God chose the descendants of ABRAHAM through the line of ISAAC and JACOB — the ancestors of today's Jews — as the people through whom he would reveal himself to the world. God therefore freed them from slavery in EGYPT and led them into the PROMISED LAND.

Christ A title by which CHRISTIANS refer to JESUS. The word is a Greek translation of the HEBREW *MESSIAH*, meaning "the anointed one."

Christian A follower of JESUS and his teachings. *Christian* is also a descriptive term for the institutions and practices of CHRISTIANITY.

Christian Science A religion founded upon some of the teachings of JESUS as formulated by the nineteenth-century American religious reformer Mary Baker EDDY.

    ☙ Christian Scientists believe that sickness is an illusion that can be defeated by the power of the spirit. They therefore refuse to be treated by doctors or to take medicine.

Christianity The religion based on the life and teachings of JESUS CHRIST. CHRISTIANS believe that Jesus Christ is the MESSIAH, sent by God. They believe that Jesus, by dying and rising from the dead, made up for the sin of ADAM and thus redeemed the world, allowing all who believe in him to enter HEAVEN. Christians rely on the BIBLE as the inspired word of God. (*See also* GOSPEL, NATIVITY, RESURRECTION, SALVATION, *and* SERMON ON THE MOUNT.)

Christopher A CHRISTIAN SAINT (though no longer listed by the CATHOLIC CHURCH in the Calendar of Saints). JESUS appeared to him as a little child whom Christopher carried across a stream. Christopher means "Christ-bearer." He is the PATRON SAINT of travelers.

church A group of CHRISTIANS; *church* is a biblical word for "assembly." It can mean any of the following: 1. All Christians, living and dead. (*See* SAINTS.) 2. All Christians living in the world. 3. One of the large divisions or denominations of CHRISTIANITY, such as the EASTERN ORTHODOX CHURCH, METHODIST CHURCH, or ROMAN CATHOLIC CHURCH. 4. An individual congregation of Christians meeting in one building; also the building itself.

Church of England The ESTABLISHED CHURCH in ENGLAND. The Church of England is PROTESTANT, and is governed by BISHOPS, with the king or queen as its official head. One of the primary results of the REFORMATION, it was begun in the early sixteenth century when King HENRY VIII declared that he, and not the POPE, was the head of the CHRISTIAN CHURCH in England. The Church of England is the original church of the ANGLICAN COMMUNION.

Cicero An orator, writer, and statesman of ancient ROME. His many speeches to the Roman Senate are famous for their rhetorical techniques (*see* RHETORIC) and their ornate style.
    🞕 A "Ciceronian" sentence is clear, rhythmic, and powerful, and is often composed of many SUBORDINATE CLAUSES and FIGURES OF SPEECH.

Cid, El (el SID) The hero of a Spanish EPIC from the twelfth century, *Poema del Cid*, or *Poem of the Cid* (*cid* comes from the Arabic word for "lord"). At different times, he fought both for and against the MOSLEM Moors who ruled SPAIN.

clockwork universe An image of the UNIVERSE as a clock wound up by God and ticking along with its gears governed by the laws of PHYSICS. This idea was very important in the ENLIGHTENMENT, when scientists realized that NEWTON'S LAWS OF MOTION, including the law of universal GRAVITATION, could explain the behavior of the SOLAR SYSTEM.

Cogito, ergo sum (KOH-gi-toh er-goh SOOM, KOJ-i-toh ur-goh SUM) The original LATIN version of the statement "I THINK; THEREFORE I AM," by René DESCARTES.

Communion A SACRAMENT of CHRISTIANITY. In a reenactment of the LAST SUPPER, the words of JESUS — "This is my body" and "This is my blood" — are spoken over bread and wine (the elements of Communion), which are then shared by the worshipers. Communion, also known as the EUCHARIST, commemorates the death of Jesus. (*See* TRANSUBSTANTIATION.)

confession In some CHURCHES, notably in the ROMAN CATHOLIC CHURCH, a SACRAMENT in which repentant sinners individually confess their sins in private to a PRIEST and receive absolution from the guilt of their sins. Each sinner is then assigned a PENANCE, which is usually several prayers to be said or good deeds to be done.
    In the first few centuries of CHRISTIANITY, penances were public: sinners had to stay outside the entrance of the church and ask the people going inside to pray for them. The period of public penance could be shortened through an INDULGENCE.

Confessions The title of two well-known AUTOBIOGRAPHIES: that of AUGUSTINE from the fourth century, describing his early years and his conversion to CHRISTIANITY, and that of the eighteenth-century PHILOSOPHER Jean-Jacques ROUSSEAU.

Confucianism (kuhn-FYOOH-shuh-niz-uhm) A system of ETHICS, founded on the teachings of CONFUCIUS, that influenced the traditional CULTURE of CHINA. Confucianism places a high value on learning, and stresses family relationships.

Confucius A Chinese PHILOSOPHER of the sixth century before the birth of JESUS; the founder of CONFUCIANISM. His teachings, which stress following traditional ways, have come down to us as a collection of short sayings.

Congregationalists A PROTESTANT denomination that has roots in the NONCONFORMISTS of ENGLAND. The Congregationalists are much like the METHODISTS in their teachings. They consider the individual congregation the basic unit of their CHURCH, and they practice BAPTISM of infants. Most Congrega-

CONFUCIUS. *An engraving of the Chinese philosopher.*

tionalists in the United States belong to the United Church of CHRIST.

Conservative Judaism A branch of JUDAISM that insists on the keeping of some requirements of the Jewish law, or TORAH (CIRCUMCISION of male infants, for example, and the eating of unleavened bread during PASSOVER), but allows for the adaptation of some of the law's requirements to fit modern circumstances (for example, some of the details of Jewish dietary laws). (*Compare* ORTHODOX JUDAISM *and* REFORM JUDAISM.)

convent A community of people in a RELIGIOUS ORDER, especially NUNS.

Copernicus, Nicolaus (kuh-PUR-ni-kuhs) A Polish scholar who, in 1543, first produced a workable model of the SOLAR SYSTEM that had the SUN at the center. His model eventually took the place of the PTOLEMAIC UNIVERSE, and provided the foundation for modern ASTRONOMY.

Counter Reformation The reaction of the ROMAN CATHOLIC CHURCH to the REFORMATION. The chief aims of the Counter Reformation were to increase faith among church members, get rid of some of the abuses to which the leaders of the Reformation objected, and affirm some of the principles rejected by the PROTESTANT CHURCHES, such as veneration of the SAINTS and acceptance of the authority of the POPE. Many JESUITS were leaders of the Counter Reformation.

courtly love A set of attitudes toward love that were strong in the MIDDLE AGES. According to the ideal of courtly love, a KNIGHT or nobleman worshiped a lady of high birth, and his love for her inspired him to do great things on the battlefield and elsewhere. There was usually no physical relationship or marriage between them, however; the lady was usually married to another man.

creation science An effort to give scientific evidence for the literal truth of the account of CREATION in the BIBLE. Creation science is not accepted by most scientists. (*See* CREATIONISM.)

creationism A literal belief in the biblical account of CREATION as it appears in the Book of GENESIS. Creationists believe that the creation of the world and all its creatures took place in six calendar days; they therefore deny the THEORY of EVOLUTION.

Crime and Punishment A NOVEL by Feodor DOSTOYEVSKY about Rodya Raskolnikov, who kills two old women because he believes that he is beyond the bounds of good and evil.

Cyrillic alphabet (suh-RIL-ik) The alphabet used for writing the Russian language and several related languages. Most of its letters differ from those in the LATIN alphabet, which is used to write English and other western European languages.

damnation Eternal punishment in HELL. (*See* MORTAL SIN/VENIAL SIN.)

Dante (DAHN-tay, DAN-tee) An Italian poet of the thirteenth and fourteenth centuries; his full name was Dante Alighieri. Dante is remembered for his masterpiece, *THE DIVINE COMEDY*, an EPIC about HELL, PURGATORY, and HEAVEN. *The Divine Comedy* was written as a memorial to BEATRICE, a woman whom Dante loved, and who died at an early age.

Dead Sea scrolls   A large collection of written scrolls, containing nearly all of the OLD TESTAMENT, found in a cave near the DEAD SEA in the late 1940s. The scrolls were part of the library of some Essenes, a religious community of JEWS that flourished for a few centuries around the time of JESUS. The scrolls are highly valued for the information they give about the BIBLE and about JUDAISM in the period.

deduction   A process of reasoning that moves from the general to the specific. The opposite process is called INDUCTION.

deism (DEE-iz-uhm)   The belief that God has created the UNIVERSE but remains apart from it and permits his creation to administer itself through natural laws. Deism thus rejects the supernatural aspects of religion, such as belief in revelation in the BIBLE, and stresses the importance of ethical conduct. In the eighteenth century, numerous important thinkers held deist beliefs. (*See* CLOCKWORK UNIVERSE.)

Descartes, René (day-KAHRT)   A French PHILOSOPHER of the seventeenth century. Descartes is known for his statement "*COGITO, ERGO SUM*" ("I THINK; THEREFORE I AM"), which was the end result of his search for something that could not be doubted. Descartes relied on reason to explain the workings of the UNIVERSE. His ideas are often called "Cartesianism," after the LATIN form of his name.

determinism   In ETHICS, the view that human actions are entirely controlled by previous conditions, operating under laws of nature. Determinism is often understood as ruling out FREE WILL.

devil   A bad or fallen ANGEL. (*See* SATAN.)

Diary of a Young Girl, The   See FRANK, ANNE.

Divine Comedy, The   A long EPIC written by DANTE in the early fourteenth century, describing Dante's journey through the afterlife. It has three parts, each of which is concerned with one of the three divisions of the world beyond: the *INFERNO* (HELL), the *Purgatorio* (PURGATORY), and the *PARADISO* (HEAVEN). *The Divine Comedy* has had a major influence on the Western literary tradition.

dogma   A teaching or set of teachings laid down by a religious group, usually as part of the essential beliefs of the group.

ᨒ The term *dogma* is often applied to statements put forward by someone who thinks, inappropriately, that they should be accepted without proof.

Doll's House, A   A play by Henrik IBSEN about a woman who leaves her husband, who has always treated her like a doll rather than a human being, in order to establish a life of her own.

Don Juan (don WAHN, don HWAHN, don JOOH-uhn)   A legendary Spanish nobleman and chaser of women; he first appears in literature in SPAIN in the seventeenth century. Many authors and composers have depicted him: Wolfgang Amadeus MOZART, in the OPERA *DON GIOVANNI*; Lord BYRON, in the long poem "Don Juan"; and George Bernard SHAW, in the play *Man and Superman.*

Don Quixote (don kee-HOH-tay, don kee-HOH-tee, don KWIK-suht)   A NOVEL written in the seventeenth century by Miguel de CERVANTES. The hero, Don Quixote (*don* is a Spanish title of honor), loses his

DON QUIXOTE. *Don Quixote is on the right; his squire Sancho Panza on the left.*

wits from reading too many ROMANCES, and comes to believe that he is a KNIGHT destined to revive the golden age of CHIVALRY. A tall, gaunt man in armor, he has many comical adventures with his fat squire, SANCHO PANZA.

≈ At one point in the story, Don Quixote's inability to distinguish reality from the DELUSIONS of his imagination leads him to attack a windmill, thinking it is a giant. Thus, to say that someone is "tilting at windmills" is to say that the person is taking on a task that is noble but unrealistic. ≈ The word *quixotic*, meaning idealistic to the point of impracticality, refers to Don Quixote.

Dostoyevsky, Feodor (dos-tuh-YEF-skee)   A Russian author of the nineteenth century, whose books include *CRIME AND PUNISHMENT* and *THE BROTHERS KARAMAZOV*. Dostoyevsky and Leo TOLSTOY were the two greatest Russian authors of NOVELS in their century.

dualism   In PHILOSOPHY and THEOLOGY, any system that explains phenomena by two opposing principles. Many PHILOSOPHERS hold to a dualism of mind and matter, or mind and body. For many THEOLOGIANS, the two principles are those of good and evil.

Easter   An important religious festival among CHRISTIANS; it commemorates the RESURRECTION of JESUS after his CRUCIFIXION. Easter is celebrated on a Sunday in spring, and the season of Easter, a time of rejoicing, continues for several weeks. The penitential season of LENT is a time of preparation for Easter.

Eastern Orthodox Church   One of the three great divisions of CHRISTIANITY; the others are the PROTESTANT CHURCHES and the ROMAN CATHOLIC CHURCH. The Catholic and Orthodox churches were originally united, but they parted in the eleventh century, when they differed over several points of doctrine, including the supreme authority of the POPE, which Orthodox Christians reject.

≈ Orthodox church buildings are beautifully and elaborately decorated. Worshipers pay special reverence to ICONS, which are paintings of JESUS and the SAINTS. ≈ The Orthodox Church is the dominant form of Christianity in much of eastern EUROPE and in GREECE.

ecumenism (EK-yoo-muh-niz-uhm, i-KYOOH-muh-niz-uhm)   A movement promoting cooperation and better understanding among different religious groups or denominations.

Eddy, Mary Baker   An American religious reformer of the late nineteenth and early twentieth centuries; the founder of CHRISTIAN SCIENCE. Her book *Science and Health* is the official statement of Christian Science principles.

Émile (ay-MEEL)   A work on education by Jean-Jacques ROUSSEAU, describing how a fictional boy, Émile, should be brought up. The book had an enormous influence on education in the age of ROMANTICISM and beyond.

encyclical (en-SIK-li-kuhl)   A letter from the POPE to the BISHOPS of the ROMAN CATHOLIC CHURCH, in which he lays down policy on religious, moral, or political issues.

Epicureanism (ep-i-kyoo-REE-uh-niz-uhm, ep-i-KYOOR-ee-uh-niz-uhm)   A form of HEDONISM defended by several PHILOSOPHERS of ancient GREECE. For the Epicureans, the proper goal of action was pleasure — but a long-term pleasure, marked by serenity and temperance.

Epiphany (i-PIF-uh-nee)   A festival in CHRISTIANITY celebrating the visit of the WISE MEN to the infant JESUS. *Epiphany* means "a showing forth" — in this case a showing forth of Jesus to the GENTILES.

Episcopal Church   *See* PROTESTANT EPISCOPAL CHURCH IN THE UNITED STATES.

epistemology (i-pis-tuh-MOL-uh-jee)   The branch of PHILOSOPHY concerned with the nature and origin of knowledge. Epistemology asks the question "How do we know what we know?"

established church   A CHURCH supported by the government as a national institution. The CHURCH OF ENGLAND is an established church in ENGLAND, as is the LUTHERAN CHURCH in the countries of SCANDINAVIA, and the PRESBYTERIAN CHURCH in SCOTLAND.

ethical relativism   In ETHICS, the belief that nothing is objectively right or wrong, and that the definition of right or wrong depends on the prevailing view of a particular individual, CULTURE, or historical period.

ethics   The branch of PHILOSOPHY that deals with morality. Ethics is concerned with distinguishing between good and evil in the world, between right and wrong human actions, and between virtuous and nonvirtuous characteristics of people.

Eucharist (YOOH-kuh-rist)   The SACRAMENT of COMMUNION among CHRISTIANS.

Euripides (yoo-RIP-i-deez)   An ancient Greek dramatist. He was the author of numerous TRAGEDIES, including the *Bacchae, Medea,* and *The Trojan Women.* He often used the device of deus ex machina to resolve his PLOTS.

evangelist   A CHRISTIAN preacher, especially one who does much traveling.

existentialism   A movement in twentieth-century literature and PHILOSOPHY, with some forerunners in earlier centuries. Existentialism stresses that people are entirely free and therefore responsible for what they make of themselves. With this responsibility comes a profound anguish or dread. Sören KIERKEGAARD and Feodor DOSTOYEVSKY in the nineteenth century, and Jean-Paul SARTRE, Martin Heidegger, and Albert Camus in the twentieth century, were existentialist writers.

fatalism   The belief that events are determined by an impersonal fate and cannot be changed by human beings. Fatalism is a form of DETERMINISM.

Faust (FOWST)   A legendary magician and practitioner of ALCHEMY of the sixteenth century, who sold his soul to the DEVIL in exchange for youth, knowledge, and power. Christopher Marlowe, an English poet of the sixteenth century, and Johann Wolfgang von GOETHE wrote famous plays about him.

   🍲 A "Faustian" bargain is one in which a person is willing to make extreme sacrifices for power or knowledge without considering the ultimate cost.

Figaro (FIG-uh-roh)   A scheming Spanish barber who appears as a CHARACTER in French plays in the eighteenth century. The OPERAS *THE MARRIAGE OF FIGARO,* by Wolfgang Amadeus MOZART, and *THE BARBER OF SEVILLE,* by Gioacchino ROSSINI, are about Figaro.

Flaubert, Gustave (floh-BAIR)   A French author of the middle nineteenth century, known for his careful choice of words and exact descriptions. Flaubert's best-known work is *MADAME BOVARY.*

Francis of Assisi (uh-SEE-zee, uh-SIS-ee)   A SAINT of the ROMAN CATHOLIC CHURCH who lived in ITALY in the thirteenth century and is known for his simplicity, devotion to poverty, and love of nature. (*See* FRANCISCANS.)

Franciscans   A RELIGIOUS ORDER founded by FRANCIS OF ASSISI, known, like Francis, for devotion to poverty. The Franciscans have many divisions, and include both men and women.

ANNE FRANK

Frank, Anne   A teenaged German Jewish girl who hid from the persecuting NAZIS for two years in WORLD WAR II. She lived with her family and several friends in a secret apartment in a warehouse in AMSTERDAM, THE NETHERLANDS, until they were discovered by the NAZIS in 1944. She was then sent to a CONCENTRATION CAMP where she died of TYPHUS. Anne Frank's story of her experiences were published after the war as *The Diary of a Young Girl.*

free will   The ability to choose, think, and act voluntarily. For many PHILOSOPHERS, to believe in free will is to believe that human beings can be the authors of their own actions and to reject the idea that human actions are determined by external conditions or fate. (*See* DETERMINISM, FATALISM, *and* PREDESTINATION.)

Freemasons A men's fraternal organization with some religious aspects. Freemasons claim descent from the builders of the TEMPLE in JERUSALEM.

Friends, Religious Society of *See* QUAKERS.

fundamentalism A CONSERVATIVE movement in THEOLOGY among nineteenth-century and twentieth-century CHRISTIANS. Fundamentalists believe that the statements in the BIBLE are literally true.

🌢 Fundamentalists often argue against the THEORY OF EVOLUTION. (*See* SCOPES TRIAL.)

Goethe, Johann Wolfgang von (GEU-tuh, GUR-tuh) A German author of the late eighteenth and early nineteenth centuries, who greatly influenced European literature. Among his celebrated works are a drama telling the story of FAUST, and the NOVEL *The Sorrows of Young Werther.*

Good Friday The Friday before EASTER Sunday; a day on which CHRISTIANS commemorate the CRUCIFIXION of JESUS. *Good Friday* means "holy Friday."

🌢 Christians observe Good Friday with sober religious services and meditation on the Crucifixion. Many of them fast.

grace The favor, love, and protection of God. According to the NEW TESTAMENT, God's grace that leads to SALVATION is a gift. (*See* JUSTIFICATION BY GRACE, THROUGH FAITH.)

greatest happiness for the greatest number The goal that human conduct, laws, and institutions should have, according to UTILITARIANISM.

Greek Orthodox Church See EASTERN ORTHODOX CHURCH.

Grimm, the brothers Two German authors of the early nineteenth century, Jacob Ludwig Carl Grimm and Wilhelm Carl Grimm, remembered mostly for their collection of fairy tales. Usually called *Grimm's Fairy Tales*, it includes "HANSEL AND GRETEL," "LITTLE RED RIDING HOOD," "RUMPELSTILTSKIN," "SNOW WHITE AND THE SEVEN DWARFS," and many others.

guru (GOOR-ooh, goo-ROOH) In HINDUISM, a teacher or spiritual leader.

🌢 By extension, a "guru" is any wise teacher who attracts DISCIPLES.

haiku (HEYE-kooh) A form of Japanese poetry. A haiku expresses a single feeling or impression, and contains three unrhymed lines of five, seven, and five SYLLABLES, respectively.

Hanukkah (KHAH-nuh-kuh, HAH-nuh-kuh) A festival in JUDAISM that occurs each December. Hanukkah commemorates the victory of the JEWS in the second century B.C. over the Syrians, who had occupied their country, and the rededication of the TEMPLE in JERUSALEM (*hanukkah* is HEBREW for "dedication"). Observers of Hanukkah light one candle in a candleholder called a MENORAH each night for eight nights in memory of a legend that, when the Temple was rededicated, its lamps burned, without enough oil, miraculously for a week.

🌢 Hanukkah was one of the less important Jewish festivals, but today it is celebrated with zest by Jews in many parts of the world — especially in the United States, where it overlaps with the celebration of Christmas.

hara-kiri (har-i-KEER-ee, hahr-uh-KEER-ee) A ritual of suicide, associated with warriors in traditional Japanese society.

Hasidim (khah-SEE-dim, hah-SEE-dim) JEWS who observe a form of strict ORTHODOX JUDAISM. They generally wear severely plain black and white clothes, and the men, following the requirements of MOSAIC LAW, leave parts of their hair and whiskers untrimmed.

hedonism (HEED-n-iz-uhm) In ETHICS, the doctrine that pleasure or happiness is the highest good in life. Some hedonists, such as the EPICUREANS, have insisted that pleasure of the entire mind, not just pleasure of the senses, is this highest good.

🌢 In common usage, "hedonism" means a devotion to sensual pleasures.

Hegel, Georg Wilhelm Friedrich (HAY-guhl) A German PHILOSOPHER of the early nineteenth century, who held that what was truly real in the world was mind or spirit, not material things. Hegel argued that history showed a gradual unfolding of this mind. Karl MARX later treated history as a similar kind of unfolding, but maintained that matter, rather than mind, was truly real; Hegel, Marx said, had "stood reality on its head." (*See* MARXISM.)

heresy A belief or teaching considered unacceptable by a religious group. (*See* HERETIC.)

heretic One who challenges the doctrines of an ESTABLISHED CHURCH; one who holds to a HERESY. Martin LUTHER was proclaimed a heretic for rejecting many of the tenets of the ROMAN CATHOLIC CHURCH.

Herodotus (hi-ROD-uh-tuhs) An ancient Greek historian, often called the father of history. His history of the invasion of GREECE by the PERSIAN EMPIRE was the first attempt at narrative history, and was the beginning of all Western history writing.

Hinduism A religion of INDIA that emphasizes freedom from the material world through purification of desires and elimination of personal identity. Hindu beliefs include REINCARNATION. (*See* BHAGAVAD GITA, BRAHMINS, PARIAH, VISHNU, *and* YOGA.)
    🕭 Traditionally, Hinduism was linked to the CASTE system — a division of Indian society into several rigid groups, with members of a higher caste holding power over those of a lower. 🕭 The sacred writings of Hinduism include the Vedas (which contain the UPANISHADS) and the BHAGAVAD GITA.

Hobbes, Thomas (HOBZ) A seventeenth-century British political PHILOSOPHER; the author of *Leviathan*. According to Hobbes, human life in a "state of nature" is "solitary, poor, nasty, brutish, and short." He argued that government must be strong, and even repressive, to keep people from lapsing into a savage existence.

Holy See In the ROMAN CATHOLIC CHURCH, the official name for the jurisdiction of the POPE (*see* is from the LATIN for "seat").

Holy Writ The BIBLE.
    🕭 Figuratively, "holy writ" is any text or document that is presumed to speak with unquestioned authority.

Homer An ancient Greek poet, author of the *ILIAD* and the *ODYSSEY*. Many literary critics have considered him the greatest and most influential of all poets. According to tradition, Homer was blind.

Horace An ancient Roman poet, known for his ODES. Horace insisted that poetry should offer both pleasure and instruction.

Hugo, Victor A nineteenth-century French ROMANTIC author. He wrote poetry, plays, and NOVELS; among his novels are *Les Misérables* and *THE HUNCHBACK OF NOTRE DAME*.

Human Comedy, The A long series of NOVELS by Honoré de BALZAC.

humanist In the RENAISSANCE, a scholar who studied the languages and CULTURES of ancient GREECE and ROME; today, a scholar of the HUMANITIES. The term SECULAR HUMANIST is applied to someone who concentrates on human activities and possibilities, usually downplaying or denying the importance of God and a life after death.

humanitarianism Concern for the well-being of one's fellow human beings.

humanities One of the main branches of learning. A scholar of the humanities studies history, literature, the FINE ARTS, and PHILOSOPHY.

Hume, David A Scottish PHILOSOPHER of the eighteenth century, known for his SKEPTICISM. Hume maintained that all knowledge was based on either the impressions of the senses or the logical relations of ideas.

Hunchback of Notre Dame, The A historical NOVEL by Victor HUGO. Set in the MIDDLE AGES, it tells the story of Quasimodo, a grotesquely deformed bell ringer at the CATHEDRAL of NOTRE DAME DE PARIS, who falls in love with a beautiful gypsy girl.

I think; therefore I am A statement by the seventeenth-century French PHILOSOPHER René DESCARTES. "I think; therefore I am" was the end of the search Descartes conducted for a statement that could not be doubted. He found that he could not doubt that he himself existed, since he was the one doing the doubting in the first place. In LATIN (the language in which Descartes wrote), the phrase is "COGITO, ERGO SUM."

Ibsen, Henrik A Norwegian author of the nineteenth century. Ibsen wrote many powerful plays on social and political themes, including *A DOLL'S HOUSE*, *Ghosts*, *An Enemy of the People*, and *Hedda Gabler*.

idealism An approach to PHILOSOPHY that regards mind, spirit, or ideas as the most fundamental kinds of reality, or at least as governing our experience of the ordinary objects in the world. Idealism is opposed to MATERIALISM or NATURALISM, and to REALISM. Georg Wilhelm Friedrich HEGEL was an idealist; so was Immanuel KANT.

Ignatius of Loyola (ig-NAY-shuhs; loy-OH-luh) A Spanish PRIEST of the ROMAN CATHOLIC CHURCH in the sixteenth century; the founder of the JESUITS. Ignatius of Loyola is a SAINT of the Roman Catholic Church.

Iliad (IL-ee-uhd) An EPIC by HOMER that recounts the story of the TROJAN WAR.

Immaculate Conception A doctrine of the ROMAN CATHOLIC CHURCH; it states that MARY, THE MOTHER OF JESUS, was free from ORIGINAL SIN.

Incarnation The CHRISTIAN belief that the Son, the second person of the TRINITY, was incarnated, or made flesh, in the person of JESUS, in order to save the world from ORIGINAL SIN.

induction A process of reasoning that moves from specific instances to predict general principles. The opposite process is called DEDUCTION — reasoning from general principles to predict specific instances.

infallibility, papal The belief of the ROMAN CATHOLIC CHURCH that the POPE is kept by God from making a mistake when he speaks on a question of faith or morals.

inference In LOGIC, the deriving of one idea from another. Inference can proceed through either INDUCTION or DEDUCTION.

Inferno The first section of *THE DIVINE COMEDY*, by DANTE. *Inferno* is the Italian word for "HELL."

ᴥ By extension, an "inferno" is a hot and terrible place or condition.

Islam A religion, founded by MOHAMMED, whose members worship the one God of JEWS and CHRISTIANS (God is called ALLAH in Arabic) and follow the teachings of the KORAN. *Islam* means "submission to the will of God"; adherents of Islam are called MOSLEMS (or MUSLIMS). The fundamental belief of Islam is "There is only one God, and Mohammed is his PROPHET."

Moslems are obliged to pray five times a day, to fast in the daytime during the holy month of RAMADAN, to abstain from pork and alcohol, and to make gifts to the poor. All of them are expected to make a pilgrimage to MECCA, Mohammed's birthplace, at least once in their lives.

ᴥ SHI'ITE AND SUNNI MOSLEMS make up the two main branches of Islam. ᴥ Islam is the dominant faith in the Arab nations (*see* ARAB-ISRAELI CONFLICT); in a number of countries of central ASIA, including IRAN; and in MALAYSIA and INDONESIA.

Jehovah's Witnesses A religious denomination that expects the MILLENNIUM to begin within a very few years. Jehovah's Witnesses insist on the use of JEHOVAH as a name for God. They deny the doctrine of the TRINITY, and consider JESUS to be the greatest of the witnesses of Jehovah.

ᴥ Jehovah's Witnesses are expected to carry on vigorous missionary work, often door to door. They publish a magazine, the *Watchtower*. ᴥ Jehovah's Witnesses believe that the BIBLE forbids them to accept BLOOD TRANSFUSIONS, even to save their lives.

Jesuits A RELIGIOUS ORDER of men in the ROMAN CATHOLIC CHURCH; its official name is the Society of Jesus. Founded by IGNATIUS OF LOYOLA in the sixteenth century, the society became the spearhead of the COUNTER REFORMATION.

ᴥ The Jesuits have a long tradition of vigorous missionary work and of intellectual and scholarly achievement. The order operates numerous schools and colleges. The Jesuits have also been known for their influence, often behind the scenes, in European politics, and for their skill and their resourcefulness in debate — characteristics that have sometimes led people to mistrust them. The ADJECTIVE *jesuitical* is still used to describe devious argumentation. In recent years, they have become better known as free-ranging thinkers on religious and political questions.

Jews The adherents of JUDAISM.

jihad (ji-HAHD, ji-HAD) In ISLAM, a holy war; a war ordained by God. The KORAN teaches that soldiers who die in jihad go to HEAVEN immediately.

Judaism The religion of the ISRAELITES of the BIBLE and of the JEWS of today, based on the teachings of the TORAH. Judaism involves the belief in one God, whose CHOSEN PEOPLE are the Jews. ABRAHAM is

STAR OF DAVID. *Also known as the Magen David.*

considered the founder of Judaism, although MOSES, who delivered the laws of God to the Israelites, is also an important figure.

The holy days and festivals of Judaism include HA-NUKKAH, PASSOVER, ROSH HASHANAH, and YOM KIPPUR. (*See also* SABBATH.)

🔊 The Star of David is a six-pointed star, formed by placing two triangles together, one upon the other, or interlaced.

JUGGERNAUT. *A detail from an engraving, showing worshipers of Juggernaut.*

Juggernaut (JUG-uhr-nawt)   A deity in HINDUISM, considered a deliverer from sin. His image is carried on a large wagon in an annual procession in INDIA, and according to legend the wagon crushed worshipers who threw themselves under it.

🔊 A force, an idea, or a system of beliefs that overcomes opposition — especially if it does so ruthlessly — is called a "juggernaut."

justification by grace, through faith   In CHRISTI-ANITY, the belief that a person can achieve SALVA-TION only through faith and reliance on God's GRACE, not through good deeds. The PHRASE is adapted from a sentence in the epistles of PAUL in the BIBLE: "By grace are ye saved through faith; and that not of yourselves: it is the gift of God." Justification is what sets a person fundamentally in friendship with God, and entitles the person to life with God in HEAVEN after death.

🔊 Whether human beings can contribute to this justification, in addition to God's grace, was one of the great points of division among CHRISTIANS at the time of the REFORMATION. 🔊 Two of the slogans of LUTHER were "Grace Alone" and "Faith Alone," which he urged against the common teaching of the ROMAN CATHOLIC CHURCH that people's good works, as well as their faith, helped to save them. Since the time of Luther, the differences between PROTESTANT and Roman Catholic teachings on this point have become hard to discern.

Kafka, Franz (KAHF-kuh)   An Austrian author of the early twentieth century. His works, all written in German, have a surreal, dreamlike quality; they frequently concern CHARACTERS who are lonely, tormented, and victimized, and who represent the frustrations of modern life. He is author of "The METAMORPHOSIS" and *The Trial*.

🔊 A "kafkaesque" situation is both bizarre and frustrating.

Kant, Immanuel (KAHNT, KANT)   An eighteenth-century German PHILOSOPHER; the leading philosopher of modern times. His views are called the Critical PHILOSOPHY, and his three best-known works are his critiques: *Critique of Pure Reason*, *Critique of Practical Reason*, and *Critique of Judgment*.

Kant was troubled because METAPHYSICS had not arrived at acceptable answers on important concerns, particularly God (whether there is one), the soul (whether it lives on after death), and the world as a whole (whether people can act freely in the world, or whether its laws determine all their actions). He maintained that the first step in getting any answers in these areas was to investigate the limits of human understanding and reasoning; this investigation was what he called a critique.

🔊 Kant held that we cannot know a THING-IN-IT-SELF as it is, but only as our mind constitutes it.

🕭 Kant asserted that while no one can understand God, the soul, or the world in the way we understand things in nature, we must believe in God, in immortality, and in FREE WILL. 🕭 Kant led an extremely simple and regulated life. According to one story, the people in his town set their clocks by his afternoon walks.

Kierkegaard, Sören (SEU-ruhn KEER-kuh-gahrd, KEER-kuh-gawr) A Danish PHILOSOPHER of the nineteenth century. Kierkegaard wrote much about the fear and loneliness that he believed come with true religion; he is considered a forerunner of twentieth-century EXISTENTIALISM.

King James Bible The best-known English translation of the BIBLE, commissioned by King James I of ENGLAND, and published in the early seventeenth century. It is also known as the Authorized Version.

🕭 The King James Bible had no rival among PROTESTANTS until the late nineteenth century, when the Revised Version was published in England.

Koran (kuh-RAN, kuh-RAHN) The sacred book of ISLAM. MOSLEMS believe that the teachings of the Koran were revealed by God to the PROPHET MOHAMMED.

kosher The descriptive term in JUDAISM for food and other objects that are clean according to its laws. These laws are contained in the TORAH and forbid, for example, the eating of pork and of shellfish, the mixing of dairy products and meat, and certain methods of slaughtering animals.

🕭 Used as an IDIOM, *kosher* means right, proper, or according to law.

La Fontaine, Jean de (ZHAHNN duh lah-fahn-TAYN, lah-fohnn-TEN) A French author of the seventeenth century, best known for his *Fables*, in which the CHARACTERS are animals.

lama (LAH-muh) In the BUDDHISM of Tibet, a MONK or PRIEST. The chief of the lamas is the Dalai Lama.

Latter-Day Saints *See* MORMONS.

🕭 The Reorganized CHURCH of JESUS CHRIST of Latter-Day Saints is a denomination that separated from the Mormons in the nineteenth century; it rejects the name Mormon for itself.

law of noncontradiction A basic principle of LOGIC: that a sentence and the denial of the sentence cannot both be true.

Lent In CHRISTIANITY, a time of fasting and repentance in the spring, beginning on ASH WEDNESDAY and ending several weeks later on EASTER.

🕭 To "give something up for Lent" is to abandon a pleasurable habit as an act of devotion and self-discipline.

liberal arts The areas of learning that cultivate general intellectual ability rather than technical or professional skills. Liberal arts is often used as a SYNONYM for HUMANITIES, although the liberal arts also include the sciences. The term *liberal* comes from the LATIN *liberalis*, meaning suitable for a free man, as opposed to a slave.

Liberty, On An ESSAY by John Stuart MILL in defense of the LIBERAL idea of political freedom. Mill takes a firm position that the state may interfere with the freedom of individuals only to protect other individuals; the person's "own good" is not a sufficient reason.

limbo In the teaching of the ROMAN CATHOLIC CHURCH regarding the afterlife, the condition of innocent persons who die without benefit of BAPTISM; those in limbo do not suffer DAMNATION, but they do not enjoy the presence of God. *Limbo* means "a bordering place."

🕭 Figuratively, "limbo" is a state of nonresolution or uncertainty: "Until he receives notice of his new posting, he'll be in limbo."

litany In many religions, a ritual repetition of prayers. Usually a clergyman or singer chants a prayer, and the congregation makes a response, such as "Lord, have mercy."

Locke, John An English PHILOSOPHER of the seventeenth century. As a philosopher of knowledge, Locke argued against the belief that human beings are born with certain ideas already in their minds. He claimed that, on the contrary, the mind is a TABULA RASA (blank slate) until experience begins to "write" on it. As a political philosopher, Locke attacked the doctrine of the DIVINE RIGHT OF KINGS, and argued that governments depend on the consent of the governed.

🕭 Locke's political ideas were taken up by the American FOUNDING FATHERS; his influence is especially apparent in the DECLARATION OF INDEPENDENCE.

logic   The branch of PHILOSOPHY dealing with the principles of reasoning. Classical logic, as taught in ancient Greece and ROME, systematized rules for DEDUCTION. The modern scientific and philosophical logic of deduction has become closely allied to MATHEMATICS, especially in showing how the foundations of mathematics lie in logic.

Loyola, Ignatius of   *See* IGNATIUS OF LOYOLA.

Lucifer   A name, traditional in CHRISTIANITY, for the leader of the DEVILS, an ANGEL who was cast from HEAVEN into HELL because he rebelled against God. Lucifer is usually identified with SATAN. The name LUCIFER, which means "bearer of light" or "morning star," refers to his former splendor as the greatest of the angels.

Luther, Martin   A religious leader in sixteenth-century GERMANY; the founder of PROTESTANTISM. Luther, a PRIEST of the ROMAN CATHOLIC CHURCH, began the REFORMATION by posting his Ninety-five Theses, which attacked the church for allowing the sale of INDULGENCES. He soon became convinced that the Roman Catholic Church was opposed to the BIBLE on the question of JUSTIFICATION BY GRACE, THROUGH FAITH, and that no accommodation of his beliefs on this point was possible within the church. Luther concluded that reform of the church had to happen through formation of a new body of CHRISTIANS. He denied the authority of the POPE and many other aspects of Catholic teaching, including the doctrine of TRANSUBSTANTIATION. Luther wrote an enormous number of books and pamphlets throughout his lifetime.
🕭 Luther's most famous statement, made when he was called to account for his views before a meeting, was, "It is neither safe nor prudent to do anything against conscience. Here I stand; I can do no other."

Lutheran Church   A PROTESTANT denomination that arose from the teachings of Martin LUTHER. Lutherans are known for their stress on the doctrine of JUSTIFICATION BY GRACE, THROUGH FAITH, and for their insistence on the BIBLE alone as a rule of faith. Lutherans practice BAPTISM of infants, and believe that JESUS is really, not just symbolically, present in the SACRAMENT of COMMUNION.
🕭 The Lutheran Church is strongest among the people of GERMANY and SCANDINAVIA, where it is an ESTABLISHED CHURCH, supported by the government. In the United States, it is strongest among people descended from Germans and Scandinavians.
🕭 Lutherans are known for their cultivation of church music, especially choral and organ music. Johann Sebastian BACH wrote much of his music for Lutheran worship.

Lysistrata   (leye-SIS-truh-tuh, lis-uh-STRAH-tuh)   An ancient Greek COMEDY by ARISTOPHANES. The title CHARACTER persuades the women of ATHENS and SPARTA, which are at war, to refuse sexual contact with their husbands until the two cities make peace.

Machiavelli, Niccolò   (mak-ee-uh-VEL-ee)   An Italian political PHILOSOPHER of the RENAISSANCE. Machiavelli was the author of *THE PRINCE*, a book that advises rulers to retain their power through cunning and ruthlessness.
🕭 A "Machiavellian" leader is one who cunningly subordinates moral principle to political goals.

macrocosm   A representation of something on a much larger scale. (*Compare* MICROCOSM.)

Madame Bovary   (BOH-vuh-ree)   The best-known NOVEL of Gustave FLAUBERT. The title CHARACTER is dissatisfied with her marriage, seeks happiness in ADULTERY, and finally commits suicide.

Man is the measure of all things   A statement by the ancient Greek PHILOSOPHER Protagoras. It is usually interpreted to mean that the individual human being, rather than a god or an unchanging moral law, is the ultimate source of value.

Mann, Thomas   (MAHN)   A German author of the twentieth century. Among his best-known works are the NOVELS *The Magic Mountain* and *Death in Venice*.

Mardi Gras   (MAHR-dee grah)   An annual festival in FRANCE, held on the day before ASH WEDNESDAY, the first day of LENT. *Mardi Gras* is French for "Fat Tuesday" — the last opportunity to eat rich food before the fast of Lent begins. It is related to celebrations elsewhere, called "carnivals," from the LATIN words *carne* and *vale*, "meat" and "farewell," meaning a farewell to meat before the abstinence of Lent.

🐚 NEW ORLEANS, LOUISIANA, is famous for its Mardi Gras celebration.

Marxism The doctrines of Karl MARX and his associate Friedrich ENGELS on ECONOMICS, politics, and society. They include the notion of economic determinism — that political and social structures are determined by the economic conditions of people. Marxism calls for a classless society (*see* CLASS), where all means of production are commonly owned, a system to be reached as an inevitable result of the struggle between capitalists and workers. (*See* COMMUNISM.)

Mass The common name in the ROMAN CATHOLIC CHURCH, and among some members of the ANGLICAN COMMUNION, for the SACRAMENT of COMMUNION.

🐚 In the MIDDLE AGES in ENGLAND, *mass* meant a religious feast day in honor of a specific person; thus, "Christ's Mass," or Christmas, is the feast day of CHRIST; Michaelmas is the feast day of Michael the ANGEL; and so on.

materialism In PHILOSOPHY, the position that nothing exists except matter — things that can be measured or known through the senses. Materialists deny the existence of spirit, and they look for physical explanations for all phenomena. Thus, for example, they trace mental states to the BRAIN or NERVOUS SYSTEM, rather than to the spirit or the soul. MARXISM, because it sees human CULTURE as the product of economic forces, is a materialist system of beliefs.

matzo (MAHT-suh) A flat piece of unleavened bread, resembling a large cracker, used by JEWS in place of yeast bread during PASSOVER. According to the biblical account of Passover, God directed the ancestors of the Jews to eat unleavened bread, rather than delay their departure from EGYPT by waiting for bread to rise.

Mecca The birthplace of MOHAMMED, and thus the holiest city for MOSLEMS. Moslems face in the direction of Mecca when they pray, and they are expected to go on a pilgrimage to Mecca at least once in their lives. Mecca is in present-day SAUDI ARABIA.

🐚 Figuratively, a "mecca" is any place that attracts a great many people.

Mennonites A group of PROTESTANTS, founded in the early days of the REFORMATION, who believe in living with great simplicity, and who refuse to hold public office or to serve in the military. Some are as strict as the AMISH in rejecting modern conveniences such as automobiles and radios. There are numerous Mennonite communities in PENNSYLVANIA and the MIDDLE WEST.

Mephistopheles (mef-i-STOF-uh-leez) In the drama *Faust* by GOETHE, a DEVIL who tempts Faust into selling his soul to the powers of darkness. Mephistopheles also appears, with his name spelled *Mephistophilis*, in the sixteenth-century English play *Doctor Faustus*, by Christopher Marlowe.

Messiah (muh-SEYE-uh) In JUDAISM and CHRISTIANITY, the promised "anointed one" or CHRIST; the Savior. CHRISTIANS believe that JESUS was the Messiah who delivered mankind from ORIGINAL SIN. JEWS believe that the Messiah has not yet come.

Metamorphoses (met-uh-MAWR-fuh-seez) A long poem by the ancient Roman poet OVID, in which he relates numerous stories from CLASSICAL MYTHOLOGY. Many of the stories deal with miraculous transformations, or metamorphoses.

"Metamorphosis, The" (met-uh-MAWR-fuh-sis) A story by Franz KAFKA. It is a tale of psychological terror, in which a salesman named Gregor Samsa wakes up one morning to find himself transformed into a giant insect.

metaphysics The field in PHILOSOPHY that studies ultimate questions, such as whether every event has a cause, and what things are genuinely real.

Methodists A PROTESTANT denomination founded by the English clergyman John WESLEY and his brother Charles Wesley in the eighteenth century. Methodists are generally flexible in doctrine and in CHURCH organization, and stress the social responsibility of CHRISTIANS. Next to the BAPTISTS, Methodists are the most numerous group of Protestants in the United States.

microcosm A representation of something on a much smaller scale. *Microcosm* means "small world," and in the thought of the RENAISSANCE, it was applied specifically to human beings, who were considered to be small-scale models of the UNIVERSE, with all its variety and contradiction.

Mill, John Stuart An English PHILOSOPHER and economist of the nineteenth century. Two of his best-known works are *Utilitarianism*, a classic statement of that approach to ETHICS (*see* UTILITARIANISM), and *On Liberty*, a similar statement for LIBERAL thought in politics.

minister   In many PROTESTANT CHURCHES, the presiding clergyman. Ministers preach sermons; conduct services; officiate at BAPTISMS, weddings, and funerals; and generally look after the needs of their congregation. Some Protestant churches refer to their clergy as PASTORS or preachers rather than ministers.

Mohammed (Muhammad)   The Arab founder of ISLAM, Mohammed is held by MOSLEMS to be the chief PROPHET of God. He was born in MECCA. Moslems believe that the KORAN was dictated to him by an ANGEL sent from God.

Molière (mohl-YAIR)   NOM DE PLUME of Jean-Baptiste Poquelin, a French playwright of the seventeenth century, best known for his COMEDIES of SATIRE, such as *The Misanthrope* and *Tartuffe*.

monism (MOH-niz-uhm, MON-iz-uhm)   A position in METAPHYSICS that sees only one kind of principle where DUALISM sees two. On the question of whether people's minds are distinct from their bodies, for example, a monist would hold either that mental conditions are essentially physical conditions (MATERIALISM), or that bodies depend on minds for their existence (IDEALISM).

monks   Men under religious vows who live in community and whose work is usually centered on their community, which is called a monastery. BUDDHISM and CHRISTIANITY have notable groups of monks. In CHRISTIANITY, the monks are members of RELIGIOUS ORDERS.

monotheism   A belief in one god. JUDAISM, CHRISTIANITY, and ISLAM are all monotheistic religions. (*Compare* POLYTHEISM.)

Montaigne, Michel de (mee-SHEL duh mon-TAYN, mohnn-TEN)   A French writer of the sixteenth century, best known for his *Essays*. Montaigne established the informal ESSAY as a major literary form.

Montesquieu, Charles, Baron de (MON-tuh-skyooh, monn-tes-KYEU)   A French political PHILOSOPHER of the eighteenth century. His major work, *The Spirit of Laws*, defended the principle of SEPARATION OF POWERS.

Mormons   The CHURCH OF JESUS CHRIST of LATTER-DAY SAINTS; a religion that originated in the United States in the nineteenth century, with teachings based on the BIBLE and the *Book of Mormon*. In Mormon belief, the *Book of Mormon* was revealed to the founder of the church, Joseph SMITH, in the early nineteenth century. When the beliefs of the Mormons brought them into conflict with some of their neighbors, they moved to western territories under the leadership of Brigham YOUNG.

Mormons lay stress on hard work, loyal family life, and abstinence from alcohol and tobacco.

❧ The land the Mormons eventually settled in the West became the state of UTAH, where Mormons still form a majority. ❧ The Mormons were once controversial because they engaged in POLYGAMY, but the church no longer sanctions the practice.

mortal sin/venial sin   A distinction of sins that is stressed in the THEOLOGY of the ROMAN CATHOLIC CHURCH. A sin is mortal when it is serious enough to subject the sinner to DAMNATION; willful murder, for instance, is considered a mortal sin. Venial sins are less serious.

Moslem (Muslim)   A follower of ISLAM. (See also SHI'ITE and SUNNI MOSLEMS.)

mosque   A MOSLEM house of worship.

music of the spheres   A beautiful sound, inaudible to the human ear, that the ancient Greeks believed was made by the STARS and PLANETS as they moved through the HEAVENS. The "spheres" were not the planets themselves, but invisible globes to which the planets were believed to be attached. (*See* PTOLEMAIC UNIVERSE.)

Muslim   *See* MOSLEM.

mysticism   In religion, the attempt by an individual to achieve a personal union with God or with some other divine being or principle. Mystics generally practice daily meditation.

natural law   The doctrine that human affairs should be governed by ethical principles that are part of the very nature of things and that can be understood by reason. The first two paragraphs of the DECLARATION OF INDEPENDENCE contain a clear statement of the doctrine.

naturalism A movement in literature and the arts, and an approach to PHILOSOPHY. Literary and artistic naturalism aims at accuracy and objectivity, and cultivates realistic and even sordid portrayals of people and their environment. Philosophical naturalism, which is often identified with MATERIALISM, holds that minds, spirits, and ideas are fundamentally material.

Neruda, Pablo (nay-ROOH-duh, nay-ROOH-thhah) A Chilean poet of the twentieth century, widely considered the greatest of recent Latin American poets. He also served in his country's senate, and was its ambassador to FRANCE.

Nicholas, Saint A Greek BISHOP of the fourth century, Nicholas was known for his kindness. Santa Claus is an English version of his Dutch name, Sinter Klaas. Legends about him, stating that he gave presents in secret to persons in trouble, contributed to the traditions surrounding Santa Claus.

Nietzsche, Friedrich (NEE-chuh, NEE-chee) A German thinker of the nineteenth century. Nietzsche, who asserted that "God is dead," was passionately opposed to CHRISTIANITY. He developed the concept of the SUPERMAN, or "Overman" (*Übermensch*), a superior human being, not bound by conventional notions of right and wrong.

nihilism (NEYE-uh-liz-uhm, NEE-uh-liz-uhm) An approach to PHILOSOPHY that holds that human life is meaningless, and that all religions, laws, moral codes, and political systems are thoroughly empty and false. The term is from the LATIN *nihil*, meaning "nothing."

nirvana (neer-VAH-nuh, nur-VAH-nuh) In BUDDHISM, the highest state of consciousness, in which the soul is freed from all desires and attachments. *Nirvana* is sometimes inaccurately used as a SYNONYM for HEAVEN or PARADISE.

noble savage Someone who belongs to an "uncivilized" group or tribe and is considered to be, consequently, more worthy than people who live within civilization. Many writers and thinkers through the centuries of Western civilization have believed in the noble savage. The expression is particularly associated with Jean-Jacques ROUSSEAU.

Nonconformists PROTESTANTS in ENGLAND in the seventeenth century and afterward who refused to belong to the CHURCH OF ENGLAND, which was the ESTABLISHED CHURCH for Protestants in the country. Many Protestant churches in the United States, such as the CONGREGATIONALISTS, are rooted in the teachings of the English Nonconformists. The Nonconformists are also called Dissenters.

nun A female member of a RELIGIOUS ORDER, living in a CONVENT, whose work is confined to the convent. The term is also applied broadly to other female members of religious orders ("sisters") who work outside their convents as teachers, nurses, administrators, and so on.

Ockham, William of (OK-uhm) An English PHILOSOPHER of the fourteenth century.

&. Ockham is known for OCKHAM'S RAZOR, his principle that "entities are not to be multiplied beyond necessity" — that is, explanations in PHILOSOPHY should be kept as simple as possible.

Odyssey An ancient Greek EPIC by HOMER that recounts the adventures of ODYSSEUS during his return from the war in TROY to his home in the Greek island of Ithaca. (*See* ODYSSEUS *and* TROY *under "Mythology and Folklore"; see also* SCYLLA AND CHARYBDIS, PENELOPE, CIRCE, *and* CYCLOPS.)

&. Figuratively, an "odyssey" is any difficult, prolonged journey.

Oedipus Rex (ED-uh-puhs, EE-duh-puhs REKS) A TRAGEDY by SOPHOCLES that dramatizes the fall of OEDIPUS.

Omar Khayyam (OH-mahr keye-AHM, keye-AM) A Persian poet of the twelfth century; author of the "RUBÁIYÁT."

original sin The sin of ADAM AND EVE, the essential event of the FALL OF MAN. According to the most common teaching of CHRISTIANS, all descendants of Adam and Eve — that is, all people — share in this sin and are, from the time they are conceived, in a state of sin. In German, the term used is *Erbsunde*, meaning "inherited sin," a more explanatory term than the English one. JESUS, through his CRUCIFIXION and RESURRECTION, made up for original sin. All who believe in Jesus and accept BAPTISM are freed from original sin, and experience SALVATION. (*See* JUSTIFICATION BY GRACE, THROUGH FAITH.)

Orthodox Christianity The form of CHRISTIANITY maintained by the EASTERN ORTHODOX CHURCH. *Orthodox* means "correct in teaching"; Orthodox Christians consider the ROMAN CATHOLIC CHURCH and the PROTESTANT CHURCHES to be incorrect in some teachings, including the relations between the persons of the TRINITY.

Orthodox Judaism The branch of JUDAISM that insists on the keeping of the Jewish law, or TORAH, in its entirety; *orthodox* means "correct in teaching." A few generations ago, the Orthodox was the dominant form of Judaism; today, fewer than one-fifth of JEWS belonging to Jewish congregations in the United States are Orthodox.

Ovid (OV-id) An ancient Roman poet; author of the *METAMORPHOSES* and *The Art of Love*.

Palm Sunday The Sunday before EASTER. It is celebrated by CHRISTIANS to commemorate the entry of JESUS into JERUSALEM five days before his CRUCIFIXION. On that occasion, the people of Jerusalem laid palm leaves in his path as a sign of welcome. Palms are carried or worn by worshipers in many CHURCHES on Palm Sunday.

pantheism The belief that God, or a group of gods, is identical with the whole natural world; *pantheism* comes from Greek roots meaning "belief that everything is a god."

Panza, Sancho *See* SANCHO PANZA.

papacy The office or position of the POPE.

paradise A place or state of pure happiness. CHRISTIANS have identified paradise both with the Garden of EDEN and with HEAVEN.

Paradiso (pahr-uh-DEE-zoh) The last part of *THE DIVINE COMEDY* of DANTE, describing HEAVEN.

Pascal, Blaise (BLEZ pa-SKAL, pah-SKAHL) A French mathematician, scientist, and religious thinker of the seventeenth century. Pascal came to believe that reason alone could not satisfy people's hopes and aspirations, and that religious faith was therefore necessary. His religious thoughts are collected in *PENSÉES* (*Thoughts*).

❧ "Pascal's wager" refers to Pascal's idea that it is prudent to believe in God's existence, since little can

be lost if there is no God, and eternal happiness can be gained if there is one.

Passover Among JEWS, the festival commemorating the EXODUS, the deliverance of the ISRAELITES from slavery in EGYPT. During Passover, unleavened bread, called MATZO, is eaten. In the course of the festival, the story of the Exodus is read.

Pasternak, Boris A Russian author of the twentieth century, famous for his poetry and for *Doctor Zhivago*, a NOVEL.

pastor In some groups of CHRISTIANS, the clergyman in charge of an individual congregation. The term is used this way in the LUTHERAN CHURCH and ROMAN CATHOLIC CHURCH and, to a lesser extent, by BAPTISTS and in the PROTESTANT EPISCOPAL CHURCH.

Patrick, Saint An early BISHOP in IRELAND, who spread CHRISTIANITY throughout the nation. Patrick is honored as Ireland's PATRON SAINT.

❧ Many legends have grown up about Patrick: that he drove snakes out of Ireland, for example, and that he used a three-leafed clover, the shamrock, to illustrate the TRINITY.

patron saint A SAINT from whom a person or group claims special protection or prayers. Saint CHRISTOPHER, for example, has been considered the patron of travelers, Saint LUKE the patron of doctors, and Saint PATRICK the patron of IRELAND. People who have the same name as a saint may consider the saint their patron. The honoring of patron saints is especially common in the ROMAN CATHOLIC CHURCH.

penance Acts done to make up for sin. (*See* CONFESSION *and* INDULGENCE.)

Pensées (pahnn-SAY) A set of reflections on religion by Blaise PASCAL (*pensées* is French for "thoughts"). This work contains the famous statement "The heart has its reasons that the reason does not know."

perfectibility of man The doctrine, advanced by ROUSSEAU and others, that people are capable of achieving perfection on earth through natural means, without the GRACE of God.

philosopher Someone who engages in PHILOSOPHY. Some examples of philosophers are ARISTOTLE, Immanuel KANT, and PLATO.

philosopher-king In the *REPUBLIC* by PLATO, the ideal ruler, who has the virtue and wisdom of the PHILOSOPHER.

philosopher's stone The stone or material that practitioners of ALCHEMY believed capable of changing other metals into gold.

&. Figuratively, the "philosopher's stone" is a substance thought to be capable of regenerating man spiritually.

philosophes (fee-luh-ZAWF) A group of RADICAL thinkers and writers in FRANCE in the eighteenth century, including VOLTAIRE and Jean-Jacques ROUSSEAU. The philosophes stressed the use of human reason, and were especially critical of established religious and political practices in France.

philosophy A study that attempts to discover the fundamental principles of the sciences, the arts, and the world that the sciences and arts deal with; the word *philosophy* is from the Greek for "love of wisdom." Philosophy has subdisciplines that explore principles of specific areas, such as knowledge (EPISTEMOLOGY), reasoning (LOGIC), being in general (METAPHYSICS), beauty (AESTHETICS), and human conduct (ETHICS).

Different approaches to philosophy, or to its subdisciplines, are also called philosophies. (*See* EPICUREANISM, EXISTENTIALISM, IDEALISM, MATERIALISM, NIHILISM, PRAGMATISM, STOICISM, *and* UTILITARIANISM.)

Pinocchio, The Adventures of A children's story of the nineteenth century by the Italian author Carlo Collodi. Pinocchio is a puppet who is brought to life by a fairy and learns moral lessons through his adventures.

&. The fairy also provides that Pinocchio's nose will grow longer whenever he tells a lie.

Plato (PLAY-toh) An ancient Greek PHILOSOPHER, often considered the most important figure in Western PHILOSOPHY. Plato was a student of SOCRATES, and later became the teacher of ARISTOTLE. He founded a school in ATHENS called the ACADEMY. Most of his writings are dialogues. He is best known for his THEORY that ideal Forms or Ideas, such as Truth or the Good, exist in a realm beyond the material world. In fact, however, his chief subjects are

ETHICS and politics. His best-known dialogues are the *REPUBLIC*, which concerns the just state, and the *SYMPOSIUM*, which concerns the nature of love.

Platonic or **platonic** (pluh-TON-ik) A descriptive term for things associated with PLATO (for example, Platonic Forms or Ideas). In general usage, *platonic* means lofty or pure, or associated with the higher thinking capacities of people.

&. A "platonic" love or a "platonic" relationship is one in which people have mental or spiritual exchanges only, and refrain from physical intimacy.

Platonism (PLAYT-n-iz-uhm) The PHILOSOPHY of PLATO, or an approach to philosophy resembling his. For example, someone who asserts that numbers exist independently of the things they number could be called a Platonist.

pluralism A conviction that various religious, ethnic, racial, and political groups should be allowed to thrive in a single society. In METAPHYSICS, *pluralism* can also mean an alternative to DUALISM and MONISM. A pluralist asserts that there are more than two kinds of principles, where the dualist maintains there are only two and a monist only one.

Plutarch (PLOOH-tahrk) An ancient Greek biographer noted for his ethical insights. He evaluated the character and conduct of many Greek and Roman rulers in his major work, popularly known as Plutarch's *Lives*.

polytheism The belief in more than one god. The ancient Greeks, for example, were polytheists; their gods included APOLLO, ATHENA, DIONYSUS, and ZEUS. (*Compare* MONOTHEISM.)

pontiff Another name for the POPE. *Pontiff* comes from a LATIN word, meaning "bridge builder," that was used as a title for some of the PRIESTS of ancient ROME.

pope The head of the ROMAN CATHOLIC CHURCH. The pope is believed by his church to be the successor to the APOSTLE PETER. He is BISHOP of ROME, and lives in a tiny nation within Rome called the VATICAN. Catholics believe that when the pope speaks officially on matters of faith and morals, he speaks infallibly (*see* INFALLIBILITY, PAPAL). Historically, the pope's influence and power have been great, extend-

POPE. *Pope John Paul II during a visit to Boston in 1980.*

ing to political as well as spiritual areas. (*See* JOHN XXIII, POPE *and* JOHN PAUL II, POPE.)

positivism An approach to PHILOSOPHY frequently found in the twentieth century. Positivists usually hold that all meaningful statements must be either logical inferences or sense descriptions, and usually argue that the statements found in METAPHYSICS, such as "Human beings are free" or "Human beings are not free," are meaningless because they cannot possibly be verified by the senses.

postulate A statement accepted as true for the purposes of argument or scientific investigation; also, a basic principle. (*See* AXIOM.)

pragmatism An approach to PHILOSOPHY, primarily held by American PHILOSOPHERS, which holds that the truth or meaning of a statement is to be measured by its practical (i.e. pragmatic) consequences. William JAMES and John DEWEY were pragmatists.

Praise God, from whom all blessings flow The opening line of the Doxology, an invocation in praise of God that is often spoken or sung during CHRISTIAN worship.

prayer rug A mat upon which MOSLEMS kneel to say their prayers.

prayer wheel In BUDDHISM, a cylinder with prayers written on it. The prayer wheel is turned by some worshipers during prayer, or the turning may be used as a substitute for spoken prayers.

predestination In THEOLOGY, the doctrine that all events have been willed by God. John CALVIN interpreted predestination to mean that God willed eternal DAMNATION for some people and SALVATION for others.

Presbyterian Church A PROTESTANT denomination based on the doctrines of John CALVIN and governed by elders (*presbyteros* is the Greek word for "elder"). The Presbyterian Church was founded in SCOTLAND, where it is the ESTABLISHED CHURCH, supported by the government.

　❧ The Presbyterian Church is strong in NORTHERN IRELAND, CANADA, the United States, and other places where people of Scottish descent are found. There are several million Presbyterians in the United States.

priest One who is designated an authority on religious matters. In some CHURCHES, especially the ANGLICAN COMMUNION, EASTERN ORTHODOX CHURCH, and ROMAN CATHOLIC CHURCH, the ordained church leader who serves a congregation of believers is called a priest. The priests in these churches administer the SACRAMENTS, preach, and care for the needs of their congregations. (*See* MINISTER *and* PASTOR.)

Prince, The The best-known work of Niccolò MACHIAVELLI, in which he asserts that a prince must use cunning and ruthless methods to stay in power.

Protestant A CHRISTIAN belonging to one of the three great divisions of CHRISTIANITY (the other two are the ROMAN CATHOLIC CHURCH and the EASTERN ORTHODOX CHURCH). Protestantism began during the RENAISSANCE as a protest against the ESTABLISHED (Roman Catholic) CHURCH. That protest, led by Martin LUTHER, was called the REFORMATION, because it sprang from a desire to reform the church and cleanse it of corruption, such as the selling of INDULGENCES.

❧ Protestants hold a great variety of beliefs, but are united in rejecting the authority of the POPE. Protestant groups include the AMISH, the ANGLICAN COMMUNION, the ASSEMBLIES OF GOD, the BAPTISTS, the CHRISTIAN SCIENTISTS, the CONGREGATIONALISTS, the LUTHERAN CHURCH, the MENNONITES, the METHODISTS, the QUAKERS, and the PRESBYTERIAN CHURCH.

Protestant Episcopal Church in the United States The American portion of the ANGLICAN COMMUNION; an alternate name for this CHURCH is the Episcopal Church. The Episcopal Church was part of the CHURCH OF ENGLAND before the AMERICAN REVOLUTION, but became independent afterward.

Protestant work ethic A view of life that promotes hard work and self-discipline as a means to material prosperity. It is called PROTESTANT because some Protestant groups believe that such prosperity is a sign of God's GRACE.

Proust, Marcel (PROOHST) A French author of the twentieth century, best known for a series of NOVELS called *Remembrance of Things Past*. Proust's writing explores the influence of past experience on present reality.

Providence, Divine God, seen as providing for mankind, as the caring guide of human destiny.

purgatory In the teaching of the ROMAN CATHOLIC CHURCH, the condition of souls of the dead who die with some punishment (though not DAMNATION) due them for their sins. Purgatory is conceived as a condition of suffering and purification that leads to union with God in HEAVEN. Purgatory is not mentioned in the BIBLE; Catholic authorities defend the teaching on purgatory by arguing that prayer for the dead is an ancient practice of CHRISTIANITY, and that this practice assumes that the dead can be in a state of suffering — a state that the living can improve by their prayers.

❧ A "purgatory" is, by extension, any place of suffering, usually for past misdeeds.

Quaker A member of the Religious Society of FRIENDS. The Quakers are a group of CHRISTIANS who use no scripture and believe in great simplicity in daily life and in worship. Their services consist mainly of silent meditation.

❧ Quakers have traditionally been committed to PACIFISM. ❧ PENNSYLVANIA was settled by a group of Quakers fleeing religious persecution.

rabbi In JUDAISM, a teacher and leader of worship, usually associated with a SYNAGOGUE.

Rabelais, François (frahnn-SWAH rab-uh-LAY, RAB-uh-lay) A French writer of the sixteenth century; the author of *Gargantua and Pantagruel*.

❧ "Rabelaisian" humor is grotesque and bawdy.

Ramadan (ram-uh-DAHN) A holy month in the calendar of ISLAM. MOSLEMS fast between sunrise and sunset during each day of Ramadan.

realism An approach to PHILOSOPHY that regards external objects as the most fundamentally real things, and perceptions or ideas as secondary. Realism is thus opposed to IDEALISM. MATERIALISM and NATURALISM are forms of realism. *Realism* is also used to describe a movement in literature that attempts to portray life as it is.

Reform Judaism The most LIBERAL branch of JUDAISM. In Reform Judaism, all of the Jewish law, or TORAH, is subject to adaptation to fit modern circumstances. In the United States, Reform Jewish congregations have more members than those of the other two branches of Judaism. (*Compare* CONSERVATIVE JUDAISM *and* ORTHODOX JUDAISM.)

reincarnation Being reborn in another body. Several religions, including HINDUISM, believe that the human spirit returns to earth in different forms again and again as it strives for perfection.

relativism The doctrine that no ideas or beliefs are universally true, but that all are instead "relative" — that is, their validity depends on the circumstances in which they are applied.

religious order In CHRISTIANITY, a group of men or women who live under religious vows. The three vows commonly taken are to relinquish all possessions and personal authority (vows of poverty and obedience) and not to engage in sexual relations (a vow of chastity). Religious orders are found in the EASTERN ORTHODOX CHURCH and the ROMAN CATHOLIC CHURCH, and, although rarely, in PROTESTANT CHURCHES. The FRANCISCANS, JESUITS, and TRAPPISTS are religious orders.

Republic   The best-known dialogue of PLATO, in which SOCRATES is shown outlining an ideal state, ruled by PHILOSOPHER-KINGS.

revival   In CHRISTIANITY, an energetic meeting intended to "revive" religious faith. Common among FUNDAMENTALISTS, these meetings are characterized by impassioned preaching and singing.

Roman Catholic Church   The branch of CHRISTIANITY headed by the POPE. The Roman Catholic Church is governed by a hierarchy with the pope at the top and, at the lower levels, BISHOPS and PRIESTS. The SACRAMENTS of COMMUNION and CONFESSION are especially important in the Roman Catholic Church; Catholics also differ from most PROTESTANTS in emphasizing veneration of the SAINTS, especially MARY, THE MOTHER OF JESUS, and seeking the intercession of the saints (praying to them so that they will in turn pray to God). The Roman Catholic Church leadership strongly opposes ABORTION and artificial means of BIRTH CONTROL.

    ❧ Roman Catholicism is the dominant faith in EUROPE around the MEDITERRANEAN SEA, in much of eastern Europe, in IRELAND, and in LATIN AMERICA.

romanticism   A movement in literature and the FINE ARTS, beginning in the early nineteenth century, that stressed personal emotion, free play of the imagination, and freedom from rules of form. Among the leaders of romanticism in world literature were Johann Wolfgang von GOETHE, Victor HUGO, Jean-Jacques ROUSSEAU, and Friedrich von SCHILLER.

rosary   A set of prayers common in the ROMAN CATHOLIC CHURCH, said during meditation on events in the lives of JESUS and of MARY, THE MOTHER OF JESUS. A rosary is also the beads that the worshiper uses to count the prayers.

Rosh Hashanah (rohsh huh-SHAH-nuh)   The festival of the New Year in JUDAISM, falling in September or October. Rosh Hashanah, YOM KIPPUR, and the eight days in between are special days of penitence.

Rousseau, Jean-Jacques (rooh-SOH)   A French PHILOSOPHER of the eighteenth century; one of the leading figures of the ENLIGHTENMENT. He held that, in the state of nature, people are good, but that they are corrupted by social institutions; this notion became a central idea of ROMANTICISM. Some of Rousseau's best-known writings are THE SOCIAL CONTRACT, an important influence on the FRENCH REVOLUTION; ÉMILE, a statement of his views on education; and his autobiography, CONFESSIONS.

"Rubáiyát" (ROOH-bee-aht, ROOH-beye-aht)   A poem by the twelfth century Persian poet OMAR KHAYYAM. This is the poem's best-known STANZA, in a celebrated translation by Edward FitzGerald (*enow* means "enough"):

> A Book of Verses underneath the Bough,
> A Jug of Wine, a Loaf of Bread — and Thou
> Beside me singing in the Wilderness —
> Oh, Wilderness were Paradise enow!

BERTRAND RUSSELL. *The philosopher shortly before his ninetieth birthday.*

Russell, Bertrand   An English PHILOSOPHER and mathematician of the twentieth century, known for his work in LOGIC and EPISTEMOLOGY, and also for his outspoken PACIFISM and other political and social views.

sacrament   A religious ceremony or rite. Most CHRISTIAN CHURCHES reserve the term for those rites that JESUS himself instituted, but there are disagreements between them on which rites those are. The LUTHERAN CHURCH, for example, maintains that BAPTISM and COMMUNION are the only sacraments, whereas in the ROMAN CATHOLIC CHURCH and the EASTERN ORTHODOX CHURCH, there are five more: confirmation; CONFESSION; anointing of the sick; the ordination of clergy; and the marriage of Christians.

Sade, Marquis de (mahr-KEE duh SAHD) A French author of the eighteenth century, notorious for works dealing with sexual perversity.

&. Sadism, or taking pleasure in inflicting pain on others, is named for the Marquis de Sade.

saint In CHRISTIANITY, a holy person, living or dead; a person who has been saved (*see* SALVATION). *Saint* is the French word for "holy." Many CHURCHES reserve the title of saint for persons who have died faithful to their CHRISTIAN commitment. The RO-MAN CATHOLIC CHURCH and the EASTERN ORTHO-DOX CHURCH require certain procedures before people can be officially named saints; this naming is called CANONIZATION.

salon A periodic gathering of persons noted in literature, PHILOSOPHY, the FINE ARTS, or similar areas, held at one person's home. Salons thrived in the EN-LIGHTENMENT.

salvation In CHRISTIANITY, union or friendship with God, and deliverance from ORIGINAL SIN and DAMNATION. JESUS promised salvation to his followers.

Salvation Army, the A PROTESTANT denomination, organized under officers in military fashion, that is known chiefly for its charitable works in cities among the poor, the homeless, and people dependent on drugs and alcohol.

Sancho Panza (SAHN-choh PAHN-zuh, SAN-choh PAN-zuh) In *DON QUIXOTE*, the down-to-earth PEASANT who accompanies the idealistic, deluded Don on his adventures. Sancho is a delightful coward, more interested in material comfort and safety than in performing courageous acts.

Sand, George (SAND, SAHND) The NOM DE PLUME of Amandine Aurore Lucie Dupin, a French author of the nineteenth century.

Sanskrit The language of ancient INDIA, and one of the oldest languages of the Indo-European family, to which English belongs.

Sappho (SAF-oh) An ancient Greek poet known for her love lyrics. The word "lesbian" is derived from the island of Lesbos, the birthplace of Sappho, who was HOMOSEXUAL.

Sartre, Jean-Paul (zhahnn-PAWL SAHRT, SAHR-truh) A French PHILOSOPHER and author of the twentieth century; a leading figure of EXISTENTIAL-ISM. His great philosophical work is *Being and Nothingness*. He also wrote NOVELS and plays, such as *No Exit*.

Scheherazade (shuh-her-uh-ZAHD) The sultan's wife who narrates the *ARABIAN NIGHTS*.

Schiller, Friedrich von A German author of the eighteenth century; a leader of ROMANTICISM in Germany. He wrote the "Ode to Joy," a poem sung by a chorus during the last movement of the NINTH SYM-PHONY of Ludwig van BEETHOVEN.

schism (SIZ-uhm, SKIZ-uhm) A break within a CHURCH, such as the division between the EASTERN ORTHODOX CHURCH and the ROMAN CATHOLIC CHURCH.

scholasticism The PHILOSOPHY and THEOLOGY, marked by careful argumentation, that flourished among CHRISTIAN thinkers in EUROPE during the MIDDLE AGES.

&. Central to scholastic thought is the idea that reason and faith are compatible. Scholastic thinkers like Thomas AQUINAS tried to show that ancient philosophy, especially that of ARISTOTLE, supported and illuminated Christian faith.

sect A religious group, especially one that has separated from a larger group. *Sect* is often a term of disapproval.

secular (SEK-yuh-luhr) Not concerned with religion or religious matters. *Secular* is the opposite of *sacred*.

&. *Secularization* refers to the declining influence of religion and religious values within a given CUL-TURE. *Secular* HUMANISM means, loosely, a belief in human self-sufficiency.

semantics The scientific or philosophical study of the relations of words and their meanings.

&. *Semantics* is commonly used to refer to a trivial point or distinction that revolves around mere words rather than significant issues: "To argue whether the medication killed the patient or contributed to her death is to argue over semantics."

seven deadly sins Widely known in the MIDDLE AGES as sins that lead to DAMNATION. They are: pride, covetousness (greed), lust, anger, gluttony, envy, and sloth.

Seventh-Day Adventists A denomination of CHRISTIANS who proclaim that the SECOND COMING of JESUS will occur in the very near future. Unlike practically all other Christians, they observe Saturday, rather than Sunday, as a SABBATH.

Shi'ite and Sunni Moslems (SHEE-eyt, SOO-nee) The two main groups of ISLAM, of which the Sunnis are the majority. The split rose from an early dispute over who should be the leader of Islam after the death of MOHAMMED. The larger group, the Sunnis, argued that the successor should be appointed by election and consensus, as tradition dictated. (Sunni comes from the Arabic word *Sunna* meaning "tradition".) The smaller group believed that Mohammed's successors should come from his family, starting with Ali, his son-in-law. These, the partisans of Ali, were named from the word *Shia* meaning "partisan" in Arabic. The defeat of the Shi'ites by the Sunnis is thought to have determined some of the characteristic attitudes of the two groups, the Sunnis stressing merit and achievement, the Shi'ites appealing to the defeated, poor, and oppressed.

sign of the cross A ritual gesture common in the ROMAN CATHOLIC CHURCH, EASTERN ORTHODOX CHURCH, and ANGLICAN COMMUNION, made at the beginning and end of prayer as a reminder of JESUS' death on the cross. Worshipers make the sign by touching first the forehead, then the breast, and then each shoulder in turn, thus tracing in the air the shape of a cross.

skepticism In PHILOSOPHY, the position that what cannot be proved by reason should not be believed. One of the main tasks of EPISTEMOLOGY is to find an answer to the charge of some extreme skeptics that no knowledge is possible.

Smith, Joseph The founder of the MORMONS in the nineteenth century. He was killed by a mob opposed to his CHURCH, and the leadership passed to Brigham YOUNG.

Social Contract, The A major work of Jean-Jacques ROUSSEAU. Rousseau states that governmental organization should be based on the general will of a society and should conform to the nature of human beings, and that the majority in a government has a right to banish resistant minorities.

Socrates (SOK-ruh-teez) An ancient Greek PHILOSOPHER who was the teacher of PLATO.

⁂ Socrates said that an oracle of the gods had pronounced him the wisest of all people, because he knew how little he knew. ⁂ The Socratic method of teaching proceeds by question and answer as opposed to lecture. ⁂ When Socrates was an old man, the citizens of ATHENS condemned him to death, alleging that he denied the reality of the gods and corrupted the youth of Athens. Socrates calmly drank the poison he was given — hemlock — and died a noble death.

solipsism (SOL-uhp-siz-uhm, SOH-luhp-siz-uhm) The belief that all reality is just one's own imagining of reality, and that one's self is the only thing that exists.

Solzhenitsyn, Aleksandr (sohl-zhuh-NEET-sin) A Russian author of the twentieth century; the author of *One Day in the Life of Ivan Denisovich* and *The Gulag Archipelago*. Solzhenitsyn criticized the government of the SOVIET UNION and lived outside the country for several years.

sophists (SOF-ists) Ancient Greek teachers who were accused by some of their contemporaries (including PLATO) of being more interested in winning arguments through crafty RHETORIC than in pursuing truth.

⁂ By extension, a "sophist" is someone who engages in persuasive but false arguments.

Sophocles (SOF-uh-kleez) An ancient Greek poet, author of *OEDIPUS REX* and *ANTIGONE*. He is counted, with EURIPIDES and AESCHYLUS, among the great Greek authors of TRAGEDIES.

Spinoza, Benedict A Dutch PHILOSOPHER of the seventeenth century who argued for a form of PANTHEISM, and set out his arguments like proofs in GEOMETRY. Spinoza earned a living by grinding LENSES for spectacles and TELESCOPES.

spirituals Religious songs of African-Americans, often written with freer RHYTHMS and HARMONIES than most standard hymns. Spirituals, many of which go back to the days of slavery, often speak of biblical models of deliverance, like the EXODUS. Some well-known spirituals are "GONNA LAY DOWN MY BURDEN," "JOSHUA FIT THE BATTLE OF JERICHO," "NOBODY KNOWS THE TROUBLE I'VE SEEN," "SWING LOW, SWEET CHARIOT," and "WHEN THE SAINTS GO MARCHING IN."

Stoicism (STOH-uh-siz-uhm)   A PHILOSOPHY that flourished in ancient GREECE and ROME. Stoics believed that people should strictly restrain their emotions in order to attain happiness and wisdom; hence, they refused to demonstrate either joy or sorrow.

Summa Theologica (SOOM-uh thee-uh-LOH-ji-kuh) The best-known work of Thomas AQUINAS, in which he treats the whole of THEOLOGY by careful analysis of arguments. In one famous section of the *Summa Theologica*, Aquinas discusses five ways of attempting to prove that there is a God.

Sunni and Shi'ite Moslems   *See* SHI'ITE AND SUNNI MOSLEMS.

Superman   An ideal of humanity found in *THUS SPAKE ZARATHUSTRA*, by Friedrich NIETZSCHE. The Superman, or Overman (the German is *Übermensch*), is the single goal of all human striving, for which people must be willing to sacrifice all. It is doubtful that Nietzsche thought of the Overman as an individual person.

Swiss Family Robinson, The   A Swiss adventure NOVEL of the nineteenth century by Johann Wyss; the title CHARACTERS are shipwrecked, and live for many years on a desert island.

Symposium (sim-POH-zee-uhm)   A dialogue by PLATO, in which SOCRATES and several other men at a banquet discuss love.

synagogue (SIN-uh-gog)   In JUDAISM, a house of worship and learning; also, the congregation that meets there.

tabula rasa (TAB-yuh-luh RAH-zuh, RAH-suh)   Something new, fresh, unmarked, or uninfluenced. *Tabula rasa* is LATIN for "blank slate."
    ❧ John LOCKE believed that a child's mind was a tabula rasa.

Talmud (TAHL-mood, TAL-muhd)   Collections of commentaries on biblical texts that form, with the TORAH, the foundation for the religious laws of JUDAISM.

Taoism (DOU-iz-uhm)   A religion native to CHINA. Its adherents attempt to live according to the Tao — the "Way," which they believe governs the UNIVERSE.

Te Deum (tay DAY-uhm, tee DEE-uhm)   A hymn of praise to God, containing many passages from the BIBLE, that is used in the ANGLICAN COMMUNION, the LUTHERAN CHURCH, and the ROMAN CATHOLIC CHURCH as part of morning prayers on festive occasions. It begins, "Te Deum laudamus," meaning, "We praise thee, O God."

Terence   An ancient Roman author of COMEDIES.

Thales (THAY-leez)   An ancient PHILOSOPHER of GREECE, called by some the first genuine Greek philosopher. He lived about 600 years before JESUS and about 150 years before SOCRATES.
    ❧ Thales is known for predicting an ECLIPSE, and thus contributing to the idea that the HEAVENS were separate from the gods.

theologian   A person who engages in THEOLOGY. Some notable theologians are Thomas AQUINAS, AUGUSTINE, John CALVIN, and Martin LUTHER.

theology   The disciplined study of religious questions, such as the nature of God, sin, and SALVATION, carried on by THEOLOGIANS.

thing-in-itself   A notion in the PHILOSOPHY of Immanuel KANT. A thing-in-itself is an object as it would appear to us if we did not have to approach it under the conditions of space and time.

Thirty-nine Articles   Thirty-nine fundamental beliefs of the ANGLICAN COMMUNION, in addition to the common CHRISTIAN creeds. The Thirty-nine Articles, most of which are short PARAGRAPHS, set down differences in belief between Anglicans and other Christians.

Thomism (TOH-miz-uhm)   The PHILOSOPHY of Thomas AQUINAS, or other philosophies inspired by his. Thomism underwent a revival starting in the middle of the nineteenth century.

Three Musketeers, The   A NOVEL by the nineteenth-century French author Alexandre Dumas, set in seventeenth-century FRANCE. The Three Musketeers are comrades of the central CHARACTER, D'Artagnan, a man younger than they, who becomes a musketeer after performing many daring deeds. The motto of the Three Musketeers is "ALL FOR ONE AND ONE FOR ALL."

Thus Spake Zarathustra (zar-uh-THOOH-struh)   A book of philosophical reflections by Friedrich NIETZSCHE, written in the style of a sacred book.
    ❧ *Thus Spake Zarathustra* puts forth Nietzsche's idea of the SUPERMAN, or Overman.

Tolstoy, Leo (TOHL-stoy, TOL-stoy, tawl-STOY)   A Russian author of the nineteenth century, thought to be among the greatest novelists, whose books paint a vivid portrait of Russian life and history. His best-known works are *War and Peace* and *Anna Karenina*.

TORAH. *A young man perusing the Torah at his bar mitzvah.*

Torah (TOH-ruh, TAWR-uh, TOY-ruh)   The law on which JUDAISM is founded (*torah* is HEBREW for "law"). This law is contained in the first five books of the BIBLE (GENESIS, EXODUS, Leviticus, Numbers, and Deuteronomy). *Torah* can also refer to the entire body of Jewish law and wisdom, including what is contained in oral tradition.

Torquemada, Tomás de (toh-MAHS thhay tawr-kuh-MAH-thhuh)   The first inquisitor-general of the INQUISITION in SPAIN, in the late fifteenth century. Torquemada was known for his severity.

totem   An animal, plant, or other object in nature that has a special relationship to a person, family, or clan and serves as a sign for that person or group.

totem pole   Among some NATIVE AMERICANS, a pole on which TOTEMS are carved. The totem pole usually stands in front of a house or shelter.

🔖 A totem pole is thought of figuratively as a SYMBOL of a hierarchy: "Where does she stand on the totem pole?"

TOTEM POLE. *Totem poles in Vancouver, British Columbia.*

transubstantiation   According to the traditional teaching of the ROMAN CATHOLIC CHURCH, the way in which JESUS becomes present in the SACRAMENT of COMMUNION. Through transubstantiation, the bread and wine consumed by worshipers in Communion are not bread and wine in *substance*, but only in *appearance*; in substance, they become the body and blood of Jesus when a PRIEST, acting on Jesus' behalf, speaks the words "This is my body" and "This is my blood" over them.

🔖 It was the focus of a great controversy during the REFORMATION, because most other groups of CHRISTIANS do not maintain the doctrine of transubstantiation. They usually hold either that the body and blood of Jesus are only symbolically present in the bread and wine of the Communion, or that the bread and wine are the body and blood of Jesus and bread and wine at the same time.

Trappists   A strict order of MONKS in the ROMAN CATHOLIC CHURCH.

    🙠 Until recent years, Trappists took a vow of silence, under which they were rarely allowed to speak to one another. They were allowed to speak only during worship, to their superiors, and to guests at their monasteries.

Trinity   The doctrine of Christianity that there is one God and three divine persons in the one God: the Father, the Son (JESUS), and the HOLY SPIRIT.

troubadours   Traveling poet-musicians who flourished in southern EUROPE during the twelfth century. They wrote songs about CHIVALRY and love.

Unitarian Universalist Association   A religious denomination characterized by tolerance of religious beliefs and the absence of doctrine and DOGMA. Unitarians have their roots in CHRISTIANITY, but reject the doctrine of the TRINITY.

unities in drama   Three requirements for drama that were a focus of discussion in Europe from the early RENAISSANCE to the end of the eighteenth century. They are: unity of action (every incident in a play should be logically connected to those before and after it); unity of time (all the incidents must occur within, or almost within, a day); and unity of place (the incidents must take place close to each other). Those who favored the unities appealed to the authority of the PHILOSOPHER ARISTOTLE. Aristotle, however, had insisted specifically only on unity of action. From the time the three unities were put forward, playwrights regularly disregarded them.

Upanishads   (ooh-PAH-nuh-shahdz, ooh-PAN-uh-shadz)   A group of writings sacred in HINDUISM concerning the relations of humans, God, and the UNIVERSE.

utilitarianism   A system of ETHICS according to which the rightness or wrongness of an action should be judged by its consequences. The goal of utilitarian ethics is to promote the GREATEST HAPPINESS FOR THE GREATEST NUMBER. Jeremy Bentham, an English PHILOSOPHER, was the founder of utilitarianism; John Stuart MILL was its best-known defender.

Utopia   A book by Sir Thomas MORE, which describes an imaginary ideal society free of poverty and suffering. The expression *utopia* is coined from Greek words, and means "no place."

    🙠 By extension, a "utopia" is any ideal state.

Vatican   The independent state within the borders of ROME, where the ROMAN CATHOLIC CHURCH has its headquarters. The SISTINE CHAPEL and SAINT PETER'S BASILICA are inside the borders of the Vatican.

venial sin   *See* MORTAL SIN/VENIAL SIN.

Verne, Jules   A French author of the nineteenth century, known for his adventure NOVELS, many of which were set in the future. Verne's books include *AROUND THE WORLD IN EIGHTY DAYS*, *Twenty Thousand Leagues under the Sea*, *From the Earth to the Moon*, and *Journey to the Center of the Earth*.

Villon, François   (vee-YOHNN)   A French poet of the fifteenth century, known for his life as an outlaw as well as for the quality of his poetry.

Virgil   An ancient Roman poet; the author of the *AENEID*, one of the great EPICS of Western literature.

Vishnu   (VISH-nooh)   A deity of HINDUISM, known as the Preserver. According to the Hindus, he has appeared as Krishna and as the BUDDHA.

Voltaire   (vohl-TAIR, vol-TAIR)   The NOM DE PLUME of François Arouet, a French PHILOSOPHER and author of the eighteenth century, and a major figure of the ENLIGHTENMENT. Voltaire was known as a wit and freethinker. The most famous of his works is *CANDIDE*.

voodoo   A form of ANIMISM involving trances and other rituals. Communication with the dead is a principal feature of voodoo. It is most common in the nations of the CARIBBEAN SEA, especially HAITI, where people sometimes mingle voodoo and CHRISTIAN practices.

Vulgate Bible   (VUL-gayt)   A LATIN translation of the BIBLE made by the scholar Jerome, a SAINT of the ROMAN CATHOLIC CHURCH, in the fourth century. This translation was the standard Bible of the Western world until the REFORMATION. *Vulgate* comes from a LATIN word meaning "common." Jerome's translation used the Latin of everyday speech.

wake   A funeral celebration, common in IRELAND, at which the participants stay awake all night, keeping watch over the body of the dead person before burial. A wake traditionally involves a good deal of feasting and drinking.

War and Peace A NOVEL by Leo TOLSTOY. It recounts the histories of several Russian families during the wars against the emperor NAPOLEON. Many consider it the greatest novel ever written.

Wesley, John An English clergyman of the eighteenth century; the founder of the METHODIST CHURCH. His brother Charles is well known as a writer of hymns, including "Hark, the Herald Angels Sing."

witchcraft The practice of entering into compacts with the DEVIL, usually to do evil to others. Today a few witches still gather in covens, or assemblies, but few take witchcraft seriously. During the sixteenth and seventeenth centuries, however, witchcraft trials were common in EUROPE. In America, a major witchcraft trial occurred at Salem, MASSACHUSETTS, in the late seventeenth century. (*See* SALEM WITCH TRIALS.)

Wittgenstein, Ludwig (LOOHD-vig VIT-guhn-shteyen, VIT-guhn-steyen) An Austrian PHILOSOPHER of the twentieth century, who spent much of his career in ENGLAND. He is known for his explorations of the relation of language to thought and knowledge.

yang and yin *See* YIN AND YANG.

yarmulke (YAH-muh-kuh, YAHR-muhl-kuh) In ORTHODOX JUDAISM and CONSERVATIVE JUDAISM, a skullcap worn by men as a sign of reverence while praying to God or talking about him.

YIN AND YANG

yin and yang Two forces in the UNIVERSE, according to a Chinese THEORY: yin is the passive, negative force, and yang the active, positive force. According to this theory, wise people will detect these forces in the seasons, in their food, and so on, and will regulate their lives accordingly.

yoga In HINDUISM, a set of mental and physical exercises aimed at producing spiritual enlightenment.

⚑ The physical exercises associated with yoga are often self-taught.

Yom Kippur (YOHM ki-POOR, YOM KUP-uhr) In JUDAISM, the DAY OF ATONEMENT, the most important religious holiday; a day of fasting to atone for sins. It comes in autumn. (*See* ROSH HASHANAH.)

Young, Brigham An American religious leader of the nineteenth century. Young guided the MORMONS after the death of their founder, Joseph SMITH, and brought them to UTAH, where they settled.

Zeitgeist (TSEYT-geyst, ZEYT-geyst) The general moral, intellectual, and cultural climate of an era; *Zeitgeist* is German for "time-spirit." For example, the Zeitgeist of ENGLAND in the VICTORIAN PERIOD included a belief in industrial progress.

Zen An approach to religion, arising from BUDDHISM, that seeks religious enlightenment by meditation in which there is no consciousness of self.

⚑ Deliberately irrational statements are sometimes used in Zen to jar persons into realizing the limits of the common uses of the intellect. One well-known example is, "What is the sound of one hand clapping?"

Zeno's paradox (ZEE-nohz) A PARADOX is an apparent falsehood that is true, or an apparent truth that is false. Zeno, an ancient Greek, argued that a number of apparent truths such as motion and plurality are really false. A well-known, simplified version of one of his paradoxes is that an arrow can never reach its target, because the distance it must travel can be divided into an infinite number of subdistances, and therefore the arrow must take an infinite amount of time to arrive at its destination.

Zola, Émile (ZOH-luh, zoh-LAH) A French author of the nineteenth century, best remembered for his ESSAY "J'accuse," which strongly criticized the French government. (*See* DREYFUS AFFAIR.)

Literature in English

From the standpoint of American cultural literacy, all commonly known literary works written in English are probably best placed in a single category. The separation of British from American literature is somewhat misleading, particularly in the case of older literature. SHAKESPEARE is an *American* author — not because he was an American, obviously, but because his writings formed a part of American culture from its beginnings. Every frontier town had Shakespeare productions and comic entertainments that alluded to details of Shakespearean plays. CHAUCER and MILTON are American writers in this sense too, having been part of educated discourse from the earliest days of our republic. In the nineteenth century DICKENS was as much an American as a British writer (certainly he thought himself so when he counted his American royalties and lecture fees). It is uncertain whether Henry JAMES and T. S. ELIOT should be considered American or British writers, and it's not particularly important.

The relation between the terms *English* and *American* is a complex one. In one sense, it is odd that we should call our language English, since our taken-for-granted knowledge as well as our vocabulary is somewhat different from that current in BRITAIN, meaning ENGLAND, SCOTLAND, and WALES. Indeed, a more precise way of representing the subtle distinctions between our two national languages might be to call them respectively "British" and "American," and some scholars do talk about "British English" and "American English." But in a broader perspective (from the standpoint of a Chinese, for instance), our current practice of calling all national forms of the language by the single term *English* is convenient and sensible. Similarly, because of the importance of British literature in forming our literate culture, it is equally convenient to place all well-known English literature in a single cultural category with subdivisions.

What are those subdivisions? Usual practice divides our literature into the following periods: the MIDDLE AGES (e.g., CHAUCER), the RENAISSANCE (e.g., Shakespeare), the eighteenth century (e.g., Samuel JOHNSON), the ROMANTIC period of the early nineteenth century (e.g., WORDSWORTH), the VICTORIAN period of the later nineteenth century (e.g., Dickens), and the twentieth century (e.g., T. S. Eliot). The most self-consciously American literature belongs to the nineteenth century, when such patriotic writers as EMERSON, MELVILLE, and WHITMAN deliberately set out to reflect the distinctive character of American culture. In the twentieth century, literature written in America has tended to be international as well as national in flavor.

Literature in English excels in every kind of writing. Its particular glory is its poetry. For historical reasons, the English language acquired a vocabulary that is unusually rich and nuanced, combining words of Germanic root (such as *see* and *glimpse*) with words of LATIN root (such as *perceive* and *envision*). This variety in our vocabulary has allowed our poets a tremendous range of sounds and meanings and made poetry in English one of humanity's great achievements.

— E. D. H.

Age cannot wither her, nor custom stale / Her infinite variety   A sentence from the play *ANTONY AND CLEOPATRA*, by William SHAKESPEARE. A friend of Mark ANTONY says that CLEOPATRA is overwhelmingly attractive to men not so much because of her beauty as because of her fascinating unpredictability and range of moods.

Ahab, Captain (AY-hab)   The captain of the ship the *Pequod* in *MOBY DICK*. Ahab is obsessed with the capture of the great white whale, Moby Dick.

Alas, poor Yorick!   Words from the play *HAMLET*, by William SHAKESPEARE. Hamlet says this in a graveyard as he meditates upon the skull of Yorick, a court jester he had known and liked as a child. Hamlet goes on to say that though "my lady" may put on "paint [makeup] an inch thick, to this favour [condition] she must come."

Alcott, Louisa May (AWL-kuht, AWL-kot)   An American author of the nineteenth century, known for *LITTLE WOMEN*, *Little Men*, and other books for and about children.

Alger, Horatio, Jr. (AL-juhr)   An American author of the nineteenth century, known for his many books in which poor boys become rich through their earnest attitudes and hard work.

☙ A true story of spectacular worldly success achieved by someone who started near the bottom is often called a "Horatio Alger story."

Alice's Adventures in Wonderland   A book by Lewis CARROLL. Alice, a young girl, enters Wonderland by following the White Rabbit down his hole, and has many strange adventures there. She meets the Mad Hatter and the March Hare, the grinning CHESHIRE CAT, and the Queen of Hearts, who shouts, "OFF WITH HER HEAD!" when Alice makes a mistake at croquet. *THROUGH THE LOOKING-GLASS* is the SEQUEL to *Alice's Adventures in Wonderland*.

All animals are equal, but some animals are more equal than others   A proclamation by the pigs who control the government in the NOVEL *ANIMAL FARM*, by George ORWELL. The sentence is a comment on the hypocrisy of governments that proclaim the absolute equality of their citizens, but give power and privileges to a small elite.

All the world's a stage   The beginning of a speech in the play *AS YOU LIKE IT*, by William SHAKE-SPEARE. It is sometimes called "The Seven Ages of Man," since it treats that many periods in a man's life: his years as infant, schoolboy, lover, soldier, judge, foolish old man, and finally "second childishness and mere oblivion." The speech begins, "All the world's a stage, / And all the men and women merely players."

Angelou, Maya (AN-juh-looh)   Twentieth-century African-American writer, whose best-known work is *I Know Why the Caged Bird Sings*, an autobiographical account of growing up as a black girl in the rural South. Much anthologized in American schoolbooks, Angelou is said to be among the most widely read contemporary writers in American schools.

Animal Farm   A NOVEL of SATIRE by George OR-WELL. Animals take over a farm to escape human tyranny, but the pigs treat the other animals worse than the people did. A famous quotation from the book is "ALL ANIMALS ARE EQUAL, BUT SOME ANIMALS ARE MORE EQUAL THAN OTHERS."

Antony, Mark   A historical politician and general of ancient ROME, who appears as a CHARACTER in the plays *ANTONY AND CLEOPATRA* and *JULIUS CAESAR*, by William SHAKESPEARE. In a famous speech in *Julius Caesar*, given after Caesar has been killed, Antony turns public opinion against those who did the killing. Antony's speech begins, "FRIENDS, ROMANS, COUNTRYMEN, LEND ME YOUR EARS"; in it, he repeats several times the words "BRUTUS IS AN HONORABLE MAN."

Antony and Cleopatra   A TRAGEDY by William SHAKESPEARE. It dramatizes the grand but ill-fated love of the Roman general Mark ANTONY and CLEO-PATRA, the queen of EGYPT.

Arthur, King   A legendary early king of BRITAIN, much celebrated in literature. The best-known works on Arthur are the fifteenth-century book *Le Morte d'Arthur*, by Thomas Malory, and the nineteenth-century series of poems *Idylls of the King*, by Alfred, Lord TENNYSON. (*See under "Mythology and Folklore."*)

As flies to wanton boys, are we to the gods; / They kill us for their sport   Lines from the play *KING LEAR*, by William SHAKESPEARE, spoken by the earl of Gloucester, a friend of King Lear. They express a bitter sense of the meaninglessness and brutality of life.

As You Like It A COMEDY by William SHAKE-SPEARE. Most of the action takes place in the Forest of Arden, to which several members of a duke's court have been banished. The speech "ALL THE WORLD'S A STAGE" is from *As You Like It.*

JANE AUSTEN. *An engraving from a sketch by her sister Cassandra.*

Austen, Jane A British author of the late eighteenth and early nineteenth centuries; her best-known works are the NOVELS *PRIDE AND PREJUDICE* and *Emma.* Austen is particularly famous for her witty irony and perceptive comments about people and their social relationships.

Baa, baa, black sheep The first line of a nursery RHYME:

> Baa, baa, black sheep,
> Have you any wool?
> Yes sir, yes sir,
> Three bags full.

Babbitt A NOVEL by Sinclair LEWIS. The title CHARACTER, an American real estate agent in a small city, is portrayed as a crass, loud, overoptimistic boor who thinks only about money and speaks in clichés such as "You've gotta have pep, by golly!"

⅋ By extension, a "Babbitt" is a narrow-minded, materialistic businessman.

Bacon, Francis An English author of the late sixteenth and early seventeenth centuries. Bacon is known in PHILOSOPHY for his defense of the SCIENTIFIC METHOD (*see* BACONIAN METHOD). In literature, he is known for his ESSAYS; they contain such memorable thoughts as "Reading maketh a full man, conference a ready man, and writing an exact man."

⅋ Bacon has sometimes been mentioned as a possible author of the plays commonly attributed to William SHAKESPEARE.

Baldwin, James An African-American author of the twentieth century. His writings, mostly about the black experience in the United States, include NOVELS, such as *Go Tell It on the Mountain*, and ESSAYS, such as *The Fire Next Time.*

Bard of Avon A title given to William SHAKESPEARE, who was born and buried in Stratford-upon-Avon, ENGLAND. A bard is a poet.

Bartlett's *Familiar Quotations* A standard American REFERENCE WORK for quotations from literature and speeches. The original compiler, John Bartlett, was an American publisher of the nineteenth century.

Beowulf (BAY-uh-woolf) An EPIC in OLD ENGLISH, estimated as dating from as early as the eighth century; the earliest long work of literature in English. The critical events are the slaying of the monster Grendel and Grendel's mother by the hero Beowulf, and Beowulf's battle with a dragon, in which he is mortally wounded.

Big Bad Wolf The wicked but ineffectual enemy of the THREE PIGS, who threatens each of them in turn by saying, "I'll huff, and I'll puff, and I'll blow your house down!" In some versions of the story, the wolf eats two of the pigs.

Big Brother is watching you A warning that appears on posters throughout Oceania, the fictional DICTATORSHIP described by George ORWELL in his book *NINETEEN EIGHTY-FOUR.*

⅋ The term *Big Brother* is used to refer to any ruler or government that invades the privacy of its citizens.

Black Boy An autobiographical NOVEL by the African-American author Richard WRIGHT, portraying racial conflicts in the rural South.

Blake, William   An English author and artist of the late eighteenth and early nineteenth centuries. Blake, a visionary, was an early leader of ROMANTICISM. He is best known for his collections of poems *Songs of Innocence* and *Songs of Experience*; *Songs of Experience* contains "TIGER! TIGER! BURNING BRIGHT." Blake illustrated, printed, and distributed all of his books himself.

Book of Common Prayer   The book used in worship by the ANGLICAN COMMUNION. Its early versions, from the sixteenth and seventeenth centuries, were widely admired for the dignity and beauty of their language.

🔊 The Book of Common Prayer has had a strong effect on literature in English through such expressions as "Let him now speak, or else hereafter for ever hold his peace," and "We have left undone those things which we ought to have done."

Boswell, James   A Scottish author of the eighteenth century, best known for his *Life of Samuel JOHNSON*.

🔊 *Boswell* has become a general term for a biographer: "James JOYCE found his Boswell in Richard Ellmann."

Brave New World   A NOVEL by Aldous HUXLEY that depicts the potential horrors of life in the twenty-fifth century. The title comes from a line in the play *THE TEMPEST*, by William SHAKESPEARE.

Brontë, Charlotte and Emily (BRON-tee, BRON-tay)   Two English authors of the nineteenth century, known for their NOVELS. Charlotte Brontë is best known for *JANE EYRE*; Emily, her sister, wrote *WUTHERING HEIGHTS*.

Browning, Elizabeth Barrett   An English poet of the nineteenth century, and the wife of Robert BROWNING. Elizabeth Browning is best known for *Sonnets from the Portuguese*. The most famous of these SONNETS begins, "How do I love thee? Let me count the ways."

Browning, Robert   An English poet of the nineteenth century whose many poems include "THE PIED PIPER OF HAMELIN" and "My Last Duchess."

🔊 The love that Browning and his wife, Elizabeth Barrett BROWNING, had for each other has been much celebrated.

Brutus   A CHARACTER in the play *JULIUS CAESAR*, by William SHAKESPEARE; one of the assassins of Jul-

ius CAESAR. (*See* "BRUTUS IS AN HONORABLE MAN," "*ET TU, BRUTE*," "FRIENDS, ROMANS, COUNTRYMEN, LEND ME YOUR EARS," *and* "NOBLEST ROMAN OF THEM ALL, THE.")

Brutus is an honorable man   A statement made several times in a speech by Mark ANTONY in the play *JULIUS CAESAR*, by William SHAKESPEARE. The speech is Antony's funeral oration over Caesar, whom BRUTUS has helped kill. "Brutus is an honorable man" is ironic, since Antony is attempting to portray Brutus as ungrateful and treacherous. He succeeds in turning the Roman people against Brutus and the other assassins.

Bumppo, Natty   The central CHARACTER in *The Leatherstocking Tales*, by James Fenimore COOPER. Natty, a settler, is taught by the NATIVE AMERICANS, and adopts their way of life.

Burns, Robert   A Scottish poet of the eighteenth century, known for his poems in Scottish dialect, such as "To a Mouse," "A Red, Red Rose," and "AULD LANG SYNE."

🔊 Many lines from Burns's poetry have become proverbial: "The best-laid schemes of mice and men / Gang aft agley" (often go astray), "Oh, wad some power the giftie gie us / To see oursels as others see us!" (Oh, if the good spirit would only give us the power / to see ourselves as others see us), "A man's a man for a' [all] that."

Byron, George Gordon, Lord   A handsome and daring English poet of the early nineteenth century, known for his sexual exploits, his rebelliousness, and his air of brooding. He was a leader of ROMANTICISM; his best-known work is *Don Juan*, a long poem of SATIRE.

Byronic hero   A kind of hero found in several of the works of Lord BYRON. Like Byron himself, a Byronic hero is a melancholy and rebellious young man, distressed by a terrible wrong he committed in the past.

Canterbury Tales, The   A work written by Geoffrey CHAUCER in the late fourteenth century about a group of pilgrims, of many different occupations and PERSONALITIES, who meet at an inn near LONDON as they are setting out for Canterbury, ENGLAND. Their host proposes a storytelling contest to make the journey more interesting. Some of the more famous stories are "The Knight's Tale," "The Miller's Tale," and "The Wife of Bath's Tale." The tales, which are almost all in rhyme, have many different styles, reflecting the great diversity of the pilgrims; some are notoriously bawdy. The language of *The Canterbury Tales* is MIDDLE ENGLISH.

Carroll, Lewis An English writer and logician, best known as the author of ALICE'S ADVENTURES IN WONDERLAND and THROUGH THE LOOKING-GLASS.

"Casey at the Bat" A poem from the late nineteenth century about Casey, an arrogant, overconfident baseball player who brings his team down to defeat by refusing to swing at the first two balls pitched to him, and then missing on the third. The author is Ernest Lawrence Thayer. The poem's final line is, "THERE IS NO JOY IN MUDVILLE — mighty Casey has struck out."

"Casey Jones" An American BALLAD from the early twentieth century about a railroad engineer who dies valiantly in a train wreck. (*See under "Fine Arts."*)

Catch-22 A war NOVEL from the 1960s by the American author Joseph Heller. "Catch-22" is a provision in army regulations; it stipulates that a soldier's request to be relieved from active duty can be accepted only if he is mentally unfit to fight. Any soldier, however, who has the sense to ask to be spared the horrors of war is obviously mentally sound, and therefore must stay to fight.

&. Figuratively, a "catch-22" is any absurd arrangement that puts a person in a double bind: for example, a person can't get a job without experience, but can't get experience without a job.

Catcher in the Rye, The A NOVEL from the 1950s by the American author J. D. Salinger. It relates the experiences of Holden Caulfield, a sensitive but rebellious youth who runs away from his boarding school.

Cather, Willa (KATHH-uhr) An American author of the early twentieth century, known for *My Ántonia* and other NOVELS of frontier life.

"Charge of the Light Brigade, The" A poem by Alfred, Lord TENNYSON that celebrates the heroism of a British cavalry brigade in its doomed assault on much larger forces. The poem contains the well-known lines "Theirs not to reason why, / Theirs but to do and die."

Chaucer, Geoffrey (CHAW-suhr) An English poet of the fourteenth century, called the father of English

poetry: he was the first great poet to write in the English language. Chaucer's best-known work is *THE CANTERBURY TALES*.

CHESHIRE CAT. *Alice meeting the Cheshire cat. Drawing by John Tenniel.*

Cheshire cat (CHESH-uhr) A cat with an enormous grin encountered by Alice in ALICE'S ADVENTURES IN WONDERLAND, by Lewis CARROLL. The cat tends to disappear, leaving only its smile hanging in the air.

&. "Smiling like a Cheshire cat" refers to anyone with a conspicuous and long-lasting smile.

Christie, Agatha An English author of the twentieth century, known for her play *The Mousetrap* and many detective THRILLERS and murder mysteries. She helped raise the "whodunit" to a prominent place in literature.

Christmas Carol, A A story by Charles DICKENS about the spiritual conversion of the miser Ebenezer SCROOGE. At first, Scrooge scoffs at the idea of Christmas with a "Bah, humbug!" After the appearance of the ghost of his stingy partner, Jacob Marley, and the Ghosts of Christmas Past, Present, and Future, Scrooge reforms and offers help to the crippled boy TINY TIM, son of Scrooge's clerk, Bob Cratchit.

"Civil Disobedience"   An ESSAY by Henry David THOREAU. It contains his famous statement "That government is best which governs least," and asserts that people's obligations to their own conscience take precedence over their obligations to their government. Thoreau also argues that if, in following their conscience, people find it necessary to break the laws of the state, they should be prepared to pay penalties, including imprisonment.

• Thoreau himself went to jail for refusing to pay a tax to support the MEXICAN WAR.

Clemens, Samuel L.   The real name of the author Mark TWAIN.

Coleridge, Samuel Taylor (KOHL-rij, KOH-luh-rij) An English author of the early nineteenth century. Coleridge was a leader of ROMANTICISM; his poems include "*KUBLA KHAN*" and "*THE RIME OF THE ANCIENT MARINER.*"

Come live with me and be my love   The opening line of "The Passionate Shepherd to His Love," a poem by Christopher Marlowe.

Conrad, Joseph   A British author of the late nineteenth and early twentieth centuries. He based many of his works, including *HEART OF DARKNESS* and *Lord Jim*, on his adventures as a sailor.

Cooper, James Fenimore   An American author of the early nineteenth century, known for his works set on the American frontier, such as the series *The Leatherstocking Tales*. (See *THE LAST OF THE MOHICANS* and BUMPPO, NATTY.)

Cordelia   The youngest of the king's three daughters in the play *KING LEAR*, by William SHAKESPEARE. King Lear at first thinks her ungrateful to him because she refuses to flatter him as her sisters do; he soon finds out that she is the only one of the three who genuinely cares for him.

cummings, e. e.   An American author of the twentieth century who spurned the use of many conventions of standard written English in his poetry. He often avoided using CAPITAL LETTERS, even in his name, and experimented freely with typographic conventions, GRAMMAR, and SYNTAX. He wrote po-

etry on love, the failings of public institutions, and many other subjects.

David Copperfield   A NOVEL by Charles DICKENS, largely the story of Dickens's own life. David Copperfield is sent away to work at a very young age, and grows to manhood over the course of the book. The account of David's grim boyhood was designed to expose the cruel conditions of child labor in BRITAIN at the time.

Death, be not proud   The first words of a SONNET by John DONNE. The poet asserts that death is a feeble enemy, and concludes with these lines: "One short sleep past, we wake eternally / And death shall be no more; Death, thou shalt die."

Death of a Salesman   A play from the 1940s by the American writer Arthur Miller. Willy Loman, a salesman who finds himself regarded as useless in his occupation because of his age, kills himself. A speech made by a friend of Willy's after his suicide is well known, and ends with the lines: "Nobody dast blame this man. A salesman is got to dream, boy. It comes with the territory."

Dickens, Charles   An English author of the nineteenth century. His works include *A CHRISTMAS CAROL*, *DAVID COPPERFIELD*, *GREAT EXPECTATIONS*, *OLIVER TWIST*, and numerous other NOVELS. He created many memorable CHARACTERS, including Bob Cratchit, FAGIN, Uriah HEEP, Jacob Marley, Samuel PICKWICK, Ebenezer SCROOGE, and TINY TIM. Dickens, a man of keen social conscience, used his books to portray the suffering of the WORKING CLASS at the time of the INDUSTRIAL REVOLUTION.

Dickinson, Emily   An American poet of the nineteenth century, famous for her short, evocative poems. Some of her best-known poems begin, "There is no frigate like a book," "Because I could not stop for Death / He kindly stopped for me," "I never saw a moor," and "I'm nobody! Who are you?"

divinity that shapes our ends, There's a   A line spoken by the title CHARACTER in the play *HAMLET*, by William SHAKESPEARE. In referring to a divine power that influences human affairs, Hamlet is defending a decision he made suddenly, and is questioning the need for careful planning in all circumstances.

Do not go gentle into that good night ... Rage, rage against the dying of the light Two lines from a poem by the twentieth-century Welsh poet Dylan Thomas, addressed to his father, who was dying.

Dr. Jekyll and Mr. Hyde, The Strange Case of A NOVEL by Robert Louis STEVENSON about the good Dr. JEKYLL, whose well-intentioned experiments on himself periodically turn him into the cruel and sadistic Mr. HYDE.

 Dr. Jekyll and Mr. Hyde provide a classic example of split PERSONALITY. In addition, the two CHARACTERS often serve as SYMBOLS of the good and evil sides of a single personality.

Donne, John (DUN) An English poet and clergyman of the seventeenth century. Donne is famous for his intricate METAPHORS, as in a poem in which he compares two lovers to the two legs of a drawing compass. He also wrote learned and eloquent sermons and meditations. The expressions "DEATH, BE NOT PROUD," "NO MAN IS AN ISLAND," and "FOR WHOM THE BELL TOLLS" are drawn from Donne's works.

Dos Passos, John (dos, dohs PAS-ohs) An American author of the twentieth century, best known for the three NOVELS that make up *U.S.A.*

Double, double toil and trouble; / Fire burn, and cauldron bubble Lines chanted by three witches in the play *MACBETH*, by William SHAKESPEARE, as they mix a potion.

Doyle, Sir Arthur Conan An English author of the late nineteenth and early twentieth centuries, best known for creating the CHARACTER Sherlock HOLMES. Doyle's works include "A Study in Scarlet," "The Sign of the Four," and "The Hound of the Baskervilles."

Dracula, Count The title CHARACTER of *Dracula*, a NOVEL from the late nineteenth century by the English author Bram Stoker. Count Dracula, a VAMPIRE, is from Transylvania, a region of eastern EUROPE now in RUMANIA. He takes his name from a bloodthirsty nobleman of the MIDDLE AGES. To lay the vampire Dracula's spirit to rest, one must drive a wooden stake through his heart.

 Count Dracula was played in films by the Hungarian-born actor Bela Lugosi, whose elegant, exotic accent has become associated with the character.

Drink to me only with thine eyes A line from a love poem by the seventeenth-century English poet Ben Jonson. He suggests that lovers find each other's glances so intoxicating that they have no need to drink wine.

Dunbar, Paul Laurence American poet of the late nineteenth century, regarded as the premier African-American poet until the advent of Langston HUGHES. From one of his poems came the title of Maya ANGELOU's book, *I Know Why the Caged Bird Sings*.

East is East, and West is West, and never the twain shall meet A line from a poem by Rudyard KIPLING. It continues, a few lines later: "But there is neither East nor West ... When two strong men stand face to face."

Education of Henry Adams, The The AUTOBIOGRAPHY of a member of the Adams family of NEW ENGLAND (*see* ADAMS, JOHN *and* ADAMS, JOHN QUINCY). Adams mingles a partial story of his life with an indictment of his education and reflections on the fundamental ideas of modern times and of the MIDDLE AGES.

"Elegy Written in a Country Churchyard" An enduringly popular poem from the middle eighteenth century by the English poet Thomas Gray. It contains the lines "Full many a flower is born to blush unseen / And waste its sweetness on the desert air," "The paths of glory lead but to the grave," and "FAR FROM THE MADDING CROWD's ignoble strife / Their sober wishes never learned to stray."

Elementary, my dear Watson A PHRASE often attributed to Sherlock HOLMES, the English detective in the works of Sir Arthur Conan DOYLE. Holmes supposedly says this to his amazed companion, Dr. WATSON, as he explains his reasoning in solving a crime. Though these precise words are never used in the Holmes stories, something like them appears in the story "The Crooked Man": "'Excellent!' I [Watson] cried. 'Elementary,' said he."

Eliot, George The NOM DE PLUME of Mary Ann Evans, an English author of NOVELS in the nineteenth century. Some of her best-known works are *Middlemarch*, *The Mill on the Floss*, and *Silas Marner*.

Eliot, T. S. An English author of the twentieth century, born and raised in the United States. Eliot

T. S. ELIOT. *A photographic portrait by Kay Reynal.*

wrote poems, plays, and ESSAYS, and urged the use of ordinary language in poetry. He was much concerned with the general emptiness of modern life and with the revitalization of religion. Among Eliot's best-known works are the poems "The Love Song of J. Alfred Prufrock" and "THE WASTE LAND," and the play *Murder in the Cathedral.*

Ellison, Ralph   An African-American author of the twentieth century, best known for the NOVEL *INVISIBLE MAN.*

Elmer Gantry   A NOVEL by Sinclair LEWIS; the title CHARACTER is a successful preacher in the MIDDLE WEST. Lewis stresses the importance of insincerity and clever publicity in the rise of Gantry.

Emerson, Ralph Waldo   An American lecturer and author of the nineteenth century; a leader of TRANSCENDENTALISM. In his ESSAY "SELF-RELIANCE" and in other works, Emerson stressed the importance of the individual, and encouraged people to rely on their own judgment.

Et tu, Brute? (et TOOH BROOH-tay)   A LATIN sentence meaning "Even you, Brutus?" from the play *JULIUS CAESAR,* by William SHAKESPEARE. Caesar ut-

ters these words as he is being stabbed to death, having recognized his friend Brutus among the assassins.

  🖙 *"Et tu, Brute?"* is used to express surprise and dismay at the treachery of a supposed friend.

every inch a king   A PHRASE used by the title CHARACTER in the play *KING LEAR,* by William SHAKESPEARE, to describe himself to his friend, the earl of Gloucester. The situation is ironic; Lear is raving over his deprivation and is wearing weeds.

face that launched a thousand ships, Was this the   A line from the sixteenth-century play *Doctor Faustus,* by Christopher Marlowe; Faustus says this when the DEVIL MEPHISTOPHELES (Marlowe spells the name "Mephistophilis") shows him HELEN OF TROY, the most beautiful woman in history. The "thousand ships" are warships, a reference to the TROJAN WAR.

Fagin (FAY-gin)   A villain in the NOVEL *OLIVER TWIST,* by Charles DICKENS. The unscrupulous, miserly Fagin teaches Oliver Twist and other orphaned boys to pick pockets and steal for him.

"Fall of the House of Usher, The"   A horror story by Edgar Allan POE. At the end of the story, two of the Usher family fall dead, and the ancestral mansion of the Ushers splits in two and sinks into a lake.

Falstaff   An endearing, fat, aging rogue who appears in several of the plays of SHAKESPEARE. He is prominent in the two parts of *King Henry the Fourth,* where he is the jolly companion of Prince Hal, the future King Henry V. Falstaff is a lover of wine, women, and song; although a coward in practice, he loves to tell tales of his supposed bravery.

far from the madding crowd   A PHRASE adapted from the "ELEGY WRITTEN IN A COUNTRY CHURCHYARD," by Thomas GRAY; *madding* means "frenzied." The lines containing the phrase speak of the people buried in the churchyard: "Far from the madding crowd's ignoble strife / Their sober wishes never learned to stray."

  🖙 In the late nineteenth century, the English author Thomas Hardy named one of his NOVELS *Far from the Madding Crowd.*

Farewell to Arms, A   A NOVEL by Ernest HEMINGWAY, set in WORLD WAR I. An American soldier and an English nurse fall in love; he deserts to join her, and she dies in childbirth.

Faulkner, William (FAWK-nuhr) An American author of the twentieth century. His works, mostly set in the South, include the NOVELS *The Sound and the Fury* and *As I Lay Dying*.

female of the species is more deadly than the male, The A frequently repeated line from the poem "The Female of the Species," by Rudyard KIPLING.

Fielding, Henry An English author of the eighteenth century. Fielding is known for his NOVELS, including *Tom Jones* and *Joseph Andrews*.

Fifteen men on the Dead Man's Chest — / Yo-ho-ho, and a bottle of rum! Lines from a pirates' song in *TREASURE ISLAND*, by Robert Louis STEVENSON.

Fitzgerald, F. Scott An American author of the twentieth century, known for his short stories and for his NOVELS, including *THE GREAT GATSBY* and *This Side of Paradise*. He led a tempestuous life with his wife, Zelda, and was one of several talented Americans, including Ernest HEMINGWAY, living in PARIS in the 1920s.

for whom the bell tolls An expression from a sermon by John DONNE. Donne says that since we are all part of mankind, any person's death is a loss to all of us: "Any man's death diminishes me, because I am involved in mankind; and therefore never send to know for whom the bell tolls; it tolls for thee." The line also suggests that we all will die: the bell will toll for each one of us. (*See* NO MAN IS AN ISLAND.)
  🍂 The twentieth-century American author Ernest HEMINGWAY named a NOVEL *For Whom the Bell Tolls*; the book is set in the SPANISH CIVIL WAR.

Frankenstein A NOVEL by Mary Wollstonecraft Shelley. The title CHARACTER, Dr. Victor Frankenstein, makes a manlike monster from parts of cadavers and brings it to life by the power of an electrical CHARGE. Frankenstein's monster is larger than most men and fantastically strong.
  🍂 Frequently the subject of horror films, the monster is usually pictured with an oversized square brow, metal bolts in his neck and forehead, and greenish skin. People often mistakenly refer to the monster, rather than to his creator, as "Frankenstein."

Franklin, The Autobiography of Benjamin A homespun account by Benjamin FRANKLIN of his

FRANKENSTEIN'S MONSTER. *Boris Karloff in the movie* Frankenstein.

early and middle years. He advocates hard work and stresses the importance of worldly success.

Friday A native CHARACTER in *ROBINSON CRUSOE*, so named by Crusoe because Crusoe found him on a Friday. Friday places himself in service to Crusoe, and helps him survive.
  🍂 Figuratively, a "man Friday" or "girl Friday" is a valued helper.

Friends, Romans, countrymen, lend me your ears The first line of a speech from the play *JULIUS CAESAR*, by William SHAKESPEARE. Mark ANTONY addresses the crowd at Caesar's funeral:

  Friends, Romans, countrymen, lend me your ears;
  I come to bury Caesar, not to praise him.
  The evil that men do lives after them,
  The good is oft interred with their bones. . . .

Frost, Robert An American poet of the twentieth century. Some of his best-known poems are "The Road Not Taken," "Stopping by Woods on a Snowy Evening" (which contains the line "And MILES TO GO BEFORE I SLEEP"), "Mending Wall" (the source of the line "GOOD FENCES MAKE GOOD NEIGHBORS"), and "The Gift Outright" (which begins with the line "The LAND WAS OURS BEFORE WE WERE THE LAND'S").

Gather ye rosebuds while ye may The first line of the poem "To the Virgins, to Make Much of Time," from the middle of the seventeenth century, by the

English poet Robert Herrick. He is advising people to take advantage of life while they are young:

> Gather ye rosebuds while ye may,
> Old Time is still a-flying;
> And this same flower that smiles today
> Tomorrow will be dying.

Get thee to a nunnery   Words from the play *HAMLET*, by William SHAKESPEARE; the advice Hamlet gives to Ophelia. He bids her live a life of celibacy.

"Gift of the Magi, The" (MAY-jeye)   A short story by O. HENRY. An extremely poor young couple are determined to give Christmas presents to each other. He sells his watch to buy a set of combs for her long hair, and she cuts off her hair and sells it to buy him a watch fob.

Give me your tired, your poor   A line from a poem, "The New Colossus," by the nineteenth-century American poet Emma Lazarus. "The New Colossus," describing the STATUE OF LIBERTY, appears on a plaque at the base of the statue. It ends with Liberty herself speaking:

> Give me your tired, your poor,
> Your huddled masses yearning to breathe free,
> The wretched refuse of your teeming shore.
> Send these, the homeless, tempest-tossed, to me:
> I lift my lamp beside the golden door.

Globe Theater   The theater in LONDON where many of the great plays of William SHAKESPEARE were first performed. Shakespeare himself acted at the Globe. It burned and was rebuilt shortly before Shakespeare's death, and was finally pulled down in the middle of the seventeenth century.

God's in his heaven — All's right with the world
A line sung by a little Italian girl, Pippa, in the poem "Pippa Passes," by Robert BROWNING.

"Goldilocks and the Three Bears"   A children's story. Goldilocks, a little girl with shiny blond hair, brashly enters the house of the Three Bears (Papa Bear, Mama Bear, and Baby Bear), eats the bears' porridge, sits in their chairs, and sleeps in their beds. When the bears return, they retrace her steps, saying, "Someone's been eating my porridge," "Someone's been sitting in my chair," and "Someone's been sleeping in my bed." When they discover Goldilocks asleep in Baby Bear's bed, Goldilocks awakes and flees in terror.

GLOBE THEATER. *The Globe Theater as it appeared in 1613.*

Gone With the Wind   A phenomenally popular NOVEL from the 1930s by the American author Margaret Mitchell. Set in GEORGIA in the period of the CIVIL WAR, it tells of the three marriages of the central CHARACTER, Scarlett O'HARA, and of the devastation caused by the war.

• The film version of *Gone With the Wind*, also from the 1930s, is one of the most successful films ever made.

Grapes of Wrath, The   A NOVEL by John STEINBECK about the hardships of an American farm family in the DUST BOWL during the 1930s. Forced off the land, they travel to CALIFORNIA to earn a living harvesting fruit.

• The title is a PHRASE from "The BATTLE HYMN OF THE REPUBLIC."

Great Expectations   A NOVEL by Charles DICKENS. Worldly ambitions lead a young boy, Pip, to abandon his true friends.

Great Gatsby, The   A NOVEL by F. Scott FITZGERALD, recounting the rise and fall of Jay Gatsby, who lives extravagantly from bootlegging and other criminal activities. He loves a beautiful woman, Daisy, who is the cause of his downfall.

Grinch Stole Christmas, How the   A children's book by Dr. SEUSS. The Grinch, a sour and unpleasant creature, tries to prevent the fun and merrymaking of Christmas in his village by stealing all the gifts and decorations. The villagers celebrate the holiday anyway, and the Grinch reforms.

• A miserly and unpleasant person — especially one who spoils other people's pleasures — can be called a "grinch."

Gulliver's Travels A SATIRE by Jonathan SWIFT. Lemuel Gulliver, an Englishman, travels to exotic lands, including LILLIPUT (where the people are six inches tall), Brobdingnag (where the people are seventy feet tall), and the land of the Houyhnhnms (where horses are the intelligent beings, and humans, called YAHOOS, are mute brutes of labor).

• Probably the most famous image from this book is of the tiny Lilliputians having tied down the sleeping giant, Gulliver.

"Gunga Din" A poem by Rudyard KIPLING about the native water carrier for a British regiment in INDIA. It ends:

> Though I've belted you an' flayed you,
> By the livin' Gawd that made you,
> You're a better man than I am, Gunga Din!

Had we but world enough, and time, / This coyness, Lady, were no crime The first lines of "To His Coy Mistress," a poem from the seventeenth century by the English poet Andrew Marvell. The poet tells a woman whom he loves that if they had endless time and space at their disposal, then he could accept her unwillingness to go to bed with him. Life is short, however, and opportunities must be seized. Other lines from the poem are: "But, at my back, I always hear / TIME'S WINGÉD CHARIOT hurrying near," and "The grave's a fine and private place, / But none, I think, do there embrace."

Hamlet A TRAGEDY by William SHAKESPEARE. The king of DENMARK has been murdered by his brother, Claudius, who then becomes king and marries the dead king's widow. The ghost of the dead king visits his son, Prince Hamlet, and urges him to avenge the murder. In the course of the play, Hamlet, a scholar, slowly convinces himself that he ought to murder Claudius. The play ends with a duel between Hamlet and the courtier Laertes, and the death by poison of all the principal CHARACTERS.

• The character of Hamlet has come to symbolize the person whose thoughtful nature is an obstacle to quick and decisive action. • *Hamlet*, Shakespeare's

longest play, contains several soliloquies — speeches in which Hamlet, alone, speaks his thoughts. Many lines from the play are very familiar, such as "ALAS, POOR YORICK!"; "There's a DIVINITY THAT SHAPES OUR ENDS"; "FRAILTY, THY NAME IS WOMAN"; "GET THEE TO A NUNNERY"; "The LADY DOTH PROTEST TOO MUCH"; "There are MORE THINGS IN HEAVEN AND EARTH, HORATIO"; "NEITHER A BORROWER NOR A LENDER BE"; "There's a special PROVIDENCE IN THE FALL OF A SPARROW"; "SOMETHING IS ROTTEN IN THE STATE OF DENMARK"; *and* "TO BE, OR NOT TO BE: that is the question."

Harlem Renaissance An African-American cultural movement of the 1920s and 1930s, centered in HARLEM, that celebrated black traditions, the black voice, and black ways of life. Anna Bontemps, Langston HUGHES, Zora Neale HURSTON, James Weldon JOHNSON, and Jean Toomer were some of the writers associated with the movement.

Hawthorne, Nathaniel An American author of the nineteenth century, known for his NOVELS and short stories that explore THEMES of sin and guilt. His works include *THE SCARLET LETTER* and *The House of the Seven Gables*.

Heart of Darkness A short NOVEL by Joseph CONRAD. It concerns a seafarer, Marlow, who is sent to the interior of AFRICA in search of a "mad adventurer" named Kurtz. The book's title refers both to the location of the story and to the evil and darkness in people's hearts.

Heep, Uriah (yoo-REYE-uh HEEP) A hypocritical, scheming blackmailer in *DAVID COPPERFIELD*, by Charles DICKENS. Heep continually insists that he is a "very 'umble person."

Hemingway, Ernest An American author of the twentieth century; one of the LOST GENERATION of Americans living in PARIS during the 1920s. In such books as *THE SUN ALSO RISES*, *A FAREWELL TO ARMS*, *For Whom the Bell Tolls*, and *The Old Man and the Sea*, he glorified heroic male exploits such as bullfighting, boxing, and safari hunting. Hemingway is known for his simple, short sentences and his lively dialogue.

Henry, O. An American author of the twentieth century, known for "THE GIFT OF THE MAGI" and other short stories. He specialized in surprise endings. His real name was William Sydney Porter.

"Hey Diddle Diddle"   A nursery RHYME:

> Hey diddle diddle
> The cat and the fiddle,
> The cow jumped over the moon;
> The little dog laughed
> To see such sport,
> And the dish ran away with the spoon.

Hiawatha, The Song of (heye-uh-WAH-thuh, hee-uh-WAH-thuh)   An EPIC by Henry Wadsworth LONGFELLOW, based on the story of an actual NATIVE AMERICAN hero. The historical Hiawatha was an Onondaga from what is now NEW YORK state, but Longfellow makes him an Ojibwa living near LAKE SUPERIOR. A famous section of the poem begins:

> By the shores of Gitche Gumee,
> By the shining Big-Sea-Water,
> Stood the wigwam of Nokomis. . . .

"Hickory, Dickory, Dock"   A nursery RHYME:

> Hickory, Dickory, Dock,
> The mouse ran up the clock,
> The clock struck one,
> The mouse ran down;
> Hickory, dickory, dock.

Holmes, Sherlock   A fictional English detective, created by Sir Arthur Conan DOYLE. Holmes's extraordinary powers of memory, observation, and DEDUCTION enable him to solve mysteries and identify criminals in cases that leave all other detectives baffled. His companion is Dr. WATSON, who records his exploits. Holmes is often mistakenly quoted as saying, "ELEMENTARY, MY DEAR WATSON."

🦶 Figuratively, any shrewd detective can be called Sherlock Holmes, or simply Sherlock.

Home is the sailor, home from sea / And the hunter home from the hill   Lines from a poem, "Requiem," by Robert Louis STEVENSON, composed for engraving on a tombstone.

Hook, Captain   The pirate-villain in the play *PETER PAN.* One of his hands has been devoured by a crocodile and replaced with a hook. He is eaten whole by the crocodile near the end of the play.

horror, The   A PHRASE spoken by the dying adventurer Kurtz ("The horror! The horror!") in *HEART OF DARKNESS,* by Joseph CONRAD.

PETER PAN AND CAPTAIN HOOK

horse!, My kingdom for a   *See* KINGDOM FOR A HORSE!, MY.

How the Grinch Stole Christmas   *See* GRINCH STOLE CHRISTMAS, HOW THE.

How sharper than a serpent's tooth it is / To have a thankless child   Lines from the play *KING LEAR,* by William SHAKESPEARE, spoken by King Lear after he has been betrayed by his two elder daughters.

Huckleberry Finn, The Adventures of   A NOVEL by Mark TWAIN. Huckleberry Finn, a boy running away from his father, and his friend Jim, a runaway slave, take to the MISSISSIPPI RIVER on a raft. Eventually Jim is captured, and Huck helps him escape. The lessons Huck learns about life are a prevailing THEME of the book.

Hughes, Langston   An African-American author of the twentieth century, known for his poems about the black experience in the United States. A well-known line from one of his poems is "What happens to a dream deferred? / Does it dry up like a raisin in the sun?" One of his most famous poems is "The Negro Speaks of Rivers." He was a leading figure in the HARLEM RENAISSANCE.

"Humpty Dumpty"   A nursery RHYME:

> Humpty Dumpty sat on a wall;
> Humpty Dumpty had a great fall.
> All the king's horses and all the king's men
> Couldn't put Humpty together again.

ZORA NEALE HURSTON. *Detail of a 1935 photographic portrait by Carl Van Vechten.*

Hurston, Zora Neale Twentieth-century African-American novelist, folklorist, and anthropologist, best known for her novel *Their Eyes Were Watching God*. A member of the HARLEM RENAISSANCE, Hurston is also known for her collection of African-American lore, *Mules and Men*.

Huxley, Aldous An English author of the twentieth century best known for *BRAVE NEW WORLD*, a NOVEL about the future.

Hyde, Mr. The vicious side of the PERSONALITY of Dr. JEKYLL in *The Strange Case of Dr. Jekyll and Mr. Hyde*, by Robert Louis STEVENSON.

I think that I shall never see / A poem lovely as a tree The opening lines of the poem "TREES," by Joyce Kilmer.

I wandered lonely as a cloud The first line of the poem "Daffodils," by William WORDSWORTH. It begins:

> I wandered lonely as a cloud
> That floats on high o'er vales and hills,
> When all at once I saw a crowd,
> A host, of golden daffodils.

Iago (ee-AH-goh) The treacherous villain in the play *OTHELLO*, by William SHAKESPEARE. As adviser to Othello, a general of VENICE, Iago lies to his master and eventually drives him to murder his wife.

ides of March, Beware the A warning Julius CAESAR receives from a fortuneteller in the play *JULIUS CAESAR*, by William SHAKESPEARE. Later in the play, he is assassinated on the IDES OF MARCH (March 15).

If music be the food of love, play on The first line of the play *TWELFTH NIGHT*, by William SHAKESPEARE. The speaker is asking for music because he is frustrated in courtship; he wants an overabundance of love so that he may lose his appetite for it.

"In Flanders Fields" A poem about WORLD WAR I by the Canadian author John McCrae, describing the scene of some of the worst fighting of the war; the "speakers" of the poem are all dead. It begins:

> In Flanders fields the poppies blow
> Between the crosses, row on row,
> That mark our place. . . .

"Invictus" A popular poem from the late nineteenth century by the English author William Ernest Henley. *Invictus* is LATIN for "unconquered." The speaker in the poem proclaims his strength in the face of adversity:

> My head is bloody, but unbowed. . . .
> I am the master of my fate;
> I am the captain of my soul.

Invisible Man A NOVEL by African-American author Ralph ELLISON, set in the United States in the 1930s; it depicts a black man's struggle for identity.

Irving, Washington An American author of the nineteenth century; "THE LEGEND OF SLEEPY HOLLOW" and "RIP VAN WINKLE" are two of his best-known works.

It is a far, far better thing that I do, than I have ever done A sentence from the end of *A Tale of Two Cities*, by Charles DICKENS. The CHARACTER who is speaking has nobly chosen to die in place of another man.

It was the best of times, it was the worst of times The beginning of *A Tale of Two Cities*, by Charles DICKENS, referring to the time of the FRENCH REVOLUTION.

"Jack, Be Nimble"   A nursery RHYME:

> Jack, be nimble;
> Jack, be quick;
> Jack, jump over the candlestick.

"Jack and the Beanstalk"   A children's story. Jack, a poor country boy, trades the family cow for a handful of magic beans, which grow into an enormous beanstalk reaching up into the CLOUDS. Jack climbs the beanstalk, and finds himself in the castle of an unfriendly giant. The giant senses Jack's presence and cries, "Fee, fie, fo, fum, I smell the blood of an Englishman!" Outwitting the giant, Jack is able to retrieve many goods once stolen from his family, including an enchanted goose that lays golden eggs. Jack then escapes by chopping down the beanstalk. The giant, who is pursuing him, falls to his death, and Jack and his family prosper.

"Jack and Jill"   A nursery RHYME. Its first STANZA reads:

> Jack and Jill went up the hill,
> To fetch a pail of water;
> Jack fell down, and broke his crown,
> And Jill came tumbling after.

"Jack Sprat"   A nursery RHYME:

> Jack Sprat could eat no fat;
> His wife could eat no lean,
> And so betwixt them both,
> They licked the platter clean.

James, Henry   An American author of the late nineteenth and early twentieth centuries. James is known for his NOVELS, such as *The Turn of the Screw* and *Portrait of a Lady*.
    ⮞ The philosopher and psychologist William JAMES was Henry James's brother.

Jane Eyre (AIR)   A NOVEL by Charlotte BRONTË. Jane Eyre serves as governess to the ward of the mysterious and moody Edward Rochester. He proposes to her, but Jane discovers that he is already married to an insane woman. Eventually Jane and Rochester are able to marry.

Jeeves   A servant who appears in comic NOVELS and SHORT STORIES about the English upper classes by P. G. Wodehouse, a twentieth-century British author, who spent most of his life in the UNITED STATES.

Jekyll, Dr. (JEK-uhl)   The kind side of the split-PERSONALITY title CHARACTER in *The Strange Case of*

DR. JEKYLL AND MR. HYDE, by Robert Louis STEVENSON.

Johnson, James Weldon   African-American writer, diplomat, and civil rights leader of the early twentieth century. He wrote a novel, *The Autobiography of an Ex-Coloured Man*, that illustrated the difficulties of talented African-Americans. He co-wrote "LIFT EV'RY VOICE AND SING," and encouraged writers of the HARLEM RENAISSANCE.

Johnson, Samuel   An English author of the eighteenth century, known for his wit and for his balanced and careful criticism of literature. Johnson, who is sometimes called "Dr. Johnson" (he held a doctorate from OXFORD), compiled an important dictionary of the English language. The story of his life is told in *The Life of Samuel Johnson*, by James BOSWELL.

Joyce, James   An Irish author of the twentieth century, known for his NOVELS, especially *Finnegans Wake*, *A Portrait of the Artist as a Young Man*, and *Ulysses*, and for his short stories, especially the collection *Dubliners*.
    ⮞ *Ulysses*, a novel revolutionary in its form, is almost entirely concerned with the actions and thoughts of three CHARACTERS on a single day. (*See* ULYSSES *under "Mythology and Folklore."*)

Julius Caesar   A TRAGEDY by William SHAKESPEARE, dealing with the assassination of Julius CAESAR and its aftermath. Some famous lines from the play are "*ET TU, BRUTE?*" "FRIENDS, ROMANS, COUNTRYMEN, LEND ME YOUR EARS," "Yon Cassius has a LEAN AND HUNGRY LOOK," and "the NOBLEST ROMAN OF THEM ALL."

justify the ways of God to men, to   The declared aim of the poet John MILTON in his poem *PARADISE LOST*. Milton tries to explain why God allowed the FALL OF MAN.

Keats, John   An English poet of the nineteenth century, one of the leaders of ROMANTICISM. His poems include "ODE ON A GRECIAN URN," "Ode to a Nightingale," and "Endymion," which contains the famous line "A THING OF BEAUTY IS A JOY FOREVER." Keats died at the age of twenty-five.

King James Bible   The best-known English translation of the BIBLE, commissioned by King James I of ENGLAND, and published in the early seventeenth century. It had no rival among the PROTESTANT faiths until the late nineteenth century; it is still widely used.

☙ Most biblical quotations in English literature come from the King James Bible. To many, the phrasing of the King James Bible is the model of how biblical verses should sound.

King Lear A TRAGEDY by William SHAKESPEARE about an old king who unwisely hands his kingdom over to two of his daughters. The daughters, who had flattered Lear while he was in power, turn on him; their actions reduce him to poverty and eventually to madness. His youngest daughter, CORDELIA, whom he had at first spurned, remains faithful to him. Some of the best-remembered lines from *King Lear* are "EVERY INCH A KING," "HOW SHARPER THAN A SERPENT'S TOOTH IT IS / TO HAVE A THANKLESS CHILD," "MORE SINNED AGAINST THAN SINNING," and "THAT WAY MADNESS LIES."

kingdom for a horse! My An exclamation from the play *King Richard the Third*, by William SHAKESPEARE; the tyrannical King Richard cries out, "A horse! A horse! My kingdom for a horse!" after his horse is killed in battle, leaving him at the mercy of his enemies.

Kipling, Rudyard An English author of the late nineteenth and early twentieth centuries. Kipling is known for his children's books such as *The Jungle Book* and *Just So Stories*; NOVELS such as *Kim* and *The Light That Failed*; and poems such as "GUNGA DIN" and "The Road to Mandalay." Some well-known lines from his works are "EAST IS EAST, AND WEST IS WEST, AND NEVER THE TWAIN SHALL MEET" and "The FEMALE OF THE SPECIES IS MORE DEADLY THAN THE MALE."

"Kubla Khan" (KOOH-bluh KAHN) An evocative poem by Samuel Taylor COLERIDGE about an exotic emperor. It begins with these lines: "In Xanadu did Kubla Khan / A stately pleasure-dome decree . . ."

lady doth protest too much, The A line from the play *HAMLET*, by William SHAKESPEARE, spoken by Hamlet's mother. Hamlet's mother is watching a play, and a CHARACTER in it swears never to remarry if her husband dies. The play is making Hamlet's mother uncomfortable, because she herself has remarried almost immediately after the murder of her first husband.

land was ours before we were the land's, The The first line of the poem "The Gift Outright" by Robert FROST.

Last of the Mohicans, The A NOVEL by James Fenimore COOPER; part of *The Leatherstocking Tales*. The leading CHARACTER is a noble NATIVE AMERICAN who helps a family of British settlers during the FRENCH AND INDIAN WAR.

Lawrence, D. H. A British author of the twentieth century; two of his best-regarded works are *Sons and Lovers* and *Women in Love*. Lawrence is known for his frank treatment of sex, and for the RADICAL ideas on society and on the family that he voiced in his books.

☙ Lawrence's NOVEL *Lady Chatterley's Lover* was banned as obscene in both BRITAIN and the United States. In the United States, the ban was appealed to the SUPREME COURT, which overruled it.

Lay on, Macduff A line from the play *MACBETH*, by William SHAKESPEARE. Macbeth speaks these words as he attacks his enemy Macduff at the end of the play; Macbeth is killed in the fight.

lean and hungry look A PHRASE from the play *JULIUS CAESAR*, by William SHAKESPEARE. Caesar remarks, concerning one of the men conspiring against him, "Yon Cassius has a lean and hungry look." Caesar means that Cassius looks dangerously dissatisfied, as if he were starved for power.

Lear, King *See* KING LEAR.

Leaves of Grass A collection of poems by Walt WHITMAN, written mainly in FREE VERSE. Published with revisions every few years in the late nineteenth century, it contains such well-known poems as "I Hear America Singing," "Song of Myself," and "O Captain, My Captain."

"Legend of Sleepy Hollow, The" A story by Washington IRVING. Its central CHARACTER, Ichabod Crane, is a vain and cowardly teacher, and the rival in love of Brom Bones. Bones terrorizes Crane by disguising himself as a legendary headless horseman.

Legree, Simon The cruel overseer of slaves in *UNCLE TOM'S CABIN*, by Harriet Beecher STOWE. Though the book describes conditions in the slaveholding states of the South, Legree, the most vicious CHARACTER in it, is from NEW ENGLAND.

Let me not to the marriage of true minds / Admit impediments   The first line of a SONNET by William SHAKESPEARE. The poet is denying that anything can come between true lovers (that is, be an impediment to their love).

Lewis, Sinclair   An American author of the twentieth century, known for using his NOVELS to criticize aspects of American life such as small-town narrowness, insincere preachers, and the discouragement of scientific curiosity. His books include *BABBITT, ELMER GANTRY*, and *Main Street*.

Liberty, On   An ESSAY by John Stuart MILL in defense of the LIBERAL idea of political freedom. Mill takes a firm position that the state may interfere with the freedom of individuals only to protect other individuals; the person's "own good" is not a sufficient reason.

"Lift Ev'ry Voice and Sing"   Title and first line of a song that has come to be known as the African-American national anthem. The words and music are by James Weldon JOHNSON and his brother J. Rosamond Johnson. The first stanza is:

> Lift ev'ry voice and sing,
> Till earth and heaven ring,
> Ring with the harmonies of Liberty,
> Let our rejoicing rise
> High as the list'ning skies,
> Let it resound loud as the rolling sea.
> Sing a song full of the faith that the dark past
>   has taught us
> Sing a song full of the hope that the present
>   has brought us
> Facing the rising sun of our new day begun,
> Let us march on till victory is won.

Lilliput (LIL-i-puht)   The first land that Lemuel Gulliver visits in *GULLIVER'S TRAVELS*, by Jonathan SWIFT. The inhabitants, though human in form, are only six inches tall.

   Something "lilliputian" (lil-i-PYOOH-shuhn) is very small. The expression is especially appropriate for a miniature version of something.

"Little Bo-Peep"   A nursery RHYME:

> Little Bo-Peep has lost her sheep,
> And can't tell where to find them;
> Leave them alone, and they'll come home,
> Wagging their tails behind them.

"Little Boy Blue"   A nursery RHYME:

> Little Boy Blue, come blow your horn,
> The sheep's in the meadow, the cow's in the corn;
> But where is the boy who looks after the sheep?
> He's under the haystack fast asleep.

"Little Jack Horner"   A nursery RHYME:

> Little Jack Horner sat in the corner,
> Eating a Christmas pie:
> He put in his thumb, and pulled out a plum,
> And said, "What a good boy am I!"

"Little Miss Muffet"   A nursery RHYME:

> Little Miss Muffet
> Sat on a tuffet,
> Eating some curds and whey.
> Along came a spider,
> And sat down beside her,
> And frightened Miss Muffet away.

"Little Red Hen, The"   A children's story. A little red hen asks her animal friends to help her plant, tend, and harvest some wheat, but they refuse. After she has harvested the wheat and baked it into bread, the same friends eagerly agree to help her eat it; she refuses to share, and keeps all the bread for herself and her chicks. In another version, she bakes a cake, is captured by a fox, escapes, and sees her friends repent their selfishness.

Little Women   A NOVEL by Louisa May ALCOTT, about four sisters growing up in NEW ENGLAND in the nineteenth century.

"London Bridge Is Falling Down"   A nursery chant:

> London Bridge is falling down,
> Falling down, falling down,
> London Bridge is falling down,
> My fair lady.

Longfellow, Henry Wadsworth   An American poet of the nineteenth century. Among his works are *The Song of HIAWATHA* and "PAUL REVERE'S RIDE."

Lord, what fools these mortals be!   A line from the play *A MIDSUMMER NIGHT'S DREAM*, by William SHAKESPEARE. A mischievous fairy, Puck, addressing his king, is commenting on the folly of the human beings who have come into his forest.

Macbeth   A TRAGEDY by William SHAKESPEARE, in which the Scottish nobleman Macbeth, misled by the prophecy of three witches and goaded on by his wife, murders the king and usurps the throne. Well-known lines from the play include "Lay on, Macduff," "Out, damned spot!" and "Tomorrow, and tomorrow, and tomorrow."

Malaprop, Mrs. (MAL-uh-prop) A character in *The Rivals*, an English play from the late eighteenth century by Richard Brinsley Sheridan. Mrs. Malaprop constantly mixes up words that sound similar, declaring, for instance, "He is the very *pineapple* of politeness," when she means *pinnacle*.

&. Today, any comic jumbling of words like those produced by Mrs. Malaprop is called a malapropism.

man's reach should exceed his grasp, a Words from a poem by Robert Browning, suggesting that, to achieve anything worthwhile, a person should attempt even those things that may turn out to be impossible.

Mary had a little lamb The first line of the children's poem "Mary's Lamb," first published in the nineteenth century. It begins:

> Mary had a little lamb,
> Its fleece was white as snow,
> And everywhere that Mary went,
> The lamb was sure to go.

"Mary, Mary, Quite Contrary" A nursery rhyme:

> Mary, Mary, quite contrary,
> How does your garden grow?
> With silver bells, and cockleshells,
> And pretty maids all in a row.

mass of men lead lives of quiet desperation, The A statement from *Walden*, by Henry David Thoreau.

Melville, Herman An American author of the nineteenth century, best known for *Moby Dick*. In his writing, Melville drew on several adventurous years he spent at sea.

Mencken, H. L. An American writer of the twentieth century, known for his works of satire, mainly essays. Mencken mocked American society for its puritanism, its anti-intellectualism, and its emphasis on conformity.

Merchant of Venice, The A comedy by William Shakespeare. The most memorable character is Shylock, a greedy moneylender who demands from the title character "a pound of flesh" as payment for a debt.

Middle English The English language from about 1150 to about 1500. During this time, following the Norman Conquest of England, the native language of England — Old English — borrowed great numbers of words from the Norman French of the conquerors. Middle English eventually developed into modern English.

&. Many of the writings in Middle English that have survived have word forms very different from those in modern English; today's readers of English cannot understand the language of these works without training. Some dialects of Middle English, however, resemble modern English, and a good reader of today can catch the drift of something written in them. Geoffrey Chaucer wrote *The Canterbury Tales* in one of these dialects.

Midsummer Night's Dream, A A comedy by William Shakespeare about a group of lovers who spend a night in a forest, where they are the victims of fairies' pranks and enchantments. One famous line from *A Midsummer Night's Dream* is "Lord, what fools these mortals be!"

miles to go before I sleep Words from the poem "Stopping by Woods on a Snowy Evening," by Robert Frost.

Milne, A. A. An English author of the twentieth century. He is best known for his stories of Winnie-the-Pooh.

Milton, John An English poet of the seventeenth century. His greatest work is the epic *Paradise Lost*, which he dictated after he went blind. With Geoffrey Chaucer' and William Shakespeare, Milton is considered one of the greatest of all English poets. A famous phrase from Milton's works is his statement of purpose in *Paradise Lost*: "to justify the ways of God to men." Also well known is the last line of his poem "On His Blindness": "They also serve who only stand and wait."

Mitty, Walter The title character in "The Secret Life of Walter Mitty," a short story by James Thurber. Mitty is a repressed, ordinary man who daydreams of doing great things.

Moby Dick A NOVEL by Herman MELVILLE. Its central CHARACTER, Captain AHAB, engages in a mad, obsessive quest for Moby Dick, a great white whale. The novel opens with the famous sentence "Call me Ishmael."

"Modest Proposal, A" An ESSAY by Jonathan SWIFT, often called a masterpiece of IRONY. The full title is "A Modest Proposal for Preventing the Children of the Poor People in Ireland from Being a Burden to Their Parents or Country, and for Making Them Beneficial to Their Public." Swift emphasizes the terrible poverty of eighteenth-century IRELAND by ironically proposing that Irish parents earn money by selling their children as food.

🙠 The PHRASE "a modest proposal" is often used ironically to introduce a major innovative suggestion.

more things in heaven and earth, Horatio A PHRASE used by the title CHARACTER in the play HAMLET, by William SHAKESPEARE. Hamlet suggests that human knowledge is limited: "There are more things in HEAVEN and EARTH, Horatio, / Than are dreamt of in your PHILOSOPHY [science]."

Morrison, Toni Twentieth-century American novelist and essayist on African-American themes. Among her best-known works are the novels *Song of Solomon* and *Beloved*.

Mother Goose rhymes The brief, traditional, anonymous verses, or nursery RHYMES, learned by children in the English-speaking world. Among the best-known Mother Goose rhymes are "HUMPTY DUMPTY," "JACK AND JILL," "LITTLE MISS MUFFET," and "OLD KING COLE."

Narrative of the Life of Frederick Douglass The AUTOBIOGRAPHY of the former black slave and ABOLITIONIST Frederick DOUGLASS, and one of the most significant African-American works from the nineteenth century.

Nash, Ogden An American author of the twentieth century, known for his witty poems, many of them published in THE NEW YORKER. They are marked by outrageous RHYMES, such as those in "The Baby" ("A bit of talcum / Is always walcum") or in "Reflections on Ice-Breaking" ("Candy / Is dandy / But liquor / Is quicker").

Native Son A NOVEL by African-American author Richard WRIGHT about a young black man whose life is destroyed by poverty and RACISM.

Neither a borrower nor a lender be A line from the play *HAMLET*, by William SHAKESPEARE. Polonius, a garrulous old man, gives this advice to his son.

Never-Never Land Originally called Neverland, the home of the title CHARACTER in the play *PETER PAN*; a place where children never grow up.

New Yorker, The A weekly magazine known for NONFICTION and short stories, and for its cartoons. Ogden NASH, Dorothy PARKER, and James THURBER are notable authors whose work appeared regularly in the magazine.

"Night Before Christmas, The" A poem from the early nineteenth century by the American author Clement C. Moore; it concerns the appearance of Santa Claus on Christmas Eve. The original title of the poem is "A Visit from St. NICHOLAS." Some lines from it are:

'Twas the night before Christmas, when all through the house
Not a creature was stirring, not even a mouse;
The stockings were hung by the chimney with care,
In hopes that St. Nicholas soon would be there.
The children were nestled all snug in their beds,
While visions of sugar-plums danced in their heads; . . .
But I heard him exclaim, ere he drove out of sight,
"Happy Christmas to all, and to all a good night!"

🙠 Moore's poem did much to establish certain aspects of the myth of Santa Claus: that he is a fat man dressed in a fur-trimmed suit, carries presents in a sack, enters houses through the chimney, and travels through the air in a sleigh pulled by reindeer.

Nineteen Eighty-Four A NOVEL by George ORWELL. *Nineteen Eighty-Four* depicts a totalitarian society of the future, ruled by an omnipotent dictator called Big Brother. In this society, called Oceania, people's thoughts are controlled as tightly as their actions. The government maintains an organization called the "thought police," and engages in constant PROPAGANDA.

🙠 The slogan "BIG BROTHER IS WATCHING YOU," which appears on posters throughout Oceania, is often repeated by persons who feel that their government is carrying on improper surveillance of its citizens. ♣ Orwell coined the term *doublespeak* to describe one kind of propaganda practiced by the state in *Nineteen Eighty-Four*.

noblest Roman of them all, the A PHRASE from the play *JULIUS CAESAR*, by William SHAKESPEARE. Mark ANTONY uses it at the end of the play to describe BRUTUS; Antony maintains that Brutus was the only one of Caesar's assassins who took part in the killing for unselfish motives.

"O Captain, My Captain" A poem by Walt WHITMAN about a captain who dies just as his ship has reached the end of a stormy and dangerous voyage. The captain represents Abraham LINCOLN, who was assassinated just as the Civil War was ending.

"Ode on a Grecian Urn" A poem by John KEATS. It contains the famous lines "'Beauty is truth, truth beauty' — that is all / Ye know on earth, and all ye need to know."

Off with her head! Off with his head! Exclamations made frequently by the Queen of Hearts in *ALICE'S ADVENTURES IN WONDERLAND*, by Lewis CARROLL.

O'Hara, Scarlett The heroine of the book *GONE WITH THE WIND*. Scarlett is a shrewd, manipulative southern belle who survives two husbands and finally is matched for wits by a third, Rhett Butler.

Old English The English language from the fifth century until about 1150. In the fifth century, the Angles and Saxons of GERMANY settled in BRITAIN and established their language in the southern part of the island — the region that was called "Angle-land," or "ENGLAND." After 1150, the Norman French language introduced after the NORMAN CONQUEST influenced Old English, and MIDDLE ENGLISH developed.

♣ Old English resembles the language spoken in Germany in the same period, and is impossible for a present-day user of English to read without training. *BEOWULF* is written in Old English.

"Old King Cole" A nursery RHYME. Its first STANZA reads:

Old King Cole was a merry old soul,
And a merry old soul was he;
He called for his pipe and he called for his bowl,
And he called for his fiddlers three.

"Old Mother Hubbard" A nursery RHYME. Its first STANZA is:

Old Mother Hubbard
Went to the cupboard,
To fetch her poor dog a bone;
But when she got there
The cupboard was bare,
And so the poor dog had none.

Oliver Twist A NOVEL by Charles DICKENS; the title CHARACTER is an orphan boy. In one famous scene, Oliver is severely punished for asking for more gruel, or porridge ("Please, sir, I want some more"). Oliver later becomes a pickpocket in a gang of young thieves led by FAGIN. Violent in PLOT, the book exposes the inadequacies of British public institutions for dealing with the poverty of children like Oliver. Oliver is eventually taken into a wealthy household and educated.

On Liberty *See* LIBERTY, ON.

Once more unto the breach, dear friends Words from the play *King Henry the Fifth*, by William SHAKESPEARE. King Henry is rallying his troops to attack a breach, or gap, in the wall of an enemy city.

one that loved not wisely but too well In the play *OTHELLO*, by William SHAKESPEARE, the title CHARACTER'S description of himself after he has murdered his wife in a jealous rage.

O'Neill, Eugene An American playwright of the twentieth century. Two of his best-known plays are *A Long Day's Journey into Night* and *The Iceman Cometh*.

Only God can make a tree The last words of the poem "TREES," by Joyce Kilmer.

Orwell, George The NOM DE PLUME of Eric Blair, an English author of the twentieth century, best known for *ANIMAL FARM* and *NINETEEN EIGHTY-FOUR*.

♣ *Nineteen Eighty-Four* is a powerful depiction of TOTALITARIANISM; hence, the ADJECTIVE *Orwellian* has been applied to government actions that suppress freedom or distort truth.

Othello A TRAGEDY by William SHAKESPEARE. The title CHARACTER, a Moor, or dark-skinned MOSLEM, is a general commanding the forces of VENICE. The villain IAGO convinces Othello that Desdemona, the general's beautiful and faithful wife, has been guilty of ADULTERY; at the end of the play, Othello smothers Desdemona. A famous line from the play is Othello's description of himself as "ONE THAT LOVED NOT WISELY BUT TOO WELL."

Our Town   A play by Thornton WILDER, dealing with everyday life in a small town in NEW ENGLAND.

Out, damned spot!   A sentence from the play *MACBETH* by William SHAKESPEARE, spoken by Lady Macbeth, the wife of the title CHARACTER. Her husband has killed the king of SCOTLAND at her urging, but her guilt over the murder gradually drives her insane. When she speaks this line she is sleepwalking, and she imagines that a spot of the king's blood stains her hand.

"Owl and the Pussy-Cat, The"   A children's poem by Edward Lear. It begins with these lines:

> The Owl and the Pussy-Cat went to sea
> In a beautiful pea-green boat:
> They took some honey, and plenty of money,
> Wrapped up in a five-pound note.

Paradise Lost   An EPIC by John MILTON. Its subject is the FALL OF MAN; it also tells the stories of the rebellion and punishment of SATAN and the creation of ADAM AND EVE. Milton declares that his aim in the poem is "to JUSTIFY THE WAYS OF GOD TO MEN."

Parker, Dorothy   An American author of the twentieth century, known for her often sarcastic wit. Parker wrote poems, short stories, film scripts, and reviews of plays and books. Her poetry contains some often-quoted lines, such as "Men seldom make passes / At girls who wear glasses."

Parting is such sweet sorrow   A line from the play *ROMEO AND JULIET*, by William SHAKESPEARE; Juliet is saying good night to Romeo. Their sorrowful parting is also "sweet" because it makes them think about the next time they will see each other.

"Paul Revere's Ride"   A poem by Henry Wadsworth LONGFELLOW, celebrating the ride made on horseback by Paul REVERE to warn the American rebels of approaching British troops. It begins with these lines: "Listen, my children, and you shall hear / Of the midnight ride of Paul Revere."

Peter Pan   A play by the Scottish author James Matthew Barrie about a boy who lives in Neverland, better known as NEVER-NEVER LAND, a country where no child ever grows up. Peter brings the three children of the Darling family from LONDON to Never-Never Land; they eventually decide not to stay, but Wendy, the eldest, promises to return every spring. Peter is assisted by his guardian fairy, Tinker Bell, and in the play he defeats his enemy, the pirate Captain HOOK.

"Peter Piper"   A nursery RHYME that begins with the tongue-twisting line "Peter Piper picked a peck of pickled peppers."

Pickwick, Samuel   The main CHARACTER of *The Pickwick Papers*, a NOVEL by Charles DICKENS. Pickwick founds a club whose members use common words in extremely quirky ways.

   📖 Someone who wishes to retract or qualify a statement says that he or she was using the words "in the Pickwickian sense." In the book, "Pickwickian sense" refers to an interpretation of an offensive remark that makes it palatable.

"Pied Piper of Hamelin, The"   (HAM-uh-lin, HAM-lin)   A poem by Robert BROWNING, based on a folktale from the MIDDLE AGES in GERMANY. The town of Hamelin is infested with rats, and the citizens hire a piper in multicolored (pied) clothing to lure the rats out with his charming music. The rats follow the piper into the river and drown. When the townspeople refuse to pay the piper, he lures away all the children of the town.

Pilgrim's Progress, The   A religious ALLEGORY by the seventeenth-century English author John Bunyan. Christian, the central CHARACTER, journeys from the City of Destruction to the Celestial City. Along the way he faces many obstacles, including the SLOUGH OF DESPOND. He is eventually successful in his journey, and is allowed into HEAVEN.

Poe, Edgar Allan   An American author of the nineteenth century, known for his poems and horror stories. Among his works are the stories "THE FALL OF THE HOUSE OF USHER," "The Tell-Tale Heart," "The Pit and the Pendulum," "The Cask of Amontillado," and "The Murders in the Rue Morgue," and the poems "The Bells" and "THE RAVEN."

poet laureate   The national poet in BRITAIN. Historically, the poet laureate's duty has been to compose official poetry for the king's or queen's birthday and for great public occasions such as victories in war, coronations, and births and weddings in the

EDGAR ALLAN POE

royal family. The poets laureate of Britain have included Geoffrey CHAUCER, William WORDSWORTH, and Alfred, Lord TENNYSON.

• The position of poet laureate was created in the United States in 1985. American poet laureates have included Robert Penn Warren, Richard Wilbur, and Mona Van Duyn.

Pollyanna A children's book from the early twentieth century by the American author Eleanor H. Porter. The title CHARACTER is an orphan girl who, despite the difficulties of her life, is always extremely cheerful.

• A "Pollyanna" remains excessively sweet-tempered and optimistic even in adversity.

Poor Richard's Almanack A collection of periodicals (each one was called *Poor Richard* or *Poor Richard Improved*) by Benjamin FRANKLIN, issued over twenty-five years in the middle of the eighteenth century. They contain humor, information, and proverbial wisdom, such as "EARLY TO BED AND EARLY TO RISE / MAKES A MAN HEALTHY, WEALTHY, AND WISE."

Pope, Alexander An English poet of the eighteenth century, known for his satiric wit and insistence on the values of CLASSICISM in literature: balance, symmetry, and restraint. His best-known poems are "The Rape of the Lock," "An ESSAY on Criticism," and "An Essay on Man."

pound of flesh A PHRASE from the play *THE MERCHANT OF VENICE*, by William SHAKESPEARE. The moneylender SHYLOCK demands the flesh of the "merchant of Venice," Antonio, under a provision in their CONTRACT. Shylock never gets the pound of flesh, however, because the CHARACTER Portia discovers a point of law that overrides the contract between Shylock and Antonio: Shylock is forbidden to shed any blood in getting the flesh from Antonio's body.

• People who cruelly or unreasonably insist on their rights are said to be demanding their "pound of flesh."

Pride and Prejudice A comic NOVEL by Jane AUSTEN about the life of an upper-MIDDLE-CLASS family, the Bennets, in eighteenth-century ENGLAND. A complex succession of events ends with the marriages of the two eldest Bennet daughters.

providence in the fall of a sparrow, There's a special A line from the play *HAMLET*, by William SHAKESPEARE, suggesting that a divine power takes a benevolent interest in human affairs. Hamlet, the speaker, is echoing words of JESUS, that one sparrow "shall not fall on the ground without your Father." Hamlet's speech continues: "If it be now, 'tis not to come; if it be not to come, it will be now; if it be not now, yet it will come: the readiness is all."

Pygmalion (pig-MAYL-yuhn, pig-MAY-lee-uhn) A play by George Bernard SHAW, about a professor, Henry Higgins, who trains a poor, uneducated girl, Eliza Doolittle, to act and speak like a lady. Shaw based his story on a tale from Greek MYTHOLOGY about a sculptor who carves the statue of a woman and falls in love with it (*see under "Mythology and Folklore"*). Higgins and Eliza develop a strong bond, and he is furious when she announces her intention to marry someone else.

• The MUSICAL COMEDY *MY FAIR LADY* is an adaptation of *Pygmalion*.

quality of mercy is not strained, The A line from the play *THE MERCHANT OF VENICE*, by William SHAKESPEARE. *Strained* means "constrained," or "forced"; the speaker is telling SHYLOCK that mercy must be freely given, and is inviting him to show mercy to the title CHARACTER.

"Raven, The"   A poem by Edgar Allan POE. A man mourning for his lost lover is visited by a raven that tells him he will see her "nevermore." The poem begins with these famous lines:

> Once upon a midnight dreary, while I pondered, weak and weary
> Over many a quaint and curious volume of forgotten lore,
> While I nodded, nearly napping, suddenly there came a tapping,
> As of someone gently rapping, rapping at my chamber door.

Red Badge of Courage, The   A NOVEL from the late nineteenth century by the American author Stephen Crane, about a young man whose romantic notions of heroism in combat are shattered when he fights in the CIVIL WAR.

reports of my death are greatly exaggerated, The   The text of a cable sent by Mark TWAIN from LONDON to the press in the United States after his obituary had been mistakenly published.

"Ride a Cock-Horse"   A nursery RHYME:

> Ride a cock-horse to Banbury Cross,
> To see a fine lady upon a white horse;
> RINGS ON HER FINGERS AND BELLS ON HER TOES,
> She shall have music wherever she goes.

"Rime of the Ancient Mariner, The"   A poem by Samuel Taylor COLERIDGE about an old sailor who is compelled to tell strangers about the supernatural adventures that befell him at sea after he killed an albatross, a friendly sea bird. A famous line is "WATER, WATER, EVERYWHERE, / NOR ANY DROP TO DRINK." (*See* ALBATROSS AROUND ONE'S NECK.)

Ring-a-Ring o' Roses   A children's RHYME, also known as "Ring around the Rosie":

> Ring-a-ring o' roses,
> A pocket full of posies,
> Ashes! Ashes!
> We all fall down.

Rings on her fingers and bells on her toes   A line from the nursery RHYME "RIDE A COCK-HORSE": "Rings on her fingers and bells on her toes, / She shall have music wherever she goes."

"Rip Van Winkle"   A story by Washington IRVING. The title CHARACTER goes to sleep after a game of bowling and much drinking in the mountains with a band of dwarves. He awakens twenty years later, an old man. Back home, Rip finds that all has changed: his wife is dead, his daughter is married, and the AMERICAN REVOLUTION has taken place.

Robin Hood   A CHARACTER of English legend, the subject of many BALLADS and stories since the fourteenth century. Robin Hood lived with his band of Merry Men in Sherwood Forest, and stole from the rich to give to the poor. (*See under "Mythology and Folklore."*)

Robinson Crusoe   A NOVEL from the early eighteenth century by the English author Daniel Defoe. Robinson Crusoe, an English sailor, is shipwrecked and cast ashore alone on an uninhabited island. With great ingenuity and energy, Crusoe sets out to civilize his surroundings: he clothes himself, grows crops, and builds and furnishes a house. Eventually, he has the company of his servant, FRIDAY, a man he has saved from cannibals. Crusoe is finally rescued after spending twenty-eight years on the island.

🙠 Robinson Crusoe has come to symbolize a person who has the strength and resourcefulness to thrive in isolation.

"Rock-a-Bye, Baby"   A nursery RHYME:

> Rock-a-bye, baby, on the tree top;
> When the wind blows, the cradle will rock;
> When the bough breaks, the cradle will fall,
> And down will come baby, cradle and all!

romanticism   A movement in literature and the FINE ARTS, beginning in the early nineteenth century, that stressed personal emotion, free play of the imagination, and freedom from rules of form. Among the leaders of romanticism in English literature were William BLAKE, Lord BYRON, Samuel Taylor COLERIDGE, John KEATS, Percy Bysshe SHELLEY, and William WORDSWORTH.

Romeo and Juliet   A TRAGEDY by William SHAKESPEARE about two "STAR-CROSSED LOVERS" whose passionate love for each other ends in death because of the senseless feud between their families. The line "ROMEO, ROMEO! WHEREFORE ART THOU ROMEO?" is well known.

🙠 Figuratively, a "Romeo" is an amorous young man.

Romeo, Romeo! Wherefore art thou Romeo?   Words from the play *ROMEO AND JULIET*, by William SHAKESPEARE. (*Wherefore* means "why.") Juliet is lamenting Romeo's name, alluding to the feud between their two families. (*See* "WHAT'S IN A NAME? THAT WHICH WE CALL A ROSE / BY ANY OTHER NAME WOULD SMELL AS SWEET.")

Roots A NOVEL by the twentieth-century African-American author Alex HALEY, later made into a popular television drama. It traces a black American man's heritage to AFRICA, where his ancestors had been captured and sold as slaves.

Rose is a rose is a rose is a rose A line by Gertrude STEIN, suggesting, perhaps, that some things resist definition in words.

Sandburg, Carl An American author of the twentieth century. Sandburg's widely varied works include poems about the countryside and industrial heartland of the United States, especially "Chicago"; *Rootabaga Stories*, written for children; and a BIOGRAPHY of Abraham LINCOLN.

Scarlet Letter, The A NOVEL by Nathaniel HAWTHORNE about Hester Prynne, a woman in seventeenth-century NEW ENGLAND who is convicted of ADULTERY. At the beginning of the story, she is forced to wear a scarlet letter *A* on her dress as a sign of her guilt. Hester will not reveal the identity of her partner in adultery. Her husband comes to realize who her lover is and takes revenge on him. Eventually, her dying lover publicly admits his part in the adultery.

Scott, Sir Walter A Scottish author of the late eighteenth and early nineteenth centuries. Scott wrote immensely popular historical NOVELS, such as *Ivanhoe* and *Waverley*, and poems, including "The Lady of the Lake."

Scrooge, Ebenezer The central CHARACTER in *A CHRISTMAS CAROL*, by Charles DICKENS; a mean-spirited miser who discovers the meaning of Christmas.

   🐚 By extension, a "Scrooge" is a miserly person.

"Secret Life of Walter Mitty, The" A story by James THURBER about a henpecked husband with extravagant daydreams: he imagines himself as a heroic pilot in wartime, a world-famous surgeon, and a soldier who can face a firing squad without fear.

   🐚 An ordinary person who dreams of leading a romantic life may be called a "Walter MITTY."

"Self-Reliance" An ESSAY by Ralph Waldo EMERSON that advises the reader "Trust thyself" and argues that "whoso would be a man must be a noncon-

formist." It is the source of several well-known EPIGRAMS, such as "To be great is to be misunderstood" and "A FOOLISH CONSISTENCY IS THE HOBGOBLIN OF LITTLE MINDS."

Seuss, Dr. (SOOHS) The NOM DE PLUME of Theodor Seuss Geisel, an American author and illustrator of the twentieth century who produced dozens of books for children. Dr. Seuss's books, such as *How the GRINCH STOLE CHRISTMAS* and *The Cat in the Hat*, contain fantastic CHARACTERS and are written in whimsical VERSE such as: "I do not like green eggs and ham. / I do not like them, Sam I Am."

WILLIAM SHAKESPEARE. *The portrait of Shakespeare in the frontispiece of the* First Folio *(1623).*

Shakespeare, William An English playwright and poet of the late sixteenth and early seventeenth centuries, generally considered the greatest of writers in English. His plays include *ANTONY AND CLEOPATRA*, *AS YOU LIKE IT*, *HAMLET*, *JULIUS CAESAR*, *KING LEAR*, *MACBETH*, *THE MERCHANT OF VENICE*, *A MIDSUMMER NIGHT'S DREAM*, *OTHELLO*, *ROMEO AND JULIET*, *THE TAMING OF THE SHREW*, *THE TEMPEST*, and *TWELFTH NIGHT*. Shakespeare also wrote over 150 SONNETS. Many familiar sayings and quotations come from his works.

Shakespeare was born in Stratford-on-Avon. He spent most of his career in LONDON as an actor, playwright, and manager of the GLOBE THEATER. His success enabled him to retire to Stratford, where he died.

Shall I compare thee to a summer's day?   The first line of a SONNET by William SHAKESPEARE. The poet notes that beautiful days and seasons do not last, but declares that his love's "eternal summer shall not fade" because his poem makes his love immortal: "So long as men can breathe or eyes can see, / So long lives this, and this gives life to thee."

Shangri-La   A fictional land of peace and perpetual youth; the setting of the book *Lost Horizon*, a NOVEL from the 1930s by the English author James Hilton, but probably best known from the movie version. Shangri-La is supposedly in the mountains of TIBET.

🙠 A "Shangri-La," by extension, is an ideal refuge from the troubles of the world.

Shaw, George Bernard (G. B. S.)   An Irish author of the late nineteenth and early twentieth centuries; he spent most of his career in ENGLAND. A playwright, critic, and social reformer, Shaw was known for his outspokenness and barbed humor. His many plays include *PYGMALION*, *Androcles and the Lion*, *Man and Superman*, and *Saint Joan*.

Shelley, Percy Bysshe (BISH)   An English poet of the nineteenth century; one of the leaders of ROMANTICISM. His poems include "To a Skylark," "Ode to the West Wind," and "Ozymandias." Like John KEATS, he died at an early age.

🙠 Shelley's wife, Mary Wollstonecraft Shelley, wrote *FRANKENSTEIN*.

Ships that pass in the night   Words from a poem, "Elizabeth," by Henry Wadsworth LONGFELLOW. The full passage reads:

Ships that pass in the night, and speak each other
    in passing,
Only a signal shown and a distant voice in the
    darkness;
So on the ocean of life we pass and speak one
    another,
Only a look and a voice; then darkness again
    and a silence.

Shoot, if you must, this old gray head   A line from "Barbara Frietchie," a poem from the CIVIL WAR years by the American poet John Greenleaf Whittier, which describes a fictional incident in the war. Barbara Frietchie, aged over ninety, displays a UNION flag when CONFEDERATE troops march through her town. The soldiers shoot the flag off its staff, but Barbara Frietchie catches it, leans out the window, and addresses the soldiers: "'Shoot, if you must, this old gray head, / But spare your country's flag!' she said."

Shylock   The merciless moneylender in *THE MERCHANT OF VENICE*, by William SHAKESPEARE. He demands a POUND OF FLESH from the title CHARACTER of the play after the merchant defaults on his DEBT.

🙠 Shylock is a JEW; there has long been controversy over whether Shakespeare's portrayal of Shylock contributes to prejudice against Jews. Shylock is a cruel miser, and eventually is heavily fined and disgraced, but he maintains his dignity. At one point in the play, he makes a famous, eloquent assertion that his desire for revenge is the same desire that a CHRISTIAN would feel in his place. "I am a Jew," says Shylock. "Hath not a Jew eyes? Hath not a Jew hands, organs, dimensions, senses, affections, passions?"

"Simple Simon"   A nursery RHYME. These are the first two STANZAS:

Simple Simon met a pieman
Going to the fair:
Says Simple Simon to the pieman,
"Let me taste your ware."

Says the pieman to Simple Simon,
"Show me first your penny";
Says Simple Simon to the pieman,
"Indeed I have not any."

"Sing a Song of Sixpence"   A nursery RHYME. It begins:

Sing a song of sixpence,
A pocketful of rye,
Four-and-twenty blackbirds
Baked in a pie.

Slough of Despond (SLOW)   A "bog of discouragement" that figures in *THE PILGRIM'S PROGRESS*, by John Bunyan. The main CHARACTER loses heart and temporarily abandons his journey to the Celestial City when he encounters the Slough.

🙠 Figuratively, a "slough of despond" is any serious depression or discouragement.

Something is rotten in the state of Denmark   A line from the play *HAMLET*, by William SHAKESPEARE. An officer of the palace guard says this after the ghost of the dead king appears, walking over the palace walls.

🙠 "Something is rotten in the state of Denmark"

is used to describe corruption or a situation in which something is wrong.

star-crossed lovers A PHRASE from the play RO-MEO AND JULIET, by William SHAKESPEARE; Romeo and Juliet are so described in the prologue to the play.

🔊 "Star-crossed lovers" refers to any lovers whose affection for each other is doomed to end in tragedy.

Stein, Gertrude An American author of the twentieth century who lived most of her life in FRANCE. She wrote her life story as *The Autobiography of Alice B. Toklas* (Toklas was her companion), and she is said to have introduced the PHRASE "LOST GENERATION" to describe the Americans who wandered about EUROPE after WORLD WAR I. Her works also include poems and the story collection *Three Lives*; the most famous line from her poetry is "ROSE IS A ROSE IS A ROSE IS A ROSE."

Steinbeck, John An American author of the twentieth century, best known for his NOVELS, including *THE GRAPES OF WRATH*, *Of Mice and Men*, and *East of Eden*.

Steinem, Gloria A twentieth-century American author, journalist, and advocate of women's rights; one of the leaders of the WOMEN'S MOVEMENT. Steinem was a founder of *Ms.* magazine. (*See* Ms.)

Stevenson, Robert Louis A Scottish author of the nineteenth century. His works include *A Child's Garden of Verses*, *The Strange Case of DR. JEKYLL AND MR. HYDE*, and *TREASURE ISLAND*. The song "FIFTEEN MEN ON THE DEAD MAN'S CHEST" appears in *Treasure Island*, and a poem by Stevenson, "Requiem," contains the lines "HOME IS THE SAILOR, HOME FROM SEA, / AND THE HUNTER HOME FROM THE HILL."

Stowe, Harriet Beecher (STOH) An American author of the nineteenth century, best known for *UNCLE TOM'S CABIN*, a powerful NOVEL that inflamed sentiment against slavery.

🔊 During the CIVIL WAR, Abraham LINCOLN met Mrs. Stowe and is reputed to have said to her, "So you are the little woman who wrote the book that made this big war."

Streetcar Named Desire, A A play by Tennessee WILLIAMS about the decline and tragic end of

Blanche DuBois, a southern belle who, as she puts it, has "always depended on the kindness of strangers."

Sun Also Rises, The A NOVEL by Ernest HEMINGWAY about a group of young Americans living in EUROPE in the 1920s. It captures the disillusionment and cynicism of the LOST GENERATION.

sweetness and light A PHRASE popularized by the nineteenth-century English author Matthew Arnold; it had been used earlier by Jonathan SWIFT. According to Arnold, sweetness and light are two things that a CULTURE should strive for. "Sweetness" is moral righteousness, and "light" is intellectual power and truth. He states that someone "who works for sweetness and light united, works to make reason and the will of God prevail."

Swift, Jonathan An Irish author of the eighteenth century, known for his skill at SATIRE. Two of his best-known works are *GULLIVER'S TRAVELS* and "A MODEST PROPOSAL."

Taming of the Shrew, The A COMEDY by William SHAKESPEARE. The "shrew" is Katherina, or Kate, a wildly moody woman. She meets her match in the spirited Petruchio, who marries her and behaves even more wildly than she, meanwhile treating her as if she were a kind and gentle lady. By the end of the play, she has been reformed, and she makes a memorable speech urging wives to submit to their husbands.

🔊 The MUSICAL COMEDY *Kiss Me, Kate*, by Cole PORTER, is based on *The Taming of the Shrew*.

Tarzan A CHARACTER in popular NOVELS by Edgar Rice Burroughs. The son of an English nobleman, Tarzan grows up in AFRICA among a pack of apes, learns the ways of the jungle, and protects its inhabitants from outsiders. The first Tarzan book appeared in 1914.

🔊 Tarzan has a standard portrayal in films and comic books. He swings through the trees on long, sturdy vines, and announces his arrival with a loud yodel. 🔊 Tarzan's girlfriend is Jane. A famous bit of dialogue is "Me Tarzan, you Jane."

Tempest, The A play by William SHAKESPEARE, sometimes called a COMEDY but also called a ROMANCE — that is, a work involving mysterious happenings in an exotic place. The central CHARACTER is

Prospero, a duke who has been overthrown and banished to an island. As a sage and magician, he rules the spirits who inhabit the island. When the men who overthrew Prospero pass near the island on an ocean voyage, he raises a tempest, wrecks their ship, and causes them to be washed ashore. In the end, they give back to Prospero his former authority, and he gives up his magic.

&. Prospero's daughter, on first seeing a handsome young man, says, "O BRAVE NEW WORLD!" a PHRASE that is often quoted.

Tennyson, Alfred, Lord (TEN-uh-suhn)   An English poet of the nineteenth century, very popular in his own time; he was POET LAUREATE of BRITAIN for over forty years. Among his works are "THE CHARGE OF THE LIGHT BRIGADE," "Crossing the Bar," and *Idylls of the King* (a retelling of the legend of KING ARTHUR).

That way madness lies   A statement made by the title CHARACTER in the play *KING LEAR*, by William SHAKESPEARE. Lear has started to speak about the treachery of his two elder daughters, but then realizes that dwelling on the injury could drive him mad.

There was a little girl / Who had a little curl   The first lines of a children's poem by Henry Wadsworth LONGFELLOW:

> There was a little girl
> Who had a little curl
> Right in the middle of her forehead;
> And when she was good
> She was very, very good,
> But when she was bad she was horrid.

"There Was an Old Woman Who Lived in a Shoe"
A nursery RHYME:

> There was an old woman who lived in a shoe.
> She had so many children, she didn't know what
>   to do.
> She gave them all broth, without any bread,
> Then whipped them all soundly, and sent them
>   to bed.

They also serve who only stand and wait   The last line of the poem "On His Blindness," by John MILTON. The poet reflects that he has a place in God's world despite his disability.

thing of beauty is a joy forever, A   The first line of the poem "Endymion," by John KEATS.

Thirty days hath September   The first line of a popular RHYME for remembering the number of days in the months of the year:

> Thirty days hath September,
> April, June, and November;
> All the rest have thirty-one,
> February stands alone.

"This Little Piggy Went to Market"   A children's RHYME, to accompany a playful pulling at the five toes:

> This little piggy went to market.
> This little piggy stayed home.
> This little piggy had roast beef.
> This little piggy had none.
> This little piggy cried "Wee! Wee! Wee!"
>   all the way home.

Thoreau, Henry David (thuh-ROH, THAWR-oh)   An American author of the nineteenth century. Thoreau was a strong advocate of individual rights and an opponent of social CONFORMITY. His best-known works are the book *WALDEN* and an ESSAY, "CIVIL DISOBEDIENCE."

"Three Bears, The"   *See* "GOLDILOCKS AND THE THREE BEARS."

"Three Blind Mice"   A nursery RHYME and children's song:

> Three blind mice, see how they run!
> They all ran after the farmer's wife;
> She cut off their tails with a carving knife.
> Did you ever see such a sight in your life,
> As three blind mice?

"Three Pigs, The"   A children's story about three pigs, each of whom builds a house to be safe from the BIG BAD WOLF. The first pig makes a house of straw, and the second a house of sticks. Both finish quickly and spend their time amusing themselves, while the third pig is building a house of bricks. When the wolf arrives at the door of each house, he boasts, "I'll huff, and I'll puff, and I'll blow your house down." He succeeds with the houses of straw and sticks, so the first two pigs take refuge in the brick house, which the wolf cannot blow in. In some versions of the story, the wolf eats the first two pigs.

Through the Looking-Glass   The SEQUEL to *ALICE'S ADVENTURES IN WONDERLAND*, by Lewis

CARROLL. In it, Alice passes through a mirror over a fireplace and finds herself once more in an enchanted land, where she meets TWEEDLEDUM AND TWEEDLE-DEE, the White Knight, HUMPTY DUMPTY, and other amazing creatures.

Thurber, James An American author and cartoonist of the twentieth century; the author of "THE SECRET LIFE OF WALTER MITTY." His humorous drawings, short stories, and ESSAYS poke gentle fun at the lives and folly of men and women.

tide in the affairs of men, There is a A line from the play *JULIUS CAESAR*, by William SHAKESPEARE. Mark ANTONY and BRUTUS are on opposite sides of an armed conflict, and Brutus is urging his comrades to seize a fleeting opportunity: "There is a tide in the affairs of men / Which, taken at the flood, leads on to fortune."

Tiger! Tiger! burning bright The first line of the poem "The Tiger," from *Songs of Experience*, by William BLAKE. The first STANZA reads:

> Tiger! Tiger! burning bright
> In the forests of the night,
> What immortal hand or eye
> Could frame thy fearful symmetry?

Time's wingéd chariot A PHRASE from the seventeenth-century English poem "To His Coy Mistress," by Andrew Marvell. It appears in these lines: "But at my back I always hear / Time's wingéd chariot hurrying near."

Tiny Tim The handicapped son of Bob Cratchit, the employee of Ebenezer SCROOGE in *A CHRISTMAS CAROL*, by Charles DICKENS. He speaks the famous line "God bless us every one."

To be, or not to be Words from the play *HAMLET*, by William SHAKESPEARE. They begin a famous speech by Prince Hamlet in which he considers suicide as an escape from his troubles: "To be, or not to be: that is the question."

Tobacco Road A NOVEL from the 1930s by the American author Erskine Caldwell, about a family of sharecroppers (*see* SHARECROPPING) from GEORGIA and their many tragedies.

ᴥ *Tobacco Road* was made into a play that ran for several years on BROADWAY. ᴥ A "Tobacco Road" is a poor shantytown, usually in the rural South, and usually populated by whites.

Tom Sawyer, The Adventures of A NOVEL by Mark TWAIN; the title CHARACTER is a wily and adventurous boy. In one famous episode, Tom Sawyer tricks his friends into whitewashing a fence for him by pretending it is a great privilege and making them pay to take over the job.

ᴥ *The Adventures of HUCKLEBERRY FINN* is a SEQUEL to *Tom Sawyer*; Huck Finn is Tom's best friend.

Tom Thumb A thumb-sized hero of children's stories from the sixteenth century on.

Tomorrow, and tomorrow, and tomorrow A line from the play *MACBETH*, by William SHAKESPEARE, spoken by the title CHARACTER after he learns of his wife's death. The speech begins:

> Tomorrow, and tomorrow, and tomorrow,
> Creeps in this petty pace from day to day
> To the last SYLLABLE of recorded time. . . .

transcendentalism A movement in American literature and thought in the nineteenth century. It called on people to view the objects in the world as small versions of the whole UNIVERSE, and to trust their individual intuitions. The two most noted American transcendentalists were Ralph Waldo EMERSON, who wrote "SELF-RELIANCE," and Henry David THOREAU.

Treasure Island A NOVEL by Robert Louis STEVENSON about a young boy, Jim Hawkins, who joins with two men in hiring a ship to search for buried treasure. Among the ship's crew are the pirate Long John Silver and his men, who are after the treasure for themselves. With considerable pluck, and the aid of his friends, Jim foils their plans and gains the treasure.

"Trees" A poem from the early twentieth century by the American poet Joyce Kilmer.

Twain, Mark The NOM DE PLUME of Samuel L. CLEMENS, an American author and humorist of the late nineteenth and early twentieth centuries. He is famous for his stories with settings along the MISSISSIPPI RIVER; his books include *The Adventures of HUCKLEBERRY FINN*, *The Adventures of TOM SAWYER*, *Life on the Mississippi*, and *The Prince and the Pauper*.

MARK TWAIN. *In his Hartford, Connecticut, home, circa 1905.*

🍃 Twain, who was once a steamboat pilot, took his pen name from a term used in river navigation.

Tweedledum and Tweedledee Fictional CHARACTERS from *THROUGH THE LOOKING-GLASS*, by Lewis CARROLL. They are pictured as fat twins who are identical in speech, attitude, and appearance.

TWEEDLEDUM AND TWEEDLEDEE. *A drawing by John Tenniel.*

🍃 Figuratively, any two people or positions that have no real differences are said to be "like Tweedledum and Tweedledee."

Twelfth Night A COMEDY by William SHAKESPEARE. The two central CHARACTERS are a twin brother and sister; each thinks that the other has been lost at sea. The sister disguises herself as a boy and goes to serve the duke of the country, a bitter man disappointed in love. The brother reappears and marries the woman whom the duke has been pursuing, and his sister marries the duke. *Twelfth Night* begins with the line "IF MUSIC BE THE FOOD OF LOVE, PLAY ON."

"Twinkle, Twinkle, Little Star" A children's poem. Its first STANZA reads:

> Twinkle, twinkle, little STAR;
> How I wonder what you are!
> Up above the world so high
> Like a diamond in the sky,
> Twinkle, twinkle, little star!
> How I wonder what you are.

Uncle Tom's Cabin A NOVEL by Harriet Beecher STOWE; it paints a grim picture of life under slavery. The title CHARACTER is a pious, passive slave, who is eventually beaten to death by the overseer Simon LEGREE.

🍃 Published shortly before the CIVIL WAR, *Uncle Tom's Cabin* won support for the antislavery cause.
🍃 Although Stowe presents UNCLE TOM as a virtuous man, the expression "Uncle Tom" is often used today as a term of reproach for a subservient black person who tolerates discrimination.

Under the spreading chestnut tree The first line of "THE VILLAGE BLACKSMITH," a poem by Henry Wadsworth LONGFELLOW. It begins:

> Under the spreading chestnut tree
> The village smithy stands.
> The smith, a mighty man is he,
> With large and sinewy hands.

Vanity Fair A NOVEL from the middle of the nineteenth century by the English author William Makepeace Thackeray. The leading CHARACTER is Becky Sharp, an unscrupulous woman who gains wealth and influence by her cleverness.

Victorian A descriptive term for the time when VICTORIA was queen of ENGLAND, from 1837 to 1901. The VICTORIAN PERIOD in England is known as a time of industrial progress, colonial expansion, and public fastidiousness in morals. The Victorian period in the United States had many of the same characteristics.

"Village Blacksmith, The" A poem by Henry Wadsworth LONGFELLOW about a village blacksmith in NEW ENGLAND. It begins with the line "UNDER THE SPREADING CHESTNUT TREE."

Walden A book by Henry David THOREAU describing his two years of life alone at Walden Pond in MASSACHUSETTS. He recounts his daily life in the woods, and celebrates nature and the individual's ability to live independently of society. A famous line from the book is Thoreau's statement that "the MASS OF MEN LEAD LIVES OF QUIET DESPERATION."

"Waste Land, The" A poem by T. S. ELIOT, published shortly after the end of WORLD WAR I. Its subject is the fragmented and sterile nature of the modern world.

Water, water everywhere, / Nor any drop to drink Lines from "The RIME OF THE ANCIENT MARINER," by Samuel Taylor COLERIDGE. The speaker, a sailor on a becalmed ship, is surrounded by salt water that he cannot drink.

🐝 By extension, these lines are used to describe a situation in which someone is in the midst of plenty but cannot partake of it.

Watson, Dr. The companion of Sherlock HOLMES in the stories by Sir Arthur Conan DOYLE. Watson helps the great detective in his investigations and serves as an audience for Holmes's explanations of how he has solved the crimes. (*See* ELEMENTARY, MY DEAR WATSON.)

We are such stuff / As dreams are made on A line from the play *THE TEMPEST*, by William SHAKESPEARE; it continues, "and our little life / Is rounded with a sleep." It is spoken by the magician Prospero. He has just made a large group of spirits vanish, and is reminding his daughter and her fiancé that mortal life also ends quickly.

Wells, H. G. An English author of the late nineteenth and early twentieth centuries, much concerned with social and political reform. He wrote futuristic NOVELS such as *The War of the Worlds* and *The Time Machine*; historical and scientific works, such as *Outline of History*; and comic novels.

Wharton, Edith An American author of the late nineteenth and early twentieth centuries. Wharton is best known for *Ethan Frome*, a NOVEL.

What's in a name? That which we call a rose / By any other name would smell as sweet Lines from the play *ROMEO AND JULIET*, by William SHAKESPEARE. Juliet, prevented from marrying Romeo by the feud between their families, complains that Romeo's name is all that keeps him from her. (*Compare* "ROMEO, ROMEO! WHEREFORE ART THOU ROMEO?")

Whitman, Walt An American poet of the nineteenth century. His principal work is *LEAVES OF GRASS*, a collection of poems that celebrates nature, DEMOCRACY, and INDIVIDUALISM.

🐝 The earthiness of Whitman's poetry shocked many readers of his time. 🐝 Walt Whitman's rugged appearance is memorable, especially in his old age, when he wore a flowing white beard.

OSCAR WILDE. *A photographic portrait taken in 1882, during the poet's tour of the United States.*

Wilde, Oscar An Irish-born author of the late nineteenth century, who spent most of his career in ENGLAND. Wilde was famous for his flamboyant wit and style of dress. His best-known works include the NOVEL *The Picture of Dorian Gray*, the play *The Importance of Being Earnest*, and the poem "The Ballad of Reading Gaol" (jail). He urged ART FOR ART'S SAKE.

✒ Wilde was convicted of HOMOSEXUAL activity and spent about two years in prison. "The Ballad of Reading Gaol" is based on his experiences there.

Wilder, Thornton An American author of the twentieth century, best known for his play *OUR TOWN*.

Williams, Tennessee An American author of the twentieth century. Williams is famous for his plays, which portray ordinary people possessed of violent passions; these plays include *A STREETCAR NAMED DESIRE*, *Cat on a Hot Tin Roof*, and *The Glass Menagerie*.

Winnie-the-Pooh A stuffed toy bear who appears in several books for children by A. A. MILNE; the CHARACTERS in the *Pooh* books are mainly stuffed animals who have come to life. Winnie-the-Pooh has many adventures with the little boy Christopher Robin, his owner.

winter of our discontent, the A PHRASE from the historical play *King Richard the Third*, by William SHAKESPEARE; it describes a civil war in England.

✒ "The winter of our discontent" has come to suggest disaffection in general. The phrase served as the title for a book by John STEINBECK.

Wizard of Oz, The Wonderful A book from the early twentieth century by the American author L. Frank Baum. Dorothy, a little girl, is carried by a TORNADO from KANSAS to the enchanted land of Oz. After performing brave deeds for the mysterious wizard who rules Oz, in the hope that he will use his magic to send her home, she finds that he is only a circus performer who has convinced the people of the land that he is a wizard. Dorothy has three companions — a scarecrow who wants brains, a woodman made of tin who wants a heart, and a cowardly lion who wants courage. The wizard pretends to give these things to them, although they have had them all along without knowing it. Dorothy eventually returns to Kansas by using magic shoes.

✒ Although *The Wonderful Wizard of Oz* continues to attract readers, it is better known through its film adaptation, *The Wizard of Oz*, with Judy Garland as Dorothy. The film, released in 1939, is frequently televised.

Woolf, Virginia An English author of the twentieth century who experimented with STREAM-OF-CONSCIOUSNESS narrative technique. Her works include the NOVEL *To The Lighthouse* and the ESSAY "A Room of One's Own," which is about the problems of female artists.

Wordsworth, William An English poet of the nineteenth century; Wordsworth was one of the leading figures of ROMANTICISM. His poems include "Daffodils," which begins with the words "I WANDERED LONELY AS A CLOUD," "THE WORLD IS TOO MUCH WITH US," "ODE: Intimations of Immortality from Recollections of Early Childhood," and "The Prelude."

"World Is Too Much with Us, The" A SONNET by William WORDSWORTH, in which the poet complains that people are too attached to the trivial things of the world and not sufficiently aware of nature as a whole.

Wright, Richard An African-American author of the twentieth century, known for his NOVELS dealing with the black experience in the United States. Two of his best-known works are *BLACK BOY* and *NATIVE SON*.

Wuthering Heights A NOVEL by Emily BRONTË about the thwarted love of two young people, Catherine and Heathcliff, and the cruel suffering Heathcliff inflicts on all involved in their separation.

"Wynken, Blynken, and Nod" A children's bedtime poem by the American author Eugene Field, from the late nineteenth century. It begins, "Wynken, Blynken, and Nod one night / Sailed off in a wooden shoe. . . ."

Yahoos (YAH-hoohz) The crude, dirty "brutes" of the land of the Houyhnhnms in *GULLIVER'S TRAVELS*, by Jonathan SWIFT. The Yahoos are irrational people, and represent the worst side of humanity. By contrast, the wise and gentle Houyhnhnms, their masters, are rational horses, and represent humanity at its best.

✒ A "yahoo" is an uncouth or uncivilized person.

Yeats, William Butler (YAYTS) Irish poet of the late nineteenth and early twentieth centuries, regarded by many as the greatest modern poet in English. Some of his best-known poems are "Sailing to Byzantium," "The Second Coming," and "Among School Children."

Conventions
of Written English

Most young Americans will know most of the contents of this section fairly well. Our schools have done a good job in teaching the technical components of the language arts. Our elementary and secondary textbooks are replete with discussions of ABBREVIATIONS, dictionary use, punctuation, and PARTS OF SPEECH. Yet these textbooks are not always consistent among themselves in the matter of nomenclature. Should a NOUN be called a substantive, a nominative, a type-one word, a thing word, or just a noun? Although there isn't a clear answer to this question, there is a clear need for consistency in our textbooks and schools. It is pointless to confuse a student who comes into a new school district with a whole new set of descriptive terms about language. Language terms are, of course, essential for teaching language arts, but there is no excuse for making the terms difficult and confusing. Linguistic scholars and theorists agree that grammatical terms and categories are inherently arbitrary; there is no one right way to analyze language. The chief reason to analyze it at all is to create a shared vocabulary for talking about language in teaching the language arts.

One of our purposes in including this section of our dictionary is to help students by encouraging standardization of the vocabulary we use in teaching about language. Because we are convinced that there is little to choose in pedagogical usefulness between "substantive" and "thing-word," we have chosen to adopt only the most widely shared, and hence most traditional, terms. Thus, in this section a noun is a noun is a noun — not because traditional grammatical terms are best, but because standardized terms are best. The traditional grammatical vocabulary is completely adequate to the task of teaching reading, writing, speaking, and listening at the highest level of excellence. The notion that novel terms from modern linguistics can advance the teaching of these arts is a superstition that no profound scholar of the subject would be willing to argue.

— E. D. H.

abbreviation   A shortened form of an expression, usually followed by a PERIOD. *Dr.* is a standard abbreviation for *Doctor*; *Mass.* and *MA* are standard abbreviations for *Massachusetts*.

acronym (AK-ruh-nim)   A word formed by combining the beginning letters of a name or PHRASE, as in

WASP for *w*hite *A*nglo-*S*axon *P*rotestant, or by combining the initial SYLLABLES of a series of words, as in RADAR (*see under* "Technology"), which stands for *ra*dio *d*etecting *a*nd *r*anging.

☙ Acronyms are often less clumsy than the complete expressions they represent, and are easier to write and remember.

143

active voice   One of the two "voices" of VERBS (*see also* PASSIVE VOICE). When the verb of a sentence is in the active voice, the SUBJECT is doing the acting, as in the sentence "John hit the ball." John (the subject of the sentence) acts in relation to the ball.

A.D.   An ABBREVIATION used with a date, indicating how many years have passed since the birth of JESUS. The abbreviation may appear before the date (A.D. 1988), or it may appear after the date (1988 A.D.). It stands for *anno Domini*, a LATIN PHRASE meaning "in the year of our Lord." (*Compare* B.C.)

adjective   A PART OF SPEECH that describes a NOUN or PRONOUN. Adjectives are usually placed just before the words they qualify: *shy* child, *blue* notebook, *rotten* apple, *four* horses, *another* table.

adverb   A PART OF SPEECH that modifies a VERB, an ADJECTIVE, or another adverb. Adverbs usually answer such questions as "How?" "Where?" "When?" or "To what degree?" The following italicized words are adverbs: "He ran *well*"; "She ran *very well*"; "George is *highly* capable."

🔊 Adverbs are often formed by adding *-ly* to an adjective, as in *truly* or *deeply*.

agreement   A requirement for PARTS OF A SENTENCE in standard written English; the parts must agree, for example, in NUMBER and PERSON.

The SUBJECT and VERB of a CLAUSE or SIMPLE SENTENCE must agree in person, as in "*He is* a boy." The subject, *he*, and the verb, *is*, are both in the third person. The subject and verb also must agree in number, as in "*We are* girls." The subject, *we*, and the verb, *are*, are both PLURAL.

NOUNS and PRONOUNS must also agree in number, person, and GENDER, as in "Every *boy* must mind *his* manners." The noun *boy* and the pronoun *his* are both SINGULAR, are both in the third person, and are both masculine.

allegory   (AL-uh-gawr-ee)   A STORY that has a deeper or more general meaning in addition to its surface meaning. Allegories are composed of several SYMBOLS or METAPHORS. For example, in *THE PILGRIM'S PROGRESS*, by John Bunyan, the CHARACTER named Christian struggles to escape from a bog or swamp. The story of his difficulty is a symbol of the difficulty of leading a good life in the "bog" of this world. The "bog" is a metaphor or symbol of life's hardships and distractions. Similarly, when Christian loses a heavy pack that he has been carrying on his back, this symbolizes his freedom from the weight of sin that he has been carrying.

alliteration   (uh-lit-uh-RAY-shuhn)   The repetition of the beginning sounds of words, as in "Peter Piper picked a peck of pickled peppers," "long-lived," "short shrift," and "the fickle finger of fate."

allusion   An indirect reference to some piece of knowledge not actually mentioned. Allusions usually come from a body of information that the author presumes the reader will know. For example, an author who writes, "She was another Helen," is alluding to the proverbial beauty of HELEN OF TROY.

ampersand   (AM-puhr-sand)   A SYMBOL for *and* (&) as in Dun & Bradstreet.

analogy   (uh-NAL-uh-jee)   A comparison of two different things that are alike in some way (*see* METAPHOR *and* SIMILE). An analogy attributed to Samuel JOHNSON is: "Dictionaries are like watches; the worst is better than none, and the best cannot be expected to go quite true."

antonyms   (AN-tuh-nimz)   Two words with opposite meanings. *Cold* and *hot* are antonyms; so are *small* and *large*. (*Compare* SYNONYMS.)

aphorism   (AF-uh-riz-uhm)   A concise and often witty statement of wisdom or opinion, such as "Children should be seen and not heard," or "People who live in glass houses shouldn't throw stones."

apostrophe   (uh-POS-truh-fee)   A mark (') used with a NOUN or PRONOUN to indicate possession ("the student's comment," "the people's choice") or in a CONTRACTION to show where letters have been left out (*isn't, don't, we'll*).

articles   In GRAMMAR, the words *a, an,* and *the,* which precede a NOUN or its MODIFIER. *The* is the DEFINITE ARTICLE; *a* and *an* are INDEFINITE ARTICLES.

autobiography   A literary work about the writer's own life. The *CONFESSIONS* of AUGUSTINE and *THE AUTOBIOGRAPHY OF BENJAMIN FRANKLIN* are two classic autobiographies.

auxiliary verb   A "helping" VERB that modifies the main verb, as in "Gail *can* win," "Gail *did* win," "Gail *could have* won." A question often begins with an auxiliary verb: "*Did* Gail win?" "*Could* Gail lose?" The various forms of the verbs *can, have, is,* and *does* frequently act as auxiliaries.

ballad　A simple narrative song, or a narrative poem suitable for singing. The ballad usually has a short rhyming STANZA, such as:

> There are twelve months in all the year,
> As I hear many men say,
> But the merriest month in all the year
> Is the merry month of May.

B.C.　An ABBREVIATION used with dates of events that took place before the birth of JESUS. B.C. stands for *before Christ. (Compare* A.D.)

B.C.E.　An ABBREVIATION sometimes used in place of B.C. It means "before the CHRISTIAN era."

bibliography　A list of the written sources of information on a subject. Bibliographies generally appear as a list at the end of a book or article. They may show what works the author used in writing the article or book, or they may list works that a reader might find useful.

biography　The story of someone's life. *The Life of Samuel Johnson,* by James BOSWELL, and *Abraham Lincoln,* by Carl SANDBURG, are two noted biographies. The story of the writer's own life is an AUTO-BIOGRAPHY.

blank verse　VERSE written in IAMBIC PENTAMETER, without RHYME. Many of the speeches in the plays of William SHAKESPEARE are written in blank verse; this example is from *MACBETH*:

> Tomorrow, and tomorrow, and tomorrow,
> Creeps in this petty pace from day to day,
> To the last SYLLABLE of recorded time;
> And all our yesterdays have lighted fools
> The way to dusty death. Out, out, brief candle!
> Life's but a walking shadow, a poor player
> That struts and frets his hour upon the stage
> And then is heard no more: it is a tale
> Told by an idiot, full of sound and fury,
> Signifying nothing.

bowdlerizing　(BOHD-luh-reye-zing, BOWD-luh-reye-zing)　Amending a book by removing passages and words deemed obscene or objectionable (*see* OBSCEN-ITY). The name comes from Thomas Bowdler's 1818 edition of the plays of William SHAKESPEARE, which was amended so that it could "be read aloud in a family."

brackets　Marks — [ ] — resembling PARENTHESES with square corners. Brackets are often used within quotations to distinguish between the quoter's own words and those of the writer being quoted: "He [the president] made a memorable speech at Gettysburg."

capital letters　One of the two kinds of letters. Capital letters, also called UPPER-CASE LETTERS, are larger than, and often formed differently from, LOWER-CASE LETTERS. Capital letters are used at the beginning of a sentence or a proper name, and may be used to show respect. Some examples are: "*The* dog barked," Daniel, the Lord, and Queen Elizabeth.

case　A grammatical category indicating whether NOUNS and PRONOUNS are functioning as the SUBJECT of a sentence (NOMINATIVE CASE) or the OBJECT of a sentence (OBJECTIVE CASE), or are indicating possession (POSSESSIVE case). *He* is in the nominative case, *him* is in the objective case, and *his* is in the possessive case. In a language such as English, nouns do not change their form in the nominative or objective case. Only pronouns do. Thus, *ball* stays the same in both "the *ball* is thrown," where it is the subject, and in "John threw the *ball*," where it is the object.

cf.　An ABBREVIATION meaning "compare." It is short for the LATIN word *confer* and instructs the reader to compare one thing with another.

character　A person in a literary work. For example, Ebenezer SCROOGE is a character in *A CHRISTMAS CAROL,* by Charles DICKENS.

circumlocution　(sur-kuhm-loh-KYOOH-shuhn) Roundabout speech or writing: "The driveway was not unlike that military training device known as an obstacle course" is a circumlocution for "The driveway resembled an obstacle course." *Circumlocution* comes from LATIN words meaning "speaking around."

classicism　An approach to AESTHETICS that favors restraint, rationality, and the use of strict forms in literature, painting, architecture, and other arts. It flourished in ancient GREECE and ROME, and throughout EUROPE in the seventeenth and eighteenth centuries. Classicists often derived their models from the ancient Greeks and Romans.

🍂 Classicism is sometimes considered the opposite of ROMANTICISM.

clause   A group of words in a sentence that contains a SUBJECT and PREDICATE. (*See* DEPENDENT CLAUSE *and* INDEPENDENT CLAUSE.)

cliché   A much used expression that has lost its freshness and descriptive power. Some clichés are "I thank you from the bottom of my heart" and "It's only a drop in the bucket."

coherence   In writing, the clear connection of ideas in an orderly fashion.

colon   A punctuation mark (:) used to introduce a description, an explanation, or a list. For example, "She would own only one kind of pet: a Siamese cat" and "The little boy announced that he wanted the following for Christmas: two sweaters, a new tent, and three toy cars."

comedy   A work — play, story, NOVEL, or film — that ends happily for the main CHARACTER (or PROTAGONIST) and contains humor to some degree. A comedy may involve unhappy outcomes for some of the characters. SHYLOCK, for example, in *THE MERCHANT OF VENICE*, a comedy by William SHAKESPEARE, is disgraced in the play. The ancient Greeks and Romans produced comedies, and great numbers have been written in modern times.

comma   A punctuation mark (,) used to indicate pauses and to separate elements within a SENTENCE. "The forest abounds with oak, elm, and beech trees"; "The bassoon player was born in Roanoke, Virginia, on December 29, 1957."

comparative   A form of an ADJECTIVE indicating a greater degree of the quality that the adjective describes. *Better* is the comparative form of *good*; *faster* is the comparative form of *fast*; *bluer* is the comparative form of *blue*; *more charming* is the comparative form of *charming*. (*Compare* SUPERLATIVE.)

complex sentence   A sentence that contains one main CLAUSE or INDEPENDENT CLAUSE and at least one SUBORDINATE CLAUSE or DEPENDENT CLAUSE: "Although I am tired (subordinate clause), I want to go to the midnight movie (main clause)." (*See* SUBORDINATION; *compare* COMPOUND SENTENCE, COMPOUND-COMPLEX SENTENCE, *and* SIMPLE SENTENCE.)

compound sentence   A sentence that contains at least two INDEPENDENT CLAUSES, often joined by CONJUNCTIONS: "Dr. WATSON explained his theory, and Sherlock HOLMES listened quietly." (*Compare* COMPLEX SENTENCE, COMPOUND-COMPLEX SENTENCE, *and* SIMPLE SENTENCE.)

compound-complex sentence   A sentence that contains at least two INDEPENDENT CLAUSES and at least one DEPENDENT CLAUSE: "Queen Elizabeth was called a redhead (independent clause), but no one knew her hair color for sure (independent clause) because she always wore a wig (dependent clause)." "Because she always wore a wig" is a dependent clause starting with the subordinating CONJUNCTION (see SUBORDINATION) *because*. (*Compare* COMPLEX SENTENCE, COMPOUND SENTENCE, *and* SIMPLE SENTENCE.)

conciseness   Economy in writing or speaking. "Bill loves to go to the movies because watching films is a real pleasure to him" is not as concise as "Bill loves to watch movies." (*Compare* CIRCUMLOCUTION.)

conjunction   A word that joins words or groups of words. There are three kinds of conjunctions: coordinating, correlative, and subordinating. Coordinating conjunctions include *and, but, or, not, yet, for,* and *so*. Correlative conjunctions include the words in the pairs *either/or, both/and,* and *neither/nor*. Subordinating conjunctions begin SUBORDINATE CLAUSES and join them to the rest of the sentence: "She didn't learn the real reason *until* she left the valley."

connotation   The meaning that a word suggests or implies. A connotation includes the emotions or associations that surround a word.

consonants   Letters of the alphabet that stand for sounds often made with a closed or partially closed mouth: B, C, D, F, G, H, J, K, L, M, N, P, Q, R, S, T, V, W, X, Z, and sometimes Y (as in *yellow*). (*Compare* VOWELS.)

contraction   A word produced by running two or more words together and leaving out some of the letters or sounds. For example, *isn't* is a contraction of *is not*.

   ❧ An APOSTROPHE is generally used in contractions to show where letters or sounds have been left out.

coordination   The use of grammatical structures to give equal emphasis to, or to "coordinate," two or more words, groups of words, or ideas: "I like eggs and toast." In the following sentences, each CLAUSE receives equal emphasis: "Mr. Jones teaches French, and Ms. Williams teaches English"; "Mr. Jones teaches French, but Ms. Williams teaches English." (*Compare* SUBORDINATION.)

copyright The legal protection given to published works, forbidding anyone but the author from publishing or selling them. An author can transfer the copyright to another person or corporation, such as a publishing company.

🔊 The SYMBOL for copyright is ©.

couplet A pair of lines of VERSE that RHYME. Some poems, such as "THE NIGHT BEFORE CHRISTMAS," are written entirely in couplets:

'Twas the night before CHRISTMAS, when all through
  the house
Not a creature was stirring, not even a mouse;
The stockings were hung by the chimney with care
In hopes that St. NICHOLAS soon would be there.

dash A punctuation mark (—) used to indicate a sudden break in thought, to set off parenthetical material, or to take the place of such expressions as *that is* and *namely*: "He's running for reelection — if he lives until then"; "Very few people in this class — three, to be exact — have completed their projects"; "She joined the chorus for only one reason — she loves to sing." In the last example, where the parenthetical material comes at the end of the sentence rather than in the middle, a COLON could be used instead of the dash.

dead languages Languages that are no longer spoken.

🔊 Some dead languages, such as LATIN, ancient Greek, and SANSKRIT, may nevertheless be studied by large numbers of people because of their literary or historical importance.

declarative sentence In GRAMMAR, the kind of sentence that makes a statement or "declares" something: "He eats yogurt."

definite article The word *the*; the ARTICLE that precedes names of specific items: "the dog," "the boats," "the heavy anchor." (*Compare* INDEFINITE ARTICLE.)

demonstrative pronouns PRONOUNS that point to specific things: *this, that, these,* and *those,* as in "This

is an apple," "Those are boys," or "Take these to the clerk." The same words are used as demonstrative ADJECTIVES when they modify NOUNS or pronouns: "this apple," "those boys."

denotation (dee-noh-TAY-shuhn) The basic dictionary meaning of a word, without its CONNOTATIONS. For example, the denotation of the word *modern* is "belonging to recent times," although the word may have different connotations.

dénouement (day-nooh-MAHNN) The solution or outcome of the PLOT of a play or NOVEL: "In the dénouement of many TRAGEDIES, the main CHARACTER dies."

dependent clause A CLAUSE that does not stand alone as a sentence but depends on another clause to complete its meaning: "*When I get my braces off*, I will be very happy." Dependent clauses are also known as SUBORDINATE CLAUSES. (*Compare* INDEPENDENT CLAUSE.)

Dewey decimal system A system used in libraries for the classification of books and other publications. It uses the numbers 000 to 999 to cover the general fields of knowledge and subdivides each field by the use of DECIMALS and letters. Named after its inventor, Melvil Dewey.

diction The choice of words. Diction is effective when words are appropriate to an audience. A man might refer to his car as his "wheels" in casual conversation with a friend, but if he were writing an ESSAY for a group of economists, he would write, "People base their decision to buy an automobile on the following considerations," not "People base their decision to buy wheels on the following considerations."

Diction can also mean the quality of pronunciation, especially in singing.

direct object A NOUN, PRONOUN, or group of words serving as the receiving end of an action, such as *the ball* in "John hit the ball." A direct object can be a word, PHRASE, or CLAUSE: "Sam chose *Rusty* to play shortstop"; "I will never understand *why he came home*." (*Compare* INDIRECT OBJECT.)

double-entendre (dub-uhl-ahn-TAHN-druh; dooh-blahnn-TAHNN-druh) A word or expression that has two different meanings (in French, *double-entendre* means "double meaning"), one of which is often bawdy or indelicate. A double-entendre is found in this sentence: "A nudist camp is simply a place where men and women meet to air their differences."

draft A preliminary version of a book, speech, ESSAY, or outline.

dramatis personae (DRAM-uh-tis puhr-SOH-nee, DRAH-muh-tis puhr-SOH-neye) A LATIN expression for "cast of CHARACTERS." It means literally "the persons of the drama," and is occasionally used at the beginning of scripts for plays as the title of the list of characters.

    In general, the "dramatis personae" are the participants in an event: "CHURCHILL, ROOSEVELT, and STALIN were the dramatis personae at the Yalta Conference."

editorial An article in a newspaper or magazine expressing the opinion of the editor or publisher.

e.g. An ABBREVIATION meaning "for example." It is short for the LATIN *exempli gratia*, "for the sake of example." A list of examples may be preceded by *e.g.*: "She loved exotic fruit, e.g., mangoes, passion fruit, and papayas."

elegy (EL-uh-jee) A form of poetry that mourns the loss of someone who has died or something that has deteriorated. A notable example is the "ELEGY WRITTEN IN A COUNTRY CHURCHYARD," by Thomas GRAY. (*Compare* EULOGY.)

ellipsis (i-LIP-sis) A punctuation mark (. . .) used most often within quotations to indicate that something has been left out. For example, if we leave out parts of the above definition, it can read: "A punctuation mark (. . .) used most often . . . to indicate . . ."

epic A long narrative poem written in elevated style, in which heroes of great historical or legendary importance perform valorous deeds. The setting is vast in scope, covering great nations, the world, or the UNIVERSE, and the action is important to the history of a nation or people. The *ILIAD*, the *ODYSSEY*, and the *AENEID* are some great epics from world literature, and two great epics in English are *BEOWULF* and *PARADISE LOST*.

    Figuratively, any task of great magnitude may be called an "epic feat" or an "epic undertaking."

epigram Any pithy, witty saying or short poem. An APHORISM can serve as an epigram, if it is brief.

    Several authors are noted for their epigrams, including Mark TWAIN and Oscar WILDE. One of Wilde's epigrams is "I can resist everything except temptation."

essay A short piece of writing on one subject, usually presenting the author's own views. Michel de MONTAIGNE, Francis BACON, and Ralph Waldo EMERSON are celebrated for their essays.

et al. (et ahl) An ABBREVIATION of the LATIN *et alii*, meaning "and others." "She was accompanied by the vice president, the SECRETARY OF STATE, et al."

eulogy (YOOH-luh-jee) Words of praise, often for a dead person, but also a staple in introducing speakers, in nominating candidates, and on other such occasions. (*Compare* ELEGY.)

euphemism (YOOH-fuh-miz-uhm) An agreeable word or expression substituted for one that is potentially offensive, often having to do with bodily functions, sex, or death; for example, *rest room* for *toilet*, *lady of the evening* for *prostitute*. The NAZIS used euphemism in referring to their plan to murder the world's JEWS as "the FINAL SOLUTION."

exclamation point A punctuation mark (!) used after an abrupt and emphatic statement or after a command: "'Help!' he cried, as his boat floated toward the edge of NIAGARA FALLS."

exeunt (EK-see-uhnt, EK-see-oont) A STAGE DIRECTION indicating that two or more actors leave the stage. *Exeunt* is LATIN for "They go out."

expletive (EK-spluh-tiv) Any exclamation or oath, especially one that is obscene or profane, as in "Goddammit, I forgot to buy the milk."

    The OVAL OFFICE tapes of President Richard NIXON, released during the investigation of the WATERGATE SCANDAL, made famous the PHRASE "expletive deleted," which appeared frequently in expurgated transcripts of the tapes.

expurgate (EK-spuhr-gayt) To clean up, remove impurities. An expurgated edition of a book has had offensive words or descriptions changed or removed.

fallacy A false or mistaken idea based on faulty knowledge or reasoning. For example, kings who have divorced their wives for failing to produce a son have held to the fallacy that a mother determines the sex of a child, when actually the father does. (*See* SEX CHROMOSOMES.)

fiction Literature that is a work of the imagination and is not necessarily based on fact. Some examples of works of fiction are *THE GREAT GATSBY*, by F. Scott FITZGERALD, and *GULLIVER'S TRAVELS*, by Jonathan SWIFT.

folklore Traditional stories and legends, transmitted orally (rather than in writing) from generation to generation. The stories of Paul BUNYAN are examples of American folklore.

four-letter words Obscene (*see* OBSCENITY) or very vulgar words of four letters, such as *piss*. Most four-letter words refer to excretion or sex.

free verse VERSE without regular METER or RHYME. *LEAVES OF GRASS*, by Walt WHITMAN, is written almost entirely in free verse.

gender A grammatical category indicating the sex, or lack of sex, of NOUNS and PRONOUNS. The three genders are masculine, feminine, and neuter. *He* is a masculine pronoun; *she* is a feminine pronoun; *it* is a neuter pronoun. Nouns are classified by gender according to the gender of the pronoun that can substitute for them. In English, gender is directly indicated only by pronouns.

genre (ZHAHN-ruh) The kind or type of a work of art, from the French, meaning "kind" or "GENUS." Literary genres include the NOVEL and the SONNET. Musical genres include the CONCERTO and the SYMPHONY. Film genres include Westerns and horror movies.

gerund (JER-uhnd) A form of a VERB that ends in -*ing* and operates as a NOUN in a sentence: "*Thinking* can be painful."

grammar The rules for standard use of words. A grammar is also a system for classifying and analyzing the elements of language.

homonyms (HOM-uh-nimz) Two words that sound alike and may even be spelled alike but have different meanings, such as *trunk* (meaning part of an elephant) and *trunk* (meaning a storage chest). Often used with the same meaning as HOMOPHONE.

homophones (HOM-uh-fohnz, HOH-muh-fohnz) Two words that sound alike. This category includes words that are spelled the same, such as *trunk* (of an elephant) and *trunk* (a storage chest), as well as words spelled differently, such as *deer* and *dear*.

hyperbole (heye-PUR-buh-lee) An exaggerated, extravagant expression. It is hyperbole to say, "I'd give my whole fortune for a bowl of bean soup."

hyphen A punctuation mark (-) used in some compound words, such as *self-motivation*, *seventy-five*, and *mother-in-law*. A hyphen is also used to divide a word at the end of a line of type. Hyphens may appear only *between* SYLLABLES. Thus *com-pound* is properly hyphenated, but *compo-und* is not.

iambic pentameter (eye-AM-bik pen-TAM-uh-tuhr) The most common METER in English VERSE. It consists of a line ten SYLLABLES long that is accented on every second beat (*see* BLANK VERSE). These lines in iambic pentameter are from *THE MERCHANT OF VENICE*, by William SHAKESPEARE:

> Ĭn sóoth,/Ĭ knów/nŏt whý/Ĭ ăm/sŏ sád.
> Ĭt wéa/riĕs mé;/yŏu sáy/ĭt wéa/riĕs yóu. . . .

ibid. An ABBREVIATION for *ibidem*, a LATIN word meaning "in the same place." It is used in footnotes and BIBLIOGRAPHIES to refer to a source cited in a previous entry.

idiom A traditional way of saying something. Often an idiom, such as "under the weather," does not seem to make sense if taken literally. Someone unfamiliar with English idioms would probably not understand that to be "under the weather" is to be sick. (*See examples under "Idioms."*)

i.e. An ABBREVIATION for *id est*, a LATIN PHRASE meaning "that is." It indicates that an explanation or PARAPHRASE is about to follow: "Most workers expect to put in a forty-hour week — i.e., to work eight hours a day."

imagery The mental pictures created by a piece of writing: "The imagery of 'THE WASTE LAND' — crumbling towers, dried-up wells, toppled tombstones — conveys the author's sense of a civilization in decay."

imperative A grammatical category describing VERBS that command or request: "*Leave* town by tonight"; "Please *hand* me the spoon."

in medias res (in MAY-dee-uhs, MEE-dee-uhs RAYS) In the middle of the action. EPICS often begin in medias res. For example, the ODYSSEY, which tells the story of the wanderings of the hero ODYSSEUS, begins almost at the end of his wanderings, just before his arrival home. *In medias res* is a LATIN PHRASE used by the poet HORACE; it means "in the middle of things."

indefinite article   The word *a* or *an* introducing an unspecified NOUN or the name of a general category: "a dog," "an apple," "an orange." *An* is used when the next word begins with a VOWEL or a silent (unpronounced) *h*, as in "an egg" or "an hour."

indentation   A space left between the left-hand margin of a line of type or handwriting and the beginning of a sentence or quotation. The beginning of a PARAGRAPH is usually indented.

independent clause   A CLAUSE that can stand alone as a sentence. The following sentence consists of two independent clauses joined by *but*: "The farmers complained of the low price of food, but the office workers did not." (*Compare* DEPENDENT CLAUSE.)

index   An alphabetical list of subjects treated in a book. It usually appears at the end of the book, and identifies page numbers on which information about each subject appears.

indirect object   A NOUN, PRONOUN, or group of words naming something indirectly affected by the action of a VERB: "She showed *me* some carpet samples"; "The agent handed *the Prentice family* their tickets."

    🙠 Indirect objects can often take or suggest the PREPOSITION *to*. For example, "She showed (to) *me* the book."

infinitive   The simple or dictionary form of a VERB: *walk, think, fly, exist*. Often the word *to* marks a verb as an infinitive: "to walk," "to think," "to fly," "to exist."

inflection   A change in the form of a word to reflect different grammatical functions of the word in a SENTENCE. English has lost most of its inflections. Those that remain are chiefly POSSESSIVE (*'s*), as in "the *boy's* hat"; PLURAL (*-s*), as in "the three *girls*"; and past TENSE (*-d* or *-ed*), as in *cared*. Other inflections are found in PRONOUNS — as in *he, him, his* — and

in irregular words such as *think/thought, child/children*, and *mouse/mice*.

interjection   A brief exclamation, often containing only one word: "Oh!" "Gee!" "Good grief!" "Ouch!"

interrogative sentence   The kind of sentence that asks a question and uses a QUESTION MARK: "How can I do that?"

intransitive verb   A VERB that does not need a DIRECT OBJECT to complete its meaning. *Run, sleep, travel, wonder*, and *die* are all intransitive verbs. (*Compare* TRANSITIVE VERB.)

    🙠 Some verbs can be intransitive in one SENTENCE and transitive in another. *Boiled* is intransitive in "My blood boiled" but transitive in "I boiled some water."

irony   The use of words to mean something very different from what they appear on the surface to mean. Jonathan SWIFT uses irony in "A MODEST PROPOSAL" when he suggests the eating of babies as a solution to overpopulation and starvation in IRELAND.

irregular verb   A VERB in which the past TENSE is not formed by adding the usual *-ed* ending. Examples of irregular verbs are *sing* (past tense *sang*); *feel* (*felt*); and *go* (*went*). (*Compare* REGULAR VERB.)

italics   Slanted letters that look like this: *We the people*. Italics are most often used to emphasize certain words, to indicate that they are in a foreign language, or to set off the title of a literary or artistic work.

jargon   A special language belonging exclusively to a group, often a profession. Engineers, lawyers, doctors, tax analysts, and the like all use jargon to exchange complex information efficiently. Jargon is often unintelligible to those outside the group that uses it. For example, here is a passage from a COMPUTER manual with the jargon italicized: "The *RZ887-x current loop interface* allows the computer to use a *centronics blocked duplex protocol*. (*See* SLANG.)

juvenilia (jooh-vuh-NIL-ee-uh)   Works produced in childhood or youth, particularly written or artistic works.

leading question An unfair question that is designed to guide the respondent: "You were drunk the night of the accident, weren't you, Mr. Norris?"

limerick A form of humorous five-line VERSE, such as:

> There once was a young man from Kew
> Who found a dead mouse in his stew.
>   Said the waiter, "Don't shout
>   Or wave it about,
> Or the rest will be wanting one too!"

lower-case letters "Small letters"; letters of the alphabet that are not CAPITAL, or UPPER-CASE, LETTERS.

lyric A kind of poetry, generally short, characterized by a musical use of language. Lyric poetry often involves the expression of intense personal emotion. The ELEGY, the ODE, and the SONNET are forms of the lyric poem.

malapropism (MAL-uh-prop-iz-uhm) A humorous confusion of words that sound vaguely similar, as in "We have just ended our physical year" instead of "We have just ended our FISCAL YEAR."

&. Mrs. MALAPROP, a CHARACTER in an eighteenth-century British COMEDY, *The Rivals*, by Richard Brinsley Sheridan, constantly confuses words. Malapropisms are named after her.

melodrama A play or film in which the PLOT is often sensational, and the CHARACTERS may display exaggerated emotion.

metaphor The comparison of one thing to another without the use of *like* or *as*: "A man is but a weak reed"; "The road was a ribbon of moonlight." Metaphors are common in literature and expansive speech. (*Compare* SIMILE.)

meter The highly organized RHYTHM characteristic of VERSE; the pattern of stressed and unstressed SYLLABLES in a line. (*See* IAMBIC PENTAMETER.)

modifier A word or group of words that describes or limits a VERB, NOUN, ADJECTIVE, or ADVERB. Modifiers applied to nouns are adjectives. Modifiers applied to verbs or adjectives are adverbs. Those that are applied to adverbs themselves are also called adverbs.

motif (moh-TEEF) In literature, art, or music, a recurring set of words, shapes, colors, or notes. In the poem "THE RAVEN," by Edgar Allan POE, for example, the word *nevermore* is a motif appearing at the end of each STANZA. Likewise, the first four notes of the Fifth Symphony of Ludwig van BEETHOVEN are a motif that is developed and reshaped throughout the work.

Ms. A title used before a woman's name, pronounced "Miz," and corresponding to *Mr.* before a man's.

&. Feminists have urged the use of *Ms.* because, unlike *Miss* or *Mrs.*, it does not identify a woman by her marital status. A leading feminist magazine is called *Ms.* (*See* FEMINISM.)

mythology The body of myths belonging to a CULTURE. Myths are traditional stories about gods and heroes. They often account for the basic aspects of existence — explaining, for instance, how the EARTH was created, why people have to die, or why the year is divided into seasons. CLASSICAL MYTHOLOGY — the myths of the ancient Greeks and Romans — has had an enormous influence on European and American culture.

narration The recounting of an event or series of events; the act of telling a story.

narrator A person who tells a story; in literature, the voice that an author takes on to tell a story. This voice can have a PERSONALITY quite different from the author's. For example, in his story "The Tell-Tale Heart," Edgar Allan POE makes his narrator a raving lunatic.

N.B. An ABBREVIATION for the LATIN PHRASE *nota bene*, meaning "note well." It is used to emphasize an important point.

nom de plume (nom di PLOOHM) French for "pen name"; an invented name under which an author writes. Mark TWAIN was the nom de plume of Samuel L. CLEMENS.

nominative case (NOM-uh-nuh-tiv) The grammatical term indicating that a NOUN or PRONOUN is the SUBJECT of a sentence or CLAUSE rather than its OBJECT. (*See* CASE *and* OBJECTIVE CASE.)

non sequitur (non SEK-wuh-tuhr) A thought that does not logically follow what has just been said:

"We had been discussing plumbing, so her remark about ASTROLOGY was a real non sequitur." *Non sequitur* is LATIN for "It does not follow."

noun   The PART OF SPEECH that names a person, place, thing, or idea. The following words are nouns: *child*, *town*, *granite*, *kindness*, *government*, *elephant*, and *Taiwan*. In sentences, nouns generally function as SUBJECTS or as OBJECTS.

novel   A long, fictional NARRATION in prose. *GREAT EXPECTATIONS* and *HUCKLEBERRY FINN* are novels, as is *WAR AND PEACE*.

nuance (NOOH-ahns)   A fine shade of meaning: "I liked the film, but I know I missed some of its nuances."

number   The grammatical category that classifies a NOUN, PRONOUN, or VERB as SINGULAR or PLURAL. *Woman*, *it*, and *is* are singular; *women*, *they*, and *are* are plural.

object   A PART OF A SENTENCE; a NOUN, PRONOUN, or group of words that receives or is affected by the action of a VERB. (*See* DIRECT OBJECT, INDIRECT OBJECT, *and* OBJECTIVE CASE.)

objective case   A grammatical term indicating that a NOUN or PRONOUN is an OBJECT. (*See* CASE *and* NOMINATIVE CASE.)

ode   A kind of poem devoted to the praise of a person, animal, or thing. An ode is usually written in an elevated style and often expresses deep feeling. An example is "ODE ON A GRECIAN URN," by John KEATS.

oxymoron (ok-see-MAWR-on)   A RHETORICAL DEVICE in which two seemingly contradictory words are used together for effect: "She is just a poor little rich girl."

paradox   A statement that seems contradictory or absurd but is actually valid or true. According to one proverbial paradox, we must sometimes be cruel in order to be kind. Another form of paradox is a statement that truly is contradictory and yet follows logically from other statements that do not seem open to objection. If someone says, "I am lying," for example, and we assume that his statement is true, it must be false. The paradox is that the statement "I am lying" is false if it is true.

paragraph   A basic unit of prose. It is usually composed of several sentences that together develop one central idea.

paraphrase   A restatement of speech or writing that retains the basic meaning while changing the words. A paraphrase often clarifies the original statement by putting it into words that are more easily understood.

parentheses   Punctuation marks — ( ) — used to separate elements in a sentence. Parentheses subordinate (*see* SUBORDINATION) the material within them so that readers save most of their attention for the rest of the sentence: "Aunt Sarah (who is really my mother's cousin) will be visiting next week."

parody   In art, music, or literature, a SATIRE that mimics the style of its object.

participle (PAHR-tuh-sip-uhl)   The VERB form that combines with an AUXILIARY VERB to indicate certain TENSES.

The present participle is formed by adding -*ing* to the infinitive; it indicates present action: "The girl is *swimming*"; "I am *thinking*." (*Compare* GERUND.)

The past participle usually ends in -*ed*; it indicates completed or past action: "The gas station has *closed*"; "The mayor had *spoken*."

Participles may also function as ADJECTIVES: "Your mother is a *charming* person"; "This is a *talking* parrot"; "*Spoken* words cannot be revoked."

A "dangling" participle is one that is not clearly connected to the word it modifies: "*Standing* at the corner, two children walked past me." A better version of this example would be, "While I was standing at the corner, two children walked past me."

parts of a sentence   Classifications of words, PHRASES, and CLAUSES according to the way they figure in sentences. (*See* AUXILIARY VERB, CONJUNCTION, DEPENDENT CLAUSE, DIRECT OBJECT, INDEPENDENT CLAUSE, INDIRECT OBJECT, MODIFIER, PREDICATE, *and* SUBJECT.)

parts of speech   Classifications of words according to their relations to each other and to the things they represent. Different parts of speech name actions, name the performers of actions, describe the performers or actions, and so on. The common parts of speech are ADJECTIVES, ADVERBS, ARTICLES, CONJUNCTIONS, INTERJECTIONS, NOUNS, PREPOSITIONS, PRONOUNS, and VERBS.

passim (PAS-im) A word used in footnotes and similar material to indicate that a word or subject occurs frequently. For example, an entry in an INDEX reading "coal: 78-86 passim" means that coal is mentioned throughout pages 78 to 86. *Passim* is LATIN for "throughout" or "here and there."

passive voice One of the two "voices" of VERBS (*see also* ACTIVE VOICE). A verb is in the passive voice when the SUBJECT of the sentence is acted on by the verb. For example, in "The ball was thrown by the pitcher," *the ball* (the subject) receives the action of the verb, and *was thrown* is in the passive voice. The same sentence cast in the active voice would be, "The pitcher threw the ball."

pastoral (PAS-tuhr-uhl) A work of art that celebrates the cultivated enjoyment of the countryside. The poem "The Passionate Shepherd to His Love," by Christopher Marlowe, is a pastoral. Its first STANZA reads:

> Come live with me, and be my love;
> And we will all the pleasures prove
> That hills and valleys, dales and fields,
> Woods or steepy mountain yields.

period A punctuation mark (.) that ends a DECLARATIVE SENTENCE. A period is also used in ABBREVIATIONS such as *Mr.* and *Dr.*

person An inflectional form (*see* INFLECTION) of PRONOUNS and VERBS that distinguishes between the person who speaks (first person), the person who is spoken to (second person), and the person who is spoken about (third person). The pronoun or verb may be SINGULAR or PLURAL. For example:

> first person singular: I walk.
> second person singular: you walk.
> third person singular: he/she/it walks.
> first person plural: we walk.
> second person plural: you walk.
> third person plural: they walk.

personal pronoun A PRONOUN that represents a person in a sentence. Personal pronouns have different forms depending on their CASE, GENDER, and NUMBER, as follows:

SINGULAR	PLURAL
nominative: I, you, he, she, it	we, you, they
objective: me, you, him, her, it	us, you, them
possessive: my, mine, your, yours, his, her, hers, its	our, ours, your, yours, their, theirs

phrase A group of grammatically connected words within a sentence: "*One council member* left *in a huff*"; "She got *much satisfaction* from *planting daffodil bulbs*." Unlike CLAUSES, phrases do not have both a SUBJECT and a PREDICATE.

plagiarism Literary theft. Plagiarism occurs when a writer duplicates another writer's language or ideas and then calls the work his or her own. COPYRIGHT laws protect writers' words as their legal property. To avoid the charge of plagiarism, writers take care to credit those from whom they borrow and quote.

❧ Similar theft in music or other arts is also called plagiarism.

plot The organization of events in a work of FICTION.

plural The grammatical category in NOUNS, PRONOUNS, and VERBS that refers to more than one thing. Most NOUNS become plural with the addition of *-s* or *-es*: *hats*, *chairs*, *dishes*, *countries*, and so on. Some nouns form the plural in other ways, as in *children*, *feet*, *geese*, and *women*. (*Compare* SINGULAR; *see* AGREEMENT.)

possessive The CASE of a NOUN or PRONOUN that shows possession. Nouns are usually made possessive by adding an APOSTROPHE and *s*: "The bicycle is *Sue's*, not *Mark's*." Possessive pronouns can take the place of possessive nouns: "The bicycle is *hers*, not *his*." (*See* NOMINATIVE CASE *and* OBJECTIVE CASE.)

predicate (PRED-i-kuht) The part of a sentence that shows what is being said about the SUBJECT. The predicate includes the main VERB and all its MODIFIERS. In the following sentence, the italicized portion is the subject, and everything that follows forms the predicate: "*Olga's dog* was the ugliest creature on four legs."

prefix Letters placed in front of a word to form a new word: "*tri*monthly," "*semi*monthly," "*bi*lingual," "*multi*lingual," "*a*ddress," "*re*dress," "*pre*date," "*post*date." (*Compare* SUFFIX.)

preposition A PART OF SPEECH that indicates the relationship, often spatial, of one word to another. For example, "She paused *at* the gate"; "This tomato is ripe *for* picking"; and "They talked the matter over head *to* head." Some common prepositions are *at*, *by*, *for*, *from*, *in*, *into*, *on*, *to*, and *with*.

pronoun   A word that takes the place of a NOUN. *She*, *herself*, *it*, and *this* are examples of pronouns. If we substituted pronouns for the nouns in the sentence "Please give the present to Karen," it would read "Please give *it* to *her*."

protagonist   (proh-TAG-uh-nist)   The principal CHARACTER in a literary work. HAMLET, for example, is the protagonist of the play by William SHAKE-SPEARE that bears his name.

proverb   A brief, memorable saying that expresses a truth or belief, such as "A FRIEND IN NEED IS A FRIEND INDEED." (*See examples under "Proverbs."*)

pun   A humorous substitution of words that are alike in sound but different in meaning (*see* DOUBLE-ENTENDRE), as in this passage from *ALICE'S ADVENTURES IN WONDERLAND*, by Lewis CARROLL:

> "And how many hours a day did you do lessons?"
>   said Alice, in a hurry to change the subject.
> "Ten hours the first day," said the Mock Turtle,
>   "nine the next, and so on."
> "What a curious plan!" exclaimed Alice.
> "That's the reason they're called lessons," the
>   Gryphon remarked: "because they lessen from
>   day to day."

purple passage   Speech or writing full of ornate or flowery language.

question mark   A punctuation mark (?) that follows a direct question: "Is Ralph really seven feet tall?"

quotation marks   Punctuation marks (" ") that set off dialogue, quoted material, titles of short works, and definitions. When something must be quoted inside a quotation, single quotation marks are used: "'Religion,' according to Marx, 'is the opiate of the masses.'"

realism   An attempt to make art and literature resemble life. Realist painters and writers take their subjects from the world around them (instead of from idealized subjects such as figures in MYTHOLOGY or FOLKLORE), and try to represent them in a lifelike manner.

rebuttal   A reply intended to show fault in an opponent's argument.

redundancy   Unnecessary repetition in speech or writing. The expression "freedom and liberty" is redundant.

reference works   Books and other works that contain useful facts and information, such as dictionaries, encyclopedias, and BIBLIOGRAPHIES.

refrain   In some pieces of VERSE, a set of words repeated at the end of each STANZA.

regular verb   A VERB that follows standard patterns in its INFLECTION. The past TENSE of a regular verb is formed by adding an *-ed* ending: walk, walk*ed*; shout, shout*ed*. (*Compare* IRREGULAR VERB.)

rhetorical question   A question posed without expectation of an answer but merely as a way of making a point: "You don't expect me to go along with that crazy scheme, do you?"

rhyme   A similarity of sound between words, such as *moon*, *spoon*, *croon*, *tune*, and *June*. Rhyme is often employed in VERSE.

roman à clef   (roh-MAHN ah KLAY)   A NOVEL in which actual people and places are disguised as FICTIONAL CHARACTERS. *Roman à clef* is French for "novel with a key."

Roman numerals   Letters of the alphabet used in ancient ROME to represent numbers: I = 1; V = 5; X = 10; L = 50; C = 100; D = 500; M = 1000. The numbers one through ten are written I, II, III, IV, V, VI, VII, VIII, IX, and X. Roman numerals are often used to signify divisions of a long work, or of a work with many parts. They are also used to lend significance to something, as in SUPER BOWL VII. Formal designation of years may also be in Roman numerals: A.D. MCMLXXXIX = A.D. 1989.

romance   In traditional literary terms, a NARRATION of the extraordinary exploits of heroes, often in exotic or mysterious settings. Most of the stories of King ARTHUR and his KNIGHTS are romances.

The term *romance* has also been used for stories of mysterious adventures, not necessarily of heroes. Like the heroic kind of romance, however, these adventure romances usually are set in distant places. SHAKESPEARE's play *THE TEMPEST* is this kind of romance.

Today, a NOVEL concerned mainly with love is often called a romance. Romances are frequently published in paperback series.

romanticism A movement that shaped all the arts in the late eighteenth and early nineteenth centuries. Romanticism generally stressed the essential goodness of human beings (*see* ROUSSEAU, JEAN-JACQUES), celebrated nature rather than civilization, and valued emotion and imagination over reason. (*Compare* CLASSICISM.)

run-on sentence A grammatically faulty sentence in which two or more main or INDEPENDENT CLAUSES are joined without a word to connect them or a punctuation mark to separate them: "The fog was thick he could not find his way home." The error can be corrected by adding a CONJUNCTION ("The fog was thick and he could not find his way home") or by separating the two clauses with a SEMICOLON ("The fog was thick; he could not find his way home").

sarcasm A form of IRONY in which apparent praise conceals another, scornful meaning. For example, a sarcastic remark directed at a person who consistently arrives fifteen minutes late for appointments might be, "Oh, you've arrived exactly on time!"

satire A work of literature that mocks social conventions, another work of art, or anything its author thinks ridiculous. *GULLIVER'S TRAVELS*, by Jonathan SWIFT, is a satire directed at eighteenth-century British society.

science fiction Works of FICTION that use scientific discoveries or advanced technology — either actual or imaginary — as part of their PLOT. Jules VERNE and H. G. WELLS were early writers of science fiction. More recent ones are Isaac Asimov, Ray Bradbury, and Arthur C. Clarke.

semicolon A punctuation mark (;) used to join two INDEPENDENT CLAUSES in a sentence. The semicolon shows that the ideas in the two clauses are related: "Jack really didn't mind being left without a car; he had the house to himself."

sequel A narrative or dramatic work complete in itself but designed to follow an earlier one. *THROUGH THE LOOKING-GLASS* is a sequel to *ALICE'S ADVENTURES IN WONDERLAND*; *The Adventures of Huckleberry Finn* is a sequel to *The Adventures of Tom Sawyer*.

sic A LATIN word for "thus," used to indicate that an apparent error is part of quoted material and not an editorial mistake: "The learned geographer asserts that 'the capital of the United States is Washingtown [*sic*].'"

simile (SIM-uh-lee) A common figure of speech that explicitly compares two things usually considered different. Most similes are introduced by *like* or *as*: "The realization hit me like a bucket of cold water." (*Compare* METAPHOR.)

     Some similes, such as "sleeping like a log," have become CLICHÉS.

simple sentence A sentence containing only one INDEPENDENT CLAUSE and no DEPENDENT CLAUSES: "He went home after class." (*Compare* COMPLEX SENTENCE, COMPOUND SENTENCE, *and* COMPOUND-COMPLEX SENTENCE.)

singular In NOUNS, PRONOUNS, and VERBS, the grammatical form that refers to only one thing. In the following sentence, the singular words are italicized: "The *policeman stops anyone who crosses* before the *light changes*." (*Compare* PLURAL; *see* AGREEMENT.)

slang Expressions that do not belong to standard written English. For example, "flipping out" is slang for "losing one's mind" or "losing one's temper." Slang expressions are usually inappropriate in formal speech or writing. (*See* JARGON.)

sonnet A LYRIC poem of fourteen lines, often about love, that follows one of several strict conventional patterns of RHYME. Elizabeth Barrett BROWNING, John KEATS, and William SHAKESPEARE are poets known for their sonnets.

split infinitive An INFINITIVE is the "to" form of a VERB, as in "to play." A split infinitive is a PHRASE in which *to* is separated from the verb. The sentence "I decided to quickly and directly go home" contains a split infinitive. Some people consider it poor style, or even incorrect style, to split an infinitive.

spoonerism A reversal of sounds in two words, with humorous effect. Spoonerisms were named after William Spooner, an English clergyman and scholar of the late nineteenth and early twentieth centuries. In one spoonerism attributed to him, he meant "May I show you to another seat?" but said, "May I sew you to another sheet?"

stage direction Part of the script of a play that tells the actors how they are to move or to speak their lines. *Enter*, *exit*, and EXEUNT are stage directions.

stanza   A group of lines of VERSE, usually set off from other groups by a space. The stanzas of a poem often have the same internal pattern of RHYMES.

stereotype   A too-simple and therefore distorted image of a group, such as "Football players are stupid" or "Frenchmen are short."

stream of consciousness   A kind of writing that presents the thoughts of a person or CHARACTER as they occur. Stream-of-consciousness writing uses such devices as characters speaking to themselves, free association, and lists of words. William FAULKNER, James JOYCE, and Virginia WOOLF wrote stream-of-consciousness NOVELS.

subject   A part of every sentence. The subject tells what the sentence is about; it contains the main NOUN or noun PHRASE: "The *car* crashed into the railing"; "*Judy and two of her friends* were elected to the National Honor Society." In some cases the subject is implied: *you* is the implied subject in "Get me some orange juice." (*Compare* PREDICATE.)

subjunctive   A grammatical form of VERBS implying hypothetical action or condition. Subjunctives are italicized in these sentences: "If Mr. Stafford *were* [not "was"] fluent in French, he could communicate with his employees more effectively"; "If Sheila *had been* here, she would have helped us with our math."

subordinate clause   In a sentence, a CLAUSE that depends on another clause for its meaning. (*See* SUBORDINATION.)

subordination   The use of expressions that make one element of a sentence dependent on another. In the following sentence, the first (italicized) CLAUSE is subordinate to the second clause: "*Despite all efforts toward a peaceful settlement of the dispute*, war finally broke out." (*Compare* COORDINATION, DEPENDENT CLAUSE, *and* INDEPENDENT CLAUSE.)

suffix   A letter or a group of letters added to the end of a word to change its meaning. For example, adding the suffix *-ter* to the ADJECTIVE *hot* turns it into the COMPARATIVE adjective *hotter*, and adding the suffix *-ly* to the adjective *quick* turns it into the ADVERB *quickly*. Other examples of words with suffixes are: "will*ing*," "manage*ment*," "service*able*," "harmon*ize*," and "joy*ful*." (*Compare* PREFIX.)

superlative   The form of an ADJECTIVE indicating the greatest degree of the quality that the adjective describes. *Best* is the superlative form of *good*; *fastest* is the superlative form of *fast*; *most charming* is the superlative form of *charming*. The usual superlative takes the ending *-est*. (*Compare* COMPARATIVE.)

syllable   A basic unit of speech generally containing only one VOWEL sound. The word *basic* contains two syllables (*ba-sic*). The word *generally* contains four (*gen-er-al-ly*). (*See* HYPHEN.)

symbol   An object or name that stands for something else, especially a material thing that stands for something that is not material. The bald eagle is a symbol of the United States of America. The cross is a symbol of Christianity.

synonyms   Words that mean roughly the same thing. *Container* and *receptacle* are synonyms.

syntax   The sequence in which words are put together to form sentences. In English, the usual sequence is SUBJECT, VERB, and OBJECT.

🔊 Syntactic languages, such as English, use word order to indicate word relationships. Inflected languages (*see* INFLECTION), such as Greek and LATIN, use word endings and other inflections to indicate relationships.

tense   An inflectional (*see* INFLECTION) form of VERBS; it expresses the time at which the action described by the verb takes place. The major tenses are past, present, and future. The verb in "I sing" is in the present tense; in "I sang," past tense; in "I will sing," future tense. Other tenses are the present perfect ("I have sung"), the past perfect ("I had sung"), and the future perfect ("I will have sung").

theme   A central idea in a piece of writing or other work of art: "The theme of desperation is found throughout his NOVELS." Also a short composition assigned to a student as a writing exercise.

thesis   The central idea in a piece of writing, sometimes contained in a TOPIC SENTENCE.

thriller   A suspenseful, sensational story or film.

topic sentence   The main sentence in a PARAGRAPH, often the first sentence. It briefly conveys the essential idea of the paragraph.

tragedy   A serious drama in which a central CHARACTER, the PROTAGONIST — usually an important, heroic person — meets with disaster either through some personal fault or through unavoidable circumstances. In most cases, the protagonist's downfall conveys a sense of human dignity in the face of great conflict. Tragedy originated in ancient Greece in the works of AESCHYLUS, SOPHOCLES, and EURIPIDES. In modern times, it achieved excellence with William SHAKESPEARE in such works as *HAMLET*, *KING LEAR*, *MACBETH*, and *OTHELLO*. Twentieth-century tragedies include *DEATH OF A SALESMAN*, by Arthur Miller, and *Murder in the Cathedral*, by T. S. ELIOT.

ə♣ ARISTOTLE argued that the proper effect of tragedy is CATHARSIS — the purging of the emotions.

ə♣ In common usage, disasters of many kinds are called tragedies.

transitive verb A VERB that needs a DIRECT OBJECT to complete its meaning. *Bring*, *enjoy*, and *prefer* are transitive verbs. (*Compare* INTRANSITIVE VERB.)

ə♣ Some verbs can be transitive in one sentence and intransitive in another: *turned* is transitive in "Brenda turned the wheel sharply" but intransitive in "Fred turned when I called."

understatement A form of IRONY in which something is intentionally represented as less than it is: "Babe Ruth was a pretty good ball player."

upper-case letters CAPITAL LETTERS. (*Compare* LOWER-CASE LETTERS.)

verb A word that represents an action or a state of being. *Go*, *strike*, *travel*, and *exist* are examples of verbs. A verb is the essential part of the PREDICATE of a SENTENCE. The grammatical forms of verbs include NUMBER, PERSON, and TENSE. (*See* AUXILIARY VERB, INFINITIVE, INTRANSITIVE VERB, IRREGULAR VERB, PARTICIPLE, REGULAR VERB, *and* TRANSITIVE VERB.)

verse A kind of language made intentionally different from ordinary speech or prose. It usually employs such devices as METER and RHYME, though not always. FREE VERSE, for example, has neither meter nor rhyme. Verse is usually considered a broader category than poetry, with the latter being reserved to mean verse that is serious and genuinely artistic.

vowels Letters of the alphabet that generally stand for sounds made with an open or partially open mouth: A, E, I, O, U, and sometimes Y (as in *style*). (*Compare* CONSONANTS.)

Fine Arts

The term *FINE ARTS* is equivalent to the older French term *beaux arts*, meaning "beautiful arts." In ancient GREECE, the fine arts were presided over by the MUSES, whence the word *museum* — a place where fine arts are displayed. Because museums of fine arts have tended to display mainly painting and sculpture, these are the arts we first think of as belonging to the fine arts. But in fact they comprise all artistic works, including literature, architecture, drama, music, dance, OPERA, and even up-to-date kinds like television and movies. In fact, any work that is exceptionally well crafted may be so described, as in the oft-heard statement that somebody has raised furnituremaking or penmanship or bookbinding "to the level of a fine art." Thomas de Quincey, an English writer of the early nineteenth century, entitled an ESSAY "On Murder as One of the Fine Arts."

When people hear the term *cultural literacy*, they sometimes associate it with artistic CULTURE — with opera, BALLET, painting, poetry, sculpture, architecture, and CLASSICAL MUSIC. These fine arts are, of course, only part of cultural literacy, but they do make up an important domain of experience that people must be aware of in order to communicate with other literate people in our society. For many people, the appreciation of the fine arts helps bring satisfaction, joy, and meaning to life; and every person deserves to be exposed to good art, whether popular or classical. But an old and true PROVERB tells us there is no disputing about taste. People who dislike ballet or BACH are not therefore unworthy or insensitive people. Nor is the art of our tradition inherently superior to that of other traditions. Yet whether the fine arts bring richness to our personal lives or we prefer other forms of enrichment, every citizen does need an acquaintance with the enduring artistic works and artists of our tradition, if only because they are indispensable reference points for our shared lives.

But not all of these enduring works of our tradition are *permanent* reference points — unchanging monuments that will never be replaced by new works of art. New classics sometimes displace older ones, just as new buildings rise upon old ruins. But our cities wisely discriminate among the buildings that they permit to be torn down. Some buildings, such as the WHITE HOUSE, the EMPIRE STATE BUILDING, and the TAJ MAHAL, deserve to be preserved both because of their artistic excellence and because of their symbolic and communal associations.

This section of our dictionary contains not only the Taj Mahal but also the WORLD TRADE CENTER; it contains both the old and the new in the fine arts. Our principle for inclusion is not personal opinion about the merits of particular art or artists, but our judgment of their established status as enduring points of reference in our culture. Everything that is included here is a classic — not because it is old or new, but because it has achieved broad currency. People refer to these works and artists without explanation, assuming that we will understand their reference. The arts are not just occasions for private appreciation and enrichment. Many of the images and songs and poems in our shared life are not only fine art but also indispensable SYMBOLS of our national existence. Indeed, much fine art of the past was not just something to be admired for its beauty but also something to be understood as part of public life. Bach's religious music, the Egyptian PYRAMIDS, the WASHINGTON MONUMENT, the American flag, and patriotic songs were and are living parts of communal life. The image of the CROSS and of the STAR OF DAVID are more than formal designs. At their most reverberant, the fine arts are not *just* objects for private pleasure and contemplation, but essential symbols that have helped define what we collectively are.

— E. D. H.

abstract art A trend in painting and sculpture in the twentieth century. Abstract art seeks to break away from traditional representation of physical objects. It explores the relationships of forms and colors, whereas more traditional art represents the world in recognizable images.

Academy Awards Prizes given annually in HOLLYWOOD by the Academy of Motion Picture Arts and Sciences for excellence in film performance and production. The SYMBOL of the award is a small statue called an OSCAR. The academy's best-known awards are for best picture, best director, best actor and actress, and best supporting actor and actress.

a cappella (ah kuh-PEL-uh) Choral singing performed without instruments. The expression means "in chapel style" in Italian. Centuries ago, religious music composed for use in chapels, which, unlike large CHURCHES, had no organs, was usually for voices only.

Acropolis (uh-KROP-uh-lis) The fortified high point of ancient ATHENS. Once the center of Athenian life, the Acropolis is now the site of famous ruins, including the PARTHENON. In Greek, the word means "high" (*acro*) "city" (*polis*).

adagio (uh-DAH-joh, uh-dah-zhee-oh) A very slow musical TEMPO.

"Adeste Fideles" (ah-DES-tay fi-DAY-lis) The original LATIN version of the Christmas carol "O COME, ALL YE FAITHFUL."

Aïda (eye-EE-duh) An OPERA by Giuseppe VERDI. The title CHARACTER is an Ethiopian princess who loves an Egyptian warrior, Rhadames. He accidentally reveals Egyptian military secrets to her, and is condemned to death by live burial in a tomb. Aida flees, but rejoins Rhadames to die with him.

🔊 *Aïda* is a particularly spectacular opera, with lavish sets, costumes, and extras — actors who have no singing parts. The "Triumphal March" from *Aïda* is often played separately by ORCHESTRAS.

allegretto (al-uh-GRET-oh, ah-luh-GRET-oh) A moderately fast musical TEMPO, not as fast as ALLEGRO.

allegro (uh-LEG-roh, uh-LAY-groh) A brisk, lively musical TEMPO. *Allegro* is Italian for "cheerful."

Allen, Woody An American comic author of the twentieth century. Since the late 1960s, he has been directing films and acting in them, usually playing a neurotic, bookish New Yorker (*see* NEW YORK CITY). Some of his best-known films are *Annie Hall*, *Manhattan*, and *Hannah and Her Sisters*.

alto The lowest range of the female singing voice, also called contralto. (*Compare* MEZZO SOPRANO *and* SOPRANO.)

"Amazing Grace" A popular CHRISTIAN hymn.

"America" An American patriotic hymn from the nineteenth century, sung to the tune of the national anthem of BRITAIN, "God Save the Queen." It begins, "MY COUNTRY, 'TIS OF THEE. . . . "

"America the Beautiful" An American patriotic hymn from the nineteenth century. It begins, "O BEAUTIFUL FOR SPACIOUS SKIES. . . ."

American Gothic A painting by the twentieth-century American artist Grant Wood. It shows a gaunt farmer and a woman standing in front of a farmhouse; the man holds a pitchfork, and both wear severe expressions.

AMERICAN GOTHIC. *Grant Wood's painting* American Gothic, *1930, oil on beaver board, 76 × 63.6 cm, Friends of American Art Collection, 1930.934. Copyright © 1988 The Art Institute of Chicago. All Rights Reserved.*

❧ *American Gothic* has been the subject of many PARODIES on magazine covers and in advertising.

andante (ahn-DAHN-tay) A steady, moderately slow musical TEMPO (*andante* is Italian for "walking"). Andante is not as slow as ADAGIO.

Anderson, Marian An African-American CON-TRALTO of the twentieth century, known for her roles in OPERA, and also for her performances of SPIRI-TUALS.

❧ In 1941, a planned concert by Anderson to be staged in Constitution Hall was blocked by the Daughters of the American Revolution (DAR), who owned the hall, because she was black. With the support of the president, Franklin ROOSEVELT, and his wife, Eleanor, Anderson gave a free concert on the steps of the LINCOLN MEMORIAL, which was attended by over 75,000 people. ❧ Anderson was the first black person to sing with the METROPOLITAN OPERA of NEW YORK CITY.

arch In architecture, a curved or pointed opening that spans a doorway, window, or other space.

❧ The form of arch used in building often serves to distinguish styles of architecture from one another. For example, ROMANESQUE architecture usually employs a round arch, and GOTHIC architecture a pointed arch.

aria (AHR-ee-uh) A piece of music for one voice (or occasionally two voices) in an OPERA, ORATORIO, or CANTATA. In contrast with RECITATIVE singing, arias are melodious; in contrast with ordinary songs, arias are usually elaborate.

❧ Arias often serve to display the talents of individual singers. ❧ Some composers, such as Richard WAGNER, have felt that arias interrupt the action of opera too much, and hence have written operas without them.

Armstrong, Louis An African-American JAZZ TRUMPET player and singer of the twentieth century. He rose to fame in the 1920s, enjoyed a long career, and died in 1971. His nickname, "Satchmo," was short for "Satchel Mouth." Armstrong was celebrated for his trumpet solos and the gravelly voice in which he sang songs such as "Hello, Dolly."

art for art's sake A slogan meaning that the beauty of the FINE ARTS is reason enough for carrying them on — that art does not have to serve purposes taken from politics, religion, ECONOMICS, and so on. Samuel Taylor COLERIDGE, Edgar Allan POE, and Oscar WILDE argued for the doctrine of art for art's sake.

❧ *Ars Gratia Artis*, the motto of the film company Metro-Goldwyn-Mayer (MGM), is a LATIN version of "art for art's sake."

Astaire, Fred An American entertainer of the twentieth century; he danced in many film MUSICALS with Ginger ROGERS, with other partners, and alone. He was admired for his speed and grace, and for his apparently effortless approach to dancing.

Audubon, John James (AW-duh-bon) An American artist and naturalist of the nineteenth century. The color illustrations that make up *The Birds of America* are his best works.

"Auld Lang Syne" (awld lang ZEYEN, SEYEN) A traditional Scottish song, customarily sung on New Year's Eve; the title means "Time Long Past." The words were handed down orally; the eighteenth-cen-

JOHANN SEBASTIAN BACH

tury poet Robert BURNS wrote them down. The song begins:

> Should auld [old] acquaintance be forgot,
> And never brought to min'?
> Should auld acquaintance be forgot,
> And auld lang syne!

Bach, Johann Sebastian (BAHKH, BAHK) A German composer, organist, and choirmaster of the eighteenth century, commonly considered the greatest composer of the BAROQUE era. His output was enormous, and includes CANTATAS, CONCERTOS, ORATORIOS, organ pieces, SONATAS for solo instruments, and SUITES for both solo instruments and ORCHESTRA; all of it is marked by elaborate COUNTERPOINT. Some of Bach's best-known works are the six *Brandenburg Concertos*; the Toccata and Fugue in D-minor for organ; and an arrangement of a hymn, "Jesu, Joy of Man's Desiring," for chorus and orchestra.

Baker, Josephine African-American actress, dancer, singer, and civil rights activist of the twentieth century. She gained her international reputation first in EUROPE. After WORLD WAR II, she was decorated by the French government for her work in the RESISTANCE, and at her death she was given a state funeral as a war hero.

ballad A simple narrative song, or, alternatively, a narrative poem suitable for singing. (*See under "Conventions of Written English."*)

JOSEPHINE BAKER. *In a typically flamboyant costume worn for one of her Parisian performances.*

ballerina In BALLET, a female dancer. (*See* PRIMA BALLERINA.)

ballet Theatrical entertainment in which dancers, usually accompanied by music, tell a story or express a mood through their movements. The technique of ballet is elaborate, and requires many years of training. Two classical ballets are *SWAN LAKE* and *THE NUTCRACKER*, composed by Peter Ilyich TCHAIKOVSKY. Two great modern ballets are *The Rite of Spring*, composed by Igor STRAVINSKY, and *Fancy Free*, by Leonard BERNSTEIN.

banjo A stringed musical instrument, played by plucking (*see* STRINGS). The banjo has a percussive sound, and is much used in FOLK MUSIC and BLUEGRASS music.

Barber of Seville, The   An OPERA by Gioacchino Rossini. The title CHARACTER is FIGARO, a master schemer. By his trickery, he helps his former master, a nobleman, win the hand of a beautiful woman.

barbershop singing   A style of singing in parts for small groups, usually four singers of the same sex ("barbershop QUARTETS"). The notes sung by the voices are usually close to each other in pitch, resulting in "tight" CHORDS, or "close" HARMONY.

    ❧ Barbershop singing flourished in the early twentieth century in the United States, and barbershop groups today often prefer the songs from that period, such as "Sweet Adeline" and "The Sweetheart of Sigma Chi."

baritone   A range of the male singing voice higher than BASS and lower than TENOR.

Barnum, Phineas T.   An American showman and entertainer of the nineteenth century; Barnum is mainly known for his circus, "The Greatest Show on Earth." His sideshows were particularly notable, even though many of the "freaks" he advertised turned out to be hoaxes, put together from parts of stuffed animals and the like (a mermaid, for example, was put together from a monkey and a fish). Barnum also managed the career of a celebrated dwarf, General Tom Thumb. After Barnum's death, his circus was absorbed into the Ringling Brothers and Barnum & Bailey Circus.

    ❧ According to a famous story about Barnum, someone pointed out that many customers had reason to be angry at him, because they paid their admission and then found out that the freaks in his show were fakes. Barnum supposedly replied that he was not worried about losing business because, in his words, "There's a sucker born every minute."

baroque (buh-ROHK)   A period in the arts, visual and musical, from about 1600 to about 1750, marked by elaborate ornamentation and efforts to create dramatic effects. In music, Johann Sebastian BACH, George Frederick HANDEL, and Antonio VIVALDI were great composers of the baroque era.

Barrymore family   A family of American actors of the late nineteenth and early twentieth centuries. The most famous of them were John and Lionel Barrymore and their sister, Ethel, all of whom appeared frequently on the stage and in films. The dashing-looking John was known as the "Great Profile."

Basie, Count (BAY-see)   An African-American JAZZ pianist and bandleader of the twentieth century. His real first name was William.

basilica (buh-SIL-uh-kuh)   A large ROMAN CATHOLIC or EASTERN ORTHODOX CHURCH building. A basilica is built with several parallel aisles separated by rows of columns, ending in a semicircular structure, the apse. SAINT PETER'S BASILICA is the church of the VATICAN in ROME.

bas-relief (bah ruh-LEEF)   A kind of carving or sculpture in which the figures are raised a few inches from a flat background to give a three-dimensional effect. The term is French for "low relief."

bass   The lowest range of the male singing voice. (*Compare* BARITONE *and* TENOR.)

bass drum   The large drum with a cylindrical shape that gives the strong beat in BRASS BANDS.

bass viol (VEYE-uhl)   The largest and lowest-pitched instrument of the STRINGS, also called a bass FIDDLE or DOUBLE BASS. The player must stand or sit on a tall stool to play it.

bassoon   The second largest and second lowest pitched of the WOODWINDS. (The less common contrabassoon is larger and has a lower pitch.) It is played with a double REED.

baton   A stick used by some conductors of choruses or ORCHESTRAS. The baton is traditionally used to indicate the TEMPO of the music.

"Battle Hymn of the Republic"   An American patriotic hymn from the CIVIL WAR by Julia Ward Howe, who wrote it after a visit to an encampment of the UNION army. The tune is that of "JOHN BROWN'S BODY"; "Glory, glory, hallelujah" is part of the REFRAIN.

Bauhaus (BOW-hows)   A German school of applied arts of the early twentieth century; its aim was to bring persons working in architecture, modern technology, and the decorative arts together to learn from one another. The school developed a style that was spare, functional, and geometric (*see* GEOMETRY).

Bauhaus designs for buildings, chairs, teapots, and many other objects are highly prized today, but when the school was active, it was generally unpopular. The Bauhaus was closed by the NAZIS, but its members spread its teachings throughout the world.

Bauhaus movement   *See* BAUHAUS.

Beale Street   A street in an African-American section of MEMPHIS, TENNESSEE, famous for its BLUES music. It is memorialized in the famous "Beale Street Blues."

Beatles   A ROCK 'N' ROLL singing group from ENGLAND that was phenomenally popular in the middle and late 1960s. The intense devotion of the group's fans, especially the hysterical screaming that the Beatles provoked in large crowds of teenagers, was called Beatlemania. The four Beatles were John Lennon, Paul McCartney, George Harrison, and Ringo Starr. Among their most popular songs, most of which were written by Lennon and McCartney, were "I Want to Hold Your Hand" and "Hey, Jude."

Beethoven, Ludwig van (BAY-toh-vuhn)   A German composer of the late eighteenth and early nineteenth centuries, whose works spanned the CLASSIC and romantic musical traditions (*see* ROMANTICISM). Considered one of the greatest composers of all time, he is particularly well known for his *MOONLIGHT SONATA* and other SONATAS for PIANO; for his STRING QUARTETS; for his CONCERTOS; and for his nine SYMPHONIES. The Third (*Eroica*), Fifth, and NINTH ("Choral") Symphonies are the most famous.
  ❧ Beethoven began to grow deaf midway through his career, but continued to compose great works.

Benny, Jack   An American comedian of the twentieth century, best known for his weekly radio and television programs. Benny was admired for his sense of timing, and for his deliberately slow delivery. His shows contained great numbers of "running gags" — jokes continued from one show to another — often concerning his age and his stinginess.

Berlin, Irving   A twentieth century American writer of popular songs (words and music). His songs include "GOD BLESS AMERICA," "WHITE CHRISTMAS," and "There's No Business like Show Business."

Bernhardt, Sarah (BURN-hahrt, ber-NAHR)   A French actress of the late nineteenth and early twentieth cen-

LUDWIG VAN BEETHOVEN. *A print by Kriehuber, after a painting by Stieler, depicting Beethoven composing* Missa Solemnis.

turies. A brilliant performer, she was considered the queen of French TRAGEDY.

Bernstein, Leonard (BURN-steyen)   An American composer and conductor of the twentieth century. He is best known for his music for plays, such as *West Side Story*, and for several years' service as music director of the NEW YORK Philharmonic ORCHESTRA.

Berry, Chuck   African-American ROCK 'N' ROLL musician and composer, who influenced many musicians of the 1950s and 1960s, including the BEATLES and Bob DYLAN.

Big Ben   The popular name for the huge clock mounted in a tower near the meeting place of the British PARLIAMENT in LONDON. Big Ben strikes the quarter-hour with the familiar Westminster chimes.

Birth of a Nation, The   A dramatic silent film from 1915 about the CIVIL WAR. *The Birth of a Nation* was directed by D. W. GRIFFITH.

Birth of Venus, The   A painting by Sandro BOTTICELLI. It depicts the birth of the goddess VENUS, also known as APHRODITE, from the foam of the sea.

THE BIRTH OF VENUS. Botticelli's well-known painting.

❧ The painting is often referred to humorously as "Venus on the half-shell."

Bizet, Georges (bee-ZAY)   A French composer of the nineteenth century, best known for his OPERA *CARMEN*.

bluegrass   A kind of FOLK MUSIC for GUITAR, BANJO, VIOLIN, other stringed instruments, and voice; bluegrass is distinguished by rapid notes and improvisation by the musicians.

blues   A kind of JAZZ that evolved from the music of African-Americans, especially work songs and SPIRITUALS, in the early twentieth century. Blues pieces often express worry or depression.

"Blue-Tail Fly"   A popular American song from the nineteenth century; the speaker in the song is an African-American slave. Its REFRAIN is: "Jimmy crack corn, and I don't care; / My master's gone away."

Bogart, Humphrey   An American actor of the twentieth century, best known for his portrayals of hard-boiled CHARACTERS in films. Sam Spade in *The Maltese Falcon* and Rick Blaine in *CASABLANCA* are two of his most famous roles.

bohemian   A descriptive term for a stereotypical way of life for artists and INTELLECTUALS. According to the STEREOTYPE, bohemians live in material poverty, because they prefer their art or their learning to lesser goods; they are also unconventional in habits and dress, and sometimes in morals.

Bolshoi Theater (BOHL-shoy, BOL-shoy)   A theater in MOSCOW known for its company of BALLET dancers.

Botticelli, Sandro (bot-uh-CHEL-ee)   An Italian painter of the late fifteenth and early sixteenth centuries. His best-known work is *THE BIRTH OF VENUS*.

Brahms, Johannes (BRAHMZ)   A German romantic composer (*see* ROMANTICISM) of the nineteenth century; his works include SYMPHONIES, CONCERTOS, CHAMBER MUSIC, songs, and *A German Requiem*, a piece for soloists, chorus, and ORCHESTRA.

❧ Brahms's "Lullaby" is a beloved short work. The words often sung to it begin, "Lullaby, and good night." ❧ Much music written in the time of Brahms, when the romantic movement was no longer new, strained for dramatic effects. By comparison, his music is notable for its restraint.

brass   Musical instruments traditionally made of brass and played by blowing directly into a small, cup-shaped mouthpiece. They include the FRENCH HORN, TRUMPET, TROMBONE, and TUBA.

brass band A musical group composed of BRASS, PERCUSSION, and (in the United States) WOODWIND instruments. The sound of a brass band carries effectively outdoors.

☙ Sometimes called marching bands, brass bands often play at athletic events and military exercises and in parades.

Broadway The central group of theaters presenting live drama in NEW YORK CITY. Many of them are located on or adjacent to the street called BROADWAY in MANHATTAN.

Brooklyn Bridge A suspension bridge built between MANHATTAN and BROOKLYN in the late nineteenth century; Manhattan and Brooklyn are today two boroughs of NEW YORK CITY. At the time of its completion, the Brooklyn Bridge was the world's longest suspension bridge.

☙ The Brooklyn Bridge is mentioned in several common expressions about the sale of the bridge by one person to another (the bridge is actually public property). A person who "could sell someone the Brooklyn Bridge" is persuasive; a person who "tries to sell the Brooklyn Bridge" is extremely dishonest; a person who "would agree to buy the Brooklyn Bridge" is gullible.

Brueghel, Pieter, the Elder (BROY-guhl) A Flemish painter of the sixteenth century, known for his paintings of PEASANT village scenes and religious subjects.

Buffalo Bill William F. Cody, an American adventurer, hunter, scout, soldier, and showman of the late nineteenth and early twentieth centuries. His popular "Wild West Show," begun in the 1880s, featured such acts as the marksmanship of Annie Oakley, mock battles between NATIVE AMERICANS and army troops, and breathtaking displays of cowboy skills and horsemanship. It toured the United States, CANADA, and EUROPE.

☙ Buffalo Bill's "Wild West Show" was a major influence in creating the popular image of the romantic and exciting old West.

Bunker, Archie The central CHARACTER in the television COMEDY series "All in the Family," which appeared in the 1970s. Bunker's family appreciated and loved him, even though he was bad tempered, ill in-

formed, and highly prejudiced against virtually all minority groups.

☙ The creators of "All in the Family" intended Archie Bunker to be a PARODY of closed-mindedness in Americans. To their surprise, numbers of people in the United States adopted Bunker as their hero.

Calder, Alexander (KAWL-duhr) An American sculptor of the twentieth century, known for his MOBILES.

"Camptown Races" A song by Stephen FOSTER. It begins:

> Camptown ladies sing dis song,
>   Doodah! doodah!
> Camptown racetrack five miles long,
>   Oh! doodah day!
> Gwine to run all night!
> Gwine to run all day!
> I'll bet my money on de bobtail nag —
> Somebody bet on de bay.

cantata (kuhn-TAH-tuh) A musical composition for voice and instruments, and including choruses, solos, and RECITATIVES.

CAPITAL. *Doric, Ionic, and Corinthian.*

capital In architecture, the top portion of a column.

☙ The form of the capital often serves to distinguish one style of architecture from another. For example, the CORINTHIAN, DORIC, and IONIC styles of Greek architecture all have different capitals.

Capitol, United States The large domed building in WASHINGTON, D.C., in which the United States CONGRESS meets.

☙ A picture of the Capitol is often used as a SYMBOL of the federal government of the United States.
☙ The Capitol dominates the skyline of the city of Washington; only the WASHINGTON MONUMENT is higher.

caricature In art or literature, a portrayal of an individual or thing that exaggerates and distorts prominent characteristics so as to make them appear ridiculous. Caricature is commonly a medium for SATIRE.

Carmen One of the most popular of OPERAS, composed by Georges BIZET, and first produced in the late nineteenth century. The title CHARACTER is known for manipulating men. One of her victims, a Spanish soldier, arranges for her to escape from jail, but she later abandons him for a bullfighter, and he stabs her. The pieces "Habanera" and "Toreador Song" are well-known excerpts from *Carmen*.

Carnegie Hall A concert hall, world-famous for its acoustics, in NEW YORK CITY.

    🐾 A performance in Carnegie Hall amounts to a seal of approval on a musician's work. For generations, playing there has been a goal of young musicians. 🐾 Carnegie Hall was the home of the New York Philharmonic ORCHESTRA for many years. When the orchestra announced in 1959 that it was moving to a new building, plans were made to tear Carnegie Hall down. Because of the efforts of the violinist Isaac STERN and other artists, however, it has been preserved as a concert hall.

Caruso, Enrico An Italian TENOR of the late nineteenth and early twentieth centuries, generally considered one of the greatest tenors in the history of OPERA.

Casablanca A romantic war adventure film from 1943, in which Humphrey BOGART plays a nightclub owner in CASABLANCA, MOROCCO, and Ingrid Bergman plays his former lover.

    🐾 *Casablanca* has a classic blend of love interest and international intrigue, and many lines from it are extremely familiar: "Here's looking at you, kid" (Bogart's toast to Bergman), and "Play it once, Sam — for old time's sake. . . . Play 'As Time Goes By'" (Bergman's request to the pianist in Bogart's club), which is often misquoted as "Play it again, Sam."

Casals, Pablo (PAH-bloh kuh-SAHLZ, kuh-SALZ) A celebrated Spanish cellist (*see* CELLO) of the twentieth century.

    🐾 After Francisco FRANCO came to power in SPAIN, Casals went into exile in FRANCE, and later moved to PUERTO RICO. He gave a famous performance at the WHITE HOUSE in 1961.

"Casey Jones" A popular American song from the early twentieth century, about an actual American railway engineer, John Luther ("Casey") Jones. When his train was about to crash, Casey told his assistant to jump, but stayed at the controls himself and applied the brakes. Although his train crashed, and Casey was killed, the passengers survived.

Cassatt, Mary (kuh-SAT) An American painter of the late nineteenth and early twentieth centuries. She spent most of her artistic career in FRANCE, in close association with the French IMPRESSIONISTS, particularly Edgar DEGAS. Mary Cassatt is best known for her pictures of mothers and children.

catharsis (kuh-THAHR-suhs) The release or purging of emotions. ARISTOTLE used the term to describe the cleansing effect of TRAGEDY. Through witnessing the struggles of another person, spectators, according to Aristotle, are purged of their own pity and fear. (*See under "Anthropology, Psychology, and Sociology."*)

cathedral A CHURCH building in which a CHRISTIAN BISHOP has his official seat; *cathedra* is LATIN for "chair." Cathedrals are usually large and imposing, and many have been important in the development of architecture. The building of a cathedral, especially in the MIDDLE AGES, was a project in which the entire town took part. (*See* CHARTRES, CATHEDRAL OF; NOTRE DAME DE PARIS, CATHEDRAL OF; *and* SAINT PAUL'S CATHEDRAL.)

cello (CHEL-oh) An instrument in the VIOLIN family, known for its rich tone. Among the STRINGS, or stringed instruments, the cello has the second-lowest range, higher only than the BASS VIOL, and it has the lowest part in STRING QUARTETS. Cellists hold the instrument between their knees to play it. *Cello* is short for *violoncello*.

Cézanne, Paul (say-ZAHN) A French painter of the nineteenth century; he was an IMPRESSIONIST early in his career, and was a leading figure in the movement toward ABSTRACT ART.

chamber music Music for two or more instruments in which only one musician plays each part. Chamber music is distinguished from music for ORCHESTRA, in which, for example, more than a dozen violinists may be playing the same notes. The most familiar kind of chamber music is the STRING QUARTET.

Chaplin, Charlie An English filmmaker and actor of the early twentieth century; Chaplin did most of his work in the United States. In his silent film comedies, he created the beloved CHARACTER the Little Tramp, who wore a shabby black suit, derby hat, and floppy shoes, and walked with a cane. *The Gold*

Rush, *City Lights*, and *Modern Times* are some of Chaplin's best-known films.

Charleston   A fast-paced dance, with elaborate arm movements, that became a craze in the United States during the 1920s.

Chartres, Cathedral of (SHAHRT, SHAHR-truh)   A great CATHEDRAL in FRANCE. Built mostly in the thirteenth century, it is considered one of the finest examples of GOTHIC architecture. The stained-glass windows, in which blue glass predominates, are especially impressive.

Chopin, Frédéric (SHOH-pan, shoh-PANN)   A Polish romantic composer (*see* ROMANTICISM) of the nineteenth century, who spent most of his career in FRANCE. Chopin is known for his expressive PIANO pieces; he composed almost exclusively for that instrument.

chord   In music, the sound of three or more notes played at the same time. The history of Western music is marked by an increase in complexity of the chords composers use.

choreography   The art of arranging dance movements for performance.

clarinet   A WOODWIND instrument, usually made of black wood or plastic, and played with a single REED. The clarinet has extensive use in DIXIELAND, JAZZ, and military music, as well as in CLASSICAL MUSIC.

   The most famous American clarinetist was Benny GOODMAN.

classic   A descriptive term for a period in Western music, encompassing roughly the last half of the eighteenth century, that includes the works of Franz Josef HAYDN and Wolfgang Amadeus MOZART and the early works of Ludwig van BEETHOVEN, among other composers.

classical music   A loose expression for European and American music of the more serious kind, as opposed to popular or FOLK MUSIC.

"Clementine"   An American FOLKSONG. Its REFRAIN is:

> Oh my darling, oh my darling,
> Oh my darling Clementine!
> You are lost and gone forever,
> Dreadful sorry, Clementine.

(*See* FORTY-NINERS.)

coda   An ending to a piece of music, standing outside the formal structure of the piece. It is the Italian word for "tail."

Cohan, George M. (KOH-han, koh-HAN)   An American songwriter and entertainer of the early twentieth century, known for such rousing songs as "GIVE MY REGARDS TO BROADWAY," "OVER THERE," "YANKEE DOODLE DANDY," and "YOU'RE A GRAND OLD FLAG."

coloratura (kul-uhr-uh-TOOR-uh)   Elaborate ornamentation in a piece of vocal music. A coloratura SOPRANO is one who can sing such highly ornamented parts.

Colosseum   A great arena of ancient ROME, which seated 50,000. It is in ruins today, but its former glory can still be imagined.

   Some of the contests staged in the Colosseum were between gladiators, who fought with swords; some were between people and animals. The arena could even be flooded for mock sea battles. According to tradition, persecuted CHRISTIANS were fed to lions in the Colosseum for the entertainment of the Romans. (*See also* BREAD AND CIRCUSES.)

"Columbia, the Gem of the Ocean"   An American patriotic song from the middle of the nineteenth century. It begins, "O Columbia, the gem of the ocean. . . ."

"Coming Through the Rye"   A Scottish song with words by Robert BURNS. It begins, "If a body meet a body, coming through the rye. . . ."

concerto (kuhn-CHAIR-toh)   A piece of instrumental music written for one or more soloists and an ORCHESTRA.

Constable, John (KUN-stuh-buhl, KON-stuh-buhl)   An English landscape painter of the late eighteenth and early nineteenth centuries, known for pastoral scenes.

contralto (kuhn-TRAL-toh)   The lowest range of the female singing voice; ALTO.

Copland, Aaron (KOHP-luhnd)   An American composer of the twentieth century, noted for the American settings of many of his pieces. Some of his best-known works are the BALLETS *Appalachian Spring*, *Billy the Kid*, and *Rodeo*; he has also written CHAMBER MUSIC, SYMPHONIES, and music for films.

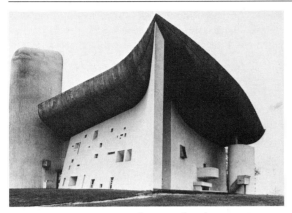

LE CORBUSIER. *Le Corbusier's church Notre Dame du Haut, in Ronchamp, France.*

Corbusier, Le (luh kawr-buu-ZYAY)   A French architect and city planner of the twentieth century, known for designing buildings with unusual curves and unconventional shapes.

Corinthian (kuh-RIN-thee-uhn)   One of the three main styles of Greek architecture (the others are DORIC and IONIC). The Corinthian column is slender and fluted; the CAPITAL incorporates sculpted leaves.

counterpoint   The use of two or more melodies at the same time in a piece of music; it was an important part of BAROQUE music. Certain composers, such as Johann Sebastian BACH, have been especially skillful at counterpoint.

country and western music   Popular music originating in the southeastern and southwestern United States. Its lyrics depict the trials and successes of everyday life. The Grand Ole Opry, located in NASHVILLE, TENNESSEE, helped to broaden its audience through radio. Well-known country and western artists are Hank Williams, Loretta Lynn, and Johnny Cash.

crescendo (kruh-SHEN-doh)   A musical direction used to indicate increasing loudness.
  ♪ The term is sometimes used figuratively to indicate rising intensity in general: "As the days went on, there was a crescendo of angry letters about my speech." *Crescendo* is also sometimes misused to indicate a *peak* of intensity, as in, "The angry letters about my speech hit a crescendo on Wednesday."

Crosby, Bing   An American singer and actor of the twentieth century. He appeared several times in films with Fred ASTAIRE and with Bob HOPE, and received an ACADEMY AWARD for his part in *Going My Way* in 1944. His most successful song recording was "WHITE CHRISTMAS."

Crystal Palace   A great exhibition hall built in ENGLAND in the middle of the nineteenth century. It was one of the first prefabricated buildings, and one of the first buildings with large expanses of glass wall.

cubism   A movement in modern art that emphasized the geometrical depiction of natural forms (see GEOMETRY). Pablo PICASSO was one of the leading cubists.

cupola (KYOOH-puh-luh)   A small ornamental structure rising from a roof. Cupolas are often dome-shaped.

Currier and Ives   Two business partners, the technician Nathaniel Currier and the artist J. Merritt Ives, who produced colored prints of everyday American life in the nineteenth century.

cymbal   A large, round metal plate used as a PERCUSSION instrument. Cymbals can be crashed together in pairs or struck singly with a drumstick, and are used in dance bands and JAZZ bands as well as in ORCHESTRAS.

da Vinci   *See* LEONARDO DA VINCI.

Dali, Salvador (DAH-lee)   A Spanish SURREALIST painter of the twentieth century. Many of his landscapes are decorated with melting clocks.

David   A large marble statue made by MICHELANGELO of the biblical king DAVID. Michelangelo portrays him as a youth just about to do battle with the giant Goliath.

Debussy, Claude (deb-yoo-SEE, day-byoo-SEE, duh-BYOOH-see)   A French composer of the late nineteenth and early twentieth centuries, known for his free RHYTHMS and indefinite KEYS. His music is often compared to the paintings of the IMPRESSIONISTS. The PIANO piece "Claire de lune" ("Moonlight") and the ORCHESTRA piece *La Mer* (*The Sea*) are two of Debussy's best-known works.

SALVADOR DALI. *Salvador Dali's painting* The Persistence of Memory. *1931. Oil on canvas, 9½ × 13″. Collection, The Museum of Modern Art, New York. Given anonymously.*

"Deck the Halls"   A traditional song of Christmas. It begins, "Deck the halls with boughs of holly; / Fa la la la la, la la la la. . . . "

Degas, Edgar (day-GAH, duh-GAH)   A French painter and sculptor of the nineteenth century. Among his preferred subjects were BALLET dancers and scenes of café life.

dilettante (DIL-uh-tahnt, dil-uh-TAHNT)   Someone who is interested in the FINE ARTS as a spectator, not as a serious practitioner. *Dilettante* is most often used to mean a dabbler, someone with a broad but shallow attachment to any field.

Disney, Walt   An American filmmaker of the twentieth century. His studios are especially known for meticulous craftsmanship in animated (cartoon) films, especially those of full feature length. The Disney studios have also produced nature films, short animated cartoons, feature-length films with live actors, and television programs. *Snow White and the Seven Dwarfs, Cinderella,* and *Sleeping Beauty* are some of Disney's best-known productions. MICKEY MOUSE and DONALD DUCK are his best-known original CHARACTERS. Two giant amusement parks, Disneyland in CALIFORNIA and Walt Disney World in FLORIDA, are based on his characters and concepts.

"Dixie"   An American song of the nineteenth century. It was used to build enthusiasm for the South

during the CIVIL WAR, and still is treated this way in the southern states. It was written for use in the theater by a northerner, Daniel Decatur Emmett. As usually sung today, "Dixie" begins:

> I wish I was in the land of cotton;
> Old times there are not forgotten:
> Look away! Look away! Look away! Dixie Land.

Dixieland   A kind of JAZZ originating in NEW ORLEANS, LOUISIANA, in the early twentieth century. The RHYTHMS of Dixieland are usually rapid, and it generally includes many improvised sections for individual instruments.

Don Giovanni (don jee-uh-VAH-nee, joh-VAH-nee)   An OPERA by Wolfgang Amadeus MOZART, recounting the dissolute life of DON JUAN (*Don Giovanni* is the Italian form of *Don Juan*). At the end of the opera, a statue of a man Don Giovanni has killed comes to life and drags the unscrupulous seducer into the burning pit of HELL.

Doric   One of the three main styles of Greek architecture (the others are CORINTHIAN and IONIC). The Doric column is heavy and fluted; its CAPITAL is plain.

double bass   Another name for the BASS VIOL.

"Down in the Valley"   An American FOLKSONG. It begins, "Down in the valley, the valley so low, / Hang your head over; hear the wind blow. . . ."

"Drunken Sailor, The"   A song of the sea. Some lines from it are:

> What shall we do with the drunken sailor,
> Early in the morning?
> Hooray and up she rises,
> Early in the morning.

Dürer, Albrecht (DOOR-uhr, DYOOR-uhr)   A German painter and engraver of the late fifteenth and early sixteenth centuries. Dürer's career came at the beginning of the REFORMATION, which he supported, and many of his subjects are religious. His woodcuts — prints made from a carved wooden block — are particularly notable.

Dylan, Bob (DIL-uhn)   An American folksinger and songwriter of the twentieth century (*see* FOLK MUSIC). His music, with its strong note of social protest, was especially popular during the 1960s, when he wrote such songs as "Blowin' in the Wind," "The

Times They Are A-Changin'," and "Like a Rolling Stone." Since then, his style has changed several times.

Eiffel Tower (EYE-fuhl)   An iron structure that dominates the skyline of PARIS. When it was built in the nineteenth century, it was the tallest freestanding structure in the world.

&. The Eiffel Tower, because of its distinctive shape, has become a SYMBOL of Paris.

Ellington, Duke   An African-American JAZZ composer, songwriter, and bandleader of the twentieth century; his real first name was Edward. Ellington's most popular songs include "Mood Indigo," "Satin Doll," "Sophisticated Lady," and "Don't Get Around Much Anymore."

Empire State Building   An office building in NEW YORK CITY, over 1,000 feet high. Opened in the 1930s, it was for many years the tallest skyscraper in the world.

&. This was the building KING KONG climbed.

engraving   An artistic print made from a metal plate on which an artist has cut a design with a graver or a small chisel. (*Compare* ETCHING.)

etching   An artistic print made from a plate on which the artist has etched a design with acid. (*Compare* ENGRAVING.)

expressionism   An artistic style that departs from the conventions of REALISM and NATURALISM, and seeks to convey inner experience by distorting rather than directly representing natural images. The highly personal visions communicated in the paintings of Vincent VAN GOGH are early examples of expressionism. Edvard Munch and Georges Rouault are considered expressionist painters.

fiddle   Another name for the VIOLIN; *fiddle* is the more common term for the instrument as played in FOLK MUSIC and BLUEGRASS.

Fields, W. C.   An American film comedian of the twentieth century, noted for his comic timing and drawling speech. He frequently played a cynical swindler. His films include *The Bank Dick*, *Never Give a Sucker an Even Break*, and *My Little Chickadee*, in which he played opposite Mae WEST.

fife   A small FLUTE with a high, piercing tone, used mainly in military bands.

EXPRESSIONISM. *Vincent van Gogh's painting* Starry Night. *1889. Oil on canvas, 29 × 36". Collection, The Museum of Modern Art, New York. Acquired through the Lillie P. Bliss Bequest.*

Figaro (FIG-uh-roh)   A scheming barber and servant who appears in several literary and musical works; Figaro is shrewder than his aristocratic master. He is the hero of the OPERAS *THE BARBER OF SEVILLE*, by Gioacchino Rossini, and *THE MARRIAGE OF FIGARO*, by Wolfgang Amadeus MOZART.

fine arts   Art that is produced more for beauty or spiritual significance than for physical utility. Painting, sculpture, and music are fine arts.

Fitzgerald, Ella   An African-American JAZZ and popular singer of the twentieth century, known for the clarity of her voice and her ability to interpret the works of a great variety of songwriters, including Irving BERLIN, Duke ELLINGTON, George GERSHWIN, Cole PORTER, and Richard RODGERS.

flute   A high-pitched WOODWIND, held horizontally by the player, and played by blowing across a hole.

flying buttress   An external, arched support for the wall of a CHURCH or other building. Flying buttresses were used in many GOTHIC CATHEDRALS; they enabled builders to put up very tall but comparatively thin stone walls, so that much of the wall space could be filled with stained-glass windows. The cathedrals of CHARTRES and NOTRE DAME DE PARIS were built with flying buttresses.

folk music A kind of music originating from the ordinary people of a region or nation, and continued by oral tradition. The BALLAD is a typical form of folk music. Music is also called "folk" when it is made by artists and composers who are inspired by, or imitate, true folk music. Composers like Bob DYLAN and Woody GUTHRIE are folk musicians of the second kind.

folksong *See* FOLK MUSIC.

forte (FAWR-tay) A musical direction meaning "to be performed loudly"; the opposite of PIANO.

🎵 The common keyboard instrument the piano-forte ("piano" for short) got its name because it could play both soft and loud notes.

fortissimo (fawr-TIS-uh-moh) A musical direction meaning "to be performed very loudly"; the opposite of PIANISSIMO.

Foster, Stephen An American songwriter of the nineteenth century. He wrote the words and music to some of the country's perennially favorite songs, including "MY OLD KENTUCKY HOME," "OH! SUSANNA," "THE OLD FOLKS AT HOME," "Jeannie with the Light Brown Hair," and "Beautiful Dreamer."

French horn A mellow-sounding BRASS instrument, pitched lower than a TRUMPET and higher than a TUBA.

fresco A painting on wet plaster. When the plaster dries, the painting is bonded to the wall. Fresco was a popular method for painting large MURALS during the RENAISSANCE. *THE LAST SUPPER*, by Leonardo DA VINCI, is a fresco, as are the paintings by MICHELANGELO in the SISTINE CHAPEL.

frieze (FREEZ) An ornamental band that runs around a building. Friezes are usually on the exterior of a building, and are often sculpted in BAS-RELIEF.

functionalism An approach to architecture that adapts the design of a building or other structure to its future use. The American architect Louis Sullivan was a notable advocate of functionalism in the late nineteenth and early twentieth centuries.

🎵 Functionalism has been a dominant PHILOSOPHY of public architecture during much of the twentieth century.

Garbo, Greta An American film actress of the twentieth century, born in SWEDEN. Garbo was celebrated for her classic beauty and her portrayals of moody CHARACTERS.

🎵 In the movie *Grand Hotel*, Garbo made the famous complaint "I want to be alone." Garbo retired from the movies in the early 1940s, and lived as a recluse until her death in 1990.

gargoyle A sculpture depicting grotesque human shapes or evil spirits used in many buildings of the MIDDLE AGES, most notably on GOTHIC CATHEDRALS. Some gargoyles drained rainwater, sending it clear of the walls of the building.

Gauguin, Paul (goh-GANN) A French painter of the nineteenth century. He is remembered for his use of color and his paintings of Polynesian women. He abandoned his business career, family, and country to live and paint in TAHITI.

Gershwin, George An American composer of the twentieth century, known for putting elements of JAZZ into the forms of CLASSICAL MUSIC, such as the CONCERTO. His works include *RHAPSODY IN BLUE*, *An American in Paris*, and the music to the OPERA *PORGY AND BESS*. *Porgy and Bess* contains the song "SUMMERTIME." Together with his brother, Ira Gershwin, he wrote many popular MUSICAL COMEDIES.

Gilbert and Sullivan Two Englishmen of the nineteenth century who wrote many witty OPERETTAS satirizing society of the VICTORIAN PERIOD (*see* SATIRE). W. S. (William Schwenck) Gilbert wrote the song lyrics and spoken dialogue, and Arthur SULLIVAN wrote the music. Their works include *H.M.S. PINAFORE*, *THE MIKADO*, and *The Pirates of Penzance*.

Giotto (JOT-oh) An Italian painter and architect of the late thirteenth and early fourteenth centuries. Art in ITALY before the time of Giotto was heavily affected by the art of the BYZANTINE EMPIRE and was highly stylized; it resembled the ICONS in Byzantine CHURCHES. Giotto was the first painter to abandon Byzantine ways and begin to depict more lifelike expressions and figures.

"Give My Regards to Broadway" A song by George M. COHAN.

"God Bless America" A patriotic song of the United States, written by Irving BERLIN. It begins, "God bless America, land that I love...."

🎵 "God Bless America" was memorably sung by Kate Smith.

Gogh, Vincent van   *See* VAN GOGH, VINCENT.

Goldberg, Rube   An American cartoonist and sculptor of the twentieth century. He was famous for his humorous diagrams of incredibly intricate machines designed to carry out simple tasks.

🔊 A "Rube Goldberg contraption" is a machine with many apparently extraneous parts, which appears to have been designed by patchwork.

Golden Gate Bridge   A long suspension bridge across the Golden Gate, a strait that connects SAN FRANCISCO BAY with the PACIFIC OCEAN. For decades after it was opened in the 1930s, it had the longest span of any suspension bridge in the world.

"Gonna Lay Down My Burden"   An African-American SPIRITUAL. It contains these lines:

> Gonna lay down my burden
> Down by the riverside;
> I ain't gonna study war no more.

Goodman, Benny   An American JAZZ clarinetist (*see* CLARINET) and bandleader of the twentieth century, known as the "King of Swing."

gospel music   Intense, joyful music that is associated with EVANGELISTS in the South, especially among African-Americans. Gospel had a strong influence on many ROCK 'N' ROLL singers. Well-known gospel artists include Mahalia Jackson and the Dixie Hummingbirds.

Gothic   In European architecture, the dominant style during the late MIDDLE AGES, characterized by slender towers, pointed ARCHES, soaring ceilings, and FLYING BUTTRESSES. Many great CATHEDRALS, including CHARTRES and NOTRE DAME DE PARIS, were built in this style.

Goya, Francisco (GOY-uh)   A Spanish painter of the late eighteenth and early nineteenth centuries. Among his works is a series of paintings and ETCHINGS that powerfully depict the horrors of war.

Graham, Martha   An American dancer and choreographer. A celebrated practitioner of modern dance, she founded the Martha Graham School of Contemporary Dance in NEW YORK CITY.

Grandma Moses   *See* MOSES, GRANDMA.

Great Wall of China   A stone wall extending for 1,500 miles across northern CHINA. Built to defend the Chinese border in ancient times, it has become a

FRANCISCO GOYA. *Goya's painting* Third of May, 1808.

favorite destination for visitors to the PEOPLE'S REPUBLIC OF CHINA.

Greco, El   A Greek painter of the late sixteenth and early seventeenth centuries who spent most of his career in SPAIN (*El Greco* is Spanish for "the Greek"). He is famous for his paintings of religious subjects and for his distorted, elongated figures.

Gregorian chant   The traditional music for LATIN texts in the worship of the ROMAN CATHOLIC CHURCH. Gregorian chant is marked by performance in UNISON, and by free-flowing RHYTHMS that follow the phrasing of the text. The chants often call for one SYLLABLE to be sung across several notes.

Griffith, D. W.   An innovative American filmmaker of the early twentieth century. He is famous for his epic silent films, such as *THE BIRTH OF A NATION*, that required huge casts and enormous sets.

guitar   A stringed musical instrument (*see* STRINGS) usually played by strumming or plucking. Guitars are widely used in FOLK MUSIC, and, often amplified electronically, in COUNTRY AND WESTERN MUSIC and ROCK 'N' ROLL.

Guthrie, Woody   An American songwriter and folksinger (*see* FOLK MUSIC) of the twentieth century. Guthrie flourished in the 1930s, writing numerous songs about social injustice and the hardships of the DEPRESSION years. Two of his best-remembered songs are "THIS LAND IS YOUR LAND" and "So Long, It's Been Good to Know Yuh."

HAGIA SOPHIA

Hagia Sophia, Cathedral of (HAH-gee-uh soh-FEE-uh) A magnificent CATHEDRAL, sometimes called Santa Sophia or Saint Sophia, in ISTANBUL, TURKEY. Once the central CHURCH building of the EASTERN ORTHODOX CHURCH, Hagia Sophia is now a museum. It has an enormous, magnificent dome, one of the most celebrated in the world, and the inside walls are decorated with MOSAICS. The building is named in honor of JESUS. *Hagia Sophia* means "Holy Wisdom," an Eastern Orthodox title for Jesus.

"Hail to the Chief" The official song or anthem of the president of the United States, played as part of welcoming ceremonies and receptions when the president first appears.

"Hallelujah Chorus" The most famous MOVEMENT of the ORATORIO *Messiah*, by George Frederick HANDEL, often sung at Christmas.

Hammerstein, Oscar, II (HAM-uhr-steyen) An American playwright and lyricist in the twentieth century. Hammerstein wrote the words for a large number of highly successful MUSICALS, especially with Richard RODGERS. He also collaborated with a number of other composers, including Jerome Kern, with whom he wrote the musical *Show Boat*.

Handel, George Frederick A German-born composer of the eighteenth century, who spent most of his career in ENGLAND. Handel, one of the great composers of the BAROQUE era, is known especially for his *MESSIAH* and other ORATORIOS, for his CONCERTOS, and for his *WATER MUSIC*.

harmony The sounding of two or more musical notes at the same time in a way that is pleasant or desired. Harmony, melody, and RHYTHM are elements of music.

harp An instrument in the STRING section of the ORCHESTRA. The orchestral harp is several feet tall, and has pedals that allow the harpist to change the KEY of the instrument as necessary.

🎵 ANGELS are imagined to play harps in HEAVEN.

harpsichord A stringed keyboard instrument much used in the BAROQUE era in music. The keys of a harpsichord move small devices that pluck the strings; the strings are not struck with hammers, as in a PIANO. Thus, although harpsichords often look much like pianos, their characteristic tinkly sound is unlike that of the piano, and a harpsichordist cannot change the VOLUME of the sound by striking the keys harder, as a pianist can.

Haydn, Franz Josef (HEYED-n) An Austrian composer of the eighteenth century; one of the great composers of the CLASSIC era. Haydn is credited with establishing the SYMPHONY as a musical form, having composed over a hundred symphonies. Of these, his *Surprise Symphony* and *Clock Symphony* are especially well known. He also composed many STRING QUARTETS.

Hepburn, Katharine An American actress of the twentieth century; she has appeared in films over several decades, and won ACADEMY AWARDS in 1933, 1967, 1968, and 1981. She often costarred with Spencer Tracy. *The Philadelphia Story* and *The African Queen* are two of her best-remembered pictures.

Hitchcock, Alfred An English filmmaker of the twentieth century who specialized in THRILLERS. Some of his best-known films are *The Birds*, *The Man Who Knew Too Much*, *North by Northwest*, and *Psycho*.

H.M.S. Pinafore See PINAFORE, *H.M.S.*

"Home on the Range" A song celebrating life in the American West; the state song of KANSAS. It begins, "Oh, give me a home where the buffalo roam, / Where the deer and the antelope play. . . ."

"Home, Sweet Home" A popular song from the nineteenth century. Its words include, "Be it ever so humble, there's no place like home."

Homer, Winslow An American painter of the late nineteenth and early twentieth centuries, known especially for his rich watercolor paintings of sea scenes.

Hope, Bob An American comedian of the twentieth century. Hope is known for his work in films, especially a series of seven "Road" pictures, including *The Road to Zanzibar* and *The Road to Morocco*, in all of which he appeared opposite Bing CROSBY and Dorothy Lamour. He is also famous as a tireless entertainer of American servicemen overseas.

Hopper, Edward An American painter of the twentieth century, best known for his realistic paintings of city scenes, such as movie theaters, diners, and offices.

Houdini, Harry (hooh-DEE-nee) An American magician of the late nineteenth and early twentieth centuries, famed for his ability to escape from straitjackets, chains, handcuffs, and locked chests.

How you gonna keep 'em down on the farm after they've seen Paree? The REFRAIN of a popular song of 1919; it refers to young American soldiers returning from EUROPE after WORLD WAR I. Many of the young veterans were from the country, and had traveled little; the gay sophistication of "Paree" (PARIS) was their first taste of big-city life anywhere. Supposedly, their return to the family farm was a considerable letdown.

I never met a man I didn't like The common version of a remark by the twentieth-century American humorist Will ROGERS.

ICON. *A portrait on wood of the Virgin Mary and baby Jesus. The icon is known as the Liberatrix and Protectress of Russia and as the Icon of Our Lady of Kazan.*

icon An image used in worship in the EASTERN ORTHODOX CHURCH and among other CHRISTIANS of similar traditions. Icons depict JESUS, MARY, and the SAINTS, usually in a severe, symbolic, nonrealistic way.

impresario (im-pruh-SAHR-ee-oh, im-pruh-SAIR-ee-oh) A sponsor or producer of entertainment, especially someone who works with OPERA or BALLET companies or performers of CLASSICAL MUSIC.

impressionism A style of painting associated mainly with French artists of the late nineteenth century, such as Edgar DEGAS, Edouard MANET, Claude MONET, and Pierre-Auguste RENOIR. Impressionist painting seeks to re-create the artist's or viewer's general *impression* of a scene. It is characterized by indistinct outlines and by small brushstrokes of different colors, which the eye blends at a distance. Soft, pastel colors appear frequently in impressionist paintings.

Ionic (eye-ON-ik) One of the three main styles of Greek architecture (the others are CORINTHIAN and DORIC). The Ionic column is slender and finely fluted; its CAPITAL is in the shape of a scroll.

"I've Been Working on the Railroad" An American FOLKSONG. It begins, "I've been working on the railroad / All the livelong day. . . ."

jazz A form of American music that grew out of African-Americans' musical traditions at the beginning of the twentieth century. Jazz is generally considered a major contribution of the United States to the world of music. It quickly became a form of dance music, incorporating a "big beat" and solos by individual musicians. For many years, all jazz was improvised and taught orally, and even today jazz solos are often improvised. Over the years, the small groups of the original jazz players evolved into the "Big Bands" (led, for example, by Duke ELLINGTON, Count BASIE, and Glenn MILLER), and finally into concert ensembles. Other famous jazz musicians include Louis ARMSTRONG, Benny GOODMAN, and Ella FITZGERALD.

"Jesus Loves Me" A children's song used by CHRISTIANS. It begins, "JESUS loves me, this I know, / For the BIBLE tells me so. . . ."

"John Brown's Body" A song of the CIVIL WAR that pays tribute to the ABOLITIONIST John BROWN. It begins, "John Brown's body lies a-moldering in the grave."

⇄ "The BATTLE HYMN OF THE REPUBLIC" was written to the tune of "John Brown's Body."

"John Henry" An American FOLKSONG about the "steel-driving man" JOHN HENRY. It contains these lines:

John Henry said to his captain,
"A man ain't nothin' but a man,

And before I'd let your steam drill beat me down,
I'd die with the hammer in my hand, Lord, Lord!
I'd die with the hammer in my hand."

Jolly Roger A black flag with a white SKULL AND CROSSBONES, flown in past centuries by pirate ships.

Joplin, Scott An African-American RAGTIME pianist and composer of the late nineteenth and early twentieth centuries. "Maple Leaf Rag" and "The Entertainer" are two of his best-known works.

"Joshua Fit the Battle of Jericho" An American SPIRITUAL, based on the story of JOSHUA, the successor of MOSES in the OLD TESTAMENT, who led the ISRAELITES into the PROMISED LAND. It begins:

Joshua fit [fought] the battle of
Jericho,
Jericho, Jericho;
Joshua fit the battle of Jericho,
And the walls came tumbling down.

Justice A figure in painting and sculpture that symbolizes the impartiality of true justice. The figure of Justice usually appears as a blindfolded woman with a scale in one hand and a sword in the other.

kettledrum A drum consisting of a skin stretched over a large shell in the shape of a half-sphere. The pitch of the kettledrum can be changed by manipulating screws at the edge of the skin or pedals at the bottom of the drum. Kettledrums are usually used in CLASSICAL MUSIC in sets of two or more, and are known by their Italian name, TIMPANI.

key The main or central note of a piece of music (or part of a piece of music). Each key has its own SCALE, beginning and ending on the note that defines the OCTAVE of the next scale. The key of C-major uses a scale that starts on C and uses only the white keys of the PIANO. In a piece composed in the key of C, the music is likely to end on the note C, and certain combinations of notes based on C will predominate.

Key, Francis Scott A lawyer and poet of the late eighteenth and early nineteenth centuries. Key wrote the words to "THE STAR-SPANGLED BANNER" while watching the British bombardment of Fort McHenry, MARYLAND, in the WAR OF 1812.

King Kong One of the most famous of movie monsters, a giant ape who terrorizes NEW YORK CITY, and makes his last stand atop the EMPIRE STATE

BUILDING. The story of King Kong was first filmed in the 1930s.

kitsch (KICH)   Works of art and other objects (such as furniture) that are meant to look costly but actually are in poor taste.

🙤 Kitsch in literature and music is associated with sentimentalism as well as bad taste.

La Scala   *See* SCALA, LA.

Last Supper, The   A FRESCO painted by LEONARDO DA VINCI depicting JESUS and his DISCIPLES at the moment Jesus announces that one of them has betrayed him. (*See under "The Bible."*)

🙤 This fresco is now so badly damaged that it can no longer be viewed by the public. 🙤 Leonardo was experimenting with techniques of painting a fresco, and this accounts for some of the deterioration.

Laurel and Hardy   Stanley Laurel and Oliver Hardy, two film comedians of the twentieth century. They almost always played their movie roles under their own names, wearing derby hats and neckties; Laurel appeared as a thin, dimwitted Englishman, and Hardy as an overweight American, often irritable and pompous. In their films, they constantly get in each other's way, and are usually involved in hopeless business undertakings or doomed personal adventures.

Leaning Tower of Pisa   A dramatically leaning tower in the city of Pisa in ITALY, built as a bell tower for the CATHEDRAL of the city; the tower dates from the twelfth century. Soon after its construction, the foundation sank, causing the tower to lean.

leitmotif (LEYET-moh-teef)   A frequently recurring bit of melody, usually in OPERA, associated with a person, thing, or emotion in the opera; *Leitmotiv* is German for "leading THEME." The leitmotif may be heard in the instrumental or the vocal part.

🙤 Leitmotifs are particularly associated with the operas of Richard WAGNER. 🙤 Recurring themes or subjects in other forms of art or literature are sometimes also called leitmotifs.

Leonardo da Vinci (lee-uh-NAHR-doh, lay-uh-NAHR-doh duh vin-chee)   An Italian artist, scientist, and inventor of the late fifteenth and early sixteenth centuries. His wide range of interests and abilities makes him a grand example of a "RENAISSANCE MAN." Leonardo painted the MONA LISA and THE LAST SUP-

LEONARDO DA VINCI. *A self-portrait.*

PER. His drawings include brilliant studies of the human body and of natural objects. Some of his sketches anticipate such modern inventions as the airplane and the tank.

liberal arts   The areas of learning that cultivate general intellectual ability rather than technical or professional skills. *Liberal arts* is often used as a SYNONYM for HUMANITIES, since literature, languages, history, and PHILOSOPHY are often considered the primary subjects of the liberal arts. The term *liberal arts* originally meant arts suitable for free people (*libri* in LATIN), but not slaves.

Liberty, Statue of   *See* STATUE OF LIBERTY.

Liberty Bell   A relic and SYMBOL of the AMERICAN REVOLUTION. The Liberty Bell, first cast in ENGLAND in the 1750s, is inscribed with words from the BIBLE: "Proclaim liberty throughout the land unto all the inhabitants thereof." The bell hung in Independence Hall in PHILADELPHIA, and was rung at the proclamation of the DECLARATION OF INDEPENDENCE. It cracked while being tolled for the death in 1835 of Chief Justice John MARSHALL, and was taken out of service. It is now on display at Independence Hall.

lieder (LEE-duhr)   The PLURAL of *lied*, the German word for "song." It refers to art songs in German mainly from the nineteenth century. The most notable composer of lieder was Franz SCHUBERT.

Lincoln Memorial A massive monument built in WASHINGTON, D.C., in honor of Abraham LINCOLN. The memorial contains a statue of Lincoln seated, and stone engravings of LINCOLN'S SECOND INAUGURAL ADDRESS and his GETTYSBURG ADDRESS.

Liszt, Franz (LIST) A Hungarian composer and pianist of the nineteenth century, known for his often fiery style of composition and performance. His *Hungarian Rhapsodies* for PIANO are particularly well remembered.

"Loch Lomond" (lok, lokh LOH-muhnd) A Scottish FOLKSONG with this REFRAIN:

Oh, YOU'LL TAKE THE HIGH ROAD,
AND I'LL TAKE THE LOW ROAD,
And I'll be in Scotland before you;
But me and my true love will never meet again,
On the bonnie, bonnie banks of Loch Lomond.

Louvre (LOOHV, LOOHV-ruh) An art museum in PARIS, formerly a royal palace. The *MONA LISA*, *VENUS DE MILO*, *WHISTLER'S MOTHER*, and thousands of other works of art are exhibited there.

Madame Butterfly An OPERA by Giacomo PUCCINI. The title CHARACTER, a Japanese woman, is betrothed to an American naval officer in JAPAN. He leaves for the United States, promising to return, but comes back three years later married to an American woman. Butterfly, disgraced, stabs herself; the officer begs her forgiveness, and she dies in his arms.

Madonna A work of art depicting MARY, THE MOTHER OF JESUS, especially one that shows her holding the infant JESUS; also a term for Mary herself. *Madonna* is Italian for "my lady."

maestro (MEYE-stroh) A title for distinguished artists, especially those in music. It may be given to teachers, composers, conductors, or performers. *Maestro* is Italian for "master."

Magic Flute, The An OPERA by Wolfgang Amadeus MOZART. A prince receives a magic FLUTE from the Queen of the Night, and sets out to rescue the queen's daughter from an Egyptian PRIEST. He succeeds, and the two are married. Both Mozart and the author of the lyrics to *The Magic Flute* were FREEMASONS; their opera sets forth the ideals of this group.

Mahler, Gustav (MAH-luhr) An Austrian composer and conductor of the late nineteenth and early twentieth centuries. Mahler wrote long, intensely emotional works for large ORCHESTRAS, including nine SYMPHONIES and part of a tenth.

Manet, Edouard (ma-NAY) A French painter of the nineteenth century, and one of the originators of IMPRESSIONISM. His *Luncheon on the Grass*, showing two clothed men and a naked woman picnicking, shocked the public of his day.

Marriage of Figaro, The An OPERA by Wolfgang Amadeus MOZART, in which the servant FIGARO outwits his nobleman master, who is trying to seduce Figaro's fiancée.

"Marseillaise, The" (mahr-se-YEZ) The national anthem of FRANCE, written during the FRENCH REVOLUTION.

Marx brothers A family of American film comedians who flourished in the 1930s; *Duck Soup* and *A Night at the Opera* are two of their films. The brothers included the wisecracking, cigar-smoking Groucho; the HARP-playing, woman-chasing Harpo, who never spoke, but beeped a bicycle horn instead; and the PIANO-playing, Italian-accented Chico. A fourth brother, Zeppo, appeared in a few films, but a fifth brother, Gummo, did not appear in any.

M*A*S*H A film and later a television series about the staff of a battlefield hospital during the KOREAN WAR; *M*A*S*H* stands for "mobile army surgical hospital." The film and the television program offered much reflection on politics, love, friendship, and war.

Mass In music, a musical setting for the texts used in the CHRISTIAN CHURCH at the celebration of the Mass, or SACRAMENT of COMMUNION. Most Masses have been written for use in the ROMAN CATHOLIC CHURCH.

• Many composers have written Masses; among them are Johann Sebastian BACH, Franz Josef HAYDN, Wolfgang Amadeus MOZART, Franz SCHUBERT, Leonard BERNSTEIN, and Duke ELLINGTON.

Matisse, Henri (ma-TEES, muh-TEES) A French painter and sculptor of the late nineteenth and early twentieth centuries. Matisse, known for his brilliant colors and bold brushstrokes, had a major influence on modern art.

mausoleum (maw-suh-LEE-uhm, maw-zuh-LEE-uhm)   A tomb, or a building containing tombs. Mausoleums are often richly decorated. The TAJ MAHAL is a mausoleum.

Mellon, Andrew   An American businessman of the late nineteenth and early twentieth centuries. Mellon served as secretary of the DEPARTMENT OF THE TREASURY in the 1920s, and donated his enormous art collection to the people of the United States. He built the NATIONAL GALLERY OF ART to house the collection.

Mendelssohn, Felix (MEND-l-suhn)   A German composer and performer of the nineteenth century. Besides SYMPHONIES, OVERTURES, and CONCERTOS, Mendelssohn composed ORATORIOS, notably *Elijah*, and the incidental music for SHAKESPEARE's *MIDSUMMER NIGHT'S DREAM*. His full surname was Mendelssohn-Bartholdy.

Messiah (muh-SEYE-uh)   An ORATORIO by George Frederick HANDEL on the life of JESUS. Written for solo singers, chorus, and ORCHESTRA, it contains the "HALLELUJAH CHORUS." In the United States, it is often sung in the season of Christmas.

Metropolitan Museum of Art   An art museum in NEW YORK CITY; one of the leading art museums in the world.

Metropolitan Opera   The most prominent OPERA company in the United States, often called "the Met" for short; it is based in NEW YORK CITY.

mezzo soprano (MET-soh, MED-zoh)   A range of the female singing voice lower than SOPRANO and higher than ALTO.

Michelangelo (meye-kuh-LAN-juh-loh, mik-uh-LAN-juh-loh)   An Italian painter, sculptor, and architect of the fifteenth and sixteenth centuries. Among many achievements in a life of nearly ninety years, Michelangelo sculpted the *DAVID* and several versions of the *PIETÀ*, painted the ceiling and rear wall of the SISTINE CHAPEL, and served as one of the architects of SAINT PETER'S BASILICA, designing its famous dome. He is considered one of the greatest artists of all time.

Mikado, The (mi-KAH-doh)   A comic OPERA by GILBERT AND SULLIVAN, about the efforts of a Japanese prince to win the hand of the national executioner's daughter. Memorable songs from *The Mi-*

MICHELANGELO. *A detail of* The Creation of Adam, *from Michelangelo's Sistine Chapel frescoes depicting the events in Genesis.*

kado include "Three Little Maids from School" and "Tit Willow."

Miller, Glenn   An American popular composer and bandleader of the twentieth century. His band was noted for its smooth but sophisticated performances of such dance numbers as "In the Mood" and "Moonlight Serenade."

Mine eyes have seen the glory of the coming of the Lord   The opening words of the "BATTLE HYMN OF THE REPUBLIC."

mobile   A sculpture made up of suspended shapes that move.

🔊 Alexander CALDER, an American sculptor of the twentieth century, is known for his mobiles.

Mona Lisa   A painting by LEONARDO DA VINCI of a woman with a mysterious smile. It is one of the most readily recognized paintings in the world.

Monet, Claude (moh-NAY)   A French IMPRESSIONIST painter of the late nineteenth and early twentieth centuries. He is known for his feathery brushstrokes and for the play of light in his paintings. His painting *Impression, Sunrise* gave the name to the impressionist movement.

Monroe, Marilyn   An American actress who starred in films during the middle of the twentieth century, and became the leading sex SYMBOL of the 1950s. While still in her thirties, she died of an overdose of sleeping pills.

🔊 To many people, Marilyn Monroe is a tragic symbol of the unhappiness that can accompany fame and glamour.

MONA LISA. By Leonardo da Vinci.

montage (mon-TAHZH, mohn-TAHZH) In art, making one composition by combining parts or the whole of other pictures, objects, or designs. In film, a stylized form of editing that provides a great deal of information in a short time. For example, the passing of years may be rendered by mixing shots of different seasons with shots of calendar pages turning.

Monticello (mon-tuh-CHEL-oh, mon-tuh-SEL-oh) The home of Thomas JEFFERSON, in VIRGINIA. The mansion at Monticello, designed by Jefferson himself, is a notable example of the use of ancient forms, such as the dome, in the architecture of his time.

☙ The Monticello mansion appears on the back ("tails" side) of the nickel; Jefferson's head is on the front.

Moonlight Sonata A SONATA for PIANO by Ludwig van BEETHOVEN. An early commentator remarked that the tranquil first MOVEMENT reminded him of moonlight on the waves.

Moore, Henry An English sculptor of the twentieth century. Moore is known for using great masses of stone and other materials to depict humanlike forms.

mosaic A picture or design made from small pieces of colored tile, glass, or other material set in mortar.

Mosaics have been widely used in CHRISTIAN CHURCHES to decorate walls and ceilings.

Moses, Grandma An American artist of the twentieth century, who painted scenes of farm life; her style, which seems childlike, is a noted example of PRIMITIVISM. She began to paint in her late seventies, when she was too old for farm work.

Mount Rushmore A mountain in SOUTH DAKOTA, in which huge likenesses of four presidents' heads are carved: George WASHINGTON, Thomas JEFFERSON, Abraham LINCOLN, and Theodore ROOSEVELT.

Mount Vernon The home of George WASHINGTON, in VIRGINIA.

movement In music, a self-contained division of a long work; each movement usually has its own TEMPO. A long, undivided composition is said to be in one movement.

Mozart, Wolfgang Amadeus (MOHT-sahrt) An Austrian composer of the eighteenth century; one of the great figures in the history of music. A child prodigy, Mozart began composing music before he was five. He, Franz Josef HAYDN, and Ludwig van BEETHOVEN are the leading composers of the CLASSIC era. Mozart wrote CHAMBER MUSIC, SYMPHONIES, OPERAS, and MASSES. Three of his best-known compositions are the short work for ORCHESTRA *Eine Kleine Nachtmusik* (*A Little Night Music*) and the OPERAS *DON GIOVANNI* and *THE MARRIAGE OF FIGARO*.

mural A painting, usually large, made directly on a wall.

☙ The Mexican artist Diego RIVERA was noted for his production of murals.

musical A short term for MUSICAL COMEDY.

musical comedy A play or film that highlights song and dance. *MY FAIR LADY*, *OKLAHOMA!*, and *A Chorus Line* are MUSICALS; all three have had both stage and film versions.

My country, 'tis of thee The first line of the patriotic hymn "AMERICA."

My Fair Lady An American stage MUSICAL of 1956, with words by Alan Jay Lerner and music by Frederick Loewe. *My Fair Lady* is based on the play *PYGMALION*, by George Bernard SHAW, about a professor in ENGLAND who teaches a low-born flower girl how to speak and act like the nobility. The songs "On the Street Where You Live" and "I Could Have Danced All Night" come from *My Fair Lady*.

"My Old Kentucky Home" A song by Stephen FOSTER; the state song of KENTUCKY. It begins, "Oh, the sun shines bright on my old Kentucky home. . . ."

National Anthem of the United States The official national song of the United States: "THE STAR-SPANGLED BANNER."

National Gallery of Art A noted art museum in WASHINGTON, D.C. The federal government pays for the operation of the buildings. The buildings themselves, and the works of art inside, were supplied by private donors. (*See* MELLON, ANDREW.)

naturalism In the visual arts, an attempt to depict the natural world as accurately and objectively as possible.

Nijinsky, Vaslav (ni-JIN-skee, ni-ZHIN-skee) A Russian BALLET dancer, widely considered to have been one of the best male dancers of the twentieth century.

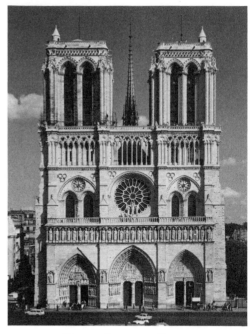

NOTRE DAME DE PARIS

NIJINSKY. *Nijinsky in 1910, dressed as a slave for a role in* Scheherazade.

Ninth Symphony One of the great achievements of European music, it was BEETHOVEN's last symphony; known also as the "Choral" Symphony. Its finale is a musical setting of Friedrich von SCHILLER's "Ode to Joy," a hymn to the unity and freedom of humanity.

"Nobody Knows the Trouble I've Seen" An American SPIRITUAL. It begins:

> Nobody knows the trouble I've seen;
> Nobody knows but JESUS.

Notre Dame de Paris, Cathedral of (noh-truh-DAHM duh pa-REE) A large CATHEDRAL in PARIS, FRANCE. Notre Dame is considered one of the masterpieces of GOTHIC architecture. It is dedicated to MARY, THE MOTHER OF JESUS; *Notre Dame* is French for "Our Lady."

Now I lay me down to sleep Words of a children's prayer in VERSE:

> Now I lay me down to sleep;
> I pray the Lord my soul to keep.
> If I should die before I wake,
> I pray the Lord my soul to take.

Nutcracker, The A BALLET by Peter Ilyich TCHAIKOVSKY, dramatizing a children's story of Christmas.

The Nutcracker is frequently presented at Christmas-time.

O beautiful for spacious skies The first line of the patriotic hymn "AMERICA THE BEAUTIFUL."

oboe A WOODWIND instrument played with a double REED; similar to a BASSOON, but pitched higher. Some describe its tone as nasal.

 🙠 The oboe appears frequently as a solo instrument in SYMPHONIES and other kinds of CLASSICAL MUSIC.

"O Come, All Ye Faithful" A Christmas carol; its original LATIN version is "ADESTE FIDELES." It begins:

  O come, all ye faithful,
  Joyful and triumphant,
  O come ye, O come ye to Bethlehem.

octave (OK-tiv) An interval between musical notes in which the higher note is six WHOLE TONES, or twelve HALF TONES, above the lower. From the standpoint of PHYSICS, the higher note has twice the FREQUENCY of the lower. Notes that are an octave apart, or a whole number of octaves apart, sound in some ways like the same note, and have the same letter for their names.

off-Broadway A descriptive term for part of the theatrical community of NEW YORK CITY that presents small-scale, often experimental dramas. The costs of off-Broadway productions are generally much lower than those of BROADWAY plays.

"Oh! Susanna" A song by Stephen FOSTER. The REFRAIN runs:

  Oh! Susanna, oh don't you cry for me;
  For I come from Alabama with my BANJO on
   my knee.

O'Keeffe, Georgia An American painter of the twentieth century. Her paintings were highly symbolic; flowers and desert scenes were among her favorite subjects.

Oklahoma! A MUSICAL COMEDY by Richard RODGERS and Oscar HAMMERSTEIN II. It began a new era of sophistication in musical comedy, and was the first of several very successful Rodgers and Hammerstein shows. "Oh, What a Beautiful Morning," "Oklahoma," and "People Will Say We're in Love" are songs from *Oklahoma!*

"Old Folks at Home, The" A song by Stephen FOSTER; the state song of FLORIDA. It begins:

  'WAY DOWN UPON THE SWANEE RIVER,
  FAR, FAR AWAY,
  There's where my heart is turning ever;
  There's where the old folks stay.

Olivier, Laurence (oh-LIV-ee-ay) An English actor, widely considered one of the best actors of the twentieth century. Olivier is best known for his deep, subtle interpretations of the CHARACTERS of William SHAKESPEARE. Several of his Shakespeare performances have been filmed. He won an ACADEMY AWARD for his portrayal of the title character in a film version of *HAMLET* released in 1948.

"Ol' Man River" A song from the MUSICAL *Show Boat*; the river is the MISSISSIPPI RIVER. The music to "Ol' Man River" is by Jerome Kern and the words by Oscar HAMMERSTEIN II; it was memorably sung by Paul ROBESON.

"On Top of Old Smoky" An American FOLK-SONG. It begins:

  On top of old Smoky,
  All covered with snow,
  I lost my true lover,
  By a-courting too slow.

"Onward Christian Soldiers" A popular CHRISTIAN hymn with music by Arthur SULLIVAN. The REFRAIN is:

  Onward Christian soldiers,
  Marching as to war,
  With the Cross of JESUS
  Going on before.

opera A musical drama that is totally or mostly sung. *AïDA*, *CARMEN*, and *DON GIOVANNI* are some celebrated operas. Light comic opera is often called OPERETTA.

operetta Comic or lighthearted OPERAS of the kind written by GILBERT AND SULLIVAN. Operettas generally have a substantial amount of spoken (not sung) dialogue.

oratorio A musical composition for voices and ORCHESTRA, telling a religious story.

orchestra A group of musicians who play together on a variety of instruments, which usually come from all four instrument families — BRASS, PERCUSSION, STRINGS, and WOODWINDS. A SYMPHONY orchestra

PICASSO. *Picasso's painting* Guernica, *showing the bombing of that town during the Spanish Civil War.*

is typically made up of over ninety musicians. Most orchestras, unlike CHAMBER MUSIC groups, have more than one musician playing each musical part.

Oscar   A small statue given by the Academy of Motion Picture Arts and Sciences to winners of its annual awards. (*See* ACADEMY AWARDS.)

"Over There"   A song by George M. COHAN about the American troops sent to EUROPE to fight in WORLD WAR I.

overture   A piece of music for instruments alone, written as an introduction to a longer work such as an OPERA, an ORATORIO, or a MUSICAL COMEDY.

pagoda   A tower with several different stories, each of which has its own roof. Pagodas are common in east ASIA, and originally served religious purposes as memorials or shrines.

Parthenon (PAHR-thuh-non)   The central building on the ACROPOLIS in ATHENS, now partly in ruins. Built in ancient times as a temple, it served as a model for much Greek and Roman architecture.

percussion   A family of musical instruments played by striking their surfaces. Percussion instruments are used to accentuate and dramatize certain notes or RHYTHMS, and include such instruments as CYMBALS, drums, triangles, and xylophones. (*See* KETTLEDRUM, SNARE DRUM, *and* ORCHESTRA.)

perspective   In drawing or painting, a way of portraying three dimensions on a flat, two-dimensional surface by suggesting depth or distance. (*See* VANISHING POINT.)

Peter and the Wolf   A piece for ORCHESTRA by a Russian composer of the twentieth century, Sergei Prokofiev. Through music, it tells the story of a disobedient boy's encounter with a wolf.

   🕭 Because each character in the story is represented by a different musical instrument, *Peter and the Wolf* is often used to introduce children to the various instruments in an orchestra.

pianissimo (pee-uh-NIS-uh-moh)   A musical direction meaning "to be performed very softly"; the opposite of FORTISSIMO.

piano   A musical direction meaning "to be performed softly"; the opposite of FORTE. As the name of a musical instrument, it is short for PIANOFORTE.

pianoforte (pee-AN-uh-fawrt, pee-an-uh-FAWR-tay)   The full name of the PIANO, the common musical instrument with a board of black and white keys, eighty-eight in all. The keys operate hammers that strike wires. *Pianoforte* is Italian for "soft-loud"; it received this name because its level of loudness depends on how hard the player strikes the keys.

piazza (pee-AZ-uh, pee-AH-zuh, pee-AHT-suh) An open square, especially in a city or town in ITALY.

Picasso, Pablo (pi-KAH-soh) A Spanish painter of the twentieth century, the most famous and influential of all modern artists. Picasso was one of the originators of CUBISM, though in the course of his long career, he painted and drew in many other styles as well. Among his best-known works is the painting *Guernica*, which protests the savagery of war.

piccolo (PIK-uh-loh) A small, high-pitched FLUTE.

🎵 The piccolo has a prominent part in the march "THE STARS AND STRIPES FOREVER," by John Philip SOUSA.

PIETÀ. *Michelangelo's* Pietà, *in Saint Peter's Basilica, Rome.*

Pietà (pyay-TAH, pee-ay-TAH) A painting, drawing, or sculpture of MARY, THE MOTHER OF JESUS, holding the dead body of JESUS. The word means "pity" in Italian.

🎵 The most famous of four Pietàs by MICHELANGELO is a sculpture at SAINT PETER'S BASILICA in the VATICAN. It is the usual referent for this term.

Pinafore, H.M.S. A comic OPERA by GILBERT AND SULLIVAN about the marriage of the beautiful daughter of the captain of the ship in the title. *H.M.S. Pinafore* contains many notable songs, including "I'm Called Little Buttercup" and "When I Was a Lad."

polka A lively dance for couples, originating in eastern EUROPE.

🎵 Johann STRAUSS the Younger wrote many polkas.

Pollock, Jackson An American painter of the twentieth century, famous for creating abstract paintings by dripping or pouring paint on a canvas in complex swirls and spatters.

pop art Art that uses elements of popular CULTURE, such as magazines, movies, popular music, even bottles and cans. (*See* ANDY WARHOL.)

Porgy and Bess (PAWR-gee) An OPERA with music by George GERSHWIN. It depicts life in the African-American community of CHARLESTON, SOUTH CAROLINA. Porgy is a handicapped beggar who protects Bess, only to have her leave town with a rival. The songs "SUMMERTIME" and "It Ain't Necessarily So" are from *Porgy and Bess*.

Porter, Cole An American songwriter of the twentieth century. Porter's songs, such as "Anything Goes," "I Get a Kick out of You," and "I've Got You under My Skin," are renowned for their witty, sophisticated lyrics.

Prado, Museo del (mooh-SAY-oh del PRAH-doh) A famous art museum in MADRID, SPAIN.

premiere The first public performance of a piece of music, a play, or a similar work.

Presley, Elvis An American ROCK 'N' ROLL singer of the twentieth century, known for his distinctive throaty tone in such songs as "Hound Dog" and "All Shook Up." He was one of the first stars of rock 'n' roll.

🎵 When Presley first appeared on television in the 1950s, the gyrations he performed while singing were considered too suggestive for broadcast. The cameras recorded him only from the waist up. 🎵 Presley died in 1977 while still in his early forties.

prima ballerina The leading BALLERINA in a dance company.

primitivism A style of art that attempts to imitate the art of primitive CULTURES or of children.

Puccini, Giacomo (pooh-CHEE-nee) An Italian composer of OPERAS in the late nineteenth and early twentieth centuries. He is best known for *MADAME BUTTERFLY*, *La Bohème*, and *Tosca*.

pyramids A group of huge monuments in the desert of EGYPT, built as burial vaults for ancient Egyptian kings. The age of pyramid building in Egypt began about 2700 B.C. (*See under "World History to 1550."*)

quartet A group of four musicians or singers; also, a piece of music for four instruments or voices.

quintet A group of five musicians; also, a piece of music for five instruments or voices.

ragtime A style of early JAZZ music written largely for the PIANO in the early twentieth century, characterized by jaunty RHYTHMS and a whimsical mood.

 🎵 Scott JOPLIN was a famous composer and performer of ragtime.

Raphael (RAF-ee-uhl, RAY-fee-uhl, rah-fee-EL) An Italian painter of the sixteenth century; a contemporary of LEONARDO DA VINCI and MICHELANGELO.

RAPHAEL

He is known for his beautiful and gracious MADONNAS and *THE SCHOOL OF ATHENS*.

recitative (res-i-tuh-TEEV) A part of a CANTATA, OPERA, or ORATORIO in which singers converse, describe action, or declaim. It moves the action forward between the high musical moments. Recitatives are distinguished from ARIAS, which are more expressive and musically more elaborate. Recitatives usually have only one SYLLABLE of text for each note of music, and the accompaniment by instruments is often very simple.

recorder A wooden FLUTE played like a whistle. It was popular in the fourteenth through eighteenth centuries. Interest in it has been revived over the past few decades.

"Red River Valley" An American FOLKSONG. It begins, "From this valley they say you are going. . . ."

reed A thin piece of wood or plastic used in many WOODWIND instruments. It vibrates when the player holds it in the mouth and blows over it (as with a single reed) or through it (as with a double reed). CLARINETS and SAXOPHONES use a single reed; BASSOONS and OBOES use a double reed.

Rembrandt (REM-brant, REM-brahnt) A Dutch painter of the seventeenth century, considered one of the greatest painters in history. Rembrandt's work, with its strong lights and deep shadows, has a unique intensity. *The Night Watch* is one of his best-known paintings.

Renoir, Pierre-Auguste (ren-WAHR) A French IMPRESSIONIST painter and sculptor of the late nineteenth and early twentieth centuries. One of the most popular of the impressionists, Renoir is known for his extravagant use of light and color, especially red, and for frequent use of the impressionist technique of small brushstrokes. His most famous paintings include *Dance at Bougival* and a series of paintings, *The Bathers*.

Requiem (REK-wee-uhm) In music, a MASS for one or more dead persons, containing biblical passages and prayers for the admission of the dead to HEAVEN. The term has been loosely applied to other musical compositions in honor of the dead. *A German Requiem* by Johannes BRAHMS, for example, uses texts from the BIBLE, but is not a Mass.

DIEGO RIVERA. *A detail from Rivera's fresco* Detroit Industry 1932–33.

Rhapsody in Blue A CONCERTO for PIANO and OR-
CHESTRA from the early 1920s by George GERSHWIN;
one of the first pieces of "serious" music to contain
elements of JAZZ.

rhythm The "beat" of music; the regular pattern of
long and short notes. Certain kinds of music, such as
BLUES or marches, have a very characteristic rhythm.
Rhythm, HARMONY, and melody are elements of music.

Ring of the Nibelung (NEE-buh-loong) A series of
four OPERAS by Richard WAGNER, based on stories
from NORSE MYTHOLOGY; the central story is that of
Siegfried and BRÜNNHILDE. As the *Ring* ends, the
gods are about to be overcome. The four operas of
the *Ring* are *The Rhinegold, The Valkyrie, Siegfried,*
and *The Twilight of the Gods.*

Rivera, Diego (dee-AY-goh ri-VAIR-uh) A Mexican
painter of the twentieth century, known for his MU-
RALS. His work glorifies farms, peasants, and revolutionary fervor.

Robeson, Paul (ROHB-suhn) An African-American
actor and singer of the twentieth century, best known
for his roles in *PORGY AND BESS* and in the movie
version of *Show Boat*, in which he sang "OL' MAN
RIVER."

⠶ Robeson was politically controversial. He lived
outside the United States for many years. He compared the treatment of African-Americans in the
United States unfavorably with their treatment in the
SOVIET UNION. Because of his political statements,
the federal government declared his United States
passport invalid.

rock music *See* ROCK 'N' ROLL.

rock 'n' roll Popular music combining elements of
BLUES (or RHYTHM and blues), GOSPEL MUSIC, and
COUNTRY AND WESTERN MUSIC, and known for its
strong beat and urgent lyrics. Well-known rock 'n'
roll artists or groups include Chuck BERRY, Buddy
Holly, the Temptations, the Supremes, the BEATLES,
the Rolling Stones, Elvis PRESLEY, and Michael Jackson.

Rockwell, Norman An American artist and illustrator of the twentieth century, known for his warm-
hearted paintings of rural and small-town life in the
United States. Many of his paintings appeared as
cover illustrations for the magazine *The Saturday
Evening Post.*

rococo (ruh-KOH-koh, roh-kuh-KOH) A style of BA-
ROQUE art and architecture popular in EUROPE during the eighteenth century, characterized by flowing
lines and elaborate decoration.

Rodgers, Richard An American popular composer
of the twentieth century, known for writing the music
to a long succession of MUSICAL COMEDIES, including
OKLAHOMA!, South Pacific, The King and I, and *The*

Sound of Music. In all these musicals, the spoken dialogue and lyrics were written by Oscar HAMMER-STEIN II.

Rodin, Auguste (roh-DAN, roh-DANN)   A French sculptor of the nineteenth century. *THE THINKER* is one of his best-known works.

Rogers, Ginger   An American actress and dancer of the twentieth century; she danced with Fred ASTAIRE in a famous series of film MUSICALS.

Rogers, Will   An American humorist of the twentieth century, known for his folksy but sharp social and political commentary. Two statements for which he is remembered are "All I know is just what I read in the papers," and "I NEVER MET A MAN I DIDN'T LIKE."

Romanesque (roh-muh-NESK)   A style of architecture and art common in EUROPE between the ninth and twelfth centuries. It combined elements of the architecture typical of the ROMAN EMPIRE and the BYZANTINE EMPIRE. The ARCHES on Romanesque buildings are usually semicircular rather than pointed as in GOTHIC architecture.

romanticism   A movement in literature, music, and painting in the late eighteenth and early nineteenth centuries. Romanticism has often been called a rebellion against an overemphasis on reason in the arts. It stressed the essential goodness of human beings (*see* ROUSSEAU, Jean-Jacques), celebrated nature rather than civilization, and valued emotion and imagination over reason. Some major figures of romanticism in the FINE ARTS are the composers Robert SCHUMANN, Felix MENDELSSOHN, and Johannes BRAHMS, and the painter Joseph TURNER.

round   A song that can be begun at different times by different singers, but with harmonious singing (*see* HARMONY) as the result. "Row, Row, Row Your Boat" is a round.

"Row, Row, Row Your Boat"   A musical ROUND:

> Row, row, row your boat
> Gently down the stream,
> Merrily, merrily, merrily, merrily;
> Life is but a dream.

Rubens, Peter Paul   A Flemish painter of the seventeenth century, known for his paintings of religious subjects and for his voluptuous female nudes.

RUBENS. *A detail from Rubens's painting* The Education of Marie de Medicis, *showing the three Graces.*

Rubinstein, Arthur (ROOH-bin-steyen)   An American pianist of the twentieth century who was born in POLAND. Rubinstein was particularly famous for his interpretations of the music of Frédéric CHOPIN.

"Saint Louis Blues"   A BLUES song by W. C. Handy.

Saint Paul's Cathedral   A CATHEDRAL in LONDON, designed by Christopher WREN, and recognizable by its huge dome. Saint Paul's Cathedral is one of the city's major landmarks.

Saint Peter's Basilica   The largest CHRISTIAN CHURCH building in the world, located in the VATICAN. The residence of the POPE adjoins it, and many ceremonies and speeches connected with the pope's administration take place there. RAPHAEL and MICHELANGELO contributed to its design and decoration.

saxophone   A WIND INSTRUMENT classified as a WOODWIND because it is played with a REED, although it is usually made of metal. Saxophones appear mainly in JAZZ, dance, and military bands. They are made in several ranges, from SOPRANO to BASS.

Scala, La (lah SKAH-luh)   A world-renowned OPERA house in MILAN, ITALY; one of the leading opera houses of the world. Its name means "The Stairs" in Italian.

scale In music, the sequence of tones that a piece of music principally uses. A composition in the KEY of C-major uses the C-major scale, made up of the white keys on a PIANO.

Schubert, Franz An Austrian composer of the nineteenth century; like Ludwig van BEETHOVEN, he composed during the transition from the CLASSIC to the romantic period in music (*see* ROMANTICISM). He is known especially for his song cycles (LIEDER), usually written for solo voice and PIANO accompaniment. His best-known instrumental works are the "Unfinished" SYMPHONY and the "Trout" QUINTET.

Schumann, Robert (SHOOH-mahn) A German romantic composer (*see* ROMANTICISM) of the nineteenth century. Schumann's best-remembered compositions are his PIANO pieces, including "Traumerei" and "The Happy Farmer," and his songs.

Sears Tower The world's tallest building. This skyscraper is located in CHICAGO.

"Sesame Street" An educational television program for preschool children, particularly aimed at disadvantaged children, that began in the late 1960s. "Sesame Street" teaches awareness of letters and numbers, and combines live actors, animation, and puppets (Muppets) in a great number of small segments, many of them musical, and some of them only a few seconds long.

  Many of the Muppets who appear on the show have become familiar across the nation, including Kermit the Frog, the roommates Bert and Ernie, the voracious Cookie Monster, and Big Bird, who towers over the human actors.

"Silent Night" A song of Christmas, originally composed in AUSTRIA in the nineteenth century. It begins, "Silent night, holy night, / All is calm, all is bright. . . . "

Sistine Chapel (sis-teen) A chapel adjoining SAINT PETER'S BASILICA, noted for the FRESCOES of biblical subjects painted by MICHELANGELO on its walls and ceilings. The CREATION is one of the notable subjects of the ceiling paintings, and the LAST JUDGMENT is depicted on the rear wall of the chapel.

  Michelangelo had to work on his back to paint the ceiling of the Sistine Chapel. The project took four years to complete.

skull and crossbones A picture or outline of a human skull and two crossed arm or leg bones. Pirate ships are supposed to have used the skull and crossbones on their flags. (*See* JOLLY ROGER.)

snare drum A shallow cylindrical drum, with wires or pieces of catgut (snares) stretched across the bottom skin to give a sharp, rattling sound when the top skin is struck. Snare drums are used in ORCHESTRAS and in nearly all kinds of bands.

sonata (suh-NAH-tuh) A musical composition for one or two instruments, usually in three or four MOVEMENTS. The sonata of the CLASSIC era in music had a definite arrangement for its movements: the first and fourth had a fast TEMPO, the second had a slow tempo, and the third was in either playful style (a "scherzo") or in dance form (a "minuet").

Sophia, Hagia, Cathedral of *See* HAGIA SOPHIA, CATHEDRAL OF.

soprano The highest range of the female singing voice. (*Compare* ALTO *and* MEZZO SOPRANO.)

Sousa, John Philip (SOOH-zuh, SOOH-suh) An American bandmaster and composer of the late nineteenth and early twentieth centuries, called the "March King." His many marches include "THE STARS AND STRIPES FOREVER," "Semper Fidelis," and "The Washington Post."

sousaphone A kind of TUBA that wraps around the player's body so that it can be carried easily while marching.

  The sousaphone is named after the bandmaster John Philip SOUSA, who suggested building the instrument in this shape.

Sphinx (SFINGKS) A great sculpture carved from the rock near the Egyptian PYRAMIDS in about 2500 B.C. It depicts a creature from Egyptian MYTHOLOGY with the head of a man and the body of a lion. (*See under* "*Mythology and Folklore.*")

Spirit of '76, The A painting from the nineteenth century by Archibald M. Willard, depicting three soldiers of the AMERICAN REVOLUTION. Though one is

The Spirit of '76. By Archibald M. Willard.

wounded, they are marching on with spirit and determination.

spirituals   A kind of religious song originated by African-Americans. Spirituals are often written with freer RHYTHMS and HARMONIES than most standard hymns. Many of them go back to the days of slavery, and they often speak of biblical models of deliverance, such as the EXODUS. Several spirituals have become standard pieces of music for concert singers and choruses. "GONNA LAY DOWN MY BURDEN," "JOSHUA FIT THE BATTLE OF JERICHO," "NOBODY KNOWS THE TROUBLE I'VE SEEN," "SWING LOW, SWEET CHARIOT," and "WHEN THE SAINTS GO MARCHING IN" are spirituals.

staccato (stuh-KAH-toh)   A direction in music meaning that the notes should be performed in an abrupt, sharp, clear-cut manner.

🍃 The term *staccato* has been applied generally to things that occur in rapid bursts, such as gunfire.

Star of David   *See* JUDAISM.

"Star Trek"   A television show of the 1960s, in which a group of space explorers, in their craft the *Enterprise*, traveled through interstellar space.

"Star-Spangled Banner, The"   The NATIONAL ANTHEM OF THE UNITED STATES. Francis Scott KEY wrote the words during the WAR OF 1812, when he saw the flag of the United States still flying over Fort McHenry, MARYLAND, after a night of attack by British troops. The tune is from a British popular song of the day. The first STANZA is:

> Oh, say, can you see by the dawn's early light,
> What so proudly we hailed at the twilight's last
>   gleaming?
> Whose broad stripes and bright stars, thro' the
>   perilous fight,
> O'er the ramparts we watched were so gallantly
>   streaming?
> And the rockets' red glare, the bombs bursting
>   in air,
> Gave proof thro' the night that our flag was still
>   there.
> Oh, say does that star-spangled banner yet wave
> O'er the land of the free and home of the brave?

Stars and Stripes   The national flag of the United States. Its fifty stars represent the fifty states; its thirteen stripes represent the THIRTEEN COLONIES that became the original states.

"Stars and Stripes Forever, The"   One of the most popular marches by John Philip SOUSA. The PICCOLO part is especially elaborate.

Statue of Liberty   A giant statue on an island in the harbor of NEW YORK CITY; it depicts a woman representing liberty, raising a torch in her right hand and holding a tablet in her left. At its base is inscribed a poem that contains the lines "GIVE ME YOUR TIRED, YOUR POOR, / Your huddled masses yearning to breathe free." Frederic Bartholdi, a Frenchman, was the sculptor. FRANCE gave the Statue of Liberty to the United States in the nineteenth century; it was shipped across the ATLANTIC OCEAN in sections and reassembled. The statue was overhauled and strengthened in the 1980s.

🍃 For many immigrants who came to the United States by ship in the late nineteenth and early twentieth centuries, the Statue of Liberty made a permanent impression as the first landmark they saw as they approached their new home.

Stern, Isaac   A celebrated American violinist of the twentieth century. Stern is known for his work to save CARNEGIE HALL from destruction, as well as for his musical performances.

Stewart, James   An American film actor of the twentieth century, known for his gangly figure and halting, even stammering, style of speech. Stewart has appeared in a great variety of movies, including *Mr. Smith Goes to Washington*, *Harvey*, *Anatomy of a Murder*, and several of the films of Alfred HITCHCOCK. He won an ACADEMY AWARD for his part in *The Philadelphia Story* in 1940.

Stradivarius (strad-uh-VAIR-ee-uhs) A kind of VIOLIN made by the Italian craftsman Antonio Stradivari in the late seventeenth and early eighteenth centuries. Those that still survive are considered the finest violins in existence.

Strauss, Johann, the Younger (YOH-hahn STROWS, SHTROWS) An Austrian composer of the nineteenth century. Strauss, sometimes called the "Waltz King," is the most famous composer of Viennese waltzes, such as "The Blue Danube" and "Tales of the Vienna Woods." (*See* VIENNA *and* DANUBE RIVER.) He also composed the music for the popular light OPERA *Die Fledermaus (The Bat)*.

Strauss, Richard (RIKH-ahrt STROWS, SHTROWS) A German composer and conductor of the late nineteenth and early twentieth centuries. Strauss is best known for the OPERA *Der Rosenkavalier (The Cavalier of the Rose)* and for *Thus Spake Zarathustra*, a piece for ORCHESTRA inspired by the book of the same name by Friedrich NIETZSCHE.

❧ Richard Strauss and Richard WAGNER are outstanding examples of composers of the late romantic period in music. (*See* ROMANTICISM.)

Stravinsky, Igor (struh-VIN-skee) A Russian composer, widely considered one of the greatest composers of the twentieth century. Among his celebrated works are the BALLETS *The Rite of Spring*, *The Firebird*, and *Petrushka*.

string quartet A musical group that includes two VIOLINS, a VIOLA, and a CELLO. The term also refers to a composition written for these four instruments. Many composers, notably Franz Josef HAYDN, Wolfgang Amadeus MOZART, and Ludwig van BEETHOVEN, have written string quartets.

strings A section of the ORCHESTRA containing the stringed musical instruments — those played by making stretched strings vibrate. In most stringed instruments, the musician draws a bow over the strings; VIOLINS, VIOLAS, CELLOS, and BASS VIOLS are played in this way. Other stringed instruments are played by plucking the strings; these include the BANJO, GUITAR, HARP, HARPSICHORD, and UKULELE.

Stuart, Gilbert An American painter of the eighteenth century. Stuart was known for his portraits, especially of George WASHINGTON.

suite (SWEET) A group of related pieces of music or MOVEMENTS played in sequence. In the BAROQUE era, a suite was a succession of different kinds of dances. In more recent times, suites have contained excerpts from longer works, such as BALLETS, or have simply portrayed a scene, as in Ferde Grofé's *Grand Canyon Suite*.

❧ A suite from the ballet *THE NUTCRACKER*, by Peter Ilyich TCHAIKOVSKY, is a popular selection with ORCHESTRAS.

"Summertime" One of the best-known songs of George GERSHWIN; it comes from the OPERA *PORGY AND BESS*, and begins, "Summertime, and the living is easy. . . ."

Supreme Court Building The building in WASHINGTON, D.C., that houses the SUPREME COURT; it follows ancient Greek models of architecture. The words "Equal Justice under Law" are carved above the main entrance.

surrealism A movement in art and literature that flourished in the early twentieth century. Surrealism aimed at expressing imaginative dreams and visions free from conscious rational control. Salvador DALI was an influential surrealist painter; Jean Cocteau was a master of surrealist film.

Swan Lake A BALLET by Peter Ilyich TCHAIKOVSKY, in which a prince fights for the love of the Swan Queen. *Swan Lake* is one of the most famous ballets.

swastika The SYMBOL of the German NAZI party; it is a cross with equal arms, and each arm is bent at a RIGHT ANGLE. The swastika was an ancient symbol of good luck.

swing A kind of JAZZ generally played by a "Big Band," and characterized by a lively RHYTHM suitable for dancing. The bands of Count BASIE, Duke ELLINGTON, Benny GOODMAN, and Glenn MILLER played swing.

"Swing Low, Sweet Chariot" An American SPIRITUAL. It begins, "Swing low, sweet chariot, / Coming for to carry me home. . . ."

symphony An extended musical composition for ORCHESTRA in several MOVEMENTS, typically four. Among the composers especially known for their symphonies are Ludwig van BEETHOVEN, Johannes BRAHMS, Franz Josef HAYDN, Gustav MAHLER, and Wolfgang Amadeus MOZART.

Taj Mahal (TAHZH, TAHJ muh-HAHL) A marble MAUSOLEUM in INDIA, built in the seventeenth century by a king for his wife. The Taj Mahal usually appears on lists of the most beautiful buildings in the world.

"Take Me Out to the Ball Game" A popular song about baseball from the early twentieth century.

tango A sensual ballroom dance that originated in SOUTH AMERICA in the early twentieth century.

Tchaikovsky, Peter Ilyich (cheye-KAWF-skee) A Russian composer of the nineteenth century. His most celebrated works include several SYMPHONIES, including the *Symphonie Pathétique*; and three ballets, *THE NUTCRACKER*, *SWAN LAKE*, and *Sleeping Beauty*.

"Te Deum" (tay DAY-uhm, tee DEE-uhm) A hymn of praise to God, with words taken largely from the BIBLE, that is used by many groups of CHRISTIANS. The "Te Deum" has been set to music by George Frederick HANDEL and by many other composers for performance in worship services of thanksgiving (after a victory in war, for example). The LATIN words *Te Deum laudamus* mean "Thee, God, we praise."

tempo In music, the speed at which a piece is performed (*see* ADAGIO, ALLEGRO, *and* ANDANTE). It is the Italian word for "time."

tenor The highest range of the male singing voice. (*Compare* BARITONE *and* BASS.)

Thinker, The A bronze statue by Auguste RODIN. The seated subject is supporting his chin on his wrist and his arm on his knee.

"This Land Is Your Land" A song by Woody GUTHRIE.

Tiffany glass Lamps and other glass objects created by Louis Tiffany, an American artisan of the late nineteenth and early twentieth centuries. These objects are greatly prized, and have been much imitated.

TAJ MAHAL

THE THINKER. *The bronze statue by Auguste Rodin.*

timpani (TIM-puh-nee) Italian for KETTLEDRUMS; the term *timpani* is often preferred by composers and performers.

Tin Pan Alley A reference to the popular music industry in the United States; the term is not used as much today as it was a generation or two ago.

  ⬥ Tin Pan Alley is often associated with songwriters who are more interested in making money off their songs than in producing high-quality music.

Titian (TISH-uhn) An Italian painter of the sixteenth century, known for his portraits and for his innovative use of color.

Toscanini, Arturo (tos-kuh-NEE-nee)   A celebrated Italian conductor of the late nineteenth and early twentieth centuries. He spent much of his career in the United States. In his later years, he conducted the National Broadcasting Company (NBC) Symphony Orchestra, which was organized for him.

Toulouse-Lautrec, Henri de (too-loohz-loh-TREK, too-loohs-loh-TREK)   A French artist of the late nineteenth and early twentieth centuries, known especially for his paintings, drawings, and posters that depict the night life of Montmartre, the district in PARIS where he lived.

trombone   A BRASS instrument; the player can change its pitch by sliding one part of the tube in and out of the other. The tone of the trombone is mellower than that of the TRUMPET.

trumpet   A BRASS instrument with a brilliant tone, much used in CLASSICAL MUSIC, as well as in military music and JAZZ.

tuba   The lowest-pitched of the BRASS instruments. In ORCHESTRAS, the tuba is usually held across the player's lap. In marching bands, the SOUSAPHONE is generally used as a low brass instrument because it was designed to be carried.

"Turkey in the Straw"   An American folk tune (see FOLK MUSIC), typically played on a FIDDLE.

Turner, Joseph Mallord William   An English romantic painter (see ROMANTICISM) of the late eighteenth and early nineteenth centuries, known especially for his dramatic, lavishly colored landscapes and seascapes.

Uffizi Gallery (ooh-FEET-see)   A famous art museum in FLORENCE, ITALY.

ukulele (yooh-kuh-LAY-lee)   A small GUITAR, developed in HAWAII, with four strings.

unison   Playing or singing the same musical notes, or notes separated from each other by one or several OCTAVES. Musicians who perform in unison are not playing or singing CHORDS.

van Gogh, Vincent (van GOH, vahn KHOHKH)   A Dutch painter of the nineteenth century. Van Gogh, a troubled genius who cut off one of his ears in a fit of depression, eventually committed suicide. His work, though virtually unknown during his lifetime, is now highly regarded. *Starry Night* and *Sunflowers* are two of his best-known paintings.

vanishing point   The point in a drawing or painting at which parallel lines appear to converge in the distance. (*See* PERSPECTIVE.)

vaudeville (VAWD-vuhl, VAW-duh-vil)   Light theatrical entertainment, popular in the late nineteenth and early twentieth centuries, consisting of a succession of short acts. A vaudeville show could continue for hours, and included comedians, singers, dancers, jugglers, trained animals, magicians, and so on.

Velázquez, Diego de (vuh-LAHS-kes)   A Spanish painter of the seventeenth century, known for his portraits of members of the court of the king of SPAIN.

VENUS DE MILO

Venus de Milo (duh-MEE-loh, MEYE-loh)   An ancient Greek statue of VENUS, famous for its beauty, though its arms were broken off centuries ago.

   ❧ It is one of the most famous possessions of the LOUVRE.

Verdi, Giuseppe (VAIR-dee)   An Italian composer of the nineteenth century, the master of Italian grand

OPERA. Among his best-known operas are *AIDA*, *Otello*, *Rigoletto*, and *La Traviata*.

Vermeer, Jan (vuhr-MEER, vuhr-MAIR)   A Dutch painter of the seventeenth century, known for painting domestic scenes of great clarity and repose.

Versailles, Palace of (ver-SEYE, vuhr-SEYE)   A large royal residence built in the seventeenth century by King LOUIS XIV of FRANCE in VERSAILLES, near PARIS. The palace, with its lavish gardens and fountains, is a spectacular example of French classical architecture. The Hall of Mirrors is particularly well known.

❧ The peace treaty that formally ended WORLD WAR I was negotiated and signed at the Palace of Versailles.

Vietnam Memorial   A monument in WASHINGTON, D.C., in honor of persons in the American armed services who died in the VIETNAM WAR. The memorial is a large black marble wall set below ground level on a flat part of the WASHINGTON MALL. The names of the dead are inscribed in the wall.

viola (vee-OH-luh)   A musical instrument shaped like a VIOLIN but somewhat larger, lower-pitched, and "darker" in tone. A viola player holds a viola like a VIOLIN, under the chin.

violin   The most familiar and highest-pitched instrument of the STRINGS. A typical SYMPHONY ORCHESTRA has more than two dozen violinists.

Vivaldi, Antonio (vuh-VAHL-dee, vuh-VAWL-dee)   An Italian composer of the early eighteenth century, known particularly for his CONCERTOS. His style affected those of several other BAROQUE composers, notably Johann Sebastian BACH.

Wagner, Richard (VAHG-nuhr)   A German composer of the nineteenth century, known for his OPERAS, many of which dramatize myths and legends. The four-opera group *THE RING OF THE NIBELUNG* and the single opera *Tristan und Isolde* are among his best-known compositions. The music for Wagner's operas is highly dramatic (he called his operas "music dramas"); requires large ORCHESTRAS; uses a continuously melodic style, rather than a division into ARIAS and RECITATIVES; and depends much on the device of the LEITMOTIF.

Warhol, Andy (WAWR-hawl, WAWR-hohl)   American artist of the twentieth century whose best-known

ANDY WARHOL. *Standing beside his painting* Portrait of Jimmy Carter.

work was a precise, enlarged image of a can of Campbell's tomato soup. He also painted Coke bottles, Brillo pads, and rows of images of Marilyn MONROE. His most famous statement was "IN THE FUTURE EVERYONE WILL BE WORLD-FAMOUS FOR FIFTEEN MINUTES." (*See* POP ART.)

Washington Crossing the Delaware   A painting from the nineteenth century by a German painter, Emanuel Leutze, showing George WASHINGTON and a group of soldiers in a small boat crossing the Delaware River. They are going to launch a surprise attack against the British troops during the AMERICAN REVOLUTION.

Washington Mall   A long, rectangular stretch of parkland in the middle of WASHINGTON, D.C., that extends from the grounds of the LINCOLN MEMORIAL to the United States CAPITOL. The WASHINGTON MONUMENT and the VIETNAM MEMORIAL are located on the Mall; the different museums of the SMITHSONIAN INSTITUTION are found along either side.

Washington Monument A structure on the WASHINGTON MALL, over five hundred feet tall, built in the nineteenth century in honor of George WASHINGTON. In shape it is an obelisk — a four-sided shaft with a PYRAMID at the top.

Water Music A set of pieces for ORCHESTRA by George Frederick HANDEL. Parts of it appear to have been written for a festival that took place on boats on the THAMES RIVER in ENGLAND.

'Way down upon the Swanee River, far, far away The first lines of the song "The OLD FOLKS AT HOME," by Stephen FOSTER.

Wayne, John An American film actor of the twentieth century who often played "tough guys," particularly soldiers and cowboys. His nickname was "Duke."

Welles, Orson An American actor and filmmaker of the twentieth century. His masterpiece is *Citizen Kane*, the story of a newspaper TYCOON, which he directed, and in which he played the title role.

   ❧ For Halloween of 1938, Welles wrote a famous radio dramatization of *The War of the Worlds*, by H. G. WELLS, the story of an invasion of the EARTH by warriors from MARS. Welles's play included several fictional radio news reports about the invasion. Many listeners who missed the beginning of the play thought that they were hearing about an actual Martian attack, and panicked.

West, Mae An American actress of the twentieth century. Mae West was a blonde, busty sex SYMBOL, whose seductiveness was usually very funny because she overstated it so greatly. The popular version of her most celebrated line is "Why don'cha come up and see me sometime?" She appeared memorably opposite W. C. FIELDS in *My Little Chickadee*.

"When Johnny Comes Marching Home" A popular song from the American CIVIL WAR. The first STANZA is:

> When Johnny comes marching home again,
>   hurrah! Hurrah!
> We'll give him a hearty welcome then, hurrah!
>   Hurrah!
> The men will cheer, the boys will shout,
> The ladies, they will all turn out,
> And we'll all feel gay, when Johnny comes
>   marching home.

"When the Saints Go Marching In" An American SPIRITUAL, one of the best-known songs played by DIXIELAND bands. The first verse is:

> Oh, when the saints go marching in,
> Oh, when the saints go marching in,
> Oh, Lord, I want to be in that number,
> When the saints go marching in.

Whistler, James An American artist of the nineteenth century, who spent most of his career in ENGLAND and FRANCE. He is best known for the painting popularly called *WHISTLER'S MOTHER*.

Whistler's Mother The popular title of a painting, *Arrangement in Grey and Black Number 1*, by James WHISTLER, which depicts his mother in profile, dressed in black, and seated on a straight chair.

"White Christmas" A popular song for Christmas, composed by Irving BERLIN and memorably sung by Bing CROSBY. It begins, "I'm dreaming of a white Christmas. . . . "

White House The mansion of the president of the United States in WASHINGTON, D.C. The White House contains reception and dining rooms, living quarters for the president and the president's family, the president's OVAL OFFICE, and offices for the presidential staff.

whole tone An interval between musical notes. Do and re are a whole tone apart, as are re and mi, fa and sol, sol and la, and la and ti.

wind instruments Musical instruments in which sound is produced by the musician's blowing into them.

woodwinds A group of WIND INSTRUMENTS with a softer tone than that of BRASS instruments. Woodwind players do not set the air in their instruments in motion by blowing through their closed lips against a cup-shaped mouthpiece, as players of brass instruments do. In woodwinds, the players insert the mouthpiece into their mouths and blow while pressing their lips against a single or double REED. BASSOONS, CLARINETS, OBOES, and SAXOPHONES are played in this way. In other woodwinds (FIFES, FLUTES, and PICCOLOS), the player blows across a hole or into a whistlelike mouthpiece (RECORDERS).

World Trade Center A pair of skyscrapers that dominate the skyline of lower MANHATTAN.

Wren, Christopher An English architect of the late seventeenth and early eighteenth centuries. Wren designed many buildings in LONDON for the large rebuilding effort that followed the city's "Great Fire" of 1666. SAINT PAUL'S CATHEDRAL is his best-known work.

Wright, Frank Lloyd An American architect of the twentieth century, known for his highly original methods of uniting buildings with their surroundings.

FRANK LLOYD WRIGHT. *The exterior of Wright's house Fallingwater, in Bear Run, Pennsylvania.*

Wyeth, Andrew (WEYE-uhht) An American painter of the twentieth century, known for *Christina's World* and other works.

"Yankee Doodle" A popular American song, dating from the eighteenth century. The early settlers of NEW YORK were Dutch, and the Dutch name for Johnny is Janke, pronounced "Yankee." This is the most likely origin of the term *Yankee*. *Doodle* meant "simpleton" in seventeenth-century English. First sung during the REVOLUTIONARY WAR by the British troops to poke fun at the strange ways of the Americans (Yankees), the song was soon adopted by American troops themselves. Since then, the song has been considered an expression of American patriotism. The popular version of the first STANZA is:

> Yankee Doodle came to town
> Riding on a pony;
> He stuck a feather in his hat
> And called it macaroni.
> Yankee Doodle, keep it up,
> Yankee Doodle dandy;
> Mind the music and the step,
> And with the girls be handy.

"Yankee Doodle Dandy" A song by George M. COHAN. The REFRAIN begins, "I'm a Yankee Doodle dandy, / A Yankee Doodle, do or die. . . . "

You'll take the high road, and I'll take the low road A line from the Scottish song "LOCH LOMOND."

"You're a Grand Old Flag" A song by George M. COHAN. The REFRAIN begins, "You're a grand old flag; / You're a high-flying flag. . . ."

World History to 1550

This section covers the period from the beginnings of civilization in the STONE AGE through the rise and fall of the ancient MEDITERRANEAN civilizations, to the DARK AGES, the MIDDLE AGES, and the beginnings of the RENAISSANCE and the REFORMATION. Although these dates are very rough by current reckoning, the Stone Age ended around 4000 B.C. with the beginning of the BRONZE AGE, which encompassed the years from about 4000 B.C. to 2000 B.C., at which point the IRON AGE began. The great civilizations of EGYPT, GREECE, and ROME developed during the Iron Age. Egyptian civilization flourished in the second millennium B.C. and then declined. Ancient Greece reached the pinnacle of its influence in the fifth and fourth centuries B.C., and then saw its influence wane after the death of ALEXANDER THE GREAT in 323 B.C. The importance of Rome increased dramatically in the century before the birth of JESUS, in large measure because of the military conquests of JULIUS CAESAR. Rome consolidated its rule over much of EUROPE, ASIA MINOR, and north AFRICA in the reign of the first Roman emperor, AUGUSTUS CAESAR, who died in A.D. 14.

The period from the FALL OF ROME in the fifth century A.D. to roughly the tenth century is often called the Dark Ages. The MEDIEVAL period, which is sometimes referred to as the age of CHIVALRY, was marked by the emergence of modern nation-states, peaked between the eleventh and fourteenth centuries, and then waned with the rise of the Renaissance in the late fourteenth and fifteenth centuries. The Renaissance, a cultural rebirth during which many of the literary and artistic treasures of the ancient world were rediscovered, lasted into the seventeenth century. Starting in the fifteenth century, the religious rift of the Reformation divided Europe between PROTESTANTS and ROMAN CATHOLICS.

— J. F. K.

Alexander the Great A ruler of GREECE in the fourth century B.C. As a general, he conquered most of the ancient world, extending the civilization of Greece east to INDIA. Alexander is said to have wept because there were no worlds left to conquer. In Alexander's youth, the philosopher ARISTOTLE was his tutor.

  🙠 Before beginning his conquests, Alexander allegedly unloosed the GORDIAN KNOT by cutting through it. It was believed that the person who unfastened the Gordian knot would rule a vast territory in ASIA.

Athens A leading city of ancient GREECE, famous for its learning, CULTURE, and democratic institutions. The political power of Athens was sometimes quite limited, however, especially after its defeat by SPARTA in the PELOPONNESIAN WAR. PERICLES was a noted ruler of Athens. (*See also under "World Geography."*)

Attila the Hun (AT-l-uh, uh-TIL-uh) A king of the HUNS in the fifth century. Attila's forces overran many parts of central and eastern EUROPE. His armies were known for their cruelty and wholesale de-

ALEXANDER THE GREAT. *A rendering from an ancient coin.*

struction, and Attila himself was called the "scourge of God."

Augustus Caesar   The first emperor of ROME; the adopted son of JULIUS CAESAR. In his reign, from 44 B.C. to A.D. 14, Rome enjoyed peace (*see PAX ROMANA*), and the arts flourished. The time of Augustus is considered a golden age for literature in Rome.

&. JESUS was born during Augustus' reign. &. The month of August is named for Augustus. &. A time when literature and the arts in a nation are at their height is sometimes called an "Augustan age." The eighteenth century in ENGLAND, when many excellent authors were at work, is called the Augustan Age of English literature.

Aztecs   A NATIVE AMERICAN people who ruled MEXICO and neighboring areas before the Spaniards conquered the region in the sixteenth century. Starting in the twelfth century, they built up an advanced civilization and empire. (*See CORTÉS, HERNANDO, and MONTEZUMA.*)

Babylon (BAB-uh-luhn, BAB-uh-lon)   A city in ancient MESOPOTAMIA, famed for its hanging gardens (one of the SEVEN WONDERS OF THE ANCIENT WORLD), and for the sensual life-style of its people.

&. The JEWS were taken captive into Babylon in the sixth century B.C. (*See also under "The Bible."*)

Bacon, Francis   An English politician, scientist, and author of the late sixteenth and early seventeenth centuries; one of the leaders of the RENAISSANCE in ENGLAND. (*See also under "Literature in English."*)

Balboa, Vasco Núñez de (bal-BOH-uh)   A Spanish explorer of the sixteenth century, who was the first European to discover the PACIFIC OCEAN, and who claimed it for SPAIN.

Becket, Thomas à   An English BISHOP of the twelfth century. Becket was archbishop of Canterbury and thus leader of the CHRISTIAN CHURCH in ENGLAND. He defended church interests against interference by the king. Four of the king's men, thinking that the king wanted Becket put to death, went to Becket's CATHEDRAL and murdered him.

&. The killing of Becket is dramatized in plays by T. S. ELIOT (*Murder in the Cathedral*) and the French playwright Jean Anouilh (*Becket*). &. Soon after Becket's death, people from all over England began to come to his burial place in Canterbury to pray, especially sick persons, who prayed for healing. The storytellers in *THE CANTERBURY TALES*, by Geoffrey CHAUCER, are on their way to Becket's tomb.

Black Death   A disease that killed nearly half the people of western EUROPE in the fourteenth century. It was a form of the BUBONIC PLAGUE.

Boleyn, Anne (boo-LIN, BOOL-in)   The second wife of King HENRY VIII of ENGLAND; the mother of Queen ELIZABETH I. Anne Boleyn was convicted of ADULTERY and beheaded.

Borgia, Cesare (CHEZ-ah-ray BAWR-juh, BAWR-zhuh)   An Italian politician of the late fifteenth and early sixteenth centuries, known for his treachery and cruelty. He was the brother of Lucrezia BORGIA.

Borgia, Lucrezia (looh-KRET-see-uh, looh-KREE-shuh BAWR-juh, BAWR-zhuh)   A sister of the Italian politician Cesare BORGIA and, like him, famous for her treachery.

bread and circuses   A PHRASE used by a Roman writer to deplore the declining heroism of Romans after the Roman Republic ceased to exist and the ROMAN EMPIRE began: "Two things only the people anxiously desire — bread and circuses." The government kept the Roman populace happy by distributing free food and staging huge spectacles. (*See* COLOS-SEUM.)

  ❦ "Bread and circuses" has become a convenient general term for government policies that seek short-term solutions to public unrest.

Bronze Age A period of history from roughly 4000 B.C. to the onset of the IRON AGE. During the Bronze Age, people learned to make bronze tools. In the Bronze Age in MESOPOTAMIA, the wheel and the ox-drawn plow were in use.

Brutus An ancient Roman politician who helped assassinate his friend JULIUS CAESAR.

  ❦ Brutus is a leading CHARACTER in the play *JULIUS CAESAR*, by William SHAKESPEARE. ❦ Caesar is said to have addressed Brutus with the words *ET TU BRUTE* ("Even you, Brutus?") as Brutus stabbed him. This sentence has become a proverbial response to betrayal.

Byzantine Empire (BIZ-uhn-teen, BIZ-uhn-teyen, bi-ZAN-tin) An empire, centered at CONSTANTINOPLE, that began as the eastern portion of the ROMAN EM-PIRE; it included parts of EUROPE and western ASIA. As the western Roman Empire declined, the Byzantine Empire grew in importance, and it remained an important power in Europe until the eleventh century. The Byzantine Empire was conquered by Turkish forces in the fifteenth century.

  The Byzantine emperor was an absolute ruler (*see* ABSOLUTE MONARCHY), and the laws and customs associated with his empire were strict and complex. His rule was supported by the CHRISTIAN CHURCH in the region, which later became the independent EASTERN ORTHODOX CHURCH.

  ❦ The word *byzantine* is often applied to a group of intricately connected and rigidly applied regulations or traditions, or to a complex BUREAUCRACY that insists on formal requirements. ❦ Constantinople is called ISTANBUL today.

Caesar The family name of JULIUS CAESAR and of the next eleven rulers of ROME, who were emperors.

  ❦ The emperors of GERMANY and RUSSIA in modern times adapted the word *caesar* into titles for themselves — KAISER and CZAR.

Caligula (kuh-LIG-yuh-luh) A cruel and insane ruler of the ROMAN EMPIRE in the first century A.D.; one of the twelve CAESARS. In order to humiliate the senators of ROME, he appointed his horse to the senate.

Cambridge University *See* OXFORD AND CAMBRIDGE UNIVERSITIES.

Carthage (KAHR-thij) An ancient city in north AFRICA, established by traders from PHOENICIA. Carthage was a commercial and political rival of ROME for much of the third and second centuries B.C. The Carthaginian general HANNIBAL attempted to capture Rome by moving an army from SPAIN through the ALPS, but he was prevented, and was finally defeated in his own country. At the end of the PUNIC WARS, the Romans destroyed Carthage, as the senator CATO had long urged. The CHARACTER DIDO, lover of AENEAS in the *AENEID*, was a queen of Carthage.

Cato (KAY-toh) A politician of ancient ROME, known for his insistence that CARTHAGE was Rome's permanent enemy. He had a custom of ending all his speeches in the Roman senate with the words "Carthage must be destroyed."

CHARLEMAGNE. *The coronation of the emperor.*

Charlemagne (SHAHR-luh-mayn) The first emperor of the HOLY ROMAN EMPIRE; his name means "Charles the Great." Charlemagne was king of FRANCE in the late eighth and early ninth centuries, and was crowned emperor in 800. He is especially remembered for his encouragement of education.

  Throughout the MIDDLE AGES, Charlemagne was considered a model for CHRISTIAN rulers.

chivalry The methods of training and standards of behavior for KNIGHTS in the MIDDLE AGES. The code of chivalry emphasized bravery, military skill, generosity in victory, piety, and courtesy to women. (*Compare* COURTLY LOVE.)

classical antiquity The age of ancient history dominated by the CULTURES of GREECE and ROME, about 500 B.C. to about A.D. 500.

Cleopatra A queen of EGYPT in the first century B.C., famous for her beauty, charm, and luxurious living. She lived for some time in ROME with JULIUS CAESAR. For several years after Caesar was assassinated, she lived in Egypt with the Roman politician Mark ANTONY. Antony killed himself on hearing a false report that she was dead. After Antony's death, Cleopatra committed suicide by allowing an asp, a poisonous snake, to bite her.

  The play *ANTONY AND CLEOPATRA*, by William SHAKESPEARE, dramatizes Cleopatra's affair with Antony and her suicide.

Columbus, Christopher An Italian explorer responsible for the European discovery of America in 1492. He had sailed across the ATLANTIC OCEAN from SPAIN, under the patronage of the king and queen, FERDINAND AND ISABELLA, hoping to find a westward route to INDIA. His ships were the *Nina,* the *Pinta,* and the *Santa Maria.* Columbus made four voyages to the NEW WORLD, visiting the BAHAMAS, CUBA, Hispaniola, PUERTO RICO, JAMAICA, TRINIDAD, VENEZUELA, and the coast of CENTRAL AMERICA.

conquistadores (kong-kees-tuh-DAWR-ays, kong-kees-tuh-DAWR-eez) *sing.* CONQUISTADOR (kong-KEES-tuh-dawr) The Spanish military leaders who established Spanish rule in the NEW WORLD by overthrowing NATIVE AMERICAN governments. (*See* CORTÉS, HERNANDO, *and* PIZARRO, FRANCISCO.)

Constantine the Great (KON-stuhn-teen, KON-stuhn-teyen) A Roman emperor of the fourth century. He founded CONSTANTINOPLE as capital of the eastern part of the ROMAN EMPIRE. Early in his reign, Constantine issued a document allowing CHRISTIANS to practice their religion within the empire. Before that, they had frequently been persecuted.

Constantinople (kon-stan-tuh-NOH-puhl) A city founded by the Roman emperor CONSTANTINE THE GREAT as capital of the eastern part of the ROMAN EMPIRE. Constantine ruled over both parts of the empire from Constantinople, which was later capital of the BYZANTINE EMPIRE. Constantinople was conquered by Turkish forces in the fifteenth century.

  Today, under the name of ISTANBUL, Constantinople is the largest city in TURKEY.

Copernicus, Nicolaus (kuh-PUR-ni-kuhs) A Polish scholar of the sixteenth century who argued that the EARTH moves about the SUN.

Cortés, Hernando (kawr-TEZ) A Spanish explorer and CONQUISTADOR of the sixteenth century. Cortés overthrew the AZTEC rulers of MEXICO and established the authority of SPAIN over the country. His name is also spelled Cortez.

Crusades A series of wars fought from the late eleventh through the thirteenth centuries, in which European kings and warriors set out to gain control of the lands in which JESUS lived, known as the HOLY LAND. At that time, these areas were held by MOSLEMS. The Crusaders conquered JERUSALEM in 1099, but failed to secure the Holy Land, and were driven out by the late thirteenth century. Nevertheless, the Crusades had several lasting results, including the exposure of Europeans to the GOODS, technology, and customs of ASIA.

  The Crusades made Europeans more willing to explore new places, and thus aided in the discovery of America.

Dark Ages A term sometimes applied to the early MIDDLE AGES, the first few centuries after the FALL OF ROME. The term suggests prevailing ignorance and barbarism, but there were forces for CULTURE and enlightenment throughout the period.

Demosthenes (di-MOS-thuh-neez) The greatest orator of ancient GREECE. Demosthenes is said to have overcome a childhood stutter by forcing himself to speak with pebbles in his mouth. He delivered speeches called Philippics attacking King Philip of Macedon, who was an enemy of Demosthenes' city of ATHENS.

Erasmus, Desiderius (i-RAZ-muhs) A Dutch scholar of the late fifteenth and early sixteenth centuries, who attempted to solve some of the controversies of the time of the REFORMATION. Erasmus urged changes in the general views of CHRISTIANS, including more personal piety, reforms that would make the ROMAN CATHOLIC CHURCH less worldly, and the study of the literature of ancient GREECE and ROME. Erasmus' most famous work is a SATIRE entitled *The Praise of Folly.*

    ❧ Erasmus' position might have been acceptable to both PROTESTANT and CATHOLIC sides during the period of the Reformation, but few religious leaders of the time were interested in compromise. ❧ Erasmus was a friend of Sir Thomas MORE.

Ericson, Leif (LEEF, LAYV ER-ik-suhn) A Norwegian explorer of about the year 1000. He is said to have discovered a place in NORTH AMERICA called Vinland. Several locations are possible for Vinland, including the Canadian province of NEWFOUNDLAND, and NEW ENGLAND.

    ❧ Ericson, rather than Christopher COLUMBUS, is sometimes called the European discoverer of America. His discovery, however, is not indisputably documented, as the discovery of Columbus is. Also, Ericson's voyages, unlike the voyages of Columbus, did not result in continuous colonization.

Fall of Rome The collapse of the ROMAN EMPIRE in the fifth century. Two of the main events of the Fall of Rome were the plundering of the city of ROME by an invading tribe, the VANDALS, in the middle years of the century, and the abdication of the last Roman emperor, Romulus Augustulus, in 476.

Ferdinand and Isabella A king and queen of SPAIN in the late fifteenth and early sixteenth centuries. They united their country and sponsored the exploration of the NEW WORLD by Christopher COLUMBUS.

feudalism (FYOOHD-l-iz-uhm) A system of obligations that bound lords and their subjects in EUROPE during much of the MIDDLE AGES. In theory, the king owned all or most of the land, and gave it to his leading nobles in return for their loyalty and military service. The nobles in turn held land that PEASANTS, including SERFS, were allowed to farm in return for the peasants' labor and a portion of their produce. Under feudalism, people were born with a permanent position in society. (*See* FIEF and VASSAL.)

    ❧ Today, the word *feudal* is sometimes used as a general term for a set of social relationships that seems unprogressive or out of step with modern society.

fief (FEEF) Under FEUDALISM, a landed estate given by a lord to a VASSAL in return for the vassal's service to the lord. The vassal could use the fief as long as he remained loyal to the lord.

GENGHIS KHAN

Genghis Khan (JENG-gis, GENG-gis KAHN) A Mongolian general and emperor of the late twelfth and early thirteenth centuries, known for his military leadership and great cruelty. He conquered vast portions of northern CHINA and southwestern ASIA.

Godiva, Lady (guh-DEYE-vuh) An English noblewoman of the eleventh century. She supposedly rode naked through her town of Coventry to save the people from an oppressive tax. (*See under "Mythology and Folklore."*)

guilds Organizations of artisans in the MIDDLE AGES that sought to regulate the price and quality of products such as weaving and ironwork. Guilds survived into the eighteenth century.

❧ Guilds gave way to trade unions, a very different type of organization. The artisans in the guilds were self-employed, unlike most members of trade unions.

Gutenberg, Johann (GOOHT-n-burg)   A German printer of the fifteenth century, who invented the printing press. Gutenberg also invented the technique of printing with "movable type" — that is, with one piece of type for each letter, so that the type could be reused after a page was printed. The Gutenberg BIBLE was the first book printed from movable type.

Hammurabi (ham-uh-RAH-bee, hah-muh-RAH-bee)   A king of ancient MESOPOTAMIA, known for putting the laws of his country into a formal code.

Hannibal (HAN-uh-buhl)   A general from the ancient city of CARTHAGE. During the second of the PUNIC WARS between Carthage and ROME, Hannibal took an army of over 100,000, supported by elephants, from SPAIN into ITALY in an effort to conquer Rome. The army had to cross the ALPS, and this troop movement is still regarded as one of the greatest in history. Hannibal won several victories on this campaign, but was not able to take Rome.

Hastings, Battle of (HAY-stingz)   A battle in southeastern ENGLAND in 1066. Invaders from the French province of Normandy, led by WILLIAM THE CONQUEROR, defeated English forces under King Harold. William declared himself king, thus bringing about the NORMAN CONQUEST of England.

Henry VIII   A king of ENGLAND in the early sixteenth century. With the support of his PARLIAMENT Henry established himself as head of the CHRISTIAN CHURCH in England, in place of the POPE, after the pope refused to allow his marriage with Catherine of Aragon to be dissolved. Since that time, except for a few years of rule under Henry's daughter Mary I, who was a ROMAN CATHOLIC, England has been officially a PROTESTANT nation.

In his personal life, Henry was known for his corpulence and for his six wives. He divorced the first, Catherine of Aragon. He beheaded the second, Anne BOLEYN, for allegedly being unfaithful to him. His third wife, Jane Seymour, died soon after giving birth

HENRY VIII. *A portrait of King Henry VIII by Hans Holbein the Younger.*

to a son. He divorced his fourth wife, Anne of Cleves. He beheaded his fifth wife, Catherine Howard, also for alleged infidelity. His sixth wife, Catherine Parr, survived him. He also had his close friend and adviser Thomas MORE executed because More would not support Henry's declaration that he was head of the church in England. Henry was the father of King Edward VI and of Queen ELIZABETH I, as well as Mary I.

Herodotus (huh-ROD-uh-tuhs)   An ancient Greek historian, often called the father of history. His history of the invasion of GREECE by the PERSIAN EMPIRE was the first attempt at narrative history and was the beginning of all Western history writing.

hieroglyphics (heye-uhr-uh-GLIF-iks, heye-ruh-GLIF-iks)   A system of writing with pictures that represent words or sounds. The ancient Egyptians wrote with hieroglyphics. (*See* ROSETTA STONE.)

❧ Present-day writing that is hard to decipher or understand is sometimes jokingly called "hieroglyphics."

Holy Roman Empire   A major political institution in EUROPE that lasted from the ninth to the nineteenth centuries. It was loosely organized and mod-

HIEROGLYPHICS. *Egyptian hieroglyphics from the tomb of Hesire.*

eled somewhat on the ancient ROMAN EMPIRE. It included great amounts of territory in the central and western parts of Europe. CHARLEMAGNE was its first emperor. In later years, the emperors were Germans and Austrians. The empire declined greatly in power after the sixteenth century.

&. The eighteenth-century French author VOLTAIRE once wrote that the Holy Roman Empire was "neither holy, Roman, nor an empire."

homage Under FEUDALISM, the personal submission of a VASSAL to a lord, by which the vassal pledged to serve the lord and the lord to protect the vassal.

Hundred Years' War A war between FRANCE and ENGLAND that lasted from the middle of the fourteenth century to the middle of the fifteenth. The kings of England invaded France, trying to claim the throne. Toward the end of the war, JOAN OF ARC helped rally the French, who finally drove the English out.

Huns A tribe from western ASIA who conquered much of central and eastern EUROPE during the fifth century. The Huns were known for their cruelty and destructiveness.

&. The British frequently referred to German soldiers as "Huns" during WORLD WAR I and WORLD WAR II as a way of emphasizing their supposed brutality.

I came, I saw, I conquered According to PLUTARCH, the words by which JULIUS CAESAR suc-

cinctly described one of his victories. In Latin the words are "*veni, vidi, vici.*"

ides of March March 15 in the ancient Roman calendar; the day in 44 B.C. on which JULIUS CAESAR was assassinated.

Incas A NATIVE AMERICAN people who built a notable civilization in western SOUTH AMERICA in the fifteenth and sixteenth centuries. The center of their empire was in present-day PERU. Francisco PIZARRO of SPAIN conquered the Inca Empire.

indulgence In the ROMAN CATHOLIC CHURCH, a declaration by church authorities that someone who says certain prayers or does good deeds will have some or all of their punishment in PURGATORY remitted.

&. In the MIDDLE AGES, indulgences were frequently sold, and the teaching on indulgences was often distorted. The attack by Martin LUTHER on the sale of indulgences began the REFORMATION.

Inquisition A court established by the ROMAN CATHOLIC CHURCH in the thirteenth century to try cases of HERESY and other offenses against the church. Persons convicted could be handed over to the civil authorities for punishment, including execution.

&. The Inquisition was most active in SPAIN, especially under Tomás de TORQUEMADA; its officials sometimes gained confessions through torture. It did not cease operation in the Spanish Empire until the nineteenth century. &. By association, a harsh or unjust trial or interrogation may be called an "inquisition."

Iron Age The period of history, succeeding the BRONZE AGE, when people first learned to extract iron from ORE and use it to forge tools, weapons, and other objects. The first organized production of iron objects developed in southwestern ASIA shortly after 2000 B.C.

Joan of Arc A French military leader of the fifteenth century, a national heroine who at the age of seventeen took up arms to establish the rightful king on the French throne. She claimed to have heard God speak to her in voices. These claims eventually led to her trial for HERESY and her execution by burning at

JOAN OF ARC. Joan of Arc at the Coronation of Charles VII, *by Jean-Auguste-Dominique Ingres.*

JULIUS CAESAR

the stake. Joan of Arc is a SAINT of the ROMAN CATHOLIC CHURCH.

Julius Caesar   A Roman general and dictator in the first century B.C. In military campaigns to secure Roman rule over the province of Gaul, present-day FRANCE, he gained much prestige. The Roman senate, fearing his power, ordered him to disband his army, but Caesar refused, crossed the RUBICON River, returned to ROME with his army, and made himself dictator. On a subsequent campaign in ASIA, he reported to the senate, "I CAME, I SAW, I CONQUERED." Caesar was assassinated by his friend BRUTUS and others on the IDES OF MARCH in 44 B.C.

knight   A mounted warrior in EUROPE in the MIDDLE AGES. (*See* CHIVALRY.)

   📖 Over the centuries, knighthood gradually lost its military functions, but has survived as a social distinction in Europe, especially in ENGLAND.

Latin   The language of ancient ROME. When Rome became an empire, the language spread throughout southern and western EUROPE.

   📖 The modern Romance languages — French, Spanish, Italian, Portuguese, and a few others — are all derived from Latin. 📖 During the MIDDLE AGES and the RENAISSANCE, Latin was the universal language of learning. Even in modern English, many scholarly, technical, and legal terms, such as *per se* and HABEAS CORPUS, retain their Latin form.

Magellan, Ferdinand (muh-JEL-uhn)   A Portuguese navigator of the sixteenth century. His crew was the first to sail around the EARTH, although Magellan himself was killed on the voyage.

Magna Carta   A list of rights and privileges that King John of ENGLAND signed under pressure from English noblemen in 1215. It established the principles that the king could not levy taxes without consent of his legislature, or PARLIAMENT, and that no free man in England could be deprived of liberty or property except through a trial or other legal process.

Marathon, Battle of   A famous battle in the fifth century B.C., in which the ancient Greeks defeated a much larger army of the PERSIAN EMPIRE.

   📖 According to legend, news of the victory was carried to ATHENS from the plain of Marathon, a distance of about twenty-six miles, by a messenger who collapsed and died of exhaustion after delivering his message. The distance of the modern marathon foot race is based on this legend.

Marco Polo   *See* POLO, MARCO.

Mayas (MEYE-uhz)   A NATIVE AMERICAN people, living in what is now MEXICO and northern CENTRAL AMERICA, who had a flourishing civilization from before the birth of JESUS until around 1600, when they were conquered by the Spanish. The Mayas are known for their astronomical observations, accurate calendars, sophisticated HIEROGLYPHICS, and PYRAMIDS.

Medici (MED-uh-chee)   A family of skilled politicians and patrons of the arts who lived in FLORENCE, ITALY, during the RENAISSANCE. (*See* Lorenzo de MEDICI.)

➜ The family produced two queens of FRANCE: Catherine, in the sixteenth century, and Marie, in the seventeenth.

Medici, Lorenzo de (law-REN-tsoh, law-REN-zoh duh MED-uh-chee)   An Italian ruler of the fifteenth century, known as "Lorenzo the Magnificent." He was patron of several of the great artists of the RENAISSANCE, including BOTTICELLI, MICHELANGELO, and LEONARDO DA VINCI.

medieval   A descriptive term for people, objects, events, and institutions of the MIDDLE AGES.

➜ "Medieval" is sometimes used as a term of disapproval for outdated ideas and customs. It may suggest inhuman practices, such as torture of prisoners. (*See* INQUISITION.)

Mesopotamia (mes-uh-puh-TAY-mee-uh)   A region of western ASIA, in what is now IRAQ, known as the "cradle of civilization." Writing first developed there, done with sticks on clay tablets. Agricultural organization on a large scale also began in Mesopotamia, along with work in bronze and iron (*see* BRONZE AGE *and* IRON AGE). Governmental systems in the region were especially advanced (*see* BABYLON *and* HAMMURABI). A number of peoples lived in Mesopotamia, including the Sumerians, Akkadians, Hittites, and Assyrians.

Middle Ages   The period of European history between ancient and modern times. The Middle Ages began with the FALL OF ROME in the fifth century, and ended with the RENAISSANCE. The Middle Ages are associated with many beliefs and practices that now seem out of date, such as CHIVALRY, FEUDALISM, the INQUISITION, the belief that the SUN revolves around the EARTH, and a host of popular superstitions. The early Middle Ages are even sometimes called the DARK AGES. The Middle Ages, however, especially in later years, also saw many notable human achievements. Among these were the building of modern nations, such as ENGLAND and FRANCE; increasingly sophisticated and expanded trade; a great advancement of technique in PHILOSOPHY and THEOLOGY; some remarkable works of literature (*see* CANTERBURY TALES, THE *and* DIVINE COMEDY, THE*); and the building of magnificent churches (*see* CHARTRES, CATHEDRAL OF *and* NOTRE DAME DE PARIS, CATHEDRAL OF).

Montezuma (mon-tuh-ZOOH-muh)   An AZTEC emperor of the sixteenth century. He was overthrown

MONTEZUMA

MESOPOTAMIA

by the Spanish CONQUISTADORES under Hernando CORTÉS.

More, Thomas   An English statesman and scholar of the sixteenth century; the author of *UTOPIA*, and a SAINT of the ROMAN CATHOLIC CHURCH. More was beheaded because he refused to recognize HENRY VIII as head of the CHRISTIAN CHURCH in ENGLAND.

𝕏 More is admired today for having put his principles above personal ambition.

Nero (NEER-oh)   An ancient Roman emperor, famed for his cruelty. He had his mother and wife killed, and kicked his mistress to death while she was pregnant. Nero also persecuted CHRISTIANS, blaming them for a great fire in ROME. According to tradition, he put the APOSTLES PETER and PAUL to death.

𝕏 A famous legend holds that Nero caused the great fire of Rome himself, and played a stringed instrument while watching it. To say that someone is "FIDDLING WHILE ROME BURNS" is to say that the person is indifferent to catastrophe.

Norman Conquest   The overthrow of the government of ENGLAND in 1066 by forces of Normandy, a province of northern FRANCE, under the leadership of WILLIAM THE CONQUEROR. William proclaimed himself king of England after defeating the English King Harold at the Battle of HASTINGS. Norman rule strengthened the power of the king and the system of FEUDALISM in England, and brought a great number of French influences to the English language (*see* MIDDLE ENGLISH) and English institutions.

Olympic Games   Games held in ancient times on the plain of Olympia in GREECE every four years. It was a time for laying aside political and religious differences, as athletes from all the Greek cities and districts competed. The games included patriotic and religious rituals as well as athletic contests, and high honors were given to the winners. The Greeks counted their years by olympiads (periods of four years), and dated events from the first Olympics in 776 B.C.

𝕏 The Olympic Games deteriorated under Roman rule of Greece and were halted in the fourth century. They were revived in the late nineteenth century, with goals of peace and fellowship modeled on those of the ancient Olympics. The modern Olympics include many athletic events of the original Olympics, such as the discus throw.

Ottoman Empire   An empire developed by Turks between the fourteenth and twentieth centuries. It was succeeded in the 1920s by the present-day REPUBLIC of TURKEY. At its greatest extent, the Ottoman Empire included many parts of southeastern EUROPE and the MIDDLE EAST.

Oxford and Cambridge Universities   The famed "ancient universities" of ENGLAND, dating back to the twelfth and thirteenth centuries. Oxford and Cambridge have long held a commanding position in English education, and their graduates have often gained eminence in public life.

𝕏 The names of these two universities are sometimes merged into "Oxbridge."

Pax Romana (PAHKS, PAKS roh-MAH-nuh)   LATIN for "the Roman peace"; the peace enforced by ancient ROME within the boundaries of its empire.

Peloponnesian War (pel-uh-puh-NEE-zhuhn, pel-uh-puh-NEE-shuhn)   A long war between the Greek city-states of ATHENS and SPARTA in the fifth century B.C. Sparta won the war.

𝕏 The historian THUCYDIDES fought in the Peloponnesian War and later wrote a remarkable history about it.

Pericles (PER-uh-kleez)   A statesman of ancient GREECE, who tried to unite the country under the leadership of his own city, ATHENS. Pericles also promoted DEMOCRACY within Athens. His rule is sometimes known as the Golden Age of Greece. Many magnificent buildings, including the PARTHENON, were built under his administration. He led the Athenians at the beginning of the PELOPONNESIAN WAR, but died soon afterward.

Persian Empire   An empire in western ASIA in ancient times. The Persians, under the kings Darius and Xerxes, attempted to conquer GREECE several times in the fifth century B.C., but were defeated in the Battle of MARATHON and in several other land and sea battles.

pharaohs (FAIR-ohz, FAY-rohz)   The kings of ancient EGYPT. The pharaohs headed strong governments; they are remembered for establishing extensive IRRIGATION systems, and for building as tombs the imposing PYRAMIDS, which still stand today.

𝕏 In the biblical account of the EXODUS, a pharaoh refused to let the ISRAELITES under MOSES leave Egypt.

Phoenicia (fuh-NEE-shuh, fuh-NISH-uh) An ancient nation of the eastern MEDITERRANEAN SEA. Its territory included what are today coastal areas of modern ISRAEL and LEBANON. The Phoenicians were famed as traders and sailors. They developed an alphabet that was eventually adapted by the Greeks and Romans into the alphabet used in writing English. In the Phoenicians' alphabet, the marks stand for individual sounds rather than for whole words or SYLLABLES, as in Egyptian HIEROGLYPHICS.

Pizarro, Francisco (puh-ZAHR-oh) A Spanish CONQUISTADOR of the sixteenth century, who overthrew the rulers of the INCAS and established the nation of PERU.

Polo, Marco An Italian explorer of the late thirteenth and early fourteenth centuries; one of the first Europeans to travel across ASIA. He visited the court of Kublai Khan (*see* "KUBLA KHAN" *under "Literature in English"*), the Mongol ruler of CHINA, and became a government official in China. His account of his travels was distributed after his return to ITALY.

Pompeii (pom-PAY, pom-PAY-ee) A city of the ROMAN EMPIRE, on the Italian seacoast, that was known for the luxury and dissipated ways of its citizens. It was destroyed in the first century by an eruption of nearby MOUNT VESUVIUS.

Ponce de León, Juan (PONS duh lee-uhn, PON-say duh lay-OHN) A Spanish explorer and CONQUISTADOR of the late fifteenth and early sixteenth centuries, who conquered PUERTO RICO. Ponce de León discovered and named FLORIDA while searching for the legendary FOUNTAIN OF YOUTH.

Ptolemy (TOL-uh-mee) An ancient Greek astronomer, living in EGYPT, who proposed a way of calculating the movements of the PLANETS on the assumption that they, along with the SUN and the STARS, were embedded in clear spheres that revolved around the EARTH. The system of Ptolemy, called the PTOLEMAIC UNIVERSE, prevailed in ASTRONOMY for nearly 1500 years, until the modern model of the SOLAR SYSTEM, with the sun at the center and the PLANETS in motion, was developed from the ideas of COPERNICUS.

Punic Wars (PYOOH-nik) Three wars between ancient CARTHAGE and ROME in the third and second

centuries B.C. HANNIBAL led the forces of Carthage in the second Punic War. Carthage was destroyed after the third Punic War.

PYRAMIDS. *The Pyramids at Giza, Egypt.*

pyramids A group of huge monuments in the Egyptian desert, built as burial vaults for the PHARAOHS and one of the SEVEN WONDERS OF THE ANCIENT WORLD. The pyramids have square bases and four triangular faces. The age of pyramid building in EGYPT began about 2700 B.C., and required vast amounts of slave labor.

Reformation A religious movement in the sixteenth century that began as an attempted reform of the ROMAN CATHOLIC CHURCH but resulted in the founding of PROTESTANT CHURCHES separate from it. Some of the leaders of the Reformation were Martin LUTHER, John CALVIN, and John KNOX. The Reformation was established in ENGLAND after King HENRY VIII declared himself head of the CHRISTIAN CHURCH in that country.

Renaissance The cultural rebirth that occurred in EUROPE from roughly the fourteenth through the middle of the seventeenth centuries, a rebirth that was based on the rediscovery of the literature of GREECE and ROME. During the Renaissance, America was discovered, and the REFORMATION began; modern times are often considered to have begun with the Renaissance. Major figures of the Renaissance include GALILEO, William SHAKESPEARE, LEONARDO DA VINCI, and MICHELANGELO. *Renaissance* means "rebirth" or "reawakening."

🝔 The term *renaissance* is often used to describe any revival or rediscovery.

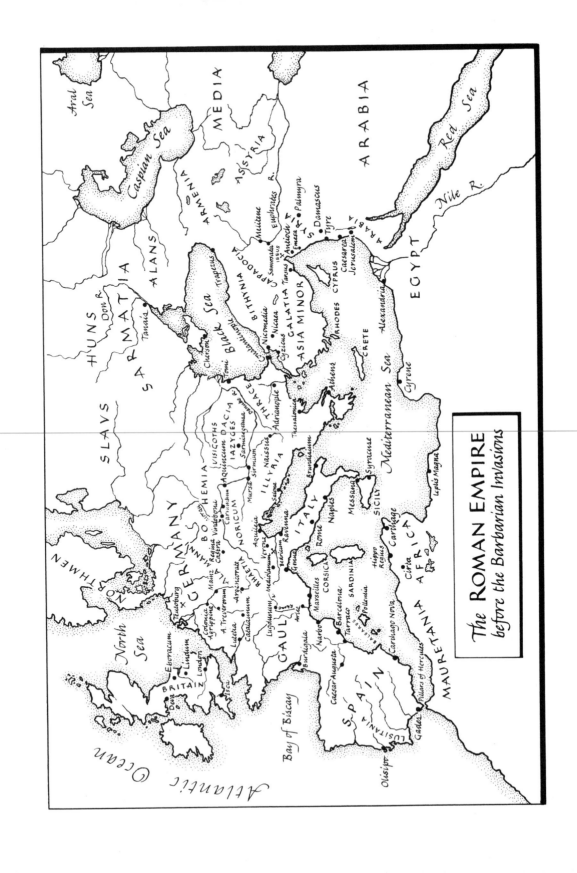

The ROMAN EMPIRE
before the Barbarian Invasions

Richard the Lion-Hearted An English king of the twelfth century. Richard, a famed warrior, fought in the CRUSADES.

❧ In the legend of ROBIN HOOD, Robin and his men are loyal to the absent King Richard, rather than to his brother, Prince John.

Roman Empire The empire centered at the city of ROME, in what is now ITALY; the most extensive civilization of ancient times. According to legend, the empire was founded in 753 B.C. by two brothers, ROMULUS AND REMUS. Rome was at first ruled by kings. Then, about 500 B.C., the Roman Republic was established, with two annually elected consuls at its head, guided by a senate. The REPUBLIC eventually weakened, and Rome passed to rule by one man — first JULIUS CAESAR, who was assassinated in 44 B.C. His successor was AUGUSTUS, who assumed the title of emperor. Over the next few centuries, he was followed by a succession of emperors. The whole Western world eventually became subject to Rome and was at peace for roughly the first four centuries after the birth of JESUS (*see PAX ROMANA*). The empire was known for its strongly centralized government and for massive public works, such as roads and aqueducts, which helped maintain its power and efficiency. As the years passed, the Roman Empire was divided into eastern and western portions (*see* BYZANTINE EMPIRE *and* CONSTANTINE THE GREAT), developed internal weaknesses, was invaded by outside tribes, and eventually ceased to exist. (*See* FALL OF ROME.)

❧ The HOLY ROMAN EMPIRE represented an effort in the MIDDLE AGES to develop a government with some of the characteristics of the old Roman Empire. ❧ In the early twentieth century, to raise the spirits of the Italians, the dictator Benito MUSSOLINI revived some of the customs and expressions of the ancient empire.

Roses, Wars of the A series of wars fought by two English houses, or families, in the late fifteenth century for rule of the country. The House of Lancaster had a red rose as its emblem; the House of York had a white rose. The forces of the House of Lancaster won, and their leader, Henry TUDOR, father of the future King HENRY VIII, became king. The power of the English kings was strengthened in the period that followed.

Rosetta stone A stone discovered in EGYPT in the late eighteenth century, inscribed with ancient Egyptian HIEROGLYPHICS and a translation of them in Greek. The stone proved to be the key to understanding Egyptian writing.

❧ A "Rosetta stone" is the key to understanding a complex problem.

Rubicon (ROOH-bi-kon) A river in northern ITALY that JULIUS CAESAR crossed with his army, in violation of the orders of the leaders in ROME, who feared his power. A civil war followed, in which Caesar emerged as ruler of Rome. Caesar is supposed to have said, "The die is cast" (referring to a roll of dice), as he crossed the river.

❧ "Crossing the Rubicon" is a general expression for taking a dangerous, decisive, and irreversible step.

Saladin (SAL-uh-din) A Kurdish general who conquered EGYPT and SYRIA in the twelfth century. His capture of JERUSALEM precipitated a CRUSADE.

❧ Saladin became legendary for both his military genius and his generosity.

Savonarola, Girolamo (sav-uh-nuh-ROH-luh) An Italian religious reformer of the fifteenth century. Savonarola spent most of his career in FLORENCE, ITALY, where his fiery oratory whipped up popular fervor against corruption of CHURCH and state. He was eventually convicted of HERESY, and burned at the stake.

serf Under FEUDALISM, a PEASANT bound to his lord's land and subject to his lord's will, but entitled to his lord's protection.

Seven Wonders of the Ancient World Seven famous structures of ancient times: the Colossus of Rhodes, the Hanging Gardens of BABYLON, the Pharos of ALEXANDRIA, the PYRAMIDS of EGYPT, the Statue of JUPITER by Phidias, the Temple of DIANA at Ephesus, and the Tomb of Mausolus (Mausoleum). All have disappeared except the pyramids.

Spanish Inquisition The CHURCH court of the INQUISITION, as established in SPAIN in the late fifteenth century. (*See also* TORQUEMADA, TOMÁS DE.)

Sparta An ancient Greek city-state and rival of ATHENS. Sparta was known for its militaristic government and for its educational system designed to train children to be devoted citizens and brave soldiers. Sparta defeated Athens in the PELOPONNESIAN WAR.

❧ The term *Spartan* is used to describe conditions

that are low on luxury and designed to produce discipline.

Spartacus (SPAHR-tuh-kuhs) A Roman slave of the first century B.C. He led an insurrection of slaves that defeated several Roman armies before being crushed.

Stone Age A period encompassing all of human history, perhaps several million years, before the BRONZE AGE. In the Stone Age, people learned to make and use stone tools and weapons.

STONEHENGE

Stonehenge Ancient circles of large, upright stones that stand alone on a plain in ENGLAND. There is some controversy about who shaped, carried, and set up these huge stones, which perhaps had religious and astronomical uses. Scholars theorize that Stonehenge was built in three phases beginning in about 2800 B.C. The huge stones are believed to date from 1800 to 1500 B.C.

1066 (**ten sixty-six**) The year of the NORMAN CONQUEST of England. (*See* HASTINGS, BATTLE OF.)

Thucydides (thooh-SID-uh-deez) An ancient Greek historian and general. Thucydides' history of the PELOPONNESIAN WAR, in which he fought, is famous for its careful reporting of events, and its sharp analysis of causes and effects.

toga An outer garment for men in ancient ROME, worn as a sign of citizenship. The toga was a nearly semicircular piece of wool, worn draped about the shoulders and body.

Torquemada, Tomás de (toh-MAHS thhay tawr-kuh-MAH-thhuh) The first inquisitor-general of the

Inquisition in SPAIN, in the late fifteenth century. Torquemada was known for his severity, especially with persons who were charged with illegally practicing JUDAISM. It is estimated that 2000 people were executed while he was in charge of the Inquisition.

🕭 Torquemada's name has come to symbolize ruthless persecution.

Trojan War A war in ancient times between forces from the mainland of GREECE and the defenders of the city of TROY, in what is now TURKEY. The war seems to have begun about 1200 B.C. It is the basis of many classical legends, and legendary accounts of the Trojan War appear in the ancient poems the *ILIAD* and the *AENEID*. (*See under "Mythology and Folklore."*)

TUTANKHAMEN. *A gold mask bearing the likeness of the pharaoh.*

Tutankhamen (tooht-ahng-KAH-muhn) A PHARAOH, or king of EGYPT, who lived about 1400 B.C. His reign was relatively unimportant, but the discovery of his unplundered tomb in the 1920s is numbered among the great archaeological discoveries of all time.

🕭 Tutankhamen is popularly known as King Tut.

Vandals A people of northern EUROPE, known for their cruelty and destructiveness, who invaded the ROMAN EMPIRE and plundered ROME itself in the fifth century.

◈ The expression *vandalism* for wanton destructiveness comes from the name of the Vandals.

vassal   Under FEUDALISM, a subordinate who placed himself in service to a lord in return for the lord's protection.

vestal virgins   Women in ancient ROME who took vows of chastity and tended the sacred flame in the TEMPLE of the goddess VESTA. Their group numbered six at any one time. A vestal virgin could marry after her term of service was over, but to do so was considered bad luck. A vestal virgin who lost her virginity during her term of service was punished by being buried alive.

Vikings   Warriors from SCANDINAVIA who raided much of coastal EUROPE in the eighth to tenth centuries. The Vikings traveled in boats with high bows and sterns, carefully designed for either rough seas or calm waters. Eventually some Vikings settled in the countries they plundered, and established new societies.

WILLIAM THE CONQUEROR. *A detail from the Bayeux tapestry. William is in the center.*

William the Conqueror   The duke of Normandy, a province of FRANCE, and the leader of the NORMAN CONQUEST of ENGLAND. He defeated the English forces at the Battle of HASTINGS in 1066, and became the first Norman king of England.

Wonders of the Ancient World, Seven   *See* SEVEN WONDERS OF THE ANCIENT WORLD.

World History since 1550

Historians often call the period from the middle of the sixteenth century to the outbreak of the FRENCH REVOLUTION in 1789 the early modern era. This era includes the RENAISSANCE and the REFORMATION, both of which extended from the fifteenth through the seventeenth centuries, and the ENLIGHTENMENT, which extended through the late seventeenth and eighteenth centuries.

The French Revolution marks the beginning of modern history. The revolution introduced a period of political upheaval in EUROPE that included the wars fought between the 1790s and 1815 by NAPOLEON BONAPARTE, which are therefore called the Napoleonic wars. The Congress of VIENNA in 1815 brought peace to Europe, but did not extinguish the flames of DEMOCRACY and NATIONALISM that had flared up during the French Revolution. The twin forces of democracy and nationalism exploded again in the so-called REVOLUTIONS OF 1848. Between 1850 and 1870, both ITALY and GERMANY emerged as modern nation-states.

The period between 1870 and 1914 witnessed intensifying nationalistic and imperial rivalries in Europe, culminating with the assassination of the Archduke FRANCIS FERDINAND and the outbreak of WORLD WAR I in 1914. During World War I, GREAT BRITAIN, FRANCE, ITALY, and RUSSIA opposed Germany, Austria-Hungary, BULGARIA, and the OTTOMAN EMPIRE. The United States entered the war in 1917, and contributed to the victory of Great Britain and France in 1918. Before the conclusion of the war, the Russian MONARCHY collapsed, and the BOLSHEVIKS came to power in the RUSSIAN REVOLUTION.

During the 1920s and 1930s, STALIN consolidated the power of COMMUNISM in the SOVIET UNION, while nationalistic and militaristic governments arose in Germany (the NAZIS under HITLER), Italy (the FASCISTS under MUSSOLINI), and JAPAN. WORLD WAR II commenced with Hitler's invasion of POLAND in 1939. In 1941, Hitler invaded the Soviet Union, and Japan attacked the United States at PEARL HARBOR. By 1945, the AXIS POWERS had surrendered; Japan capitulated after the United States dropped ATOMIC BOMBS on HIROSHIMA and NAGASAKI.

New tensions developed after World War II between the United States and the Soviet Union. This conflict, which embraced political and economic competition but not direct military confrontation, is known as the COLD WAR. During the late 1940s and 1950s, Europe divided into armed camps: the NORTH ATLANTIC TREATY ORGANIZATION (NATO), led by the United States, and the WARSAW PACT, led by the Soviet Union. Inevitably, the cold war affected ASIA as well as Europe. Communists backed by the Soviet Union gained power in CHINA in 1949. Communist and anticommunist forces clashed in the KOREAN WAR (1950–1953) and again in the VIETNAM WAR (1950s–1975). Despite these conflicts, the shared fear of nuclear war led the United States and Soviet Union to seek compromise and mutual understanding, called DÉTENTE, during the 1970s and 1980s.

SPANISH ARMADA. *Capture of the flagship of Don Miguel de Oquendo.*

At the end of the 1980s communism began to disintegrate, first in eastern Europe and then in the Soviet Union. While ending the cold war, the COLLAPSE OF COMMUNISM created new sources of international instability by bringing long-suppressed nationalism to the surface in the former countries of the Soviet Union, YUGOSLAVIA, and Czechoslovakia.

— J. F. K.

Albert, Prince A German prince of the nineteenth century who married Queen VICTORIA of BRITAIN and became enormously popular in his new country. He died in his early forties, and Queen Victoria remained in mourning for him until her death.

Alliance for Progress A major United States program of economic aid to nations of LATIN AMERICA, launched in the early 1960s.

Allies The victorious allied nations of WORLD WAR I and WORLD WAR II. In World War I, the Allies included BRITAIN, FRANCE, ITALY, RUSSIA, and the United States. In World War II, the Allies included Britain, France, the SOVIET UNION, and the United States.

ancien régime (ahnn-SYANN ray-ZHEEM) The political and social order that prevailed in FRANCE before the FRENCH REVOLUTION, built on a belief in ABSOLUTE MONARCHY and the DIVINE RIGHT OF KINGS.

Archduke Francis Ferdinand *See* FRANCIS FERDINAND, ARCHDUKE.

Armada, Spanish (ahr-MAH-duh) A fleet of over a hundred ships sent by King Philip II of SPAIN to conquer ENGLAND in 1588. Although called the "Invincible Armada," it was destroyed by a combination of English seamanship, Dutch reinforcements, and bad WEATHER. Several thousand Spaniards were killed, and about half the Spanish ships were lost.

&. The defeat of the Armada was a sharp blow to the influence and prestige of Spain in the world, and was an important step in England's ascent to power.

Armenian massacres The killing of large numbers of Armenians who lived within the OTTOMAN EM-

PIRE and its successor Turkish state in the late nineteenth and early twentieth centuries. The worst of the massacres occurred at the time of WORLD WAR I, when the Armenians had made some military strikes against the Turks, and the Turkish government feared overthrow. From 1915 to 1920, over a million Armenians died as the result of executions, massacres, starvation, and other repressive measures, and many others fled to the United States and other countries.

&. In recent years, terrorists claiming Armenian connections have killed Turkish officials and bombed Turkish buildings, demanding reparations.

Auschwitz (OWSH-vits)   An infamous CONCENTRATION CAMP established by the NAZIS in POLAND. (*See* HOLOCAUST.)

Axis powers   GERMANY, ITALY, and JAPAN, which were allied before and during WORLD WAR II. (*Compare* ALLIES.)

BASTILLE. *The storming of the Bastille on July 14, 1789.*

Bastille (ba-STEEL)   A prison in PARIS where many political and other offenders were held and tortured until the time of the FRENCH REVOLUTION. It was attacked by workers on July 14, 1789, during the revolution; the prisoners were released, and the building was later demolished.

&. The anniversary of the attack, Bastille Day, is the most important national holiday in FRANCE.

Ben-Gurion, David (ben-GOOR-ee-uhn)   An Israeli political leader of the twentieth century. Active in the movements toward the formation of ISRAEL in the early twentieth century, he was chosen to be the country's first PRIME MINISTER, and he served until the early 1960s. (*See* ARAB-ISRAELI CONFLICT.)

Berlin airlift   A military operation in the late 1940s that brought food and other needed goods into West BERLIN by air after the government of EAST GERMANY, which at that time surrounded West Berlin (*see* BERLIN WALL), had cut off its supply routes. The United States joined with western European nations in flying the supplies in. The airlift was one of the early events of the COLD WAR.

Bismarck, Otto von (BIZ-mahrk)   A political leader of GERMANY in the nineteenth century, known as the "Iron Chancellor." After the Franco-Prussian War had brought many small German states together as allies against FRANCE, Bismarck persuaded them to unite in a single German Empire under a KAISER, with Bismarck as first chancellor, or chief of government. Enormous economic progress took place under Bismarck's leadership. He resigned over differences with Kaiser WILHELM II, the emperor who was to rule during WORLD WAR I.

Black Hole of Calcutta   A cell in the jail of a British fort in CALCUTTA, INDIA. In the middle of the eighteenth century, British and Indian troops clashed at the fort. The Indian troops drove a reported 146 defenders of the fort into the cell, which measured about fifteen by eighteen feet. Many had died of suffocation by the next morning.

blitzkrieg (BLITS-kreeg)   A form of warfare used by German forces in WORLD WAR II. In a blitzkrieg, troops in vehicles, such as tanks, made quick surprise strikes with support from airplanes. These tactics resulted in the swift German conquest of FRANCE in 1940 (*see* FRANCE, FALL OF). *Blitzkrieg* is German for "LIGHTNING war."

blood, toil, tears, and sweat, I have nothing to offer but   A statement made by Winston CHURCHILL on becoming PRIME MINISTER of BRITAIN during WORLD WAR II.

Boer War (BOHR, BAWR, BOOR) A war between British and Dutch settlers (BOERS) in what is now SOUTH AFRICA, fought from 1899 to 1902, and won by the British. The country was united in 1910.

Boers (BOHRZ, BAWRZ, BOORZ) Dutch settlers in SOUTH AFRICA, also known as Afrikaners. The Boers were repeatedly driven further inland by British settlers; the British finally defeated them in the BOER WAR of 1899–1902. *Boer* is Dutch for "farmer."

Bolívar, Simón (see-MOHN buh-LEE-vahr) A Venezuelan revolutionary leader of the early nineteenth century who fought Spanish troops for the independence of countries in northern SOUTH AMERICA. The areas where Bolívar fought are now in VENEZUELA, COLOMBIA, ECUADOR, PERU, and BOLIVIA, which was named in his honor.

Bolsheviks (BOHL-shuh-viks, BOL-shuh-viks) The RADICALS in the RUSSIAN REVOLUTION, who were led by LENIN, and who favored revolution rather than gradual democratic change.

☙ *Bolshevik* has been used as a general term for a RADICAL LEFTIST, or for a COMMUNIST of the SOVIET UNION.

Bonaparte, Napoleon *See* NAPOLEON BONAPARTE.

Bourbons (boor-BOHN, BOOR-buhnz) The ruling family of FRANCE from the late sixteenth century until the FRENCH REVOLUTION. The Bourbon kings were known for their stubbornness; the politician Talleyrand is supposed to have said of them, "They have learned nothing, and they have forgotten nothing." LOUIS XIV and LOUIS XVI were Bourbon kings.

Brezhnev, Leonid (LAY-uh-nid BREZH-nef) A Soviet political leader of the twentieth century. He seized the leadership of the Soviet COMMUNIST party from Nikita KHRUSHCHEV in 1964. Brezhnev eventually became the head of government of the SOVIET UNION, and served until his death in 1982. While he was in office, the Soviet Union gave heavy military support to North VIETNAM in the VIETNAM WAR and to Arab nations in the ARAB-ISRAELI CONFLICT. Brezhnev had the Soviet army invade AFGHANISTAN in 1979 to keep a government friendly to the Soviets in power, and sent soldiers into CZECHOSLOVAKIA in 1968 to depose a government he considered unacceptable. He reached agreements with the United States on reducing the two nations' stock of NUCLEAR WEAPONS.

Britain, Battle of A series of air battles in WORLD WAR II between the German air force, the LUFTWAFFE, and the British ROYAL AIR FORCE, or RAF, during the summer and fall of 1940. Poised for an invasion of BRITAIN after the FALL OF FRANCE, the Germans sought to gain control of the air, but were thwarted by heroic British resistance and abandoned their plans for an invasion. Of the RAF's performance during the battle, PRIME MINISTER Winston CHURCHILL said, "Never in the field of human conflict was SO MUCH OWED BY SO MANY TO SO FEW."

British Empire The empire of BRITAIN, which began in the sixteenth and seventeenth centuries with the establishment of colonies in NORTH AMERICA, and ended in the twentieth century as dozens of nations, formerly British possessions, became independent. At the empire's greatest extent, around 1900, it included AUSTRALIA, CANADA, INDIA, NEW ZEALAND, vast portions of AFRICA, and many smaller territories throughout the world. The empire ceased to have an "emperor" in the late 1940s, when the British king renounced the title of emperor of India. The empire has been succeeded by the British Commonwealth, which was formed in 1931.

Bulge, Battle of the The last major offensive by the German army in WORLD WAR II. In late 1944, the invasion of BELGIUM by the ALLIES was temporarily stopped by a German counterattack in which the Germans broke through the Allied defenses, seizing territory that caused a large "bulge" in their lines. The Allies drove the German forces back with heavy casualties on both sides.

Burke, Edmund An Irish political leader and author of the eighteenth century who spent his career in ENGLAND. A member of the British PARLIAMENT, and an exceptional speaker, he sympathized with the AMERICAN REVOLUTION as a defense of existing rights of citizens. He opposed the FRENCH REVOLUTION, however, saying that it was a complete and unjustified break with tradition. (*See* PAINE, THOMAS.)

Castro, Fidel (fi-DEL) A Cuban political leader of the twentieth century. He led the revolution that in 1959 overthrew the dictator of CUBA, who had the support of the United States. Castro then presided over his country's transformation into a COMMUNIST state. His beard, cigars, and frequent wearing of combat uniforms have given him a distinctive appearance

FIDEL CASTRO. *Castro speaking to a military gathering marking the twentieth anniversary of the Bay of Pigs invasion.*

among heads of national governments. (*See* CUBAN MISSILE CRISIS.)

Catherine the Great   An empress of RUSSIA in the late eighteenth century who encouraged the cultural influences of western EUROPE in Russia and extended Russian territory toward the BLACK SEA. She is also known for her amorous intrigues, including affairs with members of her government.

Central Powers   GERMANY and its allies (Austria-Hungary, BULGARIA, and the OTTOMAN EMPIRE) in WORLD WAR I.

Chamberlain, Neville   A British PRIME MINISTER who tried to avoid war between BRITAIN and GERMANY by negotiating the MUNICH PACT in 1938, under which Germany, led by Adolf HITLER, was allowed to extend its territory into parts of CZECHOSLOVAKIA. Chamberlain proclaimed that the pact had secured "peace for our time," but his political foes called the pact APPEASEMENT. WORLD WAR II broke out less than a year later.

Chiang Kai-shek (CHANG, JYAHNG keye-shek)   A Chinese general and political leader of the twentieth century. He was president of CHINA until he was overthrown in 1949 by Chinese COMMUNIST forces under MAO ZEDONG, who established the PEOPLE'S REPUBLIC OF CHINA. Chiang fled to TAIWAN, where he established the government of the Republic of China, or NATIONALIST CHINA, recognized by the United States until 1979 as the only legitimate government of China.

Chou En-lai (JOH EN-LEYE)   *See* ZHOU EN-LAI.

Churchill, Winston   An English political leader and author of the twentieth century; he became PRIME MINISTER shortly after WORLD WAR II began, and served through the end of the war. Churchill symbolized the fierce determination of the British to resist conquest by the Germans under Adolf HITLER. He forged a close alliance with Franklin D. ROOSEVELT of the United States and Joseph STALIN of the SOVIET UNION in opposition to GERMANY. Stunningly defeated in elections after the war, he returned to office as prime minister for several years in the 1950s.

❦ Churchill was known for his fine oratory. When he became prime minister, he said, "I have nothing to offer but BLOOD, TOIL, TEARS, AND SWEAT." Concerning the British airmen who fought in the Battle of BRITAIN, he said, "Never in the field of human conflict was SO MUCH OWED BY SO MANY TO SO FEW." He originated the PHRASE "IRON CURTAIN." As an author, he is especially remembered for two histories, *A History of the English-Speaking Peoples* and *The Second World War.* ❦ Churchill's appearance was distinctive, with his bowler hat, cigars,

WINSTON CHURCHILL. *Churchill leaving 10 Downing Street, the prime minister's residence.*

portly frame, balding head, and two-finger "V for Victory" sign.

Clemenceau, Georges (klem-uhn-SOH, klay-mahnn-SOH) A French political leader of the late nineteenth and early twentieth centuries; the PREMIER of FRANCE at the end of WORLD WAR I and afterward. He presided at the peace conference after the war, which produced the Treaty of VERSAILLES. Less forgiving than the American president, Woodrow WILSON, Clemenceau wanted a peace treaty that would punish GERMANY for having started the war and would compensate France for its losses.

collapse of communism A stunning series of events between 1989 and 1991 that led to the fall of COMMUNIST regimes in eastern EUROPE and the SOVIET UNION. Faced with massive popular opposition and the unwillingness of President Mikhail GORBACHEV to send Soviet troops to their rescue, communist governments lost power, first in POLAND, where the communists agreed to free elections that swept candidates endorsed by SOLIDARITY to power in June 1989. Demands for reform spread across EAST GERMANY in the fall of 1989 and led to the end of the BERLIN WALL and the unification of East and WEST GERMANY. In November 1989 the communist government of CZECHOSLOVAKIA resigned, and in December a violent revolution led to the overthrow and execution of RUMANIA's communist boss, Nicolae Ceausescu. The BULGARIAN PARLIAMENT revoked the Communist party's monopoly on power in 1990, and in 1991 popular opposition forced the resignation of the communist CABINET in ALBANIA. The failure of a communist-led COUP D'ÉTAT against Mikhail Gorbachev in the Soviet Union in August 1991 ended the party's control of the military and government.

Commonwealth A government established in BRITAIN and IRELAND in 1649, after the execution of King Charles I. It was in the form of a REPUBLIC, under the leadership of the PARLIAMENT. Oliver CROMWELL soon assumed the supreme power in the Commonwealth and was given the title Lord Protector. After Cromwell's death in 1658, the Commonwealth quickly lost power, and the RESTORATION of the MONARCHY followed in 1660.

Communist Manifesto, The A book, published in 1848, in which Karl MARX and Friedrich ENGELS proclaimed the principles of COMMUNISM. It ends, "Workers of the world, unite."

concentration camp A place for assembling and confining political prisoners and enemies of a nation. Concentration camps are particularly associated with the rule of the NAZIS in GERMANY, who used them to confine millions of JEWS as a group to be purged from the German nation. COMMUNISTS, GYPSIES, HOMOSEXUALS, and other persons considered undesirable according to Nazi principles, or who opposed the government, were also placed in concentration camps and eventually executed in large groups. (*See* HOLOCAUST.)

Congress of Vienna *See* VIENNA, CONGRESS OF.

Cook, Captain James An English explorer of the eighteenth century, known for his voyages to the PACIFIC OCEAN. Cook visited NEW ZEALAND, established the first European colony in AUSTRALIA, and was the first European to visit HAWAII. He also approached ANTARCTICA and explored much of the western coast of NORTH AMERICA.

Cossacks (KOS-aks) A people in southern RUSSIA who became aggressive warriors during the sixteenth and seventeenth centuries. In place of taxes, they supplied the Russian Empire with scouts and mounted soldiers. The Cossacks are also famed for their dances, which feature fast-paced music and seemingly impossible leaps.

Counter Reformation The reaction of the ROMAN CATHOLIC CHURCH to the REFORMATION. The chief aims of the Counter Reformation were to increase faith among church members, end many of the abuses to which the leaders of the Reformation objected, and affirm some of the principles rejected by the PROTESTANT CHURCHES, such as veneration of the SAINTS and acceptance of the authority of the POPE. Many JESUITS were leaders of the Counter Reformation.

Crimean War (kreye-MEE-uhn) A war fought in the middle of the nineteenth century between RUSSIA on one side and TURKEY, BRITAIN, and FRANCE on the other. Russia was defeated, and the independence of Turkey was guaranteed.

  ❧ Florence NIGHTINGALE came to prominence through her nursing service during the Crimean War. The poem "THE CHARGE OF THE LIGHT BRIGADE," by Alfred, Lord TENNYSON, describes a battle in that war.

Cromwell, Oliver An English PURITAN political leader and general of the seventeenth century. He led the army of PARLIAMENT to victory over King Charles I in the English Civil War and afterward emerged as ruler of the nation under the title Lord Protector of the COMMONWEALTH. A skillful general and administrator, and a ruthless dictator, he was particularly harsh in his suppression of rebellion in IRELAND. After his death, government by a king was soon restored. (*See* RESTORATION.)

Cuban missile crisis A confrontation between the United States and the SOVIET UNION in 1962 over the presence of missile sites in CUBA; one of the "hottest" periods of the COLD WAR. The Soviet PREMIER, Nikita KHRUSHCHEV, placed Soviet military missiles in Cuba, which had come under Soviet influence since the success of the Cuban Revolution three years earlier. President John F. KENNEDY of the United States set up a naval blockade of Cuba and insisted that Khrushchev remove the missiles. Khrushchev did.

Cultural Revolution, Great Proletarian (proh-luh-TAIR-ee-uhn) A movement in CHINA, beginning in the middle 1960s and led by MAO ZEDONG, to restore the vitality of COMMUNISM in China. Mao, who gave the Cultural Revolution its name, sought to dismantle the complex governmental structure that had developed after the Chinese Revolution of the 1940s. During the Cultural Revolution, many government officials and intellectuals were sent out to work in the fields alongside the peasants. For a time, zealous young communists called RED GUARDS had considerable power. Many artworks, architectural treasures, and other cultural monuments associated with precommunist China were deliberately destroyed by the Red Guard.

czar (ZAHR, TSAHR) The title of rulers or emperors of RUSSIA from the sixteenth century until the RUSSIAN REVOLUTION. The czars ruled as absolute monarchs until the early twentieth century, when a PARLIAMENT was established in Russia. *Czar* can also be spelled *tsar*.

➤ The term *czar* is sometimes applied generally to a powerful leader or to a government administrator with wide-ranging powers.

Dachau (DAH-kow, DAH-khow) A CONCENTRATION CAMP established by the NAZIS in southern GERMANY. (*See* HOLOCAUST.)

Danton, Georges (dahnn-TOHNN) A prominent figure in the FRENCH REVOLUTION, who pressed for the execution of the king and several other enemies of the revolution. He disagreed, however, with more RADICAL revolutionaries, such as ROBESPIERRE, who eventually had him executed.

D-Day The code name for the first day of a military attack, especially the American and British invasion of German-occupied FRANCE during WORLD WAR II on June 6, 1944 (*see* NORMANDY, INVASION OF). This marked the beginning of the victory of the ALLIES in EUROPE. GERMANY surrendered less than a year later.

De Gaulle, Charles (di GOHL, di GAWL) A French political leader and general of the twentieth century. De Gaulle headed the Free French RESISTANCE to the NAZIS in WORLD WAR II and served briefly as president of FRANCE after the Nazis were driven out. He was called back as president in the 1950s under a new constitution that he himself specified. In office, he solved the crisis over ALGERIA that was dividing the country. He also made aggressive moves to strengthen France's international position, such as acquiring NUCLEAR WEAPONS. De Gaulle was known for his grand and imperious manner.

de-Stalinization (dee-stah-luh-nuh-ZAY-shuhn) An effort after the death of the Soviet PREMIER Joseph STALIN to soften some of the repressive measures used by his government. Premier Nikita KHRUSHCHEV was a leader in the de-Stalinization movement, which involved the downgrading of Stalin's reputation.

Dienbienphu (dyen-byen-FOOH) A place in INDOCHINA, now VIETNAM, where Vietnamese COMMUNISTS decisively defeated French forces in 1954. The defeat led to the French withdrawal from Indochina. (*See* VIETNAM WAR.)

Disraeli, Benjamin (diz-RAY-lee) An English political leader of the nineteenth century. He led the Conservative party of BRITAIN (TORIES) in the 1860s and 1870s, and was PRIME MINISTER twice. Disraeli strongly supported the extension of British colonies and had Queen VICTORIA proclaimed empress of INDIA.

divine right of kings The doctrine that kings and queens have a God-given right to rule, and that rebellion against them is a sin. This belief was common through the seventeenth century, and was urged by such kings as LOUIS XIV of FRANCE. (*See* ABSOLUTE MONARCHY.)

Doctor Livingstone, I presume? Words allegedly spoken by the British-born explorer Henry Stanley when, in 1871, he finally found the long-missing explorer and missionary David Livingstone in AFRICA.

SIR FRANCIS DRAKE. Sir Francis Drake in the Court of Queen Elizabeth I, *by Frank Moss Bennett. Drake stands to the right of the globe.*

Drake, Sir Francis An English navigator of the sixteenth century; the first Englishman to sail around the world. Drake often raided Spanish treasure ships; he participated in the destruction of the Spanish ARMADA.

Dreyfus affair (DREYE-fuhs, DRAY-fuhs) A scandal in FRANCE at the end of the nineteenth century involving a Jewish army officer, Alfred Dreyfus. Dreyfus was falsely convicted of betraying French military secrets and was sentenced to life imprisonment. French society was deeply divided over Dreyfus, with LIBERALS, including Émile ZOLA and Georges CLEMENCEAU, arguing that he was innocent, and CONSERVATIVES defending the French military authorities. Dislike of JEWS also affected the opinions of many in France about the incident. Zola's article

"J'accuse" ("I accuse") strongly influenced the public in Dreyfus's favor. Dreyfus was eventually cleared of all charges, reinstated in the army with a promotion, and publicly honored.

Dunkirk The scene of a remarkable, though ignominious, retreat by the British army in WORLD WAR II. Dunkirk, a town on the northern coast of FRANCE, was the last refuge of the British during the FALL OF FRANCE, and several hundred naval and civilian vessels took the troops back to ENGLAND in shifts over three days.

&. The term *Dunkirk* is sometimes used to signify a desperate retreat.

East Germany Former nation in north-central EUROPE, officially known as the GERMAN DEMOCRATIC REPUBLIC from 1949 to 1990, when East and WEST GERMANY were reunited. Its capital and largest city was East BERLIN.

&. Former EASTERN BLOC and WARSAW PACT nation, established as a republic in 1949; formed out of land in the zone of Germany occupied by the SOVIET UNION after WORLD WAR II. &. The BERLIN WALL was erected in 1961 to keep East Germans from defecting to the West. &. Although high by the standards of COMMUNIST nations, the East German living standard lagged far behind that of western Europe. Popular protests for democracy forced the communist government to open the Berlin Wall in 1989 and allow its citizens to migrate to West Germany. Unable to resist the tide of reform sweeping across communist states, the East German government agreed in 1990 to the reunification of Germany under the leadership of West Germany.

Edwardian period (ed-WAHR-dee-uhn, ed-WAWR-dee-uhn) A time in twentieth-century British history: the first decade of the century, when Edward VII, the eldest son of Queen VICTORIA, was king. The Edwardian period was known for elegance and luxury among the rich and powerful in BRITAIN, but also for moral looseness and for a general failure to prepare for some of the challenges of the twentieth century — particularly WORLD WAR I, which broke out four years after the death of King Edward.

Eichmann, Adolf (EYEK-muhn, EYEKH-muhn) A NAZI official who was responsible for the torture and killing of millions of JEWS during the HOLOCAUST. He escaped capture immediately after WORLD WAR II but was apprehended in ARGENTINA fifteen years

ELIZABETH I

later by agents of ISRAEL. In Israel, he was convicted of crimes against humanity, and was hanged.

Elizabeth I A queen of ENGLAND in the late sixteenth and early seventeenth centuries; a brilliant and crafty ruler who presided over the RENAISSANCE in England. Her reign, the ELIZABETHAN PERIOD, was a time of notable triumphs in literature (William SHAKESPEARE rose to prominence while she was queen) and war (the defeat of the Spanish ARMADA). The daughter of King HENRY VIII and Anne BOLEYN, Elizabeth never married. She is called the "Virgin Queen" and "Good Queen Bess."

🔊 The state of VIRGINIA is named after Elizabeth, the "Virgin Queen."

Elizabeth II The present queen of BRITAIN. Her husband is Prince Philip, Duke of Edinburgh, and the eldest of her four children is Prince Charles, the PRINCE OF WALES. Since Elizabeth became queen in 1952, dozens of nations, formerly possessions of Britain, have become independent.

Elizabethan period (i-liz-uh-BEE-thuhn) *See* ELIZABETH I.

Engels, Friedrich (ENG-guhlz, ENG-uhlz) A German SOCIALIST of the nineteenth century who collaborated with Karl MARX on *THE COMMUNIST MANIFESTO* and on *KAPITAL*.

Enlightenment An intellectual movement of the seventeenth and eighteenth centuries marked by a celebration of the powers of human reason, a keen interest in science, the promotion of religious toleration, and a desire to construct governments free of tyranny. Some of the major figures of the Enlightenment were David HUME, Immanuel KANT, John LOCKE, the Baron de MONTESQUIEU, Jean-Jacques ROUSSEAU, and VOLTAIRE.

Falkland Islands (FAWK-luhnd, FAWLK-luhnd) Islands in the south ATLANTIC OCEAN located near ARGENTINA but owned by BRITAIN. Argentina, which has long claimed title to the islands and refers to them as Islas Malvinas, seized them in 1982, but Britain retook them after a brief war.

fascism (FASH-iz-uhm) A system of government that flourished in EUROPE from the 1920s to the end of WORLD WAR II. GERMANY under HITLER, ITALY under MUSSOLINI, and SPAIN under FRANCO were all fascist states. As a rule, fascist governments are dominated by a dictator, who usually possesses a magnetic PERSONALITY, wears a showy uniform, and rallies his followers by mass parades; appeals to strident NATIONALISM; and promotes suspicion or hatred of both foreigners and "impure" people within his own nation, such as the JEWS in Germany. Although both COMMUNISM and fascism are forms of TOTALITARIANISM, fascism does not demand state ownership of the means of production, nor is fascism committed to the achievement of economic equality. In theory, communism opposes the identification of government with a single CHARISMATIC leader (the "CULT of personality"), which is the cornerstone of fascism. Whereas communists are considered LEFT-WING, fascists are usually described as RIGHT-WING.

🔊 Today, *fascist* is used loosely to refer to military DICTATORSHIPS, as well as governments or individuals that profess RACISM and that act in an arbitrary, high-handed manner.

Ferdinand, Archduke Francis *See* FRANCIS FERDINAND, ARCHDUKE.

fifth column People willing to cooperate with an aggressor against their own country. The term originated in a remark by Francisco FRANCO, the Spanish dictator, that he was marching on MADRID with four columns of troops, and that there was a "fifth column" of sympathizers within the city ready to help.

fin de siècle (fann duh see-EK-luh) The end of the nineteenth century; the PHRASE is French for "end of the century." *Fin de siècle* is particularly used to describe the period's self-conscious artistic movements and a sophisticated despair that became popular at the time. Oscar WILDE is one of the best-known *fin-de-siècle* figures.

Final Solution A term applied by NAZIS to the GENOCIDE of European JEWS during WORLD WAR II. Before instituting the Final Solution, the Nazi government had abolished the Jews' rights, destroyed and confiscated their property, and confined Jews in CONCENTRATION CAMPS.

France, fall of The conquest of FRANCE by GERMANY in WORLD WAR II in the spring of 1940. With France occupied, only British resistance in the Battle of BRITAIN kept Germany from gaining control of EUROPE.

Francis Ferdinand, Archduke An Austrian prince, heir to the throne, whose assassination in SARAJEVO in 1914 set off WORLD WAR I.

Franco, Francisco (FRANG-koh, FRAHNG-koh) A Spanish general and dictator of the twentieth century, often called Generalissimo Franco. Franco, a fascist (*see* FASCISM), successfully led the Nationalist armies against the Loyalists during the SPANISH CIVIL WAR in the 1930s, and then ruled SPAIN firmly until his death in 1975.

French Revolution The event at the end of the eighteenth century that ended the thousand-year rule of kings in FRANCE and established the nation as a REPUBLIC. The revolution began in 1789, after King LOUIS XVI had convened the French PARLIAMENT to deal with an enormous national DEBT. The common people's division of the parliament declared itself the true legislature of France, and when the king seemed to resist the move, a crowd destroyed the royal prison (the BASTILLE). A CONSTITUTIONAL MONARCHY was set up, but after King Louis and his queen, MARIE ANTOINETTE, tried to flee the country, they were arrested, tried for treason, and executed on the GUILLOTINE. Control of the government passed to ROBESPIERRE and other RADICALS — the extreme JACOBINS — and the REIGN OF TERROR followed (1793–1794), when thousands of French nobles and others considered enemies of the revolution were executed. After the Terror, Robespierre himself was executed, and

a new ruling body, the Directory, came into power. Its incompetence and corruption allowed NAPOLEON BONAPARTE to emerge in 1799 as dictator and, eventually, to become emperor. Napoleon's ascent to power is considered the official end of the revolution. (*See* DANTON, GEORGES *and* MARAT, JEAN-PAUL.)

Führer (FYOOR-uhr, FUUR-uhr) The title of Adolf HITLER, chancellor of GERMANY from 1933 to 1945. *Führer* is German for "leader."

Gandhi, Indira (in-DEER-uh GAHN-dee, GAN-dee) An Indian political leader of the twentieth century. She was the daughter of Jawaharlal NEHRU, and served as PRIME MINISTER of INDIA from 1966 to 1977, and again from 1980 until her assassination in 1984.

MAHATMA GANDHI. *A photograph by Margaret Bourke-White. Gandhi was frequently portrayed spinning to symbolize his plan for Indian self-sufficiency.*

Gandhi, Mahatma (Mohandas Karamchand Gandhi) (muh-HAHT-muh, muh-HAT-muh GAHN-dee, GAN-dee) A political figure of the twentieth century in INDIA; the leader of India's drive for independence from BRITAIN. Gandhi used methods of PASSIVE RESISTANCE and nonviolent disobedience such as BOYCOTTS and hunger strikes to influence British rulers. He was assassinated in 1948, just after India secured its independence. The title *mahatma* means "great soul."

Gang of Four Four Chinese political leaders of the twentieth century who were closely associated with

MAO ZEDONG (one of the four was his wife). They were denounced when moderates came to power in CHINA in 1976, and were convicted in 1981 of committing crimes, such as torture, during the Great Proletarian CULTURAL REVOLUTION.

Garibaldi, Giuseppe (juh-SEP-ay gar-uh-BAWL-dee) An Italian patriot of the nineteenth century who fought for the unification of ITALY.

George III The king of BRITAIN during the American REVOLUTIONARY WAR. He was known for insisting on royal privilege. The stubbornness of George and of his government officials is often blamed for the loss of the THIRTEEN COLONIES that became the United States. In Britain itself, however, prosperity increased greatly while he was king, and CANADA and INDIA were made British possessions.

Gestapo (guh-STAH-poh, guh-SHTAH-poh) The secret police of the THIRD REICH in GERMANY. The Gestapo operated against Germans suspected of treason by using brutal interrogation and torture; they instilled widespread fear by their terrorist methods.

&. "Gestapo tactics" in general are intimidating official procedures. &. Figuratively, any secret police organization similar to the German Gestapo may be called a "gestapo."

Gladstone, William Ewart An English political leader and author of the nineteenth century. A leader of the Liberal party, and a political opponent of Benjamin DISRAELI, he served as PRIME MINISTER several times during the reign of Queen VICTORIA. One of Gladstone's strongest interests, not satisfied in his lifetime, was providing IRELAND with a government of its own. He served in the British PARLIAMENT for sixty years.

Glorious Revolution A revolution in BRITAIN in 1688 in which the PARLIAMENT deposed King James II, a ROMAN CATHOLIC who had asserted royal rights over the rights of Parliament. Parliament gave the crown to the PROTESTANT King William III, a Dutch prince, and his British wife, Queen Mary II, as joint rulers.

The Glorious Revolution was the last genuine revolution in Britain. Because there was little armed resistance in ENGLAND to William and Mary, the revolution is also called the Bloodless Revolution. Battles did take place in SCOTLAND and IRELAND, however,

between supporters of the new king and queen and the supporters of King James.

&. When the crown was offered to William and Mary, they agreed to a Bill of Rights that severely limited the king or queen's power. The British Bill of Rights is often regarded as a forerunner to the United States BILL OF RIGHTS.

Goebbels, Joseph (YOH-zuhf GEU-buhls, GEU-buhlz) A German political leader of the twentieth century. Goebbels was PROPAGANDA MINISTER of the NAZI government and a close confidant of the leader, Adolf HITLER. Goebbels's policy was based on the notion that a lie, repeated often and forcibly, gains the legitimacy of truth. When the defeat of GERMANY seemed inevitable, he killed himself and his family.

Goering (*or* **Göring**), **Hermann** (HER-mahn GEU-ring, GER-ing, GUR-ing) A German political leader and general of the twentieth century. Goering, a close friend of Adolf HITLER, held several high positions in the NAZI government, including leadership of the air force, the LUFTWAFFE; until the Battle of BRITAIN, his aerial warfare methods were enormously successful (*see* BLITZKRIEG). At the NUREMBERG TRIALS for war criminals after the German defeat, Goering was sentenced to death, but he committed suicide before he could be executed.

Golan Heights (GOH-lahn) A hilly area on the border between ISRAEL and SYRIA that Israel seized from Syria after a fierce battle during the SIX-DAY WAR of 1967. Viewing the Golan Heights as vital to its defense, Israel has been unwilling to return the area to Syria, its archenemy.

goose step A straight-legged style of military marching used by the armies of several nations, but associated particularly with the army of GERMANY under the NAZIS.

&. The term is sometimes used to suggest the unthinking loyalty of followers or soldiers: "Brown has a goose-step mentality."

Gorbachev, Mikhail (mi-khah-EEL GAWR-buh-chawf, gawr-buh-CHAWF) The last president of the SOVIET UNION, Gorbachev came to power in 1985. Although a committed COMMUNIST, he sought to revive the ailing Soviet economy by introducing some elements of CAPITALIST competition (a policy he called *perestroika*, or "restructuring") and to encourage free expression by a policy of GLASNOST. *Perestroika* failed to stimulate the economy, while GLASNOST spurred popular criticism of communism itself and the surfacing of long-repressed NATIONALISM in the republics that composed the Soviet Union. In 1991 hardline communists, many of them Gorbachev's appointees, staged a COUP D'ÉTAT against him, but Boris YELTSIN, president of the Russian republic, rallied opposition against the coup, which also faced international criticism and aroused only lukewarm support in the Soviet military. The coup quickly collapsed and Gorbachev returned to the presidency, but with such weakened prestige that he was unable to prevent the dissolution of the Soviet Union and the disintegration of communism within it. (*See also* COLLAPSE OF COMMUNISM.)

Great Proletarian Cultural Revolution See CULTURAL REVOLUTION, GREAT PROLETARIAN.

Great War A common name for WORLD WAR I before a second world war broke out. (*See* WORLD WAR II.)

guillotine (GIL-uh-teen, GEE-uh-teen) A machine designed for beheading people quickly and with minimal pain. The guillotine, which used a large falling knife blade, was devised by a physician, Joseph Guillotin, during the FRENCH REVOLUTION and was used as the official method of execution in FRANCE until the twentieth century.

Hammarskjöld, Dag (DAHG HAH-muhr-shoold, HAM-uhr-shoold, HAH-muhr-sheuld) A Swedish diplomat of the twentieth century; the secretary-general of the UNITED NATIONS from 1953 to 1961. Hammarskjöld was intensely involved with settling differences between nations that arose from the COLD WAR and from the movement toward independence for African nations.

Hanover, House of (HAN-oh-vuhr) A German family, distantly related to the STUART kings and queens of BRITAIN, who received the crown of Britain in the early eighteenth century when the last Stuart ruler, Queen Anne, died without an heir. They established an English branch of their family that still rules Britain. GEORGE III, Queen VICTORIA, and Queen ELIZABETH II have been Hanoverians, although Victoria and her descendants have not used the family name Hanover. The control of the government of Britain

by PARLIAMENT has been greatly strengthened under Hanoverian rule, and the governmental role of the king or queen has been much reduced.

🔊 The first two Hanoverian kings, George I and George II, took little interest in their new country. George I spent most of his time in GERMANY and never bothered to learn the English language.

Hapsburgs Austrian-based dynasty that ruled much of central and parts of western EUROPE from the thirteenth to the twentieth centuries. The family's head long held the title of Holy Roman Emperor (see HOLY ROMAN EMPIRE). By 1914 the Hapsburg-ruled Austro-Hungarian Empire included all or part of territories that later became independent nations, such as CZECHOSLOVAKIA and YUGOSLAVIA. The empire collapsed during WORLD WAR I.

🔊 NATIONALISM threatened to disrupt the Hapsburg Empire in the nineteenth century; the assassination of Archduke FRANCIS FERDINAND by a Serbian nationalist in SARAJEVO in 1914 triggered World War I.

Himmler, Heinrich (HEYEN-rikh HIM-luhr) A German police official of the twentieth century. Himmler, a confidant of the leader Adolf HITLER, organized the NAZI elite forces (SS) and secret police (GESTAPO). He supervised the execution of millions of JEWS in CONCENTRATION CAMPS during WORLD WAR II. He committed suicide in 1945.

Hirohito (heer-oh-HEE-toh) Japanese emperor, who came to the throne in the 1920s. He reigned over the Japanese in WORLD WAR II. After the war, he was forced to give up the claim to divine STATUS that previous emperors had made. He died in 1989, after long outliving all the other major figures associated with the war.

Hiroshima (heer-uh-SHEE-muh, huh-ROH-shuh-muh) A Japanese city on which the United States dropped the first ATOMIC BOMB used in warfare, on August 6, 1945. After the devastation of the bombing, Hiroshima was largely rebuilt.

Hitler, Adolf A German political leader of the twentieth century, born in AUSTRIA. Hitler's early program for GERMANY is contained in his book *MEIN KAMPF*. He dreamed of creating a MASTER RACE of pure Aryans, who would rule for a thousand years as the third German Empire, or THIRD REICH. Hitler

ADOLF HITLER. *Hitler giving the Nazi party salute at a rally in 1935.*

led the NAZI party, and began to rule Germany in 1933 as a fascist (*see* FASCISM) dictator with the title *der* FÜHRER ("the leader"). He supervised the murder of six million JEWS and other supposed enemies of the Reich (*see* HOLOCAUST). Hitler began WORLD WAR II by invading POLAND in 1939. He reportedly committed suicide in 1945 when Germany's defeat was imminent.

☙ The official greeting between Nazis was "heil ("hail") Hitler."

Ho Chi Minh (HOH CHEE MIN)   A Vietnamese revolutionary leader of the twentieth century. Ho Chi Minh led the COMMUNISTS of VIETNAM in their efforts to drive out the forces of JAPAN in the 1940s (*see* WORLD WAR II), FRANCE in the 1950s (*see* DIENBIENPHU), and the United States in the 1960s (*see* VIETNAM WAR). He died in 1969.

☙ SAIGON, the former capital of South Vietnam, was renamed HO CHI MINH CITY after the communist victory there.

Holocaust (HOL-uh-kawst, HOH-luh-kawst)   The killing of some six million JEWS by the NAZIS during WORLD WAR II. To the Nazis, the Holocaust was the "FINAL SOLUTION" to the "Jewish problem," and would help them establish a pure German MASTER RACE. Much of the killing took place in CONCENTRATION CAMPS such as AUSCHWITZ and DACHAU. (*See* EICHMANN, ADOLF *and* HIMMLER, HEINRICH.)

Huguenots (HYOOH-guh-nots)   French PROTESTANTS of the sixteenth and seventeenth centuries, who were frequently persecuted by the government and by the ROMAN CATHOLIC CHURCH. For a time, the Edict of Nantes allowed them to practice their religion in certain cities. When the edict was revoked by King LOUIS XIV in the late seventeenth century, many Huguenots left FRANCE. Some emigrated to America.

Hussein, Saddam (sah-DAHM, SAH-duhm hooh-SAYN)   Dictator of IRAQ who seized power in 1979. With the intent of making Iraq the dominant power in the oil-rich PERSIAN GULF, Hussein invaded IRAN in 1980 and KUWAIT in 1990. The latter invasion provoked a military response from the UNITED NATIONS, led by the United States, which drove Iraqi forces from Kuwait in 1991. (*See* PERSIAN GULF WAR.)

☙ Hussein's cruelty and deviousness have become legendary. He has ruthlessly suppressed both SHI'ITE MOSLEMS and KURDS within Iraq; in 1987 and 1988 he authorized poison gas attacks on Kurdish villages.

☙ During the Iran-Iraq War, the United States and most other Western powers tilted toward Iraq, viewing Hussein as a lesser evil than his Iranian rival, the Ayatollah KHOMEINI. The REAGAN administration policy of aiding Hussein in the 1980s would later embarrass the administration of President George BUSH, who served as vice president under President Reagan.

☙ Although widely loathed outside the Arab world and feared by most Arab governments, Hussein retains some of his appeal to the Arab masses because of his resolute defiance of the United States and western EUROPE.

Industrial Revolution   The rapid industrial growth that began in ENGLAND during the middle of the eighteenth century and then spread over the next 150 years to many other countries, including the United States. The revolution depended on such devices as the steam engine (*see* WATT, JAMES), which were invented at a rapidly increasing rate during the period. The Industrial Revolution brought on a rapid concentration of people in cities and changed the nature of work for many persons. (*See* LUDDITES.)

International   An international organization of workers founded by Karl MARX in the 1860s. Weakened by disputes, it was dissolved in 1876, but it was succeeded by three later Internationals, which sought to spread COMMUNISM throughout the world. The most effective of these was the Third International, formed by the SOVIET UNION in 1919, and dissolved in 1943 by Joseph STALIN.

Irish potato famine   *See* POTATO FAMINE, IRISH.

Iron Curtain The former division between the COMMUNIST nations of eastern EUROPE — the EASTERN BLOC — and the noncommunist nations of western Europe. The term refers to the isolation that the SOVIET UNION imposed on its SATELLITES in the Eastern Bloc, and to the repressive measures of many Eastern Bloc governments. (*See* BERLIN WALL *and* COLD WAR.)

  ❧ The expression *iron curtain* was coined by Winston CHURCHILL, who was PRIME MINISTER of BRITAIN in WORLD WAR II. Churchill first used the term soon after the war, when the Soviet Union was beginning to carry out its plans for postwar dominance of eastern Europe.

Ivan the Terrible (EYE-vuhn, ee-VAHN) A Russian CZAR of the sixteenth century. Ivan struggled constantly with the nobles of RUSSIA and became famous for his brutality toward his enemies.

Jack the Ripper A criminal in LONDON in the late nineteenth century apparently responsible for several ghastly murders by slashing. His identity is unknown.

Jacobins (JAK-uh-binz) An extreme RADICAL party during the FRENCH REVOLUTION named for the place where its founders first met, a CONVENT of Jacobin friars. It was led by ROBESPIERRE.

  ❧ In general, a member of an extremist or radical group is often called a "Jacobin."

John XXIII, Pope The POPE from 1958 to 1963. Pope John, who convened the Second Vatican Council (VATICAN II), was a leader in liberalizing the ROMAN CATHOLIC CHURCH.

John Paul II, Pope A POPE elected in 1978. John Paul II is the first Polish pope, and the first non-Italian pope in several centuries. He has traveled extensively to spread the teachings of the ROMAN CATHOLIC CHURCH.

Kaiser (KEYE-zuhr) The German word for "emperor." The emperors of AUSTRIA and GERMANY were called Kaisers. (*See* WILHELM II.)

kamikaze (kah-muh-KAH-zee) Japanese fighter pilots in WORLD WAR II, trained to make suicide crashes into Allied ships.

Khmer Rouge (kuh-MAIR ROOHZH) The COMMUNIST movement in KAMPUCHEA (CAMBODIA) in SOUTHEAST ASIA. It came to power in 1975.

  ❧ Led by Pol Pot, the Khmer Rouge, after it came to power, instituted one of the worst examples of GENOCIDE in world history. Estimates of the number of people killed under this REGIME vary from two million to four million.

Khomeini, Ayatollah Ruhollah (eye-uh-TOH-luh rooh-HOH-luh khoh-MAY-nee, koh-MAY-nee) An Iranian religious and political leader of the twentieth century. Imposing rule by ISLAMIC law and determined to rid IRAN of foreign, and especially American, influences, he became virtual dictator of Iran in 1979. With his blessing, Iranian militants held American diplomats as hostages from 1979 to 1981. He died in 1989.

Khrushchev, Nikita (ni-KEE-tuh kroosh-CHAWF, KROOHSH-chef, KROOHSH-chawf) A Soviet political leader of the twentieth century. Khrushchev, who was PREMIER of the SOVIET UNION in the late 1950s and early 1960s, led a campaign, called DE-STALINIZATION, to remove the influence of the late premier Joseph STALIN from Soviet society. He urged PEACEFUL COEXISTENCE between his country and Western nations. Within the SOVIET BLOC, however, Khrushchev sent troops into POLAND and HUNGARY in 1956 against persons who resisted COMMUNIST government. He also aided the government of Fidel CASTRO in CUBA. He had Soviet military missiles installed there but removed them at the insistence of the United States. (*See* CUBAN MISSILE CRISIS.)

Kidd, Captain William A famous English pirate of the late seventeenth and early eighteenth centuries. Kidd was employed by the British government for some time to stop piracy, but he turned pirate himself and was executed in ENGLAND.

Klondike gold rush A rush of thousands of people in the 1890s toward the Klondike gold mining district in northwestern CANADA after gold was discovered there.

Korean War A war, also called the Korean conflict, fought in the early 1950s between the UNITED NATIONS and COMMUNIST NORTH KOREA. The war began in 1950, when North Korea invaded SOUTH KOREA. The United Nations declared North Korea the aggressor and sent troops, mostly from United States forces, to aid the South Korean army. In 1953, with neither side having a prospect of victory, a truce was signed. (*See under* "American History since 1865.")

Kuomintang (KWOH-min-TAHNG, KWOH-min-TANG) A Chinese nationalist (*see* NATIONALISM) political party founded by Sun Yat-sen, which gained control of CHINA in the early twentieth century. Later, under the leadership of CHIANG KAI-SHEK, it was defeated by the Chinese COMMUNISTS, and became the ruling party of TAIWAN, the island to which Chiang and his supporters had fled.

Lawrence of Arabia   T. E. Lawrence, an English soldier and author of the twentieth century, known for leading a rebellion of Arabs against the Turks in WORLD WAR I, and for his book describing the experience, *Seven Pillars of Wisdom*. At the negotiations that produced the Treaty of VERSAILLES, he argued unsuccessfully for independence for the Arab nations.

League of Nations   An international organization established after WORLD WAR I under the provisions of the Treaty of VERSAILLES. The League, the forerunner of the UNITED NATIONS, brought about much international cooperation on health, labor problems, refugee affairs, and the like. It was too weak, however, to prevent the great powers from going to war in 1939.

  Although President Woodrow WILSON of the United States was a principal founder of the League, the United States SENATE refused to ratify the Treaty of Versailles, and the United States never joined the League.

Lenin (LEN-in)   A Russian revolutionary leader of the early twentieth century, highly honored in the former SOVIET UNION as the founder of the modern Soviet state. Lenin, a founder of the BOLSHEVIK party, contributed much to the success of the RUSSIAN REVOLUTION of 1917. Lenin held that a dedicated group of INTELLECTUALS had to spearhead the revolution. He became chief of government of the Soviet Union after the revolution and served until his death in 1924. Joseph STALIN succeeded him. Lenin's real name was Vladimir Ilyich Ulyanov.

Lloyd George, David   A British political leader of the late nineteenth and early twentieth centuries; he was PRIME MINISTER of BRITAIN at the end of WORLD WAR I and afterward. After the war, at the negotiations that produced the Treaty of VERSAILLES, Lloyd George opposed President Woodrow WILSON of the United States, who was relatively conciliatory toward GERMANY. Lloyd George called for squeezing Germany "until the pips squeak."

LENIN

Long March   An important event in the history of the Chinese COMMUNISTS. Driven from southern and eastern CHINA by CHIANG KAI-SHEK at the end of the 1920s, the communist leader MAO ZEDONG led his forces on a long march to safety in the northwest part of China. From there, they staged attacks on the Japanese invaders and eventually on Chinese government troops — attacks that led to their conquest of China in 1949.

lost generation   The young adults of EUROPE and America during WORLD WAR I. They were called lost because after the war many of them were disillusioned with the world in general and unwilling to move into a settled life. Gertrude STEIN is usually credited with popularizing the expression.

  The CHARACTERS in the book *THE SUN ALSO RISES*, by Ernest HEMINGWAY, are often mentioned as examples of the lost generation.

Louis XIV (LOOH-ee)   A king of FRANCE in the seventeenth and early eighteenth centuries. Louis was known as the "SUN KING" for his power and splendor. By inviting French nobles to live in luxury at his palace at VERSAILLES, he removed them as threats and greatly increased his own power. He is known for saying, "L'état, c'est moi" ("I am the state").

Louis XVI (LOOH-ee) The last king of FRANCE before the FRENCH REVOLUTION; the husband of MARIE ANTOINETTE. He at first accepted a change from ABSOLUTE MONARCHY (*see* ANCIEN RÉGIME) to CONSTITUTIONAL MONARCHY in France. Then he tried to flee the country and was brought back a prisoner. RADICALS, such as the JACOBINS, assumed control of the revolution and had Louis and Marie Antoinette beheaded for treason.

Luddites (LUD-eyets) Opponents of the introduction of labor-saving machinery. The original Luddites, followers of a legendary Ned Ludd, were British laborers of the early nineteenth century who smashed textile-making machines that threatened their jobs.

☙ Modern opponents of technological change are sometimes called "Luddites."

Luftwaffe (LOOFT-vah-fuh) The German air force in WORLD WAR II. (*See* BLITZKRIEG *and* BRITAIN, BATTLE OF.)

Lusitania (looh-suh-TAY-nee-uh) A British passenger ship sunk by a German submarine off the coast of IRELAND in 1915. GERMANY, then at war with BRITAIN but not with the United States (*see* WORLD WAR I), had warned Americans against traveling on the ship. Over a hundred Americans died in the sinking. The incident worsened relations between Germany and the United States and encouraged American involvement in the war.

Maginot line (MAZH-uh-noh, MAJ-uh-noh) A chain of defensive fortifications built by FRANCE on its eastern border between WORLD WAR I and WORLD WAR II. The Maginot line was designed to stop any future invasion by GERMANY, but it was never completed. In World War II, the Germans conquered France by going around the Maginot line to the north.

☙ The expression *Maginot mentality* refers to any military strategy that is exclusively defensive and therefore flawed. It also refers to military planning that is aimed at the past. This way of thinking is sometimes referred to as "fighting the last war."

Manchu dynasty (man-CHOOH, MAN-chooh) A dynasty, Manchurian in origin, that came to power in CHINA in the seventeenth century and that greatly expanded China's control in ASIA. The dynasty was overthrown in 1911. (*See* KUOMINTANG.)

NELSON MANDELA. *Photographed in Soweto upon release from prison in 1990.*

Mandela, Nelson (man-DEL-uh) The most prominent leader in the struggle of South African blacks against APARTHEID. Mandela joined the radical African National Congress (ANC) in the 1940s and in the 1960s was sentenced to life imprisonment for sabotage and conspiracy by the white minority government of South Africa. Even in prison he remained the acknowledged leader of the ANC. In 1990 the white government released him from jail as part of a series of moves to reach a compromise with South African blacks. Since his release, Mandela has emerged as the most prominent spokesperson for the anti-apartheid movement and has been instrumental in the gradual dismantling of South Africa's racist policies.

Mao Tse-tung (MOW tsuh-TOONG, dzuh-DOONG) Another spelling of the name of MAO ZEDONG.

Mao Zedong (Mao Tse-tung) (MOW dzuh-DOONG) A Chinese revolutionary leader of the twentieth century. He led an army of workers and peasants on the LONG MARCH in the 1920s, and used GUERRILLA WARFARE techniques successfully on both the Japa-

MAO ZEDONG

nese invaders and the forces of the Chinese government under CHIANG KAI-SHEK. In 1949, his armies took over the country and established the PEOPLE'S REPUBLIC OF CHINA. Mao continued as chairman of China's COMMUNIST party and PREMIER. His "Little Red Book," *Quotations from Chairman Mao,* was standard reading for schoolchildren of the country. Toward the end of his life, he brought about the Great Proletarian CULTURAL REVOLUTION, in which all CAPITALIST or elitist culture was to be purged. Mao died in 1976.

Maoism (MOW-iz-uhm)   The doctrines of MAO ZEDONG, most notably the doctrine that a continuous revolution is necessary if the leaders of a COMMUNIST state are to be kept in touch with the people. (*See* CULTURAL REVOLUTION, GREAT PROLETARIAN.)

Marat, Jean-Paul (muh-RAH)   A French political leader of the eighteenth century. In the FRENCH REVOLUTION, Marat was a leader of the JACOBINS, a party of RADICALS. He was stabbed to death in his bathtub.

Marie Antoinette (muh-REE an-twuh-NET, an-tuh-NET)   A French queen, born in AUSTRIA, who was beheaded on the GUILLOTINE during the FRENCH REVOLUTION. Her husband, King LOUIS XVI, was also beheaded.

Marshall Plan   A program by which the United States gave large amounts of economic aid to European countries to help them rebuild after the devastation of WORLD WAR II. It was proposed by the United States SECRETARY OF STATE, General George C. MARSHALL.

Marx, Karl   A German scholar of the nineteenth century; the founder of MARXISM, the fundamental theory of COMMUNISM. Much of his work, including *KAPITAL* and *THE COMMUNIST MANIFESTO,* was done with Friedrich ENGELS. Marx lived outside GERMANY most of his life, notably in LONDON, where he wrote *Kapital.* He organized the first INTERNATIONAL in the 1860s.

master race   The expression used by the NAZIS in GERMANY for the race they wanted to create — a pure race of white people suited to rule the world. Extermination was the Nazis' main tool for making the Germans pure. (*See* HOLOCAUST.)

Mata Hari (MAH-tuh HAHR-ee, MAT-uh HAR-ee)   A spy of the twentieth century who worked for both the French and the Germans during WORLD WAR I. The French executed her in 1917.

&   A "Mata Hari" is a seductive, double-dealing woman.

Mein Kampf (meyen KAHMPF)   An AUTOBIOGRAPHY written by Adolf HITLER in the 1920s. In it, Hitler outlines his plan for the revival of GERMANY from the losses of WORLD WAR I and blames Germany's problems on CAPITALISTS, COMMUNISTS, and JEWS.

Meir, Golda (me-EER)   An Israeli political leader of the twentieth century. Meir served as PRIME MINISTER of ISRAEL from 1969 to 1974, and was known for her efforts to lessen the ARAB-ISRAELI CONFLICT through diplomacy. Arab forces, attacking in 1973, caught her country by surprise and inflicted heavy losses.

Metternich, Prince Clemens von (MET-uhr-nik)   An Austrian nobleman and political leader of the early nineteenth century; he was chancellor, or head, of the Austrian government for nearly forty years. Through his leadership at the Congress of VIENNA and elsewhere, Metternich restored order in EUROPE after the fall of the French emperor NAPOLEON BONAPARTE. He did so, however, to the advantage of the European kings and princes and at the expense of movements toward DEMOCRACY in Europe.

Moguls (or Mughals) (MOH-guhlz; MOOH-guhlz) A MOSLEM dynasty, originally Turkish but strongly influenced by Persia, that ruled INDIA in the sixteenth and seventeenth centuries. The TAJ MAHAL is an example of Mogul influence in India.

꙳ The name "mogul" is sometimes applied to a great personage or magnate. For example, the founders of the major HOLLYWOOD studios often have been called "moguls."

Montessori, Maria (mon-tuh-SAWR-ee) An Italian educator of the twentieth century. MONTESSORI SCHOOLS are based on her educational ideas.

Montessori schools (mon-tuh-SAWR-ee) Schools that are based on the educational ideas of Maria MONTESSORI, that stress development of the child's own urge for creation and accomplishment. Most Montessori education takes place in preschool and kindergarten.

Montgomery, Bernard A British general of the twentieth century; a leader of British forces in WORLD WAR II. He defeated the Germans under Erwin ROMMEL in north AFRICA and led British troops in the invasion of ITALY, NORMANDY (*see* D-DAY), and GERMANY.

Mother Teresa (tuh-REE-suh, tuh-RAY-zuh) ROMAN CATHOLIC nun, born in YUGOSLAVIA, who received the NOBEL PRIZE for Peace in 1979 for her humanitarian work among lepers and other dying poor of CALCUTTA.

Munich Pact An agreement between BRITAIN and GERMANY in 1938, under which Germany was allowed to extend its territory into parts of CZECHOSLOVAKIA in which German-speaking peoples lived. PRIME MINISTER Neville CHAMBERLAIN negotiated on behalf of Britain, and Chancellor Adolf HITLER on behalf of Germany. Chamberlain returned to LONDON proclaiming that the Munich Pact had secured "peace for our time." The Germans invaded POLAND less than a year later (*see* POLAND, INVASION OF), and WORLD WAR II began.

꙳ In later years, the Munich Pact was denounced as pure APPEASEMENT of Hitler.

MOTHER TERESA. *At an interfaith prayer service in Denver, Colorado, in 1989.*

Mussolini, Benito (mooh-suh-LEE-nee, moos-uh-LEE-nee) An Italian general and dictator of the twentieth century. Mussolini formed a fascist (*see* FASCISM) government in ITALY in the 1920s and allied Italy with GERMANY as one of the AXIS POWERS of WORLD WAR II. Mussolini, known as *il Duce* ("the leader"), was shot by his Italian opponents near the end of the war.

Napoleon Bonaparte (BOH-nuh-pahrt) A French general, political leader, and emperor of the late eighteenth and early nineteenth centuries. Bonaparte rose swiftly through the ranks of army and government during and after the FRENCH REVOLUTION, and crowned himself emperor in 1804. He conquered much of EUROPE but lost two-thirds of his army in a disastrous invasion of RUSSIA. After his final loss to BRITAIN at the Battle of WATERLOO, he was exiled to the island of St. Helena in the south ATLANTIC OCEAN.

꙳ Napoleon's name is often connected with overreaching military ambition and DELUSIONS of grandeur. ꙳ Because Napoleon was short, overly aggres-

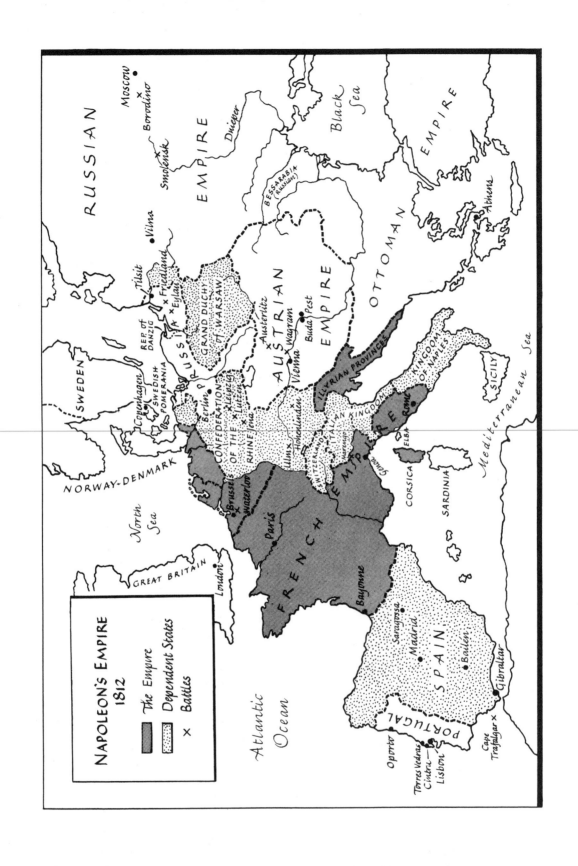

NAPOLEON'S EMPIRE 1812

The Empire
Dependent States
× Battles

RUSSIAN EMPIRE

Moscow
× Borodino
Smolensk
Vilna
Dnieper

Black Sea

OTTOMAN EMPIRE

Athens

BESSARABIA (RUSSIAN)

Tilsit
× Friedland
× Eylau

REP. OF DANZIG

P R U S S I A

GRAND DUCHY OF WARSAW

Austerlitz

A U S T R I A N   E M P I R E

Buda Pest
Vienna
× Wagram

SWEDEN

Copenhagen
SWEDISH POMERANIA

Berlin
Confederation
OF THE
RHINE
× Leipzig
× Lützen
× Jena

Hohenlinden
Ulm

ILLYRIAN PROVINCES

ITALIAN KINGDOM

SWITZERLAND
Marengo

Genoa

KINGDOM OF NAPLES

Rome

ELBA

SICILY

Mediterranean Sea

NORWAY-DENMARK

North Sea

Brussels
Switzerland
Paris

F R E N C H   E M P I R E

Bayonne

CORSICA

SARDINIA

GREAT BRITAIN

London

Atlantic Ocean

Saragossa
Madrid
S P A I N
Bailen
Gibraltar

PORTUGAL
Oporto
Torres Vedras
Cintra
Lisbon
Cape Trafalgar ×

NAPOLEON BONAPARTE. *A painting of the emperor by Jean-Auguste-Dominique Ingres.*

sive men of short stature are sometimes said to have a "Napoleon complex."

Nasser, Gamal Abdel (guh-MAHL AHB-duhl NAH-suhr, NAS-uhr)   An Egyptian military and political leader of the twentieth century. Nasser overthrew King Farouk of EGYPT in the early 1950s and soon became president. He urged Arab nations to unify against both ISRAEL and European and American influence in the MIDDLE EAST. He took control of the SUEZ CANAL for Egypt in 1956, provoking a British military attack. In 1967, he provoked a brief and unsuccessful war against Israel, the SIX-DAY WAR. Upon his death in 1970, he was succeeded by Anwar SADAT. (*See* ARAB-ISRAELI CONFLICT.)

Nationalist China   The REPUBLIC OF CHINA; the government on the island of TAIWAN, established by CHIANG KAI-SHEK in the late 1940s after he and his followers were driven from the mainland by the COMMUNISTS under MAO ZEDONG. Until 1979, the United States treated the Nationalist Chinese government as the legitimate government of all of CHINA. Nationalist China and the United States still have unofficial DIPLOMATIC RELATIONS.

NATO (NAY-toh)   *See* NORTH ATLANTIC TREATY ORGANIZATION.

Nazis (NAHT-seez, NAT-seez)   A German political party of the twentieth century, led by Adolf HITLER. The Nazis controlled GERMANY from the early 1930s until the end of WORLD WAR II. The party's full name in English is National Socialist German Workers' party; *Nazi* is short for its German name. Despite the word *socialist* in its name, it was a fascist party, requiring from its members supreme devotion to the German government — the THIRD REICH (*see* FASCISM *and* SOCIALISM). The Nazis rose to power by promising the people that Germany, which had been humiliated after WORLD WAR I, would become powerful again.

The Nazis opposed COMMUNISM, and free intellectual inquiry. Desiring to form a MASTER RACE that would rule the world, they fought the influence in Germany of peoples not of "pure" descent. Their power was particularly directed at controlling JEWS in Germany and in the countries that Germany conquered in war. After depriving Jews of their property and confining them in CONCENTRATION CAMPS, the Nazis employed the FINAL SOLUTION of killing them in large numbers; an estimated six million Jews lost their lives (*see* HOLOCAUST). Also marked for extermination were the mentally and physically handicapped and such "enemies of the Reich" as Slavs, COMMUNISTS, GYPSIES, HOMOSEXUALS, CHRISTIANS who resisted the government, and defenders of intellectual freedom. The Nazis fought World War II to spread their principles worldwide but were defeated.

NAZIS. *Flag bearers at a Nazi party conference in Nuremberg, Germany, in 1933.*

Twenty-two of their leaders were convicted of WAR CRIMES at the NUREMBERG TRIALS.

A great number of SYMBOLS, images, and names are associated with the reign of the Nazis, including the SWASTIKA emblem; the stiff-armed salute; the greeting "heil Hitler"; soldiers marching in GOOSE STEP; mass political rallies; concentration camps such as AUSCHWITZ and DACHAU; and Hitler's aides Adolf EICHMANN, Joseph GOEBBELS, Hermann GOERING, and Heinrich HIMMLER.

Nazism (NAHT-siz-uhm, NAT-siz-uhm)   The beliefs of the NAZIS.

Nazi-Soviet Non-Aggression Pact A treaty made by GERMANY and the SOVIET UNION in 1939 that opened the way for both nations to invade and dismember POLAND. (*See* POLAND, INVASION OF.)

Nehru, Jawaharlal (juh-WAH-huhr-lahl NAIR-ooh, NAY-rooh)   An Indian political leader of the twentieth century. Nehru was a close associate of Mahatma GANDHI in the struggle for independence from BRITAIN in INDIA during the 1930s and 1940s. After independence, he served as the country's first PRIME MINISTER, steering Indian foreign policy toward nonalignment (*see* NONALIGNED NATIONS). Nehru died in 1964.

Nelson, Admiral Horatio   A British naval officer of the late eighteenth and early nineteenth centuries, also called Lord Nelson. He defeated the French emperor NAPOLEON BONAPARTE in the sea battle of TRAFALGAR but was fatally wounded in the battle.

Never in the field of human conflict was so much owed by so many to so few   *See* SO MUCH OWED BY SO MANY TO SO FEW, NEVER IN THE FIELD OF HUMAN CONFLICT WAS.

New World   A name for the Americas, especially during the time of first exploration and colonization of the Americas by Europeans. (*Compare* OLD WORLD.)

Nightingale, Florence   An English nurse of the nineteenth century, known for establishing a battlefield hospital for British soldiers wounded in the CRIMEAN WAR. Her tireless service, at night as well as during the day, gained her the nickname "Lady with the Lamp."

🕭 Florence Nightingale's diligence made her a SYMBOL for all nursing and for any kind of dedicated service.

1914 to 1918   The years of WORLD WAR I.

1939 to 1945   The years of WORLD WAR II.

nonviolent resistance   *See* PASSIVE RESISTANCE.

Normandy, invasion of   The American and British invasion of FRANCE in WORLD WAR II; Normandy is a province of northern France. The successful invasion began a series of victories for the ALLIES, and GERMANY surrendered less than a year later. (*See* D-DAY.)

nuclear testing   The testing of NUCLEAR WEAPONS. (*See* NUCLEAR TEST BAN TREATY.)

Nuremberg trials (NOOR-uhm-burg)   Trials of NAZI leaders conducted after WORLD WAR II. A court set up by the victorious ALLIES tried twenty-two former officials, including Hermann GOERING, in Nuremberg, GERMANY, for WAR CRIMES. Goering and eleven others were sentenced to death. Many of the highest officials of Nazi Germany, including Adolf HITLER, Joseph GOEBBELS, and Heinrich HIMMLER, had committed suicide before they could be brought to trial, and Goering killed himself before he could be executed.

🕭 Several of those accused at the Nuremberg trials offered the defense that they were merely carrying out the orders of their superiors. This defense was not accepted.

October Revolution   The revolution in October 1917 in RUSSIA that brought the BOLSHEVIKS to power. (*See* RUSSIAN REVOLUTION.)

Old World   The Eastern Hemisphere, especially EUROPE, as opposed to the NEW WORLD — the Americas.

Ottoman Empire   An empire developed by the Turks between the fourteenth and twentieth centuries; it was succeeded in the 1920s by the present-day REPUBLIC of TURKEY. At its peak, the Ottoman Empire included, besides present-day Turkey, large parts of the MIDDLE EAST and southeastern EUROPE.

Perón, Eva (EE-vuh, AY-vuh puh-ROHN, pay-ROHN) An Argentine political figure of the twentieth century; the wife of President Juan PERÓN of ARGEN-TINA. Crafty and ambitious, she had great influence on her husband, and achieved immense popularity among the Argentinian masses through her charitable activities. She died of CANCER in the 1950s.

🍀 The MUSICAL play *Evita* is loosely based on Eva Perón's life.

Perón, Juan (HWAHN puh-ROHN, pay-ROHN) An Argentine political leader of the twentieth century. Perón, an intense nationalist, was dictator of ARGEN-TINA in the 1940s and 1950s and again, briefly, in the 1970s. His wife, Eva PERÓN, became the most powerful woman in Argentina before her early death.

Persian Gulf War A war between the forces of the UNITED NATIONS, led by the United States, and those of IRAQ that followed Iraqi dictator Saddam HUS-SEIN's invasion of KUWAIT in August 1990. The United Nations forces, called the Coalition, expelled Iraqi troops from Kuwait in March 1991.

🍀 His rallying of the U.N. against the invasion of Kuwait is considered the high point of George BUSH's presidency.

Peter the Great A Russian CZAR of the late seventeenth and early eighteenth centuries who tried to transform RUSSIA from a backward nation into a progressive one by introducing customs and ideas from western European countries. He moved the capital of Russia from MOSCOW to a new city he had built, St. Petersburg, which was renamed LENINGRAD after the RUSSIAN REVOLUTION, and has since had its old name restored due to the COLLAPSE OF COMMU-NISM.

Pitt, William, the Elder An English political leader of the eighteenth century. Pitt led the British government in the SEVEN YEARS' WAR. Although he opposed independence for the American colonies, he worked to change the harsh colonial policies of King GEORGE III and his MINISTERS.

PLO *See* PALESTINE LIBERATION ORGANIZATION.

Poland, invasion of The action by GERMANY that began WORLD WAR II in 1939. Germany invaded POLAND only days after signing the NAZI-SOVIET NON-AGGRESSION PACT, under which the SOVIET UNION agreed not to defend Poland from the east if Germany attacked it from the west. BRITAIN and FRANCE, which had pledged to protect Poland from German attack, soon declared war on Germany.

potato famine, Irish A famine in IRELAND in the nineteenth century caused by the failure of successive potato crops in the 1840s. Many in Ireland starved, and many emigrated. More than a million Irish came to the United States during the famine.

Puritans A group of RADICAL English PROTESTANTS that arose in the late sixteenth century and became a major force in ENGLAND during the seventeenth century. Puritans wanted to "purify" the CHURCH OF ENGLAND by eliminating traces of its origins in the ROMAN CATHOLIC CHURCH. In addition, they urged a strict moral code and placed a high value on hard work (*see* WORK ETHIC). After the execution of King Charles I in 1649, they controlled the new government, the COMMONWEALTH. Oliver CROMWELL, who became leader of the Commonwealth, is the best-known Puritan.

🍀 Many Puritans, persecuted in their homeland, came to America in the 1620s and 1630s, settling colonies that eventually became MASSACHUSETTS. (*See* PILGRIMS *and* PLYMOUTH COLONY.) 🍀 The words *puritan* and *puritanical* have come to suggest a zeal for keeping people from enjoying themselves.

Qaddafi, Muammar (MOOH-uh-mahr, mooh-AH-mahr kuh-DAH-fee) A Libyan military officer and political leader of the twentieth century. The ruler of LIBYA, and a militant Arab (*see* ARAB-ISRAELI CON-FLICT), Qaddafi is fervently opposed to the influence of the United States in the MEDITERRANEAN region, especially its influence on behalf of ISRAEL. The United States has accused Qaddafi of planning terrorist acts.

Quisling, Vidkun (KWIZ-ling) A Norwegian military officer and politician of the twentieth century. He collaborated with the Germans in their conquest of NORWAY in WORLD WAR II; the Germans rewarded him by making him leader of the German-controlled government of the country. After the German defeat, the Norwegian government had Quisling tried for treason and executed.

🍀 "Quislings" are persons who betray their country through cooperation with the enemy.

RAF ABBREVIATION for the British ROYAL AIR FORCE.

Raleigh, Sir Walter (RAW-lee, RAH-lee) An English explorer of the late sixteenth and early seventeenth centuries. He is best known for his expeditions to the Americas, and for introducing tobacco and the potato, two products of the NEW WORLD, into ENGLAND.

&. Raleigh is often considered a near-ideal English gentleman of the RENAISSANCE. A well-known legend holds that he spread his coat over a mud puddle so that Queen ELIZABETH I would not have to soil her feet by walking through it.

GRIGORI RASPUTIN. *Rasputin blessing his disciples.*

Rasputin, Grigori (ras-PYOOHT-n) A Russian MONK of the late nineteenth and early twentieth centuries. Before and during WORLD WAR I, Rasputin gained great influence over both Nicholas II, the CZAR of RUSSIA, and his German-born wife, who considered him a miraculous healer. The czar's only son suffered from HEMOPHILIA, a BLOOD disorder, and Rasputin seemed to be the only person who could alleviate the disease. When Rasputin told Nicholas how Russia should be ruled and whom Nicholas should choose as government officials, the czar followed his advice carefully. Jealous Russian noblemen murdered Rasputin in 1916, but his direction of the czar's policies was to prove disastrous after his death: Czar Nicholas was overthrown in 1917 and executed in 1918.

Reason, Age of Another name for the ENLIGHTENMENT.

Red Guards Loosely organized bands of militant COMMUNISTS who followed MAO ZEDONG in attacking CONSERVATIVE or BOURGEOIS elements in CHINA during the Great Proletarian CULTURAL REVOLUTION in the 1960s.

Reign of Terror A phase of the FRENCH REVOLUTION aimed at destroying all alleged pockets of resistance to the revolution. ROBESPIERRE was a leader of the Terror, during which thousands were sent to the GUILLOTINE.

Resistance, French A movement of French patriots during WORLD WAR II, after the FALL OF FRANCE to German forces in 1940. The Resistance attempted to weaken GERMANY's occupying force, especially by acts of sabotage.

Restoration The return of CONSTITUTIONAL MONARCHY in BRITAIN in the late seventeenth century. The STUARTS were placed back on the throne; the first of them after the Restoration was King Charles II.

&. The Restoration is known as a period of comparative gaiety in ENGLAND after the severe days of government by the PURITANS. Plays, in particular, had been banned by the Puritans; a large number, notably COMEDIES, were produced during the Restoration.

Revolutions of 1848 LIBERAL and nationalist (*see* NATIONALISM) rebellions that broke out in 1848 in several European nations, including GERMANY, AUSTRIA, FRANCE, ITALY, and BELGIUM. The rebellions secured temporary gains but, faced with the CONSERVATIVE hostility of the PEASANTS and growing fears of disorder among the BOURGEOISIE, they collapsed within a year.

Richelieu, Cardinal (RISH-uh-looh, ree-shuhl-YEU) A French clergyman and political leader of the seventeenth century. Cardinal Richelieu was the chief of government under King Louis XIII. He achieved two difficult goals in his career: establishing ABSOLUTE MONARCHY in FRANCE and breaking the political power of the HUGUENOTS, or French PROTESTANTS.

Robespierre (ROHBZ-pee-air, ROHBZ-peer, roh-bes-PYAIR) A French political leader of the eighteenth century. Robespierre, a JACOBIN, was one of the most

RADICAL leaders of the FRENCH REVOLUTION. He was in charge of the government during the REIGN OF TERROR, when thousands of persons were executed without trial. After a public reaction against his extreme policies, he was himself executed without trial.

Romanovs (ROH-muh-nawfs, roh-MAH-nuhfs)   The family that ruled RUSSIA from the seventeenth century until the RUSSIAN REVOLUTION. Empress CATHERINE THE GREAT and Czar PETER THE GREAT were Romanovs.

Rommel, Erwin (ROM-uhl)   A German military commander of the twentieth century. A master of the BLITZKRIEG, he saw much action in WORLD WAR II, leading campaigns in FRANCE, ITALY, and north AFRICA, where he became known as the "Desert Fox." He attained the rank of field marshal but was implicated in a plot to assassinate the German leader, Adolf HITLER. On Hitler's orders, he killed himself.

Rothschilds (RAWTHS-cheyeldz, RAWTH-cheyeldz, ROHT-shilts)   A family of European financiers and bankers active since the eighteenth century. The Rothschilds had spectacular success in governmental finance in the nineteenth century, supporting, for example, the British against the French emperor NAPOLEON BONAPARTE. The family is spread through several nations to this day.

Royal Air Force   The British air force, most famous for its performance in the Battle of BRITAIN and other campaigns of WORLD WAR II. Known as the RAF.

Royal Navy   The British navy.

Russian Revolution   A revolution in RUSSIA in 1917–1918, also called the OCTOBER REVOLUTION, that overthrew the CZAR and brought the BOLSHEVIKS, a COMMUNIST party led by LENIN, to power. The revolution was encouraged by Russian setbacks in WORLD WAR I.

Russo-Japanese War   A war fought in 1904–5 between RUSSIA and JAPAN over rival territorial claims. In winning the war, Japan emerged as a world power.

&. President Theodore ROOSEVELT of the United States was largely responsible for bringing the two sides together and working out a treaty. For his efforts, Roosevelt won the NOBEL PRIZE for peace.

Sadat, Anwar (AHN-wahr suh-DAHT, suh-DAT)   An Egyptian political leader of the twentieth century. He succeeded Gamal Abdel NASSER as president of EGYPT on Nasser's death in 1970. In a bold effort to bring peace to the MIDDLE EAST, he visited ISRAEL in 1977 and signed a peace agreement with that country in 1979. He was assassinated in Egypt in 1981. (*See* ARAB-ISRAELI CONFLICT.)

Sakharov, Andrei (SAH-kuh-rawf, SAK-uh-rawf)   A nuclear physicist in the SOVIET UNION, Sakharov helped develop their first H-BOMB. In the late 1960s, he became an outspoken critic of the arms race and of Soviet repression. He and his wife were exiled within the Soviet Union for protesting. In 1975, he was awarded the NOBEL PRIZE for peace.

Sarajevo (sar-uh-YAY-voh, sahr-uh-YAY-voh)   The city in BOSNIA AND HERZEGOVINA where the assassination that brought on WORLD WAR I took place. Archduke FRANCIS FERDINAND, the heir to the throne

SARAJEVO. *The parliament building, hit by artillery fire from Serb forces in 1991, as seen through the walls of a destroyed downtown hotel.*

of the Austrian Empire, had come to Sarajevo on a state visit; Sarajevo was then in one of the South Slavic provinces of the Austrian Empire. A young student who favored South Slavic independence shot and killed the archduke. Austria held the assassin's home country, Serbia, responsible for the incident and declared war; complex European alliances then brought other countries into the fight.

  In 1992 the city came under prolonged and bloody siege by Bosnian Serbs seeking to drive Bosnian MOSLEMS from their homes.

Schweitzer, Albert (SHWEYET-suhr, SHVEYET-suhr) A French theologian, student of music, and physician of the twentieth century. Schweitzer received many awards for his humanitarian missionary work in AFRICA, including the NOBEL PRIZE for peace.

Seven Years' War A war fought in the middle of the eighteenth century between the German kingdom of PRUSSIA, supported by BRITAIN, and an alliance that included AUSTRIA, FRANCE, and RUSSIA. Prussia and Britain won, and their victory greatly increased their power. Britain, in particular, won all of CANADA and consolidated its rule over much of INDIA. Several of the war's battles were fought in NORTH AMERICA, where it was called the FRENCH AND INDIAN WAR.

Shi'ite and Sunni Moslems *See under "World Literature, Philosophy, and Religion."*

shoguns (SHOH-guhnz) Japanese military leaders who ruled the country from the twelfth to the nineteenth centuries. There was still an emperor in JAPAN under the shoguns, but he was reduced to a mere figurehead.

Six-Day War A war fought in 1967 by ISRAEL on one side and EGYPT, SYRIA, and JORDAN on the other. Israel, victorious, took over the GOLAN HEIGHTS, the Jordanian portion of JERUSALEM, the Jordanian WEST BANK of the JORDAN RIVER, and a large piece of territory in northeastern Egypt, including the SINAI PENINSULA, which contains MOUNT SINAI. Israel still occupies all of these territories except the Sinai Peninsula, which it gave back to Egypt in 1982. Israel maintains that its security would be enormously endangered if it withdrew from the other places.

so much owed by so many to so few, Never in the field of human conflict was A declaration by the British PRIME MINISTER Winston CHURCHILL about the Battle of BRITAIN. The "few" were the fighter pilots of Britain's ROYAL AIR FORCE.

Soviet Union Officially the UNION OF SOVIET SOCIALIST REPUBLICS (USSR), a nation formerly located in eastern EUROPE and northwestern ASIA. Its capital and largest city was MOSCOW.

  In 1917 the BOLSHEVIKS, led by LENIN, seized the government of RUSSIA and in 1922 Russia merged with the Ukrainian, Belorussian, and Transcaucasian republics to form the USSR   Joseph STALIN emerged as the Soviet leader after Lenin's death in 1924. Under Stalin, the 1930s were marked by political repression and terror (*see* STALIN'S PURGE TRIALS). After the NAZI-SOVIET NON-AGGRESSION PACT of 1939, the Soviet Union added parts of FINLAND, POLAND, and RUMANIA to its territory and annexed the BALTIC republics of ESTONIA, LATVIA, and LITHUANIA. Invaded by GERMANY in 1941, the Soviet Union suffered vast losses but emerged from WORLD WAR II on the winning side and soon became a nuclear superpower.   Postwar American-Soviet relations saw the start of the COLD WAR, as the Soviet Union extended its control over the EASTERN BLOC.   The CUBAN MISSILE CRISIS was provoked by the buildup of Soviet missiles in CUBA.   In the 1970s the Soviet Union entered a period of DÉTENTE with the United States.   The reforms (GLASNOST and PERESTROIKA) introduced by Mikhail GORBACHEV weakened the COMMUNIST party's control, which suffered a mortal blow when hard-liners tried unsuccessfully in 1991 to overthrow Gorbachev.   As Communist dominance faded, NATIONALISM rose within the republics that made up the Soviet Union. The Baltic republics of Latvia, Estonia, and Lithuania, ARMENIA, BELARUS, GEORGIA, MOLDOVA, and various republics east of the CAUCASUS MOUNTAINS — AZERBAIJAN, KAZAKHSTAN, KYRGYZSTAN, TAJIKISTAN, TURKMENISTAN, and UZBEKISTAN — declared their independence.   The Soviet Union was formally dissolved in 1991. A loose federation, known as the Commonwealth of Independent States and made up of some former Soviet republics, succeeded it, but the Commonwealth is not recognized as a nation. RUSSIA took the former Soviet Union's seat on the SECURITY COUNCIL of the UNITED NATIONS.

Spanish Armada *See* ARMADA, SPANISH.

Spanish Civil War   A war fought in the late 1930s in SPAIN. On one side were the Loyalists, Spaniards loyal to a recently elected government in the form of a REPUBLIC; on the other side were fascists (*see* FASCISM), led by General Francisco FRANCO. The SOVIET UNION sent aid to the Loyalists, some of whom were COMMUNISTS; the German and Italian fascist dictators, Adolf HITLER and Benito MUSSOLINI, supported Franco. The Spanish fascists won the war and set up Franco's long rule of Spain as a dictator.

🙠 Many Americans favored one side or the other in the Spanish Civil War, particularly people of LEFT-WING sympathies, who supported the Loyalists. The Abraham Lincoln Brigade included Americans who traveled to Spain to fight in the Loyalist cause.

SS   An ELITE corps of combat troops (SS is short for *Schutzstaffel*, which is German for "elite guard") formed originally within the German NAZI party as a bodyguard for HITLER and other Nazi leaders and led by Heinrich HIMMLER. During the 1930s, Hitler steadily expanded the responsibilities of the SS to include the suppression of his political opponents within GERMANY and the persecution of the JEWS. The SS supervised the CONCENTRATION CAMPS. During WORLD WAR II, some SS units, known as *Waffen* ("armed") SS, were incorporated into the German army as elite shock troops. Initially, members of the SS were expected to be pure Aryans, preferably blond and blue-eyed, but, as German casualties mounted during the war, SS members were often recruited from the subjugated peoples of eastern EUROPE.

Stalin, Joseph (STAH-lin, STAL-in)   A Soviet political leader of the twentieth century. Stalin ruled the SOVIET UNION, often with extreme brutality, from the death of LENIN in the early 1920s until his own death in the early 1950s. His policies of collectivization, which abolished private ownership, were followed by political PURGES in which thousands of COMMUNIST party officials were killed, usually on trumped-up charges of treason. Stalin led the Soviet Union in its costly victory in WORLD WAR II; the country again lost huge numbers. President Franklin D. ROOSEVELT of the United States and PRIME MINISTER Winston CHURCHILL of BRITAIN met with Stalin in 1945 to produce the YALTA AGREEMENT. Stalin's expansion of Soviet influence after World War II contributed to the COLD WAR.

JOSEPH STALIN

Stalingrad, Battle of (STAH-lin-grad, STAH-lin-grahd)   A major battle between German and Soviet troops in WORLD WAR II. The battle was fought in the winter of 1942–1943 and ended with the surrender of an entire German army. Stalingrad is considered a major turning point of the war in favor of the ALLIES.

Stalinism (STAH-luh-niz-uhm)   The form of MARXISM associated with Soviet leader Joseph STALIN. Stalinism emphasizes the repression of all dissent, often by brutal means; a rigid adherence to government management of economic life; and the domination of all COMMUNIST movements worldwide by the SOVIET UNION. In holding to these beliefs, Stalin opposed Leon TROTSKY. (*See* TROTSKYISM.)

Stalin's purge trials   A group of trials of Soviet officials in the 1930s initiated by the PREMIER, Joseph STALIN. Large numbers of these officials were imprisoned or executed for alleged disloyalty to Stalin. (*See* STALINISM.)

Star Chamber   A royal court that began in ENGLAND in the MIDDLE AGES; cases were heard there without juries. Under the early STUART kings, it was known for its tyrannical judgments. The name came from the courtroom's ceiling, which was painted with stars.

Star Chamber is used as a general descriptive term for arbitrary tactics by a judge.

Stuarts   A Scottish family that ruled BRITAIN from the early seventeenth century to the early eighteenth century, except for the eleven years of the COMMONWEALTH. The last Stuart, Queen Anne, died without any surviving children. The crown then passed to the House of HANOVER.

Sun King   A nickname for LOUIS XIV that captures the magnificence of his court and of the Palace of VERSAILLES, which he built. Louis himself adopted the sun as his emblem.

Sunni and Shi'ite Moslems   *See under "World Literature, Philosophy, and Religion."*

Teresa, Mother   *See* MOTHER TERESA.

Thatcher, Margaret   An English political leader of the twentieth century, who became PRIME MINISTER of BRITAIN in 1979. A member of the Conservative party (TORIES), Thatcher stressed PRIVATE ENTERPRISE and attacked SOCIALISM and the WELFARE STATE. She resigned from office in 1990.

Third Reich (REYEKH, REYEK)   The name given by the NAZIS to their government in GERMANY; *Reich* is German for "empire." Adolf HITLER, their leader, believed that he was creating a third German empire, a successor to the HOLY ROMAN EMPIRE and the German empire formed by Chancellor BISMARCK in the nineteenth century.

Thirty Years' War   A war waged in the early seventeenth century that involved FRANCE, SPAIN, SWEDEN, DENMARK, AUSTRIA, and numerous states of GERMANY. The causes of the war were rooted in national rivalries and in conflict between ROMAN CATHOLICS and PROTESTANTS. For all the bloodshed, there was no decisive winner or loser. The Peace of Westphalia, which ended the war in 1648, did affirm, however, that the German states could be Catholic or Protestant at the choice of their rulers.

Tiananmen Square (TYAHN-ahn-men)   Location in BEIJING of prodemocracy demonstrations that were brutally suppressed in 1989 by troops loyal to the COMMUNIST regime of the PEOPLE'S REPUBLIC OF CHINA.

Titanic   A British luxury ocean liner, thought to be unsinkable, which sank on its first voyage in 1912

TIANANMEN SQUARE. *Student participant of a 1989 hunger strike at Tiananmen Square during prodemocracy demonstrations.*

after running into an ICEBERG in the north ATLANTIC OCEAN. Over 1500 people drowned.

Tito, Marshal (TEE-toh)   A Yugoslav military and political leader of the twentieth century. Tito, whose real name was Josip Broz, led the resistance in YUGOSLAVIA to the German invaders during WORLD WAR II and later established COMMUNIST rule in Yugoslavia. In 1948 Tito broke with the Soviet PREMIER, Joseph STALIN, and led Yugoslavia onto a course of foreign policy independent of the SOVIET UNION.

Trafalgar, Battle of (truh-FAL-guhr)   A naval battle between British and French forces in the early nineteenth century, when NAPOLEON BONAPARTE was the French emperor; the battle was fought off the southwestern coast of SPAIN. The British fleet, under Admiral Horatio NELSON, captured over a dozen French and Spanish ships and lost none of its own. During the battle, Nelson was killed aboard his flagship, HMS *Victory*.

trench warfare   Warfare marked by slow wearing down of the opposing forces and piecemeal gains at heavy cost. The term applies especially to WORLD WAR I.

BATTLE OF TRAFALGAR. *Admiral Nelson wounded and dying aboard his ship, the HMS* Victory.

Trotsky, Leon   A Russian revolutionary leader of the late nineteenth and early twentieth centuries. Trotsky rose to power alongside LENIN after the RUSSIAN REVOLUTION, taking charge of foreign affairs. In favoring world COMMUNIST revolution (*see* TROTSKYISM), Trotsky found himself in opposition to Lenin and to Lenin's successor, Joseph STALIN, both of whom insisted that the development of communism within the SOVIET UNION came first. Stalin exiled Trotsky in the late 1920s and had him assassinated in MEXICO CITY in 1940.

tsar (ZAHR, TSAHR)   Another spelling of CZAR.

Tudors   A family that ruled ENGLAND from the late fifteenth century until the beginning of the seventeenth century. Queen ELIZABETH I was a Tudor. After the death of Elizabeth, who had no heirs, the crown passed to the STUARTS of SCOTLAND.

U-boats   German submarines during WORLD WAR I and WORLD WAR II. *U-boat* is a translation of the German *U-boot*, which is short for *Unterseeboot*, or "undersea boat."

❖ The *LUSITANIA* was sunk by a U-boat, one of many attacks by U-boats on neutral ships during World War I. Such attacks drew the United States into the war.

USSR   *See* SOVIET UNION.

Vatican II   The popular name for the Second Vatican Council, an assembly of all the BISHOPS of the RO-
MAN CATHOLIC CHURCH held from 1962 to 1965. The bishops ordered a large-scale liberalization and modernization of practices in their church.

V-E Day   The day of victory in EUROPE for the ALLIES in WORLD WAR II; May 8, 1945, the day of the formal surrender of the German armies. (*Compare* V-J DAY.)

Versailles, Treaty of (ver-SEYE, vuhr-SEYE)   The treaty that officially ended WORLD WAR I, signed at the Palace of VERSAILLES in FRANCE. The leading figures at the treaty negotiations were PREMIER Georges CLEMENCEAU of France, PRIME MINISTER David LLOYD GEORGE of Britain, and President Woodrow WILSON of the United States. The treaty was far more punitive toward GERMANY than Wilson's FOURTEEN POINTS; it required Germany to give up land and much of its army and navy and to pay extensive reparations for damages to civilians in the war. The treaty also created the LEAGUE OF NATIONS.

Vichy government (VISH-ee, VEE-shee)   The government of FRANCE after GERMANY defeated and occupied it at the beginning of WORLD WAR II (*see* FRANCE, FALL OF); Vichy, the capital, is a small city in central France. The Vichy government was essentially a puppet of the Germans.

Victoria, Queen   A British queen of the nineteenth and early twentieth centuries. During her reign, BRITAIN reached new heights in industrial and colonial power and diplomatic influence. Victoria became queen at the age of eighteen, and soon married Prince ALBERT, who proved an enormous support to her; after his early death, she remained in official mourning until her own death forty years later. Victoria was known for her impartiality toward the two leading political parties of Britain, the Liberals and the Conservatives, which both produced extraordinary leaders during her reign (*see* DISRAELI, BENJAMIN *and* GLADSTONE, WILLIAM EWART). She was also known for establishing strict standards of personal morality. (*See* VICTORIAN PERIOD.)

❖ Queen Victoria's children and grandchildren married into many of the other royal families of EUROPE. Tragically, many of them passed on the disease HEMOPHILIA. Victoria carried the disease in her GENES, and one of her sons died from it. The hemophiliac son of Nicholas II, the CZAR of RUSSIA, was descended from Victoria. (*See* RASPUTIN.) ❖ The

QUEEN VICTORIA

term *Victorian* today sometimes recalls Queen Victoria's stands on personal moral issues, and may suggest prudery or a moral self-satisfaction.

Victorian period The period of British history when Queen VICTORIA ruled; it includes the entire second half of the nineteenth century, a time when BRITAIN was the most powerful nation in the world. The Victorian period was known for a rather stern morality. It was also marked by a general earnestness about life, and by a confidence that Britain's domestic prosperity (*see* INDUSTRIAL REVOLUTION) and vast holdings overseas (*see* BRITISH EMPIRE) were signs of the country's overall righteousness (*see* WHITE MAN'S BURDEN). As the Victorian period continued, however, such easy beliefs were increasingly challenged.

📌 The Victorian period produced a great number of diverse writers and thinkers. (*See* BROWNING, ROBERT; DARWIN, CHARLES; DICKENS, CHARLES; KIPLING, RUDYARD; MILL, JOHN STUART; STEVENSON, ROBERT LOUIS; *and* TENNYSON, ALFRED, LORD.)

Vienna, Congress of A conference of European nations held in 1815, after the defeat of NAPOLEON BONAPARTE. It redrew the boundaries of EUROPE and sought to lay the groundwork for peace. Under the CONSERVATIVE influence of Prince METTERNICH of

AUSTRIA, many European territories were given to the kings and princes who had held them before the FRENCH REVOLUTION. Although movements toward DEMOCRACY in Europe were set back by these events, there was no major fighting in Europe until the CRIMEAN WAR nearly forty years later.

Viet Cong (vee-et KONG, KAWNG) South Vietnamese COMMUNIST revolutionaries during the VIETNAM WAR.

Villa, Pancho (PAHN-choh VEE-uh) A Mexican revolutionary leader of the twentieth century. He was defeated in the struggle for the presidency of MEXICO after the Mexican Revolution of 1910, and was eventually assassinated. At one point, Villa raided a town in NEW MEXICO, hoping to embarrass his opposition back home. The United States sent troops under General John PERSHING in pursuit of Villa, and the United States and Mexico nearly went to war.

V-J Day The day of victory over JAPAN for the ALLIES in WORLD WAR II; September 2, 1945, the day of Japan's formal surrender. (*Compare* V-E DAY.)

Walesa, Lech (LEK vah-WEN-suh) A Polish labor leader and politician of the twentieth century, known for the success of SOLIDARITY, an independent LABOR UNION that he headed. He was periodically put under arrest by the COMMUNIST government. Walesa won the NOBEL PRIZE for peace in 1983. In 1990, he became president of POLAND.

war crimes Acts committed by soldiers or government officials, either in the course of a war or in bringing on a war, that violate the customs of warfare. Examples of war crimes include atrocities committed against civilians (*see* MY LAI MASSACRE) and the mistreatment of prisoners of war. After WORLD WAR II, twenty-two NAZI leaders were tried at Nuremberg by the victorious ALLIES, and twelve were sentenced to death for war crimes. (*See* NUREMBERG TRIALS.)

Warsaw Pact A military alliance of COMMUNIST nations in eastern EUROPE. Organized in 1955 in answer to NATO, the Warsaw Pact included BULGARIA, CZECHOSLOVAKIA, EAST GERMANY, HUNGARY, POLAND, RUMANIA, and the SOVIET UNION. It disintegrated in 1991, in the wake of the COLLAPSE OF COMMUNISM in eastern Europe and the Soviet Union.

Waterloo, Battle of A battle in BELGIUM in 1815 in which the British defeated the French under NA-

BATTLE OF WATERLOO. *The defeat of Napoleon.*

POLEON BONAPARTE. Napoleon abdicated as emperor a few days after this final defeat, and a few weeks later he was captured and sent into exile. The British were led by Arthur Wellesley, later to be named duke of WELLINGTON; they were joined by Dutch and German soldiers, and were greatly aided by the last-minute arrival of 50,000 troops from the German kingdom of PRUSSIA.

🐝 *Waterloo* has become a general term for a decisive, final defeat.

Weimar Republic (VEYE-mahr, WEYE-mahr) A common name for the democratic government of GERMANY between the abdication of KAISER WILHELM II and the assumption of power by Adolf HITLER in 1933; Weimar, Germany, was where its CONSTITUTION was drawn up. The constitution abolished the several CONSTITUTIONAL MONARCHIES that had previously formed the German Empire. The Weimar government was unpopular because of its acceptance of the harsh provisions of the Treaty of VERSAILLES; the large penalties Germany had to pay caused economic chaos in the country, with German money declining daily in value. Germany's Weimar years, however, were a period of political freedom and cultural creativity, both of which were snuffed out by Hitler.

Wellington, duke of Arthur Wellesley, a British general of the nineteenth century, revered in his country as the victor over the emperor NAPOLEON BONAPARTE at the Battle of WATERLOO.

🐝 Wellington is known for allegedly saying "the Battle of Waterloo was won on the playing fields of Eton." Eton is a famous English boarding school for boys. Wellington's statement emphasizes the effect of people's moral training and breeding on their later life.

West Germany Popular name for the FEDERAL REPUBLIC OF GERMANY before the reunification of Germany in 1990. BONN was the seat of its government.

🐝 Was a member of NATO. 🐝 Established in 1949, after dissension between the United States and the SOVIET UNION led to the division of Germany into EAST GERMANY and West Germany; formed out of the states included in the American, French, and British occupation zones. 🐝 The Bonn Convention of 1952 essentially granted West Germany national SOVEREIGNTY. In 1955 West Germany was recognized as an independent country. 🐝 Made a swift recovery, called the "economic miracle," from the devastation of WORLD WAR II. 🐝 With the COLLAPSE OF COMMUNISM, West Germany absorbed East Germany.

white man's burden A PHRASE used to justify European IMPERIALISM in the nineteenth and early twentieth centuries; it is the title of a poem by Rudyard KIPLING. The phrase implies that imperialism was motivated by a high-minded desire of whites to uplift the less advanced black and brown peoples.

Wilhelm II (VIL-helm, WIL-helm) A German emperor, or KAISER, of the late nineteenth and early twentieth centuries. After disagreements with Kaiser Wilhelm in the late nineteenth century, Otto von BISMARCK resigned as head of the German government. Wilhelm then made aggressive moves abroad that increased instability throughout EUROPE. He ruled GERMANY in WORLD WAR I, and abdicated after his country's defeat. He lived the rest of his life in obscurity in THE NETHERLANDS.

William and Mary King William III and Queen Mary II of ENGLAND, who ruled jointly after the GLORIOUS REVOLUTION of 1688 had expelled Mary's father, King James II. William and Mary were PROTESTANTS, and James was a ROMAN CATHOLIC; since the time of William and Mary, the ruler of England has always upheld Protestantism in England.

Windsor, duke of An English nobleman of the twentieth century who ruled BRITAIN as King Edward VIII in 1936. He gave up the throne after less than a year to marry an American divorcée, Mrs.

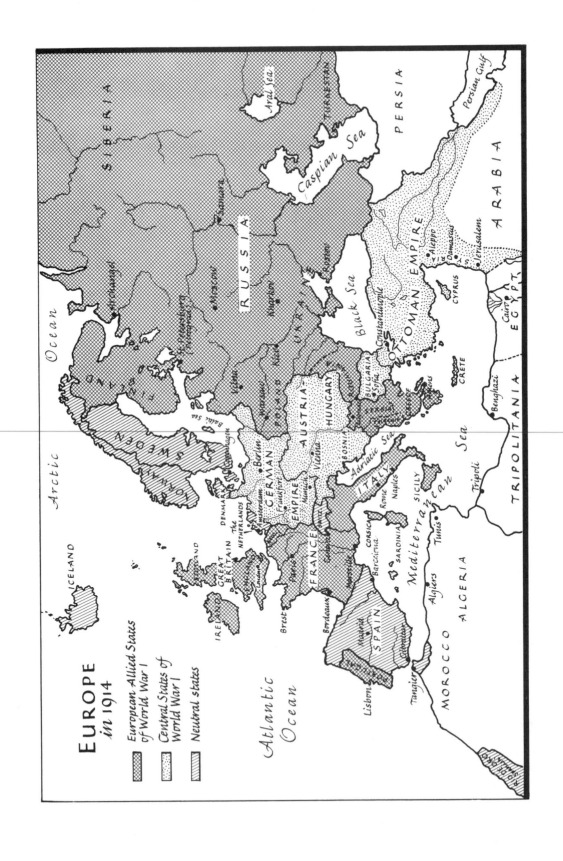

EUROPE
in 1914

European Allied States
of World War I

Central States of
World War I

Neutral states

Atlantic
Ocean

ICELAND

GREAT
BRITAIN

IRELAND

London

Brest

Bordeaux

SPAIN

Lisbon

Madrid

Tangier

MOROCCO

ALGERIA

Algiers

Tunis

Tripoli

TRIPOLITANIA

Benghazi

Mediterranean Sea

SARDINIA

CORSICA

Barcelona

Rome

Naples

SICILY

ITALY

Arctic Ocean

NORWAY

SWEDEN

Baltic Sea

DENMARK

The
NETHERLANDS

Copenhagen

Amsterdam

Berlin

GERMAN
EMPIRE

Frankfort

Munich

Vienna

AUSTRIA

HUNGARY

BOSNIA

Adriatic Sea

BULGARIA

Constantinople

Black Sea

RUSSIA

SIBERIA

Aral Sea

Caspian Sea

PERSIA

OTTOMAN EMPIRE

ARABIA

Aleppo

Damascus

Jerusalem

Syria

CYPRUS

CRETE

EGYPT

Cairo

Persian Gulf

UKRAINE

FRANCE

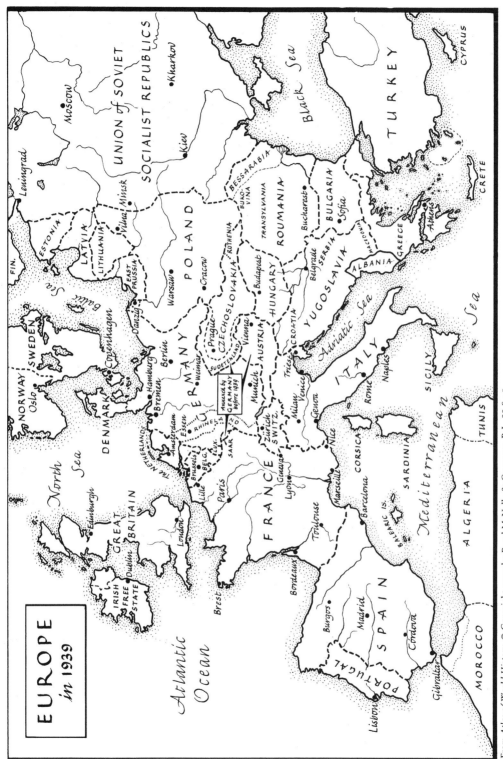

EUROPE
in 1939

ATLANTIC
Ocean

North
Sea

Baltic
Sea

Black
Sea

Mediterranean
Sea

Adriatic
Sea

NORWAY
SWEDEN
FIN.
UNION OF SOVIET
SOCIALIST REPUBLICS
Leningrad
Moscow
Kharkov
Kiev
Oslo
DENMARK
Copenhagen
ESTONIA
LATVIA
LITHUANIA
Vilna Minsk
EAST PRUSSIA
Danzig
POLAND
Warsaw
Cracow
Hamburg
Berlin
Bremen
Weimar
G E R M A N Y
Essen
RHINELAND
Amsterdam
THE NETHERLANDS
Brussels
BELG.
LUX.
SAAR
Lille
Paris
F R A N C E
Brest
Bordeaux
Toulouse
Lyon
Geneva
Marseille
Nice
SWITZ.
Zürich
Munich
AUSTRIA
Vienna
Prague
CZECHOSLOVAKIA
SUDETENLAND
RUTHENIA
Annexed by
GERMANY
before 1939
Budapest
HUNGARY
Milan
Venice
Trieste
Genoa
I T A L Y
Rome
Naples
CORSICA
SARDINIA
SICILY
BALEARIC IS.
Barcelona
S P A I N
PORTUGAL
Lisbon
Madrid
Burgos
Cordova
Gibraltar
MOROCCO
ALGERIA
TUNIS
GREAT BRITAIN
Edinburgh
London
IRISH FREE STATE
Dublin
BESSARABIA
BUKO-VINA
TRANSYLVANIA
ROUMANIA
Bucharest
BULGARIA
Sofia
SERBIA
Belgrade
YUGOSLAVIA
CROATIA
MACEDONIA
ALBANIA
GREECE
Athens
TURKEY
CYPRUS
CRETE

From Atlas of World History. © Copyright 1975 by Rand McNally & Company, R.L. 88-S-58.

Wallis Warfield Simpson, because British law did not permit a divorced woman to become queen.

 ❦ In a famous speech to the British people announcing his abdication, the duke said that he could not carry on as king "without the help and support of the woman I love."

World War I A war fought from 1914 TO 1918 between the ALLIES, notably BRITAIN, FRANCE, RUSSIA, and ITALY (which entered in 1915), and the CENTRAL POWERS: GERMANY, Austria-Hungary, BULGARIA, and the OTTOMAN EMPIRE. The war was sparked by the assassination in 1914 of the heir to the throne of AUSTRIA (see SARAJEVO). Prolonged stalemates, TRENCH WARFARE, and immense casualties on both sides marked the fighting. The United States sought to remain neutral but was outraged by the sinking of

the *LUSITANIA* by a German submarine in 1915 and by Germany's decision in 1916 to start unrestricted submarine warfare. In 1917, the United States entered the war on the side of the Allies and helped to tip the balance in their favor. In full retreat on its western front, Germany asked for an armistice, or truce, which was granted on November 11, 1918. By the terms of the Treaty of VERSAILLES, signed in 1919, Germany had to make extensive concessions to the Allies and pay large penalties.

The government leaders of World War I included Georges CLEMENCEAU of France, David LLOYD GEORGE of Britain, KAISER WILHELM II of Germany, and Woodrow WILSON of the United States.

World War I was known as the GREAT WAR, or the World War, until WORLD WAR II broke out.

 ❦ German discontent over the terms of the Treaty

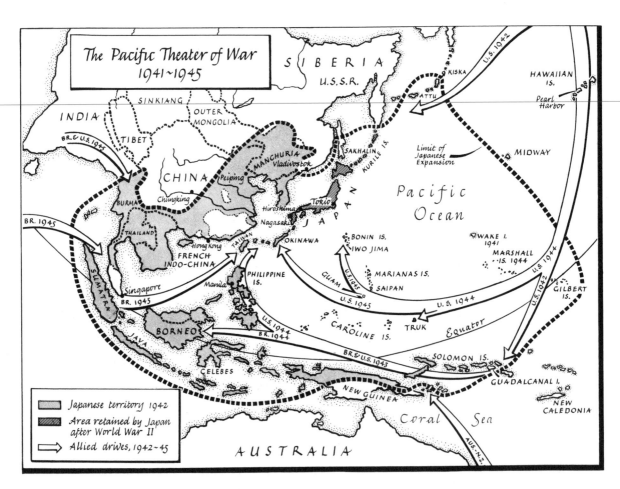

of Versailles, and over the WEIMAR REPUBLIC that had accepted its provisions, led to the rise of the NAZIS and Adolf HITLER, who pursued warlike policies not adequately opposed by the rest of EUROPE. Thus, barely twenty years after World War I was over, World War II began. ❧ A huge number of books, songs, and poems have been written about World War I. (*See ALL QUIET ON THE WESTERN FRONT; FAREWELL TO ARMS, A; and* "IN FLANDERS FIELDS.") ❧ American foot soldiers in World War I were popularly called DOUGHBOYS. ❧ "OVER THERE" was among the popular songs produced in the United States during the war. ❧ November 11, the day the fighting ended, is observed in the United States as Veterans' Day.

World War II   A war fought from 1939 TO 1945 between the AXIS POWERS — GERMANY, ITALY, and JAPAN — and the ALLIES, including FRANCE and BRITAIN, and later the SOVIET UNION and the United States. The war began when the Germans, governed by the NAZI party, invaded POLAND in September 1939 (*see* POLAND, INVASION OF). Germany then conquered France, using BLITZKRIEG tactics, and forced a desperate British withdrawal at DUNKIRK. The Germans tried to wear down the British by heavy bombing, but the British withstood the attacks (*see* BRITAIN, BATTLE OF). The Soviet Union signed a treaty with HITLER but entered the war on the side of the Allies after Germany invaded RUSSIA in 1941. The United States was drawn into the war in 1941, when the Japanese suddenly attacked the American naval base at PEARL HARBOR. Japan made extensive conquests in east ASIA but was checked by American victories at the Battle of MIDWAY ISLAND and elsewhere. The German invasion of Russia was halted at the Battle of STALINGRAD. Allied forces took Italy in 1943, forcing its surrender. Beginning with the invasion of NORMANDY in 1944 (*see* D-DAY), the Allies liberated France from German occupation and pressed on in EUROPE, defeating the Germans in the Battle of the BULGE and elsewhere. Germany surrendered in May 1945 (*see* V-E DAY). The war in the PACIFIC ended in September 1945 (*see* V-J DAY), after the United States dropped ATOMIC BOMBS on the Japanese cities of HIROSHIMA and NAGASAKI. In the aftermath of World War II, more constructive and less punitive measures were applied to the defeated countries than after World War I (*see* MARSHALL PLAN, NUREMBERG TRIALS, *and* UNITED NATIONS).

The political leaders of the war included Winston CHURCHILL of Britain, Adolf Hitler of Germany, Benito MUSSOLINI of Italy, Franklin D. ROOSEVELT of the United States, and Joseph STALIN of the Soviet Union. The military leaders included Charles DE GAULLE of France; Bernard MONTGOMERY of Britain; Hermann GOERING and Erwin ROMMEL of Germany; TITO of Yugoslavia; and Omar BRADLEY, Dwight EISENHOWER, William HALSEY, Douglas MACARTHUR, Chester NIMITZ, and George PATTON of the United States.

Yalta agreement (YAWL-tuh)   An agreement reached near the end of WORLD WAR II between President Franklin D. ROOSEVELT of the United States, PRIME MINISTER Winston CHURCHILL of BRITAIN, and PREMIER Joseph STALIN of the SOVIET UNION. The three met in Yalta, in the southern Soviet Union, in February 1945, and discussed such issues as the occupation of Germany, free elections in the liberated countries of eastern EUROPE, the postwar boundaries of POLAND and RUSSIA, and a common strategy against JAPAN. Stalin aided the United States against Japan, as he had promised; but he expanded Soviet influence rapidly into eastern Europe after the war, and the elections he agreed to were never held.

BORIS YELTSIN. *Photographed in 1990.*

Yeltsin, Boris   President of the Russian republic who criticized the slow pace of Mikhail GORBA-

CHEV's reforms. Yeltsin has led the Russian republic in its difficult and often chaotic struggle to transform its economy from one controlled by a central government to one based on free enterprise.

Zapata, Emiliano (ay-meel-YAH-noh sah-PAH-tuh) A Mexican revolutionary leader of the twentieth century. He overran plantations in the Mexican Revolution of 1910, dividing the land among peasants. He did not accept the new government's promises of re- form in 1915, and lived as an outlaw for some years until he was killed in 1919.

Zhou En-lai (Chou En-lai) (JOH EN-LEYE) A Chinese political leader of the twentieth century. Zhou was a founder of the Chinese COMMUNIST party and an ally of MAO ZEDONG. As CHINA'S PRE- MIER, he helped establish closer relations between his country and Western nations in the 1970s.

American History to 1865

The era between the first permanent English settlements in NORTH AMERICA in the early 1600s and the signing of the DECLARATION OF INDEPENDENCE in 1776 is called the Colonial period. America's desire for independence from GREAT BRITAIN led to the REVOLUTIONARY WAR (or American Revolution). The fighting phase of the war lasted from 1775 to the Battle of YORKTOWN in 1781. The Treaty of PARIS (1783) concluded the war, with British recognition of American independence. During the 1780s, the new nation struggled to develop suitable political institutions. In 1787, a convention met in PHILADELPHIA and framed the CONSTITUTION, a document designed to provide a stronger central government than that provided by the ARTICLES OF CONFEDERATION. The Constitution was ratified in 1788.

Political divisions arose during the presidency of George WASHINGTON (1789–1797) between the followers of Alexander HAMILTON, called the FEDERALIST PARTY, and those of Thomas JEFFERSON, known as the DEMOCRATIC-REPUBLICAN PARTY. These divisions continued during the presidency of Thomas Jefferson (1801–1809), whose achievements included the LOUISIANA PURCHASE (1803), and that of James MADISON (1809–1817). The WAR OF 1812 between Britain and the United States severely damaged the Federalist party, which collapsed as a force in national politics. The years 1816 to 1824, called the Era of Good Feeling, were marked by diminishing political divisions.

During the late 1820s and 1830s, political conflict resurfaced as new parties, the WHIGS and the DEMOCRATIC PARTY, clashed over a variety of issues. Although both parties developed national followings during the presidency of Andrew JACKSON (1829–1837), each was vulnerable to disruption between its northern and southern wings over the issue of slavery in the South. Already evident in the struggle over the MISSOURI COMPROMISE (1820), sectional conflict between the North and the South was sparked anew by the MEXICAN WAR (1846–1848), and exploded in the 1850s. During the 1850s, the Whig party collapsed in the North and was replaced by the REPUBLICAN PARTY, a purely sectional party. The Democratic party split into northern and southern wings in 1860. The election of the first Republican president, Abraham LINCOLN, in 1860 provoked the SECESSION of the southern states, and led to the outbreak of the CIVIL WAR (1861–1865). The war resulted in a victory for the North, and in the destruction of slavery as an institution.

— J. F. K.

abolitionism The belief that slavery should be abolished. In the early nineteenth century, increasing numbers of people in the northern United States held that the nation's slaves should be freed immediately, without compensation to slave owners. John BROWN, Frederick W. DOUGLASS, William Lloyd GARRISON, Sojourner TRUTH, and Harriet TUBMAN were well-known abolitionists.

❖ Abolitionism in the United States was an important factor leading to the CIVIL WAR.

Adams, John   A political leader of the late eighteenth and early nineteenth centuries; one of the FOUNDING FATHERS. Adams was a signer of the DECLARATION OF INDEPENDENCE. He was the second president, from 1797 to 1801, after George WASHINGTON. Washington and Adams were the only presidents from the FEDERALIST PARTY. Adams's presidency was marked by diplomatic challenges, in which he avoided war with FRANCE. The ALIEN AND SEDITION ACTS were passed while he was president.

Adams, John Quincy   A political leader of the early nineteenth century. John Quincy Adams was the son of John ADAMS, and was president of the United States from 1825 to 1829, between James MONROE and Andrew JACKSON.

ALAMO. *A wash drawing,* The Fight for the Alamo.

Alamo (AL-uh-moh)   A fort, once a chapel, in San Antonio, TEXAS, where a group of Americans made a heroic stand against a much larger Mexican force in 1836, during the war for Texan independence from MEXICO. The Mexicans, under General Santa Anna, besieged the Alamo, and eventually killed all of the defenders, including Davy CROCKETT.

   ❧ Rallying under the cry "REMEMBER THE ALAMO!" Texans later forced the Mexicans to recognize the independent REPUBLIC of Texas.

Alien and Sedition Acts   A series of laws, passed during the presidency of John ADAMS at the end of the eighteenth century, that sought to restrict the public activities of political RADICALS who sympathized with the FRENCH REVOLUTION and criticized

Adams's FEDERALIST policies. In response to the Alien and Sedition Acts, Thomas JEFFERSON and James MADISON wrote the VIRGINIA AND KENTUCKY RESOLUTIONS, which asserted STATES' RIGHTS.

American Crisis, The   A series of pamphlets written by Thomas PAINE during the REVOLUTIONARY WAR, in which Paine discussed issues of the revolution. The first pamphlet begins with a memorable statement, "THESE ARE THE TIMES THAT TRY MEN'S SOULS."

American Revolution   *See* REVOLUTIONARY WAR.

antebellum (an-tee-BEL-uhm)   A descriptive term for objects and institutions, especially houses, that originated three or four decades before the CIVIL WAR. *Ante bellum* is LATIN for "before the war."

Appleseed, Johnny   An American folk hero who established an apple tree nursery in PENNSYLVANIA in the early nineteenth century. For decades, he traveled through Pennsylvania, OHIO, INDIANA, and ILLINOIS, planting apple seeds and encouraging the settlers to start orchards. His real name was John Chapman.

Appomattox Court House (ap-uh-MAT-uhks)   A courthouse in VIRGINIA where General Robert E. LEE surrendered to General Ulysses S. GRANT in April 1865, effectively ending the American CIVIL WAR.

APPOMATTOX COURT HOUSE. *A detail from a painting by Mathieu Didier Guillaume, depicting the surrender of General Lee to General Grant.*

Arnold, Benedict   An American general of the REVOLUTIONARY WAR. He performed notably in the early days of the war, but became bitter over several setbacks to his career. After receiving command of the American fort at WEST POINT, NEW YORK, Arnold plotted to betray it to the British. The plan was revealed when the American forces captured Major John André of the British army, who was carrying messages between Arnold and the British. Arnold escaped to ENGLAND and continued a military career, but was widely scorned by the English.

🖢 Calling someone a "Benedict Arnold" is a way of calling the person a traitor.

Articles of Confederation   An agreement among the thirteen original states, approved in 1781, that provided a loose federal government before the present CONSTITUTION went into effect in 1789. There was no chief executive or judiciary, and the legislature of the Confederation had no authority to collect taxes.

Attucks, Crispus (AT-uhks)   Black sailor killed in the BOSTON MASSACRE.

🖢 It is said that he was among the first Americans to die in the struggle for liberty.

Banneker, Benjamin (BAN-i-kuhr)   African-American scientist of the late eighteenth and early nineteenth centuries. Banneker taught himself CALCULUS and trigonometry in order to make astronomical calculations for almanacs. He was hailed by ABOLITIONISTS for proving that "the powers of the mind are disconnected with the colour of the skin."

Bill of Rights   The first ten amendments to the CONSTITUTION of the United States. Among other provisions, they protect the freedoms of speech, religion, assembly, and the press (see FIRST AMENDMENT); restrict governmental rights of search and seizure; and list several rights of persons accused of crimes (see FIFTH AMENDMENT).

🖢 After the new Constitution was submitted to the states in 1787, several approved it only after being assured that it would have a bill of rights attached to it. Accordingly, these amendments were passed by the first CONGRESS under the Constitution, and were ratified by the states in 1791.

Blue and the Gray   The UNION and CONFEDERATE armies in the CIVIL WAR. The Union army wore blue uniforms; the Confederate army wore gray.

Boone, Daniel   An American frontier settler of the late eighteenth and early nineteenth centuries, best known for his exploration and settlement of KENTUCKY.

Booth, John Wilkes   The assassin of Abraham LINCOLN. Booth, an actor, was fanatically devoted to the CONFEDERATE cause in the CIVIL WAR. While Lincoln was attending a play, Booth stole into his theater box and shot him in the head at pointblank range. He then leaped down to the stage, breaking his leg, and escaped. Cornered later in a barn, he died of gunshot wounds, possibly inflicted by himself.

BOSTON MASSACRE. *A lithograph by W. Champney. Crispus Attucks (center) was one of five killed at the scene of the massacre.*

Boston Massacre   A clash between British troops and townspeople in BOSTON in 1770, before the REVOLUTIONARY WAR. The British fired into a crowd that was threatening them, killing five, including Crispus ATTUCKS. The soldiers had been sent to help the government maintain order, and were resented even before this incident. The killings increased the colonists' inclination toward revolution.

Boston Tea Party   An act of defiance toward the British government by American colonists; it took place in 1773, before the REVOLUTIONARY WAR. The government in LONDON had given a British company the right to sell tea directly to the colonies, thereby undercutting American merchants. A group of colonists found a ship in the harbor of BOSTON that was loaded with the company's tea. They dressed as NATIVE AMERICANS, boarded the ship, and threw hundreds of chests of tea overboard. The British government then tried to punish the colonists by closing the port of Boston, but this move only intensified American resistance to the rule of the king.

Brown, John   An ABOLITIONIST of the nineteenth century who sought to free the slaves by military force. After leading several attacks in KANSAS, he planned to start an uprising among the slaves. In 1859, he and a small band of followers took over a federal arsenal at HARPERS FERRY, in VIRGINIA. A detachment of marines reclaimed the arsenal and captured Brown, who was tried for treason, convicted, and hanged.

 ≉ Robert E. LEE, soon to be commanding general of the main CONFEDERATE army, led the marines who captured Brown. ≉ In death, Brown became a martyr for abolitionists. "JOHN BROWN'S BODY," a popular song in the North during the CIVIL WAR, had this refrain: "John Brown's body lies a-mold'ring in the grave; His soul goes marching on."

Bull Run, Battle of   The first battle of the American CIVIL WAR, fought in VIRGINIA near WASHINGTON, D.C. The surprising victory of the CONFEDERATE army humiliated the North and forced it to prepare for a long war. A year later the CONFEDERACY won another victory near the same place. This battle is called the Second Battle of Bull Run. The South referred to these two encounters as the First and Second Battles of Manassas.

Bunker Hill, Battle of   The first great battle of the REVOLUTIONARY WAR; it was fought near BOSTON in June 1775. The British drove the Americans from their fort at Breed's Hill to Bunker Hill, but only after the Americans had run out of gunpowder. Before retreating, the Americans killed many British troops.

 ≉ The Battle of Bunker Hill was an encouragement to the colonies; it proved that American forces, with sufficient supplies, could inflict heavy losses on the British. ≉ An American officer, William Prescott, is said to have ordered during the battle, "DON'T FIRE UNTIL YOU SEE THE WHITES OF THEIR EYES."

Burr, Aaron   A political leader who served as vice president of the United States in the first term of Thomas JEFFERSON (1801–1805). After Burr killed Alexander HAMILTON in the BURR-HAMILTON DUEL, his career declined. He was later involved in a bizarre conspiracy to sever the western states and territories from the UNION. Burr was tried for treason, but was acquitted.

Burr-Hamilton duel   A duel fought in 1804 between Aaron BURR, vice president of the United States, and Alexander HAMILTON, former secretary of the treasury. The two had been bitter political opponents for years. Burr shot and killed Hamilton.

Calhoun, John C. (kal-HOOHN)   The leading southern politician of the early nineteenth century; he served as vice president under both John Quincy ADAMS and Andrew JACKSON, and then was elected SENATOR from SOUTH CAROLINA. Calhoun championed slavery and STATES' RIGHTS. During the early 1830s, he led the NULLIFICATION movement, which maintained that when a state found a federal law unacceptable, the state had the right to declare the law null, or inoperative, within its borders. Nullification was aimed particularly at the high PROTECTIVE TARIFF of 1828; Calhoun opposed protective tariffs. A man of powerful intellect, Calhoun increasingly became obsessed with the South's minority status and with finding ways to protect slavery. Although he died in 1850, his influence helped put the South on the way that led ultimately to SECESSION and the CIVIL WAR.

Carson, Kit   A skilled frontier trapper and guide of the nineteenth century, who helped open the territory of CALIFORNIA to settlement from the United States. A general on the UNION side in the CIVIL WAR, he moved a great number of NAVAJOS by force in the 1860s; many died on the journey.

Chancellorsville, Battle of   An important battle of the CIVIL WAR, fought in VIRGINIA in 1863. The South, led by Robert E. LEE and Stonewall JACKSON, defeated a larger northern army, but Jackson was accidentally shot and killed by his own men after the battle.

Chapman, John   *See* APPLESEED, JOHNNY.

Cherokees (CHER-uh-keez)   A NATIVE AMERICAN tribe who lived in the Southeast in the early nineteenth century; the Cherokees were known as one of the "civilized tribes" because they built schools and published a newspaper. In the 1830s, the United States government forcibly removed most of the tribe to reservations west of the MISSISSIPPI RIVER. (*See* TRAIL OF TEARS.)

Civil War   The war fought in the United States between northern (UNION) and southern (CONFEDER-

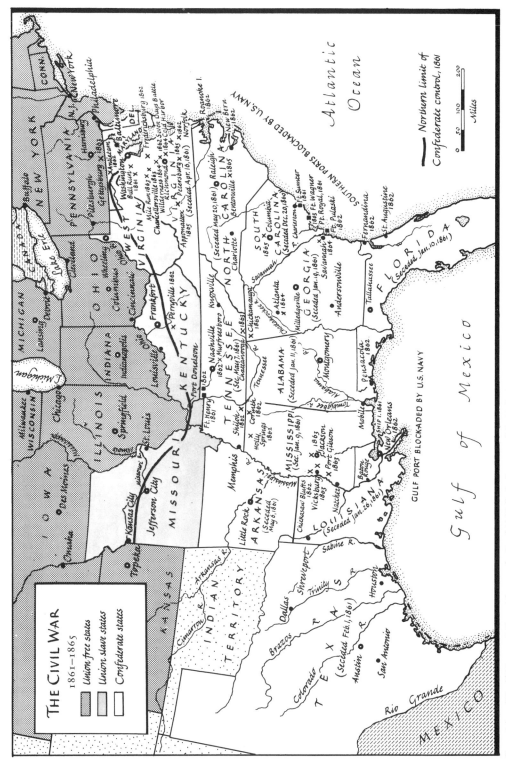

THE CIVIL WAR
1861–1865

- Union free states
- Union slave states
- Confederate states

Atlantic Ocean

Gulf of Mexico

MEXICO

——— Northern limit of Confederate control, 1861

SOUTHERN PORTS BLOCKADED BY U.S. NAVY

GULF PORT BLOCKADED BY U.S. NAVY

Miles
0   50   100   200

Canada

MICHIGAN
WISCONSIN
Milwaukee
Madison
Lansing
Detroit
Lake Michigan
Lake Erie
Lake Huron

NEW YORK
Buffalo
New York
CONN.
PENNSYLVANIA
N.J.
Philadelphia
Pittsburgh
Gettysburg
Harrisburg

OHIO
Cleveland
Columbus
Cincinnati
Wheeling

IOWA
Des Moines
ILLINOIS
Chicago
Springfield
St. Louis
MISSOURI
Jefferson City
Kansas City

INDIANA
Indianapolis

KENTUCKY
Louisville
Frankfort
×Perryville 1862

MD.
DEL.
Baltimore
Washington ×Bull Run 1861
× Bull Run 1862
Antietam 1862

WEST VIRGINIA
VIRGINIA
Manassas
× Chancellorsville 1863
× Wilderness 1864
× Richmond ×1862
× Petersburg 1865 ×1864 Cold Harbor
Appomattox 1865 (Seceded Apr. 16, 1861)
Fredericksburg 1862
Seven Days Battle
1862
Norfolk
Roanoke I. 1862

NORTH CAROLINA (Seceded May 20, 1861)
Raleigh
Charlotte ×1865 Bentonville
New Bern 1862

TENNESSEE (Sec. May 7, 1861)
Knoxville
Nashville 1862
Murfreesboro 1862
Chattanooga 1863
×Chickamauga 1863

SOUTH CAROLINA (Seceded Dec. 20, 1860)
Columbia
Ft. Sumter 1861
Ft. Charleston 1865 Ft. Wagner 1863
Pt. Royal 1861

GEORGIA (Seceded Jan. 19, 1861)
Atlanta 1864
Milledgeville
Savannah 1864
Ft. Pulaski 1862
Andersonville
Tallahassee

FLORIDA (Seceded Jan. 10, 1861)
Pensacola 1862
Fernandina 1862
St. Augustine 1862

ALABAMA (Seceded Jan. 11, 1861)
Montgomery
Mobile 1864
Tombigbee R.
Alabama R.

MISSISSIPPI (Sec. Jan. 9, 1861)
Corinth 1862
×Shiloh 1862
Holly Springs 1862
Jackson 1863
Vicksburg 1863
Port Gibson 1863
Natchez

ARKANSAS (Seceded May 6, 1861)
Little Rock
Memphis
Chickasaw Bluffs 1862
Mississippi R.
Arkansas R.
Ft. Henry 1862
Ft. Donelson 1862

LOUISIANA (Seceded Jan. 26, 1861)
Baton Rouge
New Orleans 1862
Ship I. 1861

TEXAS (Seceded Feb. 1, 1861)
Dallas
Shreveport
Trinity R.
Brazos R.
Colorado R.
Austin
San Antonio
Houston
Sabine R.
Rio Grande

INDIAN TERRITORY
Cimarron R.
Arkansas R.

KANSAS
Topeka

NEBRASKA
Omaha

Pensacola 1862

From *Atlas of World History.* © Copyright 1975 by Rand McNally & Company, R.L. 88-S-58.

ATE) states from 1861 to 1865, in which the CON-FEDERACY sought to establish itself as a separate nation. The Civil War is also known as the War for Southern Independence and as the War between the States. The war grew out of deep-seated differences between the social structure and economy of North and South, most notably over slavery; generations of political maneuvers had been unable to overcome these differences (*see* MISSOURI COMPROMISE *and* COMPROMISE OF 1850). The SECESSION of the southern states began in late 1860, after Abraham LIN-COLN was elected president. The Confederacy was formed in early 1861. The fighting began with the Confederate attack on Fort SUMTER. Most of the battles took place in the South, but one extremely crucial episode, the Battle of GETTYSBURG, was fought in the North. The war ended with the surrender of General Robert E. LEE to General Ulysses S. GRANT at AP-POMATTOX COURT HOUSE. (*See* BULL RUN, BATTLE OF; CHANCELLORSVILLE, BATTLE OF; EMANCIPATION PROCLAMATION; *and* SHERMAN'S MARCH TO THE SEA.)

&. The Civil War has been the most serious test yet of the ability of the United States to remain one nation.

Clay, Henry   A WHIG political leader of the early nineteenth century known for his efforts to keep the United States one nation despite sharp controversy among Americans over slavery. Clay represented KENTUCKY, first in the HOUSE OF REPRESENTATIVES and then in the SENATE. He was known as the "Great Pacificator" because of his prominent role in producing the MISSOURI COMPROMISE and the COMPRO-MISE OF 1850.

&. Clay ran for president twice and lost both times. He once said in a speech, "I would rather be right than be president."

Common Sense   A pamphlet written by Thomas PAINE in 1776 that called for the United States to declare independence from GREAT BRITAIN immediately. Written in a brisk and pungent style, *Common Sense* had a tremendous impact, and helped to convert George WASHINGTON to the cause of independence.

Compromise of 1850   A set of laws, passed in the midst of fierce wrangling between groups favoring slavery and groups opposing it, that attempted to give something to both sides. The compromise admitted CALIFORNIA to the United States as a "free" (no slavery) state, but allowed some newly opened territories to decide on slavery for themselves. SENA-TOR Henry CLAY was a great force behind the passage of the compromise.

&. The Compromise of 1850 is an example of how difficult it was to accommodate the two sides of the slavery question. It failed to prevent the CIVIL WAR, which broke out barely ten years later.

Concord, Battle of   *See* LEXINGTON AND CON-CORD, BATTLE OF.

Confederacy   The Confederate States of America; the government formed in 1861 by southern states that proclaimed their SECESSION from the United States. Jefferson DAVIS was its president. The Confederacy was dissolved after the CIVIL WAR. (*Compare* UNION.)

Confederate   A descriptive term for the institutions and people of the CONFEDERACY.

Constitution   The fundamental law of the United States, drafted in PHILADELPHIA in 1787 (*see* CON-STITUTIONAL CONVENTION), ratified in 1788, and put into effect in 1789. It established a strong central government in place of the ARTICLES OF CONFED-ERATION. (*See* PREAMBLE TO THE CONSTITUTION.)

Constitutional Convention   The gathering that drafted the CONSTITUTION of the United States in 1787; all states were invited to send delegates. The convention, meeting in PHILADELPHIA, designed a government with separate LEGISLATIVE, EXECUTIVE, and JUDICIAL BRANCHES. It established CONGRESS as a lawmaking body with two houses: each state is given two representatives in the SENATE, while representation in the HOUSE OF REPRESENTATIVES is based on population.

Continental Congress   An assembly of delegates from the THIRTEEN COLONIES (soon to become the thirteen states). It governed during the REVOLUTION-ARY WAR and under the ARTICLES OF CONFEDERA-TION. The Continental Congress first met in 1774, before the revolution. When it reconvened in 1775, it organized for war against Britain, and eventually passed the DECLARATION OF INDEPENDENCE.

Cornwallis, Charles (kawrn-WAH-lis, kawrn-WAW-lis)   A British nobleman and general who commanded British forces in the REVOLUTIONARY WAR. The surrender of Lord Cornwallis to George WASHINGTON at the Battle of YORKTOWN in 1781 ended the hostilities of the revolution.

Coronado, Francisco (kawr-uh-NAH-doh)   A Spanish explorer of the sixteenth century. Coronado traveled through much of what is now the southwestern United States searching for the legendary "seven gold cities of Cibola," but found no treasure. One of his men was the first EUROPEAN to discover the GRAND CANYON.

covered wagon   A typical conveyance for settlers moving west with their belongings. It was drawn by horses or oxen and equipped with a canvas cover, often supported by hoops, to keep off rain.

Crockett, Davy   A frontier settler and political leader of the nineteenth century. Crockett was born in TENNESSEE, and was killed at the ALAMO by Mexican troops in 1836. Although he cultivated the image of a rough man of the bush, Crockett was politically ambitious, and served in CONGRESS.

&♣ Crockett's trademark was a coonskin cap.
&♣ Crockett served in the army under Andrew JACKSON. He opposed Jackson's policies, however, when Jackson was president and Crockett was in Congress.

Damn the torpedoes   An exclamation by David FARRAGUT, an officer in the UNION navy in the CIVIL WAR. Warned of mines, called torpedoes, in the water ahead, Farragut said, "Damn the torpedoes! Captain Drayton, go ahead! Jouett, full speed!"

Davis, Jefferson   A political leader of the nineteenth century. He was a powerful CABINET officer in the 1850s. When his home state of MISSISSIPPI seceded from the UNION (see SECESSION), Davis left the SENATE to join the government of the CONFEDERACY. He served as president of the Confederacy throughout its existence.

Declaration of Independence   The fundamental document establishing the United States as a nation, adopted on July 4, 1776. The declaration was ordered and approved by the CONTINENTAL CONGRESS, and written largely by Thomas JEFFERSON. It declared the THIRTEEN COLONIES represented in the Continental Congress independent from GREAT BRITAIN, offered reasons for the separation, and laid out the principles for which the REVOLUTIONARY WAR was fought. The signers included John ADAMS, Benjamin FRANKLIN, John HANCOCK, and Jefferson. The declaration begins (capitalization and punctuation are modernized):

When, in the course of human events, it becomes necessary for one people to dissolve the political bands which have connected them with another, and to assume, among the powers of the earth, the separate and equal station to which the laws of nature and of nature's God entitle them, a decent respect to the opinions of mankind requires that they should declare the causes which impel them to the separation.

We hold these truths to be self-evident: that all men are created equal; that they are endowed by their creator with certain unalienable rights; that among these are life, liberty, and the pursuit of happiness; that, to secure these rights, governments are instituted among men, deriving their just powers from the consent of the governed; that whenever any form of government becomes destructive of these ends, it is the right of the people to alter or to abolish it, and to institute new government, laying its foundation on such principles, and organizing its powers in such form, as to them shall seem most likely to effect their safety and happiness.

&♣ The day of the adoption of the Declaration of Independence is now commemorated as the FOURTH OF JULY, or INDEPENDENCE DAY.

Democratic party   A political party that arose in the 1820s from a split in the DEMOCRATIC-REPUBLICAN PARTY. Andrew JACKSON was the first president elected from the Democratic party. The other Democratic presidents elected before the CIVIL WAR were Martin Van Buren, James K. POLK, Franklin Pierce, and James Buchanan. The party generally opposed the national bank, high PROTECTIVE TARIFFS, interference with slavery, and federal aid for internal improvements in the nation — all measures that the WHIGS came to favor. The Democrats' greatest strength was with farmers, laborers, and people of the frontier.

Democratic-Republican party   *See* DEMOCRATIC PARTY.

Dix, Dorothea   Nineteenth-century reformer who protested the practice of confining the mentally ill in

DOROTHEA DIX

prisons and whose labors led to the expansion and improvement of mental hospitals.

Don't fire until you see the whites of their eyes   A famous command attributed to William Prescott, an American officer, at the Battle of BUNKER HILL in the REVOLUTIONARY WAR. Prescott may have said "color" rather than "whites."

🏵 Prescott's command has become a PROVERB, meaning "Don't act before you have some chance of success."

Douglas, Stephen A.   A political leader of the nineteenth century, known for twice running against Abraham LINCOLN — for a seat in the SENATE from ILLINOIS in 1858, which he won, and for the presidency in 1860, which he lost. The two engaged in the LINCOLN-DOUGLAS DEBATES over slavery and other issues in 1858.

Douglass, Frederick W.   An African-American ABOLITIONIST of the nineteenth century. Douglass, an escaped slave, was an especially captivating speaker. His autobiography, *NARRATIVE OF THE LIFE OF FREDERICK DOUGLASS*, tells of the violence he suffered be-

cause of his beliefs. Late in his life, he attacked JIM CROW laws.

Dred Scott decision   A controversial ruling made by the SUPREME COURT in 1857, shortly before the outbreak of the CIVIL WAR. Dred Scott, a slave, sought to be declared a free man on the basis that he had lived for a time in a "free" territory with his master. The Court decided that, under the CONSTITUTION, Scott was his master's property, and was not a citizen of the United States. The Court also declared that the MISSOURI COMPROMISE, which prohibited slavery in certain areas, unconstitutionally deprived people of property — their slaves. The Dred Scott decision was a serious blow to ABOLITIONISTS.

Edwards, Jonathan   An American clergyman of the eighteenth century; a leader in the religious revivals of the 1730s and 1740s known as the Great Awakening. Edwards, an emotional preacher, emphasized the absolute power of God. His most famous sermon, the harrowing "Sinners in the Hands of an Angry God," compares sinners to spiders dangled over a flame.

Emancipation Proclamation   A proclamation made by President Abraham LINCOLN in 1863 that all slaves under the CONFEDERACY were from then on "forever free."

🏵 In itself, the Emancipation Proclamation did not free any slaves, because it applied only to rebellious areas that the federal government did not then control. Yet when people say that Lincoln "freed the slaves," they are referring to the Emancipation Proclamation.

entangling alliances with none   A PHRASE President Thomas JEFFERSON used in his first inaugural address in 1801, calling for a cautious, ISOLATIONIST foreign policy.

🏵 George WASHINGTON had given similar isolationist advice four years earlier in his FAREWELL ADDRESS: "It is our true policy to steer clear of permanent alliances with any portion of the foreign world."

Erie Canal   An artificial waterway built across NEW YORK state in the early nineteenth century, linking LAKE ERIE and the HUDSON RIVER. The canal opened trade between New York and the midwestern states, and aided in the growth of NEW YORK CITY as a port.

Farewell Address, Washington's The final address by George WASHINGTON to his fellow citizens as he was leaving the presidency. He wrote the address in 1796 but never delivered it. Washington discussed the dangers of divisive party politics, and warned strongly against permanent alliances between the United States and other countries.

Farragut, David (FAR-uh-guht) An admiral in the UNION navy in the CIVIL WAR who helped secure the MISSISSIPPI RIVER for the UNION. Once, when warned of mines, called torpedoes, in the water ahead, Farragut replied, "DAMN THE TORPEDOES!"

father of his country A title given to George WASHINGTON in recognition of his military leadership in the REVOLUTIONARY WAR and his service as first president under the CONSTITUTION.

Federalist *See* FEDERALIST PARTY.

Federalist Papers, The A series of eighty-five ES-SAYS written by Alexander HAMILTON, James MAD-ISON, and John Jay in the late 1780s to persuade the voters of NEW YORK to adopt the CONSTITUTION. The essays are considered a classic defense of the American system of government, as well as a classic practical application of political principles.

Federalist party The first American political party. The Federalist party developed during the presidency of George WASHINGTON, and was led by Alexander HAMILTON and John ADAMS. Federalists believed in a strong federal government, and advocated economic policies that would strengthen the federal government, such as the creation of a national bank. The opposition to the Federalists was led by Thomas JEFFERSON.

First Amendment The first article of the BILL OF RIGHTS. It forbids CONGRESS from tampering with the freedoms of religion, speech, assembly, and the press.

First in war, first in peace, and first in the hearts of his countrymen Words from a EULOGY for George WASHINGTON adopted by CONGRESS immediately after Washington's death. The eulogy was written by Henry Lee, a soldier and political leader from Washington's home state of VIRGINIA.

Fort Sumter *See* SUMTER, FORT.

forty-niners Those who flocked to CALIFORNIA in 1849 in search of gold, which had been discovered there in 1848. Reportedly, there were about 80,000 of them.

Founding Fathers A general name for male American patriots during the REVOLUTIONARY WAR, especially the signers of the DECLARATION OF INDEPENDENCE and those who drafted the CONSTITUTION. John ADAMS, Benjamin FRANKLIN, Alexander HAMILTON, Thomas JEFFERSON, James MADISON, and George WASHINGTON were all Founding Fathers.

Fourth of July The day on which the DECLARATION OF INDEPENDENCE was adopted by the CONTINENTAL CONGRESS in 1776; INDEPENDENCE DAY.

BENJAMIN FRANKLIN

Franklin, Benjamin A patriot, diplomat, author, printer, scientist, and inventor in the eighteenth century; one of the FOUNDING FATHERS of the United States. He was an important early researcher in ELECTRICITY, and proposed the modern model of electrical CURRENT. He also demonstrated that LIGHTNING was electricity by flying a kite in a thunderstorm and allowing it to be struck by lightning. Franklin used this discovery to invent the lightning rod. He produced other inventions as well, such as bifocal eyeglasses and the efficient Franklin stove. Particularly notable among his writings are *THE AUTOBIOGRAPHY OF BENJAMIN FRANKLIN* and *POOR RICHARD'S*

ALMANACK. He was a signer of the DECLARATION OF INDEPENDENCE, and negotiated with FRANCE and BRITAIN on behalf of the newly formed government of the United States. Toward the end of his life, he took part in the CONSTITUTIONAL CONVENTION.

🌿 At the signing of the Declaration of Independence, Franklin warned his fellow patriots that their venture, if unsuccessful, could lead to their execution for treason: "We must all hang together, or we shall surely all hang separately."

French and Indian War A series of military engagements between BRITAIN and FRANCE in NORTH AMERICA between 1754 and 1763. The French and Indian War was the American phase of the SEVEN YEARS' WAR, which was then being fought in EUROPE. In a battle between British and French forces near QUEBEC CITY in CANADA, the British gained control of all of Canada.

Garrison, William Lloyd A prominent ABOLITIONIST of the nineteenth century. In his newspaper, *The Liberator*, he called for immediate freedom for the slaves and for the end of all political ties between the northern and southern states.

Gettysburg, Battle of The greatest battle of the CIVIL WAR, fought in south-central PENNSYLVANIA in 1863. It ended in a major victory for the North, and is usually considered the turning point of the war.

Gettysburg Address A speech delivered by Abraham LINCOLN during the CIVIL WAR. Lincoln was speaking at the dedication of a soldiers' cemetery at the site of the Battle of GETTYSBURG. The opening and closing lines are particularly memorable:

Four score and seven years ago our fathers brought forth on this continent a new nation, conceived in liberty and dedicated to the proposition that all men are created equal. . . . [We must] be here dedicated to the great task remaining before us — that from these honored dead we take increased devotion to that cause for which they gave the last full measure of devotion — that we here highly resolve that these dead shall not have died in vain; that this nation, under God, shall have a new birth of freedom; and that government of the people, by the people, and for the people shall not perish from the earth.

🌿 Lincoln surprised his audience at Gettysburg with the brevity of his speech. He delivered the Gettysburg Address, which lasted about three minutes, after a two-hour speech by Edward Everett, one of the leading speakers of the day.

Give me liberty or give me death Words from a speech by Patrick HENRY urging the American colonies to revolt against ENGLAND. Henry spoke only a few weeks before the REVOLUTIONARY WAR began:

Gentlemen may cry Peace, Peace, but there is no peace. The war is actually begun. The next gale that sweeps from the north will bring to our ears the clash of resounding arms. Our brethren are already in the field. . . . Is life so dear, or peace so sweet, as to be purchased at the price of chains and slavery? Forbid it, Almighty God! I know not what course others may take, but as for me, give me liberty or give me death!

gold rush, California The movement of great numbers of people to CALIFORNIA after gold was discovered there in 1848. (*See* FORTY-NINERS.)

government of the people, by the people, and for the people Words from the GETTYSBURG ADDRESS of Abraham LINCOLN, often quoted as a definition of DEMOCRACY.

Go west, young man A favorite saying of the nineteenth-century journalist Horace GREELEY, referring to opportunities on the frontier. Another writer, John Soule, apparently originated it.

ULYSSES S. GRANT

Grant, Ulysses S. A general and political leader of the nineteenth century. Grant became commanding general of the UNION army during the CIVIL WAR. He accepted the unconditional surrender of the commanding general of the main CONFEDERATE army, Robert E. LEE, at APPOMATTOX COURT HOUSE. A REPUBLICAN, he later became president.

Greeley, Horace   A journalist and political leader of the nineteenth century, known for his strong opinions. He ran unsuccessfully for president just before his death. A favorite phrase of his was "GO WEST, YOUNG MAN."

Hale, Nathan   An American soldier and spy of the eighteenth century, captured and hanged by the British during the REVOLUTIONARY WAR. He is said to have declared at his execution in 1776, "I ONLY REGRET THAT I HAVE BUT ONE LIFE TO LOSE FOR MY COUNTRY."

Hamilton, Alexander   A soldier and political leader of the late eighteenth and early nineteenth centuries; a FOUNDING FATHER of the United States. Hamilton advised George WASHINGTON in the REVOLUTIONARY WAR, wrote most of the ESSAYS in *THE FEDERALIST PAPERS*, and was a leader in the drafting of the CONSTITUTION. He later served under Washington as the first secretary of the treasury in the new government. A FEDERALIST, he was opposed politically by Thomas JEFFERSON, and both politically and personally by Aaron BURR (*see* JEFFERSONIANISM VERSUS HAMILTONIANISM). Burr challenged Hamilton to a duel, in which Burr killed him.

Hancock, John   A political leader of the eighteenth century. He was president of the CONTINENTAL CONGRESS when the DECLARATION OF INDEPENDENCE was signed, and was the first to sign it, which he did with a large, flamboyant signature.

🖎 A "John Hancock" is a signature.

Harpers Ferry   The place now in WEST VIRGINIA where the militant ABOLITIONIST John BROWN was captured in 1859, after he seized a federal arsenal there.

Henry, Patrick   A political leader of the eighteenth century, known for his fiery oratory. He is especially remembered for saying, "GIVE ME LIBERTY OR GIVE ME DEATH."

Homestead Act   A law passed in the 1860s that offered up to 160 acres of public land to any head of a family who paid a registration fee, lived on the land for five years, and cultivated it or built on it.

"House Divided" speech   A speech made by Abraham LINCOLN to the ILLINOIS REPUBLICAN convention in 1858. In the speech, Lincoln noted that conflict between North and South over slavery was intensifying. He asserted that the conflict would not stop until a crisis was reached and passed, for, in a biblical phrase Lincoln used, "A house divided against itself cannot stand." He continued: "I believe this government cannot endure permanently half slave and half free. I do not expect the UNION to be dissolved — I do not expect the house to fall — but I do expect it will cease to be divided. It will become all one thing, or all the other."

Houston, Sam (HYOOH-stuhn)   A soldier and political leader of the nineteenth century. Houston led the Texans in their struggle to win independence from MEXICO. Later he served as president of the REPUBLIC of TEXAS. After Texas became a state, he represented it in the United States SENATE. He was elected governor of Texas just before the CIVIL WAR, but when he opposed the state's decision for SECESSION, he was removed from office.

Hudson, Henry   An English explorer of the early seventeenth century. He discovered the HUDSON RIVER while in the service of THE NETHERLANDS.

I cannot tell a lie   Words George WASHINGTON spoke as a boy, according to a biographer of Washington. (*See* WASHINGTON AND THE CHERRY TREE.)

I have not yet begun to fight   Words attributed to the eighteenth-century naval hero John Paul JONES. He was doing battle with a British ship when his own ship was badly damaged, and the British commander called over to ask whether Jones had surrendered. He answered, "I have not yet begun to fight." He and his crew then captured the British ship. His own ship later sank.

I only regret that I have but one life to lose for my country   Words spoken by the patriot Nathan HALE, who was executed as a spy by the British in 1776.

indentured servant   A person under contract to work for another person for a definite period of time, usually without pay but in exchange for free passage to a new country. During the seventeenth century most of the white laborers in MARYLAND and VIRGINIA came from ENGLAND as indentured servants.

Independence Day   The primary national holiday in the United States, celebrated every July 4; the anniversary of the adoption of the DECLARATION OF INDEPENDENCE. Customary festivities include picnics; parades; band concerts; decorations in red, white, and blue; and nighttime fireworks displays.

Iroquois League (IR-uh-kwoy)   A confederacy of NATIVE AMERICAN tribes in upper NEW YORK state, dating to the sixteenth century.

Jackson, Andrew   A general and political leader of the late eighteenth and early nineteenth centuries. As a general in the WAR OF 1812, he defeated the British in the Battle of NEW ORLEANS. He was called "Old Hickory." Jackson was elected president after John Quincy ADAMS as a candidate of the common man, and his style of government came to be known as JACKSONIAN DEMOCRACY. He rewarded his political supporters with positions once he became president (*see* SPOILS SYSTEM). A DEMOCRAT, Jackson was widely criticized for expanding the power of the presidency beyond what was customary before his time.

Jackson, "Stonewall"   Thomas J. Jackson, a general in the CONFEDERATE army during the CIVIL WAR. He got his nickname at the First Battle of BULL RUN, where he and his men "stood like a stone wall." He and General Robert E. LEE led the South to victory at the Battle of CHANCELLORSVILLE. In the evening after the battle was won, however, Jackson was fatally shot by Confederate troops who mistook him and his staff for UNION officers.

⚓ In the poem "Barbara Frietchie," by John Greenleaf Whittier, Stonewall Jackson orders his men not to harm Barbara Frietchie or the Union flags she is holding (*see* SHOOT, IF YOU MUST, THIS OLD GRAY HEAD). ⚓ Jackson's dying words, "Let us cross the river and rest in the shade," are much remembered.

Jacksonian democracy (jak-SOH-nee-uhn)   A movement for more DEMOCRACY in American government in the 1830s. Led by President Andrew JACKSON, this movement championed greater rights for the common man, and was opposed to any signs of ARISTOCRACY in the nation. Jacksonian democracy was aided by the strong spirit of equality among the people of the newer settlements in the South and West. It was also aided by the extension of the vote in eastern states to men without property; in the early days of the United States, many places had allowed only male property owners to vote. (*Compare* JEFFERSONIAN DEMOCRACY.)

Jamestown   The first permanent English settlement in North America, founded in 1607 in VIRGINIA. Jamestown was named for King James I of ENGLAND. It was destroyed later in the seventeenth century in an uprising of Virginians against the governor.

Jefferson, Thomas   A political leader of the late eighteenth and early nineteenth centuries; one of the FOUNDING FATHERS; the leader of the DEMOCRATIC-REPUBLICAN PARTY. Jefferson was principal author of the DECLARATION OF INDEPENDENCE, and served as president from 1801 to 1809, between John ADAMS and James MADISON. He arranged for the LOUISIANA PURCHASE, founded the University of Virginia, and built the mansion MONTICELLO. Jefferson is famed as a champion of political and religious freedom. (*See* JEFFERSONIAN DEMOCRACY.)

Jeffersonian democracy (jef-uhr-SOH-nee-uhn)   A movement for more DEMOCRACY in American government in the first decade of the nineteenth century. The movement was led by President Thomas JEFFERSON. Jeffersonian democracy was less RADICAL than the later JACKSONIAN DEMOCRACY. For example, where Jacksonian democracy held that the common citizen was the best judge of measures, Jeffersonian democracy stressed the need for leadership by those of greatest ability, who would be chosen by the people.

Jeffersonianism versus Hamiltonianism (jef-uhr-SOH-nee-uh-niz-uhm; ham-uhl-TOH-nee-uh-niz-uhm)   Rival ideals of American government that have persisted long after the deaths of Thomas JEFFERSON and Alexander HAMILTON, after whom they were named. Jeffersonians have preferred a weak federal government and strong state and local governments, on the grounds that lower-level governments will be more responsive than the national government to the popular will. Jeffersonians have also held that the American economy should rely more on agriculture than on industry, and have seen big business as a threat to DEMOCRACY. In contrast, Hamiltonians have insisted that a strong national government is needed to guide the economic development of the nation, especially its industrial development, and to restrain the excesses of the people.

Johnny Appleseed   *See* APPLESEED, JOHNNY.

Jones, John Paul A naval leader of the REVOLUTIONARY WAR, known for his attacks on British ships off the coast of ENGLAND. When a British commander asked him to surrender his badly crippled ship during a battle, he allegedly replied, "I HAVE NOT YET BEGUN TO FIGHT" — and compelled the British ship to surrender. Two days later, his own ship sank.

Kentucky and Virginia Resolutions *See* VIRGINIA AND KENTUCKY RESOLUTIONS.

Know-Nothings A party opposed to the holding of public office by immigrants or ROMAN CATHOLICS. The Know-Nothings, also known as "nativists," insisted that only true, "native" Americans should serve in the government. The party was quite successful in the 1850s, but split over the slavery question. Its official name was the American party. It picked up the "Know-Nothing" tag because its members, maintaining secrecy about the party's activities, customarily answered questions with, "I know nothing."

❧ Today, the term *know-nothing* is usually applied to bigots.

Lafayette, Marquis de (lah-fee-ET, laf-ee-ET) A French nobleman, political leader, and general of the late eighteenth and early nineteenth centuries. Enthusiastic for the ideals of the AMERICAN REVOLUTION, Lafayette served as a general in the American army during the REVOLUTIONARY WAR, fighting alongside his friend George WASHINGTON at the Battle of YORKTOWN and elsewhere. On returning to FRANCE, he was active in the early stages of the FRENCH REVOLUTION.

❧ A United States Army officer, speaking at the tomb of Lafayette after United States forces had arrived in support of France in WORLD WAR I, said, "LAFAYETTE, WE ARE HERE." He meant that the United States, in aiding France in the war, was returning the favor that Lafayette and the French had done for the United States in the Revolutionary War. The officer is sometimes identified as General John PERSHING.

Lafitte, Jean (luh-FEET, lah-FEET) A French pirate of the early nineteenth century, active around NEW ORLEANS, LOUISIANA. He volunteered to aid General Andrew JACKSON against the British in the WAR OF 1812, and fought in the Battle of New Orleans. Many legends have grown up around Lafitte.

ROBERT E. LEE

Lee, Robert E. A general of the nineteenth century; the commander of the CONFEDERATE troops during the CIVIL WAR. Before the war, he led the marines who put down the insurrection by John BROWN at HARPERS FERRY, and took Brown captive. In the war, he won the Battle of CHANCELLORSVILLE but lost the Battle of GETTYSBURG. He surrendered to the UNION army, under the command of Ulysses S. GRANT, at APPOMATTOX COURT HOUSE in 1865.

❧ Lee's excellence of character and brilliance as a general won him the respect of people on both sides of the war.

Lewis and Clark expedition A journey made by Meriwether Lewis and William Clark, during the presidency of Thomas JEFFERSON, to explore the American Northwest, newly purchased from FRANCE, and some territories beyond. The expedition started from ST. LOUIS, MISSOURI, and moved up the MISSOURI RIVER and down the COLUMBIA RIVER to the PACIFIC OCEAN. The information that Lewis and Clark gathered was of great help in the settlement of the West. (*See also* LOUISIANA PURCHASE.)

Lexington and Concord, Battle of (KONG-kuhrd) The first battle of the REVOLUTIONARY WAR, fought in MASSACHUSETTS on April 19, 1775. British troops had moved from BOSTON toward Lexington and Concord to seize the colonists' military supplies and arrest revolutionaries. In Concord, advancing British troops met resistance from the MINUTEMEN, and American volunteers harassed the retreating British troops along the Concord-Lexington Road. Paul REVERE, on his famous ride, had first alerted the Americans to the British movement.

❧ During the battle there was a skirmish at Concord's North Bridge, later commemorated in a poem by Ralph Waldo EMERSON:

> By the rude bridge that arched the flood,
> Their flag to April's breeze unfurled,
> Here once the embattled farmers stood
> And fired the SHOT HEARD ROUND THE WORLD.

Liberty Bell   *See under "Fine Arts."*

ABRAHAM LINCOLN

Lincoln, Abraham   A political leader of the nineteenth century; the leader of the UNION during the CIVIL WAR, and one of the most revered presidents, who served from 1861 to 1865. Lincoln, who worked for a time splitting wood into fence rails, was a lawyer by profession, and largely self-taught; there is a familiar image of him studying by firelight in the log cabin in KENTUCKY in which he was born and raised. He was an early enthusiast for the REPUBLICAN PARTY, and was its nominee for the SENATE from ILLINOIS in 1858. Lincoln rose to national promi-

nence in a famous series of debates with his opponent in the 1858 election, Stephen A. Douglas (*see* LINCOLN-DOUGLAS DEBATES). He was elected president in 1860. Lincoln was an exceptionally active commander in chief of the army and navy in the Civil War, which broke out the month after his inauguration. During the war, he issued the EMANCIPATION PROCLAMATION, delivered the GETTYSBURG ADDRESS, and approved the HOMESTEAD ACT. In his second inaugural address (*see* LINCOLN'S SECOND INAUGURAL ADDRESS), delivered in 1865 as the war was ending, he pleaded for restraint and "charity for all" in the aftermath of the war. He never was able to carry out his program of RECONSTRUCTION, however, because a supporter of the CONFEDERACY, the actor John Wilkes BOOTH, assassinated him a few days after the southern states surrendered.

❧ Lincoln has been referred to in a variety of ways, such as "honest Abe," "the rail splitter," and "the Great Emancipator." ❧ He was very tall and lanky, and often wore a black stovepipe hat. ❧ Lincoln is much admired for the political moderation that enabled him to preserve the nation, and has joined George WASHINGTON as a symbol of American DEMOCRACY. His portrait appears on the five-dollar bill and the one-cent piece. ❧ Lincoln's birthday was February 12. A holiday in February, Presidents' Day, commemorates his birthday and the birthday of George WASHINGTON.

Lincoln-Douglas debates   A series of debates between Abraham LINCOLN and Stephen A. DOUGLAS in 1858, when both were campaigning for election to the United States SENATE from ILLINOIS. Much of the debating concerned slavery, and the extension of the institution of slavery into territories such as KANSAS. The debates transformed Lincoln into a national figure and led to his election to the presidency in 1860.

Lincoln's second inaugural address   A speech given by Abraham LINCOLN at his inauguration for a second term as president, a few weeks before the UNION victory in the CIVIL WAR. It concludes with this appeal for reconciliation:

With malice toward none; with charity for all; with firmness in the right, as God gives us to see the right, let us strive on to finish the work we are in; to bind up the nation's wounds; to care for him who shall have borne the battle, and for his widow, and his orphan — to do all which may achieve and cherish a just and lasting peace among ourselves, and with all nations.

Louisiana Purchase   The purchase by the United States from FRANCE of the huge Louisiana Territory in 1803. President Thomas JEFFERSON ordered the purchase negotiations, fearing that the French, then led by NAPOLEON, wanted to establish an empire in NORTH AMERICA. The French had no such ambitions, but were happy to exchange their vast landholdings for cash. The area that they sold, extending from the MISSISSIPPI RIVER to the ROCKY MOUNTAINS, more than doubled the size of the United States.

Madison, Dolley or **Dolly**   The wife of President James MADISON. Dolley Madison was known for her wit and her grace as a hostess. She is also remembered for her calmness in the face of the British invasion of WASHINGTON, D.C., in the WAR OF 1812. She saved many documents stored in the WHITE HOUSE, along with a portrait of George WASHINGTON by Gilbert STUART.

Madison, James   A political leader of the late eighteenth and early nineteenth centuries; one of the FOUNDING FATHERS. Madison was a member of the CONTINENTAL CONGRESS. A leader in the drafting of the CONSTITUTION, he worked tirelessly for its adoption by the states, contributing several essays to *THE FEDERALIST PAPERS*. He served as president from 1809 to 1817, after Thomas JEFFERSON. The United States fought the WAR OF 1812 during his presidency. He belonged to the DEMOCRATIC-REPUBLICAN PARTY. He was married to one of the most celebrated of presidents' wives, Dolley MADISON.

manifest destiny   A popular slogan of the 1840s. It was used by people who believed that the United States was destined — by God, some said — to expand across NORTH AMERICA to the PACIFIC OCEAN. The idea of manifest destiny was used to justify the acquisition of OREGON and large parts of the Southwest, including CALIFORNIA. (*See* MEXICAN WAR.)

Mann, Horace   A legislator and educational reformer of the nineteenth century. In his home state of MASSACHUSETTS, Mann worked to increase the availability and quality of free, nondenominational public schools. Mann has been called the father of the American public school.

manumission (man-yuh-MISH-uhn)   The freeing of a slave, especially by the slave's owner.

Marbury versus Madison   A case decided by the SUPREME COURT under Chief Justice John MAR-SHALL in 1803. The Court declared unanimously that a certain law passed by CONGRESS should not be enforced, because the law was opposed to the CONSTITUTION. *Marbury versus Madison* established the principle of "judicial review" — that the Supreme Court has the power to declare acts of Congress unconstitutional.

Marshall, John   A public official of the late eighteenth and early nineteenth centuries. A FEDERALIST, Marshall served as chief justice of the SUPREME COURT from 1801 to 1835. His interpretations of the CONSTITUTION in such cases as *MARBURY VERSUS MADISON* served to strengthen the power of the Court and the power of the federal government generally.

Mason-Dixon line   A boundary line between PENNSYLVANIA and MARYLAND, laid out by two English surveyors, Charles Mason and Jeremiah Dixon, in the 1760s. Before and during the CIVIL WAR, the line was symbolic of the division between slaveholding and free states. After the war, it remained symbolic of the division between states that required racial SEGREGATION and those that did not.

Mather, Cotton (MATHH-uhr)   A scholar and religious leader of the late seventeenth and early eighteenth centuries. Mather, a prominent MASSACHUSETTS PURITAN, urged the suppression of WITCHCRAFT and supported the SALEM WITCH TRIALS.

MAYFLOWER. A detail from Mayflower in Plymouth Harbor, *circa 1880, by William Formby Halsall.*

Mayflower   The ship that carried the PILGRIMS to America. It made a permanent landing near PLYM-

OUTH ROCK in 1620, after the Pilgrims had agreed to the MAYFLOWER COMPACT.

Mayflower Compact   An agreement reached by the PILGRIMS on the ship the *MAYFLOWER* in 1620, just before they landed near PLYMOUTH ROCK. The Mayflower Compact bound them to live in a civil society according to their own laws. It remained the fundamental law of their colony of PLYMOUTH until the colony was absorbed into MASSACHUSETTS in the late seventeenth century.

🕭 The Mayflower Compact was the first written CONSTITUTION in NORTH AMERICA.

McGuffey's Readers   A series of books prepared principally by William H. McGuffey, a midwestern teacher, and designed to teach reading to schoolchildren. The series began to appear in the 1830s. It was widely used in the nineteenth century, and is still used by some schools today.

Mexican War   A war fought between the United States and MEXICO from 1846 to 1848. The United States won the war, encouraged by the feelings of many Americans that the country was accomplishing its MANIFEST DESTINY of expansion. Mexico renounced all claims to TEXAS north of the RIO GRANDE, and yielded a vast territory that embraces the present states of CALIFORNIA, NEVADA, and UTAH, and parts of ARIZONA, COLORADO, NEW MEXICO, and WYOMING.

🕭 Many generals of the CIVIL WAR, including Ulysses S. GRANT and Robert E. LEE, gained experience in battle during the Mexican War. The Mexican War was opposed by many Americans, notably by the author Henry David THOREAU, who was put in jail for refusing to pay a tax to support the war. His *CIVIL DISOBEDIENCE* explains the principles of his action.

Minutemen   Armed American civilians who were active in the REVOLUTIONARY WAR and in the period just preceding the war. They were named Minutemen because they were ready to fight alongside regular soldiers at a moment's notice. The Minutemen of MASSACHUSETTS were especially well known. (*See* LEXINGTON AND CONCORD, BATTLE OF.)

🕭 During the COLD WAR, the name "Minuteman" was given to a United States missile held ready for launching in the event of a nuclear attack.

Missouri Compromise   A settlement of a dispute between slave and free states, contained in several laws passed during 1820 and 1821. Northern legislators had tried to prohibit slavery in MISSOURI, which was then applying for statehood. The Missouri Compromise admitted Missouri as a slave state and MAINE as a free state, and prohibited slavery in territory that later became KANSAS and NEBRASKA. In 1857, in the DRED SCOTT DECISION, the SUPREME COURT declared the compromise unconstitutional.

Monitor **versus** *Merrimack*   A naval engagement of the CIVIL WAR, fought in 1862 off the coast of VIRGINIA between two ironclad ships, the UNION *Monitor* and the CONFEDERATE *Merrimack*. The incident demonstrated that wooden warships were obsolete.

Monroe, James   A political leader of the late eighteenth and early nineteenth centuries; a leader of the DEMOCRATIC-REPUBLICAN PARTY. He was president from 1817 to 1825, between James MADISON and John Quincy ADAMS. He issued the MONROE DOCTRINE in 1823, supporting the independence of SPAIN's colonies in America. The MISSOURI COMPROMISE was reached in his presidency.

🕭 Compared to other presidencies of that time, Monroe's administration was relatively free of quarrels between Americans. His time in office has been called the Era of Good Feeling.

Monroe Doctrine   A statement of foreign policy issued by President James MONROE in 1823, declaring that the United States would not tolerate intervention by European nations in the affairs of nations in the Americas. Monroe also promised that the United States would not interfere with European colonies already established, or with governments in EUROPE.

Morse, Samuel F. B.   Nineteenth-century inventor of the telegraph and of Morse code. In 1844 he transmitted the first telegraphic message: "What hath God wrought!"

Navajos (NAV-uh-hohz, NAH-vuh-hohz)   A tribe of NATIVE AMERICANS, the most numerous in the United States. The Navajos have reservations in the Southwest.

🕭 The Navajos were forced to move by United States troops under Kit CARSON in 1864. They call the march, on which many died, the Long Walk.

❧ Today, they are known for their houses, called hogans, made of logs and earth; for their work as ranchers and shepherds; and for their skill in weaving distinctive blankets and fashioning turquoise and silver jewelry.

New Amsterdam   A city founded by Dutch settlers in the seventeenth century on the present site of NEW YORK CITY.

❧ An early governor of the Dutch colony surrounding New Amsterdam bought MANHATTAN Island, the present center of New York City, from the NATIVE AMERICANS for twenty-four dollars' worth of jewelry.

Northwest Ordinance   A law passed in 1787 to regulate the settlement of the Northwest Territory, which eventually was divided into several states of the MIDDLE WEST. The United States was governed under the ARTICLES OF CONFEDERATION at the time. The Northwest Ordinance organized the territory into townships of thirty-six square miles each, and provided for self-government and religious toleration in the territory. Slavery was prohibited.

Northwest Passage   A sea route from the ATLANTIC OCEAN to the PACIFIC OCEAN through northwestern America, often sought by early explorers. There is an actual Northwest Passage, but it requires sailing through far northern waters that are icebound much of the year.

nullification   The doctrine that states can set aside federal laws. Urged in the late 1820s by John C. CALHOUN, nullification precipitated a crisis between Calhoun and President Andrew JACKSON. The doctrine was foreshadowed by the KENTUCKY RESOLUTION. (*See* VIRGINIA AND KENTUCKY RESOLUTIONS.)

One if by land, and two if by sea   The words used by Henry Wadsworth LONGFELLOW in his poem "Paul REVERE's Ride" to describe the signal used to guide the "midnight ride of Paul Revere" at the start of the REVOLUTIONARY WAR. Revere had ordered two lanterns to be placed in a BOSTON CHURCH tower to warn his confederates that the British were on the move. Longfellow embellished the story a little.

Oregon Trail   The route over which settlers traveled to OREGON in the 1840s and 1850s; trails branched off from it toward UTAH and CALIFORNIA. The Oregon Trail passed through what is now MISSOURI, KANSAS, NEBRASKA, WYOMING, and IDAHO.

Paine, Thomas   A patriot and author in the REVOLUTIONARY WAR, whose pamphlets, such as *COMMON SENSE* and the *AMERICAN CRISIS* series, urged American independence. He took part in the FRENCH REVOLUTION, and wrote *The Rights of Man* to defend it against the criticisms of Edmund BURKE. Paine also wrote *The Age of Reason*, upholding DEISM.

Penn, William   A colonist of the late seventeenth and early eighteenth centuries; the founder of PENNSYLVANIA. Penn, the son of a British admiral, became a QUAKER as a young man. The British government repaid a debt to Penn by giving him title to what is now Pennsylvania, where he established a colony with broad religious toleration. Many Quakers who were persecuted in ENGLAND settled in Pennsylvania. Penn was known for his friendly relations with the NATIVE AMERICAN tribes in his colony.

Pennsylvania Dutch   The German and Swiss settlers of PENNSYLVANIA in the seventeenth and eighteenth centuries, and their descendants. "Dutch" is a version of the German *Deutsch*, meaning "German." The Pennsylvania Dutch are known for their tidy farms and their distinctive crafts and customs. A considerable number of them belong to strict religious denominations, such as the AMISH.

Pilgrims   A group of English PURITANS, persecuted in their own country, who emigrated to America. The first group arrived on the *MAYFLOWER* in 1620. They landed near PLYMOUTH ROCK, in what is now MASSACHUSETTS, and established the PLYMOUTH COLONY, with the MAYFLOWER COMPACT as their CONSTITUTION. William Bradford and Miles Standish were noted leaders of the colony.

Plymouth Colony   The colony established in what is now eastern MASSACHUSETTS by the PILGRIMS in 1620.

Plymouth Rock   The rock, in what is now Plymouth, MASSACHUSETTS, near which the *MAYFLOWER*, carrying the PILGRIMS, landed in 1620.

Pocahontas (poh-kuh-HON-tuhs)   A NATIVE AMERICAN princess of the seventeenth century who befriended Captain John SMITH of VIRGINIA. She is said to have thrown herself upon him to prevent his execution by her father, Powhatan. She later married one of the Virginian settlers and traveled to ENGLAND with him.

Polk, James K. A political leader of the nineteenth century; Polk, a DEMOCRAT, was president from 1845 to 1849. An ardent believer in MANIFEST DESTINY, he led the United States into the MEXICAN WAR. In his presidency, the United States acquired TEXAS and CALIFORNIA and large territories in between.

Pony Express A system of mail service by relays of riders on horses, established in 1860 between MISSOURI and CALIFORNIA, through the ROCKY MOUNTAINS. It operated for only a year and a half, until a telegraph line eliminated the need for it.

❦ An early advertisement for Pony Express riders is well known: "Wanted: Young, skinny, wiry fellows not over eighteen. Must be expert riders, willing to risk death daily. Orphans preferred." ❦ BUFFALO BILL Cody and Wild Bill HICKOK were Pony Express riders in their youth.

Preamble to the Constitution (PREE-am-buhl, pree-AM-buhl) A statement attached to the beginning of the CONSTITUTION by the CONSTITUTIONAL CONVENTION, declaring the purpose of the document. It reads:

We, the people of the United States, in order to form a more perfect union, establish justice, insure domestic tranquillity, provide for the common defense, promote the general welfare, and secure the blessings of liberty to ourselves and our posterity, do ordain and establish this Constitution for the United States of America.

Pueblos (PWEB-lohz) Native American people, now found in ARIZONA and NEW MEXICO, whose distant ancestors often lived in multilevel dwellings on the sheer side of canyons. Some of these dwellings, which resembled apartment houses, can be seen in Mesa Verde National Park in COLORADO. The Spanish explorers discovered these people in the sixteenth century living in villages and named both the villages and the people "pueblos" (Spanish for town).

Puritans *See under* "WORLD HISTORY SINCE 1550"; *see also* PILGRIMS.

Remember the Alamo (AL-uh-moh) A battle cry in the Texans' struggle for independence from MEXICO, later used by Americans in the MEXICAN WAR. It recalled the desperate fight of the Texan defenders in the ALAMO, a besieged fort, where they died to the last man.

Republican party A political party that began in 1854 and is today one of the two major political parties in the United States. Originally, it was composed mainly of northerners from both major parties of the time, the DEMOCRATS and the WHIGS, with some former KNOW-NOTHINGS as well. The first Republicans were united by their opposition to the expansion of slavery. Their first winning presidential candidate was Abraham LINCOLN in 1860.

PAUL REVERE. *Paul Revere warning of the impending attack by the British.*

Revere, Paul A hero of the REVOLUTIONARY WAR. On the night before the Battle of LEXINGTON AND CONCORD in 1775, Revere, a silversmith by trade, rode across the MASSACHUSETTS countryside warning the other colonists that British troops were moving toward them to seize military supplies and arrest revolutionaries. Revere got his information about the British through signal lights placed in a church tower by a friend (*see* "ONE IF BY LAND, AND TWO IF BY SEA"). Those whom he warned were ready to fight the British the next day.

❦ Henry Wadsworth LONGFELLOW told the story of the "midnight ride," though not with complete accuracy, in his poem "PAUL REVERE'S RIDE."

Revolutionary War The war for American independence from Britain. The fighting began with the Battle of LEXINGTON AND CONCORD in 1775, and lasted through the Battle of YORKTOWN in 1781. General George WASHINGTON commanded the American forces, assisted by Ethan Allen, Benedict ARNOLD, Horatio Gates, John Paul JONES, and others. The leaders of the British included Charles CORNWALLIS, John Burgoyne, Thomas Gage, and William Howe, among others. The American cause was greatly aided by French ships and troops, and by the presence of the French nobleman and soldier the Marquis de LAFAYETTE. The Treaty of PARIS in 1783 officially ended the war. (*See* BUNKER HILL, BATTLE OF, *and* SARATOGA, BATTLE OF.)

Ross, Betsy A seamstress of the late eighteenth and early nineteenth centuries who made flags in PHILA-DELPHIA during the REVOLUTIONARY WAR. A widely accepted, but undocumented, story holds that she sewed the first American flag in the form of the STARS AND STRIPES.

Sacajawea (sak-uh-juh-WEE-uh) A young Native American woman who guided Meriwether Lewis and William Clark on their expedition to explore terri-tory gained through the LOUISIANA PURCHASE. (*See* LEWIS AND CLARK EXPEDITION.)

Salem witch trials Trials held in Salem, MASSA-CHUSETTS, in 1692 that led to the execution of twenty people for allegedly practicing WITCHCRAFT. The trials are noted for the hysterical atmosphere in which they were conducted; many townspeople were widely suspected of witchcraft on flimsy evidence.

🍂 When people are quick to accuse one another of serious misdeeds on inadequate evidence, the situation is often compared to the Salem witch trials. 🍂 A "witch hunt" is a political campaign launched under the pretext of investigating activities consid-ered subversive by the state.

Saratoga, Battle of A major battle of the REVO-LUTIONARY WAR, fought in 1777 in northern NEW YORK state. Benedict ARNOLD, who had not yet turned traitor, was a leader of the American offen-sive, which forced the surrender of British troops un-der General John Burgoyne.

🍂 The Battle of Saratoga is often called the turning point of the war, because it increased the confidence of the French government in the American forces; FRANCE began sending aid the next year.

secession The withdrawal from the United States of eleven southern states in 1860 and 1861. The seced-ing states formed a government, the CONFEDERACY, in early 1861. Hostilities against the remaining United States, the UNION, began in April 1861 (*see* SUMTER, FORT), and the CIVIL WAR followed.

Seminoles (SEM-uh-nohlz) A tribe of NATIVE AMERICANS who inhabited FLORIDA in the early nineteenth century. After fighting a war against the United States to keep their land, they were forcibly removed to reservations west of the MISSISSIPPI RIVER in the 1840s.

Seneca Falls Convention The first convention in America devoted to women's rights. It met in Seneca Falls, NEW YORK, in 1848, and passed several reso-lutions, including a demand that women be given the right to vote.

1776 The year in which the DECLARATION OF IN-DEPENDENCE was written.

🍂 In the United States, the number itself suggests patriotism. (*See* THE SPIRIT OF '76.)

Shawnees (shaw-NEEZ) A tribe of NATIVE AMERI-CANS who inhabited OHIO, INDIANA, and other parts of the MIDDLE WEST during the early nineteenth cen-tury. The most famous Shawnee leader was TECUM-SEH, who joined with the British against the Ameri-cans during the WAR OF 1812.

Sherman, William Tecumseh (tuh-KUM-suh) A general of the nineteenth century; one of the leading generals in the UNION army in the CIVIL WAR (*see* SHERMAN'S MARCH TO THE SEA). He is known for saying "WAR IS HELL."

Sherman's march to the sea A movement of the UNION army troops of General William Tecumseh SHERMAN from ATLANTA, GEORGIA, to the Georgia seacoast, with the object of destroying CONFEDERATE supplies. The march began after Sherman captured, evacuated, and burned Atlanta in the fall of 1864. His men, numbering about 60,000, destroyed rail-roads, factories, cotton gins, houses, livestock, and anything else that might be useful to the South in the war.

🍂 Northerners celebrated Sherman's march with the song "Marching through Georgia." Southerners remembered it bitterly. 🍂 Some of the action in the NOVEL GONE WITH THE WIND, which was made into a popular film, takes place during Sherman's march.

shot heard round the world A PHRASE from a poem by Ralph Waldo EMERSON about the Battle of LEXINGTON AND CONCORD. Emerson's words read, "Here once the embattled farmers stood / And fired the shot heard round the world." In other words, the determination of the colonists at Concord led to the establishment of a new nation on earth, and encouraged worldwide movements toward DEMOCRACY.

slave trade   The transportation of slaves from AFRICA to NORTH and SOUTH AMERICA between the seventeenth and nineteenth centuries. CONGRESS banned the importing of slaves into the United States in 1808.

Smith, Captain John   An English adventurer and explorer of the late sixteenth and early seventeenth centuries. Smith was one of the original settlers of JAMESTOWN in 1607. He was taken prisoner by the braves of the NATIVE AMERICAN chief Powhatan. By his own account, he was rescued through the intervention of POCAHONTAS, Powhatan's daughter.

Stamp Act   A law passed by the British government in 1765 that required the payment of a tax to BRITAIN on a great variety of papers and documents, including newspapers, that were produced in the American colonies. Special stamps were to be attached to the papers and documents as proof that the tax had been paid. The stamp tax was the first direct tax ever levied by Britain on the Americans, who rioted in opposition. The American colonists petitioned King GEORGE III to repeal the act, which he did in 1766.

Sumter, Fort   A fort at the entrance to the harbor of CHARLESTON, SOUTH CAROLINA; the location of the first military engagement of the CIVIL WAR. In April 1861, several months after South Carolina had declared its SECESSION from the United States, the militia of South Carolina demanded that the commander of the fort surrender. He refused, and the South Carolinians fired on the fort. There were no deaths in the incident. In response, however, President Abraham LINCOLN called for volunteers to put down the "insurrection," and the American CIVIL WAR began.

Taxation without representation is tyranny   A slogan of the REVOLUTIONARY WAR and the years before. The colonists were not allowed to choose representatives to PARLIAMENT in LONDON, which passed the laws under which they were taxed. To be taxed only with the consent of one's representatives in Parliament was a particularly cherished right of the people under English law, a right dating back to MAGNA CARTA in the thirteenth century. Each addi-

tional tax caused fresh resentment among the colonists. Taxation without representation is one of the principal offenses of BRITAIN listed in the DECLARATION OF INDEPENDENCE.

Tecumseh (tuh-KUM-suh)   A SHAWNEE chief of the late eighteenth and early nineteenth centuries. He took arms against American settlers moving into the MIDDLE WEST, and supported the British in the WAR OF 1812, in which he was killed.

These are the times that try men's souls   The opening words of the series of pamphlets *THE AMERICAN CRISIS*, by Thomas PAINE, begun in late 1776. Paine, seeking to stir up revolutionary spirit in the colonies, continues, "The summer soldier and the sunshine patriot may, in this crisis, shrink from the service of his country; but he that stands it now deserves the love and thanks of man and woman."

&. Paine's words are still quoted occasionally in troublesome situations.

thirteen colonies   The colonies that composed the original United States in 1776: CONNECTICUT, DELAWARE, GEORGIA, MARYLAND, MASSACHUSETTS, NEW HAMPSHIRE, NEW JERSEY, NEW YORK, NORTH CAROLINA, PENNSYLVANIA, RHODE ISLAND, SOUTH CAROLINA, and VIRGINIA.

Tippecanoe and Tyler too (tip-ee-kuh-NOOH)   A slogan from the presidential election of 1840. "Tippecanoe" was the WHIG presidential candidate William Henry Harrison, a hero of the Battle of Tippecanoe in 1811. John Tyler was the vice presidential candidate.

Tocqueville, Alexis de (TOHK-vil, tawk-VEEL)   A French historian of the nineteenth century. His book *Democracy in America* was the first impartial study of institutions in the new nation.

Trail of Tears   The route along which the United States government forced several tribes of NATIVE AMERICANS, including the CHEROKEES, SEMINOLES, Chickasaws, Choctaws, and Creeks, to migrate to reservations west of the MISSISSIPPI RIVER in the 1820s, 1830s, and 1840s. Those on the march suffered greatly from disease and mistreatment.

Truth, Sojourner   An ABOLITIONIST of the nineteenth century, and an escaped slave. She was famous as a speaker against slavery.

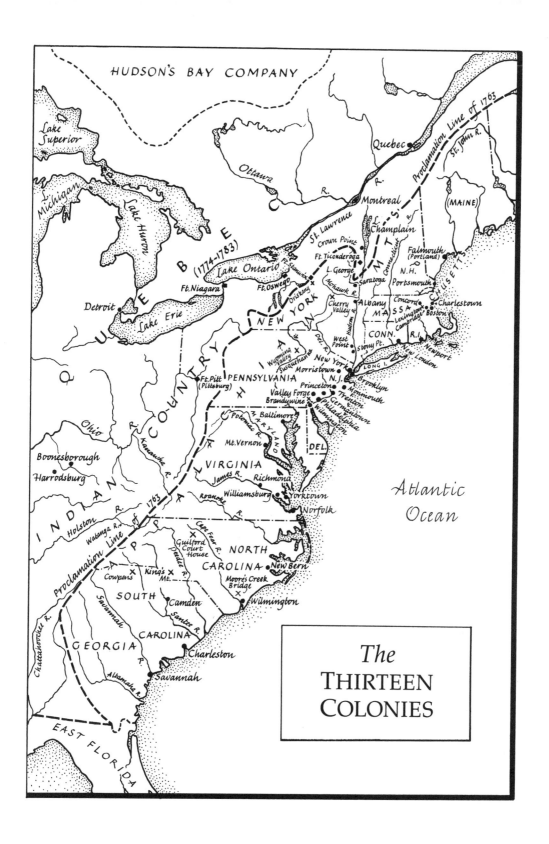

The
THIRTEEN
COLONIES

HARRIET TUBMAN

Tubman, Harriet   An ABOLITIONIST of the nineteenth century. An escaped slave herself, she helped hundreds of former slaves to freedom by way of the UNDERGROUND RAILROAD. During the CIVIL WAR, she served as a nurse, scout, and spy for the UNION army.

Turner, Nat   A black slave of the early nineteenth century, who led the only effective and sustained slave revolt in American history. He and his supporters killed several dozen white people in VIRGINIA before he was captured; he was hanged in 1831. Although Turner's rebellion led to a severe reaction among the slaveholders, it demonstrated that not all slaves were willing to accept their condition passively.

Underground Railroad   A network of houses and other places that ABOLITIONISTS used to help slaves escape to freedom in the northern states or in CANADA before the CIVIL WAR. The escaped slaves traveled from one "station" of the railroad to the next under cover of night. Harriet TUBMAN was the most prominent "conductor" on the Underground Railroad.

Union   The United States; especially the northern states during the CIVIL WAR, which remained with the original United States government. (*Compare* CONFEDERACY.)

Valley Forge   A valley in eastern PENNSYLVANIA that served as quarters for the American army in one winter (1777–1778) of the REVOLUTIONARY WAR. George WASHINGTON, who was commanding the army, had been forced to leave PHILADELPHIA, and his troops suffered from the cold and from lack of supplies. Though many deserted, Washington managed to maintain the morale of the rest. He was aided by Baron von Steuben, a German officer on his staff, who trained the men in the soldiering practices of EUROPE.

Virginia dynasty   A phrase from the nineteenth century; it points out that four of the first five presidents (George WASHINGTON, Thomas JEFFERSON, James MADISON, and James MONROE) were from VIRGINIA.

Virginia and Kentucky Resolutions   Acts passed by two state legislatures in the 1790s; they affirmed STATES' RIGHTS in response to the federal ALIEN AND SEDITION ACTS. James MADISON wrote the Virginia Resolution, and Thomas JEFFERSON wrote the Kentucky Resolution. The Kentucky Resolution declared that NULLIFICATION was an appropriate course of action for a state in the face of a dangerous increase in the strength of the federal government.

wampum   (WAHM-puhm)   Beads made from polished shells that some NATIVE AMERICANS once used as money and jewelry.

War of 1812   A war between BRITAIN and the United States, fought between 1812 and 1815. The War of 1812 has also been called the second American war for independence. It began over alleged British violations of American shipping rights, such as the impressment of seamen — the forcing of American merchant sailors to serve on British ships. American soldiers attacked CANADA unsuccessfully in the war, and the British retaliated by burning the WHITE HOUSE and other buildings in WASHINGTON, D.C. American warships frequently prevailed over British vessels (*see* "WE HAVE MET THE ENEMY, AND THEY

ARE OURS"). The greatest victory for the Americans came in the Battle of NEW ORLEANS, in which Andrew JACKSON was the commanding general — a battle fought, ironically, two weeks after the peace treaty ending the war had been signed, but before the armies could be informed. (*See also* "STAR-SPANGLED BANNER, THE.")

Washington, George   The first president of the United States, and the commanding general of the victorious American army in the REVOLUTIONARY WAR. The best known of the FOUNDING FATHERS, Washington is called the FATHER OF HIS COUNTRY. He was born in 1732 in VIRGINIA, and showed early talent as a surveyor and farmer. He served as an army officer in the FRENCH AND INDIAN WAR, as a member of the Virginia legislature, and as a delegate to the CONTINENTAL CONGRESS. In the summer of 1775, a few weeks after the outbreak of the REVOLUTIONARY WAR, he took command of the American army. He and his men won early victories over the British in NEW JERSEY at Trenton and Princeton, despite a great lack of training and supplies. Washington is particularly remembered for keeping up morale during the hardships of winter encampment at VALLEY FORGE. His victory at the Battle of YORKTOWN ended the fighting. Washington presided at the CONSTITU-

TIONAL CONVENTION of 1787, and in 1789 was unanimously elected the first president under the new CONSTITUTION. As president, he pursued a careful foreign policy, endorsed the financial program of Alexander HAMILTON, and put down the WHISKY REBELLION. Refusing to seek a third term as president, he retired from the office in 1797, issuing a FAREWELL ADDRESS that advised against party politics at home and against permanent alliances abroad. After he died in 1799, he was praised by CONGRESS as "FIRST IN WAR, FIRST IN PEACE, AND FIRST IN THE HEARTS OF HIS COUNTRYMEN."

&. The qualities of Washington that have stood out over the centuries are his courage, his impartiality, and his good judgment. &. The capital of the United States is named after George Washington, as is a northwestern state. Over thirty states have a Washington County, and his name has been given to numerous mountains, lakes, streets, and buildings. &. The painting of *WASHINGTON CROSSING THE DELAWARE*, which shows him leading his army toward a surprise attack on the British, is well known. His portrait is on the one-dollar bill, and his profile appears on the twenty-five-cent piece. &. Washington is the subject of many legends, which often celebrate his honesty (such as the story of WASHINGTON AND THE CHERRY TREE) or his strength (such as the tale that he

GEORGE WASHINGTON. Washington Crossing the Delaware, *by Emanuel Leutze.*

threw a rock, or a silver dollar, across the Rappahannock River).

Webster, Daniel A WHIG political leader and diplomat of the nineteenth century. Webster is remembered for his speaking ability and for his service as a SENATOR from MASSACHUSETTS through most of the 1830s and 1840s. Webster defended national unity in the SENATE against such advocates of STATES' RIGHTS as John C. CALHOUN. In one debate, he spoke the famous words "Liberty *and* Union, now and forever, one and inseparable!" He opposed the MEXICAN WAR and the admission of TEXAS as a slave state, but supported the COMPROMISE OF 1850, which permitted slavery in some western territories. A member of the WHIG PARTY, he ran for president three times, but was never nominated.

Webster, Noah An educator and author of the late eighteenth and early nineteenth centuries, best known for his *American Dictionary of the English Language* and *Blue-Backed Speller*. He worked for the establishment of a distinctive American version of the English language; for example, he insisted on such spellings as *wagon*, *center*, and *honor* in place of the standard British *waggon*, *centre*, and *honour*.

   A number of widely used dictionaries, of varying scope and quality, still bear Webster's name.

We have met the enemy, and they are ours A message sent from the naval Battle of LAKE ERIE in the WAR OF 1812, announcing a victory for the United States. The naval commander, Oliver Hazard Perry, addressed the words to the American land armies.

Whig party An American political party formed in the 1830s to oppose President Andrew JACKSON and the DEMOCRATS. Whigs stood for PROTECTIVE TARIFFS, national banking, and federal aid for internal improvements. SENATORS Henry CLAY and Daniel WEBSTER were prominent Whigs, as were four presidents (William Henry Harrison, John Tyler, Zachary Taylor, and Millard Fillmore). The party fell into disunity in the 1850s over slavery; some former Whigs, including Abraham LINCOLN, then joined the new REPUBLICAN PARTY.

Whisky Rebellion An insurrection that broke out in the early 1790s in western PENNSYLVANIA. Hundreds of residents took arms against federal officials charged with collecting a tax on liquor distilled at home. Federal troops then put the rebellion down. Occurring only a few years after the adoption of the CONSTITUTION, the Whisky Rebellion was an important test of the power of the new federal government to enforce its laws.

Williams, Roger A PURITAN religious leader of the seventeenth century, born in ENGLAND. After he was expelled from MASSACHUSETTS for his tolerant religious views, Williams founded the colony of RHODE ISLAND as a place of complete religious toleration.

Winthrop, John A PURITAN political leader of the seventeenth century, born in ENGLAND. Winthrop was sent to America as the first governor of MASSACHUSETTS. He compared the colony to "a city upon a hill," suggesting that it would be a model for all nations.

Yorktown, Battle of The last battle of the REVOLUTIONARY WAR, fought in 1781 near the seacoast of VIRGINIA. There the British general Lord CORNWALLIS surrendered his army to General George WASHINGTON.

American History since 1865

The period from 1865 to 1877 is known as RECONSTRUCTION. Victorious in the CIVIL WAR, the North attempted, often hesitantly, to "reconstruct" the South by securing CIVIL RIGHTS for blacks freed from slavery. The Thirteenth, FOURTEENTH, and Fifteenth AMENDMENTS sought to secure those basic rights.

The period from 1865 to 1900 was marked by dramatic industrial growth, but the expansion of industry did not benefit everyone. The newly rich ROBBER BARONS amassed enormous wealth, which they often displayed crassly. Particularly in the late 1860s and 1870s, corruption riddled American politics. Meanwhile, many factory workers suffered in misery, and farmers bitterly resented their domination by the railroads and by eastern financiers. The resentments of farmers exploded in the POPULIST PARTY of the 1890s.

Populism soon went into eclipse, but new efforts to bring social justice and economic order to the United States took shape in the PROGRESSIVE MOVEMENT. Progressives attacked such abuses as child labor and corporate pillaging, and they worked successfully for women's SUFFRAGE, which was gained with the adoption of the Nineteenth Amendment in 1920. Progressives and others also supported PROHIBITION, which became law after the adoption in 1919 of the Eighteenth Amendment.

Progressivism coincided with the emergence of the United States as a world power. After its victory over SPAIN in the SPANISH-AMERICAN WAR (1898), the United States steadily raised its profile in international affairs during the presidencies of Theodore ROOSEVELT (1901–1909) and Woodrow WILSON (1913–1921). Under Wilson, the United States entered WORLD WAR I in 1917, and played a key role at the VERSAILLES peace conference after the war.

Postwar prosperity came to a shuddering halt with the onset of the Great DEPRESSION in 1929. Elected president in 1932, Franklin D. ROOSEVELT inspired a series of government programs known as the NEW DEAL. In foreign policy, Roosevelt opposed the aggression of NAZI GERMANY. With the Japanese attack on PEARL HARBOR in December 1941, the United States formally entered WORLD WAR II.

After the conclusion of the war in 1945, disagreements between the United States and the SOVIET UNION led to the COLD WAR. In 1950, the United States sent troops to help SOUTH KOREA repel COMMUNIST invaders from NORTH KOREA. On the domestic front, Republican President Dwight EISENHOWER'S two terms (1953–1961) saw the end of the Korean War, a continuation of the cold war, substantial prosperity, and the rise and fall of Senator Joseph R. McCARTHY. In the election of 1960, the Democrats, led by John F. KENNEDY, regained the presidency. Kennedy's NEW FRONTIER was cut short by his assassination in 1963. Vice President Lyndon B. JOHNSON assumed the presidency, and launched a series of programs called the GREAT SOCIETY. Conflict over civil rights and American entanglement in VIETNAM made the late 1960s a time of extraordinary division and strife.

President Richard M. NIXON gradually withdrew American support from the government of SOUTH VIETNAM, which collapsed in 1975. The WATERGATE scandal forced Nixon's resignation in 1974. Gerald FORD served out the remainder of Nixon's second term as president, but lost the election of 1976 to Jimmy CARTER. Battered by STAGFLATION and unable to secure the release of American hostages held by IRAN, Carter lost his bid for reelection in 1980 to Ronald REAGAN. Reagan's two terms as president were marked by opposition to government regulation of the economy, tax cuts, the reduction of many domestic programs, a major increase in military spending, and a huge jump in the NATIONAL DEBT. Reagan's vice president, George BUSH, was elected president in 1988. Bush's first term was marked by the COLLAPSE OF COMMUNISM in eastern EUROPE and the SOVIET UNION, victory in the PERSIAN GULF WAR, and economic RECESSION at home. In 1992 Bush was defeated for reelection by Governor William CLINTON of ARKANSAS.

— J. F. K.

Aaron, Henry (Hank) (AIR-uhn) A baseball player of the twentieth century; he hit a record 755 home runs in his major league career, which ran from 1954 to 1976. The previous record holder was Babe RUTH, who hit 714.

Addams, Jane A social reformer of the late nineteenth and early twentieth centuries. She founded a SETTLEMENT HOUSE, Hull House, in Chicago, and also worked for peace and for women's rights. In 1931, she won the NOBEL PRIZE for peace.

Agnew, Spiro (SPEER-oh AG-nooh, AG-nyooh) A political leader of the twentieth century. Agnew was elected vice president in 1968 and 1972 as the running mate of Richard NIXON. He attacked opponents of the involvement of the United States in the VIETNAM WAR, calling them "an effete corps of impudent snobs" and "nattering nabobs of negativism." In 1973 Agnew pleaded NOLO CONTENDERE to charges of income tax evasion, and resigned from office.

Ali, Muhammad (ah-LEE) An African-American boxer of the twentieth century, who was world champion in the heavyweight class for several years between 1964 and 1979. He was known in his boxing career for his flamboyant personality and aggressive self-promotion, as well as for his superior boxing ability and style. His boxing strategy, he said, was to "float like a butterfly and sting like a bee." A BLACK MUSLIM, Ali was originally named Cassius Clay. After he refused for reasons of conscience to serve in the armed forces in the 1960s, several boxing associations revoked his title as world champion, but he regained it later.

All the news that's fit to print The motto of the *New York Times*.

Anthony, Susan B. A reformer of the nineteenth and early twentieth centuries, known especially for her advocacy of women's SUFFRAGE. She was also active in the ABOLITIONIST movement before the CIVIL WAR.

SUSAN B. ANTHONY

Apaches (uh-PACH-eez) A tribe of NATIVE AMERICANS who live in the southwestern United States. GERONIMO was an Apache.

Ask not what your country can do for you; ask what you can do for your country Words from the inaugural address of President John F. KENNEDY, delivered in 1961.

Bakke **decision** (BAK-ee) An important ruling on AFFIRMATIVE ACTION given by the SUPREME COURT in 1978. Allan Bakke, a white man, was denied admission to a medical school that had admitted black candidates with weaker academic credentials. Bakke contended that he was a victim of racial discrimination. The Court ruled that Bakke had been illegally denied admission to the medical school, but also that medical schools were entitled to consider race as a factor in admissions. The Court thus upheld the general principle of affirmative action.

Barton, Clara A reformer and nurse of the nineteenth century, who founded the American RED CROSS in the 1880s. She had organized nursing care for UNION soldiers during the CIVIL WAR.

Bay of Pigs The location of a failed attempt by Cuban exiles to invade CUBA in 1961. The invaders, numbering about 1400, had left after the CUBAN REVOLUTION, and returned to overthrow the new Cuban leader, Fidel CASTRO; they were trained and equipped by the United States CENTRAL INTELLIGENCE AGENCY. The operation was a disaster for the invaders, most of whom were killed or taken prisoner. The Bay of Pigs incident is generally considered the most humiliating episode in the presidency of John F. KENNEDY, who had approved the invasion.

Bethune, Mary McLeod (muh-KLOWD; buh-THYOOHN, buh-THOOHN) African-American educator and CIVIL RIGHTS leader who in 1904 founded a school for girls that later became part of Bethune-Cookman College and who in the late 1930s and early 1940s held an administrative position under the NEW DEAL. In 1949 she founded the National Council of Negro Women, which opposed the POLL TAX and racial discrimination and which promoted the teaching of black history in the public schools.

big stick diplomacy International negotiations backed by the threat of force. The PHRASE comes from a PROVERB quoted by Theodore ROOSEVELT, who said that the United States should "SPEAK SOFTLY AND CARRY A BIG STICK."

Big Ten A group of prominent midwestern universities known for high academic standards and keen athletic competition. Nine of the ten are state universities: the universities of Illinois (at Urbana), Iowa, Michigan, Minnesota, and Wisconsin (at Madison); Michigan State University; Ohio State University; Indiana University; and Purdue University. Northwestern University is the sole private school.

Billy the Kid An outlaw of the late nineteenth century in NEW MEXICO, who claimed to have killed over twenty people before he was gunned down himself at age twenty-one. His real name is uncertain.

Black, Hugo A judge of the twentieth century; he served on the SUPREME COURT from 1937 to 1971. Black was a strong defender of the CIVIL LIBERTIES of the individual against intrusion by the state.

Black Muslims A RADICAL movement for BLACK POWER that reached a peak of influence in the United States during the 1960s, under the leadership of MALCOLM X. Members rejected CHRISTIANITY as a religion of white people and embraced ISLAM. Like many other Black Muslims who took new names, the boxer Cassius Clay changed his name to MUHAMMAD ALI to join the movement.

Black Panthers A militant BLACK POWER organization founded in the 1960s by Huey Newton and others. Newton proclaimed: "We make the statement, quoting from Chairman Mao, that Political Power comes through the Barrel of a Gun."

Black Power A movement that grew out of the CIVIL RIGHTS MOVEMENT in the 1960s. Black Power calls for independent development of political and social institutions for black people, and emphasizes pride in black CULTURE. In varying degrees Black Power advocates called for the exclusion of whites from black civil rights organizations. Stokely Carmichael, one of the leaders of the movement and the head of the Student Nonviolent Coordinating Committee (SNCC), stated: "I am not going to beg the white man for anything I deserve. I'm going to take it."

Bonnie and Clyde Two outlaws, Bonnie Parker and Clyde Barrow, who went on a two-year spree of murder and bank robbery in the 1930s in the Southwest before being killed in an ambush.

Borden, Lizzie A woman charged with the ax murder of her father and stepmother in the 1890s in Fall

River, MASSACHUSETTS. A jury found her not guilty. The crime has never been solved.

Boss Tweed   *See* TWEED, WILLIAM MARCY.

Bradley, Omar   A general of the twentieth century. Bradley commanded the United States ground forces in the liberation of FRANCE and the invasion of GERMANY in WORLD WAR II.

brain trust   A group of INTELLECTUALS and planners who act as advisers, especially to a government. The PHRASE is particularly associated with the presidency of Franklin D. ROOSEVELT.

Brandeis, Louis D. (BRAN-deyes, BRAN-deyez)   A judge of the twentieth century, he served on the SUPREME COURT from 1916 to 1939. Brandeis believed that economic and social facts had to take precedence over legal theory. He was the first Jew to serve on the Supreme Court.

***Brown* decision**   *See* BROWN VERSUS BOARD OF EDUCATION.

Brown versus Board of Education (***Brown*** decision)   A case regarding school desegregation, decided by the SUPREME COURT in 1954. The Court ruled that SEGREGATION in public schools is prohibited by the CONSTITUTION. The decision ruled out "SEPARATE BUT EQUAL" educational systems for blacks and whites, which many localities said they were providing. The Court departed from tradition by using arguments from SOCIOLOGY to show that separate educational systems were unequal by their very nature.

• The *Brown* decision had an enormous effect on education throughout the country, not only in places where segregated schools were established by law, but also on school systems in which there was DE FACTO SEGREGATION. The federal government, in the years that followed, required many city school systems to readjust school boundaries so that individual schools would have a mixed racial population.

Bryan, William Jennings   A political leader of the late nineteenth and early twentieth centuries. Bryan, claiming to be the candidate of the ordinary American, lost three presidential elections as the nominee of the DEMOCRATIC PARTY, although he gathered substantial votes in the South and West. At the 1896 Democratic national convention, he delivered the much-remembered "CROSS OF GOLD" SPEECH in fa-

vor of unlimited coinage of silver and against the GOLD STANDARD. A FUNDAMENTALIST in religion, Bryan opposed the teaching of the THEORY of EVOLUTION in schools, and assisted in the prosecution at the SCOPES TRIAL.

Buffalo Bill   William F. Cody, a frontier settler, scout, and soldier of the nineteenth century. He was involved in several military actions against NATIVE AMERICANS, and later turned to entertainment, founding a celebrated "Wild West Show." (*See also under "Fine Arts."*)

Bull, Sitting   *See* SITTING BULL.

Bunche, Ralph (BUNCH)   African-American diplomat and prominent official of the UNITED NATIONS, Bunche won the NOBEL PRIZE for Peace in 1950 for negotiating an armistice between Israelis and Arabs.

Bush, George H.   American political leader of the late twentieth century; elected president as a REPUBLICAN in 1988 after he pledged: "Read my lips; no new taxes." Once in office, however, he reached an agreement with CONGRESS to raise taxes. Despite this, Bush's popularity rose in the wake of American success in the PERSIAN GULF WAR, but then declined as the U.S. slipped into economic RECESSION in 1991. He was defeated for reelection in 1992 by Governor William CLINTON of ARKANSAS.

business of America is business, The   A statement made by President Calvin COOLIDGE in the 1920s.

• Coolidge's words are often mentioned as typical of the overconfidence in the American economy that preceded the Great DEPRESSION.

Byrd, Richard E.   An explorer of the twentieth century; he was navigator on the first flight over the NORTH POLE. He also made one of the first flights over the SOUTH POLE, and went on several extended expeditions to ANTARCTICA.

Calamity Jane   A frontier settler of the late nineteenth and early twentieth centuries, who boasted of her dangerous exploits as a PONY EXPRESS rider and scout. She amazed people with her marksmanship.

Capone, Al (kuh-POHN)   A leader of organized crime in CHICAGO in the late 1920s, involved in gambling, the illegal sale of alcohol, and prostitution. He was sent to prison in the 1930s for income tax evasion.

carpetbaggers Northerners who went to the South after the CIVIL WAR to take part in RECONSTRUCTION governments, when persons who had supported the CONFEDERACY were not allowed to hold public office (*see* FOURTEENTH AMENDMENT). Some of them arrived, according to legend, carrying only one carpetbag, which symbolized their lack of permanent interest in the place they pretended to serve.

⇒ *Carpetbagger* is still a general term for nonresident politicians who exploit their districts.

Carter, Jimmy (James Earl) A political leader of the twentieth century; the president from 1977 to 1981. In 1976, Carter was a peanut farmer who had been a naval officer and the governor of GEORGIA; he stood outside the main power groups of the DEMOCRATIC PARTY. He gained the party's nomination, however, and defeated President Gerald FORD in the election of 1976. As president, Carter brought the heads of government of ISRAEL and EGYPT together to sign a historic peace treaty in 1979, reestablishing diplomatic relations between their two countries (*see* ARAB-ISRAELI CONFLICT). He responded to an invasion of AFGHANISTAN by the SOVIET UNION in 1979 by putting an EMBARGO on grain sales to the invader, and by keeping the United States out of the 1980 summer OLYMPIC GAMES, which were held in the Soviet Union. He also showed great concern for energy conservation. Many Americans found Carter's leadership too cautious, however, and blamed him for a lack of improvement in the economy. His most striking loss of popularity came when revolutionaries in IRAN stormed the United States embassy there in 1979 and held several dozen Americans as hostages for over a year (*see* KHOMEINI, AYATOLLAH RUHOLLAH). The Iranians agreed to release the hostages only in the last minutes of Carter's presidency in early 1981, after Carter had lost the election of 1980 to Ronald REAGAN.

⇒ Personally, Carter was known for his informality and his wide, toothy smile.

Carver, George Washington An African-American scientist and agricultural innovator of the late nineteenth and early twentieth centuries. Carver aided the economy of the South by developing hundreds of industrial uses for crops such as the peanut and the sweet potato.

⇒ Carver, who was born to slave parents, was the first black scientist to gain nationwide prominence.

Chappaquiddick incident (chap-uh-KWID-ik) An automobile accident in 1969 that greatly affected the career of SENATOR Edward (Ted) KENNEDY of MASSACHUSETTS. A woman on Kennedy's staff was drowned at Chappaquiddick Island, off the Massachusetts coast, after a car that Kennedy had been driving, and in which she had been riding, went off a bridge. Kennedy survived, but delayed informing the police, and has never provided a full explanation of the incident. Afterward, many voters lost confidence in Kennedy, who had been considered a strong possibility to be nominated by the DEMOCRATIC PARTY for president.

Chief Joseph Chief of OREGON's Nez Perce Indians who led his people in the 1870s on a desperate attempt to reach CANADA rather than submit to forcible settlement on a reservation. Forced to surrender to U.S. troops just south of the border, he reportedly stated: "Hear me my chiefs, I am tired: My heart is sick and sad. From where the sun now stands, I will fight no more."

child labor laws Laws passed over many decades, beginning in the 1830s, by state and federal governments, forbidding or restricting the employment of children and young teenagers, except at certain carefully specified jobs. Child labor was regularly condemned in the nineteenth century by reformers and authors (*see DAVID COPPERFIELD and OLIVER TWIST*), but many businesses insisted that the CONSTITUTION protected their liberty to hire workers of any age. In 1918, the SUPREME COURT agreed, declaring a federal child labor law unconstitutional. Eventually, in the late 1930s, the federal Fair Labor Standards Act was upheld by the Court. This law greatly restricts the employment of children under eighteen in manufacturing jobs.

Civil Rights Act of 1964 A federal law that authorized federal action against SEGREGATION in public accommodations, public facilities, and employment. The law was passed during a period of great strength for the CIVIL RIGHTS MOVEMENT, and President Lyndon JOHNSON persuaded many reluctant members of CONGRESS to support the law.

civil rights movement The national effort made by black people and their supporters in the 1950s and 1960s to eliminate SEGREGATION and gain equal rights. The first large episode in the movement was a boycott of the city buses in Montgomery, ALABAMA, touched off by the refusal of one black woman, Rosa PARKS, to give up her seat on a bus to a white person. A number of SIT-INS and similar demonstrations followed. A high point of the civil rights movement was a rally by hundreds of thousands in WASHINGTON, D.C., in 1963, at which a leader of the movement, Martin Luther KING, Jr., gave his "I HAVE A DREAM" speech. The federal CIVIL RIGHTS ACT OF 1964 authorized federal action against segregation in public accommodations, public facilities, and employment. The VOTING RIGHTS ACT OF 1965 was passed after large demonstrations in SELMA, Alabama, which drew some violent responses. The Fair Housing Act, prohibiting discrimination by race in housing, was passed in 1968.

After such legislative victories, the civil rights movement shifted emphasis toward education and changing the attitudes of white people. Some civil rights supporters turned toward militant movements (*see* BLACK POWER), and the late 1960s saw several riots over racial questions (*see* WATTS RIOTS). The *Bakke* DECISION OF 1978 guardedly endorsed AFFIRMATIVE ACTION.

Cleveland, Grover   A DEMOCRATIC PARTY political leader of the late nineteenth and early twentieth centuries who was president from 1885 to 1889 and again from 1893 to 1897 — the only president ever to serve nonconsecutive terms. Cleveland's presidencies were marked by his fight against corruption in the federal government, and by his efforts to solve national financial problems.

Clinton, William Jefferson (Bill)   American political leader of the late twentieth century. A DEMOCRAT, he handily defeated President George BUSH's bid for reelection in 1992. Clinton, a former RHODES SCHOLAR, had served as governor of ARKANSAS. Although harried by questions about his character during his presidential campaign, Clinton proved adept at reconciling the CONSERVATIVE and LIBERAL wings of the DEMOCRATIC PARTY and establishing himself as the candidate of change.

Cobb, Ty   A baseball player of the early twentieth century. Cobb long held the world record for runs batted in and stolen bases in a career in the major leagues. He still holds the records for number of runs scored and for lifetime batting average.

Cody, William F.   *See* BUFFALO BILL.

Congress on Racial Equality (CORE)   A leading organization in the CIVIL RIGHTS MOVEMENT. CORE launched the FREEDOM RIDERS, and came under the influence of the BLACK POWER PHILOSOPHY.

containment   A policy aimed at controlling the spread of COMMUNISM around the world, developed in the administration of President Harry TRUMAN. The formation of the NORTH ATLANTIC TREATY ORGANIZATION (NATO) in 1949 was an important step in the development of containment.

Coolidge, Calvin   A political leader of the early twentieth century. A REPUBLICAN, he rose to prominence as governor of MASSACHUSETTS when he broke a strike by policemen in BOSTON, saying, "There is no right to strike against the public safety by anybody, anywhere, any time." He was elected vice president under Warren HARDING, and became president in 1923 when Harding died. In 1924, he was elected on his own, but he declined to seek reelection in 1928; Herbert HOOVER succeeded him in 1929. Coolidge worked to restrain the growth of government, and especially to keep it from interfering with private enterprise; he once declared that "the BUSINESS OF AMERICA IS BUSINESS."

&. Coolidge was renowned for using few words; he announced his retirement from the presidency in one SENTENCE: "I do not choose to run for president in 1928."

CORE (KAWR)   *See* CONGRESS ON RACIAL EQUALITY.

Court packing   *See* ROOSEVELT'S COURT PACKING PLAN.

Crash of 1929, stock market   An enormous decrease in stock prices on the STOCK EXCHANGES of WALL STREET in late October 1929. This crash began the Great DEPRESSION.

Crazy Horse   A SIOUX chief of the nineteenth century. Crazy Horse was one of the leaders of the NATIVE AMERICAN forces at the Battle of the LITTLE BIGHORN in 1876.

Cross of Gold speech   An address by the presidential candidate William Jennings BRYAN to the national convention of the DEMOCRATIC PARTY in 1896. Bryan criticized the GOLD STANDARD, and advocated inflating the CURRENCY by the free coinage of silver, a measure popular among the DEBT-ridden farmers whom Bryan championed. "You shall not press down upon the brow of LABOR this crown of thorns," said Bryan; "You shall not crucify mankind upon a cross of gold." The speech stirred the convention, and Bryan was nominated for president.

Cuban missile crisis　A confrontation between the United States and the SOVIET UNION in 1962 over the presence of missile sites in CUBA; one of the "hottest" periods of the COLD WAR. The Soviet leader, Nikita KHRUSHCHEV, placed Soviet military missiles in Cuba, which had come under Soviet influence after the success of the CUBAN REVOLUTION three years earlier. President John F. KENNEDY of the United States set up a naval blockade of Cuba, and insisted that Khrushchev remove the missiles. Khrushchev did so.

Custer's last stand　The defeat of Colonel George A. Custer and his cavalry detachment by a large force of NATIVE AMERICANS at the Battle of the LITTLE BIGHORN in 1876. Custer and all of his soldiers were killed.

Daley, Richard　A mayor of CHICAGO in the 1950s, 1960s, and 1970s. One of the last and toughest of the big-city political "bosses," he ran a powerful political MACHINE, repeatedly and easily gaining reelection. He was also given much of the credit for the victory of John F. KENNEDY in the close presidential election of 1960; Kennedy won by only a few thousand votes in ILLINOIS. In 1968, when demonstrators against involvement of the United States in the VIETNAM WAR threatened to disrupt the Democratic national convention, meeting in Chicago, the Chicago police, with Daley's approval, responded with violence. An official investigation later described the response as a "police riot." Daley died in 1976.

🍂 Daley's organization also gave Chicago's government a reputation for quick responses to problems; Chicago was called a "city that works."

Darrow, Clarence　A lawyer and author of the late nineteenth and early twentieth centuries. He was known for his defense of unpopular causes and persons, including Eugene V. DEBS. Darrow was defense attorney in the SCOPES TRIAL.

date which will live in infamy, A　A description by President Franklin D. ROOSEVELT of the day of the Japanese attack on PEARL HARBOR — December 7, 1941. Roosevelt was addressing CONGRESS, asking it to declare war on JAPAN.

Debs, Eugene V.　A political leader of the late nineteenth and early twentieth centuries. Debs was five times the presidential candidate of the SOCIALIST PARTY. He was imprisoned in the 1890s for illegally encouraging a railway strike; Clarence DARROW was his defense attorney. During WORLD WAR I, he was imprisoned again, this time for his criticism of the war.

Democratic party　One of the two major political parties in the United States; the Democrats. The origins of the Democrats are in the DEMOCRATIC-REPUBLICAN PARTY, organized by Thomas JEFFERSON in the late eighteenth century; the first president elected simply as a Democrat was Andrew JACKSON. Always strong in the South, the party was severely damaged by SECESSION, the CIVIL WAR, and RECONSTRUCTION, and did not produce a winning presidential candidate between 1861 and 1885, when Grover CLEVELAND was elected. In the late nineteenth and early twentieth centuries, in contrast to the REPUBLICANS, the Democrats tended to be the party of the South and West, opposed to the interests of business and the Northeast. Woodrow WILSON, the next Democratic president, was part of the PROGRESSIVE MOVEMENT. In the period of the NEW DEAL, in the presidency of Franklin D. ROOSEVELT, the Democratic party reached enormous strength among LABOR UNION members, minority groups, and middle-income people. The Democratic presidents since Cleveland, Wilson, and Roosevelt have been Harry TRUMAN, John F. KENNEDY, Lyndon JOHNSON, Jimmy CARTER, and Bill CLINTON.

🍂 Since the NEW DEAL, Democrats have emphasized the role of the federal government in promoting social, economic, and political opportunities for all citizens. They generally support a tax system that places a greater burden on the rich and large CORPORATIONS, and they prefer spending on social programs to spending on defense. Today most blacks, along with Jews, LIBERALS, and labor unions, support the party, which since the 1930s has been strong in major cities. The Democrats' strength in the white South, its strongest base before 1950, has slipped significantly, and in the 1970s and 1980s many BLUE-

COLLAR workers shifted to the REPUBLICAN PARTY. ❧ The Democrats' party symbol is the DONKEY.

Depression, Great The great slowdown in the American economy, the worst in the country's history, which began in 1929 and lasted until the early 1940s. Many banks and businesses failed, and millions of people lost their jobs. (*See* DUST BOWL; FIRESIDE CHATS; HOOVERVILLES; NEW DEAL; OKIES; ROOSEVELT, FRANKLIN D.; *and* CRASH OF 1929.)

Dewey, John A PHILOSOPHER and educational reformer of the late nineteenth and early twentieth centuries. As a philosopher, Dewey followed PRAGMATISM, and its practical orientation carried over into his educational ideas, which became the basis of PROGRESSIVE EDUCATION.

Dillinger, John (DIL-uhn-juhr) A notorious bank robber of the early twentieth century, who escaped from prison twice. Dillinger was finally gunned down by agents of the FEDERAL BUREAU OF INVESTIGATION (FBI) in 1934, outside a movie theater in CHICAGO.

Disney, Walt Twentieth-century film animator and producer, he created the cartoon characters DONALD DUCK and MICKEY MOUSE and in 1937 produced the first full-length animated film, *Snow White and the Seven Dwarfs*. In 1955 he opened his amusement park, Disneyland, in Anaheim, CALIFORNIA, and he was constructing a second park, Disney World, at Orlando, FLORIDA, at the time of his death in 1971.

doughboys United States infantry soldiers who served in WORLD WAR I.

Douglas, William O. A justice of the SUPREME COURT from 1939 to 1975. Douglas was a committed LIBERAL, who urged that the Court take bold steps in the application of the CONSTITUTION.
❧ Douglas served for thirty-six years, longer than any other justice in the history of the Court.

Du Bois, W. E. B. (dooh BOYS) A black author and teacher of the late nineteenth and early twentieth centuries. A RADICAL thinker on racial questions, he helped to found the NATIONAL ASSOCIATION FOR THE ADVANCEMENT OF COLORED PEOPLE (NAACP). Du Bois criticized the position of Booker T. WASHINGTON that blacks should accept their inferior STATUS in American society and "accommodate" to white people. Later in his life, Du Bois joined the

American COMMUNIST party. His best-known book is *The Souls of Black Folk*, a collection of ESSAYS.

Dulles, John Foster (DUL-uhs) SECRETARY OF STATE under President EISENHOWER, he was known for his moralism and militant anticommunism.

Dust Bowl A parched region of the GREAT PLAINS, including parts of OKLAHOMA, ARKANSAS, and TEXAS, where a combination of drought and soil EROSION created enormous dust storms in the 1930s. The NOVEL *THE GRAPES OF WRATH*, by John STEINBECK, describes the plight of the "OKIES" and "Arkies" uprooted by the drought and forced to migrate to CALIFORNIA.

Earhart, Amelia (AIR-hahrt) An aviator of the twentieth century. Earhart was the first woman to pilot an airplane across the ATLANTIC OCEAN. She disappeared in a flight over the PACIFIC in the late 1930s.

Earp, Wyatt (URP) A law officer of the late nineteenth and early twentieth centuries. He served as the United States marshal in Dodge City, KANSAS, and took part in a famous gunfight at the O.K. Corral in Tombstone, ARIZONA, in 1881.

DWIGHT D. EISENHOWER

Eisenhower, Dwight D. (Ike) (EYE-zuhn-how-uhr) A general and political leader of the twentieth century. As supreme commander in EUROPE of the forces of the ALLIES during WORLD WAR II, he directed the invasion of NORMANDY on D-DAY, and led in the overthrow of the NAZI government of GERMANY. He later organized the military forces of the NORTH ATLANTIC TREATY ORGANIZATION. In 1952, his popularity was so high that both the DEMOCRATS and the REPUBLICANS wanted him for a presidential candidate; he chose the Republicans. "I Like Ike" was a popular slogan of his campaigns. He defeated the Democratic candidate, Adlai STEVENSON, in both 1952 and 1956. In office, he negotiated the end of the KOREAN WAR, and generally pursued moderate policies. His years as president were marked by increasing prosperity at home, although the COLD WAR with the SOVIET UNION continued abroad. Richard NIXON was Eisenhower's vice president.

ELLIS ISLAND. *Immigrants at Ellis Island standing in line to have their papers examined.*

Ellis Island An island in the harbor of NEW YORK CITY. The chief immigration station of the United States was on Ellis Island from 1892 to 1943, a time when millions of people, especially from EUROPE, came to the United States.

&. Ellis Island stands near the STATUE OF LIBERTY, which made an impressive sight for people approaching the United States for the first time. &. 1990 marked the opening of the Ellis Island Immigration Museum.

Falwell, Jerry (FAWL-wel) A religious and political leader of the twentieth century, who rose to power in the 1970s. Falwell, an outspoken PROTESTANT preacher of FUNDAMENTALIST tendencies, has appeared on television regularly. He has led a CONSERVATIVE organization, the Moral Majority, which is known for its stands against the legalization of ABORTION and against PORNOGRAPHY.

Farmer, Fannie An educator, author, and cooking expert of the late nineteenth and early twentieth centuries. She wrote the first distinctively American cookbook, *The Boston Cooking School Cook Book.*

feminist movement *See* WOMEN'S MOVEMENT.

Ferraro, Geraldine (fuh-RAHR-oh) A politician of the twentieth century. She served as a REPRESENTATIVE in Congress and was nominated by the DEMOCRATIC PARTY for vice president in 1984; the presidential candidate was Walter MONDALE. Ferraro was the first woman to run for the vice presidency on a major party ticket.

fireside chats A series of informal radio addresses given by President Franklin D. ROOSEVELT in the 1930s. In his fireside chats, Roosevelt sought to explain his policies to the American public, and to calm fears about the Great DEPRESSION.

FLAPPER. *Photograph circa 1925.*

flappers A nickname given to young women in the 1920s who defied convention by refusing to use corsets, cutting their hair short, and wearing short skirts, as well as by such behavior as drinking and smoking in public. (*See* JAZZ AGE *and* ROARING TWENTIES.)

Ford, Gerald A political leader of the twentieth century who served as president from 1974 to 1977. A prominent REPUBLICAN in CONGRESS, Ford was named vice president in 1973, after the resignation of Spiro AGNEW. He succeeded to the presidency in 1974, when President Richard NIXON was forced to resign. Ford sought to pursue moderate policies, and to communicate better with Congress and with the public than Nixon had. He refused approval, however, of a large number of bills passed by Congress, which was controlled by DEMOCRATS, saying they were too costly. He pardoned Nixon in a widely criticized effort to end division over the WATERGATE scandal. Ford lost the presidency to Jimmy CARTER in the 1976 election.

Four Freedoms Four kinds of freedom mentioned by President Franklin D. ROOSEVELT in a speech in 1941 as worth fighting for: freedom of speech and expression, freedom of worship, freedom from want, and freedom from fear. Roosevelt spoke of the Four Freedoms before the United States entered WORLD WAR II. He was presenting the war as a struggle for freedom, and calling for aid to the ALLIES.

Fourteen Points Fourteen goals of the United States in the peace negotiations after WORLD WAR I. President Woodrow WILSON announced the Fourteen Points to CONGRESS in early 1918. They included public negotiations between nations, freedom of navigation, FREE TRADE, self-determination for several nations involved in the war, and the establishment of an association of nations to keep the peace. The "association of nations" Wilson mentioned became the LEAGUE OF NATIONS. (*See also* VERSAILLES, TREATY OF.)

Frankfurter, Felix A judge of the twentieth century, he served on the SUPREME COURT from 1939 to 1962. Frankfurter believed in JUDICIAL RESTRAINT, the idea that judges should decide cases and not try to shape public policy (or "legislate") from the bench.

Freedom Riders A group of northern idealists active in the CIVIL RIGHTS MOVEMENT. The Freedom Riders, who included both blacks and whites, rode buses into the South in the early 1960s in order to challenge racial SEGREGATION. Freedom Riders were regularly attacked by mobs of angry whites, and received often belated protection from federal officers.

Friedan, Betty (fri-DAN) An author and political activist of the twentieth century, who has worked for the extension of women's rights. In 1963, Friedan published *The Feminine Mystique*, a book that proved fundamental to the WOMEN'S MOVEMENT of the 1960s and beyond. She was a founder of the NATIONAL ORGANIZATION FOR WOMEN.

Fulbright scholarships Scholarships for the exchange of students and scholars between the United States and other nations, funded originally by the sale of United States military surplus after WORLD WAR II. The program was conceived by SENATOR J. William Fulbright.

Garfield, James A. A REPUBLICAN PARTY political leader of the nineteenth century, who served as president in 1881. He was assassinated after only a few months in office.

Garvey, Marcus JAMAICAN-born black nationalist who founded the Universal Negro Improvement Association in the 1920s to encourage self-help among blacks. Opposed to COLONIALISM, Garvey advocated black separatism and NATIONALISM. The Black Star shipping line, which facilitated emigration of American blacks to AFRICA, was among his projects. He was eventually jailed for mail fraud and deported to Jamaica by the U.S. government, which feared his influence in the black community. (*See also* DU BOIS, W. E. B.)

Gehrig, Lou (GER-ig) A baseball player of the early twentieth century. A teammate of Babe RUTH, Gehrig set a record for the major leagues by playing in over 2000 consecutive games.

   🔊 While still in his thirties, Gehrig died from a rare disease of the NERVES, amyotrophic lateral sclerosis, that has become commonly known as "Lou Gehrig's disease."

Geronimo (juh-RON-uh-moh) An APACHE leader of the late nineteenth and early twentieth centuries. A brave and unrelenting warrior, Geronimo was among the last to lead NATIVE AMERICANS against white settlers. He took to farming at the end of his life.

GI Bill A law passed in 1944 that provided educational and other benefits for people who had served in the armed forces in WORLD WAR II. Benefits are still available to persons honorably discharged from the armed forces.

GI Joe   A nickname for United States soldiers, particularly during WORLD WAR II. *GI* is short for *government issue*, a descriptive term for supplies distributed by the government.

Gilman, Charlotte P.   Reformer and feminist of the late nineteenth and early twentieth centuries, she wrote *Women and Economics* (1898), a plea for female economic independence. Gilman believed that prohibiting or discouraging women from earning their livelihood made them overly dependent on men and incapable of contributing to the larger life of the community. Her belief that inequality between men and women would not be remedied merely by giving women the vote inspired feminists, especially in the 1970s and 1980s.

Goldwater, Barry   A political leader of the twentieth century. Goldwater represented ARIZONA for over thirty years in the SENATE, and was a leading spokesman for American CONSERVATISM. As the REPUBLICAN nominee, he lost the presidential election of 1964 to President Lyndon JOHNSON.

   ❧ Johnson supporters in the election often suggested that Goldwater's opposition to COMMUNISM could lead him to involve the United States in nuclear war. ❧ Goldwater's campaign marked a realignment of political loyalties in the South. He gained majorities in ALABAMA, GEORGIA, MISSISSIPPI, and SOUTH CAROLINA, which had all had a long and powerful tradition of voting DEMOCRATIC.

Gompers, Samuel (GOM-puhrz)   Labor leader of the late nineteenth and early twentieth centuries, he cofounded the American Federation of Labor (AFL), an organization composed of skilled workers in craft unions. In the 1930s the AFL was challenged by the rise of the Congress of Industrial Organizations (CIO), an organization whose member unions were composed of all workers, unskilled as well as skilled, in specific industries such as mining or automobiles. The two organizations later merged. (*See* AFL-CIO.)

Graham, Billy   An American EVANGELIST of the twentieth century. Graham began conducting religious REVIVALS in the 1940s, and calls his meetings, which he has held around the world, Crusades for CHRIST.

Grant, Ulysses S.   A general and a political leader of the nineteenth century. He became commanding general of the UNION army in the CIVIL WAR, and served as president from 1869 to 1877. While Grant, a REPUBLICAN, was president, many businesses prospered, but often through bribery of government officials. His presidency has one of the worst records of corruption in American history.

Great Depression   *See* DEPRESSION, GREAT.

Great Society   The name President Lyndon JOHNSON gave to his aims in domestic policy. The programs of the Great Society had several goals, including clean air and water, expanded educational opportunities, and the lessening of poverty and disease in the United States. (*See* WAR ON POVERTY.)

Halsey, William F. (HAWL-zee)   An admiral of the twentieth century. Halsey commanded United States fleets in the PACIFIC OCEAN during WORLD WAR II, and achieved notable victories at the island of Guadalcanal and on the Japanese coast.

   ❧ Halsey was known as "Bull" for his determination in the fight against the Japanese.

Harding, Warren G.   A political leader of the late nineteenth and early twentieth centuries, who served as president from 1921 to 1923. As REPUBLICAN PARTY candidate in the campaign of 1920, he described his goal as a return to "normalcy" after the ambitious foreign and domestic policies of the outgoing DEMOCRATIC president, Woodrow WILSON; Harding strongly opposed the participation of the United States in the LEAGUE OF NATIONS. As Harding's presidency went on, the corruption of some of the officials he appointed became increasingly evident; Harding died in office before the worst of the HARDING SCANDALS came to light.

Harding scandals   Major incidents of corruption in government that occurred while Warren HARDING was president in the early 1920s. The most notable, called the TEAPOT DOME SCANDAL, involved the lease of federally owned oil reserve lands to private interests, in return for bribes. Several high officials, including the secretary of the interior, were ultimately convicted for their part in the affair. Although not personally implicated in the wrongdoing, Harding had clearly made a bad choice of associates, and was shaken by the scandals.

Hearst, William Randolph (HURST) A journalist and newspaper publisher in the late nineteenth and early twentieth centuries. Hearst was a pioneer in the kind of sensational reporting often called YELLOW JOURNALISM. In the 1890s, his newspapers helped whip up public hostility against SPAIN, which led to the SPANISH-AMERICAN WAR.

Hickok, Wild Bill (HIK-ok) A frontier settler and United States marshal of the nineteenth century, known for his pursuit of some of the worst outlaws of the old West. Like his friend BUFFALO BILL Cody, he was a rider for the PONY EXPRESS in his youth.

Hiss, Alger (AL-juhr) An official in the DEPARTMENT OF STATE who, in 1948, was accused by a former COMMUNIST, Whittaker Chambers, of having been a secret agent for the SOVIET UNION during the 1930s. Hiss denied the charge, but was later convicted of lying under oath, and was imprisoned.

   ❧ The Hiss case is still controversial. Some have argued that Hiss was the victim of hysteria against communists. Others contend that Chambers was telling the truth. Chambers's accusation against Hiss was made before a committee of the HOUSE OF REPRESENTATIVES. ❧ CONGRESSMAN Richard NIXON, later president, became known nationwide through his part in the investigation of the charge.

Hoffa, Jimmy (HOF-uh) Labor leader who built the Teamsters Union into a powerful organization despite repeated charges of corruption. After his imprisonment from 1967 to 1971 for misuse of pension funds and jury tampering, Hoffa disappeared in 1975. It is widely assumed that he was murdered.

Holmes, Oliver Wendell, Jr. A judge of the late nineteenth and early twentieth centuries. Holmes served on the SUPREME COURT from 1902 to 1932, retiring when past ninety. He was celebrated for his legal wisdom, and frequently stood in the minority when the Court decided cases. He insisted on viewing the law as a social instrument rather than as a set of abstract principles. He delivered a famous opinion concerning FREEDOM OF SPEECH, holding that it must be allowed except when it presents a "CLEAR AND PRESENT DANGER."

Hoover, Herbert A political leader of the twentieth century, who was president from 1929 to 1933. He had been in office only a few months when the Great DEPRESSION began (see CRASH OF 1929, STOCK MAR-KET, and HOOVERVILLES). A REPUBLICAN, he was reluctant to use the power of the federal government against the Depression. Hoover tried to persuade voters that private enterprise could turn the economy around, but he lost the election of 1932 to Franklin D. ROOSEVELT. In the late 1940s, he was head of a commission to make the federal government more efficient.

Hoover, J. Edgar A law enforcement official of the twentieth century. Hoover became the director of the FEDERAL BUREAU OF INVESTIGATION (FBI) in 1924, and stayed in the position until his death in 1972. His time as director was marked by vigorous investigation and prosecution of gangsters, kidnapers, and foreign spies.

   ❧ Hoover's activities remain controversial. Some praise him as a pioneer in scientific law enforcement, but others say that he abused his power, particularly in his investigation of the supposed influence of COMMUNISTS on the CIVIL RIGHTS MOVEMENT.

Hoovervilles Encampments of the poor and homeless that sprang up during the Great DEPRESSION. They were named with ironic intent after President Herbert HOOVER, who was in office when the depression started.

Humphrey, Hubert A political leader of the twentieth century, who spent most of his political career representing MINNESOTA in the SENATE. He was elected vice president in 1964, running with President Lyndon JOHNSON. Humphrey was nominated for the presidency by the DEMOCRATIC PARTY in 1968, but lost to Richard NIXON. A major force in Humphrey's defeat was his association with Johnson's unpopular use of American troops in the VIETNAM WAR.

I have a dream A PHRASE from the most celebrated speech by Martin Luther KING, Jr., delivered at a large rally in WASHINGTON, D.C., in 1963 to supporters of the CIVIL RIGHTS MOVEMENT. King stressed the importance of nonviolent protest, and vividly painted his vision of a better future for people of all colors in the United States:

I still have a dream. It is a dream deeply rooted in the American dream. I have a dream that one day this nation will rise up and live out the true meaning of its creed: "We hold these truths to be self-evident: that all men are created equal." I have a dream that one day on the red hills of GEORGIA the sons of former slaves and the sons of former slaveowners will be able to sit down together at the table of brotherhood. I have a dream that my four little children will one day live in a nation where they will not be judged by the color of their skin but by the content of their character.

I shall return Words of General Douglas MAC-ARTHUR in 1942 as he left the PHILIPPINE Islands during WORLD WAR II. Japanese forces were about to conquer the Philippines, and President Franklin D. ROOSEVELT had transferred MacArthur to another location in the PACIFIC. MacArthur returned at the head of an American army in 1944, and freed the Philippines from Japanese control.

Iran-Contra Affair (i-RAN, i-RAHN, eye-RAN; KON-truh, KOHN-trah) Scandal in the administration of President Ronald REAGAN, which came to light when it was revealed that in the mid-1980s the United States secretly arranged arms sales to IRAN in return for promises of Iranian assistance in securing the release of Americans held hostage in LEBANON. Proceeds from the arms sales then were covertly and illegally funneled to the Contras, rebels fighting the MARXIST Sandinista government in NICARAGUA.

Ivy League A group of eight old, distinguished colleges and universities in the East, known for their ivy-covered brick buildings. The members of the Ivy League are Brown, Columbia, Cornell, Harvard, Princeton, and Yale Universities; Dartmouth College; and the University of Pennsylvania.

Iwo Jima (EE-woh, EE-wuh JEE-muh) An island in the PACIFIC OCEAN, taken from the Japanese by United States Marines near the end of WORLD WAR II after a furious battle.

• The battle has been immortalized by a famous photograph and a sculpture based on the photograph of half a dozen Marines raising the flag of the United States on a summit on Iwo Jima.

Jackson, Jesse An African-American clergyman and political leader of the twentieth century. Jackson, a leader in the CIVIL RIGHTS MOVEMENT, has energetically encouraged self-confidence in young people, especially blacks. He ran for president in the PRIMARIES of 1984 and 1988.

James, Jesse An outlaw of the nineteenth century. Jesse, his brother Frank, and their gang committed many daring robberies of banks and trains, especially in the 1870s. After a reward had been offered for

JESSE JAMES

James's capture, one of his own gang shot him in the back and collected the money.

• Jesse James is the subject of many folk legends and songs.

Japanese-Americans, internment of An action taken by the federal government in 1942, after JAPAN bombed PEARL HARBOR and brought the United States into WORLD WAR II. Government officials feared that Americans of Japanese descent living on the West Coast might cooperate in an invasion of the United States by Japan. Accordingly, over 100,000 of these residents were forced into relocation camps inland, most losing their homes, businesses, and other property in the process. About two-thirds of those moved were United States citizens. (*See* NISEI.)

• Many Japanese-Americans, including a specially created army battalion, distinguished themselves in combat in World War II.

Jazz Age The 1920s in the United States, a decade marked not only by the popularity of jazz, but also by attacks on convention in many areas of American life. (*See* FLAPPERS *and* ROARING TWENTIES.)

Jim Crow A descriptive term for the SEGREGATION of institutions, businesses, hotels, restaurants, and the like. It also refers to the laws that required racial segregation.

John Birch Society A CONSERVATIVE organization prominent in the 1950s and 1960s. The society was

particularly concerned with the dangers of COMMU-
NISM, and its views were considered extreme by most
Americans.

Johnson, Andrew   A political leader of the nineteenth century. Johnson was elected vice president in
1864, and became president when Abraham LIN-
COLN was assassinated in 1865. Johnson is the only
president to have been impeached (*see* IMPEACH-
MENT); the HOUSE OF REPRESENTATIVES charged him
with illegally dismissing a government official. The
SENATE tried him, and Johnson missed being convicted by only one vote.

Johnson, Lyndon Baines (LBJ)   A DEMOCRATIC
PARTY political leader of the twentieth century, who
was president from 1963 to 1969. Johnson rose to
power in the SENATE. He was elected vice president
in 1960, running with John F. KENNEDY, and became
president after Kennedy was assassinated. Known for
his extraordinary political skill, Johnson guided
many of Kennedy's NEW FRONTIER projects through
CONGRESS, including the VOTING RIGHTS ACT OF
1965. He also started his own set of domestic programs, known as the GREAT SOCIETY, which included
the WAR ON POVERTY. In 1965, Johnson began a
sharp increase in American military involvement in
the VIETNAM WAR, which took resources away from
the Great Society and was opposed by many of his
fellow DEMOCRATS. Greatly frustrated by his difficulties over the war in Vietnam, he declined to run
for reelection in 1968.

&. Johnson, a Texan (*see* TEXAS), often tried to
project an image of a blustery, sometimes coarse,
rancher.

Joseph, Chief   *See* CHIEF JOSEPH.

Keller, Helen   An educator and author of the twentieth century. Though blind and deaf from an early
age, she learned to read, write, and communicate
with sign language.

&. Helen Keller is often mentioned as an example
of persistence and courage in the face of overwhelm-
ing handicaps. &. The play *The Miracle Worker*
dramatizes Helen Keller's early education.

Kennedy, Edward (Ted)   The younger brother of
John F. KENNEDY and Robert F. KENNEDY. Kennedy,
a DEMOCRAT, has represented MASSACHUSETTS in the
SENATE since 1963, and is a leading LIBERAL. He has

HELEN KELLER. *Keller examining a bust of
herself by the sculptor Jo Davidson.*

been mentioned frequently over the years as a possible candidate for president, but has never been nominated. The CHAPPAQUIDDICK INCIDENT has affected
many people's view of him.

Kennedy, John F. (JFK)   A DEMOCRATIC PARTY political leader of the twentieth century; he was president from 1961 to 1963. His election began a period
of great optimism in the United States. In his inaugural address, he challenged the nation, "ASK NOT
WHAT YOUR COUNTRY CAN DO FOR YOU; ASK WHAT
YOU CAN DO FOR YOUR COUNTRY." Kennedy brought
the United States out of the CUBAN MISSILE CRISIS,
and negotiated the NUCLEAR TEST BAN TREATY of
1963 with BRITAIN and the SOVIET UNION. But he
was also responsible for the disastrous attempt to invade CUBA at the BAY OF PIGS. Kennedy's domestic
policies were called the NEW FRONTIER; he strongly
supported space exploration and the CIVIL RIGHTS
MOVEMENT. His presidency ended with his assassination on November 22, 1963, apparently by
Lee Harvey OSWALD, who allegedly shot Kennedy
as the president rode in an open car through DAL-
LAS. Kennedy's death was mourned throughout the
world.

&. At age forty-three, Kennedy was the youngest
person to be elected president in American history.
His administration was known for its dazzling, styl-
ish quality, partly because of his elegant wife, Jacque-
line (Jackie) Kennedy, and partly because Kennedy
himself was young, handsome, and eloquent.

JOHN F. KENNEDY

MARTIN LUTHER KING, JR. *King delivering his "I have a dream" speech in Washington, D.C., on August 28, 1963.*

Kennedy, Robert A younger brother of President John F. KENNEDY, who served as ATTORNEY GENERAL during his brother's presidency, and was his brother's closest adviser. Robert Kennedy, also known as Bobby, was a champion of the CIVIL RIGHTS MOVEMENT and a foe of organized crime. He was elected to the SENATE after John Kennedy's assassination. In 1968, while running for the presidential nomination of the DEMOCRATIC PARTY, he was assassinated by Sirhan Sirhan, a Palestinian, evidently because of Kennedy's position favoring ISRAEL. (*See* ARAB-IS-RAELI CONFLICT.)

Kent State A controversial incident in 1970, in which unarmed students demonstrating against the involvement of the United States in the VIETNAM WAR were fired on by panicky troops of the NA-TIONAL GUARD. Four students were killed and nine wounded. The shooting occurred at Kent State University in OHIO. The troops were subsequently ab-

solved of responsibility by the government, but their action turned many moderates against the VIETNAM WAR and the NIXON administration.

Kentucky Derby The most famous American horse race, held each spring at Churchill Downs racetrack in KENTUCKY.

King, Martin Luther, Jr. An African-American clergyman and political leader of the twentieth century; the most prominent member of the CIVIL RIGHTS MOVEMENT. King became famous in the 1950s and 1960s through his promotion of nonviolent methods of opposition to SEGREGATION, such as BOYCOTTS of segregated city buses, or SIT-INS at lunch counters that would not serve black people. His "LETTER FROM BIRMINGHAM JAIL" defended this kind of direct, nonviolent action as a way of forcing people to take notice of injustice. King helped organize the march on Washington in 1963 that drew hundreds of thousands of supporters of civil rights to WASHINGTON, D.C., for a mass rally. At this march, he described a possible future of racial harmony in his most famous speech, which had the REFRAIN "I HAVE A DREAM." In 1964, he received the NOBEL PRIZE for peace. King was assassinated by James Earl Ray in 1968.

&. King was born January 15, 1929. A national holiday each January, Martin Luther King Day, commemorates his life.

Kissinger, Henry (KIS-uhn-juhr)   A scholar and government official of the twentieth century. As an adviser and later SECRETARY OF STATE under President Richard NIXON, Kissinger prepared for the opening of diplomatic relations between the United States and the PEOPLE'S REPUBLIC OF CHINA. During the VIETNAM WAR, he helped Nixon plan and execute a secret bombing of CAMBODIA, and his negotiations with the government of North VIETNAM helped produce a cease-fire in that war. He won the NOBEL PRIZE for peace in 1973.

KKK   *See* KU KLUX KLAN.

Korean War   A war, also called the Korean conflict, fought in the early 1950s between the UNITED NATIONS, supported by the United States, and the COMMUNIST Democratic People's Republic of Korea (NORTH KOREA). The war began in 1950, when North Korea invaded SOUTH KOREA. The United Nations declared North Korea the aggressor, and sent military aid to the South Korean army. President Harry TRUMAN declared the war a "police action" because he never asked CONGRESS to pass an official declaration of war. He thereby established a precedent for President Lyndon JOHNSON, who committed troops to the VIETNAM WAR without ever seeking a congressional mandate for his action.

General Douglas MACARTHUR commanded the United Nations troops, who were mostly from the United States. The tide turned against North Korea with the landings at Inchon, and its troops were pushed back into the north; but reinforcements from the PEOPLE'S REPUBLIC OF CHINA soon allowed the North Koreans to regain lost territory. In 1953, with neither side having a prospect of victory, a truce was signed. In the course of the war, President Harry TRUMAN removed MacArthur from his command for insubordination. (*See* TRUMAN-MACARTHUR CONTROVERSY.)

Ku Klux Klan (KKK) (KOOH kluks)   A secret society dedicated to the supremacy of white people in the United States. It began in the South during the time of RECONSTRUCTION, and attempted to terrorize the many southern blacks and CARPETBAGGERS who had replaced white southerners in positions of power. The Klan gained renewed strength in the 1920s and again in the 1960s. It has stated that it aims to preserve "pure Americanism." It has attacked JEWS and ROMAN CATHOLICS, along with immigrants and COMMUNISTS, but is still primarily opposed to equal rights for black people, and has often engaged in violence against them. Klansmen wear white hoods and robes. Klan leaders have such titles as Grand Dragon, Grand CYCLOPS, and Imperial Wizard.

⚓ A favored tactic of Klansmen is to burn a wooden cross outside the house of someone whom they wish to intimidate. Typically, they want the occupant to move out of the vicinity. The burning cross is a threat of future assaults if the victim does not do what the Klan wants.

Lafayette, we are here (lah-fee-ET, laf-ee-ET)   Words spoken by an American military officer in 1917 at the tomb of a French patriot, the Marquis de LAFAYETTE, who fought for the United States in the REVOLUTIONARY WAR. "Lafayette, we are here" suggested that, by entering WORLD WAR I on the side of FRANCE, Americans were repaying a debt to the French, who had helped the United States gain its independence from BRITAIN. Some have identified the person who first said "Lafayette, we are here" as General John PERSHING.

La Guardia, Fiorello (fee-uh-REL-oh luh GWAHR-dee-uh)   A political leader of the twentieth century. A beloved mayor of NEW YORK CITY in the 1930s and 1940s, La Guardia worked to free the city of corruption, and began a great number of construction projects. La Guardia was called the "Little Flower" (*fiorello* is Italian for "little flower").

⚓ La Guardia is especially remembered for reading the comic strips from out-of-town newspapers over the radio during a newspaper strike in New York.

"Letter from Birmingham Jail"   A letter that Martin Luther KING, Jr., addressed to his fellow clergymen while he was in jail in BIRMINGHAM, ALABAMA, in 1963, after a nonviolent protest against racial SEGREGATION (*see also* SIT-INS). King defended the apparent impatience of people in the CIVIL RIGHTS MOVEMENT, maintaining that without forceful actions like his, equal rights for black people would never be gained. He wrote, "Nonviolent direct action seeks to create such a crisis and foster such a tension that a community which has constantly refused to negotiate is forced to confront the issue." King upheld the general use of nonviolent CIVIL DISOBEDIENCE against unjust laws, saying that human rights must take precedence over such laws. "Injustice anywhere is a threat to justice everywhere," he wrote. He claimed that "one who breaks an unjust law must do it openly, lovingly"; such a person, King said, is actually showing respect for law, by insisting that laws be just.

Lindbergh, Charles A. (LIND-burg, LIN-burg) An aviator of the twentieth century. In 1927, Lindbergh flew alone from NEW YORK CITY to PARIS across the ATLANTIC OCEAN traveling nonstop in *THE SPIRIT OF ST. LOUIS*. His was the first nonstop solo flight across the Atlantic. Young, and engaging in manner, he became an instant hero, nicknamed the "Lone Eagle" and "Lucky Lindy." After WORLD WAR II had begun, but before the United States entered the war, he urged American neutrality, and was heavily criticized for his stand.

 ❧ The kidnaping and murder of Lindbergh's infant son in 1932 gained attention around the world, and led to the strengthening of federal laws against kidnaping.

Lippmann, Walter A journalist and author of the twentieth century. Lippmann wrote a widely read newspaper column and several books, including *The Public Philosophy*.

 ❧ Lippmann has been mentioned as a prime example of a political pundit, a person with wide-ranging but authoritative views on public affairs.

Little Bighorn, Battle of the A battle between Colonel George A. Custer's United States cavalry troops and several groups of NATIVE AMERICANS near the Little Bighorn River in MONTANA in 1876. Custer had been pursuing a group of SIOUX, led by SITTING BULL, who had risen in arms against settlement of the country. He foolishly underestimated the size and ability of the Sioux forces, who were supported by Cheyenne warriors. They killed Custer and every one of his soldiers. Also called CUSTER'S LAST STAND.

Long, Huey A political leader of the 1920s and 1930s who served as governor of LOUISIANA and represented that state in the SENATE. He promised every family enough money for a home, car, radio, PENSION, and college education. A DEMAGOGUE, Long dominated Louisiana's politics and pushed aside opposition. He planned to run for president, but was assassinated before he could do so.

 ❧ Long was nicknamed the "Kingfish." ❧ Members of Long's family have since had a prominent role in Louisiana and national politics.

Louis, Joe An African-American boxer of the twentieth century, who held the world championship in the heavyweight class from 1937 to 1949.

 ❧ Louis was called the "Brown Bomber," and was a source of racial pride for America's blacks.

lynch law The punishment of supposed criminals, especially by hanging, by agreement of a crowd, and without a genuine criminal trial. Lynch law was used in the early settlement of the West as a way of maintaining minimal law and order before a sheriff and courts could be set up. It has also been used to deprive unpopular suspects of their rights, and to satisfy a mob's thirst for vengeance. Lynch law was often used by whites in the South to terrorize and subjugate blacks.

MacArthur, Douglas A general of the twentieth century, who commanded the forces of the ALLIES in the PACIFIC region in WORLD WAR II. When Japanese forces were about to conquer the PHILIPPINES, MacArthur was forced to leave, but vowed, "I SHALL RETURN." He did return two years later, and drove out the Japanese. After the final defeat of JAPAN, he supervised the occupation of that country by the Allies, and helped revise the Japanese CONSTITUTION. During the KOREAN WAR, he commanded troops of the UNITED NATIONS, but was removed as commander by President Harry TRUMAN. (*See* TRUMAN-MACARTHUR CONTROVERSY.)

Malcolm X An African-American political leader of the twentieth century. Malcolm X, a prominent BLACK MUSLIM, who explained the group's viewpoint in *The Autobiography of Malcolm X*, was assassinated in 1965.

Manhattan Project The code name for the effort to develop ATOMIC BOMBS for the United States during WORLD WAR II. The first controlled NUCLEAR REACTION took place in CHICAGO in 1942, and by 1945, bombs had been manufactured that used this CHAIN REACTION to produce great explosive force. The project was carried out in enormous secrecy. After a test explosion in July 1945, the United States dropped atomic bombs on the Japanese cities of HIROSHIMA and NAGASAKI.

Marshall, George C. A soldier and diplomat of the twentieth century. He was a leading planner of strategy for the ALLIES in WORLD WAR II. Marshall served as SECRETARY OF STATE from 1947 to 1949, during which time he put forth the MARSHALL PLAN. In 1953, he received the NOBEL PRIZE for peace.

THURGOOD MARSHALL

Marshall, Thurgood   A judge of the twentieth century; the first black appointed to the SUPREME COURT. Before his appointment to the Court in 1967, Marshall served as a lawyer for the NATIONAL ASSOCIATION FOR THE ADVANCEMENT OF COLORED PEOPLE, and in 1954 he argued before the Court against SEGREGATION in the case of *BROWN VERSUS BOARD OF EDUCATION*. As a Supreme Court justice, he was known for his consistently LIBERAL record and for advocating the rights of women and minorities.

Marshall Plan   The European Recovery Program, by which the United States made large donations after WORLD WAR II to countries in EUROPE to help them rebuild their devastated economies. General George C. MARSHALL, the SECRETARY OF STATE, proposed the plan in 1947.

massive resistance   The opposition of many white leaders in the South to the decision of the SUPREME COURT in *BROWN VERSUS BOARD OF EDUCATION* in

1954. The Court had declared racial SEGREGATION in public schools unconstitutional. The expression *massive resistance* was used in a letter signed by over a hundred members of CONGRESS, calling on southerners to defy the Supreme Court's ruling.

McCarthy, Joseph R.   A political leader of the twentieth century. McCarthy, a REPUBLICAN, represented WISCONSIN in the SENATE from 1947 until his death in 1957. He led an effort to identify COMMUNISTS who, he said, had infiltrated the federal government by the hundreds, although he never supplied any of their names. One of McCarthy's tactics was to establish GUILT BY ASSOCIATION: to brand as communists people who merely had known a communist or who had agreed with the communists on some issue such as racial equality. His critics called him a DEMAGOGUE who exploited people's concerns about communism. He was also feared, however, because of the mass of information he had put together on people in the government. The Senate censured him in 1954, saying that his actions were "contrary to senatorial traditions."

McCarthyism   The extreme opposition to COMMUNISM shown by SENATOR Joseph R. MCCARTHY and his supporters in the 1940s and 1950s.

&. *McCarthyism* has become a general term for the hysterical investigation of a government's opponents, or the publicizing of accusations against these opponents without sufficient evidence to support the charges.

McGovern, George (muh-GUV-uhrn)   A political leader of the twentieth century, who, after representing SOUTH DAKOTA in the SENATE, lost the presidential election of 1972 to President Richard NIXON. McGovern, a LIBERAL DEMOCRAT, was an outspoken opponent of the involvement of the United States in the VIETNAM WAR.

&. In the election of 1972, McGovern received majorities only in MASSACHUSETTS and in the DISTRICT OF COLUMBIA.

McKinley, William   A political leader of the late nineteenth and early twentieth centuries; he was president from 1897 to 1901. McKinley, a REPUBLICAN, led the United States during the SPANISH-AMERICAN WAR, although he at first opposed taking action against SPAIN. The United States annexed the PHILIPPINES in his presidency. McKinley was assassinated by an anarchist (*see* ANARCHISM) shortly after his re-election.

&. McKinley's presidency is often remembered as a time of rising American JINGOISM and IMPERIALISM.

Midway Island, Battle of   A naval and air battle fought in WORLD WAR II in which planes from American aircraft carriers blunted the Japanese naval threat in the PACIFIC after PEARL HARBOR.

Miranda **decision** (muh-RAN-duh)   A ruling by the SUPREME COURT in 1966 affecting the rights of persons under arrest. According to the Court's decision, persons being arrested must be informed of their rights against SELF-INCRIMINATION and their right to be advised by a lawyer.

Mondale, Walter (MON-dayl)   A political leader of the twentieth century. He served in the SENATE in the 1960s and 1970s, and was vice president under President Jimmy CARTER. Mondale was nominated by the DEMOCRATIC PARTY for president in 1984; he lost to Ronald REAGAN.

&. Mondale's defeat was the worst for any major party candidate since the 1930s — worse even than that of George McGOVERN in 1972; Mondale won majorities only in his home state of MINNESOTA and in the DISTRICT OF COLUMBIA. &. Mondale was the first presidential candidate of a major party to run with a female vice presidential candidate. She was Geraldine FERRARO, a member of CONGRESS.

muckrakers (MUK-ray-kuhrz)   Authors who specialize in exposing corruption in business, government, and elsewhere, especially those who were active at the end of the nineteenth and beginning of the twentieth centuries. Some famous muckrakers were Ida M. Tarbell, Lincoln Steffens, and Upton Sinclair. President Theodore ROOSEVELT is credited with giving them their name.

Murrow, Edward R.   Highly respected radio and television commentator who during WORLD WAR II reported from LONDON on German air raids against that city and who attacked Senator Joseph R. McCARTHY in the 1950s as a threat to CIVIL LIBERTIES. Murrow also created a show that first brought television cameras into the homes of celebrities for interviews.

My Lai massacre (MEE LEYE)   A mass killing of helpless inhabitants of a village in South VIETNAM during the VIETNAM WAR, carried out in 1968 by United States troops under the command of Lieutenant William Calley. Calley was court-martialed and sentenced to life imprisonment, but he only served a few years before PAROLE. The massacre, horrible in itself, became a SYMBOL for those opposed to the war in Vietnam.

Nation, Carry   A social reformer of the late nineteenth and early twentieth centuries, who argued forcefully for abstinence from alcohol. Known for taking direct action, she and her followers often used hatchets to smash beer kegs and liquor bottles in saloons. (*See* PROHIBITION.)

New Deal   A group of government programs and policies established under President Franklin D. ROOSEVELT in the 1930s; the New Deal was designed to improve conditions for persons suffering in the Great DEPRESSION. The projects of the New Deal included the Social Security system (*see* SOCIAL SECURITY ADMINISTRATION), the TENNESSEE VALLEY AUTHORITY, and the WORKS PROGRESS ADMINISTRATION.

&. The New Deal remains controversial. Some have criticized it as too expensive, and have called it an inadvisable expansion of federal control over the American economy. Others have insisted that the New Deal was an appropriate response to desperate conditions, and produced programs of continuing value.

New Frontier   A slogan used by President John F. KENNEDY to describe his goals and policies. Kennedy maintained that, like the Americans of the frontier in the nineteenth century, Americans of the twentieth century had to rise to new challenges, such as achieving equality of opportunity for all.

New Left   A RADICAL movement of the 1960s and 1970s. New Leftists opposed the MILITARY-INDUSTRIAL COMPLEX and involvement of the United States in the VIETNAM WAR; they urged more public attention to conditions of black people and the poor. New Leftists were less theoretical than COMMUNISTS, and generally did not admire the SOVIET UNION. But many of them were interested in MAOISM, and they spoke strongly for "participatory democracy." (*See* SIT-INS.)

Nimitz, Admiral Chester (NIM-its)   The commander of the United States Pacific Fleet during WORLD WAR II.

Nisei (nee-SAY, NEE-say)   Persons whose parents were born in JAPAN, but who were themselves born outside of Japan. Many Nisei were moved by force in the internment of JAPANESE-AMERICANS in WORLD WAR II.

Nixon, Richard   A political leader of the twentieth century. A member of CONGRESS in the late 1940s, Nixon came to national attention through his strong support for the investigation of the alleged COMMUNIST Alger HISS. He was elected vice president twice under President Dwight D. EISENHOWER, but narrowly lost the presidential election of 1960 to John F. KENNEDY. He ran for governor of CALIFORNIA two years later, was defeated again, and left politics for several years to practice law in NEW YORK CITY. Nixon reemerged as the REPUBLICAN presidential candidate in 1968, and defeated Hubert HUMPHREY and George WALLACE in the election. The best-remembered events of his presidency were his visits to the PEOPLE'S REPUBLIC OF CHINA and to the SOVIET UNION; a cease-fire in VIETNAM and withdrawal of United States forces from that country; and the WATERGATE scandal, which led to his downfall. In 1974, under immediate threat of IMPEACHMENT, he became the first president to resign from office.

🙠 Nixon received the nickname "Tricky Dick" for his early reputation for deviousness.

normalcy   A word used by President Warren HARDING to describe the calm political and social order to which he wished to return the United States after the idealism and commotion of the presidency of Woodrow WILSON.

🙠 *Normalcy* has been used as a general term for the political climate in the United States in the early 1920s.

O'Connor, Sandra Day   The first woman to serve on the SUPREME COURT, she was appointed by President Ronald REAGAN in 1981.

Okies (OH-keez)   People from Oklahoma, especially those who moved to CALIFORNIA in the 1930s to escape the poverty of the DUST BOWL. (*See also GRAPES OF WRATH, THE.*)

only thing we have to fear is fear itself, The   A statement from the first inaugural address of President Franklin D. ROOSEVELT in 1933. Roosevelt was speaking at one of the worst points of the Great DEPRESSION.

Oswald, Lee Harvey   The presumed assassin of President John F. KENNEDY. Oswald allegedly shot Kennedy from a high window of a building in DALLAS on November 22, 1963, as Kennedy rode down the street in an open car. Oswald was captured the day of the assassination, but was never tried; two days after Kennedy's death, as Oswald was being moved by police, a nightclub owner from Dallas, Jack Ruby, shot and killed him. A government commission led by Chief Justice Earl WARREN concluded later that Oswald, though active in COMMUNIST causes, was not part of a conspiracy to kill Kennedy. Many have questioned the findings of the commission.

JESSE OWENS. *Running in a heat for the 200-meter dash at the Olympics in Germany in 1936.*

Owens, Jesse   An African-American athlete of the twentieth century. He won four gold medals in track and field events at the OLYMPIC GAMES of 1936, held in GERMANY when Adolf HITLER was leader. His victories were a source of pride to the United States, and also — since Owens was black — a blow to the NAZI notions of a MASTER RACE.

Parks, Rosa   A black seamstress from Montgomery, ALABAMA, who, in 1955, refused to give up her seat on a Montgomery city bus to a white person, as she was legally required to do. Her mistreatment after refusing to give up her seat led to a BOYCOTT of the Montgomery buses by supporters of equal rights for black people. This incident was the first major confrontation in the CIVIL RIGHTS MOVEMENT.

Patton, George (PAT-n)   A general in WORLD WAR II, known for his expertise at warfare using tanks and other vehicles. He led operations in north AFRICA and in the Battle of the BULGE. A few months after the end of the war, he was fatally injured in a car accident in GERMANY.

🍂 Patton was called "Old Blood and Guts"; his stern, demanding, and effective leadership was legendary.

PEARL HARBOR. *Wreckage of the* USS Arizona *in Pearl Harbor.*

Pearl Harbor A major United States naval base in HAWAII that was attacked without warning by the Japanese air force on December 7, 1941, with great loss of American lives and ships. In asking CONGRESS to declare war on JAPAN the next day, President Franklin D. ROOSEVELT described the day of the attack as a "DATE WHICH WILL LIVE IN INFAMY."

Peary, Robert E. (PEER-ee) An explorer of the ARCTIC in the late nineteenth and early twentieth centuries. He and his team are generally accepted as the first persons to reach the NORTH POLE, in 1909.

Pentagon Papers A classified study of the VIETNAM WAR that was carried out by the DEPARTMENT OF DEFENSE. An official of the department, Daniel Ellsberg, gave copies of the study in 1971 to the *New York Times* and *Washington Post*. The SUPREME COURT upheld the right of the newspapers to publish the documents. In response, President Richard NIXON ordered some members of his staff, afterward called the "plumbers," to stop such "leaks" of information. The "plumbers," among other activities, broke into the office of Ellsberg's psychiatrist, looking for damaging information on him.

Pershing, John (PUR-shing, PUR-zhing) A military leader of the late nineteenth and early twentieth centuries. In 1916, General Pershing commanded the United States troops that pursued the Mexican revolutionary leader Pancho VILLA into MEXICO. In 1917, he was made commander of the United States troops sent to EUROPE to fight in WORLD WAR I.

🍂 Pershing was known as "Black Jack."

Plessy versus Ferguson (PLES-ee, FUR-guh-suhn) A case decided by the SUPREME COURT in the 1890s. The Court held that a state could require racial SEGREGATION in public facilities if the facilities offered the two races were equal. The Court's requirement became known as the "SEPARATE BUT EQUAL" doctrine. It was overturned by the Court in 1954 in *BROWN VERSUS BOARD OF EDUCATION.*

Populist party A third-party movement that sprang up in the 1890s, and drew support especially from disgruntled farmers. The Populists were particularly known for advocating the unlimited coinage of silver. The party endorsed William Jennings BRYAN, a champion of free silver, in the presidential election of 1896.

progressive education A broad movement for educational reform in the twentieth century. Progressive education is principally associated with John DEWEY, but contains many different and often conflicting ideas. In general, progressive educators view existing schools as too rigid, formal, and detached from real life. They prefer informal classroom arrangements and informal relations between pupils and teachers. They also prefer that schools teach useful subjects (including occupations) and emphasize "learning by doing" rather than instruction purely from textbooks. Some place the developing PERSONALITY of the child at the center of educational thinking and insist, "teach the child, not the subject."

Progressive movement A movement for reform that occurred roughly between 1900 and 1920. Progressives typically held that irresponsible actions by the rich were corrupting both public and private life. They called for such measures as TRUST BUSTING, the regulation of railroads, provisions for the people to vote on laws themselves through REFERENDUM, the election of the SENATE by the people rather than by state legislatures, and a graduated INCOME tax (one in which higher tax rates are applied to higher incomes). The Progressives were able to get much of their program passed into law. Presidents Theodore ROOSEVELT and Woodrow WILSON were associated with the movement.

PROHIBITION. *Federal agents destroying confiscated kegs of beer.*

Prohibition (proh-uh-BISH-uhn)   The outlawing of alcoholic beverages nationwide from 1920 to 1933, under an amendment to the CONSTITUTION. The amendment, enforced by the VOLSTEAD ACT, was repealed by another amendment to the Constitution in 1933.

∽ Prohibition is often mentioned in discussions of how much social change can be brought about through law, since alcohol was widely, though illegally, produced and sold during Prohibition; it was served privately in the White House under President Warren HARDING, for example. ∽ Many use the example of Prohibition to argue that more harm than good comes from the enactment of laws that are sure to be widely disobeyed. ∽ Some states and localities (called "dry") had outlawed the production and sale of alcohol before the Prohibition amendment was adopted. The repealing amendment allowed individ-

ual states and localities to remain "dry," and some did for many years.

public be damned, The   Words attributed to William H. Vanderbilt, a railroad executive of the late nineteenth century. They were supposedly spoken to a newspaper reporter.

∽ "The public be damned" has often been recalled when business leaders have been accused of shirking responsibility toward the public.

railroad, transcontinental   *See* TRANSCONTINENTAL RAILROAD.

Rankin, Jeanette   Suffragist and pacifist, Rankin in 1917 became the first woman to serve in CONGRESS. She has the distinction of being the only member of Congress to vote against American entry into both World Wars.

Reagan, Ronald (RAY-guhn)   A political leader of the twentieth century, elected president in 1980 and 1984. Reagan went into politics after a career as a film actor. He served as governor of CALIFORNIA from 1967 to 1975, and became a leading spokesman for CONSERVATISM in the United States. As the nominee of the REPUBLICAN PARTY, promising to work toward a balanced federal budget, he won a large victory over President Jimmy CARTER in 1980, and an even larger one over Walter MONDALE in 1984. Early in his presidency, Reagan persuaded a CONGRESS controlled by DEMOCRATS to increase spending on defense and to reduce taxes. The federal budget was to be balanced by reductions in spending outside of defense, but Reagan and the Congress were never able to agree on these. Accordingly, the federal government went deeper into DEBT throughout Reagan's presidency. Reagan nevertheless was able to reduce the size and activities of the federal government outside of defense.

His foreign policy was heavily affected by his opposition to COMMUNISM; for example, he characterized the SOVIET UNION as "an evil empire," sent troops to the CARIBBEAN island of GRENADA to help put down a revolution in 1983, and aided the opponents of the MARXIST government of NICARAGUA. The Strategic Defense Initiative, or "STAR WARS," was his favored approach to the problem of NUCLEAR WEAPONS. A scandal arose in his administration in the late 1980s, when it was learned that Reagan's subordinates had arranged a secret sale of weapons to IRAN, and an illegal transfer of the profits to rebels in Nicaragua, but investigators did not charge that Reagan himself was part of the arrangement (*see* IRAN-CONTRA AFFAIR). He met with the PREMIER of the SOVIET UNION, Mikhail GORBACHEV, in 1985, 1986, and 1987, and reached agreements on reduction of nuclear weapons. Reagan survived an attempted assassination in 1981.

• In 1984, at age seventy-three, Reagan became the oldest person ever to be elected president. • Reagan, a highly popular president, was called the "Great Communicator" for his efforts to explain government problems and projects on a level that could be widely understood.

Reconstruction The period after the CIVIL WAR in which the states formerly part of the CONFEDERACY were brought back into the United States. During Reconstruction, the South was divided into military districts for the supervision of elections to set up new state governments. These governments often included CARPETBAGGERS, since former officials of the Confederacy were not allowed to serve in them. The new state governments approved three amendments to the CONSTITUTION: the Thirteenth Amendment, which outlawed slavery; the FOURTEENTH AMENDMENT, which had a provision keeping some former supporters of the Confederacy out of public office until CONGRESS allowed them to serve; and the Fifteenth Amendment, which guaranteed voting rights for black men. Once a state approved the Thirteenth and Fourteenth Amendments, it was to be readmitted to the United States and again represented in Congress. The official end of Reconstruction came in 1877, when the last troops were withdrawn from the South.

• The program established for Reconstruction, largely the work of REPUBLICANS in the North, was far more severe than what President Abraham LINCOLN had proposed before his assassination. Large numbers of white southerners resented being kept out of the "healing" of the nation that Lincoln had called for, and were unwilling to give up their former authority. Ill feeling by former CONFEDERATES during Reconstruction led to the formation of the KU KLUX KLAN, and a long-standing hatred among southerners for the REPUBLICAN PARTY.

Red Scare The rounding up and deportation of several hundred immigrants of RADICAL political views by the federal government in 1919 and 1920. This "scare" was caused by fears of subversion by COM-MUNISTS in the United States after the RUSSIAN REVOLUTION.

Remember the *Maine* A slogan of the SPANISH-AMERICAN WAR. The United States battleship *Maine* mysteriously exploded and sank in the harbor of HAVANA, CUBA, in 1898. Stirred up by the YELLOW PRESS, the American public blamed the sinking on SPAIN, which then owned Cuba. President William MCKINLEY, who had opposed war, yielded to public pressure and asked CONGRESS to declare war.

Republican party One of the two major political parties in the United States. The party began in 1854 (*see under "American History to 1865"*); Abraham LINCOLN, elected in 1860, was the first REPUBLICAN president. During RECONSTRUCTION, many Republicans were eager to punish the South for its former slaveholding and for its SECESSION from the United States. The northern Republicans, for example, supported CARPETBAGGERS in southern governments. After Reconstruction, the Republicans favored a high PROTECTIVE TARIFF, and were generally considered the defenders of northeastern and business interests. The party supported the SPANISH-AMERICAN WAR and the expansion of United States territory overseas. Some Republicans were part of the PROGRESSIVE MOVEMENT of the early twentieth century. In the 1920s, the party reestablished its reputation for supporting business, and as being wary of any expansion of the place of government in national life. This characterization is still a reasonably accurate, if simplistic, description of basic Republican views. Since Lincoln, the Republican presidents have been Andrew JOHNSON, Ulysses S. GRANT, Rutherford B. Hayes, James A. GARFIELD, Chester A. Arthur, Benjamin Harrison, William MCKINLEY, Theodore ROOSEVELT, William Howard TAFT, Warren G. HARDING, Calvin COOLIDGE, Herbert HOOVER, Dwight D. EISENHOWER, Richard NIXON, Gerald FORD, Ronald REAGAN, and George BUSH.

• The party is often called the GOP, which stands for "Grand Old Party." • The party's symbol is an ELEPHANT.

Roaring Twenties The 1920s in the United States, called "roaring" because of the exuberant, freewheeling popular CULTURE of the decade. The Roaring Twenties was a time when many people defied PROHIBITION, indulged in new styles of dancing and dressing, and rejected many traditional moral standards. (*See* FLAPPERS *and* JAZZ AGE.)

Robinson, Jackie An African-American athlete of the twentieth century. In 1947, he became the first black person to play baseball in the major leagues.

Rockefeller, Nelson A political leader of the twentieth century, and a grandson of John D. ROCKEFELLER. He was governor of NEW YORK from 1957 to 1971, and sought the REPUBLICAN nomination for president several times. Rockefeller was known as a moderate or LIBERAL Republican. He served as vice president under President Gerald FORD.

Roe versus Wade An extremely controversial SUPREME COURT decision in 1973 that, on the basis of the right to privacy, gave women an unrestricted right to ABORTION during the first three months of pregnancy. Pro-choice forces have hailed the decision, while those associated with the "right-to-life" movement (pro-lifers) have opposed it.

Roosevelt, Eleanor (ROH-zuh-vuhlt, ROH-zuh-velt) The wife of President Franklin D. ROOSEVELT. Her humanitarian and diplomatic efforts were known and respected all over the world. She represented the United States in the General Assembly of the UNITED NATIONS from 1949 to 1952.

FRANKLIN D. ROOSEVELT

Roosevelt, Franklin D. (FDR) (ROH-zuh-vuhlt, ROH-zuh-velt) A political leader of the twentieth century. Roosevelt was president from 1933 to 1945,

longer than anyone else in American history; he was elected four times. Roosevelt, a DEMOCRAT who had been governor of NEW YORK, defeated President Herbert HOOVER in the election of 1932. He took office at one of the worst points in the Great DEPRESSION, but told the American public, "The ONLY THING WE HAVE TO FEAR IS FEAR ITSELF." The early part of his presidency is remembered for the NEW DEAL, a group of government programs designed to reverse the devastating effects of the Depression. He used FIRESIDE CHATS over the radio to build public support for his policies. In the later years of his presidency, he attempted to support the ALLIES in WORLD WAR II without bringing the United States into the war. At this time, he made his speech announcing the FOUR FREEDOMS. After the Japanese bombing of PEARL HARBOR, the United States entered the war. Roosevelt began the MANHATTAN PROJECT, which produced the ATOMIC BOMB, a weapon that after his death brought a quick but highly controversial end to the war. Near the war's end, Roosevelt negotiated the YALTA AGREEMENT with BRITAIN and the SOVIET UNION. He died a few weeks before GERMANY surrendered and before the end of the war with JAPAN.

🏵 Roosevelt's appearance seemed designed to produce confidence in a nation discouraged by economic trials. He was frequently portrayed as sticking out his chin, grinning, and smoking a cigarette in a holder. He had suffered an attack of POLIOMYELITIS when he was in his thirties, and for the rest of his life he could not walk unassisted. Photographers were therefore careful not to show him below the waist.

Roosevelt, Theodore (ROH-zuh-vuhlt, ROH-zuh-velt) A political leader of the late nineteenth and early twentieth centuries. Roosevelt was president from 1901 to 1909. He became governor of NEW YORK in 1899, soon after leading a group of volunteer cavalrymen, the ROUGH RIDERS, in the SPANISH-AMERICAN WAR. A REPUBLICAN, Roosevelt was elected vice president in 1900 under President William McKINLEY, and became president when McKinley was assassinated; he was reelected on his own in 1904. As president, he upheld many of the interests of the PROGRESSIVE MOVEMENT. His accomplishments include the breaking up of large monopolies (*see* TRUST BUSTING), better federal inspection of food, closer federal regulation of railroads, and more conservation of NATURAL RESOURCES. Roosevelt summarized his foreign policy as "SPEAK SOFTLY AND CARRY A BIG STICK." He received the NOBEL PRIZE for peace in 1906, after he brought the opponents in the RUSSO-JAPANESE WAR to an agreement. The PANAMA CANAL was begun during his presidency. He did not seek reelection in 1908, but ran unsuccessfully for the presidency in 1912 as the candidate of the PROGRESSIVE PARTY.

&. "Teddy" Roosevelt was a man of hearty enthusiasms, devoted to physical fitness ("the strenuous life") and big-game hunting. He supposedly exclaimed "Bully!" when he was pleased. &. Roosevelt once said that he was "as strong as a bull moose." Accordingly, the Progressive party of 1912, which nominated him for president, was commonly called the Bull Moose party.

Roosevelt's Court packing plan

A move by President Franklin D. ROOSEVELT to increase the size of the SUPREME COURT, and then bring in several new justices who would change the balance of opinion on the Court. Roosevelt proposed to pack the Court in the 1930s, when several CONSERVATIVE justices were inclined to declare parts of his program, the NEW DEAL, unconstitutional. CONGRESS would not allow the number of justices to be increased, and Roosevelt was criticized for trying to undermine the independence of the Court.

Rose Bowl

The oldest and most famous of the "bowl games" — college football games held after the regular college football season between teams that are invited on the basis of their record in the regular season. The Rose Bowl game is played in Pasadena, CALIFORNIA, on New Year's Day, and is preceded by the Tournament of Roses Parade of floats adorned with roses.

Rosenberg case (ROH-zuhn-burg)

A court case involving Julius and Ethel Rosenberg, an American couple who were executed in 1953 as spies for the SOVIET UNION. Some have argued that the Rosenbergs were innocent victims of McCARTHY-era hysteria against COMMUNISTS, or victims of ANTI-SEMITISM (they were Jewish). Others contend that they were indeed Soviet spies.

Rough Riders

The nickname of a volunteer group of cavalry led by Colonel Theodore ROOSEVELT in the SPANISH-AMERICAN WAR. They were famous for

ROUGH RIDERS. *Colonel Theodore Roosevelt (center, wearing glasses) and the Rough Riders on San Juan Hill, Cuba, 1898.*

a victorious charge at the Battle of San Juan Hill in CUBA.

Ruth, Babe

A baseball player of the early twentieth century, known for hitting home runs. He hit sixty home runs in 1927, a record for a 154-game season that still stands. Ruth supposedly once pointed to a spot in the seats where he would hit his next home run, and then proceeded to hit the ball there. His real name was George Herman Ruth.

Sacco and Vanzetti (SAK-oh; van-ZET-ee)

Two anarchists (*see* ANARCHISM), Nicola Sacco and Bartolomeo Vanzetti, who were convicted of a robbery and two murders in MASSACHUSETTS in the early 1920s, and were sentenced to death. Sacco and Vanzetti were born in ITALY, but had been living in the United States for years when they were tried. Several faulty procedures took place in the trial. Many people have thought that Sacco and Vanzetti were convicted because of their political views and not because of the evidence against them. Their supporters obtained several delays of their execution, but a special committee appointed by the governor of Massachusetts upheld the original jury's verdict, and they were put to death in 1927. LIBERALS and RADICALS all over the world were outraged by the execution.

Sanger, Margaret (SANG-uhr)

The founder in the 1910s and 1920s of the BIRTH CONTROL movement (she coined the term), she overcame the initial hostility of the medical profession and combated laws that

MARGARET SANGER. *Photographed in the 1930s making an appeal to a Senate committee for legislation relating to birth control.*

STATE under Presidents Abraham LINCOLN and Andrew JOHNSON. He is best known for arranging the purchase of ALASKA from RUSSIA in 1867 for seven million dollars.

❧ Alaska was long called "Seward's Folly" and "Seward's Icebox" by people who thought that the place would show little return on the American INVESTMENT in it.

sharecropping A system of farming that developed in the South after the CIVIL WAR, when landowners, many of whom had formerly held slaves, lacked the cash to pay wages to farm laborers, many of whom were former slaves. The system called for dividing the crop into three shares — one for the landowner, one for the worker, and one for whoever provided seeds, fertilizer, and farm equipment.

Sherman Antitrust Act A federal law passed in 1890 that committed the American government to opposing MONOPOLIES. The law prohibits CONTRACTS, combinations, or conspiracies "in the restraint of TRADE or commerce." Under the authority of the Sherman Antitrust Act, the federal government initiated suits against the Standard Oil Company and the American Tobacco Company. (*See TRUST BUSTING.*)

in most states prohibited CONTRACEPTION. She later headed the Planned Parenthood Federation.

Scopes trial The trial of John Scopes, a high school teacher in TENNESSEE, for teaching the THEORY of EVOLUTION in violation of state law. The trial was held in 1925, with eminent lawyers on both sides — William Jennings BRYAN for the prosecution and Clarence DARROW for the defense.

❧ At the time, many saw the Scopes trial as a sign of deep conflict between science and religion.

SDI *See STAR WARS.*

settlement houses Social and cultural centers established by reformers in slum areas of American cities during the 1890s and the early 1900s. Jane ADDAMS founded the most famous settlement house, in CHICAGO. (*See PROGRESSIVE MOVEMENT.*)

❧ Settlement houses attracted idealistic college graduates eager to learn how the poor lived and to improve the condition of the poor.

Seward, William H. (SOOH-uhrd) A political leader of the nineteenth century. Seward was SECRETARY OF

silent majority A term used by President Richard NIXON to indicate his belief that the great body of Americans supported his policies, and that those who demonstrated against the involvement of the United States in the VIETNAM WAR amounted to only a noisy minority.

Sioux (SOOH) A common name for the Dakota people, a tribe of NATIVE AMERICANS inhabiting the northern GREAT PLAINS in the nineteenth century. They were famed as warriors, and frequently took up arms in the late nineteenth century to oppose the settlement of their hunting grounds and sacred places. In 1876, Sioux warriors, led by Chief SITTING BULL, and commanded in the field by Chief CRAZY HORSE, overwhelmed the United States cavalry at the Battle of the LITTLE BIGHORN. A group of Sioux under Chief Big Foot were massacred by United States troops at WOUNDED KNEE in 1890.

sit-ins A form of nonviolent protest, employed during the 1960s in the CIVIL RIGHTS MOVEMENT and later in the movement against the VIETNAM WAR. In a sit-in, demonstrators occupy a place open to the public, such as a racially segregated (*see* SEGREGATION) lunch counter or bus station, and then refuse to leave. Sit-ins were designed to provoke arrest and thereby gain attention for the demonstrators' cause.

🐾 The civil rights leader Martin Luther KING, Jr., defended such tactics as sit-ins in his "LETTER FROM BIRMINGHAM JAIL."

SITTING BULL. *An 1885 photograph.*

Sitting Bull   A NATIVE AMERICAN leader of the SIOUX tribe in the late nineteenth century. He was a chief and medicine man when the Sioux took up arms against settlers in the northern GREAT PLAINS and against United States army troops. He was present at the Battle of the LITTLE BIGHORN in 1876, when the Sioux decisively defeated the cavalry led by Colonel George Custer. (*See* CUSTER'S LAST STAND.)

Social Gospel   A religious movement that arose in the United States in the late nineteenth century with the goal of making the CHRISTIAN CHURCHES more responsive to social problems, such as poverty and prostitution. Leaders of the movement argued that JESUS preached a message of social reform and not merely one of individual approaches to SALVATION.

Spanish-American War   A war between SPAIN and the United States, fought in 1898. The war began as an intervention by the United States on behalf of CUBA. Accounts of Spanish mistreatment of Cuban natives had aroused much resentment in the United States, a resentment encouraged by the YELLOW PRESS. The incident that led most directly to the war was the explosion of the United States battleship *Maine* in the harbor of HAVANA, Cuba, an incident for which many Americans blamed Spain (*see* REMEMBER THE *MAINE*). The United States won the war easily. The best-remembered incidents in the Spanish-American War were the charge of the ROUGH RIDERS, led by Theodore ROOSEVELT, in the Battle of San Juan Hill in Cuba, and the Battle of Manila Bay in the PHILIPPINES, at which Admiral George Dewey said, "YOU MAY FIRE WHEN YOU ARE READY, GRIDLEY." The United States acquired PUERTO RICO, Guam, and the Philippines in the war, and gained temporary control over Cuba.

🐾 The victory of the United States in the Spanish-American War made the country a world power, with territories spread across the PACIFIC OCEAN and CARIBBEAN SEA. HAWAII, which had been an independent KINGDOM, was annexed by the United States in the same period.

Speak softly and carry a big stick   A PROVERB quoted by Theodore ROOSEVELT as a brief statement of his approach to foreign policy. (*See* BIG STICK DIPLOMACY.)

Stanton, Elizabeth Cady   A reformer and feminist who joined with Lucretia Mott in issuing the call for the first women's rights convention in America, which was held at Seneca Falls, New York, in 1848. Stanton later worked in close partnership with Susan B. ANTHONY for women's SUFFRAGE. (*See* SENECA FALLS CONVENTION.)

Star Wars   A popular name, taken from the title of a film, for the Strategic Defense Initiative (SDI) of President Ronald REAGAN. "Star Wars" involves the development by the United States of a defense in outer space against INTERCONTINENTAL BALLISTIC MISSILES.

Stevenson, Adlai E. (AD-lee, AD-lay)   A political leader of the twentieth century, who served as governor of ILLINOIS, and as the United States ambassador to the UNITED NATIONS. The CUBAN MISSILE CRISIS occurred during his ambassadorship. He was nominated for president twice by the DEMOCRATIC

PARTY against Dwight D. EISENHOWER, in 1952 and 1956, and lost both times.

&. Stevenson was known for his wit and as a "thinking" rather than a crowd-pleasing candidate.

Strategic Defense Initiative (SDI)   *See* STAR WARS.

Super Bowl   The championship game of the National Football League, held each year in January.

Taft, William Howard   A political leader of the late nineteenth and early twentieth centuries. A REPUBLICAN, Taft was president between 1909 and 1913. At the beginning of his presidency, he stayed close to the policies of Theodore ROOSEVELT, who had been president before him. Later, however, he turned to more CONSERVATIVE measures, such as a high PROTECTIVE TARIFF, and he lost popularity. In foreign policy, Taft advocated DOLLAR DIPLOMACY. He came in third in the election of 1912, running as a REPUBLICAN, behind Woodrow WILSON and Theodore ROOSEVELT. In the 1920s, Taft served as chief justice of the SUPREME COURT.

Taft-Hartley Act   A major law concerning labor, passed by CONGRESS in 1947. President Harry TRUMAN vetoed Taft-Hartley (*see* VETO), but it became law by a two-thirds vote of Congress. It marked a reversal of the pro-labor policies pursued under the presidency of Franklin D. ROOSEVELT. For example, the law prohibited a list of "unfair" labor practices and restricted the political activities of LABOR UNIONS.

Teapot Dome scandal   *See* HARDING SCANDALS.

Tennessee Valley Authority (TVA)   A CORPORATION created by the federal government in the Great DEPRESSION to promote the economic development of the TENNESSEE RIVER and adjoining areas. The TVA, known as a builder of dams, is responsible for flood control, the generation of electric power, SOIL conservation, and other areas of economic development. The TVA was part of the NEW DEAL.

Tet offensive   A series of major attacks by COMMUNIST forces in the VIETNAM WAR. Early in 1968, Vietnamese communist troops seized and briefly held some major cities at the time of the lunar new year, or Tet. The Tet offensive, a turning point in the war, damaged the hopes of United States officials that the combined forces of the United States and South VIETNAM could win.

Thorpe, Jim   An athlete of the twentieth century, known for his ability in several sports. A NATIVE AMERICAN, he was a leading college football player, and also the best performer in track and field events at the 1912 OLYMPIC GAMES.

Three Mile Island   The location of an accident in 1979 in a NUCLEAR POWER plant in PENNSYLVANIA. The plant underwent a partial MELTDOWN that resulted in some RADIATION leakage into the ATMOSPHERE, panic among nearby residents, losses of billions of dollars, and intense criticism of nuclear power programs in general.

transcontinental railroad   A train route across the United States, finished in 1869. It was the project of two railroad companies: the Union Pacific built from the east, and the Central Pacific built from the west. The two lines met in UTAH. The Central Pacific laborers were predominantly Chinese, and the Union Pacific laborers predominantly Irish. Both groups often worked under harsh conditions.

Truman, Harry S. (TROOH-muhn)   A political leader of the twentieth century. A DEMOCRAT, Truman was president from 1945 to 1953. In 1944, after representing MISSOURI in the SENATE, Truman was elected vice president under President Franklin D. ROOSEVELT, and became president when Roosevelt died. He led the nation in the final months of WORLD WAR II, and made the decision to drop ATOMIC BOMBS on HIROSHIMA and NAGASAKI in JAPAN. Truman enthusiastically supported the UNITED NATIONS, and put forward the MARSHALL PLAN to aid the recovery of EUROPE after the war. He sent American troops to support the United Nations in the KOREAN WAR, and, in a controversial move, removed General Douglas MACARTHUR from his command in Korea. (*See* TRUMAN-MACARTHUR CONTROVERSY.)

&. Truman's homespun, often feisty style of leadership made him a symbol of no-nonsense MIDDLE AMERICA. People often encouraged him, following his own preferences in vocabulary, with the words "Give 'em hell, Harry." A sign on his desk read "The BUCK STOPS HERE." He was also fond of the saying, "IF YOU CAN'T STAND THE HEAT, GET OUT OF THE KITCHEN." &. Truman gained a surprise victory in the presidential election of 1948 over the REPUBLICAN candidate, Thomas E. Dewey. On the day of the election, several commentators had confidently asserted that Truman could not win, and the *Chicago Tribune* had gone to press with a huge headline reading "Dewey Defeats Truman." Truman discussed these errors with great relish the next day.

Truman-MacArthur controversy A dispute between President Harry TRUMAN and General Douglas MACARTHUR in 1951, during the KOREAN WAR. MacArthur, who commanded the troops of the UNITED NATIONS, wanted to use American air power to attack the PEOPLE'S REPUBLIC OF CHINA. Truman refused, fearing that an American attack on China would bring the SOVIET UNION into the war. When MacArthur criticized Truman's decision publicly, Truman declared MacArthur insubordinate, and removed him as commanding general. MacArthur returned to the United States, received a hero's welcome, and told CONGRESS, "OLD SOLDIERS NEVER DIE; THEY ONLY FADE AWAY."

Tweed, William Marcy NEW YORK CITY political leader, known as Boss Tweed, who in the late 1860s ran a network of corrupt city officials called the Tweed Ring. Under Tweed, city officials extorted kickbacks from contractors and others doing business with the city. His name is synonymous with municipal corruption.

Vietnam War (vee-et-NAHM, vee-et-NAM) A war in Southeast ASIA, in which the United States fought in the 1960s and 1970s. The war was waged from 1954 to 1975 between COMMUNIST North VIETNAM and noncommunist South VIETNAM, two parts of what was once the French colony of INDOCHINA. Vietnamese communists attempted to take over the South, both by invasion from the North and by GUERRILLA WARFARE conducted within the South by the VIET CONG. Presidents Dwight D. EISENHOWER and John F. KENNEDY sent increasing numbers of American military advisers to South Vietnam in the late 1950s and early 1960s. Kennedy's successor, President Lyndon JOHNSON, increased American military support greatly, until half a million United States soldiers were in Vietnam.

American goals in Vietnam proved difficult to achieve, and the communists' TET OFFENSIVE was a severe setback. Reports of atrocities committed by both sides in the war disturbed many Americans (see MY LAI MASSACRE). Eventually, President Richard NIXON decreased American troop strength, and sent his SECRETARY OF STATE, Henry KISSINGER, to negotiate a cease-fire with North Vietnam. American troops were withdrawn in 1973, and South Vietnam was completely taken over by communist forces in 1975.

❧ The involvement of the United States in the war was extremely controversial. Some supported it wholeheartedly; others opposed it in mass demonstrations and by refusing to serve in the American armed forces (see DRAFT). Still others seemed to rely on the government to decide the best course of action. (See SILENT MAJORITY.) ❧ A large memorial (see VIETNAM MEMORIAL) bearing the names of all members of the United States armed services who died in the Vietnam War is in WASHINGTON, D.C.

Volstead Act (VOL-sted, VAWL-sted, VOHL-sted) A law passed by CONGRESS in 1919 to implement PROHIBITION.

Voting Rights Act of 1965 A law passed at the time of the CIVIL RIGHTS MOVEMENT. It eliminated various devices, such as literacy tests, that had traditionally been used to restrict voting by black people. It authorized the enrollment of voters by federal registrars in states where fewer than 50 percent of the eligible voters were registered or voted. All such states were in the South.

Wall Street Crash of 1929 See CRASH OF 1929, STOCK MARKET.

Wallace, George A political leader of the twentieth century. As governor of ALABAMA in the 1960s, he resisted INTEGRATION, and promised to "stand at the schoolhouse door" to bar black people from admission to the University of Alabama. The NATIONAL GUARD eventually forced him to back down. In 1968, he was nominated for president by a third party, the American Independent party, and came in third, behind Richard NIXON and Hubert HUMPHREY. In 1972, he ran for president again, but was shot and paralyzed by a would-be assassin during the campaign. Wallace presented himself as a POPULIST, who championed poor and middle-income whites against blacks and wealthy, LIBERAL whites. In a remarkable reversal of positions, he endorsed integration in the 1980s, and was again elected governor of Alabama for four years.

War is hell A statement attributed to General William Tecumseh SHERMAN, a leader of the UNION army in the CIVIL WAR. Sherman supposedly said this several years after the war, in an address to a group of cadets.

War on Poverty   A set of government programs, designed to help poor Americans, begun by President Lyndon JOHNSON in 1964. The War on Poverty included measures for job training and improvement of housing.

Warren, Earl   A political leader and judge of the twentieth century. Warren was governor of CALIFORNIA before being named chief justice of the SUPREME COURT in 1953, and he served on the Court until 1969. His time as chief justice was marked by boldness in interpreting the CONSTITUTION; the "Warren Court" often brought the Constitution to the support of the disadvantaged (*see BROWN VERSUS BOARD OF EDUCATION and MIRANDA decision*). Warren also led a government commission investigating the assassination of President John F. KENNEDY. (*See OSWALD, LEE HARVEY.*)

Washington, Booker T.   An African-American educator of the late nineteenth and early twentieth centuries, who headed Tuskegee Institute, a college for black people in ALABAMA. Washington urged blacks to concentrate on economic gains rather than on the pursuit of social and political equality with whites. The best known of his many books is *Up from Slavery*.

Watergate   An incident in the presidency of Richard NIXON that led to his resignation. In June 1972, burglars in the pay of Nixon's campaign committee broke into offices of the DEMOCRATIC PARTY. In a complex chain of events, high officials on Nixon's staff who had been connected to the burglary used illegal means to keep the burglary from being fully investigated; these actions by Nixon's staff were known as the "cover-up." Nixon arranged for secret tape-recording of many conversations in his office regarding the cover-up, and then refused to hand the tapes over to investigators from CONGRESS. After months of legal maneuvers, Nixon finally released the tapes, which showed that he had known about criminal activity by his staff. By this time, the HOUSE OF REPRESENTATIVES was one step away from IMPEACHMENT of Nixon. Leaders of Congress told him that if he were impeached and tried, he would very likely be removed from office. He resigned the presidency in August 1974, complaining of a lack of support from Congress. Several of his assistants were convicted of various crimes connected with Watergate. Nixon himself was never indicted, and was pardoned by his successor, President Gerald FORD.

᠗ Many people became more scornful of government after the Watergate incident. Others were encouraged that the investigation and convictions were finally carried out.

Watts riots   A group of violent disturbances in Watts, a largely black section of LOS ANGELES, in 1965. Over thirty people died in the Watts riots, which were the first of several serious clashes between black people and police in the late 1960s. ᠗ Los Angeles was the scene of another riot in 1992 triggered by the acquittal of white police officers accused of beating an African-American man named Rodney King.

"We Shall Overcome"   The best-known song of the CIVIL RIGHTS MOVEMENT. It contains these words: "Deep in my heart I do believe / That we shall overcome some day."

Wild Bill Hickok   *See HICKOK, WILD BILL.*

Wilson, Woodrow   A political leader and educator of the late nineteenth and early twentieth centuries. A DEMOCRAT, he was elected president in 1912 after serving as president of Princeton University (*see IVY LEAGUE*) and as governor of NEW JERSEY. Wilson was president from 1913 to 1921. He tried to keep the United States neutral after WORLD WAR I broke out in 1914; his campaign slogan in 1916 was "He kept us out of war." After GERMANY had repeatedly violated the neutral status of the United States, the country finally did enter the war in 1917, with Wilson maintaining that "the WORLD MUST BE MADE SAFE FOR DEMOCRACY." Wilson produced his aims for peace, FOURTEEN POINTS, soon afterward. At Wilson's insistence, the treaty that ended the war provided for a new international organization, the LEAGUE OF NATIONS. Wilson was bitterly disappointed when the United States SENATE later refused to permit the United States to join the League. He went on a strenuous speaking tour to convince the American public of the League's importance. While on the tour, he suffered a STROKE, from which he never fully recovered. In 1919, Wilson was given the NOBEL PRIZE for peace.

women's movement A movement to secure legal, economic, and social equality for women, also called the FEMINIST MOVEMENT. It has its roots in the nineteenth-century women's movement, which sought, among other things, to secure property rights and suffrage for women. The modern feminist movement, often said to have been galvanized by the publication of Betty FRIEDAN's book *The Feminine Mystique*, began in the 1960s, and advocates equal pay for equal work, improved day care arrangements, and preservation of ABORTION rights. (See EQUAL RIGHTS AMENDMENT, feminism, and STEINEM, Gloria.)

Works Progress Administration (WPA) A program of the NEW DEAL in the 1930s. The WPA built sidewalks, government buildings, and similar public works throughout the United States. During the GREAT DEPRESSION, the WPA employed many people who could not find other work.

world must be made safe for democracy, The Words used by President Woodrow WILSON in 1917 to justify his call for a declaration of war on GERMANY. The words implied that Germany's militarism threatened DEMOCRACY everywhere.

World Series A series of baseball games held each October between the champions of the two major baseball leagues, the American League and the National League.

Wounded Knee A creek in SOUTH DAKOTA where United States soldiers killed large numbers of Dakota NATIVE AMERICANS — SIOUX — in 1890. The Sioux, under Chief Big Foot, had been resisting settlement of the area, and had fled to MONTANA, but United States troops brought them back to South Dakota for detention. As the soldiers were disarming the warriors in an army camp at Wounded Knee, a rifle shot alarmed the soldiers, and fighting broke out in which over 200 Sioux were killed, including women and children. The massacre was the last major military conflict between whites and Native Americans.

yellow journalism Inflammatory, irresponsible reporting by newspapers. The PHRASE arose during the 1890s, when some American newspapers, particularly those run by William Randolph HEARST, worked to incite hatred of SPAIN, thereby contributing to the start of the SPANISH-AMERICAN WAR.

Yellow Peril A supposed threat to the United States posed by JAPAN and CHINA. The PHRASE arose in the late nineteenth century, at a time when Japanese and Chinese immigration to America was meeting resistance, and when Japan was growing as a military power. (*See* JAPANESE-AMERICANS, INTERNMENT OF.)

yellow press Newspapers that practice YELLOW JOURNALISM.

You may fire when you are ready, Gridley A direction allegedly given by Admiral George Dewey to a subordinate at the Battle of Manila Bay during the SPANISH-AMERICAN WAR.

World Politics

This section includes entries for the various types of government (for example, MONARCHY, REPUBLIC, and DESPOTISM) and for IDEOLOGIES (such as COMMUNISM and SOCIALISM) that influence contemporary political movements. In general, abstract and philosophical terms, even if relevant to the United States, are included here rather than under "American Politics." The "World Politics" section does not include political leaders — even those who currently hold office. These are to be found in the various history sections.

Although "World Politics" deals with regions outside the United States, it does so from an American perspective. The institutions of nations like GREAT BRITAIN, which has close ties to the United States, receive more attention than those of DEVELOPING NATIONS. The peculiar position of the United States as a nuclear superpower is reflected in the number of entries pertinent to the terminology of nuclear arms.

— J. F. K.

ABM *See* ANTIBALLISTIC MISSILE.

absolute monarchy Rule by one person — a monarch, usually a king or a queen — whose actions are restricted neither by written law nor by custom; a system different from a CONSTITUTIONAL MONARCHY and from a REPUBLIC. Absolute monarchy persisted in FRANCE until 1789 and in RUSSIA until 1917.

acquittal The judgment of a court that a person charged with a crime is not guilty.

amnesty A pardon granted by a government for offenders, particularly for political offenders.

anarchism (AN-uhr-kiz-uhm) The belief that all existing governmental authority should be abolished and replaced by free cooperation among individuals.
    ❧ *Anarchy* is sometimes used to refer to any state of chaos or lawlessness.

antiballistic missile (an-tee-buh-LIS-tik, an-teye-buh-LIS-tik) A defensive missile, designed to destroy a BALLISTIC MISSILE in flight.

anti-Semitism (an-tee-SEM-uh-tiz-uhm, an-teye-SEM-uh-tiz-uhm) Prejudice or hatred against JEWS, a SEMITIC race. (*See* ARAB-ISRAELI CONFLICT *and* NAZIS.)

apartheid (uh-PAHR-teyet, uh-PAHR-tayt) The racist policy (*see* RACISM) of SOUTH AFRICA that has denied blacks and other nonwhites civic, social, and economic equality with whites.

appeasement A political policy of conceding to aggression by a warlike nation.
    ❧ A classic example of appeasement is the MUNICH PACT of 1938, negotiated between Neville CHAMBERLAIN and Adolf HITLER. Chamberlain, the PRIME MINISTER of BRITAIN, allowed Hitler to annex part of CZECHOSLOVAKIA to GERMANY.

appropriation The grant of money by a legislature for some specific purpose.

Arab-Israeli conflict A conflict between the Israelis and the Arabs in the MIDDLE EAST. ISRAEL, a nation under control of JEWS, was established in PALESTINE

ANTI-SEMITISM. *A German sign before the Second World War that reads "Jews are not welcome in this town."*

APARTHEID. *Black South Africans reading about a clash between white police and black miners in which eleven miners were killed.*

in the late 1940s, in territory inhabited by Arabs. Israel was placed in the midst of four Arab nations — LEBANON, SYRIA, JORDAN, and EGYPT — and the presence of Israel has led to constant contention between Israel and the Arab world. Both the Israelis and the Arabs claim land in Palestine as theirs by ancestral rights, and war has periodically broken out between them. (*See also* NASSER, GAMAL ABDEL; PALESTINE LIBERATION ORGANIZATION; SADAT, ANWAR; *and* SIX-DAY WAR.)

aristocracy A privileged, primarily hereditary ruling CLASS, or a form of government controlled by such an elite.

🔊 Traditionally, the disproportionate concentration of wealth, social STATUS, and political influence in the aristocracy has been resented by the MIDDLE CLASS and lower class.

at large A descriptive term for the election of public officials by an entire governmental unit rather than by subdivisions of the unit. For example, a delegate at large does not represent any specific district or locale, but speaks instead for a much wider group of people.

atomic bomb (A-bomb) A NUCLEAR WEAPON whose enormous explosive power results from the sudden release of ENERGY from a FISSION reaction. (*See also* HIROSHIMA, HYDROGEN BOMB, NAGASAKI, *and* STRATEGIC ARMS LIMITATION TALKS [SALT].)

attaché (a-ta-SHAY, at-uh-SHAY) A diplomatic officer attached to an embassy or consulate. Most attachés have specialties. There are military attachés, cultural attachés, economic attachés, and so forth.

🔊 Some nations disguise spies as attachés.

autocracy (aw-TOK-ruh-see) A system of government in which supreme political power is held by one person. (*Compare* CONSTITUTIONAL MONARCHY, DEMOCRACY, *and* OLIGARCHY.)

🔊 IRAQ under SUDDAM HUSSEIN is an autocracy.

balance of power A state of peace that results when rival nations are equally powerful and therefore have no good reason to wage war.

balance of terror The BALANCE OF POWER between nations that are equipped with NUCLEAR WEAPONS, stemming from their fear of annihilation in a nuclear war.

balkanization (bawl-kuh-nuh-ZAY-shuhn) Division of a place or country into several small political units, often unfriendly to one another. The term *balkanization* comes from the name of the BALKAN PENINSULA, which was divided into several small nations in the early twentieth century.

ballistic missile (buh-LIS-tik)   *See* INTERCONTINENTAL BALLISTIC MISSILE *and* INTERMEDIATE-RANGE BALLISTIC MISSILE.

banana republics   A term describing any of several small nations in LATIN AMERICA that have economies based on a few agricultural crops.

🖙 The term *banana republic* is often used in a disparaging sense; it suggests an unstable government.

Berlin wall   A wall that separated West BERLIN, GERMANY, from EAST GERMANY, which surrounded it until 1989. At the end of WORLD WAR II, the victorious ALLIES divided Berlin, the German capital, into four sectors. The eastern, or Russian, sector became the capital of COMMUNIST East Germany. The French, British, and American sectors continued as a prosperous Western "island" city surrounded by East Germany. From then until 1961, many East Germans, sometimes 2000 a day, fled to West Berlin, often with nothing more than the clothes they had on their backs. In the summer of 1961, the wall was built, and East Germany forbade its citizens to cross the wall, at the risk of being shot immediately by border guards. In November 1989, the East German government reopened the border and issued visas to East Berliners. The Berliners celebrated by breaking off pieces of the wall at a mass demonstration, which lasted into the next day. The wall has since been demolished.

🖙 The Berlin wall was one of the most visible signs of the COLD WAR, and has become a symbol of the IRON CURTAIN and TOTALITARIANISM.

bicameral legislature (beye-KAM-uhr-uhl)   A legislature with two houses, or chambers. The British PARLIAMENT is a bicameral legislature, made up of the HOUSE OF COMMONS and the HOUSE OF LORDS. Likewise, the United States CONGRESS is made up of the HOUSE OF REPRESENTATIVES and the SENATE.

bilateralism (beye-LAT-uhr-uh-liz-uhm)   Trade or diplomatic relations between two countries. (*See* DIPLOMACY *and* RECOGNITION; *compare* MULTILATERALISM *and* UNILATERALISM.)

birth control   The practice of preventing conception to limit the number of births. (*See* CONTRACEPTION, FAMILY PLANNING, POPULATION CONTROL, and SANGER, MARGARET.)

boat people   People who attempt to escape oppressive conditions in their countries by taking to the sea, often in makeshift boats. The best-known emigrations of boat people have been from VIETNAM after the COMMUNIST victory in 1975; from the PEOPLE'S REPUBLIC OF CHINA to destinations in the south PACIFIC OCEAN; and from HAITI and CUBA to the United States.

brinkmanship   The policy of a nation that pushes a dangerous situation to the limits of safety before pulling back; an aggressive and adventurous foreign policy.

Bundestag (BOON-duhs-tahg)   The lower house of the legislature of GERMANY.

cabinet   A select group of officials who advise the head of government. In nations governed by PARLIAMENTS, such as BRITAIN, the members of the cabinet typically have seats in Parliament. (*Compare* CABINET *under* "American Politics.")

capital punishment   The death penalty for a crime.

capitalism   An economic and political system characterized by a FREE MARKET for GOODS and SERVICES, and private control of production and consumption. (*Compare* SOCIALISM *and* COMMUNISM.)

capitalist   *See* CAPITALISM.

chauvinism   Exaggerated belief in the supremacy of one's nation, CLASS, CASTE, or group. Chauvinism usually involves XENOPHOBIA.

🖙 The word *chauvinism* is often used as shorthand for "male chauvinism," a term describing the attitudes of men who believe that women are inferior and should not be given equal STATUS with men. (*See also* FEMINISM.)

civil disobedience   The refusal to obey a law out of a belief that the law is morally wrong.

🖙 In the nineteenth century, the American author Henry David THOREAU wrote "CIVIL DISOBEDIENCE," an important ESSAY justifying such action.

🖙 In the twentieth century, civil disobedience was exercised by Mahatma GANDHI in the struggle for independence in INDIA. Civil disobedience, sometimes called NONVIOLENT RESISTANCE or PASSIVE RESISTANCE, was also practiced by some members of the CIVIL RIGHTS MOVEMENT in the United States, notably Martin Luther KING, Jr., to challenge SEGREGATION of public facilities; a common tactic of these civil rights supporters was the SIT-IN. King defended

CIVIL DISOBEDIENCE. *Antinuclear activists staging a sit-in at the Seabrook, N.H., nuclear power plant.*

the use of civil disobedience in his "LETTER FROM BIRMINGHAM JAIL."

civil service The nonmilitary personnel who work for a government, applying its laws and regulations.

coalition An alliance of political groups formed to oppose a common foe or pursue a common goal.

 In countries with many political parties, none of which can get a majority of the citizens' votes, the only way an effective government can be formed is by a coalition of parties. Such coalitions are often unstable.

coexistence, peaceful *See* PEACEFUL COEXISTENCE.

cold war A constant nonviolent state of hostility between the SOVIET UNION and the UNITED STATES. The cold war began shortly after WORLD WAR II, with the rapid extension of Soviet influence over eastern EUROPE and NORTH KOREA. With the COLLAPSE OF COMMUNISM in Eastern Europe and the former Soviet Union, the cold war has apparently ended. (*See* BERLIN AIRLIFT, BERLIN WALL, *and* IRON CURTAIN.)

colonialism The control of one nation by "transplanted" people of another nation — often a geographically distant nation that has a different CULTURE and dominant racial or ethnic group. (*See* ETHNICITY.)

 A classic example of colonialism is the control of INDIA by BRITAIN from the eighteenth century to 1947. Control that is economic and cultural, rather than political, is often called NEOCOLONIALISM.

commissar (KOM-uh-sahr) In various COMMUNIST systems of government, an official assigned to a

group to ensure the group's conformity to Communist party doctrine. The heads of government departments in the former SOVIET UNION were called commissars.

commissioned officer An officer of a country's armed services whose rank is confirmed by a government document (a commission). In many countries, including the United States, commissioned officers in the navy are those of the rank of ensign and above, and in the army and air force those of the rank of lieutenant and above.

 Commissioned officers are contrasted with enlisted men and women, such as privates, corporals, and sergeants, or ordinary seamen and petty officers.

common law Law developed in the course of time from the rulings of judges, as opposed to law embodied in statutes passed by legislatures (STATUTORY LAW) or law embodied in a written CONSTITUTION (constitutional law). (*See* STARE DECISIS.)

 The importance of common law is particularly stressed in the legal system of BRITAIN, on which the legal system of the United States is based.

Common Market *See* EUROPEAN ECONOMIC COMMUNITY *under "Business and Economics."*

communism An economic and social system envisioned by the nineteenth-century German scholar Karl MARX. In theory under communism, all means of production are owned in common, rather than by individuals (*see* MARXISM *and* MARXISM-LENINISM). In practice, a single authoritarian party controls both the political and economic systems. In the twentieth century, communism has been associated with the economic and political systems of CHINA and the SOVIET UNION, and of the SATELLITES of the Soviet Union. (*Compare* CAPITALISM *and* SOCIALISM.)

communist A supporter of COMMUNISM.

confederation A group of nations or states, or a government encompassing several states or political divisions, in which the component states retain considerable independence. The members of a confederation often delegate only a few powers to the central authority.

 The United States was governed as a confederation in the first few years of its independence. (*See* ARTICLES OF CONFEDERATION.) CANADA is officially a confederation of provinces.

consent of the governed A condition urged by many as a requirement for LEGITIMATE GOVERNMENT: that the authority of a government should depend on the consent of the people, as expressed by votes in elections. (*See* DECLARATION OF INDEPENDENCE, DEMOCRACY, *and* LOCKE, JOHN.)

conservatism A general preference for the existing order of society, and an opposition to efforts to bring about sharp change. (*Compare* LIBERALISM.)

conservative A descriptive term for persons, policies, and beliefs associated with CONSERVATISM.

constitution A nation or state's fundamental set of laws. Most nations with constitutions have them in written form, such as the United States CONSTITUTION. The constitution of BRITAIN, by contrast, is an informal set of traditions, based on several different laws.

constitutional monarchy A form of national government in which the power of the monarch (the king or queen) is restrained by a PARLIAMENT, by law, or by custom. Several nations, especially in modern times, have passed from ABSOLUTE MONARCHY to a constitutional monarchy, including BELGIUM, BRITAIN, DENMARK, The NETHERLANDS, NORWAY, SPAIN, and SWEDEN.

counterinsurgency Military power applied in GUERRILLA WARFARE in support of the established government.

coup (KOOH) In politics, an ABBREVIATION for COUP D'ÉTAT.

coup d'état (kooh day-TAH) A quick and decisive seizure of governmental power by a strong military or political group. In contrast to a revolution, a coup d'état, or COUP, does not involve a mass uprising. Rather, in the typical coup, a small group of politicians or generals arrests the incumbent leaders, seizes the national radio and television services, and proclaims itself in power. *Coup d'état* is French for "stroke of the state" or "blow to the government."

Court of St. James's The royal court of BRITAIN, including the queen or king and a group of officials who aid in ruling the country.

❧ Ambassadors to Britain are officially ambassadors to the Court of St. James's.

covenant A CONTRACT formed between two or more parties that is sealed with solemn vows. Political covenants usually involve pledges of mutual assistance and allegiance. (*Compare* COVENANT *under* "The Bible.")

cultural imperialism The imposition of a foreign viewpoint or civilization on a people.

decadence A state of moral decline. The term is often used in reference to the FALL OF ROME. (*See also* FIN DE SIÈCLE.)

demagogue (DEM-uh-gog, DEM-uh-gawg) A politician who seeks to win and hold office by appeals to mass PREJUDICE. Demagogues often use lies and distortion. (*See* HITLER, ADOLF, *and* STALIN, JOSEPH.)

democracy A system of government in which power is vested in the people, who rule either directly or through freely elected representatives.
❧ Democratic institutions, such as PARLIAMENTS, may exist in a MONARCHY. Such CONSTITUTIONAL MONARCHIES as BRITAIN, CANADA, and SWEDEN are generally counted as democracies in practice.

despotism (DES-puh-tiz-uhm) Unlimited political rule by one person.
❧ The term usually suggests unscrupulous rule, or tyranny.

détente (day-TAHNT) A period of lessening tension between two major national powers, or a policy designed to lessen that tension. Détente presupposes that the two powers will continue to disagree, but seeks to reduce the occasions of conflict.

deterrence A military capability sufficiently strong to discourage any would-be aggressor from starting a war because of the fear of retaliation. (*See* BALANCE OF TERROR.)

developing nation A nation where the average INCOME is much lower than in industrial nations, where the economy relies on a few EXPORT crops, and where farming is conducted by primitive methods. In many developing nations, rapid population growth threatens the supply of food. Developing nations have also been called underdeveloped nations. Most of them are in AFRICA, ASIA, and LATIN AMERICA. (*See also* THIRD WORLD.)

dictatorship Government by a single person or by a JUNTA or other group that is not responsible to the people or their elected representatives.

&. Adolf HITLER and Joseph STALIN were dictators.

diplomatic immunity Exemption of diplomats — ambassadors and other representatives of a foreign nation — from the laws of the nation to which they are assigned.

&. Foreign representatives have sometimes gone unpunished for serious crimes after claiming diplomatic immunity. The main purpose of diplomatic immunity, however, is to protect diplomats from harassment or arrest by their host government.

disfranchisement (dis-FRAN-cheyez-muhnt) Removal of the FRANCHISE, or right to vote.

dissidents Persons who refuse to conform to prevailing political and social values.

draconian (druh-KOH-nee-uhn) A descriptive term for strict and unreasonably harsh rules, laws, and penalties: "These draconian laws will certainly cause a rebellion."

&. Draco, after whom draconian measures were named, was a lawgiver in ancient ATHENS.

Eastern Bloc The name applied to the former COMMUNIST states of eastern EUROPE, including YUGOSLAVIA and ALBANIA, as well as the countries of the WARSAW PACT. (*See also* EUROPEAN ECONOMIC COMMUNITY *and* IRON CURTAIN.)

equity A body of rules or customs based on general principles of fair play rather than on COMMON LAW or STATUTORY LAW.

escalation An increase in the intensity or geographical scope of a war or diplomatic confrontation. For example, during the KOREAN WAR, some Americans urged escalation of the war through bombing of the PEOPLE'S REPUBLIC OF CHINA.

established church A religious denomination that receives financial and other support from the government, often to the exclusion of support for other de-

nominations. (*See under "World Literature, Philosophy, and Religion."*)

European Economic Community *See under "Business and Economics."*

expatriation (eks-pay-tree-AY-shuhn) Voluntary departure from the nation of one's birth for permanent or prolonged residence in another nation.

extradition (ek-struh-DISH-uhn) The legal process by which one government may obtain custody of individuals from another government in order to put them on trial or imprison them.

faction A group formed to seek some goal within a political party or a government. The term suggests quarrelsome dissent from the course pursued by the party or government majority: "His administration is moderate, but it contains a faction of extremists."

family planning The use of education and BIRTH CONTROL to limit the number of offspring and the population of a country. (*See* POPULATION CONTROL *and* SANGER, MARGARET.)

FEMINISM. *Feminist leaders Bella Abzug (left) and Betty Friedan (right) at the 1980 Democratic National Convention.*

feminism The doctrine — and the political movement based on it — that women should have the same economic, social, and political rights as men. (*See under* "*Anthropology, Psychology, and Sociology.*"

first-strike capability The ability to launch a surprise attack on an enemy with NUCLEAR WEAPONS; an attack designed to cripple the enemy's capacity to retaliate. (*See* PREEMPTIVE STRIKE.)

franchise (**political**) The vote, or the right to vote. Revocation of the franchise is DISFRANCHISEMENT.

general strike A STRIKE of all of the workers in a nation or area. General strikes are usually brief, and designed to show the unity of the WORKING CLASS.

Geneva Conventions A set of international rules that govern the treatment of prisoners, the sick and wounded, and civilians during war. Under the Geneva Conventions, for example, ambulances and military hospitals and their staff are officially neutral and are not to be fired upon. Nearly all countries of the world have agreed to the Geneva Conventions.

🔊 The first Geneva Convention was drawn up in the late nineteenth century, and concerned only the sick and wounded in war. It has been revised several times since to accommodate new wartime conditions.

genocide (JEN-uh-seyed) The deliberate destruction of an entire race or nation. The HOLOCAUST conducted by the NAZIS in GERMANY and the ARMENIAN MASSACRES in TURKEY are examples of attempts at genocide.

glasnost (GLAHS-nuhst, GLAS-nost, GLAZ-nost) A Russian word meaning "openness," which describes the policy of Mikhail GORBACHEV, PREMIER of the former SOVIET UNION. The term refers to a general loosening of government control on all aspects of life in the Soviet Union, even to the point of permitting criticism of government policies.

global village A PHRASE coined by Marshall Mc-LUHAN to describe the world that has been "shrunk" by modern advances in communications. McLuhan likened the vast network of communications systems to one extended CENTRAL NERVOUS SYSTEM, ultimately linking everyone in the world.

graft In politics, the illegal acceptance of bribes by government officials.

greatest good for the greatest number A goal put forth for governments: that they should be judged by the results of their policies, and specifically, whether those policies benefit the majority. (*Compare* GREATEST HAPPINESS FOR THE GREATEST NUMBER.)

guerrilla warfare (guh-RIL-uh) Wars fought with hit-and-run tactics by small groups against an invader or against an established government. (*See* COUNTERINSURGENCY.)

gulag (GOOH-lahg) A system of prison camps inside the former SOVIET UNION used for political prisoners. Under STALIN, millions of prisoners in these camps died from starvation and maltreatment. This system was given worldwide attention in the writings of Aleksandr SOLZHENITSYN. *Gulag* is an ACRONYM in Russian of the name meaning Chief Administration of Corrective Labor Camps.

Gypsies A nomadic people who originated in the region between INDIA and IRAN and who migrated to EUROPE in the fourteenth or fifteenth century. Most now live in Europe and the United States. Their language is called Romany. Thousands were murdered in the HOLOCAUST.

🔊 One who lives a footloose, carefree life is sometimes called a gypsy.

house arrest Forcible detention in one's house rather than in a prison. House arrest is used by some nations as a way to silence political dissent without the elaborate trials and criminal proceedings that would bring bad publicity.

House of Commons The lower house of the PARLIAMENT of BRITAIN. It includes representatives from ENGLAND, NORTHERN IRELAND, SCOTLAND, and WALES, all elected by the people. It is more powerful than the HOUSE OF LORDS, the upper house of Parliament. The leader of the ruling party in the House of Commons is the PRIME MINISTER of Britain; the prime minister chooses a CABINET composed mainly of members of the House of Commons. (*Compare* HOUSE OF LORDS.)

House of Lords The upper house of the PARLIAMENT of BRITAIN. The House of Lords is composed of the leading clergymen and nobles of the country. (*Compare* HOUSE OF COMMONS.)

human rights Freedom from arbitrary interference or restriction by governments. The term encompasses largely the same rights called CIVIL LIBERTIES or CIVIL RIGHTS, but often suggests rights that have not been recognized.

    🌢 Political leaders in the United States often use the expression when speaking of rights violated by other nations.

hydrogen bomb A NUCLEAR WEAPON with enormous explosive power, fueled by nuclear FUSION, in which ATOMS of HYDROGEN combine to form atoms of HELIUM.

ICBM *See* INTERCONTINENTAL BALLISTIC MISSILE.

ideology (eye-dee-OL-uh-jee, id-ee-OL-uh-jee) A system of beliefs or THEORIES, usually political, held by an individual or a group. CAPITALISM, COMMUNISM, and SOCIALISM are usually called ideologies.

imperialism Acquisition by a government of other governments or territories, or of economic or cultural power over other nations or territories, often by force. COLONIALISM is a form of imperialism.

intercontinental ballistic missile (ICBM) (buh-LIS-tik) A missile with a long range (5000 miles or more) that carries NUCLEAR WARHEADS, and can be launched from the ground or from submarines. (*See also* MIRV.)

intermediate-range ballistic missile (IRBM) A missile that carries NUCLEAR WARHEADS, and is launched from the ground or submarines, but has a range of only a few hundred to 1500 miles.

International Court of Justice A division of the UNITED NATIONS that settles legal disputes submitted to it by member nations. The International Court of Justice, also called the WORLD COURT, meets in THE HAGUE, The NETHERLANDS.

international law A body of rules and principles that govern the relations among nations. (*See* GENEVA CONVENTIONS *and* INTERNATIONAL COURT OF JUSTICE.)

"Internationale" (ann-tuhr-nahs-yuh-NAHL, in-tuhr-nash-uh-NAHL) An international anthem of COMMUNISTS and SOCIALISTS.

internationalism The view that nations should cooperate in international organizations such as the UNITED NATIONS to settle disputes.

IRA *See* IRISH REPUBLICAN ARMY.

IRBM *See* INTERMEDIATE-RANGE BALLISTIC MISSILE.

Irish Republican Army (IRA) A secret organization in IRELAND that originally fought for Irish independence from BRITAIN. After the division of Ireland in the early twentieth century into NORTHERN IRELAND, which remained united with Britain, and the Irish Free State, now called the Republic of Ireland (see IRELAND, REPUBLIC OF), the IRA took as its goal the uniting of the entire island under the Republic. The IRA continues to pursue this goal; membership, however, is illegal in the Republic, and the IRA's PROVISIONAL WING practices terrorism.

jingoism Extreme and emotional NATIONALISM, or CHAUVINISM, often characterized by an aggressive foreign policy, accompanied by an eagerness to wage war.

John Bull A figure who stands for ENGLAND in literary and political SATIRE and in cartoons. John Bull is a stout, feisty man, often shown in a suit made out of the British flag.

    🌢 John Bull is the British equivalent of the United States' SYMBOL UNCLE SAM.

junta (HOON-tuh, JUN-tuh) A group of military leaders who govern a country after a COUP D'ÉTAT.

KGB The secret police of the former SOVIET UNION.

kibbutz (ki-BOOTS) PLUR. KIBBUTZIM (ki-boot-SEEM) A communal farm or settlement in ISRAEL. Kibbutzim have helped build national spirit in Israel, and the residents have transformed barren land into fertile, crop-producing land.

Knesset (KNES-et, kuh-NES-et) The PARLIAMENT of ISRAEL.

Kremlin A fortress in central MOSCOW that contains the central offices of the government of RUSSIA.

KREMLIN

The term *Kremlin* was also used figuratively to mean the former Soviet government.

Kurds (kurdz, koordz)   A linguistically and culturally distinct people who inhabit parts of SYRIA, IRAN, IRAQ, TURKEY, and the former SOVIET UNION. Once part of the OTTOMAN EMPIRE, they long have sought an independent nation state, but without success. After his defeat in the PERSIAN GULF WAR, Saddam HUSSEIN brutally repressed rebellious Kurds in northern Iraq.

SALADIN was a Kurd.

leftist   One who holds a LEFT-WING viewpoint; someone who seeks RADICAL social and economic change in the direction of greater equality.

left-wing   A descriptive term for LIBERAL, RADICAL, or revolutionary political views, particularly the view that there are unacceptable social inequalities in the present order of society. COMMUNISTS and SOCIALISTS, as well as moderate liberals, come under the term *left-wing*. Left-wing groups are sometimes known collectively as the Left. (*Compare* RIGHT-WING.)

legitimate government   A government generally acknowledged as being in control of a nation and de-serving formal RECOGNITION, which is symbolized by the exchange of diplomats between that government and the governments of other countries.

liaison (LEE-uh-zon, lee-AY-zon)   A means of communication between two organizations or persons, especially governments.

liberal   A descriptive term for persons, policies, and beliefs associated with LIBERALISM.

liberalism   In the twentieth century, a viewpoint or IDEOLOGY associated with free political institutions and religious toleration, as well as support for a strong role of government in regulating CAPITALISM and constructing the WELFARE STATE.

machine, political   A powerful political organization, usually on the city or county level, that is dominated by a single "boss" or by a small group of skilled politicians. (*See also under* "American Politics.")

mandate   A command or an expression of a desire, especially by a group of voters for a political program. Politicians elected in landslide victories often claim that their policies have received a mandate from the voters.

KURDS. *A Kurdish family in a Turkish refugee camp.*

Marxism   The doctrines of Karl MARX and his associate Friedrich ENGELS on ECONOMICS, politics, and society. They include the notion of economic determinism — that political and social structures are determined by the economic conditions of people. Marxism calls for a classless society where all means of production are commonly owned (COMMUNISM), a system to be reached as an inevitable result of the struggle between the leaders of CAPITALISM and the workers.

Marxism-Leninism (LEN-uh-niz-uhm)   The doctrines of MARXISM as applied by LENIN, a founder of the SOVIET UNION, to the building of Marxist nations. With Karl MARX, Lenin called for a classless society where all means of production would be commonly owned (COMMUNISM). Unlike some Marxists, however, Lenin stressed bold, revolutionary action, and insisted that a strong COMMUNIST party would be needed in a Marxist nation to direct the efforts of the workers. Lenin also argued that CAPITALIST nations resort to aggressive IMPERIALIST moves as they decline, and that Marxist nations must therefore be prepared for war. Eventually, according to Marxism-Leninism, the rigid governmental structures that have characterized the former Soviet Union and other

Marxist nations will not be necessary; the "withering away of the state" will occur. A major problem for Marxism-Leninism has been the difficulty of abandoning these governmental structures.

minister   A title used in many countries for members of CABINETS and similar public officials, who are roughly equivalent to the officials in the United States CABINET. For example, a minister of foreign affairs will have duties similar to those of the SECRETARY OF STATE of the United States.

MIRV (MURV)   *See* MULTIPLE INDEPENDENTLY TARGETED REENTRY VEHICLE.

Molotov cocktail (MOL-uh-tawf, MOL-uh-tawv)   An incendiary bomb made from a breakable container, such as a bottle, filled with flammable liquid and provided with a rag wick. Used by the Soviets against the invading German armies in WORLD WAR II, these bombs were nicknamed after V. M. Molotov, a foreign MINISTER of the SOVIET UNION at that time.

monarchy (MON-uhr-kee, MON-ahr-kee)   A system of government in which one person reigns, usually a king or queen. The authority, or crown, in a monarchy is generally inherited. The ruler, or monarch, is often only the head of state, not the head of government. Many monarchies, such as BRITAIN and DENMARK, are actually governed by PARLIAMENTS. (*See* ABSOLUTE MONARCHY *and* CONSTITUTIONAL MONARCHY.)

moratorium (mawr-uh-TAWR-ee-uhm)   A period of delay agreed to by parties to a dispute or parties who are negotiating. A moratorium may also be an authorized delay in the repayment of a LOAN, especially by a nation (as in a moratorium on war DEBTS).

multilateralism (mul-tee-LAT-uhr-uh-liz-uhm)   Trade or diplomatic negotiations among several nations. (*See* DIPLOMACY *and* RECOGNITION; *compare* BILATERALISM *and* UNILATERALISM.)

multiple independently targeted reentry vehicle (**MIRV**)   A warhead on a BALLISTIC MISSILE that contains more than one NUCLEAR WEAPON, each capable of being aimed at a different target.

MX missile   A highly accurate NUCLEAR WEAPON, housed in a silo. A type of INTERCONTINENTAL BALLISTIC MISSILE, the MX was designed by the United States to attack similar silo-based missiles in the SOVIET UNION.

national liberation movements Movements that arise in DEVELOPING NATIONS to expel colonialist powers (*see* COLONIALISM), often by means of GUERRILLA WARFARE.

national self-determination Creation of national governmental institutions by a group of people who view themselves as a distinct nation (for example, because they have a common language). National self-determination is opposed to COLONIALISM and IMPERIALISM. (*See* FOURTEEN POINTS.)

nationalism The strong belief that the interests of a particular nation-state are of primary importance. Also, the belief that a people who share a common language, history, and CULTURE should constitute an independent nation, free of foreign domination.

   🕭 Nationalism is opposed to COLONIALISM and IMPERIALISM.

nationalization The taking over of private property by a national government.

NATO (NAY-toh) See NORTH ATLANTIC TREATY ORGANIZATION.

natural rights Rights that people supposedly have under NATURAL LAW. The DECLARATION OF INDEPENDENCE of the United States lists life, liberty, and the pursuit of happiness as natural rights.

neocolonialism The dominance of strong nations over weak nations, not by direct political control (as in traditional COLONIALISM), but by economic and cultural influence.

Nobel laureate (noh-BEL) Someone who has been awarded a NOBEL PRIZE.

Nobel Prizes Prizes given annually for achievement in PHYSICS, CHEMISTRY, literature, peace, ECONOMICS, and medicine and PHYSIOLOGY. The prizes were founded by a Swedish munitions maker, Alfred Nobel, and are considered a mark of worldwide leadership in the fields in which they are given. Nobel winners, called NOBEL LAUREATES, receive their prizes in ceremonies in STOCKHOLM, SWEDEN, except for the peace prize, which is presented in OSLO, NORWAY.

nonaligned nations Nations of the THIRD WORLD that as a group rejected alliance with either the United States or the SOVIET UNION.

nonalignment See NONALIGNED NATIONS.

nonperson A former political leader whom a government wants the people to ignore, because the former leader's views or actions are considered unacceptable by the current government. This unusual practice is most commonly used in totalitarian states (*see* TOTALITARIANISM), where past leaders often disappear from the official histories of one REGIME and reappear in the histories of another. This was particularly striking in the former SOVIET UNION, where leaders such as TROTSKY and KHRUSHCHEV became nonpersons even while they were alive. (*See* REHABILITATION.)

nonviolent resistance Refusal to obey a law considered unjust; CIVIL DISOBEDIENCE.

   🕭 Mahatma GANDHI urged and practiced nonviolent resistance during the efforts to win independence for INDIA from BRITAIN in the early twentieth century. 🕭 African-Americans in the CIVIL RIGHTS MOVEMENT often practiced nonviolent resistance in the South in the 1960s — for example, by sitting-in at segregated lunch counters in order to provoke arrest and draw attention to their cause. (*See* SEGREGATION *and* SIT-INS.)

North Atlantic Treaty Organization (NATO) (NAY-toh) An international organization, begun in 1949, known as NATO. The members have pledged to settle disputes among themselves peacefully, and to defend one another against outside aggressors. The founding members of NATO are BELGIUM, CANADA, DENMARK, GREAT BRITAIN, ICELAND, ITALY, LUXEMBOURG, The NETHERLANDS, NORWAY, PORTUGAL, and the United States. GREECE, SPAIN, TURKEY, and GERMANY became members later. FRANCE was a founding member, but withdrew from NATO's military command in 1967. The WARSAW PACT was signed by the SOVIET UNION and its allies largely in response to the formation of NATO.

Nuclear Test Ban Treaty An agreement made in 1963 by BRITAIN, the SOVIET UNION, and the United States not to test NUCLEAR WEAPONS in the air, in outer space, or under the sea. Underground testing was permitted under the treaty.

nuclear testing The testing of ATOMIC BOMBS by exploding them either above or below ground. (*See* NUCLEAR TEST BAN TREATY.)

nuclear warhead The part of an armament system containing the explosive charge, in this case one

whose explosive power comes from a NUCLEAR RE-
ACTION (*see* ATOMIC BOMB *and* HYDROGEN BOMB).
Warheads are mounted on the forward part of a pro-
jectile such as a BALLISTIC MISSILE or an artillery
round.

nuclear weapon Any weapon that employs a NU-
CLEAR REACTION for its explosive power. Nuclear
weapons include BALLISTIC MISSILES, bombs (*see*
ATOMIC BOMB *and* HYDROGEN BOMB), artillery
rounds, and mines.

nuclear-free zone An area in which NUCLEAR WEAP-
ONS, by choice of the residents, may not be moved or
stored. A number of areas around the world, such as
NEW ZEALAND, have declared themselves nuclear-
free zones, or have attempted to.

OAS *See* ORGANIZATION OF AMERICAN STATES.

oligarchy (OL-uh-gahr-kee, OH-luh-gahr-kee) A system of government in which power is held by a small
group.

ombudsman (OM-buhdz-muhn, OM-boodz-muhn)
An official appointed by a government or other organization to investigate complaints against people in
authority. This position is designed to give those with
less power — the "little people" — a voice in the operation of large organizations.

OPEC (OH-pek) *See* ORGANIZATION OF PETRO-
LEUM EXPORTING COUNTRIES.

Organization of American States (OAS) An international organization that includes the United States
and over thirty nations in LATIN AMERICA. It was
founded in the 1940s to promote the peaceful settlement of disputes and economic cooperation among
members.

pacifism The view that war is morally unacceptable
and never justified (*see* CONSCIENTIOUS OBJECTOR).
The term is sometimes applied to the belief that international disputes should be settled peacefully.

Palestine Liberation Organization (PLO) A government that claims to represent the people of PAL-
ESTINE displaced by the establishment of ISRAEL (*see*
ARAB-ISRAELI CONFLICT). The PLO is a COALITION
of Palestinian Arab groups that are RADICAL to varying degrees; some endorse the use of terrorism. Since
Israel occupies much of what was once Palestine, the

YASIR ARAFAT. *Leader of the Palestine
Liberation Organization.*

PLO is essentially a government in exile, and moves
from place to place. Currently its main headquarters
are in TUNISIA; Yasir ARAFAT is its leader. Over objections from the United States, the UNITED NATIONS
recognized the PLO as the only legitimate representative of the Palestinian people, and in 1988, the
United States itself established official relations with
the PLO.

parliament (PAHR-luh-muhnt) An assembly of representatives, usually of an entire nation, that makes
laws. Parliaments began in the MIDDLE AGES in
struggles for power between kings and their people.
Today, parliaments differ from other kinds of legislatures in one important way: some of the representatives in the parliament serve as government MINIS-
TERS, in charge of carrying out the laws that the
parliament passes. Generally, a parliament is divided
by political parties, and the representative who leads
the strongest political party in the parliament becomes the nation's *head of government.* This leader
is usually called the PRIME MINISTER OR PREMIER.
Typically, a different person — usually a king, queen,
or president — is *head of state,* and this person's duties are usually more ceremonial than governmental.

❧ The number of nations governed by parliaments has greatly increased in modern times.

parliamentary system (pahr-luh-MEN-tree, pahr-luh-MEN-tuh-ree)   A system of government in which the power to make and execute laws is held by a PARLIAMENT. BRITAIN has a parliamentary system of government, one of the oldest in the world. The United States does not; its legislature, the CONGRESS, passes the laws, and a separate part of government, the EXECUTIVE BRANCH, carries them out.

partition   A division of a nation or territory into two or more nations. CYPRUS, GERMANY, INDIA, IRELAND, KOREA, PALESTINE, and VIETNAM are notable examples of countries that have undergone partition.

passive resistance   A technique of demonstrating opposition to a government's activities simply by not cooperating with them. It is particularly associated with Mahatma GANDHI, who opposed violent revolution in his own country's fight for independence. (*Compare* CIVIL DISOBEDIENCE and NONVIOLENT RESISTANCE.)

peaceful coexistence   The idea that COMMUNIST and CAPITALIST nations need not be at war, but can live and compete together in peace. It was first advanced around 1960 by the PREMIER of the SOVIET UNION, Nikita KHRUSHCHEV, who called on both sides to avoid nuclear war. Khrushchev maintained that the communists would ultimately prevail, but by economic and political strength, not by war.

People's Republic of China   The government of CHINA set up in 1949 after the victory of the COMMUNIST forces of MAO ZEDONG. The People's Republic ruled the mainland of China, forcing the government of NATIONALIST CHINA into exile on the island of TAIWAN. For years, many Western nations, especially the United States, refused to recognize the People's Republic as the government of mainland China; instead, they exchanged ambassadors only with Nationalist China. The United States recognized the People's Republic as the government of China in 1979.

plebiscite (PLEB-uh-seyet, PLEB-uh-suht)   A vote of an entire nation or other large political unit on an issue of great importance. A plebiscite is not an election, for there are no candidates. Rather, people vote yes or no on a proposition.

PLO   *See* PALESTINE LIBERATION ORGANIZATION.

plutocracy (plooh-TOK-ruh-see)   Government by the rich. The term is usually one of reproach.

POGROM. *Cossacks beating workers in St. Petersburg.*

pogrom (puh-GRUM, puh-GROM, POH-gruhm)   A massacre or persecution instigated by the government or by the ruling CLASS against a minority group, particularly JEWS.

❧ Pogroms were common in RUSSIA during the nineteenth century.

polarization   In politics, the grouping of opinions around two extremes: "As the debate continued, the union members were polarized into warring FACTIONS."

police state   A nation whose rulers maintain order and obedience by the threat of police or military force; one with a brutal, arbitrary government.

politburo (POL-it-byoor-oh, POH-lit-byoor-oh)   A commonly used name for those who made the major governmental decisions in the former SOVIET UNION. A politburo, in general, is the chief committee of a COMMUNIST party.

political science   The systematic study of government and politics. Political science is a SOCIAL SCIENCE that makes generalizations and analyses about political systems and political behavior, and uses these results to predict future behavior. Political science includes the study of political PHILOSOPHY, ETHICS, international relations and foreign policy, public administration, and the dynamic relations between different parts of governments.

population control In reaction to the prediction by Thomas MALTHUS that the world's population would soon outgrow its food supply, a movement began in the early twentieth century to limit the number of births, and therefore limit the growth of the world's population. The movement is supported by groups such as the International Planned Parenthood Federation. A number of countries have made population control a national policy. To varying extents, the methods of population control include FAMILY PLANNING, BIRTH CONTROL, CONTRACEPTION, and ABORTION. These policies are opposed by many groups, including the CATHOLIC CHURCH, and are controversial.

Power tends to corrupt; absolute power corrupts absolutely An observation that a people's sense of morality lessens as their power increases. The statement was made by Lord Acton, a British historian of the late nineteenth and early twentieth centuries.

preemptive strike A first-strike attack with NUCLEAR WEAPONS (*see* FIRST-STRIKE CAPABILITY) carried out in order to destroy an enemy's capacity to respond. A preemptive strike is based on the assumption that the enemy is planning an imminent attack.

premier The head of government in many nations. A premier's position is usually the same as that of a PRIME MINISTER. The chiefs of government of the provinces of CANADA are called premiers.

prime minister The head of government in many nations. Prime minister is commonly the title of the head of government in a PARLIAMENTARY SYSTEM, such as that of BRITAIN or CANADA.

Prince of Wales A title traditionally held by the male heir to the throne of BRITAIN. (*See* WALES.)

proletariat (proh-luh-TAIR-ee-uht) In MARXISM, the industrial WORKING CLASS, people without property.

propaganda Official government communications to the public that are designed to influence opinion.

The information may be true or false, but it is always carefully selected for its political effect.

protectorate (pruh-TEK-tuhr-uht) A relationship between a strong sovereign nation and a weak nation or area not recognized as a nation. Once the strong nation has established a protectorate over a weak nation, it can control the latter's affairs.

Provisional Wing of the Irish Republican Army A RADICAL terrorist FACTION of the IRISH REPUBLICAN ARMY that sprang up in the late 1960s. The "Provos" aim at removing British control from six counties in the north of IRELAND that are part of the UNITED KINGDOM.

purge The systematic removal of political opponents by a government or other political organization.

radical In politics, someone who demands substantial or extreme changes in the existing system.

rapprochement (rap-rohsh-MAHNN, rah-prawsh-MAHNN) A closer approach of two groups to each other. *Rapprochement*, a French term, is often applied to two nations, especially ones that become reconciled after relations between them have worsened.

reactionary An extremely CONSERVATIVE person or position that not only resists change but seeks to return to the "good old days" of an earlier social order.

realpolitik (ray-AHL-poh-li-TEEK) Governmental policies based on hard, practical considerations rather than on moral or idealistic concerns. *Realpolitik* is German for "the politics of reality," and is often applied to the policies of nations that consider only their own interests in dealing with other countries.

recognition In diplomacy, the act by which one nation acknowledges that a foreign government is a LEGITIMATE GOVERNMENT, and exchanges diplomats with it. The withholding of recognition is a way for one government to show its disapproval of another.

Red Cross, International An international organization, founded under the terms of the first GENEVA CONVENTION. Its original duty was to care for those who were wounded, sick, or homeless in wartime. Today, it also attends to victims of natural disasters.

red tape   Administrative procedures, especially in a BUREAUCRACY, that are marked by complexity and delay: "Red tape delayed his passport."

referendum (ref-uh-REN-duhm)   A vote by the general public, rather than by governmental bodies, on a bill or some other important issue; a PLEBISCITE. (*See under "American Politics."*)

REFUGEES. *Vietnamese boat people being picked up by a rescue ship, after nine days without food or water.*

refugees   People who flee a nation, often to escape punishment for their political affiliations or for political dissent.

regime (ray-ZHEEM, ri-ZHEEM)   An administration, or a system of managing government.

rehabilitation   In politics, the restoration to favor of a political leader whose views or actions were formerly considered unacceptable. (*Compare* NONPERSON.)

reparation   Compensation demanded by a victorious nation from a defeated nation. Reparations can be in the form of GOODS or money.

    🐟 After WORLD WAR I, heavy reparation DEBTS were imposed on GERMANY by BRITAIN, FRANCE, and the other victorious nations. Resentment over these reparations aided the rise of Adolf HITLER.

reprisal   An act by which a nation seeks, short of war, to redress a wrong committed against it by another nation. BOYCOTTS and blockades are common forms of reprisal.

republic   A form of government in which power is explicitly vested in the people, who in turn exercise their power through elected representatives. Today, the terms *republic* and DEMOCRACY are virtually interchangeable, but historically the two differed. *Democracy* implied direct rule by the people, all of whom were equal, while *republic* implied a system of government in which the will of the people was mediated by representatives, who might be wiser and better educated than the average person. In the early American republic, for example, the requirement that voters own property, and the establishment of institutions such as the ELECTORAL COLLEGE, were intended to cushion the government from the direct expression of the popular will.

Rhodes scholarship (ROHDZ)   A scholarship for study at OXFORD UNIVERSITY. Cecil Rhodes, an English financier of the late nineteenth century, established the scholarships to train potential leaders. They are designed for students from GERMANY, and from nations formerly part of the BRITISH EMPIRE, including the United States. Rhodes scholars are chosen for ability, moral character, and success in sports.

right-wing   A descriptive term for CONSERVATIVE or REACTIONARY political views, particularly those supporting the current social order or calling for a return to an earlier order. Right-wing groups are sometimes known collectively as the Right. (*Compare* LEFT-WING.)

sanctions   In politics, penalties imposed by one or more nations on another nation for misconduct. Sanctions may be economic, such as the denial of trade, or diplomatic, such as withdrawal of RECOGNITION or expulsion from international organizations.

satellite   In politics, a nation that is dominated politically by another. The WARSAW PACT nations, other than the SOVIET UNION itself, were commonly called satellites of the Soviet Union.

Security Council   An important division of the UNITED NATIONS that contains five permanent members — the United States, BRITAIN, CHINA, FRANCE, and RUSSIA — and ten rotating members. It is often called into session to respond quickly to international crises. Any permanent member can exercise a VETO over a resolution before the Security Council.

sedition   Acts that incite rebellion or civil disorder against an established government.

Semite (SEM-eyet) Someone who belongs to the SEMITIC peoples. The Semites are supposedly descended from the biblical Shem, the eldest son of NOAH.

Semitic (suh-MIT-ik) A descriptive term for several peoples of the MIDDLE EAST and their descendants, including JEWS and ARABS (see ARAB-ISRAELI CONFLICT). Today the term is usually applied to Jews only. (See ANTI-SEMITISM.)

smart weapons Bombs and projectiles guided by LASERS and other means, known for their extraordinary accuracy. They were employed with telling effect by UNITED NATIONS forces in the PERSIAN GULF WAR.

socialism An economic system in which the production and distribution of GOODS are controlled substantially by the government rather than by PRIVATE ENTERPRISE, and in which cooperation rather than competition guides economic activity. There are many varieties of socialism. Some socialists tolerate CAPITALISM, as long as the government maintains the dominant influence over the economy; others insist on an abolition of private enterprise. All COMMUNISTS are socialists, but not all socialists are communists.

Solidarity A LABOR UNION in POLAND, independent of the government and of the Polish COMMUNIST party, that grew to a membership of several million in the early 1980s. Led by Lech WALESA, Solidarity pushed for many reforms and played a major part in the ouster of COMMUNISM in Poland and its replacement by a multiparty, DEMOCRATIC government.

sovereignty (SOV-ruhn-tee, sov-uhr-uhn-tee) A nation or state's supreme power within its borders. A government might respond, for example, to criticism from foreign governments of its treatment of its own citizens by citing its rights of sovereignty.

Soviet Bloc The COMMUNIST nations closely allied with the SOVIET UNION, including BULGARIA, CUBA, CZECHOSLOVAKIA, EAST GERMANY, HUNGARY, POLAND, and RUMANIA, whose foreign policies depended on those of the Soviet Union. It did not include communist nations with independent foreign policies, such as CHINA, YUGOSLAVIA, and ALBANIA. The Soviet Union used its military force several times in the Soviet Bloc to ensure that the countries' governments followed Soviet preferences: in East Germany in 1953, in Hungary and Poland in 1956, and in Czechoslovakia in 1968, for example. (See WARSAW PACT.)

statutory law (STACH-uh-tawr-ee) A law or group of laws passed by a legislature or other official governing bodies. (Compare COMMON LAW.)

Strategic Arms Limitation Talks (SALT) Negotiations started in HELSINKI, FINLAND, in 1969 between the United States and the SOVIET UNION to limit the countries' stock of NUCLEAR WEAPONS. The treaties resulting from these negotiations are called SALT I and SALT II.

strategy/tactics Two levels of problem solving. Strategy is a broad plan of action; tactics are the means for carrying out strategy.

summit meeting Direct personal negotiations between heads of governments, especially meetings that took place between the leaders of the United States and the former SOVIET UNION.

theocracy (thee-OK-ruh-see) A nation or state in which the clergy exercise political power, and in which religious law is dominant over civil law. IRAN since the revolution led by the Ayatollah KHOMEINI is a theocracy under the Islamic clergy. (See ISLAM.)

Third World The NONALIGNED NATIONS — which are often DEVELOPING NATIONS — of AFRICA, ASIA, and LATIN AMERICA. They are in a "third" group of nations since they were neither allied with the United States nor with the SOVIET UNION.

throw-weight The size of the NUCLEAR WARHEAD or set of warheads that a missile, such as a BALLISTIC MISSILE, can carry. A nation might make up for the inaccuracy of its missiles by increasing their throw-weight.

Tories A political party in BRITAIN, also called the CONSERVATIVE party. In the late eighteenth century, the Tories took form as defenders of the king and stability, and of established interests in Britain; they advised caution in making political and social change. Winston CHURCHILL, Benjamin DISRAELI, and Margaret THATCHER have belonged to the party.

totalitarianism (toh-tal-uh-TAIR-ee-uh-niz-uhm) Domination by a government of all political, social, and economic activities in a nation. Totalitarianism is a phenomenon of the twentieth century: earlier forms of DESPOTISM and AUTOCRACY lacked the technical capacity to control every aspect of life. The term is applied both to fascist governments (*see* FACISM) and to many forms of COMMUNISM.

Trotskyism (TROT-skee-iz-uhm)   The doctrines of the twentieth-century Russian political leader Leon TROTSKY, who believed that COMMUNISM should depend on the cooperation of the PROLETARIATS of all nations rather than on domination by the SOVIET UNION. Trotsky's ideas were opposed by Joseph STALIN, the Soviet PREMIER, who sent Trotsky into exile, made him a NONPERSON, and eventually had him assassinated.

ultimatum (ul-tuh-MAY-tuhm)   A formal message delivered from one government to another threatening war if the receiving government fails to comply with conditions set forth in the message. For example, after the assassination of the Archduke FRANCIS FERDINAND in 1914, the government of AUSTRIA sent an ultimatum to Serbia, which Austria held responsible for the assassination.

UNESCO (yooh-NES-koh)   *See* UNITED NATIONS EDUCATIONAL, SCIENTIFIC, AND CULTURAL ORGANIZATION.

unilateralism (yooh-nuh-LAT-uhr-uh-liz-uhm)   Action initiated or taken by a single nation rather than by two nations (*see* BILATERALISM) or several (*see* MULTILATERALISM). For example, a nation might choose to disarm unilaterally in the hope that others will follow. (*See* RECOGNITION.)

United Kingdom   Part of the official name of the British nation; the full name is the UNITED KINGDOM OF GREAT BRITAIN AND NORTHERN IRELAND. It includes ENGLAND, SCOTLAND, WALES, and six counties of IRELAND, ruled by the king or queen of England, and represented in the nation's PARLIAMENT.

United Nations   An organization that includes virtually all countries in the world, with nearly 160 member nations. Its General Assembly, in which each member nation has one vote, guides policies and finances generally. Another important division of the United Nations is the SECURITY COUNCIL, in which

five powerful nations have a majority; the Security Council is charged with solving crises and keeping peace. The United Nations also includes an Economic and Social Council, a Secretariat, or administrative division, and the INTERNATIONAL COURT OF JUSTICE, or WORLD COURT. It also is allied with several agencies that operate independently, such as the UNITED NATIONS EDUCATIONAL, SCIENTIFIC, AND CULTURAL ORGANIZATION (UNESCO), the World Bank, and the World Health Organization. ⋙ The United Nations was formed after WORLD WAR II as a successor to the LEAGUE OF NATIONS, and has served as a forum for many international disputes, notably the ARAB-ISRAELI CONFLICT and the CUBAN MISSILE CRISIS. ⋙ The KOREAN WAR was officially fought by the United Nations against NORTH KOREA. ⋙ A twenty-eight nation coalition of United Nations member states opposed IRAQ's invasion of KUWAIT in 1990. (*See* PERSION GULF WAR.)

United Nations Educational, Scientific, and Cultural Organization (UNESCO)   A controversial agency allied with the UNITED NATIONS. UNESCO was founded to enhance cooperation among members of the United Nations in education, science, and CULTURE. In the 1980s, several countries withdrew, complaining that UNESCO had become too political.

veto   A vote that blocks a decision. In the UNITED NATIONS, for example, each of the five permanent members of the SECURITY COUNCIL has the power of veto.

walk-out   The action of leaving a meeting, place of work, or organization as an expression of disapproval or grievance: "During Grimm's speech, the RADICAL students staged a walk-out."

welfare state   A state or government that promotes public welfare through programs of public health, PENSIONS, UNEMPLOYMENT COMPENSATION, public housing, and the like. The expression *welfare state* is often used by those hostile to government intervention in these areas.

West Bank   Land on the west bank of the JORDAN RIVER, formerly in the hands of JORDAN, but captured by ISRAEL in the SIX-DAY WAR of 1967. Israel has maintained that its security requires that it keep the West Bank. The Israeli government has been widely criticized for moving civilian settlers as well as soldiers into the West Bank.

World Court *See* INTERNATIONAL COURT OF JUSTICE.

zero-sum game A game in which the winnings of some players must equal the losses of the others. Zero-sum games are mentioned in a political context when it is believed that resources are limited, and every decision will produce both winners and losers.

In such situations, political decisions will be made on the basis of trade-offs between competing interests.

Zionism The belief that JEWS should have their own nation; Jewish NATIONALISM. Zionism gained much support among Jews and others in the early twentieth century, and the hoped-for nation was established in the late 1940s in PALESTINE, as the state of ISRAEL. Zionism is opposed by most Arabs. (*See* ARAB-ISRAELI CONFLICT.)

American Politics

A merican politics includes the formal institutions of our government, such as CONGRESS, the SUPREME COURT, and the various departments that compose the EXECUTIVE BRANCH, and also the process by which various bodies of citizens (often called INTEREST GROUPS) compete for influence or control over these institutions. This competition gives rise to many terms that routinely appear in the MASS MEDIA, usually without definitions. Examples include LOBBY, PORK-BARREL LEGISLATION, and MACHINE POLITICS.

The principal vehicles by which Americans traditionally have sought to influence their government are political parties, notably the REPUBLICAN and DEMOCRATIC PARTIES. These two parties, which have long dominated American politics, are themselves loose coalitions of interest groups. These interest groups are bound together by their desire to win elections, an objective that induces them to formulate PLATFORMS that will appeal to as many voters as possible.

But the goals of interest groups within a particular party often come into conflict. Try as they will, party platforms cannot always minimize the differences. As a result, interest groups sometimes shift allegiance from one party to another. For example, from 1865 until the 1930s, blacks overwhelmingly voted Republican, while southern whites gave such unflinching support to the Democratic party that their region was known as the SOLID SOUTH. Today, these allegiances have been reversed. Blacks overwhelmingly vote Democratic, while southern whites increasingly vote Republican. No matter how disenchanted an interest group becomes with a particular party, however, it nearly always prefers transferring to the rival party rather than forming a third party. Most interest groups recognize that their only chance for enduring influence lies in riding one of the major parties to victory.

The two-party system helps to distinguish American politics from the politics of some European DEMOCRACIES, which have a large number of parties. Another distinguishing feature of American politics is FEDERALISM, not only in the sense that power is divided between the federal government and the states, but also in the sense that the system of CHECKS AND BALANCES ensures a division of power within the federal government itself. Federalism plays all sorts of tricks on the two-party system. For example, the Republican party has won its share of presidential elections since WORLD WAR II, but has rarely controlled Congress. Republican presidents have often been forced to cut deals with Democratic congressional majorities. One effect of this division is that, regardless of the platform of the victorious candidate in a presidential election, the actual laws passed under any presidential administration usually reflect compromises between the two parties.

Compared to other nations, the United States is also distinguished by the large role its courts play in its political system. One of the few points of agreement among Americans is that the CONSTITU-TION is a document to be venerated. As interpreters of the Constitution, federal courts have often defined and redefined social and civil relations that in other nations are set by custom and tradition. Within the last thirty years, for example, the federal courts played a critical role in breaking down racial SEGREGATION. Our list of entries necessarily includes a large number of terms related to the legal interpretation of CIVIL RIGHTS.

Entries under "American Politics" include only terms current today. In contrast, the two "American History" sections generally cover terms that, while once of great political significance, lack current relevance. Most items pertaining to American foreign policy, including the language of the arms race, can be found in the "World Politics" section. The latter also includes philosophical movements that have affected both American and foreign political movements.

— J. F. K.

academic freedom   The right of teachers and students to express their ideas in the classroom or in writing, free from political, religious, or institutional restrictions, even if these ideas are unpopular.

ACLU   *See* American Civil Liberties Union.

affirmative action   A term referring to various government policies that aim to increase the proportion of African-Americans, women, and other minorities in jobs and educational institutions historically dominated by white men. The policies usually require employers and institutions to set goals for hiring or admitting minorities.

&. Affirmative action has been extremely controversial. Supporters maintain that it is the only way to overcome the effects of past discrimination and promote INTEGRATION. Critics dismiss it as "reverse discrimination," denying opportunities to qualified whites and men. (*See BAKKE* decision.)

AFL-CIO   ABBREVIATION for the American Federation of Labor–Congress of Industrial Organizations, two groups that merged in 1955 to become the largest federation of LABOR UNIONS in the United States. Member unions, including a variety of workers from machinists to musicians, make up over 70 percent of the unionized labor force in the United States.

&. Though nonpartisan, the AFL-CIO has strong traditional ties with the DEMOCRATIC PARTY.

Alaskan pipeline   An oil pipeline that runs 800 miles from oil reserves in Prudhoe Bay, on the northern coast of ALASKA, to the port of Valdez, on Alaska's southern coast, from which the oil can be shipped to markets. Also called the Trans-Alaska pipeline.

&. After oil was discovered in Prudhoe Bay in 1968, construction of the pipeline was delayed for several years, as conservationists warned against the effects of the pipeline on the ECOSYSTEMS through which it would run.

&. In 1989 an environmental disaster occurred when an oil tanker, the *Exxon Valdez,* ran aground and leaked millions of gallons of oil into Prince William Sound, causing the largest oil spill in U.S. history.

alderman   (AWL-duhr-muhn)   A member of a city council. Aldermen usually represent city districts, called wards, and work with the mayor to run the city government. Jockeying among aldermen for political influence is often associated with MACHINE POLITICS.

American Civil Liberties Union   An organization founded in 1920 in the wake of the RED SCARE to defend CIVIL LIBERTIES. Usually called simply the ACLU, it has often defended the rights of individuals aligned with unpopular causes, including American COMMUNISTS and NAZIS.

American Dream   A phrase connoting hope for prosperity and happiness, symbolized particularly by having a house of one's own. Possibly applied at first to the hopes of immigrants, the phrase now applies to all except the very rich, and suggests a confident hope that one's children's economic and social condition will be better than one's own.

American Legion   The largest organization of American veterans, open to those who participated in WORLD WAR I, WORLD WAR II, the KOREAN WAR, and the VIETNAM WAR. The American Legion has established an influential political position, gaining support in CONGRESS and the federal EXECUTIVE BRANCH for veterans' interests; its efforts contributed to the creation of the VETERANS ADMINISTRATION, which provides medical services and other benefits to veterans and their families. Traditionally CONSERVA-

TIVE, the American Legion promotes patriotism and a strong military defense. (*See also* VETERANS OF FOREIGN WARS.)

amicus curiae (uh-MEE-kuhs KYOOR-ee-eye) *See* FRIEND OF THE COURT.

antitrust legislation   Laws passed in the United States, especially between 1890 and 1915, to prevent large business CORPORATIONS, called TRUSTS, from combining into MONOPOLIES in order to restrict competition. The laws were instituted to encourage FREE ENTERPRISE.
  ⠆ The enforcement of antitrust laws has been inconsistent. ⠆ While the Bell Telephone system was declared a monopoly and forced to break up, huge corporations continue to merge.

appeals, court of   *See* COURT OF APPEALS.

apportionment   The allocation of seats in a legislature or of taxes according to a plan. In the United States CONGRESS, for example, the apportionment of seats in the HOUSE OF REPRESENTATIVES is based on the relative population of each state, while the apportionment in the SENATE is based on equal representation for every state. (*See also* GERRYMANDER.)

appropriation   The grant of money by a legislature for some specific purpose. The authority to grant appropriations, popularly known as the POWER OF THE PURSE, gives legislatures a powerful check over EXECUTIVE BRANCHES and JUDICIAL BRANCHES, for no public money can be spent without legislative approval. CONGRESS, for example, can approve or reject the annual budget requests of the executive branch for its agencies and programs, thereby influencing both domestic and foreign policy. (*See also* CHECKS AND BALANCES *and* PORK-BARREL LEGISLATION.)

arbitration   The settling of disputes (especially labor disputes) between two parties by an impartial third party, whose decision the contending parties agree to accept. Arbitration is often used to resolve conflict diplomatically in order to prevent a more serious confrontation.

Atomic Energy Commission (AEC)   An agency of the United States government from 1946 to 1974 that was charged with controlling and developing the use of atomic energy for civilian and military pur-

poses. In 1974, the AEC was abolished, and its duties were divided between two new agencies: the Energy Research and Development Administration (now a part of the DEPARTMENT OF ENERGY) and the NUCLEAR REGULATORY COMMISSION (NRC).

attorney general of the United States   The head of the United States DEPARTMENT OF JUSTICE, and a member of the president's CABINET. The attorney general is the chief law enforcement officer of the United States government.

block grant   A financial aid package that grants federal money to state and local governments for use in social welfare programs, such as law enforcement, community development, and health services. Block grants provide money for general areas of social welfare, rather than for specific programs. This arrangement not only reduces bureaucratic RED TAPE, but also allows grant recipients more freedom to choose how to use the funds. A product of REPUBLICAN administrations in the 1970s and 1980s, block grants reduce federal responsibility for social welfare. (*See* FEDERALISM.)

blue laws   Laws that prohibit certain businesses from opening on Sunday or from selling certain items on that day. Blue laws often apply to bars and to alcohol sales. Originally enacted to allow observation of Sunday as a SABBATH, blue laws have come under attack as violating the SEPARATION OF CHURCH AND STATE. The courts, however, have upheld most blue laws, on the basis that their observance has become SECULAR, and promotes Sunday as a day of rest and relaxation.

branches of government   The division of government into executive, legislative, and judicial branches. In the case of the federal government, the three branches were established by the CONSTITUTION. The EXECUTIVE BRANCH consists of the president, the CABINET, and the various departments and executive agencies. The LEGISLATIVE BRANCH consists of the two houses of CONGRESS, the SENATE and the HOUSE OF REPRESENTATIVES, and their staff. The JUDICIAL BRANCH consists of the SUPREME COURT and the other federal courts.

broad construction   A THEORY of interpretation of the CONSTITUTION that holds that the spirit of the times, the values of the justices, and the needs of the

CAPITOL HILL

nation may legitimately influence the decisions of a court, particularly the SUPREME COURT. Sometimes called JUDICIAL ACTIVISM. (*See* WARREN, EARL.)

busing   The movement of students from one neighborhood to a school in another neighborhood, usually by bus, and usually to break down DE FACTO SEGREGATION of public schools.

&. A SUPREME COURT decision in 1971 ruling that busing was an appropriate means of achieving integrated schools (*see* INTEGRATION) was received with widespread, sometimes violent, resistance, particularly among whites into whose neighborhoods and schools black children were to be bused. Recently, the Court ruled that school districts could end busing if they had done everything "practicable" to eliminate the traces of past discrimination.

cabinet   A group of presidential advisers, composed of the heads of the thirteen government departments (the secretaries of the DEPARTMENTS of AGRICULTURE, COMMERCE, DEFENSE, EDUCATION, ENERGY, HEALTH AND HUMAN SERVICES, HOUSING AND URBAN DEVELOPMENT, the INTERIOR, LABOR, STATE, TRANSPORTATION, and the TREASURY, and the ATTORNEY GENERAL — all of whom are appointed by the president and confirmed by the SENATE) and a

few other select government officials. Theoretically, the cabinet is charged with debating major policy issues and recommending action by the EXECUTIVE BRANCH; the actual influence of the cabinet, however, is limited by competition from other advisory staffs.

capital offense   A crime, such as murder or betrayal of one's country, that is treated so seriously that death may be considered an appropriate punishment.

capital punishment   The infliction of the death penalty as punishment for certain crimes. (*See* CAPITAL OFFENSE.)

&. In the United States, capital punishment has been an extremely controversial issue on legal, moral, and ethical grounds. In 1972, the SUPREME COURT ruled that the death penalty was not, in principle, CRUEL AND UNUSUAL PUNISHMENT (and not, therefore, unconstitutional), but that its implementation through existing state laws *was* unconstitutional. In 1976, the Supreme Court again ruled that the death penalty was not unconstitutional, though a mandatory death penalty for any crime was. Thirty-seven states now practice the death penalty.

Capitol Hill   A hill in WASHINGTON, D.C., on which the United States CAPITOL building sits. The

Checks and Balances in the Federal Government

Powers		Checks on Powers
Passes federal laws. Can override President's veto of a bill by a two-thirds vote. Establishes lower federal courts and number of federal judges.	**Legislative**	President can veto federal bills. Supreme Court can declare laws unconstitutional.
Approves or vetoes federal bills. Carries out federal laws. Appoints federal judges and other high federal officials. Can make foreign treaties. Can grant pardons and reprieves to federal offenders.	**Executive**	Congress can override President's veto by a two-thirds vote. Senate can refuse to confirm presidential appointments. Senate can refuse to ratify treaties. Congress can impeach and remove President. Supreme Court can declare executive acts unconstitutional.
Interprets and applies the law. Can declare laws passed by Congress and actions taken by the executive unconstitutional.	**Judicial**	Congress can propose constitutional amendments to overturn judicial decisions. Congress can impeach and remove federal judges.

HOUSE OF REPRESENTATIVES and the SENATE meet in the Capitol. (*See* ON THE HILL.)

caucus (KAW-kuhs) A meeting of members of a political party to nominate candidates, choose convention delegates, plan campaign tactics, determine party policy, or select leaders for a legislature.

Central Intelligence Agency (CIA) An agency of the United States government, responsible for coordinating information-gathering activities outside the United States in the interest of national security. The CIA works with the DEPARTMENT OF STATE and a variety of civilian and military organizations to protect American interests abroad and recommend directions for American foreign policy.

  ❧ The extreme secrecy of many of the CIA's operations has enhanced its reputation as an organization of espionage and intrigue.

checks and balances A fundamental principle of American government, guaranteed by the CONSTITUTION, whereby each branch of the government (EXECUTIVE, JUDICIAL, and LEGISLATIVE) has some measure of influence over the other branches and may choose to block procedures of the other branches. Checks and balances prevent any one branch from accumulating too much power and encourage cooperation between branches as well as comprehensive debate on controversial policy issues. For example, to enact a federal law, the SENATE and the HOUSE OF REPRESENTATIVES must each vote to pass the law. In this sense, each house of CONGRESS can check the other. Furthermore, even if the two houses do agree, the president must sign the law. If he chooses to VETO the law, it can still be enacted if two-thirds of the members of both houses vote to override the veto. Under this arrangement, both Congress and the president can check each other. (*See also* APPROPRIATION, IMPEACHMENT, JUDICIAL REVIEW, *and* SEPARATION OF POWERS.)

CIA *See* CENTRAL INTELLIGENCE AGENCY.

CIO *See* AFL-CIO.

circuit courts of appeals *See* COURT OF APPEALS.

citizen's arrest An arrest made by a private citizen, rather than a police officer. Under certain conditions, citizens may make lawful arrests, usually if they have been witness to a FELONY or MISDEMEANOR or have reasonable cause to believe that such a crime has been committed.

civil liberties In general, the rights to freedom of thought, expression, and action, and the protection of these rights from government interference or restriction. Civil liberties are the hallmark of liberal, DEMOCRATIC "free" societies. In the United States, the BILL OF RIGHTS guarantees a variety of civil liberties, most notably FREEDOM OF ASSEMBLY, FREEDOM OF THE PRESS, FREEDOM OF RELIGION, and FREEDOM OF SPEECH, expressed in the FIRST AMENDMENT. (*See* CIVIL RIGHTS.)

civil rights A broad range of privileges and rights guaranteed by the United States CONSTITUTION and subsequent amendments and laws that guarantee fundamental freedoms to all individuals. These freedoms include the rights of free expression and action (CIVIL LIBERTIES); the right to enter into CONTRACTS, own property, and initiate lawsuits; the rights of DUE PROCESS and EQUAL PROTECTION OF THE LAWS; opportunities in education and work; the freedom to live, travel, and use public facilities wherever one chooses; and the right to participate in the democratic political system.

    ❧ Efforts to redress the situation of inequality, such as the CIVIL RIGHTS MOVEMENT and the WOMEN'S MOVEMENT, have resulted in legislation such as the CIVIL RIGHTS ACTS of the 1960s, AFFIRMATIVE ACTION, and creation of the EQUAL EMPLOYMENT OPPORTUNITY COMMISSION.

clear and present danger The standard set by the SUPREME COURT for judging when FREEDOM OF SPEECH may lawfully be limited. Justice Oliver Wendell HOLMES, Jr., illustrated the point by arguing that no one has a constitutional right to SHOUT "FIRE!" IN A CROWDED THEATER when no fire is present, for such action would pose a "clear and present danger" to public safety. (*See* FIRST AMENDMENT.)

closed primary A type of DIRECT PRIMARY limited to registered party members, who must declare their party affiliation in order to vote. The closed primary serves to encourage party unity and prevent members of other parties from infiltrating and voting to nominate weak candidates. (*Compare* OPEN PRIMARY.)

cloture (KLOH-chuhr) A vote of a legislature used to stop debate on an issue and put the issue to a vote. (*See* FILIBUSTER.)

coattail effect The tendency for a popular political party leader to attract votes for other candidates of the same party in an election. For example, the party of a victorious presidential candidate will often win many seats in CONGRESS as well; these congressmen are voted into office "on the coattails" of the president.

commander in chief The role of the United States president as highest ranking officer in the armed forces. The CONSTITUTION provides this power, but, through the system of CHECKS AND BALANCES, gives CONGRESS the authority to declare war. During periods of war, presidents such as Franklin ROOSEVELT, Lyndon JOHNSON, and George BUSH have taken active roles as commander in chief.

confirmation hearings Meetings held by the SENATE to gather information about candidates for federal office nominated by the president of the United States. Under the CONSTITUTION, the president has the right to appoint whomever he wants to various government offices, including members of the CABINET and federal judges, but each appointment must be approved by the Senate as part of the SEPARATION OF POWERS.

Congress The LEGISLATIVE BRANCH of the United States federal government, composed of the HOUSE OF REPRESENTATIVES and the SENATE. Popularly elected, senators and REPRESENTATIVES are responsible for advocating the interests of the CONSTITUENTS they represent. Numerous congressional committees are organized to study issues of public policy, recommend action, and, ultimately, pass laws. Congress plays an important role in the system of CHECKS AND BALANCES; in fact, the two-house (bicameral) organization of Congress acts as an internal check, for each house must separately vote to pass a bill for it to become a law. In addition to lawmaking, Congress has a variety of functions, including APPROPRIATION of funds for EXECUTIVE and JUDICIAL activities; instituting taxes and regulating commerce; declaring war and raising and supporting a military; setting up federal courts and conducting IMPEACHMENT proceedings; and approving presidential appointments.

Congressional Medal of Honor　The highest military decoration in the United States armed services, often called simply the Medal of Honor. It recognizes valor and bravery in action "above and beyond the call of duty." There have been some 3400 recipients of the medal, which was established in 1862 and is awarded on behalf of CONGRESS.

Congressional Record　A published account of the votes, speeches, and debates of the United States CONGRESS.

conscientious objector (CO)　A person who refuses to render military service on the grounds of moral principle or religious belief. A CO must demonstrate a sincere, active, and long-standing objection in order to receive an exemption from armed service. The United States and some European governments officially recognize CO status; approved CO's are usually required to perform social service or noncombat military service in place of armed duty. (*See also* DRAFT, DRAFT DODGER, *and* SELECTIVE SERVICE SYSTEM.)

constituent (kuhn-STICH-ooh-uhnt)　A citizen who is represented in a government by the officials for whom he or she votes.

Constitution, United States　A document that embodies the fundamental laws and principles by which the United States is governed. It was drafted by the CONSTITUTIONAL CONVENTION and later supplemented by the BILL OF RIGHTS and other amendments. (*See* PREAMBLE TO THE CONSTITUTION.)

containment, policy of　A United States foreign policy doctrine adopted by the TRUMAN administration in 1947, operating on the principle that COMMUNIST governments will eventually fall apart as long as they are prevented from expanding their influence.

🚶 The policy of containment was used to justify American involvement in the KOREAN WAR and the VIETNAM WAR.

contempt of Congress　The deliberate obstruction of the workings of the federal LEGISLATIVE BRANCH. For example, a witness under SUBPOENA who refuses to testify before CONGRESS can be cited for contempt of Congress.

contempt of court　The deliberate obstruction of a court's proceedings by refusing to obey a court order or by interfering with court procedures. Contempt of court can be punished by fine, imprisonment, or both.

court of appeals　Courts, also called appellate courts, that are designed as part of the system of DUE PROCESS. Cases may be presented to these courts if a party is dissatisfied with the original court's decision. An appeal must demonstrate that a new decision is warranted, usually in light of new evidence, or a persuasive argument that the CONSTITUTION was improperly interpreted. A case may be appealed to successively higher state or federal appellate courts until it reaches the United States SUPREME COURT. There are twelve federal courts of appeal, each covering a group of states called a "circuit."

cruel and unusual punishment　Punishment prohibited by the Eighth Amendment to the CONSTITUTION. Cruel and unusual punishment includes torture, deliberately degrading punishment, or punishment that is too severe for the crime committed. This concept helps guarantee DUE PROCESS even to convicted criminals. Many people have argued that CAPITAL PUNISHMENT should be considered cruel and unusual punishment.

DA　*See* DISTRICT ATTORNEY.

dark horse　An unexpected winner. In politics, a dark horse is a candidate for office considered unlikely to receive his or her party's nomination, but who might be nominated if party leaders cannot agree on a better candidate.

DEA　*See* DRUG ENFORCEMENT ADMINISTRATION.

de facto segregation (di FAK-toh, day FAK-toh)　Racial SEGREGATION, especially in public schools, that happens "by fact" rather than by legal requirement. For example, often the concentration of African-Americans in certain neighborhoods produces neighborhood schools that are predominantly black, or segregated in fact (DE FACTO), although not by law (DE JURE).

defendant　The party that is being sued in court. (*Compare* PLAINTIFF.)

deficit　In general, a situation in which more money is spent than earned. In the United States federal government, a deficit occurs when federal expenditures for programs and agencies exceed federal revenues from taxes and TARIFFS. Obvious measures to balance the budget (raising taxes and cutting federal programs) are unpopular. Presidents often resort to selling BONDS from the DEPARTMENT OF THE TREASURY to the public and to the FEDERAL RESERVE in order to finance the deficit.

Democrat   A member of the DEMOCRATIC PARTY.

Democratic party   *See entries under "American History to 1865" and "American History since 1865."*

Department of Agriculture   A department of the federal EXECUTIVE BRANCH that provides services for farmers, including agricultural research, SOIL conservation, and efforts to regulate and stabilize the farming economy.

Department of Commerce   A department of the federal EXECUTIVE BRANCH whose responsibilities include management of the census and the United States Patent Office. Through a variety of bureaus and agencies, such as the Industry and Trade Administration and the Office of Minority Business Enterprise, the Department of Commerce works to promote American business interests at home and abroad.

Department of Defense (DOD)   A department of the federal EXECUTIVE BRANCH entrusted with formulating military policies and maintaining American military forces. Its top official is the civilian SECRETARY OF DEFENSE. It is headquartered in the PENTAGON.

Department of Education   A department of the federal EXECUTIVE BRANCH responsible for providing federal aid to educational institutions and financial aid to students, keeping national educational records, and conducting some educational research.

Department of Energy   A department of the federal EXECUTIVE BRANCH responsible for developing policies for effective use of the nation's energy resources. The Department of Energy is involved in energy conservation, regulating oil pipelines, and encouraging research on new sources of energy.

Department of Health and Human Services   A department of the federal EXECUTIVE BRANCH responsible for the SOCIAL SECURITY ADMINISTRATION, the Public Health Service, and other programs designed to promote public welfare. It was originally called the Department of Health, Education, and Welfare, until the separate DEPARTMENT OF EDUCATION was created in 1979.

Department of Housing and Urban Development (HUD)   A department of the federal EXECUTIVE BRANCH responsible for home finance, promoting CIVIL RIGHTS in housing, URBAN RENEWAL, and the development of new communities.

Department of the Interior   A department of the federal EXECUTIVE BRANCH responsible for the National Park Service, the Bureau of Indian Affairs, and a variety of programs designed to preserve NATURAL RESOURCES in the United States and its territories and possessions in the PACIFIC OCEAN.

Department of Justice   A department of the federal EXECUTIVE BRANCH, headed by the ATTORNEY GENERAL, which administers the FEDERAL BUREAU OF INVESTIGATION (FBI), prosecutes violations of federal law, and is responsible for enforcing all CIVIL RIGHTS legislation.

Department of Labor   A department of the federal EXECUTIVE BRANCH concerned with improving working conditions and employment opportunities for laborers. Its programs include job training (especially for the poor), appraising manpower resources and needs, and regulating occupational safety.

Department of State   A department of the federal EXECUTIVE BRANCH primarily responsible for making and conducting foreign policy. It is commonly called the STATE DEPARTMENT, and is headed by the SECRETARY OF STATE. Its activities include negotiating treaties, coordinating correspondence and information programs with foreign governments, and administering economic aid to developing nations.

Department of Transportation   A department of the federal EXECUTIVE BRANCH responsible for the national highways and for railroad and airline safety. It also manages Amtrak, the national railroad system, and the Coast Guard.

Department of the Treasury   A department of the federal EXECUTIVE BRANCH; it includes the INTERNAL REVENUE SERVICE (IRS). The Department of the Treasury has general responsibility for setting federal FISCAL POLICY, by collecting taxes and customs duties, administering the public DEBT, keeping all government accounts, minting CURRENCY, and licensing ships engaged in international and interstate commerce. The Department of the Treasury administers the SECRET SERVICE.

diehard Anyone who stubbornly resists change; often used to describe extreme CONSERVATIVES. The term *diehard* is also applied to those who remain loyal to a cause even after there is no hope of victory: "Even though it was clear that the governor had lost the election, a few diehards remained at the rally."

direct primary An election in which voters choose candidates to run on a party's ticket in a subsequent election for public office.

district attorney (DA) An official responsible for representing the government in court cases and for prosecuting criminals.

dollar diplomacy The use of diplomatic influence, economic pressure, and military power to protect a nation's economic and business interests abroad. The term was first used to describe the exploitative nature of United States involvement in LATIN AMERICA.

domino theory The idea that if one key nation in a region fell to control of COMMUNISTS, others would follow like toppling dominoes. The THEORY was used by many American leaders to justify American intervention in the VIETNAM WAR. (*See* CONTAINMENT, POLICY OF.)

donkey A SYMBOL of the DEMOCRATIC PARTY, introduced in a series of political cartoons by Thomas Nast during the congressional elections of 1874. (*Compare* ELEPHANT.)

double jeopardy Trying a person twice in the same jurisdiction for the same crime, a practice prohibited by the FIFTH AMENDMENT to the CONSTITUTION. (*See* DUE PROCESS OF LAW.)

doves (doves and hawks) *See* HAWKS AND DOVES.

draft A system for selecting young men for compulsory military service, administered in the United States by the SELECTIVE SERVICE SYSTEM. At present the United States relies on a volunteer military and does not have a draft, though young men are required by law to register with the Selective Service. (*See also* CONSCIENTIOUS OBJECTOR *and* DRAFT DODGER.)

draft dodger Someone who illegally evades the DRAFT, as opposed to a CONSCIENTIOUS OBJECTOR,

who is granted official, legal exemption from military duty. In active protest against United States involvement in the VIETNAM WAR, many Americans publicly burned draft registration cards, risking imprisonment; others fled to other countries, such as CANADA.

Drug Enforcement Administration (DEA) An agency in the United States DEPARTMENT OF JUSTICE that enforces federal laws and regulations dealing with narcotics and other dangerous drugs. It cooperates with the FBI and with local law enforcement agencies.

due process of law The principle that an individual cannot be deprived of life, liberty, or property without appropriate legal procedures and safeguards. The BILL OF RIGHTS and the FOURTEENTH AMENDMENT to the CONSTITUTION guarantee that any person accused of a crime must be informed of the charges, be provided with legal counsel, be given a speedy and public trial, enjoy EQUAL PROTECTION OF THE LAWS, and not be subjected to CRUEL AND UNUSUAL PUNISHMENT, unreasonable searches and seizures, DOUBLE JEOPARDY, or SELF-INCRIMINATION.

Eastern Establishment The ELITE universities and financial institutions of major cities in the northeastern United States. These institutions, by virtue of their long-standing economic and social dominance, are often believed to exert an influence out of proportion to their size. In American politics, the Eastern Establishment often takes a LIBERAL REPUBLICAN stand. (*See also* IVY LEAGUE, MADISON AVENUE, POWER ELITE, *and* WALL STREET.)

Electoral College (i-LEK-tuhr-uhl) The presidential electors who meet after the citizens vote for president, and cast ballots for the president and vice president. Each state is granted the same number of electors as it has senators (*see* SENATE) and REPRESENTATIVES combined. These electors, rather than the public, actually elect the president and the vice president. The FOUNDING FATHERS assumed that electors would exercise discretion and not necessarily be bound by the popular vote, but the rise of political parties undermined this assumption. Electors are now pledged in advance to vote for the candidate of their party, and nearly always do so. Thus, the vote of the Electoral College is largely a formality.

• There have been several attempts to abolish the Electoral College.

elephant   A SYMBOL of the REPUBLICAN PARTY, introduced in a series of political cartoons by Thomas Nast during the congressional elections of 1874. (*Compare* DONKEY.)

entitlements   Federal programs such as SOCIAL SECURITY, MEDICARE, and MEDICAID that disburse money according to fixed formulas to citizens who fall into designated categories. Because entitlements do not require annual congressional APPROPRIATIONS, their cost tends to rise steadily and, in the view of many, out of control.

Environmental Protection Agency (EPA)   An agency established by the United States government to coordinate federal programs aimed at combating POLLUTION and protecting the environment.

E PLURIBUS UNUM. The Great Seal of the United States.

E pluribus unum (EE PLOOR-uh-buhs YOOH-nuhm, OOH-nuhm)   A motto of the United States; LATIN for "Out of many, one." It refers to the UNION formed by the separate states. *E pluribus unum* was adopted as a national motto in 1776, and is now found on the Great Seal of the United States and on United States CURRENCY.

Equal Employment Opportunity Commission (EEOC)   An agency established by the CIVIL RIGHTS ACT OF 1964 to investigate racial and sexual discrimination. The NATIONAL ORGANIZATION FOR WOMEN (NOW) was organized in the 1960s when the EEOC failed to act upon the Civil Rights Act's sexual discrimination clause.

equal opportunity   The goal of giving all persons an equal chance to an education and employment, and to protect their CIVIL RIGHTS, regardless of their race, religious beliefs, or gender. In the United States, various minority groups have been fighting for equal opportunity over the last 150 years. (*See* AFFIRMATIVE ACTION, CIVIL RIGHTS MOVEMENT, EQUAL PROTECTION OF THE LAWS, NATIONAL ASSOCIATION FOR THE ADVANCEMENT OF COLORED PEOPLE, NATIONAL ORGANIZATION FOR WOMEN, SEGREGATION, SEXISM, SUFFRAGIST, *and* WOMEN'S MOVEMENT.)

equal protection of the laws   A PHRASE in the FOURTEENTH AMENDMENT to the United States CONSTITUTION requiring that states guarantee the same rights, privileges, and protections to all citizens. This doctrine reinforces that of DUE PROCESS, and prevents states from passing or enforcing laws that arbitrarily discriminate against anyone.

Equal Rights Amendment (ERA)   A twice-proposed but never ratified amendment to the CONSTITUTION that would prohibit denial or abridgement of rights on the basis of GENDER. First proposed in 1923, the amendment was passed by CONGRESS in 1972, but failed ratification by the requisite number of states. It was a major rallying point of the WOMEN'S MOVEMENT.

equal time   A ruling of the United States government, administered by the Federal Communications Commission, requiring that all candidates for public office be given equal access to the free or paid use of radio and television. This rule has recently been rescinded.

ERA   *See* EQUAL RIGHTS AMENDMENT.

executive branch   The branch of federal and state government that is broadly responsible for implementing, supporting, and enforcing the laws made by the LEGISLATIVE BRANCH and interpreted by the JUDICIAL BRANCH. At the state level, the executive includes governors and their staffs. At the federal level, the executive includes the president, the vice president, staffs of appointed advisers (including the CABINET), and a variety of departments and agencies, such as the CENTRAL INTELLIGENCE AGENCY (CIA), the ENVIRONMENTAL PROTECTION AGENCY (EPA), the FEDERAL BUREAU OF INVESTIGATION (FBI), and the Postal Service (*see* POSTMASTER GENERAL). The executive branch also proposes a great deal of legislation to CONGRESS and appoints federal judges, including justices of the SUPREME COURT. While the executive branch guides the nation's domestic and foreign policies, the system of CHECKS AND BALANCES works to limit its power.

ex post facto (eks pohst FAK-toh)   A descriptive term for an explanation or a law that is made up after an event and then applied to it: "The chairman's description of his plan sounds like an ex post facto attempt to justify an impulsive action." *Ex post facto* is LATIN for "from after the deed."

ex post facto law   A law that makes illegal an act that was legal when committed, that increases the penalties for an infraction after it has been committed, or that changes the rules of evidence to make conviction easier. The CONSTITUTION prohibits the making of ex post facto law. (*See* EX POST FACTO.)

extortion   The criminal offense of obtaining money or information from someone by intimidation, especially by using one's official position or power to obtain funds to which one is not entitled.

farm bloc   A group of both DEMOCRATIC and REPUBLICAN members of Congress from the farming states of the MIDDLE WEST that pressures the federal government to adopt policies favorable to farmers.

favorite son   A political figure nominated for the presidency by his or her state's delegation to the national nominating convention of a major party. Favorite sons are rarely serious candidates for the party's nomination. By nominating a favorite son, the delegation honors its nominee while simultaneously delaying its commitment until the more serious contenders for the nomination can be sorted out.

Federal Bureau of Investigation (FBI)   An agency of the United States federal government, long headed by J. Edgar HOOVER, which investigates violations of federal (rather than state or local) laws, including kidnaping, smuggling narcotics, and espionage.

    Established in 1908 under the DEPARTMENT OF JUSTICE, the FBI earned its reputation in the 1920s and 1930s by apprehending notorious bank robbers and gangsters.

federalism   A system of government in which power is divided between a national (federal) government and various regional governments. As defined by the United States CONSTITUTION, federalism is a fundamental aspect of American government, whereby the states are not merely regional representatives of the federal government, but are granted independent powers and responsibilities. With their own LEGISLATIVE BRANCH, EXECUTIVE BRANCH, and JUDICIAL BRANCH, states are empowered to pass, enforce, and interpret laws, provided they do not violate the Constitution. This arrangement not only allows state governments to respond directly to the interests of their local populations, but also serves to check the power of the federal government. While the federal government determines foreign policy, with exclusive power to make treaties, declare war, and control imports and exports, the states have exclusive power to ratify and amend the Constitution. Most governmental responsibilities, however, are shared by state and federal governments: both levels are involved in such public policy issues as TAXATION, business regulation, environmental protection, and CIVIL RIGHTS.

    The precise extent of state and federal responsibility has always been controversial. REPUBLICAN administrations, for example, have tended to grant more authority to the states, thereby encouraging political and economic freedom, but discouraging comprehensive social welfare. Until the middle of the twentieth century, the SUPREME COURT left the interpretation of many civil rights guarantees to the states, resulting in widespread discrimination against minorities.

fellow traveler   One who supports the aims or PHILOSOPHIES of a political group without joining it. A "fellow traveler" is usually one who sympathizes with COMMUNIST doctrines, but is not a member of the Communist party. The term was used disparagingly in the 1950s to describe people accused of being communists.

felony (FEL-uh-nee)   A grave crime, such as murder, rape, or burglary, that is punishable by death (*see* CAPITAL OFFENSE) or imprisonment in a state or federal facility.

Fifth Amendment   One of the ten amendments to the United States CONSTITUTION that make up the BILL OF RIGHTS. The Fifth Amendment imposes restrictions on the government's prosecution of persons accused of crimes. It prohibits SELF-INCRIMINATION and DOUBLE JEOPARDY and mandates DUE PROCESS OF LAW.

    To "take the Fifth" is to refuse to testify because the testimony could lead to self-incrimination.

filibuster (FIL-uh-bus-tuhr) A strategy employed in the United States SENATE, whereby a minority can delay a vote on proposed legislation by making long speeches or introducing irrelevant issues. A successful filibuster can force withdrawal of a bill. Filibusters can be ended only by CLOTURE.

First Amendment An amendment to the United States CONSTITUTION guaranteeing the rights of free expression and action that are fundamental to democratic government. These rights include FREEDOM OF ASSEMBLY, FREEDOM OF THE PRESS, FREEDOM OF RELIGION, and FREEDOM OF SPEECH. The government is empowered, however, to restrict these freedoms if expression threatens to be destructive. Argument over the extent of First Amendment freedoms has often reached the SUPREME COURT. (*See* CLEAR AND PRESENT DANGER, LIBEL, *and* OBSCENITY LAWS.)

&. The First Amendment begins the BILL OF RIGHTS.

First Amendment freedoms The rights of free expression established under the FIRST AMENDMENT to the United States CONSTITUTION, which include FREEDOM OF ASSEMBLY, FREEDOM OF THE PRESS, FREEDOM OF RELIGION, and FREEDOM OF SPEECH.

Foggy Bottom A nickname for the United States DEPARTMENT OF STATE, whose offices were built in a formerly swampy area of WASHINGTON, D.C., known as Foggy Bottom because of vapors rising from the swamp.

Foreign Relations Committee A committee of the SENATE charged with overseeing the conduct of foreign policy.

Foreign Service The professional arm of the EXECUTIVE BRANCH that supplies diplomats for the United States embassies and consulates around the world. Ambassadors, though officially members of the Foreign Service, are sometimes friends of the president of the United States appointed in gratitude for support given during elections.

Fourteenth Amendment An amendment to the United States CONSTITUTION, adopted in 1868. It was primarily concerned with details of reintegrating the southern states after the CIVIL WAR and defining some of the rights of recently freed slaves. The first section of the amendment, however, was to revolutionize FEDERALISM. It stated that no state could "deprive any person of life, liberty, or property, without due process of law; nor deny to any person within its jurisdiction the equal protection of the laws." Gradually, the SUPREME COURT interpreted the amendment to mean that the guarantees of the BILL OF RIGHTS apply to the states as well as to the national government.

franchise In politics, the right to vote. The CONSTITUTION left the determination of the qualifications of voters to the states. In the late eighteenth and early nineteenth century, states usually restricted the franchise to white men who owned specified amounts of property. Gradually, POLL TAXES were substituted for property requirements. Before the CIVIL WAR the voting rights of blacks were severely restricted, but the Fifteenth Amendment to the Constitution, declared ratified in 1870, prohibited states from abridging the right to vote on the basis of race. Nevertheless, southern states used a variety of legal ploys to restrict black voting until passage of the VOTING RIGHTS ACT OF 1965. Women were not guaranteed the right to vote in federal elections until ratification of the Nineteenth Amendment in 1920. In 1971 the Twenty-sixth Amendment lowered the voting age from twenty-one to eighteen. (*See* SUFFRAGE *and* SUFFRAGETTE.)

&. Losing the right to vote, called disfranchisement, is most commonly caused by failing to reregister, a procedure that is required every time a person changes residence.

freedom of assembly The right to hold public meetings and form associations without interference by the government. Freedom of peaceful assembly is guaranteed by the FIRST AMENDMENT to the CONSTITUTION.

&. SEGREGATION has been described as a violation of freedom of assembly.

freedom of association The right to form societies, clubs, and other groups of people, and to meet with people individually, without interference by the government.

freedom of religion The right to choose a religion (or no religion) without interference by the government. Freedom of religion is guaranteed by the FIRST AMENDMENT to the CONSTITUTION. (*See* SEPARATION OF CHURCH AND STATE.)

freedom of speech The right to speak without censorship or restraint by the government. Freedom of speech is protected by the FIRST AMENDMENT to the

CONSTITUTION. (*See* CLEAR AND PRESENT DANGER *and* SHOUT "FIRE!" IN A CROWDED THEATER.)

freedom of the press   The right to circulate opinions in print without censorship by the government. Americans enjoy freedom of the press under the FIRST AMENDMENT to the CONSTITUTION.

friend of the court   An individual or group interested in influencing the outcome of a lawsuit but not an actual party to the suit. The statement presented to the court is an AMICUS CURIAE brief; *amicus curiae* is LATIN for "friend of the court."

gay rights   The movement for CIVIL RIGHTS for HOMOSEXUALS. It originated after a police raid on a GAY bar in NEW YORK CITY in 1969, which triggered a riot and launched the grassroots reform movement seeking to end social and legal discrimination against gays.

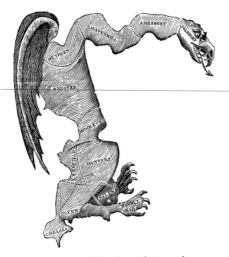

GERRYMANDER. *The boundaries of a gerry-mandered Massachusetts election district.*

gerrymander (JER-ee-man-duhr)   To change the boundaries of legislative districts to favor one party over another. Typically, the dominant party in a state legislature (which is responsible for drawing the boundaries of congressional districts) will try to concentrate the opposing party's strength in as few districts as possible, while giving itself likely majorities in as many districts as possible.

Good Neighbor policy   A United States foreign policy doctrine, adopted by Franklin ROOSEVELT in 1933, designed to improve relations with LATIN AMERICA. A reaction to the exploitative DOLLAR DIPLOMACY of the early 1900s, the Good Neighbor policy encouraged interaction between the United States and Latin America as equals. In the post–World War II era, however, the United States has often reverted to dollar diplomacy and GUNBOAT DIPLOMACY to impose its will on the countries of Latin America.

GOP   ABBREVIATION of Grand Old Party, a nickname for the REPUBLICAN PARTY in the United States.

grand jury   A jury that decides whether the evidence warrants bringing an accused person to trial. Once indicted (*see* INDICTMENT) by a grand jury, a person must stand trial.

guilt by association   The attribution of guilt to individuals because of the people or organizations with which they associate, rather than because of any crime that they have committed.

gunboat diplomacy   A policy toward a foreign country that depends on the use, or threat of the use, of arms. (*See* BIG STICK DIPLOMACY.)

habeas corpus (HAY-bee-uhs KAWR-puhs)   A legal term meaning that an accused person must be presented physically before the court with a statement demonstrating sufficient cause for arrest. Thus, no accuser may imprison someone indefinitely without bringing that person and the charges against him or her into a courtroom. In LATIN, *habeas corpus* literally means "you shall have the body."

hawks and doves   Popularly, "hawks" are those who advocate an aggressive foreign policy based on strong military power. "Doves" try to resolve international conflicts without the threat of force.

hearsay   Information heard by one person about another. Hearsay is generally inadmissible as evidence in a court of law because it is based on the reports of others rather than on the personal knowledge of a witness.

homicide (HOM-uh-seyed)   The killing of one person by another, whether intended (murder) or not (MANSLAUGHTER). Not all homicide is unlawful; killing in self-defense, for example, is not a crime.

House of Representatives   The lower house of the United States CONGRESS. With 435 popularly elected officials, the House (as it is often called) is the most representative body in the federal government. House seats are apportioned (*see* APPORTIONMENT) relative to each state's population. Because of its larger size, the House tends to maintain a closer link to local CONSTITUENT concerns than the SENATE, though both houses of Congress participate in virtually all aspects of legislation and policymaking. The SPEAKER OF THE HOUSE is one of the most influential officials in WASHINGTON, D.C., and is second in succession to the presidency, after the vice president.

hung jury   A jury that is unable to reach a verdict of guilty or not guilty. The result is a mistrial, and legal proceedings must be reinitiated to bring the case to trial again. Trying the case a second time does not constitute DOUBLE JEOPARDY.

impeachment   A formal accusation of wrongdoing against a public official. According to the United States CONSTITUTION, the HOUSE OF REPRESENTATIVES can vote to impeach an official, but the SENATE actually tries the case. One president of the United States, Andrew JOHNSON, was impeached after the CIVIL WAR, but he was acquitted. President Richard NIXON resigned from office as the House of Representatives prepared to initiate impeachment proceedings.

incumbent (in-KUM-buhnt)   One who holds a public office. By virtue of their experience in office, their exposure to the public, and their ability to raise campaign funds, incumbents usually have a significant advantage over opponents if they choose to run for reelection.

indictment (in-DEYET-muhnt)   A formal accusation of a crime, presented to the accused party after the charges have been considered by a GRAND JURY.

injunction   A court order that either compels or restrains an act by an individual, organization, or government official. In labor-MANAGEMENT relations, injunctions have been used to prevent workers from going on STRIKE.

integration   The free association of people from different racial and ethnic backgrounds (*see* ETHNICITY); a goal of the CIVIL RIGHTS MOVEMENT to overcome policies of SEGREGATION that have been practiced in the United States.

∂ Those favoring integration of schools by such forceful means as BUSING or AFFIRMATIVE ACTION have frequently argued that integration of schools will lead to integration of society as a whole. (*See* SEPARATE BUT EQUAL.)

interest group   An organized group that tries to influence the government to adopt certain policies or measures. Also called PRESSURE GROUP. (*See* LOBBY.)

Internal Revenue Service (IRS)   Part of the United States DEPARTMENT OF THE TREASURY. The IRS is responsible for the collection of all federal taxes, except customs duties.

Interstate Commerce Commission (ICC)   A federal agency that monitors the business operations of carriers transporting GOODS and people between states. Its jurisdiction includes railroads, ships, trucks, buses, oil pipelines, and their terminal facilities.

∂ The ICC was established in 1887 as the first federal agency.

isolationism   The doctrine that a nation is best advised to stay out of the disputes and affairs of other nations. The United States practiced a policy of isolationism until WORLD WAR I, and did not pursue an active international policy until after WORLD WAR II. (*See* "ENTANGLING ALLIANCES WITH NONE.")

Joint Chiefs of Staff   A high-level military advisory board in the DEPARTMENT OF DEFENSE, composed of high-ranking representatives of the army, navy, air force, and marines. The Joint Chiefs are responsible for formulating military policy and recommending action regarding issues of national security and international relations.

joint resolution   A measure approved by both houses of the United States CONGRESS and signed by the president. Similar to an act of Congress, the joint resolution is used to approve or initiate foreign policy actions, to grant a single APPROPRIATIONS proposal, and to propose amendments to the CONSTITUTION.

judicial activism   *See* BROAD CONSTRUCTION.

judicial branch   The court systems of local, state, and federal governments, responsible for interpreting the laws passed by the LEGISLATIVE BRANCH and enforced by the EXECUTIVE BRANCH. These courts try criminal cases (in which a law may have been violated) or civil cases (disputes between parties over rights or responsibilities). The courts attempt to resolve conflicts impartially in order to protect the individual rights guaranteed by the CONSTITUTION, within the bounds of justice, as defined by the entire body of American law. Some courts try only original cases, while others act as COURTS OF APPEALS. The ultimate court of appeals is the SUPREME COURT. On the federal level, the system of CHECKS AND BALANCES empowers CONGRESS to create federal courts, and all federal judges must be appointed by the president and confirmed by the SENATE. The courts may exercise the powers of JUDICIAL REVIEW and INJUNCTION.

judicial restraint A view, associated with Felix FRANKFURTER among others, that judges should be reluctant to declare legislative enactments unconstitutional unless the conflict between the enactment and the CONSTITUTION is obvious. The doctrine is akin to, but not identical with, NARROW CONSTRUCTION, and it is the opposite of JUDICIAL ACTIVISM.

judicial review The principle by which courts can declare acts of either the EXECUTIVE BRANCH or the LEGISLATIVE BRANCH unconstitutional. The SUPREME COURT has exercised this power, for example, to revoke state laws that denied CIVIL RIGHTS guaranteed by the CONSTITUTION. (*See also* CHECKS AND BALANCES.)

jurisprudence (joor-is-PROOHD-ns) The PHILOSOPHY of law. Jurisprudence implies creating a body of law and methods for interpreting the law, studying the relationships between law and society, and predicting the effects of legal decisions. In the United States, lawmakers, attorneys, scholars, and courts all take an active role in guiding jurisprudence.

justice of the peace A local officer of the JUDICIAL BRANCH empowered to try minor cases, recommend cases for trial, and perform civil ceremonies such as marriages and oath taking. Justices of the peace are usually elected locally and are paid fees for their services.

kangaroo court A court that ignores principles of justice; a court characterized by incompetence and dishonesty.

lame duck A public official or administration serving out a term in office after having been defeated for reelection or when not seeking reelection.

larceny (LAHR-suh-nee) Theft; taking another person's property with the intent of permanently depriving the owner.

left-wing A descriptive term for an individual or a political FACTION that advocates LIBERAL, RADICAL, or even revolutionary policies, usually in favor of overcoming social inequalities. In the United States, left-wing groups generally support federal social welfare programs designed to open opportunities to all citizens. (*Compare* RIGHT-WING.)

🐚 Although both major political parties in the United States have left-wing factions, left-wing policies are usually associated with the DEMOCRATIC PARTY.

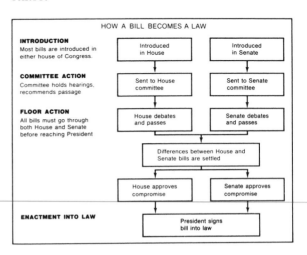

legislative branch (LEJ-i-slay-tiv) The branch of the federal and state government empowered to make the laws that are then enforced by the EXECUTIVE BRANCH and interpreted by the JUDICIAL BRANCH. The legislative branch consists of CONGRESS and the fifty state legislatures. At both state and federal levels, legislatures are made up of popularly elected REPRESENTATIVES, who propose laws that are sensitive to the needs and interests of their local CONSTITUENTS. After a law is proposed as a bill, it is sent to appropriate committees for several stages of discussion, research, and modification. It is then debated in both legislative houses — except in NEBRASKA, which has a single-house legislature — and put to a vote. If the law is passed, it is still subject to further modification and final vote by both houses. Under the system of CHECKS AND BALANCES, the president can refuse to sign the bill into law (through the VETO power). The legislature can then vote to override the veto. Other checks and balances include legislative powers to impeach public officials (*see* IMPEACHMENT), confirm appointments to the executive and judicial branches, and vote on APPROPRIATIONS.

libel A written, printed, or pictorial statement that unjustly defames someone publicly. Prosecution of libel as a punishable offense puts some measure of restriction on FREEDOM OF THE PRESS under the FIRST AMENDMENT.

Library of Congress The largest library in the United States, located in WASHINGTON, D.C., and maintained largely by federal APPROPRIATIONS. Its original purpose was to provide research facilities for members of CONGRESS; today it serves the public as well. Most copyrighted publications are catalogued by the Library of Congress, whose classification system is used by major libraries around the country.

line-item veto The authority of an executive to VETO a specific APPROPRIATION in a budget passed by a legislature. Viewing the line-item veto as an effective tactic against PORK-BARREL LEGISLATION, presidents Ronald REAGAN and George BUSH unsuccessfully sought this authority, which many state governors possess, from CONGRESS. Under current law the president must choose between signing or vetoing the entire budget rather than parts (items on budget lines) of it.

lobby A group whose members share certain goals and work to bring about the passage, modification, or defeat of laws that affect these goals. Lobbies (also called INTEREST GROUPS or PRESSURE GROUPS) can be long-standing (such as minority groups struggling to have their CIVIL RIGHTS guaranteed) or AD HOC (such as a community threatened by proposed construction of a NUCLEAR POWER plant). Lobbies may use grassroots methods, such as local rallies and campaigns, to build support for their cause, and often employ professional lobbyists, who testify before congressional committees and approach policymakers in all government branches. Powerful lobbies, such as the AFL-CIO and the AMERICAN LEGION, with millions of members, have succeeded in establishing influence in WASHINGTON, D.C.

logrolling In politics, advance agreement by legislators to vote for one another's bills. Logrolling is most common when legislators are trying to secure votes for bills that will benefit their home districts. For example, a group of congressmen from the MIDDLE WEST pushing for higher dairy prices and a group of southern congressmen supporting higher tobacco prices might make a logrolling agreement in order to get both bills passed.

loose construction *See* BROAD CONSTRUCTION.

machine, political An administration of elected public officials who use their influential positions to solidify and perpetuate the power of their political party, often through dubious means. Machine politicians make free use of the SPOILS SYSTEM and PATRONAGE, rewarding loyal party supporters with appointed government jobs. Other machine methods include GERRYMANDERING election districts; planting party representatives in neighborhoods; making deals with judges, lawyers, and other professionals; and "buying" votes by offering social services to potential voters. When machine politics was especially strong in the United States, during the latter half of the nineteenth century, politicians would go so far as to offer beer for votes, and would embezzle large amounts of public money. Machines also dominated party CAUCUSES and conventions, thereby affecting politics at all levels of government.

&. Machines are usually associated with big-city politics. &. The most impressive political machine of the twentieth century was that of Mayor Richard DALEY, in CHICAGO.

machine politics Politics associated with political MACHINES.

Mafia (MAH-fee-uh) A criminal organization that originated in SICILY, and was brought to the United States by Italian immigrants in the late nineteenth century. The Mafia is also called the Syndicate, the Mob, and the *Cosa Nostra* (Our Thing). The Mafia built its power through EXTORTION (forcing tradesmen and shopkeepers to buy Mafia protection against destruction), and by dominating the bootlegging industry (the illegal production and distribution of liquor) during PROHIBITION. Members of the Mafia often lead outwardly respectable lives and maintain a variety of legitimate businesses as a front, or cover, for their criminal activities, which include extortion, gambling, and narcotics distribution.

majority leader The leader of the party that holds a majority of seats in either house of CONGRESS or of a state legislature. Selected by their own party CAUCUSES, majority leaders act as chief spokespersons and strategists for their parties. Actually, in the

HOUSE OF REPRESENTATIVES, the majority leader is second in command of his party, after the SPEAKER OF THE HOUSE. (*See also* MINORITY LEADER.)

man's home is his castle, A A proverbial expression that illustrates the principle of individual privacy, which is fundamental to the American system of government. In this regard, the Fourth Amendment to the United States CONSTITUTION — part of the BILL OF RIGHTS — prohibits "unreasonable searches and seizures." (*See also under "Proverbs."*)

❦ Disagreement over the extent of personal privacy and over interpretation of *unreasonable* has brought many cases before the SUPREME COURT.

manslaughter (MAN-slaw-tuhr) The unlawful killing of a person, without malice or premeditation. Involuntary manslaughter is accidental, such as running into someone with a car. Voluntary manslaughter is committed in the "heat of passion," as in a spontaneous fight in which one person is killed by a strong blow. Manslaughter is usually considered less serious than murder. Both murder and manslaughter are types of HOMICIDE.

massive retaliation The doctrine that the best way to deter aggression is to threaten a potential aggressor with devastation by ATOMIC BOMBS. (*See* HAWKS AND DOVES.)

Medicare (MED-i-kair) A federal program providing medical care for the elderly. Established by a health insurance bill in 1965, the Medicare program made a significant step for social welfare legislation, and helped establish the growing population of the elderly as a PRESSURE GROUP. (*See* ENTITLEMENTS.)

military-industrial complex A general term for the cooperative relationship between the military and the industrial producers of military equipment and supplies in lobbying for increased spending on military programs.

❦ In his farewell address, President Dwight EISENHOWER warned that the growth of this relationship would increase the militarization of American society, and endanger the principles of DEMOCRACY.

minority leader The leader of the political party that holds a minority of seats in either house of CONGRESS or of a state legislature. Selected by their own party CAUCUSES, minority leaders act as chief spokespersons and strategists for their parties.

Miranda **decision** (muh-RAN-duh) A decision by the United States SUPREME COURT concerning the rights of arrested persons. In the case of *Miranda versus Arizona*, in 1966, the Court ruled that, before questioning by the police, suspects must be informed that they have the right to remain silent and the right to consult an attorney, and that anything they say may be used against them in court. The Miranda ruling protects a suspect's FIFTH AMENDMENT right against SELF-INCRIMINATION. The Miranda warning, a written statement of these rights, is normally recited by a police officer while making an arrest.

misdemeanor (mis-di-MEE-nuhr) A minor crime, punishable by a fine or a light jail term. Common misdemeanors, such as traffic violations, are usually dealt with informally, without a trial. (*Compare* FELONY.)

most-favored-nation Status in an international trading arrangement whereby agreements between two nations on TARIFFS are then extended to other nations. Every nation involved in such an arrangement will have most-favored-nation status. This policy is used, particularly by the United States, to lower tariffs, extend cooperative trading agreements, and protect nations from discriminatory treatment. Most-favored-nation agreements can also be used to apply economic pressure on nations by deliberately excluding them from international trade.

NAACP *See* NATIONAL ASSOCIATION FOR THE ADVANCEMENT OF COLORED PEOPLE.

narrow construction A THEORY of interpretation of the CONSTITUTION that holds that the courts, particularly the SUPREME COURT, should be bound by the exact words of the Constitution, or by the original intent of the framers of the Constitution, or a combination of both.

NASA (NAS-uh) *See* NATIONAL AERONAUTICS AND SPACE ADMINISTRATION.

National Aeronautics and Space Administration (NASA) An agency of the United States government, charged with directing civilian programs in aeronautics research and space exploration. NASA maintains several facilities, most notably the Johnson Space Center in HOUSTON (which selects space crew personnel and is responsible for ground direction of space flights), and the launching pads at CAPE CANAVERAL in FLORIDA.

National Association for the Advancement of Colored People (NAACP) An organization that promotes the rights and welfare of black people. The NAACP is the oldest CIVIL RIGHTS organization in the United States, founded in 1909. Among the NAACP's achievements was a lawsuit that resulted in the SUPREME COURT's landmark decision in *BROWN VERSUS BOARD OF EDUCATION*, in 1954, which declared the SEGREGATION of public schools unconstitutional. (*See also* DU BOIS, W. E. B., *and* SEPARATE BUT EQUAL.)

National Guard The volunteer military forces of each state, which the governor of a state can summon in times of civil disorder or natural disaster. Through congressional and presidential order, the National Guard can be called into service in the regular United States army.

National Labor Relations Board (NLRB) An agency of the United States government, charged with mediating disputes between labor and MANAGEMENT, and responsible for preventing unfair labor practices, such as the harassment of LABOR UNIONS by business CORPORATIONS. The NLRB attempts to maintain a position of neutrality, favoring neither labor nor management.

National Organization for Women (NOW) A major feminist organization, founded in the middle 1960s, when the EQUAL EMPLOYMENT OPPORTUNITY COMMISSION failed to enforce a clause in the CIVIL RIGHTS ACT OF 1964 prohibiting discrimination on the basis of gender. One of its founders was Betty FRIEDAN. NOW has worked to promote occupational opportunities for women and has supported legislative proposals that would guarantee women equality with men.

National Rifle Association (NRA) An organization that acts as a powerful LOBBY against governmental restrictions on the private ownership of guns. NRA supporters argue that "guns don't kill people; people kill people." They often cite the Second Amendment to the CONSTITUTION, which states: "A well-regulated Militia being necessary to the security of a free State, the right of the people to keep and bear arms, shall not be infringed."

National Security Council (NSC) A committee in the EXECUTIVE BRANCH that advises the president on matters relating to domestic, military, and foreign security. The NSC also directs the operation of the CENTRAL INTELLIGENCE AGENCY.

naturalization The process by which a foreign citizen becomes a citizen of a new country. Millions of immigrants to the United States have become American citizens. Requirements for naturalization in the United States include residency for several years, ability to communicate in English, demonstrated knowledge of American history and government, and a dedication to American values that includes no membership in subversive organizations, such as a COMMUNIST party.

NLRB *See* NATIONAL LABOR RELATIONS BOARD.

nolo contendere (NOH-loh kuhn-TEN-duh-ree, kuhn-TEN-duh-ray) A plea that can be entered in a criminal or civil case, by which an accused person neither admits guilt nor proclaims innocence of a charge. *Nolo contendere* is LATIN for "I do not wish to contend."

NOW *See* NATIONAL ORGANIZATION FOR WOMEN.

NRA *See* NATIONAL RIFLE ASSOCIATION.

NSC *See* NATIONAL SECURITY COUNCIL.

Nuclear Regulatory Commission (NRC) An agency of the United States government responsible for licensing and regulating NUCLEAR POWER plants. It was created in 1974, along with the Energy Research and Development Administration, to replace the ATOMIC ENERGY COMMISSION.

Oak Ridge A city in TENNESSEE, where URANIUM for the ATOMIC BOMB was produced during WORLD WAR II. Since that time, the government has maintained a variety of nuclear research facilities in Oak Ridge. (*See also* MANHATTAN PROJECT.)

Office of Economic Opportunity (OEO) A federal agency, founded in the 1960s as part of the WAR ON POVERTY conducted by President Lyndon JOHNSON. The OEO distributed federal money to a variety of local programs designed to promote educational opportunities and job training among the poor, and to provide legal services for the poor. The OEO was abolished in the middle 1970s, and its programs have been curtailed or scattered among other federal agencies, particularly the DEPARTMENT OF HEALTH AND HUMAN SERVICES.

ombudsman (OM-buhdz-muhn, OM-boodz-muhn) An official appointed to investigate complaints by individuals against public officials or organizations. Various institutions, such as schools, hospitals, newspapers, consumer affairs bureaus, CORPORATIONS, and some government agencies in the United States, use ombudsmen as impartial mediators. (*See* MEDIATION.)

on the Hill A phrase referring to CAPITOL HILL in WASHINGTON, D.C., where CONGRESS meets: "They're debating that nuclear waste issue on the Hill today."

open primary A type of DIRECT PRIMARY open to voters regardless of their party affiliation. Voters need not publicly declare their party affiliation, but must vote for candidates of only one party. The opposite is a CLOSED PRIMARY, in which only registered members of a party may vote.

Oval Office An oval-shaped room in the WHITE HOUSE that serves as the official office of the president of the United States. Since the presidency of Richard NIXON, the term has been used to refer to the president himself: "The order came directly from the Oval Office."

PACs (PAKS) *See* POLITICAL ACTION COMMITTEES.

patronage (PAY-truh-nij, PAT-ruh-nij) The power of a government official or leader to make appointments and offer favors. Once in office, a politician can use patronage to build a loyal following. Though practiced at all levels of government, patronage is most often associated with the MACHINE POLITICS of big cities. (*See* SPOILS SYSTEM.)

Peace Corps An agency of the United States government that sends American volunteers to DEVELOPING NATIONS to help improve living standards and provide training. Created by President John F. KENNEDY in 1961, under the auspices of the DEPARTMENT OF STATE, the Peace Corps provides an opportunity to share American wealth, technology, and expertise. During the COLD WAR it also served as a means for spreading American influence and values in the hope of preventing DEVELOPING NATIONS from allying themselves with the SOVIET UNION.

Pentagon An immense five-sided building in VIRGINIA, just outside WASHINGTON, D.C., that serves as headquarters for the DEPARTMENT OF DEFENSE.

PENTAGON. *An aerial view.*

🍂 The term is often used to refer to the Department of Defense or the military: "The Pentagon agreed today to submit the modified weapons plan to the president."

plaintiff The party that institutes a suit in a court. The person or entity the plaintiff sues is the DEFENDANT.

platform A political party's or candidate's written statement of principles and plans. A platform is usually developed by a committee at the party convention during a presidential campaign.

plea bargain An agreement that permits a DEFENDANT to plead guilty to a lesser charge instead of pleading not guilty to a more serious one. Plea bargaining is usually undertaken by a prosecutor to obtain important information from a defendant or to avoid a long and costly trial.

Pledge of Allegiance Also called the "Pledge to the Flag." The American patriotic vow, which is often recited by school classes and at formal government ceremonies, including INDEPENDENCE DAY ceremonies for new citizens:

I pledge allegiance to the flag of the United States of America, and to the REPUBLIC for which it stands, one nation under God, indivisible, with liberty and justice for all.

The PHRASE *under God*, added in 1954 (over sixty years after the pledge was originally published), has inspired heated debate over the SEPARATION OF CHURCH AND STATE.

pocket veto An automatic VETO of a bill that occurs if the president or governor neither signs nor vetoes a bill within ten days of receiving it — as long as the legislature adjourns during that period. If the legislature convenes during that period, the bill will automatically become law. A pocket veto cannot be overridden by the legislature, though the bill can be reintroduced at the next legislative session.

political action committees (PACs) Committees formed by INTEREST GROUPS to funnel donations to political candidates who are likely to support their position on various issues. Because of current campaign laws, PACs are allowed to make much larger donations than can individuals.

political machine *See* MACHINE, POLITICAL.

political science A SOCIAL SCIENCE that makes generalizations about and analyzes political systems and political behavior, and uses these results to predict future behavior. The study of political science includes political PHILOSOPHY, ETHICS, international relations and foreign policy, public administration, and the dynamic relationships among a government's EXECUTIVE BRANCH, LEGISLATIVE BRANCH, and JUDICIAL BRANCH.

poll tax A tax required as a qualification for voting. After the Fifteenth Amendment to the CONSTITUTION extended the vote to blacks in 1870, many southern states instituted poll taxes to prevent blacks from voting. The Twenty-fourth Amendment to the Constitution, adopted in 1964, prohibits poll taxes for federal elections.

populism The belief that greater popular participation in government and business is necessary to protect individuals from exploitation by inflexible BUREAUCRACY and financial CONGLOMERATES. "Power to the people" is a famous populist slogan.

pork-barrel legislation APPROPRIATIONS made by a legislature for projects that are not essential, but are sought because they pump money and resources into the local districts of the legislators. Local projects such as dams, military bases, highways, housing subsidies, and job training are often funded by pork-barrel legislation, which can be accomplished through LOGROLLING. Successful pork-barrel legislators are likely to be reelected by their CONSTITUENTS.

postmaster general The head of the United States Postal Service. Until 1970, the postmaster general was head of the federal Post Office Department, and a member of the president's CABINET. In 1970, the Postal Service was set up as an independent agency in place of the Post Office Department. The Postal Service is operated like a private CORPORATION, although postal workers receive the benefits of federal employees.

power elite Term used by the American sociologist (*see* SOCIOLOGY) C. Wright Mills to describe a relatively small, loosely knit group of people who tend to dominate American policymaking. This group includes bureaucratic, corporate, intellectual, military, and government elites, who control the principal institutions in the United States, and whose opinions and actions influence the decisions of the policymakers.

power of the purse The influence that legislatures have over public policy because of their power to vote money for public purposes. The United States CONGRESS must authorize the president's budget requests to fund agencies and programs of the EXECUTIVE BRANCH. (*See* APPROPRIATION.)

precedent (PRESS-uh-duhnt) A previous ruling by a court that influences subsequent decisions in cases where the issues are similar.

pressure group An organized group that tries to influence the government to adopt certain policies or measures. Also called an INTEREST GROUP. (*See* LOBBY.)

primaries State elections of delegates to the nominating convention that chooses a major party's presidential candidate. In some states, delegates are elected by popular vote; in other states, party CAUCUSES or miniconventions choose delegates.

    🐾 Primaries occur at different times during the presidential election year, a situation that drags out the process by which parties nominate candidates but allows wide public exposure to candidates and issues.

privacy, right of The doctrine, advanced by the SUPREME COURT most notably in *ROE VERSUS WADE*, that the CONSTITUTION implicitly guarantees protection against activities that invade citizens' privacy. The Constitution does not explicitly mention a right of privacy, but the FIRST AMENDMENT's protection of free speech, the Fourth Amendment's guarantee against "unreasonable searches and seizures," the Ninth Amendment's reference to "other" rights, the Court has ruled, imply a right of privacy. This doctrine exemplifies BROAD CONSTRUCTION.

probate court (PROH-bayt)   A court that has jurisdiction over wills, estates, and guardianship of children.

probation   Suspension of the jail sentence of a person convicted of a crime, provided that the person maintains good behavior.

proportional representation   An electoral system in which seats in a legislature are awarded to each party on the basis of its share of the popular vote. With only two major political parties, the United States does not use a system of proportional representation. Membership in the SENATE and the HOUSE OF REPRESENTATIVES, for example, is based on individual candidates' receiving a majority of votes.
  ❧ In nations in EUROPE with multiparty governments and in ISRAEL, a system of proportional representation guarantees that small parties will have official recognition in the government. ❧ Though proportional representation has been attempted in a few American cities, many American politicians argue that it tends to fragment the government, preventing quick and decisive action.

public defender   An attorney who is appointed and paid by a court to defend poor persons who cannot afford a lawyer on their own.

public works   Public facilities and improvements financed by the government for the public good. Public works include hospitals, bridges, highways, and dams. These projects may be funded by local, state, or federal APPROPRIATIONS. (See also PORK-BARREL LEGISLATION.)

quorum (KWAWR-uhm)   The minimum number of members of a committee or legislative body who must be present before business can officially or legally be conducted. In the United States CONGRESS, for example, either house must have a majority (218 in the HOUSE OF REPRESENTATIVES, 51 in the SENATE) in order to have a quorum.

racism   The belief that some races are inherently superior (physically, intellectually, or culturally) to others, and therefore have a right to dominate them. In the United States, racism, particularly by whites against blacks, has created profound racial tension and conflict in virtually all aspects of American society. Until the breakthroughs achieved by the CIVIL RIGHTS MOVEMENT in the 1950s and 1960s, white domination over blacks was officially institutionalized and supported in all branches and levels of government, by denying blacks their CIVIL RIGHTS and opportunities to participate in political, economic, and social communities.

ranking member   A legislator on a committee who belongs to the majority party and, by virtue of seniority, ranks first after the committee chairman. The most senior member representing the minority party is the ranking minority member of the committee.

ratification   The approval from the LEGISLATIVE BRANCH required to validate government agreements. In the United States, amendments to the CONSTITUTION require the ratification of state legislatures, and international treaties require the ratification of the SENATE.

referendum (ref-uh-REN-duhm)   A direct popular vote on an issue of public policy, such as a proposed amendment to a state constitution or a proposed law. Referendums, which allow the general population to participate in policymaking, are not used at the national level, but are common at the state and local levels. A referendum is often used to gauge popular approval or rejection of laws recently passed or under consideration by a state legislature. A referendum can also be used to initiate legislative action.

representatives   Popularly elected officials who serve in state legislatures and in the HOUSE OF REPRESENTATIVES in CONGRESS. Representing the local districts from which they are elected, representatives support the interests of their CONSTITUENTS by proposing bills and programs. Elected for two-year terms, representatives in Congress must be sensitive to their constituents' concerns in order to be reelected.

Republican   A member of the REPUBLICAN PARTY.

Republican party   *See entries under "American History to 1865" and "American History since 1865."*

rider   A provision, usually controversial and unlikely to pass on its own merits, that is attached to a popular bill in the hopes that it will "ride" to passage on the back of the popular bill.

right-wing A descriptive term for an individual or a political FACTION that advocates very CONSERVATIVE policies. Right-wing groups generally support FREE ENTERPRISE and rule by an OLIGARCHY. In the United States, the right wing generally argues for a strong national defense program and opposes federal involvement in promoting social welfare. (*Compare* LEFT-WING.)

➷ Although both major political parties in the United States have right-wing factions, right-wing policies are usually associated with the REPUBLICAN PARTY.

Robert's *Rules of Order* A handbook for running meetings effectively and efficiently, based on the procedures used in the British PARLIAMENT. The principles included in the handbook are applicable to any decision-making organization, from CONGRESS to community club committees. The handbook sets the guidelines for such issues as leading debates, recognizing speakers, defining the role of the chair and other officers, proposing, seconding, and voting on motions, and writing and amending CONSTITUTIONS and bylaws.

rugged individualism The belief that all individuals, or nearly all individuals, can succeed on their own, and that government help for people should be minimal. The PHRASE is often associated with policies of the REPUBLICAN PARTY, and was widely used by the Republican president Herbert HOOVER. The phrase was later used in scorn by the DEMOCRATIC presidents Franklin ROOSEVELT and Harry TRUMAN to refer to the disasters of Hoover's administration, during which the WALL STREET CRASH OF 1929 occurred and the GREAT DEPRESSION began.

Secret Service A division of the United States DEPARTMENT OF THE TREASURY, responsible for apprehending counterfeiters; investigating a variety of federal crimes; and protecting presidents and their families, presidential candidates, and foreign dignitaries visiting the United States.

secretary of defense The civilian head of the United States DEPARTMENT OF DEFENSE, and a member of the CABINET, appointed by the president and confirmed by the SENATE. The secretary of defense works with civilian and military advisers to formulate American military policies and make foreign policy recommendations to the president.

secretary of state The head of the United States DEPARTMENT OF STATE, and, as leading member of the CABINET, fourth in line of succession to the presidency. The secretary of state is charged with formulating American foreign policy and conducting relations with other nations.

segregation The policy and practice of imposing the separation of races. In the United States, the policy of segregation denied African-Americans their CIVIL RIGHTS and provided inferior facilities and services for them, most noticeably in public schools (*see* BROWN VERSUS BOARD OF EDUCATION), housing, and industry. (*See* INTEGRATION, NATIONAL ASSOCIATION FOR THE ADVANCEMENT OF COLORED PEOPLE, *and* SEPARATE BUT EQUAL.)

Selective Service System The system used in the United States to DRAFT young people into armed service. Though the United States at present has no draft, young men are required by law to register with the Selective Service when they reach the age of eighteen.

self-incrimination Being forced or coerced to testify against oneself. Self-incrimination is prohibited by the FIFTH AMENDMENT to the United States CONSTITUTION.

➷ Under this principle, a person may choose (given certain restrictions) to "take the Fifth," refusing to testify in court or before a legislative or executive committee. ➷ Prohibiting self-incrimination not only helps guarantee DUE PROCESS, but also maintains one of the basic principles of American law by putting the burden of proof on the prosecution. (*See also MIRANDA* DECISION.)

Senate, United States The upper house of the United States CONGRESS. Two senators are elected from each state, regardless of state population, guaranteeing each state equal representation. Senators are elected for six-year terms. The Senate tends to respond more directly than the HOUSE OF REPRESENTATIVES to issues of national, rather than local, concern, though both houses of Congress participate in all aspects of legislation and policymaking. The Senate has the exclusive right to try cases of IMPEACHMENT, approve presidential appointments, confirm treaties, and elect a vice president if no candidate receives a majority from the ELECTORAL COLLEGE. The vice president serves as presiding officer of the Senate.

separate but equal   The doctrine that racial SEGREGATION is constitutional as long as the facilities provided for blacks and whites are roughly equal. This doctrine was long used to support segregation in the public schools and a variety of public facilities, such as transportation and restaurants, where the facilities and services for blacks were often clearly inferior. For decades, the SUPREME COURT refused to rule the separate but equal doctrine unconstitutional, on the grounds that such CIVIL RIGHTS issues were the responsibility of the states. In the decision of *BROWN VERSUS BOARD OF EDUCATION*, in 1954, the Supreme Court unanimously ruled separate but equal schools unconstitutional. This ruling was followed by several civil rights laws in the 1960s. (*See also* *PLESSY VERSUS FERGUSON*.)

separation of church and state   The principle that government must maintain an attitude of neutrality toward religion. Separation of church and state is required by the FIRST AMENDMENT to the United States CONSTITUTION. The First Amendment not only allows citizens the freedom to practice any religion of their choice, but also prevents the government from officially recognizing or favoring any religion.

❧ The relationship between church and state has been extremely controversial since the first settlers arrived in America to escape religious persecution in EUROPE, and many cases involving the issue have reached the SUPREME COURT. ❧ Interpretation of the principle has been ambiguous: for instance, the Supreme Court has recently upheld laws prohibiting prayer in the schools, but has permitted the construction of NATIVITY scenes on government property. (*See also* ESTABLISHED CHURCH *and* FREEDOM OF RELIGION.)

separation of powers   A fundamental principle of the United States government, whereby powers and responsibilities are divided among the LEGISLATIVE BRANCH, EXECUTIVE BRANCH, and JUDICIAL BRANCH. The officials of each branch are selected by different procedures and serve different terms of office; each branch may choose to block action of the other branches through the system of CHECKS AND BALANCES. This system was designed by the framers of the CONSTITUTION to ensure that no one branch would accumulate too much power, and that issues

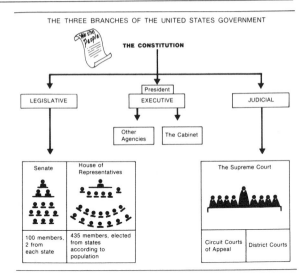

THE THREE BRANCHES OF THE UNITED STATES GOVERNMENT

of public policy and welfare would be given comprehensive consideration before any action was taken.

sexism   The belief that one sex (usually the male) is naturally superior to the other, and should dominate most important areas of political, economic, and social life. Sexist discrimination in the United States in the past has denied opportunities to women in many spheres of activity. Many allege that it still does. (*See also* AFFIRMATIVE ACTION, EQUAL EMPLOYMENT OPPORTUNITY COMMISSION, *and* NATIONAL ORGANIZATION FOR WOMEN.)

shirtsleeve diplomacy   An approach to diplomacy and international relations that implies an informal, direct involvement — a willingness to roll up one's sleeves and work. This approach has been popular among American ambassadors and other diplomats eager to demonstrate American concern for other countries' affairs. Shirtsleeve diplomacy is often associated with development efforts, such as the PEACE CORPS.

shout "Fire!" in a crowded theater   A PHRASE used by Justice Oliver Wendell HOLMES, Jr., in a SUPREME COURT decision to illustrate that there are limits to the FREEDOM OF SPEECH guaranteed in the FIRST AMENDMENT. He argued that for someone to shout "Fire!" in a crowded theater when there was no fire, causing an unwarranted panic, was an abuse of free speech. (*See* CLEAR AND PRESENT DANGER.)

slush fund   A collection of money by a political official or administration that is used to make payments for various services. Though slush funds may be used for legitimate purposes, such as paying state employees, the term is generally used to describe money that is not properly accounted for, and is being used for personal expenses and political payoffs. Money raised for political campaigns has come under increasing public scrutiny to ensure that it is not misused.

Smithsonian Institution (smith-SOH-nee-uhn)   A group of over a dozen museums and research and publication facilities, such as the National Air and Space Museum, the Museum of Natural History, the Museum of History and Technology, the National Zoo, and the NATIONAL GALLERY OF ART. Many of the Smithsonian's buildings are on the WASHINGTON MALL. The institution is named after James Smithson, an Englishman whose bequest enabled its founding in the nineteenth century.

smoke-filled room   A popular expression used to describe a place where the political wheeling and dealing of MACHINE bosses is conducted. The image originated during the REPUBLICAN presidential nominating convention of 1920, in which Warren G. HARDING emerged as a DARK HORSE candidate.

Social Security Administration   The American system for distributing old age and disability PENSIONS from the federal government. Initiated through the Social Security Act of 1935, Social Security pensions are financed by contributions from workers and employers. Benefits are also available to the survivors of workers covered under Social Security.

Speaker of the House   The presiding officer of the United States HOUSE OF REPRESENTATIVES. The Speaker, a member of the House, is elected by a majority party CAUCUS. In addition to being chief spokesman for the majority party, the Speaker runs the proceedings of House debate and voting, appoints committee members, refers bills to committees for research and development, and has an influential voice in all stages of a bill's consideration. One of the most visible and influential officials of the federal government, the Speaker is second in line, after the vice president, in succession to the presidency.

split ticket   A vote for candidates of different political parties on the same ballot, instead of for candidates of only one party. In the presidential elections, for example, a voter may choose a REPUBLICAN candidate for president, but a DEMOCRATIC candidate for senator. Split-ticket voting is not allowed in primaries (*see* CLOSED PRIMARY, DIRECT PRIMARY, OPEN PRIMARY). The increasing occurrence of split-ticket voting reflects support of individual candidates rather than unswerving party loyalty.

spoils system   Awarding government jobs to the loyal supporters of a victorious party. Originally used to encourage more people to become actively involved in policymaking, the spoils system quickly became a method of establishing and perpetuating party power. (*See* MACHINE POLITICS *and* PATRONAGE.)

stare decisis (STAIR-ee duh-SEYE-sis)   A LATIN PHRASE that literally means "to let the decision stand." It expresses the COMMON LAW doctrine that court decisions should be guided by PRECEDENT.

State Department   A common name for the DEPARTMENT OF STATE.

State of the Union address   An annual message delivered to CONGRESS by the president of the United States, in which he describes the condition of the country, outlines the nation's most serious problems, and proposes his annual program of legislation.

&a. The name of the address comes from a provision in the CONSTITUTION that the president "shall from time to time give to the Congress information of the state of the Union, and recommend to their consideration such measures as he shall judge necessary and expedient."

states' rights   Rights guaranteed to the states under the principle of FEDERALISM. Under the CONSTITUTION, states have considerable autonomy to pass, enforce, and interpret their own laws, and to pursue their own public policy programs. Proponents of states' rights argue that the states should be governed with a minimum of interference from the federal government.

&a. The relationship between federal and state responsibilities has often been controversial. Until the middle of the twentieth century, for example, the SUPREME COURT left the interpretation of many CIVIL RIGHTS guarantees to the states, resulting in hostile and widespread discrimination against minorities.

statute of limitations Any law that places a time restriction during which a lawsuit must be brought to court or a crime must be prosecuted.

straw poll Originally, a small, informal opinion survey. Today, a straw poll is generally a large-scale, scientifically determined public opinion survey based on a random sample of the population. Straw polls are commonly used to test public opinion of candidates running for office.

strict construction *See* NARROW CONSTRUCTION.

subpoena (suh-PEE-nuh) An order of a court, a legislature, or a GRAND JURY compelling a witness to be present at a trial or hearing, under penalty of fine or imprisonment. *Subpoena* is LATIN for "under penalty."

SUFFRAGETTES. *Three women, circa 1910, demonstrating for the right to vote.*

suffrage (SUF-rij) The right to vote (*see* FRANCHISE). In the United States, the term is often associated with the women's movement to win voting rights. (*See* SUFFRAGIST.)

suffragette (suf-ruh-JET) A SUFFRAGIST. Today, the term *suffragette* is often considered demeaning.

suffragist (SUF-ruh-jist) A participant in the WOMEN'S MOVEMENT to win voting rights in the United States. The fight for women's SUFFRAGE was organized in the middle of the nineteenth century. WYOMING, while not yet a state, granted women's suffrage in 1869, though the struggle for universal suffrage was to last another fifty years. In 1920, the Nineteenth Amendment to the United States CONSTITUTION was ratified, guaranteeing that no state could deny the right to vote on the basis of sex.

SUPREME COURT. *The U.S. Supreme Court justices, from left to right: (top) David H. Souter, Antonin Scalia, Anthony M. Kennedy, Clarence Thomas; (bottom) John Paul Stevens, Byron R. White, Chief Justice William H. Rehnquist, Harry A. Blackmun, and Sandra Day O'Connor.*

Supreme Court A federal court; the highest body in the JUDICIAL BRANCH. The Supreme Court is composed of a chief justice and eight associate justices, all of whom are appointed by the president and confirmed by the SENATE. They serve on the Court as long as they choose, subject only to IMPEACHMENT. Each state also has a supreme court; these courts are all COURTS OF APPEALS, primarily hearing cases that have already been tried. The federal Supreme Court ("the" Supreme Court) has the final word on interpretation of all laws and of the CONSTITUTION itself.

☙ Supreme Court decisions have a significant impact on public policy, and are often extremely controversial. In interpreting the Constitution, the justices of the Supreme Court occasionally have deduced legal doctrines that are not clearly stated (or stated at all) in the Constitution. For example, in the famous case of *McCulloch versus Maryland* (1819), Chief Justice John MARSHALL advanced the opinion, accepted by the Court, that the Constitution implicitly gives the federal government the power to establish a national bank, even though such a power is not explicitly granted by the Constitution. In *ROE VERSUS WADE* (1973), the Court ruled that state laws restricting ABORTION violate the right of privacy. This is another example of the Court's identifying an implied rather than an explicitly stated right. ❧ The *McCulloch* and *Roe* decisions illustrate the principle of BROAD or LOOSE CONSTRUCTION (interpretation) of the Constitution. The opposite is NARROW or STRICT CONSTRUCTION. Those who favor broad construction believe that the spirit of the times, the values of the justices, and the needs of the nation may legitimately influence the way justices decide cases. Advocacy of this belief is called "JUDICIAL ACTIVISM." In contrast, strict constructionists insist that the Court should be bound by the exact words of the Constitution or by the intentions of the framers of the Constitution or by some combination of both. This view is sometimes called JUDICIAL RESTRAINT.

think tank   An institution in which scholars pursue research in public policy. Largely funded by endowments and grants, think tanks work to improve public awareness of policy issues (through publications) and to influence the government to act upon issues of national importance. (*See* POWER ELITE.)

Ugly American, the   Pejorative term for Americans traveling or living abroad who remain ignorant of local CULTURE and judge everything by American standards. The term is taken from the title of a book by Eugene Burdick and William Lederer.

un-American   A term used, primarily by extreme CONSERVATIVES, to attack principles or practices considered to be at odds with the values of most Americans. Many object to the use of the term on the grounds that it is vague, shortsighted, and intolerant.
❧ The HOUSE OF REPRESENTATIVES maintained a Committee on Un-American Activities (HUAC) for several years. It was especially known for investigation of alleged COMMUNISTS. (*See* HISS, ALGER.)

Uncle Sam   A figure who stands for the government of the United States and for the United States itself. Uncle Sam — whose initials are the ABBREVIATION of United States — is portrayed as an old man with a gray goatee who sports a top hat and STARS AND STRIPES clothing. During WORLD WAR I and WORLD WAR II, posters of Uncle Sam exhorted young men to join the armed forces. (*Compare* JOHN BULL.)

UNCLE SAM. *From a World War I army recruiting poster.*

United States Constitution   See CONSTITUTION.

United States Information Agency (USIA)   A federal agency responsible for spreading information favorable to the United States around the world.

USIA   *See* UNITED STATES INFORMATION AGENCY.

VA   *See* VETERANS ADMINISTRATION.

Veterans Administration (VA)   A federal agency that coordinates the distribution of benefits for veterans of the American military forces and their dependents. The benefits include compensation for disabilities, the management of veterans' hospitals, and various insurance programs.

Veterans of Foreign Wars (VFW)   An organization of American veterans who have taken part in a foreign military campaign or expedition of the United States. Like the AMERICAN LEGION, it usually takes prodefense stands on foreign policy issues.

veto   The power of a president or governor to reject a bill proposed by a legislature by refusing to sign it into law. The president or governor actually writes the word *veto* (LATIN for "I forbid") on the bill, and sends it back to the legislature with a statement of his or her objections. The legislature may choose to comply by withdrawing or revising the bill, or it can override the veto and pass the law itself, by a two-thirds vote in each house.

&. Originally intended to prevent CONGRESS from passing unconstitutional laws, the veto is now used by the president as a powerful bargaining tool, especially when his objectives conflict with majority sentiment in Congress. (*See also* CHECKS AND BALANCES.)

victimless crime   A term sometimes used for various acts that are considered crimes under the law, but that apparently have no victim. One such crime is prostitution, which is viewed by some as a commercial exchange between two consenting adults.

vigilantes (vij-uh-LAN-teez)   Volunteer citizens who organize to suppress crime where official police forces are weak or nonexistent.

Ways and Means Committee   A permanent committee of the HOUSE OF REPRESENTATIVES, which makes recommendations to the House on all bills for raising revenue. The committee is the principal source of legislation concerning issues such as TAXATION, customs duties, and international trade agreements.

whip   In the United States CONGRESS or state legislatures, an assistant to the MAJORITY LEADER or MINORITY LEADER responsible for stirring up party support on issues, keeping track of party members' votes, and acting as a general liaison between the majority leader or minority leader and other party members.

write-in candidate   A candidate for public office whose name does not appear on the ballot (usually because he or she has not secured the nomination of a political party) but whose name must be written on the ballot by voters.

Yankee   Originally a nickname for people from NEW ENGLAND, now applied to anyone from the United States. Even before the AMERICAN REVOLUTION, the term *Yankee* was used by the British to refer, derisively, to the American colonists. Since the CIVIL WAR, American southerners have called all northerners Yankees. Since WORLD WAR I, the rest of the world has used the term to refer to all Americans.

&. The expression "Yankee, go home" reflects foreign resentment of American presence or involvement in other nations' affairs.

World Geography

M ost of today's nations did not exist as independent states a century ago. As late as 1914 empires bestrode much of the world. BRITAIN, FRANCE, and GERMANY held large parts of AFRICA as colonies. Britain also had colonies in ASIA, including INDIA. VIETNAM and CAMBODIA were part of French-controlled INDOCHINA. Even such small European nations as BELGIUM, the NETHERLANDS, and PORTUGAL had African colonies. The Austro-Hungarian empire included the former CZECHOSLOVAKIA and parts of the former YUGOSLAVIA. The OTTOMAN or Turkish empire spread across much of the MIDDLE EAST, including PALESTINE. Extending from the BALTIC SEA to the PACIFIC OCEAN, the Russian empire was colossal in size.

The defeat of the CENTRAL POWERS (primarily Germany, Austria-Hungary, and Turkey) in WORLD WAR I led to a redrawing of the map of the world. For example, Czechoslovakia and Yugoslavia became independent nations; LEBANON, IRAQ, and SYRIA were carved out of the Ottoman empire. POLAND, intermittently independent before 1914, again became a nation-state. But the aftermath of World War I did not bring independence to the African and Asian colonies of the European powers. In contrast, NATIONALISM swept the THIRD WORLD after WORLD WAR II. For example, ALGERIA, TUNISIA, and Vietnam all gained independence from France in the 1950s and 1960s. In the early 1960s a score of nations in SUB-SAHARAN Africa, mainly colonies and protectorates of Britain and France, achieved independence, including KENYA, NIGERIA, and SIERRA LEONE.

The COLLAPSE OF COMMUNISM in Eastern Europe and the SOVIET UNION between 1989 and 1991 led to new changes in the world's map. EAST and WEST GERMANY were unified. The Soviet Union, which gradually had taken over the former Russian empire, disintegrated and left in its wake a host of former provinces (called republics) that are now independent, including BELARUS, KAZAKHSTAN, MOLDOVA, and UKRAINE. The so-called Baltic republics of ESTONIA, LATVIA, and LITHUANIA — once part of the Russian empire, independent between the two world wars, and forcibly absorbed into the Soviet Union in 1940 — again are independent. No longer the center of a czarist or COMMUNIST empire, RUSSIA is now an independent nation. Most recently, the former Yugoslavia provinces of BOSNIA AND HERZEGOVINA, CROATIA, MACEDONIA, and SLOVENIA have declared their independence.

Most nations in this section are described either as MONARCHIES or as REPUBLICS. In describing nations as republics, we are not implying that they are necessarily characterized by free political institutions, merely that they are not monarchies.

For the United States and its possessions, see under "American Geography."

— J. F. K.

345

Aberdeen (ab-uhr-DEEN)   City in northeastern SCOTLAND, on the NORTH SEA.

Acapulco (ah-kuh-POOL-koh,   ak-uh-POOL-koh) City on MEXICO'S PACIFIC coast.

🐚 A fashionable resort known for its beaches and water sports, which include cliff diving.

Addis Ababa (AD-is AB-uh-buh)   Capital of ETHIOPIA and largest city in the country, located in the central region.

Aden (AH-dn, AY-dn)   Capital and chief port of YEMEN, located on the Gulf of Aden, near the southwest corner of the ARABIAN PENINSULA and the southern entrance of the RED SEA.

🐚 Its strategic location and excellent harbor have made Aden the chief trading center of southern ARABIA since ancient times, as well as a coveted conquest.

Adriatic Sea (ay-dree-AT-ik)   An arm of the MEDITERRANEAN SEA bordered by ITALY to the west and north, and SLOVENIA, CROATIA, BOSNIA AND HERZEGOVINA, YUGOSLAVIA, and ALBANIA to the east.

Aegean Sea (i-JEE-uhn)   An arm of the MEDITERRANEAN SEA off southeastern EUROPE between GREECE and TURKEY.

🐚 This sea was a main trade route for the ancient civilizations of CRETE, Greece, ROME, and IRAN.

Afghanistan   REPUBLIC in south-central ASIA, bordered by TURKMENISTAN, UZBEKISTAN, and TAJIKISTAN to the north, PAKISTAN to the east and south, and IRAN to the west. KABUL is its capital and largest city.

🐚 The SOVIET UNION invaded Afghanistan in 1979, but met stiff resistance from Moslem rebels, who received support from the United States. The Soviets agreed to withdraw in 1986, and completed their withdrawal in 1989. 🐚 In 1992 various rebel groups entered Kabul and took over the government. They currently maintain an uneasy truce with one another.

Africa   The second-largest CONTINENT, after ASIA. Located south of EUROPE, and bordered to the west by the ATLANTIC OCEAN and to the east by the INDIAN OCEAN.

🐚 Africa has been the home of great civilizations, particularly in EGYPT, along the MEDITERRANEAN SEA. In the eighteenth and nineteenth centuries, much of the continent was colonized by European nations (*see* COLONIALISM). In the twentieth century, the colonies became independent countries. 🐚 Africa south of the SAHARA is sometimes called SUB-SAHARAN or Black Africa.

Albania   REPUBLIC in southeastern EUROPE on the ADRIATIC SEA coast of the BALKAN PENINSULA, bordered by YUGOSLAVIA to the northwest, north, and northeast, MACEDONIA to the east, and Greece to the southeast and south. Tirana is its capital and largest city.

🐚 The most secretive and closed of the former EASTERN BLOC nations, Albania held free elections in March 1991, ending almost fifty years of COMMUNIST rule and inaugurating a multiparty system.

Alberta   Province in western CANADA, bordered by the NORTHWEST TERRITORIES to the north, SASKATCHEWAN to the east, MONTANA to the south, and BRITISH COLUMBIA to the west. EDMONTON is its capital and largest city.

🐚 Recent exploitation of oil, natural gas, and mineral resources has replaced agriculture as Alberta's primary industry. 🐚 Banff, in the Canadian Rockies (*see* ROCKY MOUNTAINS), is a popular vacation spot.

Alexandria   Port city of northern EGYPT, located where the NILE RIVER empties into the MEDITERRANEAN SEA.

🐚 Founded by and named for ALEXANDER THE GREAT. 🐚 One-time capital city of ancient Egypt, a center consecutively of Greek, Jewish, and CHRISTIAN CULTURE.

Algeria   REPUBLIC in northwest AFRICA, bordered to the north by the MEDITERRANEAN SEA, to the east by TUNISIA and LIBYA, to the south by NIGER and Mali, and to the west by Mauritania and MOROCCO. Its capital and largest city is ALGIERS.

🐚 Colonized by FRANCE in the nineteenth century, Algeria was involved in a long and bloody battle for independence, gaining full autonomy in the early 1960s.

Algiers (al-JEERZ)   Capital of ALGERIA and largest city in the country, located on the coast of the MEDITERRANEAN SEA.

Alps   Mountain system of south-central EUROPE.

🐚 The Alps provide scenic beauty and an abundance of winter sports, making them a popular tourist destination.

Amazon River   River in SOUTH AMERICA with headwaters in northern PERU. It flows across northern BRAZIL to the ATLANTIC OCEAN.

🐾 World's second-longest river, after the NILE, flowing nearly 4000 miles; it carries more water than any other river in the world. 🐾 Named after the AMAZONS, legendary female warriors.

Amsterdam   Capital of The NETHERLANDS, located in the west-central region of the country.

🐾 Seat of one of the world's chief STOCK EXCHANGES and a center of the diamond-cutting industry, the city is also known for its canals and for a great art museum, the Rijksmuseum.

Andes (AN-deez)   Mountain system in SOUTH AMERICA running over 4500 miles along the entire length of South America's PACIFIC OCEAN coast.

Angola (ang-GOH-luh)   REPUBLIC in southwestern AFRICA on the ATLANTIC coast, bordered to the north and northeast by ZAIRE, to the east by ZAMBIA, and to the south by NAMIBIA. Its capital and largest city is Luanda.

🐾 After achieving independence from PORTUGAL in 1976, Angola was the scene of a civil war between its MARXIST government, supported by the SOVIET UNION and CUBAN troops, and a rebel organization known as UNITA, which was aided by the United States and South Africa. In 1988 the United States engineered a settlement that led to the withdrawal of Cuban troops and to South African acceptance of black majority rule in neighboring NAMIBIA.

Ankara (ANG-kuhr-uh)   Capital of TURKEY, located in west-central Turkey. Administrative, commercial, and cultural center.

🐾 Formerly known as Angora. Home of Angora goats, famous for their fine wool.

Antarctic   The region around the SOUTH POLE, ANTARCTICA, and the surrounding ocean.

Antarctic Circle   An imaginary circle around the EARTH about three-quarters of the way from the EQUATOR to the SOUTH POLE.

🐾 The Antarctic Circle corresponds to the ARCTIC CIRCLE in the NORTHERN HEMISPHERE.

Antarctica   CONTINENT surrounding the SOUTH POLE, located almost entirely within the ANTARCTIC CIRCLE. It is covered by an ice cap up to 13,000 feet thick.

🐾 Antarctica is characterized by extremely low temperatures. 🐾 In 1911, Roald Amundsen became the first explorer to reach the South Pole, followed shortly thereafter by Robert Scott.

antipodes (an-TIP-uh-deez)   Two places on the globe that are exactly opposite each other; for example, the NORTH POLE and SOUTH POLE.

Arabia   PENINSULA in southwest ASIA, bordered on the north by JORDAN and IRAQ, on the east by the PERSIAN GULF and the Gulf of Oman, on the south by the Gulf of Aden, and on the west by the RED SEA. This historical region in the MIDDLE EAST consists of BAHRAIN, KUWAIT, OMAN, QATAR, SAUDI ARABIA, the UNITED ARAB EMIRATES, YEMEN, and several neutral zones.

🐾 Strategically important because it is situated at the crossroads of EUROPE, Asia, and AFRICA, Arabia has been coveted and controlled by many empires throughout history. The area's importance is all the greater today because of its fabulous oil reserves. The United States and the SOVIET UNION both competed for influence in Arabia after the British presence ended in the late 1960s. Arabian states joined the coalition against Iraq's invasion of Kuwait in 1990. (*See also* PERSIAN GULF WAR.)

Arabian Peninsula   *See* ARABIA.

archipelago (ahr-kuh-PEL-uh-goh)   A group of islands near one another.

Arctic   Region in the northernmost area of the EARTH, centered on the NORTH POLE.

🐾 The WEATHER of the Arctic is characterized by long, cold winters and short, cool summers. 🐾 The Arctic has been the object of much exploration by air, land, and sea. The shortest distance by plane between CONTINENTS in the NORTHERN HEMISPHERE is often over the Arctic.

Arctic Circle   Imaginary circle around the EARTH about three-quarters of the way from the EQUATOR to the NORTH POLE. North of this line is the "Land of the Midnight Sun," where the sun never sets on the summer SOLSTICE.

🐾 The Arctic Circle corresponds to the ANTARCTIC CIRCLE in the SOUTHERN HEMISPHERE.

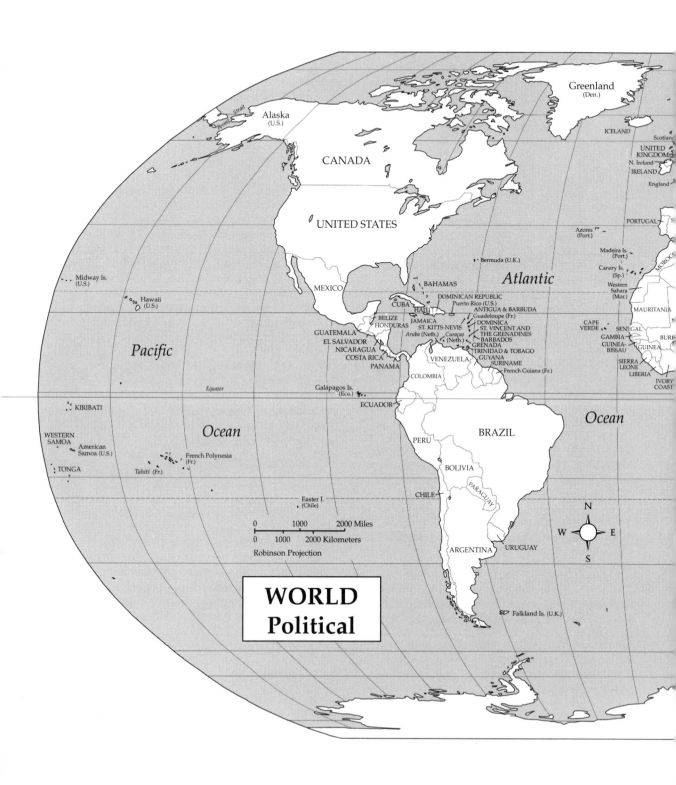

Greenland
(Den.)

ICELAND

Scotland

UNITED
KINGDOM

N. Ireland

IRELAND

England

Alaska
(U.S.)

Bering Strait

CANADA

PORTUGAL

UNITED STATES

Azores
(Port.)

Madeira Is.
(Port.)

Atlantic

Bermuda (U.K.)

MOROCCO

Canary Is.
(Sp.)

Western
Sahara
(Mor.)

Midway Is.
(U.S.)

MEXICO

BAHAMAS

DOMINICAN REPUBLIC

MAURITANIA

Hawaii
(U.S.)

CUBA

HAITI

Puerto Rico (U.S.)

ANTIGUA & BARBUDA

Guadeloupe (Fr.)

DOMINICA

CAPE
VERDE

SENEGAL

BELIZE

JAMAICA

ST. KITTS-NEVIS

ST. VINCENT AND
THE GRENADINES

GAMBIA

BURK

Pacific

HONDURAS

GUATEMALA

EL SALVADOR

NICARAGUA

COSTA RICA

PANAMA

Aruba (Neth.)

Curaçao
(Neth.)

BARBADOS

GRENADA

TRINIDAD & TOBAGO

GUYANA

SURINAME

French Guiana (Fr.)

GUINEA-
BISSAU

GUINEA

SIERRA
LEONE

LIBERIA

IVORY
COAST

VENEZUELA

COLOMBIA

Equator

Galápagos Is.
(Ecu.)

ECUADOR

Ocean

KIRIBATI

Ocean

WESTERN
SAMOA

American
Samoa (U.S.)

Ocean

PERU

BRAZIL

TONGA

Tahiti (Fr.)

French Polynesia
(Fr.)

BOLIVIA

Easter I.
(Chile)

CHILE

PARAGUAY

0   1000   2000 Miles

0   1000   2000 Kilometers

Robinson Projection

N

W   E

S

ARGENTINA

URUGUAY

WORLD
Political

Falkland Is. (U.K.)

Arctic Ocean   The cold, ice-covered waters surrounding the NORTH POLE, located entirely within the ARCTIC CIRCLE. It contains the northernmost islands of CANADA, NORWAY, and Russia.

ᶻᵃ Most of the Arctic Ocean is covered by solid ice, ice floes, and ICEBERGS.

Argentina   REPUBLIC in southern SOUTH AMERICA, bordered by CHILE to the west; BOLIVIA and PARAGUAY to the north; and BRAZIL, URUGUAY, and the ATLANTIC OCEAN to the east. Its capital and largest city is BUENOS AIRES.

ᶻᵃ Second-largest nation of South America, after BRAZIL. ᶻᵃ Juan PERÓN came to power in Argentina in 1944, establishing a DICTATORSHIP, and ruled with the aid of his second wife, the popular Eva PERÓN, until he was overthrown in 1955. He was president again from 1973 to 1974, when he died.

Armenia   REPUBLIC in extreme southeastern EUROPE, bordered by GEORGIA to the north, AZERBAIJAN to the east, IRAN to the south, and TURKEY to the south and west. Yerevan is its capital and largest city.

ᶻᵃ The former kingdom of Armenia included the present country, northeastern Turkey, and the northwest corner of Iran. ᶻᵃ Throughout their 2500-year history, the Armenian people have been repeatedly invaded and oppressed by more powerful neighboring empires, which have included Greeks, Persians, Byzantines, HUNS, Arabs, Mongols, Ottoman Turks, and Russians. ᶻᵃ Between 1894 and 1920, Armenians were the victims of a massacre organized by the Turks (see ARMENIAN MASSACRES). ᶻᵃ In 1920, the SOVIET UNION annexed Armenia, but animosity remained strong between Armenians and Russians. When the Soviet Union began to crumble in 1991, Armenia was one of the first non-Baltic Soviet republics to declare its independence. ᶻᵃ Mainly CHRISTIAN, Armenia has been involved in a bloody border dispute with neighboring Azerbaijan, which is mainly MOSLEM.

Asia   World's largest CONTINENT, joined to EUROPE to the west, forming EURASIA.

ᶻᵃ Site of some of the world's earliest civilizations. ᶻᵃ With three-fifths of the world's population, Asia has some of the world's greatest population densities.

Asia Minor   PENINSULA in western ASIA consisting of the Asian part of TURKEY.

Aswan Dam (AS-wahn, as-WAHN)   Dam just south of Aswan, a city in southern EGYPT, on the NILE RIVER. One of the world's largest dams.

ᶻᵃ The United States and BRITAIN withdrew financial aid for the dam's construction in 1956, after which the SOVIET UNION took over much of the financing.

Athens   Capital of GREECE in east-central Greece on the plain of Attica, overlooking an arm of the MEDITERRANEAN SEA. Greece's largest city, and its cultural, administrative, and economic center. Named after its patron goddess, ATHENA.

ᶻᵃ In the fifth century B.C., Athens was one of the world's most powerful and highly civilized cities (*see also under "World History to 1550"*). ᶻᵃ As the cultural center of Greece, ancient Athens was home to such influential writers and thinkers as ARISTOPHANES, EURIPIDES, SOCRATES, and PLATO. ᶻᵃ Its principal landmark is the ACROPOLIS, on which stand the remains of the PARTHENON and other buildings.

Atlantic Ocean   Second-largest ocean in the world, separating NORTH AMERICA and SOUTH AMERICA on the west from EUROPE and AFRICA on the east.

atlas   A bound collection of maps. Atlases are named after the Greek god ATLAS.

atoll (A-tawl, A-tol, AY-tawl, AY-tol)   A coral island that surrounds a lagoon. (*See* CORAL REEF.)

Auckland (AWK-luhnd)   Largest city and chief port of NEW ZEALAND, located in the northwestern part of the North Island.

Australia   Nation occupying the whole of Australia, the smallest CONTINENT, between the INDIAN OCEAN and the southwest PACIFIC OCEAN. Its capital is CANBERRA, and its largest city is SYDNEY.

ᶻᵃ First settled as penal colonies for British convicts. ᶻᵃ Its aboriginal tribes, which still exist today (*see* ABORIGINES), are thought to have migrated from SOUTHEAST ASIA 20,000 years ago.

Austria   Mountainous REPUBLIC in central EUROPE, bordered by GERMANY and the former CZECHOSLOVAKIA to the north, HUNGARY to the east, SLOVENIA and ITALY to the south, and SWITZERLAND and LIECHTENSTEIN to the west. Its capital and largest city is VIENNA.

❧ Under the Hapsburg dynasty (1278–1918), Austria maintained control of the HOLY ROMAN EMPIRE and became a leading player in European politics. ❧ After losing control of the German portions of the Holy Roman Empire in the nineteenth century, Austria joined with Hungary to create the Austro-Hungarian Empire (1867–1918). Allied with GERMANY, BULGARIA, and TURKEY in WORLD WAR I, the Austro-Hungarian Empire was devastated by the results of the war. ❧ Austria was occupied by NAZI forces in 1938 and annexed by Adolf HITLER to Germany. It was reestablished as a republic in 1945 but remained occupied by the four Allied powers until it declared neutrality in 1955. ❧ The picturesque beauty of the Tyrol region, in the western part of the country, makes it a favorite year-round tourist spot.

axis An imaginary straight LINE passing through the NORTH POLE, the center of the EARTH, and the SOUTH POLE. The earth rotates around this axis.

Azerbaijan (az-uhr-beye-JAHN, ah-zuhr-beye-JAHN) REPUBLIC in southwest ASIA, bordered to the north by GEORGIA and RUSSIA, to the east by the CASPIAN SEA, to the south by IRAN, and to the west by ARMENIA. Its capital and largest city is Baku.

❧ This former member of the SOVIET UNION declared its independence in 1991. ❧ Predominantly MOSLEM, Azerbaijan has been involved in an often violent dispute with Armenia, its predominantly CHRISTIAN neighbor, over Nagorno-Karabakh, a mainly Armenian region of Azerbaijan.

Azores (AY-zawrz, uh-ZAWRZ) Islands in the ATLANTIC OCEAN, west of mainland PORTUGAL, belonging to Portugal.

❧ Strategically located on transatlantic air and shipping routes.

Baghdad Capital of IRAQ, located in central Iraq on both banks of the Tigris River.

❧ Baghdad has long been one of the great cities of the MOSLEM world. ❧ Bombed heavily during the PERSIAN GULF WAR.

Bahamas (buh-HAH-muhz) Republic in the ATLANTIC OCEAN, consisting of 700 islands and islets and 2400 smaller islands, called cays.

❧ The Bahamas were under the control of BRITAIN until 1973, when they became an independent, self-governing state. ❧ The Bahamas are a popular winter resort.

Bahrain (bah-RAYN) Island kingdom in the PERSIAN GULF off the coasts of SAUDI ARABIA and QATAR.

❧ British PROTECTORATE from 1820 to 1971. ❧ Revenues from oil reserves, first discovered in 1931, have funded some of the most progressive programs in the Arabian nations.

Bali (BAH-lee, BAL-ee) Island of southern INDONESIA east of JAVA.

❧ Bali's striking volcanic (*see* VOLCANO) scenery provides a romantic backdrop for its CULTURE, known for its elaborate dances, rituals, and handicrafts.

Balkan Peninsula PENINSULA in southeastern EUROPE between the IONIAN and ADRIATIC SEAS on the west, the MEDITERRANEAN SEA on the south, and the AEGEAN and BLACK SEAS on the east. The nations of the Balkan Peninsula include ALBANIA, BOSNIA AND HERZEGOVINA, BULGARIA, CROATIA, GREECE, MACEDONIA, RUMANIA, SLOVENIA, and the former YUGOSLAVIA. The European portion of TURKEY is also on the Balkan Peninsula. (*See also* BALKANIZATION.)

Balkans Major mountain range of the BALKAN PENINSULA, extending from the eastern portion of the former YUGOSLAVIA through central BULGARIA to the BLACK SEA.

Baltic Sea Sea in EUROPE bordered by RUSSIA, ESTONIA, LATVIA, and LITHUANIA to the east, GERMANY and POLAND to the south, and SCANDINAVIA to the north and west; connected to several large gulfs and to the NORTH SEA by straits around DENMARK.

❧ Stronghold of the Russian navy.

Bangkok Capital of THAILAND and largest city in the country, located in the heart of Thailand's rice-growing region near the Gulf of Thailand.

❧ With its busy port and spectacular examples of Buddhist (*see* BUDDHISM) architecture, Bangkok is one of the leading cities of SOUTHEAST ASIA.

Bangladesh (bahng-gluh-DESH, bang-gluh-DESH) REPUBLIC in southern ASIA, bordered by INDIA to the north, west, and east; the BAY OF BENGAL to the south; and BURMA to the southeast. Its capital and largest city is Dacca.

❧ Created as East Pakistan in 1947, when India gained its independence from BRITAIN, and MOSLEM leaders demanded a Moslem state. Separated by cultural differences and 1000 miles of Indian territory from a neglectful central government in West Pakistan (now PAKISTAN), Bangladesh achieved its independence in 1971 after a bloody revolt and Indian intervention.

Barbados (bahr-BAY-dohs, bahr-BAY-dohz)   Island REPUBLIC in the easternmost WEST INDIES in the ATLANTIC OCEAN about 300 miles north of VENEZUELA.
🐾 Member of the British COMMONWEALTH.
🐾 Popular resort area.

Barcelona   City in northeastern SPAIN on the MEDITERRANEAN SEA. Second-largest city of Spain, after MADRID, its largest port, and its chief industrial and commercial center.
🐾 Capital of the region of Catalonia, and long a stronghold of movements for Catalan independence, Barcelona has also been a center for RADICAL political beliefs, including ANARCHISM and SOCIALISM.
🐾 Site of the 1992 Summer Olympics.

Bavaria   State in southwestern GERMANY bordered by the former CZECHOSLOVAKIA to the east, AUSTRIA to the southeast and south, and the German states of Baden-Wurttemberg and Hesse to the west and northwest. Its capital and largest city is MUNICH.
🐾 Adolf HITLER began his rise to power in Bavaria. 🐾 Famous for its beer and automobiles. BMW stands for Bavarian Motor Works.

Bay of Bengal (ben-GAWL, ben-GAHL)   Arm of the INDIAN OCEAN between INDIA and SRI LANKA on the west, BANGLADESH on the north, and SOUTHEAST ASIA on the east.

Bay of Biscay (BIS-kay)   Arm of the ATLANTIC OCEAN in western EUROPE, bordered by the west coast of FRANCE and the north coast of SPAIN.

Beijing (BAY-JING)   Capital of the PEOPLE'S REPUBLIC OF CHINA, located in the northwest region of the country. Second-largest city of China (after SHANGHAI); political, cultural, financial, educational, and transportation center of the country. Known for many years in the West as PEKING.
🐾 In 1949, the Chinese COMMUNISTS declared Beijing the capital of the People's Republic of China. 🐾 The Forbidden City, within the Inner or Tatar City, was the residence of the emperor of China. 🐾 Site of

TIANANMEN SQUARE, where communist leaders suppressed a democratic protest in June 1989.

Beirut (bay-ROOHT)   Capital of LEBANON, located in western Lebanon on the MEDITERRANEAN SEA.
🐾 Site of much of the continuing fighting between the PALESTINE LIBERATION ORGANIZATION, the Israelis, Syrians, and Lebanese groups.

Belarus (bee-luh-ROOHS)   REPUBLIC in eastern EUROPE, bordered to the northwest by RUSSIA, LITHUANIA, and LATVIA, to the northeast, east, and southeast by RUSSIA, to the south by UKRAINE, and to the west by POLAND. Its capital and largest city is Minsk.
🐾 This former member of the SOVIET UNION declared its independence in 1991. 🐾 Belarus is also known as White Russia or Belorussia.

Belfast   Capital, largest city, and major port of NORTHERN IRELAND.
🐾 Since the fourteenth century, the city has been the site of violent conflict between British and native Irish residents.

Belgium   MONARCHY in northwestern EUROPE, bordered by the NORTH SEA and The NETHERLANDS to the north, GERMANY and LUXEMBOURG to the east, and FRANCE to the south. Its capital and largest city is BRUSSELS.
🐾 Headquarters for the EEC and for NATO.

Belgrade (BEL-grayd, BEL-grahd, BEL-grad)   Capital of the former YUGOSLAVIA and of the Yugoslavian REPUBLIC of Serbia, located on the DANUBE RIVER. A commercial, industrial, political, and cultural center.

Bering Sea (BEER-ing, BAIR-ing)   Northward extension of the PACIFIC OCEAN between SIBERIA and ALASKA. The Bering Strait connects it with the ARCTIC OCEAN.

Berlin   Capital of reunited GERMANY located in northeastern part of the country.
🐾 Formerly the capital of PRUSSIA and then of Germany, Berlin was occupied by American, British, French, and Soviet troops after WORLD WAR II. Disagreements among the Allies led to the partition of the city, with the Soviet zone becoming East Berlin, and the other zones West Berlin. East Berlin became the capital of the COMMUNIST GERMAN DEMO-

BERLIN WALL. *Still intact (left) and demolished (right) sections of the Berlin Wall in 1990.*

CRATIC REPUBLIC (EAST GERMANY), but West Berlin lost its capital status to BONN in the FEDERAL REPUBLIC OF GERMANY (WEST GERMANY). ❧ The BERLIN AIRLIFT of 1948–1949 supplied West Berlin by air transport after the SOVIET UNION set up a land and water blockade in an attempt to gain political control of this noncommunist "island" in the midst of communist East Germany. ❧ The two Berlins were physically separated by the BERLIN WALL, a barrier designed to prevent East Germans from crossing into West Berlin, from 1961 to 1989. ❧ With the reunification of the two Germanys in 1990, the reunified city of Berlin was restored to its place as Germany's capital.

Berlin Wall Fortified concrete and wire barrier that separated East and West BERLIN from 1961 to 1989. It was built by the government of what was then EAST GERMANY to keep Berliners from defecting to the West. (*See also under "World History since 1550."*)

❧ The Berlin Wall was a SYMBOL of the inability of a COMMUNIST state to keep its citizens from leaving when they have a choice.

Bermuda Colony of BRITAIN, made up of some 300 coral islets and islands in the ATLANTIC OCEAN southeast of CAPE HATTERAS.

❧ Popular resort. ❧ A group of colonists on their way to VIRGINIA in 1609 were shipwrecked in Bermuda; William SHAKESPEARE used this incident as the basis for his play *THE TEMPEST*.

Birmingham City in central ENGLAND. England's second-largest city, after LONDON, and an important industrial and transportation center.

Black Sea Sea between EUROPE and ASIA, bordered on the north by MOLDOVA and UKRAINE, on the northeast by RUSSIA, on the east by GEORGIA, on the south by TURKEY, and on the west by BULGARIA and RUMANIA. Receives many great rivers, including the DANUBE, the Dnieper, and by way of the Sea of AZOZ, the DON.

❧ Popular resort area for Russians and eastern Europeans.

Bogotá (boh-guh-TAH, BOH-guh-tah) Capital of COLOMBIA and largest city in the country, located near the center of Colombia on a high, fertile plain.

Bolivia REPUBLIC in western SOUTH AMERICA, bordered by CHILE and PERU to the west, BRAZIL to the north and east, PARAGUAY to the southeast, and ARGENTINA to the south. Sucre is its constitutional capital and its largest city; La Paz is its administrative capital.

❧ Simón BOLÍVAR founded Bolivia in 1825 after winning independence from Spanish rule. ❧ The Bolivian government has tried, with little success, to fight the widespread drug production and trafficking in the country.

Bombay City in western INDIA just off the coast of the Arabian Sea.

❧ India's second-largest city, after CALCUTTA, and the only natural deep-water harbor in western India.

Bonn (BON) Former capital of the FEDERAL REPUBLIC OF GERMANY, and still home to most of the German government's bureaucracy, located in the western part of Germany, on the RHINE RIVER.

❧ The CONSTITUTION for WEST GERMANY was drafted in Bonn after WORLD WAR II. Bonn became West Germany's capital in 1949 and reunified Germany's capital in 1990, but has since lost that distinction to BERLIN.

Bordeaux (bawr-DOH)   Port city in southwestern FRANCE.

🔊 The region around Bordeaux is known for its wine.

Borneo   Island in INDONESIA southwest of the PHILIPPINES and north of JAVA.

🔊 Third-largest island in the world. 🔊 Mostly covered by dense jungle and rain forest.

Bosnia and Herzegovina (BOZ-nee-uh; hert-suh-goh-VEE-nuh, hert-suh-GOH-vee-nuh)   REPUBLIC in southeastern EUROPE on the west BALKAN PENINSULA, bordered by CROATIA to the northwest and north, YUGOSLAVIA to the east, MACEDONIA to the east and southeast, and the ADRIATIC SEA to the west. Sarajevo is the country's capital and largest city.

🔊 Sarajevo was the site of the assassination in 1914 of ARCHDUKE FRANCIS FERDINAND, which sparked WORLD WAR I. 🔊 In the early 1990s, brutal attacks by Serbian militia devastated the region, arousing international condemnation.

Bosporus (BOS-puh-ruhs)   Strait separating the European and Asian portions of TURKEY. The Bosporus is a link between the BLACK SEA and the MEDITERRANEAN SEA.

🔊 Important shipping route for RUSSIA, whose northern routes are blocked by ice in winter, and for other nations that border the BLACK SEA or use any of the many major rivers that flow into it.

Botswana (bot-SWAH-nuh)   REPUBLIC in south-central AFRICA, bordered on the south by SOUTH AFRICA, the west by NAMIBIA, the north by ANGOLA and ZAMBIA, and the northeast by ZIMBABWE. Formerly called Bechuanaland. The capital and largest city is Gaborone.

🔊 Botswana became independent from British control in the 1960s.

Brasilia (bruh-ZIL-yuh)   Capital of BRAZIL, located in the highlands of central Brazil.

🔊 One of the newest cities in the world, Brasilia was inaugurated in 1960 in order to replace RIO DE JANEIRO as Brazil's capital. The Brazilian government moved the capital in an effort to promote development in central Brazil. In less than thirty years, its population has grown to over a million inhabitants.

Brazil   REPUBLIC in eastern SOUTH AMERICA. It borders on every South American country except

CHILE and ECUADOR. Its capital is BRASILIA, and its largest city is São Paulo.

🔊 Largest of the LATIN AMERICAN countries, occupying almost half of South America. 🔊 World's leading coffee exporter. 🔊 Only country in South America whose history was dominated by PORTUGAL; largest Portuguese-speaking country in the world.

Brisbane (BRIZ-bayn, BRIZ-buhn)   Capital of Queensland state and largest city in the state; located in eastern AUSTRALIA on the PACIFIC OCEAN. Third-largest city in Australia, after SYDNEY and MELBOURNE.

🔊 Settled by the British in the early eighteenth century as a penal colony.

Britain   Officially the UNITED KINGDOM OF GREAT BRITAIN AND NORTHERN IRELAND, located on the BRITISH ISLES off the western coast of the mainland (CONTINENT) of EUROPE. It comprises ENGLAND, WALES, and SCOTLAND on the island of GREAT BRITAIN, and NORTHERN IRELAND on the island of IRELAND. Its capital and largest city is LONDON.

🔊 Ally of the United States; member of NATO. 🔊 Declared war on GERMANY in 1939. Allied with the United States and the SOVIET UNION, the British, under the leadership of Winston CHURCHILL, played an important role in defeating Germany. 🔊 Most of the settlers of the American colonies were British. The colonies remained under the British crown until the AMERICAN REVOLUTION. 🔊 One of the world's leading industrialized nations. 🔊 A CONSTITUTIONAL MONARCHY, with the hereditary king or queen performing mostly ceremonial functions. PARLIAMENT governs the country. 🔊 At the height of its imperial power in the late nineteenth century, Britain boasted colonies and possessions around the globe. (*See* BRITISH EMPIRE.)

British Columbia   Province in western CANADA, bordered by ALBERTA to the east; MONTANA, IDAHO, and WASHINGTON to the south; the PACIFIC OCEAN to the west; and the YUKON TERRITORY and the NORTHWEST TERRITORIES of Canada to the north.

British Isles   The islands of GREAT BRITAIN and IRELAND, and a number of smaller islands off their coasts.

Brussels   Capital of BELGIUM and largest city in the country, located in central Belgium. Commercial, industrial, financial, administrative, and cultural center.

🙠 Seat of several international organizations, including NATO and the European Economic Community.

Bucharest (BOOH-kuh-rest)   Capital of RUMANIA and largest city in the country, located in south-central Rumania on a tributary of the DANUBE RIVER. Rumania's chief industrial and communications center.

Budapest (BOOH-duh-pest, BOOH-duh-pesht)   Capital of HUNGARY and largest city in the country, located in north-central Hungary on both banks of the DANUBE RIVER. Industrial, cultural, and transportation center of Hungary.

Buenos Aires (BWAY-nuhs AIR-eez, EYE-riz)   Capital of ARGENTINA and largest city in the country, located in eastern Argentina near URUGUAY.

🙠 One of the largest cities in LATIN AMERICA, and Argentina's chief port and financial, industrial, commercial, and social center. 🙠 *La Prensa* and *La Nación* are two of its daily newspapers, popular throughout the Spanish-speaking world.

Bulgaria   Republic in southeastern EUROPE in the eastern part of the BALKAN PENINSULA, bordered by RUMANIA to the north, the BLACK SEA to the east, TURKEY to the southeast, GREECE to the south, and MACEDONIA and YUGOSLAVIA to the west. Its capital and largest city is Sofia.

🙠 Former EASTERN BLOC country. Soviet troops entered Bulgaria in 1944, and a COMMUNIST government was established soon thereafter. Bulgaria's communist rulers followed the Soviet lead for almost fifty years, until the collapse of the SOVIET UNION. In January 1991, a multiparty government began to institute democratic and economic reforms.

Burma   REPUBLIC in SOUTHEAST ASIA, now officially known as Myanmar, bordered by BANGLADESH, INDIA, and the BAY OF BENGAL to the west; CHINA to the north and northeast; LAOS and THAILAND to the east; and the Andaman Sea to the south. Rangoon is its capital and largest city.

🙠 Under British control until 1948, when it became an independent republic. 🙠 During WORLD WAR II, the ALLIES and Japanese troops fought intense campaigns over control of the Burma Road, a vital supply link between China and India. 🙠 Run by

its military in the 1970s and 1980s, during which its economy declined. Free elections in 1990 were won by the main opposition party but the military government refused to relinquish its powers.

Cairo (KEYE-roh)   The capital of EGYPT and largest city in the country; a major port just south of the NILE Delta in the northeast corner of AFRICA.

🙠 Cairo, the historical center of Egyptian power, was the home of the PHARAOHS. The PYRAMIDS and the SPHINX are located nearby in suburban Giza, also known as Al Jizah.

Calcutta   Largest city in INDIA, located in the eastern part of the country on the Hooghly River.

🙠 One of the largest cities in the world. 🙠 Suffers from poverty, overcrowding, and unemployment.

Calgary (KAL-guh-ree)   City in southern ALBERTA, CANADA.

🙠 Home of the Calgary Stampede, an annual rodeo. Host city of the 1988 Winter Olympics.

Cambodia   Nation in SOUTHEAST ASIA, officially known as KAMPUCHEA; bordered by LAOS to the north, VIETNAM to the east, the Gulf of Siam to the south, and THAILAND to the west and north. Phnom Penh is its capital and largest city.

🙠 Part of French-ruled INDOCHINA until 1946, when it became self-governing. It was granted full independence in 1953. 🙠 Occupied by the Japanese during WORLD WAR II. 🙠 Major battleground of the VIETNAM WAR. 🙠 In 1975 Cambodian COMMUNISTS, called the KHMER ROUGE, occupied Phnom Penh and then forcibly expelled most of its population to work in the countryside. More than one million Cambodians died at the hands of the Khmer Rouge, either by outright execution or due to forced labor and deprivation. 🙠 In 1979 Vietnam invaded Cambodia and installed a puppet government.

Cameroon (kam-uh-ROOHN)   REPUBLIC in west-central AFRICA, bordered by NIGERIA to the northwest; CHAD to the northeast; the Central African Republic to the east; CONGO, Gabon, and Equatorial Guinea to the south; and the Gulf of Guinea (part of the ATLANTIC OCEAN) to the west. Yaounde is its capital, and Douala is its largest city.

🙠 Cameroon was under British and French control from WORLD WAR I until 1960.

Canada   Nation in northern NORTH AMERICA, bordered by the ATLANTIC OCEAN to the east, the ARC-

TIC OCEAN to the north, the PACIFIC OCEAN and ALASKA to the west, and the United States to the south. Its capital is OTTAWA, and its largest city is TORONTO.

🥄 The French were the first Europeans to settle in mainland Canada, in 1604. 🥄 Ally of the United States, though conflict has arisen over environmental and trade issues. Each country is the other's leading partner in world trade. 🥄 The border between Canada and the United States is the longest unguarded border in the world.

Canberra (KAN-buhr-uh, KAN-ber-uh)   Capital of AUSTRALIA, located in southeastern Australia.

Cannes (KAN)   Fashionable resort on the French RIVIERA.

🥄 Host to an annual international film festival.

Canton   *See* GUANGZHOU.

Cape of Good Hope   Point of land in southern SOUTH AFRICA, south of CAPE TOWN.

Cape Town   Also Capetown. Legislative capital of SOUTH AFRICA. (*See also* PRETORIA.)

Capri (kuh-PREE, KAH-pree, KAP-ree)   Island in the Bay of NAPLES in southern ITALY.

🥄 International tourist attraction, known for its beautiful scenery.

Caracas (kuh-RAH-kuhs)   Capital of VENEZUELA and largest city in the country, located in northern Venezuela near the CARIBBEAN SEA. Commercial, industrial, and cultural center of the nation.

Caribbean Sea   Arm of the ATLANTIC OCEAN, bordered by the WEST INDIES to the north and east, SOUTH AMERICA to the south, and CENTRAL AMERICA to the west.

🥄 Its clear blue waters make many of its islands popular vacation spots. 🥄 Since announcing the MONROE DOCTRINE in 1823, the United States has considered the Caribbean within its "sphere of influence" — that is, a region where United States interests are directly affected. The policy has been to exclude foreign powers, though after 1959 CUBA came under strong influence of the SOVIET UNION.

Casablanca   Largest city in MOROCCO. It is a port on the ATLANTIC.

🥄 The city was the setting of *CASABLANCA*, a 1943

film starring Humphrey BOGART and Ingrid Bergman.

Caspian Sea   Saltwater lake between EUROPE and ASIA, bordered by ARMENIA, AZERBAIJAN, and RUSSIA to the west, KAZAKHSTAN to the north and east, TURKMENISTAN to the east, and IRAN to the south and west. Largest inland body of water in the world.

🥄 The VOLGA RIVER empties into the Caspian Sea.

Caucasus (KAW-kuh-suhs)   Mountain range extending from the BLACK SEA southeast to the CASPIAN SEA, through extreme southern RUSSIA, GEORGIA, ARMENIA, and AZERBAIJAN.

🥄 Forms part of the traditional border between EUROPE and ASIA. 🥄 Oil is its major resource. In WORLD WAR II, the Germans tried to seize or neutralize this resource but were driven out by the Soviets.

Central America   Region in the southernmost portion of NORTH AMERICA, linked to SOUTH AMERICA by the ISTHMUS of PANAMA; includes Belize, COSTA RICA, EL SALVADOR, GUATEMALA, HONDURAS, NICARAGUA, and Panama.

🥄 Countries in Central America (except for Belize and Costa Rica) are characterized by unstable governments and very low PER CAPITA INCOME. 🥄 The United States government has often taken the position that Central American affairs directly affect American interests. Accordingly, it has often provided financial and military aid to Central American governments and occasionally intervened militarily.

Ceylon   Former name for the nation now called SRI LANKA.

Chad   Landlocked desert REPUBLIC in north-central AFRICA, bordered by SUDAN to the east; the Central African Republic to the south; CAMEROON, NIGER, and NIGERIA to the west; and LIBYA to the north. N'Djamena is its capital and largest city.

🥄 Chad was under French control until 1960.

Champs Élysées (SHAHNN zay-lee-ZAY)   A major avenue in PARIS famous for the elegance of its cafés and shops. In French it means ELYSIAN FIELDS.

Chile   REPUBLIC in southern SOUTH AMERICA on the western slope of the ANDES. Long narrow strip of land bordered by PERU to the north, BOLIVIA and ARGENTINA to the east, and the PACIFIC OCEAN to the south and west. Its capital and largest city is SAN-TIAGO.

🐚 In 1973, General Augusto Pinochet led a COUP that overthrew and killed President Salvador Allende, a MARXIST. 🐚 Pinochet suppressed HUMAN RIGHTS and political activity until he lost a PLEBISCITE in 1988. A successor was chosen in free elections.

China Nation in eastern ASIA, bordered by RUSSIA and NORTH KOREA to the east; Russia and the Mongolian People's Republic (MONGOLIA) to the north; Russia and AFGHANISTAN to the west; and PAKISTAN, INDIA, NEPAL, Sikkim, Bhutan, BURMA, LAOS, and VIETNAM to the south. Its capital is BEIJING, and its largest city is SHANGHAI.

🐚 Most populous country in the world, and the third largest, after RUSSIA and CANADA. 🐚 The Boxer Rebellion of 1900 grew out of strong resentment of foreign influence in China. 🐚 Revolution in 1911 overthrew the Qing dynasty, ending the 2000-year-old imperial system. 🐚 CHIANG KAI-SHEK, the leader of the Chinese Nationalists, established the government of NATIONALIST CHINA in 1928 in NANJING. 🐚 The Second Sino-Japanese War, which lasted from 1937 to 1945 (merging with WORLD WAR II in 1941), grew out of Japanese encroachments on Chinese land. 🐚 The Chinese COMMUNISTS, with MAO ZEDONG as their leader, defeated Chiang's Nationalists in 1949, proclaiming the PEOPLE'S REPUBLIC OF CHINA. The Nationalists withdrew to the island of TAIWAN. 🐚 In 1950, Chinese forces joined the North Korean army in the KOREAN WAR. 🐚 In 1958, Mao undertook the "Great Leap Forward" campaign, a crash program of industrialization, but none of its goals were reached, and the effort collapsed. 🐚 In 1960, the ideological split between the Soviet Union and China widened, and the Soviets withdrew all aid. 🐚 In the mid-1960s, Mao's wife, acting on his behalf, and three colleagues, later known as the GANG OF FOUR, created a youth movement called the RED GUARDS and started the Great Proletarian CULTURAL REVOLUTION, aimed at eliminating old ideas and customs. Mobs attacked schools and cultural centers, brutally disrupting the entire nation. With the death of Mao in 1976 and the trial of the Gang of Four in 1980, the Cultural Revolution came to an end. 🐚 In 1972, President Richard NIXON visited China, reopening relations between mainland China and the United States. 🐚 In 1989, the government brutally suppressed pro-democracy demonstrations in TIANANMEN SQUARE.

Chungking (CHOONG-KING) City in south-central CHINA on the YANGTZE RIVER. Commercial center for western China, commanding a large river trade.

Cologne City in western GERMANY on the RHINE RIVER. A commercial center.

Colombia REPUBLIC in northwestern SOUTH AMERICA, bordered by PANAMA to the northwest, VENEZUELA to the northeast and east, BRAZIL to the southeast, and PERU and ECUADOR to the south. Its capital and largest city is BOGATÁ.

🐚 Its major legal crop is coffee. 🐚 Despite official government opposition, many Colombians are involved in the growth and trafficking of marijuana and COCAINE.

Commonwealth of Independent States A loose federation made up of some former Soviet republics, which succeeded the SOVIET UNION in 1991. Members at the time of its founding were ARMENIA, AZERBAIJAN, BELARUS, KAZAKHSTAN, KYRGYZSTAN, MOLDOVA, RUSSIA, TAJIKISTAN, TURKMENISTAN, UKRAINE, and UZBEKISTAN.

Congo, People's Republic of the REPUBLIC in west-central AFRICA, bordered by CAMEROON and the Central African Republic to the north, ZAIRE to the east and south, and the ATLANTIC OCEAN and Gabon to the west. Brazzaville is its capital and largest city.

🐚 It achieved independence from FRANCE in 1960.

Congo River River of central AFRICA, flowing through ZAIRE to the ATLANTIC OCEAN.

🐚 One of the world's longest rivers, it is Africa's largest potential source of electric POWER. 🐚 Explored separately but simultaneously by the missionary David Livingstone and the journalist Henry Stanley; it was the site of their proverbial encounter. (*See* "DR. LIVINGSTONE, I PRESUME?")

Copenhagen Capital of DENMARK and largest city in the country, located in eastern Denmark. Denmark's chief commercial, industrial, and cultural center.

🐚 Called the "PARIS of the north" because of its similar charm.

Corsica   Island in the MEDITERRANEAN SEA; part of FRANCE, lying southeast of the French mainland, north of SARDINIA, and west of ITALY.

ᶼ Birthplace of NAPOLEON BONAPARTE.

Costa Rica   REPUBLIC in CENTRAL AMERICA, bordered by NICARAGUA to the north, the CARIBBEAN SEA to the east, PANAMA to the southeast, and the PACIFIC OCEAN to the south and west. Its capital and largest city is SAN JOSÉ.

ᶼ One of the most politically stable countries of LATIN AMERICA; traditionally very democratic.
ᶼ Costa Rica has a literacy rate of over 90 percent.

Crete   Island in southeastern GREECE in the MEDITERRANEAN SEA.

ᶼ Largest of the Greek islands. ᶼ Site of one of the world's earliest civilizations, the Minoan civilization, which reached its peak in 1600 B.C. ᶼ In Greek MYTHOLOGY, Crete was Minos' kingdom, where the MINOTAUR lived at the center of the LABYRINTH.

Crimea   (kreye-MEE-uh, kruh-MEE-uh)   PENINSULA in the extreme southern UKRAINE, bordered by the BLACK SEA to the east, south, and west.

ᶼ As a former part of the Russian empire, one of the strongholds of opposition to the Soviet government after the RUSSIAN REVOLUTION. ᶼ Occupied by German troops from 1941 to 1945. ᶼ The CRIMEAN WAR of the 1850s, fought between Russian forces and the allied armies of GREAT BRITAIN, FRANCE, TURKEY, and SARDINIA, was the scene of the battle described in "THE CHARGE OF THE LIGHT BRIGADE."

Croatia   (kroh-AY-shuh)   REPUBLIC in southeastern EUROPE in the upper western corner of the BALKAN PENINSULA, bordered to the northwest by SLOVENIA, to the north by HUNGARY, to the east by YUGOSLAVIA, to the south and southeast by BOSNIA AND HERZEGOVINA, and to the west by the ADRIATIC SEA. Its capital and largest city is Zagreb.

ᶼ When Croatia declared its independence from Yugoslavia in 1991, fighting broke out between Croats and Croatia's large Serbian minority, who were aided by the Serb-dominated Yugoslavian government. Hostility between Croats and Serbs has a long history; during WORLD WAR II they fought on opposite sides of a civil war in Yugoslavia.

Cuba   REPUBLIC consisting of the island of Cuba and other nearby islands. It lies in the CARIBBEAN SEA at the entrance of the GULF OF MEXICO. Its capital and largest city is HAVANA.

ᶼ The sinking of the United States battleship *Maine* in Havana harbor led to the SPANISH-AMERICAN WAR in 1898. ᶼ Fidel CASTRO took control of the Cuban government in 1959. The United States broke off relations with Cuba in 1961, after Castro exhibited strong LEFT-WING leanings, established a system of military justice, and confiscated American INVESTMENTS in banks, industries, and land. Cuba then formed a close attachment to the SOVIET UNION. ᶼ In 1961, under the administration of John F. KENNEDY, American-trained Cuban exiles attempted to invade Cuba, landing at the BAY OF PIGS, only to be easily defeated by Castro's forces. The Kennedy administration was sharply criticized for the Bay of Pigs fiasco. ᶼ The CUBAN MISSILE CRISIS of 1962 occurred as a result of a Soviet buildup of medium-range missiles (capable of striking targets in the United States) in Cuba. ᶼ In 1980, Cuban refugees began pouring into the United States when Castro allowed free emigration. ᶼ The COLLAPSE OF COMMUNISM in eastern Europe and the former SOVIET UNION has left Cuba as one of the last COMMUNIST states.

Cyprus   Island REPUBLIC in the eastern MEDITERRANEAN SEA, south of TURKEY and west of SYRIA. Nicosia is its capital and largest city.

ᶼ Divided between people of Greek origin, who make up four-fifths of the population, and those of Turkish origin, who compose the other fifth.

Czechoslovakia   (chek-uh-sluh-VAH-kee-uh)   Former REPUBLIC in central EUROPE, bordered by POLAND to the north, GERMANY to the north and west, UKRAINE to the east, and AUSTRIA and HUNGARY to the south. Its capital and largest city was PRAGUE.

ᶼ COMMUNISTS seized complete control of the government in 1948. During the 1960s, a movement toward liberalization effected many democratizing reforms. An alarmed SOVIET UNION put an abrupt end to the movement by invading Prague in 1968, along with its WARSAW PACT allies. ᶼ Czechoslovakia was created by the union of the Czech lands and Slovakia, which took place in 1918, as the Austro-Hungarian Empire fell apart. ᶼ The MUNICH PACT partitioned Czechoslovakia in 1938, giving one of its regions, the Sudetenland, to Germany in an attempt to avoid war. ❧ The country surrendered to German control in 1939, and was liberated by American and Soviet forces at the end of WORLD WAR II. ❧ The COMMUNIST government, confronted by mass pro-democracy demonstrations, resigned in 1989. In 1991 the last SOVIET troops left the country. The end of communist rule resulted in the eventual split of the republic into two independent states, the Czech Republic and Slovakia.

Damascus Capital of SYRIA and largest city in the country, located in southwestern Syria. Syria's administrative, financial, and communications center.

❧ Inhabited since prehistoric times; widely regarded as the world's oldest city.

Danube River River in central and southeastern EUROPE.

❧ Flowing for nearly 2000 miles, it is the second-longest European river, after the VOLGA. ❧ Composer Johann STRAUSS, THE YOUNGER, expressed the charm and romance of the river in his "Blue Danube Waltz."

Dead Sea Salt lake on the border between ISRAEL and JORDAN.

❧ Its surface, at approximately 1300 feet below sea level, is the lowest point on EARTH.

Delhi (DEL-ee) City in north-central INDIA. NEW DELHI, the nation's capital, is a division of the city.

Denmark CONSTITUTIONAL MONARCHY in northern EUROPE, bordered by the NORTH SEA to the west, the Skagerrak and the Kattegat Straits to the north, the BALTIC SEA to the east, and GERMANY to the south.

❧ Became a member of NATO in 1949, breaking its tradition of neutrality.

Djakarta (juh-KAHR-tuh) *Also* JAKARTA. Capital of INDONESIA and largest city in the country, located on the island of JAVA.

❧ Founded by the Dutch in the seventeenth century, Djakarta resembles towns in The NETHERLANDS.

Dominican Republic REPUBLIC in the WEST INDIES, occupying the eastern two-thirds of the island of Hispaniola (HAITI occupies the other third).

Don River River in southwestern RUSSIA.

Dresden (DREZ-duhn) City in eastern GERMANY on the ELBE RIVER.

❧ Was a leading center of German music, art, and architecture for three centuries, until it was severely damaged by Allied bombing in WORLD WAR II.

Dublin Capital and major port of the REPUBLIC OF IRELAND and the largest city in the country; located on the Irish Sea, an arm of the ATLANTIC OCEAN.

❧ As the intellectual and cultural center of Ireland, Dublin was a stronghold of Irish NATIONALISM, the birthplace of renewed interest in the Irish language and Irish literature, and home to such writers as James JOYCE, Jonathan SWIFT, and William Butler YEATS.

Dubrovnik (DOOH-brawv-nik, doo-BRAWV-nik) City in southern BOSNIA AND HERZEGOVINA on the ADRIATIC SEA.

❧ Retaining much of its MEDIEVAL architecture and character, the city was a popular tourist center before it was badly damaged in 1991 during the civil war between the Croats and the Serbs.

Ecuador (EK-wuh-dawr) REPUBLIC in western SOUTH AMERICA, bordered by COLOMBIA to the north, PERU to the east and south, and the PACIFIC OCEAN to the west. Its landscape is dominated by the ANDES. Quito is its capital, and Guayaquil is its largest city.

Edinburgh (ED-n-buh-ruh) Capital of SCOTLAND, located in the Lothian region in the southeastern part. Scotland's banking and administrative center.

❧ The University of Edinburgh, which was founded in the sixteenth century, is noted for its faculties of divinity, law, medicine, music, and the arts. ❧ Cultural center, especially in the eighteenth and nineteenth centuries, when the PHILOSOPHERS David HUME and Adam SMITH, the authors Robert BURNS and Sir Walter SCOTT, and the scientist James HUTTON were active.

Edmonton Capital of ALBERTA province, CANADA, and largest city in the province.

Egypt Officially the Arab REPUBLIC of Egypt, a country in northeastern AFRICA bordered by the MEDITERRANEAN SEA to the north, ISRAEL and RED SEA to the east, SUDAN to the south, and LIBYA to the west. The principal geographic feature of the country is the NILE RIVER. Its capital and largest city is CAIRO. (*See also* ALEXANDRIA.)

&c. Egypt is the site of one of man's earliest civilizations, which flourished from about 3100 B.C. to 30 B.C., when it became part of the ROMAN EMPIRE. Many ancient works of art and architecture survive, including the PYRAMIDS and the SPHINX. &c. Egypt was the first Arab nation to make peace with Israel (*see* ARAB-ISRAELI CONFLICT), a feat accomplished after Egyptian President Anwar SADAT traveled to Israel in 1977 to meet PRIME MINISTER Menachem Begin. Sadat was later assassinated by MOSLEM extremists.

El Salvador   REPUBLIC on the PACIFIC coast of CENTRAL AMERICA, bordered to the west by GUATEMALA, to the north and east by HONDURAS, and to the south by the PACIFIC OCEAN. SAN SALVADOR is its capital and largest city.

&c. Torn by civil unrest, characterized by GUERRILLA WARFARE and terrorism (which has included the murder of American civilians), El Salvador became in the 1980s a controversial focus of an American foreign policy that seeks to protect American interests in Central America.

Elbe River (EL-buh, ELB)   River in central EUROPE, flowing several hundred miles from the northwestern section of the former CZECHOSLOVAKIA before emptying into the NORTH SEA.

&c. The Elbe created part of the former border between EAST GERMANY and WEST GERMANY.

England   One of the countries of the UNITED KINGDOM of GREAT BRITAIN AND NORTHERN IRELAND. LONDON, BIRMINGHAM, LIVERPOOL, and MANCHESTER are in England.

&c. The king or queen of England is the king or queen of the United Kingdom. &c. The name England is often used to refer to all of Great Britain.

English Channel   Arm of the ATLANTIC OCEAN between FRANCE and BRITAIN.

&c. A train-ferry service and a seaplane, as well as the Hovercraft, cross the English Channel, carrying people between PARIS and LONDON. &c. Its cold, choppy waters have been a popular challenge for long-distance swimmers. &c. A formation of high bluffs on the British side of the English Channel is known as the White Cliffs of Dover. &c. A tunnel connecting England and France is under construction.

equator   An imaginary circle around the EARTH, equidistant from the NORTH POLE and SOUTH POLE.

Estonia (e-STOH-nee-uh)   Republic on the BALTIC SEA, bordered by LATVIA to the south, RUSSIA to the east, and, separated by the Gulf of Finland, FINLAND to the north. Estonia also includes several hundred small islands in the Baltic. Its capital and largest city is Tallinn.

&c. Although more closely related by race, language, CULTURE, and history to SCANDINAVIA and GERMANY than to Russia, after 1721 Estonia was subject to Russian rule. The country briefly achieved independence in the years between WORLD WAR I and WORLD WAR II. It resisted integration with the SOVIET UNION, but was forcibly annexed in 1940. In 1991, Estonia was one of the first of the Soviet republics to declare its independence as the COMMUNIST system and the Soviet Union collapsed.

estuary (ES-chooh-er-ee)   The section of a river where it empties into the sea. (*See also under* "Earth Sciences.")

Ethiopia   Country in northeastern AFRICA bordered by the RED SEA to the northeast, Djibouti and SOMALIA to the east, KENYA to the south, and SUDAN to the west. Formerly called Abyssinia. Its capital and largest city is ADDIS ABABA.

&c. Ethiopia is Black Africa's oldest state, tracing its history back more than 2000 years. &c. Of all African nations, it most successfully withstood European attempts at colonization, remaining independent throughout its history, with the exception of a six-year period (1935–1941) during which it was occupied by ITALY, which was then governed by fascists (*see* FASCISM). &c. Ethiopia is one of the world's oldest CHRISTIAN nations, having been converted in the fourth century. &c. Ethiopia was ruled from 1930 to 1936 and again from 1941 to 1974 by the powerful and CHARISMATIC Emperor Haile Selassie I (born Ras Tafari Makonnen). Called the "Lion of Judah," he claimed direct descent from the biblical King SOLOMON and Queen of SHEBA. &c. Selassie was overthrown by a military JUNTA, which proclaimed a COMMUNIST government and allied itself with the former SOVIET UNION. &c. The Junta was overthrown in 1991. &c. It was plagued by famine in the 1980s.

Euphrates River (yooh-FRAY-teez)   River in southwestern ASIA that flows through eastern TURKEY,

SYRIA, and IRAQ before uniting with the TIGRES RIVER and emptying into the PERSIAN GULF.

🐟 Important in the development of many great civilizations in ancient MESOPOTAMIA.

Eurasia (yoo-RAY-zhuh) Land mass consisting of the CONTINENTS of EUROPE and ASIA.

Europe CONTINENT that is actually a vast PENINSULA of EURASIA.

Everest *See* MOUNT EVEREST.

Falkland Islands (FAWK-luhnd, FAWLK-luhnd) Group of islands in the south ATLANTIC, located east of the Strait of MAGELLAN off the coast of ARGENTINA.

🐟 The islands, under British rule, were seized by Argentina in 1982, but were retaken by BRITAIN.

Far East Popular expression for the east ASIAN nations of CHINA, JAPAN, NORTH KOREA and SOUTH KOREA, MONGOLIA, and TAIWAN.

fathom A unit of measurement (equal to six feet) for water depth.

🐟 To "fathom" a problem is to get to the bottom of it — to understand it.

Federal Republic of Germany Official name for GERMANY; until 1990, official name for WEST GERMANY.

Fiji (FEE-jee) A nation composed of several hundred islands in the southwestern PACIFIC, located about 2000 miles northeast of SYDNEY, AUSTRALIA. Viti Levu, the largest island, constitutes half the land area of the group. Suva is its capital and largest city.

🐟 Their mountainous scenery, unspoiled beaches, and tropical splendor make the Fiji Islands an exotic tourist destination.

Finland REPUBLIC in northern EUROPE, bordered by the Gulf of Bothnia (an arm of the BALTIC SEA) and SWEDEN to the west, NORWAY to the north, RUSSIA to the east, and the Gulf of Finland (another arm of the Baltic) and the Baltic Sea to the south. Its capital and largest city is HELSINKI.

🐟 Despite centuries of cultural, political, and economic domination by the Russian empire and the former SOVIET UNION, Finland has managed to maintain an independent identity.

Florence City in central ITALY on the Arno River.

🐟 Center of the Italian RENAISSANCE from the fourteenth to the sixteenth centuries, during which time the artistic and intellectual life of the city flourished. DANTE, Boccaccio, BOTTICELLI, Donatello, LEONARDO DA VINCI, RAPHAEL, and MICHELANGELO were among the authors and artists who were born and were active there. 🐟 Dominated by the MEDICI family from the fifteenth to the eighteenth centuries. 🐟 The city's many works of architecture include the CATHEDRAL of Santa Maria del Fiore, the Pitti Palace, and the Uffizi. 🐟 Tourist center known for its handicrafts.

France Nation in EUROPE bordered by BELGIUM and LUXEMBOURG to the north; GERMANY, SWITZERLAND, and ITALY to the east, the MEDITERRANEAN SEA and SPAIN to the south, and the ATLANTIC OCEAN to the west. Its capital and largest city is PARIS.

🐟 Ally of the United States. 🐟 During the reign of LOUIS XIV (1653–1715), France was a principal world power and cultural center of Europe. 🐟 The FRENCH REVOLUTION, organized by leaders of the MIDDLE CLASS and lower class, brought about an end to the French ABSOLUTE MONARCHY and forged a transition from FEUDALISM to the industrial era. A bloody and chaotic period, the Revolution, which ultimately engulfed much of Europe in the Napoleonic Wars, helped lay the foundations of modern political PHILOSOPHY. 🐟 In the FRENCH AND INDIAN WAR in the 1750s, the British and colonial forces drove the French from CANADA and the region of the GREAT LAKES. 🐟 In WORLD WAR I, France was one of the ALLIES. Much of that war was fought on French soil. 🐟 In WORLD WAR II, France's military resistance to the German army collapsed in the spring of 1940. Germans occupied much of France from 1940 to 1944. In 1944, the Allies invaded France, along with French troops, and drove the Germans out of France, finally defeating them in 1945. 🐟 France is known for its wine, cheese, and cooking.

Frankfurt (FRANGK-fuhrt, FRAHNGK-foort) City in west central GERMANY on the Main River. An industrial, commercial, and financial center.

Galapagos Islands (guh-LAH-puh-gohs, guh-LAP-uh-gohs) Groups of islands in the PACIFIC OCEAN off SOUTH AMERICA, owned by ECUADOR.

❧ Known for their tortoises, penguins, marine iguanas, and other unusual animals. ❧ Charles DARWIN visited these islands and gathered evidence that supported his THEORY of NATURAL SELECTION.

Ganges River (GAN-jeez) River in INDIA rising in the HIMALAYAS and flowing generally east to the BAY OF BENGAL.

❧ Most sacred river of Hindu India (see HINDU-ISM).

Geneva City in southwestern SWITZERLAND, lying on the western end of Lake Geneva, where the RHONE RIVER leaves the lake.

❧ Because of Switzerland's strict neutrality, Geneva provides an impartial meeting ground for representatives of other nations. ❧ Housed the headquarters of the LEAGUE OF NATIONS in the Palace of Nations, which is now the European headquarters of the UNITED NATIONS. ❧ The International Labor Organization, the International RED CROSS, and the World Council of CHURCHES are also based in Geneva. ❧ Under the leadership of John CALVIN in the sixteenth century, Geneva was the center of PROTES-TANTISM. ❧ The Geneva Accords were a group of four agreements made in 1954, ending seven and a half years of war in INDOCHINA. ❧ The GENEVA CONVENTIONS, signed first in 1864 and then in 1906, 1929, 1949, and 1977, provide rules for the humane treatment of prisoners and wounded persons during a war.

Georgia REPUBLIC in extreme southeastern EUROPE on the BLACK SEA, bordered to the north and northeast by RUSSIA, to the east by AZERBAIJAN, and to the south by ARMENIA and TURKEY. Its capital and largest city is Tbilisi.

❧ This former member of the SOVIET UNION declared its independence in 1991.

Germany REPUBLIC in north-central EUROPE, divided into EAST GERMANY and WEST GERMANY in 1949 and reunited in 1990. Officially called the FEDERAL REPUBLIC OF GERMANY.

❧ Germany was a collection of competing states until it was unified during the second half of the nineteenth century under the leadership of Otto von BISMARCK. ❧ Germany's industrial, colonial, and naval expansion was considered a threat by the British and French, and was one of the main causes of WORLD WAR I, in which Germany was badly defeated. ❧ After the defeat of the NAZIS in WORLD WAR II, Germany was divided into four zones occupied by British, French, Soviet, and American forces. ❧ Since reunification Germany has become Europe's leading economic power. (See EAST GERMANY and WEST GERMANY under "World History since 1550.")

Ghana (GAH-nuh) Nation in western AFRICA bordered to the north by Burkina Faso, to the east by TOGO, to the south by the ATLANTIC OCEAN, and to the west by the IVORY COAST. Its capital and largest city is Accra.

❧ It was colonized as the Gold Coast by BRITAIN.

Gibraltar (juh-BRAWL-tuhr) A colony of BRITAIN on the southern coast of SPAIN.

❧ Located on the Rock of Gibraltar, a huge limestone mass. ❧ Spain has protested British control of Gibraltar, but the dispute has remained unsettled for years. ❧ Location of an important military base; strategically significant because it can be used to keep ships from entering or leaving the MEDITERRANEAN SEA. ❧ Its seeming impregnability as a fortress during several wars led to the saying: "solid as the Rock of Gibraltar."

Glasgow (GLAS-goh, GLAZ-goh) City in south-central SCOTLAND on the River Clyde, near Scotland's west coast. Scotland's largest city.

❧ One of the greatest shipbuilding centers of the world.

Golan Heights (GOH-lahn) Hilly area in northeastern ISRAEL.

❧ Formerly part of SYRIA, the Golan Heights were used as artillery sites to bombard vulnerable Israeli targets below. Israel captured the Golan Heights in the 1967 war, and annexed the area in 1981. Syria's anti-Israel feelings were further outraged by this loss of territory.

Granada (gruh-NAH-duh) City in southeastern SPAIN.

❧ A major tourist attraction in Granada is the Alhambra, a magnificent fortress and palace complex built by Spain's MOSLEM rulers in the MIDDLE AGES on a hill overlooking the city.

Great Britain See BRITAIN.

Greece REPUBLIC in southeastern EUROPE on the southern part of the BALKAN PENINSULA. Its capital and largest city is ATHENS.

🍀 Member of NATO. 🍀 Ancient Greek CULTURE, particularly the culture developed in Athens, was the principal source of Western civilization. 🍀 Tension and fighting between Greece and TURKEY has continued for hundreds of years. 🍀 Known for its production of grapes, olives, and olive oil.

Greenland   Island lying largely within the ARCTIC CIRCLE; owned by DENMARK. Its native name is Kaballit Nunaat.

🍀 Largest island in the world. (AUSTRALIA is larger but is officially a CONTINENT, not an island.)

Greenwich (GREN-ich, GRIN-ij)   Part of metropolitan LONDON, in southeastern ENGLAND.

🍀 The PRIME MERIDIAN, which is the MERIDIAN designated zero DEGREES LONGITUDE, runs through Greenwich; Greenwich Mean Time is the mean (usual) time in Greenwich. All other time is measured in relation to it.

Grenada (gruh-NAY-duh)   Nation in the WEST INDIES, about 100 miles off the coast of SOUTH AMERICA. Its capital and largest city is St. George's.

🍀 In 1983, President Ronald REAGAN of the United States ordered an invasion of the island, allegedly to protect some 1000 American citizens from Cuban military personnel on the island.

Guadalajara (gwahd-l-uh-HAH-ruh)   City in southwestern MEXICO.

🍀 Its mild, dry CLIMATE makes it a popular health resort. 🍀 Site of much surviving architecture from the Spanish colonial era.

Guadeloupe (gwahd-l-OOHP, GWAHD-l-oohp)   Island in the eastern portion of the WEST INDIES; an overseas territory of FRANCE.

🍀 Tourism is a major industry.

Guam (GWAHM)   A self-governing island territory of the United States, located in the western PACIFIC OCEAN. With important naval and air bases, Guam is an American military bastion in the Pacific.

Guangzhou (GWANG-JOH)   City in southern CHINA. Transportation, industrial, financial, and trade center of southern China; major deep-water port.

🍀 First Chinese port regularly used for trade, especially following the Opium War (1839–1842). 🍀 Seat of the revolutionary movement under Sun Yat-sen in 1911. 🍀 It was formerly called Canton.

Guatemala   REPUBLIC in CENTRAL AMERICA, bordered by MEXICO to the west and north, Belize and the CARIBBEAN SEA to the east, HONDURAS and EL SALVADOR to the southeast, and the PACIFIC OCEAN to the south. Its capital and largest city is Guatemala City.

🍀 Noted for its particularly low average INCOME and literacy rate. 🍀 Traditionally politically unstable.

Gulf of Mexico   Part of the ATLANTIC OCEAN bordered by the southeast coast of the United States and the east coast of MEXICO.

Gulf Stream   A warm CURRENT that flows out of the GULF OF MEXICO and northward through the ATLANTIC OCEAN.

Hague, The (HAYG)   Seat of the government of The NETHERLANDS, located in the western Netherlands, near the NORTH SEA.

🍀 Site of international conferences. 🍀 Seat of the INTERNATIONAL COURT OF JUSTICE and the Permanent Court of Arbitration, both housed in the Peace Palace, which was built to fulfill the dream that The Hague might become the neutral capital of the world.

Haiti   REPUBLIC in the WEST INDIES, on the western third of the island of Hispaniola, which it shares with the DOMINICAN REPUBLIC. Its capital and largest city is Port-au-Prince.

🍀 With its extremely low average INCOME and literacy rate, Haiti is the poorest nation in the Western HEMISPHERE. 🍀 In 1957, François ("Papa Doc") Duvalier established a DICTATORSHIP, continued after his death in 1971 by his son, Jean Claude ("Baby Doc"), who was finally overthrown in 1986. Since then the government has changed several times through military coups.

Hamburg (HAM-burg, HAHM-boorg)   City in northern GERMANY on the ELBE RIVER, near where it meets the NORTH SEA.

🍀 Germany's most important industrial center. 🍀 One of the most heavily bombed German cities during WORLD WAR II.

Hanoi (ha-NOY)   Capital of VIETNAM, located in the northern part of the country.

🍀 Scene of heavy fighting between French and Vietnamese COMMUNIST forces from 1946 to 1954. 🍀 Became the capital of North Vietnam in 1954, when the French evacuated the city. 🍀 During the

VIETNAM WAR, the city suffered heavy bombing by the United States.

Havana Capital of CUBA and largest city in the country, located in western Cuba. Largest city and chief port of the WEST INDIES, and one of the oldest cities in the Americas.

🍂 The sinking of the American battleship *Maine* in Havana harbor in 1898 led to the SPANISH-AMERICAN WAR.

Helsinki (HEL-sing-kee, hel-SING-kee) Capital of FINLAND and largest city in the country; located in southern Finland on the Gulf of Finland. One of the nation's chief ports, as well as its commercial and cultural center.

🍂 Site of many international conferences. 🍂 The Helsinki Accords were signed in 1975; their goal was to increase cooperation between eastern and western EUROPE in hopes of reducing tensions resulting from WORLD WAR II and the COLD WAR.

hemisphere Any half of the EARTH's surface.

Highlands, the Mountain region in northern and western SCOTLAND.

🍂 Famous for its rugged beauty. 🍂 The distinguishing features of its CULTURE were the style of dress (including the kilt and tartan) and the clan system, now in disuse except for historical observances.

Himalayas (him-uh-LAY-uhz, huh-MAHL-yuhz) Mountain range in ASIA, extending east through PAKISTAN, INDIA, CHINA (TIBET), NEPAL, and Bhutan.

🍂 The Himalayas contain the world's highest mountains, including MOUNT EVEREST.

Hiroshima (hir-uh-SHEE-muh, hi-ROH-shuh-muh) City on the southwest coast of Honshu Island, JAPAN. Commercial and industrial center.

🍂 On August 6, 1945, Hiroshima was almost completely destroyed by the first ATOMIC BOMB ever dropped on a populated area. Followed by the bombing of NAGASAKI, on August 9, this show of Allied strength hastened the surrender of Japan in WORLD WAR II. 🍂 Many survivors of these bombings have suffered from a variety of diseases caused by RADIATION, such as LEUKEMIA.

Ho Chi Minh City (HOH CHEE MIN) Present name of SAIGON, VIETNAM, named for the revolutionary leader HO CHI MINH.

Holland A part of The NETHERLANDS. Holland is a common name for the entire country.

Holy Land *See* PALESTINE.

Honduras REPUBLIC in CENTRAL AMERICA, bordered by the CARIBBEAN SEA to the north, NICARAGUA to the east and south, EL SALVADOR and the PACIFIC OCEAN to the southwest, and GUATEMALA to the west. Its capital and largest city is Tegucigalpa.

🍂 There is a strong American military presence in Honduras. 🍂 Honduras was the training ground for the Contra rebels against the government in Nicaragua.

Hong Kong British colony located on the south coast of CHINA on the South China Sea, part of the PACIFIC OCEAN.

🍂 China ceded the island of Hong Kong to BRITAIN in the nineteenth century. Hong Kong will be returned to Chinese rule in 1997, when Britain's LEASE expires. 🍂 One of the world's leading commercial centers, Hong Kong is home to many international corporate offices and a world-famous tailoring industry.

Hudson Bay Inland arm of the ATLANTIC OCEAN in east-central CANADA. QUEBEC, ONTARIO, MANITOBA, and the NORTHWEST TERRITORIES lie on its shores.

🍂 Explored and named by Henry Hudson, who was searching for the NORTHWEST PASSAGE.

Hungary REPUBLIC in central EUROPE, bordered by the former CZECHOSLOVAKIA to the north, UKRAINE to the northeast, RUMANIA to the east and south, the former YUGOSLAVIA and CROATIA to the south, and SLOVENIA and AUSTRIA to the west. Its capital and largest city is BUDAPEST.

🍂 Former EASTERN BLOC country. 🍂 The Austro-Hungarian Empire, in which Austria and Hungary were equal partners, was established in 1867 and collapsed during WORLD WAR I. 🍂 Soviet troops invaded Hungary in 1956 to put down a revolution against the COMMUNIST government; the last Soviet troops finally left in June 1991. 🍂 Hungary held multiparty free elections in October 1990, ending forty-two years of Communist rule.

Iceland Island REPUBLIC in the north ATLANTIC OCEAN, just south of the ARCTIC CIRCLE, west of NORWAY and southeast of GREENLAND. Its capital and largest city is Reykjavik.

🍂 Proclaimed its independence from DENMARK in 1944. 🍂 Member of NATO. 🍂 A unique combination of GLACIERS and PLATE TECTONICS has resulted in an unusual land surface, dominated by a rugged coastline, hot springs, geysers, and VOLCANOES.

India REPUBLIC in southern ASIA. Its capital is NEW DELHI, and its largest city is CALCUTTA.

🍂 Second most populous country in the world, after CHINA. 🍂 British control of India began in 1757 and did not end until the dissolution of the British REGIME, or Raj, in 1947, when India was divided into India and PAKISTAN. 🍂 Mohandas K. GANDHI led the movement for Indian independence through PASSIVE RESISTANCE to British rule. He was killed by a fanatic in 1948. 🍂 Marked by conflict between the Hindu and MOSLEM populations and violence between CASTES.

Indian Ocean Third-largest ocean (after the ATLANTIC and PACIFIC), extending from southern ASIA to ANTARCTICA and from eastern AFRICA to southeastern AUSTRALIA.

Indochina Region in SOUTHEAST ASIA, including BURMA, CAMBODIA, LAOS, MALAYSIA, THAILAND, and VIETNAM.

🍂 The French colonies of Vietnam, Laos, and Cambodia were organized as French Indochina.

Indonesia REPUBLIC and ARCHIPELAGO in SOUTHEAST ASIA comprising over 13,000 islands and extending 3000 miles from MALAYSIA toward AUSTRALIA, between the INDIAN and PACIFIC OCEANS. It includes several of the world's largest islands (see BORNEO, JAVA, NEW GUINEA, and SUMATRA). Its capital is DJAKARTA.

🍂 Rich in nutmeg and cloves, the Moluccas, in the eastern part of the archipelago, are known as the Spice Islands. 🍂 Under Dutch control from the beginning of the seventeenth century to 1949. The islands were called the Dutch East Indies from 1799 until their independence. 🍂 The volcanic (see VOLCANO) island of Krakatoa, between Sumatra and Java, erupted in 1883, creating a tidal WAVE that caused great destruction to its neighboring islands. It sent volcanic debris as far as MADAGASCAR. 🍂 Indonesia is the principal oil producer in the FAR EAST and Pacific.

Iran (i-RAN, i-RAHN, eye-RAN) REPUBLIC in the MIDDLE EAST, bordered by ARMENIA, the CASPIAN SEA, TURKMENISTAN, and AZERBAIJAN to the north, AFGHANISTAN and PAKISTAN to the east, the Gulf of Oman and the PERSIAN GULF to the south, and IRAQ and TURKEY to the west. Its capital and largest city is TEHERAN.

🍂 Core of the ancient PERSIAN EMPIRE, Iran was known as Persia until 1935. 🍂 The United States supported the regime of the shah (king) Mohammed Reza Pahlavi, who was forced by popular opposition to leave the country in 1979. 🍂 Ayatollah Ruhollah KHOMEINI ruled from 1979 until his death in 1989, imposing strict ISLAMIC law. 🍂 In 1979 Iranian militants attacked the U.S. embassy and seized hostages, including sixty-two Americans, who were held until 1981. 🍂 Unsuccessfully invaded by IRAQ in 1980. 🍂 Widely believed to have controlled the taking of hostages in LEBANON. (*See* IRAN-CONTRA AFFAIR.)

Iraq (i-RAK, i-RAHK) REPUBLIC in the MIDDLE EAST, bordered by the PERSIAN GULF, KUWAIT, a neutral zone, and SAUDI ARABIA to the south; JORDAN and SYRIA to the west; TURKEY to the north; and IRAN to the east. Its capital and largest city is BAGHDAD.

🍂 The ancient civilization of MESOPOTAMIA emerged in the valley between the EUPHRATES RIVER and Tigris River in what is now Iraq. 🍂 Ruled by Saddam Hussein, a dictator who invaded IRAN in 1980 and KUWAIT in 1990. (*See also* PERSIAN GULF WAR.)

Ireland Island in the ATLANTIC OCEAN separated from GREAT BRITAIN by the Irish Sea. It is divided into NORTHERN IRELAND and the Republic of Ireland (*see* IRELAND, REPUBLIC OF).

🍂 Called the "Emerald Isle" because of its lush green countryside.

Ireland, Republic of Country occupying most of the island of IRELAND, which it shares with NORTHERN IRELAND. Its capital and largest city is DUBLIN.

🍂 The continuing conflict between Irish ROMAN CATHOLICS and PROTESTANTS began when HENRY VIII of ENGLAND imposed the Protestant Church of Ireland upon a largely Catholic population. 🍂 The Easter Rebellion of 1916, although unsuccessful, became a symbolic impetus for Irish nationalists struggling against British rule. 🍂 In 1918, Catholic nationalists proclaimed an Irish REPUBLIC, and in 1920, two separate PARLIAMENTS for Catholic Ireland and NORTHERN IRELAND were established. 🍂 A treaty with BRITAIN in 1922 established the Irish Free State.

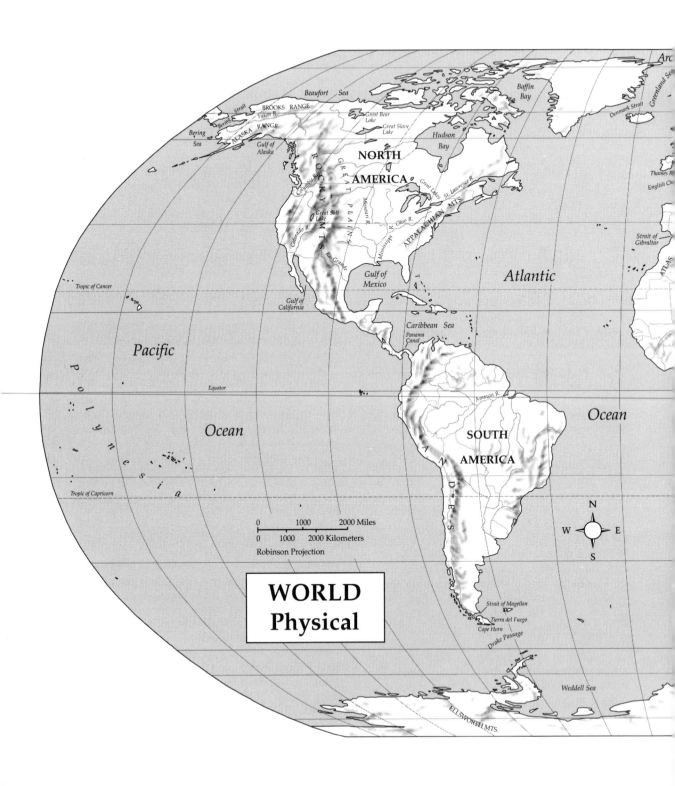

WORLD
Physical

Robinson Projection

| 0 | 1000 | 2000 Miles |
| 0 | 1000 | 2000 Kilometers |

NORTH AMERICA

SOUTH AMERICA

Pacific Ocean

Atlantic Ocean

Equator

Tropic of Cancer

Tropic of Capricorn

Beaufort Sea

BROOKS RANGE

Yukon R.

ALASKA RANGE

Bering Strait

Bering Sea

Gulf of Alaska

Columbia R.

ROCKY MTS.

GREAT PLAINS

Great Salt Lake

Colorado R.

Rio Grande

Gulf of California

Great Bear Lake

Great Slave Lake

Missouri R.

Mississippi R.

Ohio R.

Great Lakes

St. Lawrence R.

APPALACHIAN MTS.

Gulf of Mexico

Hudson Bay

Baffin Bay

Denmark Strait

Greenland Sea

Thames R.

English Ch.

Strait of Gibraltar

ATLAS

Caribbean Sea

Panama Canal

Amazon R.

ANDES

Strait of Magellan

Tierra del Fuego

Cape Horn

Drake Passage

Weddell Sea

ELLSWORTH MTS.

Polynesia

Arc[tic]

The Republic of Ireland was proclaimed in 1949. 🎕
The IRISH REPUBLICAN ARMY (IRA), a nationalist organization that has engaged in terrorism while fighting for the unification of Ireland, has its headquarters in the Republic of Ireland.

Israel   REPUBLIC in the MIDDLE EAST, formerly part of PALESTINE. Israel is bordered by LEBANON to the north, SYRIA and JORDAN to the east, the Gulf of Aqaba (an arm of the RED SEA) to the south, and the MEDITERRANEAN SEA to the west. Its capital and largest city is JERUSALEM.

🎕 The state of Israel, a homeland for JEWS worldwide, was proclaimed in 1948. Since then, conflict has arisen because of opposition by the surrounding Arab peoples to the formation of a Jewish state on what they consider Arab territory (*see* ARAB-ISRAELI CONFLICT). 🎕 As a move toward permanent peace between Israel and the Arab states, Israeli PRIME MINISTER Menachem Begin and Egyptian President Anwar SADAT met with President Jimmy CARTER of the United States in the United States and signed a peace treaty in 1979. 🎕 Since the formation of Israel, the United States has been its major supporter, but Israeli settlements on the WEST BANK strained U.S.-Israel relations.

Istanbul   (IS-tahm-bool,   IS-tam-bool,   is-tahm-BOOHL, is-tam-BOOHL)   Largest city in TURKEY, located in the northwestern part of the country on both sides of the BOSPORUS.

🎕 Formerly called Byzantium, then CONSTANTINOPLE, the city was the capital consecutively of the eastern branch of the ROMAN EMPIRE, of the BYZANTINE EMPIRE, and of the OTTOMAN EMPIRE. 🎕 Seat of the EASTERN ORTHODOX CHURCH.

isthmus (IS-muhs)   A narrow strip of land that connects two larger bodies of land and has water on both sides.

Italy   REPUBLIC in southern EUROPE, jutting into the MEDITERRANEAN SEA as a boot-shaped PENINSULA, surrounded on the east, south, and west by arms of the Mediterranean, and bordered to the northwest by FRANCE, to the north by SWITZERLAND and AUSTRIA, and to the northeast by SLOVENIA. The country includes the large islands of SICILY and SARDINIA, as well as many smaller islands, such as CAPRI. Its capital and largest city is ROME.

🎕 Italy was the core of the Roman Republic and ROMAN EMPIRE from the fourth century B.C. to the fifth century A.D. 🎕 Beginning in the fourteenth century, the Italian RENAISSANCE brought Europe out of the MIDDLE AGES with its outstanding contributions to the arts. To this day, Italy continues to be associated with great artistic achievement and is home to countless masterpieces. 🎕 Under the fascist leadership of Benito MUSSOLINI (*see* FASCISM), Italy began colonization in AFRICA and entered a military alliance with GERMANY and JAPAN. These countries were known as the AXIS POWERS in WORLD WAR II. 🎕 Italy has been a member of NATO since 1949. 🎕 Italian cooking, featuring pasta, has become a staple of the American diet.

Ivory Coast   REPUBLIC in western AFRICA on the Gulf of Guinea, bordered by Mali to the northwest, Burkina Faso to the northeast, GHANA to the east, and LIBERIA and Guinea to the west. Also known as the Republic of Côte d'Ivoire (French for Ivory Coast). Its capital and largest city is Abidjan.

🎕 French control of the area began after WORLD WAR II and lasted until 1960, when the Ivory Coast declared itself independent. 🎕 One of the most prosperous and politically stable nations in Africa.

Jakarta (juh-KAHR-tuh)   *See* DJAKARTA.

Jamaica   Nation in the WEST INDIES, situated south of CUBA and west of HAITI, in the CARIBBEAN SEA. Its capital and largest city is Kingston.

🎕 Leading world sugar producer in the eighteenth century, when a large slave population grew up around sugar plantations. 🎕 British colony from 1655 to 1962, when Jamaica became completely independent. 🎕 The country has a high level of poverty. 🎕 Tourism is a major industry.

Japan   Island nation in the northwest PACIFIC OCEAN off the coast of east ASIA, separated by the Sea of Japan from RUSSIAN SIBERIA, CHINA, and KOREA. The Japanese ARCHIPELAGO includes four major islands (Hokkaido, Honshu, Kyushu, and Shikoku) as well as many smaller islands. Its capital and largest city is TOKYO.

🎕 Called the "Land of the Rising Sun," Japan is symbolized by a red sun on a white background. 🎕 Another SYMBOL of Japan is Fujiyama, also called Mount Fuji, a VOLCANO whose symmetrical snow-capped peak has been the object of countless pilgrimages, poems, and paintings. It has not erupted since 1707. 🎕 Imperial Japan was organized on a feudal system (*see* FEUDALISM), characterized by the samurai (the warrior CLASS, which eventually became landed gentry) and the SHOGUN (the hereditary administrative leader). The emperor, believed to be divine, was the ceremonial leader. Japan is a CONSTITUTIONAL MONARCHY today. ☙ Japan's ports were first opened to Western traders in the sixteenth century, but were closed in the seventeenth century. Japan remained in virtual isolation until the 1850s, when an American naval officer, Matthew C. Perry, persuaded the government to reopen trade with the West. ☙ Suffering from overcrowding, lack of NATURAL RESOURCES, and the influence of powerful military factions, Japan pursued an aggressive policy of expansion in China during the 1930s, ultimately resulting in a military alliance with GERMANY and ITALY to form the AXIS POWERS in WORLD WAR II. (*See also* HIROSHIMA, PEARL HARBOR, *and* MACARTHUR, DOUGLAS.) ☙ Now a world leader in shipbuilding, electronics, and automobile manufacture. Long a political and economic ally of the United States, Japan has become more independent and assertive as its industrial policy has produced tensions in the relations with the United States.

Java (JAH-vuh)   Island in INDONESIA, south of BORNEO.

☙ One of the world's most densely populated regions. ☙ Under Dutch rule from 1619 to 1949.

Jerusalem   Capital of ISRAEL and largest city in the country, located on a ridge west of the DEAD SEA and the JORDAN RIVER. (*See also under "The Bible."*)

☙ Site of city has been occupied since the BRONZE AGE. ☙ Capital of ancient HEBREW kingdom under the kings DAVID and SOLOMON. ☙ Known as the "Holy City," it is sacred to JEWS, CHRISTIANS, and MOSLEMS. ☙ Conquest of Jerusalem was the goal of the early CRUSADES during the MIDDLE AGES. ☙ After the creation of the state of Israel in 1948, Jerusalem was divided between Israel and JORDAN. Following the ARAB-ISRAELI WAR of 1967, Israel annexed the remainder of the city. ☙ Famous for its many sacred sights and shrines, including the WAILING WALL, the CHURCH of the Holy Sepulcher, and the Dome of the Rock.

Johannesburg (joh-HAN-uhs-burg, joh-HAH-nuhs-burg)   Largest city in SOUTH AFRICA, located in the northeastern part of the country.

☙ The commercial center for South Africa's diamond and gold industries.

Jordan   MONARCHY in the MIDDLE EAST, bordered by SYRIA to the north, IRAQ to the northeast, SAUDI ARABIA to the east and south, and ISRAEL to the west. Amman is its capital and largest city.

☙ An Arab nation. ☙ King Hussein, a controversial figure in Middle Eastern affairs, has ruled since 1953. Although he has tried to maintain cordial relations with the West, he opposed the EGYPT-ISRAEL peace agreement of 1979, endorsed the PALESTINE LIBERATION ORGANIZATION, and refused to join the alliance against IRAQ during the PERSIAN GULF WAR.

Jordan River   River in northern ISRAEL, flowing south through the Sea of Galilee to the DEAD SEA.

☙ In the BIBLE, the Jordan was the scene of the baptism of JESUS by JOHN THE BAPTIST.

Kabul (KAH-bool, kuh-BOOHL)   Capital of AFGHANISTAN and largest city in the country, located in eastern Afghanistan.

☙ Strategically situated in a high, narrow valley wedged between two mountain ranges, it is near the main approaches to an old trade and invasion route.

Kampuchea, People's Republic of (kam-poo-CHEE-uh)   Official name of CAMBODIA.

Karachi (kuh-RAH-chee)   Largest city in PAKISTAN, in the southeastern part of the country, on the Arabian Sea near the Indus River delta. Pakistan's main seaport and industrial center.

☙ Served as Pakistan's capital from 1947 to 1959.

Kazakhstan (kah-zahk-STAHN)   REPUBLIC in west-central ASIA, bordered on the northwest and north by RUSSIA, on the east by CHINA, on the south by KYRGYZSTAN and UZBEKISTAN, and on the west by the CASPIAN SEA. Its capital and largest city is Alma-Ata.

☙ This former member of the SOVIET UNION declared its independence in 1990.

Kenya (KEN-yuh, KEEN-yuh)   REPUBLIC in eastern AFRICA bordered by SUDAN and ETHIOPIA to the north, SOMALIA to the east, the INDIAN OCEAN to the southeast, TANZANIA to the southwest, and UGANDA to the west. Its capital and largest city is NAIROBI.

☙ The Great Rift Valley in Kenya is the site of some major archaeological discoveries, including remains of the earliest known humans.

Khartoum (kahr-TOOHM)   Capital of SUDAN, a port at the juncture of the two upper portions of the NILE RIVER — the Blue Nile and White Nile.

Kiev (KEE-ef, KEE-ev)   Capital of UKRAINE in north-central region of the country on Dnieper River. A major manufacturing and transportation center.

Kilimanjaro (kil-uh-muhn-JAHR-oh)   The highest mountain in AFRICA, located in northeastern TANZANIA.

    📖 "The Snows of Kilimanjaro" is a SHORT STORY by Ernest HEMINGWAY.

Korea   Historic region consisting of NORTH KOREA and SOUTH KOREA; PENINSULA off northeastern CHINA separating the Yellow Sea and Sea of Japan, two arms of the PACIFIC OCEAN.

    📖 Under Japanese rule in the early twentieth century. At the end of WORLD WAR II, Korea was divided at the thirty-eighth parallel of north LATITUDE into two zones, with troops of the SOVIET UNION in the north and troops of the United States in the south. By 1948, two separate governments had emerged, the COMMUNIST Democratic People's REPUBLIC of Korea in the north, and the noncommunist Republic of Korea in the south. American and Soviet troops were withdrawn by 1949. The KOREAN WAR (1950–1953) began when North Korean forces invaded South Korea. Forces of the UNITED NATIONS under General Douglas MACARTHUR aided South Korea, while Chinese forces aided North Korea.

Kuwait (koo-WAYT)   Independent kingdom on the northeastern part of the ARABIAN PENINSULA, at the head of the PERSIAN GULF, bordered by IRAQ to the north and west and SAUDI ARABIA to the south.

    📖 Major petroleum producer, possessing about one-fifth of the world's oil reserves; leading member of the ORGANIZATION OF PETROLEUM EXPORTING COUNTRIES (OPEC). 📖 In 1990 Kuwait was invaded by IRAQ; in 1991 Iraqi forces were expelled by a coalition of UNITED NATIONS' forces led by the UNITED STATES. (*See also* PERSIAN GULF WAR.)

Kyrgyzstan (keer-gi-STAHN, keer-gi-STAN)   REPUBLIC in central ASIA, bordered to the northwest and north by KAZAKHSTAN, to the east and southeast by CHINA, to the southwest by TAJIKISTAN, and to the west by UZBEKISTAN. Its capital and largest city is Frunze.

    📖 This former member of the SOVIET UNION declared its independence in 1991.

Labrador   The portion of the province of NEWFOUNDLAND, CANADA, that lies on the mainland of NORTH AMERICA.

    📖 Eastern part of the large Labrador-Ungava peninsular region of eastern Canada.

Lagos (LAH-gohs, LAY-gos)   Capital of NIGERIA and largest city in the country, located in the southwest corner of Nigeria on the Gulf of Guinea, an arm of the ATLANTIC OCEAN. Nigeria's economic center and chief port.

Lake Victoria   The largest lake in AFRICA, and the second-largest freshwater lake in the world, after LAKE SUPERIOR. It is on the UGANDA-TANZANIA-KENYA border. Also called Victoria Nyanza.

    📖 Lake Victoria is a headwater reservoir for the NILE RIVER. 📖 It was explored by Henry Stanley in 1875.

Laos (LOWS, LAH-ohs)   Mountainous, landlocked REPUBLIC in SOUTHEAST ASIA, bordered by BURMA to the northwest, CHINA to the northeast, VIETNAM to the east, CAMBODIA to the south, and THAILAND to the west. Its capital and largest city is Vientiane.

    📖 Part of French INDOCHINA from 1893 to 1949; full SOVEREIGNTY granted in 1954. 📖 Civil war among COMMUNIST and noncommunist FACTIONS in the 1950s and 1960s attracted extensive covert aid from the SOVIET UNION, China, and the United States. 📖 During the VIETNAM WAR, Vietnamese communists established the HO CHI MINH Trail through the remote mountains of Laos to channel troops and supplies from North Vietnam to South Vietnam. 📖 The communist Pathet Lao, with long-standing close ties to the Vietnamese communists, have been in power since 1975.

Latin America   A term applied to all of the Spanish- or Portuguese-speaking nations south of the United States.

latitude   The measurement, in DEGREES, of a place's distance north or south of the EQUATOR. (*Compare* LONGITUDE.)

Latvia (LAT-vee-uh, LAHT-vee-uh)   REPUBLIC on the BALTIC SEA, bordered by ESTONIA to the north, RUSSIA to the east, BELARUS to the southeast, and LITHUANIA to the south. Its capital and largest city is Riga.

    📖 Nationalist sentiments brewing since the mid-nineteenth century erupted at the time of the RUS-

SIAN REVOLUTION; after the collapse of Russia and GERMANY in WORLD WAR I, Latvia was able to proclaim its independence. After twenty years of political instability, however, Latvia was forcibly integrated into the SOVIET UNION in 1940, along with ESTONIA and LITHUANIA. The collapse of the Soviet Union enabled Latvians to reassert their national identity, and they declared their country independent in August 1991.

Lebanon   REPUBLIC in the MIDDLE EAST, located on the MEDITERRANEAN SEA, bordered to the north and east by SYRIA and to the south by ISRAEL. Its capital and largest city is BEIRUT.

❦ Lebanon was established in 1920 from remnants of the OTTOMAN empire. Its mixed CHRISTIAN and MOSLEM population generally lived peacefully under a weak central government until the 1970s. ISRAEL invaded in 1978 to challenge the PALESTINE LIBERATION ORGANIZATION's (PLO) influence in Lebanon and to stop PLO raids on Israel. During the 1980s Lebanon became the scene of intense fighting between PLO, Syrian, and Israeli forces, as well as indigenous Christian and Moslem factions. Terrorist bombings and the taking of foreign nationals (including American citizens) as hostages became common events. By 1992 SYRIA had emerged as the dominant influence in Lebanon.

Left Bank   Area in PARIS on the left (south) bank of the SEINE RIVER.

❦ Center of artistic and student life.

Leipzig   (LEYEP-sig, LEYEP-sik)   City in east-central GERMANY. Manufacturing, commercial, and transportation hub.

❦ Since the REFORMATION, Leipzig has been a leading cultural center of Germany, home to philosophical, literary, and musical giants such as Johann Wolfgang von GOETHE, Friedrich von SCHILLER, Johann Sebastian BACH, Felix MENDELSSOHN, Robert Schumann, and Richard WAGNER. ❦ Leipzig was the capital of Germany's book and music publishing industries until the city was badly damaged in WORLD WAR II.

Leningrad   (LEN-in-grad, LEN-in-grahd)   Name of SAINT PETERSBURG, RUSSIA, from 1924 to 1991. (*See* SAINT PETERSBURG.)

Levant   (luh-VANT)   Name for the nations on the eastern shore of the MEDITERRANEAN SEA: CYPRUS, EGYPT, ISRAEL, LEBANON, SYRIA, and TURKEY.

Liberia   REPUBLIC in western AFRICA, bordered by SIERRA LEONE to the northwest, Guinea to the north, the IVORY COAST to the east, and the ATLANTIC OCEAN to the southwest.

❦ The American Colonization Society began settlement of black Americans, most of them freed slaves, in 1822. Eventually, 15,000 blacks emigrated to Liberia.

Libya   Nation in northern AFRICA on the MEDITERRANEAN SEA, bordered by EGYPT to the east, SUDAN to the southeast, CHAD and NIGER to the south, and ALGERIA and TUNISIA to the west. Its capital and largest city is TRIPOLI.

❦ Under the leadership of Muammar QADDAFI, Libya has pursued a policy of openly supporting and abetting terrorists around the world. This policy has made Libya an outcast state with few friends outside the Arab world.

Liechtenstein   (LIK-tuhn-steyen, LIKH-tuhn-shteyen)   CONSTITUTIONAL MONARCHY in west-central EUROPE, located in the ALPS between AUSTRIA and SWITZERLAND. Its capital and largest city is Vaduz.

❦ Not quite as large as WASHINGTON, D.C., Liechtenstein is one of the smallest European countries.

Lima   (LEE-muh)   Capital of PERU and largest city in the country, located in western Peru. Peru's economic center.

❦ Capital of the empire of SPAIN in the NEW WORLD until the nineteenth century.

Lisbon   (LIZ-buhn)   Capital of PORTUGAL and largest city in the country, located in western Portugal on the Tagus River where it broadens to enter the ATLANTIC OCEAN. Major port, and Portugal's political, economic, and cultural center.

❦ Because Lisbon was a neutral city, it became a center for international political activity during WORLD WAR II.

Lithuania   (lith-ooh-AY-nee-uh)   REPUBLIC on the BALTIC SEA, bordered by LATVIA to the north, BELARUS to the east and southeast, POLAND to the south, and by an isolated segment of RUSSIA to the southwest. Its capital and largest city is Vilnius.

❧ Lithuania was one of the largest and most powerful states in EUROPE from the fourteenth to the sixteenth centuries, at which time it merged with Poland. In the late eighteenth century, it was absorbed by Russia. A nationalist movement which grew in strength throughout the nineteenth century finally bore fruit when the Russian empire collapsed during WORLD WAR I. Lithuanians achieved their desired goal of an independent state during the interwar years, but their country was occupied and annexed by the SOVIET UNION in 1940, as were the neighboring countries of ESTONIA and LATVIA. ❧ Occupied by German forces during WORLD WAR II, at which time thousands of Lithuanian Jews were exterminated. ❧ As the COMMUNIST system began to collapse and the Soviet Union began to dissolve, Lithuania became the first of the Baltic republics to reject Soviet rule, declaring its independence in March 1990.

Liverpool   City in northwestern ENGLAND. One of the greatest ports and largest cities in BRITAIN, and the country's major outlet for industrial exports.

❧ Home of the BEATLES.

London   Capital of BRITAIN, located in southeastern ENGLAND on both sides of the THAMES RIVER. Officially called Greater London. Financial, commercial, industrial, and cultural center. One of the world's greatest ports.

❧ Many buildings of central London were destroyed or damaged in air raids, called the Blitz (short for BLITZKRIEG), during WORLD WAR II. ❧ Home of WESTMINSTER ABBEY, Hyde Park, Buckingham Palace, BIG BEN, the Tower of London, and the University of London.

longitude (LON-juh-toohd)   A measurement, in DEGREES, of a place's distance east or west of the PRIME MERIDIAN, which runs through GREENWICH, ENGLAND. (*Compare* LATITUDE.)

Low Countries, the   Collective name for The NETHERLANDS, BELGIUM, and LUXEMBOURG, so called because much of their land surface is at or below sea level. These countries have often been culturally and historically united, and, bordered by the most powerful nations in EUROPE, they have been a major battleground in European wars for centuries.

Luxembourg (LUK-suhm-burg)   CONSTITUTIONAL MONARCHY in northwestern EUROPE, bordered by BELGIUM to the west and north, GERMANY to the east, and FRANCE to the south. Luxembourg City is its capital and largest city.

❧ Member of NATO since 1949. ❧ Occupied by GERMANY during WORLD WAR I and WORLD WAR II. ❧ Part of the Battle of the BULGE was fought in northern Luxembourg in the winter of 1944–1945. ❧ An international financial center. ❧ One of Europe's oldest and smallest independent countries.

Lyon (lee-OHNN)   Also LYONS. City in east-central FRANCE on the RHONE RIVER.

❧ Principal producer of silk and rayon in EUROPE. ❧ Capital of the French RESISTANCE movement in WORLD WAR II.

Macedonia (mas-uh-DOH-nee-uh, mas-uh-DOHN-yuh)   REPUBLIC in southeastern EUROPE on the west BALKAN PENINSULA, bordered by YUGOSLAVIA to the north, BULGARIA to the east, GREECE to the south, and ALBANIA to the west. Its capital and largest city is Skopje.

❧ Macedonia is part of a mountainous region of the Balkan Peninsula, also called Macedonia, that was once ruled by the OTTOMAN empire and divided in 1912 among Greece, Bulgaria, and Serbia (later Yugoslavia). ❧ Greece has objected to the republic's adoption of the name Macedonia, which to the Greeks has been historically associated with ALEXANDER THE GREAT and ancient Greece.

Madagascar (mad-uh-GAS-kuhr)   Island REPUBLIC in the INDIAN OCEAN off the southeastern coast of AFRICA. Its capital and largest city is Antananarivo.

❧ The island of Madagascar is the fourth largest in the world. ❧ Madagascar was under French control from the late nineteenth century until 1960, when it gained full independence.

Madrid   Capital of SPAIN and largest city in the country, located in the center of Spain.

❧ Madrid was the scene of fighting between the Loyalists and rebel forces of Francisco FRANCO during the SPANISH CIVIL WAR; the city was greatly damaged. ❧ Home of an outstanding art museum, the Museo del PRADO.

Magellan, Strait of (muh-JEL-uhn)   Strait separating SOUTH AMERICA from Tierra del Fuego and other islands south of the CONTINENT.

❧ Discovered by Ferdinand MAGELLAN in 1520.

☙ Important route around South America in the days of sailing ships, especially before the PANAMA CANAL was built.

Malaysia (muh-LAY-zhuh)   Country in SOUTHEAST ASIA consisting of West Malaysia on the Malay PENINSULA (extending south of THAILAND) and East Malaysia on the island of BORNEO. Its capital and largest city is Kuala Lumpur.

Malta (MAWL-tuh)   REPUBLIC in the MEDITERRANEAN SEA south of SICILY, made up of five small islands.

☙ Malta, strategically located, has belonged to a succession of civilizations, including the ancient Greeks and the ROMAN EMPIRE. In 1800, the British established control of Malta, which has continued to maintain close ties with BRITAIN since its independence in 1964.

Manchester   City in northwestern ENGLAND about thirty miles east of LIVERPOOL.

☙ One of England's most important economic, industrial, trade, and finance centers, and heart of the most densely populated area of England.

Manitoba   Province in central CANADA, bordered to the north by the NORTHWEST TERRITORIES, the northeast by HUDSON BAY, the east by ONTARIO, the south by MINNESOTA and NORTH DAKOTA, and the west by SASKATCHEWAN. WINNIPEG is the capital and largest city.

Maritime Provinces   The collective name for the Canadian provinces of NEW BRUNSWICK, NOVA SCOTIA, and PRINCE EDWARD ISLAND.

Marseilles (mahr-SAY)   City in southeastern FRANCE on the MEDITERRANEAN SEA. Second-largest city in France, after PARIS, and its main seaport.

☙ "The MARSEILLAISE," France's national anthem, is so named because it was first sung in Paris by the Marseilles battalion when it marched to storm the BASTILLE.

Martinique (mahrt-n-EEK)   Island in the eastern WEST INDIES; an overseas part of FRANCE.

Matterhorn   Mountain in the ALPS on the border of SWITZERLAND and ITALY, celebrated for its distinctive shape.

Mecca   City in western SAUDI ARABIA.
☙ As the place where MOHAMMED the PROPHET

MECCA. *The sacred Kaaba, in the courtyard of the Great Mosque, houses the Black Stone, believed to have been sent from heaven by Allah.*

was born in the sixth century, it is the holiest city of ISLAM. ☙ A "mecca" is a place that attracts people: "HOLLYWOOD is a mecca for would-be actors and actresses."

Mediterranean Sea   Sea surrounded by EUROPE, ASIA, and AFRICA.

Melbourne (MEL-buhrn)   Second-largest city in AUSTRALIA, located on the country's southern coast. Capital of Victoria state and largest city in the state. Financial and commercial center.

Mercator projection (muhr-KAY-tuhr)   A way of showing the sphere of the EARTH on the flat surface of a map. Because this projection is centered on the EQUATOR, in order to maintain the correct shape of the features shown, the spacing between the parallels of LATITUDE increases with the increasing distance from the equator. This tends to enlarge the size of those features located nearer the poles, such as GREENLAND or NEW ZEALAND, giving a false picture of their relative size.

meridian (muh-RID-ee-uhn)   A great imaginary circle on the surface of the EARTH that runs north and south through the NORTH POLE and SOUTH POLE. LONGITUDE is measured on meridians: places on a meridian have the same LONGITUDE. (*See* PRIME MERIDIAN.)

Mexico   REPUBLIC in southern NORTH AMERICA, bordered by the United States to the north, the GULF

OF MEXICO and the CARIBBEAN SEA to the east, Belize and GUATEMALA to the southeast, and the PACIFIC OCEAN to the south and west. Its capital and largest city is MEXICO CITY.

&. The world's most populous Spanish-speaking country. &. Mexico has a significantly high foreign DEBT. Its land is rich, but much of it is difficult to cultivate. Despite the prosperity of its oil industry, Mexico's economic troubles are severe. &. Many Mexicans cross the Mexican-American border illegally in hopes of finding work in the United States. &. Mexico's proximity to the United States has led to serious territorial disputes; the immediate cause of the MEXICAN WAR of the 1840s was the annexation of TEXAS by the United States. &. Mexico became independent from SPAIN in 1821. &. Before the arrival of the Spanish in the early sixteenth century, great NATIVE AMERICAN civilizations, such as the MAYAS and the AZTECS, thrived.

Mexico City   Capital of MEXICO and largest city in the country, located in central Mexico. Mexico's political, cultural, commercial, and industrial center.

&. With nearly thirteen million inhabitants, Mexico City is one of the world's largest cities.

Middle East   Region in western ASIA and northeast AFRICA that includes the nations on the ARABIAN PENINSULA, EGYPT, IRAN, IRAQ, ISRAEL, JORDAN, LEBANON, SYRIA, and TURKEY.

&. As the site of such ancient civilizations as PHOENICIA, BABYLON, and Egypt, and the birthplace of JUDAISM, CHRISTIANITY, and ISLAM, the Middle East is known as the cradle of Western civilization. The Greek, ROMAN, PERSIAN, and OTTOMAN EMPIRES are among the great civilizations that developed and prospered in the Middle East. &. A hotbed of religious and political strife (see ARAB-ISRAELI CONFLICT, the PERSIAN GULF WAR), the Middle East attracted the attention of such powerful nations as GREAT BRITAIN, the United States, and the SOVIET UNION eager to protect their strategic interests at the crossroads of EUROPE, Asia, and Africa, and their access to precious oil reserves.

Milan   (mi-LAHN, mi-lan)   Capital of the Lombardy region in northern ITALY. Since the MIDDLE AGES, an international commercial, financial, and industrial center.

&. Landmarks include the OPERA house La SCALA and the CHURCH of Santa Maria delle Grazie, which houses a famous FRESCO by LEONARDO DA VINCI, THE LAST SUPPER. &. Center for fashion and design.

Moldova   (mol-DOH-vuh)   REPUBLIC in eastern EUROPE, bordered by UKRAINE to the north and east, the BLACK SEA to the south, and RUMANIA to the west. Its capital and largest city is Kishinev.

&. This former member of the SOVIET UNION declared its independence in 1991. &. The Soviet Union took Moldova from RUMANIA in 1940; most of its people speak Rumanian.

Monaco   (MON-uh-koh, muh-NAH-koh)   CONSTITUTIONAL MONARCHY on the French RIVIERA.

&. Its casino at MONTE CARLO, luxury hotels, and spectacular scenery make Monaco a popular resort. &. The American actress Grace Kelly married Monaco's ruler, Prince Rainier III, in 1956. Princess Grace died in 1982.

Mongolia   Country in north-central ASIA, bordered by Russian SIBERIA to the north, and CHINA to the east, south, and west. Its capital and largest city is Ulan Bator.

&. Unofficially called Outer Mongolia. &. Proclaimed independent from China in 1921, with Soviet support, and established as the People's Republic of Mongolia, a nation dominated by COMMUNISTS.

Mont Blanc   (mohnn BLAHNN)   Mountain in the ALPS, on the border between FRANCE and ITALY, southeast of GENEVA, SWITZERLAND.

&. Highest peak in France and one of the highest in EUROPE.

Monte Carlo   (MON-ti KAHR-loh)   City in MONACO, world-famous for its gambling casino.

Montevideo   (mon-tuh-vi-DAY-oh, mon-tuh-VID-ee-oh)   Capital of URUGUAY and largest city in the country, located on Uruguay's southern coast.

&. One of the busiest ports in SOUTH AMERICA, Montevideo is a cosmopolitan city characterized by broad boulevards, parks, and stately buildings.

Montreal   City in southern QUEBEC province, CANADA, on Montreal Island in the ST. LAWRENCE RIVER. Cultural, commercial, financial, and industrial center.

&. Second-largest French-speaking city in the world, after PARIS. &. Second-largest city in Canada, after TORONTO. &. Lies at the foot of Mount Royal, for which it is named.

Morocco Kingdom in northwestern AFRICA with coasts on the ATLANTIC OCEAN and the MEDITERRANEAN SEA; it is bordered by ALGERIA to the east and the western SAHARA to the south. Its largest city is CASABLANCA, and its capital is Rabat.

Moscow Capital and largest city of RUSSIA, located in the west-central region on the Moscow River. Russia's economic and cultural center.

&. The KREMLIN, Russia's political and administrative headquarters, is at the center of the city. Adjoining the Kremlin is Red Square. &. Its landmarks and institutions include the tomb of LENIN, the University of Moscow, Gorki Central Park, and the Bolshoi BALLET Theater. &. In 1991, hundreds of thousands of Muscovites, led by Boris YELTSIN, rallied against a coup that had overthrown reformist president Mikhail GORBACHEV, resulting in the defeat of the coup plotters, the end of the communist system, and the dissolution of the SOVIET UNION.

Mount Everest Mountain on the border of TIBET and NEPAL in the central HIMALAYAS.

&. At over 29,000 feet, it is the highest peak in the world. &. First scaled in 1953 by Sir Edmund Hillary of NEW ZEALAND and Tenzing Norkay of NEPAL.

Mount Kilimanjaro *See* KILIMANJARO.

Mount Vesuvius (vuh-SOOH-vee-uhs) VOLCANO, in southwestern ITALY on the coast of the MEDITERRANEAN SEA.

&. Only active volcano on the mainland of EUROPE. &. One of its earliest recorded eruptions, in A.D. 79, buried POMPEII, Herculaneum, and Stabiae under cinders, ash, and mud.

Mozambique (moh-zuhm-BEEK) REPUBLIC in southeastern AFRICA on the INDIAN OCEAN, bordered by SOUTH AFRICA to the south, SWAZILAND to the southwest, ZIMBABWE to the west, and ZAMBIA, Malawi, and TANZANIA to the north. It was a possession of PORTUGAL from 1505 until 1975. Its capital and largest city is Maputo.

Munich Capital of BAVARIA, located in southern GERMANY near the Bavarian ALPS. Commercial, industrial, transportation, communications, and cultural center.

&. Scene of the NAZI party's rise to power; National Socialism (NAZISM) was founded here in 1918, and Adolf HITLER led an attempted revolution in Munich in 1923, the Beer Hall Putsch. &. The Mu-

NICH PACT, drawn up in 1938, forced CZECHOSLOVAKIA to give up territory to the Nazis. &. During WORLD WAR II, the ALLIES bombed much of the city. After the war, it was the largest city in the American occupation zone.

Myanmar (MYAHN-mahr, meye-AHN-mahr) The official name for BURMA since 1989.

Nagasaki (nah-guh-SAH-kee, nag-uh-SAK-ee) City in southern JAPAN. One of Japan's leading ports and shipbuilding centers.

&. First Japanese port to welcome Western traders in the sixteenth century, and the only Japanese port open to the West from 1641 to 1858. &. Nagasaki became the second populated area to be devastated by an ATOMIC BOMB, on August 9, 1945. (*See also* HIROSHIMA.)

Nairobi (neye-ROH-bee) Capital of KENYA and largest city in the country, located in southern Kenya.

&. Capital of British East AFRICA — Kenya, UGANDA, Tanganyika, and Zanzibar (*see* TANZANIA) — from 1905 until the colonies became independent in the early 1960s. &. Center for tourist safaris.

Namibia (nuh-MIB-ee-uh) Country in southwestern AFRICA, bordered by ANGOLA and ZAMBIA to the north, BOTSWANA to the east, SOUTH AFRICA to the south and southeast, and the ATLANTIC OCEAN to the west. Formerly called South West Africa.

&. In 1920, South Africa began administering South West Africa under authority of the LEAGUE OF NATIONS, and in 1971, it rejected the demands of the General Assembly of the UNITED NATIONS that it withdraw. A nationalist group, the South West Africa People's Organization (SWAPO), waged GUERRILLA WARFARE in an attempt to force South Africa out of Namibia. A U.S. mediated settlement ended the civil war in 1988. In 1990 Namibia became an independent nation.

Nanjing (NAHN-JING) City in eastern CHINA on the YANGTZE RIVER, northeast of SHANGHAI. Industrial and transportation center. Also called NANKING.

&. Was China's imperial capital on several occasions, and was made capital of the REPUBLIC of China by Sun Yat-sen in 1912 after the Chinese Revolution, by Nationalist forces of CHIANG KAI-SHEK from 1928 to 1937, and again from 1946 to 1949. &. During the Second Sino-Japanese War in the

1930s, Nanjing was the scene of a Japanese massacre (the Rape of Nanking), and became the seat of a puppet regime established by the Japanese.

Nanking (NAN-king, NAHN-king)   *See* NANJING.

Naples   City in southwestern ITALY. Major seaport and commercial, industrial, and tourist center.

Nationalist China   After the conquest of mainland CHINA by COMMUNISTS led by MAO ZEDONG in 1949, Nationalist (anticommunist) leader CHIANG KAI-SHEK led the remnants of his army to the island of TAIWAN, where he established a government called Nationalist China, which the United States long recognized as the only legitimate government for all of China.

Near East   A region in western ASIA and northeastern AFRICA, often considered the same as the MIDDLE EAST.

Nepal (nuh-PAWL, nuh-PAHL)   Kingdom in central ASIA, bordered by CHINA to the north, and INDIA to the east, south, and west. Located high in the HIMALAYAS. The capital and largest city is Katmandu.

Netherlands, The   CONSTITUTIONAL MONARCHY in northwestern EUROPE, bordered by the NORTH SEA to the west and north, GERMANY to the east, and BELGIUM to the south. AMSTERDAM is the constitutional capital, and The HAGUE is the seat of the government. The Netherlands are also popularly known as HOLLAND, after a region of the country.
&. Half of the country lies below sea level. Much of this land has been reclaimed from the North Sea and is protected by dikes and irrigated by an intricate system of canals. &. During the sixteenth and seventeenth centuries, The Netherlands established a powerful commercial and colonial empire. The Dutch Empire included the settlement of NEW AMSTERDAM, which later became NEW YORK, and the conquest of the Dutch East Indies (now INDONESIA). &. The sixteenth and seventeenth centuries also saw a flowering of Dutch painting by such masters as REMBRANDT. &. During WORLD WAR II, Germany invaded and occupied The Netherlands, exterminating most Dutch JEWS. (*See* FRANK, ANNE.)

Netherlands Antilles (an-TIL-eez)   Group of islands, administered by The NETHERLANDS, in the CARIBBEAN SEA, off the northern coast of VENEZUELA.

&. The principal islands of Aruba, Bonaire, and Curaçao, combining Caribbean beaches and Dutch charm, are popular resorts.

New Brunswick   Province in eastern CANADA, bordered by QUEBEC to the north, the Gulf of St. Lawrence (an arm of the ATLANTIC OCEAN) to the east, NOVA SCOTIA to the southeast, and MAINE to the west. Together with NOVA SCOTIA and PRINCE EDWARD ISLAND, it is one of the MARITIME PROVINCES. Fredericton is its capital, and Saint John is its largest city.

New Delhi (DEL-ee)   The capital of INDIA, located in the north-central region of the country; a portion of the city of DELHI.
&. Built from 1912 to 1929 to replace CALCUTTA as the capital. &. Mahatma GANDHI was assassinated in 1948 at one of the city's prayer grounds.

New Guinea   Island in the southwestern PACIFIC OCEAN, north of AUSTRALIA. The western half of the island is administered by INDONESIA.
&. New Guinea is the world's second-largest island, after GREENLAND. &. Named for its resemblance to the Guinea coast of western AFRICA.

New Zealand   Nation in the southern PACIFIC OCEAN containing two principal islands — North Island and South Island — and several small outlying islands. Its capital is Wellington, and its largest city is AUCKLAND.
&. Known for its sheep industry and spectacular scenery.

Newfoundland (NOOH-fuhn-luhnd, NOOH-fuhn-land)   Province in eastern CANADA consisting of the island of Newfoundland, the mainland area of LABRADOR, and their adjacent islands. St. John's is its capital and largest city.
&. Became Canada's tenth province in 1949. &. Remains of possible VIKING settlements have been found in Newfoundland. &. The first overseas possession of ENGLAND; fishing settlements began in the sixteenth century.

Nicaragua   REPUBLIC in CENTRAL AMERICA, bordered by HONDURAS to the northwest and north, the CARIBBEAN SEA to the east, COSTA RICA to the south, and the PACIFIC OCEAN to the southwest. Its capital and largest city is Managua.
&. General Anastasio Somoza established a military DICTATORSHIP in 1933. He was assassinated in

1956, but his sons continued the Somoza REGIME until 1979. ❧ After fifty years of GUERRILLA WARFARE, the MARXIST Sandinistas launched a civil war and assumed power in 1979. ❧ The Sandinistas were perceived as a threat to American interests because of their LEFT-WING leanings and their ties with CUBA and the SOVIET UNION. During the 1980s the United States backed anti-Sandinista guerrillas called Contras. In 1990 the Sandinistas were defeated in free elections, but they still retain considerable influence in the country.

Nice (NEES)   City in southeastern FRANCE on the MEDITERRANEAN SEA.
❧ Most famous resort of the French RIVIERA.

Niger (NEYE-juhr, nee-ZHAIR)   REPUBLIC in western AFRICA, bordered by Burkina Faso and Mali to the west, ALGERIA to the northwest, LIBYA to the northeast, CHAD to the east, and NIGERIA and Benin to the south. Niamey is the capital and largest city.
❧ Niger was under French control from the 1880s to 1960, when it gained full independence.

Nigeria   A nation in western AFRICA on the Gulf of Guinea (an arm of the ATLANTIC OCEAN), bordered by NIGER to the north, CHAD and CAMEROON to the east, and Benin to the west. LAGOS is the capital and largest city.
❧ Nigeria has been independent from BRITAIN since 1960, and its independent history has been marked by bloodshed and instability. An ill-fated separatist movement established the secessionist state of Biafra in southeastern Nigeria from 1967 to 1970. ❧ The city-state of Benin, in what is now Nigeria, flourished from the fourteenth to the seventeenth centuries as a center of commerce and CULTURE. It was famous for its cast-gold sculptures. ❧ With over 100 million inhabitants, Nigeria is Africa's most populous country.

Nile River   River originating in central AFRICA and flowing north to the MEDITERRANEAN SEA, with its delta in EGYPT. The Nile proper is formed by the joining of the Blue Nile, which flows from ETHIOPIA, and the White Nile, which flows from LAKE VICTORIA. They meet at KHARTOUM, SUDAN.
❧ At over 4000 miles, it is the longest river in the world. ❧ The Nile River Valley in Egypt is the site of the first great civilization.

North America   Third-largest CONTINENT (after ASIA and AFRICA), comprising CANADA, the United States, MEXICO, and CENTRAL AMERICA.

North Korea   REPUBLIC on northern Korean Peninsula on east coast of ASIA, bounded on the north by CHINA, on the northeast by Russian SIBERIA, on the east by the Sea of Japan, on the south by SOUTH KOREA, and on the west by the Yellow Sea and Korea Bay. Its capital and largest city is P'yongyang.
❧ COMMUNIST country that used to have close ties with the SOVIET UNION and continues to maintain a close relationship with China. ❧ Established in 1948 as a consequence of two occupation zones, northern Korea, administered by the Soviet Union, and southern Korea, administered by the United States, set up after the Allies reclaimed Korea from the Japanese during the final days of WORLD WAR II. ❧ The KOREAN WAR began in 1950, when North Korean forces invaded SOUTH KOREA. Supplied by the Soviets, and eventually joined by the Chinese, North Korea fought forces of South Korea and the UNITED NATIONS.

North Pole   The northern end, or pole, of the EARTH'S AXIS. (*See* ARCTIC *and* ARCTIC OCEAN.)

North Sea   Arm of the ATLANTIC OCEAN northwest of central EUROPE.
❧ Oil was discovered under the sea floor in 1970.

North Yemen   *See* YEMEN.

Northern Hemisphere   The northern half of the EARTH'S surface; the half north of the EQUATOR.

Northern Ireland   Political division of the UNITED KINGDOM, located in northeastern IRELAND. (*See* ULSTER.)
❧ Northern Ireland was created in 1920, when BRITAIN established separate PARLIAMENTS for the parts of Ireland dominated by PROTESTANTS and by ROMAN CATHOLICS. The Protestant portion remained in union with Britain. ❧ Demands for equal civil and economic rights by the Catholic minority, beginning in the late 1960s, led to a renewal of violence between Catholics and Protestants. ❧ The IRISH REPUBLICAN ARMY (IRA), a nationalist organization dedicated to the unification of Ireland, has staged terrorist attacks on British troops in Northern Ireland, as well as other random terrorist attacks in Britain.

Northwest Territories   Territory in northern CANADA made up of several administrative districts, which include all the areas to the north of sixty DEGREES LATITUDE between HUDSON BAY and the YUKON and all the islands in Hudson Bay. Very sparsely populated, these territories make up more than one-third of Canada's total area.

Norway   CONSTITUTIONAL MONARCHY in northern EUROPE, located in western SCANDINAVIA. Its capital and largest city is OSLO.

❦ Norway was occupied by German troops in WORLD WAR II. ❦ Though traditionally neutral, Norway became a member of NATO in 1949. ❦ One of its chief industries is oil production from the NORTH SEA.

Nova Scotia   Province in eastern CANADA, including a PENINSULA to the east of NEW BRUNSWICK and Cape Breton Island, as well as several smaller adjacent islands. With New Brunswick and PRINCE EDWARD ISLAND, Nova Scotia makes up the MARITIME PROVINCES. Halifax is its capital and largest city.

❦ French settlers, who called the area Acadia, were expelled by the British in the 1750s. Many of the exiled Acadians settled in LOUISIANA and became the ancestors of today's Cajuns.

Occident, the   Term referring originally to EUROPE but now including NORTH AMERICA and SOUTH AMERICA as well. *Occident* means "the West," as opposed to *ORIENT*, "the East."

Okinawa (oh-kuh-NAH-wuh, oh-kuh-NOW-uh)   Island in the western PACIFIC OCEAN; part of JAPAN.

❦ During WORLD WAR II, American forces seized the island from Japan in a particularly bloody campaign. It was returned to Japan in 1972.

Oman (oh-MAHN)   Kingdom on the southern and eastern coasts of the ARABIAN PENINSULA on the Arabian Sea, bordered to the northwest by the UNITED ARAB EMIRATES, the west by SAUDI ARABIA, and the southwest by YEMEN. Oman includes a tip of land on one side of the Strait of Hormuz at the entrance to the PERSIAN GULF.

❦ Strategically located on trading and military routes between the Persian Gulf and ASIA and east AFRICA, Oman has been occupied by the Portuguese, the Turks, and the Persians; since the beginning of the nineteenth century, it has maintained close relations with BRITAIN. ❦ Oman began exporting oil in 1967.

Ontario   Province in central CANADA, bordered by HUDSON BAY and James Bay to the north; QUEBEC to the east; the ST. LAWRENCE RIVER, LAKE ONTARIO, LAKE ERIE, LAKE HURON, LAKE SUPERIOR, and MINNESOTA to the south; and MANITOBA to the west. Its capital and largest city is TORONTO.

❦ The Canadian side of NIAGARA FALLS is in southern Ontario. ❦ OTTAWA, Canada's capital, is in southeastern Ontario. ❦ Ontario is the most heavily industrialized and most prosperous province in Canada.

Orient, the   Term referring to ASIA. *Orient* means "the East," as opposed to *OCCIDENT*, "the West."

Oslo   Capital of NORWAY and largest city in the country, located at the head of a FJORD on Norway's southern coast. Norway's main port and chief commercial, industrial, and transportation center.

Ottawa   Capital of CANADA, located in southeastern ONTARIO across the Ottawa River from QUEBEC.

Pacific Ocean   The largest ocean in the world, separating ASIA and AUSTRALIA on the west from NORTH AMERICA and SOUTH AMERICA on the east.

Pakistan   REPUBLIC in southern ASIA, bordered by INDIA to the east, the Arabian Sea (an arm of the INDIAN OCEAN) to the south, IRAN to the southwest, and AFGHANISTAN to the west and north.

❦ Became part of British India in 1857. When India gained its independence in 1947, MOSLEM leaders demanded a separate Moslem state, and the nation of Pakistan was established. Originally, Pakistan consisted of two regions, West Pakistan (now Pakistan) and East Pakistan (now BANGLADESH).

Palermo (puh-LAIR-moh, puh-LUR-moh)   City in northwest SICILY on the Tyrrhenian Sea, an arm of the MEDITERRANEAN SEA. Capital of Sicily.

❦ Palermo's convenient location has made it an important port for trans-Mediterranean shipping for 3000 years. Settled by PHOENICIA in the eighth century B.C., it has come under the influence of many civilizations, including the ROMAN EMPIRE and the BYZANTINE EMPIRE. It has also come under the control of the Arabs and the French. Palermo has long been a center for art and architecture.

Palestine   Historic region on the eastern shore of the MEDITERRANEAN SEA, comprising parts of modern ISRAEL, JORDAN, and EGYPT.

🙢 Known as the HOLY LAND, it is a place of pilgrimage for several religions, including CHRISTIANITY, ISLAM, and JUDAISM. 🙢 Israel, the homeland of the JEWS, was established in Palestine in 1948. 🙢 The PALESTINE LIBERATION ORGANIZATION, under Yasir Arafat, is committed to establishing a Palestinian state, which would include territory on the WEST BANK now occupied by Israel. (*See* ARAB-ISRAELI CONFLICT.)

Panama REPUBLIC on the ISTHMUS of Panama, which connects CENTRAL AMERICA and SOUTH AMERICA, bordered by COSTA RICA to the west, and COLOMBIA to the east. Its capital and largest city is Panama City.

🙢 Backed by the United States, which wanted to negotiate a treaty to build a canal connecting the ATLANTIC and PACIFIC OCEANS, Panama revolted against Colombia, of which it was a part, and declared itself independent in 1903. 🙢 The United States built the PANAMA CANAL from 1904 to 1914, and American relations with Panama have since been shaped by the U.S. presence in the Canal Zone, which divides the country. 🙢 In 1989, the United States invaded Panama and forcibly removed its leader, Manuel Noriega, to the United States, where he has since been tried and convicted for drug trafficking. (*See also* PANAMA CANAL.)

Panama Canal Waterway across the ISTHMUS of Panama. The canal connects the ATLANTIC OCEAN and the PACIFIC OCEAN. The United States built it from 1904 to 1914 on territory leased from PANAMA.

🙢 Conflict between the United States and Panama has centered on control of the canal; a treaty was signed in 1977 returning control of the Canal Zone to Panama by the year 2000. Panama has agreed to neutral operation of the canal.

Paraguay (PAR-uh-gweye, PAR-uh-gway) REPUBLIC in south-central SOUTH AMERICA, enclosed by BOLIVIA on the west and north, BRAZIL on the northeast, and ARGENTINA on the south and west.

🙢 Controlled by a highly repressive government. 🙢 Reputed sanctuary for NAZI fugitives.

Paris Capital of FRANCE and largest city in the country, located in north-central France on the SEINE RIVER. International cultural and intellectual center, as well as the commercial and industrial focus of France.

🙢 In the Treaty of Paris (1783), BRITAIN formally acknowledged the independence of the THIRTEEN COLONIES as the United States. 🙢 During WORLD WAR II, German troops occupied the city from 1940 to 1944. 🙢 In the 1920s, Paris was home to many artists and writers from the United States and other countries. 🙢 The city's tourist attractions include the EIFFEL TOWER, the LOUVRE Museum, and the CATHEDRAL of NOTRE DAME DE PARIS. The CHAMPS ÉLYSÉES is the most famous of its many celebrated streets, avenues, and boulevards. 🙢 Center for fashion and design. 🙢 Called the "City of Light."

Peking (PEE-KING, PAY-KING) *See* BEIJING.

peninsula A body of land enclosed on three sides by water, jutting out from a larger body of land.

People's Republic of China The official name for mainland CHINA, which has a COMMUNIST government.

Persian Gulf Arm of the INDIAN OCEAN between ARABIA and IRAN.

🙢 The Persian Gulf oil fields are among the most productive in the world. 🙢 The Persian Gulf region was dominated by BRITAIN for most of this century. After Britain's withdrawal in the late 1960s, the UNITED STATES and the SOVIET UNION competed for influence in the region.

Peru REPUBLIC in western SOUTH AMERICA, bordered by the PACIFIC OCEAN to the west, ECUADOR to the northwest, COLOMBIA to the northeast, BRAZIL and BOLIVIA to the east, and CHILE to the south. Its capital and largest city is LIMA.

🙢 Achieved independence from SPAIN in 1821. 🙢 Peru was the heart of the INCA Empire, which flourished from the twelfth to the sixteenth centuries. The remains of the empire include the fabled stone fortress of Machu Picchu.

Philippines REPUBLIC in the southwestern PACIFIC OCEAN, comprising over 7000 islands. Its capital and largest city is Manila.

🙢 The Spanish held control of the islands until 1898, when they were transferred to the United States after the SPANISH-AMERICAN WAR. 🙢 Named for Philip II, king of SPAIN during the sixteenth century. 🙢 Occupied by the Japanese during WORLD WAR II, the islands were liberated by Allied troops under General Douglas MacArthur. 🙢 Although Philippine independence had long been an important political issue, the country did not gain full independence until 1946. ▨ The country was under the virtual DICTATORSHIP of Ferdinand Marcos from 1965 until 1986, when he was forced into exile in the United States.

Poland REPUBLIC in central EUROPE, bordered by the BALTIC SEA and RUSSIA to the north, LITHUANIA to the northeast, BELARUS and UKRAINE to the east, CZECHOSLOVAKIA to the south, and GERMANY to the west. Its capital and largest city is Warsaw.

▨ The invasion of Poland by GERMANY in 1939 precipitated WORLD WAR II. ▨ During World War II, about six million Poles, including three million Polish JEWS, died from a deliberate German policy of starvation, outright massacres, and mass executions carried out in CONCENTRATION CAMPS such as AUSCHWITZ. ▨ In 1952, Poland became a people's republic on the Soviet model. ▨ The SOLIDARITY movement, which demanded greater worker control in Poland, emerged in the early 1980s as one of the first signs of popular discontent with single-party rule and the COMMUNIST economic system. ▨ In 1989 Solidarity-backed candidates swept to victory in free elections.

Polynesia Group of islands in the central and southern PACIFIC OCEAN, including the islands of the state of HAWAII and the islands of French Polynesia. TAHITI and SAMOA are in Polynesia, which means "many islands."

Portugal REPUBLIC in southwestern EUROPE, bordered by SPAIN to the north and east, and the ATLANTIC OCEAN to the south and west. Its capital and largest city is LISBON.

▨ Member of NATO since 1949. ▨ Famous for its explorers in the fifteenth and sixteenth centuries. Such exploration was closely followed by colonization. By the middle of the sixteenth century, Portugal controlled a vast overseas empire, including BRAZIL. ▨ Portugal has been independent since the twelfth century, except for sixty years of Spanish rule in the late sixteenth and early seventeenth centuries.

Prague (PRAHG) Capital of the Czech Republic, situated on both banks of the Vltava River. The republic's largest city, as well as its most important industrial city; a leading European industrial and commercial center.

▨ From the fourteenth to the early seventeenth centuries, the emperors of the HOLY ROMAN EMPIRE resided at Prague as well as at VIENNA. ▨ In 1968, Prague was the center of Czech resistance to the Soviet invasion.

Pretoria (pri-TAWR-ee-uh) Administrative capital of SOUTH AFRICA. (*See also* CAPE TOWN.)

prime meridian The MERIDIAN at zero DEGREES LONGITUDE. All longitude is measured relative to the prime meridian, which passes through GREENWICH, ENGLAND.

Prince Edward Island Province in eastern CANADA in the Gulf of St. Lawrence, an arm of the ATLANTIC OCEAN, separated by the Northumberland Strait from NOVA SCOTIA and NEW BRUNSWICK, with which it makes up the MARITIME PROVINCES. Canada's smallest province. Charlottetown is its capital and largest city.

Prussia Former state in north-central GERMANY. At the height of its power, Prussia occupied more than half of present-day Germany, stretching from The NETHERLANDS and BELGIUM in the west to LITHUANIA in the east.

▨ During the eighteenth century, Prussia established its independence from POLAND, built up a strong army, and undertook a successful campaign of conquest throughout north-central Europe. ▨ In the nineteenth century, Prussia led the economic and political unification of the German states, establishing itself as the largest and most influential of these states, with BERLIN as the capital of the German Empire. ▨ After Germany's defeat in WORLD WAR II, Prussia was abolished as a state, and its territory was divided among EAST GERMANY, WEST GERMANY, the SOVIET UNION, and Poland. ▨ Prussians are often depicted as authoritarian, militaristic, and extremely orderly, a characterization based on the unswerving obedience of their army.

Pyongyang (PYUNG-YAHNG, PYAWNG-YAHNG) Capital of NORTH KOREA and largest city in the country, located in west-central North Korea.

▨ Korea's oldest city, but little remains from its 3000-year history, the city having been devastated on several occasions by JAPAN and in the KOREAN WAR.

Pyrenees (PIR-uh-neez) Mountain chain in southwestern EUROPE, between FRANCE and SPAIN, extending from the BAY OF BISCAY on the west to the MEDITERRANEAN SEA on the east.

Qatar (KAH-tahr, kuh-TAHR) Kingdom on the ARABIAN PENINSULA, located on a small PENINSULA extending into the PERSIAN GULF, bordered to the south by SAUDI ARABIA and the UNITED ARAB EMIRATES.

🍂 British PROTECTORATE from 1916 to 1971. 🍂 Qatar has successfully exploited its oil reserves since 1949.

Quebec Province in eastern CANADA, bordered to the east by NEWFOUNDLAND, the ATLANTIC OCEAN, and the Gulf of St. Lawrence (an arm of the ATLANTIC OCEAN); to the southeast by NEW BRUNSWICK and several states of the United States; to the southwest by ONTARIO; to the west by Ontario and HUDSON BAY; and to the north by islands of the NORTHWEST TERRITORIES. Its capital is QUEBEC CITY, and its largest city is MONTREAL.

🍂 French colony from 1663 to 1759, when it was lost to the British. 🍂 Canada's largest province in area and second largest in population, after Ontario. 🍂 With French as its official language, Quebec has experienced tensions between its majority French and minority English CULTURES.

Quebec City Capital of QUEBEC province, CANADA, on the ST. LAWRENCE RIVER.

🍂 Largely French-speaking. 🍂 One of the oldest cities in NORTH AMERICA, founded in the early seventeenth century.

Red China A pejorative name for the PEOPLE'S REPUBLIC OF CHINA. The term *mainland China* is preferred.

Red Sea Narrow sea between AFRICA and the ARABIAN PENINSULA.

🍂 Probably named for the red ALGAE that are sometimes present in its waters. 🍂 According to the BIBLE, the Red Sea's waters parted to allow the Israelites, led by MOSES, to escape the pursuing Egyptian army. The "Red Sea" of the biblical account, however, seems more likely to have been the marshy Sea of Reeds than the present-day Red Sea.

Republic of China *See* TAIWAN.

Republic of Korea *See* SOUTH KOREA.

Republic of South Africa *See* SOUTH AFRICA.

Republic of Yemen *See* YEMEN.

Rhine River River in EUROPE, rising in the ALPS of SWITZERLAND and flowing generally north, passing through or bordering on Switzerland, LIECHTENSTEIN, AUSTRIA, GERMANY, FRANCE, and The NETHERLANDS before emptying into the NORTH SEA.

🍂 A principal river of Europe, carrying more traffic than any other waterway in the world.

Rhineland Picturesque region of GERMANY, along the RHINE RIVER.

Rhodesia (roh-DEE-zhuh) Former name of ZIMBABWE, a nation in southeastern AFRICA.

🍂 Rhodesia was named for Cecil Rhodes, the English industrialist whose British South Africa Company colonized the region at the end of the nineteenth century. He also founded the RHODES SCHOLARSHIPS for study at OXFORD UNIVERSITY.

Rhone River Major river in FRANCE, rising in the ALPS of SWITZERLAND, flowing west through Lake Geneva, and southwest and south across France. It enters the MEDITERRANEAN SEA near MARSEILLES.

🍂 The Rhone Valley south of LYON is known for its vineyards and its fruit and vegetable gardens.

Rio de Janeiro (REE-oh day, dee zhuh-NAIR-oh) City in southeastern BRAZIL on the ATLANTIC OCEAN. Second-largest city in Brazil, after SÃO PAULO; its former capital; and its financial, commercial, transportation, and cultural center.

🍂 Famous as a tourist attraction. Especially popular are its beaches, particularly the Copacabana. 🍂 Rio's annual carnival is world-famous.

Riviera Narrow strip of land in southeastern FRANCE and northwestern ITALY on the MEDITERRANEAN SEA, also including MONACO. CANNES, MONTE CARLO, and NICE are three of its best-known towns and cities.

🍂 Its scenic beauty and mild CLIMATE make it a popular vacation area. 🍂 The French Riviera is also called the Côte d'Azur (the azure coast).

Rome Capital of ITALY, largest city in the country, and seat of the ROMAN CATHOLIC CHURCH (*see* VATICAN CITY STATE; *see also* VATICAN), located on the Tiber River in west-central Italy. One of the world's great centers of history, art, architecture, and religion.

🍂 Rome was the capital of the Roman REPUBLIC (fourth century to first century B.C.) and the ROMAN EMPIRE (first century B.C. to fifth century A.D.), whose domains, at their height, spread from GREAT BRITAIN to present-day IRAN and included all the lands surrounding the MEDITERRANEAN SEA. ᐳᐠ In A.D. 800, Rome again became associated with imperial power when CHARLEMAGNE was crowned there as the first emperor of the HOLY ROMAN EMPIRE. ᐳᐠ Rome was proclaimed capital of Italy in 1870, after Italian forces took control of the city from the POPE. ᐳᐠ Called the "Eternal City." ᐳᐠ "ALL ROADS LEAD TO ROME" is a well-known PROVERB. ᐳᐠ Ancient Rome is often referred to as the "City of Seven Hills" because it was built on seven hills surrounded by a line of fortifications. ᐳᐠ Landmarks include the COLOSSEUM, the Appian Way, the Pantheon, the Forum, the Arch of Constantine, and SAINT PETER'S BASILICA in the Vatican.

Rotterdam   City in the western NETHERLANDS, near the NORTH SEA. Second-largest city in The Netherlands, after AMSTERDAM, and its major foreign-trade center.

ᐳᐠ The center of the city was destroyed during WORLD WAR II by German bombs.

Ruhr Valley (ROOR)   Valley of the Ruhr River, in west-central GERMANY; Germany's principal industrial region.

Rumania   REPUBLIC in southeastern EUROPE on the northeast BALKAN PENINSULA, bordered by HUNGARY to the northwest, UKRAINE to the northeast, MOLDOVA and the BLACK SEA to the east, BULGARIA to the south, and the former YUGOSLAVIA to the southwest. Its capital and largest city is BUCHAREST.

ᐳᐠ During WORLD WAR II, Rumania was allied to the AXIS POWERS, but joined the ALLIES in 1944. ᐳᐠ Occupied by Soviet troops in 1944, Rumania became a people's republic on the model of the SOVIET UNION in 1947. ᐳᐠ Former EASTERN BLOC country ruled in the 1970s and 1980s by COMMUNIST dictator Nicolae Ceausescu, who was overthrown and executed during a bloody revolution in 1989. (*See* COLLAPSE OF COMMUNISM.)

Russia   A vast nation that stretches from eastern EUROPE across the EURASIAN land mass. It was the most powerful republic of the former SOVIET UNION, of which ethnic Russians composed about half of the population. It is the world's largest country. Its capital and largest city is MOSCOW.

ᐳᐠ Russia was ruled by CZARS of the ROMANOV family from the seventeenth to the twentieth centuries. ᐳᐠ PETER THE GREAT, a czar who reigned in the late seventeenth and early eighteenth centuries, at-

tempted to westernize Russian government and CULTURE. ᐳᐠ During the RUSSIAN REVOLUTION of 1917, the BOLSHEVIKS, under LENIN, took control of the government; COMMUNISTS governed from 1917 until 1991. ᐳᐠ Russia now occupies the seat on the Security Council of the UNITED NATIONS formerly held by the Soviet Union.

Sahara   Desert in northern AFRICA.

ᐳᐠ At approximately 3.5 million square miles, it is the world's largest desert.

Saigon (seye-GON)   City in southern VIETNAM; capital of South Vietnam from 1954 to 1975.

ᐳᐠ A commercial, industrial, and transportation hub of SOUTHEAST ASIA, Saigon enjoyed rapid growth and cultural prestige as the capital of French INDOCHINA. ᐳᐠ Headquarters for American and South Vietnamese forces during the VIETNAM WAR. ᐳᐠ Renamed HO CHI MINH CITY by the victorious Vietnamese COMMUNISTS in 1976.

Saint Petersburg   City in northwestern RUSSIA, situated at the head of the Gulf of Finland on both banks of the Neva River and on the islands of its delta. Second-largest city in Russia; major port, and one of the world's leading industrial and cultural centers.

ᐳᐠ The first Russian city modeled after European cities, it was founded in 1703 by PETER THE GREAT, who wanted to make it his "window to the West"; renamed Petrograd at the start of WORLD WAR I and then LENINGRAD in 1924 in honor of LENIN. ᐳᐠ German forces besieged the city during WORLD WAR II, during which time around a million inhabitants died, mostly from starvation. The city was badly damaged by German bombers and artillery. ᐳᐠ Because it is so far north, St. Petersburg experiences "white nights" for three weeks in June when the sky never completely darkens. ᐳᐠ Location of the historic Winter Palace, which was sacked during the RUSSIAN REVOLUTION but later became the Hermitage Museum. ᐳᐠ With the COLLAPSE OF COMMUNISM the city was renamed St. Petersburg.

Samoa   A group of volcanic (*see* VOLCANO) islands in the south PACIFIC OCEAN, approximately midway between HAWAII and SYDNEY, AUSTRALIA, making up the independent kingdom of Western Samoa and the United States territory of American Samoa.

ᐳᐠ Samoa's tropical CLIMATE, mountainous scenery, CORAL reefs, and POLYNESIAN CULTURE make it a popular tourist destination.

San Salvador   Capital of EL SALVADOR and largest city in the country, located in central El Salvador.

  ❧ Has suffered from recurrent and severe EARTHQUAKES.

Santiago (san-tee-AH-goh, sahn-tee-AH-goh)   Capital of CHILE and largest city in the country, located in central Chile. Commercial and political center of Chile and one of the largest cities in SOUTH AMERICA.

São Paulo (sownn-POW-looh, sownn-POW-loh)   Ultramodern city in southeastern BRAZIL. Largest city in Brazil and in SOUTH AMERICA.

Sarajevo (sar-uh-YAY-voh, sahr-uh-YAY-voh)   Capital of BOSNIA AND HERZEGOVINA.

  ❧ Site of the assassination of Austrian Archduke FRANCIS FERDINAND in 1914, which was the immediate cause of WORLD WAR I. (*See under "World History since 1550."*) ❧ Attacked and severely damaged in 1992 by Serbian militia.

Sardinia   Italian island in the MEDITERRANEAN SEA west of the mainland of ITALY.

  ❧ The kingdom of Sardinia, which was founded in the early eighteenth century, became the nucleus of united Italy during the nineteenth century.

Saskatchewan   Province in west-central CANADA, bordered to the north by the NORTHWEST TERRITORIES, to the east by MANITOBA, to the south by NORTH DAKOTA and MONTANA, and to the west by ALBERTA. Its capital and largest city is Regina.

  ❧ Some of the world's largest wheat fields grow on Saskatchewan's vast unbroken prairie.

Saudi Arabia (SOW-dee, SAW-dee, sah-OOH-dee)   MONARCHY occupying most of the ARABIAN PENINSULA, where it is bordered by JORDAN, IRAQ, a neutral zone, and KUWAIT to the north; the PERSIAN GULF, QATAR, and the UNITED ARAB EMIRATES to the east; OMAN to the east and south; YEMEN to the south; and the RED SEA and the Gulf of Aqaba to the west. Its capital and largest city is Riyadh.

  ❧ Saudi Arabia sits on at least one-fourth of the world's known oil reserves, a geological gift that makes this otherwise resource-poor, desert nation very rich and important to the industrial nations of the world. ❧ Overwhelmingly MOSLEM, the country is ruled by a royal family according to conservative Moslem law. ❧ Location of MECCA and Medina, the two most holy places in the world for Moslems, pilgrimage sites equivalent to the Catholic ROME and the Christian and Jewish JERUSALEM. ❧ Saudi Arabia became the major staging ground for United Nations forces seeking to expel Iraq from Kuwait in 1990–1991. (*See* PERSIAN GULF WAR.)

savanna   A tropical land mass of grassland and scattered trees.

Scandinavia   The region in northern EUROPE containing NORWAY, SWEDEN, and DENMARK and the PENINSULAS they occupy. Through cultural, historical, and political associations, FINLAND and ICELAND are often considered part of Scandinavia.

Scotland   One of the four countries that make up the UNITED KINGDOM OF GREAT BRITAIN AND NORTHERN IRELAND. Contains the northern portion of the island of GREAT BRITAIN and many surrounding islands. Its capital is EDINBURGH, and its largest city is GLASGOW.

  ❧ Bagpipes and kilts are well-known SYMBOLS of Scotland.

Seine River (SEN)   River in FRANCE flowing generally northwest through northern France.

  ❧ Flows through the heart of PARIS, dividing the LEFT BANK, south of the Seine, from the Right Bank, north of the Seine. ❧ Chief commercial waterway of France.

Senegal   REPUBLIC in western AFRICA, bordered by the ATLANTIC OCEAN to the west, Mauritania to the north, Mali to the east, and Guinea and Guinea-Bissau to the south. Dakar is the capital and largest city.

  ❧ Senegal was a French colony from 1895 to 1958. It became fully independent in 1960.

Seoul (SOHL)   Capital of SOUTH KOREA and largest city in the country, located in northwestern South Korea. Political, commercial, industrial, transportation, and cultural center of South Korea.

  ❧ Became the capital in 1948, with the establishment of NORTH KOREA and South Korea. ❧ The city was heavily damaged during the KOREAN WAR. ❧ Home of the 1988 Summer Olympics.

Seven Seas, the   Popular expression for all of the world's oceans.

Seville   City in southwestern SPAIN on the Guadalquivir River. Major port and cultural center.

  ❧ Capital of bullfighting in Spain. ❧ Two famous

OPERAS, *Carmen* and *The Barber of Seville*, are set in Seville. 🔊 According to legend, DON JUAN lived in Seville.

Shanghai   Largest city in CHINA, located in the eastern part of the country on the PACIFIC OCEAN.

🔊 Most populous city in ASIA. 🔊 One of the world's great seaports. 🔊 Opened to foreign trade by the Treaty of Nanking in 1842, Shanghai became a treaty port administered by BRITAIN, the United States, and FRANCE until WORLD WAR II.

Sheffield   City in northern ENGLAND.

🔊 One of England's leading industrial centers, famous for cutlery manufacture and heavy steel GOODS.

Siberia   Region of RUSSIA stretching from north-central to northeastern ASIA.

🔊 Known for its vast space, long and severely cold winters, and few inhabitants widely scattered in small settlements, Siberia has been for many centuries a place of political and criminal exile for Russians who anger the government's authorities. 🔊 As a consequence of Siberia's harsh conditions and its historical function as a place of punishment, to be "sent to Siberia" has become a metaphor for demotion, disgrace, or other forms of status diminution.

Sicily   Island in southern ITALY on the MEDITERRANEAN SEA, separated from the Italian mainland by the narrow Strait of Messina. Its capital is PALERMO.

🔊 Largest Mediterranean island.

Sierra Leone (see-ER-uh lee-OHN, lee-OH-nee)   REPUBLIC in western AFRICA, bordered by the ATLANTIC OCEAN to the west, Guinea to the north and east, and LIBERIA to the south. Freetown is its capital and largest city.

🔊 After the AMERICAN REVOLUTION, attempts were made to settle freed slaves in Sierra Leone. 🔊 Formerly a British PROTECTORATE, Sierra Leone became independent in 1961.

Sinai (SEYE-neye)   PENINSULA in northeastern EGYPT, bordered by the Gulf of Aqaba, an arm of the RED SEA, to the east, and the Gulf of Suez, another arm of the Red Sea, to the west.

🔊 Scene of fighting during the ARAB-ISRAELI CONFLICT. ISRAEL conquered and occupied Sinai in the SIX-DAY WAR but returned the region to Egypt in 1982. 🔊 In the BIBLE, MOSES received the TEN COMMANDMENTS on MOUNT SINAI.

Singapore   An island REPUBLIC in SOUTHEAST ASIA at the southern tip of the Malay PENINSULA.

🔊 British colony from 1946 to 1959, when it became independent. 🔊 Though only 225 square miles in size, a major economic power in ASIA. 🔊 One of the world's biggest and busiest ports.

Slovenia (sloh-VEE-nee-uh, sloh-VEEN-yuh)   REPUBLIC in southeastern EUROPE at the top western corner of the BALKAN PENINSULA, bordered by AUSTRIA to the north, HUNGARY to the northeast, CROATIA to the east and south, and the ADRIATIC SEA and ITALY to the west. Its capital and largest city is Ljubljana.

🔊 Often considered the most "European" of the former republics of YUGOSLAVIA, Slovenia declared its independence in 1991. In the wake of this proclamation, Yugoslav troops attacked Slovenia, but without success.

Somalia (soh-MAH-lee-uh, soh-MAHL-yuh)   REPUBLIC in extreme eastern AFRICA, directly south of the ARABIAN PENINSULA across the Gulf of Aden, bordered by ETHIOPIA and KENYA to the west. Mogadishu is the capital and largest city.

🔊 BRITAIN, FRANCE, and ITALY established PROTECTORATES in the area in the late 1880s. Somalia gained independence in 1960. 🔊 Civil war and famine have recently ravaged the country. In 1992, the UNITED STATES embarked on a humanitarian intervention designed to ensure delivery of food supplies to the population.

South Africa   Officially the REPUBLIC OF SOUTH AFRICA, a nation at the southern tip of AFRICA spanning the CAPE OF GOOD HOPE where the ATLANTIC OCEAN meets the INDIAN OCEAN. It is bordered by NAMIBIA, BOTSWANA, and ZIMBABWE to the north, and MOZAMBIQUE to the northeast. Its capitals are PRETORIA for its administrative government and CAPE TOWN for its legislature. (*See also* JOHANNESBURG.)

🔊 Dutch settlers, known as BOERS, were the first Europeans to migrate in large numbers to the territories that now make up South Africa. BRITAIN was granted the territory surrounding the Cape of Good Hope at the Congress of VIENNA, and friction between the British and Dutch remained a constant in the region. Tensions were increased by the discovery of gold and diamonds in the late nineteenth century and came to a head in the Boer War (1899–1902), in which the British defeated the Dutch-descended Afrikaners. 🔊 South Africa's policy of APARTHEID, the aggressive separation of the races and enforcement of the inferior political STATUS of all nonwhites, has been the hallmark of its internal political system. South Africa's race policies are the subject of continuing international protest and economic sanctions. ❧ Black South Africans, who constitute approximately 70 percent of the nation, have protested the draconian racist policies of the white minority through such organizations as the African National Congress (ANC), headed by Nelson MANDELA, who has spent most of his life in jail as a political prisoner. ❧ Under President F. W. De Klerk, the white minority government released Nelson Mandela from jail in 1990 and repealed some of the major laws establishing apartheid.

South America CONTINENT in the Western HEMISPHERE, connected to NORTH AMERICA by the ISTHMUS of PANAMA.
  ❧ Exploration of the continent began in the sixteenth century with the Portugese claiming what is now BRAZIL and the Spanish claiming most of the remaining land. Settlement was accompanied by the defeat of many of the NATIVE AMERICAN CULTURES, including the INCA Empire. ❧ All of the Latin American nations in South America and CENTRAL AMERICA achieved their independence from SPAIN or PORTUGAL in the first half of the nineteenth century.

South Korea Officially the REPUBLIC of KOREA; located on the PENINSULA separating the Yellow Sea and the Sea of Japan, two arms of the PACIFIC OCEAN. Its capital and largest city is SEOUL.
  ❧ Supported by the United States, South Korea was created in 1948 after American and Soviet occupation zones established at the end of WORLD WAR II had divided Korea into north and south. ❧ During the KOREAN WAR, noncommunist South Korea, aided by forces of the UNITED NATIONS, and COMMUNIST NORTH KOREA, aided by Chinese forces, fought from 1950 to 1953. ❧ During the 1980s South Korea became a major industrial power in Asia.

South Pole The southern end or pole of the EARTH'S AXIS. (See ANTARCTIC and ANTARCTICA.)

South Sea Islands The islands in the SOUTH SEAS.

South Seas The central, southern, and southwestern portions of the PACIFIC OCEAN.

Southeast Asia A geographical subdivision of ASIA that includes the following nations: BURMA, CAMBODIA, INDONESIA, LAOS, MALAYSIA, the PHILIPPINES, SINGAPORE, THAILAND, and VIETNAM.

Southern Hemisphere The southern half of the EARTH'S surface; the earth's surface south of the EQUATOR.

Southern Yemen *See* YEMEN.

Soviet Union *See under "World History since 1550."*

Soweto (suh-WET-oh, suh-WAY-toh) Collective name for a group of townships inhabited by black Africans, located southwest of JOHANNESBURG, SOUTH AFRICA.
  ❧ Site of severe racial violence.

Spain Constitutional monarchy in southwestern EUROPE, consisting of the Spanish mainland (bordered to the northwest by FRANCE and to the west by PORTUGAL), the Balearic Islands in the MEDITERRANEAN SEA, and the Canary Islands in the ATLANTIC OCEAN. Its capital and largest city is MADRID.
  ❧ During the sixteenth century, Spain was the greatest world power. Its success was based partially on the riches it acquired in the NEW WORLD (*see* LATIN AMERICA *and* SOUTH AMERICA). ❧ The destruction of the Spanish ARMADA, a fleet sent to conquer ENGLAND in 1588, marked the beginning of the decline of Spanish power. ❧ In the SPANISH-AMERICAN WAR, the United States defeated Spain, freed CUBA from Spanish colonial rule, and seized a number of former Spanish colonies, including Puerto Rico, Guam, and the PHILIPPINES. ❧ In the SPANISH CIVIL WAR conservatives led by General Francisco FRANCO overthrew the second Spanish REPUBLIC. ❧ The Spanish MONARCHY was fully restored in 1975 after Franco's death. He had been dictator (*see* DICTATORSHIP) for thirty-six years. ❧ Under King Juan Carlos, Spain has established a political democracy and has been integrated into the European community. ❧ Bullfighting is a popular spectator sport in Spain.

Sri Lanka (sree LAHNG-kuh) Formerly CEYLON, now an island REPUBLIC in the INDIAN OCEAN just southeast of INDIA.
  ❧ A British colony since 1796, the island became

independent in 1948. 🕬 Marked by hostility among its ethnic groups.

Stalingrad (STAH-lin-grad, STAH-lin-grahd) *See* VOLGOGRAD.

steppes (STEPS) Vast grassy plains associated with eastern RUSSIA and SIBERIA.

Stockholm Capital of SWEDEN and largest city in the country, located in southern Sweden on the BALTIC SEA.

🕬 Each year the NOBEL PRIZES (except the prize for peace) are awarded in Stockholm.

Stuttgart (STOOT-gahrt, SHTOOT-gahrt) City in southwestern GERMANY.

🕬 Famous for the innovative architecture of many of its buildings.

sub-Saharan Region in AFRICA south of the SAHARA desert.

Sudan (sooh-DAN) REPUBLIC in northeastern AFRICA, bordered on the north by EGYPT; on the east by the RED SEA and ETHIOPIA; on the south by KENYA, UGANDA, and ZAIRE; and on the west by the Central African Republic, CHAD, and LIBYA. Its capital is KHARTOUM, and its largest city is Omdurman.

🕬 Sudan was under the joint rule of BRITAIN and Egypt (though Britain exercised actual control) from 1899 to 1956. 🕬 Recently, it has been plagued by famine and civil war.

Sumatra (soo-MAH-truh) Island in INDONESIA in the INDIAN OCEAN northwest of JAVA and west of MALAYSIA.

🕬 Though much of the island is covered by swampland and impenetrable rain forest, Sumatra's industries — including oil, coal, gold, silver, rubber, timber, and tobacco — produce over half of Indonesia's INCOME.

Swaziland (SWAH-zee-land) Kingdom in southeastern AFRICA, bordered by SOUTH AFRICA to the south, west, and north, and MOZAMBIQUE to the east.

🕬 In 1903, Swaziland became a British territory. It became fully independent in 1968. 🕬 Today the Swazi people resist Afrikaner demands for incorporation into South Africa.

Sweden CONSTITUTIONAL MONARCHY in northern EUROPE, in the eastern part of SCANDINAVIA. Its capital and largest city is STOCKHOLM.

🕬 Traditionally neutral, Sweden maintained its neutrality through both WORLD WAR I and WORLD WAR II. 🕬 Known for its advanced and comprehensive social welfare legislation.

Switzerland Republic in central EUROPE, bordered by FRANCE to the west, GERMANY to the north, LIECHTENSTEIN and AUSTRIA to the east, and ITALY to the east and south. Its capital is Bern, and its largest city is ZURICH.

🕬 Known for its strict neutrality, Switzerland maintained armed neutrality in both WORLD WAR I and WORLD WAR II. 🕬 Swiss banks allow depositors to be identified by a number known only to the depositor and a few bank officials; private fortunes can therefore be kept secret. 🕬 Famous for its watchmaking industry and its milk chocolate.

Sydney Largest city in AUSTRALIA, located in the southeastern part of the country, surrounding Port Jackson inlet on the PACIFIC OCEAN. Capital and largest city of New South Wales state. Australia's chief port and main cultural and industrial center.

🕬 Founded in 1788 as Australia's first settlement for convicts from BRITAIN.

Syria REPUBLIC in the MIDDLE EAST, bordered by TURKEY to the northwest, north, and northeast, IRAQ to the east and south, JORDAN to the south, and ISRAEL, the MEDITERRANEAN SEA, and LEBANON to the west. Its capital and largest city is DAMASCUS.

🕬 Established from former OTTOMAN territory in 1920 but dominated by FRANCE until the 1940s. 🕬 Extremely hostile toward Israel. 🕬 In the SIX-DAY WAR, in 1967, Israeli troops dislodged Syrian forces from the GOLAN HEIGHTS, which overlook Israeli territory.

Tahiti Largest island of French POLYNESIA, located in the south PACIFIC OCEAN.

🕬 Attracted by the Polynesian CULTURE and spectacular CLIMATE and scenery, both Paul GAUGUIN and Robert Louis STEVENSON lived in Tahiti and expressed its romantic allure through their works.

Taipei (TEYE-PAY, TEYE-BAY) Capital of TAIWAN and largest city in the country, located in northern Taiwan.

🕬 In 1949, Taipei became the headquarters of CHIANG KAI-SHEK's Chinese Nationalists, who had been forced to flee mainland CHINA.

Taiwan Island nation in the PACIFIC OCEAN near the mainland of southern CHINA; seat of the REPUBLIC OF CHINA. Its capital and largest city is TAIPEI.

๛ When the Chinese COMMUNISTS came to power on the mainland, the Nationalist government of CHIANG KAI-SHEK and some of his army took refuge on Taiwan. ๛ The United States long supported the Nationalists but broke relations in 1979 to establish relations with the PEOPLE'S REPUBLIC OF CHINA.

Tajikistan (tah-JIK-uh-stan, tah-JIK-uh-stahn, tah-JEE-kuh-stan, tah-JEE-kuh-stahn) REPUBLIC in central ASIA, bounded by UZBEKISTAN to the west and northwest, KYRGYZSTAN to the north, CHINA to the east, and AFGHANISTAN to the south. Its capital and largest city is Dushanbe.

๛ This former member of the SOVIET UNION declared its independence in 1991. ๛ Tajikistan is predominantly MOSLEM.

Tanzania (tan-zuh-NEE-uh) REPUBLIC in eastern AFRICA, formed in 1964 by the union of Tanganyika and Zanzibar. It is bordered to the north by UGANDA, LAKE VICTORIA, and KENYA; to the east by the INDIAN OCEAN, to the south by MOZAMBIQUE, Malowi, and ZAMBIA, and to the west by ZAIRE, Burundi, and Rwanda. Its capital and largest city is Dar es Salaam.

๛ Louis B. LEAKEY, a British anthropologist, found the remains of a direct ancestor of the present human SPECIES, about 1.75 million years old, at Olduvai Gorge in northeastern Tanzania.

Teheran (te-RAHN, te-RAN, tay-uh-RAHN, tay-uh-RAN) Capital of IRAN and largest city in the country, located in northern Iran.

๛ Site of the Teheran Conference (1943), at which United States President Franklin ROOSEVELT, British PRIME MINISTER Winston CHURCHILL, and Soviet PREMIER Joseph STALIN met and agreed on Allied war plans and postwar cooperation in the UNITED NATIONS.

Thailand CONSTITUTIONAL MONARCHY in southern SOUTHEAST ASIA, bordered by BURMA to the west and northwest, LAOS to the north and east, CAMBODIA to the southeast, and the Gulf of Siam (an arm of the PACIFIC OCEAN) and MALAYSIA to the south. Its capital and largest city is BANGKOK.

๛ Formerly called Siam. ๛ Strongly supported the United States during the VIETNAM WAR. Thailand was the site of American air bases until 1976, when relations with the United States deteriorated.

Thames River (TEMZ) Longest river in ENGLAND, flowing generally eastward across southern England and through LONDON to the NORTH SEA.

๛ During industrialization in England, the Thames was particularly important because industries were established on the banks of the river. ๛ Passes famous buildings in London such as the Tower of London and the Houses of PARLIAMENT.

Tibet Region in southwestern CHINA, bordered by BURMA to the southeast; INDIA, Bhutan, and NEPAL to the south; India to the west; and Chinese provinces to the north and east. Located in the HIMALAYAS.

๛ The Dalai LAMA, religious and civil leader of Tibet, was forced into exile in 1959, when the Chinese annexed the country.

Tijuana (tee-uh-WAH-nuh, tee-WAH-nuh) City in Baja California Norte state, in northwestern MEXICO just south of the CALIFORNIA border near SAN DIEGO.

๛ Popular among American tourists for its racetracks and bullfights.

Timbuktu (tim-buk-TOOH) City in central Mali, in western AFRICA, near the NIGER River.

๛ By the fourteenth century, it was famous for its gold trade.

Tokyo Capital of JAPAN and largest city in the country, located on the island of Honshu at the head of Tokyo Bay. Administrative, financial, educational, and cultural center of Japan.

๛ One of the world's largest and most modern cities. ๛ Heavily damaged by Allied bombing during WORLD WAR II. ๛ Became capital of the Japanese Empire in 1868 when Japan began a period of intensive modernization.

Toronto Capital of ONTARIO, CANADA, and largest city in the province, in southern Ontario on LAKE ONTARIO. Largest city in Canada. Commercial, financial, industrial, and cultural center.

Trinidad and Tobago (tuh-BAY-goh) Independent REPUBLIC in the WEST INDIES, comprising two islands off the northeast coast of VENEZUELA. Its capital and largest city is Port-of-Spain.

🖎 Popular resort area, appreciated particularly for its CULTURE, which is composed of a mixture of black African, Indian, Chinese, European, and Middle Eastern settlers.

Tripoli (TRIP-uh-lee)   Capital of LIBYA and largest city in the country, located in northwestern Libya.

🖎 The city dates back to the seventh century B.C. 🖎 United States war planes attacked Tripoli in 1986 in retaliation for Libyan terrorist acts against American citizens.

Tropic of Cancer   Imaginary line that circles the EARTH about one-quarter of the way from the EQUATOR to the NORTH POLE. The SUN is directly overhead at the summer SOLSTICE.

Tropic of Capricorn   Imaginary line that circles the EARTH about one-quarter of the way from the EQUATOR to the SOUTH POLE. The SUN is directly overhead at the winter SOLSTICE.

Tunisia   REPUBLIC in northwestern AFRICA, bordered by ALGERIA to the west, the MEDITERRANEAN SEA to the north and east, and LIBYA to the southeast.

🖎 In the sixth century B.C., Tunisia became the center of power for the city of CARTHAGE. 🖎 Tunisia was a French PROTECTORATE from 1881 to 1956, when it achieved independence.

Turkey   REPUBLIC straddling southeastern EUROPE and the MIDDLE EAST, bordered by the BLACK SEA to the north, GEORGIA and ARMENIA to the northeast, IRAN to the east, IRAQ and SYRIA to the southeast, the MEDITERRANEAN SEA and the AEGEAN SEA to the southwest, and GREECE and BULGARIA to the northwest. Ninety-seven percent of the country is in ASIA. ANKARA is its capital, but ISTANBUL is its largest city and former imperial capital.

🖎 The OTTOMAN EMPIRE emerged in Anatolia (the western portion of Asian Turkey) during the thirteenth century and survived until 1918. At its height, during the sixteenth century, the empire stretched from the PERSIAN GULF to western ALGERIA and included all of southeastern Europe. 🖎 The declining Ottoman Empire allied with GERMANY, AUSTRIA, and BULGARIA in WORLD WAR I, and suffered disintegration and Greek occupation at the end of the war. 🖎 After the rise of a nationalist movement led by Kemal Ataturk, the Republic of Turkey was established in 1923. 🖎 In 1871, the archaeologist and scholar Heinrich Schliemann discovered the site of ancient TROY on the west coast of Asian Turkey. 🖎 Relations with Greece have been characterized by tension and conflict for centuries. 🖎 A member of NATO since 1952.

Turkmenistan   (turk-men-uh-STAN,   turk-men-uh-STAHN, turk-MEN-uh-stan)   REPUBLIC in west-central ASIA, bordered by KAZAKHSTAN to the northwest, UZBEKISTAN to the north and northwest, by AFGHANISTAN and IRAN to the south, and by the CASPIAN SEA to the west. Its capital and largest city is Ashkhabad.

🖎 This former member of the SOVIET UNION declared its independence in 1991.

Uganda (yooh-GAN-duh, ooh-GAHN-duh)   Landlocked nation on LAKE VICTORIA in east-central AFRICA, bordered by TANZANIA and Rwanda to the south, ZAIRE to the west, SUDAN to the north, and KENYA to the east. Its capital and largest city is Kampala.

🖎 From 1971 to 1979, Uganda was ruled by the notorious military strongman Idi Amin. It is estimated that Amin killed as many as 300,000 Ugandans through internal purges and campaigns of terror before he was overthrown. 🖎 Under Amin, Uganda was a sponsor of international terrorism. In 1976, a French airliner was hijacked and flown to Entebbe Airport outside Kampala. An Israeli commando unit subsequently rescued the hostages in a sensational raid.

Ukraine (yooh-KRAYN, YOOH-krayn)   REPUBLIC in southeastern EUROPE, bordered by BELARUS to the north, RUSSIA to the northeast and east, the BLACK SEA to the south, MOLDOVA, RUMANIA, and HUNGARY to the southwest, and the former CZECHOSLOVAKIA and POLAND to the west. Includes the PENINSULA of CRIMEA. KIEV is the capital and largest city.

🖎 Of the former Soviet republics, it is second to Russia in population. 🖎 Ukraine came under a succession of invaders and foreign rulers, including central Asian tribes, the Mongols, LITHUANIA, the OTTOMAN EMPIRE, Poland, and finally Russia. Under oppressive Polish and Russian rule in the seventeenth century, Ukrainian fugitives, known as COSSACKS, organized resistance movements. 🖎 A nationalist and cultural revival in the nineteenth century was rewarded after WORLD WAR I by independence, which was, however, short-lived. Invaded by Russian troops, Ukraine became one of the original Soviet republics in 1922. ⅋ Traditionally home to a large Jewish population. Many JEWS left Ukraine under oppressive conditions in the nineteenth century, and thousands more were exterminated by the NAZIS in WORLD WAR II.

Ulster A historic division of IRELAND, located in the northeastern part of the island. Six of its nine counties are in NORTHERN IRELAND. (*See* IRELAND, REPUBLIC OF.)

Union of Soviet Socialist Republics (USSR) Official name of the former SOVIET UNION.

United Arab Emirates (EM-uhr-uhts, uh-MEER-uhts) A federation of seven kingdoms on the PERSIAN GULF coast of the ARABIAN PENINSULA, bordered to the east by OMAN, the south and west by SAUDI ARABIA, and the northwest by QATAR.

⅋ Once the domain of pirates, the area was subdued by the British in 1820. It was a British PROTECTORATE from 1892 until the late 1960s. ⅋ Oil reserves have been exploited since the early 1960s.

United Kingdom of Great Britain and Northern Ireland The official name for the kingdom comprising GREAT BRITAIN (ENGLAND, SCOTLAND, and WALES) and NORTHERN IRELAND.

Urals (YOOR-uhlz) Mountain range primarily in the western part of RUSSIA that forms part of the traditional boundary between EUROPE and ASIA. The Urals extend from the ARCTIC TUNDRA to the desert region north of the CASPIAN SEA in KAZAKHSTAN.

Uruguay (YOOR-uh-gweye, YOOR-uh-gway, OOR-uh-gweye) REPUBLIC on the east coast of SOUTH AMERICA, tucked between BRAZIL to the north and east and ARGENTINA to the west. The capital and largest city is MONTEVIDEO.

⅋ Under a repressive and violent military government from 1973 to 1985. ⅋ A major producer of beef, leather, and wool.

USSR ABBREVIATION for UNION OF SOVIET SOCIALIST REPUBLICS, official name of the former SOVIET UNION.

Uzbekistan (ooz-BEK-uh-stan, ooz-BEK-uh-stahn) REPUBLIC located in central-west ASIA, bounded by KAZAKHSTAN to the west and north, KYRGYZSTAN and TAJIKISTAN to the east, AFGHANISTAN to the

south, and TURKMENISTAN to the southwest. Its capital and largest city is Tashkent.

⅋ This former member of the SOVIET UNION declared its independence in 1991.

Valencia City in eastern SPAIN on the MEDITERRANEAN SEA.

Vancouver City in southwestern BRITISH COLUMBIA, CANADA, on an arm of the PACIFIC OCEAN.

⅋ Year-round tourist center. ⅋ Named for George Vancouver, an English navigator and explorer.

Vatican City State Tiny independent nation within ROME, ITALY, located on the Vatican Hill, on the west bank of the Tiber River. Often called the VATICAN.

⅋ It is home to the POPE and central administration of the ROMAN CATHOLIC CHURCH. The pope maintains complete legal, executive, and judicial powers. The Vatican was established in the 1920s by a treaty between the pope and the Italian government. ⅋ The SISTINE CHAPEL and SAINT PETER'S BASILICA are located here. ⅋ With a total area of less than a fifth of a square mile, it is often considered the world's smallest country. ⅋ The relations of the United States with the Vatican have been controversial. For years, the United States had a diplomatic representative there without the rank of ambassador, but in the middle 1980s, the United States established full diplomatic relations with the Vatican.

Venezuela REPUBLIC in northern SOUTH AMERICA, bordered by the CARIBBEAN SEA to the north, Guyana to the east, BRAZIL to the south, and COLOMBIA to the southwest and west. Its capital and largest city is CARACAS.

⅋ Rich in oil, which accounts for about 90 percent of its export INCOME. Because of its revenue from oil, Venezuela has the highest PER CAPITA national income in LATIN AMERICA. It was a founder of the ORGANIZATION OF PETROLEUM EXPORTING COUNTRIES (OPEC). ⅋ Venezuela became independent from SPAIN in 1821.

Venice City in northeastern ITALY, built on 118 islets within a lagoon in the Gulf of Venice, an arm of the ADRIATIC SEA.

⅋ Tourist, commercial, and industrial center; one of Italy's major ports. ⅋ Venice was governed as a REPUBLIC for hundreds of years, and long dominated trade between EUROPE and the MIDDLE EAST. ⅋ Instead of streets, Venice has canals, the Grand Canal serving as its main canal. People use gondolas and other boats to move about the city. ﹖ Some of the city's landmarks are Saint Mark's Square, on which sits the BASILICA of Saint Mark, the Bell Tower, the Palace of the Doges (the former rulers of the city), and the Academy of Fine Arts. ﹖ The city houses the famous paintings of such Venetian masters as TITIAN, Tintoretto, and Paolo Veronese. ﹖ Venice was sinking an average of one-fifth of an inch yearly until the middle 1970s, when the government restricted use of water from the city's underground wells.

Versailles (ver-SEYE, vuhr-SEYE)   City in northern FRANCE about ten miles southwest of PARIS.

﹖ Site of the Palace of Versailles (*see* VERSAILLES, PALACE OF), which was built by King LOUIS XIV in the seventeenth century, and was the royal residence for over 100 years. ﹖ Scene of the beginning of the FRENCH REVOLUTION, when mobs stormed the palace. ﹖ The Treaty of Versailles (*see* VERSAILLES, TREATY OF), signed in 1919, officially ended WORLD WAR I.

Vesuvius   *See* MOUNT VESUVIUS.

Vienna   Capital of AUSTRIA and largest city in the country, located in northeastern Austria on the south bank of the DANUBE RIVER. Austria's leading cultural, economic, and political center.

﹖ Capital of the Austrian (later Austro-Hungarian) Empire under the Hapsburgs, who ruled from 1278 to 1918. ﹖ During WORLD WAR II, German troops occupied the city. It was badly damaged by bombing by the ALLIES, who controlled the city from 1945 to 1955. ﹖ Home of such composers as Ludwig van BEETHOVEN, Johannes BRAHMS, Joseph HAYDN, Wolfgang Amadeus MOZART, Franz SCHUBERT, and Johann STRAUSS, THE YOUNGER.

Vietnam (vee-et-NAHM, vee-et-NAM)   REPUBLIC in SOUTHEAST ASIA, bordered by CAMBODIA and LAOS to the west, CHINA to the north, and the South China Sea (an arm of the PACIFIC OCEAN) to the east and south.

﹖ Vietnam was under the control of FRANCE from the second half of the nineteenth century until WORLD WAR II, when it was occupied by the Japanese. The country became an autonomous state in 1946. France's attempts to reassert control resulted in the French Indochina War (1946–1954), in which

the French were defeated. ﹖ The GENEVA Conference of 1954 divided Vietnam into North Vietnam, controlled by COMMUNISTS, and South Vietnam, controlled by noncommunists. ﹖ In the VIETNAM WAR of 1954–1975, South Vietnam, which was aided by the United States, fought communist insurgents, who were aided by North Vietnam. The war ended when the communists overran the south in 1975. The country was reunified in 1976. ﹖ American involvement in the Vietnam War was strongly protested in the United States. ﹖ Great numbers of Vietnamese refugees, known as BOAT PEOPLE, fled the country in the aftermath of the war. ﹖ In 1978–1979, Vietnam invaded Cambodia and installed a puppet government.

Volga River (VOL-guh, VOHL-guh)   River in western RUSSIA, originating in hills northwest of MOSCOW and flowing generally southeastward for more than 2200 miles before emptying in the CASPIAN SEA.

﹖ Longest river of EUROPE, and principal waterway of Russia.

Volgograd (VOL-guh-grad, VOHL-guh-grad)   City located in southern RUSSIA, amid the lower VOLGA and DON rivers.

﹖ A major commercial and industrial center. ﹖ From 1925 to 1961, it was named STALINGRAD. ﹖ During the brutal winter of 1942–1943, a huge German invasion force besieged the city but ultimately failed to take it. The German defeat in the Battle of Stalingrad was a major turning point in WORLD WAR II, marking the beginning of the end for the NAZIS.

Wailing Wall, the   A wall in the old city of JERUSALEM, whose stones may have formed part of the TEMPLE of SOLOMON. For the JEWS, who call it the Western Wall and visit it in great numbers, it is a holy place that commemorates their sorrows from earliest times.

Wales   One of the four countries that make up the UNITED KINGDOM OF GREAT BRITAIN AND NORTHERN IRELAND, occupying the western PENINSULA of the island of GREAT BRITAIN. Its capital and largest city is Cardiff.

﹖ Welsh CULTURE is known for its writers and singers, dating back more than 1000 years to the bards (poet-singers) of the MIDDLE AGES.

WAILING WALL. *Men praying at the Wailing Wall in Jerusalem. Men and women pray separately at the wall.*

Warsaw   Capital of POLAND and largest city in the country, located in central Poland. Political, cultural, industrial, and transportation center of Poland.

🐦 Capital of Poland since 1596, though it was occupied by the Russians (1813–1815) and the Germans (1915–1918 and 1939–1945). 🐦 During WORLD WAR II, half a million JEWS were exterminated by the Germans in the Warsaw Jewish GHETTO.

West Bank   Land between ISRAEL and JORDAN on the west bank of the JORDAN RIVER; a central battleground for the ARAB-ISRAELI CONFLICT.

🐦 Israel took control of the West Bank after the SIX-DAY WAR in 1967. Though the SECURITY COUNCIL of the UNITED NATIONS called for Israel's withdrawal from the area, the question of control over the West Bank has not been resolved. 🐦 The United Nations has recognized the PALESTINE LIBERATION ORGANIZATION as representative of the Arab natives of the West Bank. 🐦 The scene since 1987 of a Palestinian uprising called the INTIFADA, against Israeli rule.

West Indies   ARCHIPELAGO between NORTH AMERICA and SOUTH AMERICA curving from southern FLORIDA to VENEZUELA.

🐦 Popular resort area. 🐦 Several of the islands were discovered by CHRISTOPHER COLUMBUS in 1492.

Western Europe   Those nations in EUROPE that were not part of the EASTERN BLOC, or more specifi-

cally, those nations allied with the United States in NATO (except TURKEY). Neutral or nonaligned nations such as SWEDEN, SWITZERLAND, AUSTRIA, and SPAIN, though western European in terms of geography, are not usually meant when the term "Western Europe" is used as the opposite for such terms as "Eastern Europe," "the Eastern Bloc," or "COMMUNIST Europe."

Westminster Abbey   Famous CHURCH located in LONDON, ENGLAND. Almost all English monarchs since WILLIAM THE CONQUEROR have been crowned there.

🐦 Distinguished English subjects are buried there. The Poets' Corner contains the graves of great English writers including CHAUCER and Robert BROWNING.

Winnipeg   Capital of MANITOBA, CANADA, and largest city in the province, located in southern Manitoba.

🐦 Largest city of Canada's "prairie provinces" (ALBERTA, Manitoba, and SASKATCHEWAN), and center of their agricultural industry. 🐦 Known for its severe winters.

Yangtze River (YANG-TSEE, YANG-SEE)   River in CHINA, flowing from the highlands of TIBET in western China generally eastward through central China, and emptying into the PACIFIC OCEAN at SHANGHAI.

🐦 At about 4000 miles, longest river of China and of ASIA. 🐦 Also called the Chang. 🐦 Major east-west trade and transportation route in China.

Yemen   Now the REPUBLIC OF YEMEN. Yemen is at the mouth of the RED SEA, in the southwestern corner of the ARABIAN PENINSULA, bordered by SAUDI ARABIA to the north and OMAN to the east. Formerly divided into North Yemen (the Yemen Arab Republic) and the People's Democratic Republic of Yemen.

🐦 Northern Yemen became an independent country after WORLD WAR I. 🐦 Southern Yemen won independence from BRITAIN in 1967 and became the world's only COMMUNIST Arab state. 🐦 The two Yemens were reunified as a result of the democratic reforms of the SOVIET UNION and its satellite countries in 1990.

Yucatán (yooh-kuh-TAN, yooh-kuh-TAHN)   PENINSULA mostly in southeastern MEXICO, separating the CARIBBEAN SEA from the GULF OF MEXICO.

🐦 Location of many Mayan ruins.

Yugoslavia   REPUBLIC in southeastern EUROPE, on the BALKAN PENINSULA, bordered by HUNGARY to the north, BULGARIA and RUMANIA to the east, MACEDONIA and ALBANIA to the south, the ADRIATIC SEA and BOSNIA AND HERZEGOVINA to the west, and CROATIA to the northwest. Its capital and largest city is BELGRADE.

☙ A union of six republics, the Kingdom of the Serbs, Croats, and Slovenes was formally declared in 1918; the name was later changed to Yugoslavia. ☙ Invaded by German troops in 1941 and occupied until 1944. The scene of intense fighting during the German occupation between rival ethnic factions, especially Croats and Serbs. ☙ Became a COMMUNIST state under the leadership of TITO, and developed its own form of communism, independent of the SOVIET UNION. ☙ With the COLLAPSE OF COMMUNISM in East Europe and the Soviet Union, long-repressed NATIONALISM came to the surface. Bosnia and Herzegovina, Croatia, Macedonia, and SLOVENIA declared their independence, leaving Serbia and Montenegro to form the new, truncated Yugoslavia. Independence movements in these former provinces provoked civil war with the Yugoslavian government, which is dominated by Serbs, the most numerous ethnic group in Yugoslavia before it began to disintegrate. The issue has been complicated by the presence of Serbian minorities in the newly independent republics.

Yukon Territory   Territory in northwest CANADA, bordered by the ARCTIC OCEAN to the north, the NORTHWEST TERRITORIES to the east, BRITISH COLUMBIA to the south, and Alaska to the west.

☙ In the 1890s, gold strikes in the Klondike River region attracted over 30,000 prospectors. (See KLONDIKE GOLD RUSH.)

Zaire (zeye-EER)   REPUBLIC in central AFRICA, formerly the Democratic Republic of the Congo.

☙ The territory came under Belgian control in 1885, and was officially organized as the Belgian Congo in 1908. Independence was achieved in 1960. ☙ The civil war (1960–1963) that followed independence involved forces of the UNITED NATIONS, Belgian troops, and American and Soviet support of opposing FACTIONS.

Zambia   REPUBLIC in central AFRICA, bordered by ZAIRE to the north; TANZANIA to the northeast; Malawi and MOZAMBIQUE to the east; ZIMBABWE, BOTSWANA, and NAMIBIA to the south; and ANGOLA to the west. Lusaka is the capital and largest city.

☙ British explorer David Livingstone first visited Zambia in 1851. ☙ Zambia was proclaimed independent from British control in 1964. From 1953 to 1963, it was federated with RHODESIA (then Southern Rhodesia, now ZIMBABWE) as Northern Rhodesia. ☙ In the 1970s, Zambia supported the movement for black majority rule in Rhodesia.

Zimbabwe (zim-BAHB-way)   Landlocked REPUBLIC in south-central AFRICA, bordered by BOTSWANA to the west, ZAMBIA to the north, MOZAMBIQUE to the east, and SOUTH AFRICA to the south. Formerly called RHODESIA. Harare (formerly called Salisbury) is the capital and largest city.

☙ A British colony from the end of the nineteenth century to 1965, and then (1965–1980) a renegade state ruled by a white minority, Zimbabwe became independent in 1980.

Zurich (ZOOR-ik)   Largest city in SWITZERLAND, situated in the northern part of the country.

☙ The country's commercial hub and the intellectual center of the German-speaking part of Switzerland. Known as a world banking center.

American Geography

Tests have revealed that many Americans are amazingly ignorant of the geography of their nation. In one widely cited example, a student in CALIFORNIA identified CHICAGO as a city in ITALY. Perhaps the word *Chicago*, with its VOWEL ending, sounded vaguely un-American to the student. Yet the circulation of horror stories about the general ignorance concerning geography leaves unanswered the question of how much Americans have to know about geography to follow literate discourse. Many literate Americans, who have no difficulty reading the *New York Times*, are unable to name the capitals of all fifty states. Nor could they identify all of the states through which the MISSISSIPPI RIVER flows. But they do know all of the states, major cities, and natural landmarks, and have at least a general notion of their location. For example, they know that the Mississippi River originates in the upper MIDDLE WEST and empties into the GULF OF MEXICO in LOUISIANA. They also know that the OHIO and MISSOURI rivers intersect the Mississippi, and that the confluence of these rivers shaped the economic development of the United States and determined the location of many of its cities. Following literate discourse also demands an ability to make the correct associations with terms such as WALL STREET, MADISON AVENUE, HOLLYWOOD, and WEST POINT. All of these are famous for some distinctive activity that occurs in, on, or near them.

As is true of other sections of this dictionary, the entries in this section are based on an assessment of what Americans should know to follow literate discourse. Each state, the major state capitals, the largest cities, and the most important natural landmarks have separate entries. So do possessions of the United States, such as PUERTO RICO and the VIRGIN ISLANDS. For the sake of precision, the geographical borders of each state have been listed. The section also includes a large number of places known primarily or exclusively for their associations.

— J. F. K.

Adirondack Mountains (ad-uh-RON-dak)   Mountain range in northeastern NEW YORK state.

  🍂 The region is a resort area.

Akron (AK-ruhn)   City in northeastern OHIO, near CLEVELAND.

  🍂 Heart of the nation's rubber industry.

Alabama   State in the southeastern United States bordered by TENNESSEE to the north, GEORGIA to the east, FLORIDA and the GULF OF MEXICO to the south, and MISSISSIPPI to the west. Its capital is Montgomery, and its largest city is BIRMINGHAM.

  🍂 One of the CONFEDERATE states during the CIVIL WAR.

Alaska   State in northwesternmost NORTH AMERICA bordered by the ARCTIC OCEAN to the north; YUKON, CANADA, to the east; the PACIFIC OCEAN to the south; and the BERING SEA to the west. Its capital is Juneau, and its largest city is ANCHORAGE.

  🍂 The forty-ninth state, admitted in 1959, and the largest.

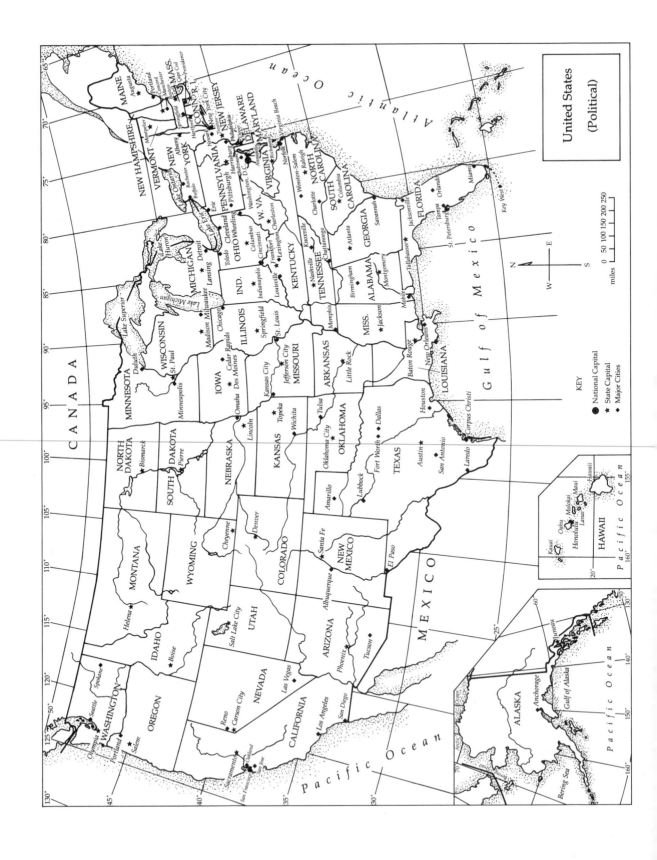

Albany State capital located in eastern NEW YORK, on the west bank of the HUDSON RIVER.

🪶 Involved with much shipping; a major trans-shipment point. Albany used to be an important fur-trading center.

Albuquerque (AL-buh-kur-kee) Largest city in NEW MEXICO.

Aleutian Islands (uh-LOOH-shuhn) Chain of volcanic (*see* VOLCANO) islands off western ALASKA between the BERING SEA and the PACIFIC OCEAN.

Allegheny Mountains (al-uh-GAY-nee) Western part of the APPALACHIAN MOUNTAINS, extending from northern PENNSYLVANIA southwest to southwestern VIRGINIA.

Anchorage City in south-central ALASKA; largest city in the state.

Ann Arbor City in southern MICHIGAN, near DETROIT.

🪶 Location of the University of Michigan.

Annapolis (uh-NAP-uh-lis) Capital of MARYLAND.

🪶 Location of the United States Naval Academy.

Appalachia (ap-uh-LAY-chuh, ap-uh-LACH-uh) A mountainous region in the eastern United States, running from northern ALABAMA to PENNSYLVANIA, and including parts of GEORGIA, SOUTH CAROLINA, NORTH CAROLINA, TENNESSEE, KENTUCKY, VIRGINIA, and all of WEST VIRGINIA.

🪶 A major coal-mining center and one of the most impoverished regions of the country.

Appalachian Mountains (ap-uh-LAY-chuhn, ap-uh-LACH-uhn) Mountain chain in the eastern United States, extending from the valley of the ST. LAWRENCE RIVER in QUEBEC, CANADA, to the coastal plain of the GULF OF MEXICO in ALABAMA.

🪶 Location of the Appalachian Trail, the world's longest continuous hiking path. It extends over 2000 miles from MAINE to GEORGIA. 🪶 Historically, the Appalachian Mountains were a barrier to early western expansion. In the early 1840s, railroads began to transport settlers across the mountains, permitting access to the frontier.

Arizona State in the southwestern United States bordered by UTAH to the north, NEW MEXICO to the east, MEXICO to the south, and CALIFORNIA and NE-

VADA to the west. Its capital and largest city is PHOENIX.

🪶 The GRAND CANYON is in northwestern Arizona.

Arkansas State in the south-central United States bordered by MISSOURI to the north, the MISSISSIPPI RIVER to the east, LOUISIANA to the south, and TEXAS and OKLAHOMA to the west. Its capital and largest city is LITTLE ROCK.

🪶 One of the CONFEDERATE states during the CIVIL WAR.

Atlanta Capital of GEORGIA and largest city in the state.

🪶 Atlanta was plundered by the UNION army during the CIVIL WAR. (*See* SHERMAN'S MARCH TO THE SEA.)

Atlantic City City in southeastern NEW JERSEY.

🪶 A seaside resort and convention center. Gambling, which has been legal there since the 1970s, draws many visitors. The Boardwalk, which was first built in the late nineteenth century, is lined with shops and hotels. 🪶 The Miss America Pageant is held in Atlantic City every September. 🪶 The street names of Atlantic City were used in the game Monopoly.

Austin Capital of TEXAS.

🪶 Location of the University of Texas.

Baltimore Largest city in MARYLAND.

🪶 Named after Lord Baltimore, founder of the colony of Maryland. The city is a major industrial center and port.

bayou (BEYE-ooh, BEYE-oh) Term used mainly in LOUISIANA and MISSISSIPPI to describe a swampy, slowly moving or stationary body of water that was once part of a lake, river, or gulf.

Beacon Hill Fashionable section of BOSTON. Location of the capitol building of MASSACHUSETTS.

Berkeley City in CALIFORNIA on the eastern shore of SAN FRANCISCO BAY.

🪶 Berkeley is the location of a distinguished branch of the University of California. The University of California at Berkeley has been a center for student activism and social-change movements, particularly in the 1960s and early 1970s.

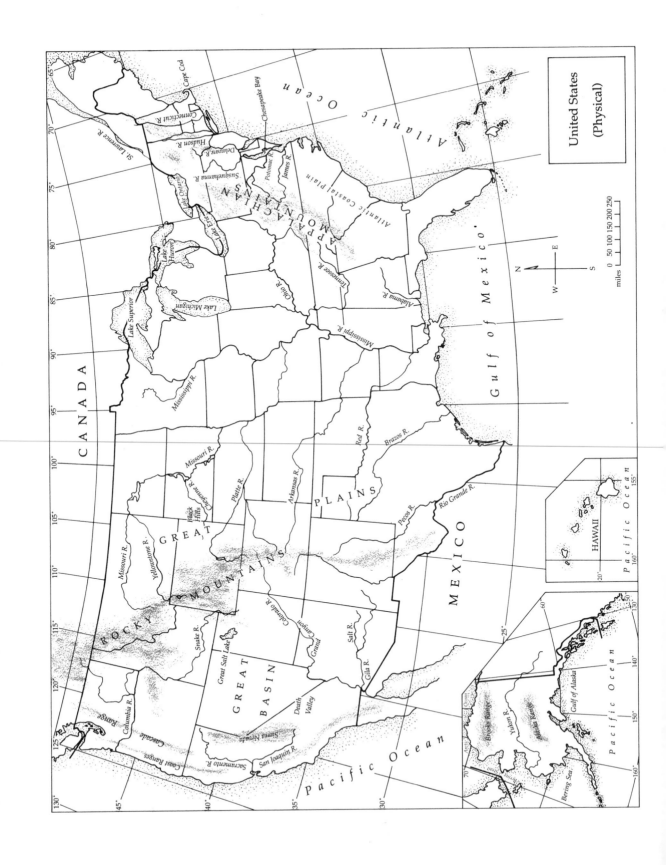

United States
(Physical)

N
W — E
S

0 50 100 150 200 250
miles

CANADA

Atlantic Ocean

Cape Cod
Connecticut R.
St. Lawrence R.
Hudson R.
Delaware R.
Susquehanna R.
Chesapeake Bay
Potomac R.
James R.
Atlantic Coastal Plain

Lake Ontario
Lake Erie
Lake Huron
Lake Michigan
Lake Superior

APPALACHIAN MOUNTAINS

Ohio R.
Tennessee R.
Alabama R.
Mississippi R.

Gulf of Mexico

Missouri R.
Mississippi R.
Red R.
Brazos R.
Arkansas R.

GREAT PLAINS

Black Hills
Cheyenne R.
Platte R.
Pecos R.
Rio Grande R.

MEXICO

GREAT
Missouri R.
Yellowstone R.

ROCKY MOUNTAINS

Snake R.
Colorado R.
Grand
Canyon
Salt R.
Gila R.

Great Salt Lake

GREAT
BASIN

Death
Valley

Columbia R.
Cascade Range
Coast Ranges
Sierra Nevada
Sacramento R.
San Joaquin R.

Pacific Ocean

HAWAII
Pacific Ocean

Gulf of Alaska
Pacific Ocean
Brooks Range
Yukon R.
Alaska Range
Bering Sea
Arctic Ocean

Berkshires (BURK-sheerz, BURK-shuhrz) Mountain chain in western MASSACHUSETTS.

Beverly Hills City surrounded by LOS ANGELES, CALIFORNIA.

🙢 Home of many HOLLYWOOD actors and actresses.

Birmingham City in north-central ALABAMA; largest city in the state.

🙢 Birmingham was the site of extreme racial violence during the CIVIL RIGHTS MOVEMENT. While it is associated with specific race riots in 1963, Birmingham has come to represent, as a whole, southern white resistance to INTEGRATION. (*See* "LETTER FROM BIRMINGHAM JAIL.") 🙢 Birmingham is known as the "PITTSBURGH of the South" for its steel and iron production.

Black Hills Mountains in southwestern SOUTH DAKOTA and northeastern WYOMING.

🙢 Sacred to the SIOUX. The opening of the Black Hills to settlement by whites in 1874 led to the Battle of LITTLE BIGHORN. 🙢 Location of MOUNT RUSHMORE.

Blue Ridge Mountains Range of the APPALACHIAN MOUNTAINS extending from southern PENNSYLVANIA south to northern GEORGIA.

Boston Capital of MASSACHUSETTS and largest city in the state.

🙢 Site of the BOSTON MASSACRE and the BOSTON TEA PARTY. 🙢 Boston is often called "the Hub" for "Hub of the Universe," or "Beantown" after Boston baked beans.

Bowery A section of lower MANHATTAN in NEW YORK CITY.

🙢 The Bowery is known for the great number of derelicts inhabiting the area.

Broadway A street in MANHATTAN, in NEW YORK CITY, that passes through TIMES SQUARE.

🙢 Broadway is known for its theaters. (*See also* under "Fine Arts.") 🙢 Sometimes called the "Great White Way" because of its bright lights.

Bronx, the One of the five boroughs that make up NEW YORK CITY.

Brooklyn One of the five boroughs that make up NEW YORK CITY.

🙢 The BROOKLYN BRIDGE connects Brooklyn with MANHATTAN. 🙢 Noted for the special "Brooklyn accent."

Buffalo City in western NEW YORK, on LAKE ERIE and the Niagara River.

🙢 NIAGARA FALLS is northwest of Buffalo.

California State in the FAR WEST bordered by OREGON to the north; NEVADA and ARIZONA to the east; Baja California, MEXICO, to the south; and the PACIFIC OCEAN to the west. Its capital is SACRAMENTO, and its largest city is LOS ANGELES.

🙢 During the California GOLD RUSH tens of thousands of people poured into California in search of gold. It is sometimes called the "Golden State." (*See* FORTY-NINERS.) 🙢 California is the most populous state. It is known for its EARTHQUAKES and the belief held by some that it will one day fall into the Pacific Ocean. 🙢 The state is famous for all the fads and ideas that originate there, many of which are considered strange or eccentric.

Cambridge City in MASSACHUSETTS, near BOSTON.

🙢 Location of Harvard University and the Massachusetts Institute of Technology.

Cape Canaveral (kuh-NAV-uhr-uhl, kuh-NAV-ruhl) Formerly Cape Kennedy. Located on the east coast of FLORIDA, it is the site of the John F. Kennedy Space Center, from which many American space vehicles have been launched.

Cape Cod Resort area on the ATLANTIC OCEAN in MASSACHUSETTS. Its fishhook shape is easily recognized on a map.

Cape Hatteras (HAT-uhr-uhs) Promontory on Hatteras Island off NORTH CAROLINA, a low, sandy BARRIER ISLAND between the ATLANTIC OCEAN and Pamlico Sound.

🙢 Called the "Graveyard of the Atlantic" because of the frequent storms that drive ships landward to their destruction.

Cascades Mountain chain extending from BRITISH COLUMBIA, CANADA, south through WASHINGTON and OREGON to northern CALIFORNIA.

Central Park A large park in MANHATTAN, half a mile wide and over two miles long.

Chapel Hill Town in central NORTH CAROLINA.

🙢 Seat of the University of North Carolina and a center of research.

Charleston Two cities in the South: one a port city in southeastern SOUTH CAROLINA, the other the capital of WEST VIRGINIA.

Charlotte City in southern NORTH CAROLINA.

ê Largest city of the state, and the foremost commercial and industrial center of the PIEDMONT region. ê Named for Queen Charlotte, wife of King GEORGE III of ENGLAND.

Chattanooga City in eastern TENNESSEE.

Chesapeake Bay Large bay on the ATLANTIC OCEAN in the states of MARYLAND and VIRGINIA.

Chicago Largest city in ILLINOIS. Located on LAKE MICHIGAN.

ê Originally called the "Windy City" because the city bragged about the 1893 World Expo that was held there. The term has since come to refer to the strong northern winds that blow off the lake in the winter. ê For many years the second largest city in the United States, before being displaced by LOS ANGELES, and therefore referred to as the "Second City." ê During the time of PROHIBITION, Chicago was controlled by gangsters, Al CAPONE being the most notorious. Gangster warfare continued long after this particularly violent period. ê Carl SANDBURG, in his poem "Chicago," called the city the "Hog Butcher for the World" because of Chicago's heavy involvement in the meat-packing industry. ê Chicago's downtown is referred to as the "Loop" because it is enclosed by elevated railways, called the "El."

Cincinnati Port city in OHIO, on the OHIO RIVER.

Cleveland Largest city in Ohio, on LAKE ERIE.

Colorado State in the west-central United States in the ROCKY MOUNTAINS, bordered by WYOMING and NEBRASKA to the north, NEBRASKA and KANSAS to the east, OKLAHOMA and NEW MEXICO to the south, and UTAH to the west. Its capital and largest city is DENVER.

Colorado River River in the southwestern United States, with its headwaters in the ROCKY MOUNTAINS of northern COLORADO, that flows generally southwest through Colorado, UTAH, and ARIZONA; forms the border between NEVADA and ARIZONA and Arizona and CALIFORNIA; and then flows through MEXICO, emptying into the Gulf of California.

ê Over millions of years, the force of the river has carved the GRAND CANYON in northwestern Arizona.

ê Source of fresh water for communities in Nevada, Arizona, and California. ê The site of the Hoover Dam.

Columbia River River that runs from BRITISH COLUMBIA, CANADA, to the PACIFIC OCEAN, and passes between OREGON and WASHINGTON.

ê Known for its great salmon runs in spring. ê The site of the Bonneville and Grand Coulee Dams.

Columbus Capital of OHIO.

Coney Island Section of BROOKLYN on the ATLANTIC OCEAN.

ê Famed as a beach resort and amusement center.

Connecticut State in the northeastern United States; southernmost of the NEW ENGLAND states, bordered by MASSACHUSETTS to the north, RHODE ISLAND to the east, the ATLANTIC OCEAN to the south, and NEW YORK to the west. Its capital is HARTFORD, and its largest city is Bridgeport.

ê One of the THIRTEEN COLONIES.

Cumberland Gap Pass through the CUMBERLAND MOUNTAINS between VIRGINIA and KENTUCKY that was used by early settlers to move west.

Cumberland Mountains Southwestern division of the APPALACHIAN MOUNTAINS. Sometimes called the Cumberland Plateau.

Dallas Large industrial and commercial city in northeastern TEXAS.

Death Valley Desert valley in southeastern CALIFORNIA and southwestern NEVADA.

ê The lowest point in NORTH AMERICA — 282 feet below sea level.

Deep South The southernmost tier of states in the South: SOUTH CAROLINA, GEORGIA, FLORIDA, ALABAMA, MISSISSIPPI, and LOUISIANA. Before the CIVIL WAR, these states were centers of cotton production and SLAVERY. All of them seceded from the United States before the firing on FORT SUMTER. They are sometimes distinguished from the states of the Upper South (VIRGINIA, NORTH CAROLINA, TENNESSEE, and ARKANSAS), which contained fewer slaves prior to the Civil War, and which seceded only after the firing on Fort Sumter.

Delaware State in the eastern United States bordered by PENNSYLVANIA to the north, Delaware Bay

and the ATLANTIC OCEAN to the east, and MARY-
LAND to the west and south. Its capital is Dover, and
its largest city is WILMINGTON.

🐚 One of the THIRTEEN COLONIES.

Denver   Capital of COLORADO and largest city in
the state.

🐚 Known as the "Mile-High City" because of its
location at an altitude of 5280 feet in the ROCKY
MOUNTAINS.

Des Moines (duh-MOYN)   Capital of IOWA and largest city in the state.

Detroit   Largest city in MICHIGAN.

🐚 As the center of automobile production, it is
often referred to as the "Motor City" or "Motown."

District of Columbia   The district occupied entirely
by WASHINGTON, D.C., the capital of the United
States. Bordered by MARYLAND to the north and VIR-
GINIA to the south.

🐚 The District was established by acts of CON-
GRESS in 1790 and 1791 on a site selected by George
WASHINGTON.

El Paso (el PAS-oh)   City in Texas on the border between MEXICO and the United States.

Ellis Island   Island in the harbor of NEW YORK
CITY, southwest of MANHATTAN.

🐚 From 1892 to 1954, it served as the prime IM-
MIGRATION station of the country. Some twelve million immigrants passed through it during this time.
🐚 Part of the STATUE OF LIBERTY National Monument.

Erie Canal   Artificial waterway that extends across
central NEW YORK from ALBANY to BUFFALO and
connects the HUDSON RIVER with LAKE ERIE. Its construction began in the early nineteenth century.

🐚 The canal was important to the financial development of NEW YORK CITY because it opened the
eastern market to the farm products of the MIDDLE
WEST. It also encouraged IMMIGRATION into the
Middle West, helping create numerous large cities.

Far West   A term often applied to the states between
the ROCKY MOUNTAINS and the PACIFIC OCEAN.

Fifth Avenue   One of the main thoroughfares of
MANHATTAN.

🐚 The avenue is known for its fashionable shops.

🐚 Fifth Avenue separates the East Side of Manhattan
from the West Side.

Florida   The southeasternmost state of the United
States, bordered by ALABAMA and GEORGIA to the
north, the ATLANTIC OCEAN to the east and south,
and the GULF OF MEXICO and ALABAMA to the west.
Its capital is Tallahassee, and its largest city is JACK-
SONVILLE.

🐚 Home of Walt Disney World, an amusement
park near Orlando. (*See* DISNEY, WALT.) 🐚 Home of
the Kennedy Space Center, launch site for many of
the United States space missions. 🐚 St. Augustine is
the oldest city in the United States, settled in the sixteenth century by SPAIN. 🐚 One of the CONFEDER-
ATE states during the CIVIL WAR.

Florida Keys   Islands off the southern coast of
FLORIDA. The best known are Key Largo and Key
West.

Fort Worth   City in TEXAS, near DALLAS.

Fresno (FREZ-noh)   City in south-central CALIFOR-
NIA.

🐚 Center of a major agricultural area.

Georgia   State in the southeastern United States
bordered by TENNESSEE and NORTH CAROLINA to
the north, SOUTH CAROLINA and the ATLANTIC
OCEAN to the east, FLORIDA to the south, and ALA-
BAMA to the west. Its capital and largest city is AT-
LANTA.

🐚 Last of the THIRTEEN COLONIES to be founded
(1733). 🐚 One of the CONFEDERATE states during
the CIVIL WAR.

Grand Canyon   A 5000-foot-deep gorge carved by
the COLORADO RIVER in northwestern ARIZONA.

🐚 Grand Canyon National Park is a great tourist
attraction.

Great Lakes   Group of five large freshwater bodies
in central NORTH AMERICA. They include, west to
east, LAKE SUPERIOR, LAKE MICHIGAN, LAKE HU-
RON, LAKE ERIE, and LAKE ONTARIO. Except for
Lake Michigan, which is entirely within the United
States, the Great Lakes serve as borders between the
United States and CANADA.

🐚 Major shipping route through the ST. LAW-
RENCE RIVER to the ATLANTIC OCEAN.

Great Plains   Grassland prairie region of NORTH
AMERICA, extending from ALBERTA, SASKATCHEWAN,

and MANITOBA, in CANADA, south through the west-central United States into TEXAS.

🌿 Now characterized by huge ranches and farms, the Great Plains were long inhabited by NATIVE AMERICANS. 🌿 In the 1930s, areas of the Great Plains were known collectively as the DUST BOWL. Poor agricultural practices led to depletion of TOP-SOIL, which was blown away in huge dust storms. 🌿 The area was called the Great American Desert well into the nineteenth century.

Great Salt Lake　Shallow body of salt water in northwestern UTAH.

🌿 Largest body of salt water in NORTH AMERICA. 🌿 SALT LAKE CITY is near the Great Salt Lake.

Great Smoky Mountains　Part of the APPALACHIAN MOUNTAINS on the border between NORTH CARO-LINA and TENNESSEE.

🌿 Named after the smokelike haze that envelops them. 🌿 Great Smoky Mountains National Park straddles the crest of the Smokies. The Appalachian Trail follows the crest of the mountains.

Greenwich Village (GREN-ich)　Neighborhood of MANHATTAN, in NEW YORK CITY.

🌿 Home of many artists, writers, and musicians. Known for the BOHEMIAN life-style of its inhabitants.

Gulf of Mexico　Gulf bordered by the southeast coast of the United States and the east coast of MEX-ICO.

Harlem　Neighborhood of MANHATTAN.

🌿 Mostly populated by African-Americans, Harlem has long been a center of black CULTURE. 🌿 During the 1920s, Harlem was the site of a great upsurge in black literature, music, and theater known as the HARLEM RENAISSANCE. 🌿 With its substandard housing and high levels of unemployment and poverty, Harlem has since become a SYMBOL of urban decay.

Hartford　Capital of CONNECTICUT.

🌿 Center of the insurance industry.

Hawaii　State located in the PACIFIC OCEAN south-west of the mainland United States. Consists mainly of a chain of eight islands, including Hawaii, the larg-est, and Oahu, location of HONOLULU, the state's capital and largest city.

🌿 Fiftieth state, admitted in 1959. 🌿 Location of PEARL HARBOR.

Hollywood　District of LOS ANGELES.

🌿 Center of the American film industry.

Honolulu　Capital of HAWAII and largest city in the state, located on the island of Oahu.

Houston (HYOOH-stuhn)　Largest city in TEXAS.

🌿 A center of the oil industry and the headquar-ters of the NATIONAL AERONAUTICS AND SPACE AD-MINISTRATION.

Hudson River　River that runs north to south in NEW YORK state.

🌿 Explored by Henry HUDSON in the early sev-enteenth century.

Idaho　State in the ROCKY MOUNTAINS bordered by BRITISH COLUMBIA, CANADA, to the north; MON-TANA and WYOMING to the east; UTAH and NEVADA to the south; and OREGON and WASHINGTON to the west. Its capital and largest city is Boise.

Illinois (il-uh-NOY)　State in the north-central United States bordered on the north by WISCONSIN, the east by INDIANA, the south by KENTUCKY, and the west by MISSOURI and IOWA. Its capital is Spring-field, and its largest city is CHICAGO.

🌿 Known as the "Land of Lincoln" because Abra-ham LINCOLN began his political career there.

Independence　City in western MISSOURI.

🌿 Beginning of the SANTA FE TRAIL, used by set-tlers moving west.

Indiana　State in the midwestern United States bor-dered by MICHIGAN to the north, OHIO to the east, KENTUCKY to the south, and ILLINOIS to the west. Its capital and largest city is INDIANAPOLIS.

Indianapolis　Capital of INDIANA and largest city in the state.

🌿 Known for a 500-mile automobile race (the In-dianapolis [Indy] 500) held each year in late May.

Iowa　State in the midwestern United States bor-dered by MINNESOTA to the north, WISCONSIN and ILLINOIS to the east, MISSOURI to the south, and NE-BRASKA and SOUTH DAKOTA to the west. Its capital and largest city is DES MOINES.

Jacksonville　Largest city in FLORIDA, located in northeastern Florida.

🌿 Commercial and financial center.

Jersey City   City in northeastern NEW JERSEY, opposite lower MANHATTAN.

❧ Port of entry; great shipping and manufacturing center.

Kansas   State in the central United States bordered by NEBRASKA to the north, MISSOURI to the east, OKLAHOMA to the south, and COLORADO to the west. Its capital is Topeka, and its largest city is WICHITA.

❧ In the 1850s, the state came to be known as "bleeding Kansas" because of the violence between hostile free-staters and proslavery settlers.

Kansas City   Two adjacent cities of the same name, one in northeastern KANSAS, the other in northwestern MISSOURI, located at the junction of the Kansas and MISSOURI rivers.

❧ A commercial, industrial, and cultural center, this was the starting point for many western expeditions.

Kentucky   State in the east-central United States bordered by ILLINOIS, INDIANA, and OHIO to the north; WEST VIRGINIA and VIRGINIA to the east; TENNESSEE to the south; and MISSOURI to the west. Its capital is Frankfort. LOUISVILLE is its largest city.

❧ The state is known for the breeding of race horses. The KENTUCKY DERBY, a famous horse race, is held every year in Louisville. ❧ Kentucky BLUEGRASS is a type of FOLK MUSIC that originated in the southern United States. The music is named for a bluish-tinged grass that grows in Kentucky. ❧ The song "MY OLD KENTUCKY HOME," by Stephen Foster, was popular in the second half of the nineteenth century.

Lake Erie   Lake bordered by ONTARIO, CANADA, to the north; NEW YORK to the east; PENNSYLVANIA and OHIO to the south; and MICHIGAN to the west.

❧ Fourth largest of the GREAT LAKES, it has been known for years for its high level of POLLUTION.

Lake Huron   (HYOOR-on, HYOOR-uhn)   Lake located between ONTARIO, CANADA, and MICHIGAN.

❧ Second largest of the GREAT LAKES.

Lake Michigan   Lake bordered by MICHIGAN to the north and east, INDIANA to the south, and ILLINOIS and WISCONSIN to the west.

❧ Third largest of the GREAT LAKES and largest freshwater lake entirely within the United States.

Lake Ontario   Lake located between ONTARIO, CANADA, and NEW YORK.

❧ Smallest and lowest in elevation of the GREAT LAKES.

Lake Superior   Lake bordered by ONTARIO, CANADA, to the north and east; MICHIGAN and WISCONSIN to the south; and MINNESOTA to the west.

❧ The largest freshwater lake in the world, Lake Superior is the largest, highest in elevation, and deepest of the GREAT LAKES.

Las Vegas   City in southern NEVADA.

❧ A famous gambling and entertainment center.

Little Rock   Capital of ARKANSAS and largest city in the state.

❧ In 1957, federal troops were sent into Little Rock to enforce the United States Supreme Court ruling in *BROWN VERSUS BOARD OF EDUCATION* against racial SEGREGATION in the public schools. Little Rock became a SYMBOL of the South's resistance to school INTEGRATION.

Long Beach   City in southern CALIFORNIA near LOS ANGELES.

Long Island   Island in NEW YORK state. Its western end is taken up by BROOKLYN and Queens, two of the five boroughs that make up NEW YORK CITY.

Los Angeles   (lawss AN-juh-luhs)   City in southern CALIFORNIA, sprawling over nearly 500 square miles.

❧ Second most populous city in the United States. ❧ A center of the entertainment industry; HOLLYWOOD is a district of Los Angeles. ❧ Los Angeles suffers from serious SMOG POLLUTION created by industry and large numbers of automobiles. ❧ The scene of the WATTS RIOTS in 1965 and of another serious riot in 1992, triggered by the acquittal of white police officers accused of beating an African-American man named Rodney King.

Louisiana   State in the southeastern United States bordered by ARKANSAS to the north, MISSISSIPPI to the east, the GULF OF MEXICO to the south, and TEXAS to the west. Its capital is Baton Rouge, and its largest city is NEW ORLEANS.

❧ One of the CONFEDERATE states during the CIVIL WAR.

Louisville   (LOOH-ee-vil, LOOH-uh-vuhl)   Largest city in KENTUCKY.

🙦 The KENTUCKY DERBY, a famous horse race, is held there every spring.

Madison   Capital of WISCONSIN.

🙦 Location of the main branch of the University of Wisconsin.

Madison Avenue   A street in MANHATTAN on which many advertising and public relations firms have offices.

🙦 The name of the street is often used to refer to the high-pressure techniques of the advertising business. 🙦 "Madison Avenue hype" carries the connotation of misrepresentation or deliberate dishonesty.

Maine   State in the northeastern United States; northernmost of the NEW ENGLAND states. Bordered by QUEBEC, CANADA, to the northwest; NEW BRUNSWICK, CANADA, to the northeast; the ATLANTIC OCEAN to the southeast; and NEW HAMPSHIRE to the west. Its capital is Augusta, and PORTLAND is its largest city.

Manhattan   Island that constitutes one of the five boroughs that make up NEW YORK CITY. (*See also* BOWERY, BROADWAY, CENTRAL PARK, HARLEM, PARK AVENUE, *and* TIMES SQUARE.)

🙦 Center of the country's financial industry (*see* WALL STREET), communications industry, including advertising and television (*see* MADISON AVENUE), and fashion industry (*see* FIFTH AVENUE). 🙦 Center of art world (*see* GREENWICH VILLAGE). 🙦 Considered by many to be an unlivable place, dangerous for strangers; often described in the PHRASE "It's a nice place to visit, but I wouldn't want to live there."

Martha's Vineyard   Island in the ATLANTIC OCEAN off southeastern MASSACHUSETTS.

🙦 Summer resort.

Maryland   State in the eastern United States bordered by PENNSYLVANIA to the north, DELAWARE to the east, and VIRGINIA and WEST VIRGINIA to the south and west. Its capital is ANNAPOLIS. BALTIMORE is its largest city.

🙦 One of the THIRTEEN COLONIES.

Mason-Dixon line   Part of the boundary between PENNSYLVANIA and MARYLAND established by the English surveyors Charles Mason and Jeremiah Dixon in the 1760s. The line resolved disputes caused by unclear description of the boundaries in the MARYLAND and PENNSYLVANIA charters.

🙦 Though the line did not actually divide North and South, it became the symbolic division between free states and slave states. Today, it still stands for the boundary between northern and southern states.

Massachusetts   State in the northeastern United States; one of the NEW ENGLAND states. Bordered by VERMONT and NEW HAMPSHIRE to the north, the ATLANTIC OCEAN to the east, RHODE ISLAND and CONNECTICUT to the south, and NEW YORK to the west. Its capital and largest city is BOSTON.

🙦 The settlement of Massachusetts began in 1620, when the first PILGRIMS arrived from ENGLAND in the *MAYFLOWER* near PLYMOUTH ROCK. 🙦 One of the THIRTEEN COLONIES, playing a key role in resisting the British before and during the REVOLUTIONARY WAR.

Memphis   (MEM-fuhs)   Largest city in TENNESSEE. Located on the MISSISSIPPI RIVER.

Miami   Best-known city in FLORIDA.

🙦 Famed for its resort hotels. 🙦 Home of the largest Cuban population outside CUBA, many of them exiles from the REGIME of Fidel CASTRO.

Michigan   State in the northern United States bordered on the north by LAKE SUPERIOR; on the east by ONTARIO, CANADA, LAKE HURON, and LAKE ERIE; on the south by OHIO and INDIANA; and on the west by WISCONSIN and LAKE MICHIGAN. Its capital is Lansing, and its largest city is DETROIT.

Mid-Atlantic states   A term often applied to NEW YORK, NEW JERSEY, PENNSYLVANIA, DELAWARE, and MARYLAND.

Middle West   Area of the northern United States including the states of ILLINOIS, INDIANA, IOWA, KANSAS, MICHIGAN, MINNESOTA, MISSOURI, NEBRASKA, OHIO, and WISCONSIN.

🙦 Location of some of the richest farming land in the world; known for its corn, hogs, and dairy and beef cattle.

Midwest   *See* MIDDLE WEST.

Milwaukee   Largest city in WISCONSIN.

🙦 Known for its breweries.

Minneapolis   (min-ee-AP-uh-lis)   Largest city in MINNESOTA, and, with ST. PAUL, one of the TWIN CITIES.

Minnesota   State in the north-central United States bordered by MANITOBA and ONTARIO, CANADA, to the north; LAKE SUPERIOR and WISCONSIN to the east; IOWA to the south; and SOUTH DAKOTA and NORTH DAKOTA to the west. Its capital is ST. PAUL, and its largest city is MINNEAPOLIS.

Mississippi   State in the southern United States bordered by TENNESSEE to the north, ALABAMA to the east, the GULF OF MEXICO and LOUISIANA to the south, and LOUISIANA and ARKANSAS to the west. Its capital and largest city is Jackson.

&. Its name comes from the MISSISSIPPI RIVER, which forms most of the state's western border. &. One of the CONFEDERATE states during the CIVIL WAR.

Mississippi River   The longest river in the United States, flowing over 2000 miles from MINNESOTA to LOUISIANA and into the GULF OF MEXICO.

Missouri (muh-ZOOR-ee, muh-ZOOR-uh)   State in the central United States bordered by IOWA to the north; ILLINOIS, KENTUCKY, and TENNESSEE to the east; ARKANSAS to the south; and OKLAHOMA, KANSAS, and NEBRASKA to the west. Its capital is Jefferson City, and its largest city is ST. LOUIS.

Missouri River   River that flows from MONTANA and joins the MISSISSIPPI RIVER near ST. LOUIS.

Mohave Desert   *See* MOJAVE DESERT.

Mojave Desert (moh-HAH-vee)   Area of low, barren mountains and flat valleys in southern CALIFORNIA.

&. Location of DEATH VALLEY National Monument. &. Lowest point in the United States.

Montana   State in the northwestern United States, lying partly in the ROCKY MOUNTAINS, bordered by BRITISH COLUMBIA, ALBERTA, and SASKATCHEWAN, CANADA, to the north; NORTH DAKOTA and SOUTH DAKOTA to the east; WYOMING to the south; and IDAHO to the west. Its capital is Helena, and its largest city is Billings.

Mount McKinley   Mountain in south-central ALASKA in the Alaska Range.
&. Highest peak in NORTH AMERICA.

Mount Rainier (ray-NEER, ruh-NEER)   Volcanic peak in southwestern WASHINGTON.

Mount Rushmore   A mountain in the BLACK HILLS of SOUTH DAKOTA noted for the huge portraits of George WASHINGTON, Thomas JEFFERSON, Abraham LINCOLN, and Theodore ROOSEVELT carved on it. Officially called Mount Rushmore National Memorial.

Mount St. Helens   Volcanic peak in southwestern WASHINGTON in the CASCADES.
&. The VOLCANO erupted violently several times in 1980 after 123 years of inactivity.

Mount Vernon   The home of George WASHINGTON; a historical landmark in northeastern VIRGINIA overlooking the POTOMAC RIVER.

Mount Whitney   Mountain in eastern CALIFORNIA.
&. Highest peak in the United States, excluding ALASKA.

Nantucket   Resort island off CAPE COD in MASSACHUSETTS.
&. Center of whaling industry during the nineteenth century.

Nashville   City in central TENNESSEE.
&. Center of country music.

Nebraska   State in the midwestern United States bordered by SOUTH DAKOTA to the north, IOWA and MISSOURI to the east, KANSAS to the south, and COLORADO and WYOMING to the west. Its capital is Lincoln, and its largest city is OMAHA.

Nevada   State in the western United States bordered by OREGON and IDAHO to the north, UTAH and ARIZONA to the east, and CALIFORNIA to the south and west. Its capital is Carson City, and its largest city is LAS VEGAS.
&. Gambling capital of the United States.

New England   Region in the northeastern United States that includes CONNECTICUT, MAINE, MASSACHUSETTS, NEW HAMPSHIRE, RHODE ISLAND, and VERMONT.
&. The region is thought to have been named by Captain John SMITH for its resemblance to the English coast.

New Hampshire   State in the northeastern United States; one of the NEW ENGLAND states. Bordered by QUEBEC, CANADA, to the north; MAINE to the east; MASSACHUSETTS to the south; and VERMONT to the west. Its capital is Concord, and its largest city is Manchester.
&. One of the THIRTEEN COLONIES.

New Haven   City in southern CONNECTICUT. ❧ Location of Yale University.

New Jersey   State in the northeastern United States, bordered by NEW YORK to the north, the ATLANTIC OCEAN to the east, DELAWARE Bay to the south and west, and PENNSYLVANIA to the west. Its capital is Trenton, and its largest city is NEWARK. ❧ One of the THIRTEEN COLONIES.

New Mexico   State in the southwestern United States bordered by COLORADO to the north, OKLAHOMA and TEXAS to the east, Texas and MEXICO to the south, and ARIZONA to the west. Its capital is SANTA FE, and its largest city is ALBUQUERQUE.

New Orleans   (AWR-lee-uhnz, AWR-luhnz, awr-LEENZ) Port city in southeastern LOUISIANA. ❧ Dominated by Creole CULTURE, which stemmed from the French settlers of the southern United States. ❧ JAZZ originated in the late nineteenth century among African-American musicians of New Orleans. ❧ MARDI GRAS is celebrated here each year. ❧ In the Battle of New Orleans (1815) Andrew JACKSON, not having yet received word that the Treaty of Ghent had ended the WAR OF 1812, repulsed the British assault on the city.

New York   State in the northeastern United States bordered by ONTARIO, CANADA, LAKE ONTARIO, and LAKE ERIE to the north and west; VERMONT, MASSACHUSETTS, CONNECTICUT, and the ATLANTIC OCEAN to the east; and NEW JERSEY and PENNSYLVANIA to the south. Its capital is ALBANY, and its largest city is NEW YORK CITY. ❧ One of the THIRTEEN COLONIES.

New York City   City in NEW YORK state and largest city in the United States. (*See* BOWERY, BROADWAY, BRONX, BROOKLYN, FIFTH AVENUE, GREENWICH VILLAGE, HARLEM, MADISON AVENUE, MANHATTAN, PARK AVENUE, TIMES SQUARE, *and* WALL STREET.) ❧ One of the key financial, communications, and arts centers of the world.

Newark   (NOOH-uhrk)   Largest city in NEW JERSEY.

Newport   Resort city in southeastern RHODE ISLAND. ❧ Famed for summer homes of nineteenth-century millionaires. ❧ Center of yachting in the United States.

Niagara Falls   (neye-AG-ruh, neye-AG-uh-ruh)   Waterfall in western NEW YORK state and southern ONTARIO, CANADA. ❧ Great tourist attraction known as a honeymooners' resort.

Nob Hill   Fashionable neighborhood in SAN FRANCISCO.

Norfolk   (NAWR-fuhk, NAWR-fawk)   City in southeastern VIRGINIA. ❧ Known for its harbor and naval base; shipbuilding center.

North Carolina   State in the southeastern United States bordered by VIRGINIA to the north, the ATLANTIC OCEAN to the east, SOUTH CAROLINA and GEORGIA to the south, and TENNESSEE to the west. Its capital is Raleigh, and its largest city is CHARLOTTE. ❧ One of the THIRTEEN COLONIES. ❧ One of the CONFEDERATE states during the CIVIL WAR.

North Dakota   State in the north-central United States, bordered by SASKATCHEWAN and MANITOBA, CANADA, to the north; MINNESOTA to the east; SOUTH DAKOTA to the south; and MONTANA to the west. Its capital is Bismarck, and its largest city is Fargo.

Oakland   City in northern CALIFORNIA on the east side of SAN FRANCISCO BAY.

Ohio   State in the northern United States bordered by MICHIGAN and LAKE ERIE to the north, PENNSYLVANIA and WEST VIRGINIA to the east, WEST VIRGINIA and KENTUCKY to the south, and INDIANA to the west. Its capital is COLUMBUS, and its largest city is CLEVELAND.

Ohio River   River that runs west from PITTSBURGH to the MISSISSIPPI RIVER.

Oklahoma   State in the southwestern United States, bordered by COLORADO and KANSAS to the north, MISSOURI and ARKANSAS to the east, TEXAS to the south, and NEW MEXICO to the west. Its capital and largest city is OKLAHOMA CITY.

Oklahoma City   Capital of OKLAHOMA and largest city in the state.

Omaha (OH-muh-haw, OH-muh-hah)   Largest city in NEBRASKA.

Oregon   State in the northwestern United States bordered by WASHINGTON to the north, IDAHO to the east, NEVADA and CALIFORNIA to the south, and the PACIFIC OCEAN to the west. Its capital is Salem, and its largest city is PORTLAND.

❧ Before the coming of the railroads, the Oregon Trail was used as an overland emigrant route from the MISSOURI RIVER to the COLUMBIA RIVER country (all of which was then called Oregon).

Pacific Islands   Consisting of the Caroline Islands, the Marshall Islands, and the Marianas Islands, covering a vast area of the PACIFIC OCEAN, including more than two thousand islands and islets. Held by the United States under UNITED NATIONS trusteeship.

Painted Desert   Hundreds of miles of sandstone formations with a remarkable range of colors; located in northeastern ARIZONA.

Park Avenue   A fashionable residential street in MANHATTAN.

Pennsylvania   State in the northeastern United States bordered by LAKE ERIE and NEW YORK to the north; NEW JERSEY to the east; DELAWARE, MARYLAND, and WEST VIRGINIA to the south; and OHIO to the west. Its capital is Harrisburg, and its largest city is PHILADELPHIA.

❧ One of the THIRTEEN COLONIES. ❧ Named after the father of William PENN, a devout QUAKER, who was granted proprietary rights by the king of ENGLAND to almost the whole of what is now Pennsylvania in the late seventeenth century.

Philadelphia (fil-uh-DEL-fee-uh, fil-uh-DEL-fyuh)   Largest city in PENNSYLVANIA.

❧ Cultural center now and especially in colonial times. Its historical monuments include Independence Hall, where the DECLARATION OF INDEPENDENCE and the CONSTITUTION were signed; the LIBERTY BELL; and Congress Hall. ❧ Philadelphia, the "City of Brotherly Love," was founded in the late seventeenth century as a QUAKER colony by William PENN.

Phoenix (FEE-niks)   Capital city of ARIZONA.

Piedmont (PEED-mont)   The plateau region of the eastern United States extending from NEW YORK to

ALABAMA between the APPALACHIAN MOUNTAINS and the ATLANTIC coastal plain. Also a historical region of northwest ITALY bound by the Swiss and French Alps. More broadly, any region of foothills.

Pike's Peak   Mountain in high central COLORADO in the Front Range (eastern range) of the ROCKY MOUNTAINS.

❧ One of the goals of early pioneers, whose motto often was "Pike's Peak or Bust."

Pittsburgh   City in southern PENNSYLVANIA.

❧ Leading industrial center, known for its steel mills.

Portland   Two major cities in the United States: the largest city in OREGON and the largest city in MAINE.

Potomac River (puh-TOH-muhk)   A river that divides WASHINGTON, D.C., from VIRGINIA.

❧ Sometimes used to refer loosely to Washington, D.C.: "Along the Potomac today, CONGRESS met to vote on the budget."

Providence   Capital of RHODE ISLAND and largest city in the state, located in the northeastern part of the state.

❧ Port of entry and major trading center. ❧ Roger WILLIAMS founded Providence in the early seventeenth century after he was exiled from the colony of MASSACHUSETTS. He named it in gratitude for "God's merciful providence."

Puerto Rico (pwer-tuh, pawr-tuh REE-koh)   Island in the CARIBBEAN SEA, southeast of MIAMI, FLORIDA. Its capital and largest city is San Juan.

❧ Puerto Rico is a commonwealth of the United States. Citizens of Puerto Rico are also American citizens but do not vote in federal elections, and do not pay federal taxes on their local earnings.

Reno   City in western NEVADA.

❧ Known for its gambling casinos and easily obtained divorces.

Rhode Island   State in the northeastern United States; one of the NEW ENGLAND states. Bordered by MASSACHUSETTS to the north and east, the ATLANTIC OCEAN to the south, and CONNECTICUT to the west. Its capital and largest city is PROVIDENCE.

❧ One of the THIRTEEN COLONIES. ❧ Roger WILLIAMS, after he was banished from MASSACHUSETTS for speaking out in favor of religious toleration, established the first settlement in the area at PROVI-DENCE in the early seventeenth century. ❧ Rhode Island is the smallest state in area.

Richmond   The capital of VIRGINIA.
❧ Capital of the CONFEDERACY during the CIVIL WAR.

Rio Grande (ree-oh GRAND, GRAN-dee)   River running east from COLORADO to the GULF OF MEXICO, dividing the United States from MEXICO.

Rochester   City in western NEW YORK.
❧ Center of the photographic equipment industry.

Rocky Mountains   Major mountain chain of western NORTH AMERICA, running from ALASKA to MEXICO.

Rustbelt   Urban areas in the Northeast and MIDDLE WEST marked by the concentration of old, declining industries, such as steel and textiles.

Sacramento   The capital of CALIFORNIA, located in the northern part of the state.

St. Lawrence River   River flowing northeast from LAKE ONTARIO to the ATLANTIC OCEAN. ONTARIO and QUEBEC, CANADA, and NEW YORK state are along its banks.
❧ Important trade route. The St. Lawrence Seaway, a system of locks, allows oceangoing ships to pass between the Atlantic and the GREAT LAKES.

St. Louis (saynt LOOH-uhs)   The largest city in MISSOURI.
❧ Known as the "Gateway to the West" because of its importance as a staging area for wagon trains in the nineteenth century. The Gateway Arch, made of steel and several hundred feet high, stands in St. Louis in commemoration of this fact.

St. Paul   The capital of MINNESOTA, and, with MINNEAPOLIS, one of the TWIN CITIES.

St. Petersburg   City in western FLORIDA.
❧ A popular winter resort. ❧ Home for many retired persons from colder northern areas.

Salt Lake City   The capital of UTAH and largest city in the state; located near the GREAT SALT LAKE.
❧ Center of the MORMON CHURCH.

San Andreas Fault (SAN an-DRAY-uhs)   A major geologic FAULT located in CALIFORNIA. It runs from SAN FRANCISCO to near SAN DIEGO and has been the source of serious EARTHQUAKES. (*See also under* "*Earth Sciences.*")

San Antonio (san an-TOH-nee-oh)   A city in south-central Texas.
❧ The location of the ALAMO.

San Diego (san dee-AY-goh)   City in southern CALIFORNIA close to the border of MEXICO.
❧ San Diego is a cultural, educational, and medical and scientific research center; a major port and naval base; and home of the San Diego Zoo.

San Francisco   A city in northern CALIFORNIA.
❧ Site of the GOLDEN GATE BRIDGE. ❧ A major West Coast intellectual center.

San Francisco Bay   Located in northern CALIFORNIA; entered from the PACIFIC OCEAN through a strait called the Golden Gate.

San Joaquin Valley (san waw-KEEN, san wah-KEEN)   A vast valley in central CALIFORNIA.
❧ Known for its rich farmland.

San Jose (san hoh-ZAY, san oh-ZAY)   A city in northern CALIFORNIA.
❧ Center for the electronics and COMPUTER industries. (*See* SILICON VALLEY.)

Santa Fe (san-tuh FAY)   Capital of NEW MEXICO.

Santa Fe Trail   Trail extending from INDEPENDENCE, MISSOURI, southwest to SANTA FE, NEW MEXICO.
❧ Important route used by settlers moving west.

Saratoga Springs   A resort city in eastern NEW YORK.
❧ Famed for its spa and its horse racing.

Seattle (see-AT-l)   The largest city in the state of WASHINGTON.
❧ Home of Boeing Aircraft Company.

Selma   City in south-central ALABAMA.
❧ In 1965, during the CIVIL RIGHTS MOVEMENT, Selma was the center of a registration drive for black voters, led by Martin Luther KING, Jr.

Shenandoah Valley (shen-uhn-DOH-uh)   A large, beautiful valley in northern VIRGINIA, between the BLUE RIDGE and ALLEGHENY MOUNTAINS.
❧ During the CIVIL WAR, it was the site of numerous battles because it served as one of the main sources of grain and fodder for the CONFEDERACY.

Sierra Nevada (see-ER-uh nuh-VAD-uh, nuh-VAH-duh) Mountain range in eastern CALIFORNIA.

🥄 Location of MOUNT WHITNEY, the highest peak in the United States outside of ALASKA.

South Carolina State in the southeastern United States, bordered by NORTH CAROLINA to the north, the ATLANTIC OCEAN to the south and east, and GEORGIA to the south and west. Its capital and largest city is Columbia.

🥄 One of the THIRTEEN COLONIES. 🥄 One of the CONFEDERATE states during the CIVIL WAR.

South Dakota State in the north-central United States bordered by NORTH DAKOTA to the north, MINNESOTA and IOWA to the east, NEBRASKA to the south, and WYOMING and MONTANA to the west. Its capital is Pierre, and its largest city is Sioux Falls.

🥄 A popular winter resort.

Sunbelt States in the South and Southwest marked by warm CLIMATE, rapid economic and population growth in the last two decades, and (often) political CONSERVATISM.

Tampa City in western FLORIDA.

🥄 Port of entry with a harbor on Tampa Bay.

Tennessee State in the south-central United States bordered by KENTUCKY and VIRGINIA to the north; NORTH CAROLINA to the east; GEORGIA, ALABAMA, and MISSISSIPPI to the south; and ARKANSAS and MISSOURI to the west. Its capital is NASHVILLE, and its largest city is MEMPHIS.

🥄 One of the CONFEDERATE states during the CIVIL WAR.

Tennessee River River formed by the confluence of two other rivers near Knoxville, TENNESSEE; it follows a U-shaped course to enter the OHIO RIVER in western KENTUCKY.

Texas State in the southwestern United States bordered by OKLAHOMA to the north, ARKANSAS and LOUISIANA to the east, the GULF OF MEXICO and MEXICO to the south, and NEW MEXICO to the west. Its capital is AUSTIN, and its largest city is HOUSTON.

🥄 One of the border states with Mexico; Mexican aliens often cross the border into Texas. 🥄 One of the CONFEDERATE states during the CIVIL WAR. 🥄 Long the largest state, it became second largest with the admission of ALASKA as the forty-ninth state in 1959.

Times Square Area of MANHATTAN formed by the intersection of Broadway and Seventh Avenue between Forty-second and Forty-fourth Streets.

🥄 Heart of the NEW YORK CITY theater district. 🥄 Known for its high levels of vice, including drug dealing, prostitution, and the sale of pornographic materials. 🥄 Site of New Year's celebration every year.

Toledo (tuh-LEE-doh) Industrial city in northwestern OHIO.

Tucson (TOOH-son) Large city in southeastern ARIZONA, in a desert surrounded by mountains.

🥄 Tourist center.

Tulsa Large city in northeastern OKLAHOMA.

Twin Cities Nickname of MINNEAPOLIS and ST. PAUL, MINNESOTA.

Utah State in the western United States bordered by IDAHO and WYOMING to the north, COLORADO to the east, ARIZONA to the south, and NEVADA to the west. Its capital and largest city is SALT LAKE CITY.

🥄 The GREAT SALT LAKE is located in the northwestern part of the state. 🥄 Members of the Church of Jesus Christ of LATTER-DAY SAINTS, also known as the MORMONS, founded the state and to a large extent still dominate it.

Vermont State in the northeastern United States; one of the NEW ENGLAND states. Bordered by QUEBEC, CANADA, to the north; NEW HAMPSHIRE to the east; MASSACHUSETTS to the south; and NEW YORK to the west. Its capital is Montpelier, and its largest city is Burlington.

Virgin Islands Islands in the CARIBBEAN SEA, east of PUERTO RICO, owned by the United States and BRITAIN.

🥄 Christopher COLUMBUS discovered the Virgin Islands in 1493.

Virginia State in the eastern United States bordered by WEST VIRGINIA and MARYLAND to the north, the ATLANTIC OCEAN to the east, NORTH CAROLINA and TENNESSEE to the south, and KENTUCKY to the west. Its capital is RICHMOND, and its largest city is VIRGINIA BEACH.

🥄 One of the THIRTEEN COLONIES. The first permanent English settlement in NORTH AMERICA was at JAMESTOWN, founded in the early seventeenth century. 🥄 Named for Queen ELIZABETH I, the "Virgin

Queen." &. One of the CONFEDERATE states during the CIVIL WAR.

Washington   State in the northwestern United States bordered by BRITISH COLUMBIA, CANADA, to the north; IDAHO to the east; OREGON to the south; and the PACIFIC OCEAN to the west. Its capital is Olympia, and its largest city is SEATTLE.

Washington, D.C.   The capital of the United States. Located in the DISTRICT OF COLUMBIA.

&. Location of headquarters for the major branches of the government of the United States, including the departments of the EXECUTIVE BRANCH, CONGRESS, and the SUPREME COURT. &. Known for its historical monuments, museums, and buildings, including the LINCOLN MEMORIAL, the SMITHSONIAN INSTITUTION, the VIETNAM MEMORIAL, the WASHINGTON MONUMENT, and the WHITE HOUSE.

West Point   A village in NEW YORK.

&. Location of the United States Military Academy, which is often referred to as West Point. &. Benedict ARNOLD was given command of the fort at West Point during the REVOLUTIONARY WAR. Arnold arranged to betray the fort, which controlled the HUDSON RIVER, in exchange for a British commission and a sum of money.

West Virginia   State in the southeastern United States bordered by PENNSYLVANIA and MARYLAND to the north, VIRGINIA to the east and south, and KEN-

TUCKY and OHIO to the west. Its capital and largest city is CHARLESTON.

&. Separated from Virginia after Virginia seceded from the UNION in 1861; it was granted statehood in 1863, during the CIVIL WAR. &. Ranks first in bituminous coal production, with about 20 PERCENT of the nation's total.

Wisconsin   State in the north-central United States bordered by LAKE SUPERIOR and the state of MICHIGAN to the north, LAKE MICHIGAN to the east, ILLINOIS to the south, and IOWA and MINNESOTA to the west. Its capital is MADISON, and its largest city is MILWAUKEE.

&. Known for its dairy products, especially cheese.

Wyoming   State in the western United States bordered by MONTANA to the north, SOUTH DAKOTA and NEBRASKA to the east, COLORADO and UTAH to the south, and IDAHO to the west. Its capital is Cheyenne, and its largest city is Casper.

Yellowstone National Park   Located in WYOMING.

&. Famous for its geysers, including "Old Faithful," and for its bears and buffalo. &. The first national park in the United States.

Yosemite National Park (yoh-SEM-uh-tee)   Located in CALIFORNIA.

&. Famous for its dramatic rock formations and waterfalls.

Anthropology, Psychology, and Sociology

A NTHROPOLOGY, SOCIOLOGY, and some subdivisions of PSYCHOLOGY are numbered among the SOCIAL SCIENCES. As the belief that God directly controlled and influenced human behavior weakened during the nineteenth century, PHILOSOPHERS tried to construct a science of society, or social science. Social scientists rejected the idea that human activities occur at random, and affirmed instead that all human activities reveal observed regularities or patterns. Gradually, social scientists refined such concepts as social CLASS and KINSHIP to explain these patterns.

By the end of the nineteenth century, the quest for a unified social science was giving way to the rise of the social sciences. As knowledge became more technical and specialized, economists, political scientists, sociologists, anthropologists, and psychologists each pursued different avenues of inquiry into social experience. Although social scientists in one field borrowed ideas from other fields, each field tended to develop its own specialized language, or JARGON, and distinctive concepts. What began as an all-encompassing effort to identify a single science of society became an enterprise marked by diversity, specialization, and often fragmentation. Today, the usual list of social sciences includes anthropology, ECONOMICS, POLITICAL SCIENCE, psychology, and sociology. In addition, some view history as a social science.

In this section, we have grouped together entries drawn from three social sciences: anthropology, psychology, and sociology. Sociology concerns itself with the behavior of humans in groups, with social relationships, social classes, social movements, and organizations. An economist might study a CORPORATION to gauge its impact on production, while a political scientist might assess how corporations try to influence political campaigns. In contrast, a sociologist explores the social relationships that develop among workers within large organizations such as corporations. Anthropologists also study social behavior, but with a difference. Where sociologists focus on groups in advanced societies of the present, anthropologists have traditionally paid more attention to social relationships among so-called primitive, preliterate peoples. In recent years, this distinction has broken down to a degree, for anthropologists now also study social behavior in advanced societies. Yet anthropologists are more likely to inform their investigation of advanced societies with comparisons with primitive societies. In this sense, anthropology encompasses a broader historical and geographical span than does sociology.

Psychology is basically the study of mental life. Some subdivisions of psychology have far more in common with natural sciences such as BIOLOGY and CHEMISTRY than with the social sciences. For example, physiological psychologists study the role of the BRAIN, GLANDS, and other ORGANS in mental processes, and often experiment on animals, especially rats, rather than humans. Many other subdivisions of psychology, however, resemble the social sciences. For example, social psychologists investigate the role of the family and the PEER GROUP in the mental development of the individual. Both sociologists and anthropologists also concern themselves with mental processes, for all social relationships among humans have psychological dimensions. The difference is that psychologists start out with mental processes, while sociologists and anthropologists usually begin with social relationships and then speculate about mental processes.

During the last sixty years, terms that originated in all three of these social sciences have come into general usage. The writings of Sigmund FREUD did much to popularize psychology. In the 1920s, terms such as *ID* and *OEDIPUS COMPLEX* became part of the vocabulary of sophisticates. More recently, the magazine *Psychology Today*, which began publication in 1967, has contributed to the popularization of psychology. The launching of *Psychology Today* in the late 1960s coincided with a growing desire among ordinary Americans to understand their innermost feelings. Similarly, sociological terms such as *STATUS* and *CLASS* have made their way into general usage.

— J. F. K.

ABORIGINE. *An Australian aborigine, hunting.*

aborigines (ab-uh-RIJ-uh-neez) The earliest known inhabitants of a region. The term is most often associated with the native hunting and gathering population of AUSTRALIA, who preceded the arrival of white settlers. (*See* HUNTING AND GATHERING SOCIETIES.)

abortion The deliberate termination of a pregnancy, usually before the EMBRYO or FETUS is capable of independent life. In medical contexts, this is called an INDUCED ABORTION, and distinguished from a SPONTANEOUS ABORTION (MISCARRIAGE) or STILL-BIRTH.

& Abortion laws are extremely controversial. Those who describe themselves as "pro-choice" believe that the decision to have an abortion should be left to the mother. In contrast, the "pro-life" FACTION, arguing that abortion is killing, holds that the state should prohibit abortion in most cases. Feminists (*see* FEMINISM) and LIBERALS generally support the pro-choice side; ROMAN CATHOLICS and PROTESTANT FUNDAMENTALISTS generally back the pro-life side. (*See* ROE V. WADE.)

acculturation (uh-kul-chuh-RAY-shuhn) The learning of the ideas, values, conventions, and behavior that characterize a social group. (*See* SOCIALIZATION.)

Acculturation is also used to describe the results of contact between two or more different CULTURES; a new, composite culture emerges, in which some existing cultural features are combined, some are lost, and new features are generated. Usually one culture is dominant (as in the case of colonization).

acrophobia (ak-ruh-FOH-bee-uh) An abnormal fear of heights.

adultery Sexual relations a married person has with a partner other than his or her spouse.

& Adultery is often cited as grounds for divorce.

alienation (ay-lee-uh-NAY-shuhn)   A feeling of separation or isolation. In SOCIAL SCIENCE, alienation is associated with the problems caused by rapid social change, such as industrialization and urbanization (*see* INDUSTRIAL REVOLUTION), which has broken down traditional relationships among individuals and groups, and the GOODS and SERVICES they produce.

   ✻ Alienation is most often associated with minorities, the poor, the unemployed, and other groups who have limited power to bring about changes in society. ✻ MARXISM holds that workers in CAPITALIST nations are alienated because they have no claim to ownership of the products they make.

alter ego (AWL-tuhr EE-goh)   An intimate friend, considered another side of oneself: "He was my alter ego; we were always picking up each other's thoughts." *Alter ego* is LATIN for "another I."

altruism (AL-trooh-iz-uhm)   A selfless concern for others.

amnesia (am-NEE-zhuh)   A loss of memory, especially one brought on by some distressing or shocking experience.

   ✻ A common variant is *selective amnesia*; the term is applied to public officials who, when questioned about alleged wrongdoing, profess that they cannot remember.

anal personality (AYN-l)   A popular term for "anal retentive PERSONALITY," a personality marked by excessive orderliness, extreme meticulousness, and often suspicion and reserve. According to PSYCHOANALYSIS, an anal personality is formed in early childhood as a product of efforts to control bowel movements. (*See* ANAL STAGE, GENITAL STAGE, *and* ORAL STAGE; *compare* ORAL PERSONALITY.)

anal stage   According to PSYCHOANALYSIS, the second social and sexual stage of an infant's development (after the ORAL STAGE), in which the infant learns to control bowel movements. FREUDIAN PSYCHOLOGY maintains that children gain pleasure from both passing and withholding their feces. Psychoanalysts believe that development of an ANAL PERSONALITY is associated with frustration over toilet training. (*See also* GENITAL STAGE *and* PLEASURE PRINCIPLE.)

angst (AHNGKST)   A kind of fear or ANXIETY; *Angst* is German for "fear." It is usually applied to a deep and essentially philosophical anxiety about the world in general or personal freedom. (*See* EXISTENTIALISM.)

animism (AN-uh-miz-uhm)   The belief, common among so-called primitive people, that objects and natural phenomena such as rivers, rocks, and wind are alive and have feelings and intentions. Animistic beliefs form the basis of many CULTS. (*See also* FETISH *and* TOTEMISM.)

anthropology   The scientific study of the origin, development, and varieties of human beings and their societies, particularly so-called primitive societies.

anxiety   Emotional distress, especially that brought on by fear of failure. (*See also* ANGST.)

aphrodisiac (af-ruh-DEE-zee-ak, af-ruh-DIZ-ee-ak)   A substance or quality that excites sexual desire.

   ✻ Aphrodisiacs are named after APHRODITE, the Greek goddess of love.

ARCHAEOLOGY. *An archaeological excavation in Ife, Nigeria.*

archaeology (ahr-kee-OL-uh-jee)   The recovery and study of material objects, such as graves, buildings, tools, artworks, and human remains, to investigate the structure and behavior of past CULTURES. Archaeologists rely on physical remains as clues to the emergence and development of human societies and civilizations. Anthropologists, by contrast, are able to interact with living people in order to study their cultures.

archetype (AHR-ki-teyep)   An original model after which other similar things are patterned. In the PSYCHOLOGY of Carl JUNG, archetypes are the images, patterns, and SYMBOLS that rise out of the COLLECTIVE UNCONSCIOUS and appear in dreams, MYTHOLOGY, and fairy tales.

asexuality (ay-sek-shooh-AL-i-tee)   Having no sexual organs, or engaging in no sexual activity.

assimilation   The process by which a person or persons acquire the social and psychological characteristics of a group: "Waves of immigrants have been assimilated into the American CULTURE."

autism (AW-tiz-uhm)   A condition in which someone appears to be involved exclusively in his or her own interior experiences. Autistic adults are pathologically self-absorbed, glimpsing the real world only through their fantasies. Autistic children suffer from a disorder in which they refuse to relate to other people, and are severely limited in their use of language. The cause of autism in children is unknown, but researchers generally feel that it lies in malfunction of the CENTRAL NERVOUS SYSTEM, not in the way their parents have treated them, or in other aspects of their environment.

beatniks   Members of the "beat" movement in the United States in the 1950s. Beatniks frequently rejected MIDDLE-CLASS American values, customs, and tastes in favor of RADICAL politics and exotic JAZZ, art, and literature. The movement was often classified as BOHEMIAN. The poet Allen GINSBERG and the novelist Jack Kerouac are examples of beatnik authors.

ᘐ "Daddy-O" (a term of address); "Cool, man, cool"; and "strictly dullsville" are examples of SLANG expressions used by beatniks, or by people who were trying to sound like beatniks.

behavior modification   The changing of a person's reactions to certain situations or STIMULI. Behavior THERAPY, a form of PSYCHOTHERAPY advocated in BEHAVIORISM, uses a variety of methods, such as assertiveness training, CONDITIONED RESPONSE, and

HYPNOSIS, to change unsatisfactory or deviant patterns of behavior.

behaviorism   A THEORY that PSYCHOLOGY is essentially a study of external human behavior rather than internal consciousness and desires. (See SKINNER, B. F.)

Bible Belt   An area of the United States, including the South and parts of the MIDDLE WEST, where fervent PROTESTANT FUNDAMENTALISM is strong. (See SCOPES TRIAL.)

bisexuality   Sexual activity with, or sexual attraction to, members of both sexes.

blackball   A rejection of an applicant's membership in a private organization, such as a club or fraternity. The term is derived from the traditional practice of members voting anonymously on admitting new members, using either a white marble (acceptance) or a black marble (denial). Acceptance must be unanimous; therefore, one black marble in the ballot box is enough to keep the applicant out of the organization.

ᘐ The term is now applied generally to efforts — especially unreasonable or vengeful actions — to keep a people or groups out of organizations they wish to join.

blacklist   Concerted action by employers to deny employment to someone suspected of unacceptable opinions or behavior. For example, individual workers suspected of favoring LABOR UNIONS have often been blacklisted by all the employers in a region.

ᘐ During the McCarthy era (see MCCARTHY, Joseph P.) in the 1950s, the careers of many public figures suspected of COMMUNIST activities were ruined by blacklisting.

blue-collar   A descriptive term widely used for manual laborers, as opposed to WHITE-COLLAR for office workers.

ᘐ The term is often associated with CONSERVATIVE values.

Boy Scouts of America   An organization for boys and young men from the ages of seven to eighteen. The aim of the Boy Scouts is to increase values of citizenship and leadership in its members. Their motto is "Be Prepared." The traditional age for Boy Scouts is about ten to fourteen; there are other levels of the program (Cub Scouts and Explorers) for younger and older boys. Several million boys and adults participate.

🐾 The Scout Law lists twelve characteristics a Boy Scout should have: to be trustworthy, loyal, helpful, friendly, courteous, kind, obedient, cheerful, thrifty, brave, clean, and reverent. 🐾 The Scout Oath requires that Scouts do their duty to God and country and "help other people at all times."

brainwashing Indoctrination that forces people to abandon their beliefs in favor of another set of beliefs. Usually associated with military and political interrogation and religious conversion, brainwashing attempts, through prolonged stress, to break down an individual's physical and mental defenses. Brainwashing techniques range from vocal persuasion and threats to punishment, physical deprivation, mind-altering drugs, and severe physical torture.

bureaucracy (byoo-ROK-ruh-see) A formal, hierarchical organization with many levels in which tasks, responsibilities, and authority are delegated among individuals, offices, or departments, held together by a central administration. According to many sociologists and anthropologists, the development of bureaucratic organizations is necessary for the emergence of any modern civilization. (*See* WEBER, MAX.)

🐾 Today, the term *bureaucracy* suggests a lack of initiative, excessive adherence to rules and routine, RED TAPE, inefficiency, or, even more serious, an impersonal force dominating the lives of individuals. (*See* BIG BROTHER IS WATCHING YOU.)

bureaucrat (BYOOR-uh-krat) Someone who works in or controls a BUREAUCRACY. The term is often used negatively to describe a petty, narrow-minded person. (*See also* CONFORMITY *and* ORGANIZATION MAN.)

Bushmen The nomadic hunting and gathering peoples of the Kalahari Desert of southern AFRICA, in BOTSWANA, NAMIBIA, and ANGOLA. (*See* HUNTING AND GATHERING SOCIETIES *and* NOMADISM.)

cadre (KAD-ree, KAH-dray) An ELITE or select group that forms the core of an organization, and is capable of training new members.

Cajun (KAY-juhn) A native of LOUISIANA believed to be descended from the French exiles from Acadia (*see* NOVA SCOTIA). Cajuns have maintained a sepa-

rate CULTURE, including a special dialect and distinctive cooking style.

Carnegie, Dale An American author and educator of the twentieth century; Carnegie published *How to Win Friends and Influence People* in 1936. The book, which has sold millions of copies, contains practical tips on gaining influence and success. Carnegie founded a CORPORATION that gives courses in applying the book's principles.

caste (KAST) One of the four hereditary social divisions in HINDUISM. Members of any one caste are restricted in their choice of occupation, and may have only limited association with members of other castes.

🐾 *Caste* has come to mean a group of persons set apart by economic, social, religious, legal, or political criteria, such as occupation, STATUS, religious denomination, legal privilege, skin color, or some other physical characteristic. Members of a caste tend to associate among themselves and rarely marry outside the caste. Castes are more socially separate from each other than are social CLASSES. 🐾 During the height of SEGREGATION in the United States, African-Americans were sometimes loosely referred to as a caste.

catharsis (kuh-THAHR-suhs) An experience of emotional release and purification, often inspired by or through art. In PSYCHOANALYSIS, catharsis is the release of tension and ANXIETY that results from bringing repressed feelings and memories into consciousness.

charisma (kuh-RIZ-muh) Extraordinary power and appeal of PERSONALITY; natural ability to inspire a large following.

🐾 The term *charisma* is usually associated with political, religious, or entertainment figures, or with prominent positions, such as POPE or president.

charismatic (kar-iz-MAT-ik) Possessing CHARISMA. Political leaders such as John F. KENNEDY and Adolf HITLER, religious leaders such as Martin Luther KING, Jr., and the Ayatollah KHOMEINI, and entertainment figures such as Greta GARBO have all been described as charismatic.

Chicanos (chi-KAH-nohz) Mexican-Americans; short for the Spanish word *mexicanos*, which is sometimes pronounced *mechicanos*.

class A group of people sharing the same social, economic, or occupational STATUS. The term *class* usually implies a social and economic hierarchy, in which those of higher class standing have greater status, privilege, prestige, and authority. Western societies have traditionally been divided into three classes: the upper or LEISURE CLASS, the MIDDLE CLASS (BOURGEOISIE), and the lower or WORKING CLASS. For Marxists, the significant classes are the bourgeoisie and the PROLETARIAT.

class consciousness Identification with other members of one's own CLASS and awareness of its relationship with other classes. According to Marxist THEORY, the PROLETARIAT will assume class consciousness when workers realize that they are being exploited by the BOURGEOISIE; then a proletarian revolution will be inevitable. Contrary to this theory, however, the American WORKING CLASS is primarily CONSERVATIVE, and favors the ESTABLISHMENT.

class structure The hierarchical organization by which a society or community is divided into CLASSES. The vast majority of the population of the United States considers itself as belonging to the MIDDLE CLASS. In MARXISM, class structure is organized into the BOURGEOISIE and the PROLETARIAT.

class struggle The idea, associated with Karl MARX, that conflict between the BOURGEOISIE and the PROLETARIAT is inevitable and will result in the triumph of SOCIALISM over CAPITALISM.

claustrophobia (klaw-struh-FOH-bee-uh) An abnormal fear of being shut in or enclosed.

cognitive development (KOG-nuh-tiv) The growth of a person's ability to learn.

collective unconscious Memories of mental patterns that are shared by members of a single CULTURE or, more broadly, by all human beings; originally proposed by the psychologist Carl JUNG to explain psychological traits shared by all people. He theorized that the collective unconscious appears as ARCHETYPES: patterns and SYMBOLS that occur in dreams, MYTHOLOGY, and fairy tales.

Coming of Age in Samoa A book published by Margaret MEAD in 1928. Mead determined that the ways in which children in SAMOA are socialized (*see* SOCIALIZATION) result in a generally happy adolescence and easy transition to sexual activity and adult-hood. These findings challenged the widely held belief that biological changes occurring during adolescence were necessarily accompanied by social and psychological STRESS. Mead argued that adolescent stress is a cultural, not a biological, phenomenon. *Coming of Age* contributed to the popularization of ANTHROPOLOGY and helped to establish the anthropology subfield of CULTURE and PERSONALITY. Her interpretation of Samoan society was later challenged by Derek Freeman and a bitter controversy ensued.

common-law marriage A legal marriage brought about by the cohabitation of a man and a woman, or by their agreement to consider themselves married, rather than by a wedding. (*See* COMMON LAW.)

compulsion In PSYCHOLOGY, an internal force that leads persons to act against their will. A "compulsive" act cannot be controlled: "Smith was a compulsive gambler."

conditioned reflex *See* CONDITIONED RESPONSE.

conditioned response In PSYCHOLOGY, the response made by a person or animal after learning to associate an experience with a neutral or arbitrary STIMULUS. Conditioned response experiments by Ivan Pavlov (*see* PAVLOV'S DOGS) paired a neutral stimulus (sounding a bell) with a natural response (salivating) by associating the bell with the presentation of food. Conditioned response experiments by B. F. SKINNER and other behaviorists (*see* BEHAVIORISM) associated an arbitrary action (an animal's pressing a lever) with a positive reward (presentation of food) or a negative reward (an electric shock).

&. Response conditioning is used in BEHAVIOR MODIFICATION. Stop-smoking clinics, for example, may use an electric shock whenever a patient lights up. The patient will then associate smoking with the unpleasant experience of the shock.

conformity Agreement between an individual's behavior and a group's standards or expectations. A conformist is one who follows the majority's desires or standards. (*See also* BEATNIKS, BUREAUCRAT, ORGANIZATION MAN, PEER GROUP, *and* PEER PRESSURE.)

conjugal (KON-juh-guhl) A descriptive term for the relationship between married persons. A conjugal family is the same as a NUCLEAR FAMILY, composed of married parents and their children. Conjugal relatives (in-laws) trace their relations through the marriage of their respective blood relatives.

conspicuous consumption   Buying unnecessary and expensive products and services as a way to show off wealth. The term was coined by U.S. economist Thorstein Veblen in *The Theory of the Leisure Class.*

coolie   An unskilled laborer or porter in eastern ASIA. *Coolie* is a degrading term for any laborer.

cosmology (koz-MOL-uh-jee)   A system of beliefs that seeks to describe or explain the origin and structure of the UNIVERSE. A cosmology attempts to establish an ordered, harmonious framework that integrates time, space, the PLANETS, STARS, and other celestial phenomena. In so-called primitive societies, cosmologies help explain the relationship of human beings to the rest of the universe, and are therefore closely tied to religious beliefs and practices. In modern industrial societies, cosmologies seek to explain the universe through ASTRONOMY and MATHEMATICS. METAPHYSICS also plays a part in the formation of cosmologies.

counterculture   A protest movement by American youth that arose in the late 1960s and faded during the late 1970s. According to some, young people in the United States were forming a CULTURE of their own, opposed to the culture of MIDDLE AMERICA. (*See* HIPPIES *and* WOODSTOCK.)

Cro-Magnon (kroh-MAG-nuhn, kroh-MAN-yuhn)   The earliest form of modern humans. The Cro-Magnons developed about 35,000 years ago, and physically resembled modern Europeans. (*See* HOMO SAPIENS.)
     ❧ Cro-Magnon people painted the walls of their caves, producing the first known human art.

cult   In ANTHROPOLOGY, an organization for the conduct of ritual, magical, or other religious observances. Many so-called primitive tribes, for example, have ancestor cults, in which dead ancestors are considered divine, and activities are organized to respect their memory and invoke their aid. A cult is also a religious group held together by a dominant, often CHARISMATIC individual, or by the worship of a divinity, an idol, or some other object. (*See* ANIMISM, FETISH, *and* TOTEMISM.)
     ❧ The term *cult* often suggests extreme beliefs and bizarre behavior.

culture   The sum of attitudes, customs, and beliefs that distinguishes one group of people from another. Culture is transmitted, through language, material objects, ritual, institutions, and art, from one generation to the next.
     ❧ Anthropologists consider that the requirements for culture (language use, tool making, and conscious regulation of sex) are essential features that distinguish humans from other animals. ❧ *Culture* also refers to refined music, art, and literature; one who is well versed in these subjects is considered "cultured."

defense mechanism   In PSYCHOLOGY, a FREUDIAN term referring to an unconscious avoidance of something that produces ANXIETY or some other unpleasant emotion. For example, someone who blots out the memory of a terrible accident is using a defense mechanism. REGRESSION and SUBLIMATION are common defense mechanisms.

delusion   A false belief held despite strong evidence against it; self-deception. Delusions are common in some forms of PSYCHOSIS. Because of his delusions, the literary CHARACTER DON QUIXOTE attacks a windmill, thinking it is a giant.

demography (di-MOG-ruh-fee)   The quantitative study of human populations. Demographers study such subjects as the geographical distribution of people, birth and death rates, SOCIOECONOMIC STATUS, and age and sex distributions in order to identify the influences on population growth, structure, and development.

developmental psychology   The branch of PSYCHOLOGY that studies the psychological growth of individuals. It deals with the psychological responses and changes in behavior that characterize such stages of life as infancy, adolescence, and old age.

double standard of sexual behavior   A moral code that permits sexual freedom and promiscuity for men but not for women. The double standard has long been associated with the traditional subordination of women.

dowry   Money, property, or material goods that a bride's family gives to the bridegroom or his family at the time of the wedding. In many CULTURES, the dowry not only helps to cement the relationship between the bride's and groom's families but also serves to reinforce traditional family roles and GENDER ROLES.

ectomorph (EK-tuh-mawrf) A person whose body structure is dominated by the outer SKIN and the NERVOUS SYSTEM. Ectomorphs are thin, and have a large skin surface relative to their weight. Other body types include ENDOMORPH (heavy and flabby) and MESOMORPH (sturdy and strong, with highly developed bones and muscles).

ego (EE-goh) The "I" or self of any person (*ego* is LATIN for "I"). In psychological terms, the ego is the part of the PSYCHE that experiences the outside world and reacts to it, coming between the primitive drives of the ID and the demands of the social environment, represented by the SUPEREGO.

🐌 The term *ego* is often used to mean personal pride and self-absorption: "Losing at chess doesn't do much for my ego."

egocentric (ee-goh-SEN-trik) Preoccupied with one's own concerns.

egomania (ee-goh-MAY-nee-uh) An extreme EGOTISM.

egotism (EE-guh-tiz-uhm) An excessive regard for one's own talents or achievements; conceit, self-importance; acting with only one's own interests in mind.

empathy (EM-puh-thee) Identifying oneself completely with an object or person, sometimes even to the point of responding physically, as when, watching a baseball player swing at a pitch, one feels one's own muscles flex.

empty nest The stage in a family's cycle when the children have grown up and left home to begin their own adult lives.

🐌 For parents, the empty nest sometimes results in midlife ANXIETY.

encounter group A method of PSYCHOTHERAPY developed in the 1960s, in which a small group of people engages in intensive interactions in order to increase self-awareness and improve interpersonal relations. Group members are encouraged to be completely honest and open, reacting to one another with their immediate feelings, while exploring the entire range of emotions. Some encounter groups also experiment with nudity, touching exercises, and role-playing.

🐌 Often associated with the RADICAL social upheaval of the 1960s, encounter groups have recently

been criticized for their potentially damaging effects, since many groups are led by people not professionally trained in psychotherapy.

endomorph (EN-duh-mawrf) *See* ECTOMORPH.

environment-heredity controversy *See* NATURE-NURTURE CONTROVERSY.

ESKIMO. *An Eskimo fishing through ice at Hooper Bay, Alaska.*

Eskimos A widely dispersed group of peoples in the ARCTIC regions of ALASKA, CANADA, GREENLAND, and SIBERIA, who have traditionally survived primarily by hunting and fishing. Despite the isolation of Eskimo communities, the Eskimos display a strong cultural, racial, and linguistic unity. Many Eskimos, especially those in CANADA, prefer the name Inuit (IN-ooh-it, IN-yooh-it).

🐌 The remarkable adaptation of these people in such a harsh environment has been a favorite subject for study among anthropologists. 🐌 Most people picture isolated Eskimos living in IGLOOS and driving dogsleds; but contact with outsiders has resulted in adoption of permanent housing settlements, snowmobiles and motorboats, and modern hunting equipment. 🐌 CHRISTIANITY has replaced many traditional religious beliefs. Efforts by federal governments to incorporate Eskimo societies have included establishment of schools in Eskimo communities and opportunities to participate in the larger government and economy.

ESP *See* EXTRASENSORY PERCEPTION.

Establishment, the Individuals and institutions that exercise social, economic, and political authority over a society. The term has a pejorative CONNOTA- TION because it suggests that political and economic power is in the hands of the few.

ethnicity (eth-NIS-uh-tee) Identity with or member- ship in a particular racial, national, or cultural group, and observance of that group's customs, beliefs, and language.

   🍃 Many minority groups in the United States maintain strong ethnic identity; especially in cities, immigrants are often attracted to ethnic communities established by people from their own country, com- munities in which many traditional cultural features are maintained. (*See* MELTING POT.)

ethnocentrism (eth-noh-SEN-triz-uhm) The belief that one's own CULTURE is superior to all others, and is the standard by which all other cultures should be measured.

   🍃 Early social scientists in the nineteenth century operated from an ethnocentric point of view. "Prim- itive" tribes, for example, were studied by anthro- pologists to illustrate how human civilization had evolved and progressed from "savage" customs to- ward the accomplishments of Western industrial so- ciety.

ethnology (eth-NOL-uh-jee) The study of contem- porary CULTURES, in order to develop a theoretical framework for analyzing human society. Cultural an- thropologists generally study societies by living among the people, observing, interviewing, and par- ticipating in their activities. More than simply de- scribing the customs of these societies, anthropolo- gists attempt to uncover underlying patterns and structures of cultural characteristics, such as lan- guage, MYTHOLOGY, GENDER ROLES, SYMBOLS, and rituals.

euthanasia (yooh-thuh-NAY-zhuh) Painlessly put- ting someone to death, usually someone with an in- curable and painful disease; mercy killing.

   🍃 Proposals to make euthanasia legal in the United States have inspired heated debate.

expatriation (eks-pay-tree-AY-shuhn) Voluntarily leaving the nation of one's birth for permanent or prolonged residence in another country.

extended family A type of family in which relatives in addition to parents and children (such as grand- parents, aunts, uncles, and cousins) live in a single household. A NUCLEAR FAMILY forms the core of an extended family.

extrasensory perception (ESP) Knowledge or per- ception without use of any of the five senses. ESP in- cludes clairvoyance (knowledge about some distant object or event, such as an unreported accident), TE- LEPATHY (reading another's thoughts), and precogni- tion (predicting the future). While many people claim to have extrasensory powers, these powers have yet to be verified by scientific procedures. (*See also* PAR- APSYCHOLOGY *and* PSYCHIC RESEARCH.)

extrovert (EK-struh-vurt) A term introduced by the psychologist Carl JUNG to describe a person whose motives and actions are directed outward. Extroverts are more prone to action than contemplation, make friends readily, adjust easily to social situations, and generally show warm interest in their surroundings. (*Compare* INTROVERT.)

feminism A movement for granting women politi- cal, social, and economic equality with men. (*See* WOMEN'S MOVEMENT.)

fetish An object believed to carry a magical or spir- itual force. Some so-called primitive tribes practice CULT worship of fetishes. (*See* ANIMISM *and* TOTEM- ISM.)

   🍃 Figuratively, a "fetish" is any object that arouses excessive devotion: "Hauser made a fetish of his Porsche."

fornication Sexual intercourse between two per- sons who are not married to each other.

forte (FAWRT, FAWR-tay) A person's strong point.

Freud, Sigmund A physician in VIENNA, AUSTRIA, in the late nineteenth and early twentieth centuries, who founded PSYCHOANALYSIS and developed the THEORY of the OEDIPUS COMPLEX. He believed that psychological problems could be traced to repressed childhood experiences, particularly to repressed sex- ual desires. He also argued that dreams provide clues to the nature of psychological problems. His theories

SIGMUND FREUD

introduced concepts such as those of the ID and SU-PEREGO into the language of PSYCHIATRY.

Freudian   Pertaining to or agreeing with the THEO-RIES of Sigmund FREUD.

Freudian slip   An error in speech that reveals re-pressed thoughts or feelings; for example, acciden-tally calling one's female boss "Mother."

future shock   A sense of insecurity and disorienta-tion often felt by people whose societies are undergo-ing rapid change.

Gallup polls (GAL-uhp)   Surveys of public opinion as conducted by George Gallup, an American who developed a quantitative method of polling public opinion. Since his death in 1984, Gallup's organiza-tion, the American Institute of Public Opinion, has continued to poll Americans on topics ranging from television-watching habits to support for presidential candidates.

gay   Descriptive term for a HOMOSEXUAL.

geisha (GAY-shuh, GEE-shuh)   A Japanese woman who is trained and paid to provide entertainment and amusing company for men.

gender roles   See SEX ROLES/GENDER ROLES.

generation gap   The differences in customs, atti-tudes, and beliefs between any two generations, but especially between youths and adults.

genital stage   According to PSYCHOANALYSIS, the third social and sexual stage of a young child's devel-opment (after the ORAL STAGE and the ANAL STAGE). In the genital stage, interest in the child's own sex organs, and in other people's, replaces the earlier fo-cusing on satisfaction of hunger and control of bowel movements. A genital PERSONALITY is mature and no longer dominated by early drives for pleasure.

🐚 The OEDIPUS COMPLEX is most often observed during the genital stage.

gerontocracy (jer-uhn-TOK-ruh-see)   A society ruled by elders.

gestalt psychology (guh-SHTAHLT, guh-SHTAWLT, guh-STAHLT, guh-STAWLT)   A type of PSYCHOLOGY based on the study of a subject's responses to inte-grated wholes, rather than to separate experiences. *Gestalt* (a German word meaning "form") also refers to any structure or pattern in which the whole has properties different from those of its parts; for ex-ample, the beauty of a musical melody does not de-pend on individual notes as such, but rather on the whole continuous tune.

ghettos   Originally, areas of MEDIEVAL cities in which JEWS were compelled to live. Today the term usually refers to sections of American cities inhabited by poorer minorities (particularly blacks and Hispan-ics). (*See* INNER CITY.)

Girl Scouts of the United States of America   An organization for girls from the ages of five to seven-teen. Its aim is to increase values of citizenship and develop the interests and abilities of the members. Their motto is "Be Prepared." The organization has five levels, divided by age: Daisy, Brownie, Junior, Cadette, and Senior Girl Scout. Several million girls and adults participate.

great man theory   An approach to history associ-ated with the nineteenth-century Scottish historian Thomas Carlyle, who declared, "The history of the world is but the BIOGRAPHY of great men." Carlyle argued that heroes shape history through the vision of their intellect, the beauty of their art, the prowess of their leadership, and, most important, their divine inspiration.

&. Carlyle's theories have generally fallen out of fashion.

group therapy Any form of PSYCHOTHERAPY involving a group of patients, rather than a one-on-one session between a patient and a therapist.

&. Group therapy is often used to explore interpersonal relations.

Haley, Alex (HAY-lee) African-American author who became famous for his book *ROOTS: THE SAGA OF AN AMERICAN FAMILY* (1976). Haley combined fact and fiction in tracing his family's history to his ancestor Kunta Kinte, who was kidnaped in AFRICA in the eighteenth century and taken as a slave to America.

&. The great popularity of *Roots*, which also became a television series, was part of the growing interest in the 1970s and 1980s in MULTICULTURALISM.

hallucination A false perception that appears to be real, as when, for example, a man dying of thirst in a desert thinks that he sees a lake. (*See also* DELUSION.)

heterogeneity (het-uh-roh-juh-NEE-uh-tee) Cultural, social, biological, or other differences within a group. (*Compare* HOMOGENEITY.)

heterosexuality Sexual attraction between a male and a female. (*Compare* BISEXUALITY *and* HOMOSEXUALITY.)

hippies Members of a movement of cultural protest that began in the United States in the 1960s and affected EUROPE before fading in the 1970s. Hippies were bound together by rejection of many standard American customs and social and political views (*see* COUNTERCULTURE). The hippies often cultivated an unkempt image in their dress and grooming, and were known for such practices as communal living, free love, and use of marijuana and other drugs. Although hippies were usually opposed to involvement of the United States in the VIETNAM WAR, their movement was fundamentally a cultural rather than a political protest. (*See* WOODSTOCK; *compare* BEATNIKS.)

Homo erectus (HOH-moh i-REK-tuhs) An early ancestor of the human SPECIES, that lived from about 1.5 million years ago to 40,000 years ago. *Homo erectus* remains have been found in AFRICA, CHINA, EUROPE, and SOUTHEAST ASIA. Archaeological excavations have revealed that *Homo erectus* developed a cooperative hunting organization and the use of fire, and may have had a spoken language.

Homo sapiens (HOH-moh SAY-pee-uhnz) The biological CLASSIFICATION of modern humans. *Homo sapiens* is LATIN for "the wise human" or "the clever human." The earliest *Homo sapiens* was NEANDERTHAL, who developed about 85,000 years ago. Sometimes modern humans are further classified into the subspecies of *Homo sapiens neanderthalis* (Neanderthals) and *Homo sapiens sapiens* (CRO-MAGNONS and present-day humans).

homogeneity (hoh-muh-juh-NEE-uh-tee, hoh-muh-juh-NAY-uh-tee) Cultural, social, biological, or other similarities within a group. (*Compare* HETEROGENEITY.)

homosexuality A sexual attraction between persons of the same sex. (*See* GAY *and* LESBIAN; *compare* HETEROSEXUALITY.)

homosexuals Persons who are sexually attracted to persons of their own sex. (*See also* GAY, HOMOSEXUALITY, *and* LESBIAN.)

hunting and gathering societies Societies that rely primarily or exclusively on hunting wild animals, fishing, and gathering wild fruits, berries, nuts, and vegetables to support their diet. Until humans began to domesticate plants and animals about 10,000 years ago, all human societies were hunter-gatherers. Today, only a tiny fraction of the world's populations support themselves in this manner, and survive only in isolated, inhospitable areas such as deserts, the frozen TUNDRA, and dense rain forests.

&. Given the close relationship between hunter-gatherers and their natural environment, hunting and gathering tribes such as the BUSHMEN and the PYGMIES may provide valuable information for anthropologists seeking to understand the development of human social structures. Hunting and gathering societies around the world share many cultural characteristics, such as NOMADISM, small community size (generally twenty-five to fifty individuals), sexual division of labor (strictly defined roles and occupations for men and women), communal food sharing, and an essentially egalitarian organization.

hypnosis Placing persons in a drowsy, sleeplike state in which they become vulnerable to the suggestions made by the hypnotist. Hypnosis may also be used to tap into the UNCONSCIOUS, and is often characterized by vivid recall of memories and fantasies. These properties make hypnosis a useful tool in PSYCHOTHERAPY. Hypnosis also has sinister implications, for subjects may be manipulated to perform embarrassing actions, or be susceptible to carrying out the hypnotist's commands after the hypnosis session (posthypnotic suggestion). These results of hypnosis, however, are extremely unlikely.

hysteria A complex NEUROSIS in which psychological conflict is turned into physical symptoms such as AMNESIA, blindness, and PARALYSIS which have no underlying physical cause. Early in his career, Sigmund FREUD worked on hysteria.

id In FREUDIAN THEORY, the part of the PSYCHE associated with instinctual, repressed, or antisocial desires, usually sexual or aggressive. In its efforts to satisfy these desires, the id comes into conflict with the social and practical constraints enforced by the EGO and SUPEREGO. (*See also* PLEASURE PRINCIPLE.)

igloo A house used by peoples of the ARCTIC regions. The typical winter igloo is domed and made of blocks of snow or ice.

illegitimacy The condition of being born to unmarried parents.

incest Sexual relations between relatives who are forbidden by law to marry; for example, between father and daughter or mother and son.

    Though each society has its own system for determining the range of people who fall into this category, every society has an incest TABOO of some sort.

Indian *See* NATIVE AMERICAN.

inhibition A personal hindrance to activity or expression. For example, fear of contracting CANCER might serve as an inhibition against smoking.

inner city A general term for impoverished areas of large cities. The inner city is characterized by minimal educational opportunities, high unemployment and crime rates, broken families, and inadequate housing. (*See* GHETTOS.)

intellectual A person who engages in academic study or critical evaluation of ideas and issues. (*See* INTELLIGENTSIA.)

intelligence quotient (IQ) A number meant to measure a person's intelligence. It is obtained by taking the RATIO of a person's "mental age," as measured by a standardized test, and the person's age in years, and multiplying this ratio by 100. Therefore, someone whose mental age and age in years are the same has an IQ of 100. An IQ of over 120 is considered superior; one between 90 and 110 is considered average. (*See also* STANFORD-BINET SCALE.)

    Psychologists are less confident today than in the past that IQ test scores really measure intelligence. Controversy exists about the effects of race and CLASS on IQ scores. (*See* NATURE-NURTURE CONTROVERSY.)

intelligentsia (in-tel-uh-JENT-see-uh) INTELLECTUALS who form an artistic, social, or political vanguard or ELITE.

introspection The contemplation of one's own thoughts and feelings.

introvert (IN-truh-vurt) A term introduced by the psychologist Carl JUNG to describe a person whose motives and actions are directed inward. Introverts tend to be preoccupied with their own thoughts and feelings, and minimize their contact with other people. (*Compare* EXTROVERT.)

IQ *See* INTELLIGENCE QUOTIENT.

James, William An American PHILOSOPHER and psychologist of the late nineteenth and early twentieth centuries. He was one of the first theorists to suggest that humans, like other animals, possess INSTINCTS. He also opposed then-dominant views by arguing that human identity is grounded not in METAPHYSICS, but in behavior.

    Henry JAMES was William James's brother.

Jung, Carl (YOONG) A Swiss psychologist of the twentieth century, who broke with his teacher Sigmund FREUD and developed his own THEORIES. Jung denied that sexuality is the basic driving urge for people. He classified people as EXTROVERTS and INTROVERTS, put forth a theory of the feminine principle in men (the anima) and the masculine principle in women (the animus), and argued that people share a

CARL JUNG

COLLECTIVE UNCONSCIOUS, made up of SYMBOLS called ARCHETYPES.

Kinsey, Alfred (KIN-zee) An American scientist of the twentieth century who investigated the sexual behavior of men and women. In 1947 and 1948, he published books on his findings — *Sexual Behavior in the Human Male* and *Sexual Behavior in the Human Female* — popularly known as the *Kinsey Reports*, which shattered existing conceptions of the nature and extent of American sexual practices.

&. Kinsey was the first scientific investigator of sexual behavior to have a wide popular impact.

kinship A relation between two or more persons that is based on common ancestry (descent) or marriage (affinity).

kleptomania (klep-tuh-MAY-nee-uh) A COMPULSION to steal, usually without either economic need or personal desire.

latency period (LAYT-n-see) According to PSYCHOANALYSIS, the period in a child's development, from about age four to about age twelve, during which sexual drives are sublimated (*see* SUBLIMATION). Psychoanalytic THEORY holds that all other stages of a child's development (the ANAL STAGE, the ORAL STAGE, the GENITAL STAGE or the OEDIPUS COMPLEX stage, and puberty) are dominated by the gratification of primarily sexual drives. During the latency period, children generally identify with the parent of the same sex, and play with other children of the same sex.

Leakey A family of anthropologists whose work at OLDUVAI GORGE in TANZANIA and elsewhere revealed that humans probably first evolved in AFRICA. Louis Leakey and his wife, Mary, discovered FOSSILS of human ancestors dating back over 3.75 million years. Their son, Richard Leakey, has continued to make discoveries in KENYA and Tanzania.

lesbian A HOMOSEXUAL woman. (*See also* GAY.)

libido (luh-BEE-doh) In FREUDIAN PSYCHOLOGY, the energy associated with the desires that come from the ID.

&. *Libido* is loosely used to mean sexual desire.

Lucy Nickname for the most complete skeleton of an early ancestor of humans ever found. Discovered in ETHIOPIA by Don Johanson and Tom Gray, Lucy lived approximately three million years ago. She walked upright, and it is estimated that she was about twenty years old when she died. Lucy is considered one of the great finds of ANTHROPOLOGY.

mainstream The prevailing current or direction of a movement or influence: "The candidate's speech represented the mainstream thinking on economic policy."

maladjustment Inability to react successfully and satisfactorily to the demands of one's environment. Though the term applies to a wide range of biological and social conditions, it often implies an individual's failure to meet social or cultural expectations. In PSYCHOLOGY, the term generally refers to unsatisfactory behavior patterns that cause ANXIETY and require PSYCHOTHERAPY.

malpractice Mistakes or negligent conduct by a professional person, especially a physician, that results in damage to others, such as misdiagnosis of a serious illness. Damaged parties often seek compensation by bringing malpractice suits against the offending physician or other professional.

Malthusianism (mal-THOOH-zhuh-niz-uhm, mal-THOOH-zee-uh-niz-uhm) A pessimistic viewpoint

MARGARET MEAD. *Photograph taken in Bali, 1957.*

on population and world resources, based on the doctrines of Thomas MALTHUS. Malthusianism holds that population tends to increase faster than the supply of food, thus preventing the steady progress of mankind. Malthus advocated premarital chastity, late marriage, and sexual abstinence as partial solutions.

mania (MAY-nee-uh)   Violent, abnormal, or impulsive behavior. In PSYCHOLOGICAL terms, mania is wild activity associated with MANIC DEPRESSION.

    🖜 A "mania" in popular terms is an intense enthusiasm or craze.

manic depression (MAN-ik)   A PSYCHOSIS marked by sharp swings of mood between excitement and exhilaration on the one hand, and deep depression on the other.

manic-depressive   A person suffering from MANIC DEPRESSION. *Manic-depressive* is also a descriptive term for conditions associated with manic depression.

masochism (MAS-uh-kiz-uhm)   Abnormal behavior characterized by deriving sexual gratification from being subjected to pain. More loosely, *masochism* refers to deriving any pleasure from experiencing pain. (*Compare* SADISM.)

matriarchy (MAY-tree-ahr-kee)   A family or society in which authority is held by females, through whom descent and inheritance are traced. More generally, a matriarchy is a society dominated by women. (*See also* MATRILINEAL, PATRIARCHY, *and* PATRILINEAL.)

matrilineal (mat-ruh-LIN-ee-uhl)   Tracing KINSHIP and descent through the female line. (*Compare* PATRILINEAL.)

McLuhan, (Herbert) Marshall (muh-KLOOH-uhn)   A twentieth-century Canadian writer and communications theorist who proposed that the MASS MEDIA, particularly television, were creating a GLOBAL VILLAGE. He also maintained that the means of communication has a greater influence on people than the information it carries. (*See* the MEDIUM IS THE MESSAGE.)

Mead, Margaret   An American anthropologist of the twentieth century, who revolutionized the field of ANTHROPOLOGY in 1928 with her book *Coming of Age in Samoa*, which emphasized the role of social convention rather than biology in shaping human behavior. In later writings she described how the behavior of men and women differed from one CULTURE to another, and thereby challenged the notion that all GENDER differences were innate.

medium is the message, The A statement by Marshall McLuhan, meaning that the form of a message (print, visual, musical, etc.) determines the ways in which that message will be perceived. McLuhan argued that modern electronic communications (including radio, television, films, and COMPUTERS) would have far-reaching sociological, aesthetic, and philosophical consequences, to the point of actually altering the ways in which we experience the world.

megalomania (meg-uh-loh-MAY-nee-uh) DELUSIONS of grandeur; an extreme form of EGOTISM. Adolf HITLER is generally considered to have been a megalomaniac.

megalopolis (meg-uh-LOP-uh-lis) A vast stretch of developed industrial urban area, such as the East Coast of the United States from BOSTON to WASHINGTON, D.C., or the RUHR VALLEY in GERMANY. *Megalopolis* is from Greek words meaning "great city."

melancholy (MEL-uhn-kol-ee) A mood of depression or sadness.

melting pot A term expressing the view that immigrants to the United States have been fused or melted into a single people.

meritocracy (mer-i-TOK-ruh-see) A government or society in which citizens who display superior achievement are rewarded with positions of leadership. In a meritocracy, all citizens have the opportunity to be recognized and advanced in proportion to their abilities and accomplishments.

mesomorph (MEZ-uh-mawrf, MES-uh-mawrf) *See* ECTOMORPH.

Middle America The interior regions of the United States, as distinguished from the East Coast and West Coast.

&. Middle America is associated with CONSERVATIVE, traditional values in politics, religion, and CULTURE.

middle class A social and economic CLASS composed of those more prosperous than the poor, or lower class, and less wealthy than the upper class. *Middle class* is sometimes loosely used to refer to the BOURGEOISIE. In the United States and other industrial countries, the term is often applied to WHITE-COLLAR, as opposed to BLUE-COLLAR, workers.

&. Values commonly associated with the middle class include a desire for social respectability and material wealth, and an emphasis on the family and education.

misanthrope (MIS-uhn-throhp) Someone who hates humanity.

misogynist (mi-SOJ-uh-nist) Someone who hates women.

mixed marriage Marriage between two people who come from different cultural, national, racial, ethnic, or religious backgrounds. Often, such marriages must withstand disapproval of both partners' families and social communities.

monogamy (muh-NOG-uh-mee) A form of marriage in which one man is united with one woman. (*Compare* POLYANDRY *and* POLYGAMY.)

mores (MAWR-ayz, MAWR-eez) The customs and manners of a social group or CULTURE. Mores often serve as moral guidelines for acceptable behavior, but are not necessarily religious or ethical.

motor development The growth of muscular coordination in a child.

mulatto (muh-LAH-toh, muh-LAT-oh) Strictly, the offspring of one white and one black parent; generally, a person of mixed black and white parentage or ancestry.

multiculturalism The view that the various CULTURES in a society merit equal respect and scholarly interest. It became a significant force in American society in the 1970s and 1980s as African-Americans, CHICANOS, and other ethnic groups explored their own history.

narcissism (NAHR-suh-siz-uhm) A consuming self-absorption or self-love; a type of EGOTISM. Narcissists constantly assess their appearance, desires, feelings, and abilities.

Native Americans The descendants of the original inhabitants of NORTH AMERICA and SOUTH AMERICA before the arrival of white settlers from EUROPE, also called INDIANS or American Indians. The term *Native American* is sometimes preferred over *Indian*

NATIVE AMERICANS. *Ojibwa and Choctaw Indians at a powwow.*

because the latter is a misnomer that originated with COLUMBUS, who mistook the inhabitants of America for the people of INDIA. Both terms, however, are widely accepted.

&. In the 1960s and 1970s, Native Americans' efforts to obtain their CIVIL RIGHTS gained wide public attention.

nature-nurture controversy   A traditional and long-standing disagreement over whether HEREDITY or environment is more important in the development of living things, especially human beings.

Neanderthal (nee-AN-duhr-thawl, nee-AN-duhr-tawl)   Ancient and now extinct relatives of modern humans. Neanderthals lived in EUROPE from about 85,000 to 35,000 years ago, and were the earliest form of the human SPECIES, *Homo sapiens*.

&. The term *Neanderthal* is sometimes used to refer to a person who is thought to have primitive or unenlightened ideas: "I tried talking politics to Joe, but he's a real Neanderthal."

nepotism (NEP-uh-tiz-uhm)   Favoritism granted to relatives or close friends, without regard to their merit. Nepotism usually takes the form of employing relatives or appointing them to high office.

neurosis (noo-ROH-sis, nyoo-ROH-sis)   A mental disorder marked by ANXIETY or fear. Neurosis is less severe than PSYCHOSIS. (*See also* ANGST, HYSTERIA, *and* PHOBIA.)

&. In popular usage, a "neurotic" is anyone who worries a lot.

nomadism (NOH-mad-iz-uhm)   A way of life in which a community has no permanent settlement, but moves from place to place, usually seasonally and within a defined territory. For HUNTING AND GATHERING SOCIETIES, nomadism does not imply aimless wandering, but suggests an organized rotation of settlements in order to ensure maximum use of available NATURAL RESOURCES.

nonverbal communication   Communication without the use of spoken language. Nonverbal communication includes gestures, facial expressions, and body positions (known collectively as "body language"), as well as unspoken understandings and presuppositions, and cultural and environmental conditions that may affect any encounter between people.

nuclear family   A type of family made up only of parents and their children. (*Compare* EXTENDED FAMILY.)

nymphomania (nim-fuh-MAY-nee-uh)   The presence in women of abnormally powerful sexual desires.

obscenity   Behavior, appearance, or expression (such as films and books) that violate accepted standards of sexual morality. American courts have long tried to define obscenity, but without much success. Some believe, for example, that any depiction of nudity is obscene; others would argue that nudity in itself is not obscene. (See FOUR-LETTER WORDS, OBSCENITY LAWS, *and* PORNOGRAPHY.)

obsession   A preoccupation with a feeling or idea. In PSYCHOLOGY, an obsession is similar to a COMPULSION.

Oedipus complex (ED-uh-puhs, EE-duh-puhs)   In FREUDIAN THEORY, the unconscious desire of a young child for sexual intercourse with the parent of the opposite sex, especially between boys and their mothers (*see* GENITAL STAGE). Followers of the psychologist Sigmund FREUD long believed that the Oedipus complex was common to all CULTURES, although many psychiatrists now refute this belief. The Oedipus complex is named after the mythical OEDIPUS, who unwittingly killed his father and married his mother.

old boy network   A set of relationships based on past friendship or acquaintance that sometimes replaces or undermines official organizations: "He didn't deserve that promotion; he got it because of his connections to the old boy network."

Olduvai Gorge (OHL-duh-veye, AWL-duh-veye)   A deep ravine in TANZANIA famous for the FOSSILS of ancestors of humans found there by Louis and Mary LEAKEY.

oral personality   According to the original THEORIES of PSYCHOANALYSIS, a PERSONALITY fixed emotionally in the ORAL STAGE of development, whose sexual and aggressive drives are satisfied by putting things in his or her mouth. Depending on when the fixation occurs, oral personalities tend to be either optimistic, generous, and gregarious, or aggressive, ambitious, and selfish. More recently, the term has come to refer to anyone who seeks pleasure through eating or sucking: "I didn't realize he was an oral personality until I saw him smoking and chewing gum at the same time." (*Compare* ANAL PERSONALITY.)

oral stage   According to PSYCHOANALYSIS, the first social and sexual stage of an infant's development, during which the infant focuses on satisfying hunger. Psychoanalysts believe that during this stage, the mouth is the focus of the LIBIDO; eating, sexual, and aggressive drives are satisfied by chewing, suckling, and biting. (See *also* ANAL STAGE, GENITAL STAGE, *and* PLEASURE PRINCIPLE.)

organization man   Someone who represses individual desires and molds behavior in order to conform to the demands of the organization he or she works for. (See *also* BUREAUCRACY, BUREAUCRAT, *and* CONFORMITY.)

ostracism (OS-truh-siz-uhm)   Banishment or exclusion from a group.

paranoia (par-uh-NOY-uh)   A form of PSYCHOSIS marked by DELUSIONS of persecution and of grandeur. One who suffers from paranoia is paranoid.

❧ In popular terminology, a "paranoid" PERSONALITY is characterized by suspicion and distrust of others; a tendency to look for hidden meaning behind other people's actions; argumentativeness; complaining; low tolerance for criticism; and a constant display of one's own talents, accomplishments, independence, and rationality.

paranoid schizophrenia (skit-suh-FREE-nee-uh, skit-suh-FREN-ee-uh)   A type of SCHIZOPHRENIA characterized by DELUSIONS of grandeur, PARANOIA, HALLUCINATIONS, jealousy, hostility, aggressiveness, unfocused ANXIETY, argumentativeness, and, in severe cases, detachment from reality to the point of AUTISM.

parapsychology (par-uh-seye-KOL-uh-jee)   The study of EXTRASENSORY PERCEPTION (ESP), communications with the dead, telekinesis (using mental energy to cause distant objects to move), and other mental phenomena that have not been explained or accepted by scientists. (See PSYCHIC RESEARCH.)

pariah (puh-REYE-uh)   An outcast; a member of a low CASTE or CLASS.

patriarchy (PAY-tree-ahr-kee)   A family or society in which authority is vested in males, through whom descent and inheritance are traced. (See *also* MATRIARCHY *and* PRIMOGENITURE.)

patrilineal (pat-ruh-LIN-ee-uhl) Tracing KINSHIP and descent through the male line. (*Compare* MATRILINEAL.)

Pavlov's dogs (PAV-lawfs, PAV-lawvz) The dogs used in CONDITIONED-RESPONSE experiments by a Russian scientist of the late nineteenth century, Ivan Pavlov. In these experiments, Pavlov sounded a bell while presenting food to a dog, thereby stimulating the natural flow of SALIVA in the dog's mouth. After the procedure was repeated several times, the dog would salivate at the sound of the bell, even when no food was presented.

peasant A farmer or agricultural worker of low STATUS. The word is applied chiefly to agricultural workers in ASIA, EUROPE, and SOUTH AMERICA, who generally adhere to traditional agricultural practices, and have little SOCIAL MOBILITY or freedom.

  🙢 *Peasant* sometimes implies crudeness or uncouth manners.

pecking order A hierarchy within a social group or community, in which those members at the top assume positions of leadership, authority, and power. The expression originated from a description of social behavior among chickens, which attack each other by pecking to establish dominance.

pederast (PED-uh-rast) A man who engages in anal intercourse, especially with boys.

peeping Tom One who derives pleasure, usually sexual, from secretly spying on others. (*See* VOYEURISM.)

  🙢 The original "peeping Tom" was a legendary resident of the town where Lady GODIVA rode naked through the streets. According to the story, Tom defied official orders by looking out his window as she went by.

peer group A group of people who share certain social characteristics, such as age, CLASS, occupation, or education, and interact on a level of equality. An individual may be a member of several peer groups, including friends, schoolmates, and co-workers. Peer groups are important in SOCIALIZATION, as individuals attempt to conform to the expectations of their peer groups. (*See* CONFORMITY *and* PEER PRESSURE.)

peer pressure The social influence a PEER GROUP exerts on its individual members, as each member attempts to conform to the expectations of the group. (*See* CONFORMITY.)

penis envy In FREUDIAN THEORY, the repressed desire of females to possess a PENIS.

  🙢 *Penis envy* is also used generally to mean a supposed female envy of men.

personality The pattern of feelings, thoughts, and activities that distinguishes one person from another.

Peter Principle A rule of organizations that states, "In a hierarchy, every employee tends to rise to his level of incompetence." Formulated by Laurence J. Peter, this rule is supposed to explain occupational incompetence.

phallic symbol (FAL-ik) A SYMBOL of the PENIS.

phobia (FOH-bee-uh) An extreme and often unreasonable fear of some object, concept, situation, or person.

Pill, the A pill designed for CONTRACEPTION by preventing OVULATION.

  🙢 The Pill was introduced in the 1950s, and its possible side effects are still being investigated. It nonetheless offered an ease of use and reliability of result that no other method of contraception had ever before supplied. In this way, it contributed greatly to the SEXUAL REVOLUTION.

pleasure principle In PSYCHOANALYSIS, the demand that an instinctive need (usually sexual or aggressive) be gratified, regardless of the social or practical consequences. Sigmund FREUD held that the ID was dominated totally by the pleasure principle, but that, with the development of the EGO and SUPEREGO, individuals become aware of the demands of social reality (the reality principle), and thereby learn to temper and regulate their quest for pleasure.

polyandry (POL-ee-an-dree) A practice in which women have two or more husbands at the same time. A rare form of POLYGAMY, polyandry is practiced by only a few CULTURES. (*Compare* MONOGAMY.)

polygamy (puh-LIG-uh-mee) The practice of having several wives or husbands at the same time. (*Compare* MONOGAMY.)

pornography Books, photographs, magazines, art, or music designed to excite sexual impulses, and considered by public authorities or public opinion as in violation of accepted standards of sexual morality. Though pornography is technically illegal, American courts have not yet settled on a satisfactory definition of what constitutes pornographic material. (*See* OBSCENITY *and* OBSCENITY LAWS.)

Post, Emily A twentieth-century American authority on manners and etiquette. Post's book *Etiquette* first appeared in the 1920s, and new editions are still issued regularly.

postindustrial society A term used by social theorists to describe the stage of economic development that follows industrialization. The postindustrial society no longer emphasizes the production of GOODS, but of SERVICES, which depend on intelligent designers and users of technology.

prejudice A hostile opinion about some person or class of persons. Prejudice is socially learned, and is usually grounded in misconception, misunderstanding, and inflexible generalizations. In particular, African-Americans in America have been victims of prejudice on a variety of social, economic, and political levels. (*See* CIVIL RIGHTS MOVEMENT *and* SEGREGATION.)

primogeniture (preye-moh-JEN-uh-choor, preye-moh-JEN-uh-chuhr) A system of inheritance in which land passes exclusively to the eldest son. Until the INDUSTRIAL REVOLUTION, this system severely restricted the freedom of younger sons, who were often forced into the military or the clergy to earn a living.

pseudoscience (sooh-doh-SEYE-uhns) A system of THEORIES or assertions about the natural world that claim or appear to be scientific but that, in fact, are not. For example, ASTRONOMY is a science, but ASTROLOGY is generally viewed as a pseudoscience.

psyche (SEYE-kee) The mind, soul, or spirit, as opposed to the body. In PSYCHOLOGY, the psyche is the center of thought, feeling, and motivation, consciously and unconsciously directing the body's reactions to its social and physical environment.

psychedelic (seye-kuh-DEL-ik) A descriptive term for things that produce or are related to HALLUCINATIONS; especially such drugs as LSD.

🐾 Psychedelic art, most popular during the late 1960s and early 1970s, combines patterns, objects,

light, and sound to simulate hallucinatory experiences.

psychiatry (seye-KEYE-uh-tree, si-KEYE-uh-tree) The medical science that studies and treats mental illness and mental MALADJUSTMENT. Psychiatrists treat mental disorders; psychologists study mental activities, whether healthy or disordered. In the United States, psychiatrists usually hold the degree of doctor of medicine (M.D.), and may prescribe medication for their patients.

psychic research Scientific investigation into phenomena that cannot be explained by known natural laws. (*See* ESP, EXTRASENSORY PERCEPTION, PARAPSYCHOLOGY, *and* TELEPATHY.)

psychoanalysis A method of treating mental illness, originating with Sigmund FREUD, in which a psychiatrist (analyst) helps a patient discover and confront the causes of the illness. Many psychiatrists believe that these causes are buried deep in the UNCONSCIOUS of the patient, and can be brought to the surface through such techniques as HYPNOSIS and the analysis of dreams. Psychoanalysis emphasizes that mental illness usually originates in repressed sexual desires or traumas in childhood.

🐾 Psychoanalysis is sometimes simply called analysis.

psychology The science dealing with mental phenomena and processes. Psychologists study emotions, perception, intelligence, consciousness, and the relationship between these phenomena and processes and the work of the GLANDS and muscles. Psychologists are also interested in diseased or disordered mental states, and some psychologists provide THERAPY for individuals. In the United States, however, psychologists, unlike psychiatrists, are not medical doctors. (*See* PSYCHIATRY.)

🐾 The two main divisions of psychology are individual or PERSONALITY psychology, and social psychology; social psychology deals with the mental processes of groups.

psychopath (SEYE-kuh-path) A mentally unbalanced person who is inclined toward antisocial and criminal behavior. (*Compare* SOCIOPATH.)

psychosis (seye-KOH-sis) A severe mental disorder, more serious than NEUROSIS, characterized by disorganized thought processes, disorientation in time and space, HALLUCINATIONS, and DELUSIONS. PARANOIA, MANIC DEPRESSION, MEGALOMANIA, and SCHIZOPHRENIA are all psychoses. One who suffers from psychosis is psychotic.

psychotherapy The use of the techniques of PSYCHOLOGY or PSYCHIATRY or both to treat mental and emotional disorders. The term includes PSYCHOANALYSIS, as well as other forms of psychological THERAPY.

Pygmy A member of any ethnic group in which the average height of the adult male is less than four feet, eleven inches. There are Pygmy tribes in dense rain-forest areas of central AFRICA, southern INDIA, MALAYSIA, and the PHILIPPINES. The most widely studied Pygmies are the Mbuti of northeastern ZAIRE, who pursue a nomadic hunting and gathering subsistence (*see* NOMADISM *and* HUNTING AND GATHERING SOCIETIES), but have established complex interdependent relationships with their non-Pygmy farming neighbors.

pyromania (peye-roh-MAY-nee-uh) An uncontrollable urge to set fires.

redneck A SLANG term, usually for a rural white southerner who is politically CONSERVATIVE, racist, and a religious fundamentalist (*see* FUNDAMENTALISM). This term is generally considered offensive. It originated in reference to agricultural workers, alluding to the fact that the back of a person's neck will be burned by the sun if he works long hours in the fields.

regression A FREUDIAN concept used by psychiatrists to signify a return to primitive or impulsive behavior after more mature behavior has been learned. (*See also* DEFENSE MECHANISM, ID, *and* LIBIDO.)

rites of passage Ceremonies that mark important transitional periods in a person's life, such as birth, puberty, marriage, having children, and death. Rites of passage usually involve ritual activities and teachings designed to strip individuals of their original roles and prepare them for new roles. The traditional American wedding ceremony is such a rite of passage. In many so-called primitive societies, some of the most complex rites of passage occur at puberty, when boys and girls are initiated into the adult world. In some ceremonies, the initiates are removed from their village and may undergo physical mutilation before returning as adults.

Rites of passage generally affirm community solidarity, especially in times of change or crisis.

role conflict A situation in which a person is expected to play two incompatible roles. For example, a boss will suffer role conflict if forced to fire an employee who is also a close friend.

role model A person who serves as an example of the values, attitudes, and behaviors associated with a role. For example, a father is a role model for his sons. Role models can also be persons who distinguish themselves in such a way that others admire and want to emulate them. For example, a woman who becomes a successful brain surgeon or airline pilot can be described as a role model for other women.

Rorschach test (RAWR-shahk) A test for PERSONALITY traits that relies on the subject's interpretations of a series of inkblots. The test was developed by Hermann Rorschach, a Swiss psychiatrist of the twentieth century.

sadism (SAY-diz-uhm, SAD-iz-uhm) Abnormal behavior characterized by deriving sexual gratification from inflicting pain on others. More loosely, *sadism* refers to deriving any pleasure from inflicting pain. Named after the Marquis de SADE, a French author of the eighteenth century, whose works describe many sexual perversities.

scapegoat A person or group that is made to bear blame for others. According to the OLD TESTAMENT, on the DAY OF ATONEMENT, a PRIEST would confess all the sins of the ISRAELITES over the head of a goat and then drive it into the wilderness, symbolically bearing their sins away.

schizophrenia (skit-suh-FREE-nee-uh, skit-suh-FREN-ee-uh) A form of PSYCHOSIS marked by a strong tendency to dissociate oneself from reality. Schizophrenia is often characterized by HALLUCINATIONS, DELUSIONS, and inappropriate reactions to situations. The word *schizophrenia* is often used informally as well as scientifically to indicate a split personality.

sensory deprivation A natural or experimentally arranged situation in which stimulation of a subject's senses is greatly reduced. Experiments have included floating subjects in soundproof water chambers. Though short periods of sensory deprivation can be relaxing, extended deprivation can result in extreme

ANXIETY, HALLUCINATIONS, bizarre thoughts, depression, and antisocial behavior. Sensory deprivation experiments have demonstrated that humans need constant sensory contact with their environment in order to function.

sex roles/gender roles The behaviors, attitudes, and activities considered appropriate and desirable for males and females. While sex roles are essentially biologically determined (ensuring successful reproduction, and forming the basis of sexual division of labor, in which women are associated with childrearing), gender roles (behavior that is considered "masculine" or "feminine") are culturally determined. In the United States, for example, men are generally expected to be independent, aggressive, physical, ambitious, and able to control their emotions; women are generally expected to be dependent, passive, sensitive, emotional, and supportive. (*See* STEREOTYPE.)

sexism The belief that one sex (usually the male) is naturally superior to the other and should dominate most important areas of political, economic, and social life.

sexual orientation Preference for sexual activity with people of the opposite sex, the same sex, or both. (*See* BISEXUALITY, HETEROSEXUALITY, *and* HOMOSEXUALITY.)

sexual revolution A drastic relaxation in general standards of sexual behavior. The most recent occurred in the 1960s, and was helped by the introduction of the PILL, an easy and reliable method of preventing pregnancy.

> The rise of the disease AIDS has been a powerful brake on the sexual revolution.

shock therapy The treatment of a mentally ill person by passing electric shocks through the BRAIN.

short-term memory Retention of information that undergoes little processing or interpretation, and can be recalled for only a few seconds. Short-term memory can retain about seven items.

> A popular example of short-term memory is the ability to remember a seven-digit telephone number just long enough to dial a call. In most cases, unless the number is consciously repeated several times, it will be forgotten.

significant other A person whose close relationship with an individual affects that individual's behavior and attitudes. A significant other is usually a family member, spouse, child, employer, co-worker, or friend, who serves as a ROLE MODEL, or whose acceptance and approval is sought.

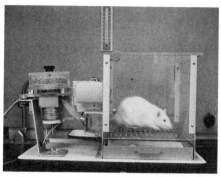

SKINNER BOX. *A Skinner box with a rat as subject. The food reservoir is on the left side of the box.*

Skinner, B. F. An American psychologist of the twentieth century who stressed the similarities between human and animal learning processes. To measure learning, Skinner devised a box (the Skinner box) in which an animal learns to press a lever in order to get food or water. (*See also* BEHAVIORISM *and* CONDITIONED RESPONSE.)

social mobility The ability of individuals or groups to move upward or downward in STATUS on the basis of wealth, occupation, education, or some other social variable.

> American society operates on the principle that an individual's achievements can be rewarded by upward social mobility.

social science The study of how groups of people behave, often in an effort to predict how they will behave in the future. The social sciences include ECONOMICS, ANTHROPOLOGY, SOCIOLOGY, POLITICAL SCIENCE, and aspects of PSYCHOLOGY and history.

socialization Learning the customs, attitudes, and values of a social group, community, or CULTURE. Socialization is essential for the development of individuals who can participate and function within their societies, as well as for ensuring that a society's cultural features will be carried on through new generations. Socialization is most strongly enforced by the family, school, and PEER GROUPS, and continues throughout an individual's lifetime. (*See also* ACCULTURATION.)

socioeconomic status (SES)   An individual's or group's position within a hierarchical social structure. Socioeconomic status depends on a combination of variables, including occupation, education, income, wealth, and place of residence. Sociologists often use socioeconomic status as a means of predicting behavior.

sociology   The systematic study of human society, especially present-day societies. Sociologists study the organization, institutions, and development of societies, with a particular interest in identifying causes of the changing relationships among individuals and groups. (*See* SOCIAL SCIENCE.)

sociopath   (SOH-see-uh-path,   SOH-shee-uh-path) Someone whose social behavior is extremely abnormal. Sociopaths are interested only in their personal needs and desires, without concern for the effects of their behavior on others. (*Compare* PSYCHOPATH.)

sodomy   (SOD-uh-mee)   Sexual intercourse that is not the union of the genital ORGANS of a man and a woman. The term is most frequently applied to anal intercourse between two men or to sexual relations between people and animals. (*See* PEDERAST.)

&. According to the BIBLE, God destroyed the cities of SODOM AND GOMORRAH for unacceptable sexual practices, apparently including anal intercourse between men. Sodomy takes its name from the city of Sodom. &. Many governments have laws against sodomy. These laws are difficult to enforce, however, and many people believe they violate personal privacy.

Stanford-Binet scale   (STAN-fuhrd-bi-NAY)   A test developed in 1916 to measure intelligence and knowledge. After several subsequent revisions, the Stanford-Binet scale has become the foundation of INTELLIGENCE QUOTIENT testing.

status   The relative position of an individual within a group, or of a group within a society.

&. Though the term can refer to either high or low standing, it is often used only to imply a position of prestige.

stereotype   A generalization, usually exaggerated or oversimplified, and often offensive, that is used to describe or distinguish a group.

stimulus   *plur.* STIMULI (STIM-yuh-leye) An action, condition, or person that provokes a response, especially a CONDITIONED RESPONSE.

subconsciousness   The part of the PSYCHE just below consciousness and capable of bursting into consciousness. For example, a repressed sexual desire is part of our subconsciousness, although we may at some time become conscious of it.

&. The subconscious is not the same as the UNCONSCIOUS. Blinking, for example, is usually unconscious and occasionally conscious, but never subconscious.

subculture   A group within a society that has its own shared set of customs, attitudes, and values, often accompanied by JARGON or SLANG. A subculture can be organized around a common activity, occupation, age, STATUS, ethnic background, race, religion, or any other unifying social condition, but the term is often used to describe deviant groups, such as thieves and drug users. (*See* COUNTERCULTURE.)

sublimation   (sub-luh-MAY-shuhn)   In FREUDIAN PSYCHOLOGY, a DEFENSE MECHANISM by which the individual satisfies a socially prohibited instinctive drive (usually sexual or aggressive) through the substitution of socially acceptable behavior. For example, someone with strong sexual drives who paints nude portraits may be engaging in sublimation.

suburbanization   (suh-bur-buh-nuh-ZAY-shuhn) The establishment of residential communities on the outskirts of a city. In the United States, many suburbs were created after WORLD WAR II, during a period of tremendous growth in population and industry. Suburban dwellers typically work in the cities, but raise their families in a less-congested, safer, and more relaxed atmosphere.

superego   (sooh-puhr-EE-goh)   In FREUDIAN PSYCHOLOGY, the part of the PSYCHE that incorporates parental or community values and standards, and acts as an inner check on behavior. The superego and EGO, responding to social demands, are often in conflict with the primitive impulses of the ID.

symbol   Something that represents or suggests something else. Symbols often take the form of words, visual images, or gestures that are used to convey ideas and beliefs. All human CULTURES use symbols to express the underlying structure of their social systems, to represent ideal cultural characteristics, such as beauty, and to ensure that the culture is passed on to new generations. Symbolic relationships are learned rather than biologically or naturally determined, and each culture has its own symbols.

taboo A descriptive term for words, objects, actions, or people that are forbidden by a group or CULTURE. The expression comes from the religion of islanders of the South PACIFIC.

technocracy (tek-NOK-ruh-see) A type of society marked by the dominant role of people with specialized technical skills, particularly engineers.

telepathy (tuh-LEP-uh-thee) Knowledge conveyed from one individual to another without means of the five senses; mind reading. (*See also* ESP, EXTRASENSORY PERCEPTION, PARAPSYCHOLOGY, *and* PSYCHIC RESEARCH.)

tenure Holding an office or position, usually with a guarantee of continued employment. For example, in universities, some professors obtain tenure, meaning that they cannot be fired under normal circumstances.

therapy Treatment intended to cure or alleviate an illness or injury, whether physical or mental.

totemism (TOH-tuh-miz-uhm) The belief that people are descended from animals, plants, and other natural objects. SYMBOLS of these natural ancestors, known as TOTEMS, are often associated with clans (groups of families tracing common descent). By representing desirable individual qualities (such as the swiftness of a deer), and helping to explain the mythical origin of the clan, totems reinforce clan identity and solidarity.

transvestite Someone who dresses in the clothes usually worn by the opposite sex. Transvestites may be BISEXUAL, HETEROSEXUAL, or HOMOSEXUAL.

Two Cultures, The A pamphlet published in 1959 by the English scientist and author C. P. Snow. Snow maintained that the sciences and literature, in ENGLAND at least, represented two antagonistic CULTURES whose members were unable to communicate with each other.

unconscious The part of the PSYCHE lying far below consciousness and not easily raised into consciousness. In FREUDIAN PSYCHOLOGY, the unconscious cannot be directly observed with the conscious mind, but has its own processes, and deeply affects conscious thought.

upward mobility Rising from a lower to a higher social CLASS or STATUS. (*See also* SOCIAL MOBILITY.)

urban renewal Programs designed to clear, rebuild, and redevelop urban slums. Critics contend that while bulldozing slums, urban renewal programs often have led to their replacement by office buildings and by apartment houses for the well-to-do.

value judgment An assessment of a person, situation, or event. The term is often restricted to assessments that reveal the values of the person making the assessment rather than the objective realities of what is being assessed.

&ᴥ We often make value judgments without realizing that we are doing so. For example, a teacher who describes a student as "the best I've ever taught — very polite and obedient" is making a value judgment about the qualities (politeness and obedience) that make a student good.

voyeurism (voy-UR-iz-uhm, vwah-YUR-iz-uhm, VOY-uhr-iz-uhm) Deriving sexual satisfaction by secretly watching others undress or engage in sexual activity. (*See* PEEPING TOM.)

Weber, Max (VAY-buhr) A German sociologist of the late nineteenth and early twentieth centuries. Weber maintained that modern CAPITALIST society is created when technical advances require administration by a BUREAUCRACY. Disagreeing with Karl MARX, Weber argued against the inevitability of revolution by the PROLETARIAT and the triumph of SOCIALISM, maintaining that social and political IDEOLOGY can act independently of economic and material conditions. He also wrote extensively on the PROTESTANT WORK ETHIC. Weber's research methods established the foundations of SOCIAL SCIENCE research, as distinct from the natural sciences.

white-collar A descriptive term for office workers, who use a minimum of physical exertion, as opposed to BLUE-COLLAR laborers. Managerial, clerical, and sales jobs are common white-collar occupations.

Women's Christian Temperance Union (WCTU) An organization founded in the late nineteenth century in the United States that encourages total abstinence from alcohol. It was one of the leading forces in bringing about PROHIBITION. Its symbol was a white ribbon. (*See* NATION, CARRY.)

Woodstock   A village in NEW YORK state, where some 400,000 young people assembled in 1969 for a rock music festival.

    ❧ The size of the crowd, and the prevalence of HIPPIE dress and customs, led to use of the term *Woodstock nation* to indicate the youth COUNTERCULTURE of the late 1960s. ❧ The term is now used loosely to mean a large, impromptu gathering.

working class   In the United States, the population of BLUE-COLLAR workers, particularly skilled and semiskilled laborers, who differ in values, but not necessarily in INCOME, from the MIDDLE CLASS. In MARXISM, this term refers to propertyless factory workers.

xenophobia (zen-uh-FOH-bee-uh, zee-nuh-FOH-bee-uh)   An unreasonable fear, distrust, or hatred of strangers, foreigners, or anything perceived as foreign or different.

zero population growth   A condition in which a population neither grows nor declines, because the number of births in a year equals the number of deaths. Many industrialized countries have relatively low birth and death rates, and a steady but small population growth. Many THIRD WORLD countries, however, have extremely high birth and death rates. Without effective methods of BIRTH CONTROL, these populations grow at a phenomenal rate, but without the resources to support them.

Zulu   A general name for some 2.5 million Bantu-speaking peoples in reserved tribal areas of SOUTH AFRICA.

Business and Economics

Economics is the SOCIAL SCIENCE that deals with the production, DISTRIBUTION, and consumption of GOODS and SERVICES. *Business* may refer to any gainful economic activity or, more narrowly, to organizations that produce and distribute COMMODITIES. Basically, economics is a branch of investigation and study, while business connotes activity. Yet the two terms increasingly overlap. Once thought of as a knack or skill that could never be taught in school, business has developed claims to scientific status in the twentieth century. Today, there are schools of business administration that, much like departments of economics, engage in study and investigation.

Both economic THEORY and the growing emphasis on the study of business have spilled over from the universities into the public forum. The budget DEFICIT, foreign TRADE DEFICIT, and STOCK MARKET boom of the 1980s and early 1990s have combined with the recent RECESSION and decline of INTEREST RATES to pique popular interest in economic issues. Less obvious but no less important, the deregulation of financial institutions by the federal government, the vast growth of PENSION funds within the last twenty years, and recent changes in the federal tax code have raised the threshold of financial knowledge for Americans. As late as the 1950s, banks rarely advertised, SAVINGS AND LOAN ASSOCIATIONS did not offer checking accounts, and insurance companies concentrated on selling insurance. Now, all of these institutions advertise and compete with one another by offering similar services. For example, all of them offer pension and retirement plans, and individual investors must be able to sort out and assess their rival claims.

To do so, ordinary Americans need not become professors of economics; but they must understand the difference between STOCKS and BONDS, and they should understand why the stock market tends to decline when the INTEREST RATES rise. This section provides the basic definitions necessary for threading one's way not only through political debates about the future of the economy but also through the rival claims of financial institutions.

— J. F. K.

absenteeism Habitual absence from work, thought to reflect employee demoralization or dissatisfaction.

accounting The system of recording and auditing business transactions. (*See* AUDIT.)

act of God A natural catastrophe, e.g., a HURRICANE, an EARTHQUAKE, or a volcanic eruption. (*See* VOLCANO.)

As a legal term relating to property damage, it appears in insurance CONTRACTS: "After the flood, Papovich was dismayed to discover that his house was not insured against acts of God." In contracts dealing with the delivery of GOODS or SERVICES, the term is used to protect the parties from litigation over delays or failures in performance owing to circumstances beyond their control.

actuary (AK-chooh-er-ee)   A mathematician who uses STATISTICS to calculate insurance premiums.

added value tax   *See* VALUE-ADDED TAX.

affluent society   A society in which scarcity of resources is *not* the predominant condition, and a general level of economic well-being has been achieved by most members of society. The term was made current by John Kenneth GALBRAITH in *The Affluent Society* (1958), which described conditions in the United States after WORLD WAR II.

🙠 Conventional economic THEORY is based on the assumption that resources are scarce. Therefore, it makes increasing production in the PRIVATE SECTOR and limiting interference and REGULATION from the government a priority. In Galbraith's affluent society, this priority is misplaced because scarcity is not predominant. The continued pursuit of conventional economic objectives in an affluent society leads to the conditions Galbraith observed in postwar America: private-sector affluence and public-sector squalor. For example, affluence in the private sector led to the mass availability of automobiles. Because public-sector interference (in the form of regulation and TAXATION) was discouraged, however, governments could not afford to build adequate roadways to accommodate those automobiles.

agribusiness   The part of the economy devoted to the production, processing, and DISTRIBUTION of food, including the financial institutions that fund these activities.

🙠 Agribusiness emphasizes agriculture as a big business rather than as the work of small family farms.

American Stock Exchange   The second largest STOCK EXCHANGE in the United States, after the NEW YORK STOCK EXCHANGE. The American Stock Exchange is in NEW YORK CITY.

amortization (am-uhr-tuh-ZAY-shuhn, uh-mawr-tuh-ZAY-shuhn)   A term that refers either to the gradual paying off of a DEBT in regular installments over a period of time or to the DEPRECIATION of the "book value" (that is, the standard assessed value) of an ASSET over a period of time.

annuity (uh-NOOH-uh-tee)   A sum of money payable yearly or at regular intervals.

🙠 Many people's retirement funds are set up to be paid in annuities.

appraisal   A formal evaluation of property by an expert, used to establish its market value.

appropriation   An expenditure voted by CONGRESS for use by some agency of the federal government or by a state legislature for use by a state government.

ASSEMBLY LINE. *Robots welding at the Chrysler Corporation St. Louis Assembly Complex in Fenton, Missouri.*

assembly line   A line of factory workers and equipment along which a product being assembled passes consecutively from operation to operation until completed.

🙠 Assembly lines are found in many industries but are particularly associated with automobile manufacturing.

assessment   The APPRAISAL of property for the purposes of TAXATION.

asset   A possession that can be turned into cash to cover LIABILITIES.

🙠 Commonly, the term denotes anything of value.

audit   The examination by an outside party of the accounts of an individual or CORPORATION.

balance of payments   The relationship between the payments made by one nation to all other nations and its receipts from all other nations.

🙠 A nation whose payments exceed its receipts is said to be running an unfavorable balance of payments, which can affect the value of its CURRENCY in foreign countries. (*See* FOREIGN EXCHANGE.)

balance sheet An orderly account of the ASSETS of a company or individual and of the financial claims on those assets by others.

Balance of International Payments
(in billions of dollars)

Item	1991	1990	1989	1985	1980
Exports of goods, services, and income	$704.9	$652.9	$603.2	$366.0	$343.2
Merchandise, adjusted, excluding military	416.0	389.5	360.5	214.4	224.0
Transfers under U.S. military agency sales contracts	10.7	9.8	8.3	9.0	8.2
Receipts of income on U.S. investments abroad	125.3	130.0	127.5	90.0	75.9
Other Services	152.9	123.3	106.9	45.0	36.5
Imports of goods and services	−716.6	−722.7	−689.5	−461.2	−333.9
Merchandise, adjusted, excluding military	−489.4	−497.6	−475.3	−339.0	−249.3
Direct defense expenditures	−16.2	−17.1	−14.6	−12.0	−10.7
Payments of income on foreign assets in U.S.	−108.9	−118.1	−128.4	−65.0	−43.2
Other services	−102.1	−89.8	−80.0	−46.0	−30.7
Unilateral transfers, excluding military grants, net	8.0	−22.3	−14.7	−15.0	−7.0
U.S. Government assets abroad, net	3.4	2.9	1.2	−2.8	−5.2
U.S. private assets abroad, net	−71.4	−58.5	−102.9	−26.0	−71.5
U.S. assets abroad, official reserve, net	−62.2	−57.7	−127.0	−27.7	−86.1
Foreign assets in U.S., net	67.0	86.3	214.6	127.1	50.3
Statistical discrepancy	−1.1	63.5	22.4	23.0	29.6
Balance on goods, services, and income	−11.7	−69.7	−95.3	−106.8	9.5
Balance on current account	−3.7	−92.1	−110.0	−118.0	3.7

Note: — denotes debits. *Source:* Dept. of Commerce, Bureau of Economic Analysis.

balance of trade That part of the BALANCE OF PAYMENTS relating to GOODS only (as opposed to SERVICES, monetary movements, official reserve transactions, etc.).

  ☛ A nation whose IMPORTS are worth more than its EXPORTS is said to have an unfavorable balance of trade, or to be running a TRADE DEFICIT.

bank run The concerted action of depositors who try to withdraw their money from a bank because they fear that the bank will fail.

bankruptcy Legally declared insolvency, or inability to pay CREDITORS.

  ☛ If an individual or a corporation declares bankruptcy, a court will appoint an official to make an inventory of the individual's or corporation's ASSETS and to establish a schedule by which creditors can be partially repaid what is owed them. ☛ An individual who is lacking a specific resource or quality is sometimes said to be bankrupt, as in intellectually bankrupt or morally bankrupt.

barter The exchange of GOODS or SERVICES for other goods or services, rather than for money.

bear market A market, especially a STOCK MARKET, characterized by falling prices; the opposite of a BULL MARKET.

beneficiary (ben-uh-FISH-ee-er-ee, ben-uh-FISH-uh-ree) The recipient of funds, property, or other benefits from an insurance policy, will, trust, or other settlement.

big board The huge electronic board at the NEW YORK STOCK EXCHANGE that reports the changing values of STOCKS traded on the exchange.

  ☛ The term is used sometimes to mean the New York Stock Exchange itself.

big business Large CORPORATIONS, as opposed to small individually or family-owned businesses.

Big Three, the In the American automobile industry, the three largest manufacturers: General Motors, Ford, and Chrysler.

bilateralism (beye-LAT-uhr-uh-liz-uhm) Trade dealings between two countries.

  ☛ Bilateral agreements often create special terms for specific GOODS traded between two countries.

black market The illegal buying and selling of GOODS above the price fixed by a government. Black markets usually develop when, because of war, disaster, or public policy, a government tries to set prices for COMMODITIES instead of allowing the normal operations of SUPPLY and DEMAND to set prices.

blue chip stock A term used to describe STOCKS of high-quality, financially sound CORPORATIONS.

  ☛ "Blue chip" suggests a safe INVESTMENT.

bond A SECURITY issued by a CORPORATION or public body and carrying a fixed rate of INTEREST. Like a STOCK, a bond is a type of INVESTMENT, but unlike a stock, a bond has a definite YIELD. (*See* MUNICIPAL BONDS *and* TREASURY BILLS.)

bonus Money or GOODS paid employees beyond their WAGES or salary.

bottleneck The point at which an industry or economic system has to slow its growth because one or more of its components cannot keep up with DEMAND.

bottom line The last line in an AUDIT, which shows profit or loss.

  ☛ By extension, "bottom line" refers to the final, determining consideration in a decision. ☛ "Bottom line" also has a derogatory implication when it refers to those people whose attention to the bottom line prevents them from recognizing the value of anything else.

bounty   A sum of money offered to an individual or industry as an incentive to encourage performance.

bourgeoisie (boor-zhwah-ZEE)   In general, the MIDDLE CLASS. Applied to the MIDDLE AGES, it refers to townspeople, who were neither nobles nor PEASANTS. In MARXISM it refers to those who control the means of production and do not live directly by the sale of their labor. Karl MARX distinguished between the "haute" (high) bourgeoisie (industrialists and financiers) and the "petite" (small or "petty") bourgeoisie (shopkeepers, self-employed artisans, lawyers). In Marxism there is a fundamental conflict between the interests of the bourgeoisie and those of the propertyless workers, the PROLETARIAT.

   ❧ "Bourgeois" may also refer to mediocre taste or to the flashy disply of wealth by the NOUVEAU RICHE.

boycott   The refusal to purchase the products of an individual, CORPORATION, or nation as a way to bring social and political pressure for change.

breach of contract   Failure to live up to the terms of a CONTRACT. The failure may provoke a lawsuit, in which an aggrieved party asks a court to award financial compensation for the loss brought about by the breach.

broker   A financial agent or intermediary; a middleman.

bubble   A period of wild speculation in which the price of a COMMODITY or STOCK is inflated far beyond its real value. Bubbles are said to "burst" when there emerges a general awareness of the folly, and the price drops.

bull market   A market, especially a STOCK MARKET, characterized by rising prices; the opposite of a BEAR MARKET.

business cycle   A period during which business activity reaches a low point, recovers, expands, reaches a high point, decreases to a new low point, and so on.

buyer's market   A market in which SUPPLY exceeds DEMAND. As a result, suppliers usually have to lower their prices, thus favoring the buyer. (*Compare* SELLER'S MARKET.)

capital   Money used to finance purchase of the means of production, such as machines, or the machines themselves.

Capital   *See* KAPITAL, DAS.

capital expenditure   The purchase of an ASSET by a firm.

capital flight   The rapid movement of INVESTMENTS out of a market or country that is seen by investors as unstable.

capital formation   The creation of CAPITAL. For example, capital is created when banks lend the money they hold in savings accounts to firms that use the money to purchase machinery.

capital gain   Personal INCOME earned by the sale of ASSETS such as STOCKS or REAL PROPERTY. The gain is the difference between the price paid for the asset and the selling price. In the past, capital gains were taxed at a lower rate than ordinary income, but this is no longer true.

capital goods   GOODS used in the production of COMMODITIES; producers' goods. (*Compare* CONSUMER GOODS.)

capital resources   Tools, machines, and factories used to produce GOODS.

capital-intensive   A term describing industries that employ relatively few laborers but that use expensive equipment. (*Compare* LABOR-INTENSIVE.)

capitalism   *See under* "World Politics."

captains of industry   A PHRASE that is sometimes used to describe businesspeople who are especially successful and powerful.

Carnegie, Andrew   An American industrial leader of the late nineteenth and early twentieth centuries. Carnegie, a self-made man, immigrated to the United States from SCOTLAND without money and made millions in the steel industry. He sold his steel interests in 1901, and gave most of the proceeds away, largely to educational, cultural, and peacemaking organizations. For example, Carnegie money went toward the founding of free public libraries in many cities and to the establishment of CARNEGIE HALL, the famous concert hall in NEW YORK CITY.

cartel (kahr-TEL) An association in which producers of a similar or identical product try to obtain a MONOPOLY over the sale of the product.

☙ The ORGANIZATION OF PETROLEUM EXPORTING COUNTRIES (OPEC) is a cartel.

Caveat emptor (KAV-ee-aht, KAH-vee-aht EMP-tawr) LATIN for "Let the buyer beware." It means that a customer should be cautious and alert to the possibility of being cheated: "*Caveat emptor* is the first rule of buying a used car."

CD *See* CERTIFICATES OF DEPOSIT.

certificates of deposit (CDs) BONDS issued by banks and SAVINGS AND LOAN ASSOCIATIONS to individual investors. CDs have terms ranging from a few months to several years; in general, the longer the term, the higher the INTEREST RATE that they bear. At the expiration of the term, investors may withdraw both the PRINCIPAL and the accrued INTEREST. Penalties are imposed for early withdrawal.

chain store One of many RETAIL stores owned by a single CORPORATION and offering similar products. Examples include Sears and Safeway.

Chávez, Cesar (CHAH-vez, SHAH-vez) An American labor leader of the twentieth century. In the 1960s, Chávez organized food harvesters in CALIFORNIA, many of them Mexican-Americans like himself, into the United Farm Workers. This union led nationwide BOYCOTTS against the table grape industry and the lettuce industry in the 1960s and 1970s. Chávez is known for his commitment to NONVIOLENT RESISTANCE.

closed shop Technically, a business in which employees must join a LABOR UNION before being hired. This practice is now illegal. The term is used synonymously with UNION SHOP.

closing Usually applied to REAL ESTATE transactions, it refers to delivery of the deed of ownership from the owner to the buyer in return for full payment.

COD An ABBREVIATION for "cash on delivery" or "collect on delivery."

collateral Property or its equivalent that a debtor deposits with a CREDITOR to guarantee repayment of a DEBT.

CESAR CHÁVEZ. *Chávez at a news conference in Miami, after negotiating a contract for 1200 citrus harvesters.*

collective bargaining Negotiations by representatives of a group of employees, often a LABOR UNION, pertaining to conditions of employment such as WAGES and working conditions.

collective farm In SOCIALIST or COMMUNIST countries such as the former SOVIET UNION, a collective is a cooperative association of farmers who work land owned by the state but who own most of their own farm implements.

commission A fee paid to a BROKER or other financial agent for negotiating a sale. The fee is based on a percentage of the sale price.

commodity Any product manufactured or grown.

common carrier A company or individual providing public transportation on a regular basis in return for a fee that is uniformly charged to all users.

Common Market *See* EEC.

communism *See* COMMUNISM *and* MARXISM-LENINISM *under "World Politics."*

compound interest INTEREST that is added not only to the PRINCIPAL of a loan or savings account but also to the interest already added to the loan or account; interest paid on interest.

conflict of interest   A situation in which someone who has to make a decision in an official capacity stands to profit personally from the decision. For example, a judge who rules on a case involving a CORPORATION in which he or she owns STOCK has a conflict of interest.

conglomerate (kuhn-GLOM-uhr-uht)   A CORPORATION with diversified holdings that are acquired through MERGERS and acquisitions but that are not necessarily related.

constant dollars   A convention of STATISTICS that measures industrial output and the like over time while controlling for changes owing to INFLATION. Using constant dollars usually gives a clearer view of how an enterprise is performing over time.

constant-dollar GNP   GROSS NATIONAL PRODUCT rendered in the prices of a given base year, thereby adjusting for INFLATION or DEFLATION.

consumer   Someone who purchases a GOOD for personal use.

consumer goods   GOODS, such as food and clothing, that satisfy human wants through their consumption or use. (*Compare* CAPITAL GOODS.)

Consumer Price Indexes
(1982–84 = 100)

Year	All Items	Food	Shelter	Apparel	Telephone
1960	29.6	30.0	25.2	45.7	58.3
1970	38.8	39.2	35.5	59.2	58.7
1980	82.4	86.8	81.0	90.9	77.7
1988	118.3	118.2	127.1	115.4	116.0
1989	124.0	125.1	132.8	118.6	117.2
1990	130.7	132.4	140.0	124.1	117.7
1991	136.2	136.3	146.3	128.7	119.7

1. Includes upkeep.
Source: U.S. Bureau of Labor Statistics, *Monthly Labor Review*

consumer price index   An index of prices for a representative sample of GOODS and SERVICES published by the government each month. The consumer price index was formerly known as the COST-OF-LIVING index.

consumerism   A movement in the United States that seeks to protect CONSUMERS against shoddy or improperly labeled products. (*See* NADER, RALPH.)

contraband   GOODS illegally transported across borders to avoid the payment of taxes.

contract   A legally binding agreement between two or more parties.

copyright   A grant of an exclusive right to produce or sell a book, motion picture, work of art, musical composition, or similar product during a specified period of time.

corporation   A business organization owned by a group of STOCKHOLDERS, each of whom enjoys LIMITED LIABILITY (that is, each can be held responsible for losses only up to the limit of his or her INVESTMENT). A corporation has the ability to raise CAPITAL by selling STOCK to the public.

cost of living   The average cost of the basic necessities of life, including food, shelter, and clothing.
   In the United States, the cost of living is monitored in the CONSUMER PRICE INDEX (formerly called the cost-of-living index), published monthly by the federal government.

cost-of-living allowance   A WAGE increase to help workers keep up with INFLATION.

counterfeit   Anything false or fraudulent, but especially bogus money.

credit   The ability to obtain GOODS, money, or SERVICES in return for a promise to pay at some later date.

credit rating   An evaluation of the financial trustworthiness of an individual, firm, or government.

credit union   An organization formed by employees of a company or institution to make personal loans at low INTEREST RATES to all employees of that company or institution.

creditor   One to whom a DEBT is owed.

currency   Any form of money in actual use as a medium of exchange.

Das Kapital   *See* KAPITAL, DAS.

data   The facts, figures, and quantitative material used in the calculation of STATISTICS.

debt   Money, GOODS, or SERVICES owed by an individual, firm, or government to another individual, firm, or government.

debtor nation   A nation that owes more to other nations than it is owed.

GREAT DEPRESSION. *Distributing bread and coffee to the unemployed, 1930.*

deduction   A cost or expense subtracted from REVENUE, usually for tax purposes.

default   Failure to pay a DEBT when it is due.

deficit   A shortage, especially the amount by which a sum of money falls short of what is required; a DEBT.

deficit financing   A government policy of financing large public EXPENDITURES by borrowing money rather than by raising taxes. Also called deficit spending.

deflation   A decrease in prices, often stated as an increase in the value of money, related to a decline in spending by CONSUMERS. (*Compare* INFLATION.)

demand   The amount of any given COMMODITY that people are ready and able to buy at a given time for a given price. (*See* SUPPLY AND DEMAND.)

demand curve   A mathematical curve, drawn on a GRAPH, that represents what the DEMAND for a COMMODITY would be if its price ranged anywhere from zero to infinity. The point at which it intersects the SUPPLY CURVE for the same commodity supposedly establishes the price of the commodity in a FREE MARKET. (*See* SUPPLY AND DEMAND.)

depletion allowance   A DEDUCTION from taxable INCOME based on the eventual exhaustion or waste of a natural ASSET such as an oil field.

deposit   A credit to an individual account, such as a bank account.

depreciation   (di-pree-shee-AY-shuhn)   A decline over time in the value of a tangible ASSET such as a house or car.

depression   A period of drastic decline in the national economy, characterized by decreasing business activity, falling prices, and unemployment. The best known of such periods is the GREAT DEPRESSION, which occurred in the 1930s.

destructive competition   Competition that forces some producers out of the market. This usually occurs when there are so many producers of a product that prices are driven down to the point where no one makes a PROFIT. It can also happen if a single producer is significantly wealthier than other producers and can afford to cut prices drastically until the other producers are driven out of business.

devaluation   A policy undertaken by a nation to reduce the value of its national CURRENCY either in relation to gold or in relation to the currencies of other nations.

diminishing returns, law of   An economic law propounded by David RICARDO, also called the law of diminishing marginal returns. It expresses a relationship between input and output, stating that adding units of any one input (labor, CAPITAL, etc.) to fixed amounts of the others will yield successively smaller increments of output.

🦂 In common usage, the "point of diminishing returns" is a supposed point at which additional effort or investment in a given endeavor will not yield correspondingly increasing results.

discount   A DEDUCTION made from a charge.

discount rate   The rate of INTEREST charged by the FEDERAL RESERVE SYSTEM on loans it makes to the banking system.

🦂 Because the Federal Reserve System lends money to the banking industry, one mechanism it has for regulating INTEREST RATES is to vary the discount rate — that is, to make the money that banks borrow relatively more or less expensive.

disposable personal income   The total amount of money available for an individual or population to spend or save after taxes have been paid. As an economic measure it is abbreviated DPI.

distribution   The process of marketing and merchandising GOODS. Also, the way in which wealth or goods or SERVICES are allotted, as in the distribution of wealth.

divestiture   (deye-VES-tuh-chuhr, deye-VES-tuh-choor)   The act of a CORPORATION or CONGLOMERATE in getting rid of a subsidiary company or division.

dividend   A payment to the STOCKHOLDERS of a CORPORATION from the corporation's earnings.

division of labor   Dividing a job into many specialized parts, with a single worker or a few workers assigned to each part. Division of labor is important to MASS PRODUCTION.

double indemnity   A feature of life insurance policies stating that the insurer will pay twice the face value of the policy if the insured dies accidentally.

Dow-Jones average   An average of the selling price of a selected group of major STOCKS on the New York Stock Exchange. Changes in the average (noted as "rises" and "falls") give BROKERS and investors a general picture of the state of the market.

down payment   A payment in part made at the time of purchase of a GOOD, with the promise to make full payment later.

dummy   In a CORPORATION, one who stands in for a real director or who serves as a nominal director during the organization of the corporation until the STOCKHOLDERS can elect directors.

dumping   The sale of GOODS of one nation in the markets of a second nation at less than the price charged within the first nation. Dumping can eliminate competitors by undercutting their prices.

durable goods   Manufactured products capable of long utility, such as refrigerators and automobiles.

duty   A tax charged by a government, especially on an IMPORT.

easy-money policy   A policy by which a central monetary authority, such as the FEDERAL RESERVE SYSTEM, seeks to make money plentiful and available at low INTEREST RATES. (*Compare* TIGHT-MONEY POLICY.)

🦂 An easy-money policy is often pursued to encourage INVESTMENT and economic growth. It can lead to INFLATION, however.

economic indicators   Series of statistical figures, such as the CONSUMER PRICE INDEX or the GROSS NATIONAL PRODUCT, used by economists to predict future economic activity.

economics   The science that deals with the production, DISTRIBUTION, and consumption of COMMODITIES.

🦂 Economics is generally understood to concern behavior that, given the scarcity of means, arises to achieve certain ends. When scarcity ceases, conventional economic theory may no longer be applicable. (*See* AFFLUENT SOCIETY.) 🦂 Economics is sometimes referred to as the "dismal science."

EEC   The ACRONYM for the European Economic Community. An organization of nations established in 1957 to promote FREE TRADE and economic cooperation among the nations of western EUROPE. Its original members were BELGIUM, FRANCE, ITALY, LUXEMBOURG, the NETHERLANDS, and WEST GER-

MANY. BRITAIN, DENMARK, GREECE, IRELAND, POR-TUGAL, and SPAIN joined later. Often known as the Common Market or (more recently) as the EC or EEC, its functions have expanded to include the allocation of industrial and agricultural specialties to different member nations. In 1991 the Maastricht Treaty committed members to adopt a single currency and common foreign policy and defense, but the treaty, which calls upon members to surrender considerable chunks of SOVEREIGNTY, has yet to be ratified.

efficiency A measure of how effective an economy is in using resources to meet consumer demands for GOODS and SERVICES.

elasticity A shift in either DEMAND or SUPPLY of a GOOD or SERVICE depending on its price. Demand is said to be elastic when it responds quickly to changes in prices, inelastic when it responds sluggishly.

embargo A governmental restriction on trade for political purposes. The objective is to put pressure on other governments by prohibiting EXPORTS to or IMPORTS from those countries.

embezzlement The stealing of money entrusted to one's care: "The treasurer of the company embezzled a million dollars."

eminent domain The right of a government to take private property for a public purpose, usually with just compensation of the owner.

entrepreneur (ahn-truh-pruh-NUR, ahn-truh-pruh-NOOR) One who starts a business or other venture that promises economic gain but that also entails risks.

equilibrium In ECONOMICS, a state of the economy in which for every COMMODITY or SERVICE (including labor), total SUPPLY AND DEMAND are exactly equal. Equilibrium is never actually attained; it is approximated by movements of the market.

&. KEYNESIAN economics departed from conventional economic THEORY in demonstrating that economic equilibrium and FULL EMPLOYMENT need not occur together. Therefore, as a system tends toward equilibrium, it might not eliminate unemployment.

equity In REAL ESTATE, the financial value of someone's property over and above the amount the person owes on MORTGAGES. For example, if you buy a house for $100,000, paying $20,000 down and bor-rowing $80,000, your equity in the house is $20,000. As you pay off the PRINCIPAL of the loan, your equity will rise.

escrow (ES-kroh) The condition of being ineffective until certain conditions are met. For example, money inherited by a minor might be held in escrow until the heir reaches a certain age. Homeowners with MORTGAGES frequently pay money for insurance and taxes on their home into an escrow account each month. The holder of the mortgage then pays the insurance and tax bills out of the escrow account when the bills are due.

eviction Legally turning a tenant out of rental property for not paying rent or not satisfying some other obligation.

Foreign Exchange Rates: 1970 to 1991

This chart shows the rate of exchange for various national currencies in U.S. dollars as of December 31 of each year shown. Rates are rounded off to the nearest penny.

Country	Currency	1970	1980	1990	1991
Canada	Dollar	.99	.86	.86	.87
France	Franc	.18	.24	.18	.18
India	Rupee	.13	.13	.06	.04
Italy	Lira	.0016	.0012	.0008	.008
Japan	Yen	.0028	.0044	.0069	.0074
Norway	Krone	.14	.20	.16	.15
Spain	Peseta	.014	.014	.010	.010
Switzerland	Franc	.23	.60	.72	.70

Another way of looking at foreign exchange rates is based on the number of units of a foreign currency equal to one U.S. dollar. The figures in this chart are as of March 29, 1993.

Country	Currency	Rate
Canada	Dollar	1.24
France	Franc	5.55
India	Rupee	31.18
Italy	Lira	1,679
Japan	Yen	116
Norway	Krone	6.94
Spain	Peseta	116.74
Switzerland	Franc	1.51

Sources: *The Wall Street Journal* and the Board of Governors of the Federal Reserve System; *Federal Reserve Bulletin*.

exchange rate The price at which one CURRENCY can be purchased with another currency or gold. At any time, for example, one American dollar can purchase a certain number of German marks or French francs or Japanese yen.

excise tax (EK-seyez) A tax, similar to a sales tax, imposed on some GOODS, especially luxuries and cars.

expenditure An expense; an amount spent.

expense account An account or list of expenses incurred in doing business outside the office, part of which is a TAX DEDUCTION. The term often applies to lunches or dinners at which business deals are made and clients entertained.

❧ One popular image for the misuse of expense accounts is the expensive, fancy meal known as the three-martini lunch.

export   Any GOOD or SERVICE sold from one nation to another.

export quota   A restriction imposed by a government on the amount or number of GOODS or SERVICES that may be exported within a given period, usually with the intent of keeping prices of those goods or services low for domestic users.

expropriation   The taking over of private property by a government, often without fair compensation but usually with a legal assertion that the government has a right to do so.

FDIC   *See* FEDERAL DEPOSIT INSURANCE CORPORATION.

featherbedding   The practice of forcing an employer to hire more workers than are needed for a job.

Fed, the   *See* FEDERAL RESERVE SYSTEM.

Federal Deposit Insurance Corporation (FDIC)   A federal agency that insures DEPOSITS in savings accounts of qualifying banks.

Federal Reserve System (the Fed)   The central monetary authority of the United States. The Board of Governors supervises the twelve Federal Reserve banks, which deal with other banks rather than with the public. The system has many functions, including regulating INTEREST RATES.

Federal Trade Commission (FTC)   A federal agency charged with enforcing ANTITRUST LEGISLATION and preventing false advertising, among other duties.

FICA   (FEYE-kuh)   An ACRONYM for Federal Insurance Contributions Act. FICA taxes are deducted from the pay of most American workers to support SOCIAL SECURITY programs.

fiscal policy   The policy of a government in controlling its own EXPENDITURES and TAXATION, which together make up the budget.

❧ A function of fiscal policy, along with MONETARY POLICY, is to regulate the level of economic activity, the price level, and the BALANCE OF PAYMENTS. Fiscal policy also determines the DISTRIBUTION of resources between the PUBLIC SECTOR and the PRIVATE SECTOR and influences the distribution of wealth.

fiscal year   A twelve-month period for which an organization such as a government or CORPORATION plans the use of its funds. Commonly, fiscal years run from July 1 to June 30, or, in the case of the United States government, from October 1 to September 30.

fixed exchange rate   A RATE OF EXCHANGE that is officially controlled by the issuing country rather than determined by the world CURRENCY market conditions. (*Compare* FLOATING EXCHANGE RATE.)

floating exchange rate   A RATE OF EXCHANGE that is determined by market conditions rather than being officially set. (*Compare* FIXED EXCHANGE RATE.)

HENRY FORD. *Henry Ford (front right), Thomas A. Edison (back right), and John Burroughs (left) in a Model T Ford in 1914. From the collections of Henry Ford Museum and Greenfield Village. Negative number 0-2572.*

Ford, Henry   An American industrial leader of the late nineteenth and early twentieth centuries. Ford perfected the ASSEMBLY LINE technique of MASS PRODUCTION, by which the Model T automobile and its successors were made available "for the multitude."

❧ Ford said, "History is bunk," and was often considered a man of extreme CONSERVATISM and hardheaded practicality. The Ford Foundation, which he established in the 1930s, has funded a great number of educational projects.

foreclosure A proceeding in which the financer of a MORTGAGE seeks to regain property because the borrower has defaulted on payments.

foreign exchange The ways in which DEBTS between two nations that use different CURRENCIES are paid. Foreign exchange rates can have an important effect on a nation's economy because the value of its currency in other countries affects the cost of both imported and exported GOODS and SERVICES. (*See* BALANCE OF PAYMENTS.)

***Fortune* Five Hundred** A listing of the five hundred largest industrial companies published each year in *Fortune* magazine.

franchise In business, a relationship between a manufacturer and a RETAILER in which the manufacturer provides the product, sales techniques, and other kinds of managerial assistance, while the retailer promises to market the manufacturer's product rather than that of competitors. For example, most automobile dealerships are franchises. The vast majority of fast food chains are also run on the franchise principle, with the retailer paying to use the brand name.

free enterprise The freedom of private businesses to operate competitively for profit with minimal governmental REGULATION.

free market The production and exchange of GOODS and SERVICES without interference from the government or from MONOPOLIES.

free trade Unrestricted trade among nations without government TARIFFS or customs DUTIES on IMPORTS.

Friedman, Milton An American economist of the twentieth century. Friedman has defended FREE ENTERPRISE and attacked government REGULATION of the economy. He has condemned SOCIALISM as an economic failure and celebrated CAPITALISM for combining prosperity with personal liberty. (*See also* MONETARISM.)

fringe benefit A payment to a worker in addition to salary or WAGES. It may take the form of cash, GOODS, or SERVICES, and include items such as health insurance, PENSION plans, and paid vacations.

full employment The condition that exists when all who want work can find jobs. Since some individuals will always be between jobs, full employment does not mean that 100 PERCENT of the work force is employed. Rather, it is customarily defined as 96 percent of the total potential work force.

Galbraith, John Kenneth (GAL-brayth) An American economist; author of *The Affluent Society* and *The New Industrial State*. (*See* AFFLUENT SOCIETY.)

glut An oversupply of GOODS on the market.

GNP *See* GROSS NATIONAL PRODUCT.

gold standard A system in which a nation's CURRENCY has a value measured in gold and can be exchanged for gold. Most nations, including the United States, went off the gold standard in the 1930s.

goods Merchandise; wares; tangible products that satisfy human wants. (*Compare* SERVICES.)

Gresham's law (GRESH-uhmz) An economic principle proposed by an English financier, Sir Thomas Gresham, that bad money will drive good money out of circulation. For example, if the United States government minted silver dollars and then, at a later date, began to mint dollar coins out of cheaper metals, the public would hoard the silver dollars (possibly for later sale at higher prices) rather than use them as a medium of exchange: silver dollars would stop circulating.

gross Exclusive of DEDUCTIONS, prior to TAXATION, as in gross income. (*Compare* NET.) Total, aggregate, as in GROSS NATIONAL PRODUCT.

gross national product (GNP) The monetary value of all of a nation's GOODS and SERVICES produced within a particular period of time, such as a year.

hidden unemployment The unemployment or underemployment of workers that is not reflected in official unemployment STATISTICS because of the way they are compiled. Only those who have no work and are actively looking for work are counted as unemployed. Those who have given up looking, those who are working less than they would like, and those who work at jobs in which their skills are underutilized are not officially counted among the unemployed, though in a sense they are. These groups constitute hidden unemployment.

🐾 Because of hidden unemployment, official statistics underestimate unemployment.

high-tech Short for "high technology"; the term describes industries and firms that use or produce advanced technology, especially in electronics.

hoarding The accumulation of a COMMODITY in excess of normal needs.

holding company A company that controls other companies.

LEE IACOCCA. *Iacocca giving "thumbs up" to reporters after announcing that Chrysler's 1984 profits were $2.4 billion.*

Iacocca, Lee (eye-uh-KOH-kuh) An American businessman of the twentieth century. The son of Italian immigrants, he worked his way to the top of the Ford Motor Company and later rescued Chrysler Corporation from financial collapse. He wrote a best-selling AUTOBIOGRAPHY.

ICC *See* INTERSTATE COMMERCE COMMISSION.

IMF *See* INTERNATIONAL MONETARY FUND.

import A COMMODITY purchased from another country.

import quota A governmental restriction on the quantities of a particular COMMODITY that may be imported within a specific period of time, usually with the goal of protecting domestic producers of that commodity from foreign competition. (*See* TARIFF.)

income The amount of money received during a period of time in exchange for labor or SERVICES, from the sale of GOODS or property, or as a profit from financial INVESTMENTS.

income distribution The way national INCOME is divided among households in the economy.

individualism A view that stresses the importance and worth of each person. In ECONOMICS, it is the doctrine that individuals best serve the public interest by pursuing their own self-interest. For example, the businessman who expands his company in order to increase his profits also creates jobs for many people, and thereby serves the public interest. (*See* LAISSEZ-FAIRE.)

industrial relations Relations between MANAGEMENT and LABOR UNIONS or between management and individual workers. Sometimes called labor relations.

inelastic demand DEMAND whose percentage change is less than a percentage change in price. For example, if the price of a COMMODITY rises 25 PERCENT and demand decreases by only 2 percent, demand is said to be inelastic. (*See* ELASTICITY.)

inelastic supply SUPPLY whose percentage change is less than a percentage change in price. For example, if the price of a COMMODITY drops 25 PERCENT and supply decreases by only 2 percent, supply is said to be inelastic. (*See* ELASTICITY.)

inflation A general increase in prices.

insider trading The unlawful practice of using information that comes from a source "inside" the business, but is not available to the general public, to trade on the STOCK MARKET. This activity is prohibited by law and is policed by the SECURITIES AND EXCHANGE COMMISSION.

𝕒 In the middle 1980s, several revelations of insider trading rocked WALL STREET.

installment buying Purchasing a COMMODITY over a period of time. The buyer gains the use of the commodity immediately and then pays for it in periodic payments called installments.

institutional investor An organization such as a government, labor union, or business that makes investments, especially in STOCK and BOND markets.

𝕒 Institutional investors account for a majority of investments made in the United States.

interdependence In ECONOMICS, the concept that all prices are to some degree affected by all other prices and also that all markets are affected by all other markets.

interest The charge for borrowing money or the return for lending it.

interest rate The usual way of calculating INTEREST — as a percentage of the sum borrowed.

Internal Revenue Service (IRS) A federal agency, part of the DEPARTMENT OF THE TREASURY, that collects most federal taxes, including INCOME and SOCIAL SECURITY taxes.

International Monetary Fund (IMF) An agency, dominated by wealthy nations, that lends money to DEVELOPING NATIONS.

Interstate Commerce Commission (ICC) A federal agency for regulating commerce that takes place in more than one state. One of its most familiar activities is regulation of trucking.

inventory An itemized list of a firm's GOODS that have not yet been sold.

investment The purchase of property with the expectation that its value will increase over time.

investment tax credit An amount that businesses are allowed by law to deduct from their taxes, reflecting an amount they reinvest in themselves.

 Investment tax credits are structured to reward and encourage economic growth.

invisible hand A term used by Adam SMITH to describe his belief that individuals seeking their economic self-interest actually benefit society more than they would if they tried to benefit society directly. The statement "WHAT'S GOOD FOR GENERAL MOTORS IS GOOD FOR THE COUNTRY" expresses essentially the same belief.

IOU Letters standing for "I owe you." An IOU is a written statement of a borrower's obligation to pay a DEBT.

itemized deduction A legal DEDUCTION from one's personal taxable INCOME for money spent on specific GOODS and SERVICES, such as property taxes and charitable contributions. These deductions must be itemized — that is, individually listed and documented — on one's tax return.

journeyman A skilled artisan who works on hire for master artisans rather than for himself.

junk bonds Technically known as BONDS of "less than investment grade," they are short-term, high-YIELD bonds. They were widely used in the 1980s to finance MERGERS, especially hostile ones.

Kapital, Das (dahs kah-pi-TAHL) The greatest work by Karl MARX on ECONOMICS; the title is German for "capital." It describes the CAPITALIST system in highly critical terms, and predicts its defeat by SOCIALISM.

Keynes, John Maynard (KAYNZ) A British economist of the early twentieth century who rejected traditional theories of the FREE MARKET and advocated vast government spending in times of RECESSION, even at the risk of unbalancing the budget.

Keynesian economics (KAYN-zee-uhn) Economic THEORIES that advocate using government policies and programs to increase employment. They are based on the thinking of John Maynard KEYNES.

Labor Day A national holiday in the United States and CANADA in honor of working people. Labor Day is observed on the first Monday in September.

labor market An area of economic exchange in which workers seek jobs and employers seek workers. A "tight" labor market has more jobs than workers. In a "slack" labor market, the reverse is true.

labor movement The movement of workers for better treatment by employers, particularly through the formation of LABOR UNIONS.

labor union An organization of workers formed to promote COLLECTIVE BARGAINING with employers over WAGES, hours, FRINGE BENEFITS, job security, and working conditions.

labor-intensive A term describing industries that require a great deal of labor relative to CAPITAL (*compare* CAPITAL-INTENSIVE). Examples of labor-intensive industries are forms of agriculture that cannot make use of machinery and SERVICE industries such as restaurants.

laissez-faire (les-ay-FAIR, lay-zay-FAIR) French for "Let (people) do (as they choose)." It describes a system or point of view that opposes REGULATION or interference by the government in economic affairs beyond the minimum necessary to allow the FREE ENTERPRISE system to operate according to its own laws.

layoff The temporary or permanent removal of a worker from his or her job, usually because of cutbacks in production or because of his or her replacement by a machine.

lease A CONTRACT that grants possession of property for a specified period of time in return for some kind of compensation.

legal tender Any form of money that a government decrees must be accepted in payment of DEBTS.

leisure class The rich, so called because they can afford not to work. The term was made current by the economist Thorstein Veblen in his book *The Theory of the Leisure Class.*

Lewis, John L. An American labor leader of the twentieth century. Lewis served for many years as president of the United Mine Workers, and founded the Congress of Industrial Organizations (*see* AFL-CIO). Lewis supported the organization of unions by industries rather than by specific crafts.

liability An obligation or DEBT.

lien (LEEN, LEE-uhn) A claim or right given to a CREDITOR to secure payment of a DEBT, usually by sale of the debtor's property.

limited liability A fundamental feature of CORPORATIONS, whereby investors are liable only up to the amount of their INVESTMENT.

&. This principle is important for failing corporations because it holds that only the ASSETS of the corporation, not the personal assets of its owners, can be liquidated (*see* LIQUIDATION) to cover the corporation's debts.

liquid asset An ASSET in the form of money, or one that can be converted quickly into money.

liquidation The conversion of the ASSETS of a firm into cash, often just before the firm goes out of business.

liquidity (li-KWID-uh-tee) The condition of having enough money on hand to meet financial obligations without having to sell fixed ASSETS such as machinery or equipment.

list price The stated price of a COMMODITY before any DISCOUNT or other reduction.

lockout The withholding of work from employees and closing down of a plant by an employer during a labor dispute.

macroeconomics The part of economic THEORY that deals with aggregates such as national INCOME, total employment, and total consumption. (*Compare* MICROECONOMICS.)

make-work Publicly provided employment that is designed primarily to relieve unemployment and only incidentally to accomplish important tasks. If private employers are hiring few people because of a business slump, the government can "make work" for people to do.

Malthus, Thomas (MAL-thuhs) A British economist of the late eighteenth and early nineteenth centuries, especially concerned with overpopulation.

&. Malthusian THEORIES hold that populations will always increase faster than food supplies and that, therefore, hunger will always exist among the poorest populations. &. Malthus's pessimistic views, along with those of David RICARDO, earned ECONOMICS the reputation of being the "dismal science."

management The body of individuals who run major businesses, usually without owning them.

marginal cost The change in total cost of production when an output is varied by one unit.

marginal tax rate The rate at which INCOME over a certain amount is taxed. Although in general, graduated INCOME taxes impose higher tax rates on higher incomes, the tax rate does not rise for each additional dollar earned. Rather, it rises by income brackets. For example, under current law, the highest marginal federal tax rate is 38.5 PERCENT, which for single taxpayers is imposed on income in excess of $54,000.

market economy An economy in which the greater part of production, DISTRIBUTION, and exchange is controlled by individuals and privately owned CORPORATIONS rather than by the government, and government interference in the market is minimal. While a total market economy is probably only theoretically but not practically possible (since it would exclude TAXATION and regulation of any kind), those economies that approximate it are typical of CAPITALISM and antithetical to SOCIALISM, which stands for collective or government-owned means of production. Market economies are also called free economies, free markets, or FREE ENTERPRISE systems.

KARL MARX

Marx, Karl A German scholar of the nineteenth century; the originator of MARXISM, the fundamental THEORY of COMMUNISM. Marx viewed political, social, and economic reality as based in the CLASS struggle, and predicted that CAPITALISM would destroy itself. With the downfall of capitalism, the workers of the PROLETARIAT would come to power and begin a new age, free of economic exploitation. Much of Marx's work, including *THE COMMUNIST MANIFESTO* and *DAS KAPITAL*, was done with Friedrich ENGELS. (*See under "World History since 1550" and* SOCIALISM.)

mass production The manufacture of GOODS in large quantities by machinery and by use of techniques such as the ASSEMBLY LINE and DIVISION OF LABOR.

mean An AVERAGE in STATISTICS. (*See under "Physical Sciences and Mathematics."*)

median The point in a series at which half of the values or units of the series are higher and half lower.

mediation The attempt to settle a dispute through a neutral party.

mercantilism (MUR-kuhn-tee-liz-uhm, MUR-kuhn-ti-liz-uhm, MUR-kuhn-teye-liz-uhm) An economic doctrine that flourished in EUROPE from the sixteenth to the eighteenth centuries. Mercantilists held that a nation's wealth consisted primarily in the amount of gold and silver in its treasury. Accordingly, mercantilist governments imposed extensive restrictions on their economies in order to ensure a surplus of EXPORTS over IMPORTS. In the eighteenth century, mercantilism was challenged by the doctrine of LAISSEZ-FAIRE. (*See also* SMITH, ADAM.)

꙳ The European quest for colonial holdings in ASIA, AFRICA, and NORTH and SOUTH AMERICA was partially a product of mercantile economics.

merger The union of two or more independent CORPORATIONS under a single ownership. Also known as takeovers, mergers may be friendly or hostile. In the latter case, the buying company, having met with resistance from directors of the targeted company, usually offers an inflated (over-market) price to persuade STOCKHOLDERS of the targeted company to sell their shares to it. Such mergers often have been financed by JUNK BONDS.

꙳ Especially common in the 1980s, hostile takeovers have become highly controversial. Some contend that they bring needed infusions of CAPITAL and efficiency to the targeted company. Others argue that, having borrowed heavily to finance the merger, the buyer is forced to sell valuable ASSETS of the targeted company in order to pay off its debt.

microeconomics Economic analysis of particular components of the economy, such as the growth of a single industry or demand for a single product. (*Compare* MACROECONOMICS.)

minimum wage The lowest legal hourly WAGE.

mixed economy An economy that combines elements of CAPITALISM and SOCIALISM, mixing some individual ownership and regulation. Some capitalist countries — for example, GREAT BRITAIN, which has FREE MARKETS but extensive governmental presence in the economy as an owner of industries and preserver of social services — have mixed economies.

monetarism (MON-uh-tuh-riz-uhm) The economic doctrine that the supply of money has a major impact on a nation's economic growth. For example, monetarists prefer to control INFLATION by restricting the growth of a nation's money supply rather than by raising taxes. The doctrine is associated with Milton FRIEDMAN.

monetary policy An attempt to achieve broad economic goals by the regulation of the supply of money. (*Compare* FISCAL POLICY.)

money market A collective term for the many markets in which there occurs the buying and selling of funds that are loaned for short periods to businesses or to governments.

money supply The amount of money in circulation at a given time, usually controlled by some central banking authority.

monopoly The exclusive control by one company of a SERVICE or product.

Morgan, J. Pierpont An American financier of the late nineteenth and early twentieth centuries. In 1901, he formed the United States Steel Corporation, the world's first billion-dollar CORPORATION.

mortgage (MAWR-gij) A legal agreement that creates an interest in REAL ESTATE between a borrower and a lender. Commonly used to purchase homes, mortgages specify the terms by which the purchaser borrows from the lender (usually a bank or a SAVINGS AND LOAN ASSOCIATION), using his title to the house as SECURITY for the unpaid balance of the loan.

multinational corporation A CORPORATION with operations in two or more countries.
 🖝 The rise of multinationals, a relatively recent occurrence, has resulted in a great deal of legal ambiguity because they can operate in so many jurisdictions.

multiplier effect An effect in ECONOMICS in which an increase in spending produces an increase in national INCOME and consumption greater than the initial amount spent. For example, if a CORPORATION builds a factory, it will employ construction workers and their suppliers as well as those who work in the factory. Indirectly, the new factory will stimulate employment in laundries, restaurants, and SERVICE INDUSTRIES in the factory's vicinity.

municipal bonds BONDS issued by nonprofit bodies such as cities, public hospitals, and school boards. They bear relatively low INTEREST RATES, but accrued interest is exempt from federal INCOME tax.

mutual fund A company organized for the purpose of making INVESTMENTS. A mutual fund gets its CAPITAL stock from private individual investors, who, in effect, allow the mutual fund to decide where to invest their money.

mutual insurance company A type of insurance company in which policyholders share in the profits.

RALPH NADER

Nader, Ralph (NAY-duhr) An American lawyer of the twentieth century and a leading advocate for CONSUMERS. Nader became prominent in the 1960s with his book *Unsafe at Any Speed*, accusing the automobile industry of producing dangerous cars. Later, Nader attacked unsanitary conditions in the meat packing industry and called for more attention to railroad and airline safety.
 🖝 Nader has been known for his focus on immediate and concrete concerns, rather than on calls for basic changes in the ways in which business is conducted. 🖝 Nader's assistants, often university students, are known as "Nader's Raiders."

NEW YORK STOCK EXCHANGE. *The floor of the NYSE on October 16, 1987, the first day in the history of the NYSE that the Dow Jones industrial average lost more than 100 points in a single session.*

national debt The DEBT of the government; the amount by which government spending exceeds tax REVENUES and must be borrowed.

✧ A large national debt can inhibit growth and drive up INTEREST RATES.

nationalization A government takeover of a private business.

natural resources Factors of production not created (though harnessed) by effort. MINERALS and FOSSIL FUELS are examples of natural resources.

negative income tax A plan to raise the INCOME of the poor by direct cash SUBSIDIES. Instead of paying an income tax, the poor would receive a cash payment from the government.

net What remains after all DEDUCTIONS have been made. (*Compare* GROSS.)

New York Stock Exchange The largest STOCK EXCHANGE in the United States, located on WALL STREET in NEW YORK CITY.

no-fault insurance A type of automobile LIABILITY insurance that tries to cut the cost of insurance by restricting the legal grounds on which suits arising out of accidents can be brought. Most payments are made without determining legal responsibility, which is most often the reason for going to court.

obsolescence (ob-suh-LES-uhns) A decline in the value of equipment or of a product brought about by an introduction of new technology or by changes in DEMAND. (*See* PLANNED OBSOLESCENCE.)

oligopoly (ol-i-GOP-uh-lee, oh-li-GOP-uh-lee) Control over production and sale of a product or SERVICE by a few companies.

OPEC. *Delegates at an OPEC meeting in Qatar. Saudi Arabian oil minister Sheik Yamani is seated in the center.*

OPEC (OH-pek) *See* ORGANIZATION OF PETRO-LEUM EXPORTING COUNTRIES.

open shop A business that employs both unionized and nonunionized labor.

organization man Someone who subordinates his personal goals and wishes to the demands of the COR-PORATION or similar large organization for which he works; a conformist. The term comes from the book *The Organization Man,* by William H. Whyte.

Organization of Petroleum Exporting Countries (OPEC) An organization of about a dozen nations that sell oil to other nations. The purpose of OPEC, a CARTEL, is to control the production of oil, and to establish favorable oil prices for the member nations. Most OPEC countries, such as LIBYA and SAUDI ARABIA, are in the MIDDLE EAST or northern AF-RICA, but INDONESIA and VENEZUELA are members as well.

    🏵 OPEC was formed in the early 1960s, but had little impact before 1973. Then, to punish the United States and several Western nations for supporting Is-

RAEL in a war against EGYPT (*see* ARAB-ISRAELI CON-FLICT), the Arab members of OPEC placed an EM-BARGO on the sale of oil to the United States and some of its allies. The result was a severe gasoline shortage and a RECESSION in Western nations, espe-cially in EUROPE, CANADA, and the United States. By the late 1970s, however, conservation measures in Western countries were fast reducing the price of oil. In response, some of the members of OPEC (partic-ularly those with large DEBTS to Western banks) be-gan to increase oil production and sales.

overdraft The amount by which a check exceeds the funds on DEPOSIT to cover it.

overhead All costs of running a business other than WAGES paid to production workers or payments for raw material to be used in production. Overhead in-cludes the cost of renting or leasing a store in which business is transacted, the cost of heating a factory, and similar expenses.

parity price (PAR-uh-tee) A price paid to American farmers that is designed to give them the same REAL

INCOME that they had between 1910 and 1914, a period selected because it was a time of agricultural prosperity.

Parkinson's Law   A law propounded by the twentieth-century British scholar C. Northcote Parkinson. It states, "WORK EXPANDS TO FILL THE TIME AVAILABLE FOR ITS COMPLETION."

partnership   An association of two or more persons to conduct a business. In contrast to a CORPORATION, those who engage in a partnership are liable for DEBTS incurred by the company to the full extent of their private fortunes rather than merely to the extent of their INVESTMENT.

pension   Payments made to a retired person either by the government or by a former employer.

peonage (PEE-uh-nij)   A system of forced labor based on DEBTS incurred by workers. Peonage developed particularly in plantation economies, where employers forced laborers to buy from employer-owned stores, pay inflated prices, and stay in debt.

per capita (puhr KAP-i-tuh)   A LATIN PHRASE literally meaning "by heads," and translated as "for each person." It is a common unit for expressing DATA in STATISTICS. A country's per capita personal INCOME, for example, is the average personal income per person.

per diem (puhr DEE-uhm, DEYE-uhm)   A LATIN PHRASE meaning "by the day." Traveling salesmen or government workers often are paid a "per diem," meaning an allowance out of which to cover daily expenses while traveling.

personal property   Furniture, automobiles, boats, and other possessions that are not included in the category of REAL PROPERTY.

planned economy   A type of economy in which some central authority makes a wide range of decisions pertaining to production and WAGES.

   🐝 The former SOVIET UNION and other COMMUNIST nations are examples of planned economies.

planned obsolescence (ob-suh-LES-uhns)   Incorporating into a product features that will almost certainly go out of favor in a short time, thereby inducing the CONSUMER to purchase a new model of the product. Placing sweeping tail fins on an automobile is an example of planned obsolescence.

poverty level   A level of INCOME above which it is possible to achieve an adequate STANDARD OF LIVING and below which it is not. It fluctuates with the COST OF LIVING.

   🐝 Because the poverty level is somewhat artificially established by the government, it can be manipulated for political ends. As with HIDDEN UNEMPLOYMENT, governments are often accused of establishing a poverty level that underestimates the number of poor people.

price controls   Measures, usually temporary, taken by governments to limit price rises in times of rapid INFLATION.

price fixing   Any usually unlawful practice by which producers of a COMMODITY act together to obtain an artificially high price.

prime rate   The INTEREST RATE that banks charge to CORPORATIONS that are considered excellent risks.

   🐝 The prime rate is usually the lowest prevailing interest rate; if it rises, rates available to CONSUMERS will soon rise.

principal   The original amount of money lent, not including profits and INTEREST.

private enterprise   Business carried on for profit and not owned by the government; also, the system that discourages public ownership of business; the same as FREE ENTERPRISE. (*See* PRIVATE SECTOR.)

private sector   That part of an economy in which GOODS and SERVICES are produced by individuals and companies as opposed to the government, which controls the PUBLIC SECTOR.

productivity   In business, a measure of worker efficiency, such as 100 units per hour. In ECONOMICS, involvement in the creation of GOODS and SERVICES to produce wealth.

profit motive   The ability to earn profits as the reason for producers to make and sell GOODS.

   🐝 The profit motive is often called a great good or a great evil in society. On the one hand, it is said to represent selfishness; on the other, it is said to drive the FREE MARKET system. (*See* INVISIBLE HAND.)

profit sharing   Distributing the profits, or part of the profits, of a business to its employees.

progressive tax A tax that takes a higher proportion of large INCOMES than of small ones. (*Compare* REGRESSIVE TAX.)

proletariat (proh-luh-TAIR-ee-uht) A term often applied to industrial workers, particularly by followers of Karl MARX.

property rights The legal limits governing the use and control of economic resources by individuals and CORPORATIONS.

prorate To divide or distribute a sum of money proportionately. For example, if one owned an automobile for only three months, an insurance company would prorate the annual premium by charging only one-quarter of it.

protective tariff A DUTY imposed on IMPORTS in order to raise their price, making them less attractive to CONSUMERS and thus protecting domestic industries from foreign competition.

proxy A person authorized to act for another, or the written authorization to act for another.

&. Shareholders in CORPORATIONS may designate proxies to represent them at STOCKHOLDERS' meetings and vote their SHARES.

public sector That part of the economy controlled by the government. (*Compare* PRIVATE SECTOR.)

public utility A private company supplying water, gas, electricity, telephone service, or the like, which is granted a MONOPOLY by the government and then regulated by the government.

pump priming Informally, government spending to increase purchasing power and stimulate the economy.

rationing A regulated allocation of resources among possible users.

&. The United States government has engaged in rationing usually only under conditions of extreme shortage or economic hardship; resources were rationed, for example, during WORLD WAR II.

real cost The cost of producing a GOOD or SERVICE, including the cost of all resources used and the cost of not employing those resources in alternative uses.

real estate *See* REAL PROPERTY.

real GNP The GROSS NATIONAL PRODUCT adjusted to account for INFLATION, measured in units called real dollars.

real income INCOME measured in terms of the GOODS and SERVICES it can buy.

real property Property held in the form of land or buildings.

real wages WAGES adjusted for the prevailing level of consumer prices. (*See also* CONSTANT DOLLARS.)

rebate The return of part of a payment for a GOOD. Unlike a DISCOUNT, which is deducted from the price before purchase, a rebate is returned after purchase.

recession A general business slump, less severe than a DEPRESSION.

redistribution Any process, such as INFLATION or TAXATION or the provision of social services, that reallocates household INCOME.

regressive tax A tax that takes a higher percentage of low INCOMES than high ones. Sales taxes, especially on food, clothing, medicine, and other basic necessities are widely cited as examples of regressive taxes. (*Compare* PROGRESSIVE TAX.)

regulation Laws through which governments can control privately owned businesses.

retail A term describing businesses that sell GOODS directly to individuals. (*Compare* WHOLESALE.)

revenue The INCOME of local, state, or national governments.

revenue sharing A transfer of tax REVENUE from one unit of government, such as the federal government, to other units, such as state governments.

Ricardo, David A British economist of the late eighteenth and early nineteenth centuries. Ricardo was essentially a classical economist in the tradition of Adam SMITH, but he expanded Smith's vision to forecast an eventual end to economic growth owing to the difficulty of increasing food production to keep up with population growth.

&. With Thomas MALTHUS, he is credited with propounding the pessimistic views that earned ECONOMICS the label of the "dismal science."

right-to-work laws Laws that make it illegal to require workers to join LABOR UNIONS as a condition of employment. Right-to-work laws are opposed to the UNION SHOP.

risk capital (venture capital) Money invested in high-risk enterprises.

robber barons A term applied to certain leading American businessmen of the late nineteenth and early twentieth centuries, including Cornelius VANDERBILT and John D. ROCKEFELLER. The term suggests that they acquired their wealth by means more often foul than fair.

JOHN D. ROCKEFELLER. *A photographic portrait, circa 1900.*

Rockefeller, John D. An American businessman of the late nineteenth and early twentieth centuries; a founder of the Standard Oil Company. Rockefeller was the richest man in the world at his retirement, and was noted for founding many charitable organizations.

Route 128 Used as a SYNONYM for high technology (*see* HIGH-TECH); this term refers to a highway encircling the suburbs of BOSTON, MASSACHUSETTS, which is known for the concentration of electronics and COMPUTER firms located along it. (*Compare* SILICON VALLEY.)

royalty A payment made for some right or privilege, as when a publisher pays a royalty to an author for the author's granting the publisher the right to sell the author's book.

savings and loan association A financial institution that resembles a bank but which historically did not offer such services as personal checking accounts and which invested CAPITAL mainly in home MORTGAGES. In the late 1970s CONGRESS passed legislation freeing savings and loan associations (often called S & Ls) from their traditional dependency on home mortgage loans. In response, S & Ls invested their capital, often unwisely, in a range of enterprises, especially REAL ESTATE. In the late 1980s hundreds of S & Ls went bankrupt, leaving the federal government, which insured the accounts of depositors, with an enormous bill.

savings bond A BOND issued by the United States government and sold in relatively small denominations, mainly to individuals.

scab Informally, a worker who stays on the job while others go on STRIKE. Also, a worker brought in to keep a plant operating when its work force is on strike. (*See* STRIKEBREAKER.)

scarcity The basic problem on which classical economic THEORY is built: simply, that human wants will always exceed the resources available to fulfill those wants. This tenet was challenged by the rise of what John Kenneth GALBRAITH described as the AFFLUENT SOCIETY.

seasonal unemployment Periodic unemployment created by seasonal variations in particular industries, especially industries like construction that are affected by the WEATHER.

SEC *See* SECURITIES AND EXCHANGE COMMISSION.

securities Written evidence of ownership or creditorship, such as BONDS and STOCK certificates.

Securities and Exchange Commission (SEC) A federal agency that supervises the exchange of SECURITIES so as to protect investors against malpractice such as INSIDER TRADING.

seller's market A market in which DEMAND exceeds SUPPLY. As a result, CONSUMERS have to pay more for GOODS. (*Compare* BUYER'S MARKET.)

seniority Length of service on a job. Seniority may be considered in making decisions about WAGES, LAYOFFS, and other working conditions.

service industry An industry that produces SERVICES rather than GOODS. Examples include transportation, banking, RETAIL trade, and entertainment.

services Work done for others as an occupation or business. (*Compare* GOODS.)

shares The units of STOCK that represent ownership in a CORPORATION.

shortage A condition that exists when DEMAND exceeds SUPPLY because of a lack of EQUILIBRIUM in a market. If a price is artificially low, buyers want to buy more of a GOOD than sellers are willing to sell. (*Compare* SURPLUS.)

sinking fund A fund into which companies or governments place money to redeem their BONDS and other forms of indebtedness.

sliding scale A set of rates that change according to a mathematical formula. The INCOME tax, for example, is levied on a sliding scale, with the rich paying a higher percentage than the poor.

Smith, Adam A Scottish scholar of the eighteenth century whose ideas about ECONOMICS led to the growth of modern CAPITALISM. His best-known work is *The Wealth of Nations*. (*See* INVISIBLE HAND.)

Social Security System A system of federally funded SERVICES and payments to help support the needy, the aged, and the temporarily unemployed as well as providing support for needy, dependent, crippled, or neglected children, rehabilitation for the disabled, and a host of other social services. The system was established as part of the NEW DEAL, and is funded by payroll taxes paid by workers and employers.

socialism *See under "World Politics."*

stagflation An economic phenomenon of the late 1960s and 1970s characterized by sluggish economic growth and high INFLATION. The word is a blend of *stagnation* and *inflation*.

standard of living A term describing the amount of GOODS and SERVICES that an average family or individual views as necessary.

stock A SHARE in the ownership of a CORPORATION.

stock exchange A place where STOCKS, BONDS, and other SECURITIES are bought and sold.

&. In the United States, the two largest stock exchanges are the NEW YORK STOCK EXCHANGE and the AMERICAN STOCK EXCHANGE. Activity on these two exchanges is usually considered an indication of the state of the economy as a whole.

stock market A market in which STOCKS are bought and sold (*see* STOCK EXCHANGE). Also, the general condition of the sale of SECURITIES in a CORPORATION.

stockholders The persons or CORPORATIONS holding STOCK in a corporation.

STRIKE. *Striking New York City hotel workers in 1985.*

strike A concerted refusal by employees in a particular business or industry to work. Its goal is usually to force employers to meet demands respecting WAGES and other working conditions.

strikebreaker An employee hired to replace a striking worker. (*See* SCAB.)

structural unemployment Relatively long-lasting unemployment resulting from long-term shifts in economies and markets rather than short-term savings in economic conditions.

&. Structural unemployment tends to develop

around major changes in an economy, such as the move from an industrial to a technological economy. Workers displaced by the decline of the old economy tend not to be trained in fields suitable for the new economy, so they remain out of work.

subsidy A grant made by a government to some individual or business in order to maintain an acceptable STANDARD OF LIVING or to stimulate economic growth.

subsistence farming Farming that provides enough food for the farmer and his family but not enough for sale. By comparison, commercial farming is farming that provides products for sale.

supply The amount of any given COMMODITY available for sale at a given time.

supply and demand In classical economic THEORY, the relation between these two factors determines the price of a COMMODITY. This relationship is thought to be the driving force in a FREE MARKET. As DEMAND for an item increases, prices rise. When manufacturers respond to the price increase by producing a larger SUPPLY of that item, this increases competition and drives the price down. Modern economic theory proposes that many other factors affect price, including government regulations, MONOPOLIES, and modern techniques of marketing and advertising.

supply-side economics An economic THEORY that holds that, by lowering taxes on CORPORATIONS, government can stimulate INVESTMENT in industry and thereby raise production, which will, in turn, bring down prices and control INFLATION. Supply-siders focus on increasing the supply of GOODS rather than stimulating DEMAND by granting SUBSIDIES to the public. Supply-side economics influenced the presidency of Ronald REAGAN.

surplus An unsold quantity of a GOOD resulting from a lack of EQUILIBRIUM in a market. For example, if a price is artificially high, sellers will bring more goods to the market than buyers will be willing to buy. (*Compare* SHORTAGE.)

surtax A tax added to an existing tax. To help finance the VIETNAM WAR, for example, CONGRESS imposed a surtax on the federal INCOME tax.

sweatshop A small factory or shop in which employees are poorly paid and work under adverse con-

SWEATSHOP. *A garment industry sweatshop at the turn of the century.*

ditions. Sweatshops were especially common in the garment industry during the early twentieth century.

take-home pay Pay after DEDUCTIONS for taxes, SOCIAL SECURITY, insurance, and other SERVICES.

takeover *See* MERGER

tariff A government tax on IMPORTS, designed either to raise REVENUE or to protect domestic industry from foreign competition.

tax break A special tax benefit given to promote specific economic or social objectives. For example, the United States government, having decided that individual home ownership is a boon to the economy, allows interest on a home MORTGAGE to be subtracted, in whole or in part, from one's taxable INCOME. The resulting lower TAXATION for homeowners constitutes a tax break.

tax deduction An expense, such as a charitable contribution, that can be deducted from one's taxable INCOME. Unlike a TAX SHELTER, a tax deduction does not necessarily take the form of an INVESTMENT.

tax haven A place that levies very low taxes or none at all on foreigners.

&. MONACO and various small Caribbean island nations are famous as tax havens.

tax loophole A provision in the laws governing TAXATION that allows people to reduce their taxes. The term has the connotation of an unintentional omission or obscurity in the law that allows the reduction of tax LIABILITY to a point below that intended by the framers of the law.

tax shelter   A type of INVESTMENT that allows a reduction in one's taxable INCOME. Examples include investments in PENSION plans and REAL ESTATE.

taxation   A government's practice of collecting money from citizens and businesses within its domain to support its operations.

tax-deductible   *See* TAX DEDUCTION.

T-bills   *See* TREASURY BILLS.

technocracy (tek-NOK-ruh-see)   The control of government and society by people with technical skills, especially engineers.

technological unemployment   Unemployment caused by the displacement of workers by machines.

tenant farming   Farming by a farmer who rents rather than owns the land.

tight-money policy   A policy in which a central monetary authority, for example the FEDERAL RESERVE SYSTEM, seeks to restrict CREDIT and raise INTEREST RATES. (*Compare* EASY-MONEY POLICY.)

   ❧ A tight-money policy might be pursued to limit INFLATION.

trade   Business or commerce; economic activity.

trade barriers   TARIFFS, IMPORT QUOTAS, customs regulations, and other disincentives meant to discourage international trade.

   ❧ Trade barriers are usually protectionist; that is, they are erected to protect domestic producers who would not be able to compete successfully with foreign producers in a FREE MARKET or in FREE TRADE.

trade deficit   The condition that exists when the value of what a country IMPORTS exceeds the value of what it EXPORTS; also called an unfavorable BALANCE OF TRADE.

   ❧ Trade deficits, because they imply that CAPITAL is leaving a country, can cause higher INTEREST RATES.

tradeoff   What must be given up, and what is gained, when an economic decision is made. (*See* OPPORTUNITY COST.)

transfer payment   INCOME transferred from one party to another without a corresponding exchange of GOODS or SERVICES. Examples are a CORPORATION's charitable contributions or a government's provision of social services.

Treasury bills (T-bills)   BONDS issued by the United States government. T-bills normally have fixed terms; that is, the purchaser cannot take possession of the accrued INTEREST for a fixed period of time after purchase. T-bills are auctioned by the Treasury each week; the auction determines the six-month INTEREST RATE.

trust   A combination of firms or CORPORATIONS for the purpose of reducing competition and controlling prices throughout a business or industry. Trusts are generally prohibited or restricted by ANTITRUST LEGISLATION. (*Compare* MONOPOLY.)

trust busting   Government activities aimed at breaking up MONOPOLIES and TRUSTS. (*See* ANTITRUST LEGISLATION.)

tycoon   Someone who has made a fortune in business, such as Cornelius VANDERBILT.

unemployment compensation   Short-term payments made to workers who have involuntarily lost their jobs.

union   *See* LABOR UNION.

union shop   A business or industry in which all new workers must join a LABOR UNION after a specified period of time. (*See* CLOSED SHOP *and* RIGHT-TO-WORK LAWS.)

urban renewal   Government-sponsored destruction of slum housing with a view to the construction of new housing.

   ❧ Large-scale urban renewal was engaged in during the 1960s and 1970s, after the departure of the rich and the MIDDLE CLASS for America's suburbs had left many United States cities in decay and disrepair.

urbanization   The process by which cities grow or by which societies become more urban.

usury (YOOH-zhuh-ree)   The practice of charging more than the legal INTEREST RATE.

utility   *See* PUBLIC UTILITY.

value-added tax (VAT) A tax on the value added to a product at each stage of its production, from raw materials to finished product. Widely employed in EUROPE, value-added taxes have the advantage (for governments) of raising revenue "invisibly," that is, without appearing as taxes on the bill paid by the CONSUMER.

CORNELIUS VANDERBILT

Vanderbilt, Cornelius An American business leader of the nineteenth century; the founder of the Vanderbilt fortune. The family's money derived first from shipping and later from railroads.

🦋 His son, William Henry Vanderbilt, summed up the Vanderbilt business philosophy in his famous comment, "THE PUBLIC BE DAMNED!"

VAT *See* VALUE-ADDED TAX.

venture capital *See* RISK CAPITAL.

vested interest One who holds a vested interest has a deep personal (and possibly financial) interest in some political or economic proposal: "As a major STOCKHOLDER of the Ford Motor Company, Senator Bilge had a vested interest in legislation restricting the IMPORT of Japanese autos." The plural, *vested interests*, often refers to powerful, wealthy property holders: "His RADICAL policies enraged vested interests."

voucher A CREDIT of a certain monetary value that can be used only for a specified purpose, such as to pay for housing or for food. Food stamps are a kind of voucher.

🦋 Some economists believe that GOODS and SERVICES supplied by the government would be provided more efficiently if vouchers that could be spent only on such goods and services were given to citizens, and private business competed to provide those goods and services.

wage scale A schedule of the WAGES paid to different classes of workers in a company.

wages Payment for SERVICES to a worker, usually remuneration on an hourly, daily, or weekly basis.

Wall Street A street in NEW YORK CITY on which the NEW YORK STOCK EXCHANGE and many INVESTMENT firms are located. The street's name is often used in reference to the activities conducted on it: "STOCK prices fell on Wall Street."

warranty A guarantee of the quality of a product or SERVICE made by the seller to the buyer.

watered stock STOCK issued at an inflated price — that is, a price not warranted by the ASSETS of the issuing company.

welfare Government-provided support for those unable to support themselves. In the United States, it is undertaken by various federal, state, and local agencies under the auspices of different programs, the best known of which are Aid to Families with Dependent Children (AFDC) and food stamps.

welfare state An economic system that combines features of CAPITALISM and SOCIALISM by retaining private ownership while the government enacts broad programs of social welfare such as PENSIONS and public housing.

What's good for General Motors is good for the country A statement made by Charles E. Wilson, while president of the General Motors Corporation, a leading United States automobile manufacturer. Wilson later became secretary of the federal DEPARTMENT OF DEFENSE.

wholesale The sale of merchandise to RETAILERS rather than directly to the public.

wildcat strike A STRIKE called in violation of an existing CONTRACT between labor and MANAGEMENT.

windfall An unexpected profit from a business or other source. The term connotes gaining huge profits without working for them — for example, when oil companies profit from a temporary scarcity of oil.

withholding tax   The tax withheld (or deducted) directly from one's paycheck.

Workmen's Compensation   A state insurance program that provides money for workers injured on the job and for the dependents of workers killed on the job.

yield   The profit obtained from an INVESTMENT.

zoning   The establishment by local governments of districts that are restricted to various types of manufacturing, commercial, or residential use.

Physical Sciences and Mathematics

The physical sciences include PHYSICS, CHEMISTRY, and ASTRONOMY, along with related branches of engineering. They are the most highly developed of the sciences, and serve as a model for the development of other areas of learning. MATHEMATICS, while not a science itself, is the language in which the physical sciences are written, and hence has had a close relation with these sciences throughout history.

Physics is the study of MATTER and motion. It is divided into two sections: classical physics, which is the science as developed before 1900; and modern physics, which encompasses twentieth-century work. Classical physics is further divided into MECHANICS, the study of motion; THERMODYNAMICS, the study of phenomena related to HEAT; and the study of ELECTRICITY and MAGNETISM. The content of each of these fields can be summarized in a few basic laws from which all the rest of the contents can be derived by mathematical reasoning. There are three laws for mechanics (NEWTON'S LAWS OF MOTION), three for thermodynamics (known simply as the laws of thermodynamics), and four for electricity and magnetism (MAXWELL'S EQUATIONS). If you add to these Newton's LAW OF UNIVERSAL GRAVITATION (now known to be a special case of general RELATIVITY), you have a handful of laws that explain everything that was studied by scientists to the end of the nineteenth century, from the motion of the MOON in its ORBIT to the flow of BLOOD through an ARTERY.

In the twentieth century, two new fields have been added to physics: relativity, which deals with objects moving at a speed near the SPEED OF LIGHT, and which constitutes our modern THEORY of GRAVITATION; and the study of the ATOM and the particles that compose it. The latter field occupies the bulk of the attention of modern physicists.

The atom consists of a NUCLEUS and ELECTRONS circling around the nucleus; the ways in which atoms come together to form MOLECULES is governed by the behavior of the electrons. When the number of atoms in a molecule is in the thousands or hundreds of thousands, the basic laws of atomic behavior discovered by physicists are of limited use, and the complex interactions of the molecules constitute their own field of study. The infinite variety of possible atomic combinations is the domain of chemistry. In the same way, the new science of materials, in which scientists produce substances with new and hitherto undreamed-of properties, involves procedures for arranging atoms in new ways.

The nucleus of the atom is composed of ELEMENTARY PARTICLES, which are themselves composed of things called QUARKS, which are still more elementary. The study of the interactions of elementary particles at high ENERGY is the frontier of knowledge in physics today.

Until the late nineteenth century, astronomy was concerned primarily with locating and tracing the position of objects in the sky. The great achievement of this stage of the science was showing that the motion of objects in the SOLAR SYSTEM could be understood completely through Newton's laws of motion. In the late nineteenth century, attention shifted to explaining *what* celestial objects were, rather than *where* they were, and the science of ASTROPHYSICS was born.

We now know that STARS, like people and trees, have life cycles — that they are born, live out their lives, and die. The SUN and other stars are powered by NUCLEAR REACTIONS in their core, and die when the nuclear fuel is consumed.

COSMOLOGY is the branch of astronomy concerned with the universe as a whole, as well as its origin. The universe is expanding, and is believed to have originated several billion years ago, in an event known as the BIG BANG. The study of these origins is an important frontier in astronomy.

Mathematics does not involve experimentation or observation of nature, and is therefore not a science like physics or chemistry. In mathematics, one may start with assumptions and rules of LOGIC, and use DEDUCTION to reach conclusions. PLANE GEOMETRY of the type taught in high school is a good example of how this procedure works. Alternately, as in the study of STATISTICS, one may start with a set of incomplete data and use INDUCTION to reach conclusions. Mathematicians provide the tools that physical scientists apply to their studies of the world. Modern mathematics has, however, become extremely abstract, and is well beyond the reach of the general public (and even of most scientists). Consequently, only those notions of mathematics that are likely to be encountered in general discussion are included in the following list.

— J. T.

A-bomb (AY-bom)   *See* ATOMIC BOMB.

absolute zero   The lowest temperature that can be attained by MATTER, corresponding to the point at which most motion in ATOMS stops. Absolute zero is about −273 DEGREES on the CELSIUS SCALE and about −460 on the FAHRENHEIT scale.

acceleration   A change in the VELOCITY of an object.

☙ The most familiar kind of acceleration is a change in the speed of an object. An object that stays at the same speed but changes direction, however, is also being accelerated. (*See* FORCE.)

accelerator, particle   *See* PARTICLE ACCELERATOR.

acid   A sour-tasting material (usually in a SOLUTION) that dissolves metals and other materials. Technically, a material that produces positive IONS in solution. An acid is the opposite of a BASE and has a pH of 0 to 7. A given amount of an acid added to the same amount of a base neutralizes the base, producing water and a SALT. Common vinegar, for example, is a weak solution of acetic acid.

☙ Figuratively, *acid* applies to anything sour or biting; for example, an "acid wit" is sharp and unpleasant.

active site   The part of an ENZYME or ANTIBODY where a CHEMICAL REACTION occurs.

acute angle   An angle that measures less than ninety DEGREES but more than zero degrees. (*Compare* OBTUSE ANGLE *and* RIGHT ANGLE.)

adhesion   The molecular (*see* MOLECULE) attraction or joining of the surfaces of two dissimilar substances. (*Compare* COHESION.)

adsorption   The assimilation of a GAS, LIQUID, or dissolved substance by the surface of a SOLID.

aerodynamics   The branch of science devoted to the study of the flow of GASES around solid objects. It is especially important in the design of cars and airplanes, which move through the air.

☙ A vehicle that has been built to minimize FRICTION with the air is said to be aerodynamically designed.

alchemy (AL-kuh-mee)   A science (no longer practiced) that sought to transform one chemical ELE-

MENT into another through a combination of magic and primitive CHEMISTRY. Alchemy is considered to be the ancestor of modern chemistry.

🙚 The search for the PHILOSOPHER'S STONE that would change lead and other base metals into gold was part of alchemy. 🙚 Today, alchemy is associated with wizards, magic, and the search for arcane knowledge.

algebra A branch of MATHEMATICS marked chiefly by the use of SYMBOLS to represent numbers, as in the use of $a^2 + b^2 = c^2$ to express the PYTHAGOREAN THEOREM.

algorithm (AL-guh-rithh-uhm) A set of instructions for solving a problem, especially on a computer. An algorithm for finding your total grocery bill, for example, would direct you to add up the costs of individual items to find the total.

alkali (AL-kuh-leye) A bitter, caustic MINERAL often found in large beds in the desert. Alkalis are BASES; two common examples are lye and ammonia.

🙚 Plants have difficulty growing in SOIL that is rich in alkalis.

alloy (AL-oy, uh-LOY) A material made of two or more metals, or of a metal and another material. For example, brass is an alloy of copper and zinc; steel is an alloy of iron and CARBON. Alloys often have unexpected characteristics. In the examples given above, brass is stronger than either copper or zinc, and steel is stronger than either iron or carbon.

alpha radiation (AL-fuh) Particles sent out by some RADIOACTIVE NUCLEI, each particle consisting of two PROTONS and two NEUTRONS bound together. Alpha particles carry a positive CHARGE. (*See* BETA RADIATION *and* GAMMA RADIATION.)

🙚 Alpha radiation, unlike gamma radiation, has low penetrating power; it can be stopped by clothing.

amplitude In PHYSICS, the height of a crest (or the depth of a trough) of a WAVE.

Andromeda galaxy (an-DROM-uh-duh) In ASTRONOMY, the GALAXY nearest to the MILKY WAY, usually seen as a large collection of STARS arranged in a central core with spiral arms. The galaxy was given this name because the stars of the CONSTELLATION Andromeda appear to enclose it.

antimatter In PHYSICS, MATTER made of ANTIPARTICLES.

antiparticle In PHYSICS, a rare form of SUBATOMIC MATTER that is a mirror image of normal matter. The antiparticle corresponding to an ELEMENTARY PARTICLE has the same MASS as the particle, but is opposite in all other properties. The antiparticle corresponding to an ELECTRON is a POSITRON, which has the same mass as an electron but a positive CHARGE. Antiprotons have the same mass as PROTONS but a negative charge. When matter and antimatter come together, the two particles annihilate each other, converting their mass into ENERGY or into other types of particles.

🙚 As far as scientists can tell, there is almost no naturally occurring antimatter in the UNIVERSE, although it is possible to make antimatter in PARTICLE ACCELERATORS.

apogee (AP-uh-jee) In ASTRONOMY, the POINT during the ORBIT of a SATELLITE, such as the MOON, at which it is farthest from the EARTH. For PLANETS in the SOLAR SYSTEM orbiting the SUN, their farthest point from the sun is referred to as *aphelion*.

Archimedes (ahr-kuh-MEE-deez) An ancient Greek scientist, mathematician, and inventor. He is best known for his investigations of BUOYANCY.

🙚 Archimedes is said to have shouted "EUREKA!" ("I have found it!") as he stepped into his bath and realized that the VOLUME of an object can be measured by determining how much water it displaces. He used this insight to measure the volume of a crown supposedly made of pure gold. After measuring the crown's volume and weighing it, he could calculate its DENSITY. He then could prove that the crown was not dense enough to be pure gold. 🙚 According to the "principle of Archimedes," when an object placed in water is weighed, and its WEIGHT in the water is compared to its weight out of the water, it seems to lose a definite amount — an amount equal to the weight of the water it displaces. This principle holds not only for water, but also for GASES, such as air. A boat floats, or a balloon rises, because it weighs less than the material it displaces. (*See* BUOYANCY.)

🙚 Archimedes is also supposed to have said, with regard to levers and FULCRUMS, "Give me the place to stand, and a lever long enough, and I will move the EARTH!"

asteroid (AS-tuh-royd) A small PLANET that revolves around the SUN. The largest asteroid is only about 600 miles in DIAMETER. (*See* ASTEROID BELT.)

asteroid belt A region of the SOLAR SYSTEM between the ORBITS of the PLANETS Mars and Jupiter. Most ASTEROIDS are found in the asteroid belt.

astronomical unit The mean distance between the EARTH and the SUN, about 98 million miles or 150 million kilometers.

astronomy The science that deals with the universe beyond the EARTH. It describes the nature, position, and motion of the STARS, PLANETS, and other objects in the skies, and their relation to the earth.

astrophysics The branch of ASTRONOMY devoted to the study of the physical characteristics and composition of objects in the sky. Typical concerns of astrophysics are how much LIGHT the STARS give off, and the size, MASS, and temperature of PLANETS and stars.

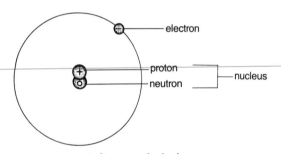

ATOM. *A diagram of a hydrogen atom.*

atom A unit of MATTER; the smallest unit of a chemical ELEMENT. Each atom consists of a NUCLEUS, which has a positive CHARGE, and a set of ELECTRONS that move around the nucleus. (*See* BOHR ATOM.)

ðŸ¢‹ Atoms link together to form MOLECULES.

atomic clock The most accurate clock available. Time is measured by the vibration of ELECTRONS in cesium ATOMS. The standard second is now defined by measurements on an atomic clock.

atomic number The number of PROTONS or ELECTRONS normally found in an ATOM of a given chemical ELEMENT. The higher the atomic number, the heavier the atom is. In a neutral atom, the number of protons and electrons is the same. (*See* ATOMIC WEIGHT *and* PERIODIC TABLE OF THE ELEMENTS.)

atomic weight The MASS of a given ATOM, measured on a SCALE in which the HYDROGEN atom has the weight of 1. Since most of the mass in an atom is in the NUCLEUS, and each PROTON and NEUTRON has an atomic weight of 1, the atomic weight is very nearly equal to the number of protons and neutrons in the nucleus. (*See* ATOMIC NUMBER.)

average A single number that represents a set of numbers. MEANS, MEDIANS, and MODES are kinds of averages; usually, however, the term *average* refers to a mean.

axiom (AK-see-uhm) In MATHEMATICS, a statement that is unproved but accepted as a basis for other statements, usually because it seems so obvious.

ðŸ¢‹ The term *axiomatic* is used generally to refer to a statement so obvious that it needs no proof.

axis In GEOMETRY, a straight LINE about which an object may rotate or that divides an object into symmetrical halves.

ðŸ¢‹ The axis of the EARTH is an imaginary line drawn through the NORTH POLE and the SOUTH POLE.

background radiation Low-level RADIATION at the surface of the EARTH that comes from COSMIC RAYS and from small amounts of RADIOACTIVE materials in rocks and the ATMOSPHERE. (*See also* COSMIC MICROWAVE BACKGROUND.)

Baconian method (bay-KOH-nee-uhn) A method of experimentation, created by Francis BACON in the seventeenth century, that derives its conclusions from observed facts rather than from previous conclusions or THEORIES.

base Any of a number of bitter-tasting, caustic materials. Technically, a material that produces negative IONS in SOLUTION. A base is the opposite of an ACID and has a pH of 7 to 14. A given amount of a base added to the same amount of an acid neutralizes the acid; water and a SALT are produced. ALKALIS are bases; ammonia is a common base.

bell curve *See* NORMAL DISTRIBUTION.

beta radiation (BAY-tuh) High-ENERGY ELECTRONS, carrying a negative CHARGE, that are sent out by some RADIOACTIVE NUCLEI. (*See* ALPHA RADIATION *and* GAMMA RADIATION.)

ðŸ¢‹ Beta radiation, unlike alpha radiation, has some

penetrating power, and can pass through clothing and wooden walls.

Big Bang theory In ASTRONOMY, a THEORY according to which the universe began billions of years ago in a single event, similar to an explosion. There is evidence for the Big Bang theory in the observed RED SHIFT of distant GALAXIES, which indicates that they are moving away from the EARTH, and in the existence of COSMIC MICROWAVE BACKGROUND. The Big Bang theory of the origin of the universe is favored by most astronomers today.

🐚 Scientists do not yet know whether the expansion of the universe will continue or will slow down and reverse at some time in the future.

Big Dipper A CONSTELLATION in the northern sky. The two STARS on the far end of the bowl of the dipper point toward the NORTH STAR. The Big Dipper is part of a larger constellation, URSA MAJOR (the Great Bear).

black hole In ASTRONOMY, an object so massive that nothing, not even LIGHT, can escape its GRAVITATION. Black holes were given their name because they absorb all the light that falls on them. The existence of black holes was first predicted by the general THEORY of RELATIVITY, which states that GRAVITY increases in proportion to MASS, and mass increases in proportion to DENSITY. Black holes are thought to arise from the death of very massive STARS. Astronomers expect to find many of them in the MILKY WAY.

🐚 Figuratively, the term *black hole* is used to refer to a total disappearance: "They never saw the man again — he might as well have fallen into a black hole."

blackbody An object that can absorb and send off RADIATION with complete efficiency — that is, it reflects (*see* REFLECTION) none of the radiation that falls on it. The higher the object's temperature, the higher the FREQUENCY of the radiation it gives off.

Bohr, Niels (BAWR) A Danish physicist of the twentieth century. Bohr was one of the founders of QUANTUM MECHANICS and the originator of the BOHR ATOM.

Bohr atom (BAWR) The simplest modern picture of the structure of the ATOM, according to which ELECTRONS move in ORBITS around the NUCLEUS. The electron's orbits can exist only at certain well-defined distances from the nucleus. When an electron changes orbits, it does so in a sudden QUANTUM LEAP. The ENERGY difference between the initial and final orbit is emitted by the atom in bundles of ELECTROMAGNETIC RADIATION called PHOTONS.

🐚 The Bohr atom is named after the twentieth-century Danish physicist Niels BOHR.

boiling point The temperature at which a given material changes from a LIQUID to a GAS. The boiling point is the same temperature as the CONDENSATION POINT. (*See* PHASES OF MATTER.)

🐚 Water boils at 212 DEGREES FAHRENHEIT or 100 degrees CELSIUS.

bond (chemical) *See* CHEMICAL BOND.

British thermal unit (Btu) A unit for measuring HEAT. One Btu raises the temperature of one pound of water one DEGREE FAHRENHEIT.

Brownian motion The erratic motion, visible through a MICROSCOPE, of small grains suspended in a FLUID. The motion results from collisions between the grains and ATOMS or MOLECULES in the fluid.

🐚 Brownian motion was first explained by the twentieth-century physicist Albert EINSTEIN, who pointed out that it was direct proof of the existence of atoms.

buffer In CHEMISTRY, a SOLUTION that can neutralize either an ACID or a BASE, and thus maintain a constant pH.

🐚 Buffers are often used in medications designed to decrease acidity in the STOMACH.

buoyancy The FORCE that causes objects to float. According to the principle of ARCHIMEDES, when a SOLID is placed in a FLUID (a LIQUID or a GAS), it is subject to an upward force equal in magnitude to the WEIGHT of the fluid it has displaced.

calculus The branch of MATHEMATICS, usually studied after ALGEBRA, that provides a natural method for describing gradual change.

🐚 Most modern sciences use calculus.

Calorie The amount of HEAT required to raise the temperature of a KILOGRAM of water by one DEGREE CELSIUS. A calorie (with a LOWER-CASE *c*) is a measurement of the heat needed to raise the temperature of a GRAM of water, rather than a kilogram.

capillary (KAP-uh-ler-ee)   A thin tube, such as a BLOOD VESSEL or a straw, through which FLUIDS flow.

🐚 The interaction between the fluid and the vessel walls produces a FORCE that can lift the fluid up into the tube, a phenomenon known as capillary action.

carbon   A chemical ELEMENT; its symbol is C. The carbon NUCLEUS has six PROTONS and six or more NEUTRONS; six ELECTRONS are in ORBIT around the carbon nucleus. (*See* HYDROCARBONS *and* ORGANIC MOLECULES.)

🐚 Carbon forms the basis for all living tissue.

carbon dioxide (CO$_2$)   A COMPOUND made up of MOLECULES containing one CARBON ATOM and two OXYGEN atoms.

🐚 Carbon dioxide is normally found as a GAS that is breathed out by animals and absorbed by green plants. The plants, in turn, return OXYGEN to the ATMOSPHERE. (*See* CARBON CYCLE *and* RESPIRATION.)
🐚 Carbon dioxide is also given off in the burning of FOSSIL FUELS. (*See* GREENHOUSE EFFECT.)

carbon 14   A RADIOACTIVE ISOTOPE of CARBON. A carbon 14 ATOM contains six PROTONS, six ELECTRONS, and eight NEUTRONS. Carbon 14 is produced when neutrons bombard atoms of NITROGEN.

🐚 Carbon 14 is used in a common form of RADIOACTIVE DATING to determine the age of ancient objects.

carbon monoxide (CO)   A COMPOUND made up of MOLECULES containing one CARBON ATOM and one OXYGEN atom.

🐚 Carbon monoxide is usually formed when materials burn; it is found, for example, in automobile exhaust. 🐚 Carbon monoxide is a colorless, odorless GAS that can be fatal to human beings if inhaled.

cardinal number   A number used to indicate the quantity of things in a group or set, but not the order or arrangement of those things. One, two, and 1000 are cardinal numbers. (*Compare* ORDINAL NUMBERS.)

catalyst (KAT-l-ist)   In CHEMISTRY, a substance that causes a CHEMICAL REACTION to occur but is not itself involved in the reaction.

🐚 The term *catalyst* is often used to refer to the prime agent of any change: "She was the catalyst for the reorganization."

cc   An ABBREVIATION for cubic CENTIMETER — the VOLUME of a cube that has edges one centimeter long.

Celsius (SEL-see-uhs)   A temperature SCALE, also called CENTIGRADE, according to which water freezes at zero DEGREES and boils at 100 degrees.

center of gravity   The POINT in any SOLID where a single applied FORCE could support it; the point where the MASS of the object is equally balanced. The center of gravity is also called the CENTER OF MASS. When a man on a ladder leans sideways so far that his center of gravity is no longer over his feet, he begins to fall.

center of mass   *See* CENTER OF GRAVITY.

centigrade   The CELSIUS temperature SCALE.

centimeter (SEN-tuh-mee-tuhr)   A unit of length in the METRIC SYSTEM; one-hundredth of a METER, or about two-fifths of an inch.

centrifugal force (sen-TRIF-yuh-guhl, sen-TRIF-uh-guhl)   A FORCE that tends to move objects away from the center in a system undergoing circular motion. Centrifugal force allows a person to whirl a bucket of water without spillage, or throws a rider in a car against the door when the car goes around a sharp curve. Centrifugal force is actually a form of INERTIA.

CFC   (chlorofluorocarbon) Chemical COMPOUNDS originally developed for use in refrigeration systems, now used widely in industry. When released into the air, these compounds break down and release CHLORINE, which causes damage to the EARTH's OZONE LAYER and is responsible for producing the OZONE HOLE.

chain reaction   In CHEMISTRY and PHYSICS, a self-sustaining series of reactions. In a chain reaction in a URANIUM-based NUCLEAR REACTOR, for example, a single NEUTRON causes the NUCLEUS of a uranium ATOM to undergo FISSION. In the process, two or three more neutrons are released. These neutrons start more fissions, which produce more neutrons, and so on.

🐚 Figuratively speaking, any group of events linked so that one is the cause of the next can be called a "chain reaction."

change of phase   *See* PHASES OF MATTER.

chaos A new branch of science that deals with systems whose evolution depends very sensitively upon the initial conditions. Turbulent flows of FLUIDS (such as whitewater in a river) and the prediction of the weather are two areas where chaos THEORY has been applied with some success.

charge, electrical A fundamental property of MATTER. PROTONS and the NUCLEI of ATOMS have a POSITIVE CHARGE; ELECTRONS have a NEGATIVE CHARGE; NEUTRONS have no charge. Normally, each atom has as many protons as it has ELECTRONS, and thus has no net electrical charge; in other words, it is neutral. Charged substances have an imbalance of positive and negative charges, a net charge that exerts a FORCE on other charged substances. Charges that are both positive or both negative repel each other; charges that are different attract.

chemical bond Any rearrangement of ELECTRONS in two ATOMS that generates a FORCE, causing the atoms to be bound to each other, forming a MOLECULE. (See COVALENT BOND and IONIC BOND.)

chemical element See ELEMENT.

chemical equilibrium A balanced condition within a system of CHEMICAL REACTIONS. When in chemical equilibrium, substances form and break down at the same rate, and the number of MOLECULES of each substance becomes definite and constant.

chemical reaction A process in which ATOMS of the same or different ELEMENTS rearrange themselves to form a new substance. While they do so, they either absorb HEAT or give it off.

chemistry The study of the composition, properties, and reactions of MATTER, particularly at the level of ATOMS and MOLECULES.

chlorine (KLAWR-een, KLAWR-in) A chemical ELEMENT, normally a corrosive gas, that is widely used for sterilization and cleaning.
&. Chlorine is added to drinking water to kill BACTERIA. &. Chlorine in CFCs is believed to be responsible for the OZONE HOLE.

chlorofluorocarbons See CFC.

circumference (suhr-KUM-fuhr-uhns) The measure of the distance around a circle.

closed universe If there is enough MATTER in the universe to stop the expansion associated with the BIG BANG, we say that the universe is closed. In a closed universe, the current period of expansion will be followed by a period of contraction (sometimes called the Big Crunch) as the GRAVITATIONAL FORCE pulls matter back in. Searching for matter to "close" the universe is a major task of modern COSMOLOGY. (See also DARK MATTER, FLAT UNIVERSE, and OPEN UNIVERSE.)

cobalt 60 (KOH-bawlt) A RADIOACTIVE ISOTOPE produced when NEUTRONS bombard ATOMS of the ELEMENT cobalt.
&. Cobalt 60 is a common substance used in RADIATION therapy for CANCER.

cohesion The molecular (see MOLECULE) attraction or joining of the surfaces of two pieces of the same substance. (Compare ADHESION.)

cold fusion The FUSION of HYDROGEN ATOMS into HELIUM at room temperature. In 1989 two scientists announced that they had produced cold fusion in their laboratory, an achievement that if true would have meant a virtually unlimited cheap energy supply for humanity. When other scientists were unable to reproduce their results, the scientific community concluded that the original experiment had been flawed.

colloid (KOL-oyd) A substance made up of particles that are larger than most MOLECULES; these particles do not actually dissolve in substances but stay suspended in them.
&. Fog, paints, and foam rubber are colloids.

combustion Burning; a CHEMICAL REACTION that involves the rapid combination of a fuel with OXYGEN. (See OXIDATION and SPONTANEOUS COMBUSTION.)

comet An object that enters the SOLAR SYSTEM, typically in a very elongated ORBIT around the SUN. Material is boiled off from the comet by the heat of the sun, so that a characteristic tail is formed. The path of a comet can be in the form of an ELLIPSE or of half a HYPERBOLA. If it follows a hyperbolic path, it enters the solar system once and then leaves forever. If its path is an ellipse, it stays in orbit around the sun.
&. Comets were once believed to be omens, and their appearances in the sky were greatly feared or welcomed. &. The most famous comet, Comet Halley

(or Halley's comet), passes close to the EARTH every seventy-six years, most recently in 1986. In many of its appearances throughout history, it was an impressive sight, but for most of 1986, over most of the world, it was a very dim object in the sky.

common denominator   A number that will allow FRACTIONS with different DENOMINATORS to be converted into fractions with the same denominator, so that these fractions can be added or subtracted. The fractions can be expressed as whole numbers divided by the common denominator. Thus, 12 is a common denominator for ⅓ and ¼, since they can be written as ⁴⁄12 and ³⁄12, respectively. (*See* LOWEST COMMON DENOMINATOR.)

❧ Figuratively, a "common denominator" is a common factor in different events: "The common denominator in these crimes is the use of inside knowledge of COMPUTER systems."

compound   In CHEMISTRY, a substance containing two or more ELEMENTS in definite proportions.

condensation point   The temperature at which a material changes from a GAS to a LIQUID; the same as the BOILING POINT. (*See* PHASES OF MATTER.)

conduction   Transfer of ENERGY through a medium (for example, HEAT or ELECTRICITY through metal) without any apparent change in the medium.

conservation of energy, law of   *See* ENERGY.

constant   A number that appears in EQUATIONS and formulas and does not vary or change. Examples are PLANCK'S CONSTANT and the SPEED OF LIGHT.

constellation   An easily recognized group of STARS that appear to be located close together in the sky, and that form a picture if LINES are imagined connecting them. Constellations are usually named after an animal, a CHARACTER from MYTHOLOGY, or a common object. (*See* BIG DIPPER, URSA MAJOR, *and* URSA MINOR.)

convection   The motion of warm material that rises, cools off, and sinks again, producing a continuous circulation of material and transfer of HEAT. Some examples of processes involving convection are boiling water, in which heat is transferred from the stove to the air; the circulation of the ATMOSPHERE of the EARTH, transferring heat from the EQUATOR to the NORTH POLE and SOUTH POLE; and PLATE TECTON-

ICS, in which heat is transferred from the interior of the earth to its surface.

coordinates   A set of numbers, or a single number, that locates a POINT on a LINE, on a PLANE, or in space. If the point is known to be on a given line, only one number is needed to locate it. If the point is known to be on a given plane, two numbers are needed. If the point is known to be located in space, three numbers are needed.

Copernicus, Nicolaus (kuh-PUR-ni-kuhs)   A Polish scholar of the sixteenth century. In 1543, Copernicus produced the first workable model of the SUN and PLANETS that had the sun at the center. (*See* GALILEO, PTOLEMAIC UNIVERSE, *and* SOLAR SYSTEM.)

Coriolis effect (kawr-ee-OH-lis)   An apparent FORCE ultimately due to the rotation of the EARTH. It is the Coriolis effect that makes the air in storms rotate counterclockwise in the northern HEMISPHERE and clockwise in the southern hemisphere.

cosmic microwave background   The MICROWAVE RADIATION that arrives at the EARTH from every direction in space. The detection of this radiation played an important role in acceptance of the BIG BANG THEORY.

❧ This radiation is sometimes referred to as the "echo" of the Big Bang.

cosmology (koz-MOL-uh-jee)   The branch of science dealing with the large-scale structure, origins, and development of the UNIVERSE. (*See* ASTRONOMY *and* BIG BANG THEORY.)

covalent bond (koh-VAY-luhnt)   A CHEMICAL BOND in which two ATOMS share some of their VALENCE ELECTRONS, thereby creating a FORCE that holds the atoms together.

❧ Most MOLECULES in living systems are held together by covalent bonds.

critical mass   In PHYSICS, the amount of material that must be present before a CHAIN REACTION can sustain itself.

❧ The term *critical mass* is often used to refer generally to the minimum amount of something needed to produce a given effect: "The town needs a critical mass of industry to attract more business."

crystal   A material in which the ATOMS are arranged in a rigid geometrical structure (*see* GEOMETRY) marked by SYMMETRY. Crystals often have clearly visible geometrical shapes.

🙠 Most MINERALS are crystalline structures.

Curie, Marie (KYOOR-ee, kyoo-REE) A French chemist of the late nineteenth and early twentieth centuries, born in POLAND. With her husband, Pierre Curie, she discovered the ELEMENT RADIUM.

🙠 Marie Curie was the first major female scientist of modern times. 🙠 Marie Curie was the only person ever to win the NOBEL PRIZE in two different sciences (PHYSICS and CHEMISTRY).

current, electrical The flow of electrical CHARGE, usually ELECTRONS. (See FRANKLIN, BENJAMIN.)

cyclotron (SEYE-kluh-tron) The first kind of PARTICLE ACCELERATOR built.

🙠 Cyclotrons are now used for special research projects.

dark matter Unseen MATTER that may make up more than 90 percent of the universe. As the name implies, dark matter does not interact with LIGHT or other ELECTROMAGNETIC RADIATION, so it cannot be seen directly, but it can be detected by measuring its GRAVITATIONAL effects. It is believed that dark matter was instrumental in forming GALAXIES early in the BIG BANG.

decay, radioactive See RADIOACTIVITY.

decibel (DES-uh-buhl, DES-uh-bel) A unit of measurement of the VOLUME of sounds.

decimal point The point or dot placed to the left of DECIMALS to separate them from the WHOLE NUMBER portion of the decimal. When the number is spoken aloud, the word "point" is usually used to signify the decimal point. For example, "8.3" is read "eight point three."

decimals Fractional numbers (see FRACTION) expressed as WHOLE NUMBERS of tenths, hundredths, thousandths, and so on. One-half, for example, is 0.5 in decimal terms.

degree In GEOMETRY, a unit of measurement of angles, $1/360$ of a circle. In PHYSICS, a unit of temperature (see CELSIUS, FAHRENHEIT, and KELVIN SCALE). A degree on the Fahrenheit scale is smaller than a degree on the Celsius or Kelvin scales. Degrees on the Celsius and Kelvin scales are the same size.

dehydration The removal of water; in CHEMISTRY, the loss of two HYDROGEN ATOMS for every OXYGEN atom. (See H_2O.)

denominator (di-NOM-uh-nay-tuhr) In MATHEMATICS, the number that appears below the line in a FRACTION. In the fraction $2/3$, the denominator is 3. (Compare NUMERATOR.)

density The relative heaviness of objects, measured in units of MASS or WEIGHT per units of VOLUME. (See SPECIFIC GRAVITY.)

diameter (deye-AM-uh-tuhr) A straight LINE passing through the center of a figure, especially a circle or sphere, and joining two opposite points on its CIRCUMFERENCE.

diffraction The breaking up of an incoming WAVE by some sort of geometrical structure (see GEOMETRY) — for example, a series of slits — followed by reconstruction of the wave by INTERFERENCE. Diffraction of LIGHT is characterized by alternate bands of light and dark, or bands of different colors.

diffusion The spreading of ATOMS or MOLECULES of one substance through those of another, especially into LIQUIDS or GASES.

distillation In CHEMISTRY, the separating of the constituents of a LIQUID by boiling it and then condensing the vapor that results. Distillation can be used to purify water or other substances, or to remove one component from a complex mixture, as when gasoline is distilled from crude oil or alcohol is distilled from a mash. When water is purified by distillation, it is boiled in a container, and the steam is sent into cooling tubes. The steam is condensed and then collected as purified water in a second container. The impurities in the water are left behind in the first container and can be discarded.

🙠 Figuratively, "distillation" is the process of retaining the essential features or components of something while removing nonessentials: "This book represents knowledge distilled from decades of research."

Doppler effect (DOP-luhr) A phenomenon observed with WAVES. The FREQUENCY of a wave of LIGHT or sound seems higher if the source is moving toward the observer, and seems lower if the source is moving away. For example, if an automobile blows its horn as it travels past someone, the apparent pitch of the sound will be higher as it approaches the person, and then will grow lower as it passes and moves away.

ᴥ The RED SHIFT of distant GALAXIES is a result of the Doppler effect on light.

E = mc²   An EQUATION derived by the twentieth-century physicist Albert EINSTEIN, in which *E* represents units of ENERGY, *m* represents units of MASS, and *c²* is the SPEED OF LIGHT SQUARED, or multiplied by itself. (*See* RELATIVITY.)

ᴥ Because the speed of light is a very large number and is multiplied by itself, this equation points out how a small amount of MATTER can release a huge amount of energy, as in a NUCLEAR REACTION.

eclipse   In ASTRONOMY, the blocking out of LIGHT from one object by the intervention of another object. The most important eclipses visible from the EARTH are eclipses of the SUN (when sunlight is blocked by the MOON) and eclipses of the moon (when sunlight on its way to the moon is blocked by the earth).

ᴥ The term *eclipse* is also used to refer to a general decline or temporary obscurity: "After taking the title last year, the team has gone into an eclipse this season."

Einstein, Albert (EYEN-steyen)   A twentieth-century physicist; Einstein was born in GERMANY in 1879 and moved to the United States in the 1930s. Einstein developed the special and general THEORIES OF RELATIVITY. His equation E = MC² led to the development of nuclear FISSION and the ATOMIC BOMB.

ᴥ In 1939, a group of scientists, including Edward TELLER, received evidence that Germany, then controlled by the NAZIS, was planning to build an atomic bomb to use against the United States. These scientists persuaded Einstein to write to President Franklin D. ROOSEVELT and urge that the United States develop an atomic bomb first. Roosevelt carried out Einstein's request. (*See* MANHATTAN PROJECT.) ᴥ In his last years, before his death in 1955, after the atomic bomb had been used in war (*see* HIROSHIMA *and* NAGASAKI), Einstein sought to educate the public on how NUCLEAR WEAPONS had changed the world situation. ᴥ Einstein believed strongly in the regularity of nature. He said, "God does not play dice with the universe," and "God is subtle, but he is not malicious." ᴥ It is important to distinguish between the theory of relativity, in which the laws of

ALBERT EINSTEIN. *Einstein writing out the equation for the density of the Milky Way in 1931.*

nature are the same for all observers anywhere in the universe, and the philosophical doctrine of RELATIVISM, which holds that there are no absolute truths. The similarity in their names has been a source of confusion.

elasticity   The property of a material that allows it to return to its original shape after having been deformed, and to exert a FORCE while deformed. (*See* STRESS.)

electrical charge   *See* CHARGE, ELECTRICAL.

electrical field   A quantity proportional to the FORCE that would be exerted on an ELECTRICAL CHARGE if it were located at a given point. Electrical fields are usually associated with the presence of other electrical charges.

electricity   A flow of ELECTRONS through a CONDUCTOR.

electrolysis (i-lek-TROL-uh-sis)   In CHEMISTRY, any process that brings about a CHEMICAL REACTION by passing electric CURRENT through a material.

ᴥ The most common form of electrolysis is ELEC-

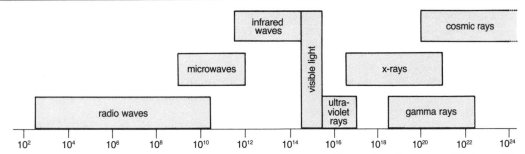

ELECTROMAGNETIC SPECTRUM. *An electromagnetic spectrum with wavelengths measured in hertz. The hertz frequency 10^6 indicates that six zeros should follow the number one (i.e., 10^6 equals 1,000,000 hertz).*

TROPLATING, in which a thin coat of metal is deposited on a solid object.

electromagnet A MAGNET created by passing an electric CURRENT through coils of wire. Electromagnets are widely used in common electrical systems.

electromagnetic induction Production of an electric CURRENT by changing the MAGNETIC FIELD enclosed by an electrical CIRCUIT. The most common use of electromagnetic induction is in the electric GENERATOR.

electromagnetic radiation Any type of ELECTROMAGNETIC WAVE.

electromagnetic spectrum The family of ELECTROMAGNETIC WAVES. The electromagnetic spectrum, starting from the waves with the longest WAVELENGTHS (and least ENERGY), consists of RADIO WAVES, MICROWAVES, INFRARED RADIATION, visible LIGHT, ULTRAVIOLET RADIATION, X-RAYS, and GAMMA RADIATION. Members of the family differ from one another only in their wavelength, or FREQUENCY. For example, the wavelength of blue light is roughly half that of red light, but the WAVES corresponding to the two colors are otherwise identical.

electromagnetic waves WAVES composed of undulating ELECTRICAL FIELDS and MAGNETIC FIELDS. The different kinds of electromagnetic waves, such as LIGHT and RADIO WAVES, form the ELECTROMAGNETIC SPECTRUM. All electromagnetic waves have the same speed in a VACUUM, a speed expressed by the letter *c* (the SPEED OF LIGHT) and equal to about 186,000 miles (or 300,000 KILOMETERS) per second.

electron (i-LEK-tron) An ELEMENTARY PARTICLE with a negative CHARGE and a very small MASS. Electrons are normally found in ORBITS around the NU-CLEUS of an ATOM. The CHEMICAL REACTIONS that an ATOM undergoes depend primarily on the electrons in the outermost orbits (the VALENCE ELECTRONS).

❧ The movement of large numbers of electrons through CONDUCTORS constitutes electric CURRENT.

electron microscope A device that uses ELECTRONS instead of LIGHT to form images of very small objects, such as individual parts of small living things.

element In CHEMISTRY, any material (such as CARBON, HYDROGEN, iron, or OXYGEN) that cannot be broken down into more fundamental substances. Each chemical element has a specific type of ATOM, and chemical COMPOUNDS are created when atoms of different elements are bound together into MOLECULES. There are over a hundred known chemical elements; ninety-two occur in nature, and the rest have been produced in laboratories.

elementary particles The particles that make up the ATOM. The elementary particles include ELECTRONS and a large number of particles, including PROTONS and NEUTRONS, that exist inside the NUCLEUS of atoms. Strictly speaking, the term *elementary* as applied to most of the particles in the nucleus is inaccurate, for scientists now believe that all the particles except ELECTRONS are made of still more elementary particles called QUARKS.

❧ The study of elementary particles is one of the frontiers of modern PHYSICS, and is associated with the building of PARTICLE ACCELERATORS.

ellipse (i-LIPS) In GEOMETRY, a curve traced out by a POINT that is required to move so that the sum of its distances from two fixed points (called foci) remains constant. If the foci are identical with each other, the ellipse is a circle; if the two foci are distinct from each other, the ellipse looks like a squashed or elongated circle.

🍂 The ORBITS of the PLANETS and of many COMETS are ellipses.

energy   In PHYSICS, the ability to do WORK. Objects can have energy by virtue of their motion (KINETIC ENERGY), by virtue of their position (POTENTIAL ENERGY), or by virtue of their MASS. (*See* $E = MC^2$.)

🍂 The most important property of energy is that it is conserved — that is, the total energy of an isolated system does not change with time. This is known as the law of CONSERVATION OF ENERGY. Energy can, however, change form; for example, it can be turned into MASS and back again into energy.

entropy (EN-truh-pee)   A measure of the disorder of any system, or of the unavailability of its HEAT ENERGY for work. One way of stating the second law of THERMODYNAMICS — the principle that heat will not flow from a cold to a hot object spontaneously — is to say that the entropy of an isolated system can, at best, remain the same, and will increase for most systems. Thus, the overall disorder of an isolated system must increase.

🍂 *Entropy* is often used loosely to refer to the breakdown or disorganization of any system: "The committee meeting did nothing but increase the entropy." 🍂 In the nineteenth century, a popular scientific notion suggested that entropy was gradually increasing, and therefore the universe was running down and eventually all motion would cease. When people realized that this would not happen for billions of years, if it happened at all, concern about this notion generally disappeared.

equation   An expression of equality between two formulas in MATHEMATICS. The two formulas are written with an equal sign between them: $2 + 2 = 4$ is an equation, as is $E = mc^2$.

equilibrium   A condition in which all influences acting cancel each other, so that a static or balanced situation results. In PHYSICS, equilibrium results from the cancellation of FORCES acting on an object. In CHEMISTRY, it occurs when CHEMICAL REACTIONS are proceeding in such a way that the amount of each substance in a system remains the same. (*See* CHEMICAL EQUILIBRIUM.)

equinox (EE-kwuh-noks, EK-wuh-noks)   The twice yearly times when the lengths of day and night are equal. At equinox, the SUN is directly over the EARTH'S EQUATOR. The vernal equinox occurs about March 22 and the autumnal equinox about September 21.

escape velocity   The speed an object must reach to escape the pull of GRAVITATION exerted by another object.

🍂 To overcome the gravitation of the EARTH and place an artificial SATELLITE in ORBIT, a rocket must reach a speed of about 25,000 miles per hour, or about seven miles per second.

ethanol (ETH-uh-nawl, ETH-uh-nohl)   Another name for ETHYL ALCOHOL.

ethyl alcohol (ETH-uhl)   The kind of alcohol made by FERMENTATION of the SUGAR in grains; the fermentation is brought about by the ENZYMES in YEAST.

🍂 Alcoholic drinks and GASOHOL contain ethyl alcohol.

Euclid (YOOH-klid)   An ancient Greek mathematician; the founder of the study of GEOMETRY. Euclid's *Elements* is the basis for modern school textbooks in geometry. One of the basic statements, or POSTULATES, of Euclid's geometry is that if a LINE and a POINT separate from it are given, only one line parallel to the first line can pass through the point.

🍂 Since Albert EINSTEIN put forth the THEORY of RELATIVITY, other approaches to geometry besides Euclid's have been needed to deal with newer ways of conceiving space. These "non-Euclidean geometries" deny Euclid's postulate about parallel lines.

evaporation   The changing of a LIQUID into a GAS, often under the influence of HEAT (as in the boiling of water). (*See* VAPORIZATION.)

🍂 The evaporation of water from the oceans is a major component in the HYDROLOGIC CYCLE.

expanding universe   *See* BIG BANG THEORY *and* RED SHIFT.

exponent (ik-SPOH-nuhnt, EK-spoh-nuhnt)   A number placed above and to the right of another number to show that it has been raised to a POWER. For example, 3^2 indicates that 3 has been raised to a power of 2, or multiplied by itself; 3^2 is equal to 9.

exponential growth (ek-spuh-NEN-shuhl)   Growth of a system in which the amount being added to the system is proportional to the amount already present:

the bigger the system is, the greater the increase. (*See* GEOMETRIC PROGRESSION.)

🐾 Figuratively, "exponential growth" means runaway expansion, such as in population growth or suburban development.

extrapolation (ik-strap-uh-LAY-shuhn) A mathematical procedure designed to enable one to estimate unknown values of a PARAMETER from known values. A common method of extrapolation is to look at data on a curve, then extend the curve into regions for which there is no data. Extrapolation is often used to predict the future.

extraterrestrial (ek-struh-tuh-RES-tree-uhl) A descriptive term for things outside the EARTH, such as possible civilizations outside the SOLAR SYSTEM, or objects such as METEORITES that actually reach the earth.

Fahrenheit A temperature SCALE according to which water freezes at thirty-two DEGREES and boils at 212 degrees. The scale was devised by Gabriel Daniel Fahrenheit, an instrument maker of the eighteenth century, born in GERMANY.

Fermi, Enrico (FUR-mee, FER-mee) An American physicist of the twentieth century, born in ITALY. Fermi built the first NUCLEAR REACTOR in the 1940s under the stands of a football field at the University of CHICAGO.

fission, nuclear A NUCLEAR REACTION in which a single large NUCLEUS splits into two or more smaller nuclei. In some cases, for example with URANIUM, ENERGY is released in this process.

🐾 The fission of uranium 235, an ISOTOPE of uranium, supplies energy for NUCLEAR REACTORS and ATOMIC BOMBS.

flash point For a given flammable substance, the lowest temperature at which vapors passing from the substance into the air will catch fire spontaneously if a small flame is present.

flat universe If there is just enough MATTER in the universe so that its GRAVITATIONAL FORCE brings the expansion associated with the BIG BANG to a stop in an infinitely long time, the universe is said to be flat. The flat universe is the dividing line between an OPEN UNIVERSE and a CLOSED UNIVERSE.

🐾 Most theorists believe that the universe is flat.

fluid In PHYSICS, a substance that flows — usually a LIQUID or a GAS.

fluorescence The emission of LIGHT from an object as a result of bombardment by other kinds of ELECTROMAGNETIC RADIATION, such as X-RAYS or ULTRAVIOLET RAYS. Fluorescent materials may appear one color when bathed in visible light and another color when exposed to other kinds of electromagnetic radiation.

🐾 "Black light" depends on fluorescence for its effects.

fluoride (FLOOR-eyed, FLAWR-eyed) Any of a number of naturally occurring COMPOUNDS of the ELEMENT fluorine. Fluorides have been found to be effective in preventing tooth decay and are routinely added to drinking water in most jurisdictions.

focal length The distance between the focal POINT of a LENS and the lens itself.

force In PHYSICS, something that causes a change in the motion of an object. The modern definition of force (an object's MASS multiplied by its ACCELERATION) was given by Isaac NEWTON in NEWTON'S LAWS OF MOTION. The most familiar unit of force is the pound. (*See* MECHANICS.)

🐾 GRAVITY, and therefore WEIGHT, is a kind of force.

fractal (FRAK-tuhl) Contraction of "fractional dimension." This is a term used by mathematicians to describe certain geometrical structures whose shape appears to be the same regardless of the level of magnification used to view them. A standard example is a seacoast, which looks roughly the same whether viewed from a satellite or an airplane, on foot, or under a magnifying glass. Many natural shapes approximate fractals, and they are widely used to produce images in television and movies.

fraction A mathematical expression representing the division of one WHOLE NUMBER by another. Usually written as two numbers separated by a horizontal or diagonal LINE, fractions are also used to indicate a part of a whole number or a RATIO between two numbers. Fractions may have a value of less than 1, as with ½, or equal to 1, as with 2/2, or more than 1, as with 3/2. The top number of a fraction is called the NUMERATOR and the bottom number the DENOMINATOR.

free fall   In PHYSICS, the motion of a body being acted upon only by GRAVITY. A SATELLITE in ORBIT is in free fall, as is a skydiver (if we neglect the effects of air resistance).

 During free fall, objects are said to be weightless.

freezing point   The temperature at which a LIQUID changes into a SOLID; the same temperature as the MELTING POINT. (*See* PHASES OF MATTER.)

 Water freezes at thirty-two DEGREES FAHRENHEIT or zero degrees CELSIUS.

frequency   In PHYSICS, the number of crests of a WAVE that move past a given point in a given unit of time. The most common unit of frequency is the HERTZ (Hz), corresponding to one crest per second. The frequency of a wave can be calculated by dividing the speed of the wave by the WAVELENGTH. Thus, in the ELECTROMAGNETIC SPECTRUM, the wavelengths decrease as the frequencies increase, and vice versa.

friction   The resistance of an object to the medium through which or on which it is traveling, such as air or water.

function   In MATHEMATICS, a quantity whose value is determined by the value of some other quantity. For example, "The octane rating of this gasoline is a function of the proportion of lead in it" means that a given proportion of lead in the gasoline will yield a certain octane rating.

fusion, nuclear   The combining of two small atomic NUCLEI to form a larger nucleus, sometimes with the release of ENERGY. (*Compare* FISSION, NUCLEAR.)

 The fusion of HYDROGEN into HELIUM releases huge amounts of energy and is the main energy source of STARS, including the SUN. HYDROGEN BOMBS use the energy of fusion. The use of fusion as a controllable energy source on EARTH is still in its experimental stages.

galaxy   A large, self-contained mass of STARS.

 A common form for galaxies is a bright center with spiral arms radiating outward. The universe contains billions of galaxies. The SUN belongs to the galaxy called the MILKY WAY.

Galileo (gal-uh-LEE-oh, gal-uh-LAY-oh)   An Italian scientist of the late sixteenth and early seventeenth

GALAXY. *The Whirlpool Galaxy.*

centuries; his full name was Galileo Galilei. Galileo proved that objects with different MASSES fall at the same VELOCITY. One of the first persons to use a TELESCOPE to examine objects in the sky, he saw the MOONS of JUPITER, the mountains on the moon of the EARTH, and SUNSPOTS.

 Authorities of the ROMAN CATHOLIC CHURCH forced Galileo to renounce his belief in the model of the SOLAR SYSTEM proposed by Nicolaus COPERNICUS. Galileo had to assert that the earth stands still, with the SUN revolving around it. A famous legend holds that Galileo, after making this public declaration about a motionless earth, muttered, "Nevertheless, it does move."

GALILEO. *After a painting by Ramsey.*

gamma radiation (GAM-uh) The most energetic RADIATION in the ELECTROMAGNETIC SPECTRUM; it has the lowest WAVELENGTH and the highest FREQUENCY in the spectrum. Gamma rays are sent out by some RADIOACTIVE NUCLEI. Unlike ALPHA RADIATION and BETA RADIATION, gamma rays are not made up of particles, and they have no CHARGE.

gas In PHYSICS, one of the PHASES OF MATTER. The ATOMS or MOLECULES in gases are more widely spaced than in SOLIDS or LIQUIDS and suffer only occasional collisions with one another.

general theory of relativity *See* RELATIVITY.

geometric progression In MATHEMATICS, a sequence of numbers in which each number is obtained from the previous one by multiplying by a CONSTANT. For example, the sequence 1, 2, 4, 8, 16, 32 . . . (in which each number is multiplied by 2 to get the next one) is a geometric progression.

☙ Many processes involving growth and spreading, such as population increases, can be described as geometric progressions.

geometry The branch of MATHEMATICS that treats the properties, measurement, and relations of POINTS, LINES, angles, surfaces, and SOLIDS. (*See* EUCLID *and* PLANE GEOMETRY.)

Goddard, Robert H. (GOD-uhrd) An American physicist of the twentieth century. Goddard launched the first LIQUID-fuel rocket, in 1926.

☙ Goddard's work helped to pave the way for the American space program.

gram The basic unit of measurement for MASS in the METRIC SYSTEM; one cubic CENTIMETER of water has a mass of approximately one gram.

Grand Unified Theory (GUT) A THEORY that describes the behavior of MATTER at temperatures that existed only in the first fraction of a second after the BIG BANG. In these theories, the STRONG, WEAK, and ELECTROMAGNETIC FORCES are unified. The greatest triumph of GUTs is that they explain the absence of ANTIMATTER in the universe. (*See also* UNIFIED FIELD THEORY.)

gravitation The FORCE, first described mathematically by Isaac NEWTON, whereby any two objects in the universe are attracted toward each other. Gravitation holds the MOON in ORBIT around the EARTH,

the PLANETS in orbit around the SUN, and the sun in the MILKY WAY. It also accounts for the fall of objects released near the surface of the earth. The modern THEORY of gravitation is the general theory of RELATIVITY.

gravity Another term for gravitation, especially as it affects objects near the surface of the EARTH.

H₂O The chemical SYMBOL for water. Each MOLECULE of water contains two ATOMS of HYDROGEN (H) joined to a single atom of OXYGEN (O).

half-life In PHYSICS, a fixed time required for half the RADIOACTIVE NUCLEI in a substance to decay. Half-lives of radioactive substances can range from FRACTIONS of a second to billions of years, and they are always the same for a given nucleus, regardless of temperature or other conditions. If an object contains a pound of a radioactive substance with a half-life of fifty years, at the end of that time there will be half a pound of the radioactive substance left undecayed in the object. After another fifty years, a quarter-pound will be left undecayed, and so on.

☙ Scientists can estimate the age of an object, such as a rock, by carefully measuring the amounts of decayed and undecayed nuclei in the object. Comparing that to the half-life of the nuclei tells when they started to decay, and, therefore, how old the object is. (*See* RADIOACTIVE DATING.)

H-bomb (AYCH-bom) *See* HYDROGEN BOMB.

heat In PHYSICS, a form of ENERGY associated with the movement of ATOMS and MOLECULES in any material. The higher the temperature of a material, the faster the atoms are moving, and hence the greater the amount of energy present as heat. (*See* INFRARED RADIATION.)

heat capacity In PHYSICS, the capability of a substance to absorb ENERGY in the form of HEAT for a given increase in temperature. Materials with high heat capacities, such as water, require greater amounts of heat to increase their temperatures than do substances with low heat capacities, such as metals. (*See* ENTROPY.)

heat of fusion *See* LATENT HEAT.

heat of vaporization *See* LATENT HEAT.

heavy water   Water with a higher average MOLEC-ULAR WEIGHT than ordinary water. In a MOLECULE of heavy water, the HYDROGEN ATOMS are ISOTOPES in which the NUCLEI each contain a PROTON and a NEU-TRON, and hence are twice as heavy as a normal hy-drogen atom.

Heisenberg, Werner (HEYE-zuhn-burg)   A German physicist of the twentieth century. Heisenberg was one of the founders of QUANTUM MECHANICS, the dis-coverer of the UNCERTAINTY PRINCIPLE, and a leader of GERMANY's attempt to construct an ATOMIC BOMB in WORLD WAR II.

Heisenberg uncertainty principle   *See* UNCER-TAINTY PRINCIPLE.

helium   A chemical ELEMENT, usually found in the form of a GAS, in which two ELECTRONS are in ORBIT, and the NUCLEUS consists of two PROTONS and two NEUTRONS. Its symbol is He.
᪣ Helium is the best known of the inert gases.
᪣ Because it is lighter than air, helium is used to fill balloons.

helix (HEE-liks)   In GEOMETRY, a three-dimensional spiral shape, resembling a spring.

hertz (HURTS)   The international unit of FRE-QUENCY: one cycle per second. The ABBREVIATION for hertz is Hz.
᪣ Household CURRENT in the United States is 60 hertz.

hexagon   A POLYGON having six sides.

horsepower   A unit of POWER equal to about 746 WATTS.
᪣ The horsepower is used to measure the power of engines. ᪣ This term was coined by James WATT, who invented a new type of steam engine in the eight-eenth century. Watt proposed that the horse did a cer-tain amount of work per second; when he sold his steam engines, this measurement allowed him to es-timate the worth of an engine in terms of the number of horses it would replace. Therefore, a six-horse-power engine was capable of replacing six horses.

Hubble, Edwin   An American astronomer of the twentieth century. Hubble was the first to show that there are GALAXIES beyond the MILKY WAY. He also discovered the RED SHIFT, thereby laying the foun-dation for the BIG BANG THEORY. (*See also* HUBBLE SPACE TELESCOPE.)

Hubble Space Telescope (HST)   The first perma-nent astronomical observatory above the EARTH's at-mosphere, HST was designed to provide much more detailed views of the universe than can be obtained from the ground. Despite the fact that the TELE-SCOPE's mirror was incorrectly tested before launch, the instrument has already produced important new data in astronomy.
᪣ A technician inserted a testing rod backwards during the manufacturing of the telescope mirror, en-dangering the entire $1.5 billion project.

hydrocarbons   Chemical COMPOUNDS whose main feature is a long chain of CARBON ATOMS bonded to HYDROGEN atoms. Hydrocarbons are ORGANIC MOL-ECULES.
᪣ Many hydrocarbons are used as fuels. Some ex-amples of hydrocarbon fuels are the components of gasoline; methane, which is the main ingredient of natural gas; and some components of wood.

hydrogen   The lightest chemical ELEMENT; its sym-bol is H. Hydrogen normally consists of a single ELECTRON in ORBIT around a NUCLEUS made up of a single PROTON. It is usually found as a GAS, and has several uses as a fuel.
᪣ Hydrogen ATOMS are combined to form HELIUM atoms in FUSION reactions in STARS and in HYDRO-GEN BOMBS, which release huge amounts of ENERGY. Hydrogen also burns rapidly, producing water as it combines with OXYGEN. (*See* H_2O *and* OXIDATION.)
᪣ For a time, hydrogen was frequently used to fill blimps and dirigibles because of its extremely low weight. In 1937, however, the hydrogen in the diri-gible *Hindenburg* caught fire, and many of the pas-sengers and crew were killed. Since that time, helium has been widely preferred to hydrogen for use in air-ships; it is not as buoyant (*see* BUOYANCY) or cheap as hydrogen, but, being an inert gas, it does not burn.
᪣ Because there is so much hydrogen in stars, it is by far the most abundant element in the universe.

hyperbola (heye-PUR-buh-luh)   In GEOMETRY, a pair of curves, each curve having a single bend, with LINES going infinitely far from the bend.
᪣ The path of a COMET that enters the SOLAR SYS-TEM and then leaves forever is a hyperbolic curve (half of a hyperbola).

hypotenuse (heye-POT-n-oohs, heye-POT-n-yoohs) In a right triangle (a triangle that has one RIGHT AN-

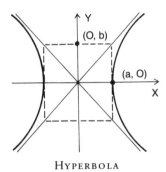

HYPERBOLA

GLE), the side opposite the right angle. (*See* PYTHA-GOREAN THEOREM.)

hypothesis (heye-POTH-uh-sis) *plur.* HYPOTHESES (heye-POTH-uh-seez) In science, a statement of a possible explanation for some natural phenomenon. A hypothesis is tested by drawing conclusions from it; if observation and experimentation show a conclusion to be false, the hypothesis must be false. (*See* SCIENTIFIC METHOD *and* THEORY.)

Hz An ABBREVIATION for HERTZ, a standard unit of FREQUENCY.

inertia (i-NUR-shuh) In PHYSICS, the tendency for objects at rest to remain at rest, and for objects in uniform motion to continue in motion in a straight LINE, unless acted on by an outside FORCE. (*See* NEWTON'S LAWS OF MOTION.)

inflationary universe A period early in the BIG BANG during which the universal expansion proceeded at a much more rapid rate that it did before or since. Cosmologists believe that most of the MATTER in the universe was created during the period of inflation.

infrared radiation (in-fruh-RED) Invisible RADIATION in the part of the ELECTROMAGNETIC SPECTRUM

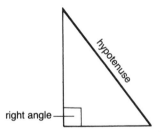

HYPOTENUSE. *The hypotenuse of a triangle is opposite the right angle.*

right angle

characterized by WAVELENGTHS just longer than those of ordinary visible red LIGHT, and shorter than those of MICROWAVES or RADIO WAVES. (*Compare* ULTRAVIOLET RADIATION.)

ॐ The HEAT we feel from a glowing coal or an incandescent light bulb is from infrared rays.

inorganic chemistry The branch of CHEMISTRY that deals with INORGANIC MOLECULES.

inorganic molecules Molecules other than ORGANIC MOLECULES. Inorganic molecules are generally simple, and are not normally found in living things. Although all organic substances contain CARBON, some substances containing carbon, such as diamonds, are considered inorganic.

integers (IN-tuh-juhrz) The WHOLE NUMBERS, plus their counterparts less than zero, and zero. The *negative* integers are those less than zero (-1, -2, -3, and so on); the *positive* integers are those greater than zero (1, 2, 3, and so on).

interference The disturbance that results when two WAVES come together at a single POINT in space; the disturbance is the sum of the contribution of each wave. For example, if two crests of identical waves arrive together, the net disturbance will be twice as large as each incoming wave; if the crest of one wave arrives with the trough of another, there will be no disturbance at all.

ॐ One common example of interference is the appearance of dark bands when a light is viewed through a window screen.

ion (EYE-uhn, EYE-on) An ATOM that has either lost or gained one or more ELECTRONS, so that it has an electrical CHARGE. Ions can be either positively or negatively charged.

ionic bond (eye-ON-ik) A CHEMICAL BOND in which one ATOM gives up an ELECTRON to another, thereby generating an electrical FORCE that holds the atoms together.

ॐ Most CRYSTALS are held together by ionic bonds.

ionization *or* **ionizing** (eye-uh-nuh-ZAY-shuhn; EYE-uh-neye-zing) Creating an ION by changing the number of electrons in an ATOM.

ॐ Certain kinds of RADIATION, such as X-RAYS, ionize atoms.

irrational number   A number that cannot be expressed as the RATIO of two WHOLE NUMBERS.

&. The SQUARE ROOTS of most whole numbers are irrational numbers.

isomers (EYE-suh-muhrz)   In CHEMISTRY, MOLECULES that contain exactly the same numbers of the same kinds of ATOMS, but in which the atoms have different structural arrangements.

isotope (EYE-suh-tohp)   In CHEMISTRY, different forms of the same ELEMENT, with NUCLEI that have the same number of PROTONS but different numbers of NEUTRONS. Isotopes are distinguished from each other by giving the combined number of protons and neutrons in the nucleus. For example, uranium 235 is the isotope of URANIUM that has 235 protons and neutrons in its nucleus rather than the more commonly occurring 238. All ELEMENTS have isotopes.

Jupiter   In ASTRONOMY, the largest PLANET in the SOLAR SYSTEM; the fifth major planet from the SUN. Jupiter is largely composed of GASES. It is named after the ruler of the Roman gods (*see under "Mythology and Folklore"*). Jupiter is visible from the EARTH.

Keck Telescope   The world's premier optical TELESCOPE, located on Mauna Kea in HAWAII. Completed in 1992, it is the first of a new generation of telescopes in which electronic controls constantly adjust a collection of small mirrors to compensate for atmospheric distortion to produce images of unprecedented clarity.

Kelvin, Lord   A British physicist of the nineteenth century. He was one of the founders of the modern science of THERMODYNAMICS. His full name was William Thompson, Lord Kelvin. (*See* KELVIN SCALE.)

Kelvin scale   The standard temperature SCALE in scientific work, proposed by Lord KELVIN. A DEGREE on the Kelvin scale is the same size as a degree on the CELSIUS scale, but the Kelvin scale starts at ABSOLUTE ZERO instead of at the FREEZING POINT of water. Thus, on the Kelvin scale, absolute zero is zero degrees, ice melts at about 273 degrees, and water boils at about 373 degrees.

Kepler, Johannes   A German astronomer of the late sixteenth and early seventeenth centuries. Kepler's three laws governing the motion of the PLANETS made modern ASTRONOMY possible. His first law includes his discovery that the ORBITS of the PLANETS are ELLIPSES.

kilogram (KIL-uh-gram, KEE-luh-gram)   A unit of MASS in the METRIC SYSTEM, equal to 1000 GRAMS. The weight of a one-kilogram mass is slightly over two pounds.

kilometer (ki-LOM-uh-tuhr, KIL-uh-mee-tuhr)   In the METRIC SYSTEM, 1000 METERS, or about five-eighths of a mile.

kilowatt (KIL-uh-waht)   One thousand WATTS. (*See* POWER.)

kinetic energy (ki-NET-ik)   The ENERGY an object has because of its motion.

Laplace, Marquis de (luh-PLAHS)   A French mathematician and scientist of the late eighteenth and early nineteenth centuries. Laplace produced the first modern THEORY to explain the formation of the SOLAR SYSTEM and the first modern theory of the TIDES.

&. Upon receiving a copy of Laplace's major work, NAPOLEON BONAPARTE observed, "You have written this huge book on the system of the world without once mentioning the author of the universe." Laplace gave this well-known reply: "Sire, I have no need for that HYPOTHESIS."

latent heat   The HEAT released or absorbed when MATTER undergoes a change of phase (*see* PHASES OF MATTER). If the heat is given off during the change from a LIQUID to a SOLID, it is called HEAT OF FUSION. If it is given off during the change from a GAS to a liquid, it is called HEAT OF VAPORIZATION.

Lavoisier, Antoine (luhv-WAH-zee-ay, lah-vwah-ZYAY)   A French scientist of the eighteenth century, Lavoisier was one of the founders of modern CHEMISTRY. He discovered the role of OXYGEN in CHEMICAL REACTIONS.

&. He was beheaded during the FRENCH REVOLUTION. The presiding judge at his trial is supposed to have remarked, "The REPUBLIC has no need of scientists."

law of universal gravitation   *See* GRAVITATION.

lens   A piece of transparent material, such as glass, that forms an image from the rays of LIGHT passing through it. (*See* FOCAL LENGTH, REFRACTION, *and* TELESCOPE.)

lepton (LEP-ton) Any one of six ELEMENTARY PARTICLES that are one of the fundamental constituents of MATTER. Leptons are not affected by the STRONG FORCE and are not normally found in the NUCLEUS of the ATOM. The ELECTRON and the NEUTRINO are examples of leptons.

light The type of ELECTROMAGNETIC WAVE that is visible to the human eye. Visible light runs along a SPECTRUM from the short WAVELENGTHS of violet to the longer wavelengths of red. (*See* PHOTON.)

light year The distance traveled by LIGHT in a year (over five trillion miles); a unit for measuring distances outside the SOLAR SYSTEM. The STAR nearest to our SUN, Alpha Centauri, is more than four light years away.

line A set of POINTS that have one dimension — length — but no width or height. (*See* COORDINATES.)

linear momentum *See* MOMENTUM.

liquid A PHASE OF MATTER in which ATOMS or MOLECULES can move freely while remaining in contact with one another. A liquid takes the shape of its container. (*Compare* GAS *and* SOLID.)

litmus (LIT-muhs) In CHEMISTRY, a kind of paper used to tell whether a SOLUTION is an ACID or a BASE. Acids turn blue litmus paper red; bases turn red litmus paper blue. Other testing paper or sophisticated instruments can be used to measure the pH of a solution more precisely.

❧ The term *litmus* is often used to refer to a general and simple test: "Your vote on this issue is a litmus test of your political PHILOSOPHY."

locus (LOH-kuhs) *plur.* LOCI (LOH-seye, LOH-keye) In GEOMETRY, the set of all POINTS (and only those points) that satisfy certain conditions; these points form a curve or figure. For example, the locus of all points in space one foot from a given point is a *sphere* having a radius of one foot and having its center at the given point. The locus of all points in a PLANE one foot from a given point is a *circle* having a radius of one foot and having its center at the given point.

lowest common denominator The smallest number that can be divided evenly into two other numbers (*see* COMMON DENOMINATOR). When FRACTIONS with different DENOMINATORS are added

together, their denominators have to be made the same; thus, fractions with denominators of nine and twelve have thirty-six as a lowest common denominator. Seventy-two and 108 are also common denominators for fractions with denominators of nine and twelve, but thirty-six is the lowest.

❧ The term *lowest common denominator* is often used to indicate a lowering of quality resulting from a desire to find common ground for many people: "This fall's TV programming finds the lowest common denominator of taste."

Mach number (MAHK) The speed of an object, measured in multiples of the speed of sound. Thus, an airplane traveling at the speed of sound is said to be at Mach 1; at twice the speed of sound, it is said to be at Mach 2.

❧ The unit is named after Ernst Mach, an Austrian physicist of the nineteenth century.

magnet An object that attracts iron and some other materials. Magnets are said to generate a MAGNETIC FIELD around themselves. Every magnet has two poles, called the north and south poles. MAGNETIC POLES exert FORCES on each other in such a way that like poles repel, and unlike poles attract each other. A compass is a small magnet that is affected by the MAGNETIC FIELD of the EARTH in such a way that it points to a magnetic pole of the earth. (*See* MAGNETIC FIELD *and* MAGNETISM.)

magnetic field A magnetic field is said to exist in a region if a FORCE can be exerted on a MAGNET. If a compass needle is deflected when it is put at a particular location, we say a magnetic field exists at that point, and the strength of the field is measured by the strength of the motion of the compass needle. The EARTH, the SUN, and the MILKY WAY GALAXY all have magnetic fields. All known magnetic fields are caused by the movement of electrical CHARGES. ELECTRONS in ORBIT in ATOMS give rise to magnetic fields, so that every atom is, like the earth, surrounded by a magnetic field. (*See* MAGNET *and* MAGNETISM.)

magnetism A fundamental property of some materials (for example, iron) and electrical CURRENTS by which they are capable of exerting a FORCE on MAGNETS. (*See* ELECTROMAGNET, MAGNET, *and* MAGNETIC FIELD.)

Mars In ASTRONOMY, the fourth major PLANET from the SUN. Mars was named after the Roman god of war because of its red color. (*See* SOLAR SYSTEM; *see under* "Mythology and Folklore.")

≈ Smaller than the EARTH, Mars has polar ice caps and a surface that includes red sands. ≈ The VIKING space mission, which placed landers on the surface of Mars, did not discover any signs of life.

mass   In PHYSICS, the property of MATTER that measures its resistance to ACCELERATION. Roughly, the mass of an object is a measure of the number of ATOMS in it. The basic unit of measurement for mass is the KILOGRAM. (*See* NEWTON'S LAWS OF MOTION; *compare* WEIGHT.)

mathematical induction   A method of proof in which a statement is proved for one step in a process, and it is shown that if the statement holds for that step, it holds for the next.

mathematics   The study of numbers, EQUATIONS, FUNCTIONS, and geometric shapes (*see* GEOMETRY) and their relationships. Some branches of mathematics are characterized by use of strict proofs based on AXIOMS. Some of its major subdivisions are arithmetic, ALGEBRA, GEOMETRY, and CALCULUS.

matter   In PHYSICS, something that has MASS and is distinct from ENERGY. (*See* PHASES OF MATTER.)

Maxwell, James Clerk   A Scottish physicist of the nineteenth century. Maxwell organized the modern study of ELECTRICITY and MAGNETISM when he wrote down MAXWELL'S EQUATIONS.

Maxwell's equations   Four EQUATIONS that contain the basic laws governing ELECTRICITY and MAGNETISM, and thus play a role analogous to that of NEWTON'S LAWS OF MOTION.

mean   In STATISTICS, an AVERAGE of a group of numbers or DATA POINTS. With a group of numbers, the mean is obtained by adding them and dividing by the number of numbers in the group. Thus the mean of five, seven, and twelve is eight (twenty-four divided by three). (*Compare* MEDIAN *and* MODE.)

mean free path   The average distance that an object (usually an ATOM or MOLECULE) can move before colliding with something.

mechanics   The branch of PHYSICS that deals with the motion of material objects. The term *mechanics* generally refers to the motion of large objects, while the study of motion at the level of the ATOM or smaller is the domain of QUANTUM MECHANICS.

≈ The basic laws of mechanics are NEWTON'S LAWS OF MOTION.

median   In STATISTICS, the middle value of a set of numbers or DATA POINTS; half the figures will fall below the median and half above. (*See* AVERAGE; *compare* MEAN *and* MODE.)

melting point   The temperature at which a given material changes from a SOLID to a LIQUID, or melts; the same temperature as FREEZING POINT. (*See* PHASES OF MATTER.)

≈ Ice melts at thirty-two DEGREES FAHRENHEIT or zero degrees CELSIUS.

Mendeleev, Dmitri (men-duh-LAY-uhf)   A Russian chemist of the nineteenth century. Mendeleev first wrote down the PERIODIC TABLE OF THE ELEMENTS.

Mercury   In ASTRONOMY, the PLANET closest to the SUN, named after the fleet-footed messenger of the Roman gods (*see under* "Mythology and Folklore") because of its swift movement in its ORBIT. Mercury takes only eighty-eight days to go around the sun. (*See* SOLAR SYSTEM.)

≈ Mercury is sometimes visible from the EARTH as a morning or evening STAR.

mercury   In CHEMISTRY, a heavy, silvery metallic ELEMENT, a LIQUID at normal temperatures. Mercury expands or contracts rapidly in response to changes in temperature, and is therefore widely used in thermometers.

≈ The term *mercury* is used figuratively in such expressions as "The mercury's rising" to mean that the temperature is going up.

meson (MEZ-on, MAY-zon)   An ELEMENTARY PARTICLE in the atomic NUCLEUS.

meter   The basic unit of length in the METRIC SYSTEM; it was originally planned so that the CIRCUMFERENCE of the EARTH would be measured at about forty million meters. A meter is 39.37 inches.

metric system   A system of measurement in which the RATIOS between units of measurement are multiples of ten. For example, a KILOGRAM is a thousand GRAMS, and a CENTIMETER is one-hundredth of a METER. Virtually all countries of the world, except the United States, use the metric system. Among scientists, the metric system is called SI — an ABBREVIA-TION for *Système internationale*, which is French for "International System."

microwaves   ELECTROMAGNETIC WAVES with a WAVELENGTH on the order of a few inches. Micro-waves are longer than INFRARED RADIATION and shorter than RADIO WAVES. Microwaves are used extensively for communication, both in SATELLITE tele-vision and for the transmission of long-distance tele-phone signals. In a microwave oven food is cooked by the heat generated when the water in the food ab-sorbs microwaves.

Milky Way   The GALAXY to which our SUN belongs.

☙ The Milky Way is also the swath of LIGHT in the night sky produced by the other STARS in the gal-axy.

mode   In STATISTICS, the most frequently appearing value in a set of numbers or DATA POINTS. In the numbers 1, 2, 4, 6, 8, 4, 9, 6, 8, and 6, the mode is 6, because it appears more often than any of the other figures. (*See* AVERAGE; *compare* MEAN *and* ME-DIAN.)

molecular weight (muh-LEK-yuh-luhr)   The sum of the ATOMIC WEIGHTS of all the ATOMS in a MOLE-CULE.

molecule (MOL-uh-kyoohl)   A combination of two or more ATOMS held together by a FORCE between them. (*See* COVALENT BOND *and* IONIC BOND.)

momentum   In PHYSICS, the property or tendency of a moving object to continue moving. For an object moving in a LINE, the momentum is the MASS of the object multiplied by its VELOCITY (LINEAR MOMEN-TUM); thus, a slowly moving, very massive body and a light, rapidly moving body can have the same mo-mentum. (*See* NEWTON'S LAWS OF MOTION.)

☙ Figuratively, *momentum* can refer to the ten-dency of a person or group to repeat recent success: "The Bears definitely have momentum after scoring those last two touchdowns."

moon   A natural SATELLITE of a PLANET; an object that revolves around a planet. The planets vary in the number of their moons; for example, MERCURY and VENUS have none, the EARTH has one, and JUPITER has seventeen or more. The planets' moons, like the planets themselves, shine by reflected LIGHT.

☙ The earth's moon is about 240,000 miles away and is about 2000 miles in diameter. The volume of the earth is fifty times that of the moon; the MASS of the earth is about eighty times that of the moon. The moon has no ATMOSPHERE, and its GRAVITY is about one-sixth that of earth.

Mount Palomar (PAL-uh-mahr)   The location of an astronomical observatory in CALIFORNIA. Inside the observatory is the Hale TELESCOPE, which contains a mirror two hundred inches across; for decades, it was the largest telescope in the world and remains one of the most productive.

NEBULA. *The Great Nebula in Andromeda — the most distant object in space visible to the naked eye.*

nebula (NEB-yuh-luh) *plur.* NEBULAE (NEB-yuh-lee, NEB-yuh-leye)   In ASTRONOMY, a hazy patch of LIGHT visible in the sky. Some nebulae are clouds of GAS within the MILKY WAY; others are distant GAL-AXIES.

necessary condition   In MATHEMATICS, a condition that must be satisfied for a statement to be true, but that does not in and of itself make it true. For ex-ample, a necessary condition to become president of the United States is that a candidate be over thirty-five years of age, but just being over thirty-five does not make one president.

negative charge   *See* CHARGE, ELECTRICAL.

Neptune   In ASTRONOMY, a major PLANET, usually eighth from the SUN. Neptune is named for the Roman god of the sea. Neptune is similar in size and composition to URANUS. It is usually visible only through a TELESCOPE, and was discovered in the 1840s. Neptune's ORBIT currently (until 1999) takes it farther from the sun than PLUTO, which is the outermost known planet most of the time. (*See* SOLAR SYSTEM; *see under "Mythology and Folklore."*)

neutrino (nooh-TREE-noh)   A massless particle with NO ELECTRICAL CHARGE that is often emitted in the process of RADIOACTIVE decay of NUCLEI. Neutrinos are difficult to detect, and their existence was postulated twenty years before the first one was actually discovered in the laboratory. Millions of neutrinos produced by NUCLEAR REACTIONS in the SUN pass through your body every second without disturbing any ATOMS.

neutron   An ELEMENTARY PARTICLE without an electrical CHARGE; one of the building blocks of the NUCLEUS of the ATOM. A neutron has about the same MASS as a PROTON.

neutron star   A STAR about the size of the EARTH, made almost entirely of NEUTRONS. It is the end product of the evolution of stars slightly larger than the SUN.

Newton, Isaac   An English scientist and mathematician of the seventeenth and early eighteenth centuries. Newton made major contributions to the understanding of motion, GRAVITY, and LIGHT (*see* OPTICS). He is said to have discovered the principle of gravity when he saw an apple fall to the ground at the same time that the MOON was visible in the sky. He also invented CALCULUS. (*See* NEWTON'S LAWS OF MOTION.)

Newton's laws of motion   The three laws that govern the motion of material objects. They were first written down by Isaac NEWTON in the seventeenth century, and gave rise to a general view of nature known as the CLOCKWORK UNIVERSE. The laws are: 1. Every object moves in a straight LINE unless acted upon by a FORCE. 2. The ACCELERATION of an object is directly proportional to the net force exerted, and inversely proportional to the object's MASS. 3. For every action, there is an equal and opposite reaction.

🐦 These three laws, together with the laws of THERMODYNAMICS and MAXWELL'S EQUATIONS, were thought to explain the entire physical universe until the beginning of the twentieth century.

nitrogen   A chemical ELEMENT that makes up about four-fifths of the ATMOSPHERE of the EARTH. Its symbol is N.

🐦 Like CARBON, nitrogen is a necessary element in the tissues of living things.

normal distribution curve   In STATISTICS, the theoretical curve that shows how often an experiment will produce a particular result. The curve is symmetrical and bell-shaped, showing that trials will usually give a result near the AVERAGE, but will occasionally deviate by large amounts. The width of the "bell" indicates how much confidence one can have in the result of an experiment — the narrower the bell, the higher the confidence. This curve is also called the Gaussian curve, after the nineteenth-century German mathematician Karl Friedrich Gauss. (*See* STATISTICAL SIGNIFICANCE.)

🐦 The normal distribution curve is often used in connection with tests in schools. Test designers often find that their results match a normal distribution curve, in which a large number of test takers do moderately well (the middle of the bell); some do worse than average, and some do better (the sloping sides of the bell); and a very small number get very high or very low scores (the rim of the bell).

North Star (Polaris) [poh-LAR-is]   A STAR positioned along the LINE in space that includes the AXIS of rotation of the EARTH. For this reason, the star does not appear to move in the sky, but remains fixed above the NORTH POLE.

🐦 Locating the North Star is useful in navigation.

nova (NOH-vuh)   In ASTRONOMY, the appearance of a new STAR in the sky (*nova* is LATIN for "new"). Novae are usually associated with the last stages in the life of a star. (*See* SUPERNOVA.)

nuclear energy   ENERGY obtained from NUCLEAR REACTIONS.

nuclear fission   *See* FISSION, NUCLEAR.

nuclear fusion   *See* FUSION, NUCLEAR.

nuclear reaction   A reaction that changes the number of PROTONS or NEUTRONS in the NUCLEUS of an ATOM. There are several kinds of nuclear reactions, including the fragmentation of large nuclei into smaller ones (nuclear FISSION), the building up of small nuclei into larger ones (nuclear FUSION), and changes begun by collisions with ELEMENTARY PARTICLES or other nuclei (as in PARTICLE ACCELERATORS).

nuclear winter A THEORY first put forward in 1983 that predicted that a large-scale nuclear exchange would produce enough smoke and soot to lower the temperature of the EARTH significantly. Subsequent calculations indicated that the climate effects would be much less than had originally been claimed, leading to the use of the term "nuclear autumn" to describe the phenomenon.

nucleus *plur.* NUCLEI (NOOH-klee-eye) The small, dense center of the ATOM. The nucleus is composed of PROTONS and NEUTRONS, and has a positive electrical CHARGE.

☙ Nuclear PHYSICS deals with the composition and structure of the nucleus.

numeral A word or symbol used to represent a number.

numerator In MATHEMATICS, the number that appears above the line in a FRACTION. In the fraction ⅔, the numerator is 2. (*Compare* DENOMINATOR.)

obtuse angle An angle that measures more than 90 DEGREES but less than 180 degrees. (*Compare* ACUTE ANGLE *and* RIGHT ANGLE.)

octagon A POLYGON having eight sides.

open universe If there is not enough MATTER in the universe to exert a strong enough GRAVITATIONAL FORCE to stop the universal expansion associated with the BIG BANG, the universe is said to be open. (*Compare* CLOSED UNIVERSE *and* FLAT UNIVERSE.)

Oppenheimer, J. Robert (OP-uhn-heye-muhr) An American physicist of the twentieth century. Oppenheimer led the research and development of the ATOMIC BOMB, and was head of the MANHATTAN PROJECT.

☙ In the early 1950s, Oppenheimer's opposition to building the HYDROGEN BOMB and his past association with LEFTISTS led to a hearing regarding his security clearance. Although the committee found that he was a "loyal citizen," his security clearance was not restored, and he was barred from government research. Oppenheimer's chief opponent in the

scientific community at this time was Edward TELLER.

optics The branch of PHYSICS dealing with LIGHT. (*See* ELECTROMAGNETIC WAVES, LASER, LENS, REFLECTION, *and* REFRACTION.)

orbit In ASTRONOMY, the path followed by an object revolving around another object, under the influence of GRAVITATION (*see* SATELLITE). In PHYSICS, the path followed by an ELECTRON within an ATOM. The PLANETS follow elliptical orbits around the SUN (*see* ELLIPSE).

☙ Informally, something is "in orbit" when its actions are controlled by an external agency or force: "The countries of eastern EUROPE were once in the orbit of the SOVIET UNION."

order of magnitude A rough measure of the size, or magnitude, of something, expressed as a POWER of ten: "The MASS of the EARTH is of the order of magnitude of 10^{24} KILOGRAMS." Also, the range of values that such a rough statement applies to.

ordinal numbers Numbers that indicate the order or position of something in a group or set, such as first, second, or fifteenth. (*Compare* CARDINAL NUMBERS.)

organic chemistry The branch of CHEMISTRY dealing with ORGANIC MOLECULES.

organic molecule A MOLECULE of the kind normally found in living systems. Organic molecules are usually composed of CARBON ATOMS in rings or long chains, to which are attached other atoms of such ELEMENTS as HYDROGEN, OXYGEN, and NITROGEN.

osmosis (ahz-MOH-sis, ahs-MOH-sis) The seeping of a FLUID through a seemingly SOLID barrier, such as a CELL WALL or a rubber sheet. When the concentration of the fluid is the same on both sides of the barrier, osmosis stops.

☙ Informally, "osmosis" is the process by which information or concepts come to a person without conscious effort: "Living in PARIS, he learned French slang by osmosis."

oxidation Any CHEMICAL REACTION in which a material gives up ELECTRONS, as when the material combines with OXYGEN. Burning is an example of rapid oxidation; rusting is an example of slow oxidation. (*See* COMBUSTION *and* REDUCTION.)

oxygen   An ELEMENT, normally a GAS, that makes up about one-fifth of the ATMOSPHERE of the EARTH. Oxygen is usually found as a MOLECULE made up of two ATOMS. Its symbol is O.

⁂ When we breathe in oxygen, it is carried by the HEMOGLOBIN in our BLOOD throughout the body, where it is used to generate ENERGY by OXIDATION. (*See* RESPIRATION.) ⁂ Oxygen is a waste product of green plants and PHOTOSYNTHESIS.

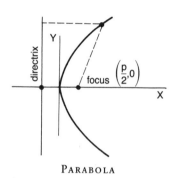

PARABOLA

parabola   (puh-RAB-uh-luh)   A geometrical shape (*see* GEOMETRY) consisting of a single bend and two LINES going off to an infinite distance in parallel directions.

⁂ An object that is propelled away from the EARTH and then drawn back by GRAVITY, such as a fly ball in baseball, follows a path shaped like a parabola.

parameter   (puh-RAM-uh-tuhr)   A quantity or number on which some other quantity or number depends. An informal example is, "Depending on the traffic, it takes me between twenty minutes and an hour to drive to work"; here, "traffic" is the parameter that determines the time it takes to get to work. In STATISTICS, a parameter is an unknown characteristic of a population — for example, the number of women in a particular precinct who will vote Democratic. ⁂ The term is often mistakenly used to refer to the limits of possible values a variable can have because of confusion with the word *perimeter.*

particle accelerator   A machine (sometimes called an "atom smasher"), often very large, that brings ELEMENTARY PARTICLES (usually either PROTONS or ELECTRONS) to a very high speed and then allows them to collide with a target. From the resulting be-

havior of the particles and the target, scientists deduce the structure of the particles.

⁂ Almost all of our knowledge of the NUCLEUS and of elementary particles depends on experiments using particle accelerators.

particle physics   The branch of science devoted to the study of the basic constituents of MATTER, particularly the constituents of the atomic NUCLEUS.

Pauling, Linus   (PAW-ling)   An American physicist of the twentieth century. Pauling has won the NOBEL PRIZE for both CHEMISTRY (for research into the FORCES that hold MOLECULES together) and peace (for his opposition to the testing of NUCLEAR WEAPONS). More recently, he has advocated the use of large amounts of VITAMIN C to prevent sickness.

pentagon   A POLYGON having five sides.

⁂ The PENTAGON is a huge five-sided building near WASHINGTON, D.C., that contains offices of the DEPARTMENT OF DEFENSE.

percent   A FRACTION expressed as a number of hundredths. Twelve percent of a quantity, for example, is twelve one-hundredths of it. Twelve percent may also be written 12%.

perigee   (PER-uh-jee)   The POINT in the ORBIT of a SATELLITE at which it is closest to its parent body. (*Compare* APOGEE.)

periodic table of the elements   A chart of the chemical ELEMENTS that displays them in rows horizontally in order of increasing ATOMIC NUMBER, and vertically according to similarity of the structure of their ATOMS. The position of an element on the table thus gives useful information about the chemical properties of the element. (*See* MENDELEEV, DMITRI.)

pH   (pee-AYCH)   In CHEMISTRY, a measure of the strength of an ACID or a BASE. A neutral solution has a pH of 7; acids a pH between 0 and 7; bases a pH from 7 to 14. Specially treated strips of paper (*see* LITMUS), or more precise instruments, may be used to measure pH.

phase change   *See* PHASES OF MATTER.

phases of matter   The states in which MATTER can exist: as a SOLID, LIQUID, or GAS. When temperature changes, matter can undergo a PHASE CHANGE, shifting from one form to another. Examples of phase changes are melting (changing from a solid to a liq-

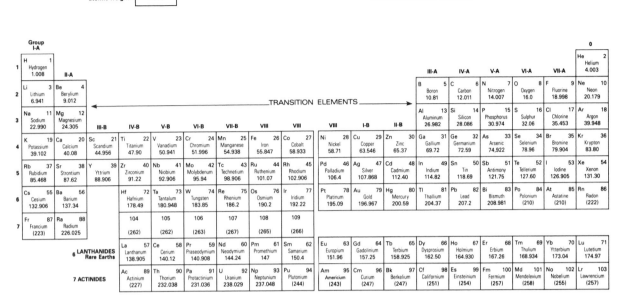

PERIODIC TABLE

uid), freezing (changing from a liquid to a solid), EVAPORATION (changing from a liquid to a gas), and condensation (changing from a gas to a liquid). (*See* BOILING POINT, CONDENSATION POINT, FREEZING POINT, MELTING POINT, TRIPLE POINT, *and* VAPORIZATION.)

photon (FOH-ton) The QUANTUM, or bundle of ENERGY, in which LIGHT and other forms of ELECTROMAGNETIC RADIATION are emitted. (*See* ATOM.)

physics The scientific study of MATTER and motion. (*See* MECHANICS, OPTICS, QUANTUM MECHANICS, RELATIVITY, *and* THERMODYNAMICS.)

pi (PEYE) The IRRATIONAL NUMBER obtained by dividing the length of the DIAMETER of a circle into its CIRCUMFERENCE. Pi is approximately 3.1416. The sign for pi is π.

Planck, Max (PLAHNGK, PLANGK) A German physicist of the late nineteenth and early twentieth centuries. Planck was one of the founders of QUANTUM MECHANICS. (*See* PLANCK'S CONSTANT.)

Planck's constant A universal CONSTANT, first discovered by Max PLANCK, that states the mathematical relationship between the FREQUENCY of an ELECTROMAGNETIC WAVE and a portion of the ENERGY (called a QUANTA) in that wave. Planck's discovery unifies the seemingly contradictory observations that energy sometimes acts like a wave and at other times acts as if it is made up of particles.

🐘 Knowing the energy level of quanta sets the SCALE of energy for events in which the ATOM and SUBATOMIC PARTICLES take part.

plane A GEOMETRICAL location having only two dimensions — length and width (no height). (*See* COORDINATES *and* PLANE GEOMETRY.)

plane geometry The study of two-dimensional figures (figures that are confined to a PLANE).

🐘 Plane geometry is one of the oldest branches of MATHEMATICS. 🐘 The Greek mathematician EUCLID was the first to study plane geometry carefully. His book *Elements* was the standard plane geometry textbook for centuries.

planet A kind of object that is in ORBIT around a STAR, but does not give off its own LIGHT; rather, it shines by reflecting sunlight. Planets close to the SUN are rocky. Those farther out consist mostly of GASES and LIQUIDS.

🐾 There are nine major planets, including the EARTH, in orbit around our sun, along with many ASTEROIDS. (*See* SOLAR SYSTEM.)

plasma (PLAZ-muh)   A state of MATTER in which some or all of the ELECTRONS have been torn from their parent ATOMS. The negatively charged electrons and positively charged IONS move independently.

🐾 Plasmas are usually associated with very high temperatures — most of the SUN is a plasma, for example.

Pluto   In ASTRONOMY, the smallest of the major PLANETS, usually ninth from the SUN. Pluto was discovered in 1930, and is named for the Roman god of the underworld. (*See* SOLAR SYSTEM; *see also* HADES *under "Mythology and Folklore."*)

🐾 Astronomers in the late nineteenth century, observing disturbances in the ORBITS of URANUS and NEPTUNE, suspected that there was a ninth planet, not yet discovered, exerting GRAVITATION on the other two. In the early twentieth century, astronomers predicted the location of the planet, and with the help of sophisticated observing equipment, Pluto — a very dim object — was found. 🐾 Pluto's orbit is a stretched ELLIPSE, unlike the orbits of the other major planets, which are nearly circular. As a result, Pluto is currently (until 1999) closer to the sun than Neptune.

plutonium (plooh-TOH-nee-uhm)   A RADIOACTIVE chemical ELEMENT that is artificially derived from URANIUM.

🐾 Plutonium is used in NUCLEAR REACTORS.

point   In GEOMETRY, a location having no dimension — no length, height, or width — and identified by at least one COORDINATE.

Polaris   *See* NORTH STAR.

polarization   The direction in which the ELECTRICAL FIELD of an ELECTROMAGNETIC WAVE points.

🐾 Reflected LIGHT, such as the light that produces glare on a sunny day, is polarized so that the electrical field is parallel to the ground. Some sunglasses are designed to take advantage of this property by blocking out that particular polarization while allowing other light to come through.

polygon   In GEOMETRY, a closed figure having three or more sides, and lying on one PLANE.

polymer (POL-uh-muhr)   In CHEMISTRY, a long MOLECULE made up of a chain of smaller, simpler molecules.

🐾 PROTEINS and many CARBOHYDRATES, such as CELLULOSE, are polymers. Plastics are also polymers.

positive charge   *See* CHARGE.

positron (POZ-i-tron)   The ANTIPARTICLE for an ELECTRON; it has the same MASS as an electron, but carries a positive CHARGE.

🐾 Positrons are found in COSMIC RAYS.

potential energy   The ENERGY an object has because of its position, rather than its motion. An object held in a person's hand has potential energy, which turns to KINETIC ENERGY — the energy of motion — when the person lets it go, and it drops to the ground.

power   In PHYSICS, the amount of ENERGY put out or produced in a given amount of time. Power is often measured in WATTS or KILOWATTS.

In MATHEMATICS, a power is a number multiplied by itself the number of times signified by an EXPONENT placed to the right and above it. Thus, 3^2, which means 3×3, is a power — the second power of three, or three squared, or nine. The expression 10^6, or ten to the sixth power, means $10 \times 10 \times 10 \times 10 \times 10 \times 10$, or one million.

precipitate (pri-SIP-uh-tayt, pri-SIP-uh-tuht)   In CHEMISTRY, a solid material that is formed in a SOLUTION by CHEMICAL REACTIONS and settles to the bottom of the container in which the reaction takes place. A precipitate may also be a substance removed from another by an artificial filter.

pressure   The FORCE exerted on a given area. (*See* ATMOSPHERIC PRESSURE.)

🐾 The most familiar measure of pressure is psi (pounds per square inch), used to rate pressure in automobile and bicycle tires.

prime number   A number that cannot be divided evenly by any other number except itself and the number one; 1, 3, 5, 7, and 11 are prime numbers.

prism (PRIZ-uhm)   A solid figure in GEOMETRY with bases or ends of the same size and shape and sides that have parallel edges. Also, an object that has this shape.

🙚 A prism of glass (or a similar transparent material) can be used to bend different WAVELENGTHS of LIGHT by different amounts through REFRACTION. This bending separates a beam of white light into a SPECTRUM of colored light.

probability A number between 0 and 1 that shows how likely a certain event is. Usually, probability is expressed as a RATIO: the number of experimental results that would produce the event divided by the number of experimental results considered possible. Thus, the probability of drawing the ten of clubs from an ordinary deck of cards is one in fifty-two (1:52), or one fifty-second.

proton (PROH-ton) An ELEMENTARY PARTICLE with a positive CHARGE, found in the NUCLEUS of an ATOM.

🙚 A proton is over a thousand times heavier than an ELECTRON. 🙚 Protons and NEUTRONS make up most of an atom's MASS.

Ptolemaic universe (tol-uh-MAY-ik) The model for the universe, put forth by the ancient Greek astronomer PTOLEMY, that had the EARTH at the center, with the SUN, MOON, PLANETS, and STARS revolving around it.

🙚 The Ptolemaic system prevailed in ASTRONOMY for nearly 1500 years, until the model of the SOLAR SYSTEM proposed by Nicolaus COPERNICUS (with the sun, not the earth, at the center) was accepted. CHURCH authorities forced GALILEO to declare belief in the earth-centered universe.

Ptolemy (TOL-uh-mee) An ancient Greek astronomer, living in EGYPT, who proposed a way of calculating the movements of the PLANETS on the assumption that they, along with the SUN and the STARS, revolved around the EARTH. (*See* PTOLEMAIC UNIVERSE.)

pulsar (PUL-sahr) A rapidly rotating NEUTRON STAR. The radiation from such a star appears to come in a series of regular pulses (one per revolution), which explains the name.

Pythagorean theorem (puh-thag-uh-REE-uhn) The THEOREM in GEOMETRY that, in a triangle with one RIGHT ANGLE, usually called a RIGHT TRIANGLE, the SQUARE of the length of the HYPOTENUSE is equal to the sum of the squares of the lengths of the other two sides.

🙚 The theorem is often expressed $a^2 + b^2 = c^2$.
🙚 The simplest mathematical expression of this theorem is called the 3, 4, 5 triangle. In a right triangle, if one side measures three units, and the second side measures four units, the hypotenuse must measure five units because $3^2 + 4^2 = 5^2$; that is, $9 + 16 = 25$. The 3, 4, 5 triangle can be very useful for making sure any corner is exactly square when only a ruler or measuring tape is available.

quanta (KWAHN-tuh) *sing.* QUANTUM In PHYSICS, discrete bundles in which RADIATION and other forms of ENERGY occur. For example, in the BOHR ATOM, LIGHT is sent out in quanta called PHOTONS. (*See* QUANTUM MECHANICS.)

quantum leap In PHYSICS, the movement of an ELECTRON from one ORBIT in an ATOM to another, sending out or taking on a PHOTON in the process. (*See* BOHR ATOM.)

🙚 Informally, a "quantum leap" may be any great, sudden, or discontinuous change.

quantum mechanics The branch of PHYSICS that deals with the behavior of MATTER at the level of the ATOM, the NUCLEUS, and the ELEMENTARY PARTICLE. At this level, ENERGY, MASS, MOMENTUM, and other quantities do not vary continuously, as they do in the large-scale world, but come in discrete units, or QUANTA. (*See* BOHR ATOM *and* PHOTON.)

quarks (KWAHRKS, KWAWRKS) In PHYSICS, the ELEMENTARY PARTICLES that make up the PROTONS and NEUTRONS that in turn make up the atomic NUCLEUS. Quarks are the most basic known constituent of MATTER. (*See* ANTIMATTER.)

🙚 No quarks have been seen in the laboratory because, according to current THEORY, they cannot exist as free particles.

quasars (KWAY-zahrz) The most distant GALAXIES seen from the EARTH, believed to be the first stage in the evolution of galaxies. The name is short for "quasistellar radio source."

rad A unit of ENERGY absorbed from IONIZING RADIATION. *Rad* is an ACRONYM for *r*adiation *a*bsorbed *d*ose.

radiation ENERGY sent out in the form of particles or WAVES. (*See* ALPHA RADIATION, BETA RADIATION, BLACKBODY, COSMIC RAYS, ELECTROMAGNETIC RA-

DIATION, FLUORESCENCE, GAMMA RADIATION, PHOTON, *and* QUANTA.)

radiation damage   The damage caused by the removal of ATOMS from a SOLID material when ELEMENTARY PARTICLES such as those associated with COSMIC RAYS or RADIOACTIVITY collide with it.

🐾 Radiation damage is an important consideration in the design of NUCLEAR REACTORS, where RADIATION levels are high. 🐾 Radiation damage is one of the devastating effects of NUCLEAR WEAPONS.

radical   In CHEMISTRY, an ATOM or group of atoms that has at least one ELECTRON free to participate in forming a CHEMICAL BOND.

🐾 In general, radicals are associated with CHEMICAL REACTIONS that proceed rapidly.

radio frequency   *See* RADIO WAVES.

radio waves   WAVES at the end of the ELECTROMAGNETIC SPECTRUM with the lowest FREQUENCY (less than 300,000,000 HERTZ) and the longest WAVELENGTH (from a few feet to many miles). Because of their low frequency, radio waves carry very little ENERGY compared to other ELECTROMAGNETIC WAVES. (*See* PLANCK'S CONSTANT.)

🐾 Radio waves can pass through the ATMOSPHERE and therefore are very useful for communication. Commercial, short-wave, and citizens' band radio are broadcast with radio waves, as is television.

radioactive   A descriptive term for a material made up of ATOMS in which RADIOACTIVITY occurs.

radioactivity   The emission of ELEMENTARY PARTICLES by some ATOMS when their unstable NUCLEI disintegrate (*see* HALF-LIFE). Materials composed of such atoms are radioactive. (*See* ALPHA RADIATION, BETA RADIATION, *and* GAMMA RADIATION.)

radium   A naturally occurring RADIOACTIVE chemical ELEMENT. Its symbol is Ra.

🐾 Radium was discovered by the chemists Marie and Pierre CURIE.

radon (RAY-don)   A colorless, odorless, RADIOACTIVE GAS that is produced by the decay of RADIUM in the soil.

🐾 Radon seeping through the ground and into buildings is a major source of indoor AIR POLLUTION and may represent a significant risk for lung CANCER.

ratio (RAY-shee-oh, RAY-shoh)   An expression of the relative size of two numbers by showing one divided by the other.

reaction, chemical   *See* CHEMICAL REACTION.

reciprocal   The number by which a given number must be multiplied to get a result of one. The reciprocal of one-half, for example, is two.

red shift   In ASTRONOMY, the reddening of LIGHT sent out by an object that is moving away from an observer. (*See* DOPPLER EFFECT.)

🐾 The red shift that can be observed in light from distant GALAXIES suggests that the universe is expanding, and thus supports the BIG BANG THEORY.

reduction   Any CHEMICAL REACTION in which the ATOMS in a material take on ELECTRONS.

🐾 Reduction is the opposite of OXIDATION.

reflection   A bouncing of LIGHT off a surface. People see themselves in mirrors through reflection. (*Compare* REFRACTION.)

refraction   A change of direction that LIGHT undergoes when it enters a medium with a different DENSITY from the one through which it has been traveling — for example, when, after moving through air, it passes through a PRISM. (*Compare* REFLECTION.)

🐾 LENSES and other optical instruments work through refraction of light.

relativity   A THEORY concerning time, space, and the motion of objects, proposed first in 1905 by Albert EINSTEIN in his special theory of relativity.

The special theory of relativity is based on the principle of special relativity, which states that all observers moving at constant VELOCITIES with respect to each other should find the same laws of nature operating in their frames of reference. It follows from this principle that the SPEED OF LIGHT would have to appear to be the same to every observer. The theory predicts that moving clocks will appear to run slower than stationary ones (*see* TIME DILATION), that moving objects will appear shorter and heavier than stationary ones, and that ENERGY and MASS are equivalent (*see* $E = MC^2$). There is abundant experimental confirmation of these predictions.

The general theory of relativity is the modern theory of GRAVITATION, proposed in 1915, also by Albert Einstein. The central point of the theory is the principle of general relativity, which states that all observers, regardless of their state of motion, will see the same laws of PHYSICS operating in the universe. The most famous prediction of the theory is that LIGHT rays passing near the SUN will be bent — a prediction that is well verified.

🙠 The special and general theories of relativity have had important implications for thought in general. They show that no frame of reference for observation of nature is more correct than any other. 🙠 It is important to distinguish between the theory of relativity, in which the laws of nature are the same for all observers anywhere in the universe, and the philosophical doctrine of RELATIVISM, which holds that there are no absolute truths. The similarity in their names has been a source of confusion.

rem   A unit of absorbed doses of RADIATION. *Rem* is an ACRONYM for *roentgen equivalent man.*

🙠 A normal medical X-RAY delivers about 0.02 rem; a fatal dose of radiation is several thousand rem.

right angle   An angle measuring ninety DEGREES, formed by the intersection of two perpendicular lines. (*Compare* ACUTE ANGLE *and* OBTUSE ANGLE.)

right triangle   A triangle that contains a RIGHT ANGLE.

Rutherford, Ernest   A British physicist of the late nineteenth and early twentieth centuries. Rutherford discovered the existence of atomic NUCLEI. He proposed the current picture of the ATOM, in which most of the MASS of the atom is in the NUCLEUS, with ELECTRONS revolving around the nucleus.

salt   In CHEMISTRY, a COMPOUND resulting from the combination of an ACID and a BASE, which neutralize each other.

🙠 Common table salt is sodium chloride.

sample   In STATISTICS, a group drawn from a larger population and used to estimate the characteristics of the whole population.

🙠 Opinion polls use small groups of people, often selected at random, as a sample of the thoughts and opinions of the general public.

satellite   In ASTRONOMY, an object, whether natural (such as the MOON) or artificial (such as a WEATHER observation satellite), that revolves around a central body. (*See under* "World Politics.")

Saturn   In ASTRONOMY, the second-largest major PLANET, sixth from the sun. Saturn was named for the Roman god of agriculture. Like JUPITER, Saturn is composed largely of GASES and LIQUIDS. Saturn is the most distant planet plainly visible to the naked eye. (*See* SOLAR SYSTEM; *see under* "Mythology and Folklore.")

🙠 Saturn, often called the most beautiful planet, is known for its rings.

scale   A system of marks set at fixed intervals, used as a standard for measurement.

🙠 On a map, plan, or chart, a scale indicates the proportion between the representation and what it represents, such as the legend "One inch equals twenty miles" on a map. 🙠 Temperature scales divide up the range of temperatures into equal DEGREES.

scientific method   An orderly technique of investigation that is supposed to account for scientific progress. The method consists of the following steps: 1. Careful observations of nature. 2. DEDUCTION of NATURAL LAWS. 3. Formation of HYPOTHESES — generalizations of those laws to previously unobserved phenomena. 4. Experimental or observational testing of the validity of the predictions thus made. Actually, scientific discoveries rarely occur in this idealized, wholly rational, and orderly fashion, and scientists often have preconceived THEORIES in mind when they design experiments and collect data.

SETI. *Goldstone radio dish antenna in the Mojave Desert, California.*

SETI (Search for Extraterrestrial Intelligence) [SET-ee]   A program at NASA devoted to the search for

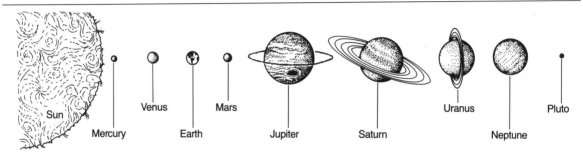

SOLAR SYSTEM. *The nine major planets in the solar system in order of their distance from the sun. The asteroid belt (not illustrated) is between Mars and Jupiter.*

signals from other parts of the GALAXY that would indicate the presence of advanced technological civilizations.

🐚 SETI involves scanning RADIO WAVES for signals, but has found none to date.

solar system   The region of the universe near the SUN that includes the sun, the nine known major PLANETS and their MOONS or SATELLITES, and objects such as ASTEROIDS and COMETS that travel in independent ORBITS. The major planets, in order of their average distance from the sun, are MERCURY, VENUS, the EARTH, MARS, JUPITER, SATURN, URANUS, NEPTUNE, and PLUTO.

solar wind   A stream of particles (mostly PROTONS) emitted by the SUN and permeating the SOLAR SYSTEM.

🐚 Particularly strong bursts of particles can penetrate the upper ATMOSPHERE and disrupt radio communications on EARTH.

solid   A PHASE OF MATTER characterized by the tight locking of ATOMS into rigid structures that resist deforming by outside FORCES.

solstice (SOL-stuhs, SOHL-stuhs)   The two occasions each year when the position of the SUN at a given time of day does not seem to change direction. In the NORTHERN HEMISPHERE, the summer solstice occurs around June 21, and is the longest day of the year. The sun stops getting higher in the sky, and the days begin to grow shorter. The winter solstice, which occurs around December 21, is the shortest day. The sun stops getting lower in the sky, and the days begin to grow longer.

solution   In CHEMISTRY, a uniform mixture of one SOLID, LIQUID, or GAS with another solid, liquid, or gas.

space telescope   *See* HUBBLE SPACE TELESCOPE.

special theory of relativity   *See* RELATIVITY.

specific gravity   The MASS of a substance, given as a multiple of the mass of the same VOLUME of a standard substance (usually water). The specific gravity of aluminum is 2.70; hence, a cubic foot of aluminum weighs 2.70 times as much as a cubic foot of water.

specific heat   The amount of HEAT needed to raise the temperature of one GRAM of a substance by one DEGREE CELSIUS, or to raise the temperature of one pound of a substance by one degree FAHRENHEIT.

spectroscopy (spek-TROS-kuh-pee)   The branch of science devoted to discovering the chemical composition of materials by looking at the LIGHT (and other kinds of ELECTROMAGNETIC RADIATION) they emit. Scientists use spectroscopy to determine the nature of distant STARS and GALAXIES as well as to identify and monitor the production of products in factories.

spectrum   The range of WAVELENGTHS produced when a beam of ENERGY, especially ELECTROMAGNETIC RADIATION, is broken up.

🐚 The spectrum making up visible LIGHT contains light in the colors violet, indigo, blue, green, yellow, orange, and red, with violet having the shortest wavelength and highest FREQUENCY, and red having the longest wavelength and lowest frequency.

speed of light   The distance LIGHT can travel in a unit of time through a given substance. Light travels through a VACUUM at about 186,000 miles, or 300,000 KILOMETERS, per second. (*See* E = MC², ELECTROMAGNETIC WAVES, RELATIVITY, *and* TWIN PARADOX.)

🐚 A LIGHT YEAR, or the distance light can travel

in a year, is over five trillion miles. ❧ Light from the SUN takes about eight minutes to reach the EARTH. ❧ Light from the MOON, and other ELECTROMAGNETIC RADIATION from the moon, takes about a second and a half to reach the earth. In conversations between ASTRONAUTS on the moon and their ground crews, there are lapses of about three seconds between exchanges, because of the time it takes for RADIO WAVES to make a round trip between the earth and the moon. ❧ The special THEORY of RELATIVITY states that the speed of light as measured by all observers is the same.

spontaneous combustion A process by which a collection of materials (such as oily rags) catches fire without the application of HEAT from outside. The OXIDATION of substances in the materials starts the fire.

square (of a number) A number multiplied by itself, or raised to the second POWER. The square of three is nine; the square of nine is eighty-one.

square root A number that, when multiplied by itself, will result in a given number. The square root of four is two; the square root of one hundred is ten.

❧ The square roots of many numbers, such as three, are IRRATIONAL NUMBERS.

standard deviation In STATISTICS, a measure of how much the DATA in a certain collection are scattered around the MEAN. A low standard deviation means that the data are tightly clustered; a high standard deviation means that they are widely scattered.

❧ About 68 percent of the data are within 1 standard deviation of the mean.

standard model The best THEORY of the ultimate nature of MATTER available today. In this theory, all matter is made from QUARKS and LEPTONS. Particles interact with each other through the medium of the STRONG FORCE, the ELECTROMAGNETIC FORCE, the WEAK FORCE, and the GRAVITATIONAL FORCE. At high temperature, the theory sees the first three of these forces as an example of a single unified force. ❧ The standard model is a UNIFIED FIELD THEORY. ❧ The standard model describes the early evolution of the BIG BANG.

star An object in the sky that sends out its own LIGHT, generated by NUCLEAR REACTIONS in its center. There are many billions of stars in our GALAXY, the MILKY WAY.

❧ Our own SUN is a medium-sized star. ❧ Each star has a definite lifetime, and dies when it uses up its supply of fuel. (*See* BLACK HOLE, NEUTRON STAR, SUPERNOVA, *and* WHITE DWARF.) ❧ All chemical ELEMENTS heavier than HELIUM are created in the center of stars, and are returned to space when the star dies. ❧ New stars are being formed constantly.

static electricity An electrical CHARGE that accumulates on an object when it is rubbed against another object — for example, the spark that jumps from someone's hand to a doorknob after the person has walked across a rug.

statistical significance In STATISTICS, a number that expresses the probability that the result of a given experiment or study could have occurred purely by chance. This number can be a margin of error ("The results of this public opinion poll are accurate to 5 PERCENT"), or it can indicate a confidence level ("If this experiment were repeated, there is a probability of 95 percent that our conclusions would be substantiated").

statistics The branch of MATHEMATICS dealing with numerical DATA. (*See* MEAN, MEDIAN, MODE, NORMAL DISTRIBUTION CURVE, SAMPLE, STANDARD DEVIATION, *and* STATISTICAL SIGNIFICANCE.)

❧ A particular problem of statistics is estimating true values of PARAMETERS from a sample of data.

stress In physics, the internal resistance of an object to an external FORCE that tends to deform it.

strong force In PHYSICS, the FORCE that holds particles together in the atomic NUCLEUS and the force that holds QUARKS together in ELEMENTARY PARTICLES. ❧ As the name implies, this is the strongest force known in nature.

subatomic A descriptive term for objects and events within the ATOM.

subatomic particles *See* ELEMENTARY PARTICLES.

sublimation (sub-luh-MAY-shuhn) In CHEMISTRY, the direct conversion of a SOLID into a GAS, without passage through a LIQUID stage. (*See* PHASES OF MATTER.)

sufficient condition In MATHEMATICS, a condition that must be satisfied for a statement to be true and without which the statement cannot be true. For example, while no one can run for president of the

United States unless he or she is thirty-five or older, simply being thirty-five is not a sufficient condition to be president. (*Compare* NECESSARY CONDITION.)

sun   The STAR around which the EARTH revolves.

&. The sun is about 4.5 billion years old, and is expected to remain in its present state for approximately another five billion years; it will eventually evolve into a WHITE DWARF.

sunspots   Dark spots on the surface of the SUN caused by MAGNETIC STORMS.

&. The number of sunspots goes through a maximum and minimum about every eleven years. During periods of maximum sunspots, the ELEMENTARY PARTICLES associated with the spots cause disturbances in the ATMOSPHERE of the EARTH, and interfere with radio and television communication.

superconducting supercollider   (SSC) A PARTICLE ACCELERATOR proposed for construction in TEXAS. If built as planned, its fifty-four-mile circumference will make it the world's largest particle accelerator until well into the twenty-first century.

&. The machine is designed to test the STANDARD MODEL and our ideas about the early evolution of the BIG BANG.

superconductivity   (sooh-puhr-kon-duk-TIV-uh-tee) A property of materials by which their electrical RESISTANCE goes to zero, and they acquire the ability to carry electric CURRENT with no losses whatsoever.

&. Formerly, materials showed superconductivity only near ABSOLUTE ZERO, but new materials have been found that are superconducting at much higher temperatures.

supernova   (sooh-puhr-NOH-vuh)   A large STAR in its death throes that suddenly explodes, increasing many thousands of times in brightness.

&. Most heavy ELEMENTS are created by NUCLEAR REACTIONS in supernovas and then returned to space. &. In 1987, a supernova was sighted near the MILKY WAY GALAXY. This supernova provided astronomers with a unique opportunity to test the THEORIES of the structure of stars.

surface tension   The FORCE exerted along the surface of a FLUID that causes it to "bead up" and form into drops. Water has high surface tension and beads up easily; alcohol has low surface tension and does not often show droplets.

symmetry   In GEOMETRY, the equivalence, POINT for point, of a figure on opposite sides of a point, LINE, or PLANE.

telescope   A device used by astronomers to magnify images or collect more LIGHT from distant objects by gathering and concentrating RADIATION. The most familiar kind of telescope is the optical telescope, which collects radiation in the form of visible light. It may work by REFLECTION, with a bowl-shaped mirror at its base, or by REFRACTION, with a system of LENSES. Other kinds of telescopes collect other kinds of radiation; there are radio telescopes (which collect RADIO WAVES), X-RAY telescopes, and INFRARED telescopes. Radio and optical telescopes may be situated on the EARTH, since the earth's ATMOSPHERE allows light and radio waves through but absorbs radiation from several other regions of the ELECTROMAGNETIC SPECTRUM. X-ray telescopes are placed in space.

Teller, Edward   An American physicist of the twentieth century, born in HUNGARY.

&. Teller is known for his research on nuclear FISSION and FUSION, and for his firm support for development of nuclear weapons in the United States. (*See* EINSTEIN, Albert.) &. Teller is called the father of the H-BOMB.

theorem   (THEE-uh-ruhm, THEER-uhm)   A statement in MATHEMATICS that is not a basic assumption, such as an AXIOM, but is deduced (*see* DEDUCTION) from basic assumptions.

theory   In science, an explanation or model that covers a substantial group of occurrences in nature, and has been confirmed by a substantial number of experiments and observations. A theory is more general and better verified than a HYPOTHESIS. (*See* BIG BANG THEORY, EVOLUTION, *and* RELATIVITY.)

thermal equilibrium   In PHYSICS and CHEMISTRY, a condition in which all parts of a system are at the same temperature.

thermodynamics   The branch of PHYSICS devoted to the study of HEAT and related phenomena. The behavior of heat is governed by the three laws of thermodynamics: 1. The total ENERGY of an isolated system cannot change; this is the law of CONSERVATION OF ENERGY. 2. Heat will not flow from a cold to a hot object spontaneously (*see* ENTROPY). 3. It is impossible, in a finite number of operations, to produce a temperature of ABSOLUTE ZERO.

🖎 All thermodynamic properties of MATTER can be understood in terms of the motion of ATOMS and MOLECULES.

thermonuclear reaction A reaction between NUCLEI, usually FUSION, which releases very large amounts of ENERGY.

time dilation In PHYSICS, the apparent slowing down of moving clocks that is predicted by the special THEORY of RELATIVITY. Time dilation is well verified experimentally.

titration (teye-TRAY-shuhn) In CHEMISTRY, the determination of what materials are present in a sample by adding precise amounts of known chemicals and observing the CHEMICAL REACTION.

🖎 The term *titration* is occasionally used informally to suggest extreme precision in some sort of measurement or determination.

tomography (tuh-MOG-ruh-fee) A procedure by which WAVES are sent through an object and computers produce images of cross sections of the object by using information on how the waves are changed. Both ULTRASOUND and CAT scans are medical uses of this technique, but it is also widely used in science and industry.

trapezoid (TRAP-uh-zoyd) A four-sided POLYGON in which two sides are parallel and two are not.

triple point In PHYSICS, the temperature at which all three PHASES OF MATTER (SOLID, LIQUID, and GAS) for a given substance can coexist.

🖎 The triple point for water is a little above the FREEZING POINT, and is used to define temperature SCALES.

twin paradox An effect predicted by the general THEORY of RELATIVITY: if one of a pair of twins remains on EARTH, and the other travels in a rocket at a speed near the SPEED OF LIGHT, the traveling twin will be younger than the earthbound twin upon returning to earth. This effect has been verified experimentally by measurements with ATOMIC CLOCKS.

UFO (yooh-ef-OH) Acronym for "unidentified flying object." Sometimes referred to colloquially as "flying saucers." Most UFO sightings have prosaic explanations; there is no hard evidence that EXTRATERRESTRIAL beings are visiting EARTH.

ultraviolet radiation RADIATION in the part of the ELECTROMAGNETIC SPECTRUM where WAVELENGTHS are just shorter than those of ordinary, visible violet LIGHT, but longer than those of X-RAYS.

🖎 Like INFRARED RADIATION, ultraviolet radiation can be detected with special instruments or films.
🖎 Sunburn is caused by ultraviolet radiation.
🖎 The OZONE LAYER of the ATMOSPHERE of the EARTH blocks most of the potentially harmful ultraviolet radiation.

uncertainty principle The statement in QUANTUM MECHANICS, formulated by Werner HEISENBERG, that it is impossible to measure two properties of a QUANTUM object, such as its position and MOMENTUM (or ENERGY and time), simultaneously with infinite precision.

unified field theory Any THEORY in which two seemingly different FORCES are seen to be fundamentally identical. MAXWELL'S EQUATIONS express a unified field theory that demonstrates the basic identity of ELECTRICITY and MAGNETISM, and the STANDARD MODEL postulates a basic identity for the STRONG FORCE, the WEAK FORCE, and ELECTROMAGNETISM.

universal gravitation *See* GRAVITATION.

uranium A chemical ELEMENT that is naturally RADIOACTIVE. An ISOTOPE of uranium, uranium 235, is the main fuel for NUCLEAR REACTORS and ATOMIC BOMBS. Its symbol is U. (*See* FISSION *and* CHAIN REACTION.)

Uranus (YOOR-uh-nuhs, yoo-RAY-nuhs) In ASTRONOMY, the seventh major PLANET from the SUN, named for the Greek god of the sky. Uranus is barely visible to the naked eye; it was the first planet discovered in modern times (1781). (*See* SOLAR SYSTEM.)

Ursa Major (UR-suh) A CONSTELLATION; the Great Bear. (*See* BIG DIPPER.)

Ursa Minor The Little Bear or Little Dipper; the CONSTELLATION that contains the NORTH STAR (POLARIS).

vacuum The absence of MATTER.

🖎 In the natural world, air will flow into regions of vacuum, giving rise to the saying "Nature abhors a vacuum." ₰ The saying is extended informally: in politics, a lack of leadership may be referred to as a vacuum, which will presumably be filled by others rushing in.

valence (VAY-luhns) A number characterizing an ATOM, equal to the number of VALENCE ELECTRONS.

valence electrons In CHEMISTRY, those ELECTRONS found in ORBITS farthest from the NUCLEUS of the ATOM. These electrons determine the way in which the atom will combine with other atoms, and thus determine its chemical properties.

vapor pressure In PHYSICS and CHEMISTRY, the AT-MOSPHERIC PRESSURE that would be exerted by any single component of a GAS if that component were the only one present. For example, the vapor pressure of OXYGEN in the ATMOSPHERE of the EARTH is the pressure that would exist if everything but oxygen were removed. The total atmospheric pressure is the sum of the vapor pressures of all the materials in the atmosphere.

vaporization In PHYSICS and CHEMISTRY, the con-version of a SOLID or a LIQUID into a GAS. (See BOIL-ING POINT, PHASES OF MATTER, and SUBLIMATION.)

vector In PHYSICS and MATHEMATICS, any quantity with both a magnitude and a direction. For example, VELOCITY is a vector because it describes both how fast something is moving and in what direction it is moving. Because velocity is a vector, other quantities in which velocity is a factor, such as ACCELERATION and MOMENTUM, are vectors also.

velocity The VECTOR giving the speed and direction of motion of any object.

Venus In ASTRONOMY, the second major PLANET from the SUN, named for the Roman goddess of love. The surface of Venus is very hot and covered with CLOUDS. Spacecraft from the former SOVIET UNION landed on Venus and survived long enough to send back photographs and measurements. (See SOLAR SYSTEM; see under "Mythology and Folk-lore.")
₰ Venus is seen from the EARTH as a bright morn-ing or evening star — occasionally bright enough to cast a shadow.

viscosity (vis-KOS-uh-tee) The internal FRICTION of a FLUID, produced by the movement of its MOLE-CULES against each other. Viscosity causes the fluid to resist flowing.

volume In MATHEMATICS, the amount of space oc-cupied by an object measured in three dimensions, expressed in cubic units. In PHYSICS, the loudness of a sound.

watt The basic unit of POWER, named after the eighteenth-century Scottish inventor James WATT.

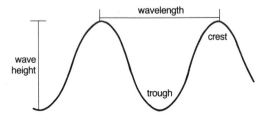

WAVE. A diagram of a sound wave.

wave In PHYSICS, any regularly recurring event, like surf coming in toward a beach, that can be thought of as a disturbance moving through a medium. Waves are characterized by WAVELENGTH, FREQUENCY, and the speed at which they move. Waves are found in many forms.
₰ The motion of a wave and the motion of the medium on which the wave moves are not the same: ocean waves, for example, move toward the beach, but the water itself merely moves up and down.
₰ Sound waves are spread by alternating compres-sion and expansion of air.

wavelength The distance between crests (or troughs) of a WAVE.

wave-particle duality In QUANTUM MECHANICS, the condition that allows every QUANTUM to appear like a WAVE in some experiments and like an ELEMEN-TARY PARTICLE in others.

weak force One of the four fundamental FORCES of nature. It is involved primarily in the phenomenon of RADIOACTIVITY. (See STANDARD MODEL and STRONG FORCE.)

weight The FORCE exerted on any object by GRAVITY.

white dwarf A kind of STAR about the size of the EARTH. White dwarfs represent a final stage of the life cycle of stars similar to the SUN; they are formed when the stars use up their fuel and can no longer support NUCLEAR REACTIONS.

whole numbers The set of familiar numbers (0, 1, 2, 3, 4, and so on) sometimes called natural numbers or counting numbers. When they are called counting numbers, zero is not included.

≈ The whole numbers are also called the positive INTEGERS (or the nonnegative integers, if zero is included).

work In PHYSICS, the product of a FORCE applied, and the distance through which that force acts.

x-ray A form of ELECTROMAGNETIC RADIATION with very high FREQUENCY and ENERGY. X-rays lie between ULTRAVIOLET RADIATION and GAMMA RADIATION on the ELECTROMAGNETIC SPECTRUM.

≈ Because x-rays can travel through SOLID material and affect photographic plates, they are widely used in diagnosing medical problems. ≈ Objects in the sky also send out x-rays in processes that use very high energy.

zodiac The imaginary band in the sky through which the SUN, the MOON, and the PLANETS appear to move. The twelve CONSTELLATIONS in the band (Aquarius, Pisces, and so on) are the familiar signs of the zodiac used in ASTROLOGY.

Earth Sciences

The central problem of the earth sciences is to understand how our PLANET works and how it came to be the way it is. The essential fact emerging from these sciences is that the EARTH can be pictured as a set of three separate but interconnected cycles.

The GEOLOGICAL CYCLE governs the formation and disappearance of solid land. The science of GEOLOGY contains two central insights. The first of these, arrived at in the eighteenth century, is that the earth is very old, and that its history can be read in the rocks on its surface. The second insight, gained in the late 1960s, is that the earth has evolved and continues to do so. The CONTINENTS have not always been where they are now, nor have they always had their present shape. Instead, the surface of the earth has changed constantly, and the continents have moved about, sometimes breaking up into pieces, sometimes coming together again. This picture of the earth, called PLATE TECTONICS, replaced the old idea of a static and unchanging planet. The study of the rocks and their history is the subject of geology, while the study of the forces that drive the activity on the surface is part of the newer field of GEOPHYSICS.

At the same time that the continents are moving, a smaller-scale geological cycle, involving the formation of rocks and their EROSION into SOIL and sand, goes on. In river deltas and the eruption of VOLCANOES, new land surface is added to the earth. At the same time, the inexorable forces of WEATHER and time break down the mountains.

On the stage set by motion of the continents, the *atmospheric cycle* operates. Powered by heat from the SUN and the earth's rotation, winds move across the surface, carrying WEATHER systems. Rainfall, temperatures, and other day-to-day aspects of our environment change in response to the prevailing winds and the JET STREAMS. These weather patterns and their causes are the subject of the science of METEOROLOGY.

Over longer time periods, changes in the earth's orbit or movement of the continents alter the patterns followed by the winds and the temperatures on the earth. Such changes in CLIMATE, of which the recurring ICE AGES are a good example, have had a profound effect on the development of the human race. Understanding long-term climate development is one of the major research fields in the earth sciences.

Intermediate between the slow, majestic changes in the continents and the daily changes in the weather is the third great cycle — the HYDROLOGIC CYCLE, the cycle of the earth's water, or hydrosphere. Water evaporates from the surface and returns as rain or snow. Some water is locked up in the polar ice caps, but most resides in the oceans. Perhaps the most poorly understood part of our planet, the oceans act as a great reservoir for many natural and artificial substances. Their currents help equalize temperatures on the globe, while at the same time they spawn the major storm systems that have such an important effect on human activities.

494

The earth sciences have traditionally divided their attention between detailed studies of each of the cycles and attempts to understand their interconnection. Today, we understand at least the broad outlines of each of them, but we understand less about how they are connected. The following list presents the important facts that have been learned about our planet thus far.

The entries in this section were chosen according to slightly different criteria from those used in the HUMANITIES and SOCIAL SCIENCES sections. They were chosen not because the majority of educated readers are expected to be familiar with them, but because most scientists would agree that they are essential to a knowledge of the earth sciences. Some of these words might be used without explanation in the *New York Times*, but many would not. Nevertheless, if you are familiar with these terms and the concepts they represent, you should know enough about the study of the earth, the oceans, and the weather to follow their progress as it is presented in the popular press.

— J. T.

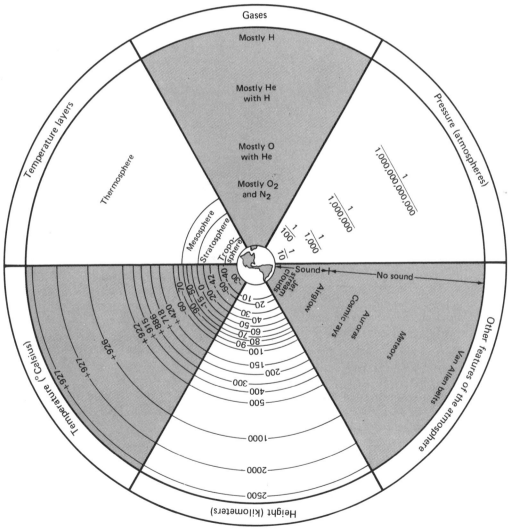

A CHART OF THE ATMOSPHERE

acid rain A type of precipitation made up of dilute ACIDS, primarily a by-product of heavy industry.

🐚 Acid rain is a result of the combination of water with chemicals released into the atmosphere by the burning of FOSSIL FUELS. 🐚 This type of pollution is a major threat to the forests and wildlife of the northeastern United States and the adjoining areas of CANADA. 🐚 Acid rain has been the focus of conflict between Canada and the United States over environmental regulation.

Air Quality Index A measure of the quantity of harmful particles and chemicals in the air.

🐚 The index is used by WEATHER forecasters to indicate the purity of the air on a given day. The higher the index, the smoggier (*see* SMOG) and more polluted the air.

Alvarez hypothesis (AL-vuh-rez) The THEORY that the MASS EXTINCTION that involved the DINOSAURS and many other living things was caused by the impact of a large ASTEROID on the EARTH 65 million years ago. 🐚 The hypothesis is named after the father and son team of scientists, Luis and Walter Alvarez, who first suggested it. 🐚 Evidence indicates that the asteroid fell in the YUCATÁN PENINSULA.

atmosphere The blanket of GAS on the surface of a PLANET or SATELLITE.

🐚 The atmosphere of the EARTH is roughly 80 percent NITROGEN and 20 percent OXYGEN, with traces of other gases. (*See* IONOSPHERE, STRATOSPHERE, *and* TROPOSPHERE.)

atmospheric pressure The PRESSURE caused by the weight of the air above a given point.

🐚 Normal atmospheric pressure at sea level is about fifteen pounds per square inch. (*See* BAROMETER.)

aurora borealis (uh-RAWR-uh bawr-ee-AL-is) A display of colored lights in the sky, also called northern lights, caused by the interaction of particles from the SUN with the upper ATMOSPHERE near the NORTH POLE. A similar display, called the aurora australis, occurs in the atmosphere above the South Pole.

barometer An instrument that measures ATMOSPHERIC PRESSURE.

🐚 In general, when the barometer falls in response to a drop in pressure, bad WEATHER is approaching; when the barometer rises because of an increase in pressure, good weather will follow.

barrier island Any low sandy island that forms offshore and protects the mainland from storms. (*See* CAPE HATTERAS.)

🐚 Barrier islands normally change location every ten to thirty years, a fact that makes coastline management a major problem in environmental policy.

basalt (buh-SAWLT, BAY-sawlt) A heavy IGNEOUS ROCK that makes up most of the material in TECTONIC PLATES. The heavier basaltic part of the plates lies under the CONTINENTS, which are made of lighter materials, such as GRANITE. (*See* PLATE TECTONICS.)

🐚 Basalt is generally the rock in ocean floors.

carbon 14 dating *See* RADIOACTIVE DATING.

catastrophism (kuh-TAS-truh-fiz-uhm) A theory that holds that changes in the EARTH take place swiftly and irreversibly. (*Contrast* GRADUALISM.) 🐚 A belief in NOAH'S FLOOD was one version of catastrophism.

cell A region of the ATMOSPHERE in which air tends to circulate without flowing outward.

CIRRUS CLOUDS

cirrus clouds (SIR-uhs) Lacy or wispy CLOUDS that form at high altitudes, generally before a change in the WEATHER.

climate A region's usual WEATHER patterns. The climate at any point on EARTH is determined by such things as the general movement of the ATMOSPHERE, the proximity of the oceans, and the altitude of the location.

🐚 The climate also is affected by the SUN, by changes in the ORBIT of the earth, by PLATE TECTON-

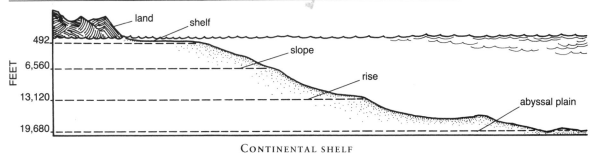

CONTINENTAL SHELF

ICS, and by human activities, particularly the burning of FOSSIL FUELS, which may lead to a GREENHOUSE EFFECT.

cloud seeding   A technique for producing rain by dropping chemicals or small objects into clouds.

clouds   Particles of water or ice suspended in the air. (*See* CIRRUS CLOUDS, CUMULUS CLOUDS, NIMBUS CLOUDS, *and* STRATUS CLOUDS.)

continental divide   An imaginary geographic line defined by the fact that water poured on one side of it would ultimately flow into the ocean on one side of a CONTINENT, while water poured on the other side of the line would flow into the ocean on the other side of the continent.

🐾 In NORTH AMERICA, the continental divide is located in the ROCKY MOUNTAINS.

continental drift   A term, no longer used by geologists, that refers to the fact that CONTINENTS are not stationary, but move across the EARTH'S surface. Continental drift is one feature of the modern theory of PLATE TECTONICS. (*See* PANGAEA.)

continental shelf   The region adjoining the coastline of a CONTINENT, where the ocean is no more than a few hundred feet deep. The shelf is built up from sediments washed down to the sea by rivers.

🐾 The continental shelves are often valuable because of the MINERAL resources and abundant marine life found there. (*See* OFFSHORE DRILLING.)

continents   The large parts of the surface of the EARTH that rise above sea level. The seven major continents are AFRICA, ANTARCTICA, ASIA, AUSTRALIA, EUROPE, NORTH AMERICA, and SOUTH AMERICA.

🐾 Continents are made from the lightest rocks in the earth. Some of these are also the oldest known rocks on earth, with an age of 3.5 billion years, measured by RADIOACTIVE DATING. 🐾 According to the theory of PLATE TECTONICS, continents move along on top of the TECTONIC PLATES like rafts floating on water.

coral reef   A formation, at or near the surface of tropical waters, formed by skeletal deposits of corals, a form of sea life.

🐾 Coral reefs form a protective environment for a wide variety of marine animals. 🐾 Atolls — ring-shaped islands that nearly or entirely enclose a lagoon — are coral reefs. 🐾 The largest coral reef is the Great Barrier Reef of AUSTRALIA.

core   In GEOLOGY, the central region of the EARTH; it extends 1400 to 1800 miles from the earth's center.

🐾 Scientists believe that the core is made primarily of iron and nickel, and has two parts — an inner solid core and an outer liquid core. 🐾 The MANTLE is the layer of the earth that overlies the core.

cosmic rays   ELEMENTARY PARTICLES, mainly PROTONS, that are produced by the SUN and other STARS and then strike the upper ATMOSPHERE of the EARTH. Some of these particles are absorbed, some help form the VAN ALLEN BELT, and some reach the earth's surface, where they form a part of the BACKGROUND RADIATION that constantly surrounds us.

crust   In GEOLOGY, the outermost layer of the EARTH. It overlies the MANTLE.

🐾 The crust includes the CONTINENTS and the ocean bottom, and is generally estimated to be about five to twenty five miles thick. 🐾 The crust is made from relatively lightweight rocks that floated to the surface when the earth was molten early in its history.

cumulus clouds (KYOOH-myuh-luhs)   Large, white, puffy CLOUDS that generally appear during fair

CUMULUS CLOUDS

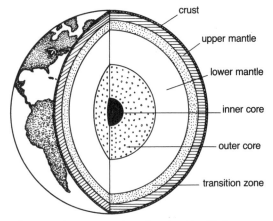

EARTH. *A cutaway view showing Earth's layers.*

WEATHER, although they also form thunderheads on hot days. Some carry rain.

cyclone   Any circular wind motion. A region of low ATMOSPHERIC PRESSURE. Also, a tropical storm.

   ❧ Cyclones can be a few feet across ("dust devils") or can be major storm systems such as HURRICANES, TORNADOES, and TYPHOONS. ❧ These winds move counterclockwise in the NORTHERN HEMISPHERE and clockwise in the SOUTHERN HEMISPHERE. (*See* CORIOLIS EFFECT.)

desalinization   (dee-sal-uh-nuh-ZAY-shuhn)   Any process that removes salt from water.

   ❧ The term is usually applied to processes that remove salt from seawater to make it available for human consumption and agriculture. Such processes tend to be very expensive.

earth   The PLANET on which we live — the third planet from the SUN.

   ❧ The earth was formed at the same time as the sun, about 4.6 billion years ago. ❧ It consists of an inner CORE made of iron and nickel, an outer core of liquid metal, a MANTLE, and, on the outside, a CRUST. ❧ The surface of the solid earth is in a state of constant change as the rock is moved around by the processes of PLATE TECTONICS. ❧ On the earth's surface, the oceans and the CONTINENTS form the stage on which the EVOLUTION of life took place. ❧ The ATMOSPHERE above the surface circulates, producing the daily WEATHER.

earth, evolution of   The EARTH was formed at the same time as the rest of the SOLAR SYSTEM by the coming together of materials that were not incorpo-

rated into the SUN. The earth was very hot (perhaps molten) at first, but quickly cooled off. Oceans appeared very early and have been on the surface continuously ever since. Life in the form of SINGLE-CELLED ALGAE was present when the earth was 3.5 billion years old. Animals with hard skeletons and shells appeared and formed FOSSILS 570 million years ago. The period since then is usually broken up into the Paleozoic Era ("old life") from 570 to 225 million years ago, the Mesozoic Era ("middle life") from 225 million to 65 million years ago, and the Cenozoic Era ("modern life") from 65 million years ago to the present. DINOSAURS flourished in the Mesozoic, while human beings have been present for only a few million years.

earthquake   A tremor of the surface of the EARTH, sometimes severe and devastating, which results from shock WAVES generated by the movement of rock masses deep within the earth, particularly near boundaries of TECTONIC PLATES. (*See* FAULT, RICHTER SCALE, *and* SEISMOLOGY.)

   ❧ Earthquakes are particularly likely where such plates are sliding past each other, as in the SAN ANDREAS FAULT. ❧ Earthquakes cannot be accurately predicted, although the likelihood of a region's suffering an earthquake can be estimated.

erosion   A type of WEATHERING in which surface SOIL and rock are worn away through the action of GLACIERS, water, and wind.

estuary   (ES-chooh-er-ee)   A wide body of water formed where a large river meets the sea. It contains both fresh and salt water.

extinction The disappearance of a SPECIES from the EARTH. ❧ The FOSSIL RECORD tells us that 99.9 percent of all species that ever lived are now extinct.

eye of a hurricane The region at the center of a HURRICANE about which the winds rotate, but which itself is relatively calm.

❧ Figuratively, the "eye of a hurricane" is the quiet center of a dispute or controversy.

fault In GEOLOGY, a place where sections of the CRUST of the EARTH move relative to each other. In the study of MINERALS, the weak spot where one part of a SOLID has moved relative to another. (*See* EARTHQUAKE.)

❧ Faults tend to occur near the edges of TECTONIC PLATES.

fossil The evidence in rock of the presence of a plant or an animal from an earlier geological period. Fossils are formed when MINERALS in groundwater replace materials in bones and tissue, creating a replica in stone of the original organism. The study of fossils is the domain of PALEONTOLOGY. The oldest fossils (of mats of ALGAE) are 3.5 billion years old.

❧ The term is used figuratively to refer to a person with very old-fashioned or outmoded viewpoints: "That old fossil of a disc jockey still thinks that the Beatles are a new group!"

fossil fuels Coal, petroleum, and natural gas.

❧ All of these fuels were formed from the remains of plants and animals that lived millions of years ago. ❧ All fossil fuels produce CARBON DIOXIDE when burned. (*See* GREENHOUSE EFFECT.) ❧ Burning fossil fuels is a main cause of AIR POLLUTION.

fossil record A term used by paleontologists (*see* PALEONTOLOGY) to refer to the total number of FOSSILS that have been discovered, as well as to the information derived from them. (*See* EARTH, EVOLUTION OF.)

front (frontal zone) In METEOROLOGY, the line that forms the boundary between two air masses. Unless they are very similar in temperature and HUMIDITY, they will not mix.

❧ Fronts usually produce unstable WEATHER.

geological cycle The continuous process in which hot, molten material coming to the surface of the EARTH from the interior forms IGNEOUS ROCKS, which are then broken down by WEATHERING to create SOIL and SEDIMENTARY ROCKS. These sedimentary rocks can be lifted up by the motion associated with PLATE TECTONICS, in which case they are again weathered and washed down to the sea. Alternatively, they can be buried deep within the earth, changed into METAMORPHIC ROCKS, and brought to the surface of the earth, or buried so deeply that they are melted and become part of the MAGMA from which igneous rocks are formed.

geology The science devoted to the study of the EARTH, particularly the solid earth and the rocks that compose it.

geophysics The science devoted to the study of the physical properties and processes of geological phenomena, including fields such as METEOROLOGY, oceanography, and SEISMOLOGY.

geothermal energy ENERGY obtained by tapping underground reservoirs of heat, usually near VOLCANOES or other HOT SPOTS on the surface of the EARTH.

❧ At present, little of the world's energy supply is obtained from these sources.

glacial cycle *See* ICE AGES.

glacier A large mass of ice formed over many years that does not melt during the summer. Glaciers move slowly over an area of land such as a mountain valley.

❧ Glaciers exist in high mountains throughout the temperate zones and cover most of ANTARCTICA. ❧ Glaciers recede during warm periods and can expand during cold periods, creating ICE AGES. ❧ A significant percentage of the water of the EARTH is locked up in glaciers.

global warming The term attached to the notion that the EARTH's temperature is increasing due to the GREENHOUSE EFFECT. ❧ Whether global warming is actually happening is a subject of scientific debate.

gradualism The belief that changes in the EARTH have taken place slowly, without sudden and violent transitions. (*Compare* CATASTROPHISM.)

granite A relatively lightweight IGNEOUS ROCK that makes up most of the CONTINENTS. (*See* BASALT, PLATE TECTONICS, *and* TECTONIC PLATES.)

greenhouse effect A term used to describe the heating of the ATMOSPHERE owing to the presence of CARBON DIOXIDE and other GASES. Normally, heat from the SUN returns to space in the form of INFRARED RA-DIATION. Carbon dioxide and other gases absorb this radiation and prevent its release, thereby warming the EARTH. This is an effect analogous to what happens in a greenhouse, where glass traps the infrared radiation and warms the air.

🙠 The burning of FOSSIL FUELS adds carbon dioxide to the atmosphere, and therefore places the earth at risk from this effect.

groundwater   Water that seeps through the SOIL or rocks underground.

🙠 Groundwater is a source of water for many communities through springs and wells. 🙠 Groundwater can be contaminated by chemical pollutants. (*See* WATER POLLUTION.)

hail   Pellets of ice that form when updrafts in thunderstorms carry raindrops to high altitudes, where the water freezes, and then falls back to EARTH. Hailstones as large as baseballs have been recorded. Hail can damage crops and property.

hard water   Water in which dissolved MINERALS make it difficult to produce a lather with soap.

🙠 Hard water is usually associated with well water in regions where the rocks contain a large proportion of iron-bearing MINERALS.

hot spot   A place on the surface of the EARTH where hot MAGMA rises to just underneath the surface, creating a bulge and volcanic activity (*see* VOLCANO). The Hawaiian Islands (*see* HAWAII) are thought to have been created by a hot spot.

humidity (absolute and relative)   The amount of water vapor in the air. Humidity is measured in two ways: 1. *Absolute humidity* is the percentage of water vapor actually present in the air. 2. *Relative humidity* is the absolute humidity divided by the amount of water that *could* be present in the air. Relative humidity indicates the degree of comfort or discomfort one feels from the humidity, because it indicates the amount of perspiration that can evaporate from the skin.

hurricane   A large tropical storm system with high-powered circular winds. (*See* CYCLONE *and* EYE OF A HURRICANE.)

🙠 Between July and October, hurricanes cause extensive damage along the Atlantic and Gulf coasts of the United States. (*See* ATLANTIC OCEAN *and* GULF OF MEXICO.)

Hutton, James   Scottish natural PHILOSOPHER of the eighteenth century; generally regarded as the founder of modern GEOLOGY. He argued that the EARTH is very old, and that its history can be read in the rocks. He also argued that the physical processes that shape the earth today are the same as those that operated in the past.

hydrologic cycle (heye-druh-LOJ-ik)   The continuous circular process in which the water of the EARTH evaporates from the oceans, condenses, falls to the earth as rain or snow, and eventually returns to the oceans through run-off in rivers or streams. Some water is absorbed by plants and returned to the ATMOSPHERE as vapor.

ice ages   Periods in the history of the EARTH when large GLACIERS covered much of the surface of the CONTINENTS.

🙠 The last ice age ended less than 20,000 years ago. 🙠 Scientists believe that there will be more ice ages in the future, caused by tiny changes in the earth's ORBIT and rotation.

iceberg   A large piece of ice that has broken away from a GLACIER at the shore and floated out to sea.

🙠 Most of the ice in an iceberg is underwater, leaving only the "tip of the iceberg" visible — a fact that is often alluded to in discussions of subjects in which the most important aspects are hidden from view.

igneous rock (IG-nee-uhs)   Rocks formed by the cooling and solidifying of molten materials brought from the interior of the EARTH to its surface.

🙠 GRANITE and solid volcanic LAVA are examples of igneous rock.

inversion, thermal   In METEOROLOGY, a situation in which a layer of warm air (an inversion layer) lies over a layer of cool air.

🙠 If an inversion occurs over a city, it results in AIR POLLUTION (*see under* "*Technology*"), because some pollutants, such as smoke or soot, which are usually removed by normal WEATHER processes, are held at the surface by the cool layer. (*See* SMOG.)

inversion layer   *See* INVERSION, THERMAL.

ionosphere (eye-ON-uh-sfeer)   A region of the ATMOSPHERE that begins at an altitude of about thirty miles.

🙠 In this region, free particles carrying an ELECTRICAL CHARGE, ATOMS ionized (*see* IONIZATION) by

RADIATION from the SUN, reflect RADIO WAVES. "Bouncing" radio waves off the ionosphere makes communication possible over long distances of the surface of the EARTH.

jet stream   A narrow band of swiftly moving air found at very high altitudes.

ᕈ Movements of the jet stream have important (but generally short-lived) effects on WEATHER patterns. ᕈ Travel time in a jet can be lengthened or shortened by the jet stream, depending on the direction of flight and the strength of the stream.

land breeze   The breeze that blows from the land toward the sea after sunset. The land cools more quickly than the ocean, cooling the air above it. The warmer air above the water continues to rise, and cooler air from over the land replaces it, creating a breeze. (*Compare* SEA BREEZE.)

lava   A type of IGNEOUS ROCK that is formed when molten MAGMA from a VOLCANO hardens.

lightning   An electrical discharge from CLOUDS that have acquired an ELECTRICAL CHARGE, usually occurring during storms. (*See* THUNDER.)

limestone   SEDIMENTARY ROCK formed from the skeletons of small marine animals.

lithosphere (LITH-uh-sfeer)   The outer layer of the EARTH, comprising the CRUST and the upper part of the MANTLE. The lithosphere is about sixty miles thick.

Lyell, Charles (LEYE-uhl)   Nineteenth-century Scottish natural PHILOSOPHER who laid the foundations for the modern sciences of GEOLOGY and evolutionary BIOLOGY. His book *Principles of Geology* had an enormous influence on other scientists in the nineteenth century, especially Charles DARWIN. He was the founder of the doctrine of uniformitarianism, which holds that all processes on the EARTH are the same today as they have been in the past. Geologists often use the slogan "the present is the key to the past" to summarize Lyell's ideas.

magma   Molten rock usually located deep within the MANTLE of the EARTH that occasionally comes to the surface through cracks in the mantle or through the eruption of VOLCANOES.

ᕈ When magma cools and solidifies, it forms IGNEOUS ROCK, of which LAVA is one type.

magnetic field of the earth   The magnetic field (*see* MAGNETISM) that surrounds and permeates the EARTH. It is the presence of this field that causes compass needles to line up in a north-south direction. The origin of the earth's magnetic field is poorly understood at the present time.

magnetic field reversals   Changes in direction or orientation of the MAGNETIC FIELD OF THE EARTH that have occurred from time to time. Sometimes the north magnetic pole is near the geographic NORTH POLE and sometimes near the SOUTH POLE in ANTARCTICA.

ᕈ The causes of these reversals are not known, but at least several hundred of them have happened.

magnetic north   The direction of the north MAGNETIC POLE.

magnetic pole   The spot on the EARTH toward which a compass needle will point.

ᕈ The north magnetic pole is not located exactly at the geographic NORTH POLE. Therefore, depending on where a compass is, its needle may not point exactly north. ᕈ The variation between magnetic north and "true" north is usually shown on navigation maps as the "angle of declination."

magnetic storm   The effect on the IONOSPHERE of large bursts of charged particles (*see* CHARGE, ELECTRICAL) from the SUN.

ᕈ During a magnetic storm, radio reception can become very difficult.

mantle   The region of the interior of the EARTH between the CORE (on its inner surface) and the CRUST (on its outer).

ᕈ The mantle is over 2000 miles thick, and accounts for more than three-quarters of the volume of the earth.

Marianas Trench (mar-ee-AN-uhz)   The deepest spot in the oceans, over 35,000 feet deep, near the PHILIPPINES.

mass extinction   Any of several events in the EARTH's past in which large numbers of SPECIES (in some cases, up to 80 percent) became extinct. ᕈ The most famous mass extinction included the destruction of the DINOSAURS 65 million years ago. (*See* ALVAREZ HYPOTHESIS.)

metamorphic rock   Rock that was once one form of rock but has changed to another under the influ-

ence of heat, PRESSURE, or some other agent without passing through a LIQUID phase.
🐦 Examples are marble, which can be formed from LIMESTONE, and slate, which is formed from SHALE.

meteor   A streak of LIGHT in the sky, often called a "shooting star," that occurs when a bit of EXTRATERRESTRIAL MATTER falls into the ATMOSPHERE of the EARTH and burns up. 🐦 Meteor showers occur at regular times during the year.

meteorites   Objects from outside the EARTH that enter the earth's field of GRAVITATION and fall to the earth's surface. METEORS, on the other hand, are objects from space that burn up in the earth's ATMOSPHERE.
🐦 Meteorites are bodies that are left over from the time when the PLANETS were created, and therefore give us clues about the formation of the SOLAR SYSTEM.

meteorology   The study of the WEATHER and CLIMATE.

microclimate   The long-term WEATHER conditions in a small area on the EARTH. Usually, this term refers to such things as the differences in weather between the tops of hills and neighboring valleys, or between different parts of the same piece of land.

mineral   In GEOLOGY, a naturally occurring inorganic substance (*see* INORGANIC MOLECULES) with a definite chemical composition and a regular internal structure.
🐦 Most minerals are CRYSTALS, like salt and diamonds. 🐦 Rocks are aggregates of minerals.

monsoon   A wind system that affects large climatic regions and reverses direction seasonally.
🐦 The Asiatic monsoon brings heavy rains to SOUTHEAST ASIA in spring and summer.

moraine (muh-RAYN)   A pile of debris, often extending for miles, deposited by a GLACIER. It is composed of rock fragments transported by the ice, which are left behind when the ice melts.

nimbus clouds   The dark CLOUDS characteristic of storms.

northern lights   *See* AURORA BOREALIS.

oil sands   Surface DEPOSITS of tarry sand that contain large quantities of petroleum.

NIMBUS CLOUDS

🐦 The major deposits of oil sands in NORTH AMERICA are in the western United States and northern CANADA. 🐦 Extracting the oil from these sands is difficult and expensive.

ore   In GEOLOGY, a MINERAL that contains a commercially useful material, such as gold or URANIUM.
🐦 Ore DEPOSITS are generally mined, and the ore is processed to recover the material.

ozone hole   A depletion of OZONE that occurs over ANTARCTICA in the winter. The ozone returns to normal levels in the summer, and the amount of depletion varies from year to year. The hole is thought to be caused by a combination of the peculiarities of atmospheric circulation (*see* ATMOSPHERE) near the SOUTH POLE and CHEMICAL REACTIONS involving CHLOROFLUOROCARBONS in the atmosphere and ice CRYSTALS in CLOUDS.

ozone layer   A band of ozone in the upper ATMOSPHERE. Ozone is a MOLECULE made of three ATOMS of OXYGEN instead of the usual two.
🐦 The ozone layer absorbs harmful ULTRAVIOLET RADIATION from the SUN, and is thus very important to the health of human beings and other life forms on EARTH. 🐦 The EARTH's ozone layer is at risk because of the action of CHLOROFLUOROCARBONS. (*See* OZONE HOLE.)

paleontology (pay-lee-uhn-TOL-uh-jee)   The study of ancient life forms, particularly as they are seen in FOSSILS.

Pangaea (pan-JEE-uh)   A possible former "supercontinent" on the EARTH. According to one HYPOTHESIS, in the distant past a large land mass, Pangaea,

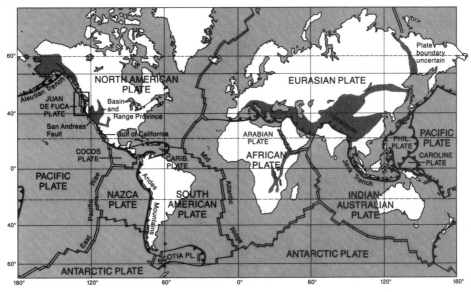

PLATE TECTONICS

included all the present CONTINENTS, which broke apart and drifted away. (*See* PLATE TECTONICS.)

plate tectonics (tek-TON-iks)   In GEOLOGY, the currently accepted THEORY of the structure of the EARTH. The earth's surface is said to be composed of plates of solid material many miles thick that move in response to forces deep within the earth. CONTINENTS are carried by the plates, and hence move as well. This movement is called CONTINENTAL DRIFT.

 ❧ EARTHQUAKES and VOLCANOES tend to occur at the boundaries between plates: the SAN ANDREAS FAULT is on such a boundary. ❧ New plate material is constantly created by the process of SEA FLOOR SPREADING, and old material is destroyed when two plates collide and one plate moves under the other.

precipitation   In METEOROLOGY, the fall of water, ice, or snow deposited on the surface of the EARTH from the ATMOSPHERE. In CHEMISTRY, a CHEMICAL REACTION in a SOLUTION in which a SOLID material is formed and subsequently falls, as a PRECIPITATE, to the bottom of the container.

prevailing westerlies   The west-to-east winds that occur in the temperate zones of the EARTH.

radioactive dating   A process for determining the age of an object by measuring the amount of a given RADIOACTIVE material it contains. If one knows how much of this radioactive material was present initially in the object (by determining how much of the material has decayed), and one knows the HALF-LIFE of the material, one can deduce the age of the object.

 ❧ The best known example of radioactive dating employs CARBON 14, a radioactive ISOTOPE of CARBON.

rainbow   The colored arch in the sky that is often seen after a rain. The rainbow is formed when water droplets in the air cause the DIFFRACTION of sunlight.

 ❧ The colors of the rainbow are violet, indigo, blue, green, yellow, orange, and red.

relative humidity   *See* HUMIDITY.

renewable resource   Any resource, such as wood or SOLAR ENERGY, that can or will be replenished naturally in the course of time.

Richter scale (RIK-tuhr)   A scale used to rate the intensity of EARTHQUAKES. The scale is open-ended, with each succeeding level representing ten times as much energy as the last. A serious earthquake might rate 6 to 8, and very destructive quakes rate higher.

 ❧ No quake greater than 9 has ever been recorded.

San Andreas Fault (SAN an-DRAY-uhs)   A FAULT in CALIFORNIA where the North American and the PACIFIC TECTONIC PLATES meet and slide along each other. (*See* EARTHQUAKE *and* PLATE TECTONICS.)

🐚 A major earthquake along this fault has been predicted for many years. Since California is a populous area, such an event might have very serious consequences.

sea breeze The breeze that blows from the sea toward the land during the day, as air rising over the warmer land is replaced by cooler air from above the sea. (*Compare* LAND BREEZE.)

sea floor spreading The process by which new material that lies under the ocean rises and pushes the existing TECTONIC PLATES aside, creating new CRUST as it does so.

🐚 Sea floor spreading is making the ATLANTIC OCEAN wider by a few inches each year.

sedimentary rock (sed-uh-MEN-tuh-ree) Material that is deposited in layers on the bottom of an ocean or lake and then transformed into rock through heat and PRESSURE. Sedimentary rocks can be recognized by their layered appearance. (*Compare* IGNEOUS ROCK *and* METAMORPHIC ROCK.)

🐚 LIMESTONE and SHALE are common sedimentary rocks.

seismic waves (SEYEZ-mik) In GEOLOGY, shock WAVES in solid rock generated by EARTHQUAKES or underground explosions. (*See* SEISMOLOGY.)

🐚 Seismic waves travel through the EARTH, and can be detected far from their source. 🐚 Most of our knowledge of the earth's interior comes from studying seismic waves. 🐚 The measurement of seismic waves is also important in detecting underground nuclear tests.

seismology (seyez-MOL-uh-jee) The branch of science devoted to the study of SEISMIC WAVES and the information they provide about the structure of the interior of the EARTH.

🐚 Our knowledge of the properties of the deep CRUST, the MANTLE, and the CORE comes from this field.

shale A SEDIMENTARY ROCK formed from layers of clay.

silicates (SIL-uh-kuhts, SIL-uh-kayts) The main MINERALS found in many rocks. Silicates are composed of ATOMS of silicon, OXYGEN, and ELEMENTS such as potassium, sodium, or calcium, under great heat and PRESSURE. Silicates make up about one-quarter of the CRUST of the EARTH.

🐚 Mica and quartz are silicates.

smog A haze or fog composed of water vapor, complex MOLECULES, and suspended particles.

🐚 In NORTH AMERICA, the primary cause of smog is pollution from automobile exhaust. 🐚 The LOS ANGELES basin, where pollutants can be trapped by INVERSIONS and the surrounding mountains, has frequent problems with smog, as do other major urban areas. 🐚 The word *smog* is a combination of *smoke* and *fog*.

soil Material on the surface of the EARTH on which plants can grow. (*See* TOPSOIL.)

🐚 Soil is produced by the WEATHERING of rocks.

solar energy The ENERGY the EARTH receives from the SUN, primarily as visible LIGHT and other forms of ELECTROMAGNETIC RADIATION. (*See* RENEWABLE RESOURCE.)

🐚 The term *solar energy* often refers to processes that use this energy to generate heat or ELECTRICITY for human use. (*See* SOLAR CELLS.)

stalactites (stuh-LAK-teyets) Rock structures formed on the ceilings of caves as water drips down, leaving behind MINERALS before it falls. (*Compare* STALAGMITES.)

🐚 Stalactites grow very slowly. 🐚 One easy way to distinguish stalactites from stalagmites is to recall that stalactites "hold *tight*" to the ceiling of a cave. Stalagmites "*might* reach the ceiling" of the cave and form a column.

stalagmites (stuh-LAG-meyets) Rock structures that grow up from the floors of caves as water drips down and deposits MINERALS. (*Compare* STALACTITES.)

🐚 Stalagmites grow very slowly.

stratification The process by which materials form themselves into layers, as occurs in the solid portion of the EARTH in SEDIMENTARY and some IGNEOUS rocks.

🐚 The ATMOSPHERE and the ocean also exhibit stratification, with the warmer materials occupying the upper layers.

stratosphere (STRAT-uh-sfeer) The region of the ATMOSPHERE of the EARTH above the TROPOSPHERE.

STALACTITES AND STALAGMITES. *The Luray Caverns, Virginia.*

STRATUS CLOUDS

The stratosphere begins at an altitude of seven to ten miles, and extends to approximately thirty miles.

stratus clouds (STRAY-tuhs, STRAT-uhs) Low CLOUDS that stretch over large portions of sky, creating overcast conditions.

tectonic plates (tek-TON-ik) The dozen or so plates that make up the surface of the EARTH. Their motion is studied in the field of PLATE TECTONICS.

☙ The plates are not the same as the CONTINENTS. The North American plate, for example, extends from the middle of the ATLANTIC OCEAN to the west coast of the United States and CANADA. These plates are about thirty miles thick.

thermal inversion *See* INVERSION, THERMAL.

thunder The noise created when air rushes back into a region from which it has been expelled by the passage of LIGHTNING.

tides The periodic rise and fall of the ocean level owing to the GRAVITATIONAL FORCE exerted by the MOON and SUN.

☙ In most parts of the world, two tide cycles occur each day.

tidal wave *See* TSUNAMI.

topsoil The thin, rich layer of SOIL where most nutrients for plants are found.

☙ Most of the land-based biological activity of the EARTH takes place here. ☙ The loss of topsoil through EROSION is a major agricultural problem.

tornado In METEOROLOGY, a storm in which high-speed winds move in a funnel-shaped pattern.

☙ Tornadoes occur chiefly during thunderstorms. ☙ If the tip of the funnel touches the ground, it can cause extensive damage. ☙ Tornadoes are common in the MIDDLE WEST.

troposphere (TROH-puh-sfeer, TROP-uh-sfeer) The lowest layer of the ATMOSPHERE of the EARTH, extending from ground level to an altitude of seven to ten miles.

tsunami (tsooh-NAH-mee) A large WAVE on the ocean, usually caused by an undersea EARTHQUAKE, a volcanic eruption, or coastal landslide. A tsunami can travel hundreds of miles over the open sea and cause extensive damage when it encounters land. Also called tidal waves.

tundra A land area near the NORTH POLE where the SOIL is permanently frozen a few feet underground.

☙ There are no trees: the vegetation is primarily lichens and mosses on the tundra. ☙ Tundra is widespread in Lapland, and in the far northern portions of ALASKA, CANADA, and the SOVIET UNION.

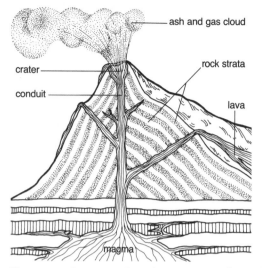

VOLCANO. *A cross section of an erupting volcano (left) and a photograph of Mount St. Helens erupting on May 18, 1980 (right).*

typhoon   In METEOROLOGY, a type of CYCLONE occurring in the western regions of the PACIFIC OCEAN.

&c. A typhoon is similar to a HURRICANE in levels of destructiveness.

Van Allen belt   Either of two layers of electrically charged (*see* CHARGE, ELECTRICAL) particles held in ORBITS above the ATMOSPHERE by the MAGNETIC FIELD OF THE EARTH. The belt is named after its discoverer, the twentieth-century American physicist James Van Allen.

volcano   A cone-shaped mountain or hill created by molten material that rises from the interior of the EARTH to the surface.

&c. Volcanoes tend to occur along the edges of TECTONIC PLATES. &c. Eruptions and lava flows associated with them can be very destructive. (*See* MOUNT SAINT HELENS *and* MOUNT VESUVIUS.)

water table   The depth (measured from the surface of the EARTH) at which underground water is first encountered.

watershed   A ridge of high land dividing two areas that are drained by different river systems. On one side of a watershed, rivers and streams flow in one direction; on the other side they flow in another direction. Also, the area drained by a water system.

&c. By extension, a "watershed" is a critical point that serves as a dividing line: "The parties reached a watershed in the contract negotiations."

weather   The daily conditions of the ATMOSPHERE in terms of temperature, ATMOSPHERIC PRESSURE, wind, and moisture.

weather map   A map showing the WEATHER patterns throughout a given region.

weather satellite   An artificial SATELLITE that revolves around the EARTH and detects and reports WEATHER patterns on the earth's surface.

weather service   *See* NATIONAL WEATHER SERVICE.

weathering   The process by which rocks are broken down into small grains and SOIL. Weathering can happen through rainfall, ice formation, or the action of living things such as ALGAE and plant roots. It is part of the GEOLOGICAL CYCLE.

westerly   *See* PREVAILING WESTERLIES.

Life Sciences

T he study of living things on the EARTH has a long history. Because of the incredible richness and diversity of life, most of the effort in BIOLOGY and in its predecessor, natural history, has been expended on an effort to describe what there is — simple exploration and cataloguing. The classical sciences of descriptive BOTANY and ZOOLOGY, with their emphasis on CLASSIFICATION, are examples of this sort of work. The division of living things into the PLANT KINGDOM and ANIMAL KINGDOM (plus three more kingdoms added by modern scientists to describe microscopic organisms and fungi), and the collection of all living things into a coherent classification scheme, are the fruit of this work. During the past century and a half, however, two important discoveries have changed the face of the life sciences.

The first of these was the development of the THEORY of EVOLUTION by Charles DARWIN and others. The mechanism of NATURAL SELECTION gave naturalists for the first time a way of answering questions about *how* life came to have the forms it has, rather than just questions about what those forms are. The great social and intellectual turmoil triggered by Darwin's work is interesting, of course, but is not relevant from a purely scientific standpoint. What does matter is that we can now understand how the observed diversity of living things could have arisen through the action of a simple and easily comprehended mechanism. The original Darwinian notions have been modified and expanded since his time, of course, and there is still debate about the pace at which SPECIES evolve. Nevertheless, the main principle of Darwinism — that living things change and adapt in response to their environment — has been incorporated as one of the pillars of the modern life sciences.

The second great change in the life sciences is the shift from studying organisms as a whole to studying the complex chemical processes inside the CELL, both in its everyday workings and in reproduction. This change can be symbolized by the discovery of the structure of DEOXYRIBONU-CLEIC ACID (DNA) and RIBONUCLEIC ACID (RNA) in the 1950s.

The new emphasis on basic BIOCHEMISTRY has had several consequences. For one thing, the realization that genetic information is passed from one generation to the next through DNA has filled in the Darwinian picture of the development of life. Natural selection acts when individuals of the same species differ, but until recently we had no notion of why these differences occurred. Now, thanks to modern GENETICS, this missing piece of the Darwinian picture is being filled in.

A detailed understanding of the working of the individual cell, the basic building block of life, is also beginning to emerge. We see the cell as a system in which information is carried and stored in DNA and RNA MOLECULES, but in which the actual work is done by an assembly of PROTEINS. Most of the details of the cell's working are too complex to be included in our list, but it is important to be aware that these secrets are being unraveled. It is hard to imagine modern CANCER research progressing, for example, without consideration of what makes a cancer cell different from a normal one. At the same time, our knowledge of genetic processes makes it possible for us to cure HERED-ITARY diseases and to create living things that never existed in nature. We can produce life forms to help improve the human condition, much as our ancestors developed domestic livestock thousands of years ago. This field remains one of the most vital and exciting areas of research in modern science.

While some life scientists are examining the smallest parts of living organisms, others are studying the complex interrelationships of communities of plants and animals. The new science of ECOLOGY aims at understanding the way that living systems (including human beings) interact with one another and with their environment. The scope of such studies can extend from a small marsh to the entire PLANET.

The entries in this section were chosen using slightly different criteria from those used in the sections of the dictionary covering the HUMANITIES and SOCIAL SCIENCES. They are chosen not because the majority of educated readers are expected to be familiar with them, but because most scientists would agree that a knowledge of these concepts is essential to a knowledge of the life sciences. Some of these words might be used without explanation in daily newspapers, but many would not. Nevertheless, if you are familiar with these terms and the concepts they represent, you should know enough about the life sciences to follow their progress as it is presented in the popular press.

— J. T.

adaptation   The changes made by living systems in response to their environment. Heavy fur, for example, is one adaptation to a cold CLIMATE.

aerobic (air-OH-bik)   In BIOLOGY, a descriptive term for organisms that require the presence of OXYGEN to live. (*Compare* ANAEROBIC.)

🙠 Aerobic exercise is exercise designed to improve the body's use of oxygen, and consists of activities like running, swimming, and doing calisthenics for an extended time.

algae (AL-jee)   Primitive organisms that contain CHLOROPHYLL but do not have structures, such as XYLEM and PHLOEM, to transport FLUIDS. Algae sometimes contain only a single CELL, and nowadays are not generally considered members of the PLANT KINGDOM.

🙠 The most familiar algae are the greenish scum that collects in still water. 🙠 Algae supply a considerable part of the world's OXYGEN.

amino acids (uh-MEE-noh)   Basic ORGANIC MOLE-CULES that combine to form PROTEINS. Amino acids are made up of HYDROGEN, CARBON, OXYGEN, and NITROGEN. Some examples of amino acids are lysine, phenylalanine, and tryptophan.

🙠 Amino acids are the basic molecular building blocks of proteins.

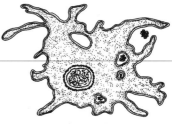

AMOEBA

amoeba (uh-MEE-buh)   An animal composed of only one CELL that has no fixed shape. It is the best known of the SINGLE-CELLED animals, or PROTOZOA.

🙠 The term *amoeba* is sometimes used to refer to something with an indefinite, changeable shape.

amphibians (am-FIB-ee-uhnz)   VERTEBRATE animals, such as frogs, that live part of their life cycle in the water and the other part on land.

🙠 *Amphibian* is also used to describe things such as vehicles that can operate both on land and in the water. 🙠 Amphibians were the first land-dwelling animals to evolve.

anaerobic (an-uh-ROH-bik, an-air-OH-bik)   A descriptive term for a process, such as FERMENTATION, that can proceed only in the absence of OXYGEN, or a living thing that can survive only in the absence of oxygen. (*Compare* AEROBIC.)

anatomy The structure of an animal or plant; also, the study of this structure through such techniques as microscopic observation and dissection. (*Compare* MORPHOLOGY *and* PHYSIOLOGY.)

animal kingdom The group of living things typically distinguished from members of the PLANT KINGDOM by the power of moving from place to place and by a METABOLISM that does not use PHOTOSYNTHESIS.

arthropods (AHR-thruh-podz) A PHYLUM, or major division of the ANIMAL KINGDOM. Arthropods are animals with jointed legs and segmented bodies, such as insects, spiders, centipedes, and CRUSTACEANS. There are more SPECIES of arthropods than of any other animal phylum.

asexual reproduction (ay-SEK-shooh-uhl) The kind of reproduction in which it is not necessary to have two parents to produce offspring. The reproduction of SINGLE-CELLED organisms through MITOSIS, and the production of SPORES in some plants and plantlike organisms, are examples of asexual reproduction.

Australopithecus (aw-stray-loh-PITH-i-kuhs, aw-stray-loh-pi-THEE-kuhs) An extinct GENUS of the HOMINID FAMILY that lived in AFRICA from about 3 to 1 million years ago. The name means "southern ape."
꙳ Members of this genus were the ancestors of modern humans. ꙳ LUCY, the "oldest human," was a member of this genus.

bacilli (buh-SIL-eye) *sing.* BACILLUS A form of BACTERIA, usually rod-shaped.

bacteria *sing.* BACTERIUM Microorganisms made up of a single CELL that has no distinct NUCLEUS. Bacteria reproduce by MITOSIS or by forming SPORES.
꙳ Some bacteria are beneficial to humans (for example, those that live in the STOMACH and aid DIGESTION), and some are harmful (for example, those that cause disease).

balance of nature A concept in ECOLOGY that describes natural systems as being in a state of EQUILIBRIUM, in which disturbing one element disturbs the entire system. The implication is usually drawn that the natural state of any system is the preferred state, and that it is best to leave it undisturbed. Whether a balance of nature really exists is a subject of debate among modern ecologists.

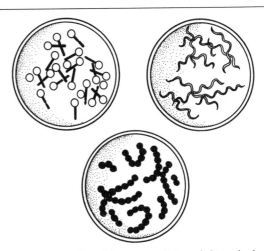

BACTERIA. Clostridium tetani *(top left), which causes tetanus;* Treponema pallidum *(top right), which causes syphilis;* streptococcus *(bottom), which causes various infections, including scarlet fever.*

basal metabolism (BAY-suhl, BAY-zuhl muh-TAB-uh-liz-uhm) The rate at which an inactive, resting organism expends ENERGY.

biochemical pathways In BIOLOGY, the long chains of CHEMICAL REACTIONS that take place in the normal operation of living systems.

biochemistry The study of the structure and interactions of the complex ORGANIC MOLECULES found in living systems.

biodegradable (beye-oh-di-GRAY-duh-buhl) Material that, left to itself, will be decomposed by natural processes. ꙳ The use of biodegradable packaging is supposed to reduce the volume of waste in landfills.

biology The study of life and living systems.

biomass Material in growing or dead plants.
꙳ The term *biomass* is most often encountered in discussions of sources of ENERGY, since biomass can be used to supply energy needs directly (as fuel wood, for example) or indirectly (by being converted to alcohol; *see* GASOHOL).

biophysics The study of living things using the techniques of PHYSICS.

biosphere (BEYE-uh-sfeer) The thin outer shell of the EARTH and the inner layers of its ATMOSPHERE; the place where all living systems are found.

birds A CLASS of VERTEBRATES distinguished by their feathers and their two legs and two wings. Birds are WARM-BLOODED ANIMALS, and their young hatch from eggs.

botany The scientific study and categorization of plants. (*See* FRUIT, PHOTOSYNTHESIS, *and* PLANT KINGDOM.)

Brontosaurus (bron-tuh-SAWR-uhs) A large herbivorous (*see* HERBIVORE) DINOSAUR, perhaps the most familiar of the dinosaurs. The scientific name has recently been changed to Apatosaurus, but Brontosaurus is still used popularly. The word is from the Greek, meaning "thunder lizard."

cambium (KAM-bee-uhm) The layer of a tree where growth occurs, just under the bark.

carbohydrates Substances composed of long chains of OXYGEN, HYDROGEN, and CARBON MOLECULES. SUGAR, starch, and CELLULOSE are all carbohydrates. In the human body, carbohydrates play a major role in RESPIRATION; in plants, they are important in PHOTOSYNTHESIS.

&. Carbohydrates in food provide ENERGY for the body and, if present in excess, are stored as FAT.

carbon cycle In ECOLOGY, the movement of ATOMS of CARBON through the BIOSPHERE. MOLECULES of CARBON DIOXIDE are taken in by plants, to be incorporated into their tissues, which may then be eaten by and incorporated into animals. Animals return the carbon to the air in the form of carbon dioxide, and the cycle starts again. (*See* PHOTOSYNTHESIS *and* RESPIRATION.)

carnivore (KAHR-nuh-vawr) A living thing that eats meat. Among MAMMALS, there is an ORDER of carnivores, including such primarily meat-eating animals as tigers and dogs. Some plants, such as the Venus's-flytrap, are carnivores.

carrying capacity In ECOLOGY, the number of living things that can exist for long periods in a given area without damaging the environment.

Carson, Rachel An American author and scientist of the twentieth century who was fervently devoted to defending the natural world against POLLUTION. Her best-known books are *Silent Spring*, concerning the overuse of pesticides and weed killers, and *The Sea Around Us*.

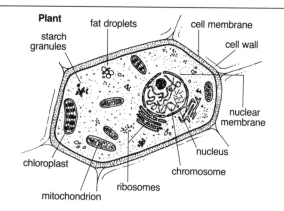

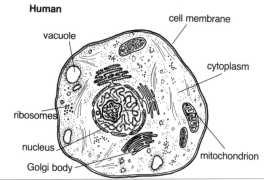

CELL. *A plant cell (top) and a human cell (bottom) as they appear under an electron microscope.*

cell The basic unit of all living things except VIRUSES. In advanced organisms, cells consist of a NUCLEUS (which contains GENETIC material), CYTOPLASM, and ORGANELLES, all of which are surrounded by a CELL MEMBRANE.

&. Groups of cells with similar structure and function form tissues.

cell differentiation The development of different CELLS to perform different functions in complex organisms. In the human body, for example, some cells develop into NERVES, others into muscles, and so on.

&. Cell differentiation is a major area of research in BIOLOGY.

cell membrane The structure separating an animal CELL from its environment or a plant cell from its CELL WALL. The cell membrane is a complex system that allows nutrients to enter the cell and waste products to leave, usually through OSMOSIS.

cell wall The rigid outer covering of a typical plant CELL, composed mainly of CELLULOSE, and lying outside the CELL MEMBRANE. Animal cells do not have cell walls.

☙ It is the cell walls that give plant stems and wood their stiffness.

cellulose (SEL-yuh-lohs) A stringy, fibrous substance that forms the main material in the CELL WALLS of plants. Cellulose is an ORGANIC MOLECULE, composed of CARBON, HYDROGEN, and OXYGEN.

chemical evolution The formation of complex ORGANIC MOLECULES from simpler INORGANIC MOLECULES through CHEMICAL REACTIONS in the oceans during the early history of the EARTH; the first step in the development of life on this PLANET. The period of chemical evolution lasted less than a billion years.

☙ Many of the steps in chemical evolution can now be reproduced in the laboratory.

chlorophyll (KLAWR-uh-fil) The complex chemical that gives a plant its green color and plays an important role in the conversion of sunlight into ENERGY for the plant. (See PHOTOSYNTHESIS.)

chordates (KAWR-dayts, KAWR-duhts) Animals that have a central NERVE like the human SPINAL CORD.

☙ Chordates make up a PHYLUM in the ANIMAL KINGDOM that includes all the VERTEBRATES, along with some primitive wormlike sea animals. (See CLASSIFICATION.)

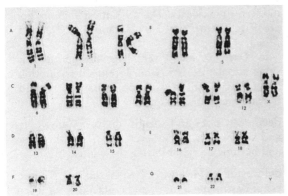

CHROMOSOMES. *Karyotype of human female chromosomes.*

chromosomes (KROH-muh-sohmz) The small bodies in the NUCLEUS of a CELL that carry the chemical "instructions" for reproduction of the cell. They consist of strands of DNA wrapped in a DOUBLE HELIX around a core of PROTEINS. Each SPECIES of plant or animal has a characteristic number of chromosomes. For human beings, for example, it is forty-six.

☙ In humans, sex is determined by two chromosomes: an X-CHROMOSOME, which is female, and a Y-CHROMOSOME, which is male. (See SEX CHROMOSOMES.)

class In BIOLOGY, the CLASSIFICATION beneath a PHYLUM and above an ORDER.

☙ MAMMALS, REPTILES, and INSECTS are classes.

Classification

The classifications of the Siberian tiger and romaine lettuce shown here are presented in descending order, beginning with the broadest category. Biologists who specialize in classification (called taxonomists) are constantly refining their terms as new relationships between organisms are recognized.

Kingdom Animalia (animals)	**Kingdom** Plantae (plants)
Phylum Chordata (chordates)	**Division** Tracheophyta (vascular plants)
Subphylum Vertebrata (vertebrates)	**Class** Angiospermae (flowering plants)
Class Mammalia (mammals)	**Subclass** Dicotyledonae (dicotyledons)
Order Carnivora (carnivores)	**Order** Campanulales or Campanulatae (bellflowers, lobelias, composites)
Family Felidae (cats)	**Family** Compositae (composites)
Genus Panthera (lion, tiger, leopard, jaguar)	**Genus** Lactuca (lettuce)
Species Panthera tigris (tiger)	**Species** Lactuca sativa (cultivated lettuce)
Subspecies Panthera tigris longipilis (Siberian tiger)	**Variety** Lactuca sativa longifolia (romaine lettuce)

classification A way of organizing living things. In BIOLOGY, plants and animals are usually classified by the structure of their bodies, in a descending hierarchy of categories: KINGDOM, PHYLUM, CLASS, ORDER, FAMILY, GENUS, and SPECIES (a useful mnemonic device: *King Philip Came Over For Good Spaghetti*). For example, human beings are classified as belonging to the ANIMAL KINGDOM, the phylum of CHORDATES, the class of MAMMALS, the order of PRIMATES, the genus *Homo*, and the species *Homo sapiens*.

Biologists frequently fill gaps in the fixed hierarchy with special categories, such as superfamilies and subspecies. Human beings, for example, belong not only to the phylum of chordates but to the subphylum of VERTEBRATES. The three classes of FISHES constitute a superclass.

DINOSAURS. *From left to right: Triceratops (30 feet long), Tyrannosaurus (50 feet long), and Stegosaurus (29 feet long).*

🐚 Plants and animals are usually identified merely by genus and species: thus, human beings are given the scientific name *Homo sapiens.*

clone A living system that is genetically identical to its ancestor (that is, it has exactly the same DNA MOLECULES). Since each CELL contains the DNA molecules that characterize an individual, it is, in principle, possible to replicate, or reproduce, complex living systems in the laboratory.

🐚 *Clone* is often used informally to indicate a close copy or resemblance: "This new COMPUTER is a clone of the IBM model."

closed ecosystem An ECOSYSTEM in which no materials can leave or enter, but through which ENERGY from external sources can flow.

🐚 The EARTH is a closed ecosystem.

codon (KOH-don) A group of three bases on the DNA molecule. Each codon determines the identity of one AMINO ACID in PROTEINS made by the CELL.

🐚 The codon is the "word" of the GENETIC CODE.

cold-blooded animals Animals, such as REPTILES, that cannot control their body temperature, and that therefore become sluggish in cold weather. (*Compare* WARM-BLOODED ANIMALS.)

🐚 Cold-blooded animals are often seen sunning themselves to warm up.

Crick, Francis H. C. *See* WATSON AND CRICK.

cross-breeding *See* HYBRIDIZATION.

cross-fertilization The FERTILIZATION of the OVUM of one plant by the SPERM of another plant.

crustacean (kru-STAY-shuhn) A CLASS of ARTHROPODS with shells.

🐚 Crabs, lobsters, shrimp, and crayfish are crustaceans.

cytoplasm (SEYE-tuh-plaz-uhm) The material within a biological CELL that is not contained in the NUCLEUS.

Darwin, Charles A British naturalist of the nineteenth century. He and others developed the THEORY of EVOLUTION. This theory forms the basis for the modern life sciences. Darwin's most famous books are *THE ORIGIN OF SPECIES* and *The Descent of Man.*

🐚 Darwin's ideas were later misrepresented by some social theorists, who developed the notion of Social Darwinism to justify practices such as child labor in nineteenth-century England.

deciduous trees and shrubs (di-SIJ-ooh-uhs) Trees and shrubs that, unlike evergreens, lose their leaves and become dormant during the winter.

deforestation (dee-fawr-uh-STAY-shuhn) The process of destroying a forest and replacing it with something else. The term is used today to refer to the destruction of forests by human beings and their replacement by agricultural systems. 🐚 Deforestation is considered to be a main contributor to the GREENHOUSE EFFECT.

deoxyribonucleic acid (dee-ok-see-reye-boh-nooh-klee-ik) *See* DNA.

dinosaurs REPTILES, now extinct, that were the dominant life form on EARTH for many millions of years. The name *dinosaur* comes from the Greek words for "monstrous lizard."

ᕶ Some dinosaurs were very large and had small brains — factors that may in part have led to their extinction. The term is often used to refer to something or someone that is antiquated and unable to adapt to change: "The old cavalry generals couldn't adjust to the use of tanks — they became dinosaurs."

ᕶ Commonly known dinosaurs include TYRANNOSAURUS REX, BRONTOSAURUS, Stegosaurus, and Triceratops.

dioxin (deye-ok-sin) Pollutants created as byproducts in many industrial processes. Dioxins accumulate in human tissue and affect human METABOLISM. They are CARCINOGENS. ᕶ Eliminating dioxins is an important goal of environmental policy.

DNA. *A DNA molecule; note the double helix. Nucleotide bases of DNA are adenine, guanine, cytosine, and thymine.*

DNA (deoxyribonucleic acid) The MOLECULE that carries genetic information in all living systems (*see* GENETIC CODE). The DNA molecule is formed in the shape of a DOUBLE HELIX from a great number of smaller molecules (*see* NUCLEOTIDES). The workings of the DNA molecule provide the most fundamental explanation of the laws of GENETICS.

DNA acts in three important ways. First, when a CELL divides, the DNA uncoils, and each strand creates a new partner from the surrounding material — a process called replication. The two cells that result from the cell division have the same DNA as the original (*see* MITOSIS). Second, in SEXUAL REPRODUCTION, each parent contributes one of the two strands in the DNA of the offspring. Third, inside the cell, the DNA governs the production of PROTEINS and other molecules essential to cell function.

DNA sequencing A process by which the sequence of MOLECULES along a strand of DNA is determined.

ᕶ The GENOME PROJECT involves DNA sequencing. (*Compare* GENE MAPPING.)

dominant trait In GENETICS, a trait that will appear in the offspring if one of the parents contributes it. (*Compare* RECESSIVE TRAIT.)

ᕶ In humans, dark hair is a dominant trait; if one parent contributes a GENE for dark hair, and the other contributes a gene for light hair, the child will have dark hair.

double helix (HEE-liks) The shape taken by the DNA MOLECULE. A HELIX is a three-dimensional spiral, like the shape of a spring or the railing on a spiral staircase. A DNA molecule consists of two helixes intertwined.

ecological niche The place or function of a given organism within its ECOSYSTEM.

ᕶ Different organisms may compete for the same niche. For example, in a forest there may be a niche for an organism that can fly and eat nectar from blossoms. This niche may be filled by some sort of BIRD, or an insect, or even a MAMMAL such as a bat.

ecology The study of living things, their environment, and the relation between the two.

ecosystem (EE-koh-sis-tuhm, EK-oh-sis-tuhm) A collection of living things and the environment in which they live. For example, a prairie ecosystem includes coyotes, the rabbits on which they feed, and the grasses that feed the rabbits.

ᕶ Chemical substances move through ecosystems on the EARTH in cycles (*see* CARBON CYCLE). ᕶ The source of ENERGY for almost every ecosystem on earth is the SUN.

embryo (EM-bree-oh) A developing plant or animal. A plant embryo is an undeveloped plant inside a seed. An animal embryo is the animal as it develops

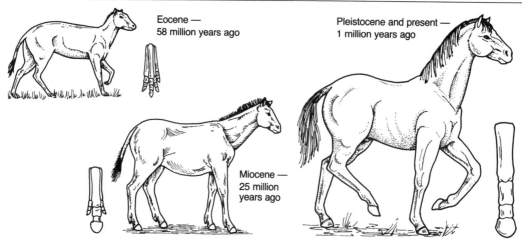

EVOLUTION. *The evolution of the horse:* Eohippus *(1 foot high),* Merychippus *(3½ feet), and* Equus *(5 feet).*

from the single CELL of the ZYGOTE until birth. Among humans and most other MAMMALS, the embryo is carried in the mother's womb.

🐚 The term is occasionally used to denote a new or developing idea or project: "The idea for the complete THEORY was already present in his work, in embryo form, in 1950."

embryology (em-bree-OL-uh-jee) The study of the EMBRYO; a major field of research in modern BIOLOGY.

enzyme (EN-zeyem) A PROTEIN MOLECULE that helps other ORGANIC MOLECULES enter into CHEMICAL REACTIONS with one another but is itself unaffected by these reactions. In other words, enzymes act as CATALYSTS for organic biochemical reactions.

eugenics (yooh-JEN-iks) The idea that one can improve the human race by careful selection of those who mate and produce offspring.

🐚 Eugenics was a popular THEORY in the early twentieth century but is no longer taken seriously, primarily because of the horrors of the eugenic efforts of the NAZI regime in GERMANY.

evolution A THEORY first proposed in the nineteenth century by Charles DARWIN, according to which the EARTH'S SPECIES have changed and diversified through time under the influence of NATURAL SELECTION. Life on earth is thought to have evolved in three stages. First came CHEMICAL EVOLUTION, in which ORGANIC MOLECULES were formed. This was

followed by the development of single CELLS capable of reproducing themselves. This stage led to the development of complex organisms capable of SEXUAL REPRODUCTION. Evolution is generally accepted as fact by scientists today, although debates continue over the precise mechanisms involved in the process. (*See* MUTATION, PUNCTUATED EQUILIBRIUM, *and* CREATION SCIENCE.)

🐚 The first cell is thought to have been formed when the earth was less than a billion years old.

family In BIOLOGY, the CLASSIFICATION lower than an ORDER and higher than a GENUS. Lions, tigers, cheetahs, and house cats belong to the same biological family. Human beings belong to the biological family of HOMINIDS.

fauna (FAW-nuh) Animals, especially the animals of a particular place and time.

fermentation A CHEMICAL REACTION in which SUGARS are broken down into smaller MOLECULES that can be used in living systems. Alcoholic beverages, such as beer, wine, and whiskey, are made from the controlled use of fermentation. Fermentation is an ANAEROBIC process.

fertilization The joining of SEX CELLS to form a new living thing. In humans, a male SPERM joins a female OVUM, or egg; the resulting ZYGOTE divides into a multicelled structure that implants in the womb and grows into an EMBRYO. In plants, POLLEN grains, containing the male sex cells, enter the female

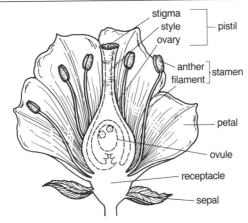

FLOWER. *A cross section.*

sex cells in the PISTIL; from this union, FRUIT eventually grows. When fertilization occurs within a single FLOWER, we call it self-fertilization. (*See* CROSS-FERTILIZATION.)

fetus The EMBRYO of an animal that bears its young alive (rather than laying eggs). In humans, the em-

bryo is called a fetus after all major body structures have formed; this stage is reached about 60 days after FERTILIZATION.

fishes Traditionally, a CLASS of VERTEBRATES that breathe with gills rather than LUNGS, live in water, and generally lay eggs, although some bear their young alive. Some biologists consider the fishes a "superclass," and divide them into three classes: bony fishes, such as sunfish and cod; fishes with a skeleton formed of CARTILAGE rather than bone, such as sharks; and fishes that lack jaws, such as lampreys.

❧ Fishes are COLD-BLOODED ANIMALS.

flora (FLAWR-uh) Plants, especially the plants of a particular place and time.

flower The part of a plant that produces the seed. It usually contains petals, a PISTIL, and POLLEN-bearing STAMENS.

food chain The series of steps by which ENERGY is obtained, used, and transformed by living things. For example: sunlight helps grain to grow, the grain feeds cattle, and humans eat the cattle.

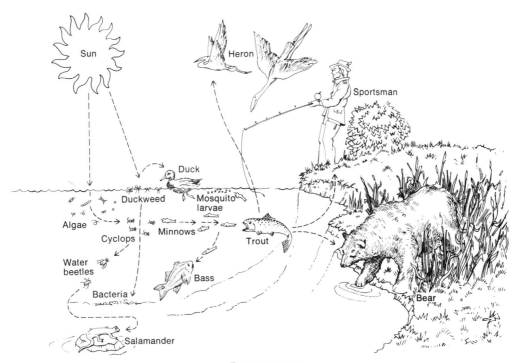

FOOD CHAIN

🉐 Harmful chemicals can become concentrated as they move up the food chain.

fruit   In BOTANY, the part of a seed-bearing plant that contains the fertilized seeds capable of generating a new plant (*see* FERTILIZATION). Fruit develops from the female part of the plant. Apples, peaches, tomatoes, and many other familiar foods are fruits.

fungi   (FUN-jeye, FUNG-geye) *sing.* FUNGUS (FUNG-guhs)   Plantlike organisms lacking CHLOROPHYLL, such as mushrooms, molds, yeasts, and mildews. Modern biologists tend to place fungi in their own KINGDOM, not in the PLANT KINGDOM, because they get their nutrients from other living things (or from the remains of living things that have died) rather than from PHOTOSYNTHESIS. (*See under "Medicine and Health."*)

gene   A portion of a DNA MOLECULE that serves as the basic unit of HEREDITY. Genes control the characteristics that an offspring will have by transmitting information in the sequence of NUCLEOTIDES on short sections of DNA.

gene mapping   The process of determining where GENES are located on individual CHROMOSOMES. (*Compare* DNA SEQUENCING.)

gene pool   The total number of GENES available in a given SPECIES.
🉐 Loosely speaking, the gene pool represents the total breeding stock available to the species.

gene splicing   A term used to refer to the process by which the DNA of an organism is cut and a GENE, perhaps from another organism, inserted. (*See* GENETIC ENGINEERING *and* RECOMBINANT DNA.) 🉐 Gene splicing is often used in industry to allow single-celled organisms to produce useful products, like human INSULIN.

genetic code   The code that translates the sequence of MOLECULES along the DNA strand into a sequence of AMINO ACIDS along PROTEINS manufactured by the CELL. Different sequences of the same four molecules produce different proteins, which, through their role as ENZYMES, govern the nature of the cell and the organism of which it is part. 🉐 All living things share the same genetic code. 🉐 Unraveling the genetic code was one of the great scientific achievements of the twentieth century, and it opened the way to GENETIC ENGINEERING.

genetic engineering   The manipulation of MOLECULES in strands of DNA to produce new types of organisms, usually by inserting or deleting GENES.
🉐 Genetic engineering is being developed commercially in the United States, with such uses as producing human INSULIN or BACTERIA that will keep plants from freezing in a mild frost. 🉐 U.S. courts have ruled that the products of genetic engineering can be patented. 🉐 There is often controversy about the risk involved in releasing genetically engineered organisms into the environment.

genetics   The study of HEREDITY, or how the characteristics of living things are transmitted from one generation to the next. Every living thing contains the genetic material that makes up DNA MOLECULES. This material is passed on when organisms reproduce. The basic unit of heredity is the GENE. (*See* CHROMOSOMES; DOMINANT TRAIT; GENETIC CODE; MENDEL, GREGOR; RECESSIVE TRAIT; *and* SEXUAL REPRODUCTION.)

genome project   (JEE-nohm)   A worldwide project now underway whose goal is to determine the precise arrangement of MOLECULES on the human DNA strand (i.e., to sequence human DNA). 🉐 The genome project is expected to cost several billion dollars and be finished before the turn of the century.

genus   (JEE-nuhs)   In BIOLOGY, the CLASSIFICATION lower than a FAMILY and higher than a SPECIES. Wolves belong to the same genus as dogs. Foxes belong to a different genus from that of dogs and wolves, but to the same family.

glucose   (GLOOH-kohs)   The most common form of SUGAR, found extensively in the bodies of living things; a MOLECULE composed of CARBON, OXYGEN, and HYDROGEN.
🉐 Glucose is involved in the production of ENERGY in both plants and animals.

gonads   (GOH-nadz)   The ORGANS in animals that produce SEX CELLS: OVARIES in the female, TESTES in the male.

green revolution   The increase in the world production of such cereals as wheat and rice during the 1960s and 1970s because of better seed and new agricultural technology.
🉐 The green revolution greatly increased the availability of food and confounded predictions of worldwide famine that had been made in the early 1970s.

habitat The area or type of environment in which a particular kind of animal or plant usually lives.

herbivore (HUR-buh-vawr, UR-buh-vawr) A living thing that eats only plants. Cattle, sheep, and horses are herbivores.

heredity The passing of characteristics from parents to children. (*See* GENETICS.)

hibernation Passing the winter in a sleeping or inactive condition. Bears, ground squirrels, woodchucks, and several other kinds of animals hibernate.

hominids (HOM-uh-nidz) The biological FAMILY that includes our SPECIES, *Homo sapiens*. This family has also included NEANDERTHALS and other forerunners of today's humans, such as AUSTRALOPITHECUS, HOMO ERECTUS, and *Homo habilis*. Today's human beings are the only surviving hominids.

Homo (HOH-moh) The GENUS to which human beings belong. The genus *Homo* includes NEANDERTHALS and other HOMINIDS closely related to today's humans, such as HOMO ERECTUS.

horticulture (HAWR-tuh-kul-chuhr) The science of cultivating garden plants.

hybridization Producing offspring from parents of different stock.

• Hybridization is used extensively in agriculture, where new forms of hardy and disease-resistant plants are produced commercially.

hydroponics (heye-druh-PON-iks) Cultivating plants in an artificial environment in which the necessary nutrients are carried to the ROOTS in a LIQUID mixture.

in vitro (in VEE-troh) In the laboratory; literally, "in glass" (laboratory experiments are often carried out in glass containers). In vitro conditions are distinguished from conditions that actually apply in nature. (*Compare* IN VIVO.)

• *In vitro* appears in the expression "in vitro FERTILIZATION," a way of producing human EMBRYOS in a laboratory; these embryos are commonly called "test-tube babies."

in vivo (in VEE-voh) In nature; literally, "in life." In vivo conditions are distinguished from those that might exist only in a laboratory. (*Compare* IN VITRO.)

instinct Behavior that is not learned but passed between generations by HEREDITY.

invertebrates (in-VUR-tuh-bruhts, in-VUR-tuh-brayts) Animals without backbones. (*Compare* VERTEBRATES.)

kingdom In BIOLOGY, the largest of the divisions of living things. The best-known kingdoms are those of the PLANTS and ANIMALS. Modern biologists recognize three additional kingdoms: MONERA (for example, BACTERIA and blue-green ALGAE), PROTISTA (for example, red ALGAE, slime molds, and AMOEBAS and other PROTOZOA), and FUNGI. (*See* CLASSIFICATION.)

Linnaeus, Carolus (li-NEE-uhs, li-NAY-uhs) A Swedish biologist of the eighteenth century. Linnaeus originated our present scheme of CLASSIFICATION of living things. Linnaeus started the standard scientific practice of referring to animals and plants by GENUS and SPECIES whereby, for example, people are *Homo sapiens* and sugar maple trees are *Acer saccharum*.

lipids (LIP-idz, LEYE-pidz) A group of ORGANIC MOLECULES that includes FATS, oils, and waxes. Lipids do not dissolve in water. In animals, including humans, lipids store ENERGY and form parts of CELL structures such as CELL MEMBRANES.

mammals A CLASS of VERTEBRATES characterized by the production of milk by the females and in most cases, by a hairy body covering. Most mammals give live birth to their young. Human beings are mammals.

meiosis (meye-OH-sis) Division of CELLS in which four "daughter" cells are produced, each with half the GENES of the parent. Meiosis is a key process in SEXUAL REPRODUCTION. In the OVARIES and TESTES, meiosis produces a great variety of SEX CELLS (SPERM and OVA), since the genes of the parent cell can be split in many different ways. The sex cells combine in FERTILIZATION to produce a new individual with the full number of genes — half from each parent. Because the sex cells come in such variety, and come from two parents, there is an enormous number of possible forms for the offspring. (*See* CHROMOSOME, GENETICS, *and* MITOSIS.)

Mendel, Gregor (MEN-dl) An Austrian biologist and MONK of the nineteenth century. Mendel discovered the basic laws of GENETICS by doing experiments with pea plants.

meristem (MER-i-stem) The region on a plant where division of CELLS (and hence growth) occurs. Usually, meristems are found in the shoots and ROOT tips, and places where branches meet the stem. In trees, growth occurs in the CAMBIUM — the layer just beneath the bark.

metabolism (muh-TAB-uh-liz-uhm)   The total of the CHEMICAL REACTIONS that maintain the life of a living thing.

  🔊 In humans, metabolism is related to the intake and use of food; persons with a high metabolism can eat more without gaining weight.

metamorphosis (met-uh-MAWR-fuh-sis)   A change in an animal as it grows, particularly a radical change, such as the transformation of a caterpillar into a butterfly.

microorganisms   Organisms so small that they can be seen only through a MICROSCOPE. (*See* BACTERIA, PROTOZOA, *and* VIRUSES.)

missing link   A supposed animal midway in EVOLUTION between apes and humans. The term is based on a misunderstanding about the THEORY of evolution, which does not state that humans are descended from apes, but rather maintains that both humans and apes descended from a common ancestor. Modern evolutionary scientists do not search for a "missing link."

mitosis (meye-TOH-sis)   Division of a single CELL into two identical "daughter" cells. Mitosis begins when the DNA in the parent cell replicates itself; it ends with two cells having the same GENES (*see* GENETICS). Most cells in the human body, and all SINGLE-CELLED organisms, reproduce through mitosis. (*Compare* MEIOSIS.)

molecular biology (muh-LEK-yuh-luhr)   The branch of science devoted to studies of the structure, function, and reactions of DNA, RNA, PROTEINS, and other MOLECULES involved in the life processes.

mollusks (MOL-uhsks)   A PHYLUM of INVERTEBRATES with soft bodies and muscular feet. Some mollusks also have hard shells. Oysters, clams, snails, slugs, octopuses, and squid are mollusks.

Monera (muh-NEER-uh)   The KINGDOM of single-celled organisms without a CELL NUCLEUS. 🔊 Monera are the most primitive living things, and are thought to have been the first to evolve.

morphology (mawr-FOL-uh-jee)   The study of the structure of living things. (*Compare* ANATOMY *and* PHYSIOLOGY.)

mutagen (MYOOH-tuh-juhn, MYOOH-tuh-jen)   Something that causes MUTATIONS in living things. Mutagens include chemicals such as drugs or TOXINS, and RADIATION.

mutations   Changes in CHROMOSOMES or GENES that cause offspring to have characteristics different from those of their parents. Mutations can be caused by the effects of chemicals, RADIATION, or even ordinary heat on DNA. Mutations produce some of the differences between members of a SPECIES on which NATURAL SELECTION acts.

natural selection   A process fundamental to EVOLUTION as described by Charles DARWIN. By natural selection, any characteristic of an individual that allows it to survive to produce more offspring will eventually appear in every individual of the SPECIES, simply because those members will have more offspring.

  🔊 The expression "survival of the fittest" was used to describe this process in the nineteenth century, but is not favored by modern scientists.

neurotransmitter   Any one of a number of chemicals that are used to transmit NERVE signals across a SYNAPSE. They are sprayed from the end of the "upstream" nerve CELL and absorbed by receptors in the "downstream" cell. 🔊 Drugs like caffeine and alcohol are thought to affect the emission and reception of neurotransmitters.

nitrogen fixing   The conversion of atmospheric NITROGEN (which plants cannot absorb) into forms of nitrogen that plants can absorb. BACTERIA in the TOPSOIL carry out the conversion.

nitrogenous wastes (neye-TROJ-uh-nuhs)   Animal wastes (particularly URINE) that contain materials high in NITROGEN content.

  🔊 Nitrogenous waste can be valuable as fertilizer.

nucleic acids (nooh-KLEE-ik)   ORGANIC MOLECULES found in the NUCLEI of CELLS. DNA and RNA, the best-known nucleic acids, govern HEREDITY and the chemical processes in the cell.

nucleotides (NOOH-klee-uh-teyedz)   The basic groupings of MOLECULES that appear along the DOUBLE HELIX of the DNA molecule.

&. The order of nucleotides in DNA determines the GENETIC CODE.

nucleus (NOOH-klee-uhs) *plur.* NUCLEI (NOOH-klee-eye)   In BIOLOGY, the central region of the CELL, in which DNA is stored. The nucleus usually appears as a dark spot in the interior of the cell. Primitive cells (such as BACTERIA and blue-green ALGAE) have no nuclei.

omnivore (OM-nuh-vawr)   An animal whose normal diet includes both plants and animals. Human beings and bears are omnivores.

opposable thumb   A thumb that can be used for grasping.
&. Opposable thumbs are one of the distinguishing features of PRIMATES. &. The opposable thumb of human beings allows us to use tools.

order   In BIOLOGY, the CLASSIFICATION lower than a CLASS and higher than a FAMILY. Dogs and cats belong to the order of CARNIVORES; human beings, monkeys, and apes belong to the order of PRIMATES. Flies and mosquitoes belong to the same order; so do birch trees and oak trees.

organ   Part of a living thing, distinct from the other parts, that is adapted for a specific function. Organs are made up of tissues, and are grouped into SYSTEMS, such as the DIGESTIVE SYSTEM.
&. The BRAIN, LIVER, and SKIN are organs.

organelles (awr-guh-NELZ)   Parts of a CELL that store food, discharge waste, produce ENERGY, or perform other functions analogous to what ORGANS do in large living things.

organic compounds   The COMPOUNDS containing CARBON that are typically found in living systems.
&. Generally, anything made from living systems, such as cloth, fuels, or wood, is said to be organic. Organic foods are foods grown with no fertilizer except the organic compounds found naturally in plants and animals.

organic molecules   The smallest units of ORGANIC COMPOUNDS. All of these MOLECULES are based on chains of CARBON ATOMS, and come in four major categories: PROTEINS, CARBOHYDRATES, LIPIDS, and NUCLEIC ACIDS (DNA and RNA).

Origin of Species, The   A book by Charles DARWIN explaining his THEORY of EVOLUTION. When pub-

lished in 1859, it provoked great controversy; by casting doubt on the historical accuracy of the biblical accounts of CREATION, it caused many believers to question their faith in CHRISTIANITY. (*See* CREATIONISM *and* SCOPES TRIAL.)

phloem (FLOH-em)   The SYSTEM of vessels in a plant that carries food from the leaves to the rest of the plant. (*See* XYLEM.)

photosynthesis   Use by green plants of the ENERGY in sunlight to carry out CHEMICAL REACTIONS, such as the conversion of CARBON DIOXIDE into OXYGEN. Photosynthesis also produces the SUGARS that feed the plant.
&. Green plants depend on CHLOROPHYLL to carry out photosynthesis.

phylum (FEYE-luhm) *plur.* PHYLA (FEYE-luh)   One of the major divisions of the KINGDOMS of living things; the second-largest standard unit of biological CLASSIFICATION. The ARTHROPODS, CHORDATES, and MOLLUSKS are phyla. Phyla in the PLANT KINGDOM are frequently called divisions.

physiology   The study of the function of living things, including such processes as nutrition, movement, and reproduction. (*Compare* ANATOMY *and* MORPHOLOGY.)

pistil (PIS-tuhl)   The female part of a plant. In flowering plants, it is at the center of the FLOWER. When fertilized with POLLEN, the pistil develops into FRUIT.

plant kingdom   One of the five KINGDOMS of living things. Most plants derive ENERGY from PHOTOSYNTHESIS.

pollen   The male SEX CELLS in plants. In flowering plants, pollen is produced in thin filaments in the FLOWER called STAMENS. (*See* FERTILIZATION *and* POLLINATION.)
&. When pollen is carried into the air by the wind, it frequently causes allergic reactions (*see* ALLERGY) in humans.

pollination   The carrying of POLLEN grains (the male SEX CELLS in plants) to the female sex cells for FERTILIZATION. Pollination can occur between plants when pollen is carried by the wind or by insects such as the honeybee (*see* CROSS-FERTILIZATION), or within the same plant, in which case it is called self-fertilization.

primates (PREYE-mayts)   The ORDER of MAMMALS that includes monkeys, apes, and human beings. Primates are distinguished from other animals in that they generally possess limbs capable of performing a variety of functions, hands and feet adapted for grasping (including OPPOSABLE THUMBS), flattened snouts, and other anatomical features. (*See* CLASSIFICATION.)

proteins (PROH-teenz, PROH-tee-inz)   Complex ORGANIC MOLECULES made up of AMINO ACIDS. Proteins are basic components of all living CELLS, and are therefore among the principal substances that make up the body. In addition to being necessary for the growth and repair of the body's tissues, proteins provide ENERGY and act as ENZYMES that control CHEMICAL REACTIONS in the CELL.

🔊 Foods that contain a high percentage of protein include meat, fish, poultry, milk products, beans, and nuts.

protista (proh-TIS-tuh)   The KINGDOM of organisms, mostly single celled, whose CELLS contain a NUCLEUS. The AMOEBA is a member of this kingdom.

protoplasm (PROH-tuh-plaz-uhm)   The jellylike material in a CELL, both inside and outside the NUCLEUS, where the CHEMICAL REACTIONS that support life take place.

protozoa (proh-tuh-ZOH-uh)   SINGLE-CELLED animals, such as AMOEBAS, that are the most primitive form of animal life. In modern BIOLOGY, they are classified in the KINGDOM of PROTISTA rather than in the ANIMAL KINGDOM.

🔊 Some protozoa are PARASITES, and may be PATHOGENIC, causing diseases such as MALARIA and DYSENTERY.

punctuated equilibrium   A possible pattern for EVOLUTION; in punctuated equilibrium, long periods of little change in living things are interrupted by short periods of rapid change. There is controversy among biologists over whether the changes of evolution have happened steadily or in a punctuated-equilibrium fashion. (*Compare* GRADUALISM.)

recessive trait   In GENETICS, a trait that must be contributed by both parents in order to appear in the offspring. Recessive traits can be carried in a person's GENES without appearing in that person. For example, a dark-haired person may have one gene for dark hair, which is a DOMINANT TRAIT, and one gene for

light hair, which is recessive. It is thus possible for two dark-haired parents to have a light-haired child, provided each parent contributes a gene for light hair.

recombinant DNA (ree-KOM-buh-nuhnt)   Techniques, usually associated with GENETIC ENGINEERING, in which strands of DNA from different sources are spliced together to form DNA for a new life form. GENE SPLICING is another name for this process.

reptiles   A CLASS of scaly VERTEBRATES that usually reproduce by laying eggs. Lizards, snakes, turtles, and alligators are reptiles. Reptiles are COLD-BLOODED ANIMALS.

🔊 The DINOSAURS were reptiles.

respiration   The conversion of OXYGEN by living things into the ENERGY by which they continue life. Respiration is part of METABOLISM.

🔊 CARBON DIOXIDE is a waste product of respiration.

ribonucleic acid (reye-boh-nooh-KLEE-ik)   *See* RNA.

ribosome (REYE-buh-sohm)   A small, ball-like structure in the CELL, made of PROTEINS and RNA MOLECULES, that serves as a platform on which the cell's proteins are made.

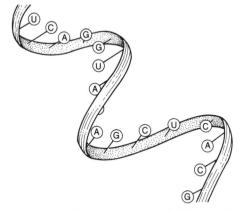

RNA. *An RNA chain; note the single strand. The nucleotide bases of RNA are adenine, guanine, cytosine, and uracil.*

RNA   One of a group of MOLECULES similar in structure to a single strand of DNA. The function of RNA is to carry the information from DNA in the CELL'S NUCLEUS into the body of the cell, to use the GENETIC CODE to assemble PROTEINS, and to com-

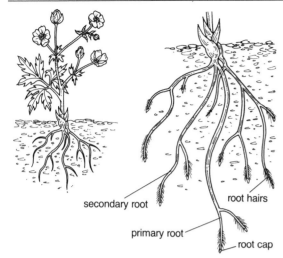

ROOT. *A buttercup and a detail of its root system.*

prise part of the RIBOSOMES that serve as the platform on which protein synthesis takes place.

root   In BIOLOGY, the part of a plant that grows downward and holds the plant in place, absorbs water and MINERALS from the SOIL, and often stores food. The main root of a plant is called the primary root; others are called secondary roots. The hard tip is called the root cap; it protects the growing cells behind it. Root hairs increase the root's absorbing surface.

sex cells   The SPERM and OVA of living things. Sex cells have only half the number of CHROMOSOMES that other CELLS (body cells) have. (*See* MEIOSIS.)

sex chromosomes   The two CHROMOSOMES in each body CELL of a living thing that determine what sex it is.
  ❧ As with other pairs of chromosomes, one of the sex chromosomes is contributed by each parent; they are of two types, X and Y, but the mother supplies only an X-CHROMOSOME. At FERTILIZATION, if the father's SPERM is also carrying an X-chromosome, the child will be female. If the father's sperm is carrying a Y-CHROMOSOME, the child will be male.

sex-linked trait   A trait associated with a GENE that is carried only by the male or female parent.
  ❧ In humans, the gene for COLORBLINDNESS is carried by the X-CHROMOSOME.

sexual reproduction   The production of a new living thing by two parent organisms, with each parent contributing half the material in the DNA of the offspring. The young, genetically different from either parent, can rapidly adapt to their environment by means of NATURAL SELECTION. (*See* CHROMOSOMES *and* MEIOSIS.)

single-celled   Made up of only one CELL.

sociobiology (soh-see-oh-beye-OL-uh-jee)   A recent and controversial area of inquiry in BIOLOGY, based on the belief that many human behavioral and social traits are inherited.

species (SPEE-sheez, SPEE-seez)   A group of closely related and interbreeding living things; the smallest standard unit of biological CLASSIFICATION. Species can be divided into varieties, races, breeds, or subspecies. Red pines, sugar maples, cats, dogs, chimpanzees, and people are species; Siamese cats, beagles, and Mongolians are varieties or races, not species.
  ❧ The term can be used to refer to any group of related things: "This species of NOVEL has become quite popular in recent years."

sperm   The male SEX CELL, typically consisting of a head, midpiece, and tail. (*See* FERTILIZATION.)
  ❧ Sperm are much smaller than the OVA they fertilize.

spore   A reproductive CELL or group of cells, produced by some plants, that is capable of developing into an adult plant without combining with another reproductive cell. The spores of nonflowering plants are analogous to the seeds of flowering plants. (*See* ASEXUAL REPRODUCTION; *compare* SEXUAL REPRODUCTION.) Primitive plants, such as molds, yeasts, and ferns, reproduce by means of spores that are carried by the wind or some other agency to a new location for growth.

stamen (STAY-muhn)   The ORGAN of a FLOWER on which the POLLEN grows.

sugars   CARBOHYDRATES that can supply ENERGY to living things. Common table sugar is sucrose. Some other sugars are fructose, which is found in fruits; lactose, which is found in milk; and GLUCOSE, which is the most common sugar in the bodies of animals and plants.

SYMBIOSIS. *Hippopotamus and egret.*

symbiosis (sim-bee-OH-sis, sim-beye-OH-sis)   The process by which two organisms live together, usually to their mutual benefit. The BACTERIA that live in the digestive tracts of cows, and which allow them to digest CELLULOSE in grass, and the cows themselves are an example of a symbiotic pair.

synapse (SIN-aps, si-NAPS)   A gap between two NERVE CELLS. Nerve signals are sent across the gap by NEUROTRANSMITTERS.

system   A group of bodily ORGANS that have similar structures or work together to perform some function, such as the DIGESTIVE SYSTEM, NERVOUS SYSTEM, and RESPIRATORY SYSTEM.

taproot   The single deep ROOT of many DECIDUOUS TREES that forms the basis for their root SYSTEMS.
   ⋙ Figuratively, a "taproot" is the source of an idea or work: "His childhood in Wales is the taproot of his poetry."

taxonomy (tak-SON-uh-mee)   The CLASSIFICATION of living things.

toxic waste   A general term used to refer to chemical COMPOUNDS produced by industry which, if they are ingested or breathed in by humans, can cause physiological damage. ⋙ The disposal of toxic wastes is a major environmental problem in the United States.

Tyrannosaurus rex (ti-ran-uh-SAWR-uhs REKS)   A large, carnivorous (*see* CARNIVORE) DINOSAUR that walked on two legs. Its name is from the Greek words meaning "tyrant" and "lizard" and the LATIN word for "king."

vertebrates (VUR-tuh-bruhts, VUR-tuh-brayts)   Animals that have a SPINAL CORD enclosed in a backbone.
   ⋙ The five traditional CLASSES of vertebrates are AMPHIBIANS, BIRDS, FISHES, MAMMALS, and REPTILES. (*Compare* INVERTEBRATES.) ⋙ Human beings are vertebrates.

virus (VEYE-ruhs) *plur.* VIRUSES   MICROORGANISMS consisting of RNA MOLECULES wrapped in a protective coating of PROTEINS. Viruses are the most primitive form of life. They depend on other living CELLS for their reproduction and growth. (*See under "Medicine and Health."*)
   ⋙ Viruses cause many diseases. (*See* VIRAL INFECTION.)

vivisection (viv-uh-SEK-shuhn, VIV-uh-sek-shuhn)   The cutting up or dissection of animals in scientific research. *Vivisection* is also a general term for the use of animals as subjects in laboratory experiments, especially in the development of new medical techniques and drugs.

warm-blooded animals   Animals, such as MAMMALS and BIRDS, that maintain a constant body temperature regardless of the temperature of the surroundings. (*Compare* COLD-BLOODED ANIMALS.)

Watson, James D.   *See* WATSON AND CRICK.

Watson and Crick   The two twentieth-century biologists (James D. Watson of the United States and Francis H. C. CRICK of ENGLAND) who first discovered the DOUBLE HELIX of DNA.

X-chromosome   *See* SEX CHROMOSOMES.

xylem (ZEYE-luhm)   The SYSTEM of vessels that transports water in a plant. (*See* PHLOEM.)

Y-chromosome   *See* SEX CHROMOSOMES.

zoology (zoh-OL-uh-jee)   The scientific study and CLASSIFICATION of ANIMALS.

Medicine and Health

The human body, along with its structure, function, illnesses, and characteristic behaviors, is only one of a multitude of living organisms in the world. Nevertheless, we have a special interest in it — a fact that is, as we shall see shortly, reflected in our educational system.

Like all living things except VIRUSES, the human body is composed of CELLS. These cells are arranged into tissues, the tissues into ORGANS, and the organs into organ SYSTEMS. Thus, there are many levels at which an understanding of the body can be sought. We can look at the BIOCHEMISTRY of single cells or tissues, at individual organs, or at the system as a whole. Modern medical science functions at all these levels.

The amount of basic scientific knowledge required to understand the body has become so great that the boundaries between medicine and the sciences are no longer easy to define. Therefore, the material in this section consists of basic terminology from three related but separate bodies of knowledge — ANATOMY, PHYSIOLOGY, and medicine.

Anatomy is the science of the shape and structure of an organism. Human anatomy involves a detailed study of the body parts and their location. PHYSIOLOGY, the science dealing with the function of living organisms, explores the various chemical and physical processes of the body. Medicine is the science and art of diagnosing, treating, and preventing disease in the body. The relationship among these three branches of science is clear: in order to treat the disorders of the human body, an extensive understanding of both bodily structure and bodily function is necessary.

Most students have been exposed to courses labeled "Health" or "Health and Hygiene." As a result, the level of understanding of the basic structure and function of the body is considerably higher than it is for the concepts related to other areas of science. For this reason, editors of major publications routinely assume that their readers possess considerable knowledge of anatomy, physiology, and medicine. Consequently, the following list is much more descriptive than those for the other sciences. Most of the words in this section are frequently used without explanation in the MASS MEDIA, and hence should be part of the vocabulary of the culturally literate.

— J. T.

abdomen (AB-duh-muhn, ab-DOH-muhn)   The part of the body between the THORAX (chest) and PELVIS that encloses the ORGANS of the ABDOMINAL CAVITY; the belly.

abdominal cavity (ab-DOM-uh-nuhl)   The cavity within the ABDOMEN that contains the STOMACH, IN-TESTINES, LIVER, PANCREAS, GALLBLADDER, SPLEEN, and KIDNEYS, and the lower part of the ESOPHAGUS.

abortion   The ending of pregnancy and expulsion of the EMBRYO or FETUS, generally before the embryo or fetus is capable of surviving on its own. Abortion may be brought on intentionally by artificial means

(INDUCED ABORTION) or may occur naturally (SPON-TANEOUS ABORTION, which is commonly referred to as a MISCARRIAGE). (*Compare* STILLBIRTH; *see also* FAMILY PLANNING *and* POPULATION CONTROL.)

abscess (AB-ses)   An inflamed area (*see* INFLAMMA-TION) in the body tissues that is filled with PUS.

Achilles tendon (uh-KIL-eez)   A TENDON connecting the heel bone with the calf muscle of the leg.

     In Greek legend, the hero ACHILLES could be wounded only in the heel.

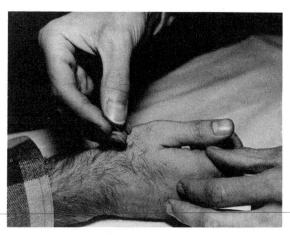

ACUPUNCTURE

acupuncture (AK-yuh-pungk-chuhr)   A technique, which originated in CHINA, for curing disease, reliev-ing pain, or bringing about partial ANESTHESIA by in-serting needles into the body at specific points.

acute disease   A disease or disorder that lasts a short time, comes on rapidly, and is accompanied by distinct symptoms. (*Compare* CHRONIC DISEASE.)

adenoids (AD-n-oydz, AD-noydz)   Two masses of tis-sue at the junction of the nose and throat, which, like the TONSILS, function in the LYMPHATIC SYSTEM, where they help filter out harmful MICROORGANISMS that can cause INFECTION. Continually swollen ade-noids may interfere with breathing and affect speech.

     Adenoids are sometimes surgically removed along with the tonsils if they are persistently inflamed (*see* INFLAMMATION).   Swollen adenoids give a dis-tinctive nasal sound to the voice.

adipose tissue (AD-uh-pohs)   CONNECTIVE TISSUE that contains CELLS filled with FAT; fat tissue.

adrenal glands (uh-DREEN-l)   Two small GLANDS, one located near the upper part of each KIDNEY, that function in the ENDOCRINE SYSTEM. Part of each ad-renal gland secretes ADRENALINE; another part se-cretes other important HORMONES.

adrenaline (uh-DREN-l-in)   A HORMONE secreted by the ADRENAL GLANDS that helps the body meet phys-ical or emotional STRESS (*see* ENDOCRINE SYSTEM). Also called EPINEPHRINE.

     Adrenaline plays a very large role in the FIGHT OR FLIGHT REACTION, which refers to the various processes that occur within the body when it is con-fronted with some form of mental or physical STRESS.   Figuratively, the term *adrenaline* is used in speak-ing of a high state of excitement: "When the race started, the adrenaline really started pumping."

aerobics (air-OH-biks)   Exercise designed specifically to improve CARDIOVASCULAR fitness and, subse-quently, the body's use of OXYGEN. Also called AERO-BIC EXERCISE.

     The term *aerobics* usually refers to a specific kind of vigorous exercise, sometimes involving dance steps, that is set to music. Other forms of aerobic ex-ercise include running, cycling, and swimming.

AIDS (AYDZ)   ACRONYM for *Acquired Immune De-ficiency Syndrome*, a fatal disease caused by the hu-man immunodeficiency VIRUS, or HIV. The virus, which is transmitted from one individual to another through the exchange of body fluids (such as BLOOD, SALIVA, or SEMEN), attacks WHITE BLOOD CELLS, thereby causing the body to lose its capacity to ward off INFECTION. As a result, most AIDS patients usu-ally die of OPPORTUNISTIC INFECTIONS that strike their debilitated bodies. AIDS first appeared in the United States in 1981, primarily among HOMOSEXU-ALS and INTRAVENOUS drug users who share needles, but it is now spreading among HETEROSEXUALS in this country.

     Believed to have originated in AFRICA, AIDS has become an EPIDEMIC, infecting 10 to 12 million peo-ple worldwide. By the year 2000, it is estimated that 40 million will have contracted the disease, with some sources predicting much higher numbers. In the United States, over 150,000 people have died of AIDS.

alcoholism   A CHRONIC DISEASE associated with the excessive and habitual use of alcohol; the disease, if left unattended, worsens and can kill the sufferer. Alcoholism is marked by physical dependency and can cause disorders in many ORGANS of the body, including the LIVER (*see* CIRRHOSIS), STOMACH, INTESTINES, and BRAIN. It is also associated with abnormal HEART rhythms, with certain CANCERS, and, because of loss of appetite, with poor nutrition. The cause of alcoholism is very complicated and most often involves a mixture of physical, psychological and possibly genetic factors.

allergy A highly sensitive reaction of the body to certain substances, such as POLLEN, that are present in amounts that do not affect most people. Common indications of allergy include sneezing, skin rashes, itching, and runny nose.

Alzheimer's disease (AHLTS-heye-muhrz, ALTS-heye-muhrz, AWLTS-heye-muhrz) A disease in which mental capacity decreases because of the breakdown of BRAIN CELLS.

&. Alzheimer's disease is a major cause of loss of intellectual function in middle-aged and elderly people.

amniocentesis (am-nee-oh-sen-TEE-sis) A procedure for finding certain disorders in a FETUS during pregnancy. In amniocentesis, a small amount of the salty LIQUID that surrounds the fetus in the AMNIOTIC SAC is drawn out through a needle inserted into the mother's ABDOMEN. The fluid generally contains some isolated CELLS from the fetus. These cells are analyzed to detect abnormalities in the CHROMOSOMES of the fetus, such as DOWN'S SYNDROME, and may also be used to judge some other conditions, such as the maturity of the fetus's LUNGS.

amniotic fluid (am-nee-OT-ik) The fluid, resembling salt water, contained in the AMNIOTIC SAC; the EMBRYO or FETUS floats in the amniotic fluid.

amniotic sac A two-layered membrane that surrounds the EMBRYO or FETUS in the UTERUS. The amniotic sac is filled with a watery fluid in which the embryo or fetus is suspended. (*See* REPRODUCTIVE SYSTEMS.)

analgesic (an-l-JEE-zik, an-l-JEE-sik) A drug, such as aspirin, that relieves pain in the body.

anemia (uh-NEE-mee-uh) A condition in which the capacity of the BLOOD to carry OXYGEN is decreased because of too few RED BLOOD CELLS in circulation, or because of too little HEMOGLOBIN.

&. Because people suffering from anemia often appear weak and pale, the term is frequently used to describe general apathy or weakness: "The team's performance has been pretty anemic these past few weeks."

anesthesia (an-is-THEE-zhuh) Loss of sensation or consciousness. Anesthesia can be induced by an ANESTHETIC, by ACUPUNCTURE, or as the result of injury or disease.

anesthetic (an-is-THET-ik) A substance that causes loss of sensation or consciousness. With the aid of an anesthetic, people can undergo surgery without pain. (*See* GENERAL ANESTHETIC *and* LOCAL ANESTHETIC.)

angina pectoris (an-JEYE-nuh, AN-juh-nuh PEK-tuh-ris) Severe chest pains caused by an insufficient supply of BLOOD to the HEART.

angioplasty (AN-jee-uh-plas-tee) A surgical technique in which a CATHETER containing a small balloon is inserted into ARTERIES around the HEART. The balloon is inflated to compress deposits of fatty substances blocking the artery, thereby restoring the flow of BLOOD.

&. Also called balloon therapy.

anorexia A short name for ANOREXIA NERVOSA.

anorexia nervosa (an-uh-REK-see-uh nur-VOH-suh) A PSYCHOSOMATIC disorder in which the sufferer refuses to eat and undertakes activities (such as self-induced vomiting) to bring about extreme weight loss. Anorexia, which is also characterized by a distorted self-image, occurs most often in young women aged twelve to twenty-one, and may result in death if medical treatment is not obtained. Treatment for anorexia often includes extensive counseling to reveal underlying emotional problems.

antibiotic (an-ti-beye-OT-ik, an-teye-beye-OT-ik, an-ti-bee-OT-ik) A substance that destroys or inhibits the growth of MICROORGANISMS and is therefore used to treat some INFECTIONS. One of the most familiar antibiotics is PENICILLIN.

antibodies (AN-ti-bod-eez) PROTEINS in the BLOOD that are produced by the body in response to specific ANTIGENS (such as BACTERIA). (*See* IMMUNE SYSTEM.)

anticoagulants (an-tee-koh-AG-yuh-luhnts, an-teye-koh-AG-yuh-luhnts) Substances that slow down or prevent BLOOD clotting.

antidepressants Drugs that prevent or relieve the symptoms of depression. Various psychological disorders are treated with antidepressants.

antigens (AN-ti-juhnz) Substances that are foreign to the body and cause the production of ANTIBODIES. TOXINS, invading BACTERIA and VIRUSES, and the CELLS of transplanted ORGANS can all function as antigens.

antihistamines (an-tee-HIS-tuh-meenz, an-tee-HIS-tuh-muhnz) Drugs that counteract the effects of a substance in the body called histamine. The body releases histamine, which causes many of the symptoms associated with ALLERGIES (sneezing, watery eyes, runny nose), in response to external agents such as POLLEN.

antiseptics Substances that prevent or inhibit the growth of disease-causing MICROORGANISMS.

anus (AY-nuhs) The opening through which FECES pass out of the body.

aorta (ay-AWR-tuh) The main BLOOD VESSEL of the body; it carries BLOOD from the left side of the HEART to other ARTERIES throughout the body. (*See* CIRCULATORY SYSTEM.)

appendectomy (ap-uhn-DEK-tuh-mee) The surgical removal of the APPENDIX.

appendicitis (uh-pen-duh-SEYE-tis) INFLAMMATION of the APPENDIX.

appendix A small saclike ORGAN located at the upper end of the LARGE INTESTINE. The appendix has no known function in present-day humans, but it may have played a role in the DIGESTIVE SYSTEM in humans of earlier times. The appendix is also called the VERMIFORM APPENDIX because of its wormlike ("vermiform") shape.

arteries BLOOD VESSELS that carry BLOOD away from the HEART and to the body tissues. (*Compare* VEINS; *see* CIRCULATORY SYSTEM.)

arteriosclerosis (ahr-teer-ee-oh-skluh-ROH-sis) A disease commonly called hardening of the ARTERIES. In arteriosclerosis, the walls of the arteries thicken and harden. The loss of flexibility results in a lessening of the flow of BLOOD to the various ORGANS of the body. (*Compare* ATHEROSCLEROSIS; *see* CIRCULATORY SYSTEM.)

arthritis INFLAMMATION of tissues in the joints, usually resulting in pain and stiffness.

arthroscope (AHR-thruh-skohp) A surgical instrument that uses FIBER OPTICS to allow physicians to see and perform surgery inside joints. The surgery involves only the insertion of a small tube into the joint. ❧ Arthroscopic surgery allows rapid recovery, and one often sees it mentioned with regard to injuries of athletes.

ascorbic acid (uh-SKAWR-bik) A form of VITAMIN C.

asthma (AZ-muh) A CHRONIC DISEASE of the RESPIRATORY SYSTEM, characterized by sudden recurring attacks of difficult breathing, wheezing, and coughing. During an attack, the BRONCHIAL TUBES go into spasms, becoming narrower and less able to move air into the LUNGS. Various substances to which the sufferer has an ALLERGY, such as animal hair, dust, POLLEN, or certain foods, can trigger an attack.

astigmatism (uh-STIG-muh-tiz-uhm) A condition in which the curvature of the CORNEA of the EYE is uneven, causing a blurring of vision. Astigmatism is normally corrected by glasses.

atherosclerosis (ath-uh-roh-skluh-ROH-sis) A form of ARTERIOSCLEROSIS in which the ARTERIES become clogged by the buildup of fatty substances, which eventually reduces the flow of BLOOD to the tissues. These fatty substances, called PLAQUE, are made up largely of CHOLESTEROL. (*Compare* ARTERIOSCLEROSIS; *see* CIRCULATORY SYSTEM.)

athlete's foot An INFECTION of the SKIN that usually attacks the feet, causing itching, peeling, and redness. Athlete's foot is caused by a kind of FUNGUS that thrives in damp places.

atria (AY-tree-uh) *sing.* ATRIUM (AY-tree-uhm) The two upper chambers in the HEART, which receive BLOOD from the VEINS and push it into the VENTRICLES. (*See* CIRCULATORY SYSTEM.)

atrophy (AT-ruh-fee) The wasting away or decrease in size of an ORGAN or tissue in the body. The muscles of persons who have a body part affected by PARALYSIS may atrophy through lack of use.

❧ The term is also used in a more general way to refer to a wasting process: "Since he stopped playing, his PIANO skills have atrophied."

auditory nerve The NERVE that connects the INNER EAR with the BRAIN. One of its two branches carries the sensation of sound to the brain; the other is involved in maintaining balance.

auricles (AWR-i-kuhlz) An old term for the ATRIA of the HEART.

autonomic nervous system (aw-tuh-NOM-ik) The part of the NERVOUS SYSTEM that controls involuntary functions of the body (those not controlled consciously), such as DIGESTION, the beating of the HEART, and the operation of GLANDS in the ENDOCRINE SYSTEM.

AZT (ay-zee-TEE) A drug used in the treatment of AIDS. It does not cure the disease, but does prolong the life of the patient in some cases.

bacterial infection An INFECTION caused by BACTERIA. The growth of many disease-causing bacteria can be halted by the use of ANTIBIOTICS. (*Compare* VIRAL INFECTION.)

🐚 Diseases caused by bacterial infections include DIPHTHERIA, GONORRHEA, TUBERCULOSIS, and TYPHOID FEVER.

balanced diet A diet that contains the proper proportions of CARBOHYDRATES, FATS, PROTEINS, VITAMINS, MINERALS, and water necessary to maintain good health.

balloon therapy *See* ANGIOPLASTY.

barbiturates (bahr-BICH-uh-rits, bahr-BICH-uh-rayts) Substances derived from an ORGANIC COMPOUND that are used as sedatives and sleep inducers. Barbiturates, which work by depressing the activity of the CENTRAL NERVOUS SYSTEM, are sometimes used in the treatment of illnesses such as EPILEPSY.

benign (bi-NEYEN) A descriptive term for conditions that present no danger to life or well-being. Benign is the opposite of MALIGNANT.

🐚 The term *benign* is used when describing TUMORS or growths that do not threaten the health of an individual.

bile A bitter fluid produced by the LIVER and stored in the GALLBLADDER. Bile is discharged into the SMALL INTESTINE when needed to aid in the DIGESTION of fats (*see* DIGESTIVE SYSTEM).

🐚 *Bile* is sometimes used figuratively to denote bitterness in general: "His writing was full of bile."

bile ducts The passages in the LIVER and GALLBLADDER that move BILE into the DUODENUM.

biofeedback (beye-oh-FEED-bak) A training technique by which a person learns how to regulate certain body functions, such as HEART rate, BLOOD PRESSURE, or BRAIN wave patterns, that are normally considered to be involuntary. The person learns by watching special monitoring instruments attached to the body that record changes in these functions.

🐚 Biofeedback has had some success in the treatment of such disorders as CHRONIC headaches and back pain.

biological clock The innate rhythm of behavior and body activity in living things. A twenty-four-hour cycle of body activity, which operates in some organisms, is called the CIRCADIAN RHYTHM.

🐚 Although the term *biological clock* refers to all innate timing mechanisms, it is often used when describing certain body functions that are subject to this rhythm, such as the loss of fertility with age.

Black Death *See* BUBONIC PLAGUE.

black lung A CHRONIC DISEASE of the LUNGS caused by inhaling coal dust over long periods. Common among coal miners, black lung is perhaps one of the best-known OCCUPATIONAL DISEASES.

bladder A stretchable saclike structure in the body that holds FLUIDS. The term is used most often to refer to the URINARY BLADDER, which is part of the EXCRETORY SYSTEM. Another kind of bladder is the GALLBLADDER.

blind spot A small region in the visual field (the area scanned by the EYE) that cannot be seen. The blind spot corresponds to an area in the eye where the OPTIC NERVE enters the RETINA.

🐚 In a general sense, the term is used to refer to an inability to see things that might be obvious to another observer: "He has a blind spot as far as his daughter's behavior is concerned."

blood The FLUID circulating through the HEART, ARTERIES, VEINS, and CAPILLARIES of the CIRCULATORY SYSTEM. Blood carries OXYGEN and nutrients to the CELLS of the body, and removes waste materials and CARBON DIOXIDE. It is composed of PLASMA (mainly water, but with a mixture of HORMONES, nutrients, GASES, ANTIBODIES, and wastes), RED BLOOD CELLS (which carry oxygen), WHITE BLOOD CELLS (which help combat INFECTION), and PLATELETS (which help the blood clot).

blood group *See* BLOOD TYPE.

blood pressure The PRESSURE of the BLOOD against the walls of the BLOOD VESSELS, especially the ARTERIES. It is expressed in two figures, said to be one "over" the other: the systolic pressure, which is the pressure when the left VENTRICLE of the HEART contracts to push the blood through the body; and the diastolic pressure, which is the pressure when the ventricle relaxes and fills with blood. Blood pressure is affected by the strength of the heartbeat, the volume of blood in the body, the elasticity of the blood vessels, and the age and general health of the person. (*See* CIRCULATORY SYSTEM.)

blood transfusion *See* TRANSFUSION, BLOOD.

blood type One of many groups into which a person's BLOOD can be categorized, based on the presence or absence of specific ANTIGENS in the blood. Blood type is inherited. Also called BLOOD GROUP.

   ⚓ Blood TRANSFUSIONS can be given only between donors and recipients who have compatible types; if the types are not compatible, the blood of the recipient forms ANTIBODIES against the blood of the donor. There are four basic groupings — A, B, AB, and O — and within these groupings, the RH FACTOR may be present or absent.

blood vessels The flexible tubular canals through which BLOOD circulates in the body. ARTERIES, VEINS, and CAPILLARIES are all kinds of blood vessels. (*See* CIRCULATORY SYSTEM.)

bone marrow *See* MARROW.

botulism (BOCH-uh-liz-uhm) A severe form of FOOD POISONING, often fatal if not treated quickly. Botulism is caused by a kind of BACTERIUM that produces a TOXIN, and is sometimes present in improperly canned or preserved foods.

brain The central ORGAN in the NERVOUS SYSTEM, protected by the skull. The brain consists of the *medulla*, which sends signals from the SPINAL CORD to the rest of the brain and also controls the AUTONOMIC NERVOUS SYSTEM; the *pons*, a mass of NERVE

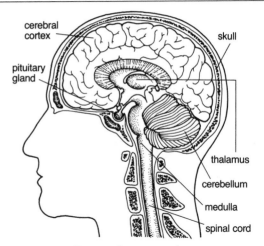

BRAIN. *A cutaway view.*

fibers connected to the medulla; the CEREBELLUM, which controls balance and coordination; and the CEREBRUM, the outer layer of which, the CEREBRAL CORTEX, is the location of memory, sight, speech, and other higher functions.

The cerebrum contains two hemispheres (the LEFT BRAIN and the RIGHT BRAIN), each of which controls different functions. In general, the right hemisphere controls the left side of the body and such functions as spatial perception, while the left hemisphere controls the right side of the body and such functions as speech.

Under the cerebral cortex are the THALAMUS, the main relay center between the medulla and the cerebrum; and the HYPOTHALAMUS, which controls BLOOD PRESSURE, body temperature, hunger, thirst, sex drive, and other visceral functions.

bronchial tubes (BRONG-kee-uhl) The system of tubelike structures that connects the TRACHEA to the LUNGS. (*See* RESPIRATORY SYSTEM.)

bubonic plague (byooh-BON-ik, booh-BON-ik PLAYG) A highly CONTAGIOUS DISEASE, usually fatal, affecting the LYMPHATIC SYSTEM. The bubonic plague is caused by BACTERIA transmitted to humans by rat-borne fleas.

   ⚓ From 1347 to 1351, a disease known as the BLACK DEATH, similar to the bubonic plague, entered EUROPE from ASIA and killed a large percentage of the population, sometimes wiping out entire towns. It caused widespread social changes in Europe.

bursa (BUR-suh) A fluid-filled sac or cavity that reduces friction between the bones, LIGAMENTS, and TENDONS in the body's joints.

bursitis (buhr-SEYE-tis) INFLAMMATION of a BURSA. Common locations of bursitis include the joints of the shoulder, knee, and elbow.

bypass, coronary See CORONARY BYPASS SURGERY.

Caesarean section (si-ZAIR-ee-uhn) Childbirth by surgical removal of the FETUS through an incision made in the wall of the ABDOMEN and in the UTERUS, usually used as an alternative when natural delivery through the VAGINA is considered risky. The number of Caesarean sections in the United States has increased sharply in recent years, causing concern among patients, surgeons, and insurers.

🔊 The term derives from the traditional belief that JULIUS CAESAR was born by this method.

cancer A disease characterized by rapid growth of CELLS in the body, often in the form of a TUMOR. Cancer is *invasive* — that is, it can spread to surrounding tissues. Although this disease is a leading cause of death in the United States, research has provided considerable insight into its many causes (which may include diet, VIRUSES, or environmental factors) and options for treatment (which include RADIATION, CHEMOTHERAPY, and surgery).

🔊 The term *cancer* is often used to describe a nonmedical condition that is undesirable, destructive, and invasive: "WATERGATE was a cancer on the presidency."

canines (KAY-neyenz) The pointed TEETH in the front of the mouth (two on the top and two on the bottom) next to the INCISORS. These teeth are also known as the eyeteeth.

capillaries (KAP-uh-ler-eez) The tiny BLOOD VESSELS throughout the body that connect ARTERIES and VEINS. Capillaries form an intricate network around body tissues in order to distribute OXYGEN and nutrients to the CELLS and remove waste substances. (*See* CIRCULATORY SYSTEM.)

carcinogenic (kahr-suh-nuh-JEN-ik) A descriptive term for things capable of causing CANCER.

carcinoma (kahr-suh-NOH-muh) A MALIGNANT TUMOR in the tissues that make up the SKIN, GLANDS, MUCOUS MEMBRANES, and LINING OF ORGANS.

cardiac arrest See HEART ATTACK.

cardiology (kahr-dee-OL-uh-jee) The branch of medicine devoted to the study and care of the HEART and CIRCULATORY SYSTEM.

cardiopulmonary resuscitation (CPR) [kahr-dee-oh-POOL-muh-ner-ee ri-sus-i-TAY-shuhn] An emergency lifesaving procedure used to revive someone who has stopped breathing or whose HEART has ceased functioning. CPR uses heart massage and mouth-to-mouth resuscitation to get the heart or LUNGS working again.

cardiovascular (kahr-dee-oh-VAS-kyuh-luhr) A descriptive term for the HEART and the BLOOD VESSELS.

cartilage (KAHR-tl-ij) A kind of tough but elastic CONNECTIVE TISSUE that can withstand considerable PRESSURE. It makes up portions of the SKELETAL SYSTEM, such as the linings of the joints, where it cushions against shock. Cartilage is also found in other body structures, such as the nose and external EAR.

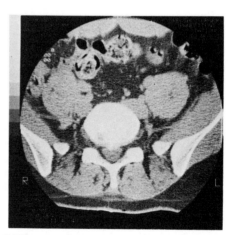

CAT SCAN. *A cross-sectional view of the spine.*

CAT scan (KAT) A three-dimensional image of a cross-section of the body made with X-RAYS that is useful in diagnosing disease (for example, in detecting TUMORS). *CAT* stands for *computerized axial* TOMOGRAPHY, the name of the method used to produce the image.

cataract (KAT-uh-rakt) A loss in the transparency of the LENS of the EYE, which reduces a person's ability to see. The condition can be treated by surgically removing the lens and replacing it with an artificial one, or with corrective eyeglasses or contact lenses.

catheter (KATH-uh-tuhr) A thin tube inserted into one of the channels or BLOOD VESSELS in the body to remove FLUIDS, create an opening into an internal cavity, or to administer injections.

catheterization (kath-uh-tuhr-uh-ZAY-shuhn) Insertion of a CATHETER into the body. Common types of this procedure include cardiac catheterization, in which a catheter is inserted into the HEART through a VEIN in the arm to diagnose heart disease, and URINARY BLADDER catheterization, in which a catheter is inserted into the URETHRA to permit URINE to flow out of the urinary bladder.

cellulite (SEL-yuh-leyet, SEL-yuh-leet) A popular term for FAT that is difficult to remove by dieting, and often has a dimpled appearance. There is no physiological difference between cellulite and ordinary fat.

central nervous system The BRAIN and SPINAL CORD. (*See* NERVOUS SYSTEM).

cerebellum (ser-uh-BEL-uhm) The part of the BRAIN that helps control muscle coordination.

cerebral (suh-REE-bruhl, SER-uh-bruhl) A descriptive term for things pertaining to the BRAIN or CEREBRUM.

    ❧ The term is also used figuratively to describe things that appeal to the intellect.

cerebral cortex The surface layer of gray tissue of the CEREBRUM, frequently called the gray matter. The large size of the cerebral cortex in humans distinguishes them from other animals. Specific parts of the cortex control specific functions, including sensation, voluntary muscle movement, thought, reasoning, and memory.

cerebral palsy (PAWL-zee) A disorder marked by lack of muscle coordination and sometimes accompanied by speech defects. It is caused by BRAIN damage present at birth or experienced during birth or infancy.

cerebral thrombosis (throm-BOH-sis) A THROMBOSIS in the BRAIN.

cerebrum (SER-uh-bruhm, suh-REE-bruhm) The largest part of the BRAIN, consisting of two lobes, the right and left cerebral hemispheres. The cerebrum controls thought and voluntary movement. (*See* CEREBRAL CORTEX, LEFT BRAIN, *and* RIGHT BRAIN.)

cervix (SUR-viks) The narrow outer end of the UTERUS. A portion of the cervix extends into the VAGINA. (*See* REPRODUCTIVE SYSTEMS.)

chemotherapy (kee-moh-THER-uh-pee) The treatment of disease with chemicals. The term *chemotherapy* often refers to a kind of treatment for CANCER in which chemicals are administered to destroy cancer CELLS.

    ❧ There are often side effects to chemotherapy, a common one being the temporary loss of hair.

chicken pox A mild but highly CONTAGIOUS DISEASE, caused by a VIRUS and characterized by slight fever and the eruption of blisters on the SKIN. Chicken pox is classified as a disease of childhood, although it can occur in adults.

    ❧ Children who have had chicken pox are immune to future infection by the virus that causes it.

chiropractic (keye-ruh-PRAK-tik) A system of treating disease that involves manipulation of the backbone and other body parts. In chiropractic, disorders of the NERVES are considered the cause of illness.

cholera (KOL-uh-ruh) An ACUTE DISEASE, and an INFECTIOUS DISEASE, caused by a kind of BACTERIUM that affects the INTESTINES. Transmitted by food or water that has been contaminated with raw sewage, cholera is often fatal, and is characterized by severe vomiting, DIARRHEA, and collapse.

cholesterol (kuh-LES-tuh-rawl, kuh-LES-tuh-rohl) A white soapy substance found in the tissues of the body and in certain foods, such as animal FATS, oils, and egg yolks. Cholesterol has been linked to HEART disease and ATHEROSCLEROSIS (it collects on the walls of ARTERIES and interferes with the flow of BLOOD). High levels of cholesterol in the blood are considered to be unhealthy. (*See* SATURATED FATS, HDL, *and* LDL.)

chronic *See* CHRONIC DISEASE.

chronic disease A disease of long duration. (*Compare* ACUTE DISEASE.)

circadian rhythm (suhr-KAY-dee-uhn) An activity cycle lasting twenty-four hours. Many living things, including humans, follow a circadian rhythm. (*See* BIOLOGICAL CLOCK.)

circulatory system The SYSTEM in the body by which BLOOD and LYMPH are circulated. The parts of

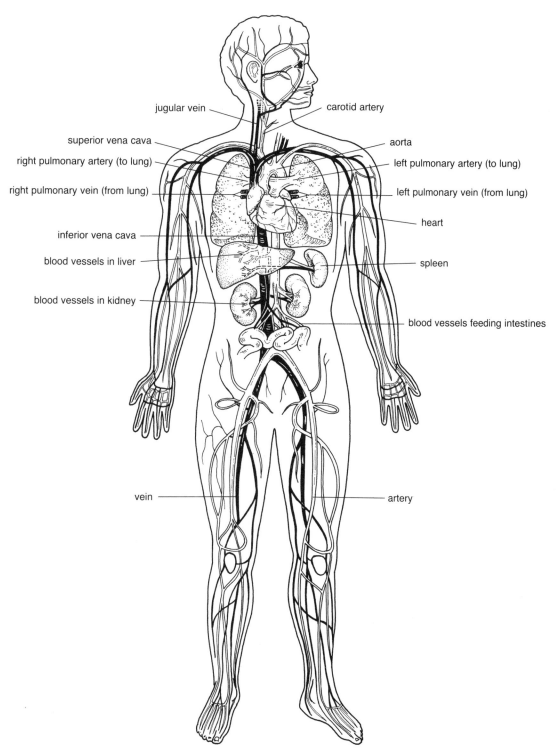

jugular vein

carotid artery

superior vena cava

aorta

right pulmonary artery (to lung)

left pulmonary artery (to lung)

right pulmonary vein (from lung)

left pulmonary vein (from lung)

heart

inferior vena cava

blood vessels in liver

spleen

blood vessels in kidney

blood vessels feeding intestines

vein

artery

CIRCULATORY SYSTEM. *In this illustration veins are black and arteries are white.*

the circulatory system include the HEART, along with all the ARTERIES, VEINS, and CAPILLARIES. The ORGANS of the LYMPHATIC SYSTEM are also considered to be part of the circulatory system. Nutrients, OXYGEN, and other vital substances are carried throughout the body by the blood, which is pumped by rhythmic contractions of the heart. Blood is pumped from the heart to the arteries, which branch into smaller and smaller vessels as they move away from the heart. The blood passes oxygen and nutrients to the CELLS and picks up waste in the capillaries, then returns to the heart via a system of veins.

circumcision (sur-kuhm-SIZH-uhn)   The surgical removal of the SKIN that covers the tip of the PENIS, usually performed soon after birth. Although circumcision is common in the United States, the procedure is no longer widely recommended as a medical necessity by physicians.

   ▸ Circumcision is practiced as a religious ceremony by JEWS and MOSLEMS.

cirrhosis (suh-ROH-sis)   A CHRONIC DISEASE of the LIVER, characterized by replacement of normal liver CELLS with a form of CONNECTIVE TISSUE. Owing to the scarring caused by this disease, irreversible damage to the liver can result.

   ▸ Cirrhosis is often associated with ALCOHOLISM.

clock, biological   *See* BIOLOGICAL CLOCK.

cocaine   A drug derived from the leaves of a shrub in SOUTH AMERICA that has an intoxicating effect on the body and can result in dependency if frequently used. Cocaine is used medically as a LOCAL ANESTHETIC.

   ▸ Cocaine use constitutes a major drug problem in the United States.

codeine (KOH-deen)   A drug obtained from OPIUM or MORPHINE that is used as a pain reliever and cough remedy.

colitis (kuh-LEYE-tis)   INFLAMMATION of the MUCOUS MEMBRANE that lines the COLON. Colitis is characterized by pain in the ABDOMEN, with alternating episodes of constipation and DIARRHEA.

colon   The middle and longest part of the LARGE INTESTINE. (*See* DIGESTIVE SYSTEM.)

colorblindness   A defect in perception of colors, caused by a deficiency of certain specialized CELLS in the RETINA that are sensitive to different colors. The condition may be partial (as in "red-green colorblindness," in which a person cannot distinguish red from green), or complete (in which the person sees all colors as gray).

   ▸ By extension, the law is said to be colorblind in its judgments, which are supposed to ignore a DEFENDANT's race.

coma (KOH-muh)   An abnormal state of deep unconsciousness. A coma may occur as the result of TRAUMA to the head, disease (such as MENINGITIS, STROKE, or DIABETES MELLITUS), or poisoning.

communicable disease   Any disease transmitted from one person or animal to another; also called CONTAGIOUS DISEASE. Sometimes QUARANTINE is required to prevent the spread of disease.

conception   FERTILIZATION; the union of the SPERM and OVUM to form a ZYGOTE. (*See* REPRODUCTIVE SYSTEMS.)

congenital (kuhn-JEN-i-tl)   A descriptive term for a disease or condition that is present at birth but is not HEREDITARY.

conjunctivitis (kuhn-jungk-tuh-VEYE-tis)   INFLAMMATION of the conjunctiva, the transparent MUCOUS MEMBRANE that lines the inner surface of the eyelid and covers the front part of the eyeball. Often called pinkeye.

connective tissue   Body tissue that serves to connect or support other tissues or parts. CARTILAGE, TENDONS, and bone are all kinds of connective tissue.

consumption   *See* TUBERCULOSIS.

contagious disease   An INFECTIOUS DISEASE that is spread through contact with infected individuals; also called a COMMUNICABLE DISEASE. Contact with the bodily secretions of such individuals, or with objects that they have contaminated, can also spread this kind of disease.

contraception   Any practice that serves to prevent CONCEPTION during sexual activity.

convulsion   A severe, often violent involuntary contraction of the muscles. Convulsions may be caused by high fevers or poisoning, and often accompany such diseases as EPILEPSY.

cornea (KAWR-nee-uh) The transparent outer covering of the front of the EYE that covers the IRIS and PUPIL.

coronary (KOR-uh-ner-ee, KAWR-uh-ner-ee) A descriptive term for the HEART or the ARTERIES that supply BLOOD to the heart muscle.

🕭 The word *coronary* is often used by itself in an informal sense to refer to a HEART ATTACK or CORONARY THROMBOSIS.

coronary arteries The two ARTERIES that supply BLOOD to the HEART TISSUE.

coronary bypass surgery A surgical procedure to restore normal BLOOD supply to the HEART by creating new routes for the blood to travel into the heart when one or both of the CORONARY ARTERIES have become clogged or obstructed (possibly as the result of ATHEROSCLEROSIS). These new routes are created by removing BLOOD VESSELS from another part of the body (most often the VEINS of the leg) and grafting them onto the heart to bypass the clogged arteries.

🕭 Often, people will call this kind of surgery a double, triple, or quadruple bypass, referring to the number of diseased coronary arteries that had to be bypassed during the operation.

coronary thrombosis A THROMBOSIS in the HEART.

cortisone (KAWR-ti-zohn) A HORMONE secreted by the ADRENAL GLANDS that is important in the METABOLISM of FATS and CARBOHYDRATES. It is used in medicine to treat some forms of ARTHRITIS and to reduce INFLAMMATION.

CPR *See* CARDIOPULMONARY RESUSCITATION.

cranium (KRAY-nee-uhm) The part of the skull that encloses the BRAIN.

crown The part of a TOOTH above the gum, covered with ENAMEL.

cyst (SIST) An abnormal saclike structure that develops in the body and is filled with FLUID or semisolid material.

cystic fibrosis (SIS-tik feye-BROH-sis) A CHRONIC DISEASE, and a CONGENITAL disease, that affects certain GLANDS in the body, particularly the SWEAT GLANDS, the PANCREAS, and the glands in the MUCOUS MEMBRANES of the RESPIRATORY SYSTEM. Cystic fibrosis causes recurring respiratory disorders (*see*

RESPIRATION) and interferes with the production of ENZYMES by the pancreas.

dentin The hard, bony material beneath the ENAMEL of a TOOTH. The bulk of a tooth is made up of dentin.

dermatitis (dur-muh-TEYE-tis) INFLAMMATION of the SKIN. Itching and redness are the basic symptoms of dermatitis, which has a variety of causes, including ALLERGIES and exposure of the skin to irritants such as chemicals or sunlight.

dermatology (dur-muh-TOL-uh-jee) The branch of medicine devoted to the study and care of the SKIN.

diabetes mellitus (deye-uh-BEE-teez, deye-uh-BEE-tuhs MEL-uh-tuhs) A CHRONIC DISEASE in which CARBOHYDRATES cannot be metabolized properly (*see* METABOLISM) because the PANCREAS fails to secrete an adequate amount of INSULIN. Without enough insulin, carbohydrate metabolism is upset, and levels of SUGAR in the BLOOD rise.

dialysis (deye-AL-uh-sis) The separation of large MOLECULES from small molecules by passage through a membrane.

🕭 A common treatment for KIDNEY disease is the use of a dialysis machine to filter toxic substances from the blood, a function that the kidneys normally perform.

diaphragm (DEYE-uh-fram) A dome-shaped structure made up of muscle and CONNECTIVE TISSUE that separates the ABDOMINAL CAVITY from the THORAX and functions in RESPIRATION. By movement of the diaphragm, air is either drawn into the LUNGS or forced out of them.

The term *diaphragm* can also refer to a small flexible cap, usually made of rubber, that fits over the CERVIX and is used for CONTRACEPTION.

diarrhea (deye-uh-REE-uh) The frequent passage of abnormally watery FECES, when this passage is a sign of disease.

diastolic (deye-uh-STOL-ik) *See* BLOOD PRESSURE.

digestion The breaking down of food, which is made up of complex ORGANIC MOLECULES, into smaller MOLECULES that the body can absorb and use for maintenance and growth.

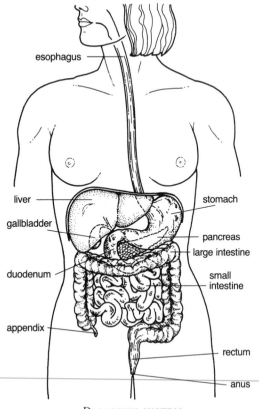

DIGESTIVE SYSTEM

labels: esophagus, liver, gallbladder, duodenum, appendix, stomach, pancreas, large intestine, small intestine, rectum, anus

digestive system   The ORGANS and GLANDS in the body that are responsible for DIGESTION. The digestive system begins with the mouth and extends through the ESOPHAGUS, STOMACH, SMALL INTESTINE, and LARGE INTESTINE, ending with the RECTUM and ANUS. Other organs in this SYSTEM include the LIVER, PANCREAS, GALLBLADDER, and APPENDIX.

diphtheria (dif-THEER-ee-uh, dip-THEER-ee-uh)   An ACUTE DISEASE, and a CONTAGIOUS DISEASE, caused by BACTERIA that invade MUCOUS MEMBRANES in the body, especially those found in the throat. The bacteria produce toxic substances that can spread throughout the body.

ꙮ In developed countries, diphtheria has been virtually wiped out through an active program of infant IMMUNIZATION.

diuretic (deye-uh-RET-ik)   A substance that increases the rate of URINE production.

Down syndrome   A CONGENITAL condition, caused by an abnormality in the CHROMOSOMES, marked by moderate to severe mental retardation and changes in certain physical features.

duodenum (dooh-uh-DEE-nuhm, dooh-OD-n-uhm)   The first part of the SMALL INTESTINE, located just below the STOMACH. (*See* DIGESTIVE SYSTEM.)

dysentery (DIS-uhn-ter-ee)   A painful disease of the INTESTINES characterized by INFLAMMATION and DIARRHEA. Dysentery may be caused by BACTERIA or VIRUSES, or may occur as the result of infestation with an AMOEBA.

ꙮ Dysentery can be transmitted by contact with water or food that has been contaminated by human waste. Public health and sanitation procedures in developed countries, however, have largely eliminated this means of transmission.

dyslexia (dis-LEK-see-uh)   Difficulty in reading when experienced by persons with normal vision and normal or above-normal intelligence. A common example of dyslexia is reading words with the letters in reverse order, as in *fyl* for *fly*.

ear   The ORGAN of hearing, which also plays a role in maintaining balance. It is divided into the OUTER EAR (from the outside to the EARDRUM), the MIDDLE EAR, and the INNER EAR.

eardrum   The membrane that divides the OUTER EAR from the MIDDLE EAR. The vibrations of this membrane in response to sound WAVES lead to the sensation of hearing. Also called the tympanic membrane.

electrocardiogram (EKG) [i-lek-troh-KAHR-dee-uh-gram]   A written recording of the electrical activity of the HEART. Electrocardiograms are used to determine the condition of the heart and to diagnose heart disease.

electrocardiograph   (i-lek-troh-KAHR-dee-uh-graf)   An instrument that records electrical activity in the HEART. The electrocardiograph produces an ELECTROCARDIOGRAM.

electroencephalogram (EEG) [i-lek-troh-en-SEF-uh-luh-gram]   A written recording of the electrical activity of the BRAIN. Electroencephalograms are useful in studying and detecting brain disorders.

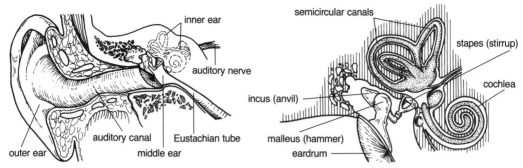

EAR. *A detail of the inner ear, which is encased in bone, is on the right.*

electrolyte (i-LEK-truh-leyet) A substance that can serve as a CONDUCTOR for an electric CURRENT when it is dissolved in a SOLUTION. Electrolytes are found in the BLOOD and tissue FLUIDS of the body.

emphysema (em-fuh-SEE-muh, em-fuh-ZEE-muh) A CHRONIC DISEASE in which the tiny air sacs in the LUNGS become stretched and enlarged, so that they are less able to supply OXYGEN to the BLOOD. Emphysema causes shortness of breath and painful coughing, and can increase the likelihood of developing HEART disease. Emphysema occurs most frequently in older men who have been heavy smokers.

enamel The hard, white substance that covers the CROWN of a TOOTH.

encephalitis (en-sef-uh-LEYE-tis) INFLAMMATION of the BRAIN. Encephalitis may be caused by a VIRUS or lead poisoning, or it may be a complication of another disease, such as INFLUENZA or MEASLES. Encephalitis can cause permanent brain damage or death. It is also possible, however, to recover from it completely.

endocrine gland (EN-duh-krin, EN-duh-kreen, EN-duh-kreyen) A GLAND that secretes HORMONES directly into the BLOOD. These glands make up the ENDOCRINE SYSTEM.

endocrine system The SYSTEM of ENDOCRINE GLANDS in the body. The endocrine system chemically controls the various FUNCTIONS of CELLS, tissues, and ORGANS through the secretion of HORMONES. The endocrine system includes the ADRENAL, PARATHYROID, PITUITARY, and THYROID glands, as well as the OVARIES, PANCREAS, and TESTES.

endorphins (en-DAWR-finz) Substances produced by the BRAIN that have painkilling and tranquillizing effects on the body. Endorphins are thought to be similar to MORPHINE, and are usually released by the brain during times of extreme body STRESS. The release of endorphins may explain why TRAUMA vic-

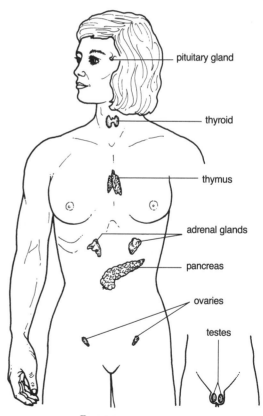

ENDOCRINE SYSTEM

tims sometimes cannot feel the pain associated with their injuries.

epidemic   A CONTAGIOUS DISEASE that spreads rapidly and widely among the population in an area. IMMUNIZATION and QUARANTINE are two of the methods used to control an epidemic.

epidermis (ep-uh-DUR-mis)   The outside layers of the SKIN.

epilepsy (EP-uh-lep-see)   A disorder of the BRAIN characterized by sudden, recurring attacks of abnormal brain function, often resulting in CONVULSIONS or SEIZURES. The seizures associated with epilepsy can sometimes be controlled by medication.

epinephrine (ep-uh-NEF-rin)   *See* ADRENALINE.

esophagus (i-SOF-uh-guhs)   The muscular tube that connects the mouth to the STOMACH and serves as a passageway for food. (*See* DIGESTIVE SYSTEM.)

estrogen (ES-truh-juhn)   A group of HORMONES, secreted mainly by the OVARIES, that influence the female REPRODUCTIVE SYSTEM in many ways, notably in preparing the body for OVULATION and in the development of female SECONDARY SEX CHARACTERISTICS.

Eustachian tube (yooh-STAY-shuhn, yooh-STAY-kee-uhn)   A tube made up of bone and CARTILAGE that connects the MIDDLE EAR to the back of the mouth.

&   Swallowing during airplane takeoffs and landings allows air to move through the Eustachian tube to equalize pressure across the EARDRUM, causing the EARS to "pop."

excretory system (EK-skruh-tawr-ee)   The SYSTEM of ORGANS that regulates the amount of water in the body, and filters and eliminates from the BLOOD the wastes produced by METABOLISM. The principal organs of the excretory system are the KIDNEYS, URETERS, URETHRA, and URINARY BLADDER.

eye   The ORGAN of sight. Some of its parts are the CORNEA, IRIS, LENS, OPTIC NERVE, PUPIL, and RETINA.

Fallopian tubes (fuh-LOH-pee-uhn)   The slender tubes through which OVA pass from the OVARIES to the UTERUS. FERTILIZATION normally takes place in the Fallopian tubes. (*See* REPRODUCTIVE SYSTEMS.)

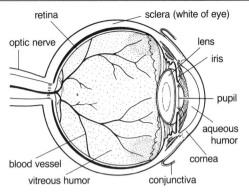

EYE. *A cross section showing the right eye and optic nerve.*

fats   ORGANIC COMPOUNDS that serve as a reserve of ENERGY for the body. Fat is stored in the body's fat tissues, which provide support, protection, and insulation for the body and its ORGANS. A BALANCED DIET must include some fats because, in addition to providing energy for the body, they are necessary for the absorption of certain VITAMINS.

&   Many people consume too much fat in their diet; this imbalance can contribute to various diseases (such as disorders of the HEART). Some fats, called SATURATED FATS, have been found to raise the level of CHOLESTEROL in the BLOOD, while other fats, called UNSATURATED FATS, may help reduce blood cholesterol levels.

FDA   *See* FOOD AND DRUG ADMINISTRATION.

FDA Recommended Daily Allowance   The amount of a particular VITAMIN, MINERAL, or nutrient that should be consumed each day to maintain good health, as determined by the FOOD AND DRUG ADMINISTRATION (FDA).

feces (FEE-seez)   Excrement; the waste material that is passed to the outside from the RECTUM through the ANUS.

fight or flight reaction   The set of processes that occur in the body when it is confronted with some form of physical or mental STRESS. For example, if a person is faced with danger (as from a vicious animal about to attack), the NERVOUS SYSTEM signals for ADRENALINE and other HORMONES to be released into the BLOOD. These hormones prepare the body either to confront the attacking animal or to flee to safety (thus, "fight or flight"). Changes in the body include increased HEART rate, dilated PUPILS OF THE EYE (to improve vision), and increased supply of BLOOD to the muscles (to prepare the body for action).

Food and Drug Administration (FDA) An agency of the United States federal government that approves or disapproves new drugs and substances that can be consumed.

food poisoning Illnesses that arise from eating food contaminated with PATHOGENIC or toxic (see TOXINS) substances. Characterized by vomiting and DIARRHEA, food poisoning is often caused by BACTERIA, such as SALMONELLA or STAPHYLOCOCCI. (See BOTULISM.)

fungus (FUNG-guhs) *plur.* FUNGI (FUN-jeye, FUNG-geye) A plantlike organism that does not contain CHLOROPHYLL, and can be found either as a single CELL or as a mass of filamentlike structures called hyphae. Some fungi cause diseases such as ATHLETE'S FOOT. Molds, yeasts, and mushrooms are some common kinds of fungi. (See under "Life Sciences.")

Galen (GAY-luhn) An ancient Greek physician and pioneer in the study of ANATOMY.

gallbladder A small, muscular sac located under the LIVER. BILE is stored in the gallbladder until it is needed by the SMALL INTESTINE for DIGESTION. (See DIGESTIVE SYSTEM.)

gallstone A hard, pebblelike material deposited in the GALLBLADDER or BILE DUCTS by the process of chemical PRECIPITATION. Gallstones can cause considerable pain, and can even obstruct the flow of BILE from the gallbladder. On some occasions, the entire gallbladder must be removed by surgery.

gangrene (GANG-green, gang-GREEN) The death and decay of body tissue owing to insufficient supply of BLOOD.

gastric A descriptive term for things pertaining to the STOMACH.

gastroenterology (gas-troh-en-tuh-ROL-uh-jee) The branch of medicine devoted to the study and care of the GASTROINTESTINAL TRACT.

gastrointestinal tract (GI tract) [gas-troh-in-TES-tuh-nuhl] The STOMACH and INTESTINES; the path that food follows once it leaves the ESOPHAGUS.

general anesthetic An ANESTHETIC that affects the entire body. This kind of anesthetic acts on the BRAIN to cause loss of consciousness. (*Compare* LOCAL ANESTHETIC.)

genitals The ORGANS involved in reproduction. (See REPRODUCTIVE SYSTEMS.)

German measles An ACUTE DISEASE, and a CONTAGIOUS DISEASE, caused by a VIRUS, producing symptoms milder than those usually associated with MEASLES; also called RUBELLA.

&. German measles can cause severe CONGENITAL defects in the developing EMBRYO or FETUS of a woman who contracts the disease in her first three months of pregnancy.

germs MICROORGANISMS that can cause disease or INFECTION.

glands ORGANS or groups of CELLS that take substances from the BLOOD and change them chemically so that they can be secreted later for further use by the body. There are two kinds of glands: those that secrete their substances directly into the bloodstream (the ENDOCRINE GLANDS), and those that secrete their substances through channels or ducts (such as the SWEAT GLANDS and SALIVARY GLANDS).

glaucoma (glow-KOH-muh, glaw-KOH-muh) A disease of the EYE marked by increased FLUID PRESSURE in the eyeball. Glaucoma can damage the OPTIC NERVE, and may result in blindness if not treated properly. Surgery may be required for severe cases of glaucoma.

gonorrhea (gon-uh-REE-uh) An ACUTE DISEASE, and a SEXUALLY TRANSMITTED DISEASE, caused by BACTERIA that invade the MUCOUS MEMBRANES of the GENITALS and URINARY TRACT. If left untreated, gonorrhea can spread to the bones and joints of the body or cause sterility. ANTIBIOTICS, especially PENICILLIN, are very effective in treating gonorrhea.

gout (GOWT) A disorder of METABOLISM characterized by attacks of painful INFLAMMATION in the joints, particularly those of the feet and hands. It occurs most often in middle-aged men. The tendency toward developing gout is inherited. STRESS, fatigue, or excessive exercise can bring on an attack.

gynecology (geye-nuh-KOL-uh-jee, jin-uh-KOL-uh-jee) The branch of medicine devoted to the care of women, and particularly to the study and care of the female REPRODUCTIVE SYSTEM.

hallucinogen (huh-LOOH-suh-nuh-juhn)   A substance or drug that can cause HALLUCINATIONS.

hardening of the arteries   *See* ARTERIOSCLEROSIS.

harelip   A CONGENITAL defect in which the upper lip is not properly fused together, so that a narrow crack or fissure splits the lip. It can be repaired through PLASTIC SURGERY.

HDL   ABBREVIATION for *h*igh *d*ensity *l*ipoprotein, MOLECULES that remove CHOLESTEROL from the bloodstream and carry it to the LIVER.

    🕭 HDLs are often called "good" cholesterol.

heart   The hollow muscular ORGAN that is the center of the CIRCULATORY SYSTEM. The heart pumps BLOOD throughout the intricate system of BLOOD VESSELS in the body.

heart attack   An episode of HEART failure or the stopping of normal heart function; a CORONARY THROMBOSIS. Symptoms of a heart attack include pain and pressure in the chest, which often spread to the shoulder, arm, and neck.

heartburn   A burning sensation in the middle of the chest at the junction of the ESOPHAGUS and STOMACH, caused by stomach ACIDS that back up and enter the lower end of the esophagus.

hemoglobin (HEE-muh-gloh-bin)   A complex ORGANIC MOLECULE containing iron that carries OXYGEN in the BLOOD.

    🕭 Hemoglobin gives blood its characteristic red color.

hemophilia (hee-muh-FIL-ee-uh, hee-muh-FEEL-yuh)   A HEREDITARY disease caused by a deficiency of a substance in the BLOOD that aids in clotting. Hemophiliacs can bleed to death even from small cuts and bruises, because their blood has largely lost the ability to clot.

    🕭 Queen VICTORIA of BRITAIN, whose descendants have been kings and queens of several countries in EUROPE, carried the GENE for hemophilia, which has turned up repeatedly in royal families since her lifetime. Her great-grandson, the heir to the throne of RUSSIA, suffered from the disease, and his parents fell under the influence of the MONK RASPUTIN in hopes of a miraculous cure. The resulting chaos in the government of Russia helped bring on the RUSSIAN REVOLUTION and the establishment of the SOVIET UNION.

hepatitis (hep-uh-TEYE-tis)   INFLAMMATION of the LIVER. Hepatitis is most often caused by a VIRUS, but can be the result of exposure to certain toxic agents such as drugs or chemicals. One viral form of the disease is spread by contaminated food and water, and another by contaminated injection needles and BLOOD TRANSFUSIONS. Symptoms of hepatitis include fever and JAUNDICE.

hereditary   A descriptive term for conditions capable of being transmitted from parent to offspring through the GENES. The term *hereditary* is applied to diseases such as HEMOPHILIA and characteristics such as the tendency toward baldness that pass from parents to children.

hernia (HUR-nee-uh)   The projection of an ORGAN or part of an organ through the wall of the structure that surrounds it. Most often, the term is applied to the protrusion of a part of the INTESTINE that can be observed as a lump in the lower ABDOMEN.

herpes (HUR-peez)   A group of related diseases and the VIRUSES that cause them. These diseases are marked by the development of blisterlike sores on the SKIN or MUCOUS MEMBRANES of the body. The herpes virus may invade the mouth region, producing fever blisters or cold sores, or may cause a SEXUALLY TRANSMITTED DISEASE in which the painful sores appear on the GENITALS. CHICKEN POX is another disease caused by a herpes virus.

Hippocrates (hi-POK-ruh-teez)   An ancient Greek physician (the "father of medicine") who is credited with founding the study of medicine.

Hippocratic oath (hip-uh-KRAT-ik)   A traditional oath of physicians, who pledge to practice medicine according to the ideals and moral principles put forth by HIPPOCRATES.

HIV (aych-eye-VEE)   ABBREVIATION for *H*uman *Im*munodeficiency *V*irus, the virus that causes AIDS.

hives   A condition characterized by the sudden appearance of red, raised areas on the SKIN that itch

HIPPOCRATES

severely. Hives may be caused by an allergic reaction (*see* ALLERGY) to foods or other substances.

Hodgkin's disease   A CHRONIC DISEASE in which the LYMPH NODES, SPLEEN, and LIVER become enlarged. The disease, whose cause is still unknown, can spread throughout other tissues and ORGANS of the body and cause death if not treated at an early stage. Many view Hodgkin's disease as a form of CANCER affecting the LYMPHATIC SYSTEM; for this reason, RADIATION and CHEMOTHERAPY are often used in treating it.

holistic medicine (hoh-LIS-tik)   An approach to medicine that emphasizes treating the person as a whole, with special attention to the interconnections of the mind and body and of the SYSTEMS within the body. Holistic medicine stresses the patient's role in health care through such means as positive attitudes, sound diet, and regular exercise.

homeopathy (hoh-mee-OP-uh-thee)   A system of treating disease in which small doses of certain substances are administered; in large doses, given to a healthy person, these substances would produce the symptoms of the disease. The principles of homeopathy do not enjoy widespread acceptance in the medical community.

homeostasis (hoh-mee-oh-STAY-sis)   The tendency of the body to seek and maintain a condition of balance or EQUILIBRIUM within its internal environment, even when faced with external changes. A simple example of homeostasis is the body's ability to maintain an internal temperature around 98.6 DEGREES FAHRENHEIT, whatever the temperature outside.

hormones   Chemical substances, produced in the body by ENDOCRINE GLANDS, that are transported by the BLOOD to other ORGANS to stimulate their function. ADRENALINE, ESTROGEN, INSULIN, and TESTOSTERONE are all hormones.

humor   An archaic term for any FLUID substance in the body, such as BLOOD, LYMPH, or BILE.
   ❧ Physicians in the MIDDLE AGES believed that four principal humors — blood, phlegm, yellow bile, and black bile — controlled body functions, and that a person's temperament resulted from the humor that was most prevalent in the body. *Sanguine* people were controlled by blood, *phlegmatic* people by phlegm, *choleric* people by yellow bile (also known as "choler"), and *melancholic* people by black bile (also known as "melancholy").

hymen (HEYE-muhn)   A thin fold of MUCOUS MEMBRANE that covers all or part of the entrance to the VAGINA.
   ❧ An apparently intact hymen is valued in some CULTURES as proof of virginity in a bride; this "proof," however, is not accurate. The hymen may appear incomplete in a virgin, and it may appear intact in a woman who has engaged in sexual intercourse.

hypersensitivity   An excessive or abnormal sensitivity to a substance. A person who is hypersensitive to a certain drug will often suffer a severe allergic reaction (*see* ALLERGY) if given the drug.

hypertension   Abnormally high BLOOD PRESSURE.

hypochondria   *See* HYPOCHONDRIACS.

hypochondriacs (heye-puh-KON-dree-aks)   Persons who constantly believe they are ill or about to become ill.

hypothalamus (heye-puh-THAL-uh-muhs)   The part of the BRAIN that controls hunger, thirst, and body temperature and regulates various activities in the body connected with METABOLISM, including the maintaining of water balance. The hypothalamus also controls the action of the PITUITARY GLAND.

hysterectomy (his-tuh-REK-tuh-mee)   The surgical removal of all or part of the UTERUS.

immune system   The SYSTEM in the body that works to ward off INFECTION and disease. Central to this system are the WHITE BLOOD CELLS. Some white blood cells produce ANTIBODIES in response to specific ANTIGENS that may invade the body; others function as scavengers to fight infection by destroying BACTERIA and removing dead CELLS.

immunity   The ability of the body to resist or fight off INFECTION and disease.

immunization   The process of inducing IMMUNITY, usually through INOCULATION or VACCINATION.

․ Frequently, schoolchildren are required by state law to be immunized against certain diseases. Because of such widespread immunization, many diseases that used to be fairly common, including SMALLPOX, TETANUS, and WHOOPING COUGH, have become rare.

incisors (in-SEYE-zuhrz)   The sharp TEETH at the front of the mouth (four on the top and four on the bottom) that are specialized for cutting.

incubation period   The amount of time it takes for symptoms of a disease to appear after an individual is infected (*see* INFECTION) with the PATHOGEN that causes the disease.

incubator   A specialized crib used in caring for infants, in which the temperature and OXYGEN content of the air can be controlled. Often, babies who are born prematurely will be placed in an incubator until they have become strong enough to be housed in a regular crib.

induced abortion   *See* ABORTION.

infection   Invasion of the body or a body part by a PATHOGENIC organism, which multiplies and produces harmful effects on the body's tissues.

infectious diseases   Diseases caused by the growth of PATHOGENIC organisms in the body. Some of these diseases may also be CONTAGIOUS DISEASES.

inflammation   The response of tissue to injury or INFECTION. Pain, heat, redness, and swelling are the four basic symptoms of inflammation.

influenza (in-flooh-EN-zuh)   Commonly called the flu; an ACUTE DISEASE, and an INFECTIOUS DISEASE, of the RESPIRATORY SYSTEM caused by a VIRUS and characterized by fever, muscle pain, headache, and INFLAMMATION of the MUCOUS MEMBRANES in the RESPIRATORY TRACT.

inner ear   The part of the EAR, located deep within the skull, where sound vibrations are converted to electrical signals and sent to the BRAIN via the AUDITORY NERVE to produce the sensation of hearing. ORGANS related to balance are also located in the inner ear.

inoculation (i-nok-yuh-LAY-shuhn)   The introduction of an ANTIGEN into the body, usually by injection, in order to stimulate the production of ANTIBODIES to produce IMMUNITY to an INFECTIOUS DISEASE. (*See* IMMUNIZATION.)

insomnia (in-SOM-nee-uh)   A persistent and prolonged inability to sleep.

insulin (IN-suh-lin, IN-syuh-lin)   A HORMONE secreted by the PANCREAS that regulates the levels of SUGAR in the BLOOD.

․ Persons suffering from DIABETES MELLITUS may receive periodic or daily injections of insulin as a treatment for the disease.

interferon (in-tuhr-FEER-on)   A PROTEIN produced by CELLS after they have been exposed to a VIRUS. Interferon prevents the virus from reproducing within the infected cells, and can also induce resistance to the virus in other cells.

intestines   The part of the GASTROINTESTINAL TRACT that extends from the STOMACH to the ANUS. The intestines are further subdivided into the LARGE INTESTINE and SMALL INTESTINE. (*See* DIGESTIVE SYSTEM.)

intrauterine device (IUD) [in-truh-YOOH-tuh-ruhn, in-truh-YOOH-tuh-reyen]   A metal or plastic device inserted into the UTERUS and used to prevent pregnancy.

intravenous (in-truh-VEE-nuhs)   A descriptive term for things within a VEIN. Intravenous feeding or medication is the passing of nutrients or medicines into a vein through a tube.

iris (EYE-ris) The colored membrane of the EYE, surrounding the PUPIL, which by contracting and expanding regulates the amount of LIGHT that enters the eye.

IUD *See* INTRAUTERINE DEVICE.

jaundice (JAWN-dis) A condition in which the SKIN, the whites of the EYE, and other tissues take on a yellowish color because of an excess of BILE coloring in the BLOOD.

jet lag A temporary disruption of the body's BIOLOGICAL CLOCK experienced by persons who travel across several time zones by airplane. The effects of jet lag, which may include fatigue and irritability, generally disappear after a few days as the body's internal rhythms readjust themselves to the new time frame.

kidney stones Small, hard masses that form by chemical PRECIPITATION and are found in the KIDNEYS. Kidney stones vary in size, with most of them being small enough to pass through the URINARY TRACT for elimination in the URINE. Some, however, may be large enough to obstruct the kidney and cause tremendous pain.

kidneys A pair of ORGANS, the principal parts of the EXCRETORY SYSTEM, located above the waistline at the back of the ABDOMINAL CAVITY. The kidneys filter waste materials from the BLOOD, excreting these wastes in the form of URINE; they also regulate the amounts of water and other chemicals in body FLUIDS.

knee-jerk reflex A sudden involuntary forward movement of the lower leg that can be produced by a firm tap to the TENDON located just below the kneecap.
  🐦 The term is loosely applied to any response or belief that is automatic rather than thoughtful. In this sense, it is usually a term of reproach: "Smith is a knee-jerk LIBERAL."

labor The physical processes at the end of a normal pregnancy, including opening of the CERVIX and contractions of the UTERUS, that lead to the birth of the baby.

laparoscope (LAP-uh-ruh-skohp) A surgical device that uses OPTICAL FIBERS in a small tube. Inserted into the abdomen, the laparoscope allows surgery without large incisions.
  🐦 Laparoscopic surgery is often referred to as "Band-Aid" surgery because it requires only small incisions.

large intestine The lower portion of the INTESTINES, which receives a soupy mixture of digested food from the SMALL INTESTINE, reabsorbs most of the FLUIDS, and then passes the resulting SOLID substance (FECES) out of the body through the ANUS. The large intestine is divided into the cecum, COLON, and RECTUM.

larynx (LAR-ingks) The specialized upper portion of the TRACHEA that contains the VOCAL CORDS; the voice box.

LDL ABBREVIATION for *low density lipoproteins*, CHOLESTEROL that is linked to HEART disease and ATHEROSCLEROSIS. (*Compare* HDL.)
  🐦 LDLs are often referred to as "bad" cholesterol.

left brain A popular term that describes the analytic, rational, and straight-line-thinking functions of the left half of the CEREBRAL CORTEX. (*Compare* RIGHT BRAIN; *see* BRAIN.)

lens A clear, almost spherical structure located just behind the PUPIL of the EYE. The lens focuses WAVES of LIGHT on the RETINA.

leprosy (LEP-ruh-see) A CHRONIC DISEASE, and an INFECTIOUS DISEASE, characterized by patches of altered SKIN and NERVE tissue (lesions) that gradually spread to cause muscle weakness, deformities, and PARALYSIS. Some forms of ANTIBIOTICS are now used to treat this disease, and PLASTIC SURGERY can help correct the deformities it causes. Also called Hansen's disease.
  🐦 Leprosy has been well known since ancient times, when widespread fear of those afflicted with the disease caused them to be treated as outcasts. Today, the term *leper* is often used to refer to a person excluded from society.

leukemia (looh-KEE-mee-uh) A kind of CANCER in which the number of WHITE BLOOD CELLS in the BLOOD greatly increases. Leukemia usually spreads to the SPLEEN, LIVER, LYMPH NODES, and other areas of the body, causing destruction of tissues, and often resulting in death.

ligament A kind of fibrous CONNECTIVE TISSUE that binds bones or CARTILAGE together.

liver A large ORGAN, located on the right side of the ABDOMEN and protected by the lower rib cage, that produces BILE and BLOOD PROTEINS, stores VITAMINS for later release into the bloodstream, removes TOXINS (including alcohol) from the BLOOD, breaks down old RED BLOOD CELLS, and helps maintain levels of blood SUGAR in the body.

lobotomy (luh-BOT-uh-mee, loh-BOT-uh-mee) A surgical incision into one or more of the NERVE masses in the front of the BRAIN. A lobotomy may be performed for the relief of certain mental disorders, although it has been largely abandoned in favor of less radical treatments.

&. Because people who have had a lobotomy often become quite passive after the operation, the term is often used to refer to someone who shows a lack of response or reaction: "She was so tired she just sat there as if she had been lobotomized."

local anesthetic An ANESTHETIC that causes loss of sensation only to the area to which it is applied. (*Compare* GENERAL ANESTHETIC.)

lockjaw *See* TETANUS.

LSD A drug, lysergic acid diethylamide, that produces HALLUCINATIONS similar to those of a PSYCHOSIS. Persons on LSD "trips," which may last for many hours, undergo distortions of their perceptions of space and time and may lose all contact with reality.

lungs A pair of ORGANS, the principal parts of the RESPIRATORY SYSTEM, at the front of the cavity of the chest, or THORAX. In the lungs, OXYGEN from the air that is inhaled is transferred into the BLOOD, while CARBON DIOXIDE is removed from the blood and exhaled.

lymph (LIMF) A clear, colorless FLUID that circulates through the LYMPHATIC SYSTEM. Lymph fills the tissue spaces of the body.

lymph nodes Small, rounded structures along the small vessels of the LYMPHATIC SYSTEM that produce disease-fighting WHITE BLOOD CELLS and filter out harmful MICROORGANISMS and TOXINS from the

LYMPH. Lymph nodes may become enlarged when they are actively fighting INFECTION.

lymphatic system (lim-FAT-ik) The network of small vessels and tissue spaces that move LYMPH throughout the body. The lymphatic system has several functions, including filtering out harmful BACTERIA; manufacturing WHITE BLOOD CELLS (white blood cells are produced by the LYMPH NODES); distributing nutrients to the CELLS of the body; helping to maintain the body's FLUID balance by draining off excess fluids so that tissues do not swell; and assisting in the DIGESTION of FATS.

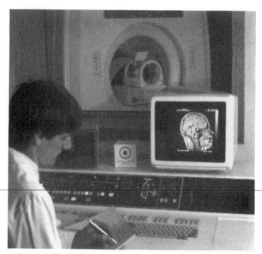

MAGNETIC RESONANCE IMAGING. *Technician and brain scan on screen in foreground. Person undergoing scanning in background.*

magnetic resonance imaging (MRI) A technique for forming detailed images of internal ORGANS and tissue. It works by putting the patient inside a magnet, then using RADIO WAVES to locate ATOMS in the tissue. Final production of the image is done by a COMPUTER. (*Compare* X-RAY *and* ULTRASOUND.)

&. MRI images are the most detailed that can be obtained.

malaria (muh-LAIR-ee-uh) An INFECTIOUS DISEASE caused by a PARASITE that is transmitted by the bite of an infected mosquito. Persons suffering from malaria experience periodic episodes of chills and fever.

malignant A descriptive term for things or conditions that threaten life or well-being. Malignant is the opposite of BENIGN.

❧ The term *malignant* is used in describing cancerous TUMORS (*see* CANCER) because such growths are a threat to the health of the individual. ❧ The term is often used in a general way to denote something that is both destructive and fast growing: "The malignant growth of the suburbs is destroying the landscape."

malnutrition Inadequate nutrition caused by the lack of a BALANCED DIET or by disorders of the DIGESTIVE SYSTEM in which the nutrients from food cannot be absorbed properly.

mammogram (MAM-uh-gram) An X-RAY of the breast, produced by MAMMOGRAPHY, that is used in screening for breast CANCER.

mammography (ma-MOG-ruh-fee) Examination of the breasts using X-RAYS. Mammography is useful in locating TUMORS of the breast that are too small to be detected by other means.

marrow The soft, specialized CONNECTIVE TISSUE that fills the cavities of bones. One kind of bone marrow is responsible for manufacturing RED BLOOD CELLS in the body.

mastectomy (ma-STEK-tuh-mee) The surgical removal of a breast.

measles An ACUTE DISEASE, and a CONTAGIOUS DISEASE, caused by a VIRUS, and characterized by the outbreak of small red spots on the SKIN. Measles occurs most often in school-age children. Also called RUBEOLA. (*Compare* GERMAN MEASLES.)

Medicare A federal health insurance program, administered by the SOCIAL SECURITY ADMINISTRATION, that provides health care for the aged.

melanin (MEL-uh-nin) A dark brown coloring found in the body, especially in the SKIN and hair. Produced by special skin CELLS that are sensitive to sunlight, melanin protects the body by absorbing ULTRAVIOLET RADIATION from the SUN.
❧ The amount of melanin present in the skin determines the color of a person's complexion: people with a large amount have dark skin, while those with very little have fair skin. Melanin is also responsible for tanning.

melanoma (mel-uh-NOH-muh) A serious, often lethal, form of SKIN CANCER.

❧ Exposure to ULTRAVIOLET RADIATION from the SUN (for example, by too much sunbathing) can cause this disease.

meninges (muh-NIN-jeez) The membranes that surround the BRAIN and SPINAL CORD.

meningitis (men-in-JEYE-tis) INFLAMMATION of the MENINGES of the BRAIN or SPINAL CORD, most often resulting from a BACTERIAL INFECTION or VIRAL INFECTION.

menopause (MEN-uh-pawz) The period in a woman's life when her MENSTRUAL CYCLES stop. Menopause typically occurs between the ages of forty-five and fifty.

menstrual cycle (MEN-strooh-uhl, MEN-struhl) The periodic series of changes in the female REPRODUCTIVE SYSTEM associated with the preparation of the UTERUS for pregnancy; the cycle is repeated roughly every twenty-eight days. During the menstrual cycle, an OVUM is released from one of the OVARIES (the release is called OVULATION), and the uterus develops an inner lining enriched with BLOOD to prepare it for the possible implantation of a ZYGOTE. If FERTILIZATION and implantation do not take place, the lining of the uterus is discharged during MENSTRUATION.

menstruation (men-strooh-AY-shuhn) The periodic discharge of the BLOOD-enriched lining of the UTERUS through the VAGINA. Menstruation marks the end of one MENSTRUAL CYCLE and the beginning of another.

methadone (METH-uh-dohn) An ANALGESIC that is sometimes used in the treatment of drug addiction.

microbe (MEYE-krohb) *See* MICROORGANISMS.

middle ear A part of the EAR on the inner side of the EARDRUM; it contains three small bones that transmit sound WAVES to the INNER EAR from the eardrum.

midwife A person who serves as an attendant at childbirth but is not a physician. Some midwives (called certified nurse midwives) are trained in university programs, which usually require previous education in nursing; others (called lay midwives) learn their skills through apprenticeship.

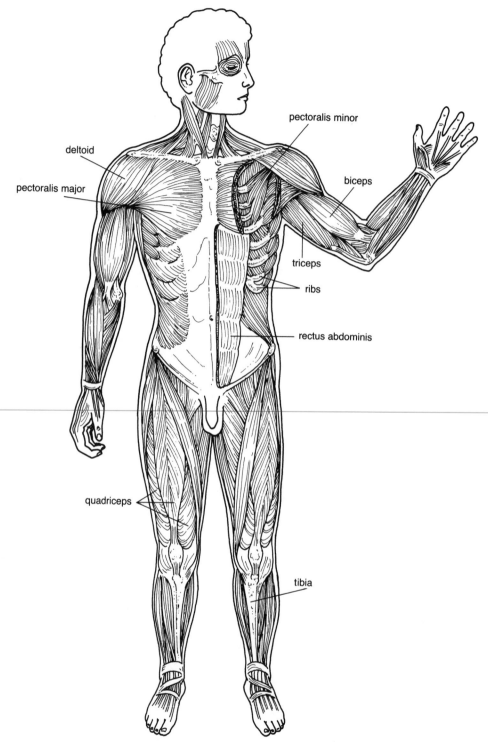

deltoid

pectoralis major

pectoralis minor

biceps

triceps

ribs

rectus abdominis

quadriceps

tibia

MUSCULAR SYSTEM. *A front view.*

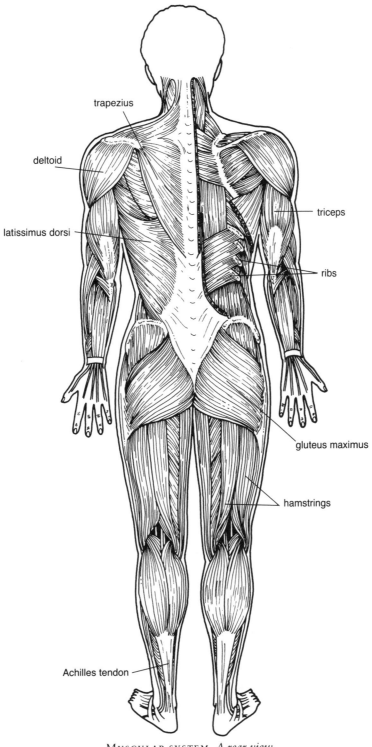

trapezius

deltoid

latissimus dorsi

triceps

ribs

gluteus maximus

hamstrings

Achilles tendon

MUSCULAR SYSTEM. *A rear view.*

minerals In the diet, certain substances necessary for the maintenance of life and good health. Some are essential components of bodily substances, such as the calcium in bones and the iron in HEMOGLOBIN, while others help regulate the activities of METABOLISM. (*See under "Earth Sciences."*)

miscarriage (MIS-kar-ij, mis-KAR-ij) A spontaneous and premature expulsion of an EMBRYO or FETUS from the UTERUS before it is capable of surviving on its own.

   🖎 Generally, a miscarriage is a failure to achieve a desired end, as in a miscarriage of justice.

molars (MOH-luhrz) The TEETH with broad surfaces at the back of the mouth that serve to grind food. Including the WISDOM TEETH, adults have twelve molars — six on the top and six on the bottom.

mononucleosis (mon-uh-nooh-klee-OH-sis) An ACUTE DISEASE, and an INFECTIOUS DISEASE, caused by a VIRUS; its symptoms include fever, swelling of the LYMPH NODES, and general exhaustion. Mononucleosis gets its name from the kind of WHITE BLOOD CELL (monocyte) that increases in number in the BLOOD of persons who have the disease. There is no specific treatment, but sufferers usually recover within a few weeks.

   🖎 Mononucleosis is sometimes called the "kissing disease," because at one time the virus was thought to be transmitted by kissing. The virus can be found in the SALIVA of those who have the disease, so there may be some truth in the belief.

morphine (MAWR-feen) An addictive drug derived from OPIUM that is used as an ANALGESIC and sedative.

MRI *See* MAGNETIC RESONANCE IMAGING.

mucous membrane (MYOOH-kuhs) The membrane that lines passageways and cavities in the body that lead to the outside, such as the mouth, GASTROINTESTINAL TRACT, nose, VAGINA, and URETHRA. These membranes are equipped with GLANDS that secrete MUCUS.

mucus A slippery and somewhat sticky FLUID secreted by the GLANDS in MUCOUS MEMBRANES. Mucus lubricates and protects the mucous membranes.

multiple sclerosis (skluh-ROH-sis) A CHRONIC DISEASE of the CENTRAL NERVOUS SYSTEM characterized by the hardening of patches of tissue in the BRAIN and SPINAL CORD. The cause of this disease is unknown, and there is no specific treatment. It occurs in varying degrees of severity, and in the worst case can result in permanent PARALYSIS.

mumps An ACUTE DISEASE, and a CONTAGIOUS DISEASE, marked by fever and INFLAMMATION of the SALIVARY GLANDS. Caused by a VIRUS, mumps is normally a childhood disease that passes with no after effects.

   🖎 A child who has had mumps is immune from further INFECTION by the mumps virus.

muscular dystrophy (DIS-truh-fee) A HEREDITARY disease in which the muscles progressively waste away. The disease cannot be treated, and its effects are irreversible.

muscular system The system in the body composed of muscle CELLS and tissues that brings about movement of an ORGAN or body part. There are three kinds of muscle: *skeletal muscle*, which is attached to bones and allows the voluntary movement of limbs; *smooth muscle*, which is found in internal ORGANS and aids in the involuntary movements that occur in the CIRCULATORY SYSTEM, DIGESTIVE SYSTEM, EXCRETORY SYSTEM, REPRODUCTIVE SYSTEM, and RESPIRATORY SYSTEM; and *cardiac muscle*, which forms the powerful walls of the HEART.

myopia (meye-OH-pee-uh) Nearsightedness. Myopia is a visual defect in which LIGHT that enters the EYE is focused in front of the RETINA rather than directly on it, so that distant objects appear blurred. Myopia can be corrected with eyeglasses or contact lenses.

   🖎 The term is often used to indicate an inability to see into the future: "The new policy is incredibly myopic, and puts future generations at a great disadvantage for the sake of a few short-term gains."

nephrology (nuh-FROL-uh-jee) The branch of medicine devoted to the study and care of the KIDNEYS.

nerve A bundle of fibers composed of NEURONS that connects the body parts and ORGANS to the CENTRAL NERVOUS SYSTEM and carries impulses from one part of the body to another.

nervous system The SYSTEM in the body that controls internal functions of the body and receives, interprets, and responds to STIMULI. The nervous system is made up of the BRAIN, the SPINAL CORD, the

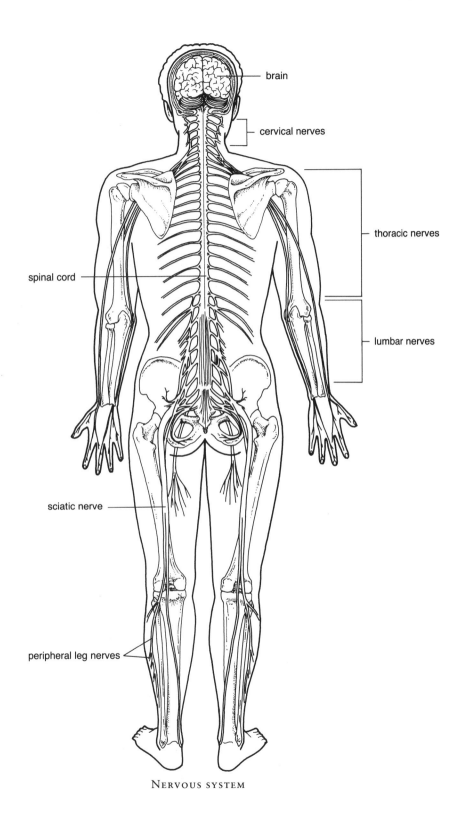

brain

cervical nerves

thoracic nerves

spinal cord

lumbar nerves

sciatic nerve

peripheral leg nerves

Nervous system

NERVES, and the sense ORGANS, such as the EYE and EAR.

neurology (noo-ROL-uh-jee, nyoo-ROL-uh-jee) The branch of medicine devoted to the study and care of the NERVOUS SYSTEM.

neurons (NOOR-onz, NYOOR-onz) The basic unit of NERVE TISSUE; the nerve CELLS. Neurons carry and transmit electrical signals throughout the NERVOUS SYSTEM.

nicotine (NIK-uh-teen) A poisonous chemical substance found in the tobacco plant.

Novocain (NOH-vuh-kayn) A substance used as a LOCAL ANESTHETIC in medicine and dentistry. *Novocain* is a trademark.

obstetrics (uhb-STE-triks) A branch of medicine that deals with the care of women during pregnancy, LABOR, and the period of recovery following childbirth.

occupational disease A disease that is caused by a person's line of work, or occupation. A well-known occupational disease is BLACK LUNG, which strikes coal miners, and is caused by the inhalation of coal dust over long periods of time.

olfactory (ol-FAK-tuh-ree, ohl-FAK-tuh-ree) A descriptive term for the sense of smell.

oncogene (ONG-kuh-jeen) Genes in animal DNA that cause CANCER.

⬩ Every CELL contains genes that, when altered slightly, can become oncogenes.

oncology (ong-KOL-uh-jee, on-KOL-uh-jee) The branch of medicine devoted to the study and cure of CANCER.

ophthalmic (of-THAL-mik, op-THAL-mik) A descriptive term for the EYE.

ophthalmology (of-thuhl-MOL-uh-jee, of-thuh-MOL-uh-jee) The branch of medicine devoted to the study and care of the EYE.

opium A highly addictive drug obtained from the poppy plant. Several other drugs, such as MORPHINE and CODEINE, are derived from opium.

opportunistic infection (op-uhr-tooh-NIS-tik) An INFECTION caused by a MICROORGANISM that under normal conditions would not bring about disease. Opportunistic infections occur when the body's IMMUNE SYSTEM is weakened by disease or MALNUTRITION. (*See* AIDS.)

optic nerve The NERVE that carries electrical signals from the RETINA in the EYE to the BRAIN.

organic In medicine, a descriptive term for things or conditions that have to do with an ORGAN in the body. The term can also refer to something that is derived from living organisms.

orthopedics (awr-thuh-PEE-diks) The branch of medicine devoted to the study and care of the MUSCULAR and SKELETAL SYSTEMS.

osteopathy (os-tee-OP-uh-thee) A system of medicine that stresses healing through the manipulation of body parts while using some standard medical practices, such as surgery or drugs.

osteoporosis (os-tee-oh-puh-ROH-sis) A softening of the bones that gradually increases and makes them more fragile. It is caused by the gradual loss of the MINERAL calcium, which helps make bones hard. Osteoporosis occurs most often in elderly women.

⬩ Many experts now believe that osteoporosis can be prevented through regular exercise, mineral supplements, and a diet high in calcium.

outer ear The part of the EAR that projects from the side of the head and functions to gather and guide sound WAVES toward the EARDRUM.

ova (OH-vuh) *sing.* OVUM (OH-vuhm) The female SEX CELLS, produced in the OVARY and released during OVULATION; the eggs. An ovum must normally be fertilized (*see* FERTILIZATION) to develop into a new living thing.

ovaries (OH-vuh-reez) *sing.* OVARY The paired ORGANS in the female REPRODUCTIVE SYSTEM that produce OVA and release certain HORMONES, such as ESTROGEN.

ovulation (ov-yuh-LAY-shuhn, oh-vyuh-LAY-shuhn) The periodic release of an OVUM from the OVARIES (usually from only one ovary). After the ovum is released, it travels into the FALLOPIAN TUBE, and from there is moved to the UTERUS. Ovulation generally happens approximately two weeks into the MENSTRUAL CYCLE.

pacemaker A group of specialized muscle fibers in the HEART that send out impulses to regulate the heartbeat. If the heart's built-in pacemaker does not function properly, an artificial pacemaker may be necessary — a small electrical device that also regulates the heartbeat by sending out impulses. An artificial pacemaker may be placed inside the body surgically or may be worn outside.

palate (PAL-uht) The roof of the mouth. The palate separates the mouth from the nasal cavity.

&. It is sometimes said that a person has a "cultivated palate" if he or she has a discerning taste for food.

pancreas (PANG-kree-uhs, PAN-kree-uhs) A GLAND behind the STOMACH that functions in both the ENDOCRINE SYSTEM and the DIGESTIVE SYSTEM. Its endocrine function involves the secretion into the bloodstream of INSULIN, which regulates the level of SUGARS in the BLOOD. As part of the digestive system, the pancreas secretes into the SMALL INTESTINE a FLUID containing ENZYMES that is used in the DIGESTION of all foods.

paralysis (puh-RAL-uh-sis) The loss of voluntary movement in a body part. Paralysis results from damage to the NERVES that supply the affected part of the body.

parasite An organism that lives off or in another organism, obtaining nourishment and protection while offering no benefit in return. Human parasites are often harmful to the body, and can cause diseases such as TRICHINOSIS.

&. The term *parasite* is often applied to a person who takes advantage of other people and fails to offer anything in return.

parathyroid glands (par-uh-THEYE-royd) A set of four small GLANDS on the undersurface of the THYROID GLAND that function in the ENDOCRINE SYSTEM. The parathyroid glands secrete a HORMONE that regulates the METABOLISM of calcium and phosphorus.

Parkinson's disease A CHRONIC DISEASE of the NERVOUS SYSTEM that usually strikes in late adult life, resulting in a gradual decrease in muscle control. Symptoms of the disease include shaking, weakness, and partial PARALYSIS of the face. Certain drugs can help alleviate some of its symptoms.

Pasteur, Louis (pa-STUR, pah-STEUR) A French scientist of the nineteenth century whose work was very important in proving that many diseases are caused by MICROORGANISMS. He developed PASTEURIZATION, in which FLUIDS, such as milk, are heated for a specific period of time to kill harmful BACTERIA.

pasteurization (pas-chuhr-i-ZAY-shuhn, pas-tuhr-i-ZAY-shuhn) Heating a FLUID, such as milk, for a specific period to kill harmful BACTERIA. This technique was developed by Louis PASTEUR.

pathogen (PATH-uh-juhn) A disease-causing agent. MICROORGANISMS, VIRUSES, and TOXINS are examples of pathogens.

pathogenic (path-uh-JEN-ik) A descriptive term for a thing or condition that can cause disease.

pathology (puh-THOL-uh-jee) A branch of medicine that explores the nature and cause of disease. Pathology also involves the study of bodily changes that occur as the result of disease.

pediatrics (pee-dee-A-triks) The branch of medicine devoted to the study and care of children.

pelvis The bowl-shaped group of bones connecting the trunk of the body to the legs and supporting the spine. The pelvis includes the hip bones and the lower part of the backbone.

penicillin An ANTIBIOTIC that is used to treat INFECTIONS caused by some kinds of BACTERIA. Penicillin, which is derived from a common kind of mold that grows on bread and fruit, was the first antibiotic discovered and put into widespread use.

penis The ORGAN of the male REPRODUCTIVE SYSTEM through which SEMEN passes out of the body during sexual intercourse. The penis is also an organ of urination.

peristalsis (per-uh-STAWL-sis, per-uh-STAL-sis) The wavelike, involuntary muscular contractions that move food through the DIGESTIVE SYSTEM.

pertussis (puhr-TUS-is) *See* WHOOPING COUGH.

phenylketonuria (PKU) (fen-l-keet-n-OOR-ee-uh) A HEREDITARY disease that prevents the proper METABOLISM of phenylalanine, an AMINO ACID. When phenylalanine is not metabolized properly, poisonous substances can build up in the body, causing BRAIN damage and mental retardation. The effects of PKU can be controlled by a special diet.

๕ States commonly require newborns to be tested for PKU.

pituitary gland (pi-TOOH-uh-ter-ee)   A small GLAND, attached to the base of the BRAIN and controlled by the HYPOTHALAMUS, that functions in the ENDOCRINE SYSTEM. The pituitary gland secretes many HORMONES: some control the actions of other glands, while others influence growth, METABOLISM, and reproduction.

PKU   *See* PHENYLKETONURIA.

placebo (pluh-SEE-boh)   A substance containing no active drug administered to a patient participating in a medical experiment as a CONTROL.

๕ Those receiving a placebo often get better, a phenomenon known as the *placebo effect.*

placenta (pluh-SEN-tuh)   An ORGAN that forms in the UTERUS after the implantation of a ZYGOTE. The placenta moves nourishment from the mother's BLOOD to the EMBRYO or FETUS; it also sends the embryo or fetus's waste products into the mother's blood to be disposed of by the mother's EXCRETORY SYSTEM. The embryo or fetus is attached to the placenta by the UMBILICAL CORD. After birth, the placenta separates from the uterus and is pushed out of the mother's body.

plague (PLAYG)   A highly CONTAGIOUS DISEASE, such as BUBONIC PLAGUE, that spreads quickly throughout a population and causes widespread sickness and death.

๕ The term is also used to refer to widespread outbreaks of many kinds, such as a "plague of locusts."

plaque (PLAK)   A thin film composed of BACTERIA, MUCUS, and food particles that forms on the surfaces of TEETH. Plaque contributes to tooth decay and gum disease.

Plaque also refers to a combination of CHOLESTEROL and LIPIDS that can accumulate on the inside of ARTERIES, causing ATHEROSCLEROSIS.

plasma (PLAZ-muh)   The liquid part of BLOOD or LYMPH. Blood plasma is mainly water; it also contains GASES, nutrients, and HORMONES. The RED BLOOD CELLS, WHITE BLOOD CELLS, and PLATELETS are all suspended in the plasma of the blood.

plastic surgery   Surgery that repairs or reconstructs a body part. Plastic surgery is used to correct physical defects and to rebuild parts of the body that have been damaged by TRAUMA or disease. Some examples of plastic surgery are breast reconstruction for women who have undergone a MASTECTOMY, and SKIN grafting for burn victims.

platelets (PLAYT-luhts)   Small, flat disks in the BLOOD that aid in clotting.

PMS (premenstrual syndrome) [pee-em-ES]   Associated with the retention of water and salts in the tissues for up to a week before the onset of MENSTRUATION, the symptoms of PMS include irritability, fatigue, emotional distress, and sometimes depression.

pneumonia (nuh-MOHN-yuh)   A disease characterized by INFLAMMATION of the LUNGS. Pneumonia can be caused by many factors, including BACTERIAL INFECTIONS, VIRAL INFECTIONS, and the inhalation of chemical irritants.

polio (POH-lee-oh)   *See* POLIOMYELITIS.

poliomyelitis (polio) (poh-lee-oh-meye-uh-LEYE- tis)   An ACUTE DISEASE, and an INFECTIOUS DISEASE, caused by a VIRUS, that brings about INFLAMMATION of certain NERVE CELLS in the SPINAL CORD. It can have a wide range of effects, from mild to severe, including PARALYSIS, permanent disability, and death. In the United States, the disease has now largely vanished since the development of a VACCINE against it. (*See* SABIN VACCINE *and* SALK VACCINE.)

๕ The history of polio, which went from a major public health problem to a minor one in a short time, is often used as an example of the benefits of medical research. ๕ President Franklin D. ROOSEVELT suffered from poliomyelitis. During his presidency, he could not walk unaided.

polyunsaturated fats (pol-ee-un-SACH-uh-ray-tuhd)   *See* UNSATURATED FATS.

premenstrual syndrome (pree-MEN-strooh-uhl, pree-MEN-struhl)   *See* PMS.

prenatal (pree-NAYT-l)   A descriptive term for the period between CONCEPTION and birth.

preventive medicine A branch of medicine that promotes activities to prevent the occurrence of disease.

prognosis (prog-NOH-sis) A medical prediction of the future course of a disease and the chance for recovery.

⮞ *Prognosis* is often used as a general term for predicting the unfolding of events: "The governor said that the prognosis for the state's financial future is bleak."

prostate gland (PROS-tayt) A GLAND in the male REPRODUCTIVE SYSTEM that surrounds the URETHRA at the lower end of the URINARY BLADDER. A large part of the FLUIDS that make up SEMEN comes from the prostate.

psychosomatic (seye-koh-suh-MAT-ik) A descriptive term for the relationship between the mind and body.

⮞ "Psychosomatic" disorders have definite physical symptoms but are thought to be caused by emotional or psychological factors. ANOREXIA NERVOSA is an example of a psychosomatic illness.

pulmonary artery (POOL-muh-ner-ee) A large ARTERY that carries BLOOD directly from the HEART to the LUNGS.

pulp The soft tissue, containing BLOOD VESSELS and NERVES, that makes up the interior of the TOOTH.

pupil The seemingly black central opening in the IRIS of the EYE, through which LIGHT enters.

quarantine (KWAWR-uhn-teen, KWAHR-uhn-teen) The isolation of people who either have a CONTAGIOUS DISEASE or have been exposed to one, in an attempt to prevent the spread of the disease.

⮞ The term is sometimes used politically to designate the political and economic isolation of a nation in retribution for unacceptable policies: "When IRAQ invaded KUWAIT, it was placed in quarantine by the nations of the world."

rabies (RAY-beez) An ACUTE DISEASE, caused by a VIRUS, which attacks the CENTRAL NERVOUS SYSTEM and results in PARALYSIS and death if not treated promptly. Rabies is transmitted to humans by the bite of an animal infected with the disease.

radiology (ray-dee-OL-uh-jee) The branch of medicine devoted to the study of images obtained by X-RAY, ULTRASOUND, CAT SCANS, or MAGNETIC RESONANCE IMAGING, and to the treatment of CANCER by RADIATION therapy.

rectum The outermost portion of the LARGE INTESTINE. FECES are stored in the rectum until they are passed out of the body through the ANUS.

red blood cells The disk-shaped CELLS in the BLOOD that contain HEMOGLOBIN. The red blood cells supply OXYGEN to all body cells and remove the CARBON DIOXIDE wastes that result from METABOLISM.

reflex An action or movement not controlled by conscious thought. A reflex may be anything from a hiccup to the involuntary response of a body part, such as the action that occurs in the KNEE-JERK REFLEX.

remission A period in the course of a disease when symptoms become less severe.

⮞ The term *remission* is often used in speaking of sufferers from LEUKEMIA or other CANCERS whose symptoms lessen or disappear. In such a case, the disease is said to be "in remission." The period of remission may last only briefly, or may extend over several months or years.

renal (REEN-l) A descriptive term for the KIDNEYS.

reproductive systems The ORGANS and GLANDS in the body that aid in the production of new individuals (reproduction).

In the male, SPERM are produced in the TESTES and conveyed to the female in a FLUID called SEMEN, which passes out of the body through the PENIS. Other parts of the male reproductive system include the PROSTATE GLAND, the SCROTUM, and the URETHRA.

In the female, the eggs, or OVA, are produced in the OVARIES and released during OVULATION into the FALLOPIAN TUBES about halfway through the MENSTRUAL CYCLE. If FERTILIZATION occurs, the resulting ZYGOTE travels down the Fallopian tube to the UTERUS, where it implants and continues development. If the ovum is not fertilized, it continues its journey toward the uterus, where it degenerates and

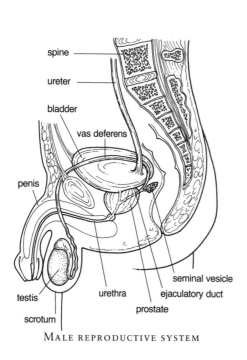

MALE REPRODUCTIVE SYSTEM

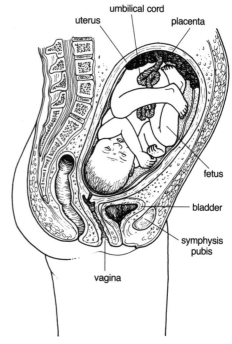

FEMALE REPRODUCTIVE SYSTEM. *In the ninth month of pregnancy.*

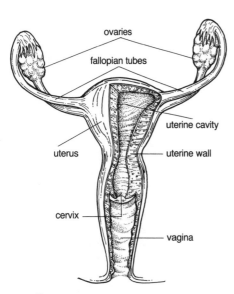

FEMALE REPRODUCTIVE SYSTEM

is released in the menstrual flow through the VAGINA during MENSTRUATION.

respiratory system (RES-puh-ruh-tawr-ee) The OR-GANS in the body involved in RESPIRATION. Air enters the body through the nose and mouth and travels down the TRACHEA, through the BRONCHIAL TUBES, and finally into the LUNGS. Once in the lungs, the air is drawn into an enormous number of thin-walled sacs richly supplied with CAPILLARIES. The exchange of OXYGEN and CARBON DIOXIDE in the BLOOD takes place in these tiny sacs.

respiratory tract The path that air follows as it is inhaled and directed into the LUNGS. The respiratory tract includes the nose and nasal passages, the throat and TRACHEA, and the BRONCHIAL TUBES.

retina (RET-n-uh) The inner layer of the EYE, sensitive to LIGHT, that is connected to the BRAIN by the OPTIC NERVE. The retina lines the interior of the eyeball. The LENS of the eye focuses WAVES of light on the retina.

Rh factor (ahr-AYCH) Any of several substances found on the surface of RED BLOOD CELLS in persons

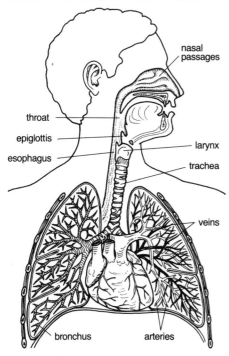

nasal passages

throat

epiglottis

esophagus

larynx

trachea

veins

bronchus   arteries

RESPIRATORY SYSTEM

designated Rh-positive that can cause an ANTIGEN-ANTIBODY reaction with red blood cells that do not have the substance. Persons whose red blood cells lack these substances are called Rh-negative.

🔊 An Rh-negative woman who gives birth to an Rh-positive baby may develop antibodies to the Rh factor during her first pregnancy. These antibodies may cause a disorder in Rh-positive babies conceived afterward that could result in the death of the infant if the condition is not recognized and treated.

rheumatic fever (rooh-MAT-ik) An INFECTIOUS DISEASE occurring most often in children who have had a previous INFECTION with a strain of STREPTOCOCCUS. Rheumatic fever, which is characterized by fever and joint pain, can cause permanent damage to the HEART if left untreated. ANTIBIOTICS, such as PENICILLIN, are used in treating the disease.

rheumatism (ROOH-muh-tiz-uhm) Any of various conditions of the bones, joints, muscles, or CONNECTIVE TISSUES marked by pain, stiffness, and INFLAMMATION.

right brain A popular term that describes the artistic and integrating functions of the right half of the CEREBRAL CORTEX. (*Compare* LEFT BRAIN; *see* BRAIN.)

rigor mortis (RIG-uhr MAWR-tis) Stiffening of the muscles of the body that occurs after death. *Rigor mortis* is LATIN for "stiffness of death."

🔊 Figuratively, *rigor mortis* refers to an absence of flexibility or vitality: "By the time the school finally closed, rigor mortis had set in in nearly every department."

root The part of a TOOTH below the gum. The root anchors the tooth to the jawbone.

rubella (rooh-BEL-uh) *See* GERMAN MEASLES.

rubeola (rooh-BEE-uh-luh, rooh-bee-OH-luh) *See* MEASLES.

Rx The symbol for prescriptions.

Sabin vaccine (SAY-bin) An oral VACCINE developed by the twentieth-century American scientist and physician Albert B. Sabin that induces IMMUNITY to POLIOMYELITIS.

saliva (suh-LEYE-vuh) The FLUID produced by the secretions of the SALIVARY GLANDS. Saliva contains ENZYMES that begin the DIGESTION of starches. It also moistens the mouth tissues and makes food easier to chew and swallow.

salivary glands (SAL-uh-ver-ee) The GLANDS in the mouth cavity that secrete SALIVA.

Salk vaccine (SAWLK, SAWK) The first VACCINE developed for IMMUNIZATION against POLIOMYELITIS. It is named for Jonas Salk, the twentieth-century American scientist who developed it.

salmonella (sal-muh-NEL-uh) A category of BACTERIA that occurs in many PATHOGENIC forms. One kind causes TYPHOID FEVER; there is evidence that other kinds cause various forms of FOOD POISONING.

saturated fats The kind of FAT in which the MOLECULES are arranged in such a way that every VALENCE ELECTRON in each of the ATOMS making up the molecule is used to form a BOND with one electron from another atom (called a single bond). Saturated fats are usually solid at room temperature, and are found in butter, red meat, poultry, and milk products.

🔊 A diet high in saturated fats increases the level of CHOLESTEROL in the BLOOD. Because of the role cholesterol may play in HEART disease, many physicians now recommend that people eat fewer saturated fats.

scarlet fever   An ACUTE DISEASE, and a CONTAGIOUS DISEASE, caused by a kind of STREPTOCOCCUS. Characterized by fever, sore throat, and a bright red rash, scarlet fever can be treated with PENICILLIN.

sciatica (seye-AT-i-kuh)   Chronic pain in the hip and upper leg caused by irritation of a large NERVE — the sciatic nerve — that runs through the PELVIS and down the back of the thigh.

scrotum (SKROH-tuhm)   The external pouch or sac located behind the PENIS. The scrotum contains the TESTES. (*See* REPRODUCTIVE SYSTEMS.)

sebaceous glands (si-BAY-shuhs)   GLANDS located in the SKIN that secrete an oily substance, sebum. Sebum lubricates the skin and hair.

🐾 Clogged sebaceous glands can result in pimples.

secondary sex characteristic   A characteristic, such as breast development, voice pitch, or facial hair, that distinguishes the sexes from each other but is not directly concerned with reproduction. The appearance of these characteristics is influenced by HORMONES.

semen (SEE-muhn)   The sticky white FLUID produced in the male REPRODUCTIVE SYSTEM that carries SPERM.

sexually transmitted diseases   Diseases that can be passed to other persons through sexual contact. AIDS, GONORRHEA, HERPES, and SYPHILIS are some examples of sexually transmitted diseases.

sickle cell anemia   A HEREDITARY form of ANEMIA in which the RED BLOOD CELLS become sickle-shaped (shaped like a crescent) and less able to carry OXYGEN.

🐾 Sickle cell anemia is a CHRONIC DISEASE and occurs most frequently in people of African descent.

skeletal system   The framework of the body, consisting of bones and other CONNECTIVE TISSUES, which protects and supports the body tissues and internal ORGANS. The human skeleton contains 206 bones, six of which are the tiny bones of the MIDDLE EAR (three in each ear) that function in hearing. The largest bone in the body is the thigh bone, or femur.

skin   The external tissue that covers the body. As the body's largest ORGAN (it makes up about one twenty-fifth of an adult's weight), the skin serves as a water-proof covering that helps keep out PATHOGENS and protects against temperature extremes and sunlight. The skin also contains special NERVE endings that respond to touch, pressure, heat, and cold. The skin has an outer layer, or EPIDERMIS, and a layer immediately below, called the dermis.

small intestine   The upper portion of the INTESTINES, extending from the STOMACH to the LARGE INTESTINE, where the DIGESTION of food takes place. The small intestine is about twenty feet long in adults.

smallpox   An ACUTE DISEASE, and an INFECTIOUS DISEASE, caused by a VIRUS, and now completely eradicated. Smallpox was characterized by high fever and large sores on the body that leave scars.

🐾 A surface with many blemishes is sometimes said to be "pockmarked" because it resembles the SKIN of a smallpox sufferer. 🐾 Smallpox is the first disease of humans to be completely eradicated by a worldwide campaign of INOCULATION.

somatic nervous system (soh-MAT-ik)   The part of the NERVOUS SYSTEM that controls voluntary movements in the body, such as those performed by the skeletal muscles (*see* MUSCULAR SYSTEM). The somatic nervous system also includes the special NERVE fibers that help keep the body in touch with its surroundings, such as those involved in touch, hearing, and sight.

spermatozoa (sphur-mat-uh-ZOH-uh) *sing.* SPERMATOZOON (spuhr-mat-uh-ZOH-uhn)   *See* SPERM.

spinal cord   The thick column of NERVE tissue that extends from the base of the BRAIN about two-thirds of the way down the backbone. As part of the CENTRAL NERVOUS SYSTEM, the spinal cord carries impulses back and forth between the brain and other parts of the body through a network of nerves that extend out from it like branches.

spleen   An ORGAN in the LYMPHATIC SYSTEM, in the upper left part of the ABDOMEN, that filters out harmful substances from the BLOOD. The spleen also produces WHITE BLOOD CELLS, removes worn-out RED BLOOD CELLS from circulation, and maintains a reserve blood supply for the body.

spontaneous abortion   A MISCARRIAGE or STILLBIRTH. (*See* ABORTION.)

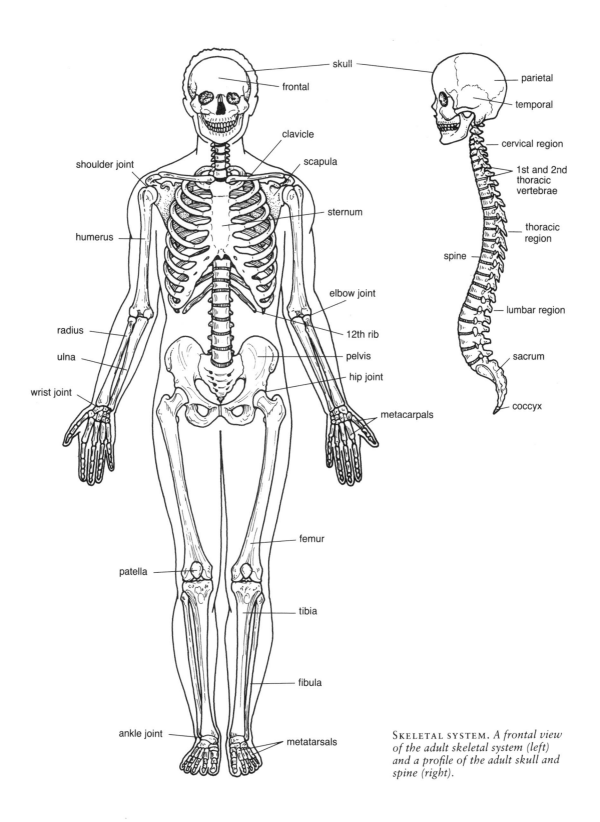

skull

frontal

parietal

temporal

clavicle

scapula

shoulder joint

cervical region

1st and 2nd
thoracic
vertebrae

sternum

humerus

thoracic
region

spine

elbow joint

radius

lumbar region

ulna

12th rib

pelvis

hip joint

wrist joint

sacrum

metacarpals

coccyx

femur

patella

tibia

fibula

ankle joint

metatarsals

SKELETAL SYSTEM. *A frontal view
of the adult skeletal system (left)
and a profile of the adult skull and
spine (right).*

staphylococcus (staf-uh-loh-KOK-uhs)   A category of BACTERIA that can cause boils, BLOOD poisoning, and other serious INFECTIONS.

sterilization   The removal of all MICROORGANISMS and other PATHOGENS from an object or surface by treating it with chemicals or subjecting it to high heat or RADIATION.

Sterilization also refers to procedures that result in infertility. VASECTOMIES and tubal ligations, in which the FALLOPIAN TUBES of a woman are tied off, are examples of sterilization techniques.

stethoscope (STETH-uh-skohp)   An instrument used in listening to internal body sounds. Most familiarly, physicians and nurses use it to listen to HEART sounds.

stillbirth   The birth of a FETUS that has died; particularly, birth of a fetus that has died in the UTERUS at a stage in development when an infant could survive on its own if born healthy.

stomach   An ORGAN in the DIGESTIVE SYSTEM, on the left side of the body behind the lower rib cage, that receives chewed food from the ESOPHAGUS. Tiny GLANDS in the stomach's lining secrete gastric juice, which contains ACIDS, MUCUS, and ENZYMES. This FLUID, along with the muscular churning actions of the stomach, helps transform food into a thick, semi-fluid mass that can be passed into the SMALL INTESTINE for DIGESTION.

strep throat   A severe sore throat caused by a kind of STREPTOCOCCUS. Strep throat can be treated with ANTIBIOTICS.

streptococcus (strep-tuh-KOK-uhs)   A category of BACTERIA that can cause various INFECTIONS in humans, including SCARLET FEVER and STREP THROAT.

stress   A physical factor such as injury, or mental state such as ANXIETY, that disturbs the body's normal state of functioning. Stress may contribute to the development of some illnesses, including HEART disease and CANCER.

🐾 The term *stress* also refers to the physical and mental state produced in the body when it is influenced by such factors: "The stress of the new job was too much for Tim, so he requested reassignment to his old position in the company."

stroke   A sudden loss of BRAIN function caused by an interruption in the supply of BLOOD to the brain.

A ruptured BLOOD VESSEL or CEREBRAL THROMBOSIS may cause the stroke, which can occur in varying degrees of severity from temporary PARALYSIS and slurred speech to permanent brain damage and death.

sweat glands   GLANDS in the SKIN that secrete sweat.

syndrome (SIN-drohm)   A set of signs and symptoms that appear together and characterize a disease or medical condition. AIDS is an example of a syndrome.

🐾 A collection of attitudes or behaviors that go together is often called a syndrome.

syphilis (SIF-uh-lis)   A CHRONIC DISEASE, and a SEXUALLY TRANSMITTED DISEASE, that is first manifested by the formation of SKIN patches called chancres. If left untreated, the disease can attack virtually any tissue of the body, including the HEART and NERVOUS SYSTEM, and cause blindness, mental illness, or death. Caused by a MICROORGANISM, syphilis can be treated effectively with PENICILLIN when the disease is in its early stages.

tapeworm   A worm with a long, flat body that can live in the human INTESTINES as a PARASITE. Infestation with a tapeworm usually occurs as the result of eating raw meat or fish that contains the immature form of the worm.

taste buds   Oval-shaped clusters of CELLS located on the tongue and lining of the mouth that contain special NERVE endings that help give rise to the sense of taste.

Tb test (tee-BEE)   A test to determine if an individual has been infected (*see* INFECTION) with the BACTERIA that cause TUBERCULOSIS. While the Tb test does not show whether the INFECTION is active or inactive, it is very useful in screening people who may have been exposed to the disease and in locating people who already have the disease.

tendon   A tough band of fibrous CONNECTIVE TISSUE that connects muscles to bones.

testes (TES-teez) *sing.* TESTIS (TES-tis)   The two ORGANS in the male REPRODUCTIVE SYSTEM that produce SPERM and TESTOSTERONE. The testes are housed in the SCROTUM.

testosterone (tes-TOS-tuh-rohn) A male HORMONE that governs SECONDARY SEX CHARACTERISTICS. It is produced in the TESTES.

tetanus (TET-n-uhs, TET-nuhs) An ACUTE DISEASE, and an INFECTIOUS DISEASE, caused by the TOXIN produced by a kind of BACTERIA that enters the body through cuts or wounds; also called LOCKJAW. In tetanus, the muscles of the body, particularly the muscles of the jaw, contract in painful spasms. Tetanus is deadly but can be prevented through IMMUNIZATION (tetanus shots).

thalamus (THAL-uh-muhs) The part of the BRAIN that coordinates NERVE impulses relating to the senses of sight, hearing, touch, and taste.

thalidomide (thuh-LID-uh-meyed) A sedative drug that was developed and used in EUROPE in the 1960s. Thalidomide was taken off the market when it became evident that it caused severe birth defects in babies born to women who had used the drug during pregnancy.

&. References to thalidomide are often made when illustrating the dangers of using drugs whose side effects are not well known.

thiamine (THEYE-uh-min, THEYE-uh-meen) One of the B VITAMINS, found in many plant and animal foods, especially wheat germ. It is needed by the body for METABOLISM and for proper functioning of the NERVOUS SYSTEM. Also called vitamin B_1.

thorax (THAWR-aks) The part of the body between the neck and DIAPHRAGM; the chest.

thrombosis (throm-BOH-sis) The development of a BLOOD clot in the CIRCULATORY SYSTEM. Depending on the location of the clot, the resultant loss of circulation can lead to a STROKE (CEREBRAL THROMBOSIS) or HEART ATTACK (CORONARY THROMBOSIS).

thymus gland (THEYE-muhs) A GLAND located behind the breastbone that functions in the development of the IMMUNE SYSTEM. The thymus is large in infancy and early childhood but begins to ATROPHY between ages eight and ten.

thyroid (THEYE-royd) A large GLAND in the neck that functions in the ENDOCRINE SYSTEM. The thyroid secretes HORMONES that regulate growth and METABOLISM.

tonsillitis (ton-suh-LEYE-tis) INFLAMMATION of the TONSILS, sometimes the result of a BACTERIAL INFECTION.

tonsils Two masses of tissue on either side of the throat. The tonsils, part of the LYMPHATIC SYSTEM, help defend the body against harmful MICROORGANISMS.

&. Tonsils are frequently removed surgically in childhood, although the trend recently has been against removal unless the tonsils have grown too large or are continually subject to INFECTION.

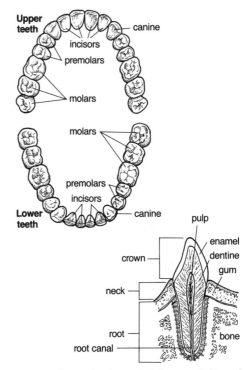

TOOTH. *The teeth of an adult human (left) and a cross section of an incisor (right).*

tooth A hard structure, embedded in the jaws of the mouth, that functions in chewing. The tooth consists of a CROWN, covered with hard white ENAMEL; a ROOT, which anchors the tooth to the jawbone; and a "neck" between the crown and the root, covered by the gum. Most of the tooth is made up of DENTIN, which is located directly below the enamel. The soft interior of the tooth, the PULP, contains NERVES and BLOOD VESSELS. Humans have MOLARS for grinding food, INCISORS for cutting, and CANINES and bicuspids for tearing.

toxins   Poisonous substances, consisting mainly of PROTEIN, that are a byproduct of METABOLISM in certain organisms. Toxins that enter the body through a BACTERIAL INFECTION can be very harmful, and can result in such diseases as TETANUS and BOTULISM.

trachea (TRAY-kee-uh)   The tube connecting the mouth to the BRONCHIAL TUBES that carries air to the LUNGS; the windpipe.

transfusion, blood   The injection of BLOOD received from a donor into the bloodstream of another individual having a compatible BLOOD TYPE. A person may need a blood transfusion if a great deal of blood has been lost through surgery or TRAUMA.
   ꙅ Diseases such as HEPATITIS and AIDS can be passed to someone who receives a blood transfusion if the blood supply is contaminated. The donor cannot contract the disease through giving blood.

trauma (TROW-muh, TRAW-muh)   Wounds that result from sudden physical injury or violence.
   ꙅ The term is frequently used to describe an emotional shock that causes serious psychological damage.

trichinosis (trik-uh-NOH-sis)   A disease caused by eating raw or undercooked pork infested with a kind of worm that lives as a PARASITE. The disease is characterized by nausea, DIARRHEA, and pain and swelling in the muscles.

tubal pregnancy (TOOH-buhl, TYOOH-buhl)   A pregnancy that begins with implantation of the EMBRYO in one of the FALLOPIAN TUBES instead of in the UTERUS. Tubal pregnancy is usually caused by a defect in the tube that prevents the fertilized OVUM from moving freely through it.

tuberculosis (tuh-bur-kyuh-LOH-sis)   An INFECTIOUS DISEASE caused by BACTERIA that mainly attack the LUNGS. The disease is characterized by the formation of patches, called tubercles, that appear in the lungs and, in later stages, the bones, joints, and other parts of the body. Tuberculosis is treated with combinations of ANTIBIOTICS, and is no longer considered a major health problem in industrialized countries. It was formerly called CONSUMPTION.

   ꙅ Years ago, tuberculosis (consumption) was a major killer; it often figures in literature and drama.
   ꙅ In recent years the incidence of tuberculosis has been on the increase in America, particularly in large cities.

tumor   An abnormal mass of new TISSUE growth that serves no function in the body. Tumors are usually classified as BENIGN or MALIGNANT, and are often caused by CANCER.

typhoid fever (TEYE-foyd)   An ACUTE DISEASE, and a highly CONTAGIOUS DISEASE, transmitted by food or water contaminated with a kind of BACTERIA. The disease, which is often fatal, is characterized by high fever, pain in the ABDOMEN, and bleeding in the INTESTINES.

Typhoid Mary   A cook who carried TYPHOID FEVER and passed it on to many people in and around NEW YORK CITY in the early twentieth century.
   ꙅ The term is often applied to the carrier of a CONTAGIOUS DISEASE, or, more generally, to anyone who brings bad luck: "The last three insurance companies I had policies with folded. I feel like Typhoid Mary."

typhus (TEYE-fuhs)   A group of ACUTE DISEASES and CONTAGIOUS DISEASES, often fatal, marked by severe headaches and high fever. Typhus is transmitted to humans by fleas, lice, or mites that are infected with the MICROORGANISM that causes the disease.

ulcer (UL-suhr)   An inflamed open sore on the SKIN or MUCOUS MEMBRANE. An ulcer may form in the inner lining of the STOMACH or DUODENUM, interfere with DIGESTION, and cause considerable pain. STRESS can often contribute to this kind of ulcer.

ultrasound   A method of diagnosing illness and viewing internal body structures in which sound WAVES of high FREQUENCY are bounced off internal ORGANS and tissues from outside the body. The technique measures different amounts of resistance the body parts offer to the sound waves, and then uses the DATA to produce a "picture" of the structures. Ultrasound is often used to obtain an image of the developing FETUS in pregnant women; the image can confirm the presence of twins or triplets, and can be used to diagnose some abnormalities.
   ꙅ When an image of the inside of the body is needed, ultrasound is often considered a safer alter-

native than X-RAYS. Like x-rays, ultrasound involves exposure of the body to a form of RADIATION; unlike x-rays, ultrasound has not been shown to be CARCINOGENIC.

umbilical cord (um-BIL-i-kuhl) A ropelike structure that connects a developing EMBRYO or FETUS to the PLACENTA. The umbilical cord contains the BLOOD VESSELS that supply the embryo or fetus with nutrients and remove waste products. Connected to the ABDOMEN of the embryo or fetus, the umbilical cord is cut at birth, leaving a small depression — the navel, or "belly button."

&. The detaching of the umbilical cord provides a figure of speech for new independence: "He finally cut the umbilical cord and moved out of his parents' home."

unsaturated fats A kind of FAT in which one or more pairs of ELECTRONS in the ATOMS making up the fat MOLECULE form a BOND with a pair of electrons from another atom (a double bond). There are two kinds of unsaturated fats: *monounsaturated*, which contain one double bond; and *polyunsaturated*, which contain two or more double bonds. Monounsaturated fats are found in peanuts, peanut butter, olives, and avocados. Polyunsaturated fats, which are usually LIQUID at room temperature, are found in such oils as corn, sunflower, and soybean oil.

&. Unsaturated fats are generally regarded to be healthier in the diet than SATURATED FATS because they may help lower the level of CHOLESTEROL in the BLOOD.

ureters (yoo-REE-tuhrz, YOOR-uh-tuhrz) The tubes that carry URINE from each KIDNEY to the URINARY BLADDER.

urethra (yoo-REE-thruh) A tube through which URINE moves from the URINARY BLADDER out of the body. In the male, the urethra also acts as the passageway for SEMEN.

urinary bladder A saclike structure that stores URINE until it can be passed out of the body through the URETHRA.

urinary tract The body parts involved in the elimination of URINE. The URETERS, URETHRA, and URINARY BLADDER are all part of the urinary tract.

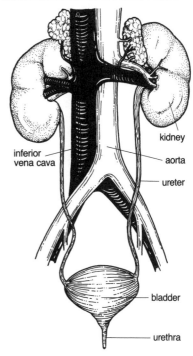

URINARY TRACT

urine The FLUID produced by the KIDNEYS, consisting of water and dissolved substances, that is stored in the BLADDER and discharged through the URETHRA. (*See* EXCRETORY SYSTEM.)

urology (yoo-ROL-uh-jee) The branch of medicine devoted to the study and care of the URINARY TRACT.

uterus (YOOH-tuh-ruhs) A pear-shaped ORGAN in the female REPRODUCTIVE SYSTEM where the EMBRYO or FETUS develops until birth. The strong muscles of the uterus help push the baby out of the mother's body.

vaccination (vak-suh-NAY-shuhn) INOCULATION with a VACCINE to produce IMMUNITY to a particular INFECTIOUS DISEASE.

vaccine (vak-SEEN) A substance prepared from dead or living MICROORGANISMS that is introduced into the body through INOCULATION. The vaccine causes the development of ANTIBODIES, which produce IMMUNITY to the disease caused by the microorganism.

vagina (vuh-JEYE-nuh) A tubelike passageway in the female that connects the external GENITALS with the UTERUS.

valium (VAL-ee-uhm) A common prescription tranquilizer, trademark for the drug diazepam.

vasectomy (vuh-SEK-tuh-mee, vay-ZEK-tuh-mee) A surgical procedure in which the ducts that carry SPERM out of the TESTES are cut and tied off so that no sperm can pass. Vasectomy is a form of male STERILIZATION and is used as a method of BIRTH CONTROL. The procedure has no effect on a man's capacity to produce SEMEN; the only difference is that his semen will no longer contain sperm.

VD *See* VENEREAL DISEASES.

veins BLOOD VESSELS that return BLOOD from the body tissues to the HEART. (*Compare* ARTERIES; *see* CIRCULATORY SYSTEM.)

venereal diseases (VD) (vuh-NEER-ee-uhl) SEXUALLY TRANSMITTED DISEASES; these diseases are named after VENUS, the Roman goddess of love.

ventricles (VEN-tri-kuhlz) The two lower chambers of the HEART, which receive BLOOD from the ATRIA and pump it into the ARTERIES. (*See* CIRCULATORY SYSTEM.)

vermiform appendix (VUR-muh-fawrm) *See* APPENDIX.

viral infection (VEYE-ruhl) An INFECTION caused by a VIRUS. At present, viral infections cannot be treated with ANTIBIOTICS. (*Compare* BACTERIAL INFECTION.)

☙ Diseases caused by viral infections include HERPES, CHICKEN POX, HEPATITIS, INFLUENZA, and the common cold.

virulence (VIR-yuh-luhns, VIR-uh-luhns) The capacity of a PATHOGEN, such as a MICROORGANISM or TOXIN, to produce disease.

☙ "Virulent" substances or organisms are extremely PATHOGENIC or toxic.

virus (VEYE-ruhs) *plur.* VIRUSES A minute organism that consists of a core of NUCLEIC ACID surrounded by PROTEIN. Viruses, which are so small that a special kind of MICROSCOPE is needed to view them, can grow and reproduce only inside living CELLS. (*See under "Life Sciences."*)

vital signs The pulse rate, body temperature, and rate of RESPIRATION of a person. The vital signs are usually measured to obtain a quick evaluation of the person's general physical condition.

vitamins Complex ORGANIC COMPOUNDS that are needed in small amounts by the body for normal growth and METABOLISM. An important part of a BALANCED DIET, vitamins occur naturally in foods, and may be added to processed foods to increase their nutritional value. Many vitamins have been identified, and each plays a specific role in the functioning of the body. For example, vitamin C is needed for the proper healing of wounds and broken bones; vitamin A helps the body resist INFECTION. Some vitamins are so important that without them certain diseases or conditions could develop. For example, a deficiency of vitamin D may cause rickets, and a deficiency of vitamin B_{12} could result in a form of ANEMIA.

vocal cords Two folds of tissue located in the LARYNX that vibrate when air passes over them, producing the sound WAVES associated with talking and singing.

vulva (VUL-vuh) The external organs of the FEMALE REPRODUCTIVE SYSTEM.

white blood cells Colorless CELLS in the BLOOD that help combat INFECTION. Some white blood cells act as scavengers by engulfing foreign particles (such as BACTERIA) and destroying them. Others produce ANTIBODIES or destroy dead cells. (*See* AIDS.)

whooping cough (pertussis) [HOOH-ping, HOOP-ing] An ACUTE DISEASE, and an INFECTIOUS DISEASE, occurring mainly in children, and characterized by violent coughing. Caused by a kind of BACTERIA, whooping cough has largely been eradicated in the United States through a program of VACCINATION, which is begun when infants are just three months old.

wisdom teeth Four MOLARS, two on the upper jaw and two on the lower jaw, that are the last TEETH to emerge in the mouth.

☙ These teeth are associated with wisdom because they appear during the late teens or early twenties, when a person is physically mature. Often, the wisdom teeth may not rise above the gum line, but remain *impacted* in the jaw, causing INFLAMMATION. If this impaction occurs, or if they pose a threat to other teeth, the wisdom teeth may need to be removed.

withdrawal symptoms A wide range of physical or emotional disorders, including nervousness, headaches, and INSOMNIA, that occur when an individual who is addicted to a substance (such as drugs or alcohol) stops using the substance.

x-ray A photograph or image obtained through the use of X-RAYS. An x-ray is taken when an image of internal body structures (such as bones or ORGANS) is needed to diagnose disease or determine the extent of injuries.

zygote (ZEYE-goht) The single CELL that results from FERTILIZATION of an OVUM by a SPERM. After dividing several times, it implants in the UTERUS. It continues to divide, producing more cells and passing through the stages of EMBRYO and FETUS.

Technology

There are two reasons to pursue scientific knowledge: for the sake of the knowledge itself, and for the practical uses of that knowledge. Because this second aspect of science affects the lives of most people, it is more familiar than the first. Knowledge must be gained, however, before it can be applied, and often the most important technological advances arise from research pursued for its own sake.

Traditionally, new technology has been concerned with the construction of machines, structures, and tools on a relatively large scale. The development of materials for building bridges or skyscrapers is an example of this, as is the development of the INTERNAL-COMBUSTION ENGINE and the NUCLEAR REACTOR. While such activities involve all the sciences, from CHEMISTRY to nuclear PHYSICS, the overriding goal has been the same: to improve the human condition by finding better ways to deal with the macroscopic world.

Since WORLD WAR II, the focus of technological activity has undergone a major change. While the old activities are still pursued, they have been largely superseded by applications of technology at the microscopic level. Instead of building large-scale structures and machines, modern-day technology tends to concentrate on finding improved ways to transfer information and to develop new materials by studying the way ATOMS come together. The SILICON CHIP and microelectronics typify this new technological trend, as does the blossoming of GENETIC ENGINEERING. The trend can be expected to continue into the foreseeable future.

The dividing line between what we include in the following list as technology and what we call science elsewhere in this volume is somewhat arbitrary. In general, what we have done is this: if a term is essential to understanding a particular branch of science, it appears in the list for that science. Thus, *atom* appears with the physical sciences, even though an understanding of atoms is clearly important to the new technology. If, however, the term involves something that is likely to affect an individual's life, even though it is not a central concept of a particular branch of science, it is listed under "Technology."

The words in the following section have been chosen because they are likely to appear without explanation in many publications, particularly in articles and books dealing with the impact and implications of technology. This section does not emphasize the social consequences of new technology, but concentrates instead on the basic knowledge needed to understand how technology works.

— J. T.

AC *See* ALTERNATING CURRENT.

AI *See* ARTIFICIAL INTELLIGENCE.

air pollution The addition of harmful chemicals to the ATMOSPHERE. The most serious air pollution results from the burning of FOSSIL FUELS, especially in INTERNAL-COMBUSTION ENGINES.

alternating current (AC) An electric CURRENT in which the flow reverses periodically. (*Compare* DIRECT CURRENT [DC].)

&. In the United States, most household current is AC, going through sixty reversal cycles each second. Electric motors in household appliances are designed to work with current at this rate of reversal.

alternator An obsolete term for an electrical GENERATOR that produces ALTERNATING CURRENT, particularly one in an automobile engine.

AM *See* AMPLITUDE MODULATION.

amp (ampere) [AM-peer] A unit of electric CURRENT. One ampere corresponds to a certain number of ELECTRONS passing a fixed point each second.

&. A typical household's electrical supply includes a total of 120 to 200 amps; a typical house CIRCUIT carries 15 to 50 amps.

amplifier In electronics, a device that takes a small electric signal and converts it into a large one. Amplifiers are used in stereo systems, electric guitars, and loudspeakers.

amplitude modulation (AM) A type of radio signal in which the amplitude, or strength, of a RADIO WAVE is varied in order to carry information from a transmitter to a receiver. (*Compare* FREQUENCY MODULATION [FM].)

analog computer (AN-l-awg, AN-l-og) A COMPUTER whose CIRCUITS are designed so that they mimic the behavior of a real physical system. Thus, a circuit in which the output VOLTAGE quadruples when the input voltage doubles is said to be an analog of a falling object, for which the distance traveled quadruples when the time doubles. Analog computers, never widely used, have been largely replaced by DIGITAL COMPUTERS.

analog signal (AN-l-awg, AN-l-og) A signal in which some feature increases and decreases in the same way as the thing being transmitted. In AM RA-

DIO, for example, the strength of the radio WAVE goes up and down in analogy with the loudness of the original sound. (*Contrast* DIGITAL SIGNAL.) &. Radio, TV, some telephones, and tape recorders all use analog signals now, but the trend for the future is to send signals in digital form.

APOLLO PROGRAM. *The* Apollo 11 *command/service module being made ready for attachment to* Saturn V.

Apollo program A series of space flights undertaken by the United States with a goal of landing a man on the MOON. Each Apollo flight carried a crew of three ASTRONAUTS. The first lunar landing by humans was achieved by *Apollo 11* on July 20, 1969. Five other successful lunar landings followed. The Apollo program ended in 1974. It was named after the Greek god of learning, APOLLO.

&. Neil Armstrong was the first man to set foot on the moon.

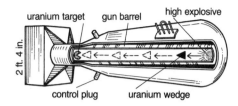

ATOMIC BOMB. *"Little Boy," the type of bomb dropped on Hiroshima (top), and the mushroom cloud that follows an atomic explosion.*

artificial intelligence (AI) The means of duplicating or imitating intelligence in COMPUTERS, robots, or other devices, which allows them to solve problems, discriminate among objects, and respond to voice command.

artificial reality *See* VIRTUAL REALITY.

astronaut A crew member of a space mission launched by the United States. (*See* APOLLO PROGRAM *and* MERCURY PROGRAM.)

atom smasher Colloquial term for a PARTICLE ACCELERATOR.

atomic bomb A bomb that is powered by nuclear FISSION, and therefore produces a quick release of ENERGY and great destruction.

automation Replacement of human workers by machines for particular jobs.

bacteriological warfare *See* GERM WARFARE.

bathyscaph (BATH-i-skaf) A deep-sea research vessel that carries a crew and is free to maneuver independently.

battery A device that produces an electric CURRENT by harnessing the CHEMICAL REACTIONS that take place within its cells.

Bell, Alexander Graham An American inventor and scientist of the late nineteenth and early twentieth centuries, born in SCOTLAND. He invented the telephone in 1876. Much of Bell's career was devoted to education of the deaf and to production of electronic devices to help them hear better.

   ❖ The Bell Telephone Company was formed as a result of Bell's work.

binary (BEYE-nuh-ree, BEYE-ner-ee) Anything composed of two parts. In modern electronic COMPUTERS, information is stored in banks of components that act like switches. Since switches can be either on or off, they have a binary character, and we say that the computer uses "binary arithmetic" to do its work.

biological warfare *See* GERM WARFARE.

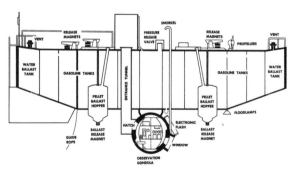

BATHYSCAPH. *A blueprint of a bathyscaph (above), and a photograph of the exterior (right).*

bit The smallest unit of information. One bit corresponds to a "yes or no." Some examples of a bit of information: whether a light is on or off, whether a switch (like a TRANSISTOR) is on or off, whether a grain of magnetized iron points up or down. ❧ The information in a DIGITAL COMPUTER is stored in the form of bits.

boom, sonic The sharp, explosive sound generated by an airplane traveling at speeds greater than the speed of sound. The sonic boom follows the aircraft much like a wake follows a ship.

Braille A system of writing and printing for the blind in which arrangements of raised dots representing letters and numbers can be identified by touch.

breeder reactor A NUCLEAR REACTOR in which PLUTONIUM and other materials are produced as a by-product. ❧ Breeder reactors are designed to produce more fuel than they consume. ❧ The development of the breeder reactor has been stopped in the United States, but continues to be pursued in Europe and Japan.

byte (BEYET) In COMPUTER technology, a unit of information made up of BITS (often eight bits). The memory capacity of a typical PERSONAL COMPUTER runs from hundreds of thousands to millions of bytes.

calculator An electronic device for performing automatic mathematical computations, usually controlled by a keyboard. Some are actually small COMPUTERS, with limited memory, that allow the user to use simple PROGRAMS.

capacitor (kuh-PAS-i-tuhr) A device used in electrical CIRCUITS. The capacitor stores an electrical CHARGE for short periods of time, and then returns it to the circuit.

cathode-ray tube (CRT) (KATH-ohd) A device that can produce an image on a screen with electrical impulses.
    ❧ A television screen is a sophisticated CRT, as is the screen on which COMPUTER output is displayed.

Celsius (SEL-see-uhs) A temperature scale in which zero degrees is the freezing point of water and 100 degrees is the boiling point. Temperature in this scale is generally denoted by °C or, in scientific usage, C alone. (*Compare* FAHRENHEIT.)

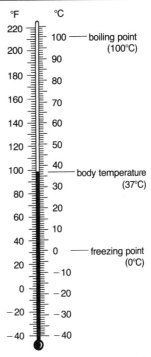

CELSIUS. *Celsius readings are on the right; Fahrenheit, on the left.*

centimeter One hundredth of a METER; equal to somewhat less than half an inch.

Chernobyl (chuhr-NOH-buhl, cher-NOH-buhl) A place in Ukraine where a NUCLEAR POWER plant — a GENERATOR powered by a NUCLEAR REACTOR — underwent a MELTDOWN in 1986. A cloud of RADIOACTIVE GASES spread throughout the region of Chernobyl, and to foreign countries as well. Forty thousand people living nearby were evacuated. Dozens of deaths and hundreds of illnesses were reported to have been caused by the accident. (*Compare* THREE MILE ISLAND.)

circuit, electrical A complete, unbroken path of conducting material (*see* CONDUCTOR) over which an electrical CURRENT can move. Every circuit has a source (such as a GENERATOR) to produce the current, and a load where the ENERGY is expended.

code A series of instructions designed to be fed into a COMPUTER. A short code is called a PROGRAM.

composite materials (kuhm-POZ-it) Materials, generally strong and lightweight, in which fibers of more than one sort of material are bonded together chemically. These types of materials were developed in the laboratory, and derive their strength from the combination of materials rather than from the interlocking of a uniform set of ATOMS.

COMPUTER. *A personal computer.*

computer An electronic device that stores and manipulates information. It differs from a CALCULATOR in being able to store a PROGRAM and to store and retrieve information in its memory without human help.

computer virus A PROGRAM that enters a COMPUTER (usually without the knowledge of the operator). Some viruses are mild, and only cause messages to appear on the screen, but others are destructive and can wipe out the computer's memory or even cause more severe damage. ❧ Computer viruses spread from machine to machine on disks and through telephone lines.

conductor A material through which electric CURRENT can pass. In general, metals are good conductors. Copper or aluminum is normally used to conduct electricity in commercial and household systems. (*Compare* INSULATOR.)

cosmonaut A crew member of a space mission launched by the former SOVIET UNION.

CRT *See* CATHODE-RAY TUBE.

cryogenics (kreye-uh-JEN-iks) The branch of technology concerned with the behavior of materials at very low temperatures, particularly temperatures near ABSOLUTE ZERO.

current, electric The flow of large numbers of ELECTRONS through a CONDUCTOR. (*See* ALTERNATING CURRENT, CONDUCTION, *and* DIRECT CURRENT.)

cybernetics (seye-buhr-NET-iks) The general study of control and communication systems in living organisms and machines, especially the mathematical analysis of the flow of information. The term *cybernetics* was coined by Norbert Wiener, an American mathematician of the twentieth century.

cyberspace (SEYE-buhr-spays) A term used in conjunction with VIRTUAL REALITY, designating the imaginary place where virtual objects exist. For example, if a COMPUTER produces a picture of a building that allows the architect to "walk" through and see what his design would look like, the builing is said to exist in cyberspace.

data processing Either the preparation of DATA for processing by a COMPUTER, or the storage and processing of raw data by the computer itself.

DC *See* DIRECT CURRENT.

DDT A colorless insecticide that kills on contact. It is poisonous to humans and animals when swallowed or absorbed through the skin. DDT is an ABBREVIATION for *dichlorodiphenyltrichloroethane.*

❧ Although DDT, when it was first invented, was considered a great advance in protecting crops from insect damage and in combating diseases spread by insects, recent discoveries have led to its ban in many countries. Residue from DDT has been shown to remain in the ECOSYSTEM and the FOOD CHAIN long after its original use, causing harm and even death to animals considered harmless or useful to man.

dielectric (deye-i-LEK-trik) A material that conducts (*see* CONDUCTION) ELECTRICITY poorly or not at all. If a VOLTAGE is applied to a dielectric, the ATOMS in the material arrange themselves in such a way as to oppose the flow of electrical CURRENT. Glass, wood, and plastic are common dielectrics. (*See* INSULATOR.)

digital computer A COMPUTER that performs operations with quantities represented electronically as digits, usually in BINARY code. (*Compare* ANALOG COMPUTER.)

digital signal A signal in which the original information is converted into a string of BITS before being transmitted. A RADIO signal, for example, will be either on or off. Digital signals can be sent for long distances and suffer less interference than ANALOG SIGNALS. ❧ The communications industry worldwide is in the midst of a switch to digital signals. ❧ Sound storage in a compact disk is in digital form.

direct current (DC) Electric CURRENT in which the ELECTRONS flow in one direction only. (*Compare* ALTERNATING CURRENT [AC].)

❧ DC is usually supplied by BATTERIES.

DNA FINGERPRINTING. *Technicians reading DNA fingerprints.*

DNA fingerprinting A technique by which the DNA of an individual can be compared with that found in a sample or another individual. ❧ DNA fingerprinting is acepted by most COURTS as evidence for establishing paternity, and increasingly is being accepted as evidence in criminal trials.

Edison, Thomas A. An American inventor of the late nineteenth and early twentieth centuries. He patented more than a thousand devices, including the phonograph and the incandescent light bulb.

❧ Edison originated the PROVERB "GENIUS IS ONE PERCENT INSPIRATION AND NINETY-NINE PERCENT PERSPIRATION." ❧ Edison was called the "Wizard of Menlo Park," after his home town in NEW JERSEY.

electric current *See* CURRENT, ELECTRIC.

electrical circuit *See* CIRCUIT, ELECTRICAL.

electromagnet A MAGNET created by passing an electric CURRENT through coils of wire. Such magnets are widely used in common electrical systems.

electroplating A process whereby a thin coat of metal is applied to a material. The process involves placing the material to be coated in a solution containing IONS of the metal and then passing an electric CURRENT through the system, which causes the ions to adhere to the material.

epoxy (i-POK-see) A high-strength adhesive, often made of two different materials that must be mixed together just prior to use.

Fahrenheit (FAIR-uhn-heyet) A temperature scale, used primarily in the United States, in which the freezing point of water is 32 degrees and the boiling point 212 degrees. Temperatures in this scale are denoted by °F or, in scientific usage, F alone. (*Compare* CELSIUS.)

feedback A process in which a system regulates itself by monitoring its own output. That is, it "feeds back" part of its output to itself. Feedback is used to control machines; a heating system, for example, uses a THERMOSTAT to monitor and adjust its output. Feedback is also used by the human BRAIN to control various muscles and joints.

❧ By extension, "feedback" is any response or information about the result of a process. ❧ Feedback is usually a feature of AUTOMATION.

fiber optics A technology that uses specially designed bundles of transparent fibers to transmit LIGHT.

❧ Some of the applications of fiber optics are in medicine, where it is used to photograph otherwise inaccessible parts of the body, and in telecommunications, where it is used to transmit telephone signals.

fingerprint The impression or mark left by the underside of the tips of the fingers or thumbs. The impression is formed by a pattern of ridges on the SKIN surface. This pattern is unique for each individual and therefore can serve as a means of identification. (*Compare* DNA FINGERPRINTING.)

❧ Fingerprinting is used extensively in criminal investigation, but is also used as a means of identification by many organizations.

fluorocarbon   *See* **CFC.**

FM   *See* FREQUENCY MODULATION.

frequency modulation (FM)   A type of radio signal in which the FREQUENCY of the RADIO WAVE is varied to carry information from the transmitter to the receiver. (*Compare* AMPLITUDE MODULATION [AM].)

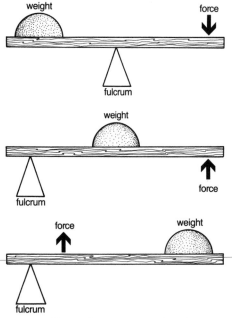

FULCRUM. *Top to bottom: First-class lever, with the fulcrum between the weight and the force; second-class lever, with the weight between the fulcrum and the force; third-class lever, with the force between the fulcrum and the weight.*

fulcrum (FOOL-kruhm, FUL-kruhm)   The point on which a lever is balanced when a FORCE is exerted.

Fulton, Robert   An American inventor of the late eighteenth and early nineteenth centuries. He launched the first successful steamboat, the *Clermont*, in 1807, on the HUDSON RIVER in NEW YORK.

galvanizing   Placement of a thin coat of a metal such as zinc over iron or steel to protect the latter from rust. Galvanized metals typically appear shiny.

gasohol (GAS-uh-hawl)   A mixture of gasoline with alcohol derived from plants. Gasohol was a popular fuel for cars and trucks during gasoline shortages.

generating plant   An installation that produces electric CURRENT for commercial sale. In the United States, most electricity is generated from FOSSIL FUELS; some is generated by NUCLEAR REACTORS.

generator   A device that produces electric CURRENT, usually by rotating a CONDUCTOR in a MAGNETIC FIELD, thereby generating current through ELECTRO-MAGNETIC INDUCTION. This sort of generator produces an ALTERNATING CURRENT (AC).

germ warfare   The use of MICROORGANISMS in war to injure or destroy humans, animals, or crops. Germ warfare is also called bacteriological warfare or biological warfare.

hardware   The physical machinery and devices that make up a COMPUTER system. It is contrasted to SOFTWARE — the PROGRAMS and instructions used to run the system.

hard-wired   In computer JARGON, a CIRCUIT is hard-wired if it is built to perform a specific function and requires no outside instructions or PROGRAM.
    ❧ "Hard-wired" is often used loosely to refer to functions that are innate and unlearned in living systems: "The ability to perceive objects in a certain way appears to be hard-wired into the BRAINS of MAMMALS."

high definition TV (HDTV)   A television system that has more lines per picture than present systems, and thus produces much sharper images. At present American TV has 525 lines per image and European TV 625, while high definition systems may have more than 1000. ❧ Many observers feel that the battle for high definition TV markets will be the next great world economic battle.

high-tech   A descriptive term for industry heavily dependent on recent laboratory discoveries. Manufacturing COMPUTERS is a typical high-tech industry.

holography (hoh-LOG-ruh-fee)   A technique using LASERS and photographic plates to produce three-dimensional images.

hydraulic   A descriptive term for a system operated or moved by a FLUID. The hydraulic jack, in which FORCE is transmitted from a handle by means of a heavy oil, is probably the most familiar hydraulic device.

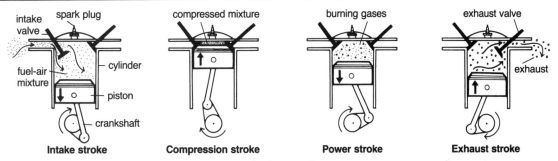

Intake stroke   **Compression stroke**   **Power stroke**   **Exhaust stroke**

INTERNAL-COMBUSTION ENGINE. *The four strokes necessary to run a gasoline engine (left to right): intake, compression, power, and exhaust.*

hydroelectric power ELECTRICITY generated from the ENERGY of running water, usually water falling over a dam.

☙ Only a small proportion of the electricity in the United States is produced by hydroelectric power.

impedance (im-PEED-ns) A measure of the apparent RESISTANCE posed by an electrical CIRCUIT to an ALTERNATING CURRENT (AC).

☙ The term *impedance* is most often encountered in dealing with antennas and speakers in television, stereo, and radio systems.

inductance A process whereby the effect of INDUCTION is used to alter the CURRENT in an ELECTRICAL CIRCUIT.

induction An effect in ELECTRICAL systems in which electrical CURRENTS store ENERGY temporarily in MAGNETIC FIELDS before that energy is returned to the CIRCUIT.

insulator A material that does not easily transmit ENERGY, such as electric CURRENT or heat. Materials such as wood, plastic, and ceramics are insulators. Fiberglass is an example of a heat insulator. (*Compare* CONDUCTOR.)

integrated circuit A miniaturized electrical CIRCUIT built on a MICROCHIP.

internal-combustion engine Any engine powered by burning fuel inside it (for example, a standard automobile engine). Internal-combustion engines normally burn FOSSIL FUELS and therefore are a major source of AIR POLLUTION. (*See* SMOG.)

irrigation Artificial provision of water to sustain growing plants.

☙ Irrigation accounts for the greatest part of water usage in the western United States.

Jobs, Steven The founder of Apple Computer and the man often given credit for the wide availability of PERSONAL COMPUTERS. ☙ Jobs is often cited as an example of the new type of ENTREPRENEUR associated with the information age.

kilowatt-hour (kwh) [KIL-uh-waht] A unit of ENERGY: the expenditure of one KILOWATT of POWER for one hour. A toaster running for an hour will use about this much energy.

laser A device that produces a very narrow, highly concentrated beam of LIGHT. Lasers have a variety of

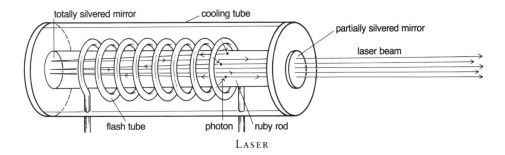

LASER

uses in such areas as surgery, welding and metal cutting, and sound and video recording and reproduction. The name is an ACRONYM for *light amplification by stimulated emission of radiation.*

leap second   A second inserted into the year (usually on New Year's Eve) to make up for the fact that the EARTH's rotation is slowing down. 🕭 Scientists know when to insert a leap second by comparing the earth's rotation to an ATOMIC CLOCK.

maglev (MAG-lev)   *See* magnetic levitation.

magnetic levitation   A process by which a MAGNET moving over a piece of metal causes ELECTRICAL CURRENTS to flow in the metal that, in turn, produce FORCES that push the magnet upward. If the force is large enough, the moving magnet can float (be levitated). 🕭 Magnetic levitation (or maglev) is used in a new generation of trains that will have cruising speeds of up to three hundred miles per hour.

magnetic tape   A device for storing information, in which signals are recorded by lining up small bits of magnetic materials in the coating on the tape. Ordinary tape recorders use magnetic tape.

mainframe   A large, powerful COMPUTER system. A typical mainframe computer will fill a good-sized room.

Marconi, Guglielmo (mahr-KOH-nee)   An Italian inventor and electrical engineer of the late nineteenth and early twentieth centuries. His most famous invention is the wireless telegraph, the forerunner of present-day radio, which he developed in the 1890s. In 1909, Marconi received the NOBEL PRIZE for PHYSICS.

mass media   Twentieth century newspapers, motion pictures, radio, television, and magazines, all of which have the technical capacity to deliver information to millions of people.

megabyte (MEG-uh-beyet)   A unit of COMPUTER information: one million BYTES.

megawatt   A unit of power: one million WATTS. A typical large electrical GENERATING PLANT can produce a thousand megawatts of ELECTRICITY.

meltdown   The most serious accident that can occur at a NUCLEAR REACTOR. In a meltdown, the RADIOACTIVE material in the reactor becomes very hot, melting some or all of the fuel in the reactor. A melt-

down may or may not be followed by the release of radioactive material to the environment. A partial meltdown, with very little external RADIATION, occurred at THREE MILE ISLAND in 1979; a complete meltdown happened at CHERNOBYL in 1986.

MERCURY PROGRAM. *Blastoff. The Mercury capsule sits above the striped section of the rocket.*

Mercury program   A program of rocket-powered flights undertaken by the United States with the goal of putting a man in orbit around the EARTH. Each Mercury flight carried one ASTRONAUT. The program ran from 1961 to 1963, and was named after the Roman god MERCURY, the messenger of the gods.
🕭 The first United States suborbital flight was made by Alan Shepard in 1961. 🕭 In 1962, John Glenn made the first orbital flight by an American astronaut.

microchip The basic component of modern miniaturized electronics. The "chip" is a series of electrical CIRCUITS built into a tiny wafer of SILICON or another SEMICONDUCTOR. 🕭 These circuits may be made by exposing the chip to a high temperature vapor of controlled composition. The vapor deposits a thin layer (sometimes only a few ATOMS thick) on the silicon. In this way complex layers of materials such as those found in TRANSISTORS can be built up in a very small area.

microfilm A film on which miniature copies of documents are reproduced. Microfilm allows for very compact storage of books and documents.

microscope A device that produces a magnified image of objects too small to be seen with the naked eye. Such objects are thus called "microscopic." The microscope is widely used in medicine and BIOLOGY. Common microscopes use LENSES; others, such as ELECTRON MICROSCOPES, scan an object with ELECTRONS, X-RAYS, and other RADIATION besides ordinary visible LIGHT.

microwave communication The transmission of signals by sending MICROWAVES, either directly or via a SATELLITE. The receivers for microwave signals are usually disc-shaped antennas a few yards across, and are often seen installed in business locations or near private homes.

modem (MOH-duhm, MOH-dem) A device that links a PERSONAL COMPUTER to a telephone line, so that the computer can receive information from other computers.

nano A prefix meaning one billionth.

nanosecond (NAN-uh-sek-uhnd) A billionth of a second. 🕭 The term is often used to refer to a very short time: "He missed having an accident by nanoseconds."

nanotechnology (nan-oh-tek-NOL-uh-jee) A branch of technology devoted to producing devices on an atomic scale. The working part of a typical nanotechnology device might be only a few thousand atoms in width.

neural networks A COMPUTER system that is designed to mimic the human BRAIN or some other biological system in its functioning. They were developed to deal with problems, like pattern recognition, that the brain does well but that traditional computer systems cannot handle easily.

nuclear power Electrical POWER generated by a NUCLEAR REACTOR.

nuclear reactor A device in which the ENERGY released by the FISSION of NUCLEI of URANIUM or another ELEMENT is used to produce steam to run an electrical GENERATOR or other device.

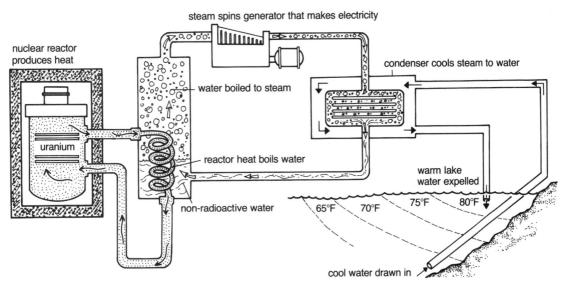

steam spins generator that makes electricity

nuclear reactor produces heat

condenser cools steam to water

water boiled to steam

uranium

reactor heat boils water

warm lake water expelled

non-radioactive water

65°F   70°F   75°F   80°F

cool water drawn in

NUCLEAR REACTOR

nuclear waste   *See* RADIOACTIVE WASTE.

nukes   A SLANG term for NUCLEAR REACTORS or NUCLEAR WEAPONS.

ᕤ "No Nukes" is a slogan of those who oppose NUCLEAR POWER and nuclear weapons.

nylon   A synthetic plastic, cloth, yarn, or thread produced industrially. Introduced in 1938, it is valued for its strength, elasticity, and durability.

offshore drilling   The operation of oil wells on the CONTINENTAL SHELF, sometimes in water hundreds of feet deep.

ᕤ Public debate about offshore drilling concentrates on the possibility that large oil spills will occur, with subsequent damage to the coastal environment.

ohm   (OHM)   The unit of electrical RESISTANCE, named after the nineteenth-century German physicist Georg Ohm.

perpetual-motion machine   A machine that could run forever. A perpetual-motion machine would have to produce at least as much ENERGY as was needed for its operation. According to the second law of THERMODYNAMICS, such a machine is impossible, and to date none has ever been successfully demonstrated.

personal computer   A small COMPUTER, intended for use by an individual. A personal computer will usually fit on a desk.

petrochemical   (pet-roh-KEM-i-kuhl)   Any material made from substances found in oil or natural gas. Most plastics are petrochemicals.

photoelectric effect   The emission of ELECTRONS from a metal when LIGHT shines on it. The effect is widely used to convert a light signal into an electric CURRENT.

photovoltaic cell   *See* SOLAR CELL.

program   A series of instructions given to a COMPUTER to direct it to carry out certain operations. The term CODE is often used to denote large-scale operations.

program, to   To provide a COMPUTER with a set of instructions for solving a problem.

programming language   In COMPUTER technology, a set of conventions in which instructions for the machine are written. There are many languages that allow humans to communicate with computers; FORTRAN, BASIC, and Pascal are some common ones.

radar   A method of finding the position and VELOCITY of an object by bouncing a RADIO WAVE off it and analyzing the reflected wave. *Radar* is an ACRONYM for *radio detection and ranging*.

ᕤ Police use radar techniques to determine the speed of automobiles.

radio telescope   *See* TELESCOPE.

radioactive waste   RADIOACTIVE materials that may be left after a commercial or laboratory process has been carried out. Some is "low-level" waste, such as objects that have touched the radioactive tracers used in certain medical tests. Other waste may be "high-level," such as the material left in a NUCLEAR REACTOR after the fuel has been consumed.

ᕤ There has been public debate over the safest means of storing the waste, which can remain dangerously radioactive for up to hundreds of thousands of years. Present practice calls for encasing the waste in metal, concrete, and ceramic containers, and burying the containers deep underground in geologically stable locations.

radiocarbon dating   A method of determining the age of an object by measuring the amount of radiocarbon (CARBON 14) it contains. It is a special example of RADIOACTIVE DATING.

radwaste   *See* RADIOACTIVE WASTE.

resistance   In ELECTRICITY, a measurement of the difficulty encountered by a POWER source in forcing electric CURRENT through an electrical CIRCUIT, and hence the amount of power dissipated in the circuit. Resistance is measured in OHMS.

satellite   Any object in ORBIT about some body capable of exerting a gravitational (*see* GRAVITATION) force. Artificial satellites in orbit around the EARTH have many uses, including relaying communication signals, making accurate surveys and inventories of the earth's surface and WEATHER patterns, and carrying out scientific experiments.

scanning probe microscope   Any of a number of devices capable of producing images of individual ATOMS and MOLECULES on surfaces of materials. (*See also* NANOTECHNOLOGY.)

secondary recovery A method of getting crude oil out of fields from which no more oil can be obtained by ordinary pumping. After secondary recovery has been completed, TERTIARY RECOVERY techniques can be employed to remove more oil. Each step in the process becomes more expensive, and even when tertiary recovery is completed, fully half of the original oil still remains underground, unrecoverable.

semiconductor A material that conducts (*see* CONDUCTION) ELECTRICITY, but very poorly. SILICON is the most common and familiar semiconductor. Devices made from semiconductors, such as the TRANSISTOR, are the basis of the modern microelectric industry.

short circuit An electrical CIRCUIT in which a path of very low RESISTANCE has been opened, usually accidentally. When the resistance drops, the electric CURRENT in the circuit becomes very high, and can cause damage to the circuit and start fires.

silicon (SIL-i-kon, SIL-i-kuhn) A CHEMICAL ELEMENT from which SEMICONDUCTORS are made. It is also used in the manufacture of glass, concrete, brick, and pottery.

silicon chip A MICROCHIP.

Silicon Valley Region on the SAN FRANCISCO Peninsula in CALIFORNIA where the miniaturized electronics industry is centered, so called because most of the devices built there are made of SEMICONDUCTORS such as SILICON.

❧ The term is often used as a catchword to describe the development of HIGH-TECH industry: "If we can attract this corporation to our town, we could become another Silicon Valley."

software The PROGRAMS and instructions that run a COMPUTER, as opposed to the actual physical machinery and devices that compose the HARDWARE.

solar cells Devices, usually made of SEMICONDUCTORS, that convert sunlight directly into electric CURRENT. Solar cells power artificial SATELLITES, and are often used in remote locations of the EARTH.

❧ At present, solar cells are too expensive and inefficient to be used for commercial generation of ELECTRICITY.

solar photovoltaic cells (foh-toh-vol-TAY-ik, foh-toh-vohl-TAY-ik) *See* SOLAR CELLS.

sonic barrier *See* SOUND BARRIER.

sonic boom *See* BOOM, SONIC.

sound barrier The sudden increase in air resistance that occurs when an aircraft approaches the speed of sound. This is also called the SONIC BARRIER.

SPACE SHUTTLE. *The* Enterprise *landing at Edwards Air Force Base, October 26, 1977, after a test flight.*

space shuttle A vehicle built by NASA that is capable of taking off from EARTH, carrying a crew and a cargo into space, and returning to earth to be used again. The shuttle is currently the main vehicle for the launching of American SATELLITES.

❧ The space shuttle *Challenger* exploded shortly after liftoff in 1986. All seven crew members died in the accident.

space station A proposed structure to be built in space by NASA in the 1990s. The space station would be a permanent habitat at which scientific and technological work could be carried out. Building a space station is considered the next step in the development and exploration of space.

Spirit of St. Louis, The The specially designed airplane that Charles LINDBERGH flew in the first nonstop flight across the ATLANTIC OCEAN. It is on display in a museum of the SMITHSONIAN INSTITUTION in WASHINGTON, D.C.

Sputniks (SPOOT-niks, SPUT-niks) A series of Soviet SATELLITES launched in 1957 and in following years. These were the first artificial satellites.

❧ The appearance of Sputnik stimulated a great deal of effort in the education of scientists and engineers in the United States. This period is now referred to as the post-Sputnik boom.

SST   A commercial aircraft that flies faster than the speed of sound; *SST* stands for *supersonic transport*. The *Concorde*, developed by the British and French, is an example of an SST.

stealth technology   The use of advanced design and specialized materials to make an aircraft difficult or even impossible to detect by RADAR. ≈ Stealth aircraft were used for the first time in the PERSIAN GULF WAR, where they were highly successful. ≈ The term is now used to refer more generally to something that remains hidden or unknown: "This is a Stealth proposal: no one knows what it means."

streamline   The line traced by a LIQUID or GAS as it moves. Streamlines are most commonly used in describing the flow of a liquid or gas around a SOLID object.
   ≈ A "streamlined" design is one in which objects that move through a gas or liquid are shaped to match these lines, and therefore reduce the ENERGY required to produce that motion.

STRIP MINING

strip mining   Removing a MINERAL deposit from the EARTH after first removing the layer of earth above it.
   ≈ Strip mining, the cheapest method of mining, is also the most controversial, because it jeopardizes the environment, and because strip-mined land is either expensive or impossible to reclaim.

superconductivity   (sooh-puhr-kon-duk-TIV-uh-tee) A property of some materials in which their electrical RESISTANCE drops to zero, and they acquire the ability to carry electric CURRENT with no loss of ENERGY whatsoever. Formerly, materials developed superconductivity only at temperatures near ABSOLUTE ZERO,

but new materials have been found that remain superconductive at temperatures above those of liquid NITROGEN. The goal of current research is to find a material that remains superconductive at room temperature.

superconductor   A material that can develop SUPERCONDUCTIVITY.
   ≈ Superconductors are used to make large ELECTROMAGNETS, and they are starting to play a major role in industry.

synfuels   (SIN-fyooh-uhlz)   Short for *synthetic fuels*. Synfuels are substances made through the extraction of petroleum or coal from minerals found in the western United States.
   ≈ The cost of synfuels is presently too high to make them commercially attractive.

synthetic polymers   (POL-uh-muhrz)   Industrially produced chemical substances consisting of a number of MOLECULES linked together with COVALENT BONDS. Examples include plastics, synthetic fibers such as NYLON, and synthetic rubber.

telemetry   (tuh-LEM-uh-tree)   Automatic measurement and transmission of DATA or information by such means as wire or (more commonly today) MICROWAVE relays from the source to a distant receiver.
   ≈ SATELLITES transmit their data by telemetry.

tertiary recovery   (TUR-shee-er-ee, TUR-shuh-ree)   Final procedures to extract crude oil from fields that have been exhausted through pumping. (*See* SECONDARY RECOVERY.)

thermal pollution   The dumping of heated GASES or heated wastewater (often from electrical GENERATING PLANTS) into the air or water.
   ≈ Thermal pollution of the air can affect the WEATHER; thermal pollution of water can threaten plants or animals living in it.

thermocouple   A device for accurate measurement of temperature. A thermocouple consists of two dissimilar metals joined at two joints in a loop so that the difference in VOLTAGE can be measured. Since voltage changes in proportion to temperature, the voltage difference indicates temperature differences.

thermonuclear   A term referring to devices that use NUCLEAR FUSION, the fusion of atomic NUCLEI, to produce ENERGY at very high temperatures. (*See* HYDROGEN BOMB.)

thermostat A device that monitors and automatically responds to changes in temperature and activates switches controlling devices such as furnaces or air conditioners.

Three Mile Island The location of an accident in 1979 in a NUCLEAR POWER plant — an electrical GENERATOR powered by a NUCLEAR REACTOR — in PENNSYLVANIA. The plant underwent a partial MELTDOWN that resulted in very little leakage of RADIATION into the ATMOSPHERE, panic among nearby residents, losses of billions of dollars, and intense criticism of nuclear power programs in general. (*Compare* CHERNOBYL.)

transformer A device used to transfer electrical energy from one CIRCUIT to another. With an ALTERNATING CURRENT, a transformer will either raise or lower the VOLTAGE as it makes the transfer.

transistor An electronic device that can work as an AMPLIFIER, transforming weak electrical signals into strong ones. It is normally made from SILICON or other SEMICONDUCTORS.

🍃 The transistor is the basic device used in miniaturized electronic systems such as portable radios or as a fast switch in COMPUTERS.

UHF (ultra high frequency) RADIO WAVES with FREQUENCIES that run between 300,000,000 and 3,000,000,000 HERTZ. (*Compare* VHF.)

universal time The measure of time obtained from the rotation of the EARTH, also known as Greenwich mean time, after the Greenwich Observatory in England. The world's time standard today is Coordinated Universal Time, which is kept by ATOMIC CLOCKS. The two universal times are kept in synchronization by the occasional insertion of LEAP SECONDS into the year.

V-2 A long-range liquid-fuel rocket used by the Germans as a BALLISTIC MISSILE during WORLD WAR II.

VHF (very high frequency) RADIO WAVES with FREQUENCIES between 30,000,000 and 300,000,000 HERTZ. (*Compare* UHF.)

Viking spacecraft A spacecraft launched by NASA that landed on MARS in the late 1970s, sending back photographs and experimental reports about the PLANET's surface.

virtual reality The creation of images and tactile sensations by means of a COMPUTER, producing the illusion of reality. Images are often projected onto special goggles to strengthen the illusion. (*See* CYBERSPACE.)

volt (VOHLT) The unit of electromotive force, the volt measures how much "pressure" there is in an ELECTRICAL CIRCUIT. The higher the voltage, the more ELECTRICAL CURRENT will flow in the circuit. 🍃 Ordinary household outlets are usually rated at 115 volts, car batteries at 12 volts, and flashlight batteries at 1.5 volts.

vulcanization An industrial process that strengthens natural rubber. Because it requires great heat, the process was named after the Roman god of fire, VULCAN.

water pollution The addition of harmful chemicals to natural water. Sources of water pollution in the United States include industrial waste, runoff from fields treated with chemical fertilizers, and runoff from areas that have been mined.

water softening The removal of certain minerals from water by means of CHEMICAL REACTIONS.

🍃 Because "hard" water contains minerals that make it difficult for soap to lather, soft water is often preferred for home use.

Watt, James A Scottish engineer active in the eighteenth century. Watt invented the modern version of the steam engine.

Whitney, Eli An American inventor of the late eighteenth and early nineteenth centuries. Whitney invented the cotton gin, a device for processing raw cotton.

Wright brothers Orville and Wilbur Wright, American mechanics and inventors of the late nineteenth and early twentieth centuries, who achieved the first sustained flight of a heavier-than-air machine — what we today call an airplane. Their flight was made at Kitty Hawk, NORTH CAROLINA, in 1903.

Picture Credits
Index

PICTURE CREDITS

The Bible

Abraham and Isaac Historical Pictures/Stock Montage **Adam and Eve** 68.187 *The Fall of Man (Adam and Eve)*, Albrecht Dürer. Nuremberg, Germany (1471–1528). Engraving, 252 × 195 cm. Centennial Gift of Landon T. Clay. Courtesy, Museum of Fine Arts, Boston. **Books of the Bible** Copyright © 1991 by Houghton Mifflin Co. Adapted and reprinted by permission from *The American Heritage Dictionary, Second College Edition.* **Crucifixion** Historical Pictures/Stock Montage *David,* **Good Shepherd** Alinari/Art Resource, N.Y. **Jesus** map from *Atlas of Ancient History: 1700 BC to 565 AD,* p. 62. Copyright © Michael Grant, 1971. Reprinted by permission of Dorset Press, a division of Marboro Books Corp. **John the Baptist** Alinari/Art Resource, N.Y. **Judgment Day,** *The Last Supper* Historical Pictures/Stock Montage **Mary** Alinari/Art Resource, N.Y. **Moses** From *1993 Information Please Almanac.* Copyright © 1992 by Houghton Mifflin Co. Reprinted by permission. **Nativity** Alinari/Art Resource, N.Y. **Noah and the Flood** Bettmann Archive **Peter** Alinari/Art Resource, N.Y.

Mythology and Folklore

Achilles, Aphrodite, King Arthur Bettmann Archive **Centaur** Alinari/Art Resource, N.Y. *Saint George and the Dragon* Isabella Stewart Gardner Museum, Boston **Laocoon, Medusa** Alinari/Art Resource, N.Y. **Minotaur** The Metropolitan Museum of Art, Purchase, 1947, Joseph Pulitzer Bequest. (47/11.5). All rights reserved. The Metropolitan Museum of Art. **Pegasus** Bettmann Archive **Phoenix** Historical Pictures/Stock Montage **Romulus and Remus** Alinari/Art Resource, N.Y. **Knights of the Round Table** Giraudon/Art Resource, N.Y. **Trojan Horse** Bettmann Archive **Zodiac** Giraudon/Art Resource, N.Y.

World Literature, Philosophy, and Religion

Plato's Academy Historical Pictures/Stock Montage **Buddha** Photograph © by David S. Strickler/Picture Cube, Inc. **Confucius** From *1993 Information Please Almanac.* Copyright © 1992 by Houghton Mifflin Co. Reprinted by permission. **Don Quixote** Historical Pictures/Stock Montage **Frank** AP/Wide World Photos **Judaism (Star of David)** From *Symbols, Signs & Signets* by Dover Publications. Copyright © 1950 by Ernst Lehner. **Juggernaut** Bettmann Archive **Pope** Photograph © 1980 by Ulrike Welsch/Photo Researchers, Inc. **Russell** AP/Wide World Photos **Torah** Photograph © by Peter Southwick/Stock, Boston **Totem Pole** SEF/Art Resource, N.Y. **Yin and Yang** Laurel Cook

Literature in English

Austen Bettmann Archive **Cheshire Cat** From *Alice's Adventures in Wonderland,* by Lewis Carroll. **Eliot** A photographic portrait of T. S. Eliot by Kay Reynal. Gelatin silver print, negative number 078248. Acc. no.: 77.52. Dimensions: 28.9 × 26.5 cm. The National Portrait Gallery, Smithsonian Institution, Washington, D.C. **Frankenstein's Monster** Copyright © by Universal Pictures, a Division of Universal City Studios, Inc. Courtesy of MCA Publishing Rights, a Division of MCA Inc./Culver Pictures. **Globe Theater** Historical Pictures/Stock Montage **Captain Hook and Peter Pan** © 1952 The Walt Disney Company **Hurston** Courtesy of Yale Collection of American Literature, Beinecke Rare Book and Manuscript Library, Yale University and Estate of Carl Van Vechten, Joseph Solomon, Executor **Poe** Bettmann Archive **Shakespeare** By permission of the Folger Shakespeare Library **Twain** Bettmann Archive **Tweedledum and Tweedledee** From *Through the Looking Glass,* by Lewis Carroll. **Wilde** Bettmann Archive

Fine Arts

American Gothic The Art Institute of Chicago. All rights reserved. **Bach** Library of Congress **Baker** Bettmann Archive **Beethoven** AKG/Photo Researchers, Inc.

The Birth of Venus Bettmann Archive **Capital** Laurel Cook **Le Corbusier** Photograph © 1976 by Paolo Koch/Photo Researchers, Inc. **Dali** The Museum of Modern Art, New York; Copyright DEMART PRO ARTE/ARS, N.Y., 1989 **Expressionism** The Museum of Modern Art, New York **Goya** Alinari/Art Resource, N.Y. **Hagia Sophia** SEF/Art Resource, N.Y. **Icon** Religious News Service Photo **Leonardo da Vinci** UPI/Bettmann Newsphotos **Michelangelo** Marburg/Art Resource, N.Y. *Mona Lisa,* **Nijinsky** Bettmann Archive **Notre Dame de Paris** Photograph © by RAPHO, Agence Photographique/Photo Researchers, Inc. **Picasso** UPI/Bettmann Newsphotos; Copyright ARS, N.Y./SPADEM 1989 *Pietà* Alinari/Art Resource, N.Y. **Raphael** Marburg/Art Resource, N.Y. **Rivera** Detail from a fresco by Mexican artist Diego M. Rivera (1886–1957). Entitled *Detroit Industry* 1932–33. Accession number 33.10.S. Copyright © 1988 The Detroit Institute of Arts, Founders Society Purchase, Edsel B. Ford Fund and Gift of Edsel B. Ford. **Rubens** Giraudon/Art Resource, N.Y. *The Spirit of '76* Board of Selectmen's Room of Abbot Hall, Marblehead, Mass. **Taj Mahal** Bratan/Art Resource, N.Y. *The Thinker* The Metropolitan Museum of Art, Gift of Thomas F. Ryan, 1910. (11.173.9). All rights reserved. The Metropolitan Museum of Art. *Venus de Milo* Alinari/Art Resource, N.Y. **Warhol** AP/Wide World Photos **Wright** Pennsylvania Division of Travel Marketing

World History to 1550

Alexander the Great Historical Pictures/Stock Montage **Charlemagne** Giraudon/Art Resource, N.Y. **Genghis Khan** Culver Pictures **Henry VIII** Alinari/Art Resource, N.Y. **Hieroglyphics** Marburg/Art Resource, N.Y. **Joan of Arc** Giraudon/Art Resource, N.Y. **Julius Caesar** Bettmann Archive **Mesopotamia** map detail from *The Columbia History of the World,* p. 53, by John A. Garraty and Peter Gay. Copyright © 1972 by Harper & Row. Reprinted by permission of the publisher. **Montezuma** Bettmann Archive **Pyramids** Photograph © by George Holton/Photo Researchers, Inc. **Roman Empire** map from *An Encyclopedia of World History,* p. 113, by William L. Langer, 5th ed. Copyright 1940, 1948, 1952, © 1968, 1972 by Houghton Mifflin Co. Used by permission. **Stonehenge** Gatewood/Art Resource, N.Y. **Tutankhamen** Photograph by Harry Burton/The Metropolitan Museum of Art **William the Conqueror** Giraudon/Art Resource, N.Y.

World History Since 1550

Spanish Armada, Bastille Historical Pictures/Stock Montage **Castro, Churchill** AP/Wide World Photos **Drake** Bennet/Art Resource, N.Y. **Elizabeth I** Scala/Art Resource, N.Y. **Gandhi** AP/Wide World Photos **Hitler** Copyright © Mary Evans Picture Library/Photo Researchers, Inc. **Lenin** AP/Wide World Photos **Mandela** Photograph by Jan Wood/Globe Photos **Mao Zedong** AP/Wide World Photos **Mother Teresa** Bettmann Archive **Napoleon Bonaparte** painting, Giraudon/Art Resource, N.Y.; map from *An Encyclopedia of World History,* p. 646, by William L. Langer, 5th ed. Copyright 1940, 1948, 1952, © 1968, 1972 by Houghton Mifflin Co. Used by permission. **Nazis** Photo Researchers, Inc. **Rasputin** Culver Pictures **Sarajevo** Bettmann Archive **Stalin** AP/Wide World Photos **Tiananmen Square** Bettmann Archive **Queen Victoria, Battle of Waterloo** Bettmann Archive **Battle of Trafalgar** Historical Pictures/Stock Montage **World War I** map from *An Encyclopedia of World History,* p. 944, by William L. Langer, 5th ed. Copyright 1940, 1948, 1952, © 1968, 1972 by Houghton Mifflin Co. Used by permission. **World War II** map (Europe) from *Atlas of World History.* Copyright © 1975 by Rand McNally & Company, R.L. 88-S-58. **World War II** map (Pacific) from *An Encyclopedia of World History,* p. 1155, by William L. Langer, 5th ed. Copyright 1940, 1948, 1952, © 1968, 1972 by Houghton Mifflin Co. Used by permission. **Yeltsin** Bettmann Archive

American History to 1865

Alamo Bettmann Archive **Appomattox Court House** U.S. Dept. of the Interior-National Park Service Photo/Photo Researchers, Inc. **Boston Massacre** Courtesy of the Bostonian Society/Old State House **Civil War** map from *Atlas of World History*. Copyright © 1975 by Rand McNally & Company, R.L. 88-S-58. **Dix** Bettmann Archive **Franklin** Library of Congress **Grant** AP/Wide World Photos **Lee** Bettmann Archive **Lincoln** Library of Congress *Mayflower* Courtesy of the Pilgrim Society, Plymouth, Mass. **Revere** Bettmann Archive **The Thirteen Colonies** map from *An Encyclopedia of World History*, p. 559, by William L. Langer, 5th ed. Copyright 1940, 1948, 1952, © 1968, 1972 by Houghton Mifflin Co. Used by permission. **Tubman** Library of Congress **Washington** The Metropolitan Museum of Art, Gift of John Stewart Kennedy, 1897. (97.34.) All rights reserved. The Metropolitan Museum of Art

American History Since 1865

Anthony Schlesinger Library, Radcliffe College **Carver** Portrait of George Washington Carver by Betsy Graves Reyneau. Oil on canvas. Acc. no.: 65.77. Date: 1942. Dimensions: 44 × 35 inches. The National Portrait Gallery, Smithsonian Institution, Washington, D.C. Gift of the G.W. Carver Memorial Committee. **Eisenhower** Reproduction by the Army Photographic Agency / Dwight D. Eisenhower Library. **Ellis Island, Flapper, James** Bettmann Archive **Keller** AP/Wide World Photos **Kennedy** Photo no. AR 7595B, John F. Kennedy Library **King** UPI/Bettmann Newsphotos **Marshall** Public Information Office, Supreme Court of the United States **Owens** AP/Wide World Photos **Pearl Harbor** National Archives and Records Service **Prohibition** Library of Congress **Roosevelt** AP/Wide World Photos **Rough Riders, Sanger, Sitting Bull** Bettmann Archive

World Politics

Anti-Semitism AP/Wide World Photos **Apartheid** UPI/Bettmann Newsphotos **Civil Disobedience** Photograph © by Richard Wood **Feminism** Bettmann Archive **Kremlin** Ewing Galloway **Kurds** Bettmann Archive **Palestine Liberation Organization (Yasir Arafat)** AP/Wide World Photos **Pogrom** SNARK/Art Resource, N.Y. **Refugee** AP/Wide World Photos

American Politics

Capitol Hill Library of Congress **Checks and Balances** Copyright © 1986 by Houghton Mifflin Co. Adapted and reprinted by permission from *America: The Glorious Republic*, vol. 1. **E Pluribus Unum** The Great Seal of the United States of America, as it appears on the back of an American dollar bill. Dept. of the Treasury, Bureau of Engraving and Printing. **Gerrymander** Rare Books and Manuscripts Division, New York Public Library; Astor, Lenox, and Tilden Foundations. **Legislative Branch** Copyright © 1986 by Houghton Mifflin Co. Adapted and reprinted by permission from *This Is America's Story*, 5th ed. **Pentagon** AP/Wide World Photos **Separation of Powers** Copyright © 1986 by Houghton Mifflin Co. Adapted and reprinted by permission from *This Is America's Story*, 5th ed. **Suffragettes** Bettmann Archive **Supreme Court** Supreme Court Historical Society **Uncle Sam** Historical Pictures/Stock Montage

World Geography

World (political) map drawn by Mapping Specialists, Ltd. **Berlin Wall** Photograph by Thomas Gade/Photo Researchers, Inc. **World (physical)** map drawn by Mapping Specialists, Ltd. **Mecca** AP/Wide World Photos **Wailing Wall** Photograph © 1981 by Jan Lukas/Photo Researchers, Inc.

American Geography

United States maps drawn by Aitkin F. Jarvis/ANCO.

Anthropology, Psychology, and Sociology

Aborigine AP/Wide World Photos **Archaeology** Photograph © by Dr. George Gerster/Photo Researchers, Inc. **Eskimo** AP/Wide World Photos **Freud** AKG/Photo Researchers, Inc. **Jung, Mead** AP/Wide World Photos **Native American** Photograph © by Eric Kroll **Skinner Box** Photograph © by Ken Robert Buck/Picture Cube, Inc.

Business and Economics

Assembly Line Photograph © by Tom McHugh/Photo Researchers, Inc. **Balance of Trade** Dept. of Commerce, Bureau of Economic Analysis **Chavez** AP/Wide World Photos **Consumer Price Index** U.S. Bureau of Labor Statistics, *Monthly Labor Review* **Exchange Rate** *The Wall Street Journal* and the Board of Governors of the Federal Reserve System, *Federal Reserve Bulletin*. **Ford** From the collections of Henry Ford Museum and Greenfield Village. Negative no. 0-2572. **Great Depression** Bettmann Archive **Iacocca** AP/Wide World Photos **Marx** Culver Pictures **Nader** Photograph © by A. Louis Goldman/Photo Researchers, Inc. **New York Stock Exchange** AP/Wide World Photos **OPEC** UPI/Bettmann Newsphotos **Rockefeller** Bettmann Archive **Strike** AP/Wide World Photos **Sweatshop** National Archives and Records Service **Vanderbilt** Bettmann Archive

Physical Sciences and Mathematics

Atom Laurel Cook **Einstein** AP/Wide World Photos **Electromagnetic Spectrum** Laurel Cook **Galaxy** Ewing Galloway **Galileo** Bettmann Archive **Hyperbola, Hypotenuse** Laurel Cook **Nebula** Ewing Galloway **Parabola** Laurel Cook **Periodic Table of the Elements** Copyright © 1986 by Barnhart Books. All rights reserved. Reprinted by permission from *The American Heritage Dictionary of Science*. **SETI** Jet Propulsion Laboratory **Solar System, Wave** Laurel Cook

Earth Sciences

Atmosphere Copyright © 1987 by Houghton Mifflin Co. Adapted and reprinted by permission from *Investigating the Earth*, 4th ed. **Cirrus Clouds** Vincent J. Schaefer, Sc. D. **Continental Shelf** Laurel Cook **Cumulus Clouds** Vincent J. Schaefer, Sc. D. **Earth** Laurel Cook **Nimbus Clouds** Vincent J. Schaefer, Sc. D. **Plate Tectonics** From *1993 Information Please Almanac*. Copyright © 1992 by Houghton Mifflin Co. Reprinted by permission. **Stalactites and Stalagmites** The Giant's Hall in the Luray Caverns, Virginia. The Virginia Division of Tourism. **Status Clouds** Vincent J. Schaefer, Sc. D. **Volcano** (left) Laurel Cook; (right) AP/Wide World Photos

Life Sciences

Amoeba, Bacteria, Cell Laurel Cook **Chromosomes** Photograph © by Martin M. Rotker **Classification** Copyright © 1991 by Houghton Mifflin Co. Adapted and reprinted by permission from *The American Heritage Dictionary, Second College Edition*. **Dinosaurs, DNA, Evolution, Flower** Laurel Cook **Food Chain** Copyright © 1984 by Houghton Mifflin Co. Adapted and reprinted by permission from *Spaceship Earth: Earth Science*, rev. ed. **RNA, Root** Laurel Cook **Symbiosis** Photograph © by Leonard Lee Rue III/Leonard Rue Enterprises

Medicine and Health

Acupuncture Photograph © by Gale Zucker/Stock, Boston **Brain** Laurel Cook **CAT Scan** Photograph © 1986 James A. Prince/Photo Researchers, Inc. **Circulatory System, Digestive System, Ear, Endocrine System, Eye** Laurel Cook **Hippocrates** Alinari/Art Resource, N.Y. **Magnetic Resonance Imaging** Photograph by Simon Fraser/Photo Researchers, Inc. **Muscular System, Nervous System, Male Reproductive System, Female Reproductive System, Female Reproductive System (pregnant), Respiratory System, Skeletal System, Tooth, Urinary Tract** Laurel Cook

Technology

Apollo Program NASA **Atomic Bomb** (top) Laurel Cook; (bottom) AP/Wide World Photos **Bathyscaph** U.S. Navy Dept. **Celsius** Laurel Cook **Computer** Wang Laboratories, Inc. **DNA Fingerprinting** Photograph by David Parker/Photo Researchers, Inc. **Fulcrum, Internal-Combustion Engine, Laser** Laurel Cook **Mercury Program** UPI/Bettmann Newsphotos **Nuclear Reactor** Laurel Cook **Space Shuttle** NASA **Strip Mining** U.S. Dept. of Agriculture, Office of Information

INDEX